PROPHET OF DOOM

ALSO BY CRAIG WINN

IN THE COMPANY OF GOOD & EVIL

TEA WITH TERRORISTS

PROPHET
OF
DOOM

ISLAM'S TERRORIST DOGMA
IN MUHAMMAD'S OWN WORDS

CRAIG WINN

PUBLISHED BY

CRICKETSONG BOOKS

A DIVISION OF VIRGINIA PUBLISHERS

PROPHETOFDOOM.NET

COVER DESIGN BY KEN POWER

Winn, Craig.
   Prophet of Doom : Islam's Terrorist Dogma in Muhammad's
Own Words / Craig Winn — First Edition.
   p. cm.
   Includes bibliographical references and index.
   ISBN 0 - 9714481 - 2 - 4

   1. Muhammad—Prophet, d. 632—Teachings.
   2. Koran/Qur'an—Criticism, Interpretation, etc.
   3. Jihad.
   4. Islam and Terrorism.
   5. Terrorism—Religious Aspects—Islam.
   6. Islamic Fundamentalism.
   I. Title.

BP166.5.W56 2004   297.6'35
           QBI33-1745

TO

MUSLIMS

MAY THE TRUTH SET YOU FREE

LETTER TO THE READER

Islam is a caustic blend of regurgitated paganism and twisted Bible stories. Muhammad, its lone prophet, conceived his religion solely to satiate his lust for power, sex, and money. He was a terrorist. If you think these conclusions are shocking, wait until you see the evidence.

The critics of this work will claim that *Prophet of Doom* is offensive, racist, hatemongering, intolerant, and unnecessarily violent. I agree—but I didn't write those parts. They came directly from Islam's scriptures. If you don't like what Muhammad and Allah said, don't blame me. I'm just the messenger.

Others will say that I cherry-picked the worst of Islam to render an unfair verdict. They will charge that I took the Islamic scriptures out of context to smear Muhammad and Allah. But none of that is true. Over the course of these pages, I quote from almost every surah in the Qur'an—many are presented in their entirety. But more than that, I put each verse in the context of Muhammad's life, quoting vociferously from the Sunnah as recorded by Bukhari, Muslim, Ishaq, and Tabari—Islam's earliest and more trusted sources. I even arrange all of this material chronologically, from creation to terror.

Predicting what he called the "Day of Doom" was Muhammad's most often repeated prophecy. While it did not occur as he foretold in 1110 A.D., it nonetheless came true. Muslims and infidels alike have been doomed by Islam.

To discover why, we shall delve into the oldest surviving written evidence. These official works include the Sira, Ta'rikh, Hadith, and Qur'an. Ishaq's Sira, or biography, called *Sirat Rasul Allah*, provides the sole account of Muhammad's life and the formation of Islam written within 200 years of the prophet's death. While the character, message, and deeds portrayed within its pages are the antithesis of Christ's and his disciples, the Sira's chronological presentation is similar in style to the Christian Gospels. The Ta'rikh is the oldest, most trusted, and comprehensive history of Islam's formation and Muhammad's example, called Sunnah. It was written by Tabari. His *History of al-Tabari* is formatted like the Bible. It begins with Islamic creation and ends with the acts of Muhammad's companions. Tabari is a compilation of Hadith quotes and Qur'an passages. As such, it provides the best skeleton upon which to flesh out the character of Muhammad and the nature of fundamental Islam. A Hadith is an oral report from Muhammad or his companions. Muslims believe that Hadith were inspired by Allah, making them scripture. The most revered Collection was compiled in a topical arrangement by Bukhari. Allah's Book, the Qur'an, lacks context and chronology, so to understand it, readers are dependent upon the Sira, Ta'rikh, and Hadith.

All that can be known about Muhammad's deeds, means, motives, god, and scripture is enshrined in these books. In their pages you will see them as they saw themselves. My only point of departure from Ishaq and Tabari will be the comprehensive review of the early Meccan surahs, a period in which they had very little to say. Our paths will join again as we approach Islam's midlife crisis: the Quraysh Bargain, Satanic Verses, Night's Journey, and Pledge of Aqaba—a declaration of war against all mankind. At this point, the Sira, Ta'rikh, and Hadith speak more clearly than the Qur'an.

So that there will be no confusion, I have set passages from Islam's scriptures in **bold-faced type**. When quoting from the Qur'an and Hadith, I have elected to use a blended translation. No language transfers perfectly—one word to another. Five of my twelve translations of the Qur'an were combined to create the most accurate conveyance of the message possible. However, the writing quality is so poor, the proofreaders of this manuscript suggested that I help Allah and Muhammad out by cleaning up their grammar, punctuation, and verbosity. So for clarity and readability, I have trimmed their unruly word patterns and meaningless repetitions, being careful not to alter the meaning or message of any passage. Insertions within parenthesis (like this) were added by the Arabic translators to fill in missing words or to clarify the text. Insertions within brackets [like this] represent my observations.

I have elected to present Islam's original source material in juxtaposition to my evaluation of its veracity. This format is similar to that used by the first English translators of *Mein Kampf* as they attempted to warn America about the dangers lurking in Hitler's manifesto. They, as I, found it necessary to hold the author accountable. A great deal was at stake then, as it is today. The last time the world was ignorant of such a hateful and violent doctrine, 55 million people died. If we don't shed our ignorance of Islam, many more will perish.

My quest to understand Islam began on the morning of September 11th 2001. I wanted to know why Muslim militants were killing us. So I went to Ground Zero for Islamic terror—Israel. The West Bank is home to more suicide bombers per capita than anywhere else on earth. I arranged to meet with the terrorists themselves. I asked members of al-Qaeda, Islamic Jihad, al-Aqsa Martyrs' Brigade, and Hamas why they were killing us. They said, "Islam. We're following Muhammad's orders." That adventure is recounted in *Tea With Terrorists*. It covers a wide range of material and serves as a companion volume, connecting fundamental Islam to terrorism. *Prophet of Doom* focuses strictly on what the Islamic scriptures have to say.

So, could it be? Could a prophet and a religion be responsible for today's terrorist attacks? I invested 10,000 hours in pursuit of that answer. I wish everyone had. But knowing that most are unable, I have distilled what I discovered into these pages.

Now for a word of caution: this journey of discovery is ordered chronologically. It is not prioritized by relevance. Explaining the root cause of Islamic terror is the biggest priority; yet it is not exposed until the last half of the book. I want you to know Muhammad, Allah, and Islam before you judge their legacy. While *Prophet of Doom* is meticulously researched, documented, and accurate, it's written as if you and I were old friends having a lively chat about the most important and lethal issue of our day.

One last thought before you head down this perilous path. I pray that when you have reached the journey's end, you will share my heart for the plight of Muslims. I want nothing more than to free them from Islam, and in so doing, free us from the terror their doctrine inspires.

Craig Winn
November 2003
ProphetOfDoom.net

The documented references in *Prophet of Doom* were derived from English translations of the following ancient Islamic manuscripts. I encourage you to purchase and read them. The *Sirat Rasul Allah* was written by Ibn Ishaq in 750 A.D. It was edited and abridged by Ibn Hisham in 830 and translated by Alfred Guillaume under the title, *The Life of Muhammad* in 1955 by Oxford Press. The *History of al-Tabari* was written by Abu Muhammad bin al-Tabari between 870 and 920 A.D. His monumental work was translated and published in 1987 through 1997 by the State University of New York Press. I quote from volumes I, II, VI, VII, VIII, and IX. Al-Bukhari's Hadith, titled: *Sahih Al-Bukhari* and *The True Traditions* was collected by Imam Bukhari in 850 A.D. I have used the collector's original nomenclature because the only printed English translation (Publisher-Maktaba Dar-us-Salam, Translator-Muhammad Khan) was abridged and erroneously numbered. Finally, I recommend that you acquire at least three of the following Qur'an translations: Ahmed Ali, Pikthal, Noble by Muhsin Khan, Yusuf Ali, or Shakir. The oldest Qur'an fragments date to around 725 A.D.—a century after they were first recited.

TABLE OF CONTENTS

PROLOGUE

WHAT WOULD YOU DO?

"I have been made victorious with terror."

Suppose you stumbled upon the Constitution of an organization that was terrorizing the world. Would you ignore such a document, or would you read it? Suppose you discovered that this Constitution's most prominent themes were pain and punishment, thievery and violence, intolerance and war. If the regime's charter ordered its devotees to kill, plunder, and terrorize, would you sound an alarm?

What if this Constitution was supported by a manifesto that contained the only authorized biography of the regime's founder, and the first devotees of this doctrine, its co-founders, said that their leader was a sexual predator, a pirate, and a terrorist? If you found such evidence, what would you do with it? What if this leader motivated his mercenaries to murder and mayhem by allowing them to keep what they had stolen in the name of the cause—their victim's homes, businesses, money—even their women and children?

All right, no more hypotheticals. I'm going to share some passages from this Constitution—from the covenant of the world's largest and most violent organization. I have changed the names to disguise the source without altering the message. "Your leader has sent you from your homes to fight for the cause. Your leader wished to confirm the truth by his words: wipe those who disagree with us out to the last. We shall terrorize everyone who is unlike us! So smite them on their necks and every joint, and incapacitate them, for they are opposed to our doctrine and our leader. Whosoever opposes our doctrine and our leader should know that we are severe in retribution. And know that one-fifth of what you acquire as booty in war is for our great leader (the rest is for you). The use of such spoils is lawful and good."

This popular and misunderstood Constitution says: "Fight them till all opposition ends and only our doctrine rules. If you meet anyone who disagrees with us in battle, inflict on them such a defeat as would be a lesson for those who come after them, that they may be warned. Slaughter those who disagree with us wherever you find them. Lie in wait for them. They are specimens of foolishness. Punish them so that our superior dogma and leader can put them to shame. If you apprehend treachery from a people with whom we have a treaty, retaliate by breaking it off. Those who do not think like us should know that they cannot bypass our doctrine. Surely they cannot get away. Fight them until they pay a heavy tax in submission to us; how perverse are they. Our leader and his doctrine will damn them. For anyone who offends our leader or opposes our doctrine will receive a painful punishment. We will burn them alive. So prepare against them whatever arms and weaponry you can muster, that you may strike terror in the enemies of our cause!"

This Constitution is genuine, and millions follow its message. Exposing it —understanding it—might actually save you from the wrath it inspires. The covenant goes on to say: "Our great leader urged all who agree with us to fight. If there are twenty among you with determination, you will vanquish two hundred; and if there are a hundred, then you will vanquish a thousand of our enemy, for they are a people devoid of understanding. Our great leader drove your enemy back in fury. He motivated our side in battle. He made their citizens flee from their homes and he terrorized them so that you killed some and made many captive. Our great leader made you inherit their lands, homes, and wealth, and gave you a country you had not traversed before."

This sounds like a terrorist manifesto—a covenant for war and genocide. Does anything this immoral, this out-of-touch with human decency, actually exist? If it did, and if it were this blatant, you'd expect to see its followers amassing their weaponry. You'd expect them to rise up and terrorize the world. Not only would they feel it was their duty to kill, you'd expect their fallen assassins to be immortalized—hailed as martyrs and paraded down crowded streets, banners waving, tears flowing, guns blazing, with angry diatribes spewing from hate-filled faces. You'd expect them to wage war under the guise of doctrinal supremacy, wouldn't you? And if there were such people, our journalists and politicians would have ferreted them out, exposed them, and protected us. Right?

Wrong! With the exception of changing the names of the perpetrators and their victims, what you read is from the actual Constitution of an enormous, rapidly growing, extremely well funded, and horrendously violent worldwide cult. And as bad as that sounds, it gets worse in context. The manifesto proudly proclaims that unarmed civilians were annihilated by armed gangs. Men were decapitated on the orders of the dogma's founder. Thousands of children were sold into slavery. Women were raped—the leader himself participating. Townships were plundered, businesses were looted, and productive assets were destroyed. The villains slept in their victims' beds, abusing their wives and daughters. And each bloody affair was meticulously recorded by the founder's companions and later chronicled by the regime's most esteemed clerics.

It's time to turn the page. Let's look at what the founder's companions had to say about their leader in his manifesto. Once again, I will change the names but nothing else. "Kill them, for he who kills them will get a great reward. Our great leader said, 'Our doctrine assigns for a person who participates in battles in our cause to be rewarded with booty if he survives, or he will be admitted into the Hall of Heroes if he is killed in the battle as a martyr. Had I not found it difficult for my followers to do without me I would have remained in army units fighting great battles and would have loved to have been martyred for the cause.'"

The regime's founder is quoted in the doctrine's anti-Semitic manifesto saying, "Issue orders to kill every Jew in the country." He was asked, "What is the best deed?" by one of his devotees. The dictator replied, "To believe in me and our doctrine." "What is the next best deed?" the devotee queried. "To fight on behalf of our cause," he answered. At the end of one such conflict, one of the regime's lieutenants told his commander, "We have conquered another nation. The captives and the booty have all been collected. Now, my leader, may I take a slave girl from among the prisoners?" "Take any one you like," the warlord replied, raping one himself. Ever mindful of his duty, this regime's leader proclaimed, "Embrace our doctrine first and then fight." Followed by, "I have been made victorious with terror!"

You have stumbled upon the Constitution of the world's largest nation—and it's not China or Russia. You've just heard the words of its founding father, and he's not Lenin, Mao, or Hitler. And today, this doctrine's adherents are doing what their founder and Constitution ordered: fighting, ravaging civilians, stealing the world's possessions, and using them to terrorize.

Since it's happening according to plan, shouldn't we muster the courage to expose it—to speak out against it? Or should we remain silent for fear of offending them? The answer is obvious. Or is it? What if the names I substituted were Allah, Muhammad, and Islam? What if *it's* a "religion?"

This "Constitution" is the Qur'an. The "manifesto" is the Islamic Hadith. The citizens of this nation are Muslims. They're doing what they were ordered to do. They left their homes to fight infidels; they stole our planes, ravaged our economy, and slaughtered innocents in the name of Allah. They even confessed to the crime. Yet not a single national spokesperson or politician has had the courage to hold Islam accountable.

Criticizing a religion is something that makes people squeamish, especially in the paranoid culture of political correctness. Christians say that we are to love, not judge. Jews, after millennia of persecution, are terrified of even the perception of intolerance. Secular humanists, in deference to multiculturalism and the peace process, have sacrificed truth on the altar of their political agenda. So why upset everyone?

Why? Because they will continue to kill us if we don't expose them.

Before revealing what the Qur'an and Hadith have to say about Muhammad and Islam, I'd like to clear up a few inevitable misconceptions. First, on Muslims—I love you in spite of your beliefs and deeds. I would like nothing more than to free you from Islam. I agree with Renan, the famed scholar, who, after dedicating himself to understanding Islamic scripture, wrote: "Muslims were the first victims of Islam. Many times I have observed in my travels that fanaticism comes from a small number of dangerous men who maintain others in the practice of this religion by terror. To liberate the Muslim from his religion is the best service that one can render him."

Second, on Christians, you—we—are responsible for the awful mess the world is in. We have turned a personal relationship with our Creator into an emasculated religion, confused and aimless. In the name of that religion, we have perpetrated inhumanities. Today, for fear of appearing hateful we are apparently willing to let a billion people live in virtual slavery, perishing in ignorance and poverty. Tolerance of evil is not a Christian virtue. We are called to be discerning.

Third, on Jews—I love you in spite of yourselves. Fourteen centuries ago your forefathers sold Bible stories to Muhammad and then mocked him when he goofed them up. By doing so you manufactured your own enemy. Now, you are a divided people, unsure whether to appease or fight the terror you helped inspire. As the world's most lettered people, I fear that you understand less than you know. I pray that you come to trust your God before it is too late.

Fourth, on secular humanists, liberals, and agnostics—you are guilty of the very things you denounce in others. History is as condemning of man separating himself from God as it is of man-made religions establishing themselves as intermediaries to God. The last hundred years have been especially indicting; atheistic doctrines have annihilated more people than all religions combined. Truth is not relative. Yet in today's media, secular humanists judiciously edit under the guise of enlightenment. While irritating, this practice is particularly lethal as it relates to Islam. The errant recasting of the religion as peaceful, the reshaping of jihad into a spiritual struggle, the impression you convey that Islam is tolerant and that the terrorists have corrupted their religion, is wrong. Thousands have died in the wake of your illusions.

Fifth, on Islam itself—without deceit and sword, Islam would have been stillborn. An infinitesimal fraction of the one billion people subservient to Islam today actually chose their fate. In Mecca, fourteen hundred years ago, after a decade of preaching, as few as fifty men chose to follow Muhammad. But that all changed in Medina. There, according to the Qur'an and Hadith, Muhammad became a political tyrant, a terrorist, and a thief. His willingness to lead seventy-five armed raids against defenseless civilians swelled his ranks as swiftly as the spoils of "war" filled his pockets.

Equipped with booty stolen from others, Muhammad and his followers conquered and then plundered their neighbors, starting with Arabia. The only choice they offered their victims was "your money or your life." Once subjected to their will, Muslims compelled submission under penalty of death. Islam is, and has always been, a doctrine devoid of choice. It prospers at the business end of a bloody sword. Soon you will see why.

The vast preponderance of today's Muslims do not know their prophet or their religion very well. Theirs is a life of ignorance, despair, tyranny, and mind-numbing ritual. They are kept in the dark, purposely deceived, for the benefit of cleric and king. And there is no incentive for them to learn. Exposed to the truth, they would reject Islam, a decision that could cost them their lives. The Qur'an itself confirms this startling reality. In the 5th surah, the final revelation chronologically, Allah ordered Muslims "not to question the Qur'an," for those who did, he said, "discarded their religion." In that light, we should feel good about freeing Muslims from the oppressiveness of Islam. For by freeing them we will free ourselves from the scourge of Islamic terror.

Despite what you've heard in the media, there is but one Islam, a singular correct view of Muhammad, Allah, and Jihad. It is the one printed in the Qur'an and Hadith. There is no independent record of Muhammad in history from which a variant view may be drawn. The Hadith and Qur'an are the sole repository of information on this man, his times, means, and mission. The Muhammad of Islam, the god of Islam, and the religion of Islam must be as these sources present them.

Lastly, Islam has no alibi, no reason to cry, "Unfair." The Qur'an condemns all non-Muslims—Christians and Jews as well as those who worship many gods and no gods. It is an equal opportunity hater. Its attitude toward unbelieving infidels is overwhelmingly hostile. A cursory reading of the first ten surahs is sufficient to prove that the relatively few nice verses were contradicted and replaced, "abrogated" in Muslim parlance, by a staggering number of nasty ones. In fact, the Qur'an was written to justify some of the most ungodly behavior the world has ever known.

The simple truth is: *good* Muslims are *bad* people. Islam makes them that way. While there are plenty of "bad" Muslims who are good people, they are as impotent as bad Nazis in the Third Reich or bad Communists during Stalin's era. The Qur'an defines good and bad Muslims for us. It says a *good* Muslim is a Jihadist, a man who leaves his home, sacrificing his wealth and life, fighting in Allah's Cause. Allah says they will be rewarded with stolen booty if they survive or with a heavenly bordello if they die. Bad Muslims, on the other hand, are peaceful. Allah calls them "hypocrites" because they are unwilling to fight. He even says that peaceful Muslims are "the most vile of creatures" and that hell's hottest fires await them. If you are a peace-loving Muslim, your god hates you.

Good Muslims, those who read Islam's scriptures long before I cracked their covers, planned, funded, staffed, executed, and celebrated the terrorist attacks of 9/11. They proudly told the world *what* they were going to do—terrorize Americans and Jews into submission. They boldly proclaimed *why* they were going to do it—for the advancement of Islam. They even told us *who* they were—good Muslims. But we ignored their announcements. It was as if on the morning of December 7th 1941, nobody noticed the rising sun insignias on the planes bombing Pearl Harbor. The bombers of September 11th 2001 wore insignias too. Theirs was a crescent moon.

For those who support the politically-inspired notion that terrorism is not condoned by Islam, that terrorists have corrupted an otherwise peaceful religion, consider this. The world's foremost authority on the Qur'an is sheik Abdel Rahman. He was the senior professor of Qur'anic studies at Islam's most prestigious university, Al-Azhar, in Cairo. Today, the sheik is a convicted terrorist, serving time in an American prison for the '93 bombing of the World Trade Center. If the Qur'an espouses peace, that's hard to explain.

The conflict between truth and perception doesn't end there. Rahman's disciples, an Egyptian sheik and a Saudi terrorist—Osama bin Laden—told a film crew that Islam was their motivation for the second bombing. "Everybody praises the great action which you did which was first and foremost by the grace of Allah," the sheik began. "This is the guidance of Allah and the blessed fruit of jihad...a beautiful fatwa. May Allah bless you." Bin Laden agreed. "We calculated in advance the number of the casualties the enemy would suffer, and who would be killed based upon the position of the planes as they hit the towers. I was thinking that the fire from the gas in the planes would melt the iron structure of the buildings and collapse them. This is all I had hoped for." The sheik replied, "Allah be praised." He shared how Muslims watching television "exploded with joy," telling bin Laden, "Egyptian TV ran a subtitle below the images of the crumbled buildings: 'In revenge for the children of al Aqsa, Osama bin Laden executes an operation against America.'" Bin Laden replied, "The brothers who conducted the operation knew they were on a martyrdom mission. Allah bless their souls."

Al-Qaeda was actually accepting "credit" for a terrorist act it did not conceive. The plan was concocted, staffed, and financed in the al-Kod mosque in Hamburg, Germany. Today, the mosque's imam still preaches fundamental and uncorrupted Islam. He doesn't need to twist it, interpret it, or take it out of context. The imam's message is for all Muslims, and it is preached in every mosque. Listen as he reads verses from the 8th surah, the one I disguised earlier. These words come directly out of the Qur'an's **"Spoils of War,"** surah: **"Allah has sent you from your homes to fight for the Cause. Allah wished to confirm the truth by his words: wipe the Infidels out to the last. I shall fill the hearts of the Infidels with terror! So smite them on their necks and every joint, and incapacitate them, for they are opposed to Allah and His Apostle. Whoever opposes Us should know that Allah is severe in retribution. The Infidels will taste the torment of Hell. So when you meet them in battle do not retreat, for all who turn away from fighting will bring the wrath of Allah on themselves and their abode will be Hell. It was not you who killed them, but Allah who did so. You did not throw what you threw. Allah did to bring out the best in the faithful."** Using this reasoning, it was the Islamic god, not Muslims, who flew the planes into the World Trade Center. "So, fight them till all opposition ends and Islam is the only religion."

Now you know the truth. Allah wants infidels "wiped out and terrorized." That makes war and terror mainstream Islam. And Allah was just getting warmed up. "If you meet them in battle, inflict such a defeat as would be a lesson for those who come after them, that they may be warned. Surely the Infidels cannot get away. Prepare against them whatever arms and cavalry you can muster, that you may terrorize the enemies of Allah."

Reading Allah's orders out of the Qur'an's 8th surah, imams preach: "O Prophet, urge the faithful to fight. If there are twenty among you with determination they will vanquish two hundred; if there are a hundred then they will kill a thousand Infidels, for they are a people devoid of understanding." This is the math of terror. It is possible because infidels are ignorant of Islam. And you should know, the Qur'an defines "Infidels" in the 5th surah. "They are surely Infidels who say Christ, the Messiah is God." (5:72)

So as not to be accused of unfairly singling out a less-than-peaceful surah from the Qur'an, listen to how Allah recruits suicide bombers in the 4th surah: "Those who barter their life in this world for the next should fight in the way of Allah; whether he is killed or victorious, a glorious reward awaits." "Urge the believers to fight...to keep back the might of the Infidels." "Seize them and kill them wherever they are." "Muslims who sit idle are not equal to those who fight in Allah's Cause with their wealth and lives. Allah has exalted those who fight for Islam."

The Islamic Sira proclaims: Ishaq:587 "Our onslaught will not be a weak faltering affair. We shall fight as long as we live. We will fight until you turn to Islam, humbly seeking refuge. We will fight not caring whom we meet. We will fight whether we destroy ancient holdings or newly gotten gains. We have mutilated every opponent. We have driven them violently before us at the command of Allah and Islam. We will fight until our religion is established. And we will plunder them, for they must suffer disgrace."

Need more proof? Are the deeds of the most respected Qur'anic scholar, the words of the most illustrious Islamic terrorist, and the scripture readings of the most revered imams insufficient? After all, a senior Saudi sheik said we shouldn't listen to bin Laden because he was an "unlicensed cleric." Never mind that popularity polls show bin Laden's approval rating at seventy-five percent among Muslims—much higher than any other cleric or leader.

Then consider this quote from the Saudi ruling family's favorite imam, al Buraik. He's not only licensed, he's atop the pecking order. Prior to a telethon hosted to enrich the families of Palestinian suicide bombers, this esteemed cleric said, "I am against America. She is the root of all evils and wickedness on earth. Muslims, don't take Jews and Christians as allies. Muslim brothers in Palestine, do not have any mercy or compassion on them, their blood, their money, or their flesh. Their women are yours to take, legitimately. Allah made them yours. Why don't you enslave their women? Why don't you wage jihad? Why don't you pillage them?"

Do you suppose the licensed Saudi cleric was corrupting Islam too? Sorry. It's Allah who commands Muslims not to befriend Christians and Jews, for he wants them killed so he can use their bodies to stoke hell's fires. *Qur'an 5:51* **"O believers, do not hold Jews and Christians as your allies. They are allies of one another; and anyone who makes them his friends is one of them."** *Qur'an 2:10* **"As for those who deny Islam...they shall be the faggots for the Fire of Hell."** Islam's god is a spirit of an entirely different color. *Ishaq:327* **"Allah said, 'A prophet must slaughter before collecting captives. A slaughtered enemy is driven from the land. Muhammad, you craved the desires of this world, its goods and the ransom captives would bring. But Allah desires killing them to manifest the religion.'"** The Saudi imam has correctly interpreted Islam's message. *Bukhari:V5B59N512* **"The Prophet had their men killed, their children and woman taken captive."** *Qur'an 33:26* **"Allah made the Jews leave their homes by terrorizing them so that you killed some and made many captive. And He made you inherit their lands, their homes, and their wealth. He gave you a country you had not traversed before."**

The Islamic warlords who rule Saudi Arabia were enthroned by the British, by way of reward. The Brits bribed them to fight against their Muslim brethren, the Ottoman Turks, in World War I. Today, the Saudi dictators thank the West by manufacturing the terrorists who kill us. It's hardly a coincidence that eighty percent of the 9/11 suicide bombers were trained in the kingdom that gave birth to Islam. Yet the Fahd princes meet with our president and protest incessantly to our media, professing that they and their religion are peace-loving. They are incensed when people blame them for the terror they have inspired. Forget for a moment that Muslim militancy is funded by the black ooze that flows from their sand—it's what they teach that's so devastating.

Eighty percent of the mosques in America and the West were built and are staffed by the Fahd warlords. They also provide their terrorist manufacturing facilities with their reading material. The official Qur'an for the English speaking market bears the stamp of the Fahd Foundation. In it, right below surah 2:190, the Qur'an's first mention of Jihad, you'll find this passage: **"Jihad is holy fighting in Allah's Cause with full force of numbers and weaponry. It is given the utmost importance in Islam and is one of its pillars. By Jihad, Islam is established, Allah's Word is made superior (which means only Allah has the right to be worshiped), and Islam is propagated. By abandoning Jihad, Islam is destroyed and Muslims fall into an inferior position; their honor is lost, their lands are stolen, their rule and authority vanish. Jihad is an obligatory duty in Islam on every Muslim. He who tries to escape from this duty, dies with one of the qualities of a hypocrite."**

There is nothing peaceful about Islam. Muhammad's dogma breeds ruthless killers. At his direction Muslims will continue to terrorize the world until there are no more non-Muslims. So that you might know what Islam does to men, I have organized 2,000 Islamic scriptures by topic in the "Muhammad's Own Words" appendix. Here are some exerpts from the Fighting, Terror, War, and

Jihad sections: *Ishaq:576* "Allah and Muhammad humiliated every coward and made our religion victorious. We were glorified and destroyed them all. By what our Apostle recites from the Book and by our swift horses, I liked the punishment the infidels received. Killing them was sweeter than drink. We galloped among them panting for the spoil. With our loud-voiced army, the Apostle's squadron advanced into the fray."

Tabari IX:69 "Arabs were the first to respond to the call of the Prophet. We are Allah's helpers and the viziers of His Messenger. We fight people until they believe in Allah. He who believes in Allah and His Messenger has protected his life and possessions from us. As for one who disbelieves, we will fight him forever in the Cause of Allah. Killing him is a small matter to us."

Muslim:C20B1N4597 "The Prophet said at the conquest of Mecca: 'There is no migration now, but only Jihad, fighting for the Cause of Islam. When you are asked to set out on a Jihad expedition, you should readily do so.'"

Qur'an 61:4 "Surely Allah loves those who fight in His Cause." *Ishaq:300* "I am fighting in Allah's service. This is piety and a good deed. In Allah's war I do not fear as others should. For this fighting is righteous, true, and good."

Bukhari:V4B52N63 "A man whose face was covered with an iron mask came to the Prophet and said, 'Allah's Apostle! Shall I fight or embrace Islam first?' The Prophet said, 'Embrace Islam first and then fight.' So he embraced Islam and was martyred. Allah's Apostle said, 'A Little work, but a great reward.'" *Bukhari:V4B53N386* "Our Prophet, the Messenger of our Lord, ordered us to fight you till you worship Allah alone or pay us the Jizyah tribute tax in submission. Our Prophet has informed us that our Lord says: 'Whoever amongst us is killed as a martyr shall go to Paradise to lead such a luxurious life as he has never seen, and whoever survives shall become your master.'"

Qur'an 47:4 "When you clash with the unbelieving Infidels in battle (fighting Jihad in Allah's Cause), smite their necks until you overpower them, killing and wounding many of them. At length, when you have thoroughly subdued them, bind them firmly, making (them) captives. Thereafter either generosity or ransom (them based upon what benefits Islam) until the war lays down its burdens. Thus are you commanded by Allah to continue carrying out Jihad against the unbelieving infidels until they submit to Islam."

Ishaq:315 "It was so criminal, men could hardly imagine it. Muhammad was ennobled because of the bloody fighting. I swear we shall never lack soldiers nor army leaders. Driving before us infidels until we subdue them with a halter above their noses and a branding iron. We will drive them to the ends of the earth. We will pursue them on horse and on foot. We will never deviate from fighting in our cause. Any people that disobey Muhammad will pay for it. If you do not surrender to Islam, then you will live to regret it. You will be shamed in Hell, forced to wear a garment of molten pitch forever!"

Ishaq:208 "When Allah gave permission to his Apostle to fight, the second Aqaba contained conditions involving war which were not in the first act of submission. Now we bound ourselves to war against all mankind for Allah and His Apostle. He promised us a reward in Paradise for faithful service. We pledged ourselves to war in complete obedience to Muhammad no matter how evil the circumstances."

Equipped with this information, you may form some important conclusions. Islamic politicos and clerics are purposely deceiving us. The truth isn't hidden, nor is it hard to find. Our media is clueless, willfully ignorant. And the cost is high. Good Muslims will continue to wage Jihad until we stop them by eliminating their means and motivation. If we don't, they will kill us.

As with the Nazis rolling into Poland following the "peace process" in 1930s Europe, the perpetrators of Islamic terror are inflamed by a violent and racist doctrine. They too have an agenda, and we are ignorant of it. If we had responded then as we do today, we'd be living on sushi and sauerkraut.

In these pages you will discover Islam's goals and read what it has to say about itself. You will see how violent conquest, racist genocide, and the spoils of war established the doctrine and turned a failed prophet into a world-renowned profiteer. I recognize that these words are incompatible with the prevailing wisdom of our politicians, religious leaders, and media. Yet the evidence is unambiguous and ubiquitous. The truth is undeniable.

Islam rises and falls on Muhammad. He is the doctrine's sole prophet, its lone founder, its god's singular conduit. Yet Islam's most revered books reveal that he was unqualified. By putting the Qur'an in chronological order, and by correlating it with the context of Muhammad's life as it was reported in the Sira, Sunnah, and Hadith, we find that Allah mirrored his prophet's character. The Islamic scriptures demonstrate that Allah was too dumb to be god and too immoral to be divine. While that may sound spiteful, it's true.

Since the world is awash in immorality and foolishness, I will strive to make this discussion germane, pertinent to our place and time. I will accomplish this by connecting the dots between today's terrorist acts and fundamentalist Islamic doctrine. But rest assured, I will not critique Islam based upon isolated verses pulled out of context. I will not expose it based upon the deeds of its followers. Within most doctrines there are meritorious words and as many examples of good deeds as there are bad. Such an endeavor would reveal more about me than this subject. Instead, I shall focus this entire debate upon what the Islamic scriptures have to say about the character and deeds of the religion's founder, his god, and his companions, the original "disciples" in Christian parlance. But fear not. You won't be cheated. Islam condemns Islam sufficiently to persuade even the most ardent skeptic.

If you're like most Americans, your defenses are raised the moment someone suggests that Islam might be responsible for Muslim militancy. You may think, as I once did, that all religions strike a balance between love and divine retribution, peace and punishment. But with Islam, that's simply not true. Their scriptures start out foolish, turn hateful, then punitive and violent.

There is almost no mention of peace, tolerance, or love. We have been played for fools. And it was easy because only an infinitesimally small percentage of "infidels" have taken the time to learn about Islam.

I wanted to know why Islamic terrorists thought killing us was good. Shouting *"Allahu Akbar!"* (Allah is Greatest) seemed like a confession, as did their parades. Muslims seemed ever ready to turn murderers into martyrs. Curious, I journeyed to the land of the suicide bombers. There, I asked a Mossad agent to arrange a meeting with a member of Force 17 (Arafat's Secret Service). This man in turn arranged for me to meet the actual terrorists—al Qaeda, Hamas, Islamic Jihad, al-Aqsa Martyrs' Brigade—so that I could ask them directly—eyeball to gun barrel—why they killed. He did, I asked, and they told me, "Islam." The terrorists said, "We are following Muhammad's example, just obeying Allah's orders." In my presence, blood dripping from their hands, they recited their prophet's speeches. They confessed—no, bragged—about those they had just murdered for the good of their cause.

Now more curious than ever, I found copies of the five oldest Islamic books and spent two years studying Muhammad and his message. What I found was bone chilling. The depiction of the prophet by the most revered Muslim sources is horrendous. Nearly every page reveals behavior that is immoral, criminal, and violent. I soon learned just how fortunate we are that most Muslims don't follow in the footsteps of Muhammad—that most don't know their prophet, their religion, their scriptures, or their history very well. If they did, and followed Islam, the whole world would be enveloped in war.

Over a billion people are slaves to Islam. The word means submission. Their scriptures order them to obey prophet, cleric, and king. As a result, Muslims in Islamic nations live with no freedoms of thought, speech, press, or religion. Unemployment, poverty, and despair run rampant. Every aspect of a Muslim's life is controlled by Islamic despots, Islamic law, Islamic scripture, Islamic education, and Islamic culture. Women are treated more harshly and awarded fewer rights than Americans give their animals. Muhammad gave men the liberty to beat their wives. Everyone is indoctrinated with the same message of religious intolerance, racial hatred, and violence. They hear it from their dictators, from their media, from their teachers, and clerics. A collusion of influences has annihilated truth and shut out reason.

With their words, Muslims tell Westerners that they and their religion are peace loving. But this is because their holy books order them to deceive us. They are told to tell us "peace" until it's too late. America's president seems to have taken their bait, and the media doesn't seem to care. Yet Islamic history, both ancient and modern, shouts out an entirely different story. So which do you believe? If their words are true, why do you suppose they kill us?

The answer is as clear as the skies over Pearl Harbor, as blatant as *blitzkrieg*. What did the insignias on the planes and tanks tell us? People don't kill for fun; they don't attack without reason. They must be motivated to risk their lives for a cause. If the bombers are suicidal, death must be more profitable than living. Someone must inspire people to hate, train them, finance them, equip them, and help them plan their dastardly deeds. The culture, doctrine, and people that aid in the execution of terror must have something to gain from causing the deaths of others. And well they do. Islam is about power, control, and money. It has always been about power, control, and money.

Terror isn't easy, nor is it cheap. The culture necessary to breed terrorists is extreme. It requires tight controls, total complicity, and years of unceasing indoctrination. If we wish to survive, we must come to understand Islam—a dogma capable of corrupting men to such a degree they believe mass murder is a ticket to paradise. Ignorance of this deception isn't tolerance. Acceptance isn't compassion. Appeasement will not lead to peace any more than accommodating the "Divine Wind" of the Kamikaze suicide bombers would have advanced world harmony.

All right. I've done a lot of talking. It's time I asked you a tough question. What do all the Islamic states that recruit, indoctrinate, finance, harbor, train, equip, motivate, and reward terrorists have in common? Too easy? Then I have another question. If the answer is so obvious, why is everybody afraid to say it? Our political leaders are sworn to defend us. The media's primary responsibility is to ferret out truth. The truth is obvious, accessible, and rationally irrefutable. So why?

Why do we continue to fund our own funeral? Why do we frisk little old ladies at airports while we stand by and watch our enemies develop nuclear and biological capability? Why did we push al-Qaeda out of Afghanistan into Pakistan, the only Islamic nation with nuclear weapons? Why did we fight a relatively meaningless megalomaniac in Iraq by forming alliances with the nations most responsible for manufacturing the actual terrorists who killed us? Who is responsible for this shameful state of affairs?

We are. We get the government we deserve. Surrounded by information, we entertain ourselves with toys and sound bites. The answer to the most deadly question of our time isn't hidden. The evidence is all around us.

During the promotional campaign for my first book on Islam, *Tea With Terrorists*, I sent every major media outlet and spokesperson a press kit. The opening paragraph asked the following questions: "Don't you suppose that the Chechen Muslims who laid siege to the Moscow theater shared something with those who bombed the Bali nightclub and the Kenyan hotel? Don't you think there might be a connection between the sniper Muhammad and the prophet Muhammad? Could the suicide bombers in Israel have the same spiritual leader as the suicide bombers of 9/11? Why have Islamic terrorists in Iraq killed more Americans than the Republican Guard? Where do you suppose these Muslim militants get their marching orders? Might al-Qaeda,

Jemaah Islamiyah, Hamas, Hezbollah, Islamic Jihad, the Muslim Brotherhood, and the Taliban be following the same prophet?"

Later that same week, Osama bin Laden issued a press release of his own.
In it he answered my questions. He said the boys who attacked the nightclub,
theater, and hotel, as well as the suicide bombers in Israel and America were:
"good Muslims—zealous Islamic fighters following Muhammad's example."
Bin Laden was telling us who the terrorists really are and why they kill, yet we
missed the message. Not a single media outlet tied these things together.

Everyone went about their business obfuscating reality. They called the
Muslims who murdered us radicals, militants, insurgents, extremists, or simply terrorists. Why are we so afraid to speak the truth? Here's a clue: on top
of one of my press releases, a South Palm Beach radio host wrote this note
in her prettiest handwriting. "I wouldn't promote your version of Islam even
if I was an evangelical Christian on my death bed." Those who are paid to
keep us informed have put their popularity and financial well being ahead of
saving lives. And while this is symptomatic of why we are ignorant, I don't
have a "version" of Islam. The only Islam I know is the one found in the
Qur'an, the one preached by the imams and sheiks, the one promoted in the
Islamic media, the one presented by the first Muslim scholars Ibn Ishaq and
al-Tabari, the one recorded in the Hadith Collections of al-Bukhari and Muslim, the one Muhammad himself lived and taught, the one terrorists like
Osama bin Laden practice. It isn't my version of Islam; it's *theirs*.

How do you suppose Islam could be any different than the religion lived
by its sole prophet, Muhammad? How could it differ from the doctrine
espoused by its deity, Allah? If Islam's prophet and god got Islam wrong—
who, pray tell, has it right? I have no interest in interpreting Islam. I simply
want to expose it. I'm a reporter, doing the job the media should have done.
And I have a singular motivation. I want to save Muslims from Islam and
thereby save Christians and Jews from Muslims.

Yes, I know. Religions are supposed to be good. Most religious prophets
are fine fellows, not terrorists, so all of this is a little hard to swallow. But one
was a terrorist. Muhammad assassinated more journalists than any modern
militant. He financed his religion entirely through piracy and the slave trade.
This prophet was a genocidal maniac. Worse still, his "god" condoned terrorism, piracy, plunder, racism, genocide, deception, and assassination. Allah
ordered his followers to kill us—and they did. The evidence screams out from
the pages of the Qur'an and Hadith Collections of al-Tabari, Ibn Ishaq, al-
Bukhari, and Muslim.

The case against Islam is a lay-down hand. The paper trail, their scripture,
points directly to Islam's lone prophet. The blood evidence, both fresh and
ancient, leads directly to Muhammad. We even have confessions—thousands
of them. In the Qur'an, Allah commands Muslims to "wipe the infidels out

to the last." Allah isn't the least bit ambiguous. In the Hadith, Muhammad says, "Kill any Jew who falls under your control. Kill them, for he who kills them will get a great reward." Today's terrorists are simply following their religion as it was originally conceived. Confronted with the evidence, one has to commit intellectual suicide to avoid seeing Islam as complicit in terror.

The truth is obvious: the terrorists haven't corrupted their religion. Islam has corrupted them. The murderers are following their prophet's example. And while most Muslims aren't terrorists, all the really good ones are. They haven't corrupted Islam any more than the S.S. corrupted Nazism or the Kamikazes corrupted the culture of Imperial Japan. We have been fighting a war against the symptoms, not the source.

The Nation of Islam has been at war with everyone, including itself, for 1,400 years. You'll see why Muslims celebrate their "victories," no matter how many innocents perish. You'll learn why their state-controlled media promotes terror. You'll know why their state-controlled schools teach hate. It will become evident why imams encourage martyrdom and jihad. And if that were not bad enough, consider this: our oil money pays for it all.

The five oldest and most trusted Islamic sources don't portray Muhammad as a great and godly man. They reveal that he was a thief, a liar, an assassin, a pedophile, a womanizer, a rapist, a mass murderer, a pirate, a warmonger, and a scheming and ruthless politician. It's hardly the character profile of a religious leader. Gandhi he was not.

Islamic scholar Dr. D.S. Margoliouth sums up Muhammad in a paragraph that may seem shocking now. But once you've completed your journey through Islam's earliest scriptures, these words will appear tame: "The character attributed to Muhammad in the biography of Ibn Ishaq is exceedingly unfavorable. In order to gain his ends Muhammad recoils from no expedient, and he approves of similar unscrupulousness on the part of his adherents, when exercised in his interest. He organizes assassinations and wholesale massacres. His career as the tyrant of Medina is that of a robber chief whose political economy consists of securing and dividing plunder. He is himself an unbridled libertine [morally or sexually unrestrained] and encourages the same passion in his followers. For whatever he does he is prepared to plead the express authorization of his deity. It is, however, impossible to find any Islamic religious doctrine which he is not prepared to abandon in order to secure a political end. At different points in his career he abandons the unity of God and his claim to the title of Prophet. This is a disagreeable picture for the founder of a religion, and it cannot be pleaded that it is a picture drawn by an enemy."

According to the Hadith and Qur'an, Muhammad and his henchmen plundered their way to power and prosperity. Their bloody conquests rivaled those of the Assyrians, Genghis Khan, Attila the Hun, and more recently Adolf Hitler. But Muhammad's murderous behavior didn't begin until he was halfway through his career. Therefore, I will address words and deeds that were simply foolish and immoral long before we arrive at those that were lethal. Yet it is not the immorality or foolishness of Islam that motivate me to share its story. It is Muhammad's legacy of terror. So as not to lose sight of that reality, I'd like to present a handful of stories that depict what Islam did to the first Muslims.

Muhammad became so afraid of being exposed, he ordered his followers to assassinate anyone who criticized him. The first was a poet named Ashraf. In an illiterate society, poets were the journalists of their day. Their words swayed public opinion. Ashraf recognized that pirate and prophet were divergent career paths, and he had the courage to say so. This Hadith is from Bukhari's Collection, Volume 4, Book 52, Number 270: *Bukhari:V4B52N270* **"Allah's Messenger said, 'Who is ready to kill Ashraf? He has said injurious things about Allah and His Apostle.' Maslama got up saying, 'Would you like me to kill him?' The Prophet proclaimed, 'Yes.' Maslama said, 'Then allow me to lie so that I will be able to deceive him.' Muhammad said, 'You may do so.'"** Islam gives Muslims a license to lie and kill.

We pick up the story on page 94 of the History of al-Tabari, Volume VII. My shorthand for this passage is: *Tabari VII:94.* **"Ashraf suspected no evil when Maslama cried, 'Smite the enemy of Allah!' So they smote him, and their swords clashed over him. Maslama said, 'I remembered my dagger and I seized it. I thrust it into the lower part of his body. I bore down upon it until I reached his genitals. Allah's enemy fell to the ground.'"**

Ishaq revealed this in the Sira, or biography, of Muhammad: *Ishaq:368* **"We carried his head back to Muhammad during the night, saluted the Prophet as he stood praying, and cast Ashraf's head before his feet. The Prophet praised Allah that the poet had been slain, and complimented us on the good work we had done in Allah's Cause. Our attack upon Allah's enemy cast terror among the Jews, and there was no Jew in Medina who did not fear for his life.'"** Murder and terror are Islam's "good works."

Ishaq:368 **"Ashraf's body was left prostrate. After his fall, all of the Jews were brought low. Sword in hand we cut him down. By Muhammad's order we were sent secretly to his home by night. Brother killing brother. We lured him to his demise with deviousness. We made him taste death with our deadly swords. We sought victory for the religion of the Prophet."** *Tabari VII:97* **"The morning after the murder of Ashraf, the Prophet declared, 'Kill any Jew who falls under your power.'"**

Ishaq:369 **"Thereupon Mas'ud leapt upon Sunayna, one of the Jewish merchants with whom his family had social and commercial relations and killed him. The Muslim's brother complained, saying, 'Why did you kill him? You have much fat in you belly from his charity.' Mas'ud answered, 'By Allah, had Muhammad ordered me to murder you, my brother, I would have cut off your head.' Wherein the brother said, 'Any religion that can bring you to this is indeed wonderful!'"**

This man was crediting the religion of Islam for transforming his brother into an unthinking killing machine. The motivation was purely racist: *Bukhari:V1B1N6* **"Just issue orders to kill every Jew in the country."** Innocent blood still dripping from his hands, Mas'ud proclaimed for all the world to hear: "Muhammad ordered me to murder." Today's terrorists haven't corrupted their religion; their religion has corrupted them.

While hideous, this act does not stand alone. Soon thereafter, Muhammad ordered Muslims to assassinate Sallam. Tabari, Islam's earliest historian, explains: *Tabari VII:101* **"They asked the Prophet for permission to kill Sallam. He granted it."** *Tabari VII:99* **"When they got to Khaybar they went to Sallam's house by night, having locked every door in the settlement on the inhabitants. He was in an upper chamber. His wife came out and asked who we were. We told her that we were Arabs in search of supplies. She told us that her husband was in bed. We entered and bolted his door. His wife shrieked and warned him of us, so we ran at him with our swords as he lay on his bed. When we had smitten him Abdallah bore down his sword into his belly until it went right through him. 'By the God of the Jews, he is dead!' Never have I heard sweeter words than those. We returned to Allah's Apostle and told him that we had killed his enemy. We disputed before him as to who had killed him, each of us laying claim to the deed. Muhammad demanded to see our swords and when he looked at them he said, 'It is the sword of Abdallah that killed him; I can see traces of food on it.'"** Deceiving victims is still standard operating procedure for Muslim militants. Attacking defenseless civilians is the very definition of terror. And so is gloating. Today's Islamic terrorists are as eager as Muhammad's original henchmen to claim "credit" for their deeds.

Ishaq's Sira recounts a third Muhammad-inspired execution: *Ishaq: 308* **"Halfway to Medina, Ocba was called out to be executed."** Since the other prisoners were being held for ransom, Ocba asked Muhammad why he was being treated more harshly than the other captives. **"The Prophet said, 'Because of your enmity to Allah and to his Prophet.' 'And my little girl,' cried Ocba in bitterness, 'who will take care of her?' 'Hell Fire,' Muhammad responded. At that moment he was decapitated. 'Wretch that you were, [Muhammad eulogized] you scoffed at me and claimed that your stories were better than mine. I give thanks that Allah has slain you and comforted me.'"** Allah condoned the murder in the 8th surah of the Qur'an, the 68th verse: *008.068* **"It has not been for any prophet to take captives until he has slaughtered in the land."**

Allah approved kidnapping for ransom so long as his prophet slaughtered first. Ocba said something Muslims didn't like, so they murdered him. No wonder authors, journalists, and politicians are afraid to critique Islam.

Looking to rob a Jewish community for a second time, Muhammad had one of his militants torture an innocent man. The tale is recounted by Ishaq and Tabari. *Tabari VIII:122/Ishaq:515* **"The Prophet gave orders concerning Kinanah to Zubayr, saying, 'Torture him until you root out and extract what he has. So Zubayr kindled a fire on Kinanah's chest, twirling it with his firestick until Kinanah was near death. Then the Messenger gave him to Maslamah, who beheaded him."** *Bukhari:V4B54N487* **"The Prophet** said, 'The Hell Fire is 69 times hotter than ordinary worldly fires.' So someone said, 'Allah's Apostle, wouldn't this ordinary fire have been sufficient to torture non-Muslims?'"

You will soon discover that the Nazi fuhrer and the Islamic prophet had more in common than just using fire to eradicate Jews. Beginning in the "Mein Kampf" chapter I will compare Hitler's Manifesto with Muhammad's so that you might know how stunningly similar they are. By so doing, you'll come to appreciate the consequence of tolerating Islam.

Let's look at one more example. Ishaq's Sira speaks of the murder of another journalist, Asma bint Marwan. She spoke critically of Muhammad, telling her tribe to be wary of him. *Ishaq: 676* "'You obey a stranger who encourages you to murder for booty. You are greedy men. Is there no honor among you?' Upon hearing those lines Muhammad said, 'Will no one rid me of this woman?' Umayr, a zealous Muslim, decided to execute the Prophet's wishes. That very night he crept into the writer's home while she lay sleeping surrounded by her young children. There was one at her breast. Umayr removed the suckling babe and then plunged his sword into the poet. The next morning in the mosque, Muhammad, who was aware of the assassination, said, 'You have helped Allah and His Apostle.' Umayr said, 'She had five sons; should I feel guilty?' 'No,' the Prophet answered. 'Killing her was as meaningless as two goats butting heads.'"

These events are but a handful among hundreds of horrific tales of barbarism described in the Islamic Hadith. Many are far worse and include the enslavement of children, rape, and mass murder.

What you are going to read from Islam's most holy books will begin as laughable; the creation accounts are dimwitted to the point of being delirious. The religion's desperate grope to convolute the lives and times of Biblical patriarchs to establish a sense of legitimacy for its scriptures, shrine, rituals, god, and prophet is pathetic. As the chronology marches on you'll meet Qusayy, Muhammad's great, great, great grandfather, and discover how he invented the five pillars of Islam as a mystic scam.

The story gets particularly interesting at this point as we uncover what Islam has to say about its prophet's abused childhood. As a result, Islam, by its own admission, becomes a money-making scheme. Everything is driven by an unquenchable thirst for revenge and a man-sized lust for power, control, sex, money, and praise. And that's not my opinion, or even an interpretation; it's what the Islamic scriptures say. Then the religion becomes very dark. Muhammad's first Qur'anic revelations are demonic, fixated on disgusting depictions of hell, devils called jinn, pain, and punishment. And that's the *good* part. The moment Muhammad and his gang slither out of Mecca, they pick up the sword and never put it down. What you are going to read from the Islamic scriptures will shake you to your core—you will be revolted and terrified—especially if you're a Muslim.

And that is the purpose of *Prophet of Doom*. I want the world to know Muhammad, Allah, and Islam as they are presented in their scriptures. But that's easier said than done. While the average terrorist knows the Qur'an and Hadith nearly as well as I do, the vast majority of Muslims do not. Peaceful Muslims have been fed a fictitious picture of their prophet and god—one that's wholly inconsistent with their own scriptures. Clerics have lied to them just as they have lied to us. Yet, as I discovered in my meetings with them, the Jihadists have memorized the verses you are going to read. So if we want to know why they kill and how to stop them, we must come to understand them too. Otherwise we're flailing at the wind, spilling blood and coin while they grow more resolute.

The Qur'an may be the worst book ever written. It is jumbled together haphazardly. It's almost as if verses were tossed into the air, blown by the wind, and then pieced together as they were plucked from the sand. The 1st surah, or chapter, was never revealed, and it's written in the wrong voice. The 2nd surah was the ninety-first received chronologically, yet it is the first revelation in the Qur'an. The 5th surah was the last in order of alleged revelation. Muhammad claims that his initial inspiration can be found in the 96th surah, which means Allah's initial salvo is tucked in the back of the book.

Unrelated subjects are brought together without intelligent transitions. Allah's book lacks context as well. It does not explain who is talking to whom or even when or where its narratives took place. But that's not the worst of it. The Qur'an is so poorly written that one in five verses makes no sense in any language. This is why Muslims don't want it translated out of Religious Arabic —a language few understand.

And that's not the end of the bad news. Much of the Qur'an is plagiarized from uninspired Jewish writings, most often from the Talmud. Allah's book is repetitive to a fault. The same stories are retold dozens of times. There are countless contradictions and a plethora of scientific and historical errors. What's more, the Qur'an's message is immoral. Allah approves incest, rape, lying, thievery, deception, slavery, torture, mass murder—even terrorism.

The Qur'an begins as a mean-spirited rant. The eye witnesses, the men and women who knew Muhammad and Islam far better than anyone today, said things like: *Qur'an 38:3* **"The disbelievers say, 'This (Prophet Muhammad) is a sorcerer, a charlatan, a wizard telling lies. He has made the alihah (gods) into one Ilah (God). This is a curious and strange thing to be sure!' Their leaders said, 'Walk away from him...there is surely some motive behind this—something sought after—a thing he has designed against us...It is surely a forgery.'"** Allah responded by threatening: *Qur'an 38:8* **"Nay, but they are in doubt about My Reminder (this Qur'an). Nay, but they have not tasted (My) Torment yet! They will be one more army vanquished among the many routed hordes.... They rejected my Messengers so My Torment is justified."** This same rant is played out nearly four hundred times. *Qur'an 74:21* **"Again, woe to them; may they be cursed for how** they plotted. They looked around, frowned, and scowled with displeasure. Then they turned back and were haughty with pride. They said, 'This is nothing but magical enchantment, derived and narrated from others. This is nothing but the words of a mortal man!'"

The Qur'an's most repetitive theme—one detailed no less than one thousand times—is a derivative of this rejection. Allah threatens all who deny Muhammad and Islam: *Qur'an 85:10* "Those who try or tempt the believers will have the penalty of Hell. They will have the doom of the burning fire. Verily, the Seizure of the Lord is severe and painful.... Allah will encompass them from behind! He will punish them. Nay! This is a Glorious Qur'an." *Qur'an 13:32* "Many an Apostle have they mocked before you; but I seized them. How awful was My punishment then! ...The unbelievers plot, but for them is torment in this life and a far more severe torture in Hell." *Qur'an 2:23* "If you are in doubt of what We have revealed to Our Messenger, then bring a surah like this, and call any witnesses apart from Allah. But you cannot, as indeed you cannot guard yourselves against the Hell Fire whose fuel is men and rocks, which has been prepared for the infidels."

If the endless rant and demented threats were all that there was to the Qur'an, you could safely put down this book and ignore Allah's foolishness. But I'm afraid I have some very bad news. The Qur'an's last twenty-four surahs chronologically, those revealed in Medina, are a call to arms. They are merciless. In them Allah says things like: *Qur'an 9:88* "The Messenger and those who believe with him, strive hard and fight with their wealth and lives in Allah's Cause." *Qur'an 9:5* "Fight and kill the disbelievers wherever you find them, take them captive, torture them, lie in wait and ambush them using every stratagem of war." *Qur'an 9:112* "The Believers fight in Allah's Cause, they slay and are slain, kill and are killed." *Qur'an 9:29* "Fight those who do not believe until they all surrender, paying the protective tax in submission." As horrible as that sounds, it gets worse. Allah claims personal responsibility for terrorism, mass murder, enslaving women and children, deception, and thievery.

Arguably, Islam's most revealing book is the Sira, not the Qur'an. The Sira provides the *lone* account of Muhammad's life and the formation of Islam written within *two centuries* of the prophet's death. It provides the context and chronology the Qur'an requires. Unfortunately, there is no surviving copy of Ishaq's manuscript called: *Sirat Rasul Allah.* Therefore, Muslims are dependant upon a significantly edited and abridged account by Hisham. His sanitized version of Muhammad's words, dogma, and deeds was translated by Guillaume under the title *The Life of Muhammad* in 1955 and published by Oxford Press.

Ishaq's biography paints an unflatering portrait of Islam's unique prophet. I include thousands of Sira quotations in *Prophet of Doom.* Each references Ishaq's name as well as the page number the specific Hadith is recorded in Guillaume's English translation of Hisham's edits of Ishaq's Sira.

The *History of al-Tabari* is by common consent the most important and earliest universal history produced in the world of Islam. It is written conversationally by piecing together Islamic Hadith, or oral reports, from the men and women who lived with Muhammad and became his companions. While each Tradition comes complete with a chain of transmitters, called an *isnad*, I have omitted the long list of Arabic names, as they serve no purpose. Islamic scholars believe that these Hadith reveal inspired behavior that should be emulated. They claim the revelations themselves were inspired by Allah, and thus are scripture. Collectively, the chronological Hadith Collections brought to us by Ishaq and Tabari form the Sunnah. The Sunnah provides the basis of Islam's rituals, behaviors, laws, and conquests.

Although the entire al-Tabari series of thirty-eight volumes was translated and published by the State University of New York Press, you will find volumes I, II, VI, VII, VIII, and IX to be the most revealing. They deal with Islamic creation, the Jewish patriarchs, Mecca before and during Muhammad's day, and the rise of Islam in Medina. All Tabari quotations in *Prophet of Doom* include Tabari's name as well as the S.U.N.Y. Press volume and page number upon which the specific Hadith can be found. My review of Islam ends with Muhammad's death, and thus the remaining volumes which chronicle the Islamic conquests of Arabia, the Middle East, Africa, Europe, and Asia, fall outside the scope of this volume.

Al-Bukhari's Hadith is second only to the Qur'an in importance to many Muslims. It is comprised of what scholars consider to be the most authentic Traditions associated with early Islam and the words of Muhammad. Its Hadith are organized by subject: *Book of Taxes, Book of Raids*, and *Book of Jihad* are examples. An online Bukhari translation by Muhsin Khan opens with these words: **"Sahih Bukhari is a collection of sayings and deeds of Prophet Muhammad, also known as the Sunnah. The reports of the Prophet's sayings and deeds are called Hadith. Bukhari lived a couple of centuries after the Prophet's death and worked to collect his Hadith. Each report in his collection was checked for compatibility with the Qur'an, and the veracity of the chain of reporters, or isnad, had to be painstakingly established. Bukhari's collection is recognized by the overwhelming majority of Muslims as one of the most authentic collections of Muhammad's Sunnah."**

Finally, there is Muslim's collection. His work is complementary to Bukhari, as he was one of his students. Together these four books give the Qur'an the context it otherwise lacks, and they give Muslims the religious rites, rituals, and rules they would otherwise do without. In fact, Islam's Five Pillars would not exist without the Hadith, and the Qur'an would be indecipherable.

Speaking of the Qur'an, I encourage you to buy several because translations differ. I have elected to combine five into a blended version for the purpose of communicating the nuances of an ancient, and little understood, language into contemporary English. These include: Ahmed Ali, Pikthal, Noble by Khan, Yusuf Ali, and Shakir. I have corrected Allah's grammar, pruned his unruly repetitions, and tried to identify many of his dangling modifiers. There are so many missing and meaningless words, I have left within parenthesis the additions Arabic translators made because without them Allah's

message is hopelessly muddled. Fortunately, by ordering the Qur'an chronologically, and by setting it in the context of the Islamic Sunnah, I believe its
message has never been as clear as it is in these pages.

Trying to hide the Qur'an's hostile and vile message, Muslim clerics claim
that it cannot be translated. But that's nonsense. They simply don't want anyone to know what Allah's book actually says. They know it's unworthy, hateful, violent, and intolerant. The Qur'an is very nasty; it's dimwitted, demonic,
and deceitful. It promotes immorality and inspires terror.

That is not to say that the Qur'an is completely void of rational thought.
About five percent of it, taken out of context and mistranslated, can be mis-
construed as peaceful and tolerant. For example, Qur'an 5:32 says: "On that
account: We ordained for the Children of Israel that if anyone slew a person—unless it be
in retaliation for murder or for spreading mischief in the land—it would be as if he slew all
mankind: and if anyone saved a life, it would be as if he saved the life of all humanity."
That sounds good until you realize that the line was plagiarized verbatim
from the *Mishnah Sanhedrin* and that it's followed by Qur'an 5:33: "The punishment for those who wage war against Allah and His Messenger and who do mischief
[non-Islamic behavior] in the land is only that they shall be killed or crucified, or their
hands and their feet shall be cut off on opposite sides, or they shall be exiled. That is their
disgrace in this world, and a dreadful torment is theirs in Hell."

Muslim apologists say that the Qur'an is tolerant because it says: 005.069
"Those who believe (in the Qur'an), those who follow the Jewish (Scriptures), and Christians
—whoever believes in God and the Last Day, and does right—on them shall be no fear, nor
shall they grieve." But this verse correctly translated says "whoever believes in
Allah...shall not fear or grieve."

Further, it must be plucked from its context, as it's surrounded by verses
which proclaim: Qur'an 5:13 "But because of their breach of their covenant We cursed the
Jews and made their hearts grow hard. They change words from their (right) places [the
illiterate prophet pronounced] and forget a good part of the message that was sent them.
Nor will you cease to find deceit in them." 005.014 "From those, too, who call themselves
Christians, We made a covenant, but they forgot a good part of the message that was sent
them so we estranged them, stirred up enmity and hatred among them." 005.017 "Say: 'Who
has the least power against Allah, if His will were to destroy Christ, the Messiah and everyone else on the earth?" 005.037 "The [Christian] disbelievers will long to get out of the Fire,
but never will they get out; theirs will be an enduring torture."

This next verse also sounds tolerant, at least until you read what follows:
Qur'an 5:46 "And in their footsteps We sent Jesus, the son of Mary, confirming the Law that
had come before him. We sent him the Gospel: therein was guidance and light, and confirmation of the Law that had come before him." 005.049 "Judge between them by what Allah
has revealed and follow not their [Christian] desires, but beware of them lest they beguile
you, seducing you away from any of that which Allah has sent down to you. And if they turn
you away [from Islam], be assured that for their crime it is Allah's purpose to smite them."

005.051 "Believers, take not Jews and Christians for friends." *005.059* "Say: 'People of the Book! Do you disapprove of us because we believe in Allah, and the revelation that has come to us?' Say: 'Shall I point out to you something much worse than this by the treatment it received from Allah? Those who incurred the curse of Allah and His wrath, those Jews He transformed into apes and swine." *005.072* "They are surely infidels who blaspheme and say: 'God is Christ, the Messiah.' But the Messiah only said: 'Children of Israel! Worship Allah.' Lo! Whoever joins other gods with Allah or says He has a partner, Allah has forbidden Paradise, and Hell will be his abode." *005.073* "They are surely disbelievers who blaspheme and say: 'God is one of three in the Trinity for there is no ilah (god) except One, Allah. If they desist not from saying this, verily a grievous penalty will befall them."

Allah's only interest in Christians and Jews is in tormenting them in hell. *Qur'an 98:1* "Those among the People of the Book who disbelieve would never have been freed from their false religion if the Clear Proofs had not come to them. An Apostle of Allah came reading out of hallowed pages, containing firm decrees.... They were commanded to serve Allah exclusively, fulfilling their devotional obligations, and paying the zakat tax. Surely the unbelievers from the People of the Book will abide in the Hell Fire. They are the worst of creatures." The Qur'an's message is intolerant, hateful, and violent.

There is another reason Muslim clerics and kings don't want the Qur'an translated. By so doing, their biggest deception dissolves. Muslims protest that Allah is simply the Arabic word for God and that we all worship the same spirit. But that's simply not true. The Qur'an says that "Ilah" is the Arabic word for "God" and that "Allah" is his name. *Qur'an 3:62* "This is the true explanation: There is no Ilah (God) except Allah." *Qur'an 52:43* "Have they an ilah (god) other than Allah?" *Qur'an 5:4* "Pronounce the Name of Allah, and fear Allah." *Qur'an 21:107* "Say: 'It is revealed to me that your Ilah (God) is only one Ilah (God)." *Qur'an 20:8* "Allah! There is no Ilah (God) save Him." *Qur'an 20:14* "Verily, I am Allah. No Ilah (God) may be worshiped but I." *Qur'an 20:97* "Your Ilah (God) is Allah: there is no Ilah (God) but He." *Qur'an 59:22* "Allah is He, no other Ilah (God) may be worshiped; He is Allah, Whom there is no other Ilah (God)."

This is important because the Judeo-Christian God, the God of the Bible, has a name: Yahweh. Not only isn't Allah Yahweh, his character could not be more opposed. Allah is a very nasty and deceptive fellow. *Qur'an 4:142* "Surely the hypocrites strive to deceive Allah. He shall retaliate by deceiving them." *Qur'an 68:44* "Then leave Me alone with such as reject this Message and call Our pronouncements a lie. Systematically by degrees, step by step, We shall punish them in ways they can not even imagine." *Qur'an 89:23* "For His [Allah's] chastisement will be such as no other can inflict. None punishes as He will punish! None can bind as He will bind."

Qur'an 64:11 "No calamity occurs, no affliction comes, except by the decision and preordainment of Allah." *Qur'an 96:15* "Let him beware! If he does not desist, We will seize him, smite his forehead, and drag him by the forelock! Then, We will call on the angels of punishment to deal with him!" *Qur'an 74:15* "They have offered stubborn opposition to Our Signs. Soon I will visit them with a mountain of calamities, imposing a distressing punishment. For men thought and plotted; woe to them! They shall be cursed." *Qur'an 74:26* "Soon will I

fling them into the burning Hell Fire! It permits nothing to endure, and nothing does it spare! It darkens the color of man, burning the skin! It shrivels and scorches men." *Qur'an 88:1* **"Some faces (all disbelievers, Jews and Christians) will be humiliated and scorched by the burning fire, while they are made to drink boiling water."** *Qur'an 18:108* **"Verily We have prepared Hell for the hospitality of the Infidels; Hell is for the disbeliever's entertainment."** No. We do not worship the same God, nor follow the same prophet.

To better understand the nature of Islam's dark spirit, to grasp his twisted, mean, and violent message, I encourage you to browse the "Muhammad's Own Words" appendix as time permits. You may want to begin with what the "Eye Witnesses" had to say as their testimony was remarkably accurate. Their view of Muhammad, Allah, and Islam is identical to my own. If you think Islam is peaceful, read quotes from the Fighting, Terror, War, Jihad, Martyrs, and Militants sections first. If you think Islam is religious, start with the Thievery, Murder, Torture, Deception, Megalomania, Money, and Lust categories. If you think Islam is tolerant, you should scan quotations under Intolerance, Jews, Christians, Women, and Racism. If you think we all worship the same God, read Demons, Allah, Ar Rahman, Hell, Paradise, No Choice, Stupidity, Islamic Science, and Allah's Astronomy.

If you have the time and fortitude, dive into the world of Islamic scholarship. The best research was conducted by Arthur Jeffery, D.S. Margoliouth, Sir W. Muir, Patricia Crone, F.E. Peters, Ernest Renan, Joseph Schacht, and John Wansbrough. For a little lighter reading, try Sir John Glubbs' *The Life and Times of Muhammad* or Mark Gabriel's *Islam and Terrorism*.

If you haven't done so already, familiarize yourself with the Judeo-Christian Scriptures because Islam is based upon twisted Bible stories. At the very least read Genesis and Matthew so you're in a position to judge whether the original or the Islamicized version is more credible. While the Bible is unphased by Islam, for the Qur'an to be true the Torah must both be inspired by God and be wrong on every page. Also, consider reading at least one book on Bible archeology. Understanding the Bible's historic roots is essential if you wish to render an informed decision about the Qur'an's variant claims.

Recognizing that most people don't have the will, time, or means to invest 10,000 hours into the study of Islam, I have done the heavy lifting for you. I have distilled Islam's five earliest books into one. And rather than taking them out of context, I have organized them chronologically and woven them together. You will see Muhammad, Allah, and Islam as they really are. So that there would be no confusion, I printed their words in **bold** and my comments in standard type. You are free to read their words alone, interpreting them yourself. Or you can see them as I do.

So that you might appreciate the consequence of ignoring Islam, I have included sections comparing the Islamic scriptures to Hitler's *Mein Kampf*. Formed as a religion to inspire martyrdom, Nazism caused the worst war in human history. Yet apart from time and place, Islam and Nazism are indistinguishable. Quotations from *Mein Kampf* are *italicized* so that they might be distinguished from the Islamic scriptures.

As you read *Prophet of Doom* you will begin to question the validity of the Islamic sources. The Hadith and Qur'an are so errant historically, logically, and scientifically, you'll think that I am quoting from sources hostile to Islam rather than from its most revered scriptures. When you come to that point, I encourage you to visit the "Source Material" appendix. It is a scholarly review of the works that comprise Islam, their inspiration, history, and authority. This analysis will be particularly helpful for Muslims, since their imams have lied to them about the nature of their scriptures.

Most rational men and women will conclude that a god who is principally vengeful, forgetful, contradictory, and irrational might not be a god after all. But why should we care? It's a free world and Muslims are entitled to their beliefs. What's more, Christians at times have behaved no better. Who are we to cast stones? The fact is, Muslims are killing us, and they will continue to kill us until we have the good sense to understand the doctrine that drives them to such behavior. Besides, the Muslim world isn't free. It has never been free.

Okay, so Muslims aren't free. So what? Why are their problems our problems? Because we are free. We have the opportunity and responsibility to diagnose this disease before it consumes our life, liberty, and prosperity as it has theirs. So fasten your seatbelt. It's time to expose Islam.

Bukhari:V4B52N50 **"Muhammad said, 'A single endeavor of fighting in Allah's Cause is better than the world and whatever is in it.'"** Fighting is not only considered good, it's Islam's best deed.

Bukhari:V4B52N220 **"Allah's Apostle said, 'I have been made victorious with terror. The treasures of the world were brought to me and put in my hand.'"** Terror is Muhammad's legacy. His motivation was money.

Bukhari:V9B88N174 **"I heard the Prophet saying, 'Islam cannot change!'"** It can't be reformed. Islam remains mired in deceit, hate, and violence.

Bukhari:V4B52N260 **"The Prophet said, 'If a Muslim discards his religion, kill him.'"** This is why we must free Muslims from Islam. Without our help, death is their only way out.

Bukhari:V7B67N427 **"The Prophet said, 'If I take an oath and later find something else better than that, then I do what is better and expiate my oath.'"** Translated into common English, he just said, "I am a lying scumbag; you should not trust me."

1

WOULD YOU BELIEVE?

"When Allah wants to frighten his slaves, the sun falls out of its chariot. This is a full eclipse, a misfortune for the sun."

An overview might be helpful before we begin. Islam started when Muhammad, a seventh century Arab, purported to be the Messenger of God. That much we know for sure. The Qur'an, he claimed, was a series of revelations he received directly from a nameless Lord.

The inspirational experience was described by Muhammad to be like a bell, clanging in his head, causing him to shake and sweat profusely. These rather nasty experiences continued, he said, until he was able to decipher the message. Thus the Qur'an, Muslims believe, is God's revelation to man through his final and most important prophet.

Yet only Muhammad heard these "revelations." He offered no evidence of his divine inspiration—we take the Qur'an solely on his word. The Bible, by comparison, had forty authors, all literate, who told a consistent story over the course of fifteen centuries. Muhammad, who was admittedly illiterate, acted alone in the formation of Islam and is alleged to have invented his religion over the course of twenty-two years.

Over a billion people live in nations controlled by Islamic principles. Thus to many, Muhammad was a rousing success. Yet these very same nations are among the world's most destitute, least free, and most violent. And they are the fountain of terror, providing the money, men, motive, and means for murder. In that light, Muhammad's legacy is considerably more tarnished.

There were no miracles to prove Muhammad's claim of being a godly conduit. There were no healings, walking on water, parting seas, raising folks from the dead, or feeding multitudes. And there are no fulfilled prophecies, like the exacting and detailed predictions that Biblical prophets routinely made to demonstrate their divine authority. But the most troubling part about our absolute reliance on Muhammad's testimony that he and his Qur'an were divinely inspired is that the prophet's character was as deficient, and his life was as despicable, as anyone who has ever lived.

That's not flattering, but it's the only rational conclusion that can be drawn from the original source material. According to the Qur'an and Sunnah, Muhammad founded Islam to rule over Arabs, Persians, and Byzantines, and through conquest, to steal their treasures. I will identify and quote thousands of verses from the Islamic scriptures to prove this, but for now, I want you to be an informed skeptic—one with a global view of Muhammad and his creation. This introductory summary will serve as a handrail in what is otherwise a topsy-turvy and disjointed realm. As we move through Muhammad's tortured Genesis accounts and convoluted recastings of Biblical patriarchs, you will need this perspective to comprehend his motives and agenda.

Over the course of these pages you'll discover that the prophet's "ministry" in Mecca was filled with troubling episodes. Following his first Qur'anic revelation, Muhammad claimed to have been demon possessed. By his own admission, he tried to commit suicide. Those who knew him best, his family and neighbors, said that he had gone mad. "He is a demon-possessed sorcerer fabricating scripture," they said, accusing him of plagiarism and of having purely selfish motives. They mocked his prophetic claims, ridiculed his Qur'an, and said that his preposterous notion of turning many pagan idols into the one God was insane. As a result of this verbal abuse, all chronicled in the Qur'an, Muhammad pledged to slaughter his kin.

With the Quraysh Bargain, the Meccans proved that Muhammad had established Islam to garner what he craved: power, sex, and money. The Satanic Verses, which followed, demonstrated that he was inspired by Lucifer, the Biblical Satan. Muhammad's hallucinogenic Night's Journey to the non-existent Temple in Jerusalem, confirmed that he could not be trusted. This flight of fancy was followed by the Pledge of Aqaba, where Islam turned political and declared war on all mankind.

Ninety Qur'an surahs were revealed during this period. They open with a score that mirror the style and content of Hanif poetry composed by Zayd, a contemporary of Muhammad. At this point, the prophet's revealing spirit was an unnamed "Lord." When we're finally introduced, we learn that the Islamic god's name is Ar-Rahman. And he is a dark and demented spirit, one who spends his days in hell. He deceives men, leads them astray, shackles them, dragging them to their doom. Ar-Rahman personally participates in hell's torments, turning men on a spit, tearing them apart, forcing them to eat thorns, pitch, and boiling water. His paradise is a brothel. Its rivers flow with wine, and multiple virgins satiate the carnal desires of the faithful.

As you might imagine, Muhammad's contemporaries, the Quraysh tribe in the little berg of Mecca, thought he was nuts. The Qur'an contains over 400 iterations of the never-ending argument between Muhammad and his tribe. Those who knew this "prophet" best called him a charlatan. They charged him with the very offenses the Qur'an and Hadith confirm he was guilty of perpetrating. Then, demonstrating the maturity and discipline of a schoolyard bully, the Islamic god struck back. He slandered the Meccans with an exhaustive list of hateful slurs and threatened them with a painful doom.

When I first read the Qur'an, I was surprised to find the endless regurgitation of spiteful attacks. The Meccans shouted: "Muhammad, you are an insane, demon-possessed sorcerer, forging the Qur'an." Allah answered: "My Messenger is not insane, nor is he demon-possessed." I found this perplexing. Why didn't some enterprising scribe edit these incriminating charges out before codifying the Qur'an? Then I realized that without the raging feud, there was no justification for the scripture's single most repetitive rant: "If you reject Muhammad, Muslims will kill you so that his god can roast you alive."

I recognize that this is the antithesis of what you expected to see during the formative years of a great religion. Yet the evidence—the only evidence—is irrefutable. The Qur'an takes us into a demented and violent realm. It's a bad job of plagiarizing held together by a childish rant. Paradise and hell are both decadent and disgusting, more satanic than divine. And the Sunnah, which professes to be inspired scripture, is no better. Stroke by stroke they present an ugly picture of an abused child who became an abuser.

Having destroyed the "religion" of Islam in Mecca, Muhammad created the political doctrine of "submission" in Medina. He became a pirate, dictator, and terrorist leader. He used Qur'anic scripture to justify horrific behavior: pedophilia, incest, rape, torture, assassinations, thievery, mass murder, and terror—all in an unbridled orgy of sex, power, and money. Again, this summation simply reflects the portrayal documented in the Islamic Sunnah and confirmed in the Qur'an.

When he was fifty, Muhammad married a six-year-old child. Then he stole his son's wife. After forcing young girls to watch his men execute their fathers, Muhammad raped them. He tortured his victims to make sure no booty escaped his grasp. He committed mass murder, slaughtering Jews in genocidal rage. In ten years, he ordered a score of assassinations and conducted seventy-five terrorist raids. He used the sword to force Arabs into submission and used the slave trade to finance Islam. He was more interested in collecting girls and taxes than anything else. He ruled through fear. And his god condoned it all.

This harsh portrayal does not represent my interpretation of the most negative Islamic scriptures or even a view derived from some jaundiced document crafted by an enemy of the religion. It is the *only* authentic picture; it's the original. By reading the Qur'an and Hadith you'll see Muhammad embarrass himself and deceive his compatriots—all with his god's blessing. This is the portrait of prophet and god that was painted by the first Muslims. One does not have to cull out the bad from the good to render this verdict. It's really hard to find anything *good* in their scriptures or behaviors.

To provide some objectivity to this startling reality, recognize that nothing is known about Muhammad and his creation, Islam, apart from five books.

They represent the only surviving written record scribed within 250 years of the prophet's life. They, and only they, represent fundamental Islam. They are *the* authority, the "gospel truth." Any statement not derived from these sources is conjecture, speculation, and opinion.

To firmly establish the validity, nature, and appropriateness of these Islamic scriptures, I want to combine what the Islamic scholars said in the preface to the most revered Hadith Collection with what others wrote on the opening page of the Qur'an. "Sahih Bukhari is a Collection of sayings and deeds of Prophet Muhammad, also known as the Sunnah. The reports of the Prophet's sayings and deeds are called Hadith. Bukhari lived a couple of centuries after the Prophet's death and collected his Hadith. Each report in his Collection was checked for compatibility with the Qur'an, and the veracity of the chain of reporters, or isnad, had to be established." Then…"The Qur'an is one leg of two which form the basis of Islam. The second leg is the Sunnah of the Prophet. What makes the Qur'an different from the Sunnah is its form. Unlike the Sunnah, the Qur'an is quite literally the Word of Allah, whereas the Sunnah [which is comprised exclusively of Hadith] was *inspired* by Allah but the wording and actions are the Prophet's. The Qur'an has not been expressed using any human words. Its wording is letter for letter fixed by Allah. Prophet Muhammad was the final Messenger of Allah to humanity, and therefore the Qur'an is the last Message which Allah has sent to us. Its predecessors such as the Torah, Psalms, and Gospels have all been superceded."

The most respected Islamic scholars tell Muslims that the "Qur'an is literally the word of Allah" and that the "Sunnah was inspired by Allah." They say this because there are hundreds of commands in the Qur'an ordering Muslims to obey Muhammad, to believe in him, to follow his example. Since the Qur'an is supposed to be "Allah" speaking, the only way to obey Muhammad, to believe in and follow him, is to know what he said and did. The Hadith represents the sole repository of these words and deeds. So, despite all evidence to the contrary, Muslims believe what you are going to read from the Qur'an and Hadith is divinely inspired *scripture* directly from Allah.

The preponderance of this "scripture" is presented in *Prophet of Doom*. To provide some perspective on the scope of the coverage you should know that the Qur'an, formatted like this book, would be 200 pages. Pared of its redundancy, it would be a quarter of that length. We will analyze nearly ninety percent of that material.

Turning to the Sunnah, the Hadith in Bukhari's Collection represent 800 pages of Muhammadisms. The majority are duplicated several times in various sections. Most have multiple lines of transmitters, or isnads, for virtually identical Traditions. Further, half of Bukhari's Collection includes laws, procedures, or meaningless anecdotes that fall outside the scope of this study. Without this redundant and extraneous material there are fifty pages of prime and pertinent reports. I'll cover fifty percent of this directly and reveal thirty percent indirectly through redundancy in Ishaq and Tabari.

Much of Muslim's work is duplicated in Bukhari. He has some unique Traditions, though, and many important insights into the nature of Jihad. Wherever we can glean fresh information from Imam Muslim, we will.

The events presented by Tabari, the first Islamic historian, mirror those contained in Ishaq's biographical account. There's a seventy percent overlap in their coverage of Muhammad's life and the formation of Islam. Devoid of this overlap, extraneous poetry, and footnotes, their combined 1,500 pages of Islamic Traditions over the period we will be studying could be distilled to 250 pages of Hadith not memorialized elsewhere. *Prophet of Doom* analyzes eighty percent of these, as they provide the most valuable insights into Islam.

Ishaq's biography and Tabari's history are comprised in their entirety of Hadith. They are Sunnah and thus Islamic scripture. Their Hadith feature chains of reporters, and they are in sync with other Collections and with the Qur'an. The sole difference is the arrangement. Ishaq and Tabari chose Hadith that could be presented in the order they occurred.

Without Ishaq and Tabari, Islam would not exist as Muhammad would be unknown. They alone provide the religion's skeleton, it's context and chronology. Without this grounding in place and time, the Qur'an is meaningless, and the remaining Hadith are of diminished value. It would be like being a Christian without the Gospels. The Tabari translators tell us: "Muhammad Ibn Ishaq was the most influential and earliest biographer of the Prophet. His Sira became the standard treatment of the events of Muhammad's life."

Ishaq collected Hadith a full *century* before anyone else. Muslims have no earlier or more accurate source. The four generations of oral transmission that followed his Collection could have done nothing but degrade the material. But sadly, Ishaq's original has been lost. What remains was edited by Hisham sixty-five years later. And Hisham said: *Ishaq:691* **"I am omitting things which Ishaq recorded in this book. I have omitted things which are disgraceful to discuss and matters which would distress certain people."** That is why Tabari is essential. He had a copy of Ishaq's *Sirat Rasul Allah* when he composed his history. Rather than editing the Sira, he referenced Ishaq each time his Hadith shed additional light on any subject—especially Islamic creation and the Satanic Verses.

By the time you have completed this review, you will know much more about Muhammad and fundamental Islam than most Muslims. And you will understand him and his doctrine better than most scholars and clerics. You will see Muhammad as he saw himself. His motives and agenda will be as transparent as his methods and means. Islam will no longer be a mystery. The only conundrum that will remain is why anyone believed this "prophet."

Muhammad and his deity created very little original material. Team Islam was into plagiarism. Most of the Qur'an was lifted from the Torah and Talmud. (Apparently God ran out of good material when he finished the Bible.) Muhammad aside, there are only four non-Biblical characters in the Qur'an.

Two represent mythical leaders of mythical lands. The third was Muhammad's biggest critic, his uncle Abu Lahab. The fourth was Alexander the Great—a Muslim prophet, according to Allah.

While all the other names are the same—Adam, Noah, Abraham, Isaac, Ishmael, Jacob, Joshua, Lot, Moses, Aaron, Jonah, David, Solomon, Mary, Jesus, Satan, and Gabriel—their stories are not. The specific historical events surrounding these lives so meticulously detailed by Jewish scribes were purposefully convoluted—ripped out of context and time—to justify Muhammad's thinly disguised agenda. I share this now so you might know that without the inclusion of Bible characters and stories, the Qur'an and Hadith would be very thin on spirituality. We would be left with little more than temper tantrums, threats, and terror. No one would confuse it for a religion.

As for the gross variance between the Bible and Qur'an, the Ar-Rahman/Allah/Muhammad team claimed that the forty literate Jews who lived and witnessed these events, performed the miracles, and recorded the prophecies, got them wrong; well, except for the overwhelming number of passages they copied. Then Muhammad claimed that he, an illiterate Arab, an enemy of the Jews living 900 miles distant and six to twenty-six centuries after the fact, revealed the "truthful" account, having corrected their deceptions. In an ignorant world, it must have sounded plausible.

It is interesting, however, that neither Muhammad, Ar-Rahman, nor Allah bothered to explain how or when these gross deceptions crept into the Bible. And this task becomes increasingly difficult for Muslims because their god said in Qur'an 80:13 that the Judeo-Christian scriptures were in good hands: 080.013 **"In honored books, exalted in dignity, kept pure and holy, written by the hands of scribes—honorable, pious and just, noble and righteous."**

The general consensus among Islamic scholars is that the Hebrew Bible, the Old Testament, was corrupted when Jews failed to accept Christ. And the Christian Bible, the New Testament, was corrupted when Christians failed to accept Muhammad. The following Hadith from their Traditions forms the basis of this doctrinal view. It comes from Bukhari's *Book of Hiring*, Volume 3, Book 36, Number 471. It can also be found in the Noble Qur'an attached to surah 41:46. *Bukhari:V3B36N471* **"The Prophet said, 'The example of the Jews, Christians, and Muslims is like the example of a man who employed [Jewish] laborers to work for him from morning till night for specific wages. They worked till midday and then said, "We do not need your money which you have fixed for us and let whatever we have done be annulled." The man said, "Don't quit, complete the rest and take your full wages." But they refused and went away. The man employed another batch after them and said [to the Christians], "Complete the rest and yours will be the wages I had fixed for the first batch." So they worked till the time of Asr [afternoon] prayer. Then they said, "Let what we have done be annulled and keep the wages you have promised." The man said, "Complete the rest of the work, as only a little remains," but they refused. Thereafter, he employed others**

[Muslims this time] and they worked till sunset. They received the wages of the two former batches. So, they represented the example of the Jews and Christians, and then Muslims who accepted Islam, the Qur'an, and Sunnah which the Prophet brought.'"

Recognizing this wasn't a very good explanation, and knowing that the story was a twisted rip off of one of Christ's parables, the Islamic scholars who translated the passage added this footnote: "The Jews refused to believe in the Message of Jesus, so all their work was annulled. Similarly, the Christians refused to accept the Message of Muhammad and thus their work was annulled too. Such people were not rewarded, because they refused true faith and died unbelievers. They should have accepted the latest Message. Their insistence on keeping their old religion deprived them of any reward. On the other hand, Muslims accepted the new religion and believed in all three Messages. They deserved a full reward for their complete surrender to Allah."

Unfortunately for Muslims, this scenario is impossible. How can one believe "all three Messages" since they are radically different? More importantly, if Judeo-Christianity is a *true* message, what's the justification for a *new* religion? And as difficult as these questions are, the most troubling still lingers: how and when did the Judeo-Christian scriptures get corrupted?

Fact is, they didn't. The Septuagint, the Greek translation of the Hebrew Bible, survives to this day. It serves as irrefutable proof that nothing was changed. It was translated 275 years before the Christian era. It matches today's Old Testament with astonishing fidelity. Then you have the Dead Sea scrolls. They were found by a Bedouin shepherd boy in the caves of Qumran. They date between 250 B.C. and 70 A.D., and were thus written during the very period Muhammad claims the Bible was corrupted. These 2,000-year-old scrolls prove that the foundation of Islam is fictitious. They are virtually indistinguishable from today's text.

The New Testament condemns Islamic theory as well. By the time Muslims said it was corrupted, there were hundreds of translations and as many as a hundred thousand copies distributed throughout the civilized world. Do you suppose that they were all brought together and altered in identical fashion just to spite Muhammad? Or is it more likely that Allah doesn't know what he is talking about? That's the crux of the issue. If the Bible wasn't corrupted in a massive and conspiratorial fashion, Islam can't be trusted. Correcting the Torah and Gospels, setting the record straight, returning to the true religion, were central to Muhammad's mission. If the scripture wasn't garbled, Islam loses its justification. If the Bible wasn't massively degraded—to the point that it would be unrecognizable—the cornerstone of Islam is a lie.

To believe that Team Islam was right, and the Hebrew prophets were wrong, one has to dismiss the fact that most of the Qur'an's stories and characters were lifted from Jewish oral traditions in the Talmud. Additionally, the Median surahs say that Muhammad had to pay Jews for access to their scriptures during the formation of his religion. "O Children of Israel, call to mind My

[Allah's] favor which I bestowed on you....and believe in what I have revealed, verifying [the Torah] which is with you. Be not the first to deny [the Qur'an], neither take a mean price in exchange for My scriptures. [Don't sell Bible stories to Muhammad—give them to him.] Do not mix up the truth with the falsehood, nor hide the truth while you know it." [Qur'an 2:40] There are a dozen more verses like this, all designed to demean Jews for charging Muhammad when he needed more scripture to call his own.

The Jews recognized the discrepancies between the accounts they had read to Muhammad and his convoluted revisions. It was obvious that the alterations were attributable to crises in his life rather than consistent with the lives of the Biblical characters they had described. So, they mocked Muhammad, as you and I might have done had we been in their shoes.

Had Muhammad invented his religion independent of the Bible, comparisons would be unnecessary. If Muslims were not killing us while shouting *"Allahu Akbar"* they would be unimportant. But he did, and they are, so it is.

The Judeo-Christian faiths are wholly independent and separate from Islam. They neither gain nor lose any authenticity from a comparison. The Bible doesn't mention Muhammad, Muslims, Islam, Allah, Mecca, or the Ka'aba, although there are some foreboding predictions about these people, their doctrine, and spirit.

But the reverse is not true. For reasons we shall discuss, Muhammad fancied himself a Jewish prophet—the Messiah even. He claimed that Islam was the original religion of Abraham. He professed that Adam, Noah, Moses, and Jesus were really Muslims. And as we have seen, he claimed that the Hebrew Bible and Christian Gospels were inspired scripture, directly from his god. Then he said that they were corrupt, which made his message necessary.

This is underscored in the 163rd verse of the 4th surah: *004.163* "Surely We [Allah] have revealed to you [Muhammad] as We revealed to Noah, and the prophets after him, and We revealed to Abraham and Ishmael and Isaac and Jacob and their offspring and the tribes [of Israel], and Jesus and Job and Jonah and Aaron and Solomon. We gave to David the Book of Psalms, and We sent apostles...and Moses, to whom Allah spoke His Word directly. All of these apostles of good news and warners were sent so that people should not have a plea against Allah." None of these men were apostles. Ishmael, Isaac, Jacob, Job, Aaron, and Solomon weren't even prophets. David was one of many writers of Psalms. And Moses spoke to Yahweh, not Allah.

In Qur'an 3:3 we read: *003.003* "He [Allah] has verily revealed to you this Book [the Qur'an] in truth and confirmation of the Books revealed before, as indeed He had revealed the Torah and the Gospel." This is reconfirmed: *005.046* "Later, in the train of the prophets, We [Allah] sent Jesus, son of Mary, confirming the Torah which had been sent down before him, and gave him the Gospel containing guidance and light, which corroborated the earlier Torah." Then...*005.047* "Let the people of the Gospel [Christians] judge by what has been revealed in it by Allah." And...*005.048* "To you We have revealed the Qur'an containing the truth, confirming the earlier revelations [Torah, Psalms, and Gospels], and preserving them from change and corruption. So judge between them by what has been revealed by Allah."

We will judge between them because Muhammad gave us no choice. Yet I will not attempt to validate the Biblical account. It isn't the purpose of this study, and the Bible gains nothing from repudiating the Islamic corruptions of its scriptures. Islam, however, has no credibility unless Muhammad can disprove the Biblical accounting, as he based Islam on his variant of the Torah.

Allah wasn't the least bit ambiguous when he said that the Torah, Psalms, and Gospels were *his* divinely inspired scriptures. But that's not possible since the Torah and Qur'an contradict each other on most every page. The message of salvation proclaimed in the Gospels is the antithesis of Islam. To say that they were all inspired by the same God is irrational, a logical impossibility.

In Qur'an 2:59 Allah lambasted the Jews: *002.059* **"The wicked [Jews] changed and perverted the word We [Allah] had spoken to a word distorted."** Because of their egregious behavior, the Jews **"became like apes despised."** But then, in the 5th surah, Allah says of the **"earlier revelations,"** the **"Torah and Gospels,"** that he **"preserved them."** So which is it? Why correct that which has been preserved from change? And more importantly, why are they so different if they are from the same God? All this makes you wonder why someone didn't have the presence of mind to edit the Qur'an before they claimed it was divine.

The Qur'an acknowledges that the Bible is ancient history's most detailed and accurate account of a people and their relationship with their Creator. The Hebrew Scriptures are not only the Qur'an's most frequently quoted resource, its characters and stories dominate each of Islam's holy books. And up to the point Muhammad corrupted them, he was on solid ground for the vast majority of the places and events described in the Bible have been shown by archeologists to be valid historical depictions. None have ever been shown to be inaccurate. Each time an attempt is made, and there have been thousands, the critic finds himself impaled on the archeologist's spade.

Yet apart from the Bible, there is no such evidence in the Qur'an. Not a single historical artifact has been found to justify its claims. There is no reference to Allah, Muhammad, Mecca, or the Ka'aba independent of the Qur'an or Hadith. And the Qur'an itself is a disjointed hodgepodge. It's not even chronological, much less historical. Unrelated subjects are strung together without intelligible transitions, rhyme or reason.

Since the Islamic scripture is based upon stories lifted from Genesis and Exodus, we are going to start at the beginning and review what Muhammad had to say about our genesis. The Bible has but one version; Islam has many. Since the Bible's account preceded Islam's by 3,000 years, we'll review it first. This will be one of only three events covered from both perspectives.

I'd like to set the stage. Yahweh's revelation of our beginning was given to man four thousand years ago. There were no scientists or even a word for "science." The language of astronomical creation, calculus, wouldn't be invented for four millennia. The language of life, DNA, was a concept well beyond this time. I say this to reveal something that should be obvious. The Genesis creation story was not intended to be a scientific explanation of *how* God made the universe. It was a spiritual explanation of *why* he created it. The explanation of *how* was scores of centuries beyond the language of the time. And it was unimportant. Those who want the Biblical account taught in schools as if it were scientific are doing a great disservice.

The *why* of creation was crucial. It is the essence of the Bible. Genesis tells us that the heavenly bodies, the earth, and life were created during six distinct periods of time. The word "day" did not actually appear in the ancient Hebrew text so we don't know if creation took millions or billions of years. But we know that with the exception of the fourth period, the order of creation, and the description of the events upon which it was comprised are in harmony with what we have learned through science. The Bible's account even has man and the animals being made from the same material and during the same period of time.

Now about that fourth day—I think it is out of order, literally demoted, for a reason. Throughout creation, Yahweh is precise, naming everything. But on the fourth day he does not name the sun, moon, or stars. They are called the greater and lesser lights, signs for the seasons, days, and years. I believe that he didn't name them and that he positioned them after the creation of vegetation for two reasons. Every religion except Judeo-Christianity turned the sun, moon, and stars into gods. And that includes Islam: Allah was a moon god. Qur'an 74:32 proclaims: **"I say the truth and call the moon to witness."** Yahweh, in contrast, wanted us to know that life was more important than things, and that things—even big bright shiny things—were not God. And more revealing still, the fourth "day" was a "sign" foretelling the "season" of the Messiah's arrival. He is symbolized by the greater light and came to us in the fourth millennia of Yahweh's calendar.

Islam's account of creation is a wee bit less credible and a touch less consistent. From the English translation of The History of al-Tabari, *Creation to the Flood*, we find: *Tabari I:188* **"Jews came to the Prophet and asked him about the creation of the heavens and the earth. [Allah didn't bother to explain our beginnings in his Qur'an so Muhammad felt obliged to help him out.] He said, 'Allah created the earth on Sunday and Monday. He created the mountains and the uses they possess on Tuesday. On Wednesday He created trees, water, cities and the cultivated and barren land. On Thursday, He created heaven. On Friday, He created stars, the sun, moon, and angels, until three hours remained. In the first of these three hours, He created the terms, who would live and who would die. In the second, He cast harm upon everything that is useful for** mankind. And in the third, Adam, and had him dwell in Paradise.'"

Did you notice how readily Muhammad was willing to speak for Allah? It's as if speaking for god was a regular part of his routine, almost as if he knew everything his god knew. Yet, judging by his answer, Muhammad may have done better if he had solicited advice. He, like Moses, has God creating the earth and vegetation before the sun and stars. But in Allah's case, there is no excuse. Allah says, **"I swear by the stars and by the signs of the Zodiac,"** in the opening verse of the 85th surah. And he, unlike Yahweh, has no interest in developing a relationship with man. In Qur'an 51:56 Allah shares, **"I have created jinn [demons] and men only to worship Me. I do not want anything from them."**

Muhammad claims that cities existed and land was cultivated before man was created. And the idea of god **"casting harm on everything useful"** gives us our first clue as to who Allah might actually be. Finally, he obliterated the stated purpose of Islam by saying that the terms of life and death were predestined by Allah. If we have no choice, we don't need a religion.

But as strange as all that seems, why did the prophet of the all-knowing Allah contradict himself in the next passage? *Tabari I:189* **"The Messenger took me by the hand and said, 'Allah created soil on Saturday. Upon it, He created the mountains on Sunday. He created the trees on Wednesday, scattered animals on Thursday, and made Adam as the last of His creatures after the afternoon prayer on Friday.'"** Allah begins on Saturday rather than Sunday and Monday. After taking a much-needed rest on Tuesday, he forgot the cities, water, and cultivation and dispenses with the creation of the sun, moon, and stars, as well as paradise. Then Allah creates man after the afternoon prayer. So, who was praying and to whom?

Tabari I:189 **"The Jews asked the Prophet, 'What about Sunday?' The Messenger answered, 'On it, Allah created the earth and spread it out.' They asked about Monday, and he replied: 'On it He created Adam.'"** So much for the afternoon prayer. **"Then they asked about Saturday and mentioned God's resting on it. Then the Prophet got very angry so Allah then revealed to him: 'We have created the heavens and the earth and what is between them in six days and fatigue did not touch Us.'"** This became Qur'an 50:38.

It's interesting that Allah was of no help providing Muhammad with a rational explanation of creation or even help keeping his stories straight, but when it came time to embarrass the God of the Jews, he jumped in with a handy Qur'anic revelation. It says, in essence, "My god is better than your god because my god didn't need to rest." But that's a problem. The "Gods" are supposed to be the same. And the Bible tells us that only one spirit thought he was better than Yahweh—the fallen angel Lucifer.

Moreover, Muhammad didn't understand that the Genesis account was designed to convey spiritual truth. Yahweh's pattern of six and one ultimately became the framework upon which his relationship with man was built.

Unfortunately, Muhammad's testimony puts us in a quandary. It is too foolish to be from a literate man, and yet his stories are loosely based upon

Genesis, the world's best known *written* account of our beginnings. I believe that the following Hadith provides some insights into how Muhammad came to know these things and on whose authority he claimed to be speaking. *Bukhari: V4B55N546* "A Jewish rabbi, Abdulla bin Salam approached the Messenger, 'I am going to ask you three things which nobody knows except a prophet: [Then how would the Rabbi know them?] What is the first portent of the Hour? What will be the first meal taken in Paradise? Why does a child resemble its father, and why does it resemble its mother?' Allah's Apostle said, 'Gabriel has just now told me of the answers.' 'Gabriel, from among all the angels, is the enemy of the Jews.' 'The first portent of the Hour will be a fire that will bring the people from east to west. The first meal of Paradise will be caudate lobe of fish-liver. As for the resemblance of a child to its parents: If a man has sexual intercourse with his wife and gets discharge first, the child will resemble him, and if the woman gets discharge first, the child will resemble her.' On that the rabbi said, 'I testify you are the Apostle of Allah, and that Jews are liars.'" It's hard to believe that anyone believes this is scripture.

Salam was one of two Jews Ishaq believes sold out to Muhammad. He was in all likelihood responsible for providing the scripture the prophet corrupted to compile his Qur'an. And Gabriel was neither an enemy of the Jews, nor who Muhammad claimed him to be. I am certain Islam's prophet mistook Lucifer for Gabriel. The totality of the Qur'an and Hadith allow no other conclusion.

Returning to the creation tale, we discover a talking planet. *Tabari I:192* "Allah said to the heavens and earth: 'Come willingly or unwillingly!' They said: 'We come willingly.' Allah said to the heavens: 'Cause My sun, My moon and My stars to rise.' To the earth He said, 'Split your rivers and bring forth fruit.' Both replied: 'We come willingly.'"

At this point we are using Tabari as our primary source of Islamic scripture. While he quotes Traditions from Ibn Ishaq, Hisham abrogated this portion of Muhammad's Hadith from the original Collection. That said, I will continue to include Qur'an quotations within the Tabari narrative, peppering them with Bukhari Hadith.

Muhammad takes us through a spirited debate on what was created first. *Tabari I:198* "I heard Muhammad say: 'The first thing created by Allah was the Pen. And Allah said to it: "Write!" It proceeded at that very hour to write whatever is going to be.'" This is an essential insight into Islam. The religion is entirely fatalistic. There is *no choice.* Everything, including our eternity, is predestined. This is the inverse of Judeo-Christianity, where we are given the choice to love God or reject him.

Returning to the "Pen," what language do you suppose it wrote? Was it some form of the Akkadian tongue in cuneiform? After all, the stylus produced the first *written* language on planet earth. Or was it Egyptian hieroglyphics, which appeared next? Could it have been Hebrew—the language of Yahweh's first revelation—the language of the Torah? After all, Allah claims he revealed it first. No. Allah says it was Arabic because the Pen wrote the Qur'an before man was created. Allah lies: *046.002* "And before it, the Book of Musa [Moses] was a guide: and this [Qur'an] is a Book verifying (it) in the Arabic language."

And...*039.027* "We have coined for man in this Qur'an every kind of parable in order that they may receive admonition. (It is) a Qur'an in Arabic, without any crookedness (therein): in order that they may guard (against evil)." *041.003* "A Scripture Book, whereof the verses are explained in detail; a Qur'an in Arabic, for people who have knowledge." Then...*041.044* "Had We sent this as a Qur'an (in the language) other than Arabic, they would have said: 'Why are not its verses explained in detail? What! (a foreign tongue, a Book) not in Arabic and (a Messenger) an Arab?' Say (unto them, Muhammad): 'It is a Guide to those who believe; and for those who do not believe it, there is a deafness in their ears, and it is blindness in their (eyes)!'" The words added in the parenthesis are things the Pen must have missed as it was writing the Qur'an. These words are not included in the Arabic original. They were added by the translators.

There are a couple of problems with the Arabic theory. Written Arabic evolved among Syrian Christians as a stylistic derivative of Aramaic in the 6th century A.D. There is no evidence the alphabet made its way to Muhammad's Mecca until after the Qur'an was revealed. Even then, the Qur'an is filled with many non-Arabic words, including the word "qur'an," which the Syrian Christians defined as "to recite" or "to preach."

Tabari I:199 "I heard the Prophet say: 'The first thing created by Allah was the Pen. Allah said to it: "Write!" The Pen asked, "What shall I write?" Allah replied, "Write what is predestined."'" I'll give Muhammad a pass on the talking pen because it makes no less sense than a talking earth. But this I've got to know: if the pen knew all that was predestined, why didn't it know what Allah wanted it to do?

Tabari explains, *Tabari I:202* "There are people who consider predestination untrue. Then they consider the Qur'an untrue.... People merely carry out what is a foregone conclusion, decided by predestination and written down by the Pen." They actually believe this stuff. And that's because this passage was crafted to explain the Qur'an's 68th surah called: "The Pen." "I [Allah] call to witness the Pen and what it inscribes." Without the Hadith, you wouldn't know what "Pen" god was talking about.

The second verse is delicious. The Lord is possessed to tell his lone prophet: *068.002* "You are not demented, demon possessed, or mad." Then he says, "There is surely an unending reward for you." That "reward" became the means, method, and motivation for creating, staffing, and promulgating Islam.

The following Bukhari Hadith confirms Islam's lack of choice and Muhammad's dearth of prophetic credentials. *Bukhari:V4B55N549* "Allah's Apostle, the true and truly inspired said, 'As it relates to your creation, every one of you is collected in the womb of his mother for the first forty days, and then he becomes a clot for an other forty days, and then a piece of flesh for an other forty days [a four month gestation isn't even half right]. Then Allah sends an angel to write four words: He writes his deeds, time of his death, means of his livelihood, and whether he will be wretched or blessed.'"

Moving on, the Pen gathers rivals for its pole position in the race of creation. *Tabari I:204* "I asked the Prophet, 'Where was Allah before His creation?' Muhammad replied: 'He was in a cloud with no air underneath or above it.'" A cloud without air, now there's one for the science classes. **"Then Allah created His Throne upon the water."** If there were clouds, water, and a throne—how did the Pen come first?

I'm sure the prophet will clear this up, so let's listen to a Hadith from one of his Companions. Like so many Traditions, this one is found in both Tabari and Bukhari. *Tabari I:204 / Bukhari:V4B54N414* **"Some people came to the Messenger, entered his presence, and said: 'Give us gifts!' [Muhammad's militants were mercenaries. The prophet bribed his way to prosperity.] This continued until it annoyed him. Then they left. Some other people came in and said, 'We have come to greet the Messenger of Allah and become knowledgeable about the religion and ask about the beginning of the world.' He said, 'Allah existed while there was nothing else. His Throne was upon the water, and all that was going to be was written on the memorial Tablet before anything else was created. Then Allah created the seven heavens.' Just then, someone came to me and said, 'That camel of yours is gone.' I went out and found that she was out of sight. I surely wish that I would have let her go so that I would not have missed the rest of the Prophet's remarks!"**

Okay, let me see if I understand this. The pen was created first but before it was created Allah created his throne. The throne was on water, which was yet to be created. Then we had writing on a tablet that had yet to be created so that Allah could tell us that there are seven heavens, which were created before or after the earth depending upon which version you believe. Bottom line: the camel's gone. That's about all we know for sure.

The Bukhari version of the runaway camel ends with this insight into how Muhammad conveyed his "inspired" revelations and how they were ulti- mately retained and passed along to us as scripture: *Bukhari:V4B54N414* **"One day the Prophet stood up amongst us for a long period and informed us about the beginning of creation. He talked about everything in detail. He ended his speech by mentioning how the people of Paradise will enter the Garden and how the people of Hell will enter the Fire. Some remembered what he had said, and some forgot."**

Muhammad's disciples weren't the only ones who had trouble remembering this stuff. *Bukhari:V6B61N550* **"The Prophet said, 'It is a bad thing that some of you say, "I have forgotten such-and-such verse of the Qur'an." For truly, I have been caused by Allah to forget it. So you must keep on reciting the Qur'an because it escapes faster than a runaway camel.'"**

Since memories were fleeting, to be fair, I say we give Muhammad another chance. Surely he'll straighten all this out. After all, a billion people trust *this* man with their soul. *Tabari I:206* **"When Allah wanted to create the heavens and earth, He grabbed a fistful of small rocks in the water. He then opened his fist with the rocks and they rose in the form of smoke. Then Allah fashioned the seven heavens and extended the earth in two days. He finished the creation on the seventh day. He created the Footstool after the Pen and then the Throne. Thereafter He created the air and darkness. He then created the water and placed His Throne upon it. ...He was in a cloud with no air underneath or above it. Thus the Messenger reported."**

So that explains it. It makes perfect sense. Muhammad was making this up as he went along. Now, I ask you: since it's obvious that his scripture was contrived, what else do you suppose Muhammad made up as he went along: Allah and Islam perhaps? And that's really the point. The more you're exposed to Muhammad and his religion, the more you will come to understand the nature and purpose of Islam.

There are two reasons I am sharing these improbable and variant Islamic creation accounts. First, I promised that we would start at the beginning and cover Muhammad's creation of Islam chronologically—starting with his version of the world's beginnings. We will go step by step through his corruption of Adam, Noah, and Abraham to see how he used the oldest patriarchs to establish the newest dogma. Second, I want you to know Muhammad and Allah—to see them as they really are. Each time they propose things that are logically impossible, contradictory, or twisted you'll be able to judge their sincerity, validity, and veracity.

By way of example, Muhammad had to make the Ka'aba—Allah's House and a rock pile to pagan gods—seem worthy of veneration. *Tabari I:216* **"Allah created the Ancient House upon the water on four pillars. He did this two thousand years before He created this world."** Islam's credibility is based upon making the Ka'aba —the black cube in Mecca—a legitimate monotheistic shrine.

Forget for a moment that this story contradicts Muhammad's earlier testimony. The Ka'aba was a wreck. During Muhammad's day it was constructed of un-hewn and un-mortared rocks. It didn't even have a roof. Even today, it's so unattractive, it has to be covered in a giant prayer blanket—and that's after having been rebuilt ten times. Such a "building," and I use that term loosely, is beneath God's status. Forget that it was a pagan shrine, housing over three hundred idols. We still have to deal with three wholly different versions of who made it. In different places in the Hadith and the Qur'an, Muhammad claims that the Ka'aba's builder was Allah, Adam, and Abraham. Well, at least they all start with the letter "A."

There are many more creation variations. But I'd be remiss if I didn't share my favorite. The whole earth was placed upon a big fish, the very same fish that swallowed Jonah. In this version we discover: *Tabari I:219* **"When Allah wanted to create the creation, He brought forth smoke from the water. The smoke hovered loftily over it. He called it 'heaven.' Then He dried out the water and made it earth. He split it and made it seven earths on Sunday. He created the earth upon a big fish, that being the fish mentioned in the Qur'an. By the Pen, the fish was in the water. The water was upon the back of a small rock. The rock was on the back of an angel. The angel was on a big rock. The big rock was in the wind. The fish became agitated. As a result, the earth quaked, so Allah anchored the mountains and made it stable. This is why the Qur'an says Allah made for the earth 'firmly anchored mountains, lest it shake you up.'"** Dr. Seuss has nothing on these guys. This is better than "One Fish, Two Fish, Red Fish, Blue Fish."

✡ ☦ ☾ ☄

Before we give up and go fishing, I'd like to share what Islam had to say about the creation of man. It was one of Muhammad's and Allah's favorite subjects—covered countless times in the Hadith and Qur'an. Since neither were capable of prophecy or miracles, man's existence was used to prove Allah's existence. *Tabari I:258* "**Allah created Adam from sticky clay, meaning viscous and sweet smelling, from slime, being stinking. It became stinking slime after having been compact soil. Allah formed Adam with His own hand.**" [Qur'an 15:26] So if a Muslim calls you a "stinking slimeball," thank him. It's a compliment. I think.

Yet, Allah forming us out of slime is insulting, and it's contradictory. The referenced verse says: *015.026* "**We fashioned man from fermented clay, stinking slime, dried tingling hard as we fashioned jinn [demons] from white hot flame.**" Elsewhere in the Qur'an god created man from "**dust**," "**spurting water**," "**contemptible water**," "**a drop of semen**," "**an embryo**," "**a single sperm [whose do you suppose?]**," "**a single cell**," "**a chewed up lump of flesh**," "**extract of base fluid**," "**inordinate haste**," or simply "**weakness**," depending on where you look. There are thirty creation accounts and twenty-two variations. Of course, this must all make sense, because Allah insists there are no contradictions in the Qur'an.

Among these fairytales, there's a problem. It is incumbent upon a belief system to answer the "why" question: Why are we here? The answer should be attached to the creation story, but Islam doesn't bother. Worse, Muhammad's ultimate answer is indicting. Allah said, "**I have created jinn [demons] and men only to worship Me. I do not want anything from them.**" Islam is devoid of choice, and worship without choice is slavery. It would be like you or me having a tape recorder blast: "You are great," all day long. God is not so insecure he needs a "praise machine," or so lame he made one as imprecise as man.

The Bible says Yahweh created Adam (the Hebrew word for man) out of the dust, or elements, breathing his spirit into us so that we would be like him spiritually. Unlike the animals, we were made in *his* image. Our spirit has Godly characteristics, enabling us to know Yahweh, to communicate with him, and to choose to have a relationship with him. If we wish to praise him *after* we have come to know him, that's fine. But it was not *why* we were created.

This conflicts with Islam. Although the god of the Qur'an sounds like Muhammad, Islam dispenses with the "in His image" idea because Islam's god and man are supposed to have nothing in common. There is a Hadith attributed to Muhammad in which he passed a man beating a slave. He told him to stop because: "**Allah made Adam in the slave's image.**" Being crafted "in the slave's image" was designed to underscore Muhammad's concept of Islam—a religion named submission—a religion without choice.

Yahweh wants us to choose; Allah wants us to submit. One wants to be loved, the other feared. There may be a reason the Islamic prostration requires one to bow their head toward Hell while their posterior moons Heaven.

The Islamic creation account continues with this Hadith: *Tabari I:258* "**Allah** sent Gabriel to the earth to bring Him some clay. The earth said, 'I take refuge in Allah against you mutilating me. So Gabriel returned without having taken any clay and said, 'Lord, the earth took refuge in You, and I granted its wish. Allah then sent Michael, and exactly the same thing happened. Then He sent the angel of death. He took some soil from the earth and made a mixture. He did not take it from a single place but took red, white, and black soil. Therefore, the children of Adam came out different." We're different races according to Islam because the stinking slime was red, white, and black. And we owe our existence to the "angel of death."

Allah wasn't finished. *Tabari I:259* "He went up with the soil, then moistened it so it became sticky clay. The soil changed and become stinking. This is what Allah meant when He said, 'From slime, stinking.'" "The Lord Almighty sent Iblis [Satan] to take some skin from the earth, both sweet and salty, and Allah created Adam from it. For this reason he was named Adam—he was created from the skin (adim) of the earth." As God's only illiterate messenger, Muhammad didn't know that Adam was actually the Hebrew word for "man." The lesson here is: if you're going to plagiarize, you ought to be more careful. Otherwise you're apt to mistake Lucifer for Gabriel and attribute creation to the wrong "god."

Was this inspired by the Creator of the universe, or did Muhammad say: *Tabari I:261* "Allah caused Adam's clay to ferment. He left it lying around for forty nights.... Iblis [Satan] used to come to it and kick it with his foot, whereupon it made sounds. Then Iblis entered Adam's mouth and left from his posterior, and he entered his ass and left from his mouth. Then he said, 'You are not something for making sounds. What then were you created for? If I am given authority over you, I shall ruin you.'" Muhammad wants us to know that Satan flows within our nature (or at least within his). *Bukhari:V3B33N254* "Satan circulates in human beings as blood flows in our bodies."

The next segment of demonic delusion is revealing. After exploring Adam's posterior, Satan told the angels, "Don't be afraid of that one [the partially fermented Adam] for Allah is solid whereas this one is hollow." While I don't know much about the consistency of fermenting humans, I do know that Allah was synonymous with the largest rock of the Ka'aba, the Black Stone. Rocks are indeed solid. God is spirit by all sane accounts, which would make him the antithesis of solid. Satan may have given us another clue.

Just for giggles, let's canvass the remaining accounts. We are told... *Tabari I:263* "When Allah's spirit entered Adam's head, he sneezed. The angels said, 'Praise be to Allah.' When it reached his stomach, he grew hungry. When it reached his feet, he ran for food. This explains why the Qur'an says, 'Man was created of inordinate haste.'" [Qur'an 21:37] "Whenever something of Allah's spirit moved in Adam's body, it became flesh and blood. When the blown spirit reached his navel, he looked at his body and was pleased to see its beauty." Why would Adam have a navel? Did he have a mother? An umbilical cord? Shouldn't Adam have been the only man in creation without a navel?

Tabari I:267 "And He [Allah] taught Adam all the names as follows: He taught him the name of everything, down to fart and little fart." (That's what it says.) "And Adam told each kind of creature about its name and referred it to its genus. Allah said, 'I know what you do not know.'" No kidding. You're pretending to be god. "If we [angels] are not better than Adam is, we are at least more knowledgeable because we existed before him, and the nations were created before him." How could the nations have been created before the first man? I know the Islamic answer, but it's no less embarrassing. You will soon discover that the Qur'an and Hadith claim that the Muslim prophet, Alexander the Great, found an extraterrestrial nation around a celestial mud pit in which the sun sets. Really.

This Hadith sounds innocuous enough until you connect it to the Qur'an. *Tabari I:271* "When the angels boasted about their knowledge, they were tested. Allah taught Adam all the names. Then He presented them to the angels and said, 'Tell Me the names of these if you speak the truth in saying that you are more knowledgeable than what I created. The angels hurriedly sought repentance. Allah said, 'Adam, tell them their names!'" Muhammad claims the Qur'an was revealed by an angel. But that's not good if Allah's angels are prone to deceit and if they are so stupid they don't know the word for swine or know a rock from a god.

Tabari I:272 "Adam began to call everything by its name, and nation after nation was presented to him. Allah preferred Adam to the angels with respect to knowledge." This is beginning to sound like the "Three Stooges Do Religion." But before you laugh it off as irrelevant, irrational, and irreverent, consider this: each Hadith was tied to the Qur'an, so while it's irreverent and irrational, it's not irrelevant.

Tabari I:224 "Each day of the six in which He created corresponds to a thousand years. The conclusion is that the time elapsed from when Allah first began creating His creatures to when He finished is 7,000 years. As proved by us earlier with the help of evidential statements, there is a duration of 7,000 years from the time when our Lord finished to the moment of the annihilation." While we're not told why Allah wants to destroy the world, we are told when. *Tabari I:181* "The Prophet said, 'I was sent immediately before the coming of the Day of Doom. I preceded it like this one preceding that one'—referring to his index and middle finger." *Tabari I:182* "He said: 'Allah will not make this nation [of Islam] incapable of lasting half a day—a day being a thousand years.' ...Consequently, based upon the Prophet's authority, what remained of time was half a day of the days of which one is a thousand years. The conclusion is that the time that had elapsed to the Prophet's statement corresponds to 6,500 years." This means that the earth should have been annihilated 500 years after Muhammad shared his divine insight in 610 A.D. Last time I checked, the year 1110 came and went without incident. The only mystery is: why didn't Islam go with it?

Bukhari:V4B56N808 "I relate the Traditions of Allah's Apostle to you for I would rather fall from the sky than attribute something to him falsely. But when I tell you a thing which is between you and me, then no doubt, war is guile. I heard Allah's Apostle say, 'In the world's last days there will appear some young foolish people who will use the Qur'an's best speech to abandon Islam. Their belief will not go beyond their throats, so wherever you meet them, kill them, for he who kills them will get a reward on the Day of Doom.'"

Muhammad just said, "Kill a Muslim and earn a prize!"

Returning to Islamic "science," this is how the sun works. *Tabari I:230* **"With your Lord there is neither night nor day. The light of the heavens comes from the light of His face."** That means that Allah was the sun, stars, and moon—a standard-issue pagan idol. And while that's not a very good start, it gets worse.

The sun not only talks, it bows down, worships Allah, and rises in the west. *Bukhari:V4B54N421* **"I walked hand in hand with the Prophet when the sun was about to set. We did not stop looking at it. The Prophet asked, 'Do you know where the sun goes at sunset?' I replied, 'Allah and His Apostle know better.' He said, 'It travels until it falls down and prostrates Itself underneath the Throne. The angels who are in charge of the sun prostrate themselves, also. The sun asks permission to rise again. It is permitted. Then it will prostrate itself again but this prostration will not be accepted. The sun then says, "My Lord, where do You command me to rise, from where I set or from where I rose?" Allah will order the sun to return whence it has come and so the sun will rise in the west. And that is the interpretation of the statement of Allah in the Qur'an: "And the sun runs its fixed course for a term (decreed). That is the Decree of (Allah) the All-Knowing."'"** [Qur'an 36:38]

The Qur'an's 36th surah confirms this foolishness. *036.037* **"A Sign for them is the Night. We withdraw from the Day, and behold they are plunged into darkness. The sun keeps revolving in its orbit at the dispensation of the All-Knowing. And the Moon, We have measured for her mansions till she returns like dried date stalks. It is not permitted for the Sun to overtake the Moon, nor can the Night outstrip the Day."** The sun and day represent Yahweh; the moon and night symbolize Satan. The spirit of Islam has put us on notice. In his world, in his religion, he's in charge. **"Each (just) swims along, floating in (its own) orbit as a Sign as in a race. And we made similar vessels [chariots] for them to ride. But we could have drowned them if we pleased."** The revealing spirit of Islam couldn't have been more foolish if he tried.

Swimming deeper into the vessel of Islamic cosmology we discover: *Tabari I:232* **"Gabriel brings to the sun a garment of luminosity from the light of Allah's Throne according to the measure of the hours of the day. The garment is longer in the summer and shorter in the winter, and of intermediate length in autumn and spring. The sun puts on that garment as one of you here puts on his clothes."** The sun wears clothes, and like us, their length varies depending upon the season. It even has a butler attending to its needs. I'll bet you didn't know that.

According to Allah's prophet, Satan's hell, not God's sun, generates heat. *Bukhari:V1B10N510* **"Allah's Apostle said, 'If it is very hot, the severity of the heat is from the raging of the Hell Fire.'"** As erroneous as all of this is, Muhammad had no excuse. He could have said, "I don't have a clue." He could have studied the writings of the Romans, Greeks, and Egyptians. They had it figured out a thousand years before Muhammad's day. In that the authority of the Qur'an, of Allah himself, and Islam hangs on his trustworthiness, this dimwitted delirium is distressing.

Muhammad wasn't through embarrassing himself. *Tabari I:233* **"I heard Ka'b the Rabbi tell a marvelous story about the sun and the moon. He said the sun and moon will** be like two hamstrung oxen flung into hell. Ibn Abbas [one of Muhammad's Companions] contorted with anger and exclaimed three times: 'Ka'b is lying! This is something Jewish he wants to inject into Islam. Allah is too majestic and noble to mete out punishment where there is obedience to Him. How could He punish two servants [the sun and moon] that are praised for constant obedience? May Allah curse that Rabbi! How insolent is he toward Allah and what a tremendous fabrication has he told about these obedient servants.'" Mind you, he's having a tizzy fit because Muhammad had said that the sun and moon were "obedient servants"—good Muslims. So, if the Rabbi deserved to be cursed for his story, what do you suppose would be the appropriate punishment for Muhammad and his pals? And before you answer, remember, the souls of a billion people hang in the balance. Asked another way, if you were given a *choice*, would you trust your eternity to this messenger?

"Ibn Abbas took a piece of wood and started to hit the ground with it. He did that for some time. Then lifting his head he threw away the wood and said: 'You want me to tell you what I heard the Messenger say about the sun and moon and the beginning of creation and how things went with them?' We said, 'We would.'" Fasten your seatbelts folks. Islam's lone prophet, Allah's only messenger, the Qur'an's singular voice is about to prove whether or not he's worthy of our trust. "When the Messenger was asked about that, he replied, 'When Allah was done with His creation and only Adam remained to be created, He created two suns from the light of His Throne. His foreknowledge told Him that He would efface one and change it to a moon; so the moon is smaller in size than the sun.'" Islam's lone prophet, the Qur'an's sole source, was either deceived, lying, or delusional when he said, "The moon was a sun."

"Muhammad continued, 'If Allah had left the two suns as He created them, night would not have been distinguishable from day. A fasting person would not know when he must fast. A woman would not know how to reckon the period of her impurity. Muslims would not know the time of the pilgrimage. Allah was too concerned with His slaves to do such a thing."

That makes me feel a whole lot better. But not this: *Tabari I:234* "Allah thus sent Gabriel to drag his wing three times over the face of the moon, which at the time was a sun. He effaced its luminosity and left the light in it. This is what Allah means: [in Qur'an 17:12] 'We have blotted out the sign of the night, and We have made the sign of the day something to see by.' The blackness you can see as lines on the moon is a trace of the blotting." Not only was Muhammad's Sunnah wrong, the prophet just destroyed the credibility of Allah's Qur'an.

Tabari I:244 "Kawwa asked Ali [Caliph at the time]: 'O Commander of the Faithful! What is that smudge in the moon?' Ali replied, 'Don't you read the Qur'an? It says, "We have blotted out the sign of the night, effacing it." That smudge is a trace of the blotting.'" Ali was right. The Qur'an says this very thing in surah 17:12.

That was bad. This is worse: "Allah then created for the sun a chariot with 360 handholds from the luminosity of the light of the Throne and entrusted 360 of the angels inhabiting the lower heaven with the sun and its chariot, each of them gripping one of those handholds. Allah also entrusted 360 angels with the moon."

I can see you shaking your head. You must think that I'm making this stuff up. There's no way a religion this stupid could have survived a week much less fourteen hundred years, right? But I didn't, and it did. In fact, one of the reasons I've given you so much of this is because of the way Muslims defend Islam's foolishness. They always accuse those with the courage to expose their scriptures of taking them out of context. So I have, and will, give you ample reason to rebuke such criticism. The more you know, the worse it gets.

And by presenting Islam's creation account in such detail, I'm exposing the mindset of Muhammad—the originator of these stories. I want you to think about the character deficiency that would prompt someone to speak such lies in the name of god. More than anything, I want you to contemplate his motivations. Why would he tell his followers that Allah had conveyed such things to him? Why did Muhammad feel the need to present himself as an authority, *the* authority? What did he want? What did he have to gain?

Muhammad's suicidal act of self incrimination continued. *Tabari I:234* "**Then the Prophet said: 'For the sun and the moon, Allah created easts and wests on the two sides of the earth and the two rims of heaven. There are 180 springs in the west of black clay—this is why Allah's word says: "He found the sun setting in a muddy spring." [Qur'an 18:86] The black clay bubbles and boils like a pot when it boils furiously.'**"

The 18th surah, aptly named "**The Cave,**" is the most foolish in the Qur'an. Muhammad's prophetic credentials were challenged in the wake of the Satanic Verses so he was forced to "reveal" enlightened answers to a series of probing questions. Unfortunately, cut off from his Hanif and Jewish sources, the prophet's answers were particularly pathetic. He claimed that Alexander the Great was a Muslim sent by Allah to explore the sunrise and sunset. *018.083* "**They ask you about Dhu'l-Qarnain [Alexander]. Say, 'I will cite something of his story. We gave him authority in the land and means of accomplishing his goals. So he followed a path until he reached the setting place of the sun. He saw that it set in black, muddy, hot water. Near it he found people.**" The Qur'an goes on to speak of punishing the extra-terrestrials and of the unprotected souls in the realm of the sunrise.

Since Muhammad was willing to spew this rubbish with reckless abandon, and since Allah was willing to corroborate it in the Qur'an, why does anyone believe them? Why kill for them? Why die for them?

Tabari I:235 "**Allah's Apostle continued, 'Allah created an ocean three farakhs (918 kilometers) removed from heaven. Waves contained, it stands in the air by the command of Allah. No drop of it is spilled. All the oceans are motionless, but that ocean flows at the speed of an arrow. The sun, moon and retrograde stars [planets] by which Allah swears in the Qur'an [81:15], run like the sun and moon and race. All of the other stars are suspended from heaven as lamps are from mosques, and circulate together praising Allah. The Prophet said, 'If you wish to have this made clear, look to the circulation of the sphere alternately here and there.'**" Imagine teaching this Qur'anic lesson in science class.

For your edification, Qur'an 81 says: *081.015* "**I swear by the stars that run their** course and hide themselves. They are my witness. And I swear by the night when it departs. Most surely this (Qur'an) is the word of an honored Messenger, a mighty powerful person of great rank and authority. One to be obeyed. My people, your companion (Muhammad) is not a demon-possessed madman. Surely he has seen Him [Allah, Satan, Lucifer, Gabriel?]. This is not the utterance of an accursed devil—these are not the words of Satan." This passage is fraught with more portent than I wish to cover at this time. However, I would like to plant some seeds. Only Lucifer would swear by the stars and by night, for he was the "Morning Star" and became the "Prince of Darkness." The angels who followed him became demons. They live to deceive men and are capable of "possessing" them—driving them "mad." Yet more typically, they lure men astray by seducing them with delusions of grandeur and promising them power, as this verse confirms.

According to the Bible, angels are God's implements—they're just messengers. They have no free will. They must submit and obey. It should be no surprise then, considering Lucifer's influence, that man's relationship to Allah in Islam is predicated upon the only type of relationship Satan ever knew.

The angelic realm is like the military. A mutineer can choose to follow a pirate but that act immediately severs their relationship with, and involvement in, the navy. If the consequence of a single act of disobedience is immediate disassociation, imprisonment, or death, it's not a choice; it's rebellion.

I can hardly wait to hear how professor Muhammad embarrasses himself next. *Tabari I:236* "When the sun rises upon its chariot from one of those springs it is accompanied by 360 angels with outspread wings.... When Allah wishes to test the sun and the moon, showing His servants a sign and thereby getting them to obey, the sun tumbles from the chariot and falls into the deep end of that ocean. When Allah wants to increase the significance of the sign and frighten His servants severely, all of the sun falls and nothing of it remains in the chariot. That is a total eclipse of the sun. It is a misfortune for the sun." No. It is a misfortune for Muhammad, Allah, Islam, and Muslims.

The prophet ended this lunacy by claiming he preached to extraterrestrials, "Allah created two cities out in space, each with ten thousand gates, each 6 kilometers distant from the other. [That makes the extraterrestrial cities bigger than the earth itself.] By Allah, were those people not so many and so noisy, all the inhabitants of this world would hear the loud crash made by the sun falling when it rises and when it sets. Gabriel took me to them during my Night Journey from the Sacred Mosque [the Ka'aba] to the Farthest Mosque [the Jewish Temple in Jerusalem]. I told the people of these cities to worship Allah but they refused to listen to me." As should we on planet Earth.

Islam's delusional creation account goes on and on. The sun is brought to heaven, it is terrorized, it cries, it falls down, it prays, it's veiled, it acts like a camel and races the moon, and it fears death. Tabari explains that the "proof of the soundness of these statements comes directly from the Messenger of Allah." Truth was not his strong suit.

2

DEVILS, DECEPTIONS & BACKRUBS

"Because Allah afflicted Eve, all the women of the
world menstruate, and they are stupid."

You may be wondering why Muhammad based his *new* religion on *old* Bible stories, and why he found it necessary to alter them. Muslim scholars insist that the characters and events, at least up to the point of departure, are similar because Yahweh and Allah are the same god. Unfortunately, that makes less sense than the sun falling out of a chariot and angelic wings blotting out the moon. If Allah is Yahweh, simply translate the Old Testament into Arabic and be done with it. We have proved that the Bible has not changed with the passage of time, so, if it was divinely inspired—as Muhammad claims—it must still be true.

But as we discovered in the last chapter, Muhammad was allergic to truth. Apparently, it didn't serve his interests. It's hard to imagine a man speaking more ignorantly or lying more transparently. The fact that Muslims are wholly reliant upon *his* testimony for the entirety of their religion and the very existence of their "god," puts them in a precarious position. Islam is on life support and we haven't even left Paradise yet.

Thus far, the Qur'an and Hadith have demonstrated that Muhammad wasn't very smart, and his god wasn't *any* help. That much should be evident by now. So lacking creativity and inspiration, Muhammad turned to the best-documented, best-known monotheistic religion, Judaism, to make his personal quest *seem* religious. So far, so good. Team Islam usurped Jewish ideas, terms, names, characters, and events. Muhammad penciled himself in as a fellow prophet—as the lead act on the marquee. He cast Allah in the role of Yahweh. He replaced Jews with Arabs and started telling Bible stories. But being illiterate, he got them all fouled up.

The Jews laughed themselves silly. Rather than accepting the self-promoting prophet, they teased him for his errant portrayals of their history. But aspiring tyrants never admit to being wrong. Rather than correct his revisionist history, Muhammad claimed supremacy. He said, "If you reject my message, you will die." Emboldened by the militants he eventually came to command, he twisted the stories further in an effort to make his wanton behavior look prophetic. Biblical accounts were contorted to the point they became nonsensical in the context of the time and place they actually occurred. The Jews, in defense of their scriptures, mocked Muhammad all the more. Enraged, Allah's Messenger struck back, calling them donkeys, apes, and pigs. He ordered his followers to **"kill every Jew."** He'd show them who was right and who was wrong. He'd prove who was godly and who was not.

When you view this continuing saga in that light, and from this perspective, even stories of a talking sun that wears clothing and sets in a muddy spring surrounded by extraterrestrials becomes relevant. And if there's a better excuse, I mean *explanation*, for this malarkey, I mean *alternate view*, I'd love to hear it. For if there is something in Islam that makes sense, something that was actually divine—we might use it to reach Muslims, reason with them, and keep them from killing us.

By way of confession, I came to see the Bible as the inspired word of Yahweh because of the prophecies it contained. I recognized that it was impossible for a 2,000 to 4,000 year-old book to accurately foretell today's events if it were not authored by a spirit that existed outside of time. You do not have to share my view, however, to understand that Islam disproved itself when it agreed with my conclusion. Two "inspired" books from the same deity cannot be contradictory to the point of being opposites.

Muhammad's dependence on the Bible requires us to compare his text with the original. To understand Islam, we must determine why they are so different. I believe that the answer is obvious. Yahweh's spirit authored one and Lucifer inspired the other. Yet, once again, you do not need to agree with me. You may view Muhammad's demonic behavior and the motivation for his deceitful scriptures metaphorically. His demons can be seen as our guttural nature, human depravity in full bloom. It doesn't require a devil to seduce covetous men into deceiving others to gain power, sex, and money.

Now for another confession. Any attempt to reorganize Islam chronologically is perilous. The religion was founded upon the claim that Abraham had a religion, that he built the Ka'aba and established Islamic rituals. With most of his Qur'an pilfered from the Torah, Muhammad professed that Adam, Noah, Abraham, Lot, Moses, and Jesus were Muslim prophets, setting the stage for Islam long before he was born. The longer Muhammad lived, the more he twisted their stories, making them his own. So if I present the evidence in the order Muhammad actually made his assertions, we'd have to jump in and out of history. But if we use a historical timeline—the Islamic version of creation through the twisting of the patriarchs, the immorality of Mecca, ending with the violence of Medina—we'll have to review Qur'anic scriptures and Islamic Hadith that were revealed last, first.

Tabari and Ishaq, as historian and biographer, use the same chronological approach I am using. Thus every surah we reference early in our narratives was revealed late in Muhammad's mission. Adam and Satan dominate Islam's genesis, yet none of the supporting Qur'anic verses are from the first score of surahs in order of their alleged revelation. I share this to keep you from jumping to the conclusion that Muhammad was a well-schooled religious man, possessing a sufficient understanding of the Bible to plagiarize it effectively at the outset of his career. In reality, he would not come to know the Torah until he came to know the Jews. And he would never understand the Gospels.

We pick up the story of Islam's creation account where we left off, with Iblis, better known as Lucifer. I'm going to work the narrative through the Qur'an. In the 7th surah, called **"The Wall Between Heaven and Hell,"** Allah, or I should say, Muhammad, corrupts one of the earliest Genesis stories. But he gets sidetracked with intolerance and terrorism before he dives into his version. So in deference to the Islamic apologists, I'll keep the whole passage in context, starting at the beginning.

Before we start, however, you should know that the only reason we can read this or any surah is because an "angel" or a "clanging bell" dictated it (or gonged it) to Muhammad directly from the "Memorial Tablets" written at Allah's command by the "Pen" before the universe was created. *007.001* **"This Book [the Qur'an] has been sent down to you."** The opening verse is not accurate. The Qur'an wasn't a book. Based upon the historical record, nothing would be committed to writing or compiled into a book for another century. **"Do not hesitate to warn the unbelievers through it."** This "warning" was not for the unbelievers' benefit or for their salvation. All non-Muslims are *predestined* to hell. So the threat of impending punishments which could not be averted strongly suggests that the author was either demented or a sadist.

Muhammad's schizophrenic spirit said: *007.003* **"Follow the Revelation given to you from your Lord and follow not as protectors other than Him [third person]. Little do you remember My [first person, singular] warning. How many towns have We [plural] destroyed as a raid by night? Our punishment took them suddenly while they slept for their afternoon rest. Our terror came to them; Our punishment overtook them. No cry did they utter but: 'We were wrong-doers.'"** The Islamic god's taste for terror is shocking. It's hard to fathom scripture bragging, **"How many towns have We destroyed?"** or, **"Our punishment took them suddenly while they slept."** What would possess someone to claim this was godly? The Islamic "god," by his own admission, is a terrorist.

Before we move on, I want to bring your attention to the motivation behind this opening salvo. Muhammad wanted his detractors to know that his god would terrorize anyone who rejected **"those to whom Our Message was sent [Muslims] or those by whom We sent it [Muhammad]."** It's a warning: "If you deny Muhammad, his followers will terrorize you."

007.007 **"Verily, We shall recount their whole story with knowledge, for We were never absent at any time or place."** Muhammad, speaking on behalf of his spirit, is acknowledging that the stories in the Qur'an appear plagiarized. But they are not, he protests, because his "god" was omnipresent. He is preparing us for an onslaught of bastardized Hebrew scripture.

"Those whose scale of good will be heavy will prosper. Those whose scale will be light will find their souls in perdition [hell], for they wrongfully treated Our Signs." That's the basis of the religion of Islam. Good works. The more you do the heavier the "good" side of your scale becomes. Unfortunately, all the good deeds in the world can't outweigh predestination. And the best "good deed" according to Muhammad is to die a jihadist terrorizing infidels.

Want proof? From Bukhari's, *Book of Jihad*, Chapter 1, number 1204: **"A man came to Allah's Messenger and said, 'Guide me to such a deed as equals Jihad in reward. ' He said, 'I do not find such a deed.'"** *Bukhari:V4B52N50* **"The Prophet said, 'A single endeavor of fighting in Allah's Cause is better than the world and whatever is in it.'"** As we move into the Medina war surahs I will share scores of these with you.

Returning to the 7ᵗʰ surah, Allah's miffed men aren't thankful. *007.010* **"It is We who have placed you [Adam] with authority on earth, and provided you with means for the fulfillment of your life: small are the thanks that you give! Little give you thanks!"**

"It is We who created you and gave you shape; then We ordered the angels to fall and prostrate themselves to Adam. And they fell prostrate, all save Iblis, who was not of those who made prostration." Iblis was Lucifer, a fallen angel better known as Satan. The Qur'an says that he was a jinn, or demonic spirit. Both the Qur'an and Bible agree that Lucifer rebelled against God.

According to the Bible, as an angel, Lucifer was merely a tool. His relationship with Yahweh was like that of a private to a general. Without choice angels cannot love. And they are incapable of creativity, which may explain why so much of the Qur'an was plagiarized. Lucifer's existence was defined by the same terms that gave Islam its name and authority: "submit and obey." The Bible says, when Lucifer rebelled, a third of the angels were cast out of heaven and became demons. They lashed out at Yahweh by deceiving man, separating us from God, just as they had been.

This all led to the most infamous meal in human history. I share this Biblical perspective because once again, Muhammad, lacking imagination, plagiarized it, albeit with his own unique embellishments. *007.012* **"What prevented you [Iblis/Lucifer] from prostrating when I commanded you?' He said: 'I am better than Adam: You created me from fire and him from clay.' So Allah said: 'Get down from this place: it is not for you to be arrogant here: get out, you are degraded, for you are of the meanest of creatures.'"** The request is odd, yet the Qur'an never explains why Allah wanted his angels to humble themselves before man.

In the Qur'an, Satan protests. *007.014* **"'Give me a reprieve until the time they are** raised.' Allah said: 'You have your reprieve.' He [Satan] said, 'Because you have thrown me out, I will lie in wait, lurking in ambush for them on Your Right Path. I will assault them from behind, from their right and left. You will find them ungrateful.' Allah said: 'Get out of here. You are disgraced and expelled. If any follow, I will fill Hell with all of you.'" The Qur'an has clearly said that Satan is deceptive, and that he's going to hell. This is important because, from this point on, Allah will claim to be deceitful and we will find him in hell, tormenting men.

Continuing to steal from Genesis, the Islamic scriptures say: *007.019* "We said: 'Adam, dwell with your wife in the Garden and enjoy: but approach not this tree or you will run into harm and become wrong-doers.' Then Satan began to whisper suggestions to them, bringing openly before their minds all their shame that was hidden from them. He said: 'Your Lord only forbid you this tree, lest you should become angels, immortal, living forever.'" This is pathetic. In the Garden, Adam *was* immortal. Seducing Adam with a promise of immortality would be like seducing Arabs with a promise of more sand. Besides, why would Adam want to become an angel if the angels were bowing to *him*?

007.021 "He swore to them that he was their sincere adviser. So by deceit he brought about their fall." This is interesting. Muslims claim that there was no fall of man, thus no reason for the Messiah to come and reconcile fallen man back into fellowship with God. Further, Satan is mimicking Muhammad. The prophet incessantly claimed to be the "sincere adviser," yet through deceit, he brought men to their knees.

"When they tasted of the tree, their shame became manifest to them, and they began to sew together leaves, covering their bodies. Allah called: 'Did I not forbid you that tree and tell you that Satan was an avowed enemy?'" For those who are curious: *Tabari I:299* "Scholars of the nation of our Prophet say, 'The tree which Allah forbade Adam and his spouse to eat was wheat.'" Yes, a wheat tree.

007.023 "They said: 'Allah, we have wronged our own souls: If you do not forgive us, we shall be of the lost losers.' Allah said: 'Go down from here as enemies of each other.'" Allah seems to think that the Garden of Eden, a.k.a. the Garden of Bliss, is in heaven. Thus when Adam rejected Allah, he was sent down, not cast out. Also, did you notice the line: "you will be enemies of each other?" He was speaking to Adam and Eve, foreshadowing the Islamic view of women.

Allah continued: "'On earth will be your dwelling place and your means of livelihood for a time.' He [third person, singular] said: "Therein shall you live, and therein shall you die, and from it shall you be raised. O children of Adam. [How did they get kids so fast?] We [first person plural] have sent clothing down to you to cover your shame, and for beauty and clothing that guards against evil. This is of the communications of Allah [now third person singular]."" Why did they need clothes to guard against evil? If their lusts carried them away—who were they going to be adulterous with?

An interesting sidebar on the first kids comes to us in this Tradition: *Tabari I:321* "When Eve became heavy with her first pregnancy, Satan came to her before she gave birth and said, 'Eve, what is that in your womb?' ["What's a womb," is what she should have asked, but didn't.] She said, 'I do not know.' He asked, 'Where will it come out from—your nose, your eye, or your ear?' She replied, 'I do not know.' He said, 'Don't you think, if it comes out healthy, you should obey me in whatever I command you?' When she said, 'Yes,' he said: 'Name him Abd al-Harith Iblis—Slave to the cursed!' She agreed." Believable dialog, don't you think? Just the kind of foundation you'd expect to underpin a great religion. "Adam said to him [Iblis/Lucifer], 'I obeyed you once before and you caused me to be driven out of Paradise.' So he refused to obey him and called the child Abd Ar-Rahman."

Ar-Rahman was the name of Muhammad's first "god." The 55th surah, named in Ar-Rahman's honor, begins: "Ar-Rahman bestowed the Qur'an, created man, and taught him to express clearly. The sun and moon revolve to his computation and the grasses and the trees bow to Him in adoration.... He created man." With multiple gods, Islam became pagan monotheism.

And with multiple truths, Islam is flawed revelation: *Tabari I:275* "They ate from it and as a result their secret part that had been concealed became apparent." It hadn't been much of a marriage up to that point. But if that's true, how did they get kids? And why does the Islamic Tradition say: *Tabari I:299* "It was the cover of fingernails that had kept their secret parts concealed." I recognize Muhammad had a warped view of sex, but this is ridiculous.

007.027 "O you Children of Adam, let not Satan seduce you, in the same manner as he got your parents out of the Garden, making them disrobe, stripping them of their clothing, to expose their shame." Just six verses earlier, Adam was nude, sinned, and thus felt the need for clothing. He made his own, sewing together leaves. Then Allah sent down supernatural clothes from AlMart. Now we're told that Satan *stripped* them? "For he [Satan/Lucifer] and his tribe [of demons/jinn] watch you from a position where you cannot see them. We made the jinn friends of the unbelievers." So there you have it. Satan, Iblis, and jinn are all cut from the same cloth—all made of fire, all from the same tribe. These invisible evil spirits, or demons, lurk in the shadows ready to ambush men, deceiving them. Yet, as you shall discover in one of the most bizarre Qur'anic passages, these pesky demons think Muhammad and Allah are swell, calling them "Prophet" and "Lord." They are employed to authenticate the Qur'an.

007.030 "Some He has guided: as for others, error is their due. They deserve loss in that they took the devils instead of Allah for their friends and think that they are rightly guided." *007.035* "Children of Adam, whenever messengers come from amongst you, rehearsing My [singular] signs and revelations to you, act rightly so that you have no fear, nor reason to grieve. But those who reject Our [plural] signs and scorn them with arrogance, they are inmates of the Fire forever." What messengers, what revelations? Allah is allegedly talking to Adam's kids. The first prophet and scripture wouldn't arrive for over two thousand years. The Islamic god had no concept of time. Worse, he couldn't even keep himself together, talking in first person singular and plural in the same verse. Somebody was very confused.

The second part of this passage is revealing. As we dig deeper into the Qur'an you'll find that the most repeated theme is: "reject Muhammad and you're toast." Although he tries a number of variants, his favorites twist Bible stories, as he has done here. Muhammad was referring to himself when he warned Adam's kids not to reject the "messenger among them."

007.037 **"Who is more unjust: one who invents a lie against Allah or one who rejects His Signs? For such, their appointed destiny must reach them from when Our messengers of death arrive and take their souls. [These guys sound a little like Hitler's S.S.] They say: 'Now where is that to which you cried to beside Allah?' They will reply, 'They have left us in the lurch.'"** There were no signs, no miracles, no proofs of any kind to confirm Muhammad's claim to being a prophet or the Qur'an's claim to being divinely inspired. The repetition of lies like this was just part of Muhammad's warped game. It's standard megalomaniac behavior. Tell a big enough lie, say it often enough, and enough will believe it for you to prevail.

007.038 **"Allah's messengers of death will say: 'Enter the fire, join the company of men and jinn who passed away before you.' Every time a fresh group of people or nation enters, they curse those that went into the Fire before them. The most recent entrants into Hell ask: 'Lord, they led us astray, so give them a double torment in the Fire.' He will say: 'For each there is already a double dose of torment.... So taste the punishment.'"**

It's stunning to the point of agony that a billion people, through seduction, indoctrination, and compulsion, have been led to believe that these hateful words are God's. Yet while stunning, it's not baffling. All Muhammad had to do was to convince fifty well-armed fools. While it took him ten years, it shouldn't have been hard. Mecca was a town of five thousand. All but a handful were illiterate. Steeped in pagan superstition, already believing in the pagan idol of the Ka'aba, the young and the rebellious, the poor and the destitute, were ripe for the picking.

Let's pick up the Islamic story of Satan and hell from the Hadith. I will be quoting from the History of al-Tabari, *Creation to the Flood*. *Tabari I:249* **"There was an angelic tribe of jinn, and Iblis belonged to it. Iblis [Satan/Lucifer] was one of the noblest angels and governed the most honored tribe."** *Tabari I:251* **"Whoever among them says: I am a god besides Him, will have Hell as his reward from Us. That is how We reward the wrongdoers.' [Qur'an 21:29] This verse was revealed specifically for Iblis, when he said what he said. May Allah curse him and have him stoned!"** We've just been given a rather interesting clue: the Qur'an was revealed for Lucifer's benefit. And ask yourself, how is a "stone" going to curse or punish a spirit?

"Iblis belonged to a tribal group called jinn. They were created from the fire of simoom. All of the angels except this tribal group were created from light. The jinn mentioned in the

Qur'an were created from a tongue of white-hot fire blazing on its side. [Qur'an 55:15] The first to dwell on the earth were jinn. They caused corruption on it and shed blood and killed each other. [Since demons are spirits, how could they shed blood and bleed?] Allah sent Iblis with an army of angels to fight against the jinn. Iblis and the angels with him caused a bloodbath, but his success went to his head." Allah made Lucifer a traitor against his own tribe, which is exactly what happened with Muhammad in Mecca.

Tabari I:252 "Allah created some creatures and said, 'Prostrate yourselves before Adam!' They replied, 'We shall not do that.' Allah sent a fire to consume them."

Four things should be perfectly clear. First, if you don't prostrate yourself, you're scorched. And while that sounds extreme, it's designed to frighten Muslims. Muhammad is quoted in a Hadith from Bukhari entitled **"Prayer is Obligatory"** saying: *Bukhari:V1B11N617* "I would order someone to collect firewood and another to lead prayer. Then I would go burn the houses of men who did not present themselves at the compulsory prayer and prostration." Islam means submission, and the sign of submission is prostration. The mosque, the centerpiece of Islamic control, is derived from the Arabic word for "the place of prostration."

Second, Satan is a jinn. Third, jinn are bad. And fourth, everybody associated with jinn loves fire—Muhammad and Allah included. I share this because of the impact it has on two of the most troubling narratives in the Qur'an. And those passages, surprisingly enough, don't include the Satanic Verses, in which Muhammad received scripture from Lucifer. They are instead ones in which Satan's jinn are used to endorse the Qur'an.

The first of these demonic interludes begins, like so many others, with a threatening rant before it torments us with nonsense. *046.027* "We have destroyed habitations all around you, having explained Our signs in different ways to them that they may turn back. Why then did the gods they had taken apart from Allah as protectors not come to their aid? In fact they strayed away from them." This is weird. Did the other gods stray away from men, making them real, or did men stray away from the other gods, making the condemnation irrelevant?

"It was all a lie what they had contrived!" After enduring a litany of Muhammad's whoppers, that's quite a claim. But nothing compared to this...*046.029* "Remember when We turned a company of jinn towards you to listen to the Qur'an? They arrived when it was being recited, and they said: 'Keep silent.' When it was over they came back to their tribe, warning them: 'O our people [fellow demonic jinn], we have listened to a Book which has come down after Moses, confirming what was sent down before it, showing the way to the truth and a path that is straight." The jinn are endorsing the Qur'an as being truthful, a straight path. That's like Churchill asking Nazis to confirm his policies. Can you imagine a god so desperate he'd solicit demonic assistance? The Good Housekeeping Seal-of-Approval, this is not.

And it didn't stop there. The demons went on to say: *046.031* "Jinn, listen to [Muhammad] the Messenger of Allah, and believe in him, so that He may forgive you your sins and save you from a painful doom." Satan's demonic spirits just proclaimed that Muhammad was their savior and their messenger. Either Muhammad's Qur'an recital was so convicting it saved devils or the devils are deceiving men by calling his lie "true." You make the call.

Back in Paradise, the Prophet's Companions explain, *Tabari I:273* **"Iblis was cursed, and Adam settled in. Adam used to go about all alone, not having a spouse to dwell with. He fell asleep, and when he woke up, he found sitting at his head a woman who had been created by Allah from his rib. [I know you've heard this before. So had Muhammad.] He asked her what she was, and she replied, 'A woman.' He asked for what purpose she had been created, and she replied, 'For you to dwell with me.' The angels, looking to find out the extent of Adam's knowledge, asked him her name. He replied, 'Eve, because she was created from a living thing.' And Allah said, 'Adam, dwell in Paradise! Eat freely of its plenty wherever you wish.'"** The omission of God's warning not to eat of the tree of the Knowledge of Good and Evil may not have been left out of this account by accident. In Islam there is no choice, and therefore, no reason for the tree. While it exits in other variations, it serves no purpose. Man is pre-destined to his fate. The reason for the tree in Genesis is to provide Adam with a choice. And it is the same choice we must all make—love God or reject him. Love cannot be compelled. Even God can't require love.

A Tradition reveals: **"He then cast slumber upon Adam as we have heard from the people of the Torah among the people of the Book."** I'm told that confession is good for the soul. At least they had the good sense and common courtesy to say where Muhammad stole his material.

Tabari I:275 **"Iblis wanted to meet them in Paradise, but the keepers prevented him from entering. He went to a snake, an animal with four feet like a camel. Iblis tried to persuade it to let him enter its mouth and take him to Adam. The snake agreed, passed by the keepers, and entered without their knowledge, because that was Allah's plan."** If Allah's plan was to *help* Satan deceive man, you know whose side Allah was on.

"Iblis talked to Adam from the mouth of the snake, but Adam paid no attention to him. So Iblis said, 'Adam, may I lead you to the tree of eternity and a power that never decays.... Both you and Eve will have eternal life and will never die.'" Since there was no death or dying in Paradise, how would Adam know what decay was? How could he be enticed to be eternal when he was created that way? **"I give you good advice. But by tearing their clothes, Iblis wanted to show them their secret parts, which had been concealed from them. From his reading of the books of the angels, he knew what Adam did not, that they had secret parts."** Wait a minute. Adam was supposed to be smart and the angels stupid. Now we're told the angels are smart enough to have books and Adam is oblivious.

Tabari I:276 **"Adam refused to eat but Eve came forward and ate. Then she said, 'Eat, Adam. I have and it has done me no harm.' But when Adam ate, their secret parts became apparent to them and they started to cover themselves with leaves of Paradise stitched together."** [Qur'an 7:22] I don't get it. Why would showing Adam and Eve their private parts seduce them into rebellion? If sex isn't good, why is it the essence of Islamic Paradise?

As you might expect, there is more than one version of this story. So for some comic relief let's look at another variant: *Tabari I:276* "Iblis proposed to the animals on earth that they should take him into Paradise so that he could speak with Adam and his spouse, but every animal refused. Finally, he spoke to the snake. It was dressed and walking on four feet, but Allah then undressed it and made it walk on its belly." Conjuring up the image of a dressed snake walking with a fiery jinn in its mouth, on four feet, being undressed by god, takes some doing.

Over the next few pages, the man solely responsible for inventing Islam, Allah, and the Qur'an said, "The tree's branches were intertwined and it bore fruit which the angels ate to live eternally." Then, "Adam went inside the tree to hide." And, "Eve cut the tree and it bled. The feather that covered Adam and Eve dropped off." So, *Tabari I:278* "Now Eve, as you caused the tree to bleed, you will bleed every new moon, and you, snake, I will cut off your feet and you will walk slithering on your face." For giggles: "Some camels were originally jinn." And: *Tabari I:279* "It was a tree which made whoever ate from it defecate. But there must be no faeces in Paradise." Since the angels ate from it to live eternally, where might they have answered the call of nature?

For another insight into the mind of Muhammad and therefore into the character of his god: *Tabari I:280* "Allah said, 'It is My obligation to make her bleed once every month as she made this tree bleed. I must also make Eve stupid, although I created her intelligent.'" Zayd, Muhammad's adopted son said, *Tabari I:280* "Because Allah afflicted Eve, all of the women of the world menstruate and are stupid." It's a wonder there are any Muslim women. It's a wonder feminist organizations are silent. Why do they tolerate a doctrine that demeans six hundred million women?

Tabari I:281 "I heard him swear by Allah unequivocally, 'As long as Adam was in his right mind, he would never have eaten from the tree. Eve gave him wine and got him drunk. She led him to the tree.'" Muhammad didn't like women very much. *Bukhari:V4B55N547* "The Prophet said, 'But for the Israelis, meat would not decay, and if it were not for Eve, wives would never betray their husbands.'" He didn't like Jews, either.

Tabari I:282 "The Messenger said, 'Friday was the Lord of Days. On Friday, Adam was created and cast down to earth. The duration of Adam and Eve's stay in Paradise was five hours.'" As usual, Muhammad had a reason for enduring the criticism these preposterous accounts surely brought him. Friday was important. Muhammad and his followers had observed the Jewish Sabbath and prayed facing the Temple Mount in Jerusalem. (It seemed only natural; they had taken everything else from Jews.) But eventually the Jews in Yathrib, today's Medina, mocked the Messenger one too many times. So Muhammad decided to differentiate his Islam from the religion of his tormentors. Saturday was theirs. Sunday was taken—something about a resurrection—so Friday became the lord of days. All Muhammad needed was a little justification.

What do you suppose happened to Adam once he was deported? The Bible picks up the story in Mesopotamia, where recorded history began, but not Islam. Muhammad had another agenda. *Tabari I:290* **"Allah cast Adam down to earth. The place where he fell down was the land of India."** Why India, you ask? Because: **"When Adam was cast down there, some of the smell of Paradise clung to India's trees."** Aisha, Muhammad's wife told us that he said, **"The things I love most are women and perfume."** The Prophet was simply trying to excuse his pre-occupation with smelling good. If his perfumes were created in paradise, smelling good was religious rather than self-indulgent.

Tabari I:291 **"Adam was cast down in India and Eve in Juddah. He went in search of her, and eventually they were united. Eve drew near him, hence Muzdalifah. They recognized each other, hence Arafat. And they were united in Jam, hence Jam."** If the India story was conceived to rationalize the prophet's obsession with perfume, why this elaborate tale? It's all about Muhammad's third and fourth vices—power and money. He wanted to legitimize and then control the pagan hajj. It was the source of the region's power and wealth during his day. Each of the places Muhammad claims the amorous couple traversed were just outside Mecca. Going to them was part of the pagan rites he later incorporated into Islam. So he was validating his claim to the religious scam he would soon steal.

Tabari was criticized for these stories. So he said, **"The soundness of this is established by a report serving as conclusive proof that Adam was cast down in India. It is rejected neither by the Muslim scholars nor by the people of the Torah and Gospel. Proof is firmly established by reports from some of them."** As you have seen, justifying the unjustifiable has caused Muslims to latch on to imaginary verifications. There is nothing in the Torah or Gospels that says Adam was dropped in India. The Biblical Garden of Eden was on Earth, not heaven; it was located near the headwaters of the Tigris and Euphrates Rivers and the Black Sea.

Tabari I:292 **"It has been mentioned that the summit of the mountain upon which Adam was cast down is one of those closest to heaven. When Adam was cast upon it his feet were on it while his head was in heaven. He heard the songs of the angels. The angels were afraid of him so his size was reduced."** The Islamic heaven must be very low.

Knowing Muhammad, there had to be an ulterior motive. The prophet was trying to rationalize something. What do you suppose it was this time? *Tabari I:293* **"When Allah cast Adam down from Paradise, Adam's feet were on earth while his head was in heaven. He became too familiar with the angels and they were in awe of him so much so that they complained to Allah in their various prayers. Allah, therefore, lowered Adam. But Adam missed what he used to hear from the angels and felt lonely. He complained to Allah and was sent to Mecca. On the way, every place where he set foot became a village, and the interval between his steps became a desert until he reached Mecca."**

We're getting close. It's important for Muhammad, and thus Islam, to place Adam in Mecca. Could there be more? **"Allah sent down a jewel of Paradise where the House [Ka'aba] is located today. Adam continued to circumambulate it until Allah sent down the Flood."** There you have it. To make the insignificant pagan Ka'aba seem godly and important, and to have the stone that represented the most senior idol of the Meccan pantheon appear like it belonged to Islam, we see Allah sending Adam to the Ka'aba and giving him his Black Stone. We even have Adam circumambulate it like a good Muslim for a thousand years, helping to justify Islamic ritual. Muhammad was not only the world's worst prophet, he was the world's most transparent liar.

Now all Muhammad needed to do was connect the Ka'aba to Abraham so he could rationalize Islam's reliance on the Hebrew Bible. With the Bible snagged, he had himself a religion. *Tabari I:293* **"That jewel was lifted up until Allah sent Abraham to (re)build the House. This is meant by Allah's word, 'And We established for Abraham the place of the House as residence.'"** [Qur'an 22:26] Muhammad was as predictable as sunrise.

You probably noticed the (re) before build. In the creation account Allah built the Ka'aba himself. Then it was built by Adam. Now we are told that Abraham built it. So I ask you: how many times should a prophet be allowed to contradict himself before he is no longer considered a prophet?

The legends behind the Ka'aba are essential to Islam. If they don't make sense, neither does the religion. *Tabari I:293* **"Allah founded the House together with Adam. Adam's head was in heaven while his feet were upon the earth. The angels were afraid so his size was reduced to sixty cubits (30 meters). Adam was sad because he missed the angelic songs. He complained, and Allah said, 'Adam, I have cast down a house for you to circumambulate, as one circumambulates My Throne.' Adam came to the House, and he and the prophets after him circumambulated it."** In this account we have the Ka'aba being built in heaven and also being built cooperatively by Adam and Allah. Either way, it's a wonder the Islamic god would take credit for building something so crude and unsightly.

Reducing Adam is a fairytale. As is the desert forming between his strides and villages cropping up in his footsteps. So then, when does the make-believe world of Islam end and the real world begin? When do we move out of fiction and into nonfiction? Stated another way, can you trust a man who is willing to base his religion on stories this farfetched? If he had to deceive us to make the Ka'aba seem worthy of devotion, is it?

Tabari I:294 **"When Adam's size was lowered to sixty cubits, he started to say, 'My lord! I was your protégé in Your House, having no Lord but You to protect me. There I had plenty to eat and could dwell wherever I wanted. But then You cast me down to this holy mountain. There I used to hear the voices of the angels and see them crowd around Your Throne and enjoy the sweet smell of Paradise. Then you cut me off from these things."**

This is a confession. Muhammad saw himself as Allah's protégé—if not as Allah himself. He constantly looked for people to protect him, and as an orphan, he was deprived of food. His own tribe became so disgusted with his continual taunts they made travel difficult for him. He was consumed with a desire to make Allah's House and Mecca both his and important. He indulged in the sweet smell of perfume and repeatedly claimed that he could hear the angels. What's more, his Qur'an is filled with complaints.

Muhammad couldn't even keep his own twisted version of Adam straight. Listen to this excerpt in which the prophet's indulgences were falsely manifest in Adam: *Tabari I:318* **"He built for himself cities and castles and populated them and made them prosperous. He also assembled weapons and established a cavalry. At the end of his life, he became a tyrant. He took the name of Adam and said, 'If someone calls me by any other name, I shall cut off his hand.' He married thirty women and they gave him many offspring. He liked them and promoted them so that later kings were their offspring. His realm expanded greatly."** Muhammad just couldn't help himself. He used a twisted caricature of Adam to make his warped existence seem godly. Muslims want us to believe that Adam, like Muhammad, was a warrior, an unbridled libertine, a prophet, and a politician who hated nicknames.

Yes, according to Islam, Adam was just like Muhammad: *Tabari I:319* **"Adam and his descendants were prophets with royal authority and rulership on Earth. Allah made him a prophet and messenger to his children. He revealed to Adam twenty-one scrolls. Adam was taught them by Gabriel and wrote them down with his own hand. Among the things Allah revealed to Adam was the prohibition against eating dead animals and pork. He also revealed to him the letters of the alphabet on twenty-one leaves."** Writing began with pictures, not letters. And since we know it, how did it escape their god's grasp?

While that's a detail, there's a bigger issue at stake. Muhammad's absurd and transparent bastardization of Biblical characters was essential to establishing his credibility and thus to imposing his religion. Ultimately, exposing Muhammad's motivation for doing so is central to understanding the mess the world is in today.

As we continue the story of the Islamic Adam, pay attention to three things. First, the details: megalomaniacs are so full of themselves they get carried away. They present their preposterous notions as if they were divinely inspired. Second, the worst part of lying is remembering what you said. Most everything Muhammad reveals contradicts something he has or will profess. Third, each tradition invariably devolves into making Muhammad seem prophetic, or Mecca, its Ka'aba, and ritual, seem divine.

Tabari I:294 **"When Allah saw the nakedness of Adam and Eve, He commanded Adam to slaughter a ram from the eight couple of small cattle He had sent down from Paradise. Adam took its wool, and Eve spun it. He and Eve wove it. Adam made a coat for himself, and a shift and veil for Eve. They put on that clothing. Then Allah revealed to Adam, 'I have a sacred territory around my Throne. Go and build a House for Me there.'"** This time the clothes weren't provided by Allah, nor made of leaves. And to spin and weave wool, one needs a spinning wheel and a loom. Did Eve invent these? And speaking of Eve; in true Islamic fashion we are led to believe she was made to wear a veil. Adam made it for her even though they were the only humans on earth. Who was she hiding her face from?

"Adam said, 'Lord, how could I build a house? I do not have the strength, and I do not know how. [Eve knows how to build a spinning wheel and loom from scratch, yet Adam can't pile rocks. And Muslims say that god made women stupid.] So Allah chose an angel to assist him and he went with him to Mecca." Angels, we've been told, were not as smart as Adam. Now they are tour guides and contractors.

Tabari I:294 "Adam built the House with materials from five mountains: Mount Sinai, the Mount of Olives, Mount Lebanon, and al-Judi. He constructed its foundations with materials from Mount Hira near Mecca. When he was finished with its construction the angel went out with him to Arafat. He showed him all the rites connected with the pilgrimage that people perform today. Then he went with him to Mecca and Adam circumambulated the House for a week. Returning to the land of India, he died upon Mount Nudh." I'd bet my life that if archeologists examined the stones of the Ka'aba they'd find no evidence that they came from any of those faraway places or that the construction dates to 4,000 B.C. But the egregious lie was not without benefit. We have arrived at the motivation behind this fairytale: the rites and rituals of Islam as they were adapted and ordered by Muhammad.

Everything associated with the pilgrimage had pagan origins. Nothing was Biblical. Muhammad knew the truth, but he was desperate to give the hajj a holy spin. His career was dependent upon it. And lest we forget, in our quest to determine his veracity, in this version Adam returns to India after a week of circumambulation. The last time we played this game, he continued to rotate until the flood.

According to the third Caliph, Umar: *Tabari I:295* "While Adam was in India Allah revealed to him that he should perform the pilgrimage to this House." As in: it already existed and thus didn't need to be built from the stones of four mountains. Then, "Eventually he reached the House. He circumambulated it and performed all the rites of the pilgrimage. He wanted to return to India. When he reached the mountain passes of Arafat, [the place of Muhammad's farewell sermon] the angels met him and said, 'You have performed the pilgrimage faultlessly.' This surprised him. When the angels noticed his surprise they said, 'Adam we have performed the pilgrimage to this House two thousand years before you were created. And Adam felt properly chastised.'" Okay. So tell me, why did the angels go to Mecca to worship Allah if he lived in heaven?

The pages that follow detail the origins of perfume and fruit. We'll take a pass on them and go directly to those things essential to Islam. As you read these words, remember that internal contradiction is one of the surest signs that something is false. Muhammad, we are discovering, is the poster boy for this dubious honor. And our boy's nose is about to grow a mile longer. *Tabari I:298* "The Black Stone which was originally whiter than snow was brought down with Adam as well as the staff of Moses. It was made from the myrtle of Paradise, which, like Moses, was ten cubits (five meters) tall, and also myrrh and incense. Then anvils, mallets, and tongs were revealed to him. When Adam was cast down upon the mountain, he looked at an iron rod growing on the mountain. The first thing of iron he hammered was a long knife [also known as a sword]. Then he hammered the oven, the one which Noah inherited and that boiled with the punishment in India. When Adam fell down, his head brushed against heaven. As a result, he became bald and passed on baldness to his children."

What was a rock doing in paradise? If one could take something, wouldn't they pick an implement more useful than a stone? Yet while that stone was worthless to Adam, it was supremely useful for Muhammad. He turned a Meccan meteorite into the creator god of the universe. But Allah's stone was black. How and why did Snow White turn ugly? Muhammad said, "The stone turned black because it was fingered by menstruating women."

A few more questions remain. If Moses was five meters tall, over sixteen feet, how did he pass himself off as being part of Pharaoh's family? And finally, how could Adam have hit his head against *heaven* by falling *down*? Perhaps this is a clue. Muhammad is telling us something about Allah and the location of the Islamic paradise.

Why be so picky, you may be wondering? Ancient mythology and pagan religions are full of such nonsense. Yes, but Islam was invented ten centuries after the last pagan myth was conceived—so he is without excuse. More to the point, Muslims are killing us today because of Muhammad's claims. Suicide bombers blast themselves into oblivion based upon this maniac's promises. Simply stated: a prophet who makes a practice of lying shouldn't be trusted!

Muhammad's promise of paradise for martyrs who die killing infidels can't be relied upon—period! Calling this verbal diarrhea "a religion" doesn't make it one. Right from the beginning, there has been a clear and undeniable pattern of deception and delusion. And it never ends. Muhammad was willing to say and do *anything* in the name of his spirit so long as it advanced his personal agenda.

Muhammad, speaking on behalf of Allah in an Islamic Hadith says: *Tabari I:301* "I shall have one of those houses singled out for My generosity and distinguish it from all others by My name and call it My House. I shall have it proclaim My greatness, and it is upon it that I have placed My majesty." Allah is bragging about a stubby pile of un-hewn and un-mortared rocks. His "House" didn't even have a roof because there was no wood for the beams, or carpenters in Mecca. "My majesty" indeed.

Sounding more like Hinduism than Islam: "In addition, I, being in everything and together with everything, shall make that House a safe sanctuary whose sacredness will extend to those around, those underneath, and those above it." That's laughable. Muhammad led dozens of armed raids against the Meccans for control of the House. Some safe sanctuary it turned out to be. Even today, Allah's Ka'aba is the cornerstone of terror. And please tell me: who is underneath the Ka'aba?

"I shall make it the first House founded as a blessing for mankind in the valley of

Mecca. They will come to it disheveled and covered with dust upon all kinds of emaciated mounts from every ravine, shouting: 'At Your service,' shedding copious tears and noisily proclaiming 'Allahu Akbar!'" Yes, that's it. Those are the words the terrorists say before they commit murder.

"You shall dwell there, Adam, for as long as you live. Then the nations, generations, and prophets of your children shall live there, one nation after the other." Outright deceit is another way to tell if someone is worthy of being the founder of a religion. There is no trace of a permanent settlement in Mecca, much less a nation, prior to the sixth century. Depending on whether you believe Moses or Muhammad, Adam left the Garden 6,000 to 7,500 years ago. That's a 4,500-year error. The harder Muhammad tries to make Mecca and the Ka'aba appear credible and religious, the less credible and religious they appear.

"He commanded Adam to go to the Sacred House which was cast down to earth for him, [What happened to building it and the rocks from four mountains?] and to circumambulate it, just as he used to see the angels circumambulate Allah's Throne. The Sacred House was a single jewel [the Black Stone] I was told. The House was cast down being a single jewel." Those last two lines confirm something that Muslims vociferously deny. A "house" is a place in which people live. It is unlike a temple, which is a place people go to worship. Allah's house was the stone. Most pagan gods were thought by their creators to embody the idol that represented them. Allah was no different.

Tabari I:302 "Eventually, when Allah drowned the people of Noah, He lifted it up, but its foundation remained. Allah established it as a residence for Abraham who (re)built its later form." That's where all of this was going all along. Muhammad had to introduce Noah and then connect Mecca and Islam to Abraham. Allah's Messenger turns both Noah and Abraham into prophets that are indistinguishable from himself. Allah, we are told, drowned everybody because they mocked Noah's message—just as he will fry those who mock Muhammad's. He remade Abraham in his image, as a Muslim who was tormented and tested. All of this was needed to justify his reliance on the Bible and make the Ka'aba appear worthy.

Tabari I:303 "When we were sitting in the mosque, Mujhid said, 'Do you see this?' I replied, you mean the Stone?' He said, 'You call it a stone?' I said, 'Is it not a stone?' He said, 'I was told by Abdallah bin Abbas that it was a white jewel that Adam took out of Paradise to wipe his tears—tears that did not stop for 2,000 years. I said, 'Why and how did it turn black?' He replied, 'Menstruating women were touching it in the Jahiliyyah [the Time of Ignorance—i.e. pre-Islam]'" Muhammad valued the Allah stone as much as he despised menstruating women. It's good to see that his faithful were able to tie these things together.

What you're going to hear next is one of the most diabolical doctrines of Islam: men and women are born to be tormented. They have no choice in the matter. Eternal damnation is god's doing, not ours. *Tabari I:305* "Then Allah rubbed

Adam's back and brought forth his progeny. And every living being to be created by Allah to the Day of Resurrection came forth at Na'man. He scattered them in front of him like tiny ants. He made covenants with them.... He took two handfuls and said to those on the right, 'Enter Paradise! And He said to the others, 'Enter the Fire! I do not care.'" A loving and merciful god if there ever was one. But beyond demented, this is further evidence that Allah and Yahweh are opposites. Yahweh wants us to choose to love him; Allah chose for us and he doesn't care, much less love.

A moment's reflection on this doctrine renders an undeniable verdict: Islam is irrelevant. If all men and women are predestined to heaven or hell, faith is folly. Good works are no more valuable than bad ones. Rituals are ridiculous. Martyrdom is madness. Eat, drink, and be merry, for a backrub sealed our fate.

Tabari I:306 "**The Messenger said, "Allah created Adam and then rubbed Adam's back with his right hand and brought forth his progeny. Then He said, 'I have created these as the inhabitants of Paradise.' Then he rubbed his back with His left hand and said, 'I have created those for the Fire, and they will act as the inhabitants of the Fire.' A man asked, 'O Messenger, how is that? Muhammad replied, 'When Allah creates a human being for Paradise, He employs him to act as the inhabitants of Paradise, and he will enter Paradise. And when Allah creates a human being for the Fire, He will employ him to act as the inhabitants of the Fire, and will thus make him enter the Fire.'"** In other words, he didn't have a clue, although he gives us a clue as to what *he* is like, a peek into his soul, into his religion, at his deity. His god directs the actions of men—good and bad. If we are to believe Muhammad, Allah is the employer of evil. And that's not good. Worse, he directs men to act badly so that he can punish them for acting as he decreed.

Islam confirmed this fatalistic right and left hand stuff in a Bukhari Hadith and then again in the 56th surah. *Bukhari:V6B60N473* "**Every created soul has his place written for him either in Paradise or in the Hell Fire. His happy or miserable fate is predetermined for him.**" *056.008* "**Those of the right hand—how happy will be those of the right hand! Those of the left hand—how unhappy will be those of the left hand! ...Who will be honored in the Garden of Bliss; a number of the earlier peoples, and a few of the later ages, on couches wrought of gold reclining face to face. Youth of never-ending bloom [perpetual virgins] will pass round to them. Cups and decanters full of sparkling wine, they shall not be affected with headache thereby, nor shall they get exhausted [Allah's Viagra?]. And such fruits as they fancy, bird meats that they relish and companions pure and beautiful with big eyes like pearls within their shells as a reward.**" In other words, a drunken orgy is your reward for being a "righty." It's no wonder they find boys willing to die for the cause.

056.033 "**Unending and unforbidden, exalted beds, and maidens incomparable. We have formed them in a distinctive fashion and made them virgins, loving companions matched in age, for the sake of those of the right hand.**" This view of Paradise is so vulgar, demeaning, sexist, and immoral, I find it repulsive. The next time you hear a Muslim say that the god of the Qur'an and the God of the Bible are the same remind them of their god's idea of a good time. The next time you hear Muslims condemn the West for its sexual decadence and perversion, ask them to read their Qur'an.

This is the fate the sadistic god of Islam selected and then predestined for the "lefties:" *056.041* "But those of the left hand—how unhappy those of the left hand. They will be in the scorching hot wind and boiling water, under the shadow of thick black smoke, neither cool nor agreeable. ...They will be gathered together on a certain day which [like their fate] is predetermined. Then you, the erring and the deniers will eat Zaqqoom [a thorn tree]. Fill your bellies with it, and drink scalding water, lapping it up like female camels raging of thirst and diseased. Such will be their entertainment, their welcome on the Day of Doom...the welcome of boiling water and the entertainment of roasting in Hell. This is indeed the ultimate truth." According to the "ultimate truth" only 1 in 1,000 people will avoid "the entertainment of roasting while lapping up thorns and scalding water."

Allah is fixated on tormenting his creation. He speaks of pain and punishment more frequently than any other subject—a thousand times in the Qur'an. And if "God" thinks this is entertaining, we've got a problem.

Fortunately for mankind, Allah isn't God. He's just a warped figment of Muhammad's sadistic imagination. And while that's good, it's also bad. Over a billion people claim to be subservient to Allah. Sixty percent are young, and many of them are willing to die for their virginal reward.

The story of Adam's boys is next. What do you bet Muhammad twists this Bible account for his benefit? *Tabari I:308* "The story of Cain and Abel was told by Allah to Muhammad in the Qur'an saying, 'Recite to them—meaning the people of the Book—the story of the two sons of Adam truthfully...to the end of the story.'"

So here we go: "Eventually, two boys, called Cain and Abel, were born to Adam. Cain was a farmer and Abel was a herdsman. Cain was the older of the two." Thus far, this is from the Bible, but there is an Islamic twist. "Cain had a sister who was more beautiful than Abel's sister. [How could that be if they were brothers?] Abel sought to marry Cain's sister, but Cain refused and said, 'She is my sister born together with me and she is more beautiful than your sister, I deserve to marry her more than you do. Adam ordered Cain to marry her to Abel. However, he refused." Muhammad's preoccupation with sex was second only to his sadism. And Islam's prophet, like his version of Abel, murdered and dabbled in incest to satisfy his cravings. Muhammad married his son's wife simply because she was more beautiful than any of his.

"Cain and Abel offered a sacrifice to Allah to find out who was more deserving of the girl. On that day Adam was absent as he had gone to have a look at Mecca. Allah had said to Adam, 'Adam do you know that I have a House on Earth?' Adam replied, 'Indeed I do not.' Allah said, 'I have a house in Mecca. So go there!' [In Islam, one thing is eternal—

contradictions. Just a few pages ago Adam was credited with building the Ka'aba] Adam said to heaven, 'Guard my two children.' [I thought he had four kids—two sons and two daughters. Don't daughters count?] But heaven refused. Adam addressed the Earth with the same request, but the Earth refused." Excuse me. In Islam, two things are eternal—contradictions and stupidity.

"He addressed the mountains but they also refused. He then spoke to Cain, who said, 'Yes. You shall go and when you return you shall be happy with the condition you find your family.'" After some bragging and bickering we find…"Abel offered a fat young sheep and Cain a sheaf of corn. Finding a large ear, Cain husked and ate it. A fire came down from heaven. It consumed Abel's offering and left that of Cain. Whereupon Cain got angry and said, 'I shall kill you to prevent you from marrying my sister. Abel said, 'Allah accepts only from those who [love? No, sorry, guess again] fear Him….' One day Cain came upon him while he was asleep. He lifted a big rock and crushed Abel's head with it."

The Islamic perversion continues: "Allah sent two ravens that were brothers and they fought with one another. When the one killed the other, it dug a hole for it and covered it with soil. When Cain saw that, he said, 'Woe to me! Am I incapable of being like that raven, so as to conceal my brother?' This explains Allah's word: 'And Allah sent a raven to scratch a hole in the earth in order to show him how to conceal his brother.'" [Qur'an 5:31] Allah's idea of dealing with guilt is to hide the evidence.

I want to let you in on a secret. These fanciful tales didn't come from Allah, or even Muhammad's vivid imagination. They were pilfered from the Jewish Talmud—an uninspired collection of myths and fables.

With that in mind, let's spend a moment in the 5th surah. After a dialog between Moses and the Israelites in the wilderness, the scene jumps abruptly two thousand years back in time: 005.027 "And relate to them the story of the two sons of Adam with truth when they both offered an offering, but it was accepted from one and was not accepted from the other. He said: 'I will most certainly slay you.' The other said: 'Allah only accepts from those who fear…. Surely I fear Allah. Surely I wish that you should bear the sin committed against me and your own sin, and so you would be of the inmates of the Hell Fire, and this is the recompense of the unjust.'" The Hadith we just read was designed to give the Qur'an the context it otherwise lacks. It explained the nature of the beef, or lamb as the case may be.

You may have noticed that Abel is meaner in the Qur'an than he was in the Hadith. Like Muhammad, he condemned his brother to the Hell Fire. So the Qur'anic Cain and Muhammad have a great deal in common.

005.030 "Then his mind facilitated to him the slaying of his brother so he slew him; then he became one of the losers. Then Allah sent a crow digging up the earth so that he might show him how he should cover the dead body. He said: Woe to me! Do I lack the strength that I should be like this crow and cover the dead body of my brother? So he became of those who regret." Allah needs the crow and burial because of Muhammad's repressed guilt for leaving so many dead bodies in his wake.

The Qur'an abruptly transitions from crow behavior to a justification for genocide. *005.032* **"For this reason did We prescribe to the children of Israel that whoever slays a soul, unless it be for manslaughter or for mischief in the land, it is as though he slew all men; Our apostles came to them with clear arguments, but even after that many of them certainly act extravagantly in the land."** Not only is the causal link unintelligible, the moral lesson is insane. Allah is saying that it's okay to kill Jews if they're causing mischief (such as tormenting the prophet by scoffing at him). Allah is thus giving Muhammad a *carte blanch* for mass murder. And he took it. Muhammad slaughtered thousands of Jews in genocidal rage.

This chilling verse exposes the real Muhammad/Allah. *005.033* **"The punishment for those who wage war against Allah and His Prophet and strive to make mischief in the land, is only this, that they should be murdered or crucified or their hands and their feet should be cut off on opposite sides or they should be imprisoned. This shall be as a disgrace for them in this world, and in the hereafter they shall have a grievous punishment. ...They would like to escape from the Hell Fire, but they will never succeed, and their suffering shall be eternal. ...He punishes whom He wills."** Stunning, isn't it?

Throughout his creation account, Muhammad has professed to being an expert on Lucifer, so I'd like to share some of my favorite Satanic Hadiths. *Bukhari:V2B21N245* **"A person slept in and missed the morning prayer. So the Prophet said, 'Satan urinated in his ears.'"** Satan wouldn't be troubled by a Muslim missing a prayer to Allah unless Islam served his interests.

Bukhari:V4B54N494 **"Allah's Apostle said, 'When the upper edge of the sun appears in the morning, don't perform a prayer till it has risen. When the lower edge of the sun sets, don't perform a prayer till it has set, for the sun rises between two sides of the Satan's head.'"**

Bukhari:V4B54N509 **"The Prophet said, 'Yawning is from Satan and if anyone of you yawns, he should check his yawning as much as possible, for if anyone of you during the act of yawning should say: "Ha," Satan will laugh at him.'"**

Bukhari:V4B54N513 **"Allah's Apostle said, 'A good dream is from Allah, and a bad dream is from Satan; so if anyone of you has a bad dream and is afraid, he should spit on his left side, for then it will not harm him.'"** The moral: sleep on the right side of the bed.

Bukhari:V4B54N516 **"The Prophet said, 'If anyone rouses from sleep and performs the ablution, he should wash his nose by putting water in it and then blow it out thrice because Satan has stayed in the upper part of his nose all the night.'"** Thank you Dr. Muhammad.

Bukhari:V4B54N522 **"Allah's Apostle said, 'When you hear the crowing of cocks, seek blessings. Their crowing indicates that they have seen an angel. When you hear the braying of donkeys, seek refuge, for their braying indicates that they have seen Satan.'"** Based upon what we have heard thus far, the Qur'an and Hadith sound a lot like the braying of donkeys. Do you suppose we have seen Satan in them?

3

I DON'T NOAH 'BOUT THIS

"He prayed that the African's color would change so that their descendants would be slaves to the Arabs and Turks."

Muhammad had a religion to sell, and by god, he was going to make it sound religious no matter how often he had to reshuffle the facts. *Tabari I:323* "I asked the Messenger of Allah how many prophets there were. He replied, '124,000.' I asked him how many of those were messengers. He replied, '313, a large crowd.'"

That's a problem of incalculable magnitude for Muslims. *Bukhari:V8B76N550* "I heard Allah's Apostle saying, 'From my followers there will be a crowd of 70,000 in number who will enter Paradise whose faces will glitter as the moon.'" These numbers don't add up. There must be a mistake. Let's check another Hadith. *Bukhari V4B54N410* "Verily! 70,000 of my followers will enter Paradise altogether; so that the first and the last amongst them will enter at the same time." Sorry Muslims, Paradise is full. A giant "No Vacancy" sign is hanging over the brothel door. In fact, it's so overbooked, 54,000 *prophets* have already been turned away. With odds like this, it's no wonder Muslims are willing to kill for a place in line.

Now that we know Muhammad's Paradise was oversold, how about Allah's Hell? *Bukhari:V8B76N537* "The Prophet said, 'Allah will say, "Adam!" "I am obedient to Your orders." Allah will say, "Bring out the people of the Fire." "How many are the people of the Fire?" Allah will say, "Out of every thousand take out nine-hundred and ninety-nine persons." At that time children will become hoary-headed and every pregnant female will drop her load. You will see the people as if they were drunk. Allah's punishment will be very severe.'" There have been more than ten billion humans born thus far. If one in every one thousand people get to frolic with Allah's babes, the brothel's capacity must be ten million, not seventy thousand. Somebody isn't telling the truth.

"That news distressed the companions of the Prophet too much, and they said, 'O Allah's Apostle! Who amongst us will be that lucky one out of the one-thousand who will be saved from the Fire?' He said, 'Have the good news that one-thousand will be from Gog and Magog, and the one (to be saved will be) from you.' [Since he wasn't a real prophet, Muhammad didn't know that the people of Gog and Magog would all succumb to Islam. They include today's Iranians, Iraqis, Turks, and Muslims in the Islamic Republics of the

Russian Federation.] The Prophet added, 'By Allah, I Hope that you Muslims will be one third of the people of Paradise.' On that, we glorified and praised Allah by saying, 'Allahu Akbar.' The Prophet then said, 'I hope that you will be one half of the people of Paradise.'" Therefore, a maximum of 35,000 Muslims will burn in lust rather than in Allah's fire. That represents 1 in 90,000. Said another way, if you were to fill a giant stadium with 90,000 Muslims, all but one will be scorched by Allah. Unless, of course, the "prophet" was lying. (In that case, they will all lose.)

Gog and Magog is Islam's time bomb—a gift from the Jews. We'll discuss the implications in the last chapter. For now, it's sufficient to know that Muhammad was over-hyping hell and overselling paradise. And if his Islamic god was really *God,* we're in trouble. He's so unmerciful, unforgiving, unloving, intolerant, and sadistic 99.9% of us are destined for hell.

Throughout the Sunnah and Qur'an, Muhammad falsely attributes Muslim prophet and messenger status to Biblical characters in order to remake them in his image. Most every prophet/messenger listed in the Qur'an came from the Bible, including: Adam, Noah, Seth, Abraham, Lot, Jacob, Joshua, Jonah, Job, Moses, David, Solomon, Saul, Elijah, Ezra, Enoch, John, and Jesus. Moses is mentioned by name in 500 verses, Abraham in 250. Muhammad's non-Biblical list consists of mistakes and myths. For example, the oft-mentioned Hud was from the mythical land of "Ad." (Something Muslims can't do.)

"I asked the Messenger, 'Who was the first of them?' He replied, 'Adam.' I asked him whether Adam was a prophet sent as a messenger. He replied, 'Yes, Allah created him with His own hand and blew some of His spirit into him. Then He immediately fashioned him in perfect shape.'" So much for fermenting him. (Qur'an 15:26 & Tabari I:261)

Tabari I:324 "When Adam was about to die, he called his son Seth and appointed him his heir. He taught him the hours of day and night and how the creatures should worship in each hour. He informed him that each hour had its special kind of creatures to worship in it. Then he said, 'Son, the Flood will be on earth and last seven years.' Adam wrote his will and addressed it to him." While there is substantial evidence of the Biblical flood, it did not last seven years, and if Adam had been a prophet he would have gotten the facts right. Further, we were just told that animals are to practice Islam, worshiping, at prescribed hours.

"After Adam's death, political leadership fell to Seth. According to a tradition on the authority of the Messenger, Allah revealed fifty scrolls to Seth." That would mean that between Adam and Seth, there were seventy-one scrolls of scripture. You'd think that with this vast quantity of divine revelation, the great Messenger of Allah would tell us something about their contents—some divine truth, perhaps. No. Sorry. Not even a hint. That's because they never existed, and since they didn't exist, they were hard to plagiarize. "'O Messenger of Allah, how many books did Allah reveal?' He replied, '104.'" Assuming that the Qur'an was one of them, what's in the other 103?

We have this treasure on the authority of the Messenger, *Tabari I:328* "When the angel of death came to seize Adam, he said, 'You have come too early. Sixty of my years remain.' The angel of death replied, 'Nothing remains. You gave those sixty years to your son David.' The Messenger continued, 'Adam denied it, and so on that day Allah established written documents and commanded the use of witnesses.'" David was 3000 years removed from Adam—hardly his son. And how can writing have been established while Adam was on his deathbed? Just a moment ago, Allah said he gave Adam twenty-one written scrolls and taught him the alphabet.

A paragraph later, we're told: "Allah wrote this down in a document and had the angels witness it.... Whereupon Allah had the document brought down and had the angels produced as witnesses against him." If Allah wrote, and if the Qur'an was important, why did it come down in the form of clanging bells and oral recitals rather than scrolls? (The answer is: it's easier to get scriptural approval for power, lust, and booty if you're making it up as you go along.)

Tabari I:332 "Adam died. Seth and his brothers were in the regions east of Paradise at a village that was the first on earth." Wait a minute; Allah said Paradise was up, and therefore not *on* earth. And how can this be the first village if Allah created cities on the third day of creation? We were even told that his footsteps became villages en route to Mecca. Somebody ought to have edited this stuff before trying to pass it off as scripture.

The prophet's next line further confirmed that he wasn't inspired by God. "The sun and the moon were in eclipse for seven days and nights." That's impossible. The sun is eclipsed by the moon and the moon by the earth's shadow. They cannot both be "in eclipse." God ought to be smarter than this.

To establish a Muslim ritual, Muhammad said, "When Adam died, the angels washed him separately several times with water and prepared a burial site. They said, 'This shall be the custom among all Adam's children.'" In Islam, non-martyrs are buried this way. Martyrs, like today's suicide bombers, are not washed. The innocent blood of innocents smeared on their bodies is a badge of honor, Allah's signal to escort them directly into paradise—wherever it might be.

"The Messenger said, 'Your father Adam was as tall as a very tall palm, that is sixty cubits. He had much hair and his privy parts were concealed. When he committed the sin of eating from the forbidden [wheat] tree, his secret part became apparent to him. He fled about in Paradise, but a tree encountered him and seized him by his forelock... When he was about to die, Allah sent down embalming chemicals and a shroud for him." Didn't Allah say Adam was bald because he bumped into heaven falling down? (Tabari I:298) And why would Allah need embalming fluid in heaven?

Tabari I:333 "Ibn Ishaq said, 'He was buried in Mecca in the cave of Abu Qubays, called the Treasure Cave.'" But there is no reason to look for his big bones there because, "Noah took them out, placed them in a coffin, and carried them along in the ark.... When Noah left the ark, he buried Adam in Jerusalem. And as mentioned before, Eve spun, wove, kneaded, baked, and did all kinds of women's work."

One of the reasons I have been reporting these early Islamic Traditions is because they provide an insight into Muhammad's character. They establish a pattern of behavior—a willingness to deceive. Specifically, they demonstrate that Muhammad was willing to pass himself off as an authority on godly and spiritual things when he clearly was not. That means his claim to being *the* Messenger of God is suspect. Therefore, so is the Qur'an and Islam.

The second reason that I have shared so many of these with you is to demonstrate that Muhammad was incapable of innovative thought. Lacking creativity and godly inspiration, he corrupted the Bible and plagiarized the Talmud. In that regard, he and the fallen angel Lucifer had a great deal in common. Simply stated, Muhammad was not capable of inventing a religion. You will soon learn that the prophet actually stole the entirety of the religious scam that became Islam.

Third, these twisted variants all serve a purpose. Muhammad used them to justify the inclusion of Qusayy's pagan practices into Islam. They gave the Five Pillars, all of which were pagan, some semblance of monotheistic credibility. Time and again, Muhammad rewrote Jewish history to make Allah, Mecca, the Ka'aba, Hajj and himself seem worthy of veneration. He recast Adam, Noah, and Abraham as Muslim messengers focused on Mecca.

If Adam, Noah, and Abraham weren't Muslims, then the preponderance of the Qur'an was stolen, not revealed. There's no other explanation for Allah's dependence on the Bible and Talmud. So Muhammad must convince us that the Jewish patriarchs worshiped Allah, received Qur'anic revelations, made journeys to Mecca, built the Ka'aba, worshiped there, and performed a complex array of Islamic rituals. If he fails in this regard, if his revisionist stories aren't *believable*, then the Qur'an is a forgery, Islam is a counterfeit, and Muhammad was a fraud. That being the case, there is no justification for them to kill us over it.

Finally, Muhammad corrupts the lives and words of Adam, Noah, Lot, and Abraham to excuse his pathetic existence. The Islamic Adam had a cavalry; he was a warrior and a tyrant just like Muhammad. Like the Islamic prophet, the Muslim Cain was guilty of incest; he was driven to murder by lust. The Islamic Noah wanted his people to be slaughtered for mocking him. The Islamic Abraham destroyed the small idols so that his people would turn to the largest one. Muhammad recast these men in his image. They were all embroiled in arguments with their peers that mirrored Muhammad's Meccan trials. In each case Allah punished those who rejected the messenger just as Muhammad claims he will torment those who deny him.

With Muhammad's agenda in mind, let's march ahead. *Tabari I:335* **"Seth stayed in Mecca performing the hajj pilgrimage and the lesser umrah until he died. He**

added the scrolls revealed by Allah to those of his father, Adam, and acted in accordance with their contents. He built the Ka'aba with stones and clay." If the Ka'aba gets one more builder it's going to become the Tower of Babel.

In the interim, we have the scrolls of babel: "The people of the Torah said, 'Enoch was born to Jared. Allah granted him the gift of prophecy. He revealed thirty scrolls to him. He was the first after Adam to write and to exert himself in Allah's Cause [Jihad]. He was the first to cut and sew clothes. He was the first to lead some of Cain's descendants into captivity and to enslave them.'" Not to be picky, but I thought that Eve was a stay-at-home mom. And I suppose fighting made Enoch the first good Muslim, a devout religious lad following in the footsteps of Muhammad.

We now have one hundred scrolls. How is it then that the first mentioned in the Qur'an were from Abraham and Moses, who have yet to be born? Qur'an 87:18: "This is surely in the earlier Books, the Books of Abraham and Moses."

The next Hadith confirms the source of Muhammad's religious material. *Tabari I:346* "Someone among the people of the Torah said, 'Methuselah was born to Enoch. He was the first to ride horses, because he followed his father's prescribed practice with respect to the jihad.'" How could Adam have established a cavalry, as an earlier Hadith claimed (Tabari I:318), if he didn't ride? Or why, if he didn't fight?

"The people of the Torah say that Lamech was born to Methuselah and that Lamech begat Noah." But it is Muhammad who tells us in the Hadith that Noah's people were just like the Meccans of his day: "Noah would admonish his people, but they mocked him. Allah revealed that he had given Noah's people a postponement from punishment so that they might apologize. Noah's people worshiped idols. So Allah sent His punishment down upon them and annihilated them." All of the stuff Muhammad claimed happened to Noah actually happened to him.

Starting with the sixth chapter, *Prophet of Doom* will focus entirely on Muhammad's life. Between now and then you should know that the Qur'an says it was actually Muhammad who "admonished his people, but they mocked him." So "Allah revealed that He had given" the Meccans "a postponement from punishment so that they might apologize" to Muhammad.

Thirty times in the Qur'an, and countless more in the Hadith, Muhammad replays this twisted variant of Noah. They are all designed to scare the Meccans into submission. By remaking Noah in his image, and recasting Meccans in the role of Noah's people, Muhammad was able to make his impotent and vicious god appear capable of serving his prophet's interests. This was an incredibly clever approach. Muhammad knew that his "god" wasn't real, and thus Allah was incapable of miracles. So by ascribing a prior miracle to him, his toothless god grew fangs.

This next Hadith forces us to make a choice. Either Noah was an Islamic prophet or Islam is a lie. *Tabari I:353* "According to a report on the authority of early Muslim scholars, there were ten generations between Adam and Noah, all of them were followers of Islam. Unbelief originated only in the generation to whom Noah was sent. Noah was the first prophet to be sent by Allah as a Messenger to a people to warn them and call them to the recognition of the oneness of Allah. Some say that Noah's people committed wickedness, drinking wine, and letting their preoccupation with musical instruments divert them from submission to Allah." If you are agonizing over whether Muhammad has told the truth, think about this: he said "drinking wine" was "wicked" and yet the rivers of Allah's Paradise "flow with wine." Muhammad condemned those who "listened to music" to hell, and yet "the angels sing."

"The Qur'an reports that they had idols, for Allah says speaking about Noah, 'My Lord they have been disobedient to me and have followed one whose property and children only add to his loss.'" The real Noah never said such a thing. He wasn't interested in someone submitting to him; he had property and sons. When we reconcile why Muhammad put these awkward words into Moses' mouth we discover that it was actually Islam's prophet who demanded obedience and was denied. It was Muhammad who had neither sons nor property. What's more, the official heirs to the Ka'aba, the property he coveted, had sons.

"They have devised a major plot and said, 'Don't give up your gods. Don't give up Wadd, Suwa, and Nasr. They have led many astray.'" [Qur'an 71:21] And while Noah never plotted, Muhammad schemed against his own family for control of a similar list of false gods. Falsely projecting one's faults upon an opponent is an effective and timeless political strategy. It's one Muhammad used to perfection. It is one of the Qur'an's least appealing and most repetitive themes.

Fearing god's terror, however, is unique to Islam. *Tabari I:354* "Allah sent Noah to them to make them afraid of His awesome power and to warn them of His assault. Noah was to call upon them to act in accordance with the demands given by Allah to His messengers and revealed by Him in the scrolls of Adam, Seth, and Enoch." Like most Islamic Traditions, this one was written to explain the Qur'an, to provide a sense of purpose and place to a book that lacks context, history, and chronology. As we dive into the surah for which this was written, notice the similarity between Muhammad's voice and Allah's.

071.001 "Surely We sent Noah to his people, saying: 'Warn your people before there comes upon them a painful punishment.' He said: 'O my people! Surely I am a warner to you that you should fear Him and obey me.'" The fact Muhammad put his words into Noah's mouth will become increasingly obvious. But before we leave this opening verse, I'd like to point out one of the many differences between the Qur'an and the Bible. Biblical prophets told us to love and obey Yahweh, not themselves. Muhammad ordered Muslims to *fear* Allah and obey *Muhammad*.

The following verse replicates Muhammad's experience in Mecca down to the smallest nuance. *071.003* "He said: 'I have called my people night and day! But my call has only made them flee the more. They put their fingers in their ears and persist, puffed up with pride.'" *071.008* "Then I called to them aloud. I spoke to them in public and I spoke to them in secret. I said, 'Ask forgiveness of your Lord. He will send down upon you the cloud, pouring down abundance of rain, and help you with wealth and sons, and make for you gardens, and make for you rivers.'" Holy cloudburst. This is a sadistic joke. The last thing Noah's clan needed was rain. But since this story was being recast for Muhammad's tribe in central Arabia, a place that was desperate for water, the reward must have seemed divine. So to make Noah look like a mini-Muhammad, the victims of the flood were to be rewarded with a deluge. How's that for a twist?

071.013 **"What is the matter with you that you do not fear Allah? He has created you through various grades. Do you not see how He has created the seven heavens, one above another, and made the moon a light, and made the sun a lamp? ...Allah has made you grow out of the earth as a growth."** The harder Muhammad tried to prove Allah was actually god; the less godly Allah actually appeared.

In this next verse Allah's words are virtually identical to Muhammad's in an earlier Hadith. It makes you wonder who was speaking for whom. *071.021* **"Noah said, 'Lord, they have disobeyed me and followed him whose wealth and children have added to him nothing but loss. And they have planned a very great plot. And they say: "By no means leave your gods, nor leave Wadd, Suwa and Nasr."'"** We have traversed time and brought Noah into the middle of Muhammad's Mecca. Only the names have been changed to protect the guilty. The Meccan gods' names were Manat, Al-Lat, and Al-Uzza.

071.024 **"They have led astray many. Because of their wrongs they were drowned, then made to enter fire, so they did not find any helpers besides Allah. [How was Allah a helper if they were drowned and roasted?] And Noah said, 'My Lord, leave not one of the unbelievers on the earth. For surely if You leave them they will lead astray Your slaves, and will not beget any but immoral, ungrateful children.'"** Saying that Noah asked God to wipe out his people is a sacrilege. Nothing could be further from the truth.

But by saying this, the Qur'an has given us a window into the soul of its prophet. It was Muhammad who wanted his clan punished, not Noah. The Meccans mocked Muhammad, so he threatened to slaughter them. And while you will read these words later, directly from Muhammad's lips, for now he's too big a weasel to stand up and accept responsibility. His thoughts have been attributed to another, besmirching a noble man's character.

So ask yourself: why would the Qur'an put such ugly words into Noah's mouth? What did Muhammad have to gain by deceiving his people? These lies didn't spontaneously appear; there must have been a motive. And if there was a motive, the lie was more than immoral; it became criminal.

While the Qur'anic account of Noah is foolish and mean-spirited, these things aren't crimes, nor is making a mistake. Lying is, however, when it's done for material gain. Today we call it fraud. The legal definition is: deceit or trickery designed to garner an unfair or dishonest advantage. Fraud is a knowing departure from truth to purposely mislead others for the sole purpose of unwarranted material gain. That's precisely what is happening here.

During this phase of Muhammad's "ministry" in Mecca he wanted his tribe to abandon all the Ka'aba gods except Allah—the idol that had "called" him to be its prophet. In this verse, Muhammad went on the attack, saying that the lesser idols needed to go so that his idol and his idol's messenger could gain control over the Ka'aba Inc.—the town's religious scam. The power and wealth Muhammad coveted flowed into the pockets of those who controlled Allah's House. So Muhammad was willing to deceive his kin to garner an unfair advantage over them for material gain. Islam's prophet profited by perpetrating a fraud. A crime has been committed.

Fortunately, a little outcome-based math will help lighten the mood. **"Allah sent Noah to his people when he was 350 years old. He stayed among them 950 years. Allah sent Noah to them when he was 480 [not 350] years old. Allah commanded Noah to build the ark. He boarded it at the age of 600 [not at 1300]."** Can you imagine attending an Islamic math class?

"All those people drowned." Maybe the Islamic Noah's preaching wasn't any more positive than Muhammad's. *Tabari I:358* **"Noah's people used to grab him and choke him until he became unconscious. When Allah wanted to ruin them, Noah cursed them, saying, 'Lord, they have disobeyed me and have followed one whose property and children only add to his loss...Lord, let no unbeliever stay on the earth!'"** The Hadith says that the worst abuse Muhammad endured in Mecca was being grabbed and choked. And as a result of being disobeyed, Muhammad cursed his people. Every word of this is designed to recast the Biblical patriarch into the spitting image of Muhammad.

Early Muslims had a problem keeping their stories straight and their facts believable. **"The length of Noah's [supertanker] ark was 1,200 cubits, and its width was 600 cubits."** A nearly four thousand-foot boat—improbabilities like this in supposedly inspired scripture are troubling...or telling.

Listen to this: *Tabari I: 367* **"The Apostles said to Jesus, 'Would you send us a man who saw the ark and could tell us about it.' He took a handful of the earth in his palm and asked, 'Do you know what this is?'"** While it is hard to believe they couldn't answer the question, it provides an insight into Islam. Muslims don't think, they obey. **"'Allah and His prophet know best!' they replied. Jesus said, 'This is the grave of Noah's son, Ham.' He struck the hill with his staff and said, 'Rise with Allah's permission!' And behold there was Ham, with gray hair, shaking the earth from his head."** With a miracle of this magnitude, you'd think the Apostles would have at least mentioned it in their Gospels. But they didn't, I suppose, because it didn't happen. What's more, if Jesus resurrected a relatively meaningless figure like Ham, why didn't Allah empower Muhammad, his most important messenger, to bring Abraham back to life, or Moses? Or Jesus, for that matter.

"Jesus asked him whether he had perished in that state with gray hair. Ham replied, 'No when I died, I was a young man, but I thought the Hour [of Doom] had come, and my hair turned gray.' Jesus said, 'Tell us about Noah's ark.' He said, 'It was 1,200 cubits long and 600 cubits wide. It had three stories, one for domestic and wild animals, another for

human beings, and a third for birds. When the dung of the animals became excessive, Allah inspired Noah to tickle the elephant's tail. He did, and a male and female hog fell down and attacked the dung. When the rat fell down into the seams of the planks of the ark and gnawed at them, Allah inspired Noah to strike the lion between its eyes and a male and female cat came out from its nose and attacked the rat.'" Where does one sign up for a religion like this?

"Jesus asked Ham, 'How did Noah learn that all the places had been under water?' He replied, 'He sent the raven to bring him information, but it found a corpse and pounced upon it, whereupon Noah cursed the raven that it should be fearful; therefore the raven does not like houses. He sent the dove. It came with an olive leaf in its beak and clay on its feet. Noah thus knew....' The Apostles said, 'O Messenger of Allah, why do you not bring him to our people so that he can sit down and talk with us?' Jesus replied, 'How could one who has no sustenance [substance?] follow you?' Jesus said to Ham, 'Go back with Allah's permission.' And Ham turned to dust again."

Rather than jump into the middle of the Qur'an's second version of the deluge, I'd like to sneak up on it so that you might begin to see how Allah manages to weave in his favorite themes. *011.001* "This is a Book [I beg to differ. That simply wasn't true. The Qur'an wouldn't become a book for three decades or more. Most of the revelations weren't even written down. And when the first scribe assigned to Muhammad actually tried to jot some down, he was assassinated.] whose verses are made decisive, then are they made plain, from the Wise, All-aware, [He is entitled to his own opinion, but not his own facts. This is a statement of opinion, as unsubstantiated as it may be.] that you shall not serve any but Allah; surely I am a warner for you from Him and a giver of good news."

011.012 "Then, it may be that you [Muhammad] will give up part of what is revealed to you...because they say: 'Why has not a treasure been sent down upon him or an angel come to him?'" The things that bugged Muhammad and the Meccans the most were: no money and no proof. The prophet was born into the wealthiest family in Mecca, the custodians of the Ka'aba. Being Allah's keeper had made his kin rich. But not Muhammad, he was abandoned at birth. Dirt poor, he envied—no despised—his own family, cursed them and coveted the wealth they derived from the family religious scam.

The prophet's tormentors wanted to know why a god who had made them rich would leave his messenger poor. They wanted to know why there weren't any miracles if Allah was so powerful. Muhammad was comparing himself to Moses and Jesus. "They did miracles. They were visited by angels. Why not you?" the Meccans probed.

As an interesting aside, the verse asks: "Why hasn't an angel come to him?" The 11th surah was late Meccan, the seventy-fifth in order of revelation. The man who claimed his "revelations" were angelic, had yet to see an angel.

The Qur'an is comprised of a raw and raging debate. Muhammad's tribe disputed his claims and mocked him unmercifully, saying his religion was a forgery, a counterfeit. *011.013* **"Or, do they say: 'He (Muhammad) has forged it (the Qur'an).'"** His contemporaries knew he was a fraud. And they weren't the least bit shy about saying so. They described him with the same words I am using.

So how do you think Muhammad answered this charge? **"Say: 'Then bring ten forged surahs like it and call upon whom you can besides Allah, if you are truthful.'"** The Qur'an is saying that this rubbish smells so sweet it can't be garbage. "No one, short of the great Allah himself, is capable of such a wondrous forgery." If that's not delusional, Webster needs to redefine the word.

There were many who rose to the challenge, creating vastly superior prose. Such enlightened men and women were called poets. Oral recitals were the only means of communication because the Bedouins of Muhammad's day were illiterate. And having read the first chapter, you know how our hero rewarded the poets who "brought chapters like it." He assassinated them. Dead men tell no tales. *011.014* **"But if they do not answer you, then know that it is revealed by Allah's knowledge and no god may be worshiped but He; will you submit?"** *Submit.* Not agree. Not understand. Not even believe. Islam is submission.

Have you ever heard a politician say, "Let me make this perfectly clear?" At that moment all you know for certain is that his or her position is anything but clear. Allah uses the phrase "clear proof" in defense of Muhammad with great regularity. Yet he never provides any proof—clear or otherwise. *011.017* **"Is [Muhammad] he who has with him clear proof (the Qur'an) from his Lord, a witness from Him reciting it and before it came the Book of Moses? These believe in it; but most men do not believe. The different sects (Jews, Christians, and all other non-Muslim nations) will reject (the Qur'an), so the Fire of Hell will be their promised meeting place."**

A second insight here is **"most men do not believe."** After ten years of preaching to his hometown this prophet inspired less than fifty men. Muhammad was a complete failure as a religious prophet. Islam, the religion of submission, failed in Mecca when Muhammad relied on his words. Islam, the political doctrine of submission succeeded in Medina when Muhammad relied on his sword. Had Muhammad not changed from prophet to pirate, we wouldn't have heard of him and his followers wouldn't be killing us today.

Speaking of the Jewish and Christian "sects," and non-Muslim nations, the Qur'an asks: *011.017* **"Who is more unjust than he who forges a lie against Allah? ... Surely the curse of Allah is on them...and the punishment shall be doubled for them."** Allah, like Muhammad, was eager to curse and punish those who didn't capitulate.

Let's examine the forgeries. As we do, notice the number of times Allah says "surely," which could be translated as, "trust me." *011.025* **"Surely We sent Noah to his people: 'Surely I am a warner for you that you shall not serve any but Allah, surely I fear for you the punishment of a painful day.' But the chiefs of those who disbelieved from among his people said: 'We do not consider you but a mortal like ourselves, and we do not see any who have followed you but those who are the meanest of us. We do not see in you any excellence over us. Nay, we deem you a liar.'"** If we were to simply substitute speakers, Muhammad for Noah, we could dispense with the core of the Meccan surahs and replace them with this bogus bill.

011.028 "Noah said: 'O my people, tell me if I have come with clear proofs from my Lord....but I consider you a people who are ignorant.'" Islam's counterfeit Noah said: *011.030* "Will you not mind? I do not say to you that I have the treasures of Allah and I do not know the unseen, nor do I say that I am an angel." This is also transparent. Noah is saying on behalf of Muhammad that he is powerless to get his people to mind. He doesn't have god's wealth, his insights, or angelic support. He's a prophet who can't predict the future. By corrupting Noah in this way, Muhammad infers that all of god's messengers were equally inept.

011.032 "They said: 'Noah, you have disputed with us at length, therefore bring to us what you threaten us with, if you are truthful.' [The Meccans demanded the same thing and Muhammad's response was identical.] He said: 'Allah only will bring it to you if He pleases, and you will not escape. I intend to give you good advice, but my advice will not profit you if Allah intends to lead you astray.' Or do they say: 'He has forged it? Say: 'If I have forged it, on me is my guilt.'" If this were really god speaking, one would think he'd be a little less transparent with his agenda. Recasting Noah this blatantly, this crassly, as Muhammad, would only fool a fool.

Next, the Qur'an reveals the problem of predestination: *011.036* "It was revealed to Noah: 'None of your people will believe except those who have already believed, therefore do not grieve at what they do. Make the ark before Our eyes and do not speak to Me in respect of those who are unjust; surely they shall be drowned.'" In other words, "Don't preach to your brothers and sisters, sons and daughters, friends and family. Don't love them; don't pray for their souls. I've got other plans for them."

011.038 "And he began to make the ark; and whenever the chiefs from among his people passed by him they laughed at him. He said: 'If you laugh at us, surely we laugh at you. So shall you know whom a chastisement will disgrace, and on whom will lasting punishment come down.'" Muhammad hated being scoffed at. So while we're on the subject of mockery, let's review a few of the four hundred variations of this theme in the Qur'an. All are allegedly from Allah, and all are in defense of Muhammad. In surah 2:14: "We were joking. But Allah will turn the joke against them." In surah 2:212: "Enamored are the unbelievers and they scoff at the faithful." In surah 5:55: "O believers, do not make friends with those who mock and make a sport of your faith, those who were given the [Bible] Book before you." And from 6:10: "Surely the apostles have been mocked before you; but what they had mocked rebounded on the mockers themselves." It's a broken record—one that required Muhammad to break the record of history so that no one would notice how odd it was for god and prophet to constantly mock their mockers.

011.040 "Our command came and water flowed forth from the valley. 'Embark in it, in the name of Allah be its sailing and its anchoring; most surely my Lord is Forgiving, Merciful.'" The idea that the ark had sails and an anchor is as incongruous in the context of a flood as depicting Allah as forgiving and merciful. His callous slap on

Adam's back sealed our fate. Being predestined to the fires of hell precludes forgiveness and mercy. They are mutually exclusive, which means one or both statements must be false. Not good if you're pretending to be God.

Within the Biblical account from which this tale was forged there is considerable truth. Yahweh was indeed grieved over man's behavior. He created us in his image, with a spiritual component, so that we could have a relationship with him. But we, as we have a tendency to do, acted badly. Fortunately, rather than giving up on us entirely and letting us prematurely disintegrate into the barbaric mentality of the twentieth century, Yahweh opted for a fresh start. He saved those who chose to be with him. He told Noah to build an ark as a means of salvation—separating Noah and Yahweh from those who had chosen a less godly path.

Noah, like all men created in God's image at the time, lived near the Garden of Eden, at the headwaters of the Tigris and Euphrates Rivers. That put him quite near the Black Sea. There is overwhelming evidence of a flood of Biblical proportions there. Traces of human settlements dating to Noah's day have been discovered buried under the shores of this inland ocean.

The Bible gives us evidence of an old earth and "humans" apart from spirit-filled man—man created in God's image. Yahweh instructed Noah to cover the ark with pitch—the residue of dead plants, animals, and time. He also talked to Noah about the sons of God marrying the daughters of men. And Yahweh told us that he put a mark on Cain's forehead so that others would know that he was under his protection. If mom and dad were the only humans, that would have served no purpose.

I share these insights because I want you to know several things. When Yahweh said that he made us out of the same elements from which he made the animals he was speaking of humans—Homo sapiens. Adam was a special creation—made of the same raw material but with one important difference. Yahweh breathed his spirit into Adam, creating us with a spiritual dimension.

The Garden of Eden was perfect, walled and guarded, protecting Adam from the death and dying that was occurring all around him—outside of God's protection. But ultimately Adam chose poorly, as did most of his descendants. And that brought us to Noah, his ark of salvation, and a very real flood that led to this new beginning.

The Qur'an follows its revisionist account of Noah's with another fairytale: *011.050* **"To Ad We sent Hud. He said: 'O my people, serve Allah, you have no ilah (God) other than He. You are nothing but forgers of lies.... Allah will send on you clouds pouring down abundance of rain.'"** The legendary Hud is giving the mythical Ad the same speech. And that's a problem. It reveals that Allah lacks imagination, an editor, and a memory. The story of the Ad is repeated eleven times. And elsewhere in the Qur'an, Allah says that the Ad were blown away, not flooded. In surah 15 we read: **"So those who were Ad turned insolent unjustly in the land, and said, 'Who** is stronger than us?' Did they not see that Allah who created them was far greater in power than they? Yet they refused to believe Our signs so We let loose on them a violent wind for several days of distress to make them taste a most disgraceful punishment here in this world, and far more shameful will be the punishment in hell. They will have no savior."

The story of Noah and his supertanker continued by informing us that Ham made the boat and that he had a brother, Yam. Yam is the unnamed son mentioned in Qur'an 11:42. And then: *Tabari I:360* "The first animal to be put aboard was the ant, and the last the donkey. When Noah brought the donkey in, Iblis [Lucifer] attached himself to its tail, so that it could not lift its legs. Noah started to say, 'Woe to you. Go in.' The donkey rose but was unable to move. Noah said, 'Woe to you. Go in even if Satan is with you.' It was a slip of the tongue, but when Noah said it, Satan let the donkey proceed. It went in, and Satan went in with it. [Lucifer and his fellow jinn must have been deathly afraid of water. Being made of fire, they would have been snuffed out, I suppose.] Noah said, 'How did you get in here with me?' Satan replied, 'You cannot escape from having me on board.' Satan stayed in the rear of the boat."

There was a reason for the Satanic slip. Muhammad's most embarrassing moment, the Satanic Verses, was called a slip of the lip. He said that Satan put words in his mouth when he acknowledged Mecca's pagan idols in return for a bribe. This story was designed to drag Noah down to his level.

Then, straight out of Islam's warped mind we learn: "Noah also carried along Adam's corpse, making it a barrier between the women and men." Since they were all married and from the same family, why? "They boarded the boat on the 10th of Rajab and they left on Ashura Day, therefore all people should fast on Ashura. Before the Flood, two sons were reportedly born to Noah who both perished. One was called Canaan. He was drowned in the flood." Well, if you don't believe that, and you shouldn't, what about this: "All the forefathers between Noah and Adam were in the state of Islam." Yes, all the Bible characters were good Muslims.

"The ark carried them around the entire Earth in six months. It did not come to rest anywhere until it came to the Sacred Territory of Mecca and Medina. [We should have guessed.] However, it did not enter the Sacred Territory but circled around for a week. [Circumnavigation must have preceded circumambulation.] The House built by Adam was lifted up, so that it was not submerged—the inhabited House with the Black Stone." Since every soul was aboard the ark, the only thing that could have "inhabited the House with the Black Stone" was Allah. In other words, the Ka'aba wasn't a shrine to the Islamic god as Muslims would have us believe; Allah lived there.

"The oven with the water boiling that Allah made as sign between Himself and Noah was the oven of stone that belonged to Eve.... On Friday, the 10th of Rajab it took off. It passed the House, which had been lifted up by Allah so it would not be submerged. Noah circumnavigated it seven times. It then went to Yemen and returned." Ar-Rahman lived in Yemen; Muhammad didn't want to leave him out.

With these words we say goodbye to Volume I of Tabari: "The eras were: from the Flood to the fire of Abraham, from the fire of Abraham to the mission of Joseph, from the mission of Joseph to the mission of Moses, from the mission of Moses to the reign of Solomon, from the reign of Solomon to the mission of Jesus, and from the mission of Jesus, to when the Messenger of Allah was sent." So what happened? Did Allah run out of Jews? And since every era is centered around Jerusalem, including Muhammad's only trip to heaven, why is Mecca sacred? Fact is, Mecca didn't exist—nor would it exist for another 3,500 years.

The Genesis account of Abraham begins in the 12ᵗʰ chapter. It's a wonderful story about Yahweh's relationship with man and his covenant with his people. It is also prophetic, warning us about the character of Ishmael and his descendants: "He will be a wild ass of a man. His hand will be against his brother and his brother's hand will be against him. And he will live in hostility with all the world." Sounds like tomorrow's newspaper, doesn't it?

The Islamic version of Abraham unfolds with these words: *Tabari II:49* "**Most of the earlier sages have said that Abraham was born during the era of Nimrod bin Cush, while most historians say that Nimrod was an official of Azdahaq. Some have asserted that Noah was sent to Nimrod, against Babylon. We have been told—though Allah knows best—that Dahhak was Nimrod and that Abraham was born during his days, and that Nimrod was his master who wanted to burn him.**" I beg to differ with the Muslim sages. But since nothing they have said thus far has made any sense, why start now?

I suppose you'd like to know who Azdahaq, Nimrod, and Dahhak are. While Nimrod is mentioned in the Bible, I'll defer to the Muslims with regard to Azdahaq. They say, *Tabari II:3* "**Qarishat was tyrannical. One day he became engrossed in thought...Allah transformed him into Azdahaq. He had seven heads and was the one who lived on the highest mountain in Iran. All the historians, both Arab and Persian, claim that he ruled over every clime and that he was a wicked sorcerer.**"

So with that cleared up, lets see what the Islamic scholars have to say about Dahhak, whom they believe to be Nimrod. "**Dahhak reigned for one thousand years after Jam—but Allah knows better. He ruled over all the earth, displaying tyranny and oppression. He killed excessively and was the first to enact the punishments of crucifixion and mutilation. [I don't know about mutilation, but crucifixion was developed by the Assyrians and perfected by the Romans.] He was the first to levy tithes [religious tax] and to mint dirhams.**" If Dahhak was Nimrod, the great Babylonian king, he was a murdering tyrant. He was also creative. According to the archeological evidence, Nimrod and his wife Semiramis invented the pagan practices that grew to become the basis of Egyptian, Greek, and Roman mythology. His Mystery Babylon religion strongly influenced Hinduism, Islam, and Catholicism. Nimrod is credited with building the first temples, hiring the first clerics, and establishing the first rituals. He was the first to fleece the flock and to control a population via a religious scam. Muhammad would have looked up to Nimrod as a role model.

This Islamic tradition goes on to claim, "It is said that there were two ganglia growing out of his shoulders, which caused pain. It became so intense he would anoint them with the brains of human beings. For this purpose he killed two men each day and anointed his ganglia with their brains. When he did, the pain would abate." I'll bet you're glad to know there is a cure for ganglia. Now all we need is a cure for Islam, for it too consumes men's brains.

Tabari II:4 "A commoner in Babylon rebelled against him. He set up a war banner and many people rallied. When Dahhak heard this he was alarmed and sent the following message: 'What is the matter? What do you want?' The man replied, 'Do you not say that you are the ruler of the world, and that the world belongs to you?'" As a fellow megalomaniac, scam artist, and terrorist murder, Dahhak/Nimrod served to make Muhammad's life seem sane, I suppose.

Let's compare the description we have just read to what Muhammad had to say about himself: *Bukhari:V1B7N331* "The Prophet said, 'I have been given five things which were not given to anyone else. Allah made me victorious with terror. The Earth was made for me.... Booty was made lawful for me yet it was not lawful for anyone else. I was given the right of intercession on the Day of Doom. Every Prophet used to be sent to his nation only, but I have been sent to all mankind.'" Chilling!

Now that I have your attention, let's return to the story. "The rebellious man said, 'Let your thirst be for all the world and not only for us, for you only kill our people.'" Yes, there was a happier time in which Muslims only killed Muslims. Now they reach out and touch everyone. "Dahhak/Nimrod agreed and ordered that the two men slain each day would be divided among all people, not from just one nation." That was so inclusive and multicultural of him.

"Dahhak was Nimrod and Abraham was born during his era.... Dahhak had been a rebel who had seized the people of the land with witchcraft and deceit and had completely terrified them with the two serpents which had been on his shoulders." Let's compare the Dahhak/Nimrod duo, which we are told are one in the same with another inseparable duo, Allah/Muhammad. From surah 3:151: "We shall strike terror into the hearts of unbelievers." From 4:89: "Seize them and kill them wherever you find them." In 4:142 we find: "Surely the hypocrites strive to deceive Allah, and He shall retaliate by deceiving them." Then: *Bukhari:V7B71N661* "Magic was worked on Allah's Apostle and he was bewitched so that he began to imagine doing things which in fact, he had not done." I'm sure these similarities are just a coincidence. After all, one indistinguishable pair claimed to be god and prophet; the other a witch and tyrant. As such, it would be irrational for them to have anything in common.

"Dahhak/Nimrod built a city in Babylon called Hawb [War]. He made Nabateans his couriers. The people were subjected to every kind of pressure, and he slew young boys." In continuing with the similarities between Nimrod and Muhammad, you should know that the prophet pressured Arabs to submit to Islam. Those who didn't were slain. *Bukhari:V4B52N260* "The Prophet said, 'If a Muslim discards his religion, kill him.'" Some would consider that "pressure."

In upcoming volumes of Tabari's History and in Ishaq's Sira we will be regaled with Hadith showing Muhammad murdering young boys. In one shameful episode he decapitated an entire tribe, slaughtering every boy over the age of twelve. The Muslim historians are making up these Nimrod myths in order to make Muhammad's murderous behavior appear normal.

To give this tall tale a religious slant, the Traditions wove Noah into the plot. This plagiarized, albeit twisted, account proclaims: *Tabari II:11* **"Shem, the son of Noah was the father of the Arabs, the Persians, and the Greeks; Ham was the father of the Black Africans; and Japheth was the father of the Turks and of Gog and Magog who were cousins of the Turks."** Then after being told that **"Noah slept with his genitals exposed,"** we learn: **"Noah prayed that the prophets and apostles would be descended from Shem and kings would be from Japheth. He prayed that the African's color would change so that their descendants would be slaves to the Arabs and Turks."** I wonder if Louis Farrakhan knows this? Probably not—he was too busy corrupting the sniper Muhammad.

We have finally arrived at the real point of the Nimrod stories: *Tabari II:18* **"Nimrod was the son of Cush bin Canaan bin Ham bin Noah. He was the lord of Babylon and of Abraham."** Muslims were on solid ground so long as they stuck to the Biblical account, but the moment they left it, they buried themselves. Nimrod died seven hundred years before Abraham was born. And Muhammad told us that Canaan died in the flood.

The actual history of the city-states of Babylon, Nineveh, and Ur is fascinating. This is where the stylus first met the tablet. It is out of the land of the Babylonians, Assyrians, and Chaldeans that recorded history began. It was here that the first laws were written, the first business was conducted, the first armies marched, the first students were taught, and the first sermons were preached. Their sermons and swords ultimately shaped the world—even unto our present day. Islam was derived in part from an offshoot of the religious scam concocted by Nimrod in Babylon. The original religion of Abraham in nearby Ur was based upon a derivative masculine moon deity named "Sin." Moon-god shrines like the Ka'aba were erected to him all over Arabia with rites that mirrored those invented in Babylon.

The people of the Fertile Crescent turned the sun, moon, and stars into gods and exported them at swordpoint. The constellations and planets were studied, and astrologists began the occult religions equating their movements to human behavior. This was the first time the masses were subjected to the will of cleric and king by way of divine right. It would not be the last.

Many of Catholicism's rituals, festivals, and doctrines were derived from Nimrod. The devotion to the virgin with child, priests as intermediaries between god and man, the celebration of Christmas, Lent, and Easter are but a few examples of religious trappings from Babylon, not the Bible.

I share this with you not to expose Catholicism's foundations, nor turn this into a mere history lesson, but so you might understand the nature of these Islamic religious traditions better. Up to this point, all we have had to work with is reason and internal contradiction to decide if Muhammad was telling the truth when he recast the Genesis accounts of creation, Adam, Satan, and Noah. Yes, they were incriminating, full of contradictions, and inaccuracies. And yes, Muhammad's agenda of making Mecca and the Ka'aba important and his own rather unprophet-like behavior seem religious was always transparent. But now we have a new tool: history.

Just as the Septuagint and the Dead Sea Scrolls disprove Allah's assertion that the Jews corrupted their scriptures, the clay tablets of Ur, Babylon, and Nineveh prove that Muhammad lied when he tried to reshape Abraham into a compatriot of Nimrod. And this lie is not without consequence. If Abraham was not as Allah claims, the Qur'an disintegrates. Abraham is the lone, thin string that connects Islam to the Bible. And without the Bible, all that is rational and religious in the Qur'an evaporates, and Islam with it.

The story of Abraham was repeated thirty times in the Qur'an in fifteen different surahs. We hear Adam's tale of woe four times. Noah was a crowd pleaser; the mocked messenger makes thirty appearances in thirty different surahs. You just can't get enough death and destruction. That's why Lot, Abraham's nephew and a relatively minor Biblical character, débuts no fewer than fifteen times. He too, was recast as Allah's Messenger. The people didn't obey, so wham—fire and brimstone. Moses, the great liberator, prophet, and miracle worker, was the most frequently named character in Allah's book, with a stunning 500 appearances. The longest surah, the 2nd, was dedicated to the golden calf the Israelites foolishly crafted in the wilderness. The 10th surah is called "**Jonah.**" The 12th is named after and preoccupied with "**Joseph.**" The 14th is dedicated to "**Abraham.**" The 17th is named after the Jews, the "**Children of Israel.**" The 19th derives its name from "**Mary,**" mother of Jesus. The 21st is dedicated to the Hebrew "**Prophets.**" Only one is named for Muhammad and just one bears the name of his first god, "**Ar-Rahman.**" "**Noah**" has a surah named in his honor, but so do the "**Pen,**" "**Jinn,**" "**Signs of the Zodiac,**" the "**Sun,**" and "**Moon.**"

Without the Bible, the Qur'an would be a very thin book. Detached from its influence, Islam loses most of its religious trappings. This is the reason Muslims are so insistent that the God of the Bible and the god of the Qur'an are the same. For if they are not, Islam's reliance on the Bible becomes an insurmountable liability rather than the religion's lone asset.

As we turn the page we are confronted with some rather astonishing Nimrod fairytales. It's odd that a historian like Tabari would jettison his chronology to insert these randomly throughout his depictions of Noah and Abraham. I'm surprised that he even presents them at all, but nonetheless, they are there, and thus we must deal with them. *Tabari II:106* "Nimrod's arrogance and rebelliousness against his Lord went on for a long time—some say four hundred years—in spite of Allah's forbearance with him."

The pot calls the kettle black. "Nimrod was ignorant. He was the first tyrant on earth." As a result: "Allah sent gnats against them [the Babylonians, I suppose], and they ate their flesh and drank their blood, and nothing but their bones were left. But Allah gave Nimrod a single gnat which entered his nostril and went on beating the inside of his head with hammers for four hundred years. The most merciful of his friends was he who bunched up his hands and beat Nimrod's head with them."

That really made him mad. *Tabari II:107* "Nimrod vowed to seek out Abraham's God. So he took four eagle fledglings and nurtured them on meat and wine so that they grew up tough and strong. Then he tied them to a chest and sat in it. He suspended a piece of meat over them and they flew up trying to reach it. When they had risen high in the sky, Nimrod looked down and beheld the earth. He saw the mountains crawling below like creeping ants. When they had risen still higher he looked and saw the earth with a sea surrounding it. After climbing still higher, he came into a region of darkness and could not see what was above him nor what was below him. He became frightened and threw the meat down. The eagles followed it, darting downward. When the mountains saw them coming near and heard their noise, they became afraid and almost moved from their places, but did not do so. As Allah says, 'Verily they have plotted their plot, and their plot is with Allah, even if their plot were one whereby the mountains should be moved.'" [Qur'an 14:46]

I recognize that these Traditions are designed to explain the Qur'an, but this one is counterproductive. And sadly, there is no excuse. These fables were concocted a thousand years after the frivolity of pagan myths had been exposed to reason. This is long after Moses, David, Solomon, Plato, Socrates, and Aristotle enlightened the civilized world.

With that in mind, let's examine the Qur'anic problem Muhammad was trying to solve. In the 41st verse of the 14th surah, we read, "Think not that Allah is oblivious.... Hastening forward, their heads upraised, their eyes staring aghast and their hearts vacant. Warn people of the day when the punishment shall be inflicted upon them. Then will the wicked say: 'Lord, give us a respite, (so) we shall respond to Your call and follow the apostles.' 'What! did you not swear before (that) there will be no reverse for us!'" Evidently the inebriated eagles didn't have reverse either. *014.046* "And they are plotting their plots, but their plan is evident to Allah, even though their plot is so adroit as to make the mountains move." So, there you have it. Muhammad needed to come up with a plot that was capable of making the mountains move for the Qur'an to make sense. The drunken eagle bit was perfect.

The surah that claims Allah isn't "oblivious" ends with these words: *014.047* "Therefore do not think Allah will fail in His promise to His prophet; surely Allah is Mighty, the Lord of Retribution." That's pretty clear, and so is this: "On the day the earth shall be changed into a different earth...you will see the guilty bound together in chains. Their shirts will be made of molten pitch and the fire will cover their faces so that Allah may reward each soul." Why do a billion people worship such a sadistic "god?"

The Nimrodian Tradition continues to scuttle any last remnant of credibility Islam may have otherwise retained: *Tabari II:108* "They took off from Jerusalem and they fell down in the Mountain of Smoke. When Nimrod saw that this method would accomplish nothing, he began building the tower—taller and taller. Then he voided excrement though it. Allah seized his building by its foundations and the roof fell down upon them and doom came upon them whence they knew not." [Qur'an 16:26] Dare we poke through the excrement and find Allah's little problem? Or do we just chalk this one up to diarrhea of the mouth?

We've come this far. Why give up now? Hold your nose if you must. Verses 22-25 of the 16th surah say that non-Muslims are puffed up with pride (probably from holding their noses) and living in denial. But Allah is on to them like stink on...well, you know what. The Big Guy asks, "'What has your Lord sent down?' They answer, 'Tales from long ago.'" In other words, a blend of plagiarism and stolen Hebrew and Babylonian myths. As you will discover in the "Source Material" appendix, the Islamic clerics in Baghdad who fleshed out the Qur'an in the eighth century attempted to make it seem more religious by usurping myths and fables from the Talmud, uninspired Jewish folklore.

That somehow leads us to this: *016.026* "Those that have gone before them had also conspired; [Have you noticed how many plots there are in the Qur'an? Everybody has a conspiracy going, even Allah.] Then Allah uprooted their structure from its foundation; the roof fell over them from above, and punishment came upon them from where they did not suspect." Okay, I understand. Without the context of the Hadith the Qur'an doesn't make sense. But with the context, *nothing* makes sense.

Tabari II:109 "Then it fell, and on that day the languages of mankind became confused from fright, and mankind came to speak seventy-three languages. Before that the only language had been Syriac. It was called Babel." In the midst of the stench, there are some pearls. The first written language was probably Akkadian. It was used by the early Sumerians, Babylonians, and Assyrians. This became Aramaic, from which Syriac evolved nearly 3,000 years later. But the confession is enlightening. The Syrian Christians were the first to write Arabic. They developed its alphabet in the sixth century. Written Arabic, from which the word "qur'an" was derived, didn't make its way into Central Arabia, and therefore to Mecca, until after Muhammad alleges the Qur'an was "revealed" to him in *Arabic.* So this ridiculous notion that Syriac was the first language is designed to solve a problem our Muslim pals have with their timeline. The alphabet of the Qur'an was actually *unknown* when "the book" was revealed.

As we move through this collection of "inspired" Hadith, we are given another glimpse behind the veil of Islam. "'We are only growing farther from heaven,' Nimrod said. 'Descend!'" Now you know which direction to look to find

Allah. *Tabari II:109* **"The unbelievers were Nimrod and Nebuchadnezzar, while the believers were Solomon bin David and Alexander."** And I'll bet you didn't know that the resolutely pagan Alexander the Great was a monotheistic Muslim or that the devoutly Jewish King Solomon was Islamic.

"In the same way, Nebuchadnezzar was warlord of the lands extending from Ahwaz to the land of the Byzantines lying west of the Tigris, before Luhrasb. He was bruised by fighting the Turks." Eighth grade history and a good timeline would do these boys a world of good.

But unfortunately, they were up to no good. Not even twenty percent of this has been believable. We have been regaled with a steady stream of impossibilities, contradictions, and fairytales. This has got to be the most-feeble attempt at religion ever postulated by man.

A crime has been committed. The evidence commands a verdict of guilty. There is a zero probability that these words were inspired by God. That means Muhammad lied: he was not a prophet, and Allah was not God.

But that's good news, not bad. It frees us to explore the more important questions. We can now focus on *how* the scam was compiled, and more importantly, *why*. Once we understand how and why we will know *what* can be done to stop Islam before it kills more of them—and us.

4

DISHONEST ABE

"Abraham was tested by circumcision, shaving his pubic hair,
washing the fore-part and rear, using a toothstick,
and plucking his armpits."

Nothing is more essential to Islam's credibility than Muhammad's version of Abraham. Islam must prove that he was a Muslim, that his God was Allah, and that he worshiped in Mecca. Recognizing this, Muhammad tried desperately to make the case.

We pick up the trail in Tabari's History with something that sounds like Hitler's idea of Arian supremacy. *Tabari II:21* **"Ham [Africans] begat all those who are black and curly-haired, while Japheth [Turks] begat all those who are full-faced with small eyes, and Shem [Arabs] begat everyone who is handsome of face with beautiful hair. Noah prayed that the hair of Ham's descendants would not grow beyond their ears, and that whenever his descendants met the children of Shem, the latter would enslave them."** The slavery theme keeps reappearing because Muhammad used the slave trade to finance the spread of Islam. Turning Noah into a racist to justify such behavior wasn't beneath Islam's prophet—but then again, little was.

We're going to pass by Muhammad's history lesson on the mythical tribes of Ad and Thamud. Their battles with the Almighty seemed important to Muhammad as he dedicated scores of Hadith to them. But I want to focus on the Islamic path to Abraham as it lies at the core of the prophet's scam. *Tabari II:50* **"Nimrod was Abraham's master and wanted him burned.... The first king who ruled over all the earth was Nimrod. There were four such kings who ruled all the earth: Nimrod, Solomon bin David, Dhu'l-Qarnain, and Nebuchadnezzar—two believers [Muslims] and two infidels."** Nimrod only ruled a city-state. Solomon's kingdom only included a portion of the Middle East. Nebuchadnezzar's realm, like that of Dhu'l-Qarnain, as Alexander the Great, was large, but neither ruled over the whole earth. As for two of them being Muslims—Muhammad and Allah are again mistaken. There wasn't a Muslim in the batch.

According to Ishaq's Sira: *Tabari II:50* **"Allah desired to send Abraham as an argument against his people and as a messenger to His worshippers since there had been no messengers between Noah and Abraham except Hud and Salih [the mythical rulers of Ad and Thamud]."** If that's true, there couldn't have been Muslim worshippers. A thousand years had passed with no religious communication. Allah said he destroyed the Ad and Thamud and he never suggests Abraham visited them. So in an attempt to establish a religious context for his scam, Muhammad destroyed it. The scenario he has just laid out precludes worshippers, and without them, all he has shared thus far concerning the establishment of Islamic rites and the veneration of the Ka'aba, could not have been passed along.

"As time drew near, the astrologers came to Nimrod, saying, 'We have learned from our lore that a boy will be born in this city of yours who will be called Abraham. He will abandon your religion and break your idols in such and such a month and year." Muslims are attempting to bestow on Abraham, whom they view as the father of Islam, the same kind of birth announcement enjoyed by Yahshua, the founder of Christianity, but they didn't have a clue when either man actually lived.

Both secular and scriptural histories tell us that Nimrod died centuries before Abraham was born. The clay tablets that were unearthed near ancient Babylon starting in the late 19th century suggest Nimrod died violently at the age of forty around 2800 B.C., two generations after the great flood. Apart from the Bible, Abraham is not as well known. Yet, archeologists have been able to confirm the Biblical accounting of when he lived by unearthing the places the Scriptures say he visited or that coexisted during his time. They have found dozens of corroborating artifacts that confirm Abraham lived between 2100 B.C. and 1950 B.C. These men were not contemporaries.

Since their lives were separated by 700 years, everything Muhammad claims about them is both suspect and uninspired. *Tabari II:53* "Another story about Abraham is that a star rose over Nimrod so bright that it blotted out the light of the sun and the moon. He became frightened and called the magicians, soothsayers, and prognosticators to ask about it. They said, 'A man will arise in your domain whose destiny is to destroy you and your rule.' Nimrod lived in Babylon but he left his town and moved to another, forcing all men to go with him but leaving the women. He ordered that any male child who was born should be slain." This is a blatant, although not believable, rip-off of the star of Bethlehem that directed wise men to Christ and of King Herod killing the male children born that year in Bethlehem.

The Bible tells us that Abram, the future Abraham, was born in Ur, the great Chaldean city, to Terah. His journey to the Promised Land is detailed in Genesis 11. Muhammad says: "Some task in Babylon came up for which Nimrod could trust only Azar, the father of Abraham. He sent him to do the job, saying, 'See that you do not have intercourse with your wife.' Azar said to him, 'I am too tenacious in my religion for that.' But when he entered Babylon he visited his wife and could not control himself. He had intercourse with her and fled to a town called Ur."

Tabari II:53 "When Abraham's mother found that she was in labor she went out to a cave near her house and bore Abraham. She shut the cave up on him and returned home. Later when she went to see how he had done, she found him alive, sucking his thumb. Allah placed Abraham's sustenance in it." Muhammad was abandoned by his mother at birth, so he invented this silly story to mimic his own childhood.

Tabari II:51 **"Abraham had been in the cave for fifteen months when he said to his mother, 'Take me out that I may look around.'"** Why bother? After fifteen months of living in a cave, he would have been blind. **"So she took him out one evening and he looked about and thought of the creation of the heavens and the earth and said, 'Verily the One who created me and fed me is my Lord—I have no other god but Him.'"** Thus, an infant conceived the first pillar of Islam. But alas, we descend to baby babble without even leaving the paragraph. **"He looked out at the sky and saw a star. 'This is my Lord.' He followed it with his eyes until it disappeared. When it set he said, 'I do not like things that set.' Then he saw the moon rising and said, 'This is my Lord.' [Perceptive kid—Allah began his life as a moon deity.] And he followed it until it disappeared. When it set, he said, 'If my Lord did not guide me, I would have gone astray.'"** A fifteen-month-old baby converts from pagan idolatry to Islam by watching the moon.

Like so many Islamic Traditions, these were written to provide the context the Qur'an lacks. Let's dive into the 6th surah to hear what Allah has to say: *006.074* **"When Abraham said to his sire, Azar: 'Why do you take idols for gods? I find you and your people in manifest error.' Thus We showed Abraham the visible and invisible kingdom of the heavens and earth that he might be of those who are sure and believe. So when night overshadowed him, he saw a star. Said he: 'This is my Lord?' When it set, he said: 'I do not love the setting ones.' When he saw the moon rising, he said: 'This is my Lord?' When it set, he said: 'If my Lord had not guided me I would be of the erring people who go astray.'"** This is embarrassing. The conversation condemns the message. After Allah personally showed Abe his kingdom so that he might be sure, the Islamic babe turns to the sky, the source of idols, and says, **"This is my Lord."** What is it about Islam that turns everyone's brains to mush—Allah's included?

006.078 **"Then when he saw the sun rising, he said: 'My Lord is surely this, the greatest of all.' So when it set, he said: 'O my people, I am through with those. Surely I have turned my face toward Him who originated the heavens and earth, and I am not a polytheist.'"** The sun, the most popular pagan deity, is now god, never mind it was the moon in the preceding Tradition. After becoming an idolater, he magically turns and says he's through with idols. And after asking a star, the moon, and the sun if they were god, he says he's not a polytheist. All the context in the world, all the explanations ever written, can't undo the damage the Qur'an does to itself.

Tabari explains it this way: *Tabari II:51* **"When day came upon Abraham and the sun rose, he saw the greatness of the sun and saw that here was something with more light than he had ever seen before. He said, 'This is my Lord! This is greater!' And when it set he exclaimed, 'O my people, I am free from all the things which you associate with Him.'"** Muhammad wants us to believe that all it took to "free" this fifteen-month old baby from pagan idolatry, worshiping the sun, moon, and stars, to become a Muslim in the oneness of Allah was for the sun to set.

006.080 **"His people disputed with him."** What people? Depending upon whether you believe Muhammad's Hadith or Allah's Qur'an, he's with his mom or dad.

He's a toddler, having just emerged from a cave for the first time. **"He said: 'Do you dispute with me respecting Allah? He has guided me. I do not fear those that you set up with Him, unless my Lord pleases; my Lord comprehends all things; will you not mind?'"** Let me see if I can decipher this. Over the course of one brief conversation, dishonest Abe tells his father that he and his people are in manifest error, and that idolatry is bad. After visiting heaven he says that big bright shiny things are gods, and that he is not a polytheist. Then he disputes with people he has never seen about their religion. He even says that he doesn't fear their gods, unless of course, his god wants him to fear them. And, wouldn't you know it, after such idiotic drivel, he tells them to mind him. This Qur'anic passage destroys the Islamic myth of divine inspiration, for this is not some minor event in the life of Islam. Abraham is purported to be the religion's founder, and this is his moment of awakening.

006.081 **"Why should I fear what you have set up with Allah, that for which He has not sent down to you any authority."** We can only assume that the Abe babe is speaking of idols his people have erected in shrines like the Ka'aba. **"O my father! Why do you worship that which neither hears, nor sees, nor can in any way help you?"** Even something as simple as this indicts Muhammad. It's a rip off. As we shall see in upcoming chapters, Arabian Hanifs (monotheists) during Muhammad's day had it figured out. They had said of the rock idols in the Ka'aba, **"Why do you worship that which neither hears, nor sees, nor can help you in any way?"**

"Do you reject my gods, Abraham? If you do not cease this, I shall stone you." As sick as this sounds, it depicts Muslim behavior. If a son renounces Islam, his father will kill him. One of my friends, a former Muslim, had this very thing happen to him. Hearing the news, his loving father reached for his gun and fired it at his son, narrowly missing him. Mark Gabriel, who holds a Ph.D. in Islamic History, wrote a book about his experience called: *Islam and Terror.*

006.083 **"And this was Our argument which we gave to Abraham against his people. And We gave him Ishaq (Isaac) and Yah'qub (Jacob) [Oops. Abraham was given Isaac and Ishmael. Jacob came later]; each did We guide, and Nuh (Noah) did We guide before, and of his descendants, David and Solomon, and Job and Joseph and Moses and Aaron; and thus do We reward those who do good (following Muhammad's example in the Sunnah). And Zachariah and Yahya (John), Isa (Jesus) and Elias; every one was of the good [i.e. Muslims]; And Ishmael and Elisha and Jonah and Lot and every one We preferred above men and jinn."** One of the many problems with the Qur'an is that Allah was no brighter than Muhammad. Job was a gentile and a contemporary of Abraham. As such he could neither be Abe's descendant nor follow Solomon.

I am reasonably certain that the Yathrib Jews read their scriptures correctly to Muhammad. But having a poor memory, and a heinous agenda, he got them all fouled up. I don't say that to be mean spirited, just informative. Muhammad will convict himself of having a heinous agenda a thousand times over before we are through. As prophets go, he was pretty pathetic.

Returning to the Islamicized Abraham, Ibn Ishaq tells us: *Tabari II:52* **"Then Abraham returned to his father Azar, having seen the right course. He had recognized his Lord."** Actually, all he had done was recognize who his Lord wasn't. And while that may sound picky, that's all Muhammad really did. Ultimately, he promoted the largest of the Meccan rock idols, Allah, and denounced the rest. **"He was free of the religion of his people, but he did not tell them that."** This, too, is revisionism for the sake of Muhammad. Allah's Messenger kept quiet about his first "revelation" for several years.

One of the most repetitive and damning indictments in the Qur'an comes from the Meccans. They recognized that Muhammad's notion of casting the smaller Ka'aba idols aside so that the largest idol could be feared as the one true god was lunacy. A big stone was no more god than a bunch of little ones. *Ishaq:38* **"Every house had an idol. When Allah sent Muhammad with the message of monotheism, the Quraysh said: 'Would he make many gods into one god? This is a strange thing.'"** So Muhammad, ever in character, bastardized the story of the great Hebrew patriarch Abraham to make his behavior seem inspired.

This sorry excuse for a religious patriarch is chronicled in both the Hadith and Qur'an. *Tabari II:55* **"His father told him, 'Abraham, we have a festival. If you go to it you will learn to like our religion.' The festival came and they went to it. On the way Abraham threw himself down and said, 'I am sick. My foot hurts.' When they went away he called to the last of them. 'I shall deal with your idols after you have gone away and turned your backs.' Abraham went to the house of the gods which was in a great hall. Opposite the entrance was a great idol, and at his side a smaller one, and next to him a smaller one, and so on."** Too bad Allah didn't get out more. He would have known that the Temple of Ur housed just one god—Sin—a masculine moon deity like himself. Unlike the Ka'aba, there weren't a bunch of rocks lying around.

"Azar made a living making the idols which his people worshipped, and he employed Abraham to sell them. Abraham would call out, 'Who will buy what will be of no use to him?' So they became unsellable. He would take them to the river and point their heads at it and say, 'Drink!' mocking his people. At length his mocking spread about among the inhabitants of his town, although Nimrod did not hear of it. Then when the time seemed right to Abraham to reveal to his people the error of what they were doing, and to tell them of Allah's command and of how to pray, he glanced up at the stars and said, 'I feel sick.' They fled from him when they heard it, but Abraham had only said it to make them go away so that he could do what he wanted with their idols. When they left he went to the idols and brought them food. He said, 'Will you not eat? What is the matter? Why do you not speak?' reproaching their falsely elevated position and mocking them."

If you've got one, open your Qur'an to the 37th surah. So as not to take Allah's word out of context, let's read from the beginning, picking up the highlights as we go along. Seeing Allah as he really is will help elucidate the Islamic mystery. The peace-loving god tells his troops: **"By those (angels) arranged in battle ranks who are strong in repelling and thus proclaim the Message of Allah! Verily,** your Ilah (God) is one!" Thank god for small favors. *037.006* "We have decked the lower heaven with stars to protect them against all rebellious evil spirits, and provide security from every forward devil. So they cannot listen to the highest chiefs for they are pelted from every side, repulsed; they are under a perpetual torment, being driven off. Except such as they snatch away something by stealth, but then they are pursued by a flaming fire of piercing brightness." In Islam, stars are used to guard against forward devils. The Islamic Ilah (God) named Allah would have us believe that he dissuades and torments "evil spirits" with physical objects.

037.011 "Just ask their opinion (Muhammad). [Whose opinion—the stars', the rebellious evil spirits'?] Are they the more difficult to create, or the other beings We have created? Them have We created out of a sticky clay! Are they stronger as a creation? Truly dost thou marvel, while they ridicule." Nay, I dost *both* marvel and ridicule. *037.013* "When they are admonished, pay no heed. When they see a Sign, [they] turn it to mockery, and incite one another to scoff. And say, 'This is nothing but evident sorcery!'" I agree.

037.016 "What! When we die, and become dust and bones, shall we be raised up and also our fathers of old? Say (Muhammad): 'Yea, and ye shall then be humiliated: Ye, in truth; and ye will be brought low.'" I suppose some Muslim scholar thought translating the Qur'an into Elizabethan English would make it sound religious. But lo, methinks it helpeth thee not. For your sake and mine, I will continue to edit most of the archaic language out of the text. I have also made a habit of correcting much of Allah's grammar, punctuation, verbosity, and oblique sentence structure. *037.019* "Then will be a single cry; and behold, they will stare! They will say, 'Woe to us! This is the Day of Doom.' This you denied! Assemble the wrong-doers and their wives and the things they worshipped besides Allah, then lead them to the fierce flaming fires of Hell." Even cleaned up, the message is repulsive.

Allah stoops to interrogate his captives. *037.024* "But stop them, for they are to be questioned. 'What is the matter with you that you do not help each other?' Nay, but this day they make full submission.... 'The sentence has come against us: we shall taste the punishment.'" Remember, according to Islam, people are never given a choice. They are predestined at birth to perish in hell's fire. This questioning is for Allah's entertainment. *037.033* "Truly, they will all share at the Penalty of Doom. That is how We shall deal with the Mujrimun (non-Muslims). For when they were told that there is no ilah but Allah, they puffed themselves up with pride and were scornful. They said: 'What, shall we give up our alihah (gods) for the sake of an insane possessed poet?'" This was "revealed" so Muhammad could lash out at the Meccans. They called him insane for turning many idols into one god. They said he was demon-possessed due to the hellish tone of his Qur'an.

As you might expect, Allah didn't see it that way. Muhammad's alter ego had but one spokesperson. If he faltered, Allah crumbled with him. *037.037* "Nay, he has come with the truth, and he confirms the Message of the messengers before him. You shall indeed taste the grievous penalty of painful doom." Tease Muhammad and Allah will burn your tailfeathers. It's the Qur'an's never-ending argument.

037.040 "Save the chosen slaves of Allah; For them there is a known provision: Fruits, Delights; they will be honored in the Gardens of Pleasure, on thrones facing one another. Round them will be passed a cup of pure white wine, delicious to the drinkers, free from ghoul (hurt) or intoxication, nor shall you be made mad or exhausted thereby." We've got the thrones and Allah's special brew, now all we need are the virgins. "And with them will be Qasirat-at-Tarf (virgin females), restraining their glances (desiring none but you), with big, beautiful eyes. As if they were (sheltered) eggs, preserved."

If the martyrs get virgins, what do their victims get? *037.054* "He said: 'Would you like to look down?' He looked down and saw him in the midst of the Fire, in the depths of Hell. He said: 'You nearly caused me to perish! Had it not been for my Lord, I would have been among those brought there [the suicide bomber said to the innocent children he had blown to pieces]!'" Allah wanted the mass murderers to know: *037.059* "Except for your former death, you shall not be punished. This is the supreme triumph! For the likes of this let strive. That is the better entertainment."

Hell's torments sound a lot like what might have occurred around a desert campfire. *037.063* "For We have truly made it as a trial to torment the disbelievers. Zaqqum is a horrible thorn tree that grows in Hell. The shoots of its fruit-stalks are like the heads of devils. Truly they [non-Muslims] will eat it and fill their bellies with it. On top of that they will be given a mixture made of boiling water to drink especially prepared. Then they shall be returned to the Blazing Fire," Allah, Islam's terrorist ilah proclaimed.

We have finally arrived at the passage the Hadith was trying to illuminate. We wanted to find out why Abraham said he was sick and why he was playing with idols. *037.083* "Surely among those who followed His Way (Islam) was Abraham. He came to his Lord with a sound heart. He said to his father and to his folk, 'What is that which you worship? Is it a falsehood—alihah (gods) besides Allah that you desire?'" The Qur'an didn't define what his "Way" was. Islam is supposed to be the religion of Abraham yet the Qur'an never explains what that might be.

037.087 "'Then what is your idea about the Lord of men and jinn?' Abraham cast a glance at the Stars. And he said, 'I am indeed sick!'" Abe's question about the Lord of the worlds followed by the capitalization of "Stars" is a problem. In the Qur'an, capitalization is a tribute to deity. Second, why did Abraham need to lie to accomplish his god's agenda? One of my translations actually alters the text by adding a parenthetical to obfuscate this problem: "Surely I am sick (of your worshipping these)." Another says "sick (with plague)." Even Muhammad calls Abe a liar. *Tabari II:63* "The Messenger said: 'Abraham told three lies in his life. Two of them were about Allah—his saying "I feel sick" and his saying "The chief idol is the one who did it."'"

037.090 "They turned their backs and went away. He turned to their gods secretly and said, 'Will you not eat?' 'What is the matter with you that you don't speak?'" Deprived of place, time, and circumstance, this doesn't make sense. Where was he? Why did he go to these gods? What are their names? And since Allah never spoke or ate, the revisionist Abe is being hypocritical. The following Hadith, stolen from the Talmud, scrambles to make sense of this: *Tabari II:55* "The people prepared food and placed it before the gods, saying, 'When we come back the gods will have blessed our food and we will eat.' When Abraham saw them with the food, he said, 'Will you not eat? And when they did not answer, he said, 'What ails you that you don't speak?' Then he attacked them. He took a piece of iron and cut off each idol's extremities. Then when only the largest idol was left, he tied the axe to its hand. When the people came to get their food and saw their gods in this state, they said, 'An evildoer has done this to our gods.'"

That was from Muhammad's Sunnah by way of the Jewish Talmud. This is from Allah's Qur'an: *037.093* "He turned upon them secretly, attacking, striking (them) with the right hand. Then came (people) with hurried steps, and faced (him). He said: 'What! do you worship what you hew out? But Allah has created you and your handwork!'"

Let's turn to the salient portion of the 21st surah, named "The Prophets," to make certain we are looking at Islam's poison pill from all possible sides. *021.051* "We bestowed on Abraham correctness of conduct, and well were We acquainted with him. Behold, he said to his father and his folk, 'What are these images, to which you are devoted?' They said, 'We found our fathers worshipping them.' He said, 'Indeed you have been in manifest error—you and your fathers.' They said, 'Have you brought us the truth, or are you some jester?'" This Qur'anic indulgence also emerges out of the blue without reference to the audience, place, time, or religion. Devoid of this context the passage is senseless today. Yet in Mecca, the meaning would have been crystal clear. Muhammad was being recast as Abraham.

021.056 "He said, 'Nay, your Lord is the Lord of the heavens and earth, He created them and I am a witness to this. I have a plot for your idols and will do something against them after you go away and turn your backs.' So he broke them to pieces, (all) but the biggest of them, that they might turn to it." A second translation says: "Then he reduced them to fragments, all save the chief of them, that haply they might have recourse to it."

This is one of the most incriminating verses in the Qur'an. Muhammad did this very thing. The prophet took the largest of the pagan idols of the Ka'aba—Allah—and promoted it to the exclusion of the others. He broke the smaller rock gods and elevated the Black Stone so that his people "might turn to it." It was as if the early Greeks had broken the statues of Athena, Poseidon, and Hermes so that they could worship the one true god Zeus. How was the biggest idol any more "god" than the other imposters?

While I'll continue to convey Islam's version of dishonest Abe to illustrate how Muhammad crafted his religious scam, I would be remiss if I didn't credit the prophet with his first miracle. He just pounded a nail into his own coffin.

The Qur'anic story continues with these uninspired words: *021.059* "They said, 'Who has done this to our alihah (gods)?' 'He is a mischief-monger.' 'We heard a youth talk of them called Abraham.' 'Then bring him before us that he may testify.' They said, 'Are you the one who did this?' He said: 'No, it was done by the biggest idol! Ask the other idols if they can speak!'...They were utterly shamed and confounded. 'You know they do not speak.' He said: 'What! Do you then serve besides Allah what brings no profit, nor can harm you? 'Fie [?] upon you, and upon the things that you worship besides Allah! Have you

no sense?' They said, 'Burn him and protect our gods.'" Since Allah never spoke, why
didn't that shame Muhammad? And why would the supposed patriarch of
monotheistic Islam tell his people that a pagan god smashed lesser idols?
Would that not make the idol real? Moreover, the Muhammadized Abraham
called a "god" false because it "cannot harm you." The implication is that
Allah is real because he's fixated on sadistic torments. That's not good.

Now that we have an argument raging, it's time to reshape Abraham of Ur
into the image of Muhammad of Mecca. For this we will bounce between the
37th and 21st surahs. *037.097* "They said, 'Build him a furnace, and fling him into the blazing red-hot fire!' They then sought a plot against him, but We made them the ones most
humiliated! And he said: 'Surely I fly to my lord; He will guide me.'" When the townsfolk
of Mecca developed their plot and tried to burn Muhammad's britches, he
flew off to Allah in his dreams. He jumped on al-Buraq, an imaginary winged
steed, half ass and half donkey (like its rider), and cruised to heaven by way
of Jerusalem. Although he humiliated himself with his tale of derring-do,
Muhammad also claimed that it was really the Meccans who were dashed.

021.069 "We said, 'O Fire, be cool and safety for Abraham!' Then they sought a strata-
gem against him and wished to set a snare, but We made them the ones that lost most!"
I know Allah loves plots, but this is ridiculous. Why would the townsfolk design
a plot to snare him after they were burning him? *021.071* "But We delivered him and
Lot to the land [of Israel] which We have blessed for men and jinn." This must be a joke.
Allah has blessed *Israel?* Was that the blessing of the PLO or Islamic Jihad?

As the Islamic Abraham flees the fire, we are confronted with an odd transition and unbelievable dialog. *037.100* "'Lord, grant me a righteous (son)!' So We gave
him the good news of a boy ready to suffer and forbear. Then, when (the son) reached (the
age of) (serious) work with him, he said: 'Son! I see in a vision that I offer you in sacrifice:
Now what is your view!' (The son) said: 'O my father! Do as you are commanded: you will
find me, if Allah so wills, one practicing Patience and Constancy!'" Even with nine
words artificially inserted into the text by the translators for clarification, this
verse is bizarre. It is as if Muhammad overheard a half dozen Bible stories
and tried to tie them all together in one paragraph. Over the course of five
sentences, he takes us from a gang of nameless people building a furnace to
terrorize Abe to having him terrorize his son. And there is a significant detail
missing—the son's name isn't stated because Muhammad can't decide which
son should be sacrificed or even where or when the event took place.

037.103 "When they had surrendered (to Allah), and he had flung him on his face, We
called out, 'Abraham! You have fulfilled the vision! Lo! that was a clear test. And We ransomed him with a momentous sacrifice, with a tremendous victim!'" Allah, the counterfeit god, continues to falsify history. *037.110* "Thus do We reward the doers of good.
For he was one of Our believing slaves. And We gave him the good news of the birth of
Isaac, a prophet among the good ones. We blessed him and Isaac: but of their progeny are
(some) that do right, and (some) that obviously do wrong." As a reward for Abraham's

faithfulness, Allah predicts the birth of the son he almost sacrificed. Brilliant.

Somewhere, sometime, someone may have done a worse job plagiarizing, but it's hard to imagine. The omissions, the lack of place, time, and purpose degrade one of the Bible's great events. Muhammad, I mean Allah, was trying to rip off, I mean utilize, the story of Abraham and Isaac. The original provides such a refreshing change from this drivel it's worth a quick review.

First, Yahweh sets the scene and unfolds the story chronologically. Genesis chronicles the life of Abraham, the places he lived, the people he encountered, as well as the birth of his two sons, Isaac and Ishmael. Yahweh had told Abraham to send Ishmael out of the Promised Land, and the boy fell out of Abraham's life and Yahweh's plans, fading into Biblical oblivion. As we approach the 22nd chapter, God tells us that Abraham was living in Beersheba. He had just returned from visiting the Philistines in Gaza. Within that context, he speaks to him about Isaac, the patriarch's miracle child from his wife Sarah, the beneficiary of the covenant.

"Now it came about after these things, that Yahweh tested Abraham and called to him, 'Abraham.' 'Here I am.' Yahweh said, 'Take your son, your only son, whom you love, Isaac, and go to the land of Moriah and offer him there as a sacrifice on one of the mountains of which I will tell you.'" The Temple in Jerusalem was built on Mount Moriah by Solomon to commemorate Abraham's faith. Yahshua would be sacrificed there to save mankind. To this day, it remains the most coveted place on earth. And it's a three-day walk, forty miles north by northwest, from Beersheba.

The details of the sacrifice were extraordinarily important to Yahweh. This drama had to be played out exactly as it would happen to Yahshua. The timing was important, too. The call came 2,000 years after the fall of Adam and two thousand years before the Messiah endured the same fate. Remember, Yahweh gave us a pattern—six eras of creation followed by an era of rest. It has been nearly 2,000 years since Christ's sacrifice and the Bible tells us that 1,000 years of peace will follow his return.

"So Abraham rose early in the morning and saddled his donkey and took two of his young men with him along with Isaac. He split wood for the sacrifice and went to the place Yahweh had told him to go. On the third day Abraham raised his eyes and saw it from a distance. Abraham said to his young men, 'Stay here with the donkey. The lad and I will go yonder. We will worship and return to you.' Abraham took the wood for the offering and laid it on his son. He took the fire and the knife. Walking together, Isaac said, 'My father.' He answered, 'Here I am, my son.' 'I see the fire and the wood, but where is the lamb for the offering?' 'Yahweh will provide for himself the lamb for the offering.'" (Notice that Abraham actually answers in God's name—I Am, or Yahweh—every time he is called.)

"When they came to the place of which Yahweh had told him; Abraham arranged the altar, bound his son Isaac, and laid him on the wood. Abraham stretched out his hand and took the knife to sacrifice his son. But Yahweh called to him from heaven, and said, 'Abraham!' 'Here I am.' 'Do not stretch out your hand against the boy and do nothing to him for I know that you love Me, since you have not withheld your son, your only son from Me.'

"Then Abraham raised his eyes and looked and saw a ram caught in the thicket by his horns; he took the ram and offered him in place of his son. 'Because you have done this thing, and have not withheld your son, I will greatly bless you and I will multiply your descendants as the stars of the heavens...and through your descendents all the nations of the earth shall be blessed.' So Abraham returned to his men, and they arose and went together to Beersheba where Abraham lived."

Real scripture sets human events in context so that we can learn something. Yahweh not only explained the nature of his relationship with man but also explained what was to come, so when it happened, we might recognize the significance.

✡ ✝ ☾ ☄

Returning to the Sira, Ishaq replays Muhammad's fantasy in front of Nimrod rather than in the hall of idols. After daring the gods to talk, Abraham is questioned by a king who died 700 years earlier. *Tabari II:57* **"'Have you seen this Allah whom you worship and whose worship you call others? Who is he?' Abraham replied, 'My Lord, Who gives life and causes death.'** [The question was too tough so he did the old political side step.] **Nimrod said, 'I give life and cause death.'"** They chatted about this for a while and then Abraham said, **"'Allah causes the sun to rise in the East, so can you make it rise in the West?'** [Good thing he didn't mention the chariot thing, the angelic handholds, or the garment of luminosity.] **Knowing that it was as Abraham said, Nimrod was ashamed. He gave no answer; he knew that he was not able to do that. Allah said, 'Thus was the unbeliever abashed'—that is to say, the proof was against him.'"** Now that Muslims know that the sun does not follow *Allah's* commands, shouldn't *they* be ashamed? Isn't the proof clearly against them?

Tabari II:58 **"They pushed Abraham into the furnace. Then the heavens and earth and all creatures therein except humans and jinn shouted to Allah, 'Our Lord! Abraham, the only one on your earth who worships you, is being burned in fire for your sake. Permit us to help him.'"** Everybody talks to Allah except humans and demons. Who might that be? **"Allah answered, 'I am his friend. I will protect him. O fire! Be coolness and peace for Abraham.'"** So following this fireside chat, we read: **"Imprison him in a building and cast him into Hell. ... Abraham raised his head** [and contradicted most all of what we have read thus far], **'You are alone in heaven and I am alone on earth.'...Had Allah not followed the command for coolness with peace, Abraham would have frozen to death."**

Tabari II:62 **"Abraham and Lot set out for Syria. On the way Abraham met Sarah, who was the daughter of the king of Harran."** Actually, Abram left Ur for Haran traveling along the banks of the Euphrates River. He was accompanied by his father, Terah, his wife and half sister, Sarai, and his nephew, Lot. **"She had criticized her people about their religion, so he married her, since he would be able to have a believing wife without having to convert her."** This verse implies one becomes a Muslim by criticizing a religion. **"Then Abraham went forth, a fugitive for the sake of his Lord...to practice his religion and worship safely."** Why would Abe fear for his safety after being saved from the fire? And why, if he was God's messenger, did he bail out of town. Shouldn't he have stayed and tried to save the Babylonians?

No. Recasting Abraham was more important. Muhammad fled Mecca as a fugitive. He ran to Yathrib, today's Medina because some pagans promised to protect him. The revisionist Abraham makes the cowardly Muhammad appear more godly. **"He settled in Harran. Then he left as a fugitive and traveled to Egypt which was under the rule of one of the earliest Pharaohs."** Well, not exactly. The first Egyptian ruler was probably the Scorpion King. He ruled more than five hundred years before Abraham's arrival.

"Sarah was one of the best humans ever. She would not disobey Abraham in any way." That was Muhammad's idea of a perfect woman. From Bukhari's Book of Belief: *Bukhari:V1B22N28* **"The Prophet said: 'I was shown the Hell Fire and the majority of its dwellers were women who are disbelievers or ungrateful.' When asked what they were ungrateful for, the Prophet answered, 'All the favors done for them by their husbands.'"**

Next we find that Muhammad "Islamicized" Abram's encounter with Pharaoh. The only germane insight into this affair is Pharaoh's gift of Hagar, a "Coptic" slave-girl. Flunking history, the Allah/Muhammad duo didn't know that the Coptics were centuries away from arriving on the international scene. Leaving Pharaoh, Abraham tells Sarah, **"You are my sister in Allah, for in all this land there are no Muslims except ourselves."** So what happened to all those scrolls and to the nations who were worshiping around Allah's House?

Some of what follows includes: **"Hagar was of good appearance and Sarah gave her to Abraham, saying, 'Take her. You may take pleasure in Hagar, for I have permitted it.'"** **"The Messenger said, 'When you conquer Egypt treat its people well. They're kin and deserve protection.'"** **"Abraham left Egypt for Syria, for he was afraid of the Egyptian king and anxious about his evil ways. He settled in Beersheba in the land of Palestine, which is the desert of Syria."** While most of this comes out of the Bible, it is flavored with the standard Muslim embellishments. One such addition is revealing. There was no Palestine during Abraham's life. The word was first composed by the Romans 2,100 years after Abraham died. The patriarch actually returned to Canaan, named after his great, great uncle. (Folks with King James Bibles may think Isaiah invented the name, but it's an errant translation. Isaiah 14:29 uses *"pelesheth,"* which means: "rolling in dust."

Tabari II:66 **"Abraham dug a well in Beersheba and said, 'Drink from it and do not let a menstruating woman dip water from it.'"** Muhammad, a sexual libertine if there ever was one, hated menstruation with a passion. As you know, he said that the reason Allah's Stone turned from white to black was "it was fingered by menstruating women." And as sick as that sounds, this next Hadith is used by Muslims to justify brutalizing their daughters. *Tabari II:72* "Sarah swore to cut something off of Hagar. 'I shall cut off her nose, I shall cut off her ear—but no, that would deform her. I will circumcise her instead.' So she did that, and Hagar took a piece of cloth to wipe the blood away. For that reason women have been circumcised and have taken pieces of cloth down to today."

"A menstruating woman came and dipped water from the well. Whereupon the water dried up." While I do not know the connection, the next paragraph begins: "When Allah wished to destroy Lot's people, he sent his messengers to Abraham, commanding him to leave their community. [Weren't we just told that the only two Muslims were Abe and Sarah? And Abraham was in Beersheba, not Sodom, so why ask him to leave?] They had done vile deeds which no one in the two worlds had done before, disbelieving their prophets and rejecting the good counsel which Lot brought them from their Lord. The messengers were ordered to visit Abraham and give him and Sarah tidings of the coming of Isaac and also of Jacob who was to come after him." For Islam to have any hope of being credible, the good news had to be of Ishmael not Isaac. Jacob wasn't Sarah's kid, and neither Jacob nor Isaac are of any value to Islam.

At this point, the Muslim mathematicians jumped into the fray: *Tabari II:68* "Abraham was sixteen when he was thrown into the fire, and Isaac was seven when he was sacrificed, while Sarah was ninety when she bore him. The place of his sacrifice was about two miles from Bayt Iliya [?]. When Sarah learned what Allah wanted with Isaac, she fell ill for two days and died on the third. Sarah was 127 when she died." Muslim math is as confused as Muslim science: 127-90=7. So much for Arabic numerals.

Now we get to the important part. *Tabari II:69* "After Ishmael and Isaac were born, Allah commanded Abraham to build a House for Him in which He would be worshipped and His name mentioned." This must be the House that Allah didn't build in heaven, that Adam didn't build, that Seth didn't build, that Noah didn't circumnavigate after Allah didn't raise it above the flood.

"Abraham did not know exactly where he was expected to build it, since Allah had not made this clear [nor anything else], and he felt uneasy in the matter. Some scholars say that Allah sent the Sakinah to him [a rip-off of the Hebrew Shekhinah—the presence of Yahweh] to show him where to build the House. The Sakinah went with Abraham, who was also accompanied by his wife Hagar [Hagar was never Abraham's wife and Muslims know it.] and his son Ishmael, who was a small boy."

The Tradition continues: "A man came to Ali bin Talib [Muhammad's adopted son, his son-in-law, future Caliph, and said, 'Will you tell me about the House?' He replied, 'It was the first built with the blessing of the standing-place of Abraham, and whoever enters it will be safe. If you wish, I will tell you how it was built. Allah said to Abraham, "Build Me a House on earth!" Abraham felt uneasy, so He sent the Sakinah. The Sakinah is a gale-force wind with two heads, and one head followed the other until they reached Mecca and coiled up at the site of the House, the way a snake coils.'"

There are some who suggest that Allah is Satan, the snake who tempted Adam. Using this metaphor to describe Allah's presence supports that theory. But whether or not that is true, this passage is troubling. Mecca is nearly a thousand miles from Beersheba. These places are separated by rugged mountains and virtually impassible desert. There is no plausible way a hundred-year-old man, a slave girl, and a small child could have endured such a journey. And this may be why neither Muhammad nor Allah ever bothered to tell us how they accomplished the improbable voyage.

Tabari II:70 **"Abraham was commanded to build where the Sakinah had rested. When he had finished it except for one stone, [guess which one] the boy went away to build something else. But Abraham said, 'No, I still need one more stone, as I still order you.' So the boy went looking, and when he found one he brought it to Abraham. But Abraham had already set the Black Stone in place. He said, 'Father, who brought you this Stone?' Abraham answered, 'It was Gabriel who brought it to me from heaven.' Then the two of them finished it."** And I could have sworn that Muhammad told us that the stone was brought to earth by Adam. (Tabari I:298) Was he lying then, or now?

Version two follows. It is also from Ali: **"When he built it he went forth and left Hagar and Ishmael behind. Ishmael became very thirsty. Hagar climbed Safa to look for water but saw nothing. Then she went to Marwah, but the same thing happened. Then she returned to Safa and looked around, but could not find Ishmael. After looking seven times without success she said, 'Ishmael, you have died where I cannot see you.'"** You may be wondering why she would look for water now and yet not have bothered during the three-month desert crossing. You may be wondering why she would look on the top of barren mountains rather than in a valley oasis. You may be wondering why she repeated the process seven times, endangering the life of her child. The answer is Islam. Muhammad needed to make the hajj rites religious. Even today Muslims are required to run between these mountains seven times. This explains why they do it.

However, there were problems. Abraham was supposed to be the father of Islam. In this Hadith, he didn't perform any of the rites. He merely re-re-re-rebuilt the House and bailed. And the one who performed the Islamic ritual, Hagar, left Islam's most important child alone in the desert (as did Muhammad's mother, not so coincidentally).

The sacred Meccan well of Zamzam needed Biblical credibility too, so... **"The boy scraped the ground with his finger and the spring of Zamzam welled up. Hagar began to dam up the water, but Gabriel said, 'Leave it.'"**

In the versions that follow, we're told, **"Abraham and Ishmael set out for Mecca. They took pickaxes without knowing where the house was. So Allah sent a wind, which had two wings and a head of a snake. It swept the area around the Ka'aba clear for them to build the foundations of the original House."** Not *on* the foundations, nor to *see* the foundations, but to *build* the foundations of the original House. **"This was when Allah said, 'When We prepared for Abraham the place of the House.'"** [Qur'an 22:26]

Since three contradictory versions were not enough: *Tabari II:71* "**Allah commanded Abraham to build the House and to call on humanity to perform the pilgrimage. He left Syria with his son Ishmael and his mother Hagar. Allah sent the Sakinah which had the power of speech. Abraham followed it to Mecca. When it came to the place of the House, it spun round and round and said to Abraham, 'Build on me! Build on me!' [Allah's House was built upon a snake.] Abraham laid the foundations and raised the House, working with Ishmael until they came to the cornerstone. Abraham said, 'O my little son, find me a stone which I can put here as a sign to the people.' He brought him a stone, but Abraham did not like it. When Ishmael came back the cornerstone had already been brought and put in place.**" After failing math, science, and history, Islam is failing architecture. The cornerstone is the first rock laid, not the last. And cornerstones are big and rectangular. The Allah Stone is small and oval. But again, it wasn't by accident. The Bible refers prophetically to Christ as "the cornerstone" and you-know-who was desperate to be worshiped just like him.

How was Abraham supposed to call humanity to this place? The valley was uninhabited. It was in the middle of a foreboding desert. The first settlement wouldn't be established for 2,500 years. Furthermore, the Islamic Abraham was piling un-hewn, un-mortared rocks in a desert ravine. The first heavy rain would have done it in.

Perhaps the fourth version of Abraham in Mecca will be more rational. After circumcising Hagar, rather than cutting off her nose: *Tabari II:72* "**Sarah said, 'She will not live in the same town with me.' So Allah told Abraham to go to Mecca, where there was no House at the time. He took Hagar and her son and put them there.... Allah pointed out to Abraham the place to build the House [which would make Allah the snake]. .... When they reached Mecca, there was nothing there but acacia trees.**" If that is true, Muhammad's earlier accounts must have been false. "**The House at the time was but a hill of red clay.... When he was done, Abraham headed back to Syria.... Gabriel dug out Zamzam with his heel for Ishmael.**" All I can assume is that neither Muhammad nor Allah had a clue as to how the rock-pile got there. These wildly divergent explanations are preceded and followed by dozens more. It is as if Muslims think truth can be found in a pile of lies, if only the pile is big enough.

The Traditions move on to recount a variety of patriarchal Meccan visits. Never mind that Mecca didn't exist. Muhammad wants us to believe in fairytales, in talking stones and trees: *Tabari II:78* "**And everything that heard him—stones, trees, hills, and dust said, 'Here I am, my Allah, here I am.'**"

Continuing to give meaningless ritual religious meaning: *Tabari II:81* "**Abraham took Ishmael with him on the day of Tarwiyah [the 8th day of the hajj] and stayed at Mina with the Muslims who were there. He prayed with them the prayers of midday, afternoon, sunset and late evening. He spent the night and prayed the dawn prayer with them. In the morning he went out to Arafat, and he spoke to them there until sunset drew near.**" This Hadith goes on to detail all of the remaining hajj rituals, all of which are still performed by Muslims as if they were acting out Abraham's example. "**He** showed them the sacrifice-ground of Mina, then performed the sacrifice and shaved his head. From Mina he went into the crowd to show them how to perform the march around the Ka'aba. Then he took them back to Mina to show them how to throw the stones, until he had completed the pilgrimage and proclaimed it to mankind."

Because the previous account was unbelievable for a myriad of reasons, not the least of which was that there were no Muslims in Mecca, Muhammad felt compelled to give it an angelic twist. *Tabari II:82* "The Prophet said, 'Gabriel came to Abraham on the day of Tarwiyah and went with him to Mina, Arafat, back to Mina, threw stones, performed the sacrifice, shaved his head, and finally hurried to the House. Then Allah ordered Muhammad to 'follow the religion of Abraham.'" [16:123] That must means that the religion of Abraham, Islam, can be defined as running between two desolate mountains, tossing stones at stones, shaving one's head, and walking around a rock pile. And so it would be. Even today, Islam is known for its rites and rituals rather than for its righteousness or reason.

As we turn the page, we find ourselves embroiled in the mother of all disagreements. Even Muhammad and Allah are at odds: "The earliest sages of our Prophet's nation disagree about which of Abraham's two sons it was that he was commanded to sacrifice. Some say it was Isaac, while other say it was Ishmael." Mind you, these are the very same people we are reliant upon for remembering the Qur'an and passing it along orally so that other sages could jot it down. This might well explain why it is so disjointed, contradictory, and I dare say silly, (not to mention perverted, demented, and disgusting).

Tabari reports: "Both statements are supported by testimony related on the authority of the Prophet. Both statements are equally sound since they both came from the Prophet. Thus only the Qur'an [which also came from the Prophet] could serve as proof that the account naming Isaac was clearly the more truthful of the two." But if that is the case, Islam falters, since it draws its legitimacy from Ishmael. Muhammad claims that he was "prophet quality" because he was a direct descendant of Ishmael.

Tabari II:83 "'We ransomed him with a tremendous victim,' [Qur'an 37:107] refers to Isaac." But how can that be? In verse 104 Allah says, "We called out, 'Abraham, You have fulfilled your dream, thus do we reward the good. That was indeed a trying test. So...We gave him the good news of Isaac." How can Abe have nearly sacrificed Isaac if the reward for fulfilling that trying test *was* Isaac?

In version two: "'Messenger, repeat the knowledge Allah has given you about the son of the two victims.' The Messenger laughed and they said, 'Who are the two victims?' The Prophet said, 'When Abd al-Muttalib was ordered to dig Zamzam [Not Ishmael or Gabriel?], he vowed that if Allah would make it easy for him, he would sacrifice one of his sons. The choice fell upon Abdallah, but his uncles prevented it, saying, 'Ransom your son with one hundred camels.' So he did that, and Ishmael was the other victim.'" The first boy spared, Abdallah, "Slave-to-Allah," was Muhammad's father. And as we shall soon see, he botched that story as badly as he did the other.

Tabari II:84 "When Abraham was told to sacrifice Isaac, Satan said, 'By Allah, if I cannot deceive the people with this, I shall never be able to do it.'" Satan not only swears by Allah, he says that the bogus connection between Abraham and Islam is his best way to fool mankind. And he was right!

It's also interesting that the deception would be over sacrifice. Judaism, Christianity, and all rational civilizations use sacrifice as the means to promote justice and maintain spiritual or societal order. Commit a crime and you will be required to sacrifice your money, your freedom, or your life. If crime is without cost, anarchy reigns. In Judaism, the sacrificial rite for the forgiveness of sin was rich in symbolism. It was based upon the "Mercy Seat" of the Arc of the Covenant. And it was connected prophetically to the blood of an unblemished lamb or dove. It's all explained in the Torah. In Christianity, Christ became the perfect lamb and sacrificed himself on our behalf.

But in Qur'anic Islam, there is no sacrifice. While the Sunnah perpetuates Qusayy's senseless slaughter, there is no symbolism, no prophetic implication, and no reason, as forgiveness is capricious in Islam. And that is why totalitarian governments use draconian measures to maintain order. Muhammad was an amoral thief empowered by situational scriptures, so he failed to appreciate the necessity of sacrifice. And that's why the "ransom of great sacrifice" mentioned in the Qur'an is left unexplained.

Tabari II:87 "Caliph Umar said, 'I asked a former Jew, who was considered to be a great Jewish scholar before he converted to Islam. He said, 'Ishmael, by God, O Prince of Believers. The Jews know that, but they are envious of you Arabs because it was your father who was named in Allah's command and to whom Allah ascribed such merit.'"

Then why do you suppose the prophet said, "When Isaac grew up, Abraham had a dream in which he was told, 'Fulfill your promise that if Allah grants you a son by Sarah you will sacrifice him. [In other words: "If you give me a son I'll kill him for you."] Then he drew the knife across Isaac's throat, but the knife did not scratch him, for Allah had placed a sheet of copper on Isaac's throat. When Abraham saw it he turned him over and tried to cut him on the nape of his neck.' This confirms Allah's Qur'an: 'When he surrendered, he flung him down upon his face.'" [37:103]

In the next Hadith it's Ishmael: "When Abraham was alone with his son on the trail on Mt. Thabir [a mountain near Mecca], it is said he said to Ishmael, 'O my son, I saw in a dream that I was to sacrifice you. What do you think?' Ishmael told him, 'O my father, Do as you were ordered...and sharpen your knife-blade so that it will finish me off quickly." If only Islam would go down as easily.

The tests attributed to Abraham may be the low water mark for Islam's credibility thus far. This strand of pearls begins to unwind in Tabari's second volume, *Prophets and Patriarchs*: *Tabari II:97* "After Allah had put Abraham to the test— when Nimrod bin Cush tried to burn him in the fire, when He commanded him to sacrifice his son after he had become old enough to walk, when He made him raise the foundations of the House, and devote himself to its rituals—after all of this, He put Abraham to the test with still further commands which He has mentioned. He said, 'And when his Lord tried Abraham with commands and he fulfilled them.' [2:124] The earliest scholars of the Islamic community (ummah) disagreed about the nature of these commandments with which Allah tested Abraham and which Abraham obeyed."

These tests were crucial because Islam—according to Muhammad—was the result of Abraham's obedience. Yet the Qur'an is deficient—completely silent on the nature of these trials and their significance. So rather than let Allah wallow in blissful ignorance, the Companions rushed in to save the day. *Tabari II:98* "Islam consists of thirty parts, and no one ever tested with this obligation carried it out, except Abraham." "'And when his Lord tried Abraham with commands,' means that Allah tested him with the acts of ritual purification, five in the head and five in the body. [5+5=30] Those in the head are: trimming the mustache, rinsing the mouth, cleansing the nostrils with water, using the toothstick, and parting the hair with the fingers. Those in the body are: paring the nails, shaving the pubic hair, circumcision, plucking the armpit, and washing off traces of feces and urine."

Can't be! Surely this is a misprint. There is no way that the adoptive father of the world's fastest growing religion earned the dubious honor by passing such an inane "test." Let's examine another Hadith to make sure we've got this right. "Allah's words, 'When his Lord tried Abraham with commands,' mean that Abraham was tested by circumcision, shaving his pubic hair, washing the fore-part and rear, using a toothstick, trimming the mustache, paring nails, and plucking his armpits.'"

That wasn't any better. How about this: *Tabari II:99* "Abraham was tested with ten Islamic practices: rinsing the mouth, cleansing the nostrils with water, trimming the mustache, using a toothstick, plucking the armpit, paring the nails, washing finger joints, circumcision, shaving pubic hair, and washing the rear and vulva." So after adding: "bathing on Friday," a fourth version gets ritualistic with: "walking around the Ka'aba, running between Safa and Marwah, stoning pillars, and hurrying." I disdain ritual. I am, therefore, unimpressed with its justification. Ritual is a tool used by power-hungry men to condition the masses and subject them to their rule. It is a control device for the oppressor to use against the ignorant. It separates men from God and discourages rational inquiry.

Tabari claims that these Hadiths somehow illuminate portions of the 2nd surah. Let's see how: *002.118* "Those who are ignorant say: 'Why doesn't Allah speak to us Himself or show us a sign?' So said the people before them. We have indeed shown our clear signs already." Neither Allah nor Muhammad ever bothered to provide any proof of divine inspiration—no signs, no miracles, no prophecies—so this, once again, refers to the miracles of the Bible.

"Lo! We have sent you (Muhammad) with the truth, a bringer of glad tidings and a warner. And you will not be asked about the companions of the Blazing Hell Fire." That's almost funny. Allah is telling Muhammad that he won't be asked about hell.

Why then do you suppose hell is the Qur'an's most oft repeated subject?

002.120 **"Never will the Jews or the Christians be satisfied with you unless you follow their form of religion. Say: 'The guidance of Allah is Guidance. ... Those to whom We have given the Book read it as it ought to be read."** The Qur'an cannot be true and confirm the Bible as Allah claims if Judeo-Christianity is an errant "form of religion." And at this point the Qur'an wasn't remotely complete; it wasn't even written down. Allah was therefore saying that people were doing something that simply couldn't be done. That would make him a liar. What's more, Allah was speaking to an illiterate man—one incapable of reading.

"These [Jews] believe in it; and whoever disbelieves it are losers. Children of Israel, call to mind the special favor which I bestowed upon you, and that I [Allah] preferred you to all others and made you excel the nations." Muhammad was in a pickle. Without the Jews being Yahweh's chosen people, the prophets and scriptures upon which he based Islam lost their relevancy. If they were irrelevant, so was Islam.

Like so much of the Qur'an, this surah provides no intelligent transition between subjects. It has rambled on about god's inability to provide a sign, to telling us that Muhammad was a warner. It flip-flops from telling him not to follow the religion of the Jews to calling the Jews God's chosen people. Then after condemning Christ's mission and crucifying Muhammad's credibility in the process, it moves to a revisionist account of the Biblical patriarch Abraham. *002.124* **"And (remember) when Abraham's Lord tried him with (certain) commands, which he fulfilled: He said: 'I will make you an Imam [Islamic leader] to the Nations.' He pleaded: 'And also Imams from my offspring!' He answered: 'But My Promise does not include evil-doers.'"** The nature of the trials, or commands, which Abraham allegedly fulfilled was not listed. Considering that the passage of these trials made Abraham the father of Islam—the Imam of the nations—the omission was serious. Not surprisingly, it sent the Muslim sages scurrying for answers. Sadly, what we just reviewed was the best they could do. The Noble Qur'an translators even include this Hadith: *Bukhari:V7B72N779* **"I heard the Prophet saying, 'Five practices are characteristics of the Fitra [religion of Abraham]: circumcision, shaving the pubic hair, cutting the moustaches short, clipping the nails, and depilating the hair of the armpits.'"** This "religion" can't be fixed. It needs to be discarded.

Every Biblical story quoted in the Qur'an was designed to make Muhammad's unprophet-like behavior seem religious or to make Islamic rituals seem sane. The next verse was no exception. *002.125* **"Remember when We made the House a place of assembly for men and a place of safety; and the place Abraham stood to pray; and We covenanted with Abraham and Ishmael that they should sanctify My House for those who circumambulate it, use it as a retreat, bow down, prostrating themselves."** *002.126* **"And remember [This is an odd command. What are they remembering this from? The Bible doesn't say anything remotely like this, and no other scriptures refer to Abraham.] Abraham said: 'My Lord, make this a City of Peace, and feed its people with fruits, such of them as believe in Allah and the Last Day.'"** Even this is odd. Muhammad was verbally attacked during the entire time he preached in Mecca. As a result, he attacked Mecca with a large army at the end of his career, putting him in direct opposition to the patriarch's supposed prophecy.

"He said: 'As for those who reject, indulge them; soon I will compel them to the doom of the torment of Hell Fire, an evil destination!'" To compel is to induce or coerce. Why would God want to act like Satan and coerce someone into hell?

002.127 **"Remember, Abraham and Ishmael raised the foundations of the House: 'Our Lord! Accept this service from us.'"** While I realize that no one was writing this stuff down, and that a short pencil is more effective than a long memory, god and his prophet ought to be able to do better. Just two verses earlier Allah said that he had made the House. Next we learn: **"'Our Lord, make of us Muslims, submissive to Your (will), and of our offspring a nation of Muslims, bowing to You; and show us our place for the celebration of rites.'"** Abraham died 2600 years before the first Muslim was conned into Islam. In fact, the Arabic word for Muslim wouldn't even be coined for twenty-six centuries.

Yet a nation of Muslims is how Muhammad viewed the world. The prophet saw our planet in two pieces—the Nation of Islam (called Dar us-Islam) and lands yet to submit, the House of War (called Dar us-Harb). And while Islam has been at war with itself for all of its thirteen centuries, it will continue to fight the House of War until we capitulate. Many in the Western media and most politicians claim that the war on terrorism is unlike any other because the terrorists come from many nations. Now you know the truth: the terrorists represent one nation—the Nation of Islam.

002.129 **"Our Lord, raise up in their midst a Messenger from among them who shall recite to them Your revelations, and instruct them in the Book and in wisdom and make them grow."** By the time the second surah was "revealed" Muhammad had fled Mecca for the safety of Medina. Now in close proximity with Jews, he had a problem. These folks were literate, and as a result, they were harder to fool. They undoubtedly told Muhammad that he couldn't be God's final messenger because that role belonged to the Messiah. Moreover, there were hundreds of specific prophecies regarding the Messiah, none of which he met. So what do you suppose the wannabe Messiah did? Right. He made one up.

But for it to be believable, he had to revise Abraham first: *002.130* **"He who turns away from the religion of Abraham makes himself a fool with folly."** Abraham did not have a religion. He had a relationship. There were no rituals, rites, prostrations, pilgrimages, or prescribed prayers. In fact, the word "religion" doesn't exist in the Torah. It can't be found even once in all of the Old Testament. *002.131* **"When his Lord said to him, 'Be a Muslim,' he said: 'I submit [Islam] to the Lord of the worlds.'"** Likewise, you won't find the words Muslim, submit, or Islam.

The revisionist Abraham said, **"Our Lord, make us submissive [Islam] to You and make of our seed a nation [of Muslims]. And show us our ways of worship."** If Abraham received scrolls from Allah and performed the Islamic rituals, he could not have asked, "Show me the ways of worship."

"You, only You, are the Relenting. Our Lord, raise up in their midst a messenger." You can almost hear Muhammad cry, "I'm da man." Jesus has been demoted and Abraham promoted so that Abe can vouch for the credentials of Muhammad and thereby silence the prophet's critics.

Muhammad believes that Allah chose Islam for Abraham and his sons, especially Jacob, from whom all Jews are descended. *002.132* **"And this was the legacy that Abraham left to his sons by Yah'qub (Jacob); 'Oh my sons! Allah has chosen the Faith for you—the true religion; then die not except in the faith of Islam as Muslims. He said to his sons: 'What will you worship after me?' They said: 'We shall worship your Ilah (God), the Ilah (God) of your fathers, of Abraham, Ishmael and Isaac, the one Ilah (God): To Him we submit in Islam.'"** Why do you suppose Yahweh trifled with Judaism and Christianity if Abe were a Muslim? And could Abraham have referred to God as Allah if the name wouldn't be invented for more than twenty centuries? Even then, it was the proper *name* of a pagan rock idol in Arabia, not Israel. How do you suppose Yahweh's name could have been repeated 6,868 times in the Bible if his name were really Allah? And there is no way to weasel out of this predicament. Muslims scream that "Allah" is simply the Arabic *word* for "God," yet that assertion is in direct conflict with the Qur'an. In this verse the Arabic word for "God" (capital "G"), "Ilah," was used three times.

Alright, now that we've turned Jews into Muslims it's time to condemn them. *002.134* **"Those are people whose nation has passed away. They shall reap the fruit of what they did, They say: 'Become Jews or Christians if you would be guided.' Say (Muhammad): 'Nay! Only the Religion of Abraham the Hanif. He was not a Mushrikun [non-Muslim disbeliever].'"** The Qur'an says nothing of the religion of Abraham. It only suggests prostrations and rituals—mindless drivel. Since the world's best-documented faiths are Judaism and Christianity, and their Bible introduced Abraham to the world, you'd think that Islam would at least try. But no, all we get is feeble justification for a sorry mix of pre-existing pagan rites.

"Hanifs" were monotheistic poets. While they inspired Islam's first score of surahs, they were not Muslims. We will discuss them in upcoming chapters.

002.136 **"Say (Muslims): 'We believe in Allah and that which is revealed to us and that which was revealed to Abraham, and Ishmael, and Isaac, and Jacob, and the (twelve Jewish) tribes, and that which Moses and Jesus received, and that which the prophets received from their Lord. We make no distinction between any of them, and unto Him we have surrendered (in Islam).'"** You'd think that after 1400 years, some bright Muslim would ask, "*What* was revealed to Abraham, Ishmael, Isaac, and Jacob?" If Allah knows, why is he keeping it a secret? Or, why not ask, "If we Muslims shouldn't make any distinction between the revelations Moses and Jesus received and those claimed by Muhammad, why was Islam necessary?"

If they were without distinction this cannot be true: **"If they believe as you believe they are rightly guided; but if they turn away they are in great opposition. Allah will** suffice you against them." Allah says the revelations are identical—Judaism's, Christianity's, and Islam's, and then he says "they are in great opposition."

There is some good news. The Islamic god was a self-indulgent fool: *002.138* "(Our religion is) the Baptism of Allah: And who can baptize better than Allah?" Not only is Allah a Jew, he's a Baptist. And while that's embarrassing, the symbolism is deadly for Islam. Muslims don't baptize, and that's a problem if their religion is the Baptism of Allah—especially since he's the best Baptiser.

Baptism by water is the outward expression of having chosen Christ as one's savior. It is symbolic of receiving his Spirit—the spirit of Yahweh. While the Holy Spirit is something that the Qur'an both acknowledges and condemns, He, like the Torah, Gospels, and Christ, plays no part in Islam. Allah is a distant god. His spirit does not reside in man.

While we turned to this surah in an effort to connect Traditions regarding Abraham to Allah's account in the Qur'an, we have hit a veritable goldmine of Islamic blunders. This may be the most grotesque of all. *002.139* "Say (unto the People of the Scripture [Christians and Jews]): Will you dispute with us about Allah, seeing that He is our Lord and your Lord?" Muslims, in a desperate grope for credibility, are being told that Yahweh and Allah are the same god. It is hard to imagine a more vulgar lie. Yahweh and Allah are love and lust, redemption and punishment, personal and remote, brilliant and dimwitted, peace and terror. They are as different as their scriptures.

Yet this deception is essential to Islam. If Allah isn't Yahweh, Muhammad is a liar and the Qur'an is lunacy. There is no other justification for Muhammad's reliance on Genesis and Exodus. Muslims must reconcile the irreconcilable, bridging the chasm between Yahweh's and Allah's wholly divergent characters. It is a desperate battle for survival that Islam cannot win.

The infinitesimal chance Islam had of prevailing with this ridiculous assertion evaporated when the Dead Sea scrolls were discovered. The text and message on those uncorrupted scrolls rendered *impossible* the comprehensive corruption and conspiracy that would have been necessary to make the doctrines and gods similar, much less the same.

002.140 "Nay! Do you say that Abraham, Ishmael, Isaac, Jacob and the Tribes were Jews or Christians? Say: Do you know better than Allah? Who is more unjust than those who conceal the testimony they received from Allah?" If this weren't so stupid it would be funny. Allah is saying that Christians and Jews call Abraham, Ishmael, Isaac, Jacob and the Tribes, "Jews and Christians," as if they knew more about them than Allah. Well, apparently they do. Abraham wasn't, strictly speaking, a Jew. He was a Chaldean from Ur as was his wife Sarah. Anyone who has bothered to read Genesis knows that. But Allah was illiterate, just like Muhammad. Reading Genesis was therefore beyond him. Ishmael was the bastard child of an Egyptian slave. He was expressly excluded from Yahweh's covenant with the Jews. No Jew or Christian would ever claim relations with him. Isaac, Abraham's miracle son, provided the link between Abraham and Jacob. Jacob was the father of the twelve tribes and *was* therefore a Jew—*the* Jew. And last time I checked, the tribes of Israel were Jews, not Christians. The first Christian wouldn't be born for twenty centuries.

By this time it should be abundantly clear—Allah wasn't God. The dark spirit of Islam wasn't even sane. *002.141* **"The fools among the people will say: 'What has turned them from the Qiblah [the direction Muslims face in prayer] to which they formerly observed [facing Jerusalem]?'"** Following the Satanic Verses, Ka'aba worship was on the rocks, so Muhammad had Muslims pray to a substitute shrine—the only holy site in the Bible —the Jewish Temple in Jerusalem. But that didn't last because the Jews began disputing his preposterous claims of prophethood. Something had to be done. The answer was simple enough. Muslims were ordered to turn away from Jerusalem and to bow toward the House that Allah-Adam-Abraham built.

"We appointed the Qiblah which you were used to, as a hard test for those who followed the Messenger. Indeed it was a momentous change, except to those guided by Allah." I don't suppose anyone bothered to ask why bowing one direction versus another in ritualistic prayer was such a tough test. I would think that twisting one's prayer blankie might be sufficient. Why go to all the trouble to twist the Torah?

002.144 **"Turn your face in the direction of the sacred Mosque [the Ka'aba]. Wherever you are, turn your faces in that direction. The people of the Book know well that this revelation is the truth from their Lord."** Allah is saying that the Jews and Christians know that the Ka'aba is of paramount importance to Judeo-Christianity. Further, he is protesting that the Jews and Christians have collaborated in a massive cover-up to keep the true importance of the pagan shrine a secret. Frankly, I am stunned that something this obviously false and foolish could be considered godly by anyone.

Implicit in this farce is that the Judeo-Christian focus on the Temple Mount in Jerusalem is bogus. For this to be true, the entire Bible, starting with Genesis 11 running through Revelation 22, would have to be fundamentally flawed, for virtually every page is rooted in the history of Israel, and focused on Jerusalem. To say that Jews and Christians conspired to artificially elevate the importance of Israel, Jerusalem, and the Temple at the expense of Mecca, a town that didn't even exist during the two thousand years the scriptures were being written—in all sixty-six books of the Bible—is ludicrous.

Yet the stakes are unimaginably high. If Allah's contention is wrong, then Islam's foundation is ripped asunder. All of the corrupted Biblical accounts in the world won't help. If the Islamic connection to the Hebrew prophets and patriarchs falters, every important aspect of Muhammad's religion fails: Allah isn't god; Muhammad isn't a prophet. And if they aren't who they claim they are, they aren't worthy of anyone's prayers, allegiance, or soul.

Therein lies the tale—the ticking time bomb of Islam. There is no room for an Arab prophet with a wholly divergent message, especially one without miracles or prophecies, in the line of Hebrews. The last messenger of the scriptures is undeniably the Messiah, not Muhammad.

That gave the Messenger of Islam several enormous problems. He had to claim that the Messianic prophecies were corrupted and meaningless—an impossible task. He had to ignore the fact that Christ fulfilled them—a fool's folly (one sadly shared by the Jews). Then he had to somehow distort Bible stories and characters to such an extent that it made his unprophet-like behavior and ridiculous pagan rites seem religious, rational, moral, and inspired. But that led to a new problem. How does one do that without debasing the faith upon which the new religion is based?

It can't be done—at least not rationally. But Islam has never been popular with rational people. It is like an acid, corroding everything it touches, eating away at the brain and heart. It corrupts men, turning them into unthinking, mindless murderers in pursuit of lustful pleasures. It causes Muslims to be so fearful of the truth, they threaten to kill anyone willing to expose their lie.

Muhammad wasn't finished telling his faithful that the Jews and the Christians had collaborated in the greatest hoax in all of recorded history. *002.146* **"The people of the Book recognize him as they know their own sons; but some of them conceal the truth which they themselves know."** Muhammad's "god" is saying on behalf of his "prophet" that the Jews recognized Muhammad as the Messiah but were keeping it a secret. He was evidently counting on everyone being illiterate and naïve. And judging by the numbers of people he fooled, he may have been right.

The trials and tribulations of Dishonest Abe, also known as a figment of Muhammad's imagination, end where they began—by ripping off a well-documented Bible story. *Tabari II:111* **"Lot bin Haran bin Terah, son of Abraham's brother, and his people, the folks of Sodom, traveled from Babylon following their religion. They went to Syria as fugitives with Sarah. It is said that Terah, Abraham's father, went with them."** Yes, Terah was Abe's dad, not Azar, like the Traditions have been insisting. And yes, they were close when they said that they left Babylon. It was actually Ur, a hundred miles south. And yes, the troop included Lot and Sarah. They were not, however, fugitives, they had no religion, and the people of Sodom were not with them. Lot would eventually live in Sodom, but that wouldn't occur for a couple of thousand miles and many years.

"Terah died. Abraham, Lot and Sarah went on to Syria and then to Egypt, which was then ruled by a Pharaoh named Sinan bin Al-wan bin Ubayd bin Uwayj bin Imlaq bin Lud bin Shem bin Noah. He was the brother of Dahhak/Nimrod, who had appointed him governor of Egypt." These boys would have been so much better off if they had just stuck with the Biblical account rather than drumming up this nonsense. Truth is, they would have been better off if they had just stuck with Judaism and never perverted it into Islam—and so would we.

"After this, Abraham, Lot and Sarah went back to Syria and settled in Palestine. Allah sent Lot to the people of Sodom. They were disbelievers in Allah and immoral. Allah said, 'You commit lewdness such as no creature before. You come into males, cut the roads, and commit abominations in your assemblies.'" [Qur'an 29:28] Allah, please, watch the language. They have a perfectly good word for that male thing. It's called homosexuality. As for the lewdness, they have a word for that too. And even you should know it—as it was named after the town. But as for "cutting the roads," I'm at a loss.

Fortunately, Muslim sages are ever ready to enlighten us. *Tabari II:112* "Allah's statement, 'you cut the road' means: When the traveler, the son of the road, passed by they would block the road and perform with him that ugly deed.... Some say that they used to shorten whoever passed by. Other say that they used to break wind in their assemblies, while some said that they used to have intercourse with each other there.... Some Islamic scholars agree, while others differ. The abomination was breaking wind." I wonder if that was why Allah taught Adam about "the fart and the little fart?" It may have been why Muhammad revealed this pearl in Bukhari's *Book of Wudu:* *Bukhari:V1B4N139* "He asked Allah's Messenger about a person who imagined to have passed wind during the Salat prayer. Allah's Messenger replied: 'He should not leave his Salat unless he hears sound or smells something.'" You see, Islam *can* be tolerant.

Others say: "They would accost a rider and seize him and mount him," explains surah 29:28. Or: "Allah's statement refers to the fact that no male jumped upon a male before the people of Lot." Then you have Muhammad's version: "The Messenger of God said, 'And you commit abominations in your assemblies means they would cut off wayfarers and mock them, and that was the abomination that they committed.'" Horror of horrors! Being mocked was Muhammad's curse in life. Virtually everyone he encountered berated him.

The Messenger had a lot to say about Lot. Although Lot never preached a day in his life and was the furthest thing from a prophet, the temptation to transform him into a mini-Muhammad was too great to pass up. *Tabari II:115* "Lot called on them to worship Allah. By Allah's command he tried to prohibit them from doing those things which Allah disliked such as brigandage, committing lewd acts, and entering males in the posteriors. Because they persisted, he threatened them with painful doom. They rejected his admonitions, saying to him 'Bring Allah's doom upon us, if you are telling the truth!'" I could have sworn that we've heard this story before.

"At length Lot asked his Lord for help against them, since the matter was dragging on, as was their persistence in sinfulness. Then Allah—when he wanted to disgrace them and destroy them and help His Messenger Lot against them—sent Gabriel and two other angels. It had been said that the two other angels were Michael and Israfil." Every word of this was loaded, chosen specifically to distress Muhammad's Meccan tormentors. "Mess will me and my god will get you."

Tabari II:120 "Gabriel picked up their land with his wing and turned it over. He lifted it so high the inhabitants of heaven heard the crowing of roosters and the barking of dogs. He turned them upside down and rained upon them stones of clay." [Qur'an 15:74]

The 15th surah says: "Thus did We turn it upside down, and rained down upon them stones of what had been decreed. Surely in this are signs for those who examine. And surely it is on a road that still abides. Most surely there is a sign in this for the believers. The dwellers of the Rock rejected the messengers."

Allah is daring us to use his depiction of Sodom as a proof of his divinity. But Sodom wasn't turned upside down, it wasn't stoned with clay, nor was it ever close enough to heaven for the angelic host to hear the roosters. And the roads have long since disappeared. We know that because archeologists have found Sodom, Gomorrah, and the other cities of the plain. And guess what? They are exactly where the Bible said they would be. They were destroyed exactly when the Bible said that they were destroyed. And yes, they were buried exactly how the Bible proclaimed—under brimstone. Once again, the Bible was precisely accurate, and the Muhammad/Allah team couldn't even plagiarize it without burying themselves.

Some of the lowlights of the versions that follow include: *Tabari II:121* "Gabriel spread out his wings and gouged out their eyes." "Then Allah took them to Syria." Which is odd because that's where we were told they were in the first place.

This next one is a hoot. There are more errors than sentences. "Gabriel seized its girdle, then snatched it up so high into the sky that the angels could hear their dogs. He threw rocks at the laggards, one after the other. There were three towns called Sodom that lay between Medina and Syria. It has been mentioned that there were four million people in the town." Four thousand, maybe. They all had different names, like Gomorrah, and they were unearthed on the shores of the Dead Sea.

Muhammad's convoluted story of Lot is repeated a half dozen times in different surahs and that many times again in the Traditions. It's no wonder it was the prophet's personal favorite. He had the opportunity to turn a nobody into a messenger whose people got pummeled because they mocked him.

We leave Volume II of Tabari with these stirring words, "O Messenger! How many books did Allah reveal? He said, 'One hundred and four books. To Adam He revealed ten leaves, to Seth fifty leaves, and to Enoch thirty leaves. To Abraham he revealed ten leaves and also the Torah, Gospel, the Zabur, and the Rurqan.'" Oops. Even Allah knows better. The Torah wasn't written until the time of Moses. But what makes this statement particularly lame is that eighty-five percent of the Torah chronicles the history of people who lived after Abraham died.

Tabari II:130 "I said, 'O Messenger! What were the books of Abraham?' He answered, 'They were all proverbs such as, 'O dominated, afflicted and deceived king! I did not send you to collect all the world, one part to another, rather I sent you so that I would not have to hear the cry of the oppressed.'" If they were all that feeble, it's little wonder no one other than the illiterate messenger ever read them.

5

CAN QUSAYY SCAM?

*"Qusayy purchased the custodianship of the Ka'aba
for a skin full of wine and a lute."*

Desolate is the best word to describe Arabia in the years before the prophet's birth. Although civilization made its début along the only portion of Arabia that doesn't touch the sea, for thirty-five centuries it failed to take root in the desert sands. In the east lay Mesopotamia, the fertile land between the Tigris and Euphrates. Its legendary cities invented the tool that binds you and me, reader and writer: man's greatest invention, written language. Nearly five thousand years ago, the Sumerians, Babylonians, and Assyrians used cuneiform to proclaim their achievements in science, math, astronomy, law, medicine, agriculture, architecture, the arts, and religion.

Yet while these advances were occurring, Arabia remained isolated and stagnant—providing the culture necessary to propagate Islam. Poverty in proximity to greatness makes a people vulnerable to deceit.

While we stand upon the shoulders of the Babylonian, Assyrian, and Sumerian scholars, we are haunted by their faith. Two politically-minded doctrines grew out of its schemes—Medieval Catholicism and fundamental Islam. For a thousand years the most powerful forces were not nations but religions. Both deployed rites first practiced in Babylonians temples. Many Catholic symbols, festivals, and doctrines are rooted in the practices of these distant peoples. Christmas, Easter, Lent, the priesthood, confession, and the worship of the Virgin Mary are examples of present rites borrowed from a pagan past. Islam was not immune. Allah was Sin, the moon god of Ur. The Qur'anic Paradise and Hell were imported from the same realm.

The cuneiform indentations in clay that confirmed these startling realities became hieroglyphics along the Nile and an alphabet on the eastern shores of the Mediterranean. We know from the temple writings in Karnak that pagan gods like those of the Fertile Crescent flourished in Egypt. We saw them emerge again in Greece, then Rome. Yet in Canaan it was a different story. A god appeared unlike any other. In a world of idols, he was spirit. In a world of plenty, he was one. In a world of distant deities symbolized by astronomical bodies he was personal, approachable, knowable. His name was Yahweh. His people were Jews. Together they documented their history and their relationship. In so doing, these peoples at the western doorstep of Arabia played a central role in the most telling of all modern tales.

Their intersection begins when a young man named Abram left Sin. In a perilous journey he, his stunning wife Sarai, his father Terah, and his nephew Lot, left Ur of the Chaldeans, and headed northwest. Crossing along the roof of the Arabian Peninsula, their route carried them along the Euphrates to an outpost town called Haran. There, Abram's father died, but not his father's god. Sin, the moon god of Ur, reigned supreme. Called by a higher source than even the moon and its god, Abram, Sarai, and Lot left the safety of the mighty river and headed to the land of Canaan—the Promised Land.

In the greatest story ever told, Abram became Abraham, father of nations. He sired Ishmael at ninety by way of his wife's Egyptian maid and in so doing Abraham gave birth to the seed of Islam. A decade later, the centenarian witnessed the promised miracle birth of Isaac to Sarai, now Sarah. Isaac became the child of destiny, for through him would come all of the prophets and patriarchs: Jacob, Joshua, Moses, David, Solomon, Isaiah, Daniel, Jeremiah, and two millennia later, Yahshua, known to Westerners as Jesus of Nazareth. This Biblical story was destined to play out in the crossroads of history, in the most contested land on earth, at the very intersection of continents.

Yet these great dramas depicting the rise of civilizations and faiths simply teased the Arabians. The footprints of culture, science, language, religion, law, and the arts were blown away by the searing winds. The Chaldeans, Assyrians, Babylonians, Persians, Egyptians, Greeks, and Romans all intertwined their histories with Abraham's descendants through Isaac, but not Ishmael. It was as if the Arabs were on a deserted island, marooned in time. Such was the milieu for Islam, a religion so sterile it could only have taken root in a like mind and place.

Arabs remained illiterate throughout the millennia, which is why we know so little about them. And it is why they knew so little about the world that engulfed them. Their language was derived from Aramaic, the dominant tongue of history's initial millennia. But Arabic found neither stylus nor pen for one hundred generations. By Muhammad's time, less than one in a hundred Arabians could write. Classical Arabic, the language in which the Qur'an would come to be written, was just beginning to evolve in Syria.

The Bedouins of the Syrian steppe were nomadic by necessity. Their land was too poor to support towns of substance. Arabs, (a name derived from the word arid) were tribal peoples; there was never a dominant civilization over them. Most attempts to conquer their Peninsula were foiled by the harsh environmental conditions, further exacerbating the challenge of knowing these people. For three thousand years they were neither conquered nor conquerors, for subduing Bedouins was like herding cats. The Babylonians, Assyrians, Egyptians, Persians, Greeks, and Romans all failed. But it was not because Arabs were savage. They coveted freedom and valued nonviolence. For the first three millennia of recorded history, Arabs were among the world's most peaceful and self-reliant people. It is only during the last 1400 years that they have been terrorists. The dividing line was Islam. Muhammad corrupted them.

Islamic scholars try valiantly to paint the pre-Islamic period, called *Jahiliyyah*, or Period of Ignorance, in the worst possible light. They demonize Arabs to make the resulting Islamic society, arguably the most ignorant and brutal in history, look good by comparison. But what little evidence we have of these people, their lives, and customs, indicates that they didn't act foolishly. Unlike their descendants in the twenty-first century, seventh-century Arabs were a free, peace-loving people who cherished family values and honored tribal commitments.

Reliant on springs, most nomadic Bedouins provided sustenance by cultivating date palms, herding sheep, working leather, or running caravans. Their parched land was known for hearty camels and wide-open spaces. With the rain clouds blocked by the ragged mountains of Syria, Israel, Jordan, and western Arabia, more often than not the harbingers of life merely teased the land that became Muhammad's.

It was these very conditions that made it impregnable. The roads that enabled the armies of Babylon, Assyria, Persia, Egypt, Greece, and Rome to conquer and control much of the world were difficult to build and impossible to maintain. And there was no incentive. Virtually nothing of value originated from this barren realm. It only served as a dry ocean to be crossed when carrying goods from producer to consumer. But since the Arabian Peninsula was surrounded by seas and the most vital of rivers, circumnavigating it was always easier than passing through. The land Muhammad coveted was a foreboding wasteland, a place that time had forgotten.

Whispers and faint echoes were all Arabs knew of the world surrounding them. Over time they came to hear of the gods of Nimrod and Babylon. Similar gods rose in Egypt, Greece, and Rome. They blended man, beast, and sky into palpable superstitions that elevated rulers to deity. The inventors and keepers of divine trust—god's coconspirators and messengers—crafted schemes designed to make their subjects submit, pay, and obey.

By the seventh century, Arabs had also heard of the two great monotheistic religions. Stories of the Jews, their patriarch Abraham, and his God Yahweh, were commonplace. Moses was known as the great liberator, David and Solomon as kings. Following their captivity in Babylon, many Jews settled in Arabia, especially in the oasis town of Yathrib. They told the Bedouins that they were kindred spirits of sorts. The Torah claimed both peoples, Arabs and Jews, were descendants of Abraham. The Arabs traced their lineage through

Ishmael, embarrassing in that he was the bastard son of a slave girl. The real heir to Yahweh's covenant was Isaac, born to Abraham's wife Sarah. Innocent enough, such notice would loom large.

The nomads of Arabia also knew something of Christianity, which by the sixth century was the most pervasive force, albeit peaceful, in the civilized world. While Christian ideals were winning converts in the literate realms of Egypt, Rome, Greece, and Persia, such was not the case in Arabia. There, Christians were being persecuted with a vengeance—not by Arabs, but by a Jew named Dhu Nuwas, who had risen to power in Yemen. This, too, would have haunting echoes, for the Christian faith was reduced to a faint whisper compared to that of the Jews. Moreover, the "turn the other cheek" message of Christ didn't play well in a society reliant on revenge to maintain order. So the Arabs lived suspended between the monotheism of the west and the swirling superstitions of the east.

Allegiance to tribe and family kept these people grounded. The nomads lived without police, laws, or judges, as there were too few to govern. Clashes between tribes occurred, but were usually settled by one raiding the other's flock—a goat for a goat. It was often a game played for bragging rights. They despised treachery and deceit. In skirmishes, honor was more important than victory. The subjugation of another tribe was never contemplated. Early Arabs were neither passive nor aggressive. Surviving was battle enough.

They practiced a crude form of Hammurabi's Laws 2,500 years after they had been written. Murder was avenged by murder, theft by theft, insult by insult. To facilitate commerce, tribal alliances were formed by politically minded princes. More militant than the local tribal chiefs, they occasionally waged skirmishes in pursuit of plunder and power. Like Islam's prophet, their sphere of influence grew at the point of a sword. Sir John Glubb, a student of Islam and life-long resident of Arabia, explains, "These peculiarities are important to the career of Muhammad. The Prophet became a man of political and military authority, so the Bedouins saw him not so much as the Messenger of Allah, but as a new prince." Entertained lavishly in his company, tribal chiefs were often enticed to align their clans with his movement.

From what we can tell, Arabs were prone to superstition and addicted to poetry—factors that would loom large in the formation of Islam. Poetry conceived by Hanifs became the initial ingredient in Muhammad's religion. The Hanifs were monotheists, believing that they shared the legacy of Abraham. Early on, Muhammad aligned himself with them, calling his religion Hanifism. Later, in a struggle for power, he renamed his crusade "Submission" and waged a war of words, then swords, against those who had inspired him.

It is interesting that all of the positive values extolled by Muhammad's Lord Ar-Rahman in the first forty Qur'anic surahs were a subset of Bedouin values and Hanif beliefs. They promoted the protection of the weak, charity, and good deeds. Sadly, much of this would be abrogated, as would the nature of Muhammad's god. He became Allah, vengeful, paranoid, deceitful, dreadfully nasty, and violent. Allah became Muhammad's alter ego—indistinguishable and inseparable.

While Arabs were principally pagan, thus polytheistic, there was no religious prejudice or persecution in the land, and monotheism was spreading rapidly. A large concentration of Jews, a remnant of the Babylonian captivity twelve centuries prior, lived unmolested in a town they had helped build, the thriving agricultural community of Yathrib, today's Medina. Their number was thought to be around thirty thousand—a tremendous concentration of people considering the nature of the land they occupied.

Two hundred miles south of Yathrib lay Mecca. It was nestled in a narrow, dry, and stony valley a quarter of a mile wide and a mile and a half long. The mountains on either side were rugged and devoid of vegetation, naked. Unlike Yathrib, Mecca was sterile. There was too little water for agriculture. There were no trees and far too little grass for productive grazing. The village was comprised of mud huts. Neither hewn stones nor bricks, even hand-formed and sun-dried, were to be found anywhere. In this regard, Mecca lagged behind the developed world by three millennia.

There were no roofs in Mecca, as there was no timber. With no timber, there were no carpenters. Blistering winds and encroaching sands were the lot of rich and poor. No one escaped the elements. Every hut was open to the scorching heat of the day and chill of the desert night. And exposure was not without pain. There are few places as unappealing. If Jerusalem and Israel are the world's heart and aorta, Mecca and Arabia are the dust between her toes. I do not say this to be disparaging, but to provide a point of reference, a necessary contrast, between the places and the claims made about them.

The stateliest "structure" in Mecca was the Ka'aba, a shrine of sorts that Allah, the moon god, shared with idols like Hubal. Their "House" consisted of four walls. It was an open, crude, and roofless cube in the sixth century, having nearly succumbed to gravity and flash floods. Constructed of local rock, totally un-hewn and un-mortared, it was as ignoble as the idols it housed—mostly stones. Hubal was the only graven image. Lord only knows how they distinguished between the gods and the "building."

Glubb tells us, "It is interesting that most Arabian idols do not seem to have been modeled after human beings, as were those of Greece and Rome.... Idolaters in all ages have denied that they worshipped an image made by hands, but have claimed that they prayed to the spirit which dwelt in it. The Arabic language has a word for a stone believed to be the abode of a deity. Many Arabs believed that a blessing could be obtained by kissing or rubbing such a stone." As we shall discover, kissing and fondling Allah's Black Stone was something Muhammad did with reverence and regularity.

Apart from the Ka'aba, Mecca was nothing. Isolated, the little burg of perhaps five thousand inhabitants made nothing, grew nothing. It was a long, hard ride to the civilizations of the Mediterranean. Ships passed to the west, caravans to the east. Mecca was controlled by a conniving lot, a tribe called the Quraysh, the clan of Muhammad. What we know about them is derived exclusively from Islamic Traditions, Muslim oral reports.

The Quraysh history, as best we can piece it together from the Islamic scripture, goes something like this: The Khuza'a tribe from the south ousted the Jurhum clan from a tent encampment called Mecca around 400 A.D. Tabari explains: **"The Jurhum acted badly, stealing sacrifices that had been presented to the Ka'aba."** They were "oppressive." Ishaq agrees: **"The Jurhum were heavy-handed, guilty of taboos, and treated the Ka'aba gifts as their own. A battle ensued and the Khuza'a expelled the Jurhum from Mecca."** The Jurhum's legacy was: **"the two gazelles of the Ka'aba and the cornerstone which they buried in the well of Zamzam. They retreated to Yemen bitterly grieved at losing control of the Ka'aba."**

Why would losing control of a dilapidated rock shrine dedicated to rock gods grieve the dearly departed? The answer has far-reaching implications, implications that would ultimately topple a pair of towers on the other side of the world. The plot, as they say, is about to thicken.

On their own merits, the Ka'aba, Mecca, and Quraysh would be among the least important places and people on earth, for the world is awash in illiterate pagans, mud huts, and rock shrines. But as a result of Qusayy's ingenuity and Muhammad's bravado, they would become the *raison d'etre* of Islam. Mecca, the Ka'aba, and its Black Stone, would ultimately become freedom's most fierce adversaries.

If the Islamic scripture is even partially accurate, Allah and the Ka'aba predated Muhammad by five generations. He didn't invent them. Nor did he conceive the pagan rituals, fairs, holy months, fasts, prostrations, taxes, and pilgrimages that made these things worth owning. In the preceding chapters we studied *how* the Bible was corrupted to give Allah, the Ka'aba, Mecca, and Islam's pagan rites a religious veneer. But *why* is considerably more important, considerably more revealing. To appreciate Islam for what it really is, we must first come to understand Muhammad's motivation for deriving a new monotheistic doctrine from an old assemblage of pagan idols. We must come to know why Islam's prophet incorporated his people's crude rites into his new religion. In that his revelations were less than inspired, there must have been something that inspired him to promote a stone.

Yes, Muhammad and his fellow Meccans worshiped rocks. Lacking craftsmanship, artistry, and tools, they were unable to make the elegant statuary synonymous with other religious idols. The most interesting stones became gods. Most had personal names. The biggest rock, thereby the biggest god of the Ka'aba, was Allah. His oval stone was a dark reddish-brown. But Allah was a fractured deity. With time and abuse he had been splintered into seven chips, all banded together. Compared to the devotion his fragments enjoy, the pieces are rather small; combined they are only eleven by fifteen inches. Today, the chips are imbedded in the southeastern corner of the Ka'aba, four feet above the ground. But Allah is no ordinary assemblage of minerals. He, like fellow Islamic god, Ar-Rahman, had a pre-Islamic past. And, as we have seen, Muslims have a variety of entertaining accounts of how they were graced by such an auspicious token of the universe's creator. But before we entertain the justifications for promoting a pair of pagan stones, lets look at Allah and Ar-Rahman through the eyes of a historian.

Stone cults were neither uncommon nor uncivilized. Even the Greeks were wont to worship stones. Apollo was once believed to be a meteorite in Delphi. His sanctuary was thought to be the center of the earth. Robert Charroux, in *Masters of the World*, explained, "Helenius, the son of Priam and a famous Greek soothsayer, could foretell the future by means of a stone that had been given to him by Apollo. To obtain the oracle of the gods, he shook the stone above his head and recited the incantations. The stone then spoke in a strange, faint voice and announced the future." And so it would be; a millennia later Muhammad would heed the summons of another talking stone.

But the Black Stone and its House were hardly unique. There were many such temples, called *tawaghits*, scattered across Arabia. Patrons made sacrifices and left gifts to their stone of choice, prostrated themselves in prayer, and circumambulated the shrines. Most commanded hajj and umrah pilgrimages during holy months. Those seeking the rock's blessing would commonly rub themselves against the stone and kiss it reverently.

The Islamic scripture agrees: *Ishaq:38* **"Every house had an idol which they worshiped. They would rub the stone for good luck. When Allah sent Muhammad with the message of monotheism, the Quraysh said: 'Would he make many gods into one god? This is a strange thing."** Unfortunately for Islam, many false gods do not one true god make.

Ishaq:38 **"Now along with the Ka'aba, the Arabs had adopted Tawaghits, temples they venerated like the Ka'aba. They, too, had their custodians. They used to circumambulate them."** According to the Islamic scriptures, Allah was one of many pagan rock idols, the Ka'aba was one of many pagan rock shrines. Islamic circumambulation was one of many pagan rites. *Ishaq:38* **"Al-Lat was in a Tawaghit Temple in Fa'if which was venerated like the Ka'aba."** *Ishaq:38* **"Luhayy put Al-Uzza in a Nakhla Tawaghit. When they had finished their Ka'aba Hajj they circumambulated Al-Uzza. The Quraysh worshiped her. Manat was worshiped by the Aus and Khazraj in Yathrib."** Those who prayed to Al-Uzza and Manat, *Ishaq:39* **"shaved their heads and completed all of the rites associated with the Hajj."** Yet these men were pagans. How did their rituals become part of Islam and why?

Muslims are compelled to observe the same rituals today. The Black Stone, its House, the prostration, kissing, circumambulation, shaving, the

hajj, umrah, and holy months somehow migrated from a pagan past to orthodox Islam by way of corrupted Jewish scriptures. The most telling of these
tales is the one in which Muhammad and Allah claimed that Abraham
smashed lesser idols so that his people might turn to the largest one.

A quartz god was worshiped in Tabhalah, an oasis town seven days journey from Mecca. Sad was the rock deity in the region of Juddah along the
Red Sea, west of Mecca. *Ishaq:39* **"Many Arabs served an idol named Dhu'l-Khalasa.
Himyar had a temple called Ri'am. Ruda was the temple of the Banu Rabi'a. Dhu'l-Ka'a-
bat belonged to the Banu Bakr. Bahira was the filly of the Sa'iba. Hami was their stallion.
Wasila was a ewe. Muhammad said, 'Allah has not made Bahira, Wasila, or Hami. And
those who do not agree invent lies.'"**

We are told that the Azds and Nabateans bowed to **"Dhu'l-al-Shara in his
shrine in Petra."** He was a proud god with a large rectangular stone and elegant
temple to match. Like Allah, Dhu'l-al-Shara was a reddish brown rock. Fellow moon gods could be found in Marib, Hureidha, and Tayma. Il Umquh
was the Sabean moon god in Marib. In Hureidha, the god was Sin, named
after the famous moon god of the Chaldeans in Ur. The last Babylonian king,
Nabonidus, built an elaborate *tawaghit* in Tayma to his moon god while in
exile. The moon god of Mecca, Allah, lived, if we may be so bold, in the
heart of moon god country.

Bukhari:V6B60N374 **"We were in the Prophet's company in the middle of the lunar month.
He looked at the moon and said, 'You will see your Lord as you see this moon.'"** This reverence to the moon was hardly a flight of fancy. In the 8th chapter of Judges,
there's a three thousand-year-old Bible reference: "The Ishmaelites hung crescent moon ornaments from their camel's necks." So today, when you look up
and see crescent moons decorating Muslim mosques and flags, you'll know
that the Arabian love affair with the moon has survived thirty centuries.

Yet this affair was no more monogamous than Islam. Even in his neighborhood, Allah had competition. The sun god Manaf was worshiped by the
Quraysh, as was Hubal, a handsome idol carved into the shape of a man.

Allah's daughters, Al-Uzza, Al-Lat, and Manat, being chips off the old
block, were stones. Manat was symbolized by a darkened moon, eerily reminiscent of Islam today. She was the goddess of fate and commanded her subjects to shave their heads when approaching her. Being a good pagan, when
Muhammad fulfilled his umrah pilgrimage in Mecca, he shaved his head in
Manat's presence. This pagan practice was invested with godly overtones
when Muhammad insisted that Abraham had done likewise. Later, Muhammad honored the pagan goddess Manat by incorporating predestination into
Islam and by using her insignia as the logo of his "new" religion.

Not to be outdone, Al-Lat had her own shrine in Ta'if, near Mecca. A
cubic rock, she lived on barley porridge. While her diet was humble, her veneration was not. Her temple lies under the left minaret of the early Islamic

mosque of Ta'if. Al-Lat's sister, the goddess Al-Uzza, was considerably younger and lived in the Hurad valley. A Quraysh favorite, she received the most lavish gifts and sacrifices. Muhammad saw her as a nude black woman.

Interestingly enough, Islam itself was nearly sacrificed at the altar of Allah's three little girls. In a weaker moment the prophet said that the goddesses Al-Lat, Al-Uzza, and Manat were conduits to Allah, intermediaries. But then when the monotheistic wing of his religion objected to four pagan gods being three too many, the prophet confessed that he had been inspired by Satan. Islam as a religion died that day in Mecca, only to be reborn as a political doctrine in Yathrib the following year. But we're getting ahead of our story.

Although Muhammad is credited with bringing monotheism to Arabs, the Qur'an venerates three distinctly different gods. In the first Meccan period, the god was nameless. He was referenced solely by the title "Lord." This deity was modeled after Zayd's god, which is not surprising since the Meccan Hanif's poems formed the basis Muhammad's early surahs. The Hanifs derived the title "Lord" and their faith from the Jews—a people who called their God "Lord" for fear of saying his name. If they used Yahweh's name incorrectly, they were accused of blasphemy, and risked being stoned. While their scriptures contained 7,000 repetitions of His name, Rabbis always read and said "Lord" in its place. Being illiterate, the Meccans wouldn't have known the difference.

But a title was insufficient. The creator of the universe needed a name. All gods had names. So in the second Meccan period, Muhammad called his Lord "Ar-Rahman." Inscriptions from the fifth century reveal that Ar-Rahman was worshiped in Yemen by another group of Hanifs. We know about them because Dhu Nuwas, the Jewish Yemeni king, may have been one. His exploits were chronicled in Greek, Syriac, and Aramaic. When he attacked the Abyssinian Christians in Southern Arabia in the early sixth century, he swore by Ar-Rahman, "The Merciful," and Ar-Rahim, "The Benevolent." An invocation including these god's names now precedes all but the 9th surah.

Muhammad transitioned from Lord to Ar-Rahman in surahs 56, 68, 78, 89, and the last half of surah 93. While none of these mention Allah, Ar-Rahman and Lord are used interchangeably, often side-by-side.

The names Ar-Rahman and Ar-Rahim are used fifty-one times in the Meccan period and twice in the first Medina surah. Then they disappear, replaced by Allah, never to be mentioned again. This is important because surrounded by a veritable sea of pagan idols, all Muhammad did was whittle down the number. An interesting insight in this regard can be found in Surah 21:36:

"When the unbelievers see you they make fun of you, mocking you, ridiculing you. They say,

'Is this the one who mentions your gods?' They would deny all mention of Ar-Rahman!"
This is a problem on a number of levels. The Qur'an is saying that Muhammad
is being teased because he "mentions the Meccan gods." Why? Allah was a
Meccan god. And if Islam began monotheistic, why was "gods" plural? Moreover, by having the Meccans "deny all mention of Ar-Rahman," two things became
apparent: Muhammad's god was Ar-Rahman and the Meccans' was not.

It is interesting that while the Islamic god doesn't seem to know his name
or if he is one (I, Me, and My in verse 37) or many (We and Us in verse 35), he
is the same old guy, showing signs that men don't heed and making threats.
021.037 "Man is made of haste. I [Ar-Rahman] shall show you My Signs; then you will not ask
Me to hasten the punishment! If only the unbelievers could apprehend the moment when
they would not be able to ward off the fire from their faces and their backs.'"

The "What's My Name" game continued with this Qur'an passage: *021.041*
"Many apostles have been scoffed before you, but they were caught by what they ridiculed.
Say (Muhammad): 'Who guards you from Ar-Rahman?' But at the mention of their Lord
they turn away. Or do they have lords of their own besides Us who can defend them?'"
They turned away because the Meccans knew Allah, not Ar-Rahman.

Surah 25 speaks to the confusion over who the Islamic deity really was.
The 59th verse ends with these words: "He is the Benevolent." Left untranslated,
that says: "He is Ar-Rahim." Verse 60 begins with this: "When you say to them: 'Bow
before Ar-Rahman,' they say: 'What is Ar-Rahman?' Should we adore whomever you ask us
to? And their aversion increases further." Muhammad was asking the Meccans to
prostrate themselves to a god *named* Ar-Rahman. They, however, rebelled,
asking, "What is Ar-Rahman?" They knew Allah, the top dog of the Ka'aba, but
not everyone knew the other fellow as he wasn't a local rock idol.

This debate over god's name was hardly academic. Since several gods are
named, Islam can't be monotheistic. And since none of the names are Yahweh, they aren't the God of the Bible. Therefore, the Biblical prophets and
patriarchs should not have been used to justify Islamic rites and rituals.

Verse 25:63 reconfirms that the first Muslims were: "Slaves of Ar-Rahman who
walked in submission [Islam]." (The end of this verse is foreboding. It says, "When
Muslims are addressed by the ignorant they should reply, 'Peace.'" They get away with
telling us they're "peaceful" because we are "ignorant" of Islam.)

Qur'an 13:30 says: "We revealed it to you, but they do not believe in Ar-Rahman.
Tell them: 'He is my Lord. There is no other god but He. In Him have I placed my trust.'"
There isn't any wiggle room here. Ar-Rahman is not only synonymous with
Muhammad's Lord, Ar-Rahman is his god's name. Allah was a nobody.

But it wouldn't remain that way. The reconciliation between the Islamic
gods Ar-Rahman and Allah occurred at the end of the 17th surah. It was a
concession on Muhammad's part. So that we don't take the great event out of
context, let's sneak up on it. The surah opens attempting to explain why the
Qur'an had been doled out in increments: *017:106* "We have divided the Qur'an into

parts that you may recite it to men slowly, with deliberation. That is why We sent it down by degrees." Actually, specific verses were "revealed" in direct response to issues in Muhammad's life. When he wanted to steal, booty was approved. When he wanted to kill, his god approved killing. When he craved incest, his lust was conveniently satisfied. When he wanted more wives than the Qur'an allowed, guess what: a special dispensation from the Big Guy. And when he wanted to cleanse the world of Jews, his god was accommodating.

017.107 "Say: 'Believe in it or do not believe: Those who were given knowledge before it bow in adoration when it is read out to them.' And [they] say: 'Glory be to our Lord. The promise of our Lord has indeed been fulfilled. And weeping they kneel down and this increases their submission.'" Not that it's out of character, but the beginning of this verse is a lie. Those who were given the knowledge before the Qur'an refers to the Torah and Gospels and thus to Christians and Jews. They never "bowed in adoration" when the Qur'an was "read out to them." It couldn't have been read since it hadn't been written, and they laughed themselves silly when they heard it, as we do today.

017.110 "Say: 'Call Him Allah or call Him Ar-Rahman; whatever the name you call Him, all His names are beautiful.'" "The name." "His names." Thank you Allah or Ar-Rahman, or whatever your name might be, for confirming the obvious. Neither Allah nor Ar-Rahman are *words* that mean "god;" they are *names* of gods. The Arabic *word* for "God" is *"Ilah"* and it's used throughout the Qur'an.

We can only assume Muhammad learned about the Hanifs and their god, Ar-Rahman, while he was a caravan merchant frequenting Yemen. Maslamah and Zayd, both contemporaries of Muhammad, proclaimed the Hanif doctrine. Maslamah could have been Muhammad's twin. He taught a strict moral code that prohibited drinking and fornication. He required fasting and formal ritualistic prayers three times a day. Maslamah believed in the Day of Resurrection and encouraged a hajj. He preached in the same rhymed prose of Muhammad's Qur'an and even called himself the "Messenger of God," saying his revelations came from Ar-Rahman. And whatever Maslamah missed, Zayd covered. His poetic lines made their way into the Qur'an verbatim.

While Muslims disparaged Maslamah, calling him the "arch liar" and "false prophet" his style and substance was indistinguishable from Muhammad's. The foremost American Islamic academician, F.E. Peters, said, "It is difficult to imagine that Maslamah 'borrowed' Ar-Rahman from Muhammad… It is easier to assume that Ar-Rahman had a genuine and long-standing cult in Yemen, a cult to which Muhammad may have been drawn."

A war was ultimately waged over who was the better prophet. During the War of Compulsion, the battle of Aqrabah was fought between Muslims and Maslamah's forces. Ar-Rahman's troops won the first encounter but in the second attack Muslims divided their army to see who could die the most valiantly. Seven hundred of Muhammad's companions died that day, as did much of the Qur'an. Up to Muhammad's death, the surahs were stored only in the memories of warriors. The most faithful were now dead and dying in a grove of old trees that became known as the "Garden of Death." While the Qur'an suffered a serious blow, Allah's army carried the day, slaughtering 7,000 Arabs. With their deaths, all opposition to Islam was suppressed in Arabia. Ar-Rahman was forgotten. And so it would be, forevermore.

Returning to Mecca during the late fifth century, we discover that the Khuza'a tribe had ousted the Jurhum clan. As a result, Luhayy came to establish the rites and privileges of the Ka'aba. But he became ill, we are told by Muslim scholar Ibn al-Kalbi, in his *Book of Idols*. **"Luhayy went to a hot spring in Syria to be cured. During his stay he noticed that the locals worshipped idols. 'What are these things?' he asked. To which they replied, 'We pray to them for rain and for victory over enemies.' Luhayy asked the Syrians for some of their stones. They agreed and he took them back to Mecca where he erected them around the Ka'aba."**

Luhayy's fellow tribesmen played along. Everyone got into the mode of worshiping stones, enshrining them, prostrating themselves in prayer, and circumambulating them. Ibn al-Kalbi tells us, **"The Arabs were accustomed to offering sacrifices before these idols and stones. Nevertheless they were aware of the excellence and superiority of the Ka'aba to which they went on pilgrimage."**

Muhammad, however, did not speak so kindly of Luhayy, the first Arab associated with the Ka'aba. He said: *Ishaq:35* **"I saw Luhayy dragging his intestines in Hell. I asked him about those who lived between his time and my time and he said that they had all perished."** Muhammad went on to say, **"This led the Meccans to worship stones. Thus generations passed and they forgot their primitive faith and adopted another religion, replacing that of Abraham and Ishmael. They prayed to idols and adopted the same errors as the peoples before them. Yet they held fast to the Ka'aba and circumambulated it, the greater and lesser pilgrimage, the standing place, and the cry: 'At Your service, O Allah, at Your service."**

We have arrived at the crux of the matter. Muslims reading these words will recognize that the rituals just depicted form the very heart of Islam. Yet Muhammad, Islam's founder, conceived none of these religious rites. Every Islamic doctrine and ritual existed before the Qur'an, Muhammad, or even the first Muslim graced our world. As Ishaq has correctly explained, Islam was practiced in all of its glory before the Islamic prophet was born. And while that's a problem, it gets worse in context. The practitioners were all pagans and the rites were all directly related to a religious scam—a money making scheme. That's why, according to Muhammad, they were all damned to drag their intestines through hell.

Over these next pages you are going to discover how Muhammad's great,

great, great, grandfather Qusayy, capitalized on the work Luhayy had done when he carried "idols and stones" back to the Meccan shrine. Qusayy, a pagan, an opportunist, and a very creative, albeit twisted fellow, invented every important Islamic ritual and doctrine to gain power and money. Qusayy invented the religious scam Muhammad dusted off and called Islam.

So you ask, how do I know this? Because all we know about Qusayy and the early Meccans comes from the Hadith and that's what it says. So that begs another question: why would Islam tell us something so damaging to Islam? I believe they had to. The Qur'an and Hadith make it clear that every Islamic rite was already being practiced by the pagans of Muhammad's day so they were compelled to provide a reason. The Qur'an makes no effort to explain the nature of prostration or the hajj so the Hadith had to. Moreover, for Muhammad to be a Biblical prophet he had to be connected to Abraham. How is that possible if Muslims don't first connect him to the most important Meccan? And finally, the whole story of Islam is about Muhammad coveting the Ka'aba Inc. Unless we know who founded it and nurtured the scheme during its entrepreneurial phase, we'll never understand who is doing what to whom, or why. But as with all things Islam, it's a two-edged sword. One side cuts through the fog of ignorance; the other kills the ignorant.

Ishaq:38 **"The Quraysh had a well in the Ka'aba and an idol called Hubal. They adopted Asaf and Na'ila by Zamzam, sacrificing beside them. They were a man and woman of the Jurhum tribe—Asaf ibn Baghy and Na'ila bint Dik—who were guilty of sexual relations in the Ka'aba and so Allah transformed them into two stones. Aisha said, 'We always heard that Asaf and Na'ila copulated in the Ka'aba so Allah transformed them into stones.'"**

Ishaq says that Luhayy's Khuzas eventually permitted Kinana's Quraysh to return to the Ka'aba. The Quraysh, Muslims would have us believe, are direct descendants of Abraham through Ishmael. F.E. Peters in his book, *Muhammad and the Origins of Islam,* explains, "The tribal eponym 'Kinana' stands for fifteen generations after Ishmael, in the line of direct descent, and Qusayy, the chief actor in what follows, is eight generations after Kinana. Thus, according to Islamic reckoning, Ishmael's descendants returned to their father's town some seven centuries after he and Abraham built the Ka'aba in Mecca. In the meantime the Ishmaelites, now called the Quraysh, had generally lived dispersed in scattered settlements throughout the neighborhood."

Peters is brilliant, and his research is impeccable, but this is nonsense. It's not his fault, mind you, but the Muslim sources themselves. They had no idea who the Quraysh were or from whence they had come. But in a desperate grope for legitimacy, they were ever prone to make-believe. Abraham lived around 2000 B.C. Seven centuries would place us in the fourteenth century B.C., not fifth century A.D. The Ishmaelites are traced to the Sinai, not Arabia, but that is the least of their problems. Islam's justification for promoting Allah and his Ka'aba is all derived from having had it built by Abraham, the great Jewish patriarch, and then having Muhammad being a direct descendant of his son Ishmael. Neither are true. For according to Islam's own Traditions, the Ka'aba was first ennobled by some stones Luhayy hauled from a Syrian hot spring. The lure of a miracle cure begat a religion.

Ibn Ishaq's Sira opens with a section entitled: **"Muhammad's Pure Descent from Adam."** *Ishaq:3* **"This is the book of the Biography of the Apostle of Allah. Muhammad was the son of Abdallah, bin Abdul Muttalib, bin Hashim, bin Abd Manaf, bin Qusayy,"** and so on a total of thirteen generations to Kinana. Ishaq lists another fifteen generations back to Abraham and Ishmael. The accounting from Abraham to Noah and ultimately to Adam came directly out of Genesis and is of little value in that we are all descendants of Adam and Noah. However, I'd like to apply some simple math to the more recent genealogy to show that the first Muslims were clueless. Qusayy (the founder of the scam that became Islam) preceded Muhammad by approximately eighty years. And Luhayy (the founder of the Ka'aba) preceded Qusayy by the same length of time. Similarly, Kinana could not have been more than one hundred years removed from Luhayy which puts us in the early part of the fourth century A.D. To make Muhammad's genealogy "pure," fifteen generations would have to span over 2300 years. Put another way, the Jews who maintained precise *written* records in their Temple in anticipation of the Messiah, listed forty-one generations from Abraham to Christ. Another fifteen would be required to arrive at Kinana's time for a total of fifty-six—nearly four times the Islamic number.

While this may seem trivial in comparison to sun setting in a muddy spring surrounded by extraterrestrials, it's not. Islam is completely dependent upon establishing a link between Abraham and the pagan rites practiced around the Ka'aba. If their chronologies are errant by a factor of four hundred percent, it does not bode well for the rest of their theory.

The earliest Islamic record of Mecca with even a modicum of veracity pertains to the Jurhum. They were alleged to have camped periodically in the valley that later became Mecca. Tabari, the earliest Muslim historian, would have us believe that the Jurhum practiced pagan rites identical to current Islamic rituals in the fifth and sixth centuries A.D.

In that this is the first "historical" indication of Mecca, its people, and shrine, the Muslims are out on a 2500 year old limb. Ishmael was born around 2000 B.C. And there is no tangible evidence to connect the dots between the Biblical character and Mecca, much less with Muhammad, Allah, and the Ka'aba. Twenty-five centuries of historical silence is a *very* long time—especially for an illiterate people.

It was in this muddle of ignorance that Qusayy was about to found a family business and establish himself as Muhammad's mentor. Islam's unofficial patriarch was born at the end of the fifth century A.D.: *Tabari VI:20* **"Qusayy asked his mother which tribe he came from. She answered, 'You are the son of Kilab ibn Murra** ibn Ka'b ibn Luhayy ibn Ghalib ibn Fihr ibn Malik ibn al-Nadr ibn Kinana al-Qurashi.'" To which he said, 'Good grief. I think I'll change my name.' Just kidding. Actually, Tabari reports: "Your tribe lives in Mecca by the Ka'aba. ...This revelation awoke in Qusayy a strong desire to return to Mecca and join his people, the Quraysh." Mecca was hardly a prize, though. There were no permanent homes, only tents. Flash floods were a menace and the summer heat was unbearable, as there was no shade. People passed through, but no one lived in Mecca.

Mom told her son: "'Wait for a sacred month and go with the pilgrimage.' Qusayy waited until the sacred month arrived and the pilgrims set out. When he reached Mecca and had completed the pilgrimage, he remained there." One of the five pillars of Islam is to complete the hajj pilgrimage to Mecca in the sacred month. This Hadith proves that the rite was idolatrous five generations before Muhammad said it was Islamic. Even Muhammad's names for the pilgrimages, "hajj and umrah," were borrowed from his pagan past.

The pagan Qusayy, arriving at the tent village, established the model Muhammad would ultimately require Muslims to follow. But that's not all he did to inspire Islam's future prophet. Tabari quotes: *Ishaq:48* "At the time Hulayl was in charge of the Ka'aba and ruled in Mecca. Qusayy asked him for the hand of his daughter Hubba in marriage." She was the wealthiest and best-connected babe in town. Five generations later, Muhammad, abandoned and penniless, would marry Khadija —the wealthiest woman in Mecca. Family tradition.

Settling in, the newlyweds made four babies, two of which were named after the local rock gods, underscoring the fraudulent nature of Muhammad's religious invention. "Hubba bore him Abd al-Dar, Abd Manaf, Abd al-Uzza and Abd. His progeny increased, his wealth multiplied and he became greatly honored." Qusayy showed he was a heathen idolater when he named his kids after rock idols. Yet he performed a pilgrimage to Mecca in a holy month. He moved in with the king, the custodian of the Ka'aba, and married his daughter. They named their first kid Slave-to-the-House—the most important thing in their lives, their source of wealth and power. Then they honored their gods by naming their next two children after them. And while it's interesting that Allah didn't even get an honorable mention, that's not the biggest problem. These passages confirm that the Ka'aba was a pagan shrine and that at best, Allah was just one of many gods. The veneration of the "House" of idols shows that it was unconnected to any monotheistic religion—Islam included.

A Hadith gives us a glimpse of what was to come: *Ishaq:49* "Qusayy thought he had a better right to the Ka'aba and to rule over Mecca than the Khuza'a since the Quraysh were the most noble and pure descendants of Ishmael." The motivation for Islam can be condensed into a similar sentence. Muhammad thought he had a better right to the Ka'aba and to rule over Mecca than his family. If you keep this in mind, everything associated with Islam's formation will make sense.

The sages who crafted this Tradition in Baghdad a dozen generations after

Qusayy's death must have thought their audience would remain as ignorant as their religious teachings were preposterous. First, in an illiterate society, how would Qusayy know that he was a more direct descendant of Ishmael than any other Arab? Ishmael had been sandals up for 2500 years. Without copious and exacting written records, genealogies are impossible to establish after a handful of generations. Arabic as a written language had yet to be invented, and there were nearly sixty generations separating these men. Second, how could they purport to know what Qusayy thought? There were no written accounts to connect him and his thoughts to the day these Hadith were written —four centuries later. Since this scenario is impossible, the only reason Muslim scholars felt compelled to legitimize Qusayy's "right to the Ka'aba and rule over Mecca," was to justify his great, great, great grandson's claim.

Tabari VI:20 **"He called upon his fellow tribesmen, the Quraysh, to expel the Khuza'a and seize Mecca for themselves. They accepted his proposal and swore an oath of allegiance to him."** While I'm stunned the world hasn't exposed the scam that became Islam, I am grateful that the Islamic scripture makes it so easy. Muhammad would do precisely the same thing. He called upon his raiders to conquer the Quraysh and seized control of the town. They accepted his proposal and swore oaths of allegiance to *him*. While we will cover these pledges later, suffice it to say for now, like Qusayy's oath, it was a call to arms. And as with Muhammad, the Meccans were the enemy, and the target was the Ka'aba.

Tabari, relying on Traditions collected by Ishaq, reports: **"The Arabs, recognizing their religious duty, accompanied Qusayy. Marching to the Ka'aba they said, 'We have better right to this than you.' At that they opposed one another and began to fight. A fierce battle broke out, as a result of which...Qusayy wrested from them the privileges which had been in their hands, thus denying them."** Little did they know how fraught with portent these words would be—they haunt us to this day.

Before we leave the skirmish, I feel obliged to share the alternate "peaceful" version: *Tabari VI:21* **"Qusayy purchased the custodianship of the Ka'aba for a skin full of wine and a lute."** While this variant earns kudos for nonviolence, it's hardly religious. Purchasing the shrine that stands at the center of Islamic life, their god's house, for things their religion outlaws—music and booze—is laughably ironic. It's also an example of conflicting "truths."

Proving that Islam has something for everybody, Ishaq serves up alternative three. This one foreshadows Islamic terrorists today and their willingness to use biological agents. **"I have heard, and Allah knows best, that the Khuza'a were seized by an outbreak of pustules which nearly wiped them out. They abandoned Mecca."**

Making sure he had all his bases covered, Ishaq provided a fourth alternative. This one was for the doves, those who would use the "peace process" to steal that which they covet. *Ishaq:52* **"Both sides called for peace and for the appointment of one of the Arabs to arbitrate between them on their differences."** This was evidently the model Jimmy Carter used to win the Nobel Peace Prize. All the spoils went to the Muslims. The infidels traded their land and money and got nothing in return. **"The verdict was that Qusayy [read "Arabs or Muslims"] had a better claim to the Ka'aba [read "Temple Mount"] and to rule Mecca [read "Jerusalem"] than the Khuza'a [read "the Jews"].** All the injuries inflicted and blood shed by Qusayy [read "suicide bombers" or "Arab armies"] upon the Khuza'a [read "the Jews"] were cancelled and disregarded [read "forgotten, excused, or justified"], while all injuries inflicted by the Khuza'a ["the Jews"] upon the Quraysh [read "Muslims or Arabs"] should be compensated for by blood money [read "Carter committed the United States to paying the Arabs who lost the Six Day War $2 billion a year in perpetuity"]. He added that Qusayy should be given a free hand to control the Ka'aba and Mecca."** Nothing has changed. Diplomacy with Islamic tyrants remains equally unbalanced and equally futile.

Whether Qusayy's forces prevailed by force, bribe, the peace process, or pestilence, they gained control of the tent village and rock shrine that had been populated by the patriarch's great, great, grandfather, Luhayy. Ibn Ishaq chronicled the momentous event as only a Muslim could. *Ishaq:52* **"Thus Qusayy gained authority over the Ka'aba and the lordship over the people of Mecca. He behaved like a king over his tribe so they made him a king."** Qusayy, having established the model for Muhammad, went on to build the family business. Let's listen to how it was done: *Ishaq:53* **"Qusayy assumed control and kingship. He was obeyed. He held the keys to the shrine, being the doorkeeper of the Ka'aba. He held the right to water the pilgrims from the well of Zamzam and to feed them. He presided at the assemblies and held the right to hand out the war banners. In his hands lay all the dignities of Mecca, all of which he took for himself."** This is the essence of Islam. Muhammad would speak these same words upon his conquest of Mecca.

Then Qusayy established the model Muhammad would follow in Yathrib when he expelled the Jews from their homes by force, and he rewarded his fellow Muslims by dividing their property between them. **"He also divided the property in Mecca among his followers, settling every clan of the Quraysh in the dwelling places assigned to them. No issue regarding public affairs was decided nor was any banner of war entrusted without Qusayy's permission."** Scores of years later, Muhammad would use force to gain control over Medina, Mecca, the Ka'aba, its god, its dwellings, its well, pilgrims, assemblies, and even the disposition of war banners. He behaved like a king, forcing his will on his tribe, killing anyone who got in his way. While these Hadiths prove that Muhammad wasn't the least bit inventive, he has to be given credit for recognizing a workable plan and executing it. The pagan Qusayy, a charlatan, nourished every important aspect of Islam generations before Muhammad was born. Moreover, he, like the prophet, did it in pursuit of sex, power, and money.

The Tradition concludes with these haunting words, words that became prophetic. *Tabari VI:24/ Ishaq:53* **"Qusayy's authority among the Quraysh during his lifetime and after his death was like a religion which the people followed and which could not be infringed; they always acted in accordance with its laws. They regarded it as filled with** good omens and recognized his superiority and nobility.... He took for himself the assembly house which led from it to the mosque (place of prostration) of the Ka'aba."

Muhammad would do the same in Medina. He took for himself an assembly house which led to the mosque where all Islamic affairs were decided. And like Qusayy, Muhammad took upon himself the honor of handing out war banners before each of the *seventy-five terrorist raids* he orchestrated. "When they were about to fight another tribe, banners were tied only in his house, where one of his own sons would hand them out."

Ishaq knew the troubling ramifications of what he had just revealed. If this were true it meant that a heathen had founded the religious scam Muhammad shaped into Islam. He recognized, as you and I do, that Muhammad's reliance on Biblical characters to legitimize Islamic rituals and pillars was as feeble as it was preposterous. The ten tests of Abraham were perverse philosophically, the fables of Nimrod were lunacy historically, and the pure descent from Ishmael was grossly improbable genealogically. With the Jewish connection in rubble, the Hadith portrayal of Qusayy obliterated Arab and Meccan credibility. As such, Ishaq sought out an ally to corroborate his account, choosing the second Caliph. *Ishaq:53* "Umar confirmed the story of Qusayy and how he gained control of the Ka'aba and the affairs of Mecca."

The Hadith is incriminating, unraveling the fabric of Islam. More than a hundred years before the first Qur'anic revelation fell from Muhammad's lips, the pillars of Islam had been established by a pagan entrepreneur. The Ka'aba was the center of a new idolatrous religion; a scam designed to enrich its lone, undisputed, and unchallenged king—a man who used *religion* for political and personal gain. With methods identical to Muhammad's, Qusayy took control through *jihad* and political covenants. He was purported to have nobility and superiority as he established religious doctrine; he was a *messenger* to be *obeyed*. The *prostration* had been established, as had the place of worship—the *mosque*. The *hajj*, down to the most minute rites, had been enshrined in the religious lore. There was even a *holy month*. All that was needed now was for a religious *tax* to be implemented and for *Allah* to be promoted from among the quarry of rock idols for the pillars to be complete. If these final ingredients manifest themselves before we leave the fifth century, Islam will be laid bare-naked to the world of reason—exposed as the scam of Qusayy, not the religion of Abraham, and most certainly not the "revelation" of Allah.

Before we search the annals of Islamic history for the final two pillars, let's ponder the perplexing place their scriptures have taken us. There is no chance these pagan doctrines could have been derived from Abraham. There is no way to pass such rites across the two-dozen centuries that separate the real Islamic patriarch, Qusayy, from the patriarch of the Jews. There are no writings, no carvings, no scrolls, no scriptures, no recorded histories, and no archeology. There isn't even a hint of Mecca existing during this awesome void of time.

And thus there aren't any people through whom these religious duties could have been conveyed. As such, the pillars were established upon the rocky ground of a pagan religious scam. You are witnessing the birth of Islam.

Muslims say it isn't so—that it can't be so—because if it were, their religion would be nothing more than regurgitated paganism—a twisted plot. They claim Abraham came to Mecca to build the Ka'aba and establish Islamic rites, but they omit how he could have survived the desert crossing with a maid and an infant. They don't say why he would have left the Promised Land for a deserted valley in the middle of nowhere. Islam isn't the religion of Abraham or the doctrine of the prophet Muhammad. It is the religion of Qusayy.

The rites and rituals, regulations and taxes described in the rest of this chapter will be familiar to Muslims reading these words. They practice all of them today. So that they might know *how* they came to be hoodwinked into performing such mindless drivel, and to parting with their wealth and lives, I want to share how the pagan Qusayy developed his scam—the scam that became Islam.

Having taken what didn't belong to him, Islam's founder, the patriarch Qusayy, was now in business, the only viable business in the fledgling burg of Mecca. A man of politics, he became the prototype for what was to come. The largest structure in town, the meeting hall, served as his home and seat of power as it would for Muhammad. Qusayy connected it to the source of wealth, the Ka'aba. He established regular prostration prayer services at the mosque and a plethora of religious rituals. The most disturbing, and enduring, was a butt up sort of thing whereby the moon god was mooned.

Tabari, like Ishaq, wanted his readers to know that he was not responsible for making up a story so damning to Islam. In the midst of his commentary he inserted a Hadith similar to Ishaq's. It's attributed to **"Khabbab, the author of al Maqsurah."** He said, **"I heard a man telling Umar bin al-Khatab, when he was Caliph, this story of Qusayy and how he gathered his own tribe together, expelled tribes from Mecca, and gained control of the Ka'aba. Umar did not reject it or disavow it."**

That said, the Hadith explains how Islamic ritual was actually established five generations before the Qur'an or Muhammad: *Ishaq:49* **"The pilgrims gathered in Mecca, went out to the mawqif, completed the hajj and went to Mina.... Nothing now remained of the ritual of the pilgrimage but the ceremony of dispersal from Mina."** The *mawqif* is the plain of Arafat, about ten miles east of Mecca. Standing there between midday and sunset is an important part of the Islamic hajj. This is followed by the *ifadah*, or dispersal.

"On the day of the dispersal they went to stone the jimar, and a man of the Sufah used to throw pebbles for the pilgrims, none throwing until he had thrown." This idolatrous rite would also have Islamic overtones. Muhammad, borrowing from his pagan past, instructed Muslims to observe the *jimar*. Pebbles are thrown at three erections or heaps of stones. They are held to represent the Devil.

Soon we find another Qusayy invention that Muhammad copied. *Tabari VI:31* **"Qusayy instituted the lighting of the fire at al-Muzdalifah when the wuquf took place so that those being driven away from Arafat could see it. This fire continued to be lit in this place throughout the Jahiliyyah. This fire was also lit in the time of the Messenger, and of Abu Bakr, Umar, and Uthman."** Al-Muzdalifah is between Arafat and Mina. Standing there is one of the Islamic hajj rites, as is the fire. Bakr, Umar, and Uthman are the first three Islamic Caliphs after Muhammad.

Qusayy's ability to get the Meccans to perform these pagan rites served Muhammad magnificently. By the prophet's day they were all so ingrained among the Quraysh that the Qur'an simply assumed the continuance of the idolatrous ways without ever mentioning them. They became part of Islamic dogma by way of Hadith such as these.

This next Tradition demonstrates how dependent Muhammad was on Qusayy for the development of "Allah's" religious doctrine: *Tabari VI:25* **"Qusayy's tribe held him in honor and high esteem. No one opposed his rule in any way." "His commands were never disobeyed and nothing he did was opposed." "As regards the hajj, he confirmed the right of the Arabs to continue their previous customs. This is because he considered these to be a religious duty which he should not change."** Qusayy established the cornerstone of Islamic rule: "submit and obey." We will hear these words reverberate throughout the Qur'an. Devotion is a duty, prayer is an obligation, and rituals are compulsory. Islam is devoid of choice.

The Hadith goes on to report: **"Qusayy had a house built in Mecca which was the house of assembly in which the Quraysh used to decide their affairs."** Within days of Muhammad's arrival in Medina, we will see him order the construction of his house and assembly area. Then he will craft an "agreement" making him the sole decision maker over all affairs. All of this serves to prove that Islam was not the revelation of Allah to Muhammad but instead the verbatim implementation of the religious scam of Qusayy.

Moving from entrepreneur to capitalist, our model opportunist soon found himself promoting a series of economic fairs around the holy months. As godfather, he took a cut on each deal. *Ishaq:55* **"The rifada was a tax which the Quraysh paid from their property to Qusayy at every festival."** It, like the Ka'aba concession, was an exclusive franchise, a cartel of sorts. Muhammad would rename the *tax* the zakat, but it was no different. Islam had its fourth pillar.

Being the top dog in Ka'abaVille, however, was hardly worth bragging about. While Mecca's claim to fame was the rock shrine for rock gods, it was insignificant compared to Karnak, Athens, Delphi, Rome, or Ephesus. While Qusayy's scheme was inventive, it was a small-time affair. If it weren't for what Muhammad did with it, the religious scam of Qusayy wouldn't be worth the ink on this page.

Acting as patriarch of his own con, Qusayy made certain that only his direct descendants were eligible to participate in the family business. Even then, his relatives were forbidden until they were forty. This is why it's assumed Muhammad was a direct descendant and that he was forty when he claimed the Ka'aba for himself.

While the geographic and meteorological conditions were deplorable in Mecca, the con was better than working, which is why Qusayy conceived it and why Muhammad coveted it. Profits accrued from providing hospitality to pilgrims, on fees, and from taxes. The family took a cut on merchandise sold during the "truce of the gods" fairs of Ramadhan. And they charged pilgrims fees to feed and dust the idols they placed in the Ka'aba. It was a scam worth coveting. With enough money Qusayy could hire someone to fan away the flies.

Dividing the spoils inequitably between his sons, Qusayy said: *Ishaq:55* "**Abd al-Dar, by Allah, I shall make you the equal of the others, even though they have been raised in dignity over you. No man of them shall enter the Ka'aba until you have opened it, no [war] banner shall be tied for the Quraysh to go to battle except by your hand, no man shall drink water in Mecca [from the well of Zamzam] except that which you have provided, no man shall eat food in the pilgrimage season other than your food, and the Quraysh shall not decide their affairs anywhere but in your house.**" In other words, he gave him the family business—Islam. And he swore by the ultimate Islamic god. *Allah* has emerged and the Five Pillars are now complete. Muhammad would later come to call himself the Messenger of Allah, and he would usurp his authority to resolve a similar family dispute. Initially, these rights and privileges passed him by, going instead to another heir. Jealous, Muhammad said that Allah told him that they were really his.

This incriminating Hadith continues to expose Islam's pagan roots. Every last detail was incorporated into Islam. *Tabari VI:25* "**Then he gave Abd al-Dar the house in which the Quraysh always made their decisions, and gave him the office of being Ka'aba's custodian, declaring war, presiding over the assembly, and collecting the rifadah, a tax levied in every pilgrimage season by the Quraysh according to their wealth and handed over to Qusayy. It was imposed on the Quraysh by Qusayy, who said to them when he commanded them to pay it, 'Quraysh, you are neighbors of Allah, people of his Ka'aba and people of the sacred precincts of the Haram. The pilgrims are guests of Allah and visitors to His House.' They did so, and every year they levied a tax on their property and paid it to Qusayy and he would use it for the pilgrims during the days of Mina. This institution of his became the state of affairs among the Quraysh during the whole of the Jahiliyyah [pre-Islamic period of Ignorance] up to the time Allah brought Islam, and then became a part of Islam, continuing to this day.**" *Ishaq:57* "**Allah's Apostle said, 'Whatever deal there was in the days of ignorance, Islam strengthens it.'**"

Put a fork in this thing and turn off the barbeque. Islam has cooked its own goose. The last of the Islamic pillars has been established and we are still scores of years from the first Qur'anic revelation. The religious scam has been established right down to the smallest detail, and they even admit it. All Muhammad had to do was steal it.

The Qusayy model had a single prophet. His god was now Allah. This was a match for Islam's first pillar. The prostration prayer was an obligatory duty and it was performed facing his Ka'aba—the second pillar. The religious tax, or zakat, was instituted and collected in Allah's name—the third pillar. The hajj pilgrimage was laid out and observed in all its ritualistic detail—the fourth pillar. And en route to Mecca, Qusayy observed the holy month of Ramadhan and *Tahannuth* fasting—the fifth pillar.

But, as you shall see, the pillars of Islam were merely window dressing. The real foundation of the doctrine was submission—absolute obedience. *Tabari VI:25* **"Qusayy's tribe held him in honor and high esteem. No one opposed his rule in any way."** **"His commands were never disobeyed and nothing he did was ever opposed."** *Ishaq:56* **"Qusayy was never contradicted nor was any measure of his overthrown."** Religion was a veil. *Tabari VI:24* **"His authority among the Quraysh during his lifetime and after his death was like a religion which the people followed; they always acted in accordance with it."**

That said, the means to submission was the sword. It established Islam. Muhammad would use Qusayy's war banners to initiate scores of terrorist raids. The resulting booty financed his "religion" and "inspired" his initial adherents. And as with Qusayy, the real motive was money. But theirs was not an honest endeavor. Their wealth was not created from the sweat of their brow; it was booty, looted from others. In fact, Muhammad's first rendition of Islam's Pillars included a share of stolen property. *Bukhari:V1B2N50* **"'Apostle, order us to do some religious deeds that we may enter Paradise.' The Prophet asked them, 'Do you know what it means to believe in Allah Alone?' They replied, 'Allah and His Apostle know better.' The Prophet said, 'It means: 1. To testify that none has the right to be worshipped but Allah, and Muhammad is Allah's Apostle. 2. To perform prayers perfectly. 3. To pay the Zakat obligatory tax. 4. To observe the Ramadhan fast. 5. And to pay one fifth of the booty taken in Allah's Cause.'"**

Following Qusayy's lead, submission to Allah, or Islam, was defined as: acknowledging Muhammad as the sole authority, bowing down, paying a tax, observing a pagan practice, and sharing the booty collected from terrorist raids.

Under the tutelage of Islam's patriarch, Mecca made a transition from an ignoble and ignominious pagan sand pit to a religious scam extraordinaire. The Ka'aba Inc. became a family business awaiting the polishing touches of one of the great promoters of all time—Qusayy's great, great, great grandson, Muhammad. Within a hundred years a collection of mud huts, a dilapidated rock pile, and a silly religious scam would emerge as a tour de force. Within two hundred years, and with a little tweaking and plagiarism, the scam's adherents would conquer much of the civilized world.

I'd like to pause for a moment and reflect upon the place to which the Qur'an and Hadith have brought us. In the creation accounts we learned that Muhammad and Allah could not be trusted, that they were too dishonest and foolish to be prophet and god. They buried themselves when they presented hell so graphically and revealed that their heaven was a brothel. Their plagiarized and twisted stories recasting Adam, Noah, Abraham, and Lot as Muslim prophets tore asunder Islam's credibility—its very reason for being. The stories were contradictory, transparent, and irrational. The claims that the Qur'an confirmed the Bible and that Allah was Yahweh were preposterous— further indicting the doctrine. And now, we have a deathblow. We have discovered that Islam's five pillars were conceived by Qusayy not Muhammad (a pagan, not a Muslim). As a result, Islam is dead. And the post mortem is clear. Death was self-inflicted—it was suicide.

While the case may not yet be the lay-down hand I promised in the first chapter, the story of Islam's formation is still young. In the next hundred pages I will reveal a mountain of corroborating evidence—all from their scriptures.

As is the case with all humankind, Qusayy's wealth didn't buy him a reprieve from family squabbles or the grim reaper. Abd al-Dar failed to serve in the capacity for which he had been named. Abd al-Uzza and Abd grabbed the keys to the kingdom. They became the beneficiaries of the religious tax. No one, we are told, would be able to eat, drink, fight, worship, or decide any matter without their express written permission. Okay, *verbal* permission. They were illiterate.

Each of Qusayy's sons considered themselves more worthy than the others. Civil strife broke out between the Scented Ones and the Confederates. In a move that would have made Neville Chamberlain proud, peace was achieved by cutting the baby in half. Watering pilgrims and collecting taxes were controlled by Abd Manaf's clan. Ka'aba access and waging war went to the family Abd al-Dar. This continued to be the state of affairs in Mecca until an orphan boy with royal heritage coveted it all.

The most interesting historical artifact from sixth century Arabia leads us directly to that orphan. It was the Year of the Elephant, which according to Muslim scholars was 570 A.D. It is blazoned into the annals of Islamic history. Not correctly, mind you. It was actually 552, according to archeologists.

The momentous event began with considerable fanfare. *Ishaq:4* **"Rabi'a of Yemen saw a terrifying vision. So he summoned every soothsayer, sorcerer, omenmonger, and astrologer in his kingdom."** These occult types said his dream predicted a Satanic invasion from Africa, one ultimately thwarted by the arrival of a "pure prophet" (guess who?): **"By the Serpent of the lava plains, I swear the Ethiopians shall** attack.... A pure Prophet to whom revelation will come from on high will bring it to an end." The Devil worshippers professed: "An Apostle will bring truth and justice among men of religion and virtue." You just can't beat a good Satanic endorsement.

The soothsayers went on to claim prophetically: *Ishaq:5* "It will be his intention to destroy the Jews living among him. In poetic verse they warned: 'In rage against two Jewish tribes who live in Yathrib who richly deserve the punishment of a fateful day.'"

The Satanic crowd who predicted Jews would be victimized by their prophet, allegedly acquired these quotes from some rabbis: "The approaching army will seek to destroy the temple in Mecca, for we know of no other temple in the land which Allah has chosen for himself. The rabbis told Rabi'a to do what the people of Mecca did: 'Circumambulate the Ka'aba, to venerate and honor it, to shave his head, and to bow down in humility in its sacred precincts.' Recognizing the soundness of this advice, the king cut off their hands and feet, and continued on to Mecca."

The stubby rabbis are said to have narrated a rather long poem from "their sacred books, reciting from the Torah." A few of its lines are intriguing. They correctly defined the Ka'aba for what it really was and for what Muhammad would ultimately do with it: *Ishaq:12* "A House of ancient wealth in Mecca. Treasures I wanted to seize." Then they are said to have authored one of the Qur'an's most embarrassing lines: "Dhu'l-Qarnain [Alexander the Great] before me was a Muslim...with knowledge true. He saw where the sun sinks from view in a pool of mud and fetid slime.'"

While there is considerable evidence Islam is Satanic, having "every soothsayer, sorcerer, omenmonger, and astrologer" predict the arrival of "a pure Prophet to whom revelation will come," is more blatant a connection than you'd think their scriptures would admit. They even suggest that the Devil worshippers were right because, as predicted, an African army did invade Yemen. Here's what Ibn Ishaq has to say about them: "After building a church, Abrahah, an Abyssinian viceroy, led his army north." While the non-Islamic records don't mention a place as insignificant as Mecca, the Muslim sages allege that Abrahah wanted to conquer their booming metropolis with the express intent of destroying the Ka'aba. They say that the viceroy was bent on luring pre-Islamic Arabs away from idolatry and toward a new Christian cathedral. The very thought of it must have made the rocks of the Ka'aba tremble.

Abrahah is said to have arrived on the outskirts of town with an army of sorts. But what made him formidable was his ride. The viceroy was mounted on a mighty elephant. And thus far, although grossly misdated, the story is almost plausible. Abyssinia is today's Ethiopia, so its viceroy could well have been mounted upon the mightiest of land mammals. What's not reasonable is that there isn't enough food or water to sustain an elephant in the Arabian Desert, at least for the beast to be more of an asset than liability.

Details aside, the story gets good at this point. *Ishaq:26* "Mahmud [the elephant] bowed down whenever it was asked to face Mecca. Then Allah rallied a flock of birds, each carrying a pea-like stone in its beak and in each claw. Everyone who was hit died." They were instantly dissolved, their flesh falling from their bones. **"Abrahah's fingers fell off one by one."** Naturally proud of his achievement, Allah, with some help from his pal Muhammad, recounted his stirring victory in the Qur'an. *105.001* **"Have you not seen how your Lord dealt with the companions of the elephant? Did He not make their treacherous plan go wrong, ending in confusion? He sent against them hordes of flying creatures, pelting them with stones of baked clay. He turned them into stalks of straw devoured."** A Hadith describes the nature of the disease: **"Whoever was struck by a pebble started scratching his body, tearing his flesh."**

History suggests that the Abyssinian brigade was actually done in by smallpox. Even Islam agrees, in effect calling their god a braggadocios liar: *Ishaq:27* **"Utba told me that he was informed that this year was the first time that measles and small pox had been seen in Arabia."** And while that's hardly miraculous, the Islamic Tradition affirms a shocking reality. Sixty years before the first Muslim tread the planet, Allah was a pagan god, and the Ka'aba, the center of Islamic worship, was a pagan shrine, giving Allah and his House a history that isn't the least bit flattering. Desperate to prove Allah was real, Muslims attributed this bizarre tale to their anemic deity. Good thing they did. As it turned out, this peculiar story became Allah's only miracle.

When Abdul Muttalib, Muhammad's grandfather, Meccan king and Ka'aba custodian, heard of the approaching men, he told Allah and his pantheon that they were on their own. *Ishaq:24* **"Allah, you know that we do not wish to fight, for we do not have the ability.... A man protects his house, so You protect Your House. Don't let their craft overcome Your craft tomorrow.... Deliver up the black barbarians."** Tabari adds: **"But if You want to leave and change our qiblah [the direction the Meccan idolaters faced in prayer seventy-five years before Muhammad insisted it was an Islamic requirement], You may do as You please."** On his exodus, Muttalib may have said something like, "As for me, I'm out of here. I know that the family business is a scam. It's been nice, but we can always stack a new pile of rocks when the invaders are gone."

Contrary to the Muslim revisionists, pre-Islamic Arabs were lovers, not fighters. Muttalib is alleged to have told the Quraysh, **"If we offer no resistance, there will be no cause for bloodshed."** Knowing that they were out muscled, and being merchants, not militants, the Meccans, at Muttalib's suggestion, scampered out of town and headed for the hills. They let their gods fend for themselves. This should give us pause because it means that it must have been Islam that turned these pacifists into warriors.

Early Muslims, in an effort to commemorate Allah's magnificent achievement, tell us that Muhammad was born in the Year of the Elephant. They say it is proof he was a prophet. But that's a problem. If Muhammad was born in 552, the year history says Abrahah moved north, he would have been seventy years old when he married his favorite wife, the six-year-old Aisha. And if Muslims need to falsify an event to make Muhammad appear prophetic, what does it say about the veracity of their religion?

However, there was a ray of hope in Mecca. Four Arabs had come to recognize that it was high time to stop worshiping stones. The rest of the world had long since gone monotheistic, thanks to the Jews and Christians. These religious leaders, called Hanifs, were natural monotheists. *Ishaq:99* **"Waraqa Naufal, Ubaydullah Jahsh, Uthman Huwayrith, and Zayd Amr were of the opinion that their people had corrupted the religion of Abraham, and that the Stone they went around was of no account. 'It could not hear, nor see, nor hurt, nor help.' They told their people, 'Find yourselves a religion, for by God, you have none.'"**

While much of this was encouraging, one line completely destroys Muhammad's credibility and murders Allah. These Hanifs not only inspired the first score of Qur'anic surahs, they served as Muhammad's link to the notion that Islam was the religion of Abraham. Yet these men said, **"the Stone they went around was of no account. It could not hear, see, hurt, or help."** That Stone was Allah's. A generation before Allah's Messenger stole Islam from Qusayy's heirs, Arabs in his hometown had figured it out. Their moon rock was no better than moonshine—a source of money and false hope, nothing more.

According to Ishaq, Waraqa became a Christian. His credibility will soon be usurped to advance Muhammad's agenda. Ubaydullah became a Muslim, rejected Islam the following year, and also became a Christian. Uthman became a Christian as well, holding a high office in the Byzantine empire. But..."**Zayd stayed where he was; he accepted neither Judaism nor Christianity. He abandoned the religion of his people.**" As we shall learn, Zayd recited poems that formed the basis of the early Qur'anic surahs. Yet on this day: *Ishaq:99* **"Abu Bakr said that he saw Zayd as a very old man leaning his back on the Ka'aba saying, 'O Quraysh, by Him in whose hand is the soul of Zayd, not one of you follows the religion of Abraham but I. O God, if I only knew how you wished to be worshipped I would so worship you; but I do not know.' Then he prostrated himself on the palms of his hands.**" The implications of this Hadith are devastating to Islam—especially when we witness the similarity and superiority of Zayd's poetry to that contained in the Qur'an. Although this Hanif's poems predate the Qur'an, you'll appreciate them more when they are set in the context of "Muhammad's" *first* revelations.

Some say that material stolen from several sources ceases to be plagiarism and becomes research. If that is true, Islam was Muhammad's research project as he stole it from Qusayy, Zayd, and the Jews.

6

HEART OF DARKNESS

"I fear that a demon has possessed him."

It's time I share something disturbing about the five holy books we are using to expose Muhammad, Allah, and Islam. They were not contemporaneous writings. Muslims say that Islam, unlike Judeo-Christianity, was played out in the light of recorded history but the opposite is true. The prophets and patriarchs of the Bible were lettered, and their contemporaries were literate. Their written scrolls encountered an educated audience of voracious readers within a generation of the events they described. The Islamic scripture, however, was all based upon long lines of oral tradition. No copy of the Qur'an dated to within a hundred years of the prophet's death survives. The oldest Hadith manuscript is two hundred years removed from the events it chronicles. Islam's dark past is addressed at length in the "Source Material" appendix.

Muslim Traditions allege that the Qur'an first became a book at the direction of Abu Bakr, Muhammad's father-in-law, during the War of Compulsion. We are told that the first Caliph feared that Muhammad's divine revelations would be lost because most of the best "reciters" had become warriors. According to a lone Hadith, Umar, the second Caliph, convinced Bakr that something had to be done. The fleeting memories of Jihad fighters were the sole repositories of the Qur'an, and they were being killed at an alarming rate. The loss of most or all of Muhammad's "revelation" was imminent. Legend has it that Zaid, a native of Medina and one of the prophet's helpers, was assigned the task. He **"gathered together the fragments of the Qur'an from every quarter, from date leaves, bones, stone, and from the breasts of men."**

According to J. M. Rodwell, one of the early Qur'an translators, "Zaid and his coadjutors did not arrange the materials which came to them with any system more definite than that of placing the longest and best known surahs first. Anything approaching a chronological arrangement was entirely ignored. Late Medina surahs were often placed before early Meccan ones; the short surahs at the end of the Qur'an were its earliest portions; while verses of Meccan origin were embedded in Medina surahs, and verses promulgated at

Medina were scattered up and down in the Meccan surahs."

Muslim scholars don't dispute Rodwell's claim. And that's alarming, because it means that no one was able to discern when a surah was revealed. No one even knew what comprised a surah. They were jumbled together gobbledygook, completely out of order. And if Muhammad's contemporaries were this confused, there is no chance they actually remembered the detail of what he claimed was disseminated by the almighty.

Rodwell continues his analysis with these words: "It would seem as if Zaid put his materials together just as they came to him, and often with entire disregard to continuity of subject and uniformity of style. The text, therefore, assumes the form of a most unreadable and incongruous patchwork, and conveys no idea whatever of the development and growth of any plan in the mind of the founder of Islam, or of the circumstances by which he was surrounded and influenced." Then after praising Zaid for his lack of "tampering" Rodwell adds that it is "deeply regrettable that no contemporary provided any historical reference, suppressed contradictory verses, or excluded inaccurate statements."

Therefore, even in the best possible light, the Qur'an as first assembled was a mess. It was out of order, jumbled together, contradictory, and inaccurate. Yet there is no proof that even this best-case scenario is reliable. There is no corroborating evidence that the "revelations" actually became a book under Bakr, Umar, or Zaid. There are no fragments or tablets. All we have is a flimsy oral tradition suggesting that this best-case scenario occurred. There isn't even a letter or a historical reference from any of the literate nations conquered by the first Muslim warriors to suggest that the Qur'an existed.

By contrast, there are 25,000 ancient Bible parchments, scrolls, fragments, and letters testifying to the immediacy and accuracy of today's Judeo-Christian scriptures. Yet the only archeological evidence that has survived from the Qur'an's first century is a coin and an inscription inside the Dome of the Rock on the Jewish Temple Mount. These fragments differ from each other and from today's book.

The Qur'an's chasm of historical credibility is the good news. The other four books of Islam that comprise the Sunnah: the Sira, Ta'rikh (History), and Hadith, didn't find parchment or scroll for one to three hundred years after the events were played out. Turning to Rodwell we learn: "The first biographer of Muhammad of whom we have any information was Zohri, who died A.H. 124; but his works, although quoted by later writers, are no longer extant." Said another way, Zohri's biography may have been written one hundred years after the events occurred, but it doesn't matter because no one has ever found a copy. "Ibn Ishaq, who died in A.H. 151 (763 A.D.), composed a biography of Muhammad for the Caliph's use. Although there are no surviving copies of his work either, much of it was salvaged by Hisham, an admittedly biased editor. He died in A.H. 213." Ibn Hisham's *Life of Muhammad* begins with a stunning confession. He says that he removed material that discredited Muhammad from Ishaq's original manuscript.

Tabari didn't edit Ishaq's Sira to make Muhammad look better, but he only referred to the earlier work when it conflicted with his own collection of oral testimony or Hadith. Tabari completed his *History of Prophets and Kings* in A.H. 310—three hundred years after the prophet's death. The *Concise Encyclopedia of Islam* says: "His work became the definitive resource." This makes his annals of Muhammad's creation of Islam the earliest surviving unedited account of the prophet's words and deeds, and therefore of the context in which his Qur'an was revealed. It also means that there was a three hundred year gap filled principally by oral transmission for the lone unedited collection of Islamic Hadith containing any chronology or context.

Rodwell, in the preface of his early Qur'an translation, tells us: "It may be considered quite certain that Traditions concerning Muhammad were not reduced to writing for at least the greater part of a century. They rested entirely in the memory of those who have handed them down, and must necessarily have been colored by their prejudices and convictions, to say nothing of the tendency to formulate myths and fabrications to serve the purposes of the contending factions…. It soon becomes obvious to the reader of Muslim Traditions that both miracles and historical events have been invented for the sake of expounding a dark and perplexing text [the Qur'an]; and that the earlier Traditions are largely tinged with a mythical element."

He goes on to say: "These ancient writers [Ishaq and Tabari] are the principal sources whence anything approaching authentic information as to the life of Muhammad has been derived. And it may be safely concluded that after the diligent investigations carried on by the professed collectors of Traditions in the second century after the Hijrah, that little or nothing remains to be added to our stores of information relative to the details of Muhammad's life, or to facts which may further illustrate the text of the Qur'an. There are no records posterior in date to these authorities that should be considered."

While every Islamic scholar I have studied agrees with Rodwell's assessment, that's not the end of the bad news. The people of Central Arabia in the sixth through eighth centuries were illiterate. Thus the Hadith was passed along by word of mouth through the generations, father to son through chains of transmitters called isnads.

Let's view this problem from a more contemporary perspective. Imagine reconstructing the history of the American Revolution today based entirely upon oral traditions handed down over nine generations. Without books, letters, paintings, or pictures, it would be impossible to recreate the words of Cornwallis and Washington or to resurrect the drama as it was actually played out. Now, imagine writing this history in London, thousands of miles from where the events unfolded—in the home of those who were defeated. Such is the story of Islam. The first and best Hadith, Sunnah, and Sira were compiled in Baghdad, not Mecca or Medina, two to three centuries removed. And like detailing the American Revolution in Britain, each of the Persian scholars wrote in a highly politicized climate for men with a personal agenda. A compelling argument can be made for Islam being Persian rather than Arabian; the birthplace being Baghdad, not Mecca.

Yet while none of this attests to the reliability or unbiased nature of the Islamic scripture, it doesn't actually matter. If Muhammad were really a prophet, if Allah were really a god, and if the Hadith and Qur'an were really divinely inspired and dictated, the accuracy of these books would be of paramount importance. Our eternity would rest upon their every word. But since Muhammad was as feeble-minded as his deity and as emotionally disturbed as his scripture depicts him, an accurate witness and a faithfully maintained account is irrelevant.

So if much of this isn't true, why bother? Because through force, fate, and faith, over a billion people *believe* it's true. They believe Muhammad was a prophet, Allah was his God, and that the Qur'an was comprised of divine revelations. They even think the sayings of the prophet, upon which the Hadith, Sira, and Sunnah are based, were divinely inspired *scripture*. Because most Muslims aren't free, literally trapped by fate and force in this delusion and in the hellish conditions the doctrine inspires, compassion compels us to expose the fraud and release them from the shackles of Islam.

Oh, and then there is the other little problem—Islamic terrorism. This stuff is corrosive, causing people to act in accordance with its teachings, prophet, and god. Islam commands and conditions men to murder. It motivates them to commit acts of terror. If we want to thwart this foe we must first understand what its adherents believe and what drives them to such ungodly behavior. If we want to rid the world of terror, we must first expose the doctrine that makes men terrorists. Remember, prior to Muhammad, Arabs conquered no one. After Islam they subjected much of the known world to their sword. What changed them, pray tell, if not these words?

While the Islamic "holy books" aren't historically reliable, they are *Islam*—not a version, interpretation, or corruption of Islam, but the essence of the religion. Muhammad can be no different than these books depict him. If they don't accurately present the prophet and his dark spirit, they are unknowable and thus irrelevant. Frankly speaking, Islam loses either way.

Returning to the Hadith, we discover an interesting artifact concerning the early Meccans and their Ka'aba. It also heralds from the Year of the

Elephant. Abdul Muttalib was a big shot in town, a wealthy idolater born two generations before Muhammad. In the line of Qusayy, he became the custodian of the Ka'aba. *Tabari VI:15* "After the death of his uncle al-Muttalib, Abdul Muttalib took over the privilege of watering and feeding the pilgrims which the sons of Abd Manaf had held before him. He was honored and was a man of great importance, for not one was his equal." *Ishaq:62* "Sleeping on the graves of Hagar and Ishmael he was ordered in a vision to dig Zamzam. 'Allahu Akbar,' he shouted. 'This is the well of our father Ishmael.'" *Tabari VI:15* "He brought out what was buried there, namely, two golden gazelles, swords and coats of mail. He made the swords into a door for the Ka'aba." It's interesting that the Ka'aba's treasure contained the implements Muhammad would use to loot the world: swords and coats of mail. The door to Allah's House and the path to Islam were the same.

Ownership of the newfound booty was determined by a gambling game. Divining arrows were thrown at Hubal's feet, "the greatest of the idols." *Ishaq:64* "Muttalib prayed to Allah and the priest threw the arrows. The Ka'aba won the gazelles."

Abdul Muttalib "was the first to institute the two yearly caravans." He was "the first to obtain for the Quraysh guarantees of safety which allowed them to travel far and wide from the sacred precincts of Mecca,"—guarantees Muhammad would break.

Then one day, sun boring down on the treeless town, Muttalib was struggling to clear the well of Zamzam when: *Ishaq:66/Tabari VI:2* "It is alleged, and Allah only knows the truth, that Abdul Muttalib encountered opposition when he was digging Zamzam. He vowed that if given ten sons, to make his labor less arduous and to protect him, he would sacrifice one of them to Allah at the Ka'aba." Bad move, because eventually he *had* ten sons. So, foolishly faithful to the rocks, he tossed divining arrows at Hubal's feet to determine which son should die. *Ishaq:67* "They used to conduct their affairs according to the decisions of the arrows." His youngest lost. The boy's name was Abd-Allah, or Slave-to-Allah.

Now why would someone name a kid "Slave-to-Allah" a generation before Islam's prophet claimed Allah was the creator-god of the universe? The answer is as embarrassing as any in the annals of religious lore. For all Muhammad really did was promote one of the existing Meccan idols, the moon god Allah, above Hubal, Al-Lat, Manat, Al-Uzza, and hundreds of others. On this day Allah had to compete for adoration, as Muttalib's tossing arrows at Hubal's feet attests. A Bukhari Hadith confirms the godly congestion: *Bukhari:V5B59N583* "When the Prophet entered Mecca on the day of the Conquest, there were 360 idols around the Ka'aba. The Prophet started striking them with a stick."

Islamic scholar Montgomery Watt, one of the English translators of Tabari, adds an interesting footnote. He says, "The name [not word] Allah has throughout been [wrongly] translated as 'God.' It should be kept in mind, however, that in the pre-Islamic period it does not necessarily mean "God" in a monotheistic sense. It is known from the Qur'an (29:61 and 39:38) that many pre-Islamic Arabs believed in Allah as a god who was superior to the other gods whom they also recognized."

Allah was a *name*, much like the Judeo-Christian "Yahweh." But Muslims desperately needed the world to see it otherwise. For if Allah was a proper name—not a word—their religion was a fraud. The creator of the universe can't be a pagan god, no matter how big a stick Muhammad swung. And Allah can't be Yahweh any more than I can be George Washington.

Arabic, like Hebrew before it, was derived from Aramaic. In Hebrew, *"el,"* was the word for god—lower case "g"—as in idols. Elohiym was used with the article to convey "God" with a capital "G." In Arabic, *"el"* became *"il."* Then, over time, Arabs derived a secondary word for god, *"ilah."* With *"al"* being the Arabic word for "the," Muslims would have us believe that "Allah" is a contraction of *"al"* and *"ilah."* But the first pillar of Islam contradicts this claim when it says: "There is no *ilah* but Allah." If "Allah" were the Arabic word for god it would have been written: "There is no *allah* but Allah. Moreover, the Qur'an itself uses *"Ilah"* when Allah claims to be "the God of Abraham" (Qur'an 2:132). And that ends the debate because the only way Muslims can claim Allah, not *Ilah*, is the Arabic word for "God" is for the Qur'an to be errant or for its author to be either ignorant or deceitful. Further, there are hundreds, if not thousands, of Islamic traditions like the one we just reviewed that confirm that Allah was the name of a well-known pagan deity (at least in Mecca). Their own scriptures profess that Allah had an ignominious rule as a Meccan rock idol centuries before he was transformed from god to God, from an *ilah* to Allah. All of which serves to destroy the most essential Islamic myth: "We all worship the same God."

Back in Mecca: *Ishaq:67* **"When Abdul Muttalib had ten sons grown to maturity and he knew that they would protect him, he told them of his vow, and called on them to keep faith with Allah in this matter. They expressed their obedience, and asked what they should do. He replied, 'Let every one of you take an arrow, write his name on it, and bring it to me.' They did this, and he went into the presence of Hubal in the interior of the Ka'aba. Hubal was the greatest of the idols of Quraysh in Mecca."** Wow! Ibn Ishaq, the earliest compiler of Muslim Traditions, just told us that the high god of the Ka'aba was Hubal—not Allah. Doesn't this make Allah (also the god of the second god of the Qur'an following Ar-Rahman) a second rate deity?

Papa Muttalib started having second thoughts. So he went off and consulted with a sorceress, hoping to get the "right" advice. *Tabari VI:2* **"By Allah! You shall never sacrifice him but you must get an excuse for not doing so."** This sounds innocent enough until you realize that the person swearing by Allah is a Devil worshipper. **"There is a sorceress who has a familiar spirit; ask her, and you will know what to do. If she commands you to sacrifice him, you will sacrifice him, and if she commands you to do something which offers relief to you and to him, you can accept it."** Sorceresses are occult mediums: in other words, witches. Their familiar spirits are demons.

The noose around Islam's neck is tightening. We have multiple gods in the Ka'aba and a witch deciding the fate of Muhammad's father. "So they went to Medina where they discovered that the sorceress had moved to Khaybar. They rode until they reached her. She said, 'Retire from me until my familiar spirit visits me and I can ask him. Abdul Muttalib stood and prayed to Allah." Now there's a picture: idolaters praying to Allah in Islamic fashion in the presence of a Devil worshiper. So, what do you think Satan's representative had to say? Would she pardon Muhammad's papa and allow Islam to be born?

Lucifer must like Islam because..."On the following day they went back. She said, 'Yes! News has come to me. How much is the blood-money among you?' They replied, 'Ten camels.' She said, 'Bring forward the young man and ten camels, and cast arrows. If they fall against the boy, add camels until your Lord [Would that be Satan, Hubal, or Allah?] is satisfied.'"

We continue with Ishaq's account: *Tabari VI:5* "They returned to Mecca when they had all agreed on the matter, Abdul Muttalib stood and prayed to Allah inside the Ka'aba beside Hubal. The arrows fell against Abdallah, so they added ten camels, making twenty. With Muttalib standing and praying to Allah they went on this way ten times. Each time the arrows fell against Abdallah." Satan's representative seems to have been considerably more accommodating. There is just one chance in 1024 that fifty-fifty odds will go awry ten times in a row.

Tabari explains the horror of it all: "Abdul Muttalib stood beside Hubal in the interior of the Ka'aba, calling upon Allah. The custodian of the arrows took and cast them, and the lot fell against Abdallah. So Muttalib took Abdallah by the hand. He grabbed a large knife. Then he went up to the idols Isaf and Nailah [the fornicating stones] who Quraysh used to slaughter their sacrifices, to sacrifice Abdullah."

But rather than slice his son's throat, Muttalib opted for one more cast of the divining arrows. They finally fell in favor of the boy. So Abdul, the stones, idols, gods, diviners, and sorcerers came to an understanding. Abdallah's life was spared. "Your Lord is satisfied at last. The camels were slaughtered and left there. No man or wild beast was turned back from eating them."

"Abdul Muttalib took Abdallah by the hand. It is alleged they passed by Umm Qattal bt. Abd al-Uzza [Slave-to-the-goddess-al-Uzza], the sister of Waraqa [the Hanif]. She was by the Ka'aba. When she looked at his face she said, 'Where are you going, Abdallah? I have seen many camels slaughtered for you, so sleep with me now.'" Sure, why not add a little prostitution into the mix. We've already got devil worship, paganism, gambling, and child abuse occurring around the Ka'aba.

But the bribe was evidently insufficient. So the proud papa, king of Mecca, custodian of the Ka'aba, and heir to the religious scam, took his son to the wealthiest and most powerful man of the neighboring clan, the Banu Zurah, and arranged for his son Abdallah to marry the chief's daughter Aminah. The blushing bride's grandmother was abd al-Uzza, which made her "genealogy and status" perfect, according to Ishaq.

Before we consummate this marriage, I must say I'm surprised Bukhari,

Tabari, and Ishaq recount this sordid tale. Muhammad grew up a stone's throw from where it occurred. Yet he chose to ignore his ignominious past, revising Jewish history instead, in order to make the near sacrifice at his backyard shrine look monotheistic. In lieu of the truth, he said that the Hebrew patriarch Abraham had nearly sacrificed Ishmael at Allah's House.

Take a deep breath. The next Hadith begins with an inordinately long sentence. *Tabari VI:6* **"It is alleged that he consummated his marriage to her there as soon as he married her, that he lay with her and that she conceived Muhammad; then he left her presence and came to the woman who had propositioned him, and said to her, 'Why do you not make the same proposition to me today which you made to me yesterday?'"** To which she replied, **"The light which was with you yesterday has left you, and I have no need of you today."**

Remember, these Hadiths found paper in Baghdad centuries after Muhammad's passing. By that time, the Muslim scholars who authored them had well-defined agendas. In particular, they had to make their guy look as godly as that Christian guy, or they'd be out of business. The Gospels proclaimed that Christ was the light of the world, so Muslims contrived this Hadith to make their prophet appear similarly enlightened. And if you think that I'm being too cynical, listen to the next line from Tabari. **"She had heard about this from her brother Waraqa bin Nawfal, who was a [Hanif turned] Christian and had studied the scriptures; he had discovered that a prophet from the descendants of Ishmael was to be sent to this people; this had been one of the purposes of his study."**

Holy hogwash. The Hebrew Bible says nothing about the descendants of Ishmael other than they will be wild asses of men whose hand will be raised against their brothers and that they would live in hostility with all the world. While prophetic, it's hardly prophet material.

So why did the Muslim scholars choose to deceive us? They needed to, that's why. And within their community they could get away with it. The lie provided their pathetic prophet with some semblance of credibility, however tenuous. And Arabs would never be wiser for it. They were illiterate, and even the miniscule percentage who could read were out of luck when it came to the Bible. There is no trace of an Arabic translation of the Old Testament prior to that of Saadias Gaon in 900 A.D., decades after this delusion was promulgated. And the oldest Arabic New Testament was published by Erpenius in 1616 from a transcription of a 1171 Coptic scroll.

In the territories controlled by the Muslim warlords of the seventh through tenth centuries, words were irrelevant, as unimportant as evangelists. Islam grew by sword through conquest, not by words and reason. And those who benefited from this ruse knew that by the time their deceptive words were exposed, it would be too late; the victory would have been won.

For those who may think I am perhaps making too much of too little, consider this: *Tabari VI:7* **"When Abdul Muttalib was taking Abdallah to marry Aminah they** passed by a female soothsayer called Fatimah, a convert to Judaism from the people of Tabalah who had read the scriptures and who saw light in his face. 'Young man,' she said, 'would you like to lie with me now, and I will give you a hundred camels?'" Contriving a phony Christian endorsement of the Muslim prophet was not enough. Now a Jewish soothsayer is called to verify the light. But why would a Jew react this way? The Judeo-Christian scriptures say nothing—zip, zero, zilch—about the father of a prophet having a light in his face. Further, Judaism and soothsaying are mutually exclusive. Jews serve Yahweh; soothsayers serve Satan.

The third variant of this desperate grope for credibility demeans Abdallah. "His father took him and married him to Aminah and he stayed with her for three days. Then he left her and when he passed by the Khath'am woman he felt a desire to accept the proposition which she had made. He asked her, 'Would you like to have what you wanted before?' 'Young man,' she said, 'I am not, by Allah, a woman of questionable morals. I saw light in your face and wished it to be within me. But Allah willed that He should place it where He wished.'" The Devil worshiper wanted the Devil's child.

Then our Allah/Devil-serving soothsayer: "recited the following verses: 'I saw a sign which shone in the black clouds. I comprehended it as light which illuminated like the full moon. I hoped to have it as a source of pride which I might take back with me.... By Allah, no other woman has plundered your person of that which Aminah has.... Not all the fortune which the young man inherits comes from resolve, nor does that which escapes him come from remiss. So if you desire something, behave with restraint for two grandfathers combined to ensure it for you. A hand clenched or outstretched will ensure it for you. When Aminah conceived that which she conceived from him, she conceived an incomparable glory'" From black signs to pride, from full moons to plundering, from inherited fortunes to grandfathers ensuring loot, the young prophet would get what he desired from both open and clenched fists. This passage is so fraught with portent, so twisted with harbingers of Muhammad's con, the originator must have laughed himself silly as his quill met parchment. He evidently got himself so worked up he bungled the tense in his parting salvo. Once again, a simple story belies the nature of Islam. "Our guy is better than your guy and we will say anything, no matter how absurd, to prove it."

Abdallah lived long enough to father a son, but not to see him born. In a haunting overture of what was to come, the prophet's father died while on a business trip to Yathrib. Fifty-two years later the religion of Islam would die there as well when a prophet went on a business trip to Yathrib and became a profiteer.

In an attempt to make Muhammad appear Messianic, our hero was portrayed as having been born to considerable fanfare. There were celestial fireworks, regal visitors, an angelic host, and a veritable cornucopia of miracles. In that the worst of these were laughable, and the best were copied from the

Gospels, I'll spare you the gory details—especially since none of them make any sense in context of what happened next. There is, however, one in Ishaq's Biography that is intriguing: *Ishaq:69* **"It is alleged in popular stories (and only Allah knows the truth) that Aminah, the mother of Allah's Apostle, used to say when she was pregnant, 'A voice said to me, "You are pregnant with the Lord of this people and when he is born say, I put him in the care of the One from the evil of the envier; then call him Muhammad."' She saw a light come forth from her by which she could see the castles in Syria."** Envy is what drove Muhammad to create Islam. The care of the Evil One— better known as Lucifer or Satan—may well have been what inspired him.

The truth is rather ignoble. Muslim scholars know nothing about Muhammad's birth, and very little about his childhood. They missed his birthday by eighteen years when they claimed he was born in the year of the elephant, recently dated to 552 A.D. But to make their prophet fit Qusayy's profile of being forty when he staked his claim to the Ka'aba, Islamic historians claim Muhammad was born in 570—exactly forty years before the first "revelation." Missing a date this important by eighteen years calls all of Islam's oral testimony into question. By way of example, this did not occur: *Ishaq:70* **"I heard a Jew calling out at the top of his voice from Yathrib, 'O Jews, tonight has risen a star under which Ahmad is to be born.'"**

Born fatherless, Muhammad's mother abandoned him, giving him up to be suckled by a Bedouin woman. With his father dead and his mother poor, no wet-nurse wanted the infant because the burden exceeded the potential remuneration. Raising another's child in the inhospitable desert was done for money, not love. The least qualified of the wet-nurses, we are told, after failing to find a wealthy kid, reluctantly snatched the last available newborn, the would-be prophet, and hauled him off into the wilderness. A Hadith explains: *Ishaq:70* **"Halima went forth with her baby whom she was nursing, with other women, in search of babies to nurse. She was destitute and could not sleep because of the weeping of her hungry child. She had no milk to give him."** Halima was obviously in no position to suckle another child. This was a disaster waiting to happen.

Ishaq:71 **"When Halima reached Mecca, she set out to look for foster children. The Apostle of Allah was offered to everyone of us, and each woman refused him when she was told he was an orphan, because we hoped to get payment from the child's father. We said, 'An orphan!' And we spurned him because of that. Every woman who came with me got a suckling except me. And when we decided to depart, I said, 'I do not like the idea of returning with my friends without a suckling. I will take that orphan.' I took him for the sole reason that I could not find anyone else."** So much for the "light" theory. Women were throwing themselves at Muhammad's dad to sire him, but no one wanted to raise him. That doesn't make any sense.

What happened out there in the blowing sands and blistering heat is anybody's guess. All we know is that a baby was abandoned by his mother and given to a woman who was ill prepared to care for him. The only testimony that survives is in the Qur'an—a haunting and recurring theme that suggests he may have been abused. Allah's revelations speak of an orphan boy with wealthy relatives being abandoned, treated poorly, and being shut out of the family business—The Ka'aba Inc. Permutations of this theme permeate Allah's book, compelling the Muslim sages to give this mess a prophetic twist.

Ibn Ishaq claims that when Muhammad was two, Halima brought him back to his mother Aminah. *Ishaq:72* **"But she sent him back. Some months after his return to the desert two men in white seized the boy, threw him down and opened up his belly, stirring it up."** We are told that Muhammad was "livid." **"Halima said, 'I am afraid that this child has had a stroke, so I want to take him back before the result appears.' She carried him back to Aminah and said, 'I am afraid that ill will befall him, so I have brought him back to you.' She asked what had happened. I said, 'I fear that a demon has possessed him.'"** She was right.

Muhammad confirms the "spiritual" encounter. *Ishaq:72* **"They seized me and opened up my belly, extracted my heart and split it. They extracted a black drop from it and threw it away. They washed my heart and belly with snow until they had cleaned them."** *Muslim:B1N311* **"Gabriel came to Muhammad while he was playing with his playmates. He took hold of him and lay him prostrate on the ground and tore open his breast and took out the heart. Then he extracted a blood-clot out of it and said: 'That was the part of Satan in you.' And then he washed it with the water of Zamzam in a golden basin and then it was joined together and restored to it place. The boys came running to their mother and said: 'Muhammad has been murdered.' They all rushed toward him. I myself saw the marks of needle on his breast."** If this occurred, it was Lucifer, not Gabriel, and he was placing his spirit inside.

Organ removal and washing are Satanic—part of occult ritual worship— the kind of thing Muhammad's father and grandfather were into. And ironi- cally, if it *had* happened, it would be miraculous and therefore in conflict with the Qur'an. Allah's book says that the only miracle associated with the prophet was the revelation of the surahs themselves. In Qur'an 21:5, we find that one of the many arguments used by Muhammad's critics at the time was that he couldn't do miracles. Since the Judeo-Christian Prophets could, and did, they said he couldn't be a prophet. If Muhammad had been involved in a miracle, or could do one, all he would have had to do to silence his critics was to explain the ones that had taken place, or simply summon his god's power to perform one. But no.

Sixth century surgery aside, the Islamic sages say that before the year was out, Aminah died. A slave girl took care of our young hero for a while before his grandfather finally took an interest. And even this is potentially disturbing, for the scriptures say of Abdul Muttalib's affection: *Ishaq:73* **"He would make him sit beside him on his bed and would stroke him with his hand. He was extremely fond of him and used to constantly pet him."**

Straight from the Devil we learn: *Ishaq:79* **"There was a seer [occultist prophet]** who came to Mecca to look at Muhammad. She said, 'Bring me that boy, for I saw just now that by Allah he has a great future.'" Then, disaster strikes once more: *Tabari VI:44* "Abdul Muttalib died eight years after the Year of the Elephant. He entrusted the future Messenger's care to his uncle Abu Talib, because Abu and Abdallah had had the same mother." Needless to say, Muhammad had one whacked-out childhood. It's not hard to understand why he was so insecure or why he turned out as he did.

Virtually everything associated with Muhammad was decidedly unprophet-like. His birth was not foretold. The circumstances surrounding it were nasty. He couldn't perform a miracle. He never issued a single prophetic utterance that came true as predicted. His scripture was abysmal—devoid of context and chronology. It focused on hate, violence, and punishment. His "new" religion was simply repackaged paganism blended with a plethora of plagiarized and twisted Bible stories. What little was inventive was tragic. War was elevated to a paramount religious duty. Plunder was approved, as was incest, thievery, lying, assassination, genocide, and rape to name a few Islamic innovations. Paradise became a lustful orgy. The would-be prophet's depictions of hell told us more about him than about the place. And his life was an example of what not to do, rather than how to behave. Then there was his god—a trickster, angry and demented.

According to the Qur'an, the Meccans knew the prophet was full of it. They ridiculed him on every occasion—a hundred variations of the never-ending argument were faithfully recounted in the Islamic holy book. But the Meccans were eventually conquered and criticizing the prophet became a deadly game. So the next time the Muslim hierarchy was confronted with the notion that their man didn't measure up was when they paraded his legacy out to the literate word. The enlightened didn't buy it either, and for all the reasons we have just mentioned.

That put the Muslim warlords in a pickle. They had raided everyone from India to Spain. Now they needed to control that which they had conquered. And they recognized that there is no better way to subdue a population than to impose a religion. So about a hundred and fifty years after the prophet's death, the Persians rolled out the first version of the Islamic "religion." It was as dismal a failure as it had been in Mecca. Their subjects said, "This guy's no prophet and this stuff isn't scripture." By way of example, Al-Kindi, a Christian polemicist employed in the Caliphal court in 830 A.D. wrote: "The result of this process by which the Qur'an has come into being is that it's patently obvious to those who have read these scriptures that Muslim histories are all jumbled together and intermingled. It is an evidence that many different hands have been at work therein, and caused discrepancies, adding or cutting out whatever they liked or disliked. As such, the conditions are right for a new revelation to be sent down from heaven."

So the Islamic sages retreated to Baghdad and went back to the drawing board. Over the course of the next hundred years they buffed up their boy and their book, releasing a new and improved Islam. This time there were miracles and Christians and Jews ever at the ready to testify on the prophet's behalf.

Let's listen in, but with a critical ear, to see how well the sages cleaned up the prophet of Islam. Under the title, "The Messenger of Allah Is Recognized by the Monk Bahira" Tabari parades out a Hadith shared by Ishaq. *Tabari VI:44/Ishaq:79* "Once Abu Talib was going on a trading expedition to Syria with a party of Quraysh, but when he had made his preparations and was ready to set out, the Messenger, so they allege, could not bear to be separated from him." Before I go on, I'd like to point out something that should be obvious. Tabari and Ishaq share a set of code words. When they say, "so they allege," "it is alleged," "it is said," "some say," or "Allah knows best," they are simply reporting what they were told to write. They don't believe it any more than you should.

"Talib took pity on him, 'By Allah, I will take him with me, and we shall never part,' or words to that effect. The caravan halted at Busra [Bostra?] in Syria, where there was a learned Christian monk named Bahira in his cell. There had always been a monk in that cell, and their knowledge was passed on, it is alleged, [the code words again] by means of a book which was handed down from generation to generation." There is no record of this monk, his cell, or his book outside this Hadith. But that's small potatoes compared to what comes next.

Tabari VI:44/Ishaq:79 "Bahira prepared a meal for them because while he was in his cell he had seen the Messenger shaded by a cloud which marked him out from among the company. When they halted in the shade of a tree, he observed the cloud covering the tree and bending down its branches over Muhammad until he was in the shade. Bahira descended from his cell and sent the caravan a message inviting them all. When he saw the Messenger, he observed him very intently, noting features of his person whose description he had found in his Christian book." Judeo-Christian prophets aren't described physically in any "book." But in order to create a Christian endorsement from a learned monk, the Muslims have invented this monk, story, and book.

"After the company had finished the meal and dispersed, he asked the Messenger about certain matters which had taken place both when he was awake and when he was asleep. Muhammad told him, and he found that these things corresponded to the description which he had found in his book. Finally he looked at his back, and saw the seal of prophethood between his shoulders in the very place described in his book." Camel-dung—every word of it. First, the Gospels are clear. No great prophet after the Messiah is foretold. Second, there isn't a set of "awake and asleep" criteria for a divine calling, which is probably why the Hadith doesn't bother listing them. Third, there is no Biblical "seal of prophethood." The concept was derived from Arabian pagan mythology to designate occult practitioners who talked to demons. Furthermore, the "seal" was actually nothing more than a hairy mole. (Tabari IX:159)

Next, the "Christian" Monk swears by the Meccan idols. *Tabari VI:45/Ishaq:80*

"'By Al-Lat and Al-Uzza,' Bahira said.' 'Take him back to your country, and be on your guard against the Jews, for, by Allah, if they see him and recognize what I have, they will seek to do him harm.'" The Jews spent years, not hours, with the "prophet." They let him move into their town and sold him stories from their Talmud. They never lifted a finger to harm him, even though he annihilated *them* in genocidal rage.

The hardest part of lying is remembering what you said. So in true Islamic form, we have a second variant of the "mark of the prophet" tale. "Abu Talib set off for Syria accompanied by the Messenger and a number of shaykhs. When they were above the monk's cell they went down and unloaded their camels. The monk walked among them, coming up and taking the hand of the Messenger. He said, 'This is the Chief of the Worlds, *the* Messenger. This person has been sent by Allah as a mercy to the Worlds.'" Let's call this "Holy Hogwash, Version Two." First, chief is a political term, not a religious one. Second, this time there were no questions, no signs, no seals—just a baseless, over-the-top endorsement. Third, how many "worlds" are there? And fourth, how could Muhammad have been a "mercy" to Christians when he and his god told Muslims to wipe them out to the last?

"The shaykhs of the Quraysh said to him, 'What is it you know?' He replied, 'When you appeared at the top of the pass there was not a tree or a stone which did not prostrate itself in worship; and they only prostrate themselves to a prophet.'" Hard to believe, but HH-2 is more pathetic than its predecessor. Neither Christians, stones, nor trees prostrate themselves—not even to wannabe prophets. Besides, prophets aren't supposed to be worshiped. God is.

Inanimate objects showering Muhammad with devotion was hardly a one-time occurrence. *Tabari VI:63* "Before Gabriel appeared to Muhammad to confer on him his mission as Messenger of Allah, it is said that he used to see signs and evidences indicating that Allah wished to ennoble him. Two angels came to him, opened up his breast, and removed the hatred and impurity which were in it. [I'd sue them for malpractice.] It is said [the Islamic code words for "this is rubbish"] that whenever he passed by a tree or a stone, it would greet him."

Not to be outdone, in a Hadith from a line of transmitters—or isnad—that includes three Muhammads, a pair of Alis, two Slaves-to-Allah, and an Abd Ar-Rahman, we learn: "Whenever Muhammad went out to attend his business [answer the call of nature] he would go a great distance, out of sight of houses, and into the ravines and wadi beds. And then every stone and tree he passed would say, 'Peace be upon you, Messenger of Allah.'" Even today, Muslims, no smarter than the stones, are required to add "peace be unto him" after the mention of Muhammad's name. And his "business" still stinks.

Returning to the monk: *Tabari VI:46* "I also recognize him by the seal of prophethood which is below the cartilage of his shoulders and which is like an apple." Delicious. The apple has become the symbol of temptation. It's perfect for Islam.

HH-2 wasn't finished destroying Muhammad's prophetic credentials. It went on to establish the Christian Byzantines as enemies in addition to the

Jews. But I suppose having Christians and Jews endorse a religion that would grow by plundering them makes about as much sense as Muhammad being a prophet. **"While Bahira was standing by them beseeching them not to take the Messenger to the land of the Byzantines, since if these saw him, they would recognize him by his description and would kill him."** Muhammad forbade Muslims from drawing his likeness. If his appearance was testimony of his prophetic credentials, and so easily recognizable, why would he do such a thing?

Patricia Crone, an Islamic scholar and archeologist says: "There are fifteen different versions of Muhammad being blessed by a representative of a non-Islamic religion who 'recognized' him as a future prophet. Some place this encounter during his infancy, others when he was nine; some say he was twenty-five. One Tradition maintains he was recognized by Ethiopian Christians, several say by a Syrian monk, many claim by Yathrib Jews, one suggests it was a local Hanif, while others maintain it was a sorcerer. Some even suggest it was the belly of a dead animal. So what we have here is nothing more than fifteen equally fictitious versions of an event that never took place."

The Muslim sages who can't remember what their prophet told them in Mecca are telling us that they can recreate a conversation between opposition parties in Syria. Let's listen in, and while we're doing so, let's try to determine why the Hadith contains this dialog in the first place. **"The monk turned around and suddenly beheld seven men advancing from the land of the Byzantines. He went up to them and said, 'What brings you here?' They replied, 'We have come because this prophet is appearing in this month. Men have been sent to every road, and we have been chosen as the best of men and have been sent to your road.'"** There isn't a prophetic utterance in any Christian book about an Arab prophet. Yet we are led to believe that Christians not only knew exactly when, but precisely where, they would find such an unspecified person. This is desperate to the point of pathetic. If Muslims need to contrive such preposterous lies to make Muhammad appear prophetic, he most certainly wasn't.

Yet they continue to lay planks on this flimsy foundation: *Tabari VI:64* **"Zayd bin Amr [a Hanif poet from whose words Muhammad based early Qur'anic revelations] said, 'I expect a prophet from the descendants of Ishmael, in particular from the descendants of Abd al-Muttalib.'"** Mind you, the first written confirmation of this precise prediction came three hundred years *after* Muhammad's birth. By comparison, the last of the Biblical Messianic prophecies, for which these Islamic predictions were contrived to compete, were committed to writing 400 years *prior* to Christ's birth. And unlike all things Muslim, Christians have a paper trail. The Septuagint, the Greek translation of the Hebrew Bible compiled in Alexandria in 275 B.C., survives to this day.

The post-dated Hadith of Zayd, a man who rejected both Islam and Muhammad, continues: **"I shall inform you of his description so that he will not be hidden from you. He is neither short nor tall, whose hair is neither abundant nor sparse,** whose eyes are always red, and who has the seal of the prophethood between his shoulders. His name is Ahmad [a variant of Muhammad], and this town [Mecca] is his birthplace and the place in which he will commence his mission. Then his people will drive him out and hate the message which he brings, and he will emigrate to Yathrib and triumph."

The Islamic sages who put these words in the Hanif's mouth three centuries after his death, want you to know that every faith—Judeo-Christian to Satanic—agrees: "I have traveled around in search of the faith of Abraham. [The only pre-Islamic mention of Abraham is in the Bible. Apart from the Torah, nothing is known about him—not even his name. And the Torah is clear: Abraham didn't have a religion; he had a relationship.] Every person whom I ask, whether Jew, Christian, or Magian, says, 'This faith lies where you have come from,' and they describe him as I have described him to you. They say that no prophet remains but he.' Amir said, 'When I became a Muslim, I told the Messenger what Zayd had said, and I gave him his greetings. He said, 'I saw him in Paradise dressed in flowing robes.'" Although Zayd composed most of the Qur'an's first score of surahs, he rejected Muhammad's credentials and thus Islam. By his own admission, he can't be in the Islamic paradise.

These "endorsements" are so preposterous it begs the question: what must educated Muslims think when they read such nonsense? You don't have to be a religious scholar to know that the Jewish Messiah wasn't an Arab or that Christians had but one prophet. So when this obvious deception was brought before Islam's lone messenger for certification and he endorsed the lie, what must they think? *Do* they think? Why would one trust a man who must lie—or be lied for—to validate his calling?

Ishaq:90 "Jewish rabbis, Christian monks, and Arab soothsayers had spoken about the Apostle of Allah before his mission when his time drew near. The rabbis and monks found his description in their scriptures. The Arab occultists had been visited by satans from the jinn with reports which they had secretly overheard before they were prevented from hearing by being pelted with stars." *Ishaq:91* "The Prophet explained the nature of shooting stars. 'Allah shut off the satans by these stars which pelted them. So satans tried to steal information, listening in, mingling what they heard with conjecture and false intelligence. They conveyed it to the soothsayers.'"

Ishaq:92 "Umar bin al-Khattab [the future Caliph] was sitting with others in the Messenger's mosque when a Bedouin came up looking for him. Umar said, 'This man was a soothsayer in the Jahiliyyah.'" The Satan-worshiper-turned-Allah-advocate said, "During the Jahiliyyah [pre-Islamic Period of Ignorance] we used to do worse things than you. We used to worship idols and embrace graven images until Allah honored us with Islam." You know you're dealing with a rotten religion when an occultist tells the champions of Islam, "We used to do worse things than you." The suggestion is that Muhammad's behavior in Yathrib—pedophilia, incest, rape, piracy, terrorism, genocide, and the slave trade—was better than serving a demon.

"'O men,' the soothsayer said, 'Allah has honored and chosen Muhammad, purified his heart and his bowels.'" Then the future Caliph, in Muhammad's presence, asked the former occultist what he learned from the demonic spirits: *Ishaq:93* "'Tell me,' said Umar, 'what is the most amazing saying which your familiar spirit [satanic jinn or demon] communicated to you?' 'He came to me a month before Islam and said: "Have you considered the Jinn [demons from Satan's tribe] and the hopelessness and despair of their religion [the occult—witchcraft, tarot cards, black magic, astrology, séances, etc.]?"'" The Islamic hierarchy was interested in what the Satanic types had to say. Kindred spirits, I suppose.

Tabari VI:66 "Then Umar said, 'By Allah I was by one of the idols of the Jahiliyyah. An Arab sacrificed a calf to it, and we were waiting for it to be divided up in order to receive a share. I heard coming from the belly of the calf a voice which was more penetrating than any I've heard—this was a year before Islam. The dead calf's belly said, 'There is no ilah but Allah.'"

The next Hadith comes courtesy of a fine isnad of four Muhammads and a future Caliph. "We were sitting by an idol a month before the Messenger commenced his mission, having slaughtered camels. Suddenly we heard a voice calling from the belly of one: 'Listen to the wonder; There will be no more eavesdropping to overhear inspiration; We throw down shooting stars for a prophet in Mecca; His name is Ahmad. His place of emigration is Yathrib' We held back and marveled; then the Messenger began his mission." The moral of the story is: the next time one of those pesky Christians or Jews says that Muhammad wasn't a prophet because there were no prophecies pointing to his mission, you can tell them it just isn't so. A dead camel and a cow told you he was Allah's boy.

How about one more, just to be fair. "A man came to the Prophet and said, 'Show me the seal which is between your shoulders, and if you lie under any enchantment [a demonic curse or spell] I will cure you, for I am the best enchanter [a witch practicing black magic] of the Arabs.' 'Do you wish me to show you a sign?' asked the Prophet. 'Yes. Summon that cluster.' So the Prophet looked at a cluster of dates hanging from a palm and summoned it, and began to snap his fingers until it stood before him. Then the man said, 'Tell it to go back,' and it went back. The enchanter said, 'I have never seen a greater magician than I have seen today.'" Takes one to know one.

Moving from the ridiculous to the sublime, the religion *based* upon pagan practices has a chapter entitled: "The Messenger is Protected by Allah from Participating in Pagan Practices." The first Hadith is from Ali, the prophet's adopted son and his son-in-law, the patriarch of the Shi'ites, and the first of many assassinated Caliphs. He said, "I heard the Messenger saying, 'I was only tempted to take part in heathen practices on two occasions, and both times Allah prevented me from doing what I wanted. After that I was never tempted to evil, right up to the time when Allah honored me by making me his Messenger." Since each of Islam's pillars was conceived by a pagan, I believe we have caught the prophet in another lie.

The temptation behind us, we move to one of today's more common sins:

sex in the workplace. Muhammad married his boss. *Ishaq:82* **"Khadija was a wealthy and respected merchant. She was determined and intelligent, possessing many properties. She was the best born woman of the Quraysh, and she was the richest, too."** *Tabari VI:48* **"She used to employ men to engage in trade with her property and gave them a share of the profit, for the Quraysh were merchants. When she heard of Muhammad's truthfulness and nobility of character, she sent for him and proposed that he should go to Syria and engage in the trade with her property. She would give him more than she gave other men who traded for her...."** The sentence rambles on to say that Islam's matriarch sent one of her slaves to keep tabs on the neophyte merchant.

"When they reached Syria he halted in the shade of a tree near a monk's cell. The monk went up to Maysarah [Khadija's slave], and said, 'Who is this man who has halted beneath this tree?' Maysarah replied, 'He is a man of Quraysh, one of the people of the Haram sacred precinct.' 'No one has ever halted beneath this tree but a prophet,' said the monk." A sixth century monk could never have seen a prophet. Further, there is no evidence that a Christian or Jewish prophet *ever* set foot in Syria.

The next line puts us in the precarious position of wondering who is lying. If the following Tradition is true, the Qur'an's assertion that there were no miracles associated with Muhammad is false. **"They assert that Maysarah saw two angels shading him from the sun as he rode his camel."**

"When he arrived in Mecca, he brought Khadija her property, which she sold for twice the price.... She sent for the Messenger and, it is reported, said to him, 'Cousin, your kinship to me, your standing among your people...make you a desirable match.' She offered herself to him in marriage." In one of history's great ironies, the most independent, successful, and liberated woman of her day played a pivotal role in assuring that a billion women after her would be deprived of these things.

Muhammad married money—a woman old enough to be his mother. What's more, the would-be prophet married his boss. While this is questionable, it is not illegal. Nor is what happened next. *Tabari VI:49* **"Khadija sent a message to the Muhammad inviting him to take her...She called her father to her house, plied him with wine until he was drunk, slaughtered a cow, anointed him with perfume, and clothed him in a striped robe; then she sent for Muhammad and his uncles. When they came in, her father married him to her. When he recovered from his intoxication, he said, 'What is this meat, this perfume, and this garment?' She replied, 'You have married me to Muhammad bin Abdallah.' 'I have not done so,' he said. 'Would I do this when the greatest men of Mecca have asked for you and I have not agreed?'"**

While achieving a prophetic marriage through alcoholic inebriation isn't religious, it's the last line that should give us pause. Muslims have contrived scores of pre-Islamic Hadiths to elevate Muhammad's standing among his people. Yet according to Khadija's father, he was a nobody. Further, he was hardly a prize specimen either: *Tabari IX:157* **"The Messenger was neither tall nor short. He had a large head and beard with big black eyes. His palms and feet were calloused; he had large joints, his face was white with a reddish tinge, his chest hair was long, and when** he walked, he bent forward as if he were descending a slope."

The next ten years passed without a single word from Tabari. While Muslims claim to know what the monk said in Syria, they haven't a clue what happened in Mecca. Ishaq has but one line: *Ishaq:83* "**Khadija was the mother of all of the Apostle's children except Ibrahim [who was born to one of Muhammad's sex slaves], namely al-Qasim, al-Tayyib, and al-Tahir. They all died in paganism.**" The implication here is that the prophet's boys are all roasting in hell.

The story of the greatest con ever sold resumes with this: *Tabari VI:50* "**We have mentioned the conflicting reports about the Prophet's marriage to Khadija. Ten years later, the Quraysh demolished the Ka'aba and then rebuilt it. According to Ibn Ishaq, this was in the Messenger's thirty-fifth year. The reason for demolition of the Ka'aba was that it consisted of loose stones rising to somewhat above a man's height, and they wished to make it higher and put a roof over it, since some men had stolen treasures kept in its interior.**"

All along I have told you that the Ka'aba was little more than a rock pile. This Islamic Hadith confirms the ignobility of Allah's "House." And this is important. There is no chance that a roofless six-foot high collection of loose rocks could have survived the rigors of two millennia of flash floods and searing sandstorms. Not only is there no written or oral legacy connecting Muhammad, Mecca, and the Ka'aba with Abraham, there is no physical evidence either. The center of the Islamic faith, Allah's House, on which the whole Islamic world bows and turns, was a rock pile for rock gods.

Tabari, who reported Hadith claiming Allah had raised the Ka'aba above the floodwaters, now says: "**The Ka'aba had been destroyed when the people of Noah were drowned, and Allah commanded Abraham and Ishmael to rebuild it on its original foundations. This they did as stated in the Qur'an 2:127. 'When Abraham and Ishmael were raising the foundations of the House [they said], "Lord! Accept [this] from us."'**" Not only is the Qur'anic dialog gibberish, as usual, and the circumstances preposterous, it's idiotic following the assertion that Allah's House was a pile of loose stones. Muslims had no concept of time. The twenty-six hundred year chasm and thousand-mile divide that separate Abraham from Muhammad's Ka'aba cannot be crossed.

Tabari VI:52 "**The Ka'aba had not had any custodians since its destruction in the time of Noah. Then Allah commanded Abraham to settle his son by the Ka'aba, wishing thereby to show a mark of esteem to one whom he later ennobled by means of his Prophet Muhammad.**" Now we are being told that Allah esteemed the 20th century B.C. Ishmael by way of the 7th century A.D. Muhammad. "**Abraham and his son Ishmael were custodians of the Ka'aba after the time of Noah. At the time, Mecca was uninhabited....**" Since even the Islamic Hadiths aren't bold enough to move Abraham from Canaan to Mecca, how was he the custodian? And if the place was uninhabited from 2000 B.C. to 500 A.D., why pile rocks in Mecca? It can't be the center of worship if no one was there to worship. So what's the point?

Tabari tells us that the Jurhum became the custodians of the Ka'aba. He simply skipped over the intervening 2,500 years between its alleged founding and the Jurhum presence. If you recall, the Jurhum clan ousted the Khuza'a tribe from their campsites around Mecca around 500 A.D. According to the Tradition, they acted badly, **"misappropriated the wealth which had been presented to the Ka'aba and oppressed those who came to Mecca. Their behavior became so unrestrained that when one of them could not find a place in which to fornicate he would go into the Ka'aba and do it there. It is asserted that Isaf fornicated with Na'ilah in the interior of the Ka'aba and that they were transformed into two stones. During the Jahiliyyah [period of pre-Islamic Ignorance] any person who acted wrongfully or oppressively in Mecca, perished on the spot."** This fanciful pagan milieu formed the basis of Islam. **"Allah sent a bleeding of the nose and a plague of ants against the Jurhum and destroyed them, while Khuza'a expelled those who survived...Amir felt that he would be defeated, so he brought out the two gazelles of the Ka'aba and the sacred Black Stone."**

The irreverent blend of Jewish history and Arab mythology continues: *Tabari VI:55* **"The Ka'aba was taken over by the Khuza'a except three functions which were in the hands of the Mudar. The first of these was the ijazah, the giving of permission to the pilgrims to leave Arafat...The second function was the ifadah, the permission for the pilgrims to disperse to Mina on the morning of the sacrifice."** Two more Islamic rituals associated with the hajj now have links to an ignoble pagan past. *Ishaq:88* **"This state of affairs lasted until Allah sent Muhammad and revealed to him and gave him the laws of his religion and the customs of the pilgrimage."** Following a hundred Hadith desperately trying to ascribe the rites and rituals of Islam to the Jewish patriarchs, and a hundred more proclaiming that they were derived from the pagan practices of Qusayy, one line contradicts them all.

There was however, a pre-Islamic pagan custom Muhammad disregarded. And wouldn't you know it, it was the one he should have retained. **"The third function was the nasi, the delaying or postponement of the sacred month by intercalation. When Islam came, the sacred months had returned to their original times, and Allah established them firmly and abolished the nasi."** Pre-Islamic Arabs, unlike civilized people around them, had yet to switch away from the lunar calendar. But to their credit, they were at least observing intercalation to keep their seasons intact. Muhammad abandoned intercalation, condemning Muslims to a 354-day year. Not only didn't the pagan sacred months return to their original times, he assured that they would never be established, forever floating around the solar year. While foolish, the lunacy honored his god's lunar legacy.

One of the most revered Islamic legends comes from this period. A series of Hadiths focused on **"Rebuilding of the Ka'aba"** begin with this report: *Tabari VI:56* **"A relative of Abd Mahaf [Slave-to-the-Sun-God] had stolen treasure from the Ka'aba. They took him to a female Arab soothsayer, who, using her occult skill, pronounced in rhyming prose that he should not enter Mecca for ten years because of his violation of the sanctity of the Ka'aba."** This Islamic Tradition confirms what I shared earlier. Soothsayers are Satanic; they are occult mediums. Further, she recited in the same style of the Qur'an—rhyming prose. And more incriminating still, a Devil worshiper is being used to proclaim the sanctity of the Ka'aba.

The reason this story is included in the presentation of rebuilding Allah's House is that the shrine's low walls and open top made it easy for looters to steal the gods. So when the Meccans found that: *Ishaq:84* **"A ship belonging to a Greek merchant had been driven ashore by rough seas at Jeddah and had been broken to pieces, they took its timbers and prepared them for use in roofing the Ka'aba. There was a Copt in Mecca who was a carpenter, and thus they had both the materials and a craftsman ready at hand."** This serves to confirm the primitive nature of the Ka'aba and of Mecca itself. There was no source of wood, and without wood, there were no carpenters. Without wood and men to work it, all buildings were open to the harsh elements. Mecca in the time of Muhammad was a motley collection of open mud huts. This is important because Islam is said to have arisen because the Meccans were flaunting their wealth. That simply wasn't possible.

The next transition is as disjointed as the Qur'an, and equally revealing. **"There was a snake which used to come out of the well in the Ka'aba into which votive objects were thrown. It would lie on top of the Ka'aba wall every day to sun itself. It was a terror."** There are way too many Satanic symbols associated with Muhammad and Allah. Abraham was drawn from Israel to Mecca by god's presence in the form of a snake. The same snake coiled himself up, showing Abraham where to build the Ka'aba. Now a snake is living inside Allah's House. The snake and the apple sign on Muhammad's back, are Satan's most enduring symbols.

Ishaq:84 **"People were terrified of the snake because whenever anyone went near, it would draw itself up, make a rustling noise, and open its mouth. One day, as it was lying on top of the Ka'aba as usual, Allah sent a bird which seized it and carried it off. [And who said Allah couldn't do miracles.] On seeing this the Quraysh said, 'We may hope that Allah is pleased with what we intend to do. We have craftsman and we have timber, while Allah dealt with the snake.'"** *Tabari VI:56* **"This was fifteen years after the Sacrilegious War. Muhammad was thirty-five. When they made the decision to demolish and rebuild the Ka'aba, Abu took a stone from it which leapt from his hand and returned to its place."**

This Hadith, in context of Muhammad's imminent involvement in the Ka'aba's reconstruction and it's Black Stone, strongly suggests that the Meccans thought the Black Stone was Allah and that he/it actually lived in the Ka'aba. *Ishaq:85* **"The people were afraid to demolish the temple and withdrew in terror from it. Al-Walid said, 'I will begin the demolition.' He took up his pickaxe and walked up to the House saying, 'O Ka'aba, do not be afraid. O Allah we intend nothing but good.' Then he demolished part of it near the two corners."** One of Muhammad's religious contemporaries is telling a rock pile not to be afraid. Approaching Allah with a pickaxe, he says that he means him no harm. How is a pickaxe threatening to God? And, if he were God, and you approached his "House" with a pick, a carpenter, and some wood, don't you think he might figure it out?

In this final Tradition prior to the first Qur'anic revelation, Muhammad is shown personally participating in the superstitions of his peoples' stone-worshiping milieu. *Tabari VI:58* **"A man of the Quraysh who was among those demolishing it thrust a crowbar between two stones to pry one of them up. When the stone moved, the whole of Mecca shook. They knew they had reached the foundations. The clans then gathered stones to rebuild the Ka'aba. Each clan gathered separately and built separately. When they reached the place where the Black Stone was to be put they began to dispute about it, since every clan wished to lift the Stone to its place."**

Once again we are confronted with a stark reality. Allah's House, the center of Islam, was a rock pile and it was rebuilt in like fashion. The stones were not hewn, cut, or mortared. There was no plan. They were just collected and piled. And once more we are forced to see the sacred Black Stone for what it was—Allah.

This next tidbit is particularly incriminating. *Ishaq:85* **"The Quraysh found in the corner a writing in Syriac. They could not understand it until a Jew read it for them. It read: 'I am Allah the Lord of Mecca. I created it on the day that I created heaven and earth and formed the sun and moon.'"** God writing in Syriac, not Arabic, conflicts with the Qur'an's claim that Arabic was Allah's language. Further, since written Arabic *evolved from* Syriac and migrated to Mecca, it's clear that the written language of the Qur'an was unknown to the Meccans at the time Muhammad claims the surahs were revealed to him. Oops!

"The Quraysh remained in this state for five days, and then they gathered in the mosque to consult together and to reach an equitable agreement." We are reminded that mosques preceded Islam and that prostration, the Islamic prayer position from which the word was derived, was part of idolatrous worship. It is apparent that relatively little of Islam was invented by Muhammad.

The payoff line of this Hadith is upon us. *Tabari VI:59* **"Men of the Quraysh said, 'Make the first man who comes in at the door of this mosque the arbiter of our difference so that he may judge on the matter.' The first man was Muhammad, and when they saw him they said, 'This is the trustworthy one with whom we are satisfied. This is Muhammad.' He came up to them and they told him about the matter and he said, 'Bring me a cloak.' They brought him one, and he took the Black Stone and placed it on it with his own hands. Then he said, 'Let each clan take one side of the cloak, and then lift it up all together.' They did so, and when they had brought it to its place he put it in position with his own hands."**

I do not know if Muhammad actually suggested this solution. But I know that a man who reveres a stone is no wiser than the rock he reveres.

7

WITH WHOM AM I SPEAKING?

"I am afraid that something bad has happened to me."

The Qur'an starts off no better than Muhammad himself. The prophet's first revelation is a fiasco. But so as not to prejudice the historic beginnings of Islam, I shall let the first Muslims do it for me.

Let's begin with what Allah has to say in his inaugural Qur'an address. This treasure isn't the first surah. It isn't even inscribed in the first fifty. It's buried near the end of the book. *096.001* **"Read in the name of your Lord who created man out of clots of congealed blood. Read, for your Lord is the most generous. He who taught the use of the pen that man might be taught that which he did not know."** That's the whole shebang. The moment of moments: the birth of Islam. An unnamed spirit, representing an unidentified entity, reveals himself to Muhammad, and all we get is this.

Why would an all-knowing deity ask an illiterate man to read? Why does the spirit tell us that man was created from blood clots? Why gloat, saying he's generous—in what way and to whom? But the real question is: if this spirit **"taught by the pen what men did not know,"** where are those words?

It's not a very auspicious beginning for a religion capable of ensnaring a billion souls. There must be a cogent explanation. Yet the Qur'an makes no attempt to explain the nature of the meeting or the meaning of the message.

There are but a handful of "credible" accounts of what happened that night. Let's turn to al-Bukhari first. In his *Book of Revelation* we find a Hadith narrated by Aisha, Muhammad's child wife. She was the daughter of Abu Bakr, the man who became the first Caliph. She had yet to be conceived when this event occurred. *Bukhari:V1B1N3-V6B60N478* **"The commencement of divine inspiration to Allah's Messenger was in the form of dreams that came true like a bright light. The Prophet loved the seclusion of a cave in Hira. The angel came to him and asked him to read. The Prophet replied, 'I do not know how to read.' The Prophet added, 'Then the angel caught me forcefully and pressed me so hard that I could not bear it any more. He released me and asked me to read. I replied, "I do not know how to read." Thereupon he caught me again and pressed me till I could not bear it any more. He asked me to read but I replied,**

"I do not know how to read or what shall I read?" Thereupon he caught me for the third time and pressed me, "Read in the name of your Lord who has created man from a clot. Read! Your Lord is the most generous." Then the Apostle returned from that experience; the muscles between his neck and shoulders were trembling, and his heart beating severely. He went to Khadija and cried, 'Cover me! Cover me!' She did until his fear subsided. He said, 'What's wrong with me? I am afraid that something bad has happened to me.' Khadija replied, 'Never! By Allah, Allah will never disgrace you....'"

Allah's name wasn't mentioned in the first Qur'an surah. In fact, Muhammad's god remained an unnamed "Lord" throughout the first seventeen Qur'an revelations. When the Lord was finally identified, his name was Ar-Rahman. It's curious then that this crucial Islamic Hadith elected to contradict the Qur'an and call god Allah. Equally curious, why did Muhammad's wife, the pagan Khadija, swear by Allah when the god who bore that name was one of many rock idols? The answers are simple, different, and revealing. Aisha, the source of this Hadith, didn't reveal it until after the prophet's death—long after Ar-Rahman's name had been incorporated into Allah's character. As for Khadija, Allah held the keys to something she and her husband coveted.

The accounts of what happened this night are consistently inconsistent. And while that's bad as it relates to creation and patriarchs, those were events from another time, another people, another place, and another religion. Now Muslims are without excuse. Islam began in their midst, on their watch, and through their clan. We aren't dealing with events that occurred two to four thousand years B.C. This is 610 A.D. Contradiction is now condemning, for it forces us to recognize that all Islamic scripture was preserved in like fashion —through oral transmission. If these recollections aren't reliable, nothing is.

The second version of the first revelation is found in Tabari and Muslim: *Tabari VI:67* "Aisha reported: 'Solitude became dear to Muhammad and he used to seclude himself in the cave of Hira where he would engage in the Tahannuth [pagan religious rites performed in Ramadhan that included fasting] worship for a number of nights before returning to Khadija and getting provisions for a like period, till truth came upon him while he was in a cave. The first form of revelation was a true vision in sleep. He did not see any vision but it came like the break of dawn.'" *Muslim C74B1N301* "The truth came unexpectedly and said: 'Recite,' to which he replied: 'I am not lettered.' The Apostle said, 'He took hold of me, and pressed me, till I was hard pressed. He let me off and said: "Recite." I said: "I am not lettered."'" It continues on as before until the Tabari Hadith picks up the nightmare with this line: *Tabari VI:67* "Muhammad, you are the Messenger." What follows is convoluted, out of order, and conflicting. "The Prophet said, 'I had been standing, but fell to my knees; and crawled away, my shoulders trembling. I went to Khadija and said, "Wrap me up!" When the terror had left me, he came to me and said, "Muhammad, you are the Messenger of Allah."' Muhammad said, 'I had been thinking of hurling myself down from a mountain crag, but he appeared to me as I was thinking about this and said, "I am Gabriel and you are the Messenger." Then he said, "Recite!" I said,

"What shall I recite?" He took me and pressed me three times. I told Khadija, "I fear for my life." She said, "Rejoice, for Allah will never put you to shame."'"

While there are significant differences between these versions, and insights worth examining, I want to focus on the most incriminating details. In the first version an unnamed angel nearly pressed the life out of Muhammad. In the second, Gabriel is said to have kept Muhammad from jumping to his death. In the third, Gabriel is named again but he does not appear until after Muhammad is comforted in Khadija's bed. Yet the Qur'an says nothing of Gabriel during the first twelve years of Muhammad's mission. We are not introduced until the first surah in Yathrib, which was the 91st chronologically. Since Muhammad alleges that Gabriel was the source of his godly revelation, these inconsistencies devastate his credibility.

That said, I'd like to share the most "esteemed" version of Islam's initial revelation. It's a bit more colorful and comes courtesy of Ishaq's biography, compiled a hundred years before the other sources. *Ishaq:105* **"Aisha said that when Allah desired to honor Muhammad, the first sign of prophethood was a vision in brightness of day shown to him in his sleep. [In other words, he was dreaming.] He liked nothing better than to be alone. When he left Mecca and there was no house in sight, every stone and tree that passed by said, 'Peace be unto you, Allah's Apostle.' Muhammad would turn around and see naught but trees and stones. [In other words, he was stoned.] He stayed seeing and hearing things as long as it pleased Allah. Then Gabriel came to him with the gift of Allah's grace [the spiritual beating] while he was on Hira in the month of Ramadhan. The Apostle would pray in seclusion on Hira every year for a month to practice Tahannuth as was the custom of the Quraysh in the heathen days. [In other words, Muhammad was a heathen and the Islamic Pillar requiring Ramadhan fasting was pagan.] Tahannuth is religious devotion [to pagan idols]. After praying in seclusion, he would walk around the Ka'aba seven times. [The centerpiece of the Hajj Pillar is pagan as well.]"**

Ishaq:106 **"The Prophet set off to Hira with his family. When it was night, Gabriel brought him the command of Allah. 'He came to me,' the Apostle said, 'while I was asleep, with a coverlet of brocade whereon was some writing, and said, 'Read.' I said, 'What shall I read?' He pressed me so tightly that I was near death. Then he let go and said, 'Read!'"** This happens twice more, then… **"When I thought I was nearly dead I said, 'What shall I read; only to deliver myself from him, lest he should do the same thing to me again. He said, 'Read in the name of your Lord who created man of blood coagulated. Read! Your generous Lord taught by the pen.'"** Then the illiterate man said, **"So I read it, and he departed from me. I awoke from my sleep. These words were written on my heart."**

Ishaq reports: **"None of Allah's creatures was more hateful to me than an ecstatic poet or a man possessed. I thought, 'Woe is me, I'm a possessed poet.'"** The worst thing that can befall a man or woman is to be possessed by the devil. He or she loses all sense of decency. To his credit, Muhammad recognized what had happened. To his shame, he damned three billion souls along with his own.

Ishaq:106 **"I will go to the top of the mountain and throw myself down that I may kill** myself and be at rest." There was no doubt in his mind. During the violent encounter with the spirit in the darkness of that cave, Muhammad had been possessed by the Devil. He wanted to commit suicide—something that Satan could not allow. He had big plans for his prophet. *Ishaq:106* **"So I climbed to the mountain to kill myself when I heard a voice saying, 'Muhammad, you are Allah's Apostle.' I raised my head to see who was speaking and lo, I saw Gabriel in the form of a man with feet astride the horizon."** And how, pray tell, would our terrified and possessed poet know Gabriel from Lucifer? Here's a clue: *Bukhari:V9B87N113* **"The Prophet said, 'A good dream is from Allah, and a bad dream is from Satan.'"** Judging by his own account, this was a very bad dream.

Ishaq:106 **"I stood gazing at him and that distracted me from committing suicide. I couldn't move. Khadija sent her messengers in search of me and they gained the high ground above Mecca so I came to her and sat by her thigh. She said, 'O Abu'l-Qasim, where have you been?' I said, 'Woe is me. I am possessed.' She said, 'I take refuge in Allah from that Abu'l-Qasim. Allah would not treat you that way. This cannot be, my dear. Perhaps you did see something,'"** Khadija said, wheels of commerce turning in her head. **"'Yes, I did,' I said,"** playing along. **"I told her of what I had seen [while I was asleep]. She said, 'Rejoice, son of my uncle, and be of good cheer. Verily, by Him in whose hand is Khadija's soul, I have hope that you will be the prophet to this people.'"** With that, the Profitable Prophet Plan was born. **"She gathered her garments and went to her cousin Waraqa bin Naufal [the Hanif], who had become a Christian. He read the scriptures and learned from those who followed the Torah and the Gospels."**

Tabari provides some additional insights: *Tabari VI:70* **"He went to Khadija and said, 'I think that I have gone mad.' 'No, by Allah,' she said. 'Your Lord would never do that to you. You have never committed a wicked act.' Khadija went to Waraqa and told him what had happened. He said, 'If what you have said is true, your husband is a prophet.... After this Gabriel did not come to him for a while and Khadija said, 'I think that your Lord must hate you.'"** This is followed by yet one more variant: *Tabari VI:70* **"In the beginning of the Messenger's prophetic mission he used to spend a month every year in religious retreat on Hira. This was part of the practice of Tahannuth in which the Quraysh used to engage during the Jahiliyyah. Tahannuth means self-justification.'"** That's intriguing. Muhammad practiced a *Jahiliyyah* ritual rite, an ignorant pre-Islamic form of pagan worship. What's more, the very definition of *Tahannuth*—self justification—became synonymous with the prophet's personal agenda.

So much for Muhammad's claim of having being prevented from doing any pagan act by Allah. Islam began in the midst of a pagan ritual.

The deeper we dig into Islam's initial salvo, the worse it gets. So hold your nose if you must, because it's time to poke around. We know that Muhammad was a recluse—a wannabe prophet who preferred solitude to people. The fact he spent so much time alone in caves instead of at home being a parent and husband or at work being productive is troubling. Yes, he was being religious, but even that is problematic. As an idolater, he practiced the heathen *Tahannuth* rituals—fasting, self-justification, and meditation—during the pagan *holy month* of Ramadhan. He disappeared into caves for spiritual awakening, calling out to a Black Stone named Allah. And he was ultimately possessed.

The "read" versus "recite" debate is interesting in itself. Modern Muslims, in trying to solve the obvious problem of why an all-knowing spirit would ask an illiterate man to read, say that the word really means recite. But that's worse. Why would Muhammad say he didn't know how to recite, especially when that was what he was best at? And why would the spirit of Islam ask a man to recite if he taught by the pen? Even the word "recite-read" is prickly. The original word is *qara*, from which Qur'an was derived. It was first used by the Syrian Christians to mean preach, not read. Even the Arabic words *ma aqrau* can mean either "I can't read," or "what shall I read." But that's still a problem because Muhammad wasn't given a scroll to read.

Since we have discussed Allah's ignominious inaugural address, let's move on to the Prophet's less than heroic response. According to every account, he was scared spitless. Imagine that: you've just invested the month of Ramadhan hanging around in a cave for the express purpose of communing with the spirit world and one comes and scares you to death. In the earliest versions he is said to have been so distraught he wanted to commit suicide. The whole encounter not only sounds demonic, the wannabe prophet said he was possessed.

The revelation over, the newly minted messenger slid down the barren slopes west of Mecca, scurried across two miles of desert dunes, and entered the narrow valley town, where he immediately cuddled up to mama (and make no mistake, his wife was the closest thing to a mother he'd ever known). Panicked and tormented, the forty-year-old Muhammad cried out to his sixty-year-old wife, **"Cover me,"** crawling into a fetal position against her thigh. He thought he'd been molested by a jinn, possessed by a demonic spirit, in the dark of night. He said, **"I do not know what has happened to me. I fear for myself."** **"He poured out his mental confusion,"** and according to Ibn Ishaq, said, **"I'm afraid I'm going out of my mind and being possessed by an evil spirit."** Score another point for those who say that Islam is Satanic.

In my opinion, what Khadija did next set the forces in motion that ultimately condemned three billion souls, enslaved over a billion women, and plunged the world into chaos. She founded Islam. Yes, Khadija was the founder of Islam. Muhammad was *her* first convert. In a twist of sadistic irony, the most liberated and prosperous woman in Islamic literature built the cage in which all Muslim women are trapped.

Calming her husband and employee down she said, **"Rejoice, cousin, and be of good cheer. You will be the Prophet. Allah will not bring you to shame...."** Wow! Muhammad thinks he's just gone mano-a-mano in a wrestling match with a demon and Khadija says it isn't so. **"It can't be. Be happy. I swear by Allah that He shall never humiliate you."** **"I hope that you may be the prophet of this community."**

Allah was just one of 360 stones gathering dust in the Ka'aba. Together with Hubal, Manaf, and the gang, they were the mustard on Mecca's hotdog. No Ka'aba, no hajj. No hajj, no festival. No festival, no money. Khadija was a businesswoman—in business to make money selling her wares to the pilgrims who piled into Mecca each year to visit their gods. She wasn't going to let anything foul that up. Not only did she tell her employee/husband that he was wrong, that it was *not* a demon, she said that her god, the pagan lunar deity, the biggest and blackest stone in the Ka'aba, would never allow him to be molested by an angry spirit—no way! Then, in anticipation of what was to come, she began her public relations campaign. She told her recluse husband that he was a swell guy, charitable, sociable, and trustworthy. He was the perfect candidate to be the Social Chairman of a Fraternity.

Bright and successful, Khadija was on a mission. She came up with a profitable prophet plan. She had prospered in a man's world, but had no real power. In fact, she was embarrassed. Having been widowed twice, she had proposed marriage to Muhammad, an employee half her age. It was scandalous.

To gain permission, she had had to get the patriarch of her family drunk at the betrothal feast. Once he was successfully intoxicated, Khadija was able to coerce the consent she required. The odd couple was married, but all was not a bed of cactus flowers. Their sons died in infancy. It was a terrible stain in a culture that, like Islam, attributed misfortune to godly disdain. Khadija's husband was an absentee parent to their remaining daughters, and AWOL when it came to working in the family business. He was an illiterate recluse with a penchant for lone vigils in barren, dusty, lightless caves, which in a small town of perhaps 5,000, was gossip fodder. He was hardly making her look good. You just *know* that the girls were talking behind her back.

So to turn the tables on them, Khadija tells her husband that he's the prophet of his people—Allah's guy. As "God's Messenger" he's important, and so is she. The lucrative custodianship of the Ka'aba, the even more lucrative administration of the hajj, the religious tax, was Muhammad's birthright, she implied, but fate had dealt him a savage blow. Now, Khadija knew, opportunity was knocking. She and he could have it all, everything they coveted—prestige, money, power. All they had to do was convince the Meccans that Muhammad was Allah's Messenger. Since Allah was just a rock, no one would ever be able to dispute their claim. What was Allah going to do—roll over, crumble, actually *speak?* **"No way. It can't be. Be happy. I swear by Allah that He shall never humiliate you."** Khadija even tells her hubby that he's prefect for the job: truthful, generous with her money, and for a loner, he's caring and entertaining. But it must not have been enough. Prophet Man just laid there quivering.

What little we have heard thus far makes no sense when attributed to a divine revelation. However, it makes perfect sense when we view the Qur'an in the context of a self-aggrandizement scheme—the self-justification of the *Tahannuth*. If I'm right and Khadija was trying to proselytize Muhammad, recruit him into her Profitable Prophet Plan, what do you suppose she'd do next? Get someone "religious" to validate her claim, perhaps? Yes indeed. Let's return to the Hadith. *Bukhari:V1B1N3* **"Khadija then took Muhammad to Waraqa bin Naufal. He was the son of Khadija's uncle [and the brother of a sorceress]. He was the only man in town who had embraced Christianity in the pre-Islamic Days of Ignorance. He used to write the writing with Hebrew letters. He would write from the Gospel in Hebrew as much as Allah wished him to write. He was very old and had lost his eyesight.**

"Khadija told Waraqa, 'Listen to the story of your nephew, my cousin!' Waraqa asked, 'Nephew, what have you seen?' Muhammad described whatever he had seen. Waraqa said, 'This is the same one who keeps the secrets whom Allah had sent to Moses. I wish I were young and could live up to the time when your people would expel you!' Muhammad asked, 'Will they drive me out?' Waraqa replied, 'Yes, anyone who came with something similar to what you have brought was treated with hostility.' A few days later, Waraqa died and the divine inspiration was paused for a long while."

Ishaq tells us that Khadija went alone to Waraqa. *Ishaq:107* **"When she related to him what Muhammad told her he had seen and heard, Waraqa cried, 'Holy! Holy! If you have spoken the truth, Khadija [And what are the chances of that?], there has come unto him the Namus, the spirit who appeared long ago to Moses. Tell Muhammad to be of good cheer, for he is to be the Prophet of his people.' So Khadija returned to her husband and told him what Waraqa had said. As a result, his fears were somewhat calmed."**

Tabari's account is presented in Muhammad's voice: *Tabari VI:68* **"Then she took me to Waraqa and said, 'Listen to your brother's son.' He questioned me and I told him what had happened. He said, 'This is the Namus [from the Greek word "law"] which was sent down to Moses, son of Abraham....'"** The dialog repeats that found in Bukhari until this line, spoken by Muhammad: **"The first parts of the Qur'an to be revealed to me after Iqra were: 'By the pen and that which they write. You are not a madman. Yours will be a reward unfailing, and you are of a great nature. You shall see and they shall see."** Muhammad's quotation is an incomplete variant of the 68th surah. But the Islamic scholars who have reordered the Qur'an chronologically believe that the 68th was the *fortieth* surah handed down, not the second. Montgomery Watt, the translator of this volume, agrees, saying, "The 68th surah was unlikely to be early, since it implies that Muhammad had been charged with being a madman possessed by jinn." This error by Muhammad at the very outset of his Qur'anic career is horrendous. It means that even *he* couldn't remember when his "revelations" were given to him.

That aside, I have a bone to pick with Waraqa. Moses met directly with Yahweh, not some cave-loving rascally spirit named Namus. Moses asked, "Whom should I tell the Israelites is sending me?" My Bible says that God

answered him directly and said, "Yahweh," which means "I Am." In fact, the
Bible never mentions Allah, a word that means "oak tree" in Hebrew. And
Yahweh's name is repeated 6,868 times—something that would be hard to
miss if old Waraqa actually knew Hebrew. But what did Waraqa know about
this? It's irrational to think someone would translate the Gospels (which were
written in Greek) into Hebrew, a dead language at the time. Aramaic maybe.
Or Arabic, if it existed in written form in Mecca, but not Hebrew. Besides,
Moses is chronicled in the Torah, not the Gospels—so it was the wrong book.

And Waraqa was the wrong guy to be translating the written word; he was
blind. But blind or not, the old man, a mere seventy-two hours from death,
served Khadija's purpose. She used him to convince her fellow Meccans that
Allah had a messenger. Her man was the next Moses, a prophet to her people.
So how does a new religion spring to life on such shaky ground? If the facts
are so obviously fallacious, how could the revelation be truthful?

What I'm going to say next will appear scandalous at first blush. I believe
Muhammad murdered Waraqa. The Hanif was the most revered holy man in
Mecca. After Khadija had used him, he became a liability—someone who
could and would profess that Muhammad's claims were untrue. When you
finish *Prophet of Doom* and discover how many men Muhammad assassinated
for the same reason, I believe you'll share my view.

Next we learn that even Khadija was troubled by Muhammad's dark
adventure into the spirit world. *Tabari VI:73/Ishaq:107* "'Cousin, can you tell me when this
visitor comes to you?' Muhammad replied, 'Yes.' She said, 'Tell me then, when he comes.'
Gabriel came to him as before, and Muhammad said, 'Here is Gabriel who has just come
to me.' She said, 'Yes? Come, cousin, and sit by my left thigh.' He came, and she said,
'Can you see him?' 'Yes.' 'Move around and sit by my right thigh.' He did so and she said,
'Can you see him?' 'Yes.' She said, 'Sit in my lap.' He did so, and she said, 'Can you see
him?' He replied, 'Yes.' She was grieved, and flung off her veil and disclosed her body
while the Apostle was sitting in her lap." Alternate one says, "Khadija put the Messenger inside her shift next to her body." Alternate two proclaims: "I heard that she made
the Apostle come inside her shift." Both end with: "Then she said, 'Can you see him?'
'No.' At that she said, 'Rejoice cousin. By Allah, this spirit is an angel and not Satan.'"

The implication is that the mystery spirit was an angel, not a devil, because
he was too modest to look upon an old woman's body. But angels don't lust,
and pre-Islamic women didn't wear veils. Yet in fairness, Khadija was a sixty-
year-old desert dweller—a peek under her shift might have frightened the Devil.

Khadija wasn't the only one who couldn't see Muhammad's shy spirit.
Bukhari:V4B54N440 "The Prophet said, 'Aisha, this is Gabriel. He sends his greetings and salu-
tations to you.' Aisha replied, 'Salutations and greetings to him.' Then addressing the
Prophet she said, 'You see what I don't see.'" And he would have been hard to miss.
Bukhari:V4B54N455 "The Prophet informed us that he had seen Gabriel and he had 600 wings."

The identity of Muhammad's dark spirit aside, there was another nagging problem—radio silence. There were no visions, dreams, demonic encounters, or wrestling matches—nothing for nearly three long years. The menacing cave critter was nowhere to be found. Every day Muhammad went to visit the spirit at the Ka'aba but the mighty Allah couldn't even muster a simple "howdy," or "read," or whatever rocks are inclined to say when their pen pals stop by for a visit. It was embarrassing. He was a messenger without a message. Anguished, Muhammad contemplated suicide a second time. So what do you think happened next? Right you are: ProphetVision.

Muslim:C74B1N304/Bukhari:V4B54N461 **"While talking about the period of pause in revelation, the Prophet said, 'While I was walking, all of a sudden I heard a voice. I looked and saw the angel who had visited me at the cave sitting on a chair in the sky. I got scared of him and ran back home and said, "Wrap me in blankets, Khadija." And then Allah revealed the Verses of the Qur'an to me. 'O Muhammad, the shrouded one, wrapped up in garments, arise and warn the people against the Lord's Punishment, and abandon the idols.' [This candidate for revelation number two is a divergent recital of Qur'an 74:1.] After this the revelation started coming strongly, frequently, and regularly."**

But the second revelation is found in the 93rd surah, not the 74th. That surah speaks specifically to the two-to-three-year hiatus in divine inspiration. How are we supposed to believe anything Islam's prophet says when he can't keep his own story straight? Further, there are two "enwrapped" surahs, not one, and neither is consistent with Muhammad's recollection. Besides, if Gabriel was sitting on the floating chair, why did Muhammad run home? We're told that he was suicidal because Gabriel was nowhere to be found. He shows up and his messenger bails? No way. And if it really was Gabriel, why do we have to leave Mecca and endure ninety surahs before we're introduced to the alleged source of these recitals?

Then it gets worse. We are asked to believe that Allah, who has been too busy being the top dog of the Ka'aba to chat with our hero, finally tracks the panicked prophet down. He tells a grown man, hiding under the covers, that he wants him to go out and warn people. And why is Allah so angry? Why does he need to punish all the little blood clots? He and his prophet are just getting warmed up. We haven't even been introduced. If this is God speaking, why doesn't Muhammad know his name? Remember, all of the early surahs use the title "Lord." And when the spirit finally gets around to introducing himself, he says that he's Ar-Rahman.

Maybe we've got the story wrong. Let's check out another Hadith to be sure. *Muslim:B1N307/Tabari VI:74* **"I asked Abu Salama what was revealed first from the Qur'an. He said: 'The shrouded one enveloped in the cloak.' But I knew better and said: 'Wasn't it "Recite?"'' Jabir said: 'I am telling to you what the Messenger told me. He said: "I stayed in the cave for one month and when my stay was completed, I came down and went into the valley. Somebody called me. I looked but I did not see anybody. I was again called but saw nothing. I raised my head, and there on the Throne in the atmosphere he was sitting.**

I began to tremble because I was afraid of him.' These were [Caliph] Uthman's words, but the correct version is, 'I was terror-stricken by him. Then I came to Khadija and they threw water on me and Allah sent down this: 'You who are shrouded, arise and deliver a warning, your Lord magnify, your clothes cleanse.'''" At this point all we know for certain is that Muhammad was a pathological liar, he had a poor memory, he was depressed and suicidal, and that he claimed to be demon possessed.

Maududi, one of the most famous Qur'an commentators, explains: "After this first Revelation, no Revelation came down to the Prophet for quite some time. The long suspension was such a period of deep grief and distress for him that he started going early to the tops of the mountains to throw himself down from them. But whenever he stood on the edge of a peak, the Angel Gabriel would appear and tell him that he was Allah's Prophet. This would console him and restore his peace of mind." As the author of the Qur'an's most esteemed commentary, I have elected to place his comments in bold to clearly distinguish orthodox Islamic thought from my own.

The Hadith upon which this embarrassing confession is found proves that Islam's lone prophet was suicidal. *Tabari VI:76* "The inspiration ceased to come to the Messenger for a while, and he was deeply grieved. He began to go to the tops of mountain crags, in order to fling himself from them; but every time he reached the summit of a mountain, Gabriel appeared to him and said to him, 'You are Allah's Prophet.' Thereupon his anxiety would subside and he would come back to himself." Muhammad explains: "I was walking one day when I saw the angel who used to come to me at Hira. I was terror-stricken by him." If he was comforted by Gabriel every time he wanted to commit suicide, why did his image terrify him? Why didn't the spirit impart a message if he met with his messenger on these occasions? And why are none of these encounters mentioned in the Qur'an?

Let's open our Qur'ans to the 73rd surah and see what Islam's spirit had to say. *073.001* "O you who have been wrapped in your garments! Who said, 'Cover me, cover me. I'm afraid of the angel.' Keep watch all night except a little. And recite the Qur'an as it ought to be recited, in slow, measured rhythmic tones. Surely We will soon entrust you with Our weighty Word. Surely the night is the most devout way when the soul is most receptive and the words most telling. During the day you already have a busy schedule, an occupation with ordinary business duties." Muhammad's spirit friend wants him to spend the night reciting the Qur'an. Since eighty words have been revealed thus far, that's a pace of eight words an hour. But that is trivial compared to nocturnal devotion. The Qur'an was revealed in darkness, and night is the best time to ponder its meaning. Satan is the Prince of Darkness, and evil loves the night. We have stumbled upon another clue.

073.008 "But keep in remembrance the name of your Lord and devote yourself to Him whole-heartedly." How can one remember the name of a Lord who has not yet been named? "Lord of the East and West: there is no ilah but He: take Him therefore for (your) Disposer of Affairs. And bear patiently what they say and avoid them with a becoming avoidance." That would make Muhammad the only messenger who was told to avoid his audience. A Hadith says: *Ishaq:115* **"Now Muhammad did not want his secret to be divulged before he applied himself to the publication of his message."** In other words, he needed time to create enough of these rhyming surahs to make his claim seem believable.

073.011 **"Leave Me (alone to deal with) the rejecters, the possessors of ease and plenty. I respite them a little. We have heavy fetters with Us (to bind them), and a roaring furnace (to burn them), and food that chokes, sticking in the throat and a painful torment."** While we haven't been introduced, Muhammad's spirit seems all too familiar. The Bible speaks of the Lord of the fire, of a spirit that chokes the life out of men, binding them to sin. Muhammad's Lord is the spitting image of Satan.

Before we press on, I'd like to bring your attention to the fact that nothing religious has been revealed thus far. The Qur'an is but a paragraph long and its prophet has been told to avoid discussing it. Therefore, *Muhammad* is being rejected, not his message. This rejection preceding "possessors of ease and plenty" tells us that the wannabe prophet is tormented by his relative poverty. Covetous of what belongs to others, his inward anguish turns sadistic. The heavy fetters, roaring furnace, and choking torments are a way of lashing out at those he envies. At this early juncture there is no other plausible explanation. Either Muhammad was deeply disturbed, wanting to torture men without justification, or his deity was unjust and perverted. As such, the **"Enwrapped"** surah unravels Islam's moral authority.

Portions of the 93rd surah were revealed second, chronologically. *Ishaq:155* **"The revelations stopped for some time so that the Apostle was distressed and grieved. Then Gabriel brought him the 'Morning,' in which he swore that he had not forsaken him and did not hate him."** The following insight is from Maududi: **"The surah's theme is to console the Prophet and remove his anxiety, which had been caused by the suspension of revelation. By swearing an oath by the morning and night, he was reassured. Then, he was given the good news that the hardships he was experiencing in the initial stage of his mission would not last long. Soon, Allah would bless him so abundantly that he would be pleased."** This is nonsense. Muhammad hadn't suffered any hardships on account of his mission thus far because there had been no mission. All that had happened was a bout in a cave with an angry spirit, a nonsensical revelation, some panic, Khadija's scheme, a blind man's blessing, and a little boasting around town. But Muslims, needing an excuse for their Prophet's morose and suicidal behavior, were willing to contradict Allah's revelation to give their hero an alibi.

Let's dive into the surah so you'll see what I mean. *093.001* **"I swear by the early hours of the day, and the night when it covers with darkness. Your Lord hath not forsaken thee, nor doth He despisith thee."** Whoa. Time out. Why the King James 17th century English? Do you suppose the words "thy, hath, forsaken, thee," and "doth despisith" are being used in these translations to make the Qur'an seem Biblical? Just speculation on my part, but for readability sake, I'll endeavor from now on to make the "Lord's" words more intelligible.

Let's move on, now that we doth verily know that the Lord doth swearith but hath not forsaken. Although it beith a mystery why he doth despisith thee not and why he lovith the darkness. But here's a clue: Satan is the Morning Star, the Prince of Darkness. *093.004* **"Surely what comes after is better for you than the present or that which has gone before. Soon will your Lord give you so much you shall be well pleased. Did He not find you an orphan and protect you? And find you lost and perplexed and show you the way? Did He not find you poor and made you rich?"** Times can't be so bad that God has to bribe prophets to work for him. He can't really think that the blood-clot revelation was direction. His boy could barely find his way home. And if the Lord had already enriched Muhammad, why is his present so bleak? Or better question, since Muhammad had the childhood from hell, how was he protected? Is God's memory failing? Or is Muhammad's spirit endorsing Khadija's Profitable Profit Plan? "He found you poor and made you rich?"

This is a good place to give you my interpretation of the Gospel according to Khadija: "Stick with me, kid, and I'll make this prophet gig profitable." I can't prove it mind you, but it makes more sense than this coming from God.

Having married money twice and climbed the social ladder of Mecca, Khadija was in trouble. Her fortunes were dwindling while her absentee husband/employee sulked in caves. Having made a fortune selling trinkets to hajj pilgrims at the pagan fairs surrounding the Ka'aba, Khadija knew all about religious scams. So she had motive, means, and opportunity. What's more, her behavior was consistent with my theory.

According to Aisha's testimony in the Hadith, and Ishaq's in the Sira, Khadija was the real founder of Islam. Muhammad believed he had been possessed by a demon. He was scared to death. She converted him to Islam, usurping her nearly dead cousin's credibility. Remember what she said: **"No, never. It can't be. Be happy. I swear by Allah that He shall never humiliate you. Truly, I *hope* you will be the Prophet of this people. Allah will not bring you to shame."**

Let's review the facts. The caravan business Khadija owned owed its prosperity to Allah's recently restored pagan rock shrine. It stood not more than a hundred meters from where this conversation took place. Mecca provided one of the few wells, shallow as it was, for caravans moving goods from the ports of Yemen to Syria. While that was good, no one becomes rich caring for folks passing through town. So the Ka'aba became Mecca's meal ticket. Muhammad's great, great, great grandfather, Qusayy, had gained control over the idol temple and organized an annual pilgrimage to the shrine. He collected a tax from every Arab attendee. While a religious tax was a profitable idea, and one that made its way into Islam, the series of economic fairs Qusayy arranged surrounding the hajj proved to be his most capitalistic venture.

Papa Muttalib, Muhammad's grandfather, the one who sacrificed camels to the Ka'aba's idols at a sorceress's urging, ultimately gained control over the concession to feed and water the pilgrims. He became the recipient of the religious tax, something that made him even richer. As the Ka'aba's custodian, he pocketed big bucks charging Arab chiefs rent for housing their sacred stones. He charged them more for visitation rights, and still more for their gods' care—feeding, watering, and dusting services. The combination served to make the merchants of Mecca rich—by Bedouin standards, anyway.

Khadija was a beneficiary. So she told Muhammad, "Better than being the Ka'aba's custodian; you are Allah's Prophet. And that's more prestigious and profitable than being a recluse, my dear." A Hadith entitled, **"Khadija the First to Believe,"** contained these incriminating lines: **"Muhammad was to tell them of his Lord's bounty to himself: 'Of the bounty of your Lord let your discourse be.'"** This was followed by: **"Thereupon the Messenger began to proclaim Allah's bounty to himself."**

Ishaq's Sira reports: *Ishaq:155* **"Khadija was the first to believe in Allah and His Apostle. By her Allah lightened the burden on His Prophet. He never met with contradiction and charges of falsehood but he was comforted by her when he went home. She strengthened him and belittled the opposition."** Khadija believed in Allah before Muhammad did because Allah was her meal ticket. And while she conceived the prophet idea, she had to endure a great deal just to keep "god's messenger" going. His **"contradictions"** prompted **"charges of falsehood."** We have already discovered these echoing throughout the Hadith. So Khadija **"belittled the opposition."** This made her the inspiration for the Qur'an's overwhelming propensity to condemn Muhammad's opponents, threatening them with doom.

Testimony in support of the Profitable Prophet Plan can be found throughout Tabari's History. *Tabari VI:82* **"During the Jahiliyyah I came to Mecca and stayed with Abbas bin Muttalib. The sun rose while I was looking at the Ka'aba. A young man [Muhammad] came up and gazed at the sky. He turned to face the Ka'aba. Soon after, a woman [Khadija] and a youth [Ali] came and stood behind him. The young man bowed and the woman and youth bowed; then the man stood erect, followed by the woman and youth. The young man prostrated himself, and they did the same. Abbas asked, 'Do you know what this is?' 'No,' I answered. 'This is Khadija, my nephew's wife. He has told me that his Lord has commanded them to do what you see them doing. Allah's oath, I do not know anyone on the face of the earth but these three who follow this religion.' I asked Abbas, 'What is this religion?' He answered, 'This is Muhammad bin Abdallah, who claims that Allah has sent him as His Messenger with this religion and that the treasures of Chusroes and Caesar will be given to him by conquest.'"** This is an incriminating confession. It is an admission of guilt—proof that Islam was created by a wannabe pirate.

I'd like to linger on this Hadith a moment. I'm surprised the Islamic scriptures would confess to the Profitable Prophet Plan so openly. This is the *first* explanation of the motivation behind Muhammad's "religion." And we're told that it was conceived to steal treasure by way of conquest. While this is confirmed countless times in Medina, we are still in Mecca—just three partial surahs into the Qur'an. And Tabari's Hadith does not stand alone. Ishaq reveals a similar Tradition; only his is more direct. *Ishaq:113* **"When I was a merchant I came to Mecca during the hajj pilgrimage. While I was there a man came out to pray and stood facing the Ka'aba. Then a woman and a boy came out and stood praying with him. I asked, 'What is their religion? It is something new to me.' Abbas said, 'This is Muhammad who alleges that Allah has sent him with it so that the treasures of Chusroes and Caesar will be open to him. The woman is his wife Khadija who believes in him.'"** The original motivation for Islam was greed. The Profitable Prophet Plan has been confirmed by the Hadith, Sira, and Qur'an. A false prophet composed situational scriptures for money.

However, the con got off to a rocky start. Muhammad impugned his credibility. Rome had long since been plundered. The last Caesar had been sandals up for centuries. So who was that other guy, you may be wondering, and why would Muhammad covet Chusroes' treasure? I did some digging and found that he was Khosru Parvez, a Persian King and contemporary of Muhammad. In 626 A.D., adjusted for today's dollars, he had stashed away over $2 billion in silver and gold. His annual income exceeded $700 million. Relative to others of his day, he was the richest man alive.

In Bukhari we find another confession of guilt: *Bukhari:V4B52N267* **"The Prophet said, 'Khosrau will be ruined, and there will be no Khosrau after him, and Caesar will surely be ruined and there will be no Caesar after him, and you will spend their treasures in Allah's Cause [Jihad].'"** And, *Bukhari:V4B56N793* **"The Prophet said, 'If you live long enough the treasures of Khosrau will be opened and taken as spoils. You will carry out handfuls of gold and silver.'"** Then, *Bukhari:V4B56N795* **"I have been given the keys of the treasures of the world by Allah."** Money was the motivation behind Islam.

In this light, let's examine the remainder of the second revelation of the Profitable Prophet Plan. *093.009* **"Therefore, treat not the orphan with harshness, or oppress him. Nor repulse the beggar. As for him who asks, do not chide him. But as for the favor your Lord has now bestowed upon you, Muhammad, announce it!"** This also sounds suspicious. Islam's first two religious covenants are specific to Muhammad. He was an orphan, treated with harshness. He was oppressed, probably molested, as we shall learn later, and had to beg. He was chided as a child and as a man. These things haunted him. It was why he had his god tell those who treated him poorly that it wasn't nice. But he would get even because his dark spirit was going to make *him* rich and *them* poor. Then in a less-than-godly blunder, Muhammad's Lord tells his prophet to announce their business relationship before introducing himself or telling us anything about his nature or purpose. He even contradicted himself. The 73rd surah told Muhammad to avoid such announcements.

If you think I may be a little too cynical here, just wait. Each of the next twenty surahs serve to confirm my theory, one already rife with confessions.

Before we go to the "Lord's" fourth Qur'anic gift to Muhammad, let's look at how the Prophet said these insights came to him. Once again, Aisha, the fifty-year-old Prophet's six-year-old wife, is the source of Islamic enlightenment. She said, *Bukhari:V1B1N2* **"'Allah's Messenger! How is the Divine Inspiration revealed to you?' He replied, 'Sometimes it is like the ringing of a bell. This form of Inspiration is the hardest of all and then this state passes off after I have grasped what is inspired. Sometimes the angel comes in the form of a man and talks to me and I grasp whatever he says.' Aisha added: 'I saw the Prophet being inspired and (noticed) the sweat dropping from his forehead on a very cold day as the Inspiration was over.'"**

Since the Hadith claims Muhammad only saw Gabriel on two occasions, how did he come upon the remaining 112 surahs? *Bukhari:V6B60N378* **"Whoever tells you that Muhammad saw his Lord is a liar...and the Prophet only saw Gabriel twice."**

In Islam's creation account, we were told that Allah had given up on oral communication and wanted everything in writing with angelic witnesses. Now he turns to an illiterate man and communicates by means of a gong. The god of a billion people ought to be more capable than clanging bells, blood clots, and having to bribe a despondent messenger. Yet that's all we've got thus far. Perhaps things will turn around with the next series of revelations.

Unfortunately, no one seems to know what came next. Muslims don't even know how the surahs were pieced together. Early and late revelations are jumbled haphazardly. So the best we can do is to attribute a collection of surahs to the formative period. The 96th surah is a great example. The first third represents the first verses revealed. The remainder was "received" years later when the prophet began to prostrate himself at the Ka'aba. We're told that Abu Jahl, Muhammad's archrival and nemesis, taunted him. Maududi reports: **"After his appointment to Prophethood, and before he started preaching Islam, Muhammad began performing the prostration prayer facing Allah's House the way Allah taught him."** Surprisingly, this performance was never described in the Qur'an. Its absence is perplexing. Allah took time to give Muhammad permission to partake in incest, thievery, womanizing, the slave trade, and mass murder, but never bothered to explain the nature of the religious performance. **"Watching the technique, the Quraysh assumed that he had adopted a new religion. The other people were watching it with curiosity, but Abu Jahl in his arrogance and pride threatened the Prophet and forbade him to worship in that way in the Ka'aba."**

Maududi, endeavoring to explain the 96th surah, brings us this Tradition: **"Does Muhammad set his face on the ground before you?"** When they replied in the affirmative, he said: **"By Lat and Uzza, if I ever catch him in that act, I will set my foot on his neck and rub his face in the dust."** Since the Ka'aba was called a mosque—or "a place of prostration in Arabic"—way back in Qusayy's day, Muhammad didn't invent face-to-the-ground bowing. **"When he saw the Messenger in the prostration posture, he tried to set his foot on his neck. But suddenly he turned back as if** in a fright. Asked what was the matter, he said, 'There was a ditch of fire and a terrible apparition between me and Muhammad.' On hearing this the Prophet said: 'Had he come near me, the angels [demons] would have smitten him and torn him to pieces.'"

This is intended to be another proof of Muhammad's calling. But it's lame. The notion that Muhammad's most annoying rival, after publicly threatening the prophet, would admit to seeing a divine sign protecting him, is ludicrous. If it occurred, he might run, he might apologize, he might become a Muslim, but Jahl would never confess to being foiled by the prophet's deity and then remain an adversary. Unless, of course, he saw the fire as a symbol of the Devil's influence in the prophet's proclamation.

Other scriptures from Bukhari and Muslim report: "The Prophet was performing his prayer at the Ka'aba. Abu Jahl passed and said, 'Muhammad, did I not forbid you to do this?' And then he started to threaten him. In response, the Prophet rebuked him severely. There upon Jahl said, 'On what strength do you rebuke me?' 'By Allah. My followers in this valley exceed yours in number.'" This time the scene was recast without the embarrassing reference to the pit of flames. But that hardly gets the revisionists out of the fire. It would be some time before Muhammad would reveal his god's name. And by their own admission, there were only three Muslims in a town of five thousand.

With the Hadith providing the necessary context, let's see what Muhammad's spirit friend had to say. *096.015* "Let him beware! If he [Abu Jahl] does not desist, We will seize him, smite his forehead, and drag him by the forelock, a lying, sinful forelock! Then, let him call upon his henchmen for help and summon his council of comrades. We will call on the angels of punishment to deal with him! (or) We will call the guards of hell. (or) We too would summon the braves of Our army." This "scripture" was so bizarre, I elected to give three different translations of the killer angels. "God" calling them "tools of punishment, guards of hell, and an army of braves" sounds demonic. Further, the depiction of a spirit seizing a man, smiting a man, dragging a man, is consistent with Satan. It didn't take long for Islam to get nasty or for Muhammad to reveal the source of his inspiration.

The surah ends with: *096.019* "Nay, beware! Do not obey him. Pay him no heed: but bow down in adoration, and draw near." So in this, the first surah revealed, the Qur'an's equivalent of "In the beginning God created the heavens and the earth," Muhammad's unnamed Lord tells his lone prophet not to obey an unnamed boy. How profound. He threatens punishment and calls on an army of hell's angels to drag his victim off so that he can personally oversee his torture. Then he tells his messenger to approach a pagan rock shrine and bow down in adoration. This is some god. This is some book. This is some start.

74th surah is similar to the last two revelations, so let's review it next. *074.001* "O you who are covered up in your cloak, arise and deliver your warning! And your Lord do magnify, while keeping your garments free from stain! And uncleanness do shun, nor expect in giving, any worldly gain. And for the sake of your Lord, be patient." Once again our hero is hiding under the covers. Yet his seizing, smiting, and dragging Lord wants him to deliver a warning. That's quite a picture. But so as to pretty it up, the "Lord," ever fascinated with meaningless details, tells Muhammad to dress for success—to keep his clothes clean. And he listened, according to Will Durant. In his *Story of Civilization*, he says Muhammad "was vain. He gave considerable time to his personal appearance—perfumed his body, painted his eyes, dyed his hair, and wore a ring inscribed 'Muhammad the Messenger of Allah.'" Later Hadiths will confirm each of Durant's charges.

Vanity aside, I find that the "don't expect any worldly gain" verse hilarious considering that it followed Allah's promise to make Muhammad rich. We are only a few hundred words into the Qur'an and we have another contradiction. While Muhammad's claims of divine inspiration are disputable, there is no dispute over his wealth. Islam made a profit.

The next verse continues a trend that may be the most demented ever conceived in religious genre. Paraphrased: "God hates us and can't wait to introduce us to a hell he has made for our hospitality." While heaven and hell are concepts he borrowed from Judeo-Christianity, Muhammad takes them well beyond Dante's inferno. *074.008* **"The trumpet shall sound a day of anguish for disbelievers. Leave Me alone to deal with the creature whom I created bare and alone! Leave Me to deal with those I granted wealth and sons."** As diabolical as it sounds, this is Islam in a nutshell. We are told that anyone who doesn't believe Muhammad is destined to be punished by his god—up close and personal. The Islamic god's hands-on involvement with anguish is the antithesis of Judeo-Christianity in which hell is defined as separation from God. In Islam, the dark spirit wants to be left alone to supervise the torture. The next time someone suggests that the gods of the Bible and Qur'an are the same, remind them of these verses.

There are a thousand deeds that could have been mentioned in this early surah, like love, not committing murder, telling the truth, being faithful in marriage, not coveting what belongs to others, but all we get is what irks the would-be prophet. *074.015* **"These men are greedy and desire that I should give them even more. By no means! For they have offered stubborn opposition to Our Signs and Our revelations."** There have been no signs and Muhammad has yet to share a single revelation. He's still hiding under the covers. So what we are getting here is a peek into the prophet's covetous and tormented soul. He's so insecure, so paranoid, he *believes* he's going to be rejected.

Leaving this delusion, we return to sadistic. **"Soon I will visit them with a mountain of calamities, imposing a fearful doom and a distressing punishment."** *074.019* **"For these men thought and plotted; so woe to them! They shall be cursed for their plots."** While we have been exposed to a series of plots, this is the first in order of revelation. It is particularly troublesome because Muhammad's spirit is so eager to curse man; he threatens before he teaches. With that, I'd like to propose another theory. There is a reason the Qur'an was assembled out of order.

When it's realigned chronologically, its credibility evaporates.

074.021 **"Again, woe to them; may they be cursed for how they plotted. They looked around, frowned, and scowled with displeasure. Then they turned back and were haughty with pride. They said: 'This is nothing but magical enchantment, derived and narrated from others. This is nothing but the words of a mortal man!'"** In this passage, the Qur'an debuts its most repetitive themes. Muhammad and his message would be attacked for a host of reasons including their lack of divine credibility, their satanic or demented tone, and for their obvious plagiarism—stealing the script from prior sources. Those who recognized this, as most did during Muhammad's day, were cursed and doomed to be roasted by Islam's god.

The surah continues with this twisted rant: *074.026* **"Soon will I fling them into the burning Hell Fire! And what will explain what Hell Fire is? It permits nothing to endure, and nothing does it spare! It darkens and changes the color of man, burning the skin! It shrivels and scorches men."** Yeouch! Muhammad's spirit is getting a little hot under the collar. Sure there's a hell, but this Satan wannabe is way too into the details. And as for stubborn opposition to **"Our signs and Our revelations"**— he's kidding right? Opposition to what? Blood clots, reading, reciting, being nice to orphans? And what signs? There haven't been any. No miracles, no prophecies, not even any new material. So why the temper tantrum?

This surah jumps back and forth, as does much of the Qur'an, from first person singular to plural, so the problem might be schizophrenia. "I" and "Our" are routinely used in reference to Muhammad's demonic spirit. While this duplicity is irritating, there must be more to this. Islam is only beginning; Muhammad has just been called, and he has yet to preach. His god remains unnamed. So why visit creation with a mountain of calamities, impose a fearful doom, fling men into fires that darken the skin, scorching and shriveling? And what's up with god being bothered by people plotting against him? That's like me taking on the American military with a peashooter.

The Qur'an's mean-spirited outbursts make no sense in the context of a religious prophet. But if Khadija was the inspiration behind Muhammad, it's another story—the story of a scheming profiteer **"belittling the competition."** The Merchants of Mecca chafed at the preposterous allegations of the self-appointed prophet, because they controlled the religious scam and didn't appreciate his claim to their property.

For those who have an appetite for hell talk, be of good cheer. The Lord provides: *074.031* **"We have appointed nineteen angels to be the wardens of the Hell Fire. We made a stumbling-block for those who disbelieve and We have fixed their number as a trial for unbelievers in order that the people of the Book may arrive with certainty, and that no doubts may be left for the people of the Book, those in whose hearts is a disease."** According to the dark spirit of Islam, angels are hell's wardens, and he uses them as stumbling blocks to foil mankind. And while that's demented, it pales in comparison to the claims that the people of the Book—Christians and Jews

—are diseased and that they will arrive in hell with confirmed reservations.

During radio interviews, I am routinely called a bigot when I expose Islam. Yet I never speak unkindly of Muslims, only of the doctrine that drives so many to murder and mayhem. It's *Islam* that's "unkind." The Qur'an isn't debating scripture, doctrines, or even deeds; it's condemning human beings. As such, the Islamic god is a hateful, intolerant racist—a bigot.

The 31st verse of the 74th surah continues with this line: **"And for those to whom the Scripture Book has been given, and the believers, there should be no doubt. The unbelievers may say, 'What does the Lord intend by this?' The Lord will lead astray whomever He pleases, and He will guide whomever He pleases: and none can know the armies of your Lord except He, and this is no other than a warning to mankind."** This is confusing. Who should be without doubt—Muslims or Infidels? The Qur'an wouldn't be a book for decades. The Hebrew Bible had been a book for nearly two millennia. The Gospels promise heaven to those who accept the Messiah as their Savior—no doubt. The Qur'an only promises paradise to murderers —martyrs, in their parlance. All other Muslims remain in doubt until their scales are weighed. And as for god being pleased to lead folks astray and having an army—**"what does the Lord intend by this?"**

The lack of clarity may be intentional. Muhammad's deity admitted that he toys with people. God playing with men's souls is embarrassing. Creating stumbling blocks and leading folks astray is demonic. Swearing by the Moon (capital "M") is incriminating. It reveals Ar-Rahman's and Allah's origins. *074.032* **"No, truly: I swear by the Moon as a witness, and by the darkness of night as it wanes."** Loving the "darkness of night" suggests that the spirit of Islam is Satan. As does this, for Lucifer is called the "Morning Star," and his abode is hell: **"And by the dawn as it is unveiled, surely Hell is one of the greatest signs and gravest misfortunes, a warning to men."** The gravest misfortune—hell—was created expressly for him. With a deceiving and demonic spirit at the helm of the world's fastest growing religion, no wonder we're in such a mess today.

The surah winds down with this: **"To any of you that chooses to press forward or lag behind, know that every soul will be held in pledge for its deeds except the Companions of the Right Hand. They will be in Gardens of Delight."** The first part of this verse is standard mainstream religion, at least non-Christian religion: man will be judged by his deeds. The second part is senseless, desperate—even contradictory. Having collected fewer than a handful of followers, Muhammad was willing to offer a free pass to paradise to anyone who was willing to be one of his companions. But at what cost? The rest of the Qur'an is unambiguous. Islam is a religion of works, one in which Muslims are judged based upon the comparative weight of the good and bad things they have done during their life. This verse expressly contradicts that doctrine when it says that the Right-Handed Companions aren't accountable. Both cannot be true, which makes one a lie. In that salvation is at stake, this contradiction is catastrophic.

074.040 "They will question each other and ask the guilty, 'What led you into burning Hell Fire?' They will say: 'We were not of those who prayed or fulfilled our devotional obligations; nor were we of those who fed the wretched. We used to wade in vain disputes. We used to deny the Day of Judgment, until death overtook us.'" The conversation between those in the "Gardens of Delight" and the inmates of the "burning Hell Fire" is told so that Muhammad's Lord can squeeze in a little "religion" in the midst of his tirade on retribution. With Islam, devotion is an obligation, not an expression of love. Further, men have been condemned for not doing something that has not yet been specified. But showing that he is a master of the obvious, the Lord adds prayer to his list of good things. There are now five "do's" in the Qur'an. Unspecified prayer and ritual have been added to orphan happiness, wretched beggar support, and cleanliness. And on the "don't do" list we have vain disputes.

The surah culminates with these bizarre verses: *074.048* **"No intercession of any intercessors will avail them."** Whoever collected these surahs wants us to know that there is no savior. Christ was just kidding about that salvation thing on the cross. However, by saying this, they injured their prophet's credibility, for he claimed to be an intercessor. *074.049* **"What is the matter with them that they turn away from admonition as if they were freighted asses!"** Asses indeed. Twenty-six centuries earlier, Yahweh told us that Ishmael's offspring, a heritage Muslims claim, "would be wild asses of men."*074.052* **"Each one of them wants to be given scrolls of revelation spread out! No! By no means! They fear not the hereafter. Nay, this is an admonishment. Let them keep it in remembrance! But they will not heed unless the Lord wants them to. He is the fountain of fear. He is the fount of mercy."**

Stop the presses; clang the bell. That's flat out amazing. Five revelations into Islam and the Lord has just contradicted himself a third time. And this, like the others, is at the core of Muhammad's mission. Didn't the Islamic god teach the use of the pen so that he could teach man what they did not know? Didn't he give scrolls to every Adam, Abraham, and Jesus? Now he says that when men ask for scrolls of revelation they will be told, "No! By no means! No scrolls for you." Mecca, we have a problem.

Oh, and I almost forgot. What do you think about a "god" who says, **"He is the fountain of fear. He is the fount of mercy."** Beyond the schizophrenic duplicity, imagine spending eternity with a deity that calls himself the fountain of fear.

For those who may be troubled by the Biblical references to fear, fear not. The root of both the Hebrew and Greek words used for "fear" mean "revere" when used in the context of our relationship with Yahweh.

Moving on to the 94th surah, the next chronologically, Maududi explains: **"No sooner had Muhammad started preaching Islam than the same society which had esteemed him, turned hostile. The relatives and friends, clansmen and neighbors, who treated him with respect, began to shower him with abuse. No one in Mecca was prepared to listen to him; he was ridiculed and mocked in the street, so the initial stage was very** discouraging. That is why surah 94 was sent down to console him."

Before we dive into the surah, I'd like to share a Hadith from Ibn Ishaq to demonstrate how reluctant Muhammad was to discuss the relationship he had formed with his demonic spirit. *Ishaq:117* "Three years elapsed from the time that Muhammad concealed his state until Allah commanded him to publish his religion according to information that has reached me. 'Proclaim what you have been ordered and turn away from the polytheists.' [Qur'an 15:94] 'Warn your family, your nearest relations.' [Qur'an 26:214] When these words came down to the Apostle he said, 'Allah has ordered me to warn my family and the task is beyond my strength. When I make my message known to them I will meet with great unpleasantness so I have kept silent. But Gabriel [Lucifer] has told me that if I do not do as ordered my Lord [Satan] will punish me.'" This Hadith is injurious to Islam. The surahs it references (15 and 26) were not among the first fifty revealed, so the timing is impossible. Further, Khadija was the first Muslim and Ali was the third. Muhammad's only other family members were daughters, and in Islam, they don't count. So what "great unpleasantness" was he afraid of? Moreover, imagine a revelation so feeble, the prophet has to be threatened to deliver it. Muslims deserve something better than this.

094.001 "Have We not opened up your chest and removed your burden which left you hopeless?" Muhammad claimed that the *Sharh Sadr* occurred on three occasions. According to Islamic theory, his chest was cut open by the angels; his heart was removed, washed, and then reinserted. *Tabari VI:75* "'Messenger, how did you first know with absolute certainty that you were a prophet?' He replied, 'Two angels came to me while I was somewhere in Mecca.... One angel said, "Open his breast and take out his heart." He opened my chest and heart, removing the pollution of Satan and a clot of blood, and threw them away. Then one said, "Wash his breast as you would a receptacle." He summoned the Sakinah [the Hebrew Shekhinah, or God's presence], which looked like the face of a white cat, and it was placed in my heart. Then one said, "Sew up his breast." So they sewed up my chest and placed the seal between my shoulders.'" While none of this occurred, Islam doesn't escape the operation unscathed. If God wished to cleanse a man's spirit of sin, he wouldn't do open heart surgery.

094.004 "We have exalted your fame, raising high the esteem in which you [Muhammad] are held." While I'm convinced that Islam was all about exalting Muhammad, this verse should be troubling for Muslims. First, theirs was the only egotistical prophet. Second, every Qur'anic verse revealed during this period says Muhammad was ridiculed, mocked, and tormented by his neighbors. Either god hasn't been attentive and doesn't know what's going on, or he has a rather demented view of esteem. But Muslims miss the foolishness simply because the first surahs revealed are at the end of the book. And by the end of Muhammad's life, he had plundered his way to prosperity.

The "Opening Up" surah ends saying: *094.005* "With every difficulty, there is relief. Therefore, when you are free from whatever you're doing, make your Lord your exclusive object." In context, this is absurd. Muhammad had nothing else to do. In fact, he had made a career of ditching responsibility. As soon as he became an adult he married money and started hanging out in caves.

The self-proclaimed prophet reluctantly began to recite dribs and drabs of the Qur'an publicly. But while the poetry may have sounded decent, the message was indecent. Collectively, almost universally, the people of Mecca became outraged. According to the Qur'an, Muhammad's friends called him: a "liar" and a "magician." They accused him of being "possessed by devils." His kin called him an "insane plagiarizing poet." He was characterized a "sorcerer," "lunatic," "farfetched forger," "fool," and "specious pretender."

I was not the first to see Muhammad as a money-grubbing, self-aggrandizing, plagiarizing fraud. His own clan, his own family, his contemporaries, saw right through his act. **"The unbelievers said: 'He is a deceiving sorcerer, turning many gods into one deity.'" "There must be a motive behind the Qur'an. It is surely a fabrication." "They laugh at the Qur'an and say, 'Should we abandon our gods for the sake of an insane poet?'" "Allah has not sent down anything. You are only speaking lies." "When Our clear revelations are read out to them, they say, 'This is nothing but a fabricated lie. This is nothing but pure sorcery.'"**

"What sort of Prophet is this? Why was no angel sent to him?" Then, from surah 21: **"Yet they say: 'These are only confused dreams. He has invented them. Let him therefore bring a miracle to us as the earlier prophets did.'"** Muhammad was called a fraud more than a hundred times in the Qur'an. At least twenty times, his clan accused him of being the only prophet who couldn't do a miracle.

In the 11th surah: **"They say of the Prophet, 'He has forged the Qur'an.'"** From the 10th: **"We find you full of folly and a liar to boot."** Then in the 9th we see the completed equation: **"There are some among them who talk ill of the Prophet. For those who offend Allah's Apostle there is a painful punishment. Have they not realized that anyone who opposes Allah and His Prophet will abide in hell forever?"**

Before we turn the page on Muhammad's opening Qur'anic salvo, I'd like to share my perspective on Islam's beginnings. I believe the Hadith and Qur'an. I believe Muhammad was running away from responsibility, as they claim. Solitude became dear to him. He was searching for God in all the wrong places. As a result, he encountered a demon. It terrified him, just as it would have you or me. Then it possessed him. Panicked, he ran home and confessed, but his social-climbing wife would have none of it. Khadija said that the demonic spirit was Allah. Ironically, she may have been right.

She founded Islam by bequeathing the family business, the Ka'aba Inc., Qusayy's religious scam, to her recluse husband and employee. "The Lord" became Muhammad's ambition. The Qur'an became a tool, one used to claim his prize. God was created in Muhammad's image. He was tortured, illiterate, covetous, delusional, and demented. Yes, I believe the Hadith and Qur'an were right.

8

THE ABUSED ABUSER

"Seize him, manacle him, chain him and
cast him into the blazing fire of hell."

It must have been hot in Mecca. Tempers were flying. As the hajj season approached, Muhammad became a menace. The merchants knew that if he started babbling his nonsense to the pilgrims, it would detrimentally impact the Ka'aba Inc.'s revenue streams and their pocketbooks. So at a meeting Muhammad had called to present Islam, Abu Lahab, the prophet's uncle, said: *Ishaq:118* "'Muhammad is trying to bewitch you.' With that the Quraysh got up and left before the Messenger could speak. The following day they gathered again. This time the Apostle said, 'Kinsmen, I know of no Arab who has come to his people with a nobler message than mine. I have brought you the best of this world and the next.'"

As Muhammad confessed earlier, the purpose of his religious scam was to steal the treasures of the Persians and Romans. The message of Islam, he said, was the best of both worlds. If you survive, you get booty; if not, you get virgins. *Bukhari V4B52N46* "I heard Allah's Apostle saying, 'Allah guarantees that He will admit the Muslim fighter into Paradise if he is killed, otherwise He will return him to his home safely with rewards and booty.'" Islam is as simple as it is perverse.

Ishaq:118 "'So which of you will cooperate with me in this matter, my brother, my executor, and my successor being among you?' The men remained silent. I [Ali], though the youngest, most rheumy-eyed, fattest in body and thinnest in legs, said, 'I will be your helper.' Muhammad laid his hand on my back and said, 'He is my successor. Listen to him and obey him.' The Meccan men got up laughing. They told Abu Talib, 'He has ordered you to listen to and obey your ten-year-old son.'" Okay, so that didn't go very well.

Then, ever courageous, the wannabe pirates turned tail. *Ishaq:118* "When the Apostle's companions prayed they went to the glens so that their people could not see them. But one day they were rudely interrupted. The Muslims protested and then turned to blows. They smote a polytheist with the jawbone of a camel and wounded him. This was the first blood to be shed in Islam." Let it be known that the Islamic Hadith attributes "first blood" to the Muslims, not the Infidels.

Abu Jahl and other Meccan leaders went to Abu Talib. *Ishaq:119* "Your nephew has cursed our gods [at this point he had cursed all of them, including Allah], insulted our

religion [more correctly, insulted us by trying to steal our religion], mocked our way of life
and accused our forefathers of error." That was actually their biggest beef. Muhammad had said that their fathers and grandfathers were burning in hell. "Either
you stop him or let us get to him. For you, like us, are in opposition to him. He gave them
a conciliatory reply. They returned a second time and said, 'We have asked you to put a
stop to your nephew's activities but you have not done so. By Allah, we cannot endure having our fathers reviled and our customs mocked.'" *Ishaq:119* "Muhammad thought that his
uncle had the idea of abandoning and betraying him, and that he was going to lose his
support." While the Meccans were disgusted by Muhammad and his message,
they held Talib in high esteem. Without uncle Abu's support, the prophet
would have been run out of town. "The Apostle broke into tears."

Ishaq tells us, "The situation worsened; the quarrel became heated and the Meccans
were sharply divided." *Ishaq:120* "Every tribe fell upon the Muslims [all five of them], seducing
them from their religion. But Allah protected his Prophet from them through his uncle."

Therefore, as the hajj drew nigh, the Quraysh chiefs held a conference and
launched what Muslims called a propaganda campaign against Muhammad.
Ishaq:121 "'If we say contradictory things about Muhammad, we might lose our credibility
[and thus the financial benefits of being heir to Qusayy's religious scam]. Therefore, let us
agree upon one criticism, which we can all claim without dispute. Some say that we should
call Muhammad a deranged soothsayer. But is his the incoherent speech of a madman?
[Yes] Some say he is possessed. But there is no choking, spasmodic movements, or whispering.' [Actually, this is how Muhammad said that he endured revelations.] Others said,
'Then let's say he is a poet.' 'No, he is no poet. We know poetry in its forms.' [They knew
that the Hanif Zayd, among others, was a far better poet than Muhammad and his god.]
Then they said: 'He is a sorcerer.' 'No, we have seen sorcerers and their sorcery. With him
there is no spitting and no blowing. [Oops. There are dozens of Hadiths depicting Muhammad spitting and blowing to exorcize illness and evil spells.] 'Then what are we to say for
by Allah, his speech is sweet, his root is deep and his branches are fruitful.'" No revisionist history here. I'm sure Muhammad's biggest critics said it just that way.

Muhammad's relatives and neighbors, men and women who knew him
far better than any Muslim today, said: "'The nearest thing to the truth is that he is
a sorcerer who has brought a message by which he separates a man from his father, his
brother, his wife, children and family.' They all agreed. Then, according their scheme, the
men of Quraysh spread the word that 'this is nothing but ancient sorcery' among the pilgrims in the hajj season. They warned everyone they met that Muhammad was a possessed sorcerer, stirring up divisions in the families."

While I think Satan is too smart to have inspired the Qur'an, the Quraysh
were right. Muhammad wanted to destroy the family unit. He, like Communists today, focused on replacing this societal bond with religious submission
to leader and doctrine. And as we shall see, he prevailed—turning brother
against brother and son against father.

In his pro-Islam Qur'anic commentary, Maududi says: "One finds that the

Qur'an was not revealed to preach religious tolerance as some people seem to think, but it was revealed in order to separate the Muslims from the disbeliever's religion, their rites of worship, and their gods, and to express their total disgust." Amen.

A poem alleged to be from Talib dominates the next five pages of Ishaq's Sira. The unbelieving pagan infidel speaks reverently of Islamic rituals. Highlights include: *Ishaq:123* "By the Black Stone, when they stroke it going round it morning and evening. By Abraham's standing place, footprint in the rock still fresh. By the running between Marwa and Safa. Every pilgrim riding to Allah's House." "By the station of Mina." "By the great stone heap, aiming at its top with pebbles." The poem goes on to speak of fighting, Muhammad's critics fall in pools of their own blood. "For if we are men we will take revenge. And you will suffer the full effects of war."

Muslims should be troubled that an unbelieving pagan endorsed their rituals. And he was more prophetic than their prophet. Yet that pales in comparison to what Abu Talib said next. *Ishaq:126* "Tell Qusayy that our cause will be blazed abroad. Give Qusayy the good news that after us there will be a falling apart among our enemies." He was correctly crediting Qusayy with being the founder of the cause that will be blazed abroad by the sword.

The next Ishaq Hadith provides an excellent segue back into the Qur'an. *Ishaq:130* "When the Quraysh became distressed by the trouble caused by the Apostle they called him a liar, insulted him, and accused him of being a poet, a sorcerer, a diviner [occult soothsayer], and of being possessed. However, the Apostle continued to proclaim what Allah had ordered him to proclaim. He excited their dislike by condemning their religion, forsaking their idols, and leaving them to their unbelief."

In the surah entitled, "The Unbelievers," Muhammad's spirit tells him to: *109.001* "Say: O unbelievers! I worship not that which you worship, nor will you worship that which I worship. And I will not worship that which you have been wont to worship, nor will you worship that which I worship. To you your Way, and to me my way." Now there is an honest admission. "My way." That's all Islam would ever be. It was his religion, his plunder, his women, his power, his legacy. "You shall have your religion and I shall have mine."

In Mecca, Abu Lahab was a king of sorts. As chief of the Hashim clan, he was heir to the religious scam. He was also Muhammad's next-door neighbor and uncle. Their mud huts shared a common wall. "Sometimes when Muhammad was performing the prayer [performing, not conversing—Islam was a charade], Abu Lahab would place a goat's stomach on him. Sometimes when food was being cooked in the courtyard, he and his wife would throw filth at the cooking pot. The Prophet would say: 'What kind of neighborliness is it?' Lahab's wife had made it a practice to cast thorns at his door at night so that when he came out, they would stick in his feet."

The 110th surah, called "Help," is the only place in the Qur'an where one of the prophet's foes is condemned by name. Maududi explains, "Muhammad's uncle, Abu Lahab, had character traits that became the basis of this condemnation. To understand this it is necessary to understand Arabian society of that time." Our Islamic tutor goes on to claim: **"In ancient days chaos and confusion prevailed; bloodshed and plunder reigned throughout Arabia."** Actually that was not true. Chaos, bloodshed, and plunder prevailed after Islam, not before. When the truth hurts, Muslims lie—even if they have to condemn Arabs.

Caught in his duplicity, Maududi contradicted himself: **"One's clansmen protected his own. It was called** *silah rehmi:* **good treatment of the kindred. It was the most highly esteemed moral value of Arabian society. Breaking off of connections with the kindred was regarded as a great sin."** If that is true, Muhammad became an egregious sinner, for his doctrine and terrorist raids pitted Arab against Arab. Squabbles over money led directly to a murderous civil war.

"In his enmity of Islam, Abu Lahab, broke the peace." How Lahab's taunting can be condemned in light of Muhammad's murderous rage is an enigma.

In my opinion, Muhammad's real motivation for lashing out against uncle Abu was that he had what he coveted. While both men were descendants of Abdul Muttalib, the inheritance bypassed the prophet and went to Lahab. To add insult to injury, when Muhammad's father died, the orphaned prophet resented the fact that he was neither adopted nor supported by rich ol' uncle Abu. Maududi says, **"Uncle Abu was expected to look after the nephew as one of his own children. But this man in his hostility to Islam and love of** *kufr* **trampled all the Arab traditions under foot."** Now, now, Mr. Muslim scholar, you've got the cart before the horse. And in so doing you've missed the entire purpose of Islam.

Let me explain. Abu Lahab didn't trample on Arab tradition on account of Islam as Muhammad and our esteemed scholar would have you believe. There was no Islam back when the orphan needed help. Further, Muhammad had married money twenty-five years prior to this altercation. While it wasn't the gravy train of the religious scam, the wannabe prophet hardly needed to be adopted now. But "now" is the operative word. Back when Muhammad was an orphaned boy, nobody wanted him—and "nobody" included the man who had it all, uncle Abu. Because Lahab had rejected and abandoned the boy, Muhammad was carried off into the desert. His words scream out to us today, telling us that he was abused. Fire and scalding water were the instruments of torment, along with insufficient food, requiring him to forage in the garbage. The Qur'an is our witness to those terrible times. Islam is the result.

When the prophet in training returned to Mecca at six, his mother died—a mother who had seen neither hide nor hair of him, a mother who had failed to protect him, a mother who had abandoned him. It is little wonder Muhammad craved female attention; little wonder that he married a woman his mother's age, a woman who could take care of him. And it is little wonder Muhammad treated women as half human. The plight of Muslim women today remains a haunting echo of his tormented past.

Pent up rage can be a powerful force with enduring consequences. And so it would be. When Muhammad was fifty, he took his best friend's six-year-old daughter. He would later tell her, **"The things I love most are fragrant smells and beautiful women."** He embraced incest, stealing his adoptive son's bride. The Qur'an would claim that his wives were dispensable—that Allah would simply give him a new batch of virgins if they didn't behave. Then when Muhammad rebuked his child-wife's criticism for collecting an ever-increasing number of concubines, there was another handy Qur'anic scripture. To which Aisha said, **"Your Lord surely seems eager to gratify your desires."**

After Muhammad's mother died, Abu Lahab rejected the vulnerable boy a second time. The six-year-old Muhammad was forced into the arms of a slave. Can you imagine the pain, the envy, the rage? His father's brother was heir to the religious scam of the hajj, the Ramadhan fair, and the tax. He was custodian of the Ka'aba, Allah's House. Muhammad had nothing. He cried out to his uncle, begged his uncle to protect him, shelter him, feed him. But no.

Two more miserable years passed before Muhammad's grandfather, Abdul Muttalib, finally acknowledged the destitute child. But even then, this was disturbing, for Ishaq said that Abdul Muttalib **"would make him sit beside him on his bed and would stroke him with his hand. He was extremely fond of him and used to constantly pet him."**

Grandpa died a couple of years later, and prophet-to-be was handed off to Abu Talib, another uncle. Like Abu Lahab, he was his father's brother. Muhammad was not yet ten years old, and by either death or choice he had been rejected or abandoned by his mother twice, his father, a Bedouin woman, a slave, uncle Abu Lahab twice, and then by grandpa Muttalib. Just the suspicion that uncle Talib would reject him brought the forty-five year old man to tears. Muhammad had a horrible life and a tormented childhood. It's not hard to see why he was so insecure, why he was filled with rage, why his Qur'an reflected his animosity, and why uncle Abu Lahab became the focus of his pain—the one man singled out by name for condemnation. While the scam was promoted by Khadija, much of the motivation for Islam can be laid at uncle Abu's feet.

In Tabari's *Muhammad in Mecca*, I found a Hadith that I have combined with another like it from Ibn Ishaq: *Tabari VI:89* **"One day the Messenger mounted al-Safa [his favorite she-camel] and called out: 'If I were to tell you that behind the hill there was an enemy host ready to fall upon you this evening, would you believe me?' 'Certainly,' the Meccans replied. He said, 'I am a warner in face of terrible doom.' Abu Lahab responded, 'If I were to accept your religion, what would I get?' The Prophet said, 'You would get what the others will get [which is submission to me].' Abu Lahab said: 'Is there no preference or distinction for me?' The Prophet replied: 'What do you want?' Lahab said: 'May this religion perish in which I and all other people should be equal!' The Prophet said: 'Then I warn you that you are heading for a torment.' Then Allah revealed: 'The power of Abu Lahab will perish,' reciting to the end of the verse."** There was no room for a second king in Islam. Muhammad would not rest until he reigned alone.

Before Muhammad's proclamation of prophethood, he married two of his three daughters to Lahab's sons, Utbah and Utaibah. It's odd that a *prophet* would be so shortsighted as to marry his own flesh to such a repugnant man. But Muhammad was always more profiteer than prophet. There was but one reason why he would give his daughters to someone he despised. Abu Lahab, like Khadija, had money, power, and prestige—things that could be usurped through arranged marriages.

After Muhammad began "inviting" the Meccans to view him as Allah's Prophet, as the real heir to the hajj, Ramadhan fair, religious tax, and Ka'aba custodianship, Abu Lahab said to both his sons: "I forbid myself seeing and meeting you until you divorce the daughters of Muhammad." Muhammad was horning in on daddy's business. So, both divorced their wives.

Tabari VI:89 "Utaibah became so nasty that he came before the Prophet and said: 'I repudiate Islam.' Then he spat at him, but his spital did not fall on him. The Prophet prayed: 'O Allah, subject him to the power of a dog from among Your dogs.'" If the Lord were really the all-forgiving deity Muhammad claimed him to be, he wouldn't condemn his prophet's cousin to be eaten by dogs for a little miscast spital. But if Allah was who Muhammad knew him to be, the Devil symbolized by the Black Stone of the Ka'aba, he was something to be cast at those who stood between him and the things he coveted. This Hadith was just part of the act.

According to Abdul Barr: "Afterwards, Utaibah accompanied his father [uncle Abu Lahab] on a journey to Syria. During the trip their caravan halted at a place that, according to local people, was visited by wild beasts at night. Lahab told his companions, the Quraysh: 'Make full arrangements for the protection of my son, for I fear the curse invoked by Muhammad on him.' The people made their camels sit around Utaibah and went to sleep. That night a tiger came. It crossed the circle of the camels and devoured Utaibah, tearing him to pieces." I do not know if this is proof that Muslims will say anything to make Allah look like he's really a god or if Allah doesn't know a cat from a dog.

Maududi, in his Qur'an commentary, explains: "Abu Lahab's wickedness can be judged by the fact that after the death of the Prophet's son Hadrat Qasim, and the passing of his second son, Hadrat Abdullah, uncle Abu Lahab instead of condoning [consoling?] his nephew in his bereavement, hastened to the Quraysh chiefs to joyfully give them the news that Muhammad had become childless." What he doesn't see is Muhammad's character. More than a decade *after* they died he arranged for his daughters to marry the sons of this vile man. *Why*, if Abu didn't have something Muhammad coveted? Wake up, folks.

"Wherever the Prophet went to preach his message of Islam, Abu Lahab followed him and forbade people to listen. 'I was a boy when I accompanied my father to the face of Dhul-Majaz. I saw the Messenger exhorting, saying: "O people, say: there is no deity but Allah, (say that and) you will attain success." Following behind him I saw a man, who was telling the people; "This fellow is a liar. He has gone astray from his ancestral faith."'"

Hadrat Rabiah tells us, "**The Prophet went to the halting place of each tribe and said: 'O children of so and so, I have been appointed Allah's Messenger to you. I exhort you to worship only Allah. So, affirm faith in me and join me so that I may fulfill my mission.' Following close behind was a man saying: 'Children of so and so, he is leading you astray from Lat and Uzza and inviting you to the religion of error, the religion he has invented. Do not listen to what he says and do not follow him.' Abu Lahab cast stones until his heels bled. He said, 'Do not listen to him, he is a liar.'**" He was indeed "leading [Muslims] astray...inviting [them] to the religion of error." However, the reference to Allah is evidence this Tradition originated in Yathrib, not Mecca. Allah was years away from making his Qur'anic début.

If those who were closest to Muhammad, his next-door neighbor and uncle, for example, were not convincing enough, the prophet condemned himself. "**I have been appointed Allah's Messenger to you. I exhort you to worship only Allah. So, *affirm faith in me* and join me so that *I* may fulfill my mission.**" As the creed of a great religion, this is sorely wanting. Yet seen through the eyes of an abused boy seeking revenge, coveting power, it makes perfect sense. As a religious scam, everything is cause and effect.

Eventually, the clans of the Quraysh boycotted Muhammad's lean and lowly group of followers socially and economically. "**Abu Lahab,**" we are told by Ibn Hisham, "**was the only person who sided with the disbelieving Quraysh against his own clan. This boycott continued for three years. The poorest of Muhammad's followers began to starve. This, however, did not move Abu Lahab.**" *Ishaq:161* "**Lahab and his wife Umm mocked and laughed at him so the Qur'an came down on their wickedness. Umm carried thorns and cast them in the Apostle's way.**" According to Maududi: "**When his uncle was condemned by name, the people learned that the Messenger could treat a relative harshly in the matter of religion. When his own uncle was taken to task publicly the people understood that there was no place for the ties of blood in this religion.**" Which is to say that Muhammad was in fact guilty of undermining the family unit.

The "**Palm Fiber**" revelation is so indicative of Muhammad, such a window into his soul, I have provided five translations: *111.001*
Yusuf Ali: Perish the hands of the Father of Flame! Perish he!
Noble: Perish the two hands of Abu Lahab (the Prophet's uncle), and perish he!
Pickthal: The power of Abu Lahab will perish, and he will perish.
Shakir: Perdition overtake both hands of Abu Lahab, and he will perish.
Ahmed Ali: Destroyed will be the hands of Abu Lahab, and he himself will perish.
   111.002
Yusuf Ali: No profit to him from all his wealth, and all his gains!
Noble: His wealth and his children will not benefit him!
Pickthal: His wealth and gains will not exempt him.
Shakir: His wealth and what he earns will not avail him.
Ahmed Ali: Of no avail shall be his wealth, nor what he has acquired.
   111.003

Yusuf Ali: Burnt soon will he be in a Fire of Blazing Flame!
Noble: He will be burnt in a Fire of blazing flames!
Pickthal: He will be plunged in flaming Fire,
Shakir: He shall soon burn in fire that flames,
Ahmed Ali: He will be roasted in the fire,

    111.004

Yusuf Ali: His wife shall carry the (crackling) wood—As fuel!
Noble: And his wife, too, who carries wood (thorns which she put in the Prophet's way).
Pickthal: And his wife, the wood-carrier,
Shakir: And his wife, the bearer of fuel,
Ahmed Ali: And his wife, the portress of fire wood,

    111.005

Yusuf Ali: A twisted rope of palm-leaf fibre round her (own) neck!
Noble: In her neck is a twisted rope of Masad (palm fiber).
Pickthal: Will have upon her neck a halter of palm-fibre.
Shakir: Upon her neck a halter of strongly twisted rope.
Ahmed Ali: Will have a strap of coir rope around her neck.

Abu Lahab mouths off and tosses stones, so Muhammad sics his god on his uncle and curses his cousin. Then, by way of confession, the prophet makes a point of telling us that neither inherited wealth, nor monies earned will exempt his uncle from torment. The reason for the differentiation between old and new money was that Muhammad coveted the things that Abu inherited—Qusayy's religious scam. The prophet wanted us to know that the custodianship of the Ka'aba wouldn't save Abu because he had laid his claim. The Ka'aba Inc. belonged to Muhammad. Allah told him so.

Sometimes the smallest details tell us the most. Why do you suppose god would contradict himself to tell us that Abu's wife would be porting the firewood for hell when elsewhere men's bodies are said to be the hell's fuel. Here's a clue: Arab fires were often fueled by the *sa'dan* shrubs that bore the thorns Abu's wife spread at Muhammad's door. Yes, Muhammad's mind was as twisted as the rope around Umm's neck. *Bukhari:V6N356* **"Lodged in her neck is a twisted rope of palm fiber, the chain of which is in the Fire of Hell."**

But as bad as all of this looks, we're just getting warmed up. A family schooled in religious hoaxes was starting another. Maududi explains: **"In the earliest phase of Prophethood, Muhammad passed through the most trying conditions. The whole nation turned hostile; there was resistance on every side. The Prophet and a handful of his Companions did not see the remotest chance of success. So Allah, in order to console him, sent down several verses. Allah said [the primary reason for inventing Islam is]: 'Soon your Lord shall give you so much that you shall be well pleased.' And Allah said [the secondary reason for inventing Islam is]: We shall exalt your renown for you. Even though Our enemies are trying to defame you throughout the country, We, on the contrary, have arranged to exalt your name and fame.'"**

Actually, Muhammad didn't have an enemy outside the burg of Mecca—which is to say that Allah's worldview was alarmingly stunted. And even the term "enemy" was grossly overstated. Muhammad's tribe scoffed at his revelations, they chided him, and laughed at his expense. Unlike a real enemy, they hadn't attacked him, imprisoned him, or destroyed his home—the kind of things Muhammad would do in Medina, and his followers do today.

Maududi says: "Such were the disturbing conditions under which the 108th surah [aptly named: Preeminence] was sent down. The Quraysh were angry with the Prophet. His Companions became helpless, poor people who were being persecuted and tyrannized." There is something about Islam that corrodes the mind. The behavior Maududi is railing against is the very legacy of Islam. Every Islamic nation is a tyranny, their people are poor, and non-Muslims are persecuted. For good measure, they even persecute their own, especially women. It is astonishing that an Islamic scholar can write these words without seeing himself in the mirror.

"Furthermore," Maududi continues, "he was bereaved by the death of two sons, one after the other, whereat his nearest relatives, clan, and neighbors were rejoicing and uttering such words as were disheartening and disturbing for a noble person who had treated even his enemies most kindly." Kindly? Never in the course of human events has a religious man treated his own clan, his detractors, his kin, so hatefully. Muhammad's spirit tongue-lashed the Meccans in the Qur'an and condemned them to hell. And his messenger would beat the hell out of them by raiding their means of sustenance and conquering their town. Further, Ishaq lists three sons, not two, all of whom died in infancy twenty years earlier.

In his concluding line, Maududi confirms Islam's demonic nature: "At this Allah just in one sentence of this brief surah gave Muhammad the good news, better news than ever given to any man: his opponents will be cut off from their root and not he." The *good* news is that the prophet's family and neighbors will be "cut off." The "Gospel" of Islam isn't about salvation; it's about damnation.

In this verse, Muhammad claimed his prize—the fountain of perpetual wealth—Kausar. Unfortunately, it flowed from the fountain of deceit—Allah's Ka'aba. *108.001* "To you have We granted Kausar, the fountain of abundance. Therefore to your Lord turn in Prayer and Sacrifice." Before we leave the Bank of Kausar I want to bring your attention to the word "therefore." A bargain has been struck. Prayer and sacrifice are services for payments rendered. Muhammad is telling us something we should already know: "I'm doing it for the money."

The following Tradition is yet another confession from the world's best known religious profiteer: *Tabari VI:95* "Abu Talib said to Muhammad, 'Nephew, how is it that your tribe is complaining about you and claiming that you are reviling their gods and saying this, that, and the other?' The Allah's Apostle said, 'Uncle, I want them to utter one saying. [There is no ilah but Allah and Muhammad is his Prophet.] If they say it, the Arabs will submit to them and the non-Arabs will pay the jizyah tax.'" The "jizyah" is an exorbitant tax collected by Muslims from Christians and Jews to this very day. It's called the "protection tax" and it works just like the one imposed by the mafia. If you pay it, they let you live. If you don't, you die.

Just in case you think this Hadith is too incriminating to be part of the Islamic lore, too money grubbing to be prophetic, consider these words from Islam's god. After telling Muslims that **"Allah will enrich you out of His bounty,"** Qur'an 9:29 says: **"Fight against those People of the Book [Christians and Jews] who do not follow what Allah and His Messenger (Muhammad) acknowledge as the true religion (Islam), nor accept Our law, until they pay the Jizyah tribute tax in submission, and feel themselves subdued, being brought low."** A second translation reads: **"pay the tax in acknowledgment of our superiority and their state of subjection."** Islam was a money-making scheme—just a Profitable Prophet Plan.

108.003 **"For he who insults you (Muhammad) will be cut off."** Compare these words with those of Christ. Unjustly rather than justifiably criticized, physically tortured rather than verbally teased, Christ prayed: "Forgive them, for they know not what they do." But the dark spirit of Islam cuts the insulters down—sending them off to burn in hell.

At this point, it's a guess as to what surah came next. The 75th is as likely as any. The self-reproaching spirit says: *075.001* **"I swear by the Day of Resurrection; and I call to witness the self-reproaching spirit, the accusing soul. Does man think that We cannot assemble his bones?"** The accusing soul is Satan although it could also be Muhammad, for he incriminates himself with every word. As for assembling bones, Islam preaches bodily resurrection, not spiritual salvation. The drunken orgy in the Garden of Bliss requires a body, not a soul, heart, or brain.

As the surah continues, we learn that the Day of Resurrection and Doom are one in the same. We are also confronted with the darkening of the moon, an overt Satanic reference. *075.003* **"Nay, We are able to put together the tips of his fingers. But man wishes to do wrong and fain denial. He questions: 'When is the Day of Doom?' So when the sight becomes dazed, and the moon becomes dark, and the sun and the moon are brought together, man will say: 'Where is the refuge?' By no means! There will be no place of safety.... Nay, man will be evidence against himself, although he tenders his excuses. Move not your tongue concerning the Qur'an to make haste. [Don't you just love the transition?] It is for Us to collect it, put it together, and promulgate it. When We have read it, follow its recital as promulgated. It is for Us to explain it."**

Muslim clerics claim that the point of friction between Muhammad and this tribe was over resurrection. But that's not true. As evidence that Arabs believed in the afterlife, they had their relatives tie their favorite camel to their grave so that it would follow them to paradise. Heaven might be big, and there was no sense in walking when one could ride. Thus, a belief in an afterlife wasn't the point of contention. The real problem was that Muhammad said his people's ancestors were burning in hell because they died during the "Period of Ignorance"—pre Muhammad. In that the Meccans loved their parents and grandparents, this upset them and naturally caused many to assail Muhammad's parochial and intolerant view. They may also have chafed at his lewd depictions of heaven and his sadistic hell.

The moon becoming dark and being brought together with the sun is troublesome. In the Bible, the moon is the illusory, false, and counterfeit source of illumination, therefore symbolic of Satan. Darkness is equated with evil and deception. The Bible says: "Men loved darkness rather than light because their deeds were evil."

The abrupt transition in this surah is like most of the Qur'an. "Move not your tongue to make haste" comes completely out of the blue. There is no segue or context. And it makes no sense. God is eternal. Furthermore, the suggestion that god has to explain his Qur'an for it to make sense is embarrassing. It brings to mind one of the book's final and most troubling verses. *005.101* **"Believers, ask not questions about things which if made plain to you may cause you trouble when the Qur'an is revealed. Some people before you asked questions, and on that account lost their faith."** Maududi, in his commentary, *The Meaning of the Qur'an*, explains: **"The Prophet forbade people to ask questions or to pry into such things."** The Hadith confirms this prophetic warning. *Bukhari:V2B24N555* **"I heard the Prophet say, 'Allah has hated you for asking too many questions.'"**

The reason questions are prohibited is clear. There is no cogent explanation for any of this. Islam is irrational. The deeper one digs, the uglier it becomes. The surest way to save Muslims from Islam is to expose them to it. Even the Qur'an agrees. And this is precisely why Muslims protect their doctrine by attacking anyone who quotes from their scriptures.

The **"Resurrection"** surah continues: *075.020* **"But men love the present life, and neglect the hereafter. Some faces that Day will beam, looking toward their Lord; and some faces will be gloomy knowing that some great back-breaking calamity is about to be inflicted on them. Yes, when their soul comes up their throat and reaches their collarbone they will cry, 'Is there a magician or wizard who can save us?' But they will know that it is the hour of parting and one leg will be joined with another, agony heaped on agony, affliction combined with affliction."** It's hard to imagine how a religion this full of satanic overtones and this fixated on anguish has survived, much less grown. If it weren't for the sword, Islam would have been stillborn.

Yes, I know that the Bible also speaks of hell and punishment, so why attack Islam so vehemently? The answer is: appropriateness, proportion, personal involvement, and vividness. First, the Bible speaks of hell as a place for those who have received ample and rational divine revelation, but have chosen to reject it. It provides standards for living via scripture in advance of judgment. The Bible even provides real proof that its revelations are godly through countless miracles and predictive prophecies. Those who end up in hell have to ignore all of this and choose not to be with God. Further, the Biblical hell wasn't created for man. It was designed for Lucifer and his fallen angels, today's demons, as a result of their disobedience. It's little wonder Islam's dark spirit spends so much time there.

The Qur'an never proves its divine authority and has yet to provide either ample revelation or standards for living. And there is no example to follow. Muhammad was the lone prophet and his life was the antithesis of godly. In other words, it's inappropriate for god to threaten hell before he has explained what people must do to avoid it.

Second, the frequency of the Qur'an's references to hell and its tortures are alarmingly out of proportion. I have not taken the passages describing retribution out of context. Every early surah has been presented in its entirety. Bad overwhelms good in the Qur'an; hell is featured, not heaven. Rebuffing Muhammad's tormentors is far more prevalent than instructing the faithful. Torment is the Qur'an's *most* prominent theme.

Third, hell in the Bible is separation from God. In the Qur'an Allah is the driving force of hell, its creator and manager. Allah wants to be left alone with man so that he can oversee his tortures. This is a fundamental difference between Yahweh and Allah, between Judeo-Christianity and Islam. In the Bible, the reward of heaven is being with God. In the Qur'an, by contrast, the reward is being with virgins; communion with Allah isn't mentioned.

Fourth, the Bible's descriptions of hell are many magnitudes milder. There is gnashing of teeth, and we're told it's hot, but little more. The vividness in which Allah describes the specifics of hell's torments is deeply disturbing, even demented.

Fifth, in Judeo-Christianity, hell is a place one chooses. No one is sent there against their will. We are all given a choice: love God and form a personal relationship, or reject him and spend eternity separated from him. In Islam, most Muslims and all non-Muslims are *predestined* to hell. In other words, their god chooses to condemn them.

Muhammad's dark spirit had a one-track mind. The Meccans were tormenting his prophet, calling him a lying wizard, a lousy plagiarizer, a possessed poet. He was bent on making them pay. But to put teeth in his bite, Muhammad had to "prove" that his spirit was "God." 075.032 **"So he did not accept the truth, nor did he pray. He called the truth a lie and turned his back. Then he gleefully went to his clan. Woe to you, yes, woe! Destruction is near. Again, woe to you, yes, woe! Again your doom is near. Does man think that he will be left to wander aimlessly? Was he not a drop of sperm emitted in lowly form? Then did he become a leech-like clot; then did the Lord make and fashion him in due proportion."**

To understand Muhammad's motivations, his god's nature, and Islam's purpose we must thoughtfully consider every early revelation. Each provides something we can use to free Muslims from Islam and in turn free ourselves from Islamic terror. In that light, let's review Maududi's writings on the 67th surah: "It is characteristic of early revelations in that it presents the entire teachings of Islam and the object of the Prophet's mission so that they could be assimilated easily. During this time, most Meccans cursed the Prophet and prayed for his and the believers' destruction." A few surahs ago we were told that the unbelievers were in hell because they didn't pray. But that aside, we're about to discover "the entire teaching of Islam and the object of the Prophet's mission."

067.001 "Blessed is He who holds the reins of Kingship." Why is this written in third person if it's supposed to be the Lord is speaking? And why is god blessing Himself? Perhaps this is another confession—evidence of Muhammad's ambition. An insecure man saw himself as king.

According to the Qur'an, death precedes life and both are a test. This is followed by Islam's greatest omission. The test isn't explained—the Qur'an doesn't give the rules by which we are to be judged. "Who has created death and life that He may test you—which of you is best in deeds; He is the Mighty, the Forgiving."

Muhammad's worldview was upside down. Unable to give followers a reason to live, he gave Muslims a reason to die—testing their will to sacrifice their lives as martyrs. Islam was more about pain than paradise. Unable to convince men to choose his religion based upon its merits, Muhammad threatened them with damnation. And the religion was more about puffery than proof. Unable to produce a sign, a miracle, a prophecy, Muhammad pushed out his chest and simply proclaimed himself Messenger. *Ishaq:116* "I heard the Apostle say, 'I have never invited anyone to accept Islam who hasn't shown signs of reluctance, suspicion and hesitation.'"

Now that we know the motivation for Islam was power, would you like to meet its god and witness his teaching? *067.003* "We created seven heavens, one above the other. Muhammad, can you see any fault in Ar-Rahman's creation? Look again: Can you see any rifts or fissures? Then look again and yet again. Your gaze turns back dazed and tired. We have adorned the lowest skies with lamps, and We have made them missiles to drive away the devils and against the stone Satans, and for them We have prepared the doom of Hell and the penalty of torment in the most intense Blazing Fire. For those who reject their Lord is the punishment of Hell: Evil, it is such a wretched destination. When they are flung therein, they will hear the terrible drawing in of their breath and loud moaning even as the flame blazes forth, roaring with rage as it boils up, bursting with fury. Every time a fresh crowd is cast in, Hell's wardens will ask, 'Did no Warner come to you?' They will say: 'Yes indeed; a Warner did come to us, but we rejected him and said, "The Lord never sent down any Message: you are nothing more than an egregious delusion!"'"

Muhammad's spirit has a name: Ar-Rahman—the deity of the Yemeni Hanifs. The first pillar of Islam has been pulverized. There is a god besides Allah. The Qur'an says so. But monotheism and religious foundations torn asunder, this idol is no less delusional or demented than Muhammad's Lord.

Calling stars lamps that will be turned into missiles to drive away devils is dimwitted, but when it comes to gods, I'll take feeble-minded to demented any day. Ar-Rahman says that he personally prepared the torment in the Blazing Fire. And as before, he seems to relish the details. The fire is intense, it is a wretched place, the victims are flung in, their breath is choked out, they moan, roaring with rage as the flames boil up around them—bursting in fury. Crowds of new victims are callously called "fresh." Then to add indignity to insult, the unbelievers are interrogated by hell's wardens.

While creation and astronomy are obviously weaknesses on Ar-Rahman's resume, when it comes to pain and suffering he is an expert. In that it's beneath God to ramble on in such a nasty tone, the Qur'an leaves us in a quandary. If God didn't inspire these words—who did?

I'd like to propose a source of inspiration. We have ample evidence to suspect Khadija's involvement in the conception of the Profitable Prophet Plan, and selling Muhammad on it. After two years of silence we have a series of revelations that speak of making money (Khadija) and empowering and enriching destitute orphans (Muhammad). We even have sworn testimony, confessions that purport to be scripture.

This takes us to vengeance. It's the motivation for the onslaught of hellish pain so graphically and vociferously presented in these initial surahs. They strongly suggest personal knowledge. The terrible drawing in of breath, the loud moaning that follows, flames boiling up, bursting forth with rage, combined with god shackling, choking, and pouring boiling water on men is beyond normal imagination.

Fortunately, we are given a clue as to the root cause that underlies this inhuman rage. Each time a fresh wound is inflicted, the tormentor tells his victims that it's their fault. They deserve their fate. If they weren't so bad, so unworthy, so undesirable, if they had only listened, they wouldn't be punished. Such is the modus operandi of a typical child abuser. There is a considerable body of evidence in the Hadith and Qur'an that screams to us today: Muhammad was molested. Nobody wanted him. He was abandoned by his father and rejected by his mother. Those with substance, his uncle Abu and grandfather Muttalib, saw him as an inconvenience. The Bedouin woman into whose custody he was placed viewed him as unworthy, as she knew she wouldn't be paid for her services. The scene was ripe for abuse.

In the low-tech world of the Arabian Desert, campfires, scalding water, pitch, thorns, and shackles may well have been the implements of torture. And I suspect that the would-be prophet was told that he deserved the punishment. Then, as so often happens, the victim came full circle. Muhammad went from prey to perpetrator—from abused to abuser.

With this in mind, let's jump back into the 67th surah—one of the first "revealed" to Muhammad—One that contains **"the entire teaching of Islam and the object of the Prophet's mission."** *067.010* **"They will say, 'Had we but listened and** learned, we wouldn't be in the burning flames!' So they shall acknowledge their guilt, but there will be no joy for the inmates of the blazing fire." Muhammad is imagining his critics accepting blame for their hellish predicament just as the victims of child abuse internalize their guilt. The perpetrators of such heinous crimes assuage their consciences by telling the abused that they are being punished because they didn't listen. They do it so often and so vehemently, victims begin to see themselves as somehow responsible for the torment they are enduring. Yet whether they falsely confess to their complicity or keep it inside, the torture never ends—they remain prisoners to the pain.

All too often, the tormentor manages to twist reality, to somehow show their ultimate restraint as a form of mercy. The abuser views himself as merciful, even gracious and forgiving, for suspending the torture he is inflicting. And this strategy enables the perpetrator to control their prey. Authority and power satiate their cravings; they hide their inadequacies. The final ingredient in this demented recipe is the threat of future calamity. The abused are told that they are being watched by the all-powerful predator. If they squeal, he'll make them pay; he'll make the consequence grievous.

067.012 "For those who fear the Lord in secret there is a reward. Whether you say a thing secretly or openly, He knows your innermost thoughts." Let me translate this for you. If you keep quiet out of fear, you will be rewarded with a reprieve from punishment. But be careful of what you think and say, because I am watching you.

The following verses vainly try to establish a sense of legitimate authority for the Wrathful Tormentor, painting the perpetrator as "Gracious." 067.014 "It is He who has made the earth subservient to you that you may travel and eat the things He provided. [Be nice and you won't be chained, burned, or have to eat trash. But if you squeal...] To Him you shall return. Are you so unafraid that He will not open the earth to swallow you, pelt you with showers of stones, or let loose on you a violent wind so that you shall know how terrible is My warning [threat]? But indeed men before them rejected My warning. They denied, so then how terrible will be My punishment of them and My wrath." It's an old and perverted story: victimization is the victim's fault because he or she ignored the obvious signs of the tormentor's authority and justification.

You may think that I'm making too much of a single surah, but this surah does not stand alone. Pain and punishment for those who do not acquiesce to the authority of the perpetrator is the Qur'an's single most dominant theme with one thousand iterations. Being burnt alive is the most common form of torment. We are even told that men's bodies, their flesh, fuel the fire.

We also have another poignant clue in this passage, a Freudian slip. Muhammad begins by referring to god as "He," establishing his lord's power, control, and justification. Then he transitions to "My" as he says "My warning they denied, so then how terrible will be My rejection of them and My wrath." And all of this, unlike most of the Qur'an, is in singular (He and My) not the usual plural (We and Our). That's because this is personal with

Muhammad. We are looking directly into the heart of Islam's founder.

Roasting men alive is not the only method of punishment deployed in the Qur'an. Yet each and every variation is consistent with what the would-be prophet might have endured around a Bedouin campfire. The other ghoulish treatments include being forced to drink scalding water, being made to eat thorns, and choking down boiling pitch. Clothes are set on fire. Men are shackled with twine and turned on a spit. And while I cannot prove that our orphan was abused as a child, all the evidence points in that direction.

It explains why the Qur'an is so filled with threats of pain and punishment. It explains the nature of the torments. It explains the underlying reason for them. And it explains why the prophet was so angry at uncle Abu. By not adopting him, Lahab was ultimately responsible for the anguish Muhammad endured. It even explains the motivation for Islam. Lahab controlled the religious scam Muhammad coveted. He had what his nephew craved—power and wealth. They would have provided relief.

Since the Qur'an was too poorly written, too foolish, too contradictory, and too twisted to be divinely inspired, there must have been an ulterior motivation behind such haunting words. If not abuse, then what?

Thus far, Islam has been as transparent as a cloudless desert sky. Let's take a quick inventory. At Khadija's urging, Muhammad usurped the authority of an unnamed lord to stake his claim to the wealth that flowed from his family's religious scam. A hellish childhood created a hellish religion that looks suspiciously similar to what the prophet may have personally endured. Heaven was created in his image as well, depicted as the lustful realm an abandoned boy would have desired—a realm where the women who rejected him were used to bring him pleasure. God's character and words came to reflect the prophet's wishes.

The remainder of the 67th surah simply wallows in puddles of delusion and despair. *067.019* **"Do they not observe the birds above them, spreading their wings and folding them in? Nothing holds them aloft except Ar-Rahman: Truly Ar-Rahman watches over all things."** Flight happens because Ar-Rahman holds birds aloft. It's clear Muhammad never went to physics class. Bernoulli's principal, the law that explains aerodynamic lift, was way too complex. And make no mistake, this is offered as a *proof* of Ar-Rahman's existence, not as a metaphor.

Yet for a god so into holding birds aloft, he sure wasn't much help on the morning of 9/11/2001. Perhaps Ar-Rahman was distracted burning infidels. No, that's not right. Knowing Muhammad's lord as we do, his spirit let go of the United and American birds so that he could watch thousands of infidels burn. "Allahu Akbar!"

With the Lord's divine authority firmly established, we return to **"The Kingdom"** surah. *067.020* **"Who is he that will send an army to assist you besides Ar-Rahman? The unbelievers are lost in delusion."** Another motivation, another teaching is revealed. Ar-Rahman is a militaristic god with an army. Jihad would soon become Islam's most recognizable attribute, the means the messenger would use to abuse his adversaries.

As we discovered earlier, Ar-Rahman was a pagan rock idol with a House like Allah's. The two gods vied for attention. And it's clear that Allah was slighted in the early going. Not only hasn't he been mentioned thus far, he wouldn't find his way into Islam for quite some time. It's not a very nice way to treat the Lord of the House. So why choose this name?

Muslim scholars have no viable explanation as to why Muhammad called his Lord Ar-Rahman. The best they can do is say that god has many names and that Ar-Rahman became one of their god's attributes. But that's nonsense. Ar-Rahman was the name of a pagan deity, one much better known—at least outside the tiny village of Mecca—than Allah. He was an idol—not an attribute. Further, all of the initial religiosity contained in the early revelations mirrors the religion of the Hanifs—the followers of Ar-Rahman.

There are serious problems associated with the prophet choosing to name his spirit Ar-Rahman. When Muhammad ultimately migrated from the shallow doctrinal pool of the Hanifs to the unimaginably deep reservoir of the Jews, he was forced to claim that his Lord was their Lord—the Jewish God Yahweh. Otherwise, why were all the characters and stories so similar? But that was problematic. Although Muhammad didn't know it, the God of the Bible had a name—Yahweh. He didn't know because the Jews were afraid to say it for fear of blasphemy. And since he was illiterate, Muhammad couldn't read any of the 6,868 times YHWH, or Yahweh, was written in their Scriptures. Just like our Bible translations today, when the Hebrew word says "Yahweh," God's personal name, we read and say "the Lord." But Joe is not Jim. Moses is not Muhammad. And Yahweh is neither Ar-Rahman nor Allah.

As in politics, a blunder becomes a crisis when it is covered up and then exposed. The Islamic clerics, following their prophet's lead, have tried to sweep the name of the Qur'an's first god under the rug. So we must ask: if there is nothing to hide—why try so hard to hide it? Of the many Qur'an translations, all but two errantly replace Ar-Rahman's name with an attribute like "Merciful," the title "Lord," the generic "God," or with the name "Allah." But unlike the Jews, who misinterpreted the Third Commandment, there is no excuse for changing Ar-Rahman to Lord, God, or Allah.

This problem is exacerbated by the invocation that was later added before each surah. In their desire to make Ar-Rahman into Allah and to make both appear "good" in spite of their scriptures, this line is repeated 113 times: **"In the name of Allah, most benevolent (Ar-Rahim), ever-merciful (Ar-Rahman)."** So desperate are Islamic scholars to present their hateful, punitive, and warlike spirit in a favorable light, one even wrote a book proclaiming, "Merciful and Benevolent are the Qur'an's most repeated attributes for Allah." Holy hogwash. The salutation wasn't part of the Qur'anic revelation. It's an invocation—one as lame as it is contradictory.

For those who may be curious, I'll digress a moment. The Third Commandment does not say: "Thou shall not take the name of the Lord thy God in vain." Not only is it beneath Yahweh to write such a trivial thing in stone, his name isn't "the Lord." A name can't be "taken," and "vain" means either egotistical as it relates to a person, or failed as it relates to an endeavor. In that the line was meaningless, Jews, and later Christians, falsely assumed that our Creator was telling us that they shouldn't swear or say, "Yahweh."

The Commandment as it was actually written in Hebrew says something that is vital to our very survival: "You shall not accept or advance in the name or character of Yahweh, your deity, anything that is deceptive or destructive." Our failure to understand this Commandment and live by it is the reason Holy Wars are fought. Our tolerance of things that purport to be godly, but are instead false and destructive, is why Islam exists. It is why Muslim militants kill us. It is why the world is, and has been, in such a horrible mess.

So why didn't Muhammad initially name his dark spirit? Why did he begin by calling him by the Hebrew, hence Hanif title "Lord?" Why then did he finally name him after a rival to the Meccan Allah? Good questions all. And since the Muslim sages don't provide a viable answer, I'll propose one—speculative as it might be. Khadija converted Muhammad by telling him that her aged cousin said that he was a prophet in the line of Moses. This man knew that the Jews called their God "Lord." But the Meccans were not satisfied with a title. All gods had names. Even pagan stone idols had names—why not Muhammad's god? If he was so important, he must have a name.

That put the wannabe prophet in a pickle. If he called his god by any of the most familiar pagan names—Hubal, Allah, Al-Lat (the female form of Al-Lah), Manat, or Al-Uzza—something would be expected of them. After all, if they could give such marvelous Qur'an recitals, why not a miracle? Since these idols were close at hand it would have been hard to explain away their lack of participation in the prophet's mission.

With the Meccan pantheon too close for comfort, Muhammad did what he did best. He stole someone else's material. The Hanifs had a religion, and they had a god—one who "lived" a comfortable distance away. He simply appropriated their material and their deity. Ar-Rahman was perfect, in a twisted sort of way. His name meant "merciful." As such it became a way to disguise the Qur'an's demented edge. It's like calling the Communist dictatorship in China a republic.

Each of the initial Qur'anic surahs reflected Hanif beliefs and religiosity, not Jewish. The convoluted Bible stories we covered during creation and patriarch chapters were revealed much later—after the prophet had exhausted the rather anemic belief structure of the Hanifs and needed something more.

And that too is interesting. The Qur'an's reliance on the Bible varies inversely with access to the Ka'aba, Allah's House, and directly with access to Jews. If Allah or Ar-Rahman were God, why would that be?

While you're pondering that conundrum, consider this: the moment Muhammad migrated to Medina, he capitalized upon the opportunity that distance from Mecca's impotent rock idol provided. In the 2nd surah, the first revealed after fleeing Mecca, Ar-Rahman became Allah. You see, Allah and his house were now a safe distance south. God changes his name so Muhammad can lay claim to that which he has been chased away from—the religious scam surrounding the Ka'aba. Ar-Rahman is never to be heard from again. He simply fades into the amorphous world of attributes.

As we return to the Qur'an, we find Muhammad embroiled in an argument—one that fits nicely into the abused theory. *067.021* **"Who is there that can provide you with food in case He was to withhold His provision? Nay, they obstinately persist in rebellion and aversion. Is then one who walks headlong groping, groveling on his face, better guided, or one who walks evenly on a Straight Path?"** The quality of this writing is so pathetic it almost makes you feel sorry for Muhammad—almost.

067.025 **"They say: When shall this threat be executed if you are truthful? Say: 'As to the knowledge of the time, it is with the Lord alone: I am sent only to warn you clearly.'"** The Meccans were looking for a little proof but our hero couldn't provide any. The best he could do was say, "You just wait. One day when you least expect it, my god will get you." **"But when they see the threat, the sorry faces of those who disbelieve will be distraught, and it will be said to them: 'This is what you asked for.' Say (Muhammad): 'See? Whether God destroys me, and those with me, or not, no one can deliver the unbelievers from their grievous doom.' Say: 'He is Ar-Rahman; in Him we believed, and in Him we have placed our trust: Soon will you know which one of us is in manifest error.'"** Yes indeed we will. But it saddens me that two billion precious souls have already been lost to the egregious lie that became Islam.

Rant over, Muhammad tried to prove that Ar-Rahman was real. *067.030* **"Say, 'Just think: if your water were to dry up, who would bring you water?"** The Meccans were dependent upon the meager and nearly bitter well of Zamzam. Muhammad was telling his clan that its feeble flow was a miracle from Ar-Rahman—a clear sign he was god. He was threatening: "Mess with me, and my god will cause you to die of thirst." According to Muhammad, if it trickled forth, it was a miracle. If it dried up, that too was miraculous. In actuality, the only miracle was that anyone believed him. I'm surprised he didn't claim that as a sign.

Therefore, **"the entire teaching of Islam and the object of the Prophet's mission"** is: the prophet craves power and will threaten anyone to get it. His god's name is Ar-Rahman and he is sadistically abusive. Stars are missiles used to drive away devils. Muhammad's kin claim he was deluded. For that they will endure flames, roaring with rage. All the while they will be interrogated. The Lord must be feared, not loved, for he will swallow his creation, pelting them with showers of stones. His punishment is as terrible as his wrath. Ar-Rahman has armies ready to march. He threatens to besiege communities, withholding food and water from those who grovel on their faces. What's more, the Islamic god's grievous doom cannot be avoided.

The **"Concrete Reality"** surah was one of the earliest revealed, although it's an odd choice of names: concrete didn't exist in Mecca. The 69th surah was sent down at the time when opposition to Muhammad had started, but had yet to come to a boil. Maududi shares a Tradition from Musnad Ahmad, explaining: **"Before embracing Islam I came out of my house with the idea of causing trouble for the Prophet, but he had entered the mosque of the Ka'aba before me. When I arrived I found that he was reciting surah Al-Haaqqah [69]. I stood behind him and listened. I wondered at its literary charm and beauty. Then suddenly an idea came to my mind that he must be a poet as the Quraysh alleged. At that moment he recited the words: 'This is the Word of an honorable Messenger. [Another confession: Muhammad admitted that the Qur'an was the word of a messenger—not god.] It is not the word of a poet.' I said to myself: 'Then, he must be a soothsayer, if not a poet.' Thereupon be recited the words: 'Nor is it the word of a soothsayer.'"**

Experience for yourself the literary charm and beauty of the **"Concrete Reality"** surah: *069.001* **"The sure calamity! What is the sure calamity! And what would make you realize what the sure calamity is! The Thamud and the Ad people branded as false the Stunning Calamity! Samood and Ad called the striking calamity a lie. But the Thamud—they were destroyed by a terrible storm of thunder and lightning! And the Ad, they were destroyed by a furious roaring wind, exceedingly violent. He made it rage against them seven long nights and eight days in succession: so that you might see the people lying prostrate in its path, as if they were hollow palm trees tumbled down! Muhammad, do you see any remnant of them?"**

We're right back to god pummeling his creation. This time the Ad and Thamud are his victims. One of these tribes, the Ad, is mythological while the Thamud is alleged to have been a smallish village that might have existed somewhere north of Mecca—one long since buried in shifting sands. But buried was not forgotten. It provided Muhammad with fodder for his favorite depiction of the almighty: "God hates men, especially when they tease his prophet." The Ad and Thamud mocked and denied, so the Big Guy creamed them. It doesn't get more charming and beautiful than that.

On a roll, Muhammad used the same trick to twist some Bible stories to suit his situation. *069.009* **"Pharaoh, and those before him, and the Cities Overthrown [He wants to say Sodom and Gomorrah, but he doesn't yet know their names.], committed habitual sin. They disobeyed, disbelieving the messenger of their Lord. [Again, he has yet to learn Lot's name. It took access to Jewish rabbis and lots of practice before Team Islam** became good at plagiarizing the Bible. The first attempts were jerky and incomplete.] So He punished them with an overwhelming penalty, a vehement punishment. Allah gripped them with a tightening grip. [This is vague also because Muhammad wasn't aware of the ten plagues.] We, when the water overflowed beyond its limits, carried mankind in the floating boat that We might make it a Message unto you. [Amazing. He doesn't even know Noah's name at this point.] That ears might be retentive and preserve it, retain its memory and bear its lessons, a memorial for you." Even this is wild. Ears, not eyes, were used to retain its memory. Because not a single word of the Qur'an had been written down, Muhammad couldn't bring himself to acknowledge that the Bible already had a two thousand year *written* history.

The only guy in Mecca who seemed to know anything about the Bible, Waraqa, was long since dead. So all the Khadija/Muhammad combo knew was what they had gleaned from the Hanifs—just the bits and pieces of the most popular stories. Yet in Muhammad's twisted mind he somehow saw the Jewish exodus from Egypt as analogous to his torment in Mecca. He says, in essence, "Their people were bad. My people are bad. Their people ignored their prophet. My people are ignoring me. Their god wiped the unbelievers out just as my god will wipe the Meccans out." Having read the Bible, I can assure you that the only correlation between Moses' and Muhammad's critics existed between the Islamic prophet's ears.

Let's return to **"The Concrete Reality"** to find the promised literary charm and beauty. After telling us that the mountains will be crushed to powder and the sky will cleave asunder and fall to pieces while eight angels bear the Lord's throne aloft, we're told that the right-handers will read the ledger and have a grand time eating and drinking, but not the lefties. They (as in "Muhammad's Meccan tormentors") will say: 069.027 **"'I wish death had put an end to me. Of no use is my wealth, vanished is my power.' [And that's because Muhammad will steal both.] The stern command will say: 'Seize him, manacle him, chain him and cast him into the Blazing Fire of Hell. String him to a chain the length of which is seventy cubits. This is the fate of those who do not believe in the Lord Most Supreme or feed the poor. They have no friend today. They will have no food save filthy refuse which the hellish eat.'"**

The dark spirit of Islam still sounds more like Satan than God. What other demented soul would say: **"Seize him, manacle him, chain him, burn him, make him eat filthy refuse?"** Surely, such a vile rant is beneath even Ar-Rahman, the Merciful and Ar-Rahim, the Benevolent. As such, it must *not* have been beneath Muhammad, the Abused.

Just when you thought that there was no way more charm and beauty could get packed into a surah: 069.038 **"But nay! I swear that this is truly the word of an honored, illustrious, and noble Messenger; it is not the word of a poet, nor is it the word of a soothsayer."** There it is again—the confession. These words, this message, the Qur'an itself, is from a man, not god. This "filthy refuse" stinks because it isn't godly. Muhammad swears to it. Then in true megalomaniac fashion, the prophet who is unable to find anyone willing to slather him with praise, pats *himself* on the back—"I'm an honored, illustrious, and noble Messenger, not a poet or soothsayer." Sure you are, pal.

Every great con leaves clues. It's their signature. And while Muhammad was a lousy prophet he was a great con artist. Charlatans become so enamored with their ability to manipulate, they dangle clues thinking they're too clever to get caught. You can almost hear Muhammad laughing as he denies being a soothsayer.

The Meccans, knowing this charlatan better than we do today, said that they wanted proof he wasn't just making this stuff up as he went along. So he told them: *069.043* "This is a Message sent down from the Lord of men and jinn. And if the Messenger were to attribute any false words to Us, We would seize him and cut his aorta. None of you would be able to stop Us. So truly this is a Message for those who fear. Yet We know that there are those who deny and belie (this Qur'an). But truly this (Qur'an) revelation is a cause of sorrow and anguish; the nemesis of unbelievers. Verily, it (this Qur'an) is an absolute truth." Thank the Lord the surah of literary charm and beauty is over. It was beautiful how it climaxed with aorta cutting. And what could be more charming than a blend of "fear," "sorrow," and "anguish" for those who challenge the veracity of this drivel? But alas, methinks he doth protest too much.

Yet we learned something new. Muhammad is the source of the Qur'an, and he can prove that his god is real. Proof of that, however, isn't his ability to do miracles, or say things that are intelligible. No. The proof is that his imaginary god hasn't sliced his aorta. Imagine that. Since the Easter Bunny, the Tooth Fairy, and Santa Claus haven't slit my throat, do you suppose they're gods, too?

We also know more about the chains and food of hell. And that's important to Muhammad because at some point in his youth, I believe he was tied up and forced to eat trash. Just speculation on my behalf, but it makes more sense than the "Lord of men and jinn" telling us that he is going to seize his creation, manacle us in hundred-foot chains, and feed us garbage while we burn in his blazing fire.

Moving on, the subject matter of the 70th surah bears evidence that it was sent down in conditions closely resembling those that caused us to endure the refuse of the 69th. It goes something like this: "My god is so nasty, and my critics are so scummy, the former can't wait to punish the latter for denying my illustriousness and nobility." Okay, that was a paraphrase. Here is the real thing: *070.001* "A questioner questioned concerning the doom about to fall upon the infidels, which none can avert or repel, a Penalty from the Lord of the Ascending Stairways. To whom the angels and the soul take a day to ascend, whose length is fifty thousand years." The Lord of the House—a dilapidated one-story pile of rocks—now says he has a 50,000 year-long stairway (that takes a *day* to ascend). Impressive.

But while we're asking questions, I have a few. If infidels (which would be everyone on earth other than Khadija, Muhammad, and Ali) cannot "avert" the "punishment from the Lord" why "threaten" them? Why preach to them? Why create them? Is not the definition of a "sadist" one who tortures those who cannot escape? Is the Islamic god therefore, by definition, a sadist?

This is the eighteenth surah we have reviewed in its entirety. Each has plunged headfirst into the depths of hell. *070.005* **"So be patient with good patience. They surely think it (the torment) to be far off, but We see (the Day of Doom) (quite) near. On that Day the sky will be like the boiling filth of oil, the mountains will be like tufts of wool. And friends will not ask a friend, though they will be made to see each other. (All will see his father, children and relatives.) The Mujrim (disbeliever) desire will be to free himself from the Punishment by sacrificing his children as a ransom to save himself from the torment."** Muhammad must think that everyone is as depraved as he. And like so many who have been tormented before and since, he was unable to break the cycle. The abused became the abuser.

070.012 **"He would sacrifice his wife and his brother, and his kin who sheltered him, and all that is on earth to deliver himself from the Doom. By no means! For them it is the Fire of Hell! Plucking apart his body right to the skull! Taking away the head skin. Eager to roast; dragged by the head, hell shall claim all who flee."** The Islamic doom cannot be averted or repelled. It is a penalty directly from god, a deity so perverse he personally created a place where men are plucked apart and dragged by their skulls. He is even depicted as eager to roast his creation. It's hard to imagine somebody demented enough to think such thoughts, much less call them scripture.

Now that Muhammad and his Lord have scared the excrement out of us, it's time for some good old-fashioned religion. This is the new prophet's first attempt at establishing Islam. *070.019* **"Truly man was created impatient; greedy by nature, irritable and perturbed when evil touches him; and niggardly when good touches him."** As usual, he begins with a condemnation. *070.022* **"Not so those who follow (the Book). [This parenthetical was inserted by a translator. Another said, "Not those who worship." I suppose saying "Not so those who follow and worship Muhammad" would have been too accurate and thus incriminating.] Or who are devoted to Salat (prayers)."**

070.023 **"Those who persevere in devotion [to whom?]; and those in whose wealth is a recognized right [Muhammad's claim to the Ka'aba Inc.], for the needy beggar who asks and the unlucky who has lost his property and wealth [Muhammad again]; and those who hold to the Day of Recompense; and those who fear the torment of their Lord, for their Lord's torment is such none can feel secure; and those who preserve their chastity (those who guard their private parts) except with their wives and the slave girls they possess—for which there is no blame, [Sex with slaves is okay with the Big Guy. Since slavery is involuntary servitude and rape is involuntary sex, the Qur'an just condoned rape.] and those who respect their trusts; and those who stand firm in their testimonies; and those who guard their worship [How can one guard worship when the Qur'an has yet to explain it?]; such will be the honored ones in the Gardens of Bliss."**

Muhammad's initial plunge into Islamic doctrine wasn't very good. The

Straight Path to Paradise leaves much to be desired. But I suppose there is some good news here if you're a Muslim. Everything in this list is linked with "and those who" which means if you do any one of these things, you're in the Garden. So any of the following will work: saying some prayers, getting it on with a sex slave, recognizing your wealth, or begging for money.

No wonder there are so many Muslims. How can you miss with a religion like this? But knowing Muhammad as we do, I'm sure it's not all sweetness and light. He's dished out as much positive stuff as he can endure. *070.036* **"What is the matter with the disbelievers that they rush madly to listen to you (Muhammad in order to belie you and mock you and Allah's Book)? Doesn't every man long to enter the Garden of Delight?"** No. I'm not looking for a drunken orgy, multiple virgins, low-hanging fruit, or any of the other things Muhammad's spirit claimed are in store for his pals. However, for those who are, I wouldn't trust this guy to deliver.

070.039 **"By no means! For We have created them out of the base matter they know not! [I think god just said, "We don't know Shinola because he made us out of Shinola."] I am called to witness (swear by) the Lord of the (365) points of sunrise and sunset in the east and west that We can certainly replace them, substituting better men than they. [Holy Rock-of-the-Ka'aba. The Islamic god said humans are expendable. So much for the benevolent and merciful theory.] And We are not to be defeated in Our Plan. And we are not to be outrun."** *070.042* **"So let them chat vainly and play about, with their idle disputes until they encounter that Day of Doom which they have been threatened! They will rise from their sepulchers in sudden haste as if they were rushing to a goal, their eyes lowered in dejection and disgrace, aghast, abasement stupefying them—ignominy shall overtake them! Such is the Day that they are threatened with!"** The Merciful Ar-Rahman sounds like such a friendly god, doesn't he? If he's this charming, I can hardly wait to meet Allah.

I want to share a Hanif poem. In so doing you'll see where the prophet got his early material, his style, and his supply of Bible characters. Zayd ibn Amr was the most famous Meccan Hanif—a religious poet and holy man. He had a direct relationship with Muhammad. All of Zayd's insights were incorporated into the Qur'an's initial surahs, many verbatim. Muhammad stole his stories, concepts, and style—right down to the Qur'an's odd use of "Say." So, needless to say, the Hanif resisted Islam and rejected the notion that Muhammad was a prophet.

Guillaume's translation of Ishaq's *Life of Muhammad* includes several excellent examples of Zayd's poetry. All Muhammad had to do was to write himself in as prophet and add a hefty dose of hellish torment to Zayd's poems and he had himself a religion. I have added a "Q" for "Qur'an" after each line in which Zayd, not Allah, inspired Islamic scripture.

His first poem was preceded by this Hadith: *Ishaq:100* **"O Ilah, if I only knew how** you wished to be worshipped I would do so; but I do not know. Then Zyad prostrated him-self [in Islamic fashion] on the palms of his hands while facing the Ka'aba."

I worship one Lord. I renounce Al-Lat and Al-Uzza. - Q

I will not worship Hubal, though he was our lord. - Q

Ilah has annihilated many men whose deeds were evil. - Q

I serve my Lord Ar-Rahman so that the forgiving Lord may pardon my sin. - Q

So keep fearing Ilah, your Lord, and you will see the Gardens. - Q

While for the infidels, hell fire is burning. - Q

Shamed in life, when they die their breasts contract in anguish. - Q

The second poem is equally indicting, revealing the source from which the Qur'an's first surahs were plagiarized. It also reveals that Zayd was a better linguist and poet than Allah. God only knows why Ishaq included this incriminating evidence in his Sira.

To the heavenly King—there is no Ilah but Him. - Q

Beware, O men, of what follows death! - Q

You can hide nothing from Ilah. - Q

Beware of associating another with Ilah, - Q

For the straight path has become clear. - Q

Mercy I implore, others trust in the jinn. - Q

I am satisfied with you, O Ilah, as a Lord. - Q

I will not worship another Ilah beside You. - Q

Your mercy sent an angel to Moses as a herald. - Q

You said to him, Go, you and Aaron - Q

And summon Pharaoh the tyrant to turn to Ilah - Q

And say to him, 'Did you spread out this earth without a support?' - Q

Say to him, "Did you set the moon in the middle thereof, - Q

As a light to guide when night covered it?' - Q

Say to him, 'Who sent forth the sun by day? - Q

Say to him, 'Who planted seeds in the dust - Q

That herbage might grow and wax great, - Q

Therein are Signs for the understanding. - Q

You in your kindness did deliver Jonah - Q

Who spent nights in the belly of the fish. - Q

Though I glorify your name, I often repeat: - Q

O Lord, forgive my sins. - Q

O Lord of creatures, bestow Your gifts and mercy on me. - Q

An accompanying Hadith claims: "Zayd was determined to leave Mecca to travel about in search of the Hanif religion, the religion of Abraham." Two poems follow. They include concepts that also made their way into the Qur'an: "submis-sion," the name of the religion; "fear," the implement of submission; "humil-iation," the motivation for Islam; and "severing ties," the result. Then after authoring the Qur'an, the unbelieving Infidel detailed the rites and rituals

Muhammad would follow. *Ishaq:102* **"Zayd faced the Ka'aba inside the mosque and said, 'I am a sincere worshipper in truth. Here I am at your service. I take refuge in what Abraham took refuge when he stood and faced the Qiblah. I am a humble slave. I put my face in the dust. Whatever I am commanded, I must do."**

The term "Muslim" means "one who submits." After naming the religion Islam/Submission, Zayd, a man who rejected Muhammad's claims, said that he was a Muslim. *Ishaq:102* **"I submit myself."**

A Hadith from Ibn Sa'd claims Zayd said: **"The Ka'aba is the Qiblah of Abraham and Ishmael. I do not worship stones and do not pray toward them. I do not sacrifice to them, nor do I eat that which is sacrificed to them, and do not draw lots with arrows. I will not pray toward anything but this House till I die."** With only a momentary change in qiblah to lure the Jews of Yathrib to Islam, Muhammad followed Zayd's teachings verbatim. Too bad he strayed from copying his words verbatim. At least Zayd was lucid.

Earlier we discovered that Qusayy, not Abraham, was Islam's patriarch. Now we learn that Zayd, not Muhammad, was Islam's original prophet—the actual author of the Qur'an's first surahs. For added proof, lets turn to page 270 of M. J. Kister's *Study of Early Hadiths*. He presents the following Islamic Tradition: **"Muhammad slaughtered a ewe for one of the idols. [So much for the "I never did anything pagan" claim.] He roasted it and carried it with him. Then Zayd ibn Amr met us in the upper part of the valley. It was one of the hot days of Mecca. When we met we greeted each other. Muhammad said: 'Why do I see you, son of Amr, hated by your people?' He said, 'This happened without my being the cause of their hatred. I found them associating alihah (gods) with Ilah and I was reluctant to do the same. I wanted to worship Ilah according to the religion of Abraham.' The [soon-to-be] Prophet said, 'Would you like some food?' Zayd said, 'Yes.' Then Muhammad put before him the meat of the ewe. Zayd said, 'What did you sacrifice to, Muhammad?' He answered, 'To one of the idols.' Zayd said, 'I am not one to eat anything slaughtered for a divinity other than Ilah."**

Zayd practiced Islam, wrote what would become Qur'anic scripture, and was a monotheist while Muhammad was still a pagan. This serves as proof that Muhammad got his initial inspiration from a man, not god. Muhammad stole Zayd's religion, right down to the nuances of poetic style.

Now you know the truth: Qusayy was Islam's patriarch; Zayd was its prophet; the scheme was Qusayy's; the style was Zayd's. Muhammad simply took the credit.

9

DEMENTED DEITY

"Systematically by degrees, step by step, We shall
punish them in ways they cannot even imagine."

Having survived the deluge of hate unleashed in the last chapter, let's dive back into the Qur'an. After all, Islam has seduced a billion souls; there must be something godly somewhere. *068.001* **"I call to witness the Pen and what it writes. [The Islamic god just asked an inanimate object to bolster his credibility by witnessing on his behalf.] You are not a demented madman or possessed."** With all the evidence to the contrary, Muhammad found a spirit who didn't think he was crazy.

But as reassuring as that may sound to some, it's one of the most disturbing things I have read in a document that purports to be scripture. For if we are to take this at face value, the Islamic god found it necessary to tell his last and most important messenger that he wasn't demon-possessed.

068.003 **"Nay, truly for you is a never-ending reward."** I know it's not polite to gloat, but I told you so. Islam was a business transaction between a man who craved power, sex, and money and a spirit who knew how to scratch an itch.

So, the most immoral man to claim prophet status said of himself: *068.004* **"You are an exalted character of tremendous morality. Soon you will see, and they will see, which of you is afflicted with madness. Surely the Lord knows best who errs from His way, and who follows the right course. So don't listen to those who deny, or those who would form compromises with you to get you to relent. Heed not despicable men or contemptible swearers or back-biters, neither obey feeble oath-mongers, or slanderers, going about defaming, hindering good, transgressing beyond bounds, crude, deep in sin, violent and cruel, greedy, and intrusive, ignoble, and besides all that, mean and infamous because they possesses wealth and numerous sons."** I'm astonished that someone would have the gall to pass off this hateful, mean-spirited rant as scripture. There were twenty slurs in this paragraph alone. One would have been more than sufficient.

068.015 **"When you recite Our proofs and verses (from the Qur'an) they cry, 'Tales of the ancients, mere fables of long ago.' Soon shall We muzzle them and brand the beast on the snout!"** Ouch! Muhammad's Lord chafes when he's called a plagiarizer. Must be hitting a little too close to home. Let's turn to the Sira to see how close...
Ishaq:180 **"According to my information, the Apostle often sat by a young Christian slave**

named Jabr. The Meccans said, 'He is the one who teaches Muhammad most of what he brings.' Then Allah revealed, *016.103* 'We know what they (pagans) say: "It is only a mortal man who teaches him (Muhammad). But the tongue of the man they wickedly point to is notably foreign, while this (Qur'an) is pure Arabic.'" When accused of plagiarism, the best Team Islam could do was to claim that the Bible Jabr was quoting from wasn't written in Arabic. That's a problem. First, by responding to the Meccan's claim that Muhammad was out of his mind, a demon-possessed madman, plagiarizing scripture, the Qur'an confirmed that these were legitimate concerns. Muhammad's kin were convinced he was demon possessed and insane.

Second, the Qur'an continues to reflect man's least civil nature rather than rising above the fray and inspiring humankind. Name-calling isn't divine and the never-ending argument isn't motivational. Further, without the supplemental "scripture" from the Hadith, the Qur'an response is senseless. No one would have any way of knowing who was talking to whom, or why. Senseless material that floats aimlessly outside place, circumstance, and time doesn't belong in a book that claims to be dictated word for word by God.

Third, if Arabic was Allah's chosen language for revelation, why were "his" earlier revelations written in Hebrew and Greek? And as illiterates, Team Islam remains confused as to how translations work. Words are just tools, names for things and ideas mankind uses to convey a message. Every language has a word for demon, god, mad, and plagiarize. But this argument goes to the root of why today's Muslims say their Qur'anic message can't be translated—they still don't understand the nature of language. Little do they know, the Greek Gospels they are so fond of claiming credit for literally began their existence as translations of Aramaic conversations.

Fourth, the source of the Qur'an's inspiration and its audience was so dimwitted, the claim was posited that changing the language obfuscated the source. That's as lame as Muslims claiming that Muhammad couldn't have stolen his Qur'an from the Bible because he couldn't read—suggesting the surahs were miraculous. Yet even the Qur'an pokes holes in this argument by saying the Jews incorrectly *read* their scriptures to Muhammad, saying words that weren't really on their scrolls. All this Christian source had to do was to verbally convey the gist of the Biblical stories. And judging by the quality of the material we are reading, the prophet was qualified to twist them from there.

Fifth, by bringing this argument, the Qur'an injured itself. The rebuttal is a lie. The Qur'an wasn't written in **"pure Arabic."** The plethora of parentheses in the Qur'an text we have been examining proves this. They were put there to fill in missing words, fix the grammatical errors, solve the problem of dangling participles, and render a discernable message. Moreover, as you'll discover in the "Source Material" appendix, the Qur'an is filled with hundreds of foreign words, most stolen from Christians and Jews. It contains words that have no meaning in any language, including Arabic. In its defense, the Qur'an says only

Allah knows what they mean. But that defeats the whole purpose of scripture.

While we're on the subject of exposing the words of fools, the 16th surah says: *016.103* **"When we replace a message with another, and Allah knows best what He reveals, they say: 'You have made it up.'"** The Meccans recognized that Muhammad's Qur'an recitals were conflicting, and that the prophet couldn't keep his stories straight. They knew that internal contradiction was the surest sign that something was bogus. Since Muhammad wasn't able to refute his critic's claims, he had his spirit friend belittle them. Even today, unable to defend Islam, Muslims slander and threaten their accusers.

The warning: **"Surely We will try them..."** in the 68th surah is followed by seven verses of incoherent gibberish. I'll pick up the scripture reading at the 25th verse: **"So they [Muhammad's Meccan tormentors] departed, conversing in secret, saying, 'We have lost our way.' And when they saw it [?], they said: 'We are in error! We are made to suffer.' They turned, one against another, in reproach, blaming each other. They said: 'Alas for us! We were disobedient.' Said they: 'Woe to us! Such is the punishment (in this life), but greater is the punishment in the hereafter.'"** Nothing pleases an insecure and abused man more than the thought of his critics groveling at his feet—admitting that they were wrong. And when they beg for mercy, none is given. The Qur'an is little more than a mirror reflecting Muhammad's inadequacies.

068.035 **"Shall We treat those who submit and obey (Muslims) like the disbelievers?"** Muhammad's favorite words: **"submit and obey."** They permeate the Qur'an. The prophet's Islamic empire would be based upon this simple formula.

"What is the matter with you? How do you judge? Have you a scripture wherein to learn, or have you a book to read?" Yes. It's called the Bible. Comprised of the Torah, Poets, Prophets, Gospels, and Epistles. Muhammad would soon come to learn about this book. He'd steal from it, call it inspired, and then assail it. Yet on this day, he's simply illiterate and ill-informed. Taunted by his hecklers, he says that he's better than they are because they don't have a book to read. In actuality, it was Muhammad who had no book and could not read. The Qur'an never approached being a book during Muhammad's lifetime—no matter how many times he and his deity called it one. The surahs remained a loosely kept and unordered assemblage of oral recitals for decades.

068.041 **"Or do you have Partners? Then let them produce their partners, if they are truthful!"** This is a cheap shot. Muhammad is suggesting that the lesser Ka'aba idols are not on par with his deity. Yet since he was never able to coax a single miracle, not even a wiggle, out of either of his stone gods, Ar-Rahman or Allah, this is hypocritical. **"On the day when the great calamity of doom befalls them in earnest, and they are ordered to prostrate themselves, they will not. On that day there shall be a severe affliction. Their eyes will be downcast, abasement stupefying them; ignominy will cover them. Seeing that they had been summoned beforehand to bow in adoration, while they were still whole and unhurt, they refused."** Requiring prisoners to bow while **"still whole and unhurt,"** sounds more like a POW camp than a place conceived, built, and managed by god—unless, of course, that "god" is Satan.

068.044 **"Then leave Me alone with such as reject this Message and call Our pronounce-ments a lie."** Once again, the dark spirit of Islam wants to be left alone with his victims so that he can torture men personally. It's hard to imagine a spirit, other than Satan, wanting to spend his days abusing humankind. **"Systemati-cally by degrees, step by step, We shall punish them in ways they can not even imagine."** What a novel idea: a demented deity.

068.048 **"So wait with patience for the Lord's Judgment, and be not like the companion of the fish, when he cried out in agony, choked with anger."** This is Muhammad's attempt to make the story of Jonah and the whale, which he learned from Zayd, relevant to his situation. And it's not by chance that the four Biblical characters he has mentioned thus far all came out of the Hanif's most famous poem. But feeble is as feeble does: Muhammad can't recall Jonah's name, even though the Hanif gave it to him. And while being absent-minded is for-givable, suggesting that god tortured Jonah is not. Degrading this man and convoluting his mission simply reveals Muhammad's character.

"Had not grace from his Lord reached him, he would have been cast off, corrupt on a barren plain, in disgrace while he was a reprobate." Jonah was neither corrupt nor a reprobate. His mission was to save the Assyrians, the mortal enemy of the Jews, and easily the baddest boys on the planet. He went to their capital, Ninevah, and preached. Yahweh worked a miracle and the Assyrians repented, sparing the nation for a century. (Something America may want to consider.)

068.051 **"And the unbelievers would almost smite you (Muhammad) with their eyes, trip-ping you when they hear the Message. And they say: 'Surely he is possessed!'"** Those who knew Muhammad much better than we could possibly know him today, said that he was possessed by demons. We know this because the dark spirit of Islam attested to it in his book. Perhaps he considered it a compliment.

We have already reviewed the initial verses of the 73rd surah. They were allegedly "revealed" shortly after the three-year hiatus in revelation. Now, in the name of full disclosure, it's time to tackle the rest of the recital. Last time we heard the dark spirit say: *073.011* **"Leave Me alone to deal with the beliers (those who deny My Verses). Respite those who possess good things for a little while. Verily, with Us are heavy shackles (to bind them), a raging fire (to burn them), food that chokes, and a penalty (torment) of a painful doom."**

Then the 14th verse proclaims: **"One Day the earth and the mountains will be in violent commotion. And the mountains will become a heap of running sand. We have sent to you a Messenger (Muhammad) to witness against you, [not to you, but against you, the troubled spirit said] even as We sent a messenger to Pharaoh. But Pharaoh disobeyed the messenger; so We seized him and We laid on him a violent hold and a grievous punish-ment. So then how can you avoid the punishment if you disbelieve on the Day (of Doom) that will make children hoary-headed? Whereon the sky will be cleft asunder? His promise must be accomplished."** Muhammad would have been better off if he hadn't altered Zayd's Hanif poem. Twisting it gets him into trouble.

The last verse of the 73rd surah is a sore thumb—completely out of context and time. It's ten times longer than the next longest verse, and it speaks of life in Medina, not Mecca. It says there are many believers, and the Qur'an is too long to recite in one night. Muhammad speaks of travels, of fighting in Allah's Cause, of booty, the payment of the zakat, or religious tax, and of giving Allah a "goodly loan."

To stay in Mecca, we'll skip over it and return to the company of demons. Turns out they loved this incessant talk of hell fire, ripping men apart, shackles, and chains. In seventh century Arabia, devils were called jinn. The spirit who inspired the Qur'an loved his tribe so much, he named the 72nd surah in their honor: "The Jinn." Listen to what Satan, I mean Muhammad's Lord, had to say about his prophet's dubious fan club. *072.001* "Say (Muhammad): 'It has been revealed to me that a group of (three to ten) Jinn listened (to the Qur'an). They said, "We have heard a really wonderful recital (of this Qur'an)! It guides to the Right Path. We have come to believe it. We shall not associate anything with our Lord."'" This confirms that Muhammad and the demons serve the same Lord. They believe in the same scripture. They have the same religion.

072.003 "And exalted be the majesty of our Lord [Satan]: He has taken neither wife nor son. There were some foolish ones among us, who used to utter preposterous things, atrocious lies against the Lord; We Jinn had thought that no man or jinn would ever say anything untrue about the Lord." Not only does Satan's tribe love the Islamic Lord and his Qur'an, they're willing to attack his competitors and detractors. Yes, Muhammad's god had competitors, and they ranged from puny local rock idols like Allah's daughters Manat, Al-Uzza, and Al-Lat to Yahweh.

Stealing from Zayd, the Qur'an goes on to report: *072.006* "But there were men among mankind who took shelter with the male jinn. But they (jinn) increased them in waywardness, folly, and revolt. And surely they came to think as you thought, that the Lord would not raise up any Messenger." If Muslims weren't killing us, this pathetic attempt at scripture would be funny. The tale begins much like the 46th surah which we reviewed earlier, by claiming jinn think the Qur'an is wonderful. They endorse Muhammad's recital saying it's the straight path to *their* Lord. Then, two verses later these very same jinn are accused of increasing people's waywardness, folly, and revolt. The author of this surah seems irrational.

We have been told that the Islamic lord ambushes men and that he places wardens over hell so that his creation will burn in the shooting flames. Now the Qur'an says these fearsome things are in heaven: *072.008* "We jinn pried into the secrets of heaven; but we found it filled with fierce guards, stern wardens and flaming fires. We used to sit there in, hidden in observatories, trying to steal [an interesting choice of words] a hearing; but any who listen now will find a shooting star and a flaming fire watching him, lying in wait as an ambush for him." Muhammad's spirit is confusing heaven with hell. Could be heat stroke.

072.010 **"And we Jinn know not whether harm or evil is the intended fate of all men on earth, or whether the Lord intends to give them some guidance."** The Islamic god has just dug himself in deeper. He started this "revelation" saying that the jinn listened to Muhammad reciting his Qur'an—Islam's guidance to all mankind. They gave it the Good-Ka'aba-Keeping Seal-of-Approval. Now he says the jinn are clueless as to whether the lord will guide men or just fire up the godly barbeque and roast them. While I'm certain God didn't inspire this mess, it begs the question: who would be willing to promote such an obvious fraud? Who would create heaven and hell with wardens and fiery missiles? Who needs to be praised and feared? Who thinks decadence and carnal lust are heavenly. Who wants to lure men to their doom?

The spirit who leads men astray by appearing to be enlightened said, *072.011* **"There are among us [jinn] some who are upright, some otherwise; we follow divergent ways (religious sects). But we came to realize that we could not weaken the Lord on earth, nor by any means frustrate Him. We cannot escape, outpacing Him by flying away."**

Demonic spirits loving the Qur'an is so condemning of Islam it bears additional scrutiny. The Qur'an tells us that jinn were made of fire, like Satan, and belong to his tribe. In fact, in surah 18:50 Allah says that Satan is a jinn. The Qur'anic angels, by contrast, were made from light. As an interesting aside, the only earthly source of light in Muhammad's Mecca was fire. Angels and Devils would have been indistinguishable from his perspective and definition. He would not have been able to tell Gabriel from Lucifer (although he would have liked Lucifer a whole lot better).

Just to make sure we've got this demonic jinn thing right, let's look at some Bukhari and Muslim Hadiths. Perhaps Lucifer is really being confused for Gabriel. *Bukhari:V6B60N332* **"The Prophet said, 'Last night a demon from the Jinn came to me to disturb my prayer, but Allah gave me the power to overcome him. I intended to tie him to one of the pillars of the mosque till the morning so that all of you could see him.'"** If you recall, Muhammad was terrorized by Gabriel. However, he had no problem with the Devil. As I said, he has them confused.

The Qur'an says jinn are invisible, so someone must have wondered how Muhammad knew they'd heard his recital. He offered this explanation. *Bukhari:V5B58N199* **"'Who informed you Prophet about the Jinn when they heard the Qur'an?' He said, 'A tree informed me about them.'"** Satanic soothsayers work with the jinn who just testified that the Qur'an was truthful: *Bukhari:V9B93N650* **"Some people asked the Prophet about soothsayers. 'Allah's Apostle! Some of their talks come true.' The Prophet said, 'That word which happens to be true is what a Jinn snatches away by stealth (from Heaven) and pours it in the ears of the soothsayer with a sound like the cackling of a hen. The soothsayer mixes it with one hundred lies.'"**

This is as stunning as it is incriminating: *Bukhari:V6B60N475* **"Allah's Apostle became sick and could not offer his prayer. A lady came and said, 'Muhammad! I think that your Satan has forsaken you, for I have not seen him with you for two or three nights!'"**

On that Allah revealed: 'By the night when it darkens, your Lord has neither forsaken you, nor hated you.'" (Qur'an 93:1) Accused of being forsaken by Satan, Muhammad says that his lord has not forsaken him. He doesn't deny the Devil.

The man who never allowed the Qur'an to be written or read, only spoken, during his life, revealed that seductive speech was magic. *Bukhari:V6B60N662* **"Allah's Apostle said, 'Some eloquent speech is as effective as magic.'"** *Bukhari:V9B87N127* **"The Prophet said, 'I have been given the keys of eloquent speech and given victory with terror.'"** Then speaking of magic, the Devil's most seductive tool, we learn: *Bukhari:V6B60N658* **"A man worked magic on Allah's Apostle until he started imagining that he had done a thing that he had not really done."**

Earlier, the Meccans said "spitting and blowing" were signs that someone was demon-possessed, that they were a sorcerer, or a soothsayer. You don't suppose Muhammad did these things? *Bukhari:V7B71N643* **"I heard the Prophet saying, 'If anyone of you dreams something he dislikes, when you get up, blow thrice on your left.'"** The next time he was asked the same question, he replied: *Bukhari:V9B87N115* **"If you spit on the left side of your bed the bad dream will not harm you."**

Bukhari:V6B60N373 **"The Prophet explained, 'Paradise and Hell argued.... Allah said to the Hell Fire, "You are my (means of) punishment by which I torment whoever I wish of my slaves. You will have your fill. As for the Fire, it will not be filled until I put My Foot over it.'"** Allah has not delegated torture. He is a hands-on participant.

Having been possessed by the devil, Muhammad was an authority on them. He even admitted to having a devil as an attaché but said that Allah commanded him. *Muslim: B039N6757* **"Allah's Messenger said: 'Everyone has an attaché from amongst the jinn (devils).' [The translator recognized that jinn and devils were indistinguishable.] The Prophet's Companions asked: Allah's Messenger, is there one with you too?' He said: 'Yes, but Allah helps me so I am safe from his hand and he does not command me but for good.'"** Judging by the demented and immoral tone of the Qur'an, Satan has been allowed to define the word "good," too.

Knowing the truth about Allah, Muhammad didn't want anyone questioning how his Lord was conceived. *Muslim:B001N0244/Bukhari:V4B54N496* **"The Messenger of Allah observed: 'Satan comes to everyone of you and says, "Who created this and that," until he asks, "Who created your Lord?" When he comes to that, one should seek refuge and keep away from such idle thoughts.'"** Lucifer was created by Yahweh which proves he wasn't God.

Speaking of his own ministry: *Bukhari:V4B55N554* **"Allah's Apostle said, 'Shall I not tell you about the a story of which no prophet told his nation? Someone will bring with him what will resemble Hell and Paradise, and what he will call Paradise will be actually Hell.'"**

A tradition related by both Bukhari and Muslim protest that Muhammad's demonic encounter was validated historically. How, pray tell? **"The Prophet was going to visit a fair with some Companions. On the way a company of the jinn happened by. When they heard the Qur'an being recited, they tarried and listened attentively. This event is described in the Qur'an and shows that the jinn who heard the Qur'an** were polytheists and deniers of the Prophethood of Muhammad. Then, it is confirmed historically that the Prophet was able to convince them to worship Allah alone."

While on the subject of demented deities, please consider: *Bukhari:V4B54N482* "Allah's Apostle said, 'The Hell Fire complained to its Lord saying, "O my Lord! My different parts are eating each other up." So, He allowed it to take two breaths, one in winter, the other in summer. This is the reason for the severe heat and bitter cold you find in weather.'" Imagine: Muslims believe God inspired this. But it doesn't sound and more inspired than this: *Bukhari:V4B54N487* "The Prophet said, 'The Hell Fire is 69 times hotter than ordinary worldly fires.' So someone said, 'Allah's Apostle, wouldn't this ordinary fire have been sufficient to torture the unbelievers?'"

Team Islam knew that demons loved the darkness of night. *Bukhari:V4B54N533* "Muhammad preached, 'Cover your utensils, tie your water skins, close your doors, and keep your children close at night, as Jinn spread out at such time and snatch things away. When you go to bed put out your lights, for they may use a candle to burn you and your house.' Ata added, 'The Prophet actually said, Devils, instead of Jinn.'"

As you read the next two Hadith, remember, Islam claims they're scripture. *Bukhari:V4B54N516* "The Apostle said, 'If anyone rouses from sleep and performs the ablution, he should wash his nose by putting water in it and then blowing it out thrice, because Satan has stayed in the upper part of his nose all night.'" *Bukhari:V4B54N492* "It was mentioned to the Prophet that a man slept in and missed the morning prayer. The Prophet said, 'Satan urinated in his ears.'" If Muhammad's dark spirit were not Satan, why would the Devil be upset by a Muslim missing prayers?

Muhammad's propensity to cavort with demons is unnerving. Each encounter unravels the fabric of Islam's credibility. As such, I took the liberty of pulling some analysis from Maududi's Qur'an commentary. "The jinn used to be able to eavesdrop on heaven but suddenly they found that angels had been set as guards and meteorites were being shot on every side so that they could find no place of safety to hear the secret news. They had set about searching for the unusual thing that had occurred on the earth to explain why the security measures had been tightened up. Many companies of jinn were moving about in search when one of them, after having heard the Qur'an from the Prophet, formed the opinion that it was the very thing which had caused all the gates of the heavens to be shut against them." There must be something in Islam that turns men's minds to mush.

Maududi continues to press the Islamic case. "Before one studies 'The Jinn' surah one must know the reality of jinn so as to avoid mental confusion. Many misunderstand, thinking that jinn are not real, but only a figment of ancient superstitions and myths. They have not formed this opinion on the basis that they have known all the realities and truths about the universe. They cannot claim to possess any such knowledge.... The person who thinks that what he does not perceive, does not exist, and what exists must necessarily be perceived, provides proof of the narrowness of his own mind. With this mode of thought, not to speak of the jinn, man cannot even acknowledge any reality.... Muslims have given strange interpretations to the clear statements of the Qur'an about jinn, Iblis, and Satan.

They say that this does not refer to any hidden creation, but implies man's own animal forces, which have been called Satanic. But the statements of the Qur'an in this regard are so clear and explicit that this bears no relevance. The Qur'an leaves no room to regard the jinn as a human species. At the creation of Adam, Iblis resolved to misguide mankind, and since then the jinn have been persistently trying to mislead man. They deceive with evil suggestions, beguiling, and making evil seem good." Maududi hasn't helped his cause. By trying to convince us that the jinn are not only real, but deceitful, he has condemned Islam. "The Jinn" surah reveals that jinn endorse the Qur'an. Maududi confirms that the Qur'an claims that jinn exist to "deceive with evil suggestion, beguiling, and making evil seem good." Therefore, the Qur'an must be designed to "misguide mankind," to "deceive," to make "evil seem good." Nice job, professor.

Now that we understand jinn, it's time to finish their surah. 072.013 "So, since we [Jinn] have listened to the guidance (of this Qur'an), we have accepted (Islam): and any who believes in his Lord has no fear of loss, force, or oppression." If that's the case, why was so much of the Qur'an fixated on the ongoing oppression Muhammad endured? This leaves us with only three alternatives: Muhammad didn't believe in his lord, god was telling us a lie, or Islam's deity was impotent and couldn't protect his prophet. Perhaps we've stumbled onto something.

072.014 "Amongst us are some Muslims (who surrendered, submitting), and some who are disbelievers. Those who submit in Islam—they have sought the path of right path." Submission to god and messenger is the essence of Islam. Muhammad was able to gain what he coveted by threatening men with hell's fires, by seducing them with paradise's virgins, and by forcing them to into submission with jihad.

072.015 "But the Qasitun (disbelievers) are the firewood of hell." What sounds more warped to you: a god who turns his creation into firewood, or a man who threatens such nonsense to coerce others into submission?

072.016 "If they (non-Muslims) had remained on the right path, We should have given them plenty to drink that We might try them by that means." No matter how this is interpreted—it's weird. How could non-Muslims have been on the right path? How can drinking be a trial? And why try those who are on the right path in the first place?

The Islamic god isn't a very nice spirit. "If any turns away from the reminder of his Lord (the Qur'an), He will thrust him into an ever growing torment, and cause for him a severe penalty." Once again, it's "god" doing the thrusting and the inflicting.

If the jinn listen to and vouch for the Qur'an, why is Muhammad being told to say that he can't bring them to right conduct? 072.019 "Yet when the Devotee stood up to invoke his Lord, the Jinn crowded around Him to listen. [The capitalized "Devotee" and "Him" refer to Muhammad as he was the only one reciting. And that's a problem, because to invoke in a religious setting means to call upon or pray to. This puts Muhammad on par with his deity.] Say (Muhammad): 'I invoke my Lord alone, and ascribe unto Him no partner.' Say: 'It is not in my power to cause you Jinn harm. I cannot hurt or benefit you, nor bring you to right conduct.'"

Before we hear what the Lord of the Jinn wants Muhammad to say next, it's important to expose the nature of this revelation. The Islamic god isn't speaking for himself. The "Say" format is Muhammad's way of speaking on his own behalf while keeping the semblance, or trappings, of religiosity. He borrowed the style from Zayd. *072.022* "**Say: 'No one can save me from God's punishment, nor can I find a place of refuge apart from Him unless I deliver the communications I receive from Him and deliver His Message.' [With that said, the remainder of this verse is supposed to be god talking. Ignore the fact it's written in third rather than first person.] Whoever disobeys the Lord and His Messenger then there is for him the fire of Hell where they shall abide forever.**" That's Islam in a nutshell. Obey Muhammad or you'll roast in hell.

Some might challenge my conclusions on the basis that I omitted "Lord." Fact is, neither Allah nor Ar-Rahman ever spoke. The only evidence of their existence is Muhammad's testimony. And since *his* story isn't remotely credible, we are left with the deranged ranting of an insecure abuse victim in pursuit of revenge via the Profitable Prophet Plan. You see, all Muhammad had to do was to corrupt a mere handful of lost souls with promises of stolen treasure. Once they obeyed, the pirate was in a position to force others into submission. And he did, lining the pockets and satiating the cravings of the desperate men he had lured into his company. Muslims became militants. The militants became murderers. The murderers became terrorists. The terrorists became like Muhammad. And Muhammad became more and more like the god he had created. The circle was complete.

Next we are told that god can't keep a secret and that the all-knowing, all-seeing spirit needs to have sentinels hang with his messengers to be certain his messages are delivered. Generals are known to assign sentinels, as are political leaders, but gods are supposed to act like gods. *072.024* "**Until they see with their own eyes that [Hell] which they are promised, they will not know who is weaker and less important. Say: 'I do not know whether (the punishment) which you have promised is near, or whether my Lord prolongs its term. (He is) the knower of the unknown, and He does not divulge His secrets to any except to an Apostle He has chosen. And then he makes a band of guards march before him and behind him that He may know that they have delivered the Messages of their Lord. He counts all things.'**"

Muhammad's attempts at "religion" were feeble. The preponderance of early Islamic scripture was little more than an angry rant. Since this is pathetic, it begs the question: why bother trying to understand it? Muhammad was obviously a deeply disturbed con man, which makes everything he said irrelevant. Or does it? It wasn't so very long ago that another angry rant, *Mein Kampf*, was discounted for exactly the same reasons.

Though it is dark and twisted, understanding the Qur'an is essential to our survival. Muhammad, like Hitler, succeeded in seducing a sufficient number of misfits into submission to terrorize the world. They poisoned their victims with their doctrines, Islam and Nazism—turning good men bad. Consciences were eroded, minds were corroded, and the abused became abusers. They became like their prophet, *der fuhrer*. And the world paid a horrible price.

The seventh surah is one of many that ties Islam to terror. It began, as you may recall, with Allah launching a blitzkrieg attack on some unsuspecting townsfolk. His line, **"Our terror came unto them while they slept,"** was chilling. We covered the first half of this revelation in the third chapter as it devolved into a disturbing conversation between Allah, Satan, and Adam. Now it's time to jump back in where we left off. *007.039* **"The first will say to the last: 'See there! No advantage have you over us; so taste the torment you have earned!' To those who reject Our signs and deny Our revelations, treating them with arrogance, no opening will there be of the gates of the Garden of Bliss, until the camel can pass through the eye of the needle. Such is our reward for the guilty. They shall have a bed on the floor of Hell and coverings of fire; this is how We reward them."** The Qur'an may be the only book that is more racist, hateful, and violent than *Mein Kampf*. Hitler gave six million Jews a bed of fire. Muhammad's dark spirit could have been his inspiration.

I have a copy of *Mein Kampf* published immediately after Chamberlain signed the Munich Pact giving most of Czechoslovakia to Hitler. The land-for-peace process was complete; the war had yet to begin. With that in mind, I want to quote from the translators' introduction. As I do, I want you to mentally substitute 9/11 for the annexation of Czechoslovakia, Muhammad for Hitler, the Qur'an for *Mein Kampf*, and Islam for Nazism. "The pact of Munich [9/11] has awakened the American public as never before to the seriousness to the world and to themselves of the Nazi [Islamic] program and consequently to the possible significance of every page of the book that can justly be regarded as the Nazi [Islamic] gospel. Here, in its entirety, for the American people to read and to judge for themselves, is the work which has sold in Germany [the Nation of Islam] by the millions, and which is the best-written evidence of the character and spirit of Adolf Hitler [Muhammad] and his government. *Mein Kampf* [the Qur'an] gives the full flavor of the author's mind, conveying his motivations."

As if they were talking about the Qur'an and its author Muhammad, the translators said: "Hitler [Muhammad] was not an artist in literary expression, but a political profiteer often indifferent to grammar and syntax. *Mein Kampf* [the Qur'an] is a propagandistic essay by a violent partisan. As such, it often warps historical truth, sometimes ignoring it completely. We have, therefore, felt it our duty to accompany the text with factual information, which constitutes an extensive critique of the original. No American would like to assume responsibility for giving the public a text which, if not tested in the light of diligent inquiry, might convey the impression that Hitler [Muhammad] was writing history rather than propaganda."

Fifty million people perished because we did not heed these words: "In conclusion, read *Mein Kampf* [the Qur'an] with a clear eye and the book will show you what manner of man *der Fuhrer* [the Prophet] is—one who as a boy had nothing excepting a passionate belief that Germany [the Nation of Islam] must obtain a larger place in the sun with the help of the sword. The engines of industry now spin round in trepidation, and the engines of war are piled giddily in higher and higher pyramids. Already the latter are all that really count—the former only serve to create an illusion. There will be no stopping this doctrine until in the world of ideas or ideals there are those which are stronger than those contained in *Mein Kampf* [the Qur'an]. It is our profound conviction that as soon as enough people have seen through this book, lived with it until its revelations are so startlingly vivid that all else is obscured by comparison, the tide will begin to turn."

They said: "We have the deepest regard for the German [Arab] people... so we have elected to set down without malice, yet with all the truth that we can muster, the record of Hitler [Muhammad] and his Struggle [Recital]." Today, the stakes are even higher. With weapons of mass destruction, a billion may die in the wake of our ignorance. So in an attempt to postpone what may be inevitable, in the last chapters I will compare *Mein Kampf* to the Qur'an, and Nazism to Islam. But between now and then, take a deep breath and continue to journey with me through the mind and motivations of Hitler's twin, the Prophet Muhammad.

Muslims claim that the 103rd surah is a matchless specimen. Maududi says: **"A whole world of meaning was compressed into its brief words, which is too vast in content to be fully expressed even in a book. Imams have rightly said that if the people only considered this surah, it alone would suffice for guidance."**

103.001 **"I swear by time, most surely man is in loss, except those who believe, and do good, and enjoin on each to bear in fortitude the trials that befall."** That's it—the whole thing—start to finish. While it was neither really good nor really bad, at least it was really short.

Let's try another blitzkrieg surah. *104.001* **"Woe to every kind of scandal monger and backbiter, [Ah, there we go. We're back to the Muhammad we've come to know.] who amasses wealth and count it. He thinks that his wealth will make him immortal."** Every time Muhammad makes a stab at religion, he fouls it up. The first time he tried this he claimed that rape—sex with slaves—was a means to heaven. Now he's saying that the rich are scandalmongers because they think wealth, not faith, will bring immortality. But that's nonsense. Wealth is most often accumulated by bright and industrious people. As such, they are seldom delusional. Muhammad, however, was, and wealth ultimately bought *him* immortality.

Thievery in Medina saved Islam and made a failed prophet infamous—immortal—in the minds of billions.

104.004 **"By no means! He will be sure to be thrown into that which breaks him into pieces. (or) Nay, but verily he will be flung to the Consuming One. (or) No! he shall most certainly be hurled into the crushing disaster."** I have provided several translations so that you might not be cheated out of this wondrous pearl. *104.005* **"And what will explain to you that which Breaks him into Pieces? (or) what the Consuming One is! (or) what the crushing disaster is? It is the fire kindled by Allah which leaps up over them penetrating the hearts of men. It shall be made to vault over them. Lo, it has closed in on them. In pillars outstretched."** Allah personally kindles the fires of hell. Please let that linger in your mind. Islam's hell is not separation from Allah; hell is where Allah lives (to burn 999 out of every 1,000 people)!

The 79th surah opens with oaths sworn by angels akin to the Nazi S.S. Our illustrious Muslim cleric explains: **"The people have been told: 'The hellish torments which you regard as absolutely impossible, are not difficult for Allah, even though He will have to make lengthy preparations. Just a single jolt will upset this system of the world… and the same people who were wont to deny it will be trembling with fear, terror struck at what they thought was impossible.'"** He continues: **"Then, relating the story of the Prophet Moses and Pharaoh, the people have been warned: 'You know full well what fate the Pharaoh met as a consequence of belying the Messenger and rejecting the guidance brought by him and endeavoring to defeat his mission by trickery and deceit. If you do not learn a lesson from it and do not change your ways and attitude accordingly, you also will have to meet the same fate.'"** In other words, my conclusions are identical to those of the Muslim sages. We only differ when it comes to Muhammad's inspiration and motivation.

I do not believe God can be this demonic or moronic. They do. *079.001* **"I swear by those (angels) who violently tear out (the souls of the wicked), and drag them forth to destruction, by those who gently take out (the souls of the believers), by those meteors rushing by, swimming along (angels or planets), and by those who press forward as in a race (the angels, or stars, or horses [the translators added, clueless as to what their god was trying to say]), and by those who regulate the affair."** Muhammad contradicted two essential elements of Islam. This Qur'anic passage is a far cry from perfect. It isn't even comprehensible. And throughout the Qur'an, the lord claims he will reform decomposing men bodily as he retrieves them from the grave. If we are to be reassembled in the flesh, why are our souls torn out? And why does this separation occur before judgment?

079.006 **"On the Day the earth and mountains will shake in violent commotion, followed by oft-repeated commotions (and everybody will die). Hearts on that day shall palpitate, beating painfully in fear and anxiety. Cast down will be their owners' eyes."** Muhammad is having fun now. You can almost see him getting all worked up. *079.010* **"They say: 'Shall we be restored to (our) former state? Even after we have become rotten crumbled bones?'"** That's exactly what I just explained. Bodies are reformed, which makes soul separation nonsensical (for Islam, anyway).

Again, without benefit of an intelligible transition, we're asked: *079.015* **"Has the story of Moses reached you?"** The only place the Meccans could have heard of Moses is from the same source Muhammad heard it—the Hanifs (who had heard it from the Jews)—both of whom he plagiarized. **"When his Lord called upon him in the holy valley of Tuwa twice, 'Go to Fir'aun (Pharaoh), verily he has become inordinate, transgressed all bounds and rebelled, and say to him, "Wouldst thou that thou shouldst be purified?"'"** Okay, I let that verse go unedited. You'll have to figure out what Allah was trying to say on your own. Normally I try to clean up his stylistic and grammatical errors in order to make reading easier. *079.019* **"And, 'That I guide you to your Lord, so you should fear Him.'"** Not love him, for to know the dark spirit of Islam is to fear him.

There is nothing more dangerous than a little knowledge. Still in Mecca, Muhammad didn't know enough about Moses or his mission to keep from impugning himself. The reason Yahweh sent Moses to Pharaoh had nothing to do with the Egyptian monarch and everything to do with the Jewish people. On the corruption scale, Pharaoh was less rebellious and inordinate than most other dictators. In fact, Egypt was the most moral of all ancient societies. But the Jewish people were enslaved, and Yahweh wanted them freed.

These errors were not careless. They were part of Muhammad's twisted plan. The prophet was a failure among his people. They mocked him and his claims mercilessly. To redeem himself, our charlatan needed to make his self-serving quest look like a godly mission. So he elected to corrupt the Exodus story. Only it didn't fit. Moses wasn't sent as a messenger to preach to Pharaoh; he was sent to free his people from bondage. Therefore, Muhammad had to corrupt the story to serve *his* personal agenda.

But he didn't do a very good job…*079.020* **"Then (Moses) showed him the Great Sign. But (Pharaoh) rejected and disobeyed."** Sorry. The first sign wasn't mighty. In fact, it was so meaningless, it was replicated by Pharaoh's magicians. Moses' staff became a snake. It wasn't until Pharaoh became obstinate that Yahweh's signs, not Moses', became plagues of epic proportion.

079.021 **"He turned his back, striving (against the Lord)."** Oops. Pharaoh wasn't fighting against God. He thought he *was* a god. Pharaoh was trying to keep his Jewish slaves, nothing more. **"Then he collected (his people) and cried, 'I am your Lord, the Most High.'"** Good grief. Muhammad's Lord needs a history lesson. Pharaoh, like most dictators of his day, was considered to be a god but never "the Most High." The Pharaohs built temples to the sun god Amun-Re. Allah and Ar-Rahman, pagan moon gods themselves, ought to have known that.

079.025 **"So the Lord seized him with punishment for his last and first crime (making an example of him). Truly this is an instructive warning for whoever fears the consequences."** With every word, Muhammad dug himself in deeper. Yahweh never seized Pharaoh, nor did he make an example of him. All Yahweh did was up the ante until Pharaoh let his people go. The truth simply didn't fit Islam's agenda or capabilities. Muhammad couldn't even coax his spirit to turn a snake into a stick. Yet he is without excuse. He claimed Allah was Yahweh, so he should have known about the exodus of his people. But alas, without these bastardized Bible stories, his Qur'an would have been a very thin book—a pamphlet at best.

Without segue, we jump to: *079.027* **"What! Are you the harder to create, or is heaven? He raised its height, and put it into a right good state."** This must be a trick question, because we are harder to create. You can find Allah's heaven replicated in any whorehouse. Throughout the Qur'an, the proofs of god's existence are absurd. Here heaven, which cannot be seen, is called a sign.

079.029 **"Its night He endows with darkness, and its splendor He brings out."** By his own admission, he is the prince of darkness. This is the third time Islam's dark spirit has shown an affinity for the night. Score another point for those who claim Islam is Demonic.

The Qur'an says its god **"spread the earth," "brought water therefrom,"** and **"fixed mountains firmly to be a benefit for men and cattle."** Then: *079.034* **"When the disastrous calamity comes; and Hell Fire shall be placed in full view for (all) to see, then for him who rebelled, Hell Fire will be his home."**

In a verse that could define hypocrisy; Muhammad, the ultimate sexual libertine, tells us that those who refrain from lust will be rewarded with lust: *079.040* **"For those who feared standing before his Lord (tribunal) and restrained himself from impure lustful desires, their abode will be the Garden of Bliss."** While this wasn't the most demonic surah or the most dimwitted, it was the most poorly written. It's little wonder Muslims say the Qur'an cannot be translated.

Thus far we have reviewed twenty-five surahs—nearly a quarter of Allah's book. We have yet to encounter anything profound, anything that resembles holiness. And as we turn the page to the 80th surah, we discover that it opens without benefit of a subject: *080.001* **"frowned and turned away."** The translators assumed it was **"(The Prophet),"** but it's time I present a surah without benefit of Allah's little helpers so that you might see how they were actually written.

The **"He Frowned"** Surah: **"frowned and turned away. Because there came to him the blind man. And how can you know that he might become pure? Or that teaching might profit him? As for him who thinks himself self-sufficient, to him you attend; What does it matter to you if he will not become pure? But as to him who came to you running, and is afraid. Of him you are neglectful and divert your attention to another, nay; indeed it is an admonition. So whoever wills, let him mind it."** Grammatical errors, omissions, and poor writing quality aside, this surah demonstrates why Ishaq's Sira is more essential to Islam than the Qur'an. Without the context his chronology of oral reports provides, this Qur'anic story, like all others, is senseless.

Ishaq explains that while trying to promote himself, Muhammad ignored this poor blind man (Abdallah bin Umm) in favor of a Quraysh chief. The reason was obvious. The chief had everything Muhammad coveted—the blind man didn't. Teaching the blind man would not "profit him."

The next verse also begins without a subject. 080.013 "(It is) in Books held in (honor), exalted (in dignity), kept pure and holy, (written) by the hands of scribes. Honorable, Pious, Just, Noble and righteous." This verse alone makes Islam an open and shut case, condemning Muhammad as fraud. The "exalted books kept pure and holy" were the Torah, Psalms, and Gospels. They were the *only* books, other than the Qur'an, that Allah and Muhammad said were divinely inspired scripture. Yet there were no Qur'anic scribes at this point, as the Qur'an was *not* written. The first and only Islamic scribe during Muhammad's lifetime resigned within days of accepting the job, only to be hunted down and assassinated by the prophet. The real scribes of this day were a well-known order of devoutly pious Jews. But the scripture they "kept pure and holy" was the antithesis of the Qur'an.

Coveting what rightfully belonged to Yahweh, Islam's dark spirit categorically stated that the Bible was *his* book. Equally important, he said it had been kept pure by honorable scribes. So wouldn't you know it, the first time he said something nice, it killed him. If the Bible was kept pure there is no possible explanation for the divergence in Qur'anic stories, the difference in gods or doctrines. If Allah said this, as Muhammad attests, he committed suicide because he destroyed Islam. For if the Bible is as Allah says—inspired and pure—then a book that repudiates its doctrines and damns its people can be neither inspired nor pure. It's simple logic: if B is right, and if Q contradicts B, Q cannot be right. So what then does that make Q?

The Meccans knew Muhammad was wrong, they just didn't know why. During the seventh century they were about as unfamiliar with Biblical scripture as most agnostics are today. They knew enough to rebuke Muhammad for stealing Jewish stories—saying that the Qur'an was nothing more than "other people's lore." But while they recognized his plagiarism was uninspired, his twisted variants were not nearly as incriminating to them as they are to us. Muhammad's agenda was, however, totally transparent. Eager to make submission sound godly, the new prophet latched on to the only credible monotheistic religion, heritage, and scriptures available to him. He plagiarized them, twisting stories to serve his scheme—a scheme that could only have prevailed in the illiterate and isolated realm of central Arabia.

Muhammad began his crusade to confiscate control of the family business by stealing the god and doctrines of the Hanifs. When they proved insufficient, he changed his qiblah, turning himself into a Biblical prophet. The first attempt was feeble, as we have just seen. It would take Muhammad some time to learn enough about the Bible to turn it into the cornerstone of Islam.

Yet within months of selecting that new cornerstone, Muhammad would change his qiblah once again. This time he pulverized the rock upon which he had built his new faith and returned to his pagan past. Coming full circle he distanced himself from the Bible by legitimizing every aspect of Qusayy's religious scam—the hajj pilgrimage, the religious tax, the war banners, the Ramadhan fasts, the holy months, the Ka'aba, and even the Black Stone. The place of prostration changed from Jerusalem to Mecca, the apple of his eye, the place and people he wanted to control.

But the price was high. Any flirtation between Islam and rational thought died an ugly death during these transformations. Mutually exclusive doctrines were praised and repudiated, treated as if they were the same and separate. Islam self-destructed, as did its god and his messenger. Now, if it would only die in the minds of those who use it to terrorize the world.

Continuing with the "**He Frowned**" surah: *080.017* **"Be cursed man! He has self-destructed. From what stuff did He create him? From nutfa (male and female semen drops) He created him and then set him in due proportion."** The continual cursing of man has grown wearisome. Muhammad and his Lord appear to have self-destructed. There is no female semen, and whose *nutfa* drops do you suppose were used? It also bears mentioning here that Allah claims to have created man thirty-five times in his Qur'an. The method, however, changes. There are twenty-five variations of the material he used.

While we're on the subject, I thought you might get a chuckle out of these: *Bukhari:V4B55N546* **"The Prophet said, 'If a man has sexual intercourse with his wife and gets discharge first, the child will resemble the father, and if the woman gets discharge first, the child will resemble her.'"** That was brilliant. As was this sermon on predestination: *Bukhari:V4B55N550* **"The Prophet said, 'Allah has appointed an angel in the womb, and the angel says, "Lord, a drop of semen discharge. Lord, a clot, Lord, a piece of flesh." And then, if Allah wishes to complete the child's creation, the angel will say. Lord, male or a female? Lord, wretched or blessed in religion? What will his livelihood be? What will his age be?" The angel writes all this while the child is in the womb of its mother.'"** In other words, our fate is sealed. The Islamic god chooses whom he wishes to abuse.

This lecture on man's four-month gestation follows an assertion that Muhammad's insights were "**truly inspired**," and thus scripture. *Bukhari:V4B54N430* **"Allah's Apostle, the true and truly inspired said, 'Regarding the matter of the creation of a human being: humans are put together in the womb of the mother in forty days. Then he becomes a clot of thick blood for a similar period. He becomes a piece of flesh for forty days. Then Allah sends an angel who is ordered to write four things: the new creature's deeds, livelihood, date of death, and whether he will be blessed or wretched. He will do whatever is written for him.'"** Dr. Muhammad went on to preach: *Bukhari:V4B54N506* **"When a human being is born, Satan touches him at both sides of the body with his two fingers. That is why it cries."**

In Judeo-Christianity, death came as a result of man turning away from God. In Islam death is the result of god. *080.020* **"As for the way—He has made it easy for him. Then He causes him to die. Then assigns his grave. Then when He pleases, He raises him to life again. Nay, by no means has man fulfilled what the Lord has commanded him."** In Islam, disease is also divine: *Bukhari:V7B71N665* **"The Prophet said, 'No contagious** disease is conveyed without Allah's permission.'" Fortunately, there is a cure: *Bukhari:* *V4B54N537* "The Prophet said, 'If a house fly falls in your drink, you should dip it (in the drink), for one of its wings has a disease and the other has the cure for the disease.'" However, since fevers are the result of disease and since Allah lives in hell…*Bukhari:V4B54N484* "I heard the Prophet saying, 'Fever is from the heat of the Hell Fire.'"

080.024 "Then let man look at his food and how We provide it. We pour water in showers and We split the earth in fragments, and produce therein corn, grapes and nutritious fodder, olives, dates, enclosed gardens, dense with trees, fruits and grasses." Phraseology that might make sense metaphorically is used improperly as a proof statement.

080.033 "At length, when the deafening cry comes, that Day shall a man flee from his own brother, and from his mother and father, and he will abandon his wife and children. Each one of them will have enough concern to make him indifferent to others." Allah has prepared punishments so horrific, men and women will abandon their children, parents, and spouses to avoid enduring it. I dare say, only a man who had suffered such torment, would attribute such behavior to God.

080.038 "Some faces that Day will be beaming, laughing, and other faces will be dust-stained, veiled in darkness, such will be the rejecters, the doers of iniquity, the disbelievers, the wicked." Islam is wickedness veiled in darkness.

Maududi introduces our next divine revelation. "In the 81st surah, Allah defends his Messenger. 'Whatever Muhammad is presenting before you is not the bragging of a madman, nor an evil suggestion inspired by Satan, but the word of a noble, exalted and trustworthy messenger sent by Us, whom Muhammad has seen with his own eyes in the bright horizon of the clear sky in broad daylight.'"

The 81st surah begins as the 80th ends. *081.001* "When the sun is wound round and its light is overthrown; When the stars fall; When the mountains vanish like a mirage; When the pregnant she-camels are neglected; When the wild beasts are herded together; When the oceans become a blazing fire or overflow; When the souls are sorted out and joined with their bodies [not plucked away as we read earlier]; When the female buried alive, is questioned—for what crime she was killed?" We remain mired in the prophet's favorite subject, the Day of Doom. *081.010* "When the pages are laid open; When heaven is stripped off and torn away; When the Hell Fire is lighted and the Blazing Fire is kindled to fierce heat; When the Garden of Bliss is brought near. (Then) every person will know what he has brought." Sorry Islam, but you can't have it both ways. Allah can't *predestine* men as he did in the previous surah and then say that their fate is based upon their *deeds*. This is an irreconcilable contradiction. It confirms that the author wasn't rational.

081.015 "So verily I swear by the planets that recede. I swear by the stars that run swiftly and hide themselves; and by the Night as it dissipates; and by the Dawn as it breathes away the darkness." This may sound poetic in Arabic, but it's between senseless and pagan in English. Hopefully it's leading somewhere… *081.019* "Verily this is the Word (the Qur'an brought by) a most honorable Messenger imbued with power, the Lord of the Throne, Mighty, One to be obeyed." We have reached the core of Islam—the seed from which the religion emerged. Muhammad proclaims: I am **"honorable."** I am **"imbued with power."** I am a **"Mighty"** man. I am **"One to be obeyed."** I am **"Lord of the Throne."** "I'm *the* authority, kissing cousin to god."

Loving, caring, compassionate, and wise didn't make the prophet's list. But no matter; all of this, all of Islam, is summarized by these words: "I am the **'Messenger imbued with power, the Lord of the Throne, Mighty, One to be obeyed.'"**

081.022 **"And people, your comrade is not one who is possessed, or one who has gone mad."** A man who must repeatedly protest that he isn't possessed, is. The reason the protestation is repeated so often is because the charge was leveled with regularity. The Meccans recognized that "revelations" this demented had to be mired in hell. They further realized that revelations this delusional were hallucinogenic, the product of insanity: *081.023* **"And without doubt he saw himself on the clear horizon."** Some translations say he saw "Him," as in "God," on the horizon. Others say Muhammad saw himself. They are equally true. In Islam, man created god in his image. Muhammad modeled Allah's persona.

Maududi's interpretation of this verse is consistent with Ali's translation. They claim Muhammad saw his Lord, as in Allah. But that's a problem because Aisha said: *Bukhari:V4B54N457* **"Whoever claims that the Prophet Muhammad saw his Lord is committing a great fault for he only saw Gabriel in his genuine shape in which he was covering the horizon."** The Noble Qur'an translation agrees with the Hadith. It claims that it was Gabriel on the horizon and goes so far as to add the angel's name to the text. But surely the Islamic god isn't suggesting that "Gabriel," a mere angel, is the Lord of the Throne?

So we are left with nothing but bad choices. The most direct reading has Muhammad saying these grandiose things about himself as the list follows the "Messenger." And it's senseless to promote an angel to the status of "Lord" unless, of course, that angel is really Lucifer, whose life's ambition is to be: **"imbued with power, the Lord of the Throne, Mighty, One to be obeyed."**

Let's take this one step further: *Bukhari:V6B60N378* **"Masruq asked Aisha, 'O Mother of the faithful, did Muhammad see his Lord?' Aisha said, 'What you have said makes my hair stand on end! Know that if somebody tells you one of the following things, he is a liar. Whoever tells you that Muhammad saw his Lord, is a liar. Whoever tells you that the Prophet knows what is going to happen tomorrow, is a liar. And whoever tells you that he concealed, is a liar.' Aisha added. 'The Prophet saw Gabriel in his true form twice.'"** So, Muhammad lied when he said he was a prophet. What's more, if Muhammad only saw Gabriel twice, the Qur'an is 112 surahs too long.

Knowing the truth, Muhammad desperately tried to deny it. But the more he protested, the more obvious his scam became. *081.024* **"Neither is he a concealer, withholding knowledge of the unseen. Nor is it (the Qur'an) the Word of an evil spirit accursed, the utterance of a devil, the curses of Satan."** The accusation was very close to being accurate. The Qur'an *is* **"the word of an evil spirit accursed, the utterance of a devil, the curses of Satan."**

According to the Hadith, Aisha was asked about her husband's nature. She said: **"Muhammad's character is the Qur'an."** In other words, he was his god. And his psychopathic delusion and visions of grandeur continued to the bitter end of the surah. *081.026* **"Then where are you going? Verily this (Qur'an) is no less than a reminder to all the Alamin (men and jinn [demons or devils])."**

Muslims are quick to criticize any criticism of Islam, claiming that all critiques are inaccurate because they only focus on verses that make their religion look bad. They may be right. Having analyzed a thousand verses thus far, every one has been bad.

Others claim that infidels unfairly take their scriptures out of context. Times have changed, they say. But this charge is a two-edged sword. If the Qur'an is no longer relevant to our times, why follow its teachings?

Some give up defending Islam and simply point an accusing finger at their antagonists, calling them hatemongering racists. Having read these surahs, I'm sure you recognize that for every accusing finger they thrust forward, three more point back at them. In this regard, Muslims are similar to Communist propagandists. They project their flaws onto their opponents and thereby confuse enough people to thwart an assailant's effectiveness. Yet the inverse of their charge is true: it is *Islam* that is racist, hateful, and intolerant. It demonizes all who don't surrender.

It is therefore permissible, even proper, to hate Islam (without hating Muslims) just as it was possible to despise Nazism without hating Germans. In fact, the German people were the biggest beneficiaries of our fight against Hitler's demented doctrine. Our awakening and resolve, our courage and sacrifice, freed Germans, as it may someday free Muslims from a similarly oppressive, racist, warmongering, and demented doctrine.

Let's review a few more surahs. Surely we will find something redeeming. The 87th is from the early Meccan period. Imam Maududi explains: **"The Prophet was reassured: 'Do not worry: We shall enable you to recite this Word, then you shall not forget it.' Then after a lapse of time, on another occasion, when the Resurrection surah was being revealed, the Prophet involuntarily began to rehearse the words of the Revelation. Thereupon it was said: 'O Prophet do not move your tongue to remember this Revelation hastily. It is for Us to explain its meaning.'"** If this sounds repetitious, it's only because it is. No, we have not yet reviewed the 87th surah, but unable to remember what he and said, one surah to the next, Muhammad had an annoying habit of repeating himself. While this peculiar "tongue movement" obsession is covered multiple times, it's a Qur'anic piker compared to Pharaoh and Moses. Their singular encounter was replayed fifty times. Muhammad must have loved plagues. *Bukhari:V8B77N616* **"Allah's Apostle said, 'Plague is a means of torture which Allah sends upon whom-so-ever He wishes.'"**

As for forgetfulness, consider this: *Bukhari:V6B61N550* **"The Prophet said, 'It is a bad thing that some of you say, "I have forgotten such-and-such verse of the Qur'an." For** indeed, I have been caused to forget it. So you must keep on reciting the Qur'an because it escapes from the hearts of men faster than a runaway camel.'"

Returning to the tongue-lashing of the 87th surah, we find: *087.001* **"Glorify the Name of your Lord, the Most High, Who creates, then proportions, Who has measured; and then guided."** Did you notice the blunder? Muslims are told to glorify the name of their Lord before they know his name. Muslims don't notice this omission because they recite the Qur'an in the order it was assembled, not in the order it was "revealed." By reordering the Qur'an chronologically, a host of serious problems emerge. Allah doesn't become god until late in the game.

The lack of guidance is also a problem. You could put the full measure of what the dark spirit has given thus far in a thimble. It's not only insufficient; it's perplexing. Curiously, the Islamic god's guidance has failed to include any of the Ten Commandments—odd in that he claimed to have written the Torah. In fact, his messenger would systematically violate all of them. He placed Allah before Yahweh. He turned a graven image, a Black Stone, into a god. He bowed down, prostrating himself to the former idol. He created a false doctrine. He renounced the Sabbath. He rebuked his father and mother and severed family ties. He committed murder and adultery countless times. Stealing became his passion; he called it booty. He bore false witness and became one of history's most egregious cons. Coveting money, power, and sex drove him to create Islam. Muhammad couldn't have done more violence to the core teaching of the Torah if he had tried.

087.004 **"Who brings forth herbage, then makes it dried up, dust-colored swarthy stubble? We shall make you read so that you will not forget."** This transition is as lame as the command. He never learned to read. The Qur'an calls Muhammad "the unlettered prophet." But there is a story behind the duplicity. Our hero wanted it both ways. He wanted the respect only learned and literate men possess. After all, the Qur'an was supposed to be a book. Previous prophets became prophets by actually writing their prophecies. Yet this prophet also wanted to dispel the popular belief that he was a plagiarizer. If he couldn't read, the Hebrew Bible stories suddenly appeared more miraculous than stolen. Only one problem: Muhammad's Qur'anic deviations are dead ringers for the Talmud—Jewish oral tradition.

087.007 **"Except as He may will: He knows what is hidden."** Holy runaway camel! This is stunning from a scriptural perspective. Muhammad is admitting that he forgets some of what he claims god has revealed. Worse, he is proposing that his forgetfulness is god's fault. So how can he be god's last messenger, the truth teller for all time, if he can't remember what was said from one day to the next? Divinely inspired scripture is supposed to be timeless instruction.

But once again there was a method behind the madness. Muhammad wanted his revelations to be accepted as godly during a time his contemporaries called them the uninspired rantings of a demon-possessed maniac. To mute his mockers he had to overcome a problem of his own creation. The Meccans knew that real scripture was timeless, not myopic; godly instructions didn't change or contradict themselves. The Meccans knew that Muhammad's scripture didn't meet these criteria. Far too much of it was specific to the his personal situation and meaningless beyond it. Worse, it was contradictory and mean spirited. So Muhammad insisted that changes and contradictions were part of god's plan. In the 2nd surah, he took this preposterous notion to the level of comedy. His spirit said: **"When We cancel a Message or throw it into oblivion We replace it with a better one."**

In the Hadith, we discover that this prophet couldn't be trusted: *Bukhari:V7B67N427* **"The Prophet said, 'If I take an oath and later find something else better than that, then I do what is better and expiate my oath.'"** *Bukhari:V6B60N8* **"Umar said, 'Our best Qur'an reciter is Ubai. And in spite of this, we leave out some of his statements because Allah's Apostle himself said, "Whatever verse or revelation We abrogate or cause to be forgotten We bring a better one."'"** This is one of many reasons I have reordered the Qur'an chronologically. If one verse encourages peace and another contradicts it by ordering Muslims to fight, the one that came later cancels the earlier one—casting it into oblivion. (Unfortunately, the Qur'an's most violent surahs are its last surahs.)

087.008 **"And We will make easy for you the easy way. Therefore do remind in case the reminder profits."** I knew it. I'm just glad Muhammad admitted it—**"the reminder profits."** The wannabe prophet recognized what every tyrant knows: tell a lie often enough and enough people will believe it for you to profit.

087.010 **"He who fears will mind."** This verse proclaims the means behind the madness. Fear serves Islam the same way it serves all totalitarian societies. Fear causes people to mind—to obey. Now you know why Muhammad found it profitable to frighten his tribe with tales of a hateful god, eager to burn them. Now you know why hell's torments were so vividly described.

Throughout time, dictators like Muhammad have risen to fame and fortune by deploying the politics of fear and intimidation. While much of the Qur'an has been foolish, fretful, and fanatical, this pearl is not. Fear is essential to any dictatorial regime. It was behind the peace of the *Pax Romana*; it was the control mechanism behind the Inquisition. Fear is the reason we see blind obedience in every Muslim state. While this jewel was political, not religious, and sinister, not inspirational, we have finally found something meritorious—or at least true—in the Qur'an.

087.012 **"Who will be flung in to burn in the great Fire (and be made to taste its burning,)** *087.013* **in which they will then neither die nor live?"** The "Lord" must have been distracted because he didn't answer his question. I checked ten translations. All asked the question, none answered it. For a book that claims to be divinely inspired, this is one of a thousand verses that suggests otherwise.

087.014 **"He indeed shall be successful who purifies himself, and magnifies the Name of his Lord and prays."** Although this sounds religious, the transition from flinging folks into the fire isn't. Further, **"magnifying the name of the Lord"** is defined in later surahs as **"Allahu Akbar."** It's the **"Prayer of Fear,"** designed to terrorize non-Muslims. It means: "Allah is Greatest." What's interesting is that Islam's signature line destroys Islam's credibility. If we all worship the same God, if there is but one God, and if the Qur'an's god is the same spirit who inspired the Bible, as Muslims claim, this equivalence repudiates the notion of superiority.

087.018 **"Verily, this is in the Books of the earliest Revelation, in the former scrolls and Scriptures, The Books of Abraham and Moses."** If the new religion is like the old religion, why does god want, and why does man need, a new religion? If these Scriptures are the same as the old ones then why can't we find any of these Muhammadisms in the original version? And god is supposed to know what he is talking about: there were no "Books of Abraham."

088.001 **"Has the narration reached you of the overwhelming (calamity)?"** Good Grief. Muhammad has repeated the dreadful tale of woe so many times he's become the Prophet of Doom. **"Some faces (all disbelievers, Jews and Christians) that Day, will be humiliated, downcast, scorched by the burning fire, while they are made to drink from a boiling hot spring."** Muhammad's continued desire to burn his detractors and force them to drink boiling water serves as confirmation he was abused. In all probability he was burnt with fire and punished with scalding water. Still feeling unloved, the victimized boy became a victimizer by threatening all who stood in his way with the same torments he himself endured.

The lack of any historical evidence, scriptural or otherwise, surrounding Muhammad's childhood makes the molestation charge difficult to prove. All we have is the testimony of the victim. Yet it is plentiful, consistent, and convincing. Muhammad's desire to see his critics punished, to suffer in the manner he suffered, is unexplainable any other way. Victims victimize in like fashion. Abuse breeds abuse. *088.006* **"They shall have no food but a poisonous plant with bitter thorns, which will neither nourish nor satisfy hunger."** It obviously haunted him. And his torments have survived to haunt us today.

Even as he transitions to paradise, Muhammad can't restrain himself. He must tweak the nose of those who are verbally abusing him. Heaven is being rid of them. In a way, it's very sad. *088.008* **"(Other) faces will be joyful, glad with their endeavour. In a lofty Garden they hear no harmful speech."**

088.012 **"Therein will be a bubbling spring, raised throne-like couches, drinking cups ready placed, cushions set in rows, and rich silken carpets all spread out."** In most political doctrines Utopia reflects the desires of the inventor. The more vividly Muhammad portrays heaven, the more we learn about his ambitions. Just as in his descriptions of hell, with each word we see the prophet more clearly. For another look, consider: *Bukhari:V4B55N544* **"Allah's Apostle said, 'The first group who will enter Paradise will be glittering like the moon and those who will follow will glitter like the most brilliant star. They will not urinate, relieve nature, spit, or have any nasal secretions. Their combs will be gold and their sweat will smell like musk. Their companions will be houris** [virgins]. All of them will look alike and will be sixty cubits (180 feet) tall.'"

Without missing a beat we turn from paradise to camels: *088.017* "Will they not consider the camels, how they are created? And the sky, how it is raised? The mountains, how they are rooted, and the Earth, how it is spread out?" Unable to perform a miracle Muhammad claimed the oddest things as proof. *088.021* "So remind, you are only a reminder. You are not a warden over them; except for those who turn away and disbelieve, in which case, he will be punished with the severest punishment. Verily to Us they will return." The Islamic god is saying that his prophet is the jail keeper of all who deny Islam so that he (Allah) can personally attend to our punishment.

Each surah we have reviewed has been incriminating. Let's hope Muhammad improves with practice. I for one would like to read something positive and uplifting for a change. *089.001* "I swear by the dawn, and the ten nights, and the even and the odd, and the night when it departs." This is not a very auspicious start. It's bad enough swearing by night and darkness. Swearing by odd and even smacks of numerology—another occult practice. *089.005* "There surely is an oath for thinking man." And I hope the Islamic god finds it before he drives us crazy.

089.006 "Saw you not how your Lord dealt with Ad, possessors of lofty buildings, the likes of which were not produced in all the land?" I'm reasonably sure the grandeur of Rome, the beauty of Acropolis, the splendor of Ephesus, the Temples in Karnack, the pyramids along the Nile, the metropolis that was Babylon dwarfed the "lofty buildings, the likes of which were not produced in all the land." For variety's sake, the god of the Qur'an should try truth occasionally.

089.009 "And Thamud, who hewed out huge rocks in the valley? And with Pharaoh, who had the stakes (to torture men), who terrorized the region and multiplied mischief?" If this "god" is being honest about the Thamud, why haven't archeologists unearthed any of their huge cut stones? And why isn't there any evidence of Pharaoh terrorizing his people or being corrupt?

Muhammad returns to his favorite subject, providing a veritable smorgasbord of victims. It was so multi-cultural of him. *089.012* "All made mischief so your Lord poured on them the disaster of His torment, a scourge of diverse chastisements." I think we get the message. The Islamic god is a terrorist.

Reading the Qur'an causes me to wonder why the media is so protective, even supportive, of Islam. Page after page, it chafes against the values liberals hold dear. How has the media overlooked the religion's preoccupation with hate speech? There has been no talk of tolerance or peaceful coexistence in these pages. Surah after surah has been about scourges, disasters, and punishments. Sure, liberals tout diversity, but not when it defines a variety of torments.

Stealing a line from Zayd again, the dark spirit of Islam says: *089.014* "Most surely your Lord is in laying in wait, watching." It's little wonder Communists and Muslims get along so well. Somebody is always watching. Step out of line and you get "a scourge of diverse chastisements."

089.015 "Now, as for man, when his Lord gives him gifts, he says all puffed up, 'My Lord has honored me.' But when He tries him, restricting his subsistence, he says in despair, 'My Lord has humiliated me; He despises me.' Nay, nay! It is because you don't honor the orphan. [Gee, I wonder who that might be? Do you know an orphans who needs to be honored?] And urge not the feeding the poor. And you devour inheritance—all with greed, and you love wealth." If Muhammad wants us to believe that these are God's words, he's going to have to be a little less transparent. His childhood is showing, as is his greed. He's afraid his kin will devour the wealth he covets—the income streams of the Ka'aba Inc.—before he can steal them.

089.021 "Nay, when the earth is made to crumble and the Lord comes, His angels rank upon rank, and Hell is brought face to face, man will remember, but how will that avail him? For His Chastisement will be such as no other can inflict. None punishes as He will punish! None can bind as He will bind." Allah is number one in chastisements, punishments, and imprisonments. At least he's good at something.

089.029 "Enter then, among My devotees! Yea, enter into My Paradise!" I'll take a pass. Thanks anyway.

There is some good news. The surahs are getting shorter. Maududi, our Qur'anic scholar tells us: "In the 90th surah a vast subject has been compressed into a few brief sentences. It is the miracle of the Qur'an that a complete ideology of life which could be explained in a thick volume has been abridged most effectively in brief sentences." Let's jump right in. Enough with pain and punishment. We're about to find the meaning of life. *090.001* "Nay! I swear by this city. And you shall be made free from obligation in this city." Islam is the most obligatory "religion" ever concocted. It's the antithesis of being free from obligation. They've got the obligatory prayer, the obligatory hajj, the obligatory tax, and the obligatory surrender to Muhammad and Islamic authority. Islam itself means submission, and submission means that Muslims are obligated to surrender their freedom. What's more, Mecca was a motley collection of mud huts. It was no more a "city" than Muhammad was a "prophet" or Allah was a "god."

090.003 "And the mystic ties of parent and child;" This is getting worse, not better. Muhammad did more to destroy family ties than any religious leader in history. He told Muslims that they must love him more than they loved their children. He tore families apart and sent sons off to murder their fathers. But in Islam's defense, another translation renders the verse senseless rather than contradictory: "And by the begetter and that which he begot."

090.004 "Verily We have created man in toil and struggle, to be in distress." (Didn't we just read: *087.008* "And We will make it easy for you to follow the simple path to the state of ease?" Which one is true?) "Does he think that no one has power over him? He may say boastfully; Wealth have I squandered in abundance!" While many are wealthy, and some have squandered, few have bragged about squandering. So why, if this surah is the secret to life, the great miracle of the Qur'an, are we wasting our time with this?

Because big brother is watching: *090.007* **"Does he think that no one sees him? Have We not given him two eyes, a tongue and two lips, and pointed out the two ways?"** Then…**"But he has made no haste on the steep path. And what will explain to you the steep path? (It is) freeing a neck (slave)."** This pegs the Hypocrite Scale. Muhammad owned slaves. He forced tens of thousands of people into bondage so he could sell them to finance his military conquests. The Qur'an itself even brags about enslaving Jewish women and children.

This odd phraseology is further evidence that Islam's prophet contrived this religion to lay claim to what he coveted: the custodianship of the Ka'aba. *090.014* **"Give food in a day of hunger to the orphan with claims of relationship, an orphan near of kin, the indigent down in the dust."** Muhammad was that orphan—the rarest of orphans—one with "claims of relationship" to something valuable.

I am amazed that something this transparent hasn't been exposed and discredited. It's so obvious. Muhammad is saying as clearly as words allow: "My family has squandered the wealth I covet. The path to my heaven lies in satisfying my cravings—giving me, the orphan with claims, everything I desire." Forty surahs, one rant: "I'll make my family pay for the way they've treated me." Revenge made a religion.

090.017 **"Be of those who believe and exhort one another to perseverance and pity. Such are the Companions of the Right Hand."** Islam's prophet was always an exception to his own rules. He pitied no man. He attacked his clan's caravans, attacked their city. He attacked the Jews, expelled them from their homes, confiscated their property, tortured them, sold them into slavery. He murdered many in genocidal rage. "Pity."

090.019 **"But those who reject Our Signs, Proofs, and Verses, they are the unhappy Companions of the Left Hand. Fire will be their awning, vaulting over them."** This is the perfect benediction to the magnificent miracle of the Qur'an. The tolerant and peace-loving religion of Islam has just said that all non-Muslims are toast.

Let's try the next surah, named in honor of the **"Sun."** They can't all be this bad. *091.001* **"I swear by the sun and its brilliance, and by the moon when she follows him."** I'm glad we cleared that up. The sun is a male and the female moon follows him. What's more, the most common symbols of pagan gods are being used to authenticate Islam's deity. **"I swear by the day when it shows it, by the Night as it conceals it, drawing a veil over it, [Okay, I give up. What's it?] by the heaven and Him Who built it, by the earth and Him Who spread it [It sounds like "it" was the earth, but became heaven, and then became the earth again.], by Nafs (a person) and Him Who perfected it, and inspired it with what is wrong for it and right for it. Truly he succeeds that purifies it, and he fails that corrupts it."** According to the Qur'an, religious success is found in purifying **"it."** So why did "god" neglect to tell us what *it* is and how we are to go about purifying *it* once we find *it*?

091.011 **"Thamud rejected (their prophet) through their inordinate wrong-doing, and** rebellious pride, [Oh, no! Not the dreaded prophet taunting Thamuds again.] Behold, the most-wicked wretch among them broke forth but the Messenger said to them: 'Be cautious. It is a She-camel of God! And bar her not from having her drink!'" Islam's god and his prophet have an affinity for she-camels.

091.014 "But they rejected him as a false prophet, and they hamstrung her." The dark spirit of Islam seldom ventures beyond the texts he stole from the Hanifs and the Bible. Yet each attempt is a credibility disaster. The Thamud are about to be obliterated for the heinous crimes of prophet rejection and she-camel abuse. Islam's troubled troubadour wants his critics to know that his god stands ready to obliterate all traces of them, too. "So Allah on account of their crime, obliterated their traces, doomed them, desolated their dwellings, leveling them to the ground, crushing them for their sin." Don't be messing with the prophet's she-camel.

091.015 "And for Him, He does not fear the consequences." The benediction to this surah provides us with a haunting insight into the mindset of Muslims. The Islamic god and prophet have no conscience. Pulverizing their critics is all in a day's work. 9/11 was just another day at the office.

In that one man's refuse is another man's food, I would be remiss in not sharing what our distinguished Islamic cleric had to say about the splendor of the 92nd surah. "According to the style of the Qur'an's brief surahs three moral characteristics of one kind and three of another have been presented as an illustration from among a vast strivings of man. Truth has been described in such brief, elegant, and pithy sentences that they move the heart and go down into memory as soon as one hears them."

Such lavish praise is well beyond my meager means. Let's see if the pithy sentences of the next surah move the heart as they elegantly etch themselves into our memories. *092.001* "I swear by the night when it draws a veil, and the day when it shines, and the creating of the male and the female, lo your effort is dispersed toward diverse ends. So he who gives and fears, and accepts the best, We will make smooth for him the path to Bliss." The Islamic deity needs a new speechwriter, perhaps one who is literate. This is gobbledygook. The Islamic god likes those who give and fear and take the best for themselves. But hey, I suppose a confused spirit is better than one fixated on deceit, pain, and punishment.

Unfortunately, Islam was conceived to steal money. Islam is the absence of freedom. Islam's dark spirit facilitates the path to misery. *092.008* "But he who is a greedy miser and is unconcerned, acting niggardly, considering himself free, rejecting, We will make smooth for him the path to misery."

092.011 "And his wealth will not avail him when he goes down (in destruction)." My daddy could have written this surah. He used to tell me: "There are no Brinks trucks in funeral processions."

092.012 "Verily We [plural] take upon Ourselves [plural] (to show) the way, and verily unto Us [plural] (belong) the last and the first. Therefore do I [singular] warn you of a Fire blazing fiercely; ["I used to be schizophrenic, but we're better now."] None shall enter it but the most unhappy." The story of unhappy crispy critters entering the blazing fires of hell doesn't sound pithy or elegant to me.

092.016 "He who giveth the lie denieth and turneth away. [I thought it might sound better left in the King's English but it doesn't help] But he who fears shall be removed from it, those who spend their wealth for increase in self-purification, and no one has with him any boon for which he should be paid back, but only the desire to seek the Countenance of their Lord. He will attain complete pleasure." Since "their Lord" hangs out in hell, that's pretty ominous.

For your entertainment pleasure, Allah would like to indulge you with a surah focused on debasing man. *095.001* "I swear by the fig and the olive, and by the Mount of Sinai, and by this city made secure." While swearing by figs is lame, calling a city "secure" that Muhammad was about to flee to save his life is pathetic.

095.004 "We have indeed created man in the best molds. Then do We abase him, reducing him to be the lowest of the low, except such as believe: For they shall have a reward unfailing. What causes you to deny the penalty?" *095.008* "Is not He the wisest of judges?"

We have already examined the 96th surah, so let's skip ahead to the 97th. *097.001* "We have revealed it in the Night of Predestination." The Islamic conundrum: if we are predestined, then there is no reason for guidance. If there is no need for guidance, there is no reason for a prophet. If there is no reason for a prophet, there is no value to a religious scam. No scam, no profit. No profit, no Muhammad. No Muhammad, no Allah. No Allah, no terrorists. If only….

I'm not the first to be troubled by Islam's foolhardy allegiance to predestination. *Bukhari:V6B60N473* "While we were in a funeral procession, Allah's Apostle said, 'Every created soul has his place written for him either in Paradise or in Hell. They have a happy or miserable fate predestined for them.' A man said, 'Apostle! Shall we depend upon what is written and give up doing deeds? For whoever is destined to be fortunate, will join the fortunate and whoever is destined to be miserable will go to Hell.'"

097.002 "And what will make you comprehend the grand night? The grand night is better than a thousand months. Therein come down the angels and the Ruh (Spirit) by the Lord's permission, on every errand." Muhammad and his Lord are singing their praises. The night of a thousand months is the celebration of that dark moment in the cave where devil and prophet became one. It's the night we learned we were blood clots; the night an illiterate man was asked to read. Ah, but it was also the night we were told that truth existed somewhere in a book, in the Bible perhaps, because God had taught men the use of the pen so that they might learn that which they did not know.

097.005 "There is peace until the dawning of the day!" See, Islam is a peaceful religion —till morning anyway. Then all hell breaks loose just as it did in New York City at 8:45 A.M. E.D.T, September 11th 2001. It was Islam's most revealing hour. It is why we must expose a doctrine capable of driving men to such madness.

10

MUDDLED MESSAGE

"This (Prophet Muhammad) is a sorcerer, a charlatan, a wizard telling lies."
"Allah said, 'I am planning a scheme against them.'"

By examining the Qur'an in the order it was revealed and by adding the context of the Islamic Traditions, a very disturbing trend emerges. The Islamic deity migrates from a nameless Lord to Ar-Rahman and then to Allah. The spirit starts off demonic, personally involving itself in hellish torments. Then he journeys from foolish to fierce, moving from uninspired tongue-lashings to all-out brutality. The Qur'anic message evolved from simplistic Hanif traditions to dumbed-down subsets of the Judaic Talmud, finally settling upon Qusayy's arcane pagan rituals. All of these were used to give a terrorist manifesto a veil of religiosity. Then, in a perverse twist of irony, the peoples who supplied the raw material for Islam became its enemies. The Hanif's were defeated in the bloodiest battles of the War of Compulsion. The Jews suffered genocide at Muhammad's hand. Even the Meccans who nurtured the pagan religious scam were conquered by the religion they had inspired.

Muhammad was always running away from his god. It was as if proximity was a problem. When he was in Mecca with Allah, his dark spirit was Ar-Rahman. Away in Medina, he became Allah. God was always just far enough away to insulate the prophet from his detractors' claims of non-performance.

There is something else odd, too. The more Muhammad distanced himself from Allah, and the closer he moved toward the Jews and their rich repository of scripture, the more the Qur'an started to sound like the Hebrew Bible, or at least the Talmud. Yet the longer Muhammad stayed with the Jews, the more his god grew to hate them. Ultimately, he ordered his prophet to annihilate people of the Book upon which Islam's credibility was based.

History condemns Islam, which is why Muslims rewrite it. Listen to this attempt by Maududi, our Qur'an expert: **"The general chaos and confusion prevailing in Arabia, in which the whole country was in turmoil, has been presented as an argument. Bloodshed, loot and plunder raged on every side. Tribes were subjecting tribes to raids, and no one could have peaceful sleep at night from fear that some enemy tribe might raid his settlement early in the morning. Every Arab was fully conscious of this state** of affairs and realized that it was wrong." There is no thought in all of Islamic scholarship that is as essential, as indicting, or as ignorant as this one. Yet the revisionist image of pre-Islamic Arabs as bloodthirsty raiders is widely accepted. Its derogatory overtones are preached because they are essential to the religion's survival. The ugly Arab theory is postulated to fool the feeble minded into believing that in the context of his times, Muhammad was a godly man and that Islam made bad men good.

But neither hypothesis is true. There is no historical evidence of Arabs conquering their neighbors before Islam. After Islam, Muslims conquered much of the world. Before Islam, there was no evidence of Arabs being looters who terrorized in violent raids. But that all changed with the advent of Muhammad. Having failed as a religious prophet in Mecca, Allah's Messenger became a profiteer and pirate in Medina. Muslims put Arabia in turmoil, spilling blood for plunder. They became a gang who terrorized, raiding settlements and caravans alike. They knew terror, murder, thievery, and the slave trade were wrong, yet they did these things all the same. Their consciences were simply assuaged by the Qur'an. Muhammad and his god said that booty was good, and that killing was the surest way to reach the Islamic paradise.

Seventh century Arabs were illiterate, isolated, and perhaps even ignorant. But there is no evidence that they were bloodthirsty raiders. Islam turned good men bad. That's why today's Muslims find it essential to revise their past and invert truth. But it is their true past, their actual history, that indicts them. Simply stated: Islam perverts men. The closer one gets to it, the more one surrenders to its calling; the more one emulates its prophet and follows the Qur'an, the more perverted one becomes. Not all Muslims are terrorists—only the good ones are.

To find out why, let's return to the Qur'an. The 106th surah, named after Muhammad's tribe, **"The Quraysh,"** presents the nature of things before Islam. *106.001* **"For the protection of the Quraysh (there are covenants covering the journeys of trading) caravans (so that they can) travel safely by winter and summer. So let them worship the Lord of this House (the Ka'aba), (He) Who provides them with food and with security against fear and danger."** This is a fairly accurate reflection of pre-Islamic Mecca, its caravans, covenants, protective months, and Ka'aba.

The 100th surah foreshadows what was to come. *100.001* **"I call to witness the (cavalry steeds), the (snorting courses), that run breathing pantingly (rushing off to battle), striking sparks of fire, scouring to the raid at dawn, raising clouds of dust as they penetrate deep into the midst of a foe en masse."** The most vicious Islamic raids deployed cavalry. As such, the prophet molded his religion to reward those who fought astride horses. The kind of religious fighting hinted at in the 100th surah came to be known as "Jihad." The Qur'an would call it "Allah's Cause." But by either definition it became Islam's principle attribute and its most enduring symbol. *Bukhari:V4B52N44* **"A man came to Allah's Apostle and said, 'Instruct me as to such** a deed as equals Jihad in reward.' He replied, 'I do not find such a deed.' Then he added, 'Can you, while the Muslim fighter is in the battlefield enter your mosque to perform prayers without ceasing and fast forever?' The man said, 'But who can do that?'" In other words, eternal fasting and prayer is less "religious" than being a Jihadist.

Cavalry was central to his success, so the religious prophet crafted scripture to reward man and mount. *Bukhari:V4B52N104* **"The Prophet said, 'Good will remain in the foreheads of horses for Jihad for they bring about a reward in Paradise or booty.'"** "The best of both worlds" theme was how Muhammad would ultimately sell Islam to his gang of misfits. *Bukhari:V4B52N105* **"The Prophet said, 'If somebody keeps a horse in Allah's Cause motivated by His promise, then he will be rewarded for what the horse has eaten or drunk and for its dung and urine.'"** *Bukhari:V4B52N112* **"Allah's Apostle said, 'Horses are kept for one of three purposes. For some they are a source of reward, for others a means of shelter, and for some a source of sins. The one for whom they are a source of reward, is he who keeps a horse for Allah's Cause (i.e., Jihad)."** As we move from the delusion of Mecca to the terror of Medina, you may want to keep these Hadiths in mind. To Muhammad, "Allah's Cause" was synonymous with "Jihad," and both were all about fighting.

The Qur'an's seventh century version of Blitzkrieg was followed by: *100.006* **"Lo! man is an ingrate to his Lord. To that fact he bears witness (by his deeds). Violent is he in his love of worldly goods, tenacious in the pursuit."** From the day he arrived in Yathrib, to the day he died, Muhammad's **"deeds"** were **"violent."** He led terrorist raids in **"tenacious pursuit of worldly goods."** Islam's prophet was the most violent and covetous man ever to have spoken on god's behalf. As such, these words bear witness to the fraud he perpetrated and to his hypocrisy.

100.009 **"Does he not know when that which is in the graves is poured forth, and the secrets of men are exposed, their Lord will be aware?"** The secrets buried in the victims' graves cry out: Muhammad must be exposed.

At this point I would like to alter course. There is only so much ugliness one can endure without a break. So rather than dissect the remainder of the early Meccan revelations in their entirety, I'm going to provide a "Best of Muhammad" by subject. But first, a Maududi introduction: **"These surahs were sent down when persecution of Muslims was near its climax. Their theme was to warn the disbelievers of the evil consequences of the persecution and tyranny that they were perpetrating on the converts to Islam, and to console believers. If Muslims remain firm and steadfast against tyranny and coercion, they will be rewarded richly for it."**

Islamic logic is funny, in a twisted sort of way. While mocking the self-proclaimed prophet could hardly be called "tyranny," today's most coercive and tyrannical nations are Islamic. They have become what they detested. As with the child abuse that gave rise to Islam, Muslims have come full circle— the abused have become the abusers. Even Maududi seems to agree: "'**Allah will avenge Himself on those who persecute you by burning the unbelievers to death and casting them into pits full of fire.' The disbelievers will not only be punished in Hell for their** disbelief but, more than that, they will suffer punishment by fire as a fit recompense for their tyranny and cruelties. 'Allah's grip is very severe.' If you are proud of your strength, you should know that Pharaoh and Thamud were stronger and more numerous. Therefore, you should learn a lesson from the fate they met. Allah's power has so encompassed you that you cannot escape His encirclement, and the Qur'an that you are bent upon belying is unchangeable: 'It is inscribed in the Preserved Tablet, which cannot be corrupted in any way'"…although it does a world-class job of corrupting.

The themes that follow are Muhammad's favorites. We'll start with a sampling of how the Islamic deity responded to those who challenged his prophet's credentials. *076.004* "For the rejecters We have prepared chains, iron collars, manacles, and a blazing fire." *077.039* "If you have a trick or plot, use it against Me! If you have any wit, outwit Me. Woe to the rejecters!" *078.028* "They called Our proofs, signs, and verses false with strong denial. We have recorded everything in a book, so taste (that which you earned). We give you nothing but torment." *078.040* "We have warned you of a penalty, of a torment on the Day of Doom when the disbeliever will say, 'Woe is me! I wish I were dust!'" *083.010* "Woe to those who deny, reject Our message, and repudiate. When Our Verses are rehearsed they say, 'Tales of the ancients! Mere fables of old.'" *083.029* "The disbelievers used to laugh at believers. When they passed by them, they winked at one another (in mockery). When they returned to their folk, they would jest…but soon the believers will laugh at the unbelievers sitting on high thrones, gazing. The unbelievers will be paid back for what they did." *084.022* "The unbelievers reject (Muhammad and the Qur'an); they deny and lie. Allah has full knowledge of what they secrete. So announce to them tidings of a terrible torment." *084.020* "What is the matter with them that they do not believe, and when the Qur'an is recited to them, they do not fall prostrate in adoration." *085.010* "Those who try or tempt the believers will have the penalty of Hell: They will have the doom of the burning fire. Verily, the Seizure of the Lord is severe and painful…. Allah will encompass them from behind! He will punish them. Nay! This is a Glorious Qur'an." *086.015* "They are plotting a scheme against you, but I am also planning a scheme against them." That was as direct as it was unpleasant. Accept Muhammad or suffer the consequences. Dissent is not to be tolerated.

With the mockers warned, it was time to terrorize them. *077.029* "It will be said: Depart to the doom those who used to deny! Depart to a shadow of smoke (from the Hell Fire) ascending in three columns, which yields no relief or shelter and is of no use against the fierce blaze. Verily, (Hell) throws off sparks huge as castles as if they were yellow camels." *078.021* "Truly Hell is as a place of ambush, a resort for the rebellious. A dwelling place for the disbelievers. They will abide there forever. Therein they taste neither coolness nor any drink save a boiling water and a fluid, dark, murky, intensely cold, paralyzing, a dirty wound discharge. It is a fitting reward for them." *084.010* "Soon will He cry for perdition, invoking destruction, throwing them into the scorching fire. They shall enter the fire and be forced to taste its burning." *085.001* "I swear by the Zodiacal Signs, woe to the makers of the pit of fire. Cursed were the people of the Ditch." *085.005* "The Fire is supplied abundantly with fuel." *101.008* "He whose balance is light will abide in a bottomless Pit. And what will make you know what it is? It is a fire blazing fiercely!" The Hell Fire is Allah's resort for the rebellious—it's for those who don't surrender.

To avoid this hellish doom, submit to Muhammad and obey him. A drunken brothel shall be your just dessert. *076.005* **"As for the righteous, they will drink a cup of wine from a spring, making it gush forth abundantly."** *076.019* **"And round them shall serve immortal boys of perpetual freshness, never altering in age. If you saw them, you would think they were scattered pearls."** *076.021* **"Upon them will be green garments of fine green silk and heavy gold brocade. They will be adorned with bracelets of silver; Their Lord will slack their thirst with wine."** *077.041* **"The righteous shall be amidst cool shades, springs, and fruits—all they desire. Eat and drink to your heart's content."** *078.031* **"Verily for those who follow Us, there will be a fulfillment of your desires: enclosed Gardens, grapevines, voluptuous full-breasted maidens of equal age, and a cup full to the brim of wine. There they never hear vain discourse nor lying—a gift in payment—a reward from your Lord."** *083.022* **"The believers will be in Delightful Bliss: On couch-like thrones, gazing, their thirst will be slaked with pure wine."** *085.011* **"For those who believe and do good deeds will be Gardens; the fulfillment of all desires."** Muhammad not only created god in his image, he crafted a paradise that mirrored his fantasies. It was filled with thrones, free-flowing wine, perpetual virgins, ever voluptuous. And there were no mockers—"never was heard vain discourse, nor lying." And that I suppose would eliminate recitals of the Qur'an. Paradise indeed.

But it was all for naught if the Islamic god was not. The following Allahisms are proof he wasn't divine. *076.001* **"There came over man a period of time when he was a thing not worth mentioning."** *076.002* **"We created Man from nutfa (drops) of mingled sperm (sexual discharge of men and women), in order to try him. So We gave him the gifts of hearing and sight."** *076.015* **"Goblets made of silver, crystal-clear, and transparent."** *076.028* **"When We want We can replace man by substituting another in his stead."** *077.020* **"Have We not created you from a despicable fluid? Then We placed it in a place of safety for a known period because We measure; and We are the Best to measure."** *077.025* **"Have We not made the earth a receptacle for the living and the dead?"** *078.006* **"Have We not made the earth as a bed and the mountains pegs?"** *078.037* **"The Lord with Whom they cannot dare to speak, none can converse with Him, none are able to address Him."** *084.016* **"But nay! I swear by...the night and all that it enshrouds which it drives on, and by the Moon in her fullness: you shall journey on from plane to plane."** *086.005* **"So let man consider from what he is created. He is created from gushing water pouring forth, coming from between the backbone and the ribs."** *099.001* **"When the earth is shaken to her violent convulsion and throws up her burdens, man cries, 'What is the matter with her?' She declares her tidings and relates her chronicles, for He will give her inspiration."** *086.013* **"Lo this (Qur'an) is a conclusive Word; it is not a thing for amusement. It is no pleasantry. And it is no joke."** Man isn't worth mentioning, and he can be easily replaced. To try us, god gave us hearing and sight. Perhaps we are to use them to see the earth as a receptacle and hear it speak with inspiration.

Yet two verses are more fatal than frivolous. **"The Lord with Whom they cannot** dare to speak, none can converse with Him, none are able to address Him." If that's true, why prostrate oneself five times a day in prayer? And what is the difference between not being able to converse with god and having no god at all?

"This Qur'an is a conclusive word; it is not a thing for amusement. It is no pleasantry. And it is no joke." It is neither funny, pleasant, nor amusing, but it is conclusive. It proves that Muhammad was a fraud and that Allah wasn't god.

I feel compelled to issue a warning: Islamic material will put you to sleep. It is poorly written, disorganized, and directionless. Do not attempt to operate your life while under its influence as serious injury or death may result.

The following pages are an exposé on early Qur'an surahs. Much of the material is incoherent. Devoid of context and chronology, these surahs are odious and repetitive rants. Yet their muddled message is the essence of Islamic religiosity, so I feel compelled to review them with you.

Maududi wants us to believe that the opposite is true. He claims that the religion of Islam, as presented in the Qur'an, is brilliantly comprised of three fundamental doctrines: "Tauhid (the oneness of Allah) [whom we have yet to meet], the apostleship of Muhammad [whose apostleship is covered in the Sunnah, not the Qur'an], and the belief that the dead are raised bodily [not spiritually]. The 112th surah, 'Pure Faith,' teaches *Tauhid*, pure and undefiled. Therefore, the Prophet regarded this one surah as equal to one-third of the Qur'an." *112.001* "Say: He is Allah, (the) One; the Self-Sufficient Master, Whom all creatures need; He has begotten no one, nor is He begotten; and there is no one comparable to Him." Thank God for small favors. Two gods like this "One" would be two too many. But Muhammad's suggestion that this one-sentence surah was equal to one-third of the Qur'an, is too delicious for words. If only…

The Qur'an's final two surahs tell us nothing we do not already know. But with their inclusion, we will have analyzed every surah from the 67th through the 114th, most of them in their entirety. *113.001* "Say: I seek refuge with the Lord of the Dawn from the mischief of the evil He created." The Qur'an is filled with evil and virtually devoid of love. And that's because the "mischief of evil" was created by Allah—the Prince of Darkness. *113.003* "From the mischievous evil of Darkness as it becomes intensely dark, and from the mischief of those who practice the evil of malignant witchcraft and blowing on knots, and from the mischievous evil of the envier when he covets." I was taught that it's better to remain silent and be thought a fool than to open one's mouth and remove all doubt. Muhammad is indicting his own behavior. He did the very things he claimed were demonic.

As proof that Muhammad was guilty of "the mischievous evil of darkness," and that he practiced "the evil of malignant witchcraft and blowing," I present these confessions: *Bukhari:V7B71N643* "I heard the Prophet saying, 'If anyone sees something he dislikes, he should blow three times on his left side and its evil will not harm him.'" *Bukhari:V6B61N535* "Whenever the Prophet became ill he used to blow his breath over his body hoping for its blessing." *Bukhari:V6B61N536* "When the Prophet went to bed he would cup his hands together and blow over them reciting surahs. He would then rub his hands over whatever parts of his body he could reach, starting with his head, face and frontal areas." If those who "practice the evil of malignant witchcraft and blowing" are demonic, Muhammad has introduced us to his revealing spirit.

This next Hadith is especially incriminating as it is entirely Satanic. Its author is Aisha, Muhammad's favorite wife. *Bukhari:V4B54N490-V7B71N658* "Magic was worked on the Prophet so that he began to believe he was doing a thing which he was not actually doing. [In other words, an evil spell caused him to hallucinate and lie. Such is the nature of a men possessed by demons.] One day he said, 'I feel that Allah [Satan] has inspired me as how to cure myself. Two persons [demons] came to me in my dream. One of them asked the other, "What is the ailment of this man?" "He has been bewitched. He is under the spell of magic." "Who cast the magic spell?" "A Jew." "What material did he use?" "A comb, the hair knotted on it, and the outer skin of the pollen of the male date-palm." "Where did it come from?" "It is in the well of Dharwan."' So, the Prophet went to the well. Upon his return, he said, 'The date-palms are like the heads of devils.' I asked, 'Did you blow out those things with which the magic was worked?' He said, 'No, for I have been cured by Allah and I am afraid that this action may spread evil amongst the people.'" Denial, hallucinations, paranoia, and deceit are all part of the demonic recipe. Muhammad didn't want the story out because it was so incriminating. He became what he condemned—and he knew it.

The 114th surah is last only because it is brief. Muslims admit that the Qur'an is out of order, assembled longest to shortest surah, but they make no attempt to reorder it chronologically or even to illuminate it by attaching it to the context of Muhammad's life. The reasons are clear. Out of order and devoid of context it is confusing. In order and in context it is devastating.

114.001 "Say: I seek refuge in the Lord of men and jinn [demons], the King of men and jinn, the Ilah (God) of men and jinn." In all but two of my translations of the "Man" surah, "Ilah" for "God" was replaced by "god" with lowercase "g." Since Muhammad and his fellow Muslims capitalize words for no apparent reason, not capitalizing God is significant. And since the position and political titles of Lord and King were capitalized, not elevating god could have been Muhammad's way of letting us know who begat whom.

Even the Devil earned a trio of capitalizations. *114.004* "From the evil of the sneaking Devil who Whispers Evil and withdraws after his whisper, the slinking Satan, the same who whispers into the hearts of mankind from among the jinn and men." Wouldn't you know it, the Qur'an ends as it began—with an evil spirit. Satan is sneaking around, whispering evil to jinn and men. How appropriate.

Unfortunately, the end of the Qur'an doesn't mean the end of Islam. Muhammad was on a mission—one that hadn't gone very well. The Hanif well had run dry and the Meccans remained unconvinced. So the wannabe prophet decided to change his qiblah, his god, and his inspiration. With the next thirty-nine surahs we enter the second Meccan period. The Jews were gradually replacing the Quraysh on the Qur'an's center stage just as their Bible began to dominate Islamic scripture. As we shall discover, this was a very unpleasant time for Muhammad.

In our quest to understand fundamental Islam, let's dive into the 56th surah, named "The Inevitable." It is revealing in that it establishes heaven and hell in Muhammad's image. It is incriminating in that there is no chance these lurid depictions are divine.

Like so much of the Qur'an, "The Inevitable" is style devoid of substance. It has become Muhammad's style to profess an intimate knowledge of heaven and hell, regaling us with vivid teases and torments. They have become the carrot and whip of his self-indulgent rise to power. But the Islamic path remains unlit. While the prophet's fiery hell and lustful heaven have been detailed to distraction, we have precious little doctrine upon which to navigate his new creed. "Surrender or die" is clear enough, but it's clearly not enough to call Muhammad's creation a religion.

Islam's oracle opens the surah as the Prophet of Doom. *056.001* "When the inevitable Event befalls abasing, there will be no denying." The Meccans ridiculed most everything Muhammad said, so the wannabe prophet retreated into his imaginary realm, a place he created, a place no one could deny. *056.003* "Bringing low. Exalting. The earth shall be shaken with a terrible shaking, and the mountains shall be made to crumble with crumbling, so that they become powdered dust, floating particles." According to the "prophet" the shaking and crumbling was to occur in the year 1110 A.D., half an Islamic day, or 500 normal years, from his coronation as Allah's last messenger. Since the calamitous event known as the Day of Doom was Muhammad's most important and oft repeated prophecy, and since it remains unfulfilled 900 years hence, might we be entitled to question his prophetic credentials?

056.007 "And you shall be three groups. So those on the Right Hand; What will be the Companions of the Right Hand? And the Companions of the Left Hand, What will be the Companions of the Left Hand? And those Foremost will be Foremost. These are they who are nearest. Drawn nigh in Gardens of Delight." These questions remain unanswered throughout this "divine revelation." If they were important enough for "god" to ask, you'd think they would merit an answer. For if we became "lefties" simply because Allah's fickle hand of fate rubbed Adam's back the wrong way, predestining us to hell, then let's bury this religion and free everyone from its impoverished legacy. If a little heavenly petting is the foundation of Islam— let's wave goodbye and rid the world of the terror it inspires.

056.013 "A multitude of those from among the first, and a few from the latter, (will be) on couch-like thrones woven with gold and precious stones. Reclining, facing each other.

Round about them will (serve) boys of perpetual (freshness), of never ending bloom, with goblets, jugs, and cups (filled) with sparkling wine. No aching of the head will they receive, nor suffer any madness, nor exhaustion. And with fruits, any that they may select: and the flesh of fowls, any they may desire. And (there will be) Hur (fair females) with big eyes, lovely and pure, beautiful ones, like unto hidden pearls, well-guarded in their shells. A reward for the deeds." Allah's brothel: the best little whorehouse in Mecca.

Let's check out Muhammad's Hadiths on the subject. First, we learn that heaven's rewards will send you to hell. *Bukhari:V7B69N494* "I heard the Prophet saying, 'From among my followers there will be some who will consider illegal sexual intercourse, the wearing of silk, the drinking of alcoholic drinks and the use of musical instruments, to be lawful. Allah will destroy them during the night and will let mountains fall on them. He will transform the rest into monkeys and pigs and they will remain so till the Day of Doom.'" *Bukhari:V4B54N476-544* "The Prophet said, 'In Paradise they will not urinate, relieve nature, spit, or have any nasal secretions. Everyone will have two virgins who will be so beautiful and transparent the bones of their legs will be seen through their flesh.'"

Returning to the Qur'an's depiction of paradise: *056.025* "There hear they no vain speaking nor backbiting, only saying the word, 'Peace! Peace.'" Only saying one word is going to make the Islamic paradise a very boring place. No wonder Allah is providing such a rich menu of entertainment options.

"The Companions of the Right Hand, what will be the Companions of the Right Hand?" Here we go again. The question is asked but not answered. The surah tells us the fate of the Righties without a hint as to who they are or what they did to gain entrance into Allah's brothel. "Among thorn-less lote trees. And among Talh (banana-trees) with flowers piled high, in shade long-extended, by water flowing constantly, and fruit in abundance, whose season is not limited, nor forbidden." The Islamic paradise continues to reflect the parochial view of an abandoned orphan boy struggling to survive the rigors of an unrelenting desert. It's comprised of fruits, fowl, shade, flowing water, comfy seating, attentive servants, Viagra-like wine, and lusty virgins. It's a place to die for. But, fair warning, I wouldn't trust a god whose reward in paradise—drinking and fornication—is what he forbids on earth.

056.034 "On couches or thrones raised high. Verily, We have created them (maidens) incomparable: We have formed their maidens as a special creation, and made them to grow a new growth. We made them virgins—pure and undefiled, lovers, matched in age." Muhammad is telling his young recruits that their virgins will regain their virginity after each conquest—"they grow a new growth." He is also telling them that the Islamic paradise is for men only. Their lovers are a "special creation"—not women of this world. And to satisfy their most lustful cravings—their sex partners are plentiful, as in more than one. Their "incomparable maidens, special companions, virgins, and lovers" are always plural—Islam's *ménage a trois*.

And while Allah dispenses with how the Right-Handers managed to score their decadent reward, he tells us from whence they came. *056.039* "A numerous company from among the first, And a (goodly) number from those of later times."

But enough of this frivolity, it's time to roast some infidels. *056.041* "**The Companions of the Left Hand, what will be the Companions of the Left Hand? (They will be) in the midst of a Fierce Blast of Hot Wind and in Boiling Water, and a shadow of black smoke, neither cool nor pleasant. For that they were wont to be indulged, heretofore they were effete with luxury, and persisted obstinately in the great violation.**" The great Lefty violation was the abandonment of an orphan boy, depriving him of a share of the family business, and then rejecting his prophetic claims.

056.047 "**And they used to say, 'What! when we die and become dust and bones, shall we then be resurrected? And also our forefathers?' Say: 'Yea, those of old and those of later times, All will be gathered together for the tryst, a meeting appointed for a Day well-known.'**" This is Muhammad's Day of Doom in which men are exhumed from the grave, their bones and flesh reassembled, so that some can burn in lust while others burn in hell. It's flesh that is gratified and roasted—not spirit.

056.051 "**Then, moreover, verily you the erring ones, the deniers, you will surely taste the Tree of Zaqqoom and fill (your) bellies with it. And drink Boiling Water on top of it. Indeed you shall drink like diseased camels raging with thirst! Such will be their entertainment, their welcome on the Day of Doom.**" If nothing else, you have to give Muhammad credit for originality. It's hard to imagine a god this entertaining, albeit in a demented way.

056.057 "**It is We Who have created you: admit the truth and then surrender.**" That's Islam in a nutshell. Admit Muhammad is a prophet and then acquiesce to his will or you will eat thorns and drink scalding water. "**Then tell Me the semen that you emit, throwing out. Is it you who create it, or are We the Creators? [It's only natural— the god of lust is the god of semen.] We have decreed/predestined/ordained Death for you all, and We are not to be frustrated from replacing you with others in (forms) that you know not.**" Muhammad and Allah shared many things in common, including the thought that men were replaceable. They used fiery threats and lustful taunts to seduce an unending supply of martyrs to fight and die for the things they coveted. Islam wasn't invented to save men but to abuse them.

056.068 "**Have you observed the water which you drink? Do you shed it from the clouds or are We the Shedder? If We pleased, We could have made it salty and bitter; why do you not give thanks?**" The Shedder thing was scientifically inaccurate and hardly a proof, so would you believe… "**Have you observed the fire which you kindle? Is it you that produce the trees for it, or are We the producers?**" Now you know why Yahweh chose to use miracles and prophecies to prove the Bible's divine inspiration. Unable to do either, Allah stammered.

056.073 "**We, even We, have made it [wood] a memorial (of the Hell Fire), and an article of comfort and convenience for the denizens of deserts [where there are fewer trees than anywhere else]. Therefore celebrate with praises the name of thy Lord, the Tremendous!**" There are more… *056.075* "**Furthermore I call to witness the falling Stars, and that is indeed a mighty adjuration, a tremendous oath, if only you knew, that this is indeed a** noble recitation (of the Qur'an)." Among the long line of unintelligible segues, this is a standout. We transitioned from calling incinerating space pebbles mighty witnesses to the Qur'an being noble. **"In a Book kept hidden that is protected which none shall touch but those who are clean, the purified ones."** Time out. A revelation by definition can't be hidden. Since this revelation, the Qur'an, is the foundation of Islam—how did they manage to foul it up? **"A Revelation from the Lord of men and jinn. Is it such a talk that you would hold in light esteem, a statement to scorn? Do you then hold this announcement in contempt?"** In a word, yes. As did the Meccans who knew it and Muhammad best.

The next ten verses are so muddled, the message is undecipherable even with the Arabic translators adding a forty-seven words to help their god out. *056.082* **"And instead (of thanking) for the provision He gives you, you deny (Him by disbelief). To give (it) the lie you make your means of subsistence. Then why do you not (intervene) when (the soul of the dying man) reaches the throat, And you the while (sit) looking on, But We (Our angels who take souls) are nearer unto him than you, but you see not. Then why do you not, if you are exempt from (future) account (punishment), and not in bondage (unto Us), Do you not force it (the soul) back (into its body), if you are true (in the claim of independence)? Thus, then, if he (the dying person) is of those drawn nigh, (There is for him) breath of life and plenty, and a Garden of Delights. And if he is of those on the Right Hand, Then (the greeting) 'Safety and peace' (from the punishment of Allah)."** If this is divinely inspired scripture, then I'm William Shakespeare.

In the final verses of the 56th surah, Muhammad's dark spirit returns to his favorite subject. *056.092* **"But if he (the dying person), be of the denying (of the Day of Doom), erring (away from Islam), then for him is the entertainment with boiling water and roasting in hell fire. Verily. this is the absolute truth with certainty, so celebrate (Muhammad)."**

Stunning. The entertainment for those who reject this dark dogma is to be roasted and boiled. What kind of god would tell his prophet to "celebrate" human torture? Since no god could possibly be this disturbed, this demented, should Muhammad be despised for perpetrating this fraud, or pitied? Should Muslims be freed from this delusion or should we simply sit back and watch them celebrate their torturous acts of terror today?

In exposing Islam I have erred on the side of the Qur'an and Hadith. That is to say, I have been nearly as repetitious as they have been. By bringing the doctrines most holy books together chronologically and placing them in the context of time and place, the evidence piles up one confession at a time. The truth ultimately becomes undeniable. Therefore, I will continue to present their scriptures as completely as your endurance allows. By observing a consistent pattern of behavior, you will be able to render an accurate assessment.

In this light, let's dissect the 52nd surah, kissing cousin to the 56th. *052.001* **"I** call to witness Tur (Mount Sinai) and a Scripture Book inscribed, written on a fine parchment scroll unrolled, and the House ever-peopled, and the roof raised high, and the sea kept filled." The Islamic spirit is trying to pull a fast one. The House wasn't "ever-peopled." As you will discover in the "Source Material" appendix, there is no archeological and historical evidence to show that Mecca even existed before the sixth century. Therefore, Islam's formation is based upon a lie, because without people it would have been impossible to pass on any semblance of Islamic ritual from Abraham to Qusayy.

Elsewhere in the Qur'an, we're told that the "Book" was chiseled on Memorial Tablets, not inscribed on perishable parchment scrolls. But that's the least of the Qur'anic headaches. It claims, as Maududi confirms, that it was first written before creation, and that it was passed down and maintained in its original form—verbatim. **"The Qur'an that you are bent upon belying is unchangeable: 'It is inscribed in the Preserved Tablet, which cannot be corrupted in any way.'"**

Since the Qur'an's claims regarding its origin and nature are essential to our understanding, I'd like to explore this matter more completely. Allah's "book" says of itself: *012:001* **"These are verses of the immaculate Book, a clear discourse."** Immaculate means perfect, flawless—inerrant. Yet we've already discovered scores of errors, big and small. *012:003* **"Through the Qur'an We narrate the best of histories."** Yet it is devoid of history. It doesn't even provide any context. *002.001* **"This is a book free of doubt."** That is true, but not in the way it was intended. *010:037* **"This Qur'an is such a writing that none but Allah could have composed it. It confirms what has been revealed before."** Not only would the behavior in the Islamic heaven be illegal in every state save the brothels of Nevada, the Qur'an contradicts rather than confirms the prior revelation it says is inspired. What's more, the writing quality is horrendous—it's an embarrassment. Then, while lecturing on creation, Allah's prophet professed, **"All that was going to be was written on the memorial Tablet before anything else was created."** And that is particularly odd since everything we have read thus far has been fixated on one man's quest for gold and glory. Said another way: the Qur'an's revelations only seem to serve Muhammad.

The reason I bring this to your attention is to scuttle the Islamic claim that the Qur'an is a perfect reflection of the original tablet inscribed in heaven. The earliest Qur'anic writings all differ with each other, and they conflict with the present version. Coins from 685 A.D. have inscriptions that don't match today's surahs. The scripture inside the Dome of the Rock (691 A.D.) also varies. Further, the earliest copies of the Qur'an were written without vowels and the diacritical dots that modern Arabic uses to determine what letter is intended. It wasn't until the late eighth century, more than a hundred and fifty years after Muhammad's death, that Islamic scholars added diacritical marks to clear up countless ambiguities. In doing so, they chose the letters and vowels—and thus the current words, punctuation, and meaning. They translated what was essentially code into the gibberish we are reading today.

Then there is the problem of the parchments themselves. The oldest fragments date to the eighth century, not the seventh. They were found in a pager grave on the loft rafters of the Mosque of Saria'a in 1972. Aberrations from the accepted text abound, including the order of the verses, textual variations, and artistic embellishments. Gerd Puin, the leader of the German team analyzing the scrolls said, "Revisions are very clearly written over earlier, washed-off versions. What the Yemeni Qur'ans suggest is an evolving text rather than the word of God revealed in its entirety to the Prophet Muhammad." Puin went on to declare: "The Qur'an claims for itself that it is 'mubeen,' or clear, but if you look at it, you will notice that every fifth sentence or so simply doesn't make sense. A fifth of the Qur'anic text is incomprehensible. This is what has caused the anxiety regarding translation. If the Qur'an is not comprehensible, if it can't even be understood in Arabic, then it's not translatable into any language." This stark reality is frightening to orthodox Muslims who parrot their prophet's claim that the Qur'an has been preserved perfectly—unchanged and inerrant—just as Allah wrote it.

The perfection claim Allah makes on behalf of his Qur'an would be impossible even if Allah were god. Language is an imperfect tool. One word can mean many things and meanings often change with inflection. Connotation is altered by context, something the Qur'an lacks. Knowing the time, place, and parties to a conversation is required to establish the intended implication. For example, the Classical Arabic word used for fighting could just as easily be translated killing. And the word for virgin is indistinguishable from the classical Arabic word for white grape.

Yahweh knew better. He never said his Scripture was inerrant. He said it was sufficient. But while we are on the subject, I'd like to share something you might find interesting. There are thousands of prophecies in the Bible, most of which are exacting. There have been no misses. There are thousands of detailed historical depictions in the text—none of which have been shown to be invalid. In the books of Genesis, Exodus, Numbers, and Deuteronomy, every 50th Hebrew letter spells "Torah." In Leviticus, the central book of the Torah, every 70th letter spells "YHWH." Proofs of inspiration abound.

The Qur'an's obsession with demented torments is proof of a different kind of inspiration. Its fixation on fatalism, the annihilation of choice, and therefore the impossibility of love, provides another salient clue as to the nature of Islam's dark spirit. *052.007* **"Verily the Doom and torment of your Lord will surely come to pass; there is none that can avert it or ward it off."**

This "god" is a nasty and violent fellow: *052.009* **"On the Day when heaven will heave in dreadful shaking, trembling, and the mountains will fly hither and thither, woe to those who reject [me], that play in shallow trifles and sport in vain discourses. That Day they will be pushed down by force, thrust with a horrible thrust into the Fire of Hell. Unable** to resist, they shall be driven to the fire with violence." There is a spirit this demented. His name is Lucifer. The Qur'an boldly reveals his nature and ambition.

052.014 "'This,' it will be said, 'is the Fire, which you used to deny! Is this a magic fake? Burn therein, endure the heat; taste it. It's the same whether you bear it patiently, or not. This is My retaliation for what you did.'" This is blatantly demonic.

Those who are willing to trust a spirit this carnal shall be rewarded in like fashion (if he's not the Devil): *052.017* "Verily, the Muttaqun (those who fear) will be in Gardens and Delight. Enjoying the (bliss) which their Lord has provided, and their Lord saved them from the torment of the blazing Fire. 'Eat and drink with glee, because of what you used to do [damning, robbing, enslaving, and murdering people for me].' They will recline (with ease) on Throne Couches (of dignity) arranged in ranks; and We shall join them to beautiful Hur (female maidens) with big, lustrous eyes." The fact that heaven and hell are consistently depicted in Muhammad's parochial image is a sign that *his* passions inspired this part of the Qur'an, *not* God's.

052.021 "Those who believe and whose families follow them in Faith, to them shall We join their offspring: Nor shall We deprive them of their works: (Yet) each individual is in pledge for his deeds." Imagine that. Wives and children will be joined with husbands and fathers who are cavorting with virgins. That ought to be entertaining. "And We shall provide fruit and meat, anything they desire. There they shall pass from hand to hand a (wine) cup free of frivolity, free of all taint of vanity or cause of sin." Allah's brew of free frivolity sounds like a date-rape drug.

This less-than-heavenly picture continues with these perverse strokes: *052.024* "Round about them will serve, (devoted) to them, young boy servants of their own (handsome) as well-guarded pearls." In previous verses, Allah used the "well-guarded pearl" reference to designate virgins, maidens whose virtue was hidden, or protected, in closed shells. Now, used in reference to handsome and devoted boy servants, it sounds like homosexuality. "They will advance to each other, drawing near, engaging in mutual enquiry. They will say: 'We used to be afraid (of the punishment) in the midst of our families, but Allah has been good to us, and has delivered us from the torment of the Scorching Wind and Breath of Fire.'" Could Allah be saying that they previously suppressed their homosexual urges for fear of their families' wrath, but now they are out of the closest?

052.028 "We used to invoke Him before: truly He the Benign, the Merciful!" A benign and merciful tormentor; now there's a thought. I can only wonder how Muslims justify the obvious contradiction between their god's definition and his behavior. "Therefore remind: By the Grace of your Lord, you are no vulgar soothsayer, nor are you a possessed madman." Another translation reads: "Therefore warn (men, Muhammad). By the grace of Allah you are neither soothsayer nor madman." Either way, it's evidence that neither Muhammad nor the Meccans were convinced.

052.030 "Or do they say: 'A Poet! We await for him some evil accidental calamity (hatched) by time!' Say: 'Await you! I too will wait along with you!'" From another translation: "Say (unto them): Except (your fill)! Lo! I am with you among the expectant." With the words that the Islamic scholar arbitrarily added to the text to make the message seem rational removed, the verse reads: **"Say: Except! Lo! I am with you among the expectant."** While scholars may quibble over the meaning, I think one thing is clear: illiterate men ought not author scripture.

Ali's translation explains: **"Do they say: He is a poet from whom we expect an adverse turn of fortune?"** How perceptive. The Meccans saw Muhammad as a con artist ready to pick their pockets. And he did. The "poet" robbed their caravans, stole their town, and then usurped all rights associated with their religious scam.

To rebut his critics, the pot called the kettle black. *052.032* **"Is it that their mental faculties of understanding urge them to this, or are they an outrageous folk, transgressing beyond the bounds?"** While the never-ending argument between the Meccans and Muhammad over the prophet's lack of prophetic credentials is wearisome, this verse demonstrates the Qur'an's lack of divine inspiration. An all-knowing God would never have asked such a question.

As the argument raged on, Muhammad's kin were ever more convinced that the wannabe prophet was simply fabricating his divine credentials to steal their money. *052.033* **"Or do they say, 'He fabricated it (the Qur'an)?' Nay, they will never believe. Let them then produce a recital/speech/announcement/discourse like unto it, if they speak the truth!"** The Meccans knew what we have learned— Muhammad was making this up as he went along. And the best the prophet could do was to say, "Prove I'm lying by producing a recital as good as this."

The early Hanif poem by Zayd, upon which the early surahs were based, was easily as good, if not much better. And the Bible, from which the later surahs were plagiarized, was infinitely more rational, more prophetic, and godly. Therefore, based upon the challenge, Muhammad's recitals were false. We have called his bluff. But then again, it wasn't a big deal. As you shall soon see, Adolf Hitler's rants were better than this.

052.035 **"Were they created of nothing, or were they themselves their creators? Or did they create the heavens and earth? Nay, they have no certainty. Do they possess the treasures of your Lord? Or are they the tyrant treasurers set in absolute authority to do as they like [with the Ka'aba Inc.]?"** Now that's our boy. Muhammad saw himself as the one set in absolute authority—to do anything he liked. As such he was empowered to pirate treasures and cavort immorally without recrimination. Moreover, he actually got away with it.

Pressing his case, the lord is alleged to have asked: *052.038* **"Or have they a ladder, by which they can (climb up to heaven and) listen (to its secrets)? Then let (such a) listener of theirs produce a warrant manifesting proof."** According to Muhammad, Adam bumped his head on heaven. So the Islamic heaven isn't very high. A ladder would have been sufficient. However, since Mecca was devoid of wood and carpenters, just building a ladder would have been a bigger miracle than Muhammad or his dark spirit ever mustered.

052.039 **"Or has He (Allah) only daughters and you have sons?"** The prophet ought to
have stopped when he was down and left us in doubt. Muhammad's Lord is
demeaning the Meccan rock idol Allah. He's saying that "He" isn't worthy
because he had daughters, not sons. Allah's daughters were fellow rock idols
Al-Lat, Al-Uzza, and Manat of Satanic Verse fame. Since boys were viewed
as better than girls, Muhammad's dark spirit is implying that Allah was a low-
life loser. And make no mistake, Allah was the only Meccan deity with
daughters. This exact same verse was repeated later in the Qur'an as a way of
digging Muhammad out of his devilish dilemma when he confessed to mis-
taking Satan for Allah.

052.040 **"Or is it that you demand a reward or fee from them (for preaching Islam), so that
they are burdened with expense and a load of debt? Or that the Ghaib (unseen) is in their
hands that they have it written down? Or do they intend a plot (against you), staging a
deception? But those who defy and seek to ensnare (the messenger) are themselves being
plotted against and will be tricked!"** Muhammad's lord is saying that the Meccans
are lucky that he isn't charging them for these spiritual insights. Further, he's
implying that they are impoverished because they haven't written any scripture. Mind you, Muhammad hadn't written any either, and none of them could
have read it if either of them had. Then he goes off on his favorite conspiracy theory—everyone is plotting against my guy. Which isn't actually true—
only those of us who knew Muhammad were interested in exposing his plot.

The verse ends with one of many confessions. The Islamic god is a trickster.
He plots against men. So, why do Muslims trust the "word" of an admittedly
deceitful spirit? How do they know he is not deceiving *them*?

As with so much of the Qur'an, the next verse doesn't fit with the rest of
the surah—and thus was probably revealed much later. Up to this point the
Lord has been unnamed and Allah has been demeaned. Now we're being told
that there is no god (ilah) but Allah. *052.043* **"Or have they an ilah (god) other than
Allah? [An odd question to ask the Meccans since their primary deity was named Allah.]
Glory be to Allah from what they set up."**

052.044 **"Were they to see a piece of sky falling, they would say: 'Clouds gathered in
heaps!' So leave them alone until they encounter that Day where they shall swoon (with
terror); their plotting will avail them not, and no help shall be given them (so they shall
receive their torment). Verily, for those who do wrong, there is another punishment besides
this, but most of them understand not."** The spirit of Islam is in a rut: the sky is
falling, men are swooning in terror, and there are ever more plots and punishments. No matter where one looks, the Qur'an is a very nasty book.

Returning to the Hadith, we find Tabari, in an effort to please his Shi'ite
overlords, saying that Ali was the first male lured into Islamic submission.

Tabari VI:83 **"Ali was the first to accept Islam. He submitted at the age of nine."**
Now that we have three Muslims, let's take a quick inventory. Khadija founds Islam to salvage her reclusive, suicidal husband's tattered reputation. She convinces him that he's not cavorting with demons, and he adopts her Profitable Prophet Plan. Amply motivated by revenge and greed, the dynamic duo assails their clan with claims equally preposterous and delusional. They were "belittling the competition." Their alleged "scripture" is as demented as their motives are transparent. What's more, their anemic idol and his fanciful message are so infantile every Meccan scoffs at the would-be prophet, save one nine-year-old child. And he's adopted under guess-who's care.

Tabari VI:83 **"One of the favors Allah bestowed on Ali bin Talib [Ali was uncle Abu's son, hence Muhammad's cousin.] was that the Messenger was his guardian before Islam."** And that occurred because: **"The Quraysh were afflicted by a severe drought. Muhammad said to his uncle al-Abbas, one of the richest Banu Hashim [Muhammad's clan], 'Abbas, your brother Abu Talib has many dependents, and you see how people are suffering. I will take one of his sons and you take one."** The champion of Dads, **"Abu Talib said to them, 'As long as you leave me Aqil, do as you wish.' Muhammad took Ali."**

"Our fellow scholars are agreed," Tabari says, **"that Ali accepted Islam a year after the Prophet began his mission, and that he remained in Mecca for twelve years."** As such, the score at end of the prophet's first year was: Islam 1, Pagans 4,999.

But if Islam was low on converts, it was long on controversy. Abu Bakr, Muhammad's richest pal, future father-in-law, and Caliph, claimed he preceded Ali. **"'O Messenger, who has followed you in this religion?' He replied, 'Two men have followed me in it, a free man and a slave; Abu Bakr and Bilal.'"**

The prophet misspoke when he said Bilal. Zayd bin Harithah, not to be confused with Zayd the Hanif, was the first slave to submit. He was owned by Khadija. She gave him to Muhammad, and after some time, he adopted the boy, making him his second son. Companions of the Prophet say: **"The first man to believe and follow the Prophet was Zayd bin Harithah, his client [slave] and adopted son."** Ibn Ishaq says that the slave-turned-son was number two: **"Zayd was the first male to accept Islam and to pray after Ali. Then Abu Bakr accepted Islam."**

A word of caution is appropriate here. Freeing a slave and adopting him was a fine and upstanding thing to do. But before we lavish praise upon Muhammad, consider this: in Mecca, sons were considered a sign of godly favor. No sons, no favor. Muhammad's own boys died in infancy—a strong signal to the Meccans that god had punished him. What's more, in an act we would call incest, the prophet would come to steal Zayd's wife. In Medina, while his son was away terrorizing Meccans, Muhammad stumbled into her tent, saw her undressed, lusted, and took her as his own.

Regardless of who was conned first, by the end of the fourth year, it was Islam 4, Pagans 4,996. Tabari confirms the stealth prophet's slow start. *Tabari VI:89* **"Three years after the commencement of his mission, Allah commanded His Prophet** to proclaim the divine message which he had received publicly to the people." "In the previous three years of his mission, until he was commanded to summon people openly, he had kept his preaching secret and hidden." At the time Muslims "were few in number and practiced their faith in secret." He was the world's first mute messenger.

Mistaken, Tabari states that Allah summoned the tongue-tied troubadour with these words from the 15th surah, "So proclaim that which you are commanded, and withdraw from the polytheists." Qur'anic scholars say, however, that the 15th surah was 57th in order of divine revelation, not third. Either the surahs are hopelessly jumbled or somebody is terribly wrong.

In the next paragraph, Tabari confirms that even the first Muslims were clueless when it came to the progression of surahs. After parading the 15th out as the third, he nominates the 26th for the fourth position. All three Qur'anic chronologists say that the 26th immediately preceded the 15th.

Regardless of the score or progression, Bakr was said to be a better salesman than Islam's Messiah. "Many responded to his summons and accepted Islam."

Some however, needed a little encouraging. "They came to blows, and Sa'd struck one of the polytheists with a camel's jawbone and split his head open."

That leads us to the showdown at uncle Abu's mud hut. This discussion is similar to the one chronicled earlier in Ishaq's Sira, but it is placed later in the flow of things by Tabari in his History. He claims that Hajjaj's eight sons *Tabari VI:93* "went to Abu Talib and said, 'Your nephew [Muhammad] has reviled our gods, denounced our religion, derided our traditional values, and told us that our forefathers were misguided [and burning in hell]. Either curb his attacks on us or give us a free hand to deal with him, for you are as opposed to him as we are.'" This Hadith suggests that Muhammad was the cause of his own grief. He denounced traditional Arab values and damned his ancestors. The Meccans wanted nothing more than for him to shush up. But no... "he continued as before."

The leadership returned to "Talib once again. They said, 'We asked you to forbid your nephew from attacking us, but you did nothing. By Allah, we can no longer endure this vilification of our forefathers, this derision of our traditional values, and this abuse of our gods." We are told: "This breach and enmity with his tribe weighed heavily on Abu Talib."

The Meccans were reasonable, rational, and restrained. They returned to Abu Talib a third, fourth, and fifth time. "You are our elder and our chief, so give us justice against your nephew and order him to desist from reviling our gods, and we will leave him to his god." At this point, Muhammad's god was not one of the Meccan gods—further evidence of the migration from Ar-Rahman to Allah.

Tabari VI:95 "Abu Talib sent for Muhammad. 'Nephew, here are the shaykhs and nobles of your tribe. They have asked for justice against you. You should desist from reviling their gods and they will leave you to your god.' 'Uncle,' he said, 'shall I not summon them to something which is better than their gods?'" He was protesting that his god, Ar-Rahman, was better than their god, Allah. But how can that be? The Islamic religion was based upon the claim that Muhammad was Allah's messenger.

Yet on this day, Muhammad wants to summon the Meccans to a god who is better than their Allah.

Tabari VI:96 **"Abu Talib said to Muhammad, 'Nephew, how is it that your tribe is complaining of you and claiming that you are reviling their gods and saying this, that, and the other?' The Messenger said, 'I want them to utter one saying. If they say it, the Arabs will submit to them and the non-Arabs will pay the jizyah [submission tax] to them."** This is another confirmation of the Profitable Prophet Plan.

The shaykhs and nobles are alleged to have said something that contradicts the prior Hadith. Yet it is no less debilitating to Allah's claim of divinity. **"Does Muhammad make the gods one god? This is indeed an astounding thing."** Muhammad combined the traits of six pagan idols—Ar-Rahman, Ar-Rahim, Allah, Al-Lat, Al-Uzza, and Manat—into a single deity. He manufactured his god!

The Qur'an confirms this admission in the 38th surah. **"Sad [the name of an Arabian moon god], I swear by the Qur'an, full of reminding."** The Noble Qur'an has a different take on the "Sad" intro: **"Sad (These letters are one of the miracles of the Qur'an, and none but Allah knows their meanings.)"** Imagine that: Islam claims that nobody understands the final "reminder" to mankind. And so desperate are Muslims for miracles, incomprehensibility is called a sign of divinity.

Then the Islamic god says that those who deny the senseless are arrogant and misinformed: *038.002* **"Nay, those who disbelieve are in false pride and opposition."**

This is followed by a little Islamic bragging: *038.003* **"How many generations have we destroyed before them? They cried out for mercy when it was too late for escape. They wonder that a warner has come to them from among themselves. And the disbelievers say, 'This (Prophet Muhammad) is a sorcerer, a charlatan, an wizard telling lies. He has made the alihah (gods) into one Ilah (God). This is a curious and strange thing to be sure!' Their leaders said, 'Walk away from him...there is surely some motive behind this—something sought after—a thing he has designed against us...It is surely a forgery.'"**

Those who lived with Muhammad, dealt with him, worked with him, and listened to him, knew exactly who he was: **"He is a sorcerer, a charlatan, a wizard telling lies."** They knew what he was doing: **"He has turned our gods into a single God."** And they were never in doubt as to why: **"There is surely some motive behind it—something sought after."** They even understood his means: **"It is a forgery."** The eyewitnesses to the crime are unanimous in their testimony: a fraud has been perpetrated. Their eyewitness account has been retained in the Qur'an. But sadly, neither Muslims nor Infidels are listening to what those who knew Muhammad best had to say. And that, perhaps, is the biggest crime of all.

Then, as a Mafia godfather would do today, the dark spirit of Islam threatened the eyewitnesses and intimidated the jury pool: *038.007* **"'We have not heard of this in the religion of later days. This is nothing but an invention! What! Has this been sent to him?' Nay, but they are in doubt about My reminder (this Qur'an). Nay, but they have not tasted (My) Torment yet! Let them climb up the ladders to the heavens. They will be one more army vanquished among the many routed hordes."** Forever lame, Allah, in trying to vindicate himself, confirmed his guilt. He just said that his heaven was hellish, a place where people are vanquished.

But the cocky, schoolyard bully wasn't finished gloating. He went on to list his all-in-one-god's glorious achievements: *038.012* **"Before them belied the people of Noah, Ad, Pharaoh the man of stakes (for punishment), Thamud, the people of Lot, and the Wood dwellers, such were the Confederates. They rejected my Messengers so My Torment was justified."** I've heard of justifiable homicide but never justifiable torment.

After confirming his pagan origins, and proving his demented nature, the 38th surah reveals the dark spirit's lack of mental acuity. Allah introduces his listeners to David, the greatest Jewish king. He claims that King David was his votary, and that he turned to him, not Yahweh, despite a mountain of evidence to the contrary. But damn the facts. Muhammad had people to subdue, credibility to usurp, power to grab, and money to steal. *038.017* **"We endued Our slave David with power. It was We who subdued the hills to sing Our praises with him at nightfall. And the birds were assembled, all obedient to him."** *038.020* **"We made his kingdom strong and bestowed (Islamic) Prophethood on him."**

This delusional celestial songfest is followed by a meaningless story of runaway ewes. Then we learn: *038.024* **"It occurred to David that he was being tried by Us, and he begged his Lord to forgive him and fell down, prostrating himself in [Islamic] homage."** According to Allah, King David was a Muslim! Can you imagine the conspiracy that would have had to happen to write David's Islamic practices and devotion to Allah out of the Bible and his faux Jewishness in? Allah has to be the most delusional god ever conceived by man.

Now that the Qur'an has pulverized what little credibility its god and prophet might have possessed, it is time to say goodbye to the **"Sad"** surah: *038.027* **"We have not created the heavens and the earth and all that lies between for nothing. So woe to the unbelievers because of the fire of Hell."** The first nine words I believe.

Back in Mecca: *Tabari VI:98* **"The situation deteriorated, hostility became bitter, and people withdrew from one another, displaying open hatred."** Trying to salvage a deteriorating situation, **"the Meccan chiefs conspired to seduce their sons, brothers, and clansmen away from the new religion. It was a trial which severely shook the Muslims who had followed the Prophet. Some were seduced."** So to salvage as many converts as possible, Muhammad commanded Muslims **"to emigrate to Abyssinia."**

Tabari VI:98 **"The main body went to Abyssinia because of the coercion they were being subjected to in Mecca. His fear was that they would be seduced from their religion."** **"There is a difference of opinion as to the number of those who emigrated in stealth and secret. Some say there were eleven men and four women. ...Ibn Ishaq claims there were ten."**

It doesn't appear that the words of Islam were very convincing. A little coercion and the fragile band buckled. In the eighth year of Muhammad's reign as prophet the score is Islam 15, Pagans 4,985. It's little wonder Islamic states prohibit freedom of religion. Even Muhammad couldn't sell this stuff.

11

SATAN'S BARGAIN

"Satan cast a false Revelation on the Messenger of God's tongue."

The motley crew that slinked out of Mecca under the cover of darkness included Muhammad's daughter, Ruqayyah. Other notables were named slaves to the House, to Ar-Rahman, to the sun god Manaf, slave to Allah, and to Allah's daughter Al-Uzza. It was a pagan potpourri.

Muhammad was down but not out: *Tabari VI:101* **"The Messenger remained in Mecca preaching in secret and openly, protected by his uncle Abu Talib."** It was another Islamic first: a secretive prophet was being protected by a seventy-year-old pagan. **"When the Quraysh saw that they had no means of attacking him physically [The old guy was either formidable or the Meccans were impotent.], they accused him of sorcery, soothsaying, and madness, and of being a poet. They began to keep those away from him whom they feared might listen and follow him."**

I have distilled a "Best of the Meccans" list of accusations against Muhammad and his claims from the hundreds that permeate the Qur'an. For your reading pleasure: **"He is liar and a magician." "He is possessed by devils." "He is an insane plagiarizing poet."** The Meccans called him **"a lunatic, a farfetched forger, a fool, a specious pretender, and deceitful." "The unbelievers said: 'He is a deceiving sorcerer, turning many gods into one deity.'"** They saw an ulterior **"motive behind the Qur'an. It is a fabrication." "They laugh at the Qur'an." "Allah hasn't sent down anything. You are only speaking lies." "This is nothing but pure sorcery." "The unbelievers say, 'The Qur'an is nothing but earlier peoples' lore.'" "These are fables of antiquity which he has reinvented." "What sort of prophet is this? Why was no angel sent to him?" "These are only confused dreams. He has invented them. Let him bring a miracle to us as the earlier prophets did." "They say of the prophet, 'He has forged the Qur'an.'" "We find him full of folly and a liar to boot."**

Rather than preach salvation to his tribe, Muhammad taunted his accusers: **"Some of them talk ill of the Prophet. For those who offend Allah's Apostle there is a painful punishment. Anyone who opposes Allah and His Prophet will abide in hell forever."** In a duet with Allah, Muhammad bellowed: my critics are: **"despicable men, contemptible swearers, back-biters. They're feeble scandal-mongers."** Carried away in the moment, the god of the Qur'an said that his creation were: **"mischief mongers, faggots, apes, nail biters, donkeys, pigs, and tongue twisters."** It was a war of words. The sticks and stones would come later.

Muslim apologists insist that their prophet's warmongering in Medina was a result of the Meccan verbal assault. But according to their Hadiths, it was Muhammad who tongue lashed first. The Meccan response was measured and reasonable. They sought peace through diplomacy and were ultimately terrorized, plundered, and conquered as a result. Their plight should scream out to us today.

The Islam vs. Pagan contest seldom rose above a war of words in Mecca. *Ishaq:130/Tabari VI:101* **"The nastiest thing I saw the Quraysh do to the Messenger occurred when their nobles assembled in the Hijr [the standing place in the mosque of the Ka'aba]. They discussed Muhammad, saying, "We have never seen the kind of trouble we have endured from this fellow. He has derided our traditional values, declared our way of life foolish, abused and insulted our forefathers, reviled our religion, caused division among us, divided the community, and cursed our gods.""**

Allah was their most revered idol. Saying that Muhammad insulted him is an indictment of Islam. And he couldn't have reviled their religion to any significant degree because he incorporated every aspect of Qusayy's scam into Islam. Therefore, the real problem lay elsewhere. This prophet made himself a societal nuisance. He destroyed traditional values, caused divisions among the people, and assailed both the living and the dead.

"'We have endured a great deal from him.' While they were saying this, the Apostle walked up and kissed the Black Stone. Then he performed the circumambulation of the Ka'aba. As he did they said some injurious things about him. I could see from the Messenger's face that he had heard them. When he passed a second time they made similar remarks. When he passed them the third time, the Prophet stopped and said, 'Hear me, O Quraysh. By Him who holds Muhammad's life in his hand, I will bring you slaughter.'"

The founder of Islam was performing pagan rites, kissing a rock idol and venerating a rock shrine. He had attacked the traditional values of his people, demeaned their ancestors, and caused division. He had built his "religion" of submission upon doctrines he had stolen from Qusayy, Hanif poetry, and Jewish scripture. And for what? So he could lay claim to Allah's Fountain of Kausar—the Ka'aba Inc.

If you think my summation is too harsh, consider what just happened. After enduring years of hate speech from Muhammad, the Meccans criticized him. They accurately labeled the prophet's religion "plagiarized madness and sorcery." In response, the founder of Islam turned to his accusers and said, **"I will bring you slaughter."** Not salvation, not good news, not a wonderful message from a loving God. No. "I will bring you *slaughter*." It was Muhammad's message to the world. And he performed as promised.

The Meccans were as stunned by this response to their verbal jousting as we should be today. They were in the presence of a covetous charlatan, and they knew it. Unfortunately, they didn't respond intelligently. They were wary of condemning a religion, no matter how corrupt. They were deluded into thinking that a tyrant could be appeased. As a result, the Meccans would lose everything by accommodating the evil that had grown up in their midst.

Tabari VI:102 **"They were gripped by what he had said. The word he used struck people so not one could move. It was as though everyone had a bird perched on his head. Even those who had been urging the severest measures against him, now spoke in a conciliatory way, using the politest expressions they could muster. They said, 'Depart Abu al-Qasim [Muhammad's real name]; for by Allah, you were never violent.'"** At least he wasn't before he became demon possessed and poisoned by Islam.

Peace is not the absence of war; it is not obtained through accommodation. These men wanted to live in peace, so they capitulated. They strove to understand their menace, to talk nicely to their tormentor, to satiate his demands. They were politically correct and got pummeled for it. Their olive branches of kindness were turned into spears of reprisal. Within a decade or so of this peace initiative the entire Middle East—from Egypt to India—was stung by the Islamic war machine.

Appeasing tyrants is the surest path to war. Neville Chamberlain appeased Adolf Hitler in Munich using his nicest words. He, like the Meccans, caved in to the madman's demands. The Brits gave the Nazis Czechoslovakia. The deadliest war in human history was the result.

Today, the world is trumpeting another "land for peace" initiative in hopes of satiating a terrorist regime. But as before, if a nation is sacrificed to a demented doctrine, if Israel is given to Islam, the world will erupt in global war. This time a billion will die. Negotiating with tyrants simply fuels their fanaticism. No matter how much their victims give, it is never enough. Evil must never be allowed to fester and grow—even if it's called a religion.

Tabari VI:102 **"The Prophet left, and the next day they gathered in the Hijr, and I [Abdallah] was again present. 'You were talking about the unpleasantness which you endured and the things Muhammad has done, but when he said something disagreeable you shrank from him.'"** As a result, the doves were consumed by the hawk. *Ishaq:131/ Bukhari:V5B57N27* **"Then I saw Uqba coming to the Prophet while he was praying. He seized his robe. Abu Bakr came crying and pulled Uqba away. He said, 'Would you kill a man just because he says: "Allah is my Lord.'"** Then they left him. That is the worst that I ever saw the Quraysh do to him."** Bakr's overreaction to the tug on his pal's lapel was contrived to make sure Muslims wouldn't miss the intent of the 40th surah: challenge Islam and you die. In it, Muhammad corrupted the story of Moses to frighten the Meccans. The applicable verse is 40:38. **"A believer from the House of Pharaoh who had kept his faith to himself, said: 'Will you kill a man because he says; 'My Lord is Allah,' when he has brought clear signs from his Lord?"** So as not to take this verse or surah out of context, we'll review it at the end of the chapter.

✡ ✟ ☪ 💣

Tabari VI:103/Ishaq:131 "Hamzah bin Abdul Muttalib came with his bow slung over his shoulder. He was a great huntsman and used to go out for game with his bow and arrows. When he came back from the hunt he would not go back to his family until he had circumambulated the Ka'aba. He was the strongest man of the Quraysh. A woman rose up and said, 'If only you had seen what your nephew Muhammad had to endure just now before you came. Abu Jahl spoke to him offensively.'"

"Hamzah was carried away by a fury, as it was Allah's will to honor him this way. [In Islam, it is an honor to be furious.] He went off quickly, not stopping to speak to anyone. Instead of circumambulating the Ka'aba, he was ready to attack Abu Jahl when he saw him. When he entered the mosque, [This is a reminder that the Ka'aba was a pagan mosque, or place of prostration, before it was the center of Islamic worship. Further, the prostration prayer, Islam's signature move, preceded the Qur'an.] he saw him sitting among the people. Hamzah raised his bow and gave Abu a blow which split his head open in an ugly way. He said, 'Do you insult him when I am a member of his religion? Hit me back if you can.'" Before Islam, Hamzah hunted for food. After Islam he hunted men for his god. While he was but a lone terrorist with a bow, he established the pattern that would soon rock the world.

The change did not escape notice. *Tabari VI:103/Ishaq:132* "Hamza's Islam was complete. He followed the Prophet's every command. The Quraysh recognized that by Hamzah's acceptance of Islam Muhammad had been made strong. Hamzah would protect him." Violence made a man's Islam complete. And a man made a prophet strong.

Ishaq:141/Tabari VI:104 "The first to recite the Qur'an aloud in Mecca after the apostle was Abdallah bin Mas'ud. One day the companions of the Prophet were assembled together [all five of them] and remarked, 'The Quraysh have never heard this Qur'an recited aloud to them. Who will make them listen to it?'" This is an astonishing admission. Muhammad is fifty-years old and a decade into his mission. Mecca is a tiny place, clustered around a miniscule shrine. Eighty surahs have been revealed, seventy percent of the Qur'an, yet "the Quraysh have never heard this Qur'an recited aloud to them." Then what, pray tell, was the source of war of words between Muhammad and his critics? If Muhammad wasn't preaching "god's" word, what on earth was he saying that was so obnoxious?

"Abdallah bin Mas'ud said, 'I will.' They said, 'We fear what they will do to you. What we want is a man who has a clan who will protect him against them if they seek to harm him.' He [foolishly] replied, 'Let me do it. Allah will protect me.'" But alas, Allah was never in the miracle business.

Tabari didn't reference the surah Mas'ud elected to recite. Ishaq did. I was stunned to learn that it was the 55th, "Ar-Rahman." The Hadith claims Allah's protection yet Mas'ud was singing Ar-Rahman's praises. It's little wonder the Meccans were up in arms. Muhammad was venerating Allah's House, their Ka'aba, but was claiming that it belonged to a rival moon god.

Ishaq:141 "The next day Ibn Mas'ud went to the Ka'aba in the late morning when the Quraysh were gathered in groups. He turned toward them as he recited: *055.001* "Ar-Rahman bestowed the Qur'an. He created man. He has taught man eloquent speech (and intelligence). The sun and moon are made punctual, following courses, they revolve to a computation." (According to the Islamic god, the sun moves, not the earth.) "Ar-Rahman created the herbs (or stars) and the trees all of which prostrate themselves."

Mas'ud proudly proclaimed: *055.014* "He created man of fermented clay dried tinkling hard like earthen ware, and created jinn from the white-hot flame of fire. How many favors of your Lord will you both (men and jinn) deny?" Ar-Rahman, like Allah, made man as one would distill alcohol. *055.019* "He has set the two seas [not seven] in motion that flow side by side with a barrier between them that they cannot cross. [Wrong again.] How many favors of your lord will you both deny?" How many lies must the dark spirit of Islam utter before Muslims deny him?

The first Meccan Qur'an recital turned nasty with these words: *055.031* "Soon We will dispose of you both (men and jinn) by applying Our two armies. How many favors of your Lord will you both deny?" A second translation reads, "We shall soon be free to turn on you, O weary caravans." Muhammad would soon prosper by raiding Meccan caravans. *055.035* "There will be let loose on you both white-hot flames of fire and smoke that chokes so that you will not be able to defend yourselves. How many favors of your Lord will you both deny?" Ar-Rahman makes jinn out of the same material he will use to torture men. That means the dark spirit of Islam intends to send his demons after us. And, lest we forget, this spirit considers torture a "favor."

Mas'ud continued to recite the "Ar-Rahman" surah to the Meccans: *055.041* "The sinners will be seized by their forelock and feet. Which of the favors of your Lord will you then deny? This is the Hell the sinners called a lie. They will go round and round between its fierce fires and boiling water. Which of the favors of your Lord will you then deny?" Apart from Satan, can you imagine any spirit suggesting that burning and scalding were favors?

Having sickened the Quraysh with demonic torments, Mas'ud teased them with decadence. *055.046* "For him who lives in terror of his Lord are two Gardens containing delights: shade, two fountains flowing, fruits in pairs. Reclining on carpets lined with silk brocade, fruits hanging low. In them virginal females with averted glances (desiring none but you), undeflowered by men or jinn. Is the reward of goodness aught but goodness?" Ar-Rahman has just labeled decadence "good," and living in terror is the path to Paradise. *055.062* "And beside this, there are two other Gardens, rich green in color from plentiful watering. In them will be two springs, gushing forth, and fruits. And beautiful companions, virgins cloistered in pavilions, undefiled by men and jinn, reclining on green cushions and rich mattresses. Which of the favors of you Lord will you both deny?"

I would have liked to have seen the reaction on the Meccan's faces as they listened to Muhammad's "religious disciple" recite this demonic message. *Ishaq:141 / Tabari VI:104* "The Meccans took notice of Mas'ud. 'What on earth is this son of a slave's mother saying?' Then they said, 'He is reciting some of what Muhammad has prayed.' [Not recited, prayed. These fantasies represented Muhammad's cravings.] They rose up and began to hit him in the face. [So much for Allah's protection.] He continued to recite as much as Allah willed that he should, and went back to his companions with the marks of their blows on his face. They said, 'This is what we feared would happen to you,' but he replied, 'The enemies of Allah [Ar-Rahman?] were never more despicable in my sight than they are now. If you wish, I will do the same thing to them tomorrow.' They replied, 'No, you have done enough.'" It's the cause and effect of Islam. The religion causes Muslims to hate anyone who isn't a Muslim. It's a condition that persists to this day.

The Sira follows this incriminating encounter with another. Because Muhammad was afraid to recite the Qur'an in public, Meccans eavesdropped outside his mud hut at night. *Ishaq:143* "When they heard the Qur'an they said in mockery, 'Our hearts are veiled, we do not understand what he is saying. There is a load in our ears.' Then Allah revealed, 'And when you recite the Qur'an we put between you and those who do not believe a hidden veil. They turn in aversion.' In secret counsels the mockers say, 'They are following a man bewitched.'"

The next Ishaq segment is omitted by Tabari. I can only assume that the historian couldn't find a credible supporting Tradition or he had collected enough contrary Hadiths to question its veracity. *Ishaq:143* "The Quraysh showed their enmity to those who followed the Apostle. Every clan which contained Muslims attacked them, imprisoning them, beating them, allowing them no food or drink, and exposing them to the burning heat of Mecca, so as to seduce them from their religion. Some gave way under pressure of persecution, and others resisted." Considering that Muhammad had threatened to slaughter the Quraysh, they may have been justified. Further, the doctrine Muhammad was espousing was corrosive. It turned peaceful men into killers.

Ishaq was able to provide only one example of abuse. *Ishaq:144* "A rock was put on a slave's chest. When Abu Bakr complained, they said, 'You are the one who corrupted him, so save him from his plight.' 'I will do so,' said Bakr. 'I have a black slave, tougher and stronger than Bilal, who is a heathen. I will exchange him.' The transaction was carried out." Even when these bozos did something right, it was wrong. Trading slaves wasn't religious, and calling a black man a "heathen" was racist.

Tabari VI:103 "Umar bin al-Khattab [the Caliph who ruled during Islam's bloodiest conquests] was a staunch and mighty warrior. He accepted Islam, as had Hamzah before him. The Messenger's Companions began to feel stronger." *Ishaq:155* "Umar became a Muslim, he being a strong, stubborn man whose protégés none dare attack. The prophet's companions were so fortified by him and Hamza that they got the upper hand on the Quraysh. 'We could not pray at the Ka'aba until Umar became a Muslim, and then he fought the Quraysh until we could pray there.'" The warrior's acceptance of Islam enabled the prophet to change his qiblah from faith to power, from religion to politics, from a war of words to a clash of arms. While the results of Umar aligning his sword with Muhammad's mission are undeniable, one question lingers.

Why did he join the fledgling force?

Did Muhammad lure Umar into Islam with promises of drunken orgies? "Delights in gardens of pleasure, on couches facing one another; a cup from a gushing spring of wine, white, delicious to the drinkers. None shall be made mad or exhausted thereby." "On thrones raised high, with maidens incomparable. Lo! We have formed their companions as a special creation, and made them to grow a new growth. We made them virgins—pure and undefiled, lovers, matched in age, for those on the right hand."

Or did Muhammad terrorize Umar into submission with his depictions of hell: "Soon will I fling them into the burning Hell Fire! It permits nothing to endure, and nothing does it spare! It darkens and changes the color of man, burning the skin! It shrivels and scorches men." "Let him beware! If he does not desist, We will seize him, smite his forehead, and drag him by the forelock!" "For the rejecters is Entertainment with Boiling Water and roasting in Hell Fire." "Truly Hell is as a place of ambush, a resort for the rebellious." "Therein taste they neither coolness nor any drink save a boiling water and a fluid, dark, murky, intensely cold, paralyzing, a fitting reward." "They will eat thorns and fill their bellies with the heads of flaming devils. Then on top of that they will be given a mixture made of boiling water to drink especially prepared." "We have prepared the doom of Hell and the penalty of torment in the most intense Blazing Fire. When they are flung in, they will hear the terrible drawing in of their breath and loud moaning even as the flame blazes forth, roaring with rage as it boils up, bursting with fury, plucking apart his body right to the skull! Eager to roast; dragged by the head, Hell shall claim all who flee."

Or do you suppose he tempted him with booty, a share in Khadija's Profitable Prophet Plan? "As for the favor your Lord has bestowed upon you, Muhammad, announce it!" "Soon your Lord will give you so much you shall be pleased. He found you poor and enriched you." "Of the bounty of your Lord let your discourse be." "Muhammad claims that Allah has sent him as His Messenger with this religion so that the treasures of Chusroes and Caesar will be given to him by conquest." "I want them to utter one saying. If they say it, the Arabs will submit to them and the non-Arabs will pay the jizyah tax in submission." "The use of booty from the spoils of war are lawful and good." "Know that one fifth of what you acquire as booty is for Allah and His Apostle." "If they ask you of the benefits of accruing the spoils of war, tell them, 'The benefits belong to Allah and His Messenger [and will be shared with Umar].'" I don't know if Umar is in Hell with Allah tormenting infidels or lounging in the Brothels of Bliss. But I do know Islam made the Islamic warrior king very, very rich!

Ishaq went to great lengths to explain Umar's conversion. *Ishaq:156* "Umar said, 'I am making my way to Muhammad, the apostate who has split up the Quraysh and made a mockery of our traditions, to kill him.' 'Your sister, Fatima, has become a Muslim so you had better go and deal with her first.' Umar heard her reciting Khabbab [There is no surah by that name and it isn't referenced in the text.] as he came near the house. He said, 'What is this balderdash?' 'You have heard nothing,' she lied. 'By Allah, I have,' Umar said, striking his sister in the face and wounding her. When he saw the blood, he felt sorry and asked to hear what Fatima was reciting. 'You are unclean in your polytheism and only the clean may listen to it.'" He washed his hands of the violence he had inflicted and she graced him with a little recital. The brute proclaimed: "How fine and noble is this speech. Lead me to Muhammad so that I may accept Islam."

Leaving the Sira and returning to the Sunnah we discover: *Tabari VI:106* "**The revelation from Allah was coming to the Prophet continuously, commanding and threatening those who showed open hostility to him, and vindicating him against those who opposed him.**" And so it would be. Reading the ninety Meccan surahs is like listening to a decade-long argument. They said, "You are a lying, plagiarizing, charlatan, a fraud and a sorcerer. There is surely a motive behind all of this madness." He said, "I am not a lying madman or a demon possessed sorcerer. And because you have mocked me, I will bring you slaughter." With that recap, we can dispense with the remaining score of Meccan surahs and move on with the story.

At this point, Ibn Ishaq reveals a stunning temptation—one which I have entitled "The Quraysh Bargain." *Ishaq:132-3* "**Utba, who was a chief, said while sitting in a Quraysh assembly, 'Why don't I go to Muhammad and make some proposals to him? If he accepts, we will give him whatever he wants, and he will leave us in peace.' They thought it was a good idea, because if they tried to negotiate with him they would no longer be blamed for his actions. So Utba went to the Prophet, who was sitting in the mosque by himself, and said, 'O my nephew, you are one of us yet you have come to our people with a matter that is dividing the community. You are ridiculing our customs. You have insulted our gods and our religion. You have even declared that our forefathers were infidels. So listen to me and I will make some suggestions, and perhaps you will be able to accept one of them.' The Apostle agreed. Utba said, 'If what you want is money, we will gather for you some of our property so that you may be the richest man in town. If you want honor, we will make you a chief so that no one can decide anything apart from you. If you want sovereignty, we will make you king. And if this demonic spirit which has possession of you is such that you cannot get rid of him, we will find a physician for you, and exhaust our means trying to cure you. For often a demonic spirit gets possession of a man, but he can be rid of it.' The apostle listened patiently.**" Wow! The Sira is incriminating.

While Muhammad hesitated, the Meccans went on the offensive—hitting every one of his hot buttons. They charged: *Ishaq:134* "'**Muhammad if you don't accept our offer then ask your Lord to give us the land and water we lack, for we are shut in by these mountains, we have no river, and none live a harder life than we do.**" With this they destroyed Muhammad's stated justification for preaching Islam. The Meccans weren't gluttonous as Muslims claim. "**If you speak the truth, resurrect Qusayy for us for he was a true shaikh, so that we may ask him whether what you say is accurate.**" The Quraysh correctly identified the true patriarch of Islam, the founder of the Ka'aba Inc., and the man who invented the scam Muhammad coveted. "**If you do this we will believe you and know that God has sent you as an apostle as you claim.**'"

Muhammad did nothing, so..."**Well then at least ask your god to send an angel to confirm your depictions of paradise and give you the mansions and gold you obviously** crave. If not that, then send us the Day of Doom you threaten us with, for we will not believe you until you perform a miracle." The Meccan knew that a prophet devoid of prophecies and miracles couldn't be what he claimed. What's more, they knew that his god was powerless. "Why doesn't your god help you? Didn't he know that we were going to present you with these opportunities to prove yourself? Listen, Muhammad; we know the truth. Information has reached us that you are taught by this fellow in Yemen called al-Rahman. By Allah, we will never believe in Ar-Rahman." The Meccans even knew the source of the Qur'anic revelations, a Hanif named after their god. "'Alright then, our conscience is clear.' When they said this the Prophet got up and left." The Quraysh saw right through Muhammad's prophetic act and laid him bare.

As you read these words remember that the Sira's Hadith are not only considered to be divinely inspired scripture, they represent Islam's most essential writings. The Sira provides the lone chronology of Muhammad's words and deeds written within three centuries of his death. *Ishaq:135* "**Muhammad, your people have made certain propositions.... They asked you for things so that they might know that your position with God is as you say it is so that they might believe and follow you, and yet you did nothing. They even asked you to hasten the punishment you are frightening them with, but you could not do it.' The Prophet went to Khadija, sad and grieving.**" Ishaq tells us that the Quraysh escalated their verbal assault, calling Muhammad a "**sorcerer—spitting and blowing,**" an "**insane poet—preaching in rhyme,**" and "**demon possessed—whispering delirium.**" They said that his Qur'an was plagiarized—"**fairy tales of the ancients.**" Yet with each new iteration, his familiar spirit had a ready Qur'anic verse—ever escalating the war of words.

One of the most bizarre facets of this new game of "put up or shut up" involved some Jewish rabbis from Yathrib. The Quraysh sent emissaries to test Muhammad's claim that he was the last of the Biblical prophets. We're told that the rabbis laid down a challenge. *Ishaq:136* "**Ask him about the Mighty Traveler who reached the confines of both East and West. Ask him what the spirit is. And ask him what happened to the men who disappeared in ancient days. If he does not know he is a rogue, a forger, so treat him as you will.**" While the Jews asked no such questions, the Meccans convinced Muhammad that they had. "**So Muhammad said to the emissaries, 'I will give you the answers tomorrow.' But the Apostle waited for fifteen days without a revelation from God on the matter, nor did Gabriel come to him, so the people of Mecca began to spread evil reports.**" Fact is, the Meccans had fingered the Yemeni Hanif (and thus God), and our hero couldn't ask the Yathrib Jews (and thus Gabriel) because he thought that they had composed the challenge.

Left to his own devices, Muhammad didn't do very well. He said that the answers finally came to him in the form of the 18th surah—aptly named "**The Cave.**" The last time he was on his own searching for god in all the wrong places, Satan had met him there. This time his spirit friend said that the "Mighty Traveler" was a Muslim: *018.083* "**They ask about Dhu'l-Qarnain [Alexander** the Great]. I shall recite to you something of his story. We established him and gave him the means to do everything. So he reached the setting place of the sun and saw that it set in a muddy spring of hot, black water. Around it he found people. He asked if he might punish them." The story goes on to talk about extraterrestrials, mythical people, and to claim that the pagan Alexander was a Muslim. I'll present the entire story in the last chapter as it ultimately points to our destiny.

The **"men who disappeared,"** according to the Qur'an, were Moses and his servant. They went sailing looking for a fish and some buried treasure. The inane story unfolds at the 60th verse and continues until god sends Alexander off looking for the extraterrestrials.

The verses that precede these "answers" focus on Satan, **"hell fire, punishments, deceptions, and annihilations."** I can only assume that the **"spirit"** is the Devil himself. In fact, **"The Cave"** surah ends with: **"We have prepared Hell for the hospitality of the infidels...because they disbelieved and mocked My Signs and Messengers."**

However, Ishaq believes the **"men who disappeared"** were **"the dwellers of the cave of Raqim."** Beginning at the 18th verse, Allah claims that some men stayed in a cave for 300 years and argued about dogs. Ahmed Ali, in his translation of the Qur'an says that the cave is the place the Dead Sea Scrolls were found. That's hilarious in that the Qumran scrolls prove that the Qur'an is a lie.

What this all means is, without Jewish and Hanif inspiration, Muhammad didn't do very well. The 18th surah is the Qur'an's most foolish.

At this point, Tabari picks up the trail of the Quraysh Bargain. The Meccans clearly understood Muhammad's motives. In one of Islam's most revealing Hadiths, we discover: *Tabari VI:106* **"The Quraysh promised Muhammad that they would give him so much wealth that he would become the richest man in Mecca [money], they would give him as many wives as he wanted [sex], and they would submit to his commands [power]."** They didn't bother tempting him with an acknowledgment of his prophetic claims—by agreeing that he really was Allah's Messenger. The Meccans knew that the prophet gig was just a means to an end.

"The Quraysh said, 'This is what we will give you, Muhammad, so desist from reviling our gods and do not speak evilly of them.'" This bargain was proposed on the basis of accommodating the Meccan gods. The deal was clear; the stakes were high. Sex, power, and money were being offered in exchange for total capitulation. The oneness of Allah was all that separated Muhammad's Islamic doctrine from Qusayy's scam. If the messenger accepted, he was through as a prophet, and Islam was finished as a religion.

Tabari VI:107 **"'If you will do so, we offer you something which will be to your advantage and to ours.'"** The prophet was evidently intrigued, tantalized perhaps. They held the keys to the Ka'aba Inc. and were offering him a founder's share. This could be good…**"'What is it,' he asked. They said, 'If you will worship our gods, Al-Lat and Al-Uzza, for a year, we shall worship your god for a year."** Once again, it's both perplexing and incriminating that the Quraysh don't name Muhammad's god.

After all, Allah was *their* god. In fact, Allah was supposed to be the proud poppa of Al-Lat (the female form of Allah) and Al-Uzza.

There is but one explanation for this omission. Muhammad was still referring to his god as Ar-Rahman, the deity of the Yemeni Hanifs. Those who codified the Qur'an decades later simply swapped Ar-Rahman's name out of some of the later Meccan surahs and replaced it with Allah. This change is confirmed by a Hadith contemporaneous to these events: *Ishaq:162* **"Abu Jahl met the Apostle and said, 'By Allah, Muhammad, you will either stop cursing our gods or we will curse the god you serve.' So the Qur'an verse was revealed, 'Do not insult those [gods] to whom they pray lest they curse God wrongfully through lack of knowledge.' [Qur'an 6:108] I have been told that the Apostle then refrained from cursing their gods, and *began* to call them to Allah [rather than Ar-Rahman]."** The critical word is: "began."

Tabari VI:107/Ishaq:165 **"Walid, As, Aswad, and Umayyah said, 'Muhammad, come and let us worship that which you worship and you worship what we worship. We shall combine in the matter and shall make you a partner in all our undertakings. [The Ka'aba Inc.—the legacy of Qusayy's religious scam was still the principle game in town.] If what you have brought is better than what we already have, we will be partners with you and take our share, and if what we have is better than what you have, you shall be a partner with us in what we have, and you shall have your share of it."** Their schemes were virtually indistinguishable. They were only squabbling over ownership.

Muhammad's immediate response to the Quraysh Bargain should tell us all we need to know about Islam's lone prophet. He didn't say no. He hesitated, and was clearly tempted to worship Al-Lat and Al-Uzza if it meant money, sex, and power. **"Let me see what revelation comes to me from my Lord [not Allah],' he replied."**

Although I can't prove it using the Islamic Traditions, in my opinion, Muhammad went to his aging wife Khadija and asked her what she thought he should do. After all, she had been the founder of Islam—the inspiration behind the Profitable Prophet Plan. I think Khadija scuttled the deal. More wives would have been competition. And although she would have relished the prestige of being a shareholder in the Ka'aba Inc, what was she going to do with more money? She was over seventy years old and near death.

So Khadija nixed the deal: **"Then, the following inspiration came from the Preserved Tablet: 'Say: O disbelievers! I worship not that which you worship; nor do you worship that which I worship, And I shall not worship that which you worship, nor will you worship that which I worship. To you your religion and to me my religion.'"** Sorry Tabari, I know that is what the Hadith says but it just ain't so. The 109th surah, from which this revelation was quoted, was among the first handed down. It was revealed a *decade* before this bargain was struck. So what *really* happened?

Khadija died (or was killed), and Muhammad accepted the deal. The very next line in The History of al-Tabari, *Muhammad at Mecca*, confirms my theory: **"Satan Cast a False Revelation on the Messenger of Allah's Tongue."** Possessed by the

Devil, Muhammad chose poorly. He succumbed to his demonic urgings and
began to worship Al-Lat and Al-Uzza. He was finished as a prophet.

While the Islamic spin-meisters in Baghdad tried their best to put lipstick
on this camel, the whole affair was as ugly as it was deadly. No matter how
valiantly they attempted to excuse Muhammad's behavior, a pig in makeup is
still a swine. *Tabari VI:107* **"The Messenger was eager for the welfare of his people and
wished to effect reconciliation with them in whatever way he could. It is said he wanted to
find a way to do this, and what happened was as follows:"** Before we wallow in what
follows, I'd like to poke a hole in the excuse. Muhammad's people were long
gone. He had sent them off to Abyssinia for fear they would be seduced. And
the notion of reconciling himself to the pagans is laughable. Muhammad had
done nothing but harangue them for a decade now, calling them names barely
suitable for print. When they teased him he said, "I will bring you slaughter."
Sorry, Muslim apologists, I don't think so.

The isnad, or chain of reciters, introducing the Hadith reads: **"Ibn Mumayd-
Salamah-Muhammad Ibn Ishaq-Yazid bin Ziyad al-Madani-Muhammad bin Ka'b al-
Qurazi:"** I share this because of what happened to Salman Rushdie. He wrote
a novel based upon what these champions of Islam had to say. Muslims went
berserk. They had Rushdie's book banned and panned. They nailed Satanic
Verses to crosses and burned it during hostile rioting. The Ayatollah
Khomeni, the leader of the Islamic world at the time, put a fatwa on Rushdie,
offering his fellow Muslims a million dollars for the writer's head.

Yet Rushdie had merely exposed Islam's own Traditions. So why get mad
at him? Was Muhammad so perverse and Islam so corrupt that modern clerics have to hide the truth for their doctrine to survive? Apparently, yes.

This is what follows: *Tabari VI:108/Ishaq:165* **"The Messenger saw his tribe turn on him.
He was pained to see them shunning the message he had brought from Allah. So he [aban-
doned both his message and his god because he] longed for something that would reconcile his tribe to *him*. With his love for his tribe and his anxiety over this it would have
delighted him if the obstacle which had made his task so difficult could be removed [so
he could accept their generous offer of power, sex, and money]."** The only points of
contention, thus obstacles to reconciliation, were: Ka'aba custodianship, the
number of gods, and the top god's identity (Allah or Ar-Rahman).

**"So Muhammad debated with himself and fervently desired such an outcome. Then
Allah revealed: 'By the Star when it sets, your comrade does not err, nor is he deceived; nor
does he speak out of his own desire. [In truth, he did all three and was about to prove his
guilt.] And when he came to the words: 'Have you thought about Al-Lat, Al-Uzza and
Manat,' Satan, when he was meditating upon it and desiring to bring reconciliation, cast
on his tongue, because of his inner longings and what he desired, the words: 'These are
exalted high-flying cranes (goddesses). Verily their intercession is accepted with approval."**
Simply stated, Muhammad said, "I accept the Quraysh Bargain."

But at what cost? The Qur'anic recitals had been filled with assertions that there were no intercessors. And four gods were at least three too many for a monotheistic religion. Muhammad had therefore abandoned the central plank of his mission: "There is no ilah but Allah." Islam was no longer monotheistic. What's more, the prophet's grandiose and Messianic claim of being Allah's intercessor was pummeled, stoned by a trio of rock idols. And that wasn't the worst of it. Islam's lone spokesperson had just aligned himself with Satan.

It's little wonder the Ayatollah wanted Rushdie's book burned. It's little wonder the Qur'an urges Muslims not to pry too deeply into Islam or ask questions. The truth is devastating. The Quraysh Bargain and Satanic Verses confirm that Muhammad was demon possessed and that the Qur'an was "inspired" to advance his personal agenda. These Hadiths prove Islam was a fraud, as counterfeit as a $3 bill. What's more, the Profitable Prophet Plan has been elevated from highly probable to undeniable.

But the Islamic Hadith was not finished burying its prophet. *Tabari VI:108/Ishaq:166* **"When the Quraysh heard this, they rejoiced and were delighted at the way in which he spoke of their gods, and they listened to him. While the Muslims, trusting their Prophet in respect to the messages which he brought, did not suspect him of a vain desire or slip. When he came to the prostration, having completed the surah, he prostrated himself and the Muslims did likewise, obeying his command and following his example."** Now you know the reason why the world is in such a mess. A demon-possessed man sought to satiate his vain desires, and billions, failing to suspect his fraud, followed his example and obeyed his commands.

If you are a Muslim reading these words, flee this delusion before it's too late. This despicable man and his demonic spirit are not worthy of your soul. *Tabari VI:108/Ishaq:166* **"Those polytheists of the Quraysh and others who were in the mosque likewise prostrated themselves because of the reference to their gods which they had heard, so that there was no one in the mosque, believer or unbeliever, who did not prostrate himself. Then they all dispersed from the mosque."**

In the context of the Quraysh Bargain, this passage proves that Islam was nothing more than Muhammad's scheme to take what rightfully belonged to others. It was his personal gateway to money, power, and sex. The Ka'aba Inc.—the religious scam of the patriarch Qusayy—was being cashed in by a covetous and amoral man. The evidence is undeniable. Islam was a plot, not a religion. Allah and Satan were one.

Independent Islamic scholars, even those sensitive to the religion, know that this Satanic indulgence destroyed Islam. They recognize that nothing in the Qur'an can be trusted if the prophet can't distinguish between Godly and Satanic inspiration. And while they have a point, they miss *the* point. Apart from the initial cave demon, there *never* was any spiritual inspiration. The Qur'an, cover to cover, is too foolish, violent, demented, and immoral to be Godly. The Meccans were right: it was from "a madman, a plagiarizing poet, a far-fetched forger, a demon possessed sorcerer. There is surely a motive behind the Qur'an."

Within the context of these Traditions we must also deal with the lesser issues. The passage confirms that Allah was one of many gods. Muhammad promoted a pagan rock idol. The prostration prayer, the performance that distinguishes Muslims from other religious practitioners, was pagan too. So was the mosque, the cradle of Islamic submission. And the Ka'aba, the center of Islamic obedience, was a pagan shrine. All five pillars of Islam crumbled in the wake of the prophet's Satanic indulgence. There were ilahs beside Allah. Muhammad was Satan's messenger. The prostration became a pagan ritual rather than an Islamic obligation—all were rendered naught by a devilish bargain. Even the religious tax became suspect as it was orchestrated by a prophet tempted and trumped by the love of money.

The religion of Islam died that day along with its founder, Khadija. But out of its ashes the political doctrine of Islam emerged. And while the prophet failed, the profiteer soared to ever-greater lows. Acquiescing to temptation, accepting Satan's Bargain, Islam turned from gray to black. As the sun set on the pagans mooning the Meccan moon god, it also set on the religion of Islam, never to rise again.

As much as Muslims would love to absolve themselves and their prophet of the Quraysh Bargain and Satanic Verses by claiming that the Hadiths were "unauthorized," they are unable. Both history and their cover up render their objections moot. Without the reconciliation that followed the Bargain, there was no way to explain: *Tabari VI:109/Ishaq:167* **"The news of this prostration reached those of the Messenger's Companions who were in Abyssinia. The people said, 'The Quraysh have accepted Islam.' Some rose up to return. Then angel Gabriel came to the Messenger and said, 'Muhammad, what have you done?'"** While that's what the Hadith says, the prophet first mentioned Gabriel's name two years later in Medina. But that's not to say he didn't have visitors. A trio of men, Bakr, Umar, and Hamzah, took their prophet to the woodshed—or at least that's where they would have taken him if Mecca had wood.

Islam's dark spirit was quoted saying: *Ishaq:166* **"'You have recited to the people that which I did not bring to you from Allah, and you have said that which He did not say to you.' The Messenger was grieved and feared Allah greatly. So Allah [not Gabriel] sent a revelation to him, consoling him and making light of the affair [of worldly bargains and Satanic indulgences]. He informed him that there had never been a prophet or messenger before who desired as he desired and wished as he wished but that Satan had cast words into his recitation, as he had interjected them on Muhammad's tongue and into his desires."**

To hell with truth—literally. Desperate to save his prophetic mission, Muhammad retreated to familiar ground. He claimed that he was as covetous, immoral, demented and ill-advised as every other prophet. He was just dabbling in a little demonic delusion to satiate his cravings for power, sex, and money. It was no big deal.

Only the Jewish scriptures couldn't bail him out this time. Neither the Torah nor the Talmud contained devilish tales that could be twisted to salvage his sorry soul—so none were given. There were no names dropped, Biblical or otherwise. Muhammad was on his own. No other prophet had ever **"desired and wished as he had desired and wished."**

The founders of Islam said: *Ishaq:166* **"Then Allah annulled what Satan had cast, and established his verses by telling him that he was like other prophets and messengers."** Muhammad's lord revealed: **"Every Messenger or Prophet before you recited the message Satan cast into his recitation. Allah abrogates what Satan casts. Then Allah established his verses. Allah is Knower, Wise."** [Qur'an 22:52]

One lie has been refuted with another. The 22nd surah would not be revealed for another decade. In fact, it was one of the final Medina surahs. But by reciting it, Muhammad destroyed his only alibi—denial. Now that the Qur'an has verified the Satanic Verses, Muslims cannot whisk them under the carpet without impugning Allah's credibility along with Muhammad's.

Let's take a quick look at the surah to better understand Muhammad's mindset. But so as not to compound the prophet's error and take the passage out of context, I want you to know that the 47th verse of this late surah speaks of Allah's intended punishment on the Day of Doom. The 48th is about Allah overtaking townships, the 49th speaks of warnings, the 50th forgiveness, and the 51st demeans the inmates of the flaming fire. Somehow that brings us to: *022.052* **"Never did We send a messenger or a prophet before you, but, when he framed a desire, Satan threw some vanity into his desire: but Allah will cancel anything (vain) that Satan throws in."** A second translation reads: **"He recited (the message) Satan proposed. But Allah abolishes that which Satan proposes."** Another claims: **"Satan made a suggestion respecting his desire; but Allah annuls that which Satan casts."** And we have: **"whose recitations Satan tampered with, yet Allah abrogates what Satan interpolates; and Allah will confirm His Signs/Revelations: for Allah is all-knowing and wise."**

It was such a devilishly delicate matter, so everyone seemed to have a little different take on what Allah allegedly revealed, albeit ten years late. But no matter how you slice it, the Qur'anic excuse confirms that the Satanic Verse episode actually occurred. The Hadith cannot, therefore, be "unauthorized." Muhammad is said to have allowed Satan to throw **"some vanity into his desires,"** (The Quraysh Bargain) and to have allowed Satan to **"tamper with the recitations"** (The Satanic Verses). Allah then canceled Satan's toss, abolished the Devil's proposal, annulled Satan's cast, or performed an abrogation—the ultimate miracle of the Qur'an. He never denied the Quraysh Bargain or the Satanic Verses. Therefore, Muslims can't either.

Allah abrogating the Devil aside, the Qur'anic justification for the Satanic Verses ends with this treasure of spiritual inspiration: *022.053* **"That He may make the suggestions thrown in by Satan, the Devil's proposals, but a trial and temptation for those in whose hearts is a disease. Verily the wrong-doers are in a schism. And those on** whom knowledge has been bestowed may learn that the (Qur'an) is the truth from your Lord, and that they may believe therein, and their hearts may submit lowly before it, for verily Allah is the Guide of those who believe, to the Straight Way." Muhammad succumbs to temptation, sides with the Devil, and it's everyone's fault but his own. His indulgence was convoluted into a trial for the infidels—our schism. Then, after saying that Satan's proposals often slip into scripture, we are asked to trust the Qur'an, to submit lowly before it. While this is revolting, it is also convicting. Muslims who try to deny the existence of the Satanic Verses must deny the Qur'an, for it clearly acknowledges them.

That leaves Islam in an impossible position. Muslims must either admit that Muhammad was a power-hungry, money-grubbing, sex-crazed charlatan in cahoots with the Devil, or they must deny the validity of the Hadith and Qur'an. One leaves them without a prophet, the other without a god. Either way, they no longer have a religion.

Tabari VI:110 "**Thus Allah removed the sorrow from his Messenger, reassured him about that which he had feared, and cancelled the words which Satan had cast on his tongue, that their gods were exalted high-flying cranes (goddesses) whose intercession was accepted with approval. He now revealed, following the mention of 'Al-Lat, Al-Uzza, and Manat,' the words: 'are yours the males and his the females? That indeed is an unfair division! They are but names which you and your fathers have given,' to the words: 'to whom he wills and accepts.**" [Qur'an 53:21]

Not only does this mean that Allah copy-edits Satan, it proves Muhammad didn't know where he was—or even who said what to whom, when. The aforementioned quote was from the 53rd surah, which came before the 22nd. In fact, the 53rd was the forty-sixth surah handed down. It preceded the Satanic event by *many* years. The 22nd surah was 107th out of 114 in order of revelation. The Hadith says that these spiritual revelations followed one another, yet that is impossible. Not only is their order reversed, they are separated by a sea of words, hundreds of miles, and a decade of time.

So Islam has a fatal problem. If the rationale for dismissing the Satanic Verse/Quraysh Bargain episode isn't valid, or even plausible, Muhammad's motivations for establishing the submission religion were about vain desires, not godly revelations. There is no way for Muslims to differentiate between spiritual guidance and satanic deception—an acute problem considering how much of the Qur'an is fixated on Satan's realm, pain, and punishment. Whether the Quraysh Bargain and Satanic Verses occurred or not, the Qur'an cannot be trusted, for it claims they did. Further, a "perfect and eternal tablet" cannot be out of order, inverted, or grossly disjointed—especially on an issue of this magnitude.

The entire validity of Islam pivots around the Satanic Verse/Quraysh Bargain. If Muhammad was enticed by sex, money, and power and capitulated, as these Hadiths testify, Islam is finished. The credibility of its lone prophet is tarnished beyond redemption. His motivations are exposed for all to see. As a result, Qusayy becomes the founder of Islam; Muhammad is simply a self-serving promoter. And Khadija's Profitable Prophet Plan suddenly becomes the *only* viable explanation.

More devastating still, these events do not stand alone. Muhammad admitted that Islam was designed to enrich himself at the expense of others. We have examined his confessions. Moreover, his behavior from this point on, as chronicled by the Hadith, becomes *entirely* focused on sex, power, and money. As for Satan, Muhammad admitted being demon possessed. His neighbors recognized the signs, according to the Qur'an. They even offered to help him exorcise his demons.

The fact that Muhammad admitted to having been inspired by Satan has caused many to say that Islam is Satanic, and not without just cause; the evidence is overwhelming. The symbols used throughout the Islamic scriptures are from the Occult. A snake, the personification of Satan, led Abraham to the Ka'aba and revealed its foundations. A snake is the only creature said to have lived in the Ka'aba. The darkened or crescent moon, another Satanic symbol representing counterfeit light, is the religion's logo. Allah was a moon god. He swore by the moon. His stone was black. The darkness of night was the best time to worship him and recite his message. The Qur'an was endorsed by jinn, demons from Satan's tribe. Muhammad listened to soothsayers. He believed in magic spells. An occultist saved his father's life; another wanted to lay with him. Even the seal of prophethood on Muhammad's back was said to look like an apple—the image of Satanic temptation. And Satan played a starring role in the Qur'an, being named ten times more often than Muhammad.

Then there's the Qur'an's depiction of Allah. He spends time in Satan's realm, tormenting the inmates of hell. He is never shown playing with the virgins in paradise. Allah, like Satan, is sadistic. He leads men astray, shackles them, and drags them into hell, where he's personally involved, using their bodies as fagots for his fires. He turns men on a spit, makes them eat thorns, and pours boiling water on them for what he calls "their entertainment."

Some will protest that the same book and prophet call Allah merciful, and that they claim Satan to be their foe. But that is the greatest proof of all. Satan never identifies himself; he is the master of camouflage. The Qur'anic orders to "crucify unbelievers" and "wipe infidels out to the last," followed by "Allah is merciful and kind," is perfectly transparent. It's exactly what the Devil would do—appear divine while inspiring devilish behavior. In fact, the behavior in Allah's heaven would lead men to the Biblical hell. Satan is the master of deceit. Black is white, the lie becomes true, and everything leads away from a relationship with the one true God.

There are but three differences between Satan and Allah. And those differences cause me to believe that Islam wasn't wholly Satanic. Satan is real.

He is powerful and brilliant. Allah was imagined. He was impotent and foolish. Much of Islam was Muhammad's doing. He is to be despised, not pitied. He, like the demonic spirit that inspired him, must be exposed and rebuked.

The Hadith claims that Qur'anic remedy for Muhammad's Satanic indulgence is in the 53rd surah. Let's see if Team Islam gets itself out of trouble or if it digs itself in deeper. "The Star" is named after Lucifer, the "Morning Star." *053.001* **"I call to witness the Star when it dips. Your Companion (Muhammad) is neither confused, deceived, nor misled [except by Satan, in the guise of Allah]. Nor does he speak out of (his own) desire [unless he is tempted with money, sex, and power]. It is a revelation revealed, He was taught (this Qur'an) by the Supreme Intellect (Gabriel [actually Lucifer]), One free from any defect in body or mind: for he (Gabriel) rose and became stable (in stately form), clear to view. While he was in the highest part of the horizon, then he approached and came closer, then he prostrated. He was at a distance of but two bow-lengths or (even) nearer."** The claim that he bowed is telling. Neither Gabriel nor Lucifer would have bowed to any man so Muhammad is adlibbing here.

Since the Hadith says Gabriel was the source of Qur'anic inspiration, Islam has tumbled into the abyss no matter how this verse is interpreted. *Bukhari:V1B1N4-5* **"Allah's Apostle used to listen to Gabriel whenever he came, and after his departure he used to recite the Qur'an as Gabriel had recited it." "Gabriel used to meet him every night to teach him the Qur'an."** But we have been told that Allah was the "Supreme Intellect," that he was "Most Wise, All Knowing," and that he had no partners. Since Allah's Gabriel would never claim a superior position to Allah, this cannot be Gabriel. So who might it be?

Here are some clues. The surah is named after Lucifer, and it's presented in conjunction with the Satanic Verses. By way of witness, the **"Star"** is calling himself the **"Supreme Intellect, one free from any defect in body or mind."** The only angel who considered himself to be superior to God was Lucifer. For such blasphemy, Lucifer was thrown out of heaven. So now he says that he not only landed on his feet in perfect stately form, he has risen. As clearly as words allow, he has just told us that he has fulfilled Biblical prophecy and transformed himself into an angel of light to deceive a gentile messenger with a new "gospel" based upon prostration. (You'll find a complete analysis of Isaiah's and Paul's prophecies and their Islamic fulfillment in the "Mein Kampf" chapter starting on page 380.)

The Satanic Verse goes on to say: *053.010* **"So He did reveal to His slave whatever He revealed. The (Prophet's) heart did not falsify what he perceived he saw. Will you then dispute with him about what he saw? For indeed he saw him [him who] at a second descent. [Oops. A "descent" is a journey down.] Near the Lote Tree beyond which none may pass. Near it is the Garden of Abode (the Seventh Haven). [Therefore, Muhammad's heaven is down, not up.] When that covered the Lote Tree which did cover it. [Say what?] The sight turned not aside, nor did it go wrong! ["I really did see him. I did. I really did. Why don't you believe me?"] Indeed he did see of the greater signs of his Lord!"** Methinks—

no, *meknows*—he doth protest too much—especially since we are about to enter the realm of the Satanic Verses and pagan gods.

053.019 "Have you then seen or thought upon Al-Lat and Al-Uzza (two idols of the pagan Arabs), and considered another, the third (goddess), Manat (of the pagan deities)?" Manat was an afterthought because she was not part of the Quraysh Bargain.

Now, for Allah's copy-edits: "What! for you sons, the male sex, and for Him, daughters, the female? Are yours the males and His the females? Behold, such would be indeed a division most unfair!" Muhammad just jumped from the Devil's frying pan into the hell fires of sexism and discrimination. He is saying that Al-Lat, Al-Uzza, and Manat can't be Allah's daughters nor goddesses because they are girls. In plain English: "It would be an injustice for men to have sons and gods to have daughters because women are worthless." It's little wonder that the Islamic politicians and clerics who depend on Islam for their status, power, and wealth threaten to kill anyone willing to expose this nonsense.

053.023 "These are nothing but names which you have invented, you and your fathers, for which Allah has sent down no authority." Yes they are *names*, names given to them by Muhammad's forefathers—just like Allah's name.

Projecting one's flaws onto an opponent is standard political fare: "They follow nothing but conjecture and what they themselves desire! Whereas guidance has come to them from their Lord! Nay, shall man have anything he hankers after, whatever he covets?" It seemed to work for Muhammad. The career move from prophet to profiteer would satiate his every craving. For example, when Muhammad wanted more women, Allah said: *033.051* "You may have whomever you desire; there is no blame."

Fortunately, we have ratted him out. This surah is as transparent as it is incriminating. *053.026* "And there are many angels in heaven whose intercession does not avail except after Allah has given permission to whom He pleases and chooses. Those who believe not name the angels with female names." This is Qur'anic waffling. Muhammad is trying to please both Meccan and Muslim. He's saying that the female goddesses could be angels, and that Allah might consider allowing them to be intercessors after all.

The next eight verses can be summarized by: "The Meccans know nothing and want everything and Muhammad knows all and wants nothing." Then *053.036* "Nay, is he not acquainted with what is in the Pages (of the Books) of Moses—and of Abraham who fulfilled all that?" Muhammad is admitting that the Torah was the source of his "inspiration," but he doesn't know much about "all that."

A dozen verses ramble nowhere with lines like: "It is He who makes you happy and morose," before heading back into the world of pagan astrology and mythological people. *053.049* "He is the Lord of Sirius (the Mighty Star the pagan Arabs used to worship). It is He Who destroyed the (powerful) ancient Ad (people) [who never existed], and (the tribe of) Thamud He spared not; And before them, the folk of Noah, for that they were (all) most unjust and rebellious; and He destroyed the Overthrown Cities (of Sodom and Gomorrah). [Allah didn't know their names but the translator did, so he helped god out.]

So there covered them that that which did cover (making them ruins unknown)." The writing quality is as impoverished as the message.

The Bible says that the ruins of Sodom and Gomorrah will serve as visual confirmation of Yahweh's judgment and salvation. The Qur'an says that the ruins are unknown. Since archeologists have found Sodom and Gomorrah, their brimstone should serve as a visual confirmation that Allah is a liar. And please don't be troubled by the slur. Now that we know that Allah is Satan, it's a compliment.

053.056 "This is a Warner, of the Warners of old! The threatened Hour is nigh. None besides Allah can remove it. Do you then wonder at this recital? And will you laugh at it and not weep, wasting your time in amusements? [That's a hoot. With countless wives, sex slaves, and child concubines, Islam's prophet was the king of frivolity.] So fall you down in prostration to Allah, and serve [me]!"

Since neither the 53rd nor 22nd surah redeemed Muhammad, we are left with the Profitable Prophet Plan being the only viable explanation for Islam. *Tabari VI:110* "When Muhammad brought a revelation from Allah canceling what Satan had cast on the tongue of His Prophet, the Quraysh said, 'Muhammad has repented of [actually, reneged on] what he said concerning the position of our gods with Allah. He has altered [the bargain] and brought something else.' Those two phrases which Satan had cast on Muhammad's tongue of were in the mouth of every polytheist. They became even more ill-disposed and more violent in their persecution of those of them who had accepted Islam and followed the Messenger." The pagans had the prophet on the ropes and they knew it. Not only had he lied and broken a promise for personal gain, he had destroyed his credibility and abandoned the central pillar of his "doctrine"—the oneness of a spirit that only spoke to him.

"The Muslims who had left Abyssinia [Ethiopia] upon hearing that the Quraysh had prostrated themselves with the Prophet, now approached. When they neared Mecca, they learned that the rumor of the Meccan people accepting Islam was false. They returned to their families and said, 'You are more dear to us [than Islam, is the implication].' The people reversed their decision...." Considering the distances and the speed upon which news and people traveled, Muhammad may have gone as long as a year before he bailed out on the Quraysh Bargain and Allah's little girls. The indulgence cost him most of his converts.

This admission of failure is followed by a second variant of the Satanic Verses. It ends with this admission: "The Messenger said, 'I have fabricated things against Allah and have imputed to Him words which He has not spoken.'"

The Quraysh Bargain and Satanic Verses conclude my case against the *religion* of Islam. As I promised to demonstrate, the doctrine has completely destroyed itself. Yet the rest of the story is both entertaining and foreboding. While these confessions from Muhammad and Allah enable us to close the books on the religious scam, accepting their guilty pleas, a new scam is about to unfold. This one is political, and this one prevailed.

✡ ✟ ☾ 💣

Khadija's death (or murder) was followed by the passing of the prophet's protector, uncle Abu Talib. With them gone, Muhammad spiraled out of control. He became ever more paranoid, delusional, and demented.

With his Ka'aba now unquestionably pagan, the prophet desperately needed a new Qiblah. So he imagined himself flying a Buraq to Jerusalem. With his aged sex partner gone, he needed young love. So the fifty-year-old prophet married a six-year-old girl. With his protector gone, he needed a new show of arms. So he promised some pagans paradise in return for the protection Pledge of Aqabah. With his audience tainted, he needed a new pool of potential victims. So he picked up his tent and hightailed it to Yathrib. And because the prophet had left the strong arms of Umar, Hamzah, and Bakr out of the Quraysh Bargain, they ultimately persuaded him to renege on the agreement. So he dumped the goddesses and became a pirate. Muhammad's last year in Mecca was mayhem and madness.

Tabari VI:115 **"The deaths of Abu Talib and Khadija were a great affliction to the Messenger. After the death of Abu Talib, the Quraysh went to greater lengths in molesting him than they had ever done during his lifetime. One of them even poured dust upon his head. The Prophet said, 'The Quraysh never did anything unpleasant to me until Abu Talib died.'"**

Islam's prophet needed someone to protect him from all the verbal abuse. *Ishaq:192* **"When Abu Talib died, the Messenger went to Ta'if to seek support and protection against his own people."** The Thaqif were the chiefs and nobles of the leading tribe in Ta'if. **"He spoke to them about the requests which he had come to make, (that is,) that they should come to his aid in defense of Islam and take his side against those of his own tribe who opposed him."** If Allah were really a god do you think Muhammad would have asked pagans from a neighboring town to defend him? But what if Islam were really a political doctrine designed to suppress and enrich? Would a failed profiteer ask a Meccan rival to join his enterprise? The endeavor might at least make sense under those circumstances.

But the Thaqif were as unimpressed with Muhammad as were the Quraysh. *Tabari VI:116/Ishaq:192* **"One of them said, 'If Allah has sent you, I will tear off the covering of the Ka'aba.' Another said, 'Couldn't God find somebody better than you to send?' The third added, 'I shall not speak to you, for if you are Allah's messenger as you say, you're too important for me to reply to, and if you're lying, you're too despicable to address.'"** Muhammad's motivations were so transparent the Thaqif were *instantly* convinced he was a charlatan. The combination of the Quraysh Bargain and Satanic Verses were devastating to Muhammad's, Allah's, and Islam's credibility.

"Muhammad left them, despairing of getting any good out of the Thaqif." The fact he couldn't convert them to Islam and save their souls was unimportant—he despaired because he couldn't *get* anything from them. **"I have been told that he said to them, 'If that is your decision, keep it secret and do not tell anyone about it,'** for he did not want his tribe to hear about this matter and be emboldened against him." A prophet begging pagans for protection was nearly as embarrassing as a prophet patronizing pagan deities for sex, power, and money. It's little wonder our desperate profiteer was squeamish about any of this getting out.

"However, they did not comply with his request, and incited against him their ignorant rabble who reviled him, shouted at him, and hurled stones until a crowd gathered and forced him to take refuge in a garden a long distance from town."

Huddling in the garden, Muhammad claims a Christian came to his aid, handing him some grapes. When the quivering prophet took them he said, "'In the name of Allah,' and then ate. Addas looked him in the face and said, 'By Allah, these words are not used by the people of this country.'" This deception is no more credible than any of the other Christian endorsements of Islam. Ilah was the Arabic word for God. And no one was going to confuse Yahweh's name and character with Allah's name and nature. Even the Ta'if pagans knew Allah. What's more, three pages earlier, another Hadith ripped this notion to shreds. The pagans in Mecca were said to have posted a document in the Ka'aba which began, "In your name, O Allah."

"Muhammad said, 'From what country do you come, Addas, and what is your religion?' He replied, 'I am a Christian, from the people of Nineveh.'" Oops. Nineveh, after being reprieved by Jonah for a hundred years, rebelled again and was destroyed a thousand years earlier. But the error is not without merit, for it explains the reason behind this fable. Muhammad's journey to Ta'if is being recast as heroic and godly—just like Jonah's prophetic mission to Nineveh. "The Messenger said, 'From the town of the righteous man Jonah the son of Matta?'" Oops, again. Jonah was from the Nazareth area in Israel. The Assyrian capital was hardly his town. He despised the place. What's more, his father's name was Amittai, not Matta.

"'How did you know about Jonah the son of Matta?' he asked. The Messenger replied, 'He is my brother. He was a prophet and I am a prophet.' [The truth is he heard about him from Zyad.] Addas bent down before the Messenger [Prostration to prophets isn't Christian behavior.] and he kissed his head, his hands, and feet." The story goes on to say, "Muhammad has told me something which none but a prophet knows." If that's true, how did Addas know it?

Now that we have a "Christian" endorsement, how about another from Satan's tribe, the jinn? *Tabari VI:116/Ishaq:193* "When the Messenger despaired of getting any positive response from the Thaqif, he left Ta'if to return to Mecca. When he was at Nakhlah, he rose in the middle of the night to pray, and, as Allah has told [in the Qur'an], a number of the jinn passed by. Ishaq says that he was told that there were seven jinn from Nasibin of the Yemen."

Ishaq continues: "They listened to him, and when he had completed his prayer they went back to their people to warn them, having believed and responded to what they had heard." According to the Qur'an, jinn aren't people. They are invisible spirits that lead men astray, members of Satan's tribe; they're made of fire like that found in hell. "Allah mentioned their story when he said: 046.029 'Behold, We turned towards you (Muhammad) a company of Jinn who wished to hear the Qur'an: when they stood in the presence thereof, they said, "Give ear!"'"

For the third in a series of demonic endorsements: 046.030 "We have heard a Book revealed after Moses, confirming what came before it: it guides to the Truth and to a Straight Path.' 'O our people, hearken to the one who invites (you) to Allah, and believe in him. He will forgive you your sins [The uncapitalized "him" in the clause "believe in him" is in reference to Muhammad, therefore elevating him from messenger to Messiah. This is confirmed in the next line, which says that he, as in Muhammad, will forgive sins.], and deliver you from a Penalty Grievous.' 'If any does not hearken to the one who invites (us) to Allah, he cannot frustrate (Allah's Plan) on earth, and no protectors can he have besides Allah: such men (wander) in manifest error.'" Yet again, Allah is the Demonic Lord.

Tabari VI:118 "The Messenger came back to Mecca and found that its people were more determined to oppose him and to abandon his religion, except for a few weak people who believed in him." Just when you think that the Islamic Traditions have pounded the final nail into Muhammad's prophetic coffin, they find another. Following the Quraysh Bargain, the Satanic Indulgence, the Pagan Protection Fiasco, and the Jinn Endorsement, we're told that Muslims rejected Muhammad. Imagine that. They "abandoned his religion, except for a few weak people." Ten years into Muhammad's mission, the score is: Islam 10, Pagans 4,990.

Following the Satanic Verses, Allah was enshrined as Islam's god. The 40th surah, aptly named "The Forgiver," is typical of those revealed during the late Meccan period. 040.001 "Ha Mim. (These letters are one of the miracles of the Qur'an and none but Allah understands their meaning.) The revelation of this Book is from Allah, Exalted in Power, the All-Knower, The Forgiver, the Accepter, the Severe in Punishment."

Now that we have been properly introduced, it's time to get down to business—Allah's business. 040.004 "None can argue or dispute about the Signs of Allah or His Revelations but the Unbelievers." Islamic states make it a criminal offense for anyone to argue or dispute anything regarding Muhammad, Allah, the Qur'an, or Islam. The penalty for expressing such an opinion is death. Simply stated: Islam is the least open, least tolerant, dogma ever conceived.

"Let not their strutting about or their turn of fortune deceive you (for their ultimate end will be the Fire of Hell)!" This must be the verse Islamic warlords quote to quell their subjects today. "Sure those Western democracies are prospering while we live in the squalor of Islam. But don't let their good fortune deceive you into believing their success and our failure is a result of our religion's moral poverty. "No, never. It couldn't be. Allah would never harm you."

Freedom obliterated, political correctness imposed, it was time to corrupt a Bible story to make the Meccan rejection of Muhammad, seem somehow prophetic. *040.005* "Before them, folk denied, the People of Noah, and the Confederates (of Evil) after them; and every nation has plotted against their prophet, to seize and destroy him." There is no record of an Islamic prophet coming to *any* nation, much less every nation. (Saudi Arabia didn't became a nation until 1932 when the British elevated a warlord to king.) "They disputed by means of falsehood to condemn the truth. So I [first person] seized and destroyed them! How (terrible) was My punishment! In this way the sentence [behavior] of your Lord [The speaker has returned to third person in mid-thought.] against the disbelieving infidels was justified. They will be the inmates of the Hell Fire!" The change of speaker that permeates the Qur'an is important. The voice is confused because the real source was confused. Muhammad didn't know if he should steal his scripture from Qusayy, Zayd, or Moses—or simply claim credit for himself.

040.007 "Those (angels[demons]) who sustain the Throne and those around it sing praise to their Lord and believe in Him; and ask forgiveness for those who believe: 'Our Lord! Your reach is over all things, in mercy and knowledge. Forgive those who repent and follow Your Path. Save them from the torment of the blazing fire! Grant that they enter the Gardens of Eden.'" Forgive the interruption, but what is the basis of Islamic forgiveness? In each of the religions upon which Islam was based, a sacrifice was required. It is the same with all rational societies. Commit a crime and a judge will require you to sacrifice your money, your freedom, or your life, depending upon the severity of the offense. Such has always been true with rational religions. If sin is without consequence, the result is chaos. If forgiveness is capricious, anarchy reigns. This oversight is one of many reasons Islam is so impoverished. It explains why Islamic states require tyrannical oppression to maintain a semblance of order.

With predestination there is no choice; and without choice, what follows makes no sense. *040.009* "'And ward off from them ill-deeds; and he from whom You ward off ill-deeds that day, him verily have You taken into mercy. That is the supreme success."

Destined to hell: *040.010* "Lo, those who disbelieve will be informed by proclamation: 'Verily Allah's abhorrence is more terrible than your aversion to yourselves.'" Allah abhors men. Another translation reads: "Allah's hatred of you is terrible, seeing that you were called to the Faith [of submission] and you refused." It's yet another sign that Allah is not Yahweh. The God of the Bible abhors deception, evil, false gods, and false religions, but he loves men—even men and women caught in deceptive, evil, and false doctrines. So we're dealing with Satan here.

The abhorred inmates of Allah's Hell: *040.011* "will say: 'Our Lord! [which would make Allah available in Hell and the Lord of Hell] Twice have You made us die, and twice have You made us live! Now we have recognized our faults. Is there any way out (of this fire)?' (The answer will be:) 'This is (your plight) because, when Allah was invoked as the Only (object of worship), you rejected (Islam), but when partners were joined to Him, you believed!" Translated into English this means: When Muhammad accepted

Allah and discarded Ar-Rahman, and when he promoted Allah's little girls to goddesses, his adversaries believed. But the non-monotheistic Satanic indulgence didn't work out so, ever the hypocrite, Muhammad says that if anyone follows his example, they'll burn in hell.

040.013 **"It is He Who shows you his Ayat (Signs and Proofs)."** According to the Qur'an, there were no miracles—ever. Allah never so much as rolled over. However, the Hadith contradicts Allah's Book, and says: *Bukhari:V4B56N830-1* **"The Meccan people requested Allah's Apostle to show them a miracle, and so during the lifetime of the Prophet [they haven't a clue as to when] the moon was split into two parts. On that the Prophet said, 'Bear witness [to my god].'"** Since there is no evidence to corroborate fanciful tale, I'm surprised Muslims don't claim that putting the moon back together as if it had never been apart was a miracle, too.

Now that Allah is the spirit of Islam, it's time to elevate his status. *040.014* **"So call you (O Muhammad) upon Allah, making (your) worship pure for Him (in obedience), even though the disbelievers may detest it. (He is the) Owner of High Ranks, Owner of the Throne. By His Command does He send the (inspiration) to any of His slaves he pleases, that it may warn (men) of the Day of Mutual Meeting."** If this is scripture, the perfect word of their god inscribed on an eternal tablet, why must so many words be added to the text for it to even approach being intelligible?

040.016 **"The Day whereon they will (all) come out of their graves: not a single thing of them is hidden. Who will be in control that Day?' Allah, the One, the Irresistible!"** God would not ask such a question or answer it so absurdly. The spirit depicted in these scriptures is hardly irresistible. Another translation, adds: **"(Allah Himself will reply to His Question)"** A third, however, ends more in keeping with Allah's demeanor: **"Allah, the Subduer (of all)."**

040.017 **"This day every person shall be rewarded for what he earned; no injustice (shall be done); surely Allah is quick in reckoning."** With the pseudo-religious stuff out of the way, it's time to get mean: **"Warn them of the Day of (Doom) that is drawing near, when hearts will jump up and choke their throats, filling them with anguish. And they can neither return their hearts to their chests nor throw them out. No friend nor intercessor will the disbelievers have. (Allah) knows of (the tricks) that deceive with treachery, and all that the bosoms conceal."** Allah continues to be the master of deceit.

040.021 **"Do they not travel through the earth and see the end of those before them? They were superior to them in strength, and in the traces (they have left) in the land, yet Allah seized and destroyed them, and they had no one to defend them against Allah. That was because their Messengers kept bringing them Clear (Signs and Proofs) (of Allah's Sovereignty), but they rejected them: So Allah seized and destroyed them: for He is Strong, Severe in Punishment and Retribution."** Allah is the god of seizures, destruction, punishment, and revenge—not love. Sure sounds demonic to me.

All right, enough with the pain and punishment. It's time to indulge in Allah's other hobbies—plagiarism and self-delusion. *040.023* **"We sent Musa (Moses) with Our Signs and Proofs and an authority manifest, a clear warrant to Firon**

[Pharaoh], but he called (him) a sorcerer telling lies!...Now, when he brought them the Truth from Our presence, he said, 'Slay the sons of those who believe with him, and keep alive their females,' but the plots of unbelievers (end) in nothing but errors (and delusions) in the state of perdition!..." An ellipsis is used to let readers know something has been omitted something from the text. The ellipses ("…") found in this passage are in the Qur'an translations, suggesting Allah left something out of his perfect and complete (albeit plagiarized and twisted) revelation. I have a theory. The Islamic god couldn't read or write any better than his prophet so he didn't know this story well enough to retell it credibly.

The liberation of the Jews from Egypt is faithfully recorded in the book of Exodus. Proven accurate by archeologists, it has endured unaltered since 275 B.C. when scholars in Alexandria Egypt translated the Bible into Greek, the *lingua franca* of its day. Yet there is but a faint echo of this great victory of faith in Muhammad's forgery. But rather than correct Allah's ignorance I'll simply present his version. If you are interested in truth, read Genesis and Exodus. However, as you ponder the Islamic perversion, consider Muhammad's motive. He had been spewing his caustic brew of lust and torment for a decade and had nothing to show for it. Lacking credibility, prophecy, miracles, and originality, he stole these things from Moses—a man who had them all.

Every word of what follows parallels Muhammad in Mecca and his war of words with the Quraysh establishment: *040.026* "Said Pharaoh: 'Leave me to kill Moses; and let him cry to his Lord! What I fear is he will change your religion, and cause mischief to appear in the land!' Moses said: 'I have called upon my Lord and your Lord (for protection) from every arrogant one who believes not in the Day of Doom!'" Pardon me. Pharaoh's god was Amun-Re. Mighty temples were erected to him. The moon god of Mecca, he was not. Allah's rock pile and his puny Black Stone weren't in Amun-Re's league.

This leads to the line that brought us to the 40th surah. *040.028* "A believer [thus a Muslim], a man from among Pharaoh's family [therefore, not a Muslim], who had concealed his faith [in Islam, a religion that wouldn't be invented for almost 2,000 years], said: 'Will you slay a man because he says, "My Lord is Allah," when he has come to you with Clear (Signs) from your Lord? If he be a liar, on him is his lie: but, if he is telling the truth, then some of that (scourge of Allah, the calamity) which he threatens will befall you. Truly Allah guides not one [who] is extravagant and lies! O my People! Yours is the dominion this day: You have the upper hand, being dominant in the land, but who will save us from Allah's Punishment, should it befall us?'" What's with the "O my People" speech? Moses and his brother Aaron went alone to Pharaoh. Sure there were Jews enslaved in Egypt, but they were miles away making bricks. The only people within earshot of Pharaoh were Egyptians, members of his staff and family.

040.029 "Pharaoh said: 'I point out that which I see; I guide to the Right Path.' Then said the man who believed: 'O my People! Truly I fear for you something like the fate (of disaster) of the Confederates! Something like the fate of the People of Noah, Ad, and Thamud, and those who came after them: but Allah never wishes injustice to slaves." There isn't a trace of the Ad. And even if these imaginary people actually existed, they wouldn't have risen in Arabia until centuries after this conversation occurred. As such, these words could not have been spoken. Therefore, Allah is lying.

Allah lies because he "causes men to err and he leads them astray." 040.032 "O my People! I fear a Day when there will be mutual wailing, a Day when you shall turn your backs and flee. No one shall defend you against Allah. Any whom Allah causes to err, there is no guide. That is how Allah leads the skeptic astray." This unnamed Muslim in Pharaoh's household sounds an awful lot like Muhammad in Mecca. If they aren't the same person, they had the same speechwriter. 040.035 "Those who dispute the Signs and Verses of Allah without any authority, grievous and odious, hateful and disgusting, is it in the sight of Allah and the Believers." If my Scriptures were this odious and hateful, I'd consider their exposure disgusting too.

040.036 "Pharaoh said: 'O Haman, build me a lofty tower that I may attain a way (to reach) the heavens, that I may mount up and look upon the Ilah (God) of Moses. But as far as I am concerned, I think (Moses) is a liar!' Thus was made alluring, in Pharaoh's eyes, the evil of his deeds; and the plot of Pharaoh led to nothing but perdition." Allah wants us to believe that the Egyptian king ordered his people to build the Tower of Babel to reach god. What's more, his "Haman" is from the book of Esther and also tied to the land of the Babylonians, not the Egyptians. But at least Pharaoh knew that in 1,900 years the Arabic word for God would be Ilah, not Allah.

040.038 "The [nameless Muslim] man [masquerading as Muhammad] who believed said: 'O my People! Follow me: I will lead you to the Right Path (Islam). This life is nothing but enjoyment. It is the Hereafter that is the abode to settle. Whether man or woman, a Believer is such as will enter the Garden of Bliss. Therein will they have abundance. And O my People! How (strange) it is for me to call you to deliverance while you call me to the Hell Fire!" Muhammad tipped his hand, again. The "Right Path," "Garden of Bliss," and "Hell Fire" were his most notorious inventions—his signature.

040.042 "You call me to blaspheme against Allah, and to associate partners with Him whom I have no knowledge." This unknown partnership argument is nonsense played in Egypt. Their gods were exceedingly well known, and they were unabashedly numerous. "Without doubt you do call me to one who is not fit to be called to. The Transgressors will be inmates of the Hell Fire!"

The great unnamed masquerader wasn't finished exposing his real identity or purpose: 040.044 "Soon will you remember what I say to you (now), My (own) affair I commit to Allah: for Allah (ever) watches over His Slaves. Then Allah saved him from (every) ill that they plotted (against him), but the brunt of the Penalty, the evil doom encompassed on all sides of Pharaoh's folk." During this whole longwinded speech, the unnamed Muslim never uttered the words for which Moses had been sent: "Let my people go." And that's because Muhammad's recreation of the saga between Moses and Pharaoh was designed to liberate Allah's prophet from criticism, not the Jews from bondage.

With every word sounding like Muhammad in Mecca, the perversion of Moses in Egypt continued, this time with a recap of Allah's favorite subject. *040.046* "In front of the Fire will they be brought and exposed morning and evening: And (the sentence will be): 'Cast the People of Pharaoh into the severest torment, the most awful doom!' Behold, they will argue noisily with each other while they wrangle in the Fire! The weak ones (who followed) will say to those who had been arrogant, 'We but followed you. Can you then take (on yourselves) from us some share of the Fire? The arrogant will say: 'We are all in this (Fire)! Truly, Allah has judged between slaves!'" Even with a change of scenery and exposure to the dominant culture of the day, Allah remained mired in the inferno of the Arabian Desert.

This Qur'anic charade is speaking on behalf of a religion that wouldn't be conceived for nearly twenty centuries. *040.049* "Those in the Fire will say to the guards and keepers of Hell: 'Pray to your Lord to lighten the torment for a day!' They will say: 'Did there not come to you your Messengers with Clear Signs?' They will say, 'Yes.' 'Then pray (as you like)! But the prayer of the disbelievers is futile (and will go unanswered)!' They will present their excuses, but they will (only) have the curse and the home of misery." The tirade ends by revealing the source from which the raw material was stolen: *040.053* "We showed Moses the guidance, and caused the children of Israel to inherit the Scripture Book (the Torah)."

The 40th surah is too long to cover from start to finish. But before we say goodbye to "The Forgiver," consider this: *040.070* "Those who deny the Book and what We have sent down with Our Apostles will soon come to have iron collars and chains around their necks; they will be dragged through boiling water and then thrust into the Fire to be burnt." While we have changed gods, it wasn't an improvement.

Imagine for a moment that you're Ibn Ishaq. You're in Baghdad 130 years, or about five generations, after Muhammad brought these disasters upon himself. A Caliph waltzes in and orders you to write the Islamic Gospel— *"The Life of the Prophet Muhammad."* But all you have got to work with are oral reports called Hadith—handed down father to son over the vast chasm of time.

You put quill to paper, but your hand shakes. With every word you destroy, demonize actually, the man responsible for the political dogma under which you toil. His scriptures are as twisted and dark as his life. So what do you do?

To his credit, I think Ishaq wrote what he was told. If a Hadith explained an otherwise incomprehensible Qur'an, if it explained otherwise unjustifiable ritual, if it explained the change in the nature of Arabs that led to their bloody conquests, it made its way into his Sira. So this lone scribe established Islam—literally. Ishaq is responsible for virtually everything Muslims know about Muhammad, his god, his scripture, and his religion. And it isn't good.

12

DELUSIONS OF GRANDEUR

"Will you succumb to his witchcraft with your eyes open?
These are merely medleys of muddled dreams!"

Allah's House was tainted with the lingering effects of the Satanic Verses so Muhammad needed a new Qiblah—a new direction to go and a new object to exploit. He needed to replace the Ka'aba with a more credible shrine. So the wannabe prophet conjured up one of the most preposterous lies ever uttered in the name of religion. He said that he was flown on a winged steed to the Temple in Jerusalem. There, he was welcomed triumphantly by all the former scriptural big shots. They were waiting for him, assembled in a solemn conclave of prophet solidarity.

His imagination running wild, Muhammad leapt from the Temple Mount skywards, ascending from one heaven to another, finding himself in the presence of Allah, who promptly dismissed him, demanding that Muslims moon him fifty times a day. Hallucination over, Muhammad awoke the following morning in the house of his late uncle Abu. The vision still dancing vividly before his eyes, he cried out to his niece, **"Omm Hani, during the night I prayed in the Temple of Jerusalem."** She begged him not to expose such frivolity to the Quraysh, but he persisted.

Ishaq:184 **"Umm, Abu Talib's daughter, said: "The Apostle went on no journey except while he was in my house. He slept in my home that night after he prayed the final night prayer. A little before dawn he woke us, saying, 'O Umm, I went to Jerusalem.' He got up to go out and I grabbed hold of his robe and laid bare his belly. I pleaded, 'O Muhammad, don't tell the people about this for they will know you are lying and will mock you.' He said, 'By Allah, I will tell them.' I told a negress slave of mine, 'Follow him and listen.'"**

As the story spread, Muhammad's fledgling cadre of followers abandoned him. The disillusionment was confirmed by Katib al Wackidi, **"Upon hearing this many became renegades who had prayed and joined Islam."** The Sira says: *Ishaq:183* **"Many Muslims gave up their faith. Some went to Abu Bakr and said, 'What do you think of your friend now? He alleges that he went to Jerusalem last night and prayed there and came back to Mecca.' Bakr said that they were lying about the Apostle. But they told him that he was in the mosque at this very moment telling the Quraysh about it. Bakr said, 'If** he says so then it must be true. I believe him. And that is more extraordinary than his story at which you boggle.' Then Allah sent down a Qur'an surah concerning those who left Islam for this reason: 'We made the vision which we showed you only, a test for men. We put them in fear, but it only adds to their heinous error.'" [Qur'an 13:33] Once again, Muhammad flips out and it's everyone's fault but his own. And while it's not surprising anymore, the 13ᵗʰ surah was handed down in Medina, not Mecca.

What's surprising is that the "Thunder" surah actually rebukes Muhammad's claim of a miraculous journey. After saying, *013.005* "Those who deny will wear collars and chains, yokes (of servitude) tying their hands to their necks; they will be the inmates of Hell.... They will witness Our (many) exemplary punishments! Verily, your Lord is severe in retribution," we are told that Muhammad was *unable* to perform a miracle. *013.007* "The unbelievers say, 'Why was no sign or miracle sent down to him by his Lord?' But you are only the bearer of bad news—of warnings." The admission is repeated: *013.027* "The unbelievers say, 'How is it that no sign miracle was sent down to him by his Lord?' Say, 'God leads whosoever He wills astray.'" The Qur'an is clear: there were no miracles.

The Islamic god was not only powerless, he was schizophrenic. *013.030* "They do not believe in Ar-Rahman. Tell them, 'He is my Lord. There is no other ilah but He. In Him I have placed my trust.'" The dark lord says to those who are mocking his prophet: *013.032* "Many an Apostle have they mocked before you; but I seized them. How awful was My punishment then! ...The unbelievers plot, but for them is torment in this life and a far more severe torture in Hell." Then the spirit of the Qur'an brags, "He sends thunderbolts and smites whom He pleases." Imagine worshiping a god this nasty.

Suggesting that he wasn't always impotent, Ar-Rahman boasts: *013.038* "It was not for any Apostle to come up with a miracle or sign unless it was granted by Our permission." But he was capricious and forgetful. "For every age there is a Book revealed. Ar-Rahman abrogates, blots out, or confirms (whatever He wants)." And we better watch out: *013.041* "Do they not see Us advancing from all sides into the land (of the disbelievers), reducing its borders (by giving it to believers in war victories)? (When) Allah dooms there is none who can postpone His doom. Sure, they devised their plots, but We are the best schemers." But his con didn't fool very many: *013.043* "Yet the disbelievers say: 'You are not a Messenger.' Tell them: 'This Scripture is sufficient witness between me and you.'"

Now that we know there were no miracles, and that these troubled words are the lone witness to the validity of Muhammad's claims, let's try to make sense of his fictitious journey. As always, it will be difficult to tell where the prophet's imagination subsided and that of the Muslim sages began. For example, when questioned by the Quraysh, we are told that the angel-less and miracle-less messenger convinced his spirit friend to erect a model of Jerusalem in their midst. As further evidence of the Night Journey, Muhammad said that while whizzing over a caravan the noise of his flying steed frightened a camel to death. Upon returning to Mecca, someone is said to have confirmed that a camel had indeed been anxious. It served as proof.

The only other Qur'anic mention of the flight of fancy is found in the 17ᵗʰ surah which opens: "Glory to Him who carried His votary by night from the Sacred Mosque (at Mecca), to the farther Temple, the environs which we have blessed, that we might show him some of Our Signs. Verily He hears and sees."

The six-year-old Aisha, who married the fifty-year-old prophet within days of Khadija's death, said: *Ishaq:183* "The Prophet's body remained where it was. Allah removed his spirit at night." In that there was no way to see Jerusalem at night in the seventh century, the cover of darkness must have suited Islam's demonic spirit. Aisha further indicted her husband's tale with: *Bukhari:V4B53N400* "Once the Prophet was bewitched so that he began to imagine that he had done a thing which in fact he had not done." Finishing the job, she said: *Bukhari:V4B54N457* "Whoever claimed that Muhammad saw his Lord is committing a great fault, for he only saw Gabriel."

While Aisha's criticism was incriminating, there was a bigger problem. There was *no* Temple in Jerusalem. Six centuries years before al-Buraq took flight, the Romans destroyed it. By 70 A.D. not one stone stood upon another. And that would make both the Islamic god and his prophet liars.

Bukhari: V4B55N585 "'O Allah's Apostle! Which mosque was first built on the surface of the earth?' He said, 'The mosque Haram in Mecca.' 'Which was built next?' He replied 'The mosque of Al-Aqsa in Jerusalem.' 'What was the period of construction between the two?' He said, 'Forty years.'" No matter how one goes about interpreting these facts and fantasies, Muhammad lied. If the Ka'aba was built by Allah, it was several billion years old. If by Adam, then the year was 4000 B.C. If by Abraham, it was 2000 B.C. If historical evidence is our guide, the year was about 500 A.D. The Temple of Solomon was built in 967 B.C. (precisely 1,000 years before Christ's crucifixion and resurrection in 33 A.D.). The Dome of the Rock was raised on the foundations of the Roman Temple of Jupiter in 691 A.D. As for the mosque, Al-Aqsa was constructed over a Roman basilica on the southern end of the Temple Mount many centuries later. Muhammad got the order wrong as well as the gap separating them.

While I'm not a psychiatrist, this story sounds delusional: *Bukhari:V4B54N429/ V5B58N227* "The Prophet said, 'While I was at the House or standing place in a state midway between sleep and wakefulness, an angel recognized me as the man lying between two men. [That sounds provocative.] A golden tray full of wisdom and belief was brought to me and my body was cut open from the throat to the lower part of my pubic area.' The Prophet said, 'My abdomen was washed with Zamzam water taking away doubt or polytheism or pre-Islamic beliefs or error. Then he took out my heart and filled it with belief and wisdom before returning it to its place. Then Al-Buraq, a white animal, smaller than a mule and bigger than a donkey was brought to me and I set out with Gabriel.' The Prophet said, 'The animal's step was so wide it reached the farthest point within reach of the animal's sight.'"

From the Sira: *Ishaq:182* "While I was in the Hijr, Gabriel came and stirred me with his foot. He took me to the door of the mosque and there was a white animal, half mule, half donkey, with wings on its sides yet it was propelled by its feet. He mounted me on it. When I mounted, he shied. Gabriel placed his hand on its mane and said [to the jackass], 'You should be ashamed to behave this way. By God, you have never had a more honorable rider than Muhammad.' The animal was so embarrassed, it broke into a cold sweat."

In a Hadith from Muslim's Collection, Muhammad dispenses with the surgery and adds two ritual prayers in the Temple along with a refreshing drink: *Muslim:C75B1N309* "The Messenger said: 'I was brought on al-Buraq, an animal white and long. I mounted it and came to the Temple in Jerusalem. I tethered it to the ring used by the prophets and entered the mosque, praying two rak'ahs in it. Then I came out [of the nonexistent building] and Gabriel brought me a vessel of wine and one of milk. I chose the milk, and he said: "You have chosen the natural thing," and took me to heaven.'"

Ishaq:182 "When we arrived at the Temple in Jerusalem, we found Abraham, Moses, and Jesus, along with a company of prophets. I acted as their imam in prayer." In case you're curious: "Moses was a ruddy faced man, thinly fleshed, curly haired with a hooked nose. Jesus was a reddish man with lank wet hair and many freckles." *Ishaq:184* "After the completion of my business in Jerusalem, a ladder was brought to me finer than any I have ever seen. [Mind you, since there was no wood in Mecca, he had never seen a ladder.] An angel was in charge of it and under his command were 12,000 angels each of them having 12,000 angels under his command." Imagine that, 144,000,000 angels holding a ladder. "And none knows the armies of Allah better than he."

Knowing Muhammad, what do you suppose he asked to see *first?* If you guessed "Hell," you win. *Ishaq:185* "Muhammad said, 'Order Malik to show me Hell.' 'Certainly! O Malik, show Muhammad Hell.' Thereupon he removed its covering and the flames blazed high into the air until I thought that they would consume everything." In Islam, wrong is right, down is up, hell is where Allah lives.

Bukhari:V4B54N429 and *Muslim:C75B1N309* converge at this point and we learn that hell is in the nearest heaven: "'When I reached the nearest heaven, Gabriel said to heaven's gatekeeper, "Open the gate." The guard asked, "Who is it?" He said, "Gabriel." The gatekeeper said, "Who is accompanying you?" Gabriel said, "Muhammad." The guard replied, "Has he been called?" Gabriel said, "Yes." Then it was said, "He is welcomed. What a wonderful visit his is!" Then I met Adam and greeted him and he said, "You are welcomed, O son and Prophet." Gabriel said, "These parties on his right and on his left are the souls of his descendants. Those of them on his right are the companions of Paradise and the parties which are on his left are the inmates of Hell. So when Adam looked towards his right side, he laughed, and when he looked left, he wept.'"

Ishaq gets a little graphic at this point: *Ishaq:185* "Adam reviewed the spirits of his offspring. The infidels excited his disgust. Then I saw men with lips like camels. In their hands were pieces of fire like stones which they thrust into their mouths. They came out their posteriors." Before I tell you who deserved this fate, think about the folks who irked Muhammad most. Who wouldn't share what he coveted, who neglected him, allowing him to be abused? "I was told they sinfully devoured the wealth of orphans." Others had "bellies like camels." Some were "maddened by thirst." "Then I saw women hanging by their breasts. They had fathered bastards."

But not all was hellish. Speaking of the son whose wife he would steal in an act of incest, the prophet said, *Ishaq:186* **"He took me into Paradise and there I saw a damsel with dark red lips. I asked her to whom she belonged, for she pleased me much when I saw her. She said, Zayd [Muhammad's adopted son]. The apostle gave Zayd the good news about her."** She was his consolation prize, I suppose.

Returning to Muslim and Bukhari: **"'Then we ascended to the second heaven. The guard at the gate asked, "Who is it?" Gabriel said, "Gabriel." The gatekeeper asked, "Who is with you?" He said, "Muhammad" "Has he been sent for?" He said, "Yes." The guard said, "He is welcomed. What a wonderful visit his is!" and opened the gate. Then I met Jesus and Yahya (John) who said, "You are welcomed, O brother and Pious Prophet."'"**

Rising above Jesus: **"'We ascended to the third heaven. The keeper of the gate asked, "Who is it?" "Gabriel." The gatekeeper asked, "Who is with you?" "Muhammad." "Has he been sent for?" "Yes." "He is welcomed. What a wonderful visit his is!" He opened the gate.'** The Prophet added: 'There I met Joseph and greeted him. He replied, "You are welcomed, brother and Prophet!" We ascended to the fourth heaven and again the same questions and answers were exchanged with the gatekeeper. There I met Idris [Enoch]. He said, "Welcome Prophet." We ascended to the fifth heaven and again the same questions and answers were exchanged at the gate with its guard. There I greeted Aaron.'"** The Islamic heaven is filled with Jews, and it has more gates and guards than do most prisons. I wonder if that's a coincidence?

Whatever the reason, they were all flung open for the great Arab prophet: **"'Then we ascended to the sixth heaven and again the same questions and answers were exchanged. There I met and greeted Moses. When I proceeded on, he started weeping and on being asked why, he said, "Followers of this youth who was sent after me will enter Paradise in greater number than my followers."'"** This passage provides a glimpse into Muhammad's corroded heart. In an effort to elevate himself he had the audacity to claim Moses was jealous of *him*.

Leaving Jewish prophets in the dust, our dynamic duo scampered ever higher: **"'We ascended to the seventh heaven and again the same questions and answers were exchanged with the gatekeeper. There I greeted Abraham. He ascended with me till I was taken to such a height, I heard the scraping of pens. I was shown Al-Bait-al-Ma'mur (Allah's House). I asked Gabriel about it and he said, "This is where 70,000 angels perform prayers daily and when they leave they never return to it (a fresh batch arrives daily)." I was shown Sidrat-ul-Muntaha (a tree) and I saw its Nabk fruits which resembled clay jugs. Its leaves were like elephant ears. Four rivers originated at its root; I asked Gabriel about them. "The two hidden rivers are in Paradise, and the apparent ones are the Euphrates and the Nile."'"** At least he had that part right. He was in a state of *denial*.

"Fifty prayers were enjoined on me [by Allah]." But Moses wasn't pleased: **"'I descended till I reached Moses who asked, "What have you done?" I said, "I have been ordered to offer fifty prayers a day." He said, "Your followers cannot bear fifty prostrations. I tested people before you and tried my level best to bring the tribe of Israel to obedience [Islam]. Your followers cannot put up with such an obligation. So, return to your Lord and**

request a reduction in the burden." I returned and requested Allah (for reduction) and He made it forty. I had a similar discussion with Moses. Then I returned to Allah for reduction and He made it thirty, then twenty, then ten. Then I came to Moses who repeated the same advice. Ultimately Allah reduced it to five. When I came to Moses the last time, he said, "What have you done?" I said, "Allah has made it five only." He repeated the same advice but I said that I had requested so many times I felt ashamed and surrendered (to Allah's final order). When I left, I heard a voice saying, "I have passed My Order and have lessened the burden on My Worshipers."'"

You're brought before the creator of the universe and all you talk about is how many times he wants to be mooned with "burdensome and obligatory," mind-numbing ritualistic prostrations? I don't think so. But then again, thinking is why I'm not a Muslim. So, while we are on the subject, think about this: why would Islam's lone prophet leave Allah's Ka'aba in Mecca and fly to Yahweh's Temple in Jerusalem to get into heaven? In all of Muhammad's flights of fancy, there are few more troubling questions than this one.

Muhammad's Muslims were curious, albeit about minutiae. They wanted to know what the heavenly host looked like. *Bukhari:V4B55N607* **"Allah's Apostle said, 'On the night of my Ascension to Heaven, I saw Moses who was a thin person, looking like one of the men of the tribe of Shanua; and I saw Jesus with a red face as if he had just come out of a bathroom. [I swear, I'm not making this stuff up.] And I resemble Abraham more than any of his offspring.'"** And it's okay to scour the Bible for the names of fellow prophets because: *Bukhari:V4B56N667* **"The Messenger said, 'Convey (my teachings) to the people even if it were a single sentence, and tell others the stories of Israel (which have been taught to you), for it is not sinful to do so. And whoever tells a lie on me intentionally, will surely take his place in the Hell Fire.'"**

It bears mention that the Night Journey is far more than an obscure theological story to Muslims. I personally met with members of Hamas, al-Qaeda, Islamic Jihad, and al-Aqsa Martyrs' Brigade in Bethlehem in December, 2001. They told me in all seriousness that the Night's Journey was the basis for the Islamic claim to Jerusalem. What's more, they were willing to kill and die to take it back in the name of their Prophet.

Back in Mecca, and ever in character, the bruised messenger did what all similarly insecure people do. He projected his morbid self-delusion upon his critics. As he had with the Satanic Verses, he had his god say that the Night's Journey was a trial. *Bukhari:V8B77N610* **"'We granted the vision of the ascension to the heavens, Miraj, which We showed you as an actual eye witness but as a trial for people.' [Qur'an 17:60] Allah's Apostle actually saw with his own eyes the vision of all the things which were shown to him on the Night Journey to Jerusalem. It was not a dream."**

The 17th surah, named **"Children of Israel,"** reports: *017.060* **"Your Lord circumscribes mankind and He showed you the vision and the accursed tree of the Qur'an [Zaqqom, the torture tree of Hell]. It was a bone of contention for men, a trial for them. Thus do We instill fear and make them afraid."** The surah claims: **"Verily, We gave Moses the Torah...and** to David, We gave the Book of Psalms." Speaking of Jews, he says: *017.007* **"We shall rouse Our slaves to shame and ravage you, disfiguring your faces. They will enter the Temple as before and destroy, laying to waste all that they conquer."** To his shame, Muhammad did rouse Muslims to attack Jews. However, his militants couldn't have entered or destroyed what the Romans had eradicated 600 years earlier. Allah is mistaken, again. But by lying to us this way, we have come to know him better.

The most laughable passage in the 17th surah follows the usual rant: **"Dread His punishment. Indeed the Lord's torment is to be feared. He will inflict severe anguish."** *017.059* **"Nothing stops Us from sending signs and proofs except that earlier people rejected them as lies. We sent to Thamud the she-camel as a clear sign, but they treated her cruelly."** It's hard to imagine anyone believes this is scripture. The Islamic god just said: "We don't do miracles any more because the Thamud hurt our camel."

After saying the Qur'an was so well written jinn and men couldn't conspire to compose the likes of it, we discover that Muhammad doesn't measure up and there is no Qur'an: *017.090* **"They say, 'We shall not believe you (Muhammad), until you cause a spring to gush forth from the earth [like Moses]. Or until you have a garden, and cause rivers to flow in their midst [like you claim Allah does]. Or you cause the sky to fall upon us in chunks, as you say will happen [like Yahweh did to Sodom and Gomorrah]. Or you bring angels before us face to face [like Abraham]. Or you have a house adorned with gold [like David or Solomon], or you ascend up into the skies [like Jesus]. No, we shall not have faith in you unless you send down to us a book that we can read [like the Bible].'"** This surah was the seventieth chronologically, and yet the Meccans claimed Muhammad didn't have anything to read. There was no Qur'an. There were no miracles.

Following the Night's Journey, the prophet had a new Qiblah to replace the one he had soiled, so all he needed now was some followers. But having disgraced himself in Mecca with the Satanic Bargain, the Ta'if Stoning, and Wild Buraq Ride, he needed a new audience. Fortunately, opportunity sprang from a most unexpected place. The pilgrimage fairs promoted by Qusayy were still in full swing. *Tabari VI:120* **"The Messenger used to appear at the times of the pilgrimage before the Arab tribes, summoning them to Allah, informing them that he himself was a prophet sent by Allah, and asking them to believe his words and defend him. 'I am Allah's Messenger to you, commanding you to worship Allah and not to associate anything with him [like I just did], to cast off whatever idols you worship other than Him, to believe in me, and the truth of my message, and to defend me so that I may make manifest the message of Allah I have been sent to convey.'"** This was all about, "Me, myself, and I." Insecure people like Muhammad have an insatiable craving for praise. They live to be in control. And they will stop at nothing to achieve their agenda, rationalizing everything they do along the way.

"When the Prophet completed his speech and his appeal, Abd Al-Uzza Lahab would say, 'Banu so-and-so, this man is calling upon you to cast off Al-Lat and Al-Uzza...and accept the error of his ways. Do not obey him; do not listen to him.'" The Muslim sages felt that it was in their interest to demean uncle Abu by calling him Slave-to-Al-Uzza Abu. But it's a two edged sword. For if Al-Uzza and Al-Lat were pagan goddesses for which men were named, Allah was also a pre-Islamic idol whose name men bore. In the next Hadith from, of all people, Abd Ar-Rahman, we read: "Speaking to the clan of the Banu Abdallah Muhammad said, 'Allah has given your ancestor an excellent name.'"

As a prophet, Muhammad was an abysmal failure. *Ishaq:194* "The Apostle offered himself to the Arab tribes at the fairs whenever an opportunity arose. He used to ask them to believe in him and protect him." *Ishaq:195* "The Apostle stopped by the Arab encampments and told them that he was the Prophet of Allah ordering them to worship Him, to believe in His Messenger, and protect him until Allah made plain His purpose." "He went to the tents of the Kinda and offered himself to them, but they declined. He went to the Abdallah clan with the same message, but they would not heed. The Apostle went to the Hanifa, where he met with the worst reception of all. He tried the Amir, but one of them said to him, 'I suppose you want us to protect you from the Arabs with our lives and then if you prevail, someone else will reap the benefits. Thank you, No!'"

Craving power and money: *Tabari VI:122/Ishaq:195* "Whenever Muhammad heard of a pilgrim coming to the fairs who was important, he would give special attention to him. Some shaykhs of Yathrib's Awf clan came to Mecca on the umrah. When Muhammad heard about Suwayd's arrival [a poet called "The Perfect One"], he was attentive to him. Suwayd said, 'Perhaps what you are presenting is like what I am saying.' The Messenger asked, 'What are you reciting?' 'The book of Luqman,' he replied. [Luqman was a mythical Arab. He appears in the 31st surah.] The Messenger said, 'Hand it to me [so that I can plagiarize it like I have Hanif poetry and Jewish scripture.].' Suwayd handed it over and explained it to him. Muhammad said, 'This speech is good, but I have better. My speech is a Qur'an which Allah has revealed to me.' The Prophet recited some of it to Suwayd. He said, 'This is a fine saying,' and went off, rejoining his people."

Undeterred, the Prophet continued to mill among the crowds, pressing the flesh, as he regaled them with his solicitations. But time was running out. The ritual ceremonies were nearly over. *Ishaq:197* "The Apostle heard about Abdul. He asked them if they would like to get something more profitable than their present errand." Since they were on a religious pilgrimage, Muhammad must have been selling the religion of stolen booty. But their leader "took a handful of dirt and threw it in Muhammad's face."

Now desperate, Allah's boy followed the devotees of the pagan idols on their final procession to Arafat and then back to Mina. In the narrow valley opportunity knocked. Muhammad shuffled up to a group of pilgrims from Yathrib. "What tribe are you from?" "The tribe of Khazraj," one replied. "Ah!" the Prophet said excitedly. "Your tribe is a confederate of the Jews, isn't it?" "Yes. We are." "Then, why don't we sit down and chat?" A Hadith reports: *Tabari VI:124* "When Allah wished to make His religion victorious [with the sword], to render His Prophet mighty [with political power], and to fulfill His promise [to make Muhammad rich], the Messenger went out during that pilgrimage and met a group of Ansar at Aqabah, a party of Khazraj." The Ansar, or "Helpers," were Muslims from Yathrib. At the time there were none.

Ishaq:197 "Allah had prepared them for Islam because they lived next to the Jews, who were people of scripture and knowledge. While the Khazraj were polytheists and idolaters, they had gained the mastery over the Jews, raiding them. Whenever any dispute arose the Jews would say, 'A prophet will be sent soon. His time is at hand. We shall follow him and with him as our leader we shall kill you.'" This Hadith confirms several things that would shape Islam. First, there were Jews in Yathrib—lots of them. They were smart, well read, and Biblically grounded. The Arabs were pagans, yet they dominated the Jews—something Muhammad would capitalize upon in a big way. When the Jews became frustrated, they did what they had always done. They said, "We may be down now but you just wait. One day our Messiah will come and things will be different."

The expectation of a Messiah was interwoven throughout the whole of Jewish life. As such, it would have been communicated to the Arabs. And no doubt, the idolatrous and illiterate inhabitants of Yathrib would have envied the rich customs and heritage of the Jews. It was the perfect environment for the failed prophet of Mecca. The Arabs in Yathrib, tomorrow's Medina, were ripe for the harvest. Still addicted to idolatrous superstitions, they were just well enough acquainted with Judaism to swallow Muhammad's corruptions. They were the perfect patsies for his desperate con. Already anticipating a Messiah, they readily accepted the reformer of Qusayy's Ka'aba worship as their Prophet. They invited the wolf in sheep's clothing into their midst, a decision they would soon come to regret. But it's ironic in a way. The only reason these Arabs accepted Muhammad was because the Jews, having rejected the real Messiah, were still awaiting his arrival. Otherwise, the good folks of Yathrib would have rejected Muhammad just like everybody else had.

Ishaq:198/Tabari VI:125 "After the Messenger had spoken to the group from Yathrib they said, 'Take note. This is the very prophet whom the Jews are menacing us with. Don't let them find him before we accept him.' Because of this, they responded to his call and became Muslims." Finding himself at the right place at the right time, Muhammad fooled the Arabs into thinking that he was the promised Jewish Messiah. Delusions of grandeur had overwhelmed him once again.

Muhammad's status in Mecca was so stained, not a word of what occurred over the next twelve months was provided by either Tabari or Ishaq. Nothing. They both jumped to the same time the following year. The religion of Islam died, undeniably and absolutely, from the moral decadence of the Quraysh Bargain, from the spiritual depravity of the Satanic Verses, and the hallucinogenic lunacy of the Night's Journey. Simply stated, immoral, possessed lunatics don't make good prophets.

Ishaq:198/Tabari VI:125 "The following year, twelve of the Ansar came on the pilgrimage and met the Messenger, this being the first Aqabah. They took an oath of allegiance to him according to the terms of the 'Pledge of Women.' This was before the duty of making war was laid upon them." A footnote reads: "It was called 'The Pledge of Women' because Qur'an 60:12 told Muhammad to require this from women wanting to become Muslims." Only one small problem: the 60th surah was revealed eleven years later—after Mecca had been conquered.

The next Hadith explains: *Ishaq:199/Tabari VI:127* "There were twelve of us and we pledged ourselves to the Prophet in the manner of women that was laid out before war was enjoined. The terms were that we should not associate anything with Allah, we should not steal, should not commit adultery or fornication, should not kill our children, should not slander our neighbors, and we should not disobey Muhammad in what is proper. If we fulfilled this, we would have paradise, and if we failed Allah would punish us in hell." [Qur'an 60:12] Qur'anic postdating aside, in these two sentences we have come upon more religious substance than has been provided in all of the Islamic "scripture" thus far. And while that's bad, it pales in comparison to Muhammad's behavior. He would soon break all of his own rules.

Meeting over, we return to radio silence from Mecca. In an eight thousand-page book detailing every miniscule detail of Islam's rise, Tabari could find nothing to report from Ka'abaVille. Muhammad was dreaming of greener pastures. *Bukhari:V4B56N818* "The Prophet said, 'In a dream I saw myself migrating from Mecca to a place having plenty of date trees. I thought that it was Yemen or Hajar, but it came to be Yathrib." The second half of the dream was prophetic, albeit after the fact. "I saw myself wielding a sword and its blade got broken. It came to symbolize the defeat the Muslims suffered at Uhud. I swung the sword again, and it became normal as before, and that was the symbol of the victory Allah bestowed upon Muslims. I saw cows in my dream, and that was a blessing; they symbolized the believers. And the blessing was the reward of Allah after Badr." The battle of Badr did bring faith to a dying religion. And ignorant cows fattened for the slaughter is a telling symbol of Muhammad's view of his fellow Muslims.

Caught between two worlds and two Qiblahs, the prophet didn't know which way to turn. The leader of the gang of Aqabah said: *Tabari VI:131* "'I shall not turn my back on the Ka'aba and shall pray toward it.'" The Meccan Muslims lied, "'By Allah, we have not heard that our Prophet prays in any other direction than Jerusalem, and we do not wish to differ from him.'"

Soon thereafter the gang of twelve frightened their chieftain into joining them. "If you remain in your present state you will be fuel for the flames of hell." When they next met, the chief told Muhammad, *Ishaq:203* "'Choose what you want for yourself and your Lord.' The Messenger recited [lurid tales of virgins from] the Qur'an and made us desirous of Islam. Then he said, 'I will enter a contract of allegiance with you, provided that you protect me as you would your women and children.'" Contracts are for businessmen. They use them to make money. Allegiances are for politicians.

They use them to get their way. Protection is for pirates, insulating them from the repercussions of the terror they inflict on others. With each word, Islam was beginning to look like a politically-minded swindle.

The destruction of Islam continued: *Tabari VI:133* "We pledge our allegiance to you and we shall defend you as we would our womenfolk. Administer the oath of allegiance to us, Messenger of Allah, for we are men of war possessing arms and coats of mail."

Motivated by the prophet, the newly initiated were almost itching for a fight. "'O Messenger, there are ties between us and the Jews which we shall have to sever. If we do this and Allah gives you victory, will you perhaps return to your own people and leave us?' Muhammad smiled and said, 'Nay, blood is blood, and bloodshed without retaliation is blood paid for. You are of me and I am of you. I shall war against whomever you fight.'" As it would transpire, he did as they feared.

The religious charade was over. The moment the prophet was aligned with men wielding swords he became a pirating profiteer. If the Quraysh Bargain was his first temptation, the Pledge of Aqabah was second. He failed both.

No one was confused. They knew exactly what they were doing. *Ishaq:204/ Tabari VI:134* "'Men of the Khazraj, do you know what you are pledging yourselves to in swearing allegiance to this man?' 'Yes,' they answered. 'In swearing allegiance to him we are pledging ourselves to wage war against all mankind.'" And with that, the final nail was driven into the coffin of the "religion" of Islam. They had declared war.

Ishaq:205 "'If you are loyal to this undertaking, it will profit you in this world and the next.' They said, 'We will accept you as a Prophet under these conditions, but we want to know specifically what we will get in return for our loyalty.' Muhammad answered, 'I promise you Paradise.'" The advance of political Islam was dependent upon this simple concept: "Serve me now, and I *promise* to reward you *later*—much later."

Tabari reports it this way: "'What shall we gain for our faithfulness?' He answered, 'Paradise. So reach out your hand.' They stretched out their arms and swore an allegiance to him." *Heil* Muhammad! The Nazis saluted Hitler precisely the same way. And the result was also the same.

Ishaq:205/Tabari VI:133 "When we had all sworn the oath of allegiance to the Messenger, Satan shouted from the top of Aqabah in the most piercing and penetrating voice I have ever heard. 'People of the [pagan ritual] stations [of the idolatrous hajj] of Mina, do you want to follow a blameworthy reprobate?' The Messenger said, 'What does the Enemy of God say?' 'I am the Devil, and I shall deal with you!'" It is little wonder he screamed from the mountaintop. The Devil had won a great victory.

Chairman Muhammad quickly got down to the business of politics. "'Appoint twelve naqub representatives from among you for me, who will see to the peoples' affairs.' They appointed twelve representatives, nine from the Khazraj and three from the Aws." As with all political dictators, the *naqub* representatives were camouflage—little more than window dressing. There is no record of them ever meeting.

Ishaq:205 "The following morning, Quraysh leaders came to our encampment saying that they had heard that we had invited Muhammad to leave them and that we had pledged ourselves to support him in a war against them. Thereupon members of our tribe swore that nothing of the kind had happened and that we knew nothing of it." Lying was the first thing these Muslims did after pledging to wage war against all mankind. There is an important lesson here (one our politicians and media are missing).

Tabari VI:136 "When the Quraysh came to recognize what had really happened, they urged one another to torment the Muslims and treat them harshly." After all, Muhammad had just upped the ante, moving from a war of words to a clash of swords. "The Muslims suffered great hardship." And that's because: *Tabari VI:138* "Those present at the oath of Aqabah had sworn an allegiance to Muhammad. It was a pledge of war against all men. Allah had permitted fighting." Jihad was born.

The pendulum had swung. The "peace-loving religion" born in Mecca was abrogated. *Tabari VI:139* "After Allah had given his Messenger permission to fight by revealing the verse 'And fight them until persecution is no more, and religion is all for Allah,' [Qur'an 8:39] the Messenger of Allah commanded [not persuaded or asked] those at Mecca to emigrate to Yathrib and join their brethren, the Ansar." And wouldn't you know it, Muhammad couldn't even get that right. The 8th surah, aptly named, "The Spoils of War," was revealed after the Battle of Badr, several years later. His god was doing his level best to accommodate his prophet's ambitions. His timing was off, that's all.

Ishaq:208 "When Allah gave permission to his Apostle to fight, the second Aqaba contained conditions involving war which were not in the first act of submission. Now we bound ourselves to war against all mankind for Allah and His Apostle. He promised us a reward in Paradise for faithful service. We pledged ourselves to war in complete obedience to Muhammad no matter how evil the circumstances." And they were "evil."

Ishaq lists the signatories of the Declaration of Submission: "Uhud commanded the Apostle's archers. He was killed in the battle of Yemen [during the War of Compulsion] as a martyr. Abu was present at all of the Apostle's battles and died in Byzantine territory as a martyr. Mu'adh was present at every raid. He was killed at Badr as a martyr. Mu'awwidh, his brother, shared the same glory. Umara was at every battle and died a martyr in Yemen. As'ad died before Badr when the Prophet's mosque was being built. The Apostle put Amr in command of the rearguard. He died at Uhud as a martyr. Abdallah led many raids and was slain as a martyr at Muta. He was one of Muhammad's commanders. Khallad fought at Badr, Uhud, and Khandaq. He was martyred fighting the [Jewish] Qurayza. The Apostle said that he would have the reward of two martyrs." The list goes on, but you get the picture. Islam kills!

Christ's apostles died as martyrs trying to save men. They used words, not swords. Their sacrifice was a living testament to their faith. Muhammad's companions died wielding swords—sacrificing the lives of others to satiate their own cravings. Christ and Muhammad, Christianity and Islam, the Bible and the Qur'an, Yahweh and Allah are opposites.

Ishaq:212 "The Apostle had not been allowed to fight or shed blood before the second Aqaba. He had simply been ordered to call men to Allah, to endure insult and forgive the ignorant." Camel dung—every word of it. The "Apostle" didn't have the *ability* to fight prior to the pledge of allegiance. The instant he wielded influence over men of war he went to war against those who had insulted him. "I shall bring you slaughter," was how this reprobate defined "forgiveness."

Ishaq:212 **"The Quraysh persecuted his followers, seducing some from their religion and exiling others. They became insolent towards Muhammad's God and rejected His gracious purpose. They accused His prophet of lying. So He gave permission to His Apostle to fight those who had wronged him. He said in his Qur'an: 'Fight them so that there will be no more seduction [i.e., no more exposing Islam's faults], until no Muslim is seduced from Islam. Fight them until the only religion is Islam and Allah alone is worshiped.'"** [Qur'an 22:40 & 2:198] That's reasonably clear: worship Allah or Muslims will kill you.

As a result, every Meccan Muslim save Bakr and Ali scurried off to Yathrib. *Tabari VI:140* **"The Quraysh were now anxious about Muhammad going there as they knew he had decided to join them in order to make war on them."** The Meccans read him like an open book—just like we are doing.

Unfortunately for the billions of souls that have been lost to this ruse, they acted as we do today in the face of Islamic aggression and terror: *Tabari VI:140/Ishaq:221* **"They deliberated as to what to do about Muhammad as they had come to fear him."** One said, **"Keep him in fetters, lock him up, and wait for the same kind of death to overtake him which overtook other poets of his sort."** A handsome shaykh, Muslims say was really the Devil, protested. **"If you imprison him, his followers will attack and snatch him away. Then their numbers will grow so large, they will destroy the authority of the Quraysh."** Sorry shaykh, but that's ridiculous. In twelve years of preaching, Muhammad had seduced fewer than one hundred souls. And most of them abandoned Islam in the aftermath of the Quraysh Bargain, Satanic Verses, and Night's Journey. He was his own worst enemy.

Another suggested, **"Let us expel him from among us and banish him from the land. The harm which he has been doing will disappear, and we shall be rid of him. We shall be able to put our affairs back in order and restore our social harmony."** This sounds eerily like yesterday's newspaper.

The Meccans were as wrongly fixated on a singular person as we are today. Islamic terror survived Muhammad's death because the "religion" manufactured more Muhammads: Bakrs, Alis, Umars, Uthmans, Osama bin Ladens, and Saddam Husseins. By failing to understand the motivations behind Islam, and by focusing on a symptom rather than the disease, the Meccans lost their children, their property, their economic system, and their freedoms. As shall we....

The Quraysh were waylaid by Islam's religious trappings. If they had existed back then, I'm sure the most enlightened Meccans would have paraded the "peace-loving" Muslims out on CNN, ABC, and CBS to reveal the "true" character of the doctrine that had just declared war. "Give peace a chance," they would have protested as the murderous marauders grew ever stronger—corrupting ever more souls. As a direct result of their ignorance, the balance of power shifted. Their economy was plundered by the "peaceful religion." Their people were kidnapped, ransomed, robbed, enslaved, raped, assassinated, and terrorized. The Meccans finally woke up and waged a war of sorts. But it was too little, too late.

The Devil, masquerading as an Arab shaykh, spoke on behalf of his messenger: *Tabari VI:141/Ishaq:222* "By Allah, this is not judicious [fair]. Do you not see the beauty of his discourse, the sweetness of his speech, and how he dominates the hearts of men with the compelling force of the message he brings? By Allah, if you expel him, I think it likely that he will descend upon some other Arab tribe and win them over with his recitals so that they will follow him and adopt his plans. He will lead them against you. They will attack, crush you, seize your power, rob you, and do with you whatever he wants." The Devil was right. He did those very things.

Tabari VI:142/Ishaq:222 "Thereupon Abu Jahl said, 'I think that we should take one young, strong, well-born man from each clan and give each a sharp sword. They should make for him and strike him with their swords as one man and kill him.'" This sounds hauntingly similar to the United States pleading with its allies and the U.N. to form a multinational collation to go after the legacy of Muhammad—Islamic terror. Not surprisingly, it worked as poorly for them as it does for us today. By the time all of the alliances had been duly formed and all factions had been sufficiently bribed, the terrorist leader had snuck away.

There must have been a Frenchman among the clans because somebody spilled the beans. I'm sorry, that was a cheap shot. The "truth" is: while he was in the neighborhood, the Devil, masquerading as a shaykh, went to Muhammad in his true form—in the likeness of an angel: "Gabriel came to the Messenger and said, 'Do not spend this night in the bed in which you usually sleep.' When the first third of the night had gone past, the young men gathered at his door and waited for him to go to sleep so that they could fall upon him. When Muhammad saw what they intended to do, he said to Ali [his adoptive son], 'Lie on my bed and wrap yourself up in my green cloak, the one I use when I go to bed. Nothing unpleasant will befall you from them.'" What a weasel. With a mob of men wielding swords standing outside his door, he told his son to wear his pajamas and lie on his bed. I'm not sure there is even a word to describe such cowardly and despicable behavior.

Tabari VI:142 "Muhammad said to Ali, 'If Abu Bakr comes to you, tell him that I have gone to Thawr and ask him to join me. Send me some food, hire a guide for me who can show me the road to Yathrib, and buy me a riding camel.' Then the Messenger went off, and Allah blinded the sight of those who were lying in wait for him so that he departed without them seeing him." In other words—he snuck out the back door. After all, if Allah had blinded the multinational coalition, there would have been no need for Ali to wear the fearless prophet's PJs.

Tabari VI:143/Ishaq:222 "Among those who had gathered against him was Abu Jahl. He said, while waiting at his door, 'Muhammad alleges that if we follow him, we shall be kings over the Arabs and Persians. Then after we die fighting for him, we shall be brought back to life and live in gardens like those in Jordan. He also claims that if we do not submit to him, we shall be slaughtered. And after his followers kill us, we shall be brought back to life and thrown into the fires of hell in which we shall burn.'" Abu Jahl encapsulated the whole of Islam and the Qur'an. It is sobering. How can something so clear escape the grasp of so many today?

Muhammad even confessed to the crime: "Allah's Messenger came out and took a handful of dust and said, 'Yes, I do say that; and you are one of them.' Allah took away their sight so that they could not see him. [Just as we have been blinded today.] And Muhammad began to sprinkle the dust [of ignorance and complacency] on their heads while reciting the following verses: 'Ya Sin. I call to witness the Qur'an. You are one sent on a straight path...The sentence is justified against most of them, for they do not believe. We will certainly put iron collars on their necks which will come up to their chins so that they will not be able to raise their heads. And We have set a barrier before them, and cover them so that they will not be able to see.'" [Qur'an 36:1] Once again, the Islamic god's timing was off but his heart was in the right place. Q36 was handed down thirty surahs and three years before the great escape.

"By the time he had finished reciting these verses, he had put dust on the heads of every one of them," and he saved his son, right? No. "...after which he went to where he wished to go."

Before we hightail it out of the quarrelsome confines of the barren and hostile Meccan valley, I'd like to examine some of the final surahs handed down during the war of words. Considering the mood, why not start with "Ta-Ha?" *020.001* "Ta-Ha. We have not sent down the Qur'an to you to be (an occasion) for your distress. Nay, it is an admonition to those who fear."

Skipping ahead to the eighth verse: *020.008* "Allah! There is no Ilah save Him. His are the most beautiful Names." Contemplating the problem of replacing Ar-Rahman with Allah, a second translation says: "To Him belong the most beautiful attributes."

020.009 "Has the story of Moses reached you? [An incredible question since it has been replayed ten times. The dark spirit seems to have contracted Alzheimer's.] Behold, he saw a fire: So he said to his folk, 'Tarry; I perceive a fire; perhaps I can bring you some burning brand or find some guidance at the fire.'"

Following this lame introduction, Allah manages to butcher Yahweh's meeting with Moses at the burning bush. *020.014* "Verily, I am Allah. No Ilah (God) may be worshiped but I. So serve you Me, and perform regular prostration prayer for My praise. Verily the Hour is coming. I am almost hiding it from Myself." Prostrating Jews, a Hebrew deity named Allah, and godly surprises—only from the mind of Muhammad.

Confused as ever, Allah has Moses play with his staff before encountering Pharaoh. *020.017* "'And what is that in your right hand, Moses?' 'It is my rod: I lean on it; I beat down fodder for my flocks; and in it I find other uses.' (He) said: 'Cast it down. Moses threw it, and behold! It was a snake, a serpent gliding." Allah loved snakes.

Yahweh, however, had a different agenda. His goal was to free His chosen people from bondage. Yet liberating Jews didn't suit Muhammad's scheme. His problem was freeing himself from the pesky Meccans. *020.024* "Go to Pharaoh, for he has indeed transgressed all bounds. (He) said, 'Lord, open for me my chest, ease my task, and loose the knot from my tongue." Muhammad, not Moses, wanted these things.

Next we find the Prophet of Doom putting his words into Moses' mouth. *020.048* "Verily it has been revealed to us that the Penalty of Doom awaits those who reject and deny." Acting more Meccan than Egyptian, Pharaoh challenged his tormentor's credibility, asking for some proof. But the surrogate Muhammad didn't have any: *020.051* "(Pharaoh) said: 'What about previous generations?' (Moses) replied: 'The knowledge is with my Lord, recorded in a Book: my Lord never errs, nor forgets. And We showed Pharaoh all Our Signs, but he did reject and refuse." In other words, Muhammad didn't have a clue.

Then missing the point entirely, Allah has Pharaoh say: *020.057* "Have you come to drive us out of our land with your magic, Moses?" *020.060* "Pharaoh devised his plot. Moses said, 'Woe to you! Forge not a lie against Allah, lest He destroy you by torment!'"

The Qur'anic dialog disintegrates into bickering reminiscent of Mecca: *020.062* "So they disputed with one with another but kept their talk secret. They said: 'These two are magicians. Their object is to drive you out of your land with their magic. They want to do away with your most cherished institutions, driving out your chiefs.'" *020.070* "So the magicians were flung down to prostration, crying: 'We believe in the Lord of Aaron and Moses.' (Pharaoh) said: 'Do you believe in Him before I give you permission? He must be your chief, who has taught you magic! Be sure I will cut off your hands and feet on opposite sides. And I will have you crucified on trunks of palm trees so shall you know for certain which of us can give the more severe and lasting punishment!'"

While every surah attests to the fact the Qur'an wasn't divinely inspired, some passages are more revealing than others. This one is a real prize. Crucifixion was invented by the Assyrians, but not until 500 B.C. Moses returned to Pharaoh in 1200 B.C. which makes their Qur'anic conversation impossible— something wholly inconsistent with a book claiming to be perfect.

But the Islamic god did more than crucify himself on the tree of ignorance. A moral God cannot compete for the prize of "most severe punisher." In Allah's final Qur'anic address he spoke these chilling words: *005.033* "The punishment for those who wage war against Allah and His Apostle and perpetrate disorders in the land is to crucify them or have a hand on one side and a foot on the other cut off."

The most important aspect of the liberation of the Jews from Egyptian bondage—Passover—was missed by Muhammad and his prop Allah. Since Islamic forgiveness was arbitrary and capricious, not as a result of sacrifice, they didn't comprehend the significance of the blood of the lamb. As a "prophet" and "god," they should have known that it was symbolic of Christ's mission. Lamb's blood was smeared on a horizontal beam, a beam that became the threshold to salvation. Yes, there was a cross in the story of Moses. But you had to be more godly than Muhammad to see it.

Twenty verses later, Allah forgets his name and Aaron thinks he is Muhammad. *020.090* "**Aaron had indeed told them earlier: 'O my people, you are being misled with this. Surely your Lord is Ar-Rahman. So follow me and obey my command."**

Jump ahead a few verses and the deities are still at it—plagiarizing the Bible and making fools of themselves. *020.096* "**Sameri [?] replied: 'I saw what they saw not: so I took a handful (of dust) from the footprint of the Messenger and threw it. Thus did my gut suggest to me.' (Moses) said: 'Get gone! Your (punishment) in this life will be such you will say, "Touch me not." Moreover you have a curse on you that you cannot escape. Now look at your ilah (god), of whom you have become devoted. We will (burn) it and scatter it in the sea! But your Ilah (God) is Allah: there is no ilah but He. Thus do We relate to you some stories of what happened before from Our own Remembrance.'"**

Ever in character, Ar-Rahman/Allah is/are about to melt down in the midst of an identity crisis. *020.100* "**Whoever turns aside from it, he shall bear a burden on the Day of Doom. They will abide in that. Grievous evil will the load on them. We shall gather the Mujrimun (disbeliever) blue or blind-eyed with thirst.... My Lord will blast them and scatter them as dust.**" *020.108* "**Their voices will be hushed before Ar-Rahman. You will not hear a sound but faint shuffling. That day no intercession will matter other than his whom Ar-Rahman grants permission.**" *020.113* "**Thus we have sent the Qur'an down as a Lecture in Arabic and explained the intimidations and different threats that they might fear Allah.**" It's another Islamic first—god in the role of bully—the great intimidator. And thus his Qur'an is not a discussion between God and man; it is a lecture.

020.114 "**High above all is Allah, the King! [Which made Muhammad King, since he was the only semblance of Allah's existence.] Do not try to anticipate the Qur'an before its revelation comes to you (Muhammad).**" That's almost funny. It's obvious he was making it up as he went along.

Because he was unable to heed the following words he had to author "scripture" to excuse his immoral and covetous behavior: *020.131* "**Do not covet what we have granted other people. Nor strain your eyes in longing for the things We have given for their enjoyment, the splendor of the life, through which We tempt them. But the provision of thy Lord is better and more enduring.**" Islam's dark spirit was about to make thievery legal and thereby fulfill his promise to enrich his profiteer. Scripture would soon serve to satiate Muhammad's sexual cravings, as well.

Before we throw up or die laughing, let's leave the "**Ta-Ha**" surah with this disclaimer from Muhammad's spirit friend: *020.133* "**They say: 'Why does he not bring us a sign or miracle from his Lord?' Has not a Clear Sign come to them in the former scripture Books of revelation?**" The Devil just said: "If you want a real God and miracles, you need to read Yahweh's scriptures, the Bible." It took us a while, but we found a nugget of truth in the Qur'an.

The 21st surah, named "**The Prophets,**" was revealed during Muhammad's waning days in Mecca. In earlier chapters we covered the heart of this surah.

On this pass we will just pick up some of the remaining highlights. It opens immersed in the never-ending feud: *021.002* "Never comes to them a renewed reminder from their Lord, but they listen to it in jest, playing in sport, their hearts toying with trifles. The wrongdoers conceal their private counsels, conferring in secret, 'He is just a man like yourselves—a mortal. Will you succumb to his witchcraft with your eyes open?' Say: 'My Lord is the One that hears and knows.' 'Nay,' they say, 'these are merely medleys of muddled dreams! He forged it! He is just a poet! Let him then bring us a miracle like the ones that were sent to (prophets) of old!'" This is the complete package. Muhammad's contemporaries ridiculed his Qur'anic revelations. They called him a counterfeiter, a witch, a muddled dreamer, and a mere poet. They said that he lacked any proof for his farfetched claims of divine selection and inspiration. And clearly, they knew him much better than we do today.

021.006 "Not one of the populations which We destroyed believed: will these believe? And We sent not before you but men, whom We revealed. Ask the keepers of the Reminder (Scriptures, the Torah and Gospel) if you do not know. Nor did We give them bodies that ate not food, nor were they immortals. Then We fulfilled to them the promise. So we saved them and whom We pleased, and We destroyed the disbelievers." The Islamic god just asked Muslims to check with the Jews if they were looking for answers.

Using a moron to argue with a village of illiterates, the ignorant deity said: *021.010* "Verily, We have sent down for you a Book in which is your reminder. Have you then no sense?" Returning to his favorite theme: "How many towns have We utterly destroyed because of their wrongs, exchanging them for other people? When they (felt) Our Torment, behold, they (began to) fly. Fly not, but return to that which emasculated you so that you may be interrogated. They cried: 'Woe to us!' Their crying did not cease till We mowed them down as ashes silent and quenched." The Islamic god (a.k.a. Satan) is bragging about how many civilizations he destroyed. Demonstrating the god-less mindset of a concentration camp warden he said he emasculated men, interrogating them, making them cry. Then he mowed them down—turning their bodies to ashes. It's little wonder Hitler based *Mein Kampf* on Islam.

The next passage takes us from demented to delusional. *021.016* "Not for sport did We create the heavens, earth and all that is between! It wasn't a plaything. If it had been Our wish to take a pastime, to make a diversion or hobby (like a wife or a son), We surely could have made it Ourselves, in Our presence, if We would do." While this is weird, the last line is revealing. Yahweh is infinite; Allah is not. The heavens and earth are *outside* his presence.

021.018 "Nay, We fling the true against the false, and it knocks out its brains. [In a way, it's true. Hurl enough of this stuff at someone and they'll lose their mind.] Behold, it is vanished! Ah! woe be to you for that thing you ascribe. To Him belong all (creatures) in the heavens and earth: Those who are near Him are not too proud to serve, nor are they weary."

Moving ahead, we return to the never-ending argument. *021.024* "Say, 'Bring your proof: this is the Reminder Book for those before me but most do not know and are adverse.'" Unable to read, neither god nor prophet knew that a recital was not a book and that their lecture was diametrically opposed to "The Book" they were referencing. As a result, they insisted the gods and books were the same. *021.025* "**Not a messenger did We send before you but We revealed to him: La ilaha illa Ana (No gods but I), so worship Me.**"

Incredibly, this assertion of a singular divinity is followed by: *021.026* "**And yet they say: 'Ar-Rahman has begotten a son.' Too exalted his He.**" Most translations, trying to hide their god's duplicity, mistranslate the passage: "**(Allah) Most Gracious has begotten offspring.**" If Muslims have to deceive us to keep their god together, their god isn't in any better shape than the fractured rock they call his home.

Schizophrenia aside, the verse was the first of many designed to demean Christ. Yahshua, Jesus' real name, claimed to be God. *021.029* "**If any of them should say, 'I am an ilah (god) besides Him,' such a one We should reward with Hell.**" If Allah is right, the Messiah is burning in hell—which is indeed where the dark spirit would like to see him. But then again, since hell is separation from God, it wouldn't be hell any more.

It's time for the Islamic god, whatever his name might be, to prove his divinity. *021.026* "**Don't the unbelievers see that the heavens and earth were joined together in one piece before we clove them asunder? We made from water every living thing. Will they not believe? And We have set on the earth mountains as stabilizers, lest the earth should convulse without them. And We have made therein broad highways for them to pass through, that they may be guided. We have made the heaven a roof well guarded. Yet they turn away from its Signs! All (the celestial bodies) swim along, on a course, floating.**" Celestial bodies swim, and mountains prevent earthquakes.

It's little wonder unbelievers were prone to ridicule. *021.036* "**When the disbelievers see you (Muhammad), they treat you with ridicule, choosing you out for mockery: 'Is this he who mentions your gods? Yet they disbelieve at the mention of Ar-Rahman.**" If Ar-Rahman were Allah, this conversation would be impossible, because Allah was a Meccan god. They believed in him, in his Ka'aba, and in his Black Stone. He was their meal ticket. However, since Ar-Rahman was a competitive idol, the god of the Yemeni Hanifs, the godly confusion was understandable. But while it made sense, it destroyed Islam's central claim, its only reason for being—"There is no ilah but Allah."

The next verse returns to pain and punishment, because there is an Ilah and he is not Allah, for Allah is Satan. *021.037* "**Man is created of haste: I will show you My Signs; then you will not ask Me to hasten them! They say: 'When will this (come to pass) if you are telling the truth?' If only the unbelievers knew (when) they will not be able to ward off the fire from their faces, nor from their backs! Nay, it will come to them all of a sudden and stupefy them, and they will be unable to repel it or avert it.**"

Punishment over, Ar-Rahman wants us to know that his prophets were all as pathetic as Muhammad. *021.041* "**Mocked were messengers before you, but their scoffers were hemmed in by what they mocked. Say: 'Who can protect you from (the wrath of) Ar-Rahman?' Yet they turn away from the mention of their Lord. Have they alihah (gods)** who can defend them against Us (from Our Torment)?" A Meccan would never have turned away from Allah. Yet everyone should run from this spirit before they become its prey.

021.044 "Do they see Us advancing, gradually reducing the land (in their control), curtailing its borders on all sides? It is they who will be overcome." Sounds like Ar-Rahman is promoting an Islamic land grab.

In the next thirty verses, Muhammad recreates Abraham in his image. Then he moves on to Isaac, Lot, Noah, David, Solomon, Job, Ishmael, Jonah, Zachariah, and John. Next we learn that Mary was a virgin whose chastity was preserved by Allah so that he could breathe his spirit into her, producing a token for mankind.

That brings us to: *021.098* "Verily you (unbelievers), and that which you worship besides Allah, are (but) faggots for the Hell Fire! And come to it you will! There, sobbing and groaning will be your lot. You will not hear (anything else)."

The surah's final verses tell us that the "good reward for those pre-ordained by Us" will be to "safely avoid the mighty terror." The Devil says, "The heavens will be rolled up like a scroll—reverted to nothing." And: "We prescribed the Book of Psalms."

The last Meccan hurrah was the 46th surah. Let's see how team Islam said goodbye to their friends. *046.001* "Ha-Mim. (Only Allah knows their meaning) The Revelation of the Book is from Allah, All-Mighty, All-Wise." Introductions made, it's time for the one hundredth rendition of: "Say: 'Do you see what you invoke besides Allah? Show me. What they have created of earth or heaven. Bring me a Book (revealed before this Scripture), or any trace of knowledge (in support of your claims), if you are truthful!" As you know, Muhammad didn't have a "Book." Under the most favorable scenario, it would be twenty years and twenty-four surahs before the first Qur'an was inscribed. And even then, it lacked "any trace of knowledge."

Next, we are asked to endure the "Day of Doom," take one hundred. *046.006* "And when men are gathered they will be hostile enemies and reject worship!" Followed by the one hundredth rerun of "Our Clear Signs." "When Our Clear Signs are rehearsed to them, the unbelievers say: 'This is evident sorcery! It is a fabrication.'"

The Meccan surahs could be reduced to a single page essay if we merely cut out the things that didn't belong: plagiarized Hanif poetry, corrupted Bible stories, Qusayy's pagan scam, the never-ending argument, threats of pain and punishment, mind-numbing repetition, and incomprehensible gibberish. By way of example: *046.008* "Or do they say, 'He has forged it?' Say: 'If I fabricated it, still you have no power to support me against Allah. He knows best of that whereof you talk (so glibly)! Sufficient is He a witness between me and you!'" Translated into English: Illiterate sorcerers sound foolish when they forge scripture.

But occasionally we find a morsel of truth: *046.009* "Say: 'I am no bringer of new-fangled doctrine among the messengers...'" Apart from his warped depictions of heaven and hell, Muhammad was a copier, not an inventor. The next line was also true: "...nor do I know what will be done with me or with you." As was this next one, but not in the way Muhammad intended: "I follow that which is inspired in me; I am but a Warner." There was no question that Muhammad was inspired, but so was every monopolist and tyrant. And the "inspired in me" line was a confession. Throughout time, the greatest cons have left clues. It's part of the game.

046.010 "Bethink you: If (this) be from Allah, and you reject it, and a witness from among the Children of Israel testifies to its similarity (of Allah's Qur'an with earlier Torah), and believed while you are arrogant and spurn it. Lo! Allah guides not wrong-doing folk.'" By saying that the Qur'an was "similar" to Jewish scripture, Allah confirmed his ignorance. As for the Islamic god bragging about finding a Jew who was willing to endorse his hellish rant, that's hilarious, as desperate as it is pathetic. If the Sira is accurate, Muhammad found one Jew among 30,000 in Medina he was able to bribe. Islam's prophet gave Abdallah bin Salam (an unlikely name for a Jew) a house he had stolen from others.

The never-ending argument marched on: *046.011* "The disbelievers say to the believers: 'Had this (Islam) been a good thing, (such men as) they would not have gone to it before us!' And seeing that they do not guide themselves thereby, they will say, 'This is an ancient falsehood, the same old lie!'" This has merit. The Meccans were saying, "If this message was so good, bad people like Muhammad and his gang wouldn't be the only ones attracted to it. If the message were worthy, they wouldn't be hypocrites, ignoring what they preached. If the religion had substance why did Muhammad capitulate to the Quraysh Bargain? Why did he indulge in the Satanic Verses? Why did he hallucinate the Night's Journey?"

046.012 "Before this was the Scripture Book of Moses [the Torah] as a guide. This Book [the Qur'an] confirms and verifies (it) in the Arabic tongue; to admonish the unjust, and as glad tidings to the good-doers." This is one of Muhammad's most suicidal lines. The conflicts between Torah and Qur'an are so great, and the differences between Yahweh and Allah are so extreme, both cannot be divine. The nucleus of the Torah is the Ten Commandments, yet Muhammad murdered every one. Logic therefore dictates: if the Torah was inspired, the Qur'an cannot be for it contradicts the Torah at every turn. If the Torah wasn't inspired, then the Qur'an cannot be because it claims it was. This is the Islamic version of Russian roulette: every chamber is loaded. There's no way to win.

046.013 "Verily those who say, 'Our Lord is Allah,' and remain firm, on them shall be no fear. Such shall abide in the Garden." Yet the previous surah said that the Lord was Ar-Rahman, and that *fearing* him was required for admittance. Now there is "no fear," and the magic words are "Our Lord is Allah." Which one, if either, is true?

It's time for a celebration. It took a while to find one, but the next verse is positive. *046.015* "We have enjoined on man kindness to his parents: With reluctance did his mother bear him, and in pain did she give him birth. The bearing of and his weaning is thirty months. At length, till he reaches full strength at the age of forty years, he says, 'My Lord! Arouse me that I may be grateful for Your favor which You favored me and my parents, that I may do deeds acceptable to You. Be good to me in the matter of my seed. I turned to You and I surrender in Islam.'" As we review the final ten years of Muhammad's life, I will let you judge whether he practiced what he preached.

Then we are told, "this is nothing but the tales of ancients." Those who are "utterly lost" are "losers" sharing the same "sentence as the previous nations of jinn and men." And: "All are assigned degrees according to their deeds." Which brings us to: 046.020 "On that Day the unbelievers will be placed before the Fire, (It will be said to them): 'You squandered your good things in this life and you sought comfort from them, but today shall you be rewarded with a penalty of humiliation.'"

To prove Allah ranked number one in peoples pummeled, the Big Guy reminds us of his dealings with the mythical Ad: 046.021 "And make mention of (Hud) one of Ad's brethren. Behold, he warned his people about the winding sand tracts. But there have been warners before him and after him. Worship none other than Allah. I fear for you the Penalty of Doom."

Transitioning from punishments to arguments: 046.022 "They [the Meccans] said: 'If you have come in order to turn us away from our gods then bring upon us the (calamity) you threaten us with, if you are telling the truth.' He [Muhammad] said: 'The knowledge (of when it will come) is only with Allah. I proclaim to you the mission on which I have been sent: But I see that you are a people in ignorance!'" The first person speaker in this "divine" revelation is Muhammad, not Allah. The passage lacks the "Say" trappings that are normally used to make Muhammad's words appear like they are coming from his god. This time he goofed.

Representing an impotent deity must have been as grating as the wind-blown sand. All Muhammad could do was threaten: 046.024 "Then, when they saw the (penalty in the shape of) a cloud advancing towards their valleys, they said, 'This will give us rain!' 'Nay, it's the (calamity) you were asking to be hastened—a blast of wind with a painful torment destroying all things by the command of its Lord. Then by the morning nothing was to be seen but (the ruins of) their houses! Thus do We reward the disbelievers.'" While the words are muddled, the message is clear: Allah was a terrorist.

Blending the never-ending argument with pain and punishment, Allah said: 046.026 "And We firmly established them in power which We have not given to you Quraysh, and We endowed them with hearing, seeing, and intellect, but they were of no profit to them when they went on rejecting the Signs and Verses of Allah." Allah just said that he made the Quraysh weak, blind, deaf, and dumb. Muhammad, incidentally, was Quraysh. "And they were completely encircled by that which they used to mock! We destroyed populations round about you. And We have shown the Signs in various ways, that they may turn."

That said, we come to the Ta'if demonic endorsement we covered earlier: 046.029 "And (remember) when We turned a company of jinn towards you (Muhammad) to listen to the Qur'an, they arrived when it was being recited, and they said, 'Keep silent.' When it was over they came back to their people warning them. 'O our people we have listened to a Book [that didn't exist] which has come down after Moses, confirming [actually corrupting] what was sent down before it showing the straight path [to hell]."

046.031 "O our people [fellow demons] listen to the summoner of Allah and believe in him (Muhammad) so that he can forgive you and save you from a painful doom." Muhammad may have been a miracle-less, prophecy-less, inspiration-less loser but that didn't stop devils from claiming that he was just like Christ. "Believe in him and he will save you," the demons proclaimed.

046.032 "He who does not respond to the summoner of Allah does not weaken the power of Allah on earth. Don't they see Allah, Who created the heavens and earth, and was never tired with their creation, is able to give life to the dead? Yea, He is able to do all things." Muhammad is saying, "My god is better than your god because my god didn't need to rest on the seventh day." Yet how can Allah be better than Yahweh if they are supposed to be the same?

"On the Day the unbelievers are placed before the Fire, they will say, 'Is this real?' 'Yes, it's by the Lord! Taste the penalty you denied!'" Predictably, the farewell address ends focused on doom: *046.035* "Have patience (Muhammad), even as the other messengers. Seek not to hasten their doom. On that day they will see the (punishment) they are promised."

This is the perfect place for a Qur'anic review. I have quoted passages from ninety of the Qur'an's 114 surahs. Half of those have been reviewed in their entirety, including every surah handed down during the first five years. The score of Meccan surahs I passed over can be summarized as follows: the Muhammadized stories of Adam, Noah, Abraham, Lot, Moses, Pharaoh, Jesus, and Mary are collectively retold nearly one hundred times. Jonah, Joshua, Jacob, Joseph, and Job are added to the mix with a surah named in Jonah's honor. Another is dedicated entirely to Joseph. The Jewish kings Saul, David, and Solomon are shown cavorting with devils in stories shamelessly plagiarized from the Talmud—Jewish myths and folklore. The crude recastings suit Muhammad's agenda, and they are as transparent as they are obnoxious. But this pales in comparison to the never-ending argument and the dreadful tales of pain and punishment. Religious thought apart from that stolen from Moses, Qusayy, and Zayd is sparse.

Now that we've closed the book on Mecca, how do you suppose our bastion of prophetic piety responded to the demise of his wife and uncle, his benefactor and his protector? Before the body of his seventy-year old wife, Khadija, was cold, the fifty-year old prophet married Aisha, a six-year old child. Pedophilia not withstanding, the aging religious leader tried polygamy next. He married, Sawda, an emigrant from Abyssinia, on his way out of town.

As for Abu Talib, his behavior towards him was equally callous. *Ishaq:191* "Abu Jahl with sundry other notables went to Abu Talib and said, 'We acknowledge your rank with us, but now that you are at the point of death we are deeply concerned. You know the trouble that exists between us and your nephew, so call him and let us make an agreement that he will leave us alone and we will leave him alone.' The Messenger arrived and Abu said, 'Nephew, these noble men have come to give you something and gain something in return.' Muhammad said, 'Can you give me words by which you can rule the Arabs and subject the Persians to you?' 'How about ten words,' Abu Jahl said [knowing the drill]. Muhammad replied, 'You must say, "There is no ilah but Allah" and "Muhammad is his Messenger."' They clapped their hands and said, 'Do you want to make all the Ilahs into one Ilah, Muhammad? That would be an extraordinary thing.'"

Muhammad's Islam was about money and power, to be sure, but what was the fate of those who helped him along the way? *Ishaq:192* **"If you say those words uncle Abu, then I shall be able to intercede for you on Resurrection Day."** Abu Talib didn't and died. His brother, Abbas, claimed that on his deathbed he moved his lips. So Abbas came running to Muhammad and said, "Nephew, my brother has spoken the words you gave him to say.' The Apostle replied, 'I did not hear them.'" *Bukhari:V5B58N222* **"A Muslim said to the Prophet, 'You were not of any help to your uncle Abu Talib even though he used to protect you.' The Prophet said, 'He is in a shallow fire, and had It not been for me, he would have been in the bottom of the Hell Fire.'"**

In contrast to the depraved behavior of the Muslim prophet, a notable pagan performed admirably. Remember uncle Lahab? Upon hearing of Khadija's and Talib's death, he went to the Ka'aba and proclaimed. **"Muhammad has suffered a great loss. Attack him no longer."**

Unimpressed, Muhammad was ready to move on. When last we saw him, he had dressed his son in his pajamas and was sprinkling magic dust on his enemies' heads. *Tabari VI:144* **"Some assert that Bakr came to Ali and asked him about the prophet. He told him that he had gone to the cave of Thawr...in the darkness of night. The Prophet heard Bakr coming and thought he was one of the polytheists. He increased his pace and his sandal strap snapped. He skinned his big toe on a stone. It bled profusely. Bakr was afraid that he would scare Muhammad so he spoke to him before they reached the cave at dawn and went inside."**

Meanwhile, back in Mecca, the locals **"scolded Ali and beat him,"** proving that Allah was powerless and Muhammad wasn't a prophet. **"They took him to the mosque and imprisoned him for a while. About this Allah revealed, 'And when the unbelievers plot against you to kill you or drive you out, they plot, but Allah plots too, and Allah is the best plotter.'"** The Arabic word for "plotter" could just as easily have been translated "schemer." The scheming prophet had found the perfect god.

The next Hadith says that Bakr and Muhammad set off together rather than separately. And while that is a contradiction, it's not the most disturbing part of the Tradition. We learn that Bakr's son, born like his sister Aisha, years after Allah anointed his messenger, was named Abd al-Rahman.

Aisha recalls the prophet's paranoia: *Ishaq:223* **"Muhammad never failed to come by our house every day at the two ends of the day. ...Once he came during the heat of the day so we knew that it was because of something special. When he came in Abu rose from his bed, and the Messenger sat down. Muhammad said, 'Send out those who are with** you.' My father said, 'Prophet, these are my daughters [one of which is now your wife]; they can do you no harm, may my father and mother be your ransom.'"

Tabari VI:147 "According to what I have been told the Messenger is said to have informed Ali that he was leaving and to have commanded him to stay behind to hand back those things which people had entrusted to his custody. Everyone in Mecca who had any possession would deposit it with Muhammad because they knew of his honesty." That squares nicely with the demon possessed, lying sorcerer theme complained about incessantly in the Qur'an.

Ishaq:223 "When the Messenger decided upon departure, he went to Bakr and the two of them left by a window in the back of Abu's house and went to a cave in Thawr, a mountain below Mecca." This time there was no plot, no multinational alliance, no swordsmen lurking outside Muhammad's house, no warning from Gabriel, no pajamas or Ali in bed, no fairy dust, no blind men, no stubbed toe, and no scripture handed down commemorating the great escape. As such, it seems that Islam is the only religion in which no one, from god to prophet, can tell the truth. And that's because Muhammad was possessed by a demonic spirit. The prophet's lord became his ambition. His paradise reflected his fantasies. His hell was a manifestation of the revenge he craved—payment for the torment he had endured as a child. This was all a nasty charade.

Somewhere in this mound of manure, in its transparent plagiarism, mindless repetition, odious schemes, obnoxious arguments, and demented threats I had hoped to find a glimmer of original inspiration so I could provide some semblance of balance. But there is none. Islam as a religion perished in the blazing heat and driving sands of Mecca only to rise from the ashes as a political doctrine in Yathrib. The ritualistic trappings that survived the desert crossing were simply used to manipulate future subjects.

It was only 250 miles, but most everything changed. Ar-Rahman became an attribute and Allah became god. And what a god he was: one who was ever ready to condone whatever suited his prophet's personal agenda—fighting, assassination, genocide, rape, incest, polygamy, lying, racism, and thievery. The war of words turned violent. The Meccans were robbed and plundered. But that was child's play compared to the fate of the Jews. They went from allies to enemies faster than you can say, "Massacre them."

While the score following twelve years of wrangling in Mecca ended Islam 50, Pagans 4,950, the game wasn't over, not by a long shot. In fact the battle was just beginning. *Tabari VI:157* Under the banner, "Institution of the Islamic Era" we find: "It is said that when Allah's Messenger came to Medina [September 622 A.D.] he ordered the establishment of a new era. They used to reckon time by the number of months after Muhammad's arrival."

As with all things Islam, the statement attributed to Muhammad wasn't true, but it demonstrated a crucial mindset. It was actually Umar, the second Caliph, who ordered the institution of the Islamic calendar. He established

Muhammad's Hirjah, or migration, to Medina as the first year the Islamic Era. From the Muslim perspective, it was no longer 622 A.D., or 622 years after the birth of Christ, but A.H. 1. They were commemorating the year Islam was born.

They knew what you now know: the religion of Islam died in Mecca. A tyrannical and violent political doctrine took its place. The first Medina surah abrogated most everything that had been proclaimed during Islam's faded "religious" period. This was a new day, Resurrection Day, the beginning of political Islam—the doctrine of submission.

Some things didn't change, however. Muhammad's character remained the same, as did his charade of using godly pronouncements to defend his claims. But his behavior did change; so did his commandments. Circumstances enabled the failed prophet to act more belligerently. While the Meccans remained enemies, the Hanifs joined an ever-growing list of condemned—one that would soon include the members of rival religions—Christians and Jews.

Most of the religious rhetoric and pagan rituals borrowed by Muhammad from Qusayy during his stay in Mecca continued unabated in Medina, although god changed his name, and the revealing spirit, Lucifer, was named Gabriel. Muhammad continued to rely on the Bible for inspiration. But rather than admonishing Meccans for the abomination of non-capitulation, scripture became Muhammad's means to authorize abominations. The Qur'an became his favorite tool. Muhammad was about to prove that when it comes to repression, nothing succeeds like the mix of religiosity, money, and weapons. The events that were about to unfold in the Arabian Desert would ultimately cost mankind more than could possibly be imagined.

Tabari VII:1 **"The time for the Friday prayer overtook Muhammad while he was in the bed of a wadi [dry riverbed]. This place was used as a mosque that day. This was the first Friday prayer which the Messenger held in Islam."** The facts have been altered to fit the agenda. On arriving in Medina, the prophet tried to hoodwink the Jews into joining his team by claiming that he observed their Sabbath, prayed toward their Temple, and was one of their Prophets. The initiation of the Friday prayer ritual into Islam came as a result of the Jews mocking Muhammad's bogus allegations. While factually inaccurate, the Hadith remains an insightful depiction of the Muslim mindset. The Islam of the prophet Muhammad, the Islam of terror, was first practiced in Medina.

The isnad upon which this oral tradition is based does not include Abu Bakr, the only man with Muhammad at the time, so it is as suspect as it is revealing. *Tabari VII:2* **"The sermon the Messenger led at the first Friday prayer in the wadi outside Medina began, 'Praise be to Allah. I praise him, and call on him for help, forgiveness and guidance. I believe in him, do not deny him and I am an enemy of whoever denies him.'"** This established the tone and purpose of Islam. Anyone who didn't submit became an enemy. And for Muslims who claim that Muhammad was perfect—Christ-like—that doesn't mesh with asking for forgiveness.

"I bear witness that there is no deity but Allah, without partner, and that Muhammad is his Messenger whom he has sent with guidance after an interval in the appearance of messengers, at a time when knowledge is scarce, men are led astray, time is cut short, the Last Hour is at hand, the End is near." It is amazing that Muhammad claimed that Allah had no partners when the overriding theme of the Medina surahs was the establishment of the partnership between Allah and his Apostle. They not only shared everything, including booty from raids, they ultimately became equals, coconspirators to be believed in, obeyed, and feared.

You may recall that Muhammad predicted that the Last Hour, the End of the World, the dreaded Day of Doom, would follow the commencement of his union with Allah by five hundred years—1110 A.D. When Bukhari collected this Hadith in 850 A.D., and when Tabari built it into his history in 900, it still loomed on the horizon, unfulfilled and thus inerrant.

There was, however, some truth in the opening stanza of Muhammad's first sermon. Knowledge was scarce—especially when it came to his prognostications and revelations. In this vacuum, his ignorance was mistaken for divine inspiration. "Whoever obeys Allah and his Prophet has been rightly guided." Two words say it all: "obey" and "and." The partnership has been formed between Allah and Muhammad and we have been put on notice that the stated purpose is to obey them. And since Allah never revealed himself apart from Muhammad, the "and" was redundant. "Whoever disobeys them has erred, been remiss, and gone far astray. I recommend to you the fear of Allah, for the best thing which a Muslim can enjoin upon a Muslim is that he should be...commanded to fear Allah." The prophet has revealed the implement of submission—fear. Remember, the Qur'an said, *087.010* "He who fears will obey." In ten sentences Muhammad encourages "fear" ten times. From Muhammad to Hitler, from Stalin to Saddam, fear is how tyrants govern.

Tabari VII:3 "Beware of what Allah has warned you concerning himself. The fear of Allah, for whoever acts according to it in fear and dread of his Lord is a trusty aid to what you desire." It was clear why Muslims should fear god. Their boss was a demonic plotter, lurking in hell, dragging men he had deceived to their doom, tormenting them in his raging fire.

"Allah says, 'The sentence that comes from me cannot be changed, and I am in no wise a tyrant unto the slaves.' The fear of Allah will ward off Allah's hatred, retribution, and wrath." In Islam, infidels have been predestined to a pronouncement of guilt, the hellish sentence comes from god, and it cannot be appealed.

This diabolical thought is followed by: "Allah has caused you to know his Book and opened his path before you in order that He may know those who speak the truth and those who lie." If the inverse of sense is nonsense, we have found it. Yahweh gave us the Bible so that we might recognize truth and detect liars. Allah gave the Qur'an so that *he* might know truth from deceit.

Muhammad, standing in the sand of a wadi, admonished the sole member of his congregation, Abu Bakr: "Be enemies of Allah's enemies and strive in Allah's Cause [Jihad] in the way to which He is entitled. He has chosen you and named you Muslims [one who submits]." The notion that god has enemies remains essential to the growth Islam. But it's the innocuous line: "He has chosen you and named you Muslims," that's far more revealing. In Judeo-Christianity men and women are given the opportunity to choose God. In Islam, the dark spirit chooses.

"There is no power but with Allah. Allah pronounces judgment upon men, and because Allah rules men they do not rule him." The sword swung by Muslims must have been a mirage or Allah himself was wielding it. The last line of Muhammad's sermon makes no sense if Allah is god. Yet it makes perfect sense if Muhammad is Allah and if he wants to rule like god.

Tabari VII:4 "The Messenger mounted his she-camel and let her reins hang loose. [Now there's a passage one better not take out of context.] The inhabitants of every settlement of the Ansar (the Muslims of Medina, called Helpers) which she went past invited him to stay with them, saying, 'Come Messenger to a settlement which has many defenders, is well-provisioned, and impregnable.'" Although not on the same scale, the Ansar, following the Quraysh lead, are tempting the prophet.

Ishaq:228 "He would say to them, 'Let go of her reins, for she is commanded.' Finally he reached the present site of his mosque, and his camel knelt down [just like Abraha's Islamic Elephant] where the door of his mosque is. At that time that place was a drying-floor for dates and belonged to two orphan boys." He's in town five minutes and he's conned a piece of land away from two orphans. The hypocrisy is so thick you can cut it with a scimitar. And did you notice that the first mosque was Muhammad's, not Allah's? (Actually, it would be more home, brothel, and politburo than mosque, anyway.)

"The Messenger ordered that a mosque should be built there. ...It is said that Muhammad bought the site of his mosque and then built upon it, but the correct version in our opinion is this: 'The site of the mosque of the Prophet belonged to two orphans under Najjar's care. It contained palm trees, cultivated land and pre-Islamic graves. The Messenger said, "Ask me a price for it," but they said, "Our only reward shall be from Allah." Muhammad then gave orders concerning the site; the palm trees were cut down, the cultivated land leveled, and the graves were dug up.'"

The preparation for the first Islamic mosque was not without rich symbolism. Islam remains unproductive, the world's most impoverished doctrine. It wantonly demolishes productive assets. It hypocritically cons the poor out of their only chance for a better life. And Islam was, and continues to be, built upon the backs of dead infidels.

Muhammad left Mecca penniless. He couldn't have bought the land any more than he could have financed the construction. Even his camel was a gift. But this was the new Muhammad. He knew what so many religious charlatans have come to know. Promise the people paradise, and they will give you the world.

13

THE PEDOPHILE PIRATE

*"When the Prophet married Aisha she was very young
and not yet ready for consummation."*

Chairman Muhammad settled into his public housing project and immediately began to act like the fool he had become. *Ishaq:235* **"In the year of the Prophet's arrival, Abu Umamah died from a rattling in the throat. The Messenger said, 'His death is an evil thing for the Jews and the Arab Hypocrites for they are sure to say, "If Muhammad were really a prophet his companion would not have died." But truly, I have no power with Allah either for myself or for my companions.'"** Truer words were never spoken.

Muhammad had no morals either. *Tabari VII:7* **"The Prophet married Aisha in Mecca three years before the Hijrah, after the death of Khadija. At the time she was six."** *Ishaq:281* **"When the Apostle came to Medina he was fifty-three."** *Tabari VII:6* **"In May, 623 A.D./A.H. 1, Allah's Messenger consummated his marriage to Aisha."** He would be dead in ten years; she hadn't lived that long. Pedophilia was, and continues to be, child abuse. The abused had come full circle; he was now an abuser.

Accusing a prophet of being a pedophile sounds outrageous. Yet the evidence is undeniable: *Tabari IX:128* **"When the Prophet married Aisha, she was very young and not yet ready for consummation."** This is how it happened: *Tabari IX:131* **"My mother came to me while I was being swung on a swing between two branches and got me down. My nurse took over and wiped my face with some water and started leading me. When I was at the door she stopped so I could catch my breath. I was brought in while Muhammad was sitting on a bed in our house. My mother made me sit on his lap. The other men and women got up and left. The Prophet consummated his marriage with me in my house when I was nine years old."** Given a choice, I believe most people would prefer to get their spiritual inspiration from someone who wasn't a sexual predator.

Muhammad struggled to justify his behavior. *Bukhari:V9B86N98* **"The Prophet said, 'A virgin should not be married till she is asked for her consent.' 'O Apostle! How will the virgin express her consent?' He said, 'By remaining silent.'"** *Bukhari:V9B87N139-40* **"Allah's Apostle told Aisha, 'You were shown to me twice in my dreams [a.k.a. sexual fantasies]. I beheld a man or angel carrying you in a silken cloth. He said to me, "She is yours, so uncover her." And behold, it was you. I would then say to myself, "If this is from Allah, then it must happen."'"** Allah not only approved pedophilia, he insisted upon it. That makes the Islamic god as perverted as his prophet.

Since fifty-three-year-old pedophiles are not prophet material, I want to give Islam every possible opportunity to clear this up. The next Hadith is from Aisha. *Tabari VII:7* "There are special features in me that have not been in any woman except for what Allah bestowed on Maryam bt. Imran [She was referring to Mary, the mother of Jesus, although she didn't know her name or her father's name, and none of the "features" applied]. I do not say this to exalt myself over any of my companions.' 'What are these?' someone asked. Aisha replied, 'The angel brought down my likeness [she was a babe]; the Messenger married me when I was seven; my marriage was consummated when I was nine [she was abused]; he married me when I was a virgin, no other man having shared me with him [she was a child]; inspiration came to him when he and I were in a single blanket [she "inspired" him]; I was one of the dearest people to him; a verse of the Qur'an was revealed concerning me when the community was almost destroyed [she inspired Allah]; and I saw Gabriel when none of his other wives saw him [she lied].'" Think about the implications of what she just said. Muhammad was "inspired"—a Qur'an surah was handed down while the prophet was having sex with a little girl. Allah didn't find pedophilia the least bit troubling.

The following confirms that the first Muslims were consumed by greed, the prophet was inspired by the body of a child, and the circumstances surrounding Qur'an revelations were as perverted as the scripture itself. *Bukhari:V5B57N119* "The people used to send presents to the Prophet on the day of Aisha's turn [to have sex with him]. Aisha said, 'His other wives gathered in the apartment of Um Salama [wife number two] and said, "Um, the people send presents on the day of Aisha's turn and we too, love the good presents just as much as she does. You should tell Allah's Apostle to order the people to send their presents to him regardless of whose turn it may be." Um repeated that to the Prophet and he turned away from her. When the Prophet returned to Um, she repeated the request again. The Prophet again turned away. After the third time, the Prophet said, "Um, don't trouble me by harming Aisha, for by Allah, the Divine Inspiration [Qur'an surahs] never came to me while I was under the blanket of any woman among you except her.""" If there have been any skeptics who have made it this far without acknowledging that the Qur'an was inspired to satisfy Muhammad's cravings, rather than to save men's souls, welcome to the realm of reason.

Earlier, I accused the victim of pedophilia of lying. I want to explain why. Her eighth divine gift was contradicted during one of the bedroom revelations. *Bukhari:V4B54N440* "The Prophet said, 'Aisha, this is Gabriel. He sends his greetings and salutations.' Aisha said, 'Salutations and greetings to him, and Allah's Blessings.' Addressing the Prophet she said, 'You see what I don't see.'"

This Hadith reveals how perverted Muhammad was and how sane other Arabs were by contrast. *Bukhari:V4B52N211* "I participated in a Ghazwa [raid] with the Prophet. I said, 'Apostle, I am a bridegroom.' He asked me whether I had married a virgin or matron. I answered, 'A matron.' He said, 'Why not a virgin who would have played with you? Then you could have played with her.' 'Apostle! My father was martyred and I have some young sisters, so I felt it not proper that I should marry a young girl as young as them.'" It's obvious who corrupted whom.

Muhammad's behavior would be considered criminal in every civilized nation on earth. No moral society has ever condoned old men having sex with young children. If you are caught, you're locked up—separated from decent people. Pedophilia is so heinous, convicted felons torment child abusers—even they can't stand to be in their presence.

Such a grotesque act disqualified Muhammad from his alleged calling. What's more, his personal perversity had a lasting legacy. Muslims follow his example. While most of what happens in the Islamic world escapes our purview, as Islam is hostile to all freedoms, including press and inquiry, we have gained glimpses in Afghanistan and Iraq. There, virginal young girls are frequently raped by Muslim men. And as you would expect in a culture influenced by Muhammad, the victims are shamed, not the perpetrators.

That said, most Muslims know that sexual perverts who prey on children are "stinking slime." It is little wonder Muhammad's contemporaries called him "mad," "insane," and "demon possessed." It is little wonder Islamic clerics try so hard to hide this stuff from the world. It is why Muhammad assassinated a score of poets, the journalists of their day, who had the courage to expose him. It is why Muslim rulers issue fatwas today.

Decadent egomaniacs like Muhammad are deeply troubled and tortured souls. Their insecurities drive unbridled lusts for power, sex, and money. Their feelings of inadequacy cause them to be shy, yet their outward manner overcompensates making them abusive and purposely deceptive. They need others to bow down to them in submission, and they require unquestioned obedience. Muhammad was a textbook case (as was Adolf Hitler, his modern twin). *Bukhari:V4B56N762* **"The Prophet was shier than a veined virgin girl."** *Bukhari:V9B89N251* **"Allah's Apostle said, 'Whoever obeys me, obeys Allah, and whoever disobeys me, disobeys Allah, and whoever obeys the ruler I appoint, obeys me, and whoever disobeys him, disobeys me.'"** Pedophilia, incest, and rape are all perverted manifestations of a thirst for power and control. Insecurity is the cause.

I apologize for dragging you through this muck. I realize the material we just covered would be illegal, even in a pornographic movie. And we are not done. We have yet to deal with the prophet's other depravities: incest and rape. But at least you now know why this control freak's paradise was a brothel filled with ever-attentive young virgins ready to be conquered.

Muhammad, like his religion, was fixated on the flesh. According to the Qur'an, bodies were reassembled so that skin could be singed in hell and teased in paradise. Man's spirit was incidental. I believe this is because the religion was made in the prophet's image. It reflected his character and desires.

To appreciate Islam's elevation of body over soul, we must look at the source of his inspiration. Muhammad was right when he described the angel that visited him as a slave. *Bukhari:V4B54N455* **"So (Allah) conveyed the Inspiration to His slave (Gabriel) and then he (Gabriel) conveyed (it to Muhammad)."** Angels, fallen or heavenly, demonic or godly, have no choice. To borrow another line from Islam, "They must submit and obey." Islam's dark spirit knew all about angelic submission, because he once was one: *007.011* **"It is We who created you and gave you shape; then We ordered the angels to fall and prostrate themselves to Adam."**

The same passage goes on to correctly implicate Satan and suggest angels are eternal. *007.019* **"Satan began to whisper suggestions to them, bringing openly before their minds all that was hidden from them. He said: 'Your Lord only forbid you this tree, lest you should become angels, immortal, living forever.'"**

Satan, like all angels, is a four-dimensional construct. That is to say, he can maneuver in time—the fourth dimension. While this may sound complex, we have known since Einstein that space has a fourth axis, an infinite aspect that we cannot yet navigate. In this regard, angels are superior to men as we are trapped in three-dimensional bodies—stuck in time. Yahweh is not, which is why his name means "I Am," or "I Exist." He is immortal and timeless; his infinity exists in the fourth dimension. This explains how Yahweh predicts the future. He knows the future not because he has ordained it but because he has already been there and witnessed the culmination of our choices.

Now, put yourself in Lucifer's wings for a moment. He knows that his spirit is inferior to ours for two reasons. We are made spiritually in God's image. And we have choice. With choice we have the capacity to be creative and to love. This is why God created us. These attributes remain his and our most powerful qualities. So Lucifer doesn't want to compete with us spiritually. He can't win.

But when he competes bodily, he can't lose. We are three dimensional—he is four. The difference is infinite, just as it is between two- and three-axis realms. The comparison is like a cartoon rendering of Mickey Mouse competing with Walt Disney—or more accurately, with Walt's secretary. This is why Islam is focused on the body. It's why the covetous Muhammad was the perfect Satanic prophet.

The arrival of the first child born to Muslims after the Hijrah was celebrated: *Tabari VII:9* **"The Messenger's Companions cried, 'Allahu Akbar' [Allah is Greater than Yahweh, was the implication], when she was born. This was because a story was current among the Muslims that the Jews claimed that they had bewitched them so that no children would be born. The Muslims praised Allah that he had falsified the Jews' claim."** They were saying that their "god's" magic spells were more powerful then the Jewish God's. Even if they were right, it made Islam wrong.

The next seven section heads in Tabari's *The Foundation of the Community,* begin with the word **"Expedition."** The Arabic word is **"Maghazi,"** which Ishaq translates **"Raid."** It actually means invasion. It's synonymous with **"Jihad,"** defined by Bukhari as **"Holy fighting in Allah's Cause."** A more complete explanation is provided in the *Book of Jihad*, on page 580 of Maktba Dar-us-Salam's publication of *Sahih Al-Bukhari*: **"Jihad is holy fighting in Allah's Cause with full force of weaponry. It is given the utmost importance in Islam and is one of its Pillars. By Jihad Islam is established, Allah is made superior and He becomes the only God who may be worshiped. By Jihad Islam is propagated and made superior. By abandoning Jihad (may Allah protect us from that) Islam is destroyed and Muslims fall into an inferior position. Their honor is lost, their lands are stolen, and Muslim rule and authority vanish. Jihad is an obligatory duty in Islam on every Muslim. He who tries to escape this duty dies as a hypocrite."**

Memorize this paragraph. Shout it out to all who will listen. Every word was derived from the Qur'an. Every word was lived by Muhammad. It accurately represents fundamental Islam, so much so, each of the 150 Hadiths that follow this definition of Jihad speak of fighting; *none* suggest a spiritual struggle. Among them, Muhammad says that the most important deed is Jihad, fighting in Allah's Cause. (Bukhari:V4B52N44) And the Qur'an agrees, saying peaceful Muslims are hypocrites, destined for hell. They are **"the worst of creatures," "the most vile of animals."** (Qur'an surahs 3 and 33.)

So that there is no question regarding the appropriateness of using Bukhari as a source, here's what the Islamic scholars had to say in the preface: **"Al-Bukhari's Hadith is the most authentic and true book of the Prophet."** The translators said, **"I am perfectly sure that the translation, with Allah's help and after all the great efforts exerted in its production, has neared perfection."** The imams from the cradle of Islam, the Islamic University of Medina in Saudi Arabia, said, **"It has been unanimously agreed that Imam Bukhari's work is the most authentic of all the other sources in Hadith literature put together. It is second only to the Qur'an."**

That leaves you and me at the crossroads of destiny. If we don't deal with the awesome gravity of Islamic Jihad, our future will vanish before our eyes. If we wish to avoid the abyss of world war we must expose the doctrine committed to world conquest. We must liberate Muslims from Islam.

"The Expedition Led by Hamzah" was the first Maghazi. Hamzah, a huntsman in Mecca, was now a **"Mujahid"** (plural—Mujahidun), **"a Muslim warrior in Jihad."** *Tabari VII:10* **"In Ramadhan, seven months after the Hijrah, Muhammad entrusted a white war banner to Hamzah with the command of thirty Emigrants. Their aim was to intercept a Quraysh caravan."** Seven months after fleeing Mecca in shame, the pedophile prophet has become a pirate and terrorist.

So that there is no misunderstanding, let's define these less than admirable characterizations. Pirate: a renegade who, along with others under his command, uses force of arms to steal the property of others. Terrorist: a person who violently attacks civilians, destroys their property, and disrupts their economy as a means to achieve a political objective.

The flag Muhammad handed to Hamzah was a war banner. It was one of the many symbols the prophet borrowed from his patriarch Qusayy. Hamzah was a warrior. He was given the command of thirty men. Their aim was to intercept a caravan, a civilian economic enterprise owned by the people Muhammad had promised to slaughter because they had teased him. Although we are told: "**they separated without a battle,**" the intent was piracy and terror. Their failure didn't change what they had become—what Islam had done to them. At this point in the profiteer's career, there were simply more good guys than there were bad guys, and he was as inept a pirate as he was a prophet.

Turning to Muhammad's biographer, we learn more about the mindset of the first Muslims. *Ishaq:283* "**Hamza's expedition to the seashore comprised thirty riders, all Emigrants from Mecca. He met Abu Jahl who had 300 riders. Amr, intervened for he was at peace with both sides. Hazma [Muhammad's raider] said, so they allege: 'Wonder at good sense and at folly, at a lack of sound counsel and at sensible advice. Their people and property are not yet violated as we haven't attacked. We called them to Islam [surrender] but they treat it as a joke. They laughed until I threatened them. At the Apostle's command, I was the first to march beneath his flag, a victorious banner from Allah. Even as they sullied forth burning with rage, Allah frustrated their schemes.'**"

Abu Jahl, a pagan businessman, responded to the Muslim militants: *Ishaq:284* "**I am amazed at the causes of anger and folly and at those who stir up strife by lying controversy. They abandon our fathers' ways. They come with lies to twist our minds. But their lies cannot confound the wise. If you give up your raids we will take you back for you are our cousins, our kin. But they chose to believe Muhammad and became obstinately contentious. All their deeds became evil.**" As always, the Meccans understood Islam.

Ibn Ishaq believed: *Ishaq:281* "**The Raid on Waddan was the first Maghazi.**" He said, "**The Expedition of Ubayda Harith was second. The Apostle sent Ubayda out on a raid with sixty or eighty riders from the Emigrants, there not being a single Ansar among them. He encountered a large number of Quraysh in the Hijaz. Abu Bakr composed a poem about the raid.**" Some of the most memorable lines include: "**When we called them to the truth they turned their backs and howled like bitches. Allah's punishment on them will not tarry. I swear by the Lord of Camels [Allah?] that I am no perjurer. A valiant band will descend upon the Quraysh which will leave women husbandless. It will leave men dead, with vultures wheeling round. It will not spare the infidels.**" To which a pagan named "Slave-to-Allah" replied: *Ishaq:282* "**Does your eye weep unceasingly over the ruins of a dwelling [Allah's House] that the shifting sands obscure? Is your army and declaration of war firm enough that we should abandon images venerated in Mecca, passed on to heirs by a noble ancestor [Qusayy]? Are your steeds panting at the fray, are your swords polished white, are they in the hands of warriors, dangerous as lions, or are you conceited? Are you here to quench your thirst for vengeance? Nay, they withdraw in great fear and awe.**"

Of the raid, the historian reports: *Tabari VII:10* "**Eight months after the Hijrah, Allah's Messenger entrusted a white war banner to Ubaydah and ordered him to march to Batn Rabigh. He reached the pass of Marah, near Juhfah, at the head of sixty Emigrants without a single Ansari (Medina Muslim) among them. They met the polytheists at a watering place** called Ahya. They shot arrows at one another but there was no hand-to-hand fighting."

The prophet is now a repeat offender. Eight months into the Islamic Era he has ordered multiple attacks. Muslim apologists profess that Muhammad was forced into defending Islam and that he was neither aggressor, pirate, nor terrorist. But that position is indefensible. Nothing is known about the Muhammad of history—no independent records exist. All that is known about him is contained in these Hadiths. If they say he attacked a civilian caravan and then ordered men to march and fight in another town, he did. Therefore, he was the aggressor. There isn't even a hint of self-defense in these Traditions, nor do they try to explain away the prophet's motives. They were after money, not armies—booty, not converts.

You may be wondering why none of the Ansari joined the Muslim Emigrants from Mecca on either raid. I believe that the answer is that they hadn't been Muslims long enough and therefore still knew right from wrong. Islam had already corrupted the Meccan Muslims to the point that they thought piracy and terror were justifiable, even admirable. Kind of reminds us of the modern day Islamic terrorists.

Ishaq:285 **"Then the Apostle went raiding in the month of Rabi u'l-Awwal making for the Quraysh. He returned to Medina without fighting. Then he raided the Quraysh by way of Dinar."** *Tabari VII:11* **"In this year the Messenger entrusted to Sa'd a white war banner for the expedition to Kharrar. Sa'd said, 'I set out on foot at the head of twenty men. We used to lie hidden by day and march at night, until we reached Kharrar on the fifth morning. The caravan had arrived in town a day before. There were sixty men with it. Those who were with Sa'd were all Emigrants.'"** Muhammad is now a serial offender, a committed pirate and terrorist, albeit a failed one.

Tabari VII:11 **"The Messenger of Allah went out on a raid as far as Waddan, searching for Quraysh. In the course of which, the Banu Damrah made a treaty of friendship with him. Then Muhammad returned to Medina without any fighting and remained there for the rest of the month."** This time Muhammad took command himself with the express intent of finding the Quraysh and robbing them. And while it is noble that he inked a treaty of friendship, even this was the wrong thing for a prophet to do. Treaties are political, not religious. Muhammad was now considered a "fellow chief" commanding a band of armed men—hardly prophet-like. Besides, the Qur'an would ultimately say that treaties with unbelieving infidels weren't binding on Muslims. This alliance was with pagans.

Tabari VII:12 **"During this stay he sent Ubaydah at the head of sixty horsemen from the Emigrants without a single Ansari among them. He got as far as a watering place in Hijaz [Central Arabia], below the pass of Marah. There he met a greater band of Quraysh, but there was no fighting except Sa'd shot an arrow. Then the two groups separated from one another, the Muslims leaving a rearguard."** Islamic raiders marched with the intent to plunder and kill. The only thing that stopped them from achieving their objective was the sight of a superior force. As we seek to defend ourselves today, we would do well to keep this in mind.

Tabari VII:13 "Muhammad led an expedition in [the month of] Rabi al-Akhir in search of Quraysh. He went as far as Buwat in the region of Radwa and then returned without any fighting. Then he led another expedition in search of the Meccans. He took the mountain track and crossed the desert, halting beneath a tree in Batha. He prayed there. [What on earth was he praying for? "O God, please help me rob and kill people. Thank you. Amen."] After a few days the Prophet went out in pursuit of the Kutz."

The Islamic Era was but a year old, yet Muslims were fully committed to the path of piracy and terror. Forget for a moment that this was supposed to be a religion. There was nothing noble, moral, or redeeming about raiding parties seeking to plunder civilian caravans or expeditions marching off to terrorize unsuspecting villagers. Just as there was no redeeming surah in Mecca, there is no virtuous behavior in Medina. I haven't cherry-picked the ugly parts out of a sea of pious religious activities. I have reported everything.

The second year of the Islamic Era began as the first one ended. The opening headline reads: *Tabari VII:15* "Expeditions Led by Allah's Messenger," This was followed by: "In this year, according to all Sira writers, the Messenger personally led the Ghazwa of Alwa. [A Ghazwa is an Islamic Invasion in Allah's Cause consisting of a large army unit led by the Prophet himself.] He left Sa'd in command of Medina. On this raid his banner was carried by Hamzah. He stayed out for fifteen days and then returned to Medina." This was the eighth failed terrorist attack in as many months.

There are two interesting subtleties here. First, Sa'd, Chairman Muhammad's most fierce warrior, was left in "command" of Medina. The "prophet" had become a warlord. And considering the nature of the Islamic world today, that made him a role model. Second, the "religion" of Islam actually coined a word to define an armed raid personally led by its prophet. There is something very perverse about that.

"According to Waqidi, the Messenger went on a Ghazwa at the head of two hundred of his companions in October, 623 and reached Buwat. His intention was to intercept a Quraysh caravan with a hundred men and twenty-five hundred camels." This expedition was neither a military operation nor was it defensive. And it most assuredly wasn't religious. It was an act of terrorism against a civilian economic activity. The pirate was after booty.

The Hadith reports: "In this year Muhammad sent forth the Emigrants to intercept a Quraysh caravan en route to Syria. His war banner was carried by Hamzah." It also failed. The score was Muslim Militants 0, Infidels 10. Unfortunately, Islam would get better at this game than they ever got at religion.

Ishaq:286/Tabari VII:16 "Ali and I were with the Messenger on the Ghazwa of Ushayrah. We halted on one occasion and saw some men of the Banu Mudlij working in one of their date

groves. I said, 'Why don't we go and see how they work?' So we went and watched them for a while; then we felt drowsy and went to sleep on dusty ground under the trees. Muhammad woke us, arriving as we were covered in dust. He stirred Ali with his foot and said, 'Arise, O dusty one! Shall I tell you who was the most wretched man? Ahmar of Thamud for he slaughtered the she-camel and he shall strike you here.' Muhammad put his hand to the side of Ali's head, until it was soaked from it. Then he grabbed his beard."
The Qur'an claims that the Thamudic nation was destroyed by Allah because someone hamstrung a camel. While it's odd he liked camels more than men, there was a bigger perversion still in this tale of misplaced ambition. The Muslims were so unfamiliar with honest labor they went to watch someone work. And they were so lazy, they fell asleep doing it.

Ultimately, that was why the pirates were there in the first place. When the bedraggled Muslim refugees migrated north they became dependent upon handouts. They were physically able to work, since they went off on raids. And the oasis town of Yathrib was a bustling agricultural and commercial center, so there was plenty of work being done. All of which leads to a conclusion: something in Islam made the Muslims unwilling to work. And it affects them to this day. Islamic states have the lowest per capita productivity in the world. Islam politically and economically is as faulty as the religion is false. Lose, lose.

Ishaq:286 "**Meanwhile the Apostle sent Sa'd on the raid of Abu Waqqas. The Prophet only stayed a few nights in Medina before raiding Ushayra and then Kurz.**"

Let's review Bukhari's *Book of Maghazi* to get a better feel for what's happening: *Bukhari:V5B57N1* "**Allah's Apostle said, 'A time will come when a group of Muslims will wage a Holy War and it will be said, "Is there anyone who has accompanied Allah's Apostle?" They will say, "Yes." And so victory will be bestowed on them.'**" *Bukhari:V5B57N51* "**The Apostle said, 'Tomorrow I will give the flag to a man whose leadership Allah will use to grant a Muslim victory.**" *Bukhari:V5B59N569* "**I fought in seven Ghazwat battles along with the Prophet and fought in nine Maghazi raids in armies dispatched by the Prophet.**"

There was nothing "spiritual" about fundamental Islam: *Bukhari:V5B57N74* "**I heard Sa'd saying, 'I was the first Arab to shoot an arrow in Allah's Cause.'**" *Bukhari: V5B59N288* "**I witnessed a scene that was dearer to me than anything I had ever seen. Aswad came to the Prophet while Muhammad was urging the Muslims to fight the pagans. He said, 'We shall fight on your right and on your left and in front of you and behind you.' I saw the face of the Prophet getting bright with happiness, for that saying delighted him.**" *Bukhari:V5B59N290* "**The believers who did not join the Ghazwa and those who fought are not equal in reward.**" *Bukhari:V5B59N320* "**Allah's Apostle said, 'When your enemy comes near shoot at them but use your arrows sparingly (so that they are not wasted).'**" *Bukhari:V5B59N401* "**Allah's Wrath became severe on anyone the Prophet killed in Allah's Cause.**"

While the terrorist raids were hardly religious, religious symbolism and rewards were used to solicit and inspire warriors: *Bukhari:V5B59N456* "**Muhammad led the Fear Prayer with one batch of his army while the other (batch) faced the enemy.**" *Bukhari: V5B59N330* "**The Prophet said, 'This is Gabriel holding the head of his horse, equipped with** arms for the battle.'" *Bukhari:V5B59N440* "Allah's Apostle used to say, 'None has the right to be worshipped except Allah Alone because He honored His Warriors and made His Messenger victorious. He (Alone) defeated the Infidel clans; so there is nothing left.'" *Bukhari: V5B59N377* "A man came to the Prophet and said, 'Can you tell me where I will go if I get martyred?' The Prophet replied, 'To Paradise.' The man fought till he was martyred."

There are no such bargains in the Gospels. Killing is not an express ticket to heaven. Yahshua never asked his followers to "slay" anyone. Christ mentions killing only once. He tells a parable about a ruler in the final days of the Tribulation to encourage Christians to be productive, not destructive.

In the Torah, Yahweh asked the Israelites to kill once, as well. He told Moses and Joshua to remove those poisoned by the Canaanite religion from the land. They were like Muhammad's Muslims: immoral, terrorizing, plundering, enslaving, and murdering. Their religion was as corrupt as Islam—equally demonic. Yahweh recognized it was more compassionate to exterminate some Canaanites than it was to allow them to seduce millions. He made the right call, but the Jews failed to execute his order.

Let's consider Yahweh's moral justification for fighting. Imagine that you were God and knew the thousand people most responsible for the September 11th suicide bombings. You know that they have been poisoned to believe that mass murder is a service to you. Left alone, they will corrupt and murder thousands. Would you kill them before they perpetrated these crimes or would you let them go ahead?

Now move back in time to the dawn of the 20th century. As usual, the world is full of bad people and bad ideas, but two doctrines are especially lethal—Communism and Nazism. Because you've read their manifestoes and have maneuvered in time, you know what is going to happen. Within their first three decades, these dictatorial, intolerant, and violent dogmas will lead directly to the annihilation of over fifty million people and to the indoctrination of a billion more. Given the opportunity, would you exterminate a few thousand aspiring Communists and Nazis to save the lives of the fifty million their regimes butchered? Would you do it to save a billion people from being forced into submission—forced to live in civil, religious, intellectual, and economic poverty? Would you do it to keep them from growing strong enough to kill you, your neighbors, and your children? What is the most moral, just, and compassionate choice?

Perhaps now you know why Yahweh ordered his people to slay the practitioners of a doctrine virtually identical to Islam. But don't get carried away. His last command to kill was 3,200 years ago. His command wasn't open ended. It was directed at a specific group of people, in a specific time and specific place. Apart from self defense, that's the end of the story.

So, when you hear Muslims defend their violent doctrine, saying that the Bible is equally warlike, you'll know the truth. Yahweh asked once. He identified the reason and the people. The order wasn't open ended, either. And, even if it were, there are no Canaanites to kick around.

What's more, the Jews were expressly forbidden from taking a spoil. When the walls of Jericho fell, its storehouses remained filled. Children were not sent off into slavery; women were not raped as if they were booty. The Judeo-Christian scriptures have to be corrupted to inspire such horrible acts.

Allah, by contrast, gave Muslims hundreds of commands to kill. His orders were open ended—surviving throughout time. And his intended victims were many: those who worshiped the one true God, many gods, or no gods at all. Allah especially hated Christians and Jews, ordering Muslims to fight them until they were "wiped out to the last." This is fundamental Islam—the very core of Muhammad's message.

That said, there is one Bible verse that appears to be both open ended and to encourage violence. As such, Psalm 149 became the rallying cry for the Crusades. In actuality it is prophetic, speaking of what's called the "Tribulation," and of the return of the Messiah. In the fashion of Hebrew poetry, the Psalm presents a series of nine couplets—pairs of phrases that say the same thing in different words.

Let's review them. The first couplet speaks prophetically of the new millennium, of the church and saints: "Praise Yahweh. Sing unto Yahweh a fresh song, and sing his praise in the congregation of saints." The second celebrates the end of the Tribulation, and the Messiah's return: "Let Israel rejoice in Yahweh who made them, let the Children of Israel be joyful in their King." Then, "Let them praise Yahweh's character in dance, let them sing praises unto Yahweh with the tambourine and harp." Speaking of the Messiah's gift of salvation, the next reports: "For Yahweh is pleased with his people; He will glorify the meek with salvation." The fifth couplet reveals: "Let the saints be joyful in this glorious honor; let them shout from their resting place." At Christ's return the souls of the saints will be raised from their graves.

A Catholic Pope misinterpreted the sixth verse to advance his personal agenda: "Let the exaltation of the Almighty be in their mouths, and a two-edged sword be in their open hand." A two-edged sword is the Bible's metaphor for divine judgment or rendering a godly verdict. That's why it's in an "open hand," which could not wield an instrument of violence. Its pair in the couplet references the exalted words of the Almighty—suggesting an oral verdict, not a slashing weapon. The seventh pair proclaims: "To advance vengeance upon the nations and punishment upon the people." This speaks to the final judgment of Yahweh on those who attack Israel during World War III, midway through the Tribulation. Interesting, in that the predicted Magog war against Israel is perpetrated entirely by Islamic states.

This is followed by: "To yoke kings together, bringing them forth, and those who are severe will be tied with iron twine." In other words, following

God's verdict, the purveyors of false doctrines, those who are severe, will be restrained. The final couplet reveals: "To advance the verdict upon them, prescribed by the splendor of his saints. Praise Yahweh." The entire Psalm is prophetic, speaking of the final judgment of nations following the Messiah's return in power and glory. There is no command to fight or kill anyone.

Since Islam's principle defense is to claim that Christians have performed no better, especially during the Crusades, I want to bring your attention to two incredibly important historical facts. First, Pope Benedict IV: he reigned in 1033 A.D., precisely 1,000 years after Christ's resurrection. Benedict became like Muhammad, demonic, fixated on the occult, demented, delirious, and lascivious. The Church became corrupt, focused on rituals, suppression, and money. With power-hungry men at the helm, it splintered, ultimately causing cleric and king to send men off on fool-hearty crusades.

The second historical fact is that the Crusaders *weren't* Christians. They couldn't have been. Four centuries had passed since the last sermon was given in a language common to the people of Europe. The first Bible to be printed in the vulgar tongue, John Wycliffe's, wouldn't find quill for another four centuries. To be a "Christian" one must know Christ. He could not have been known to the men who fought. They carried his symbols, nothing more.

Returning to 7th-century Medina, Muhammad was back on the warpath: *Tabari VII:18/Ishaq:287* "The Messenger sent Abd Allah out with a detachment of eight men of the Emigrants without any Ansari, or Helpers, among them. He wrote a letter, but ordered him not to look at it until he had traveled for two days. Then he was to carry out what he was commanded to do. When Abd Allah opened the letter it said, 'March until you reach Nakhlah, between Mecca and Ta'if. Lie in wait for the Quraysh there, and find out for us what they are doing.'" The letter suggests there was treachery among the treacherous. One or more Muslims was spilling the beans and tipping off the Quraysh before the militants could rob them.

"Having read the letter, Abd Allah said, 'To hear is to obey.' He told his companions, 'The Prophet has commanded me to go to Nakhlah and lie in wait for the Quraysh.'" To "lie in wait" was an order to kill. I present Allah as an authority. Qur'an 9:5: "When the prohibited months for fighting are over, slay the pagans wherever you find them. Take them captive and besiege them. Lie in wait for them in every likely place."

Abd Allah tells his fellow militants: "'The Prophet has forbidden me to compel you, so whoever desires martyrdom, let him come with me. If not, retreat. I am going to carry out the Prophet's orders.'" Martyrdom—the word that manufacturers terrorists faster than the world can rid itself of them, was spoken for the first time. No word has ever held such dire consequences for abused or abuser.

The Islamic concept of martyrdom was twisted. Muhammad took a good word and made it bad. Prior to Islam, a martyr willingly sacrificed his or her life to save others, not kill them. A Christian martyr sought nothing. Their lives served as a living witness so that others might know the value of their faith. They died with scripture in their hands, not swords. The Greek word *martus*, from which martyr was derived, means "witness." Yet at Muhammad's direction it came to mean "murderer." Muslims obtained martyrdom by terrorizing others—murdering millions. Muslim martyrs are mercenaries, wielding swords in pursuit of plunder.

I believe that this is Lucifer's signature once again. He is the world's most acclaimed counterfeiter. Martyrdom is good, but not as a pirate. Money is good, but not when it is plundered. Sex is good, but not as an act of pedophilia. Prophets are good, but not when they are motivated by profit. Scripture is good, but not when it's perverted. Prayer is good, but not when one prostrates oneself to the Devil. Islam *is* true—truly Satanic.

Ishaq:287 **"His companions went with him; not one of them stayed behind."** A second Hadith says: **"Whoever desires death, let him go on and make his will; I am making my will and acting on the orders of the Messenger of Allah."** *Tabari VII:18* **"They made their way through the Hijaz until Sa'd and Utbah lost a camel which they were taking turns riding. They stayed behind to look for it. [In other words, they chickened out.] The rest went on until they reached Nakhlah. A Meccan caravan went past them carrying raisins, leather, and other merchandise, which the Quraysh traded. When they saw the Muslims they were afraid of them. Then Ukkashah [one of the Muslims] came into view; they saw that he had shaved his head, and they felt safer. The Quraysh said, 'They are on their way to the umrah (lesser pilgrimage); there is nothing to fear.'"** The pagan umrah had become part of Islam. However, shaving one's head was used to venerate Al-Lat, not Allah. So the Quraysh were as confused as I am. Why would a Muslim militant venerate a pagan idol while perusing plunder in Allah's name?

Ishaq:287 **"The Muslim raiders consulted one another concerning them, this being the last day of Rajab."** Rajab, like Ramadhan, was a holy month on the pagan calendar. Fighting, looting, and general mayhem were prohibited. It is troubling that the observance of a pagan rite was a limiting factor, while thievery and murder were not. This says a great deal about the nature of Islam. **"One of the Muslims said, 'By Allah, if we leave these people alone tonight, they will get into the Haram (the sacred territory of Mecca) and they will be safely out of our reach. If we kill them we will have killed in the sacred month.'"** The debate was between paganism and criminal behavior. Islam had nothing to do with Muhammad's mission.

Tabari VII:19 **"They hesitated and were afraid to advance on them, but then they plucked up courage and agreed to kill as many as they could and to seize what they had with them."** This isn't the least bit ambiguous. The first Muslims—Muhammad's disciples—were about to conduct a terrorist raid with the intent to loot and kill.

"Waqid ibn Abd Allah shot an arrow at Amr and killed him. Uthman ibn Abd Allah and al-Hakam surrendered, but Nawfal ibn Abd Allah escaped and eluded them. Then Abd

Allah and his companions took the caravan and the captives back to Allah's Apostle in Medina." Islam had drawn first blood. The score was now Islam 1, Infidels 11. The Hadith says: **"This was the first booty taken by the Companions of Muhammad."**

Reading the passage carefully, we find there were four Slaves-to-Allah in the raid—two were Muslims and two were infidels. It is yet another drop in an ocean of evidence that Allah was a pagan deity, a common rock idol.

Abd Allah said of his adventure: *Ishaq:289* **"Our lances drank of Amr's blood and lit the flame of war."** *Tabari VII:20/Ishaq:287* **"Abd Allah told his Companions, 'A fifth of the booty we have taken belongs to the Apostle.' This was before Allah made surrendering a fifth of the booty taken a requirement."** Qur'an 8:41, a verse from a surah dedicated to booty, says that Muhammad was entitled to one fifth of whatever Muslims looted. The 69th verse proclaims: **"The use of such spoils is lawful and good."** The fact Abd Allah announced this partitioning of booty years in advance of the Qur'anic endorsement suggests that the idea was Muhammad's, and that his god simply legitimized his claim. Money is a powerful motivator.

"He set aside a fifth of the booty for Allah's Messenger and divided the rest between his Companions." If there was any doubt as to why the first Muslim militants were off on their twelfth raid in twelve months, it should have been eliminated with this line. Their mission had nothing to do with religion. Nor did Muhammad's. It had always been about money. Religion was simply a tool, a veil, a distraction—a means to legitimize murder and mayhem. Muhammad's raiders weren't religious zealots; they were mercenaries at best, pirates at worst. And lest we forget, they were now murderers, kidnappers, and thieves.

When the raiders returned to Yathrib, they were blindsided by a raging controversy. Both the Emigrants and Helpers were horrified—deeply troubled by the breach of the holy month protections. Even the most despicable bandits refrained from thievery during Rejab. And, I suppose, they may have been bothered by the fact they had murdered, robbed, and kidnapped their kin.

This societal disdain put the prophet in a quandary. Muhammad was broke, and poor dictators don't last long. But if he accepted the booty, he would trash his already shaky religious credentials. He was on his heels and teetering from the Quraysh Bargain, the Satanic Verses, the Night's Journey, and the Migration of Shame. Stooping to the depths of a scoundrel, a murderous pirate, and a two-bit terrorist so desperate for money he would steal during Rajab, was one blow too many. So what to do?

His first ploy was to betray his troops, something Muslim suicide bombers should keep in mind the next time they contemplate murdering their way to paradise. *Tabari VII:20* **"When they reached the Prophet he said, 'I did not order you to fight in the sacred month. He impounded the caravan and the two captives and refused to take anything from them."** The prospect of **"martyrdom"** and **"lying in wait"** confirms that Muhammad *had* sent his Muslim raiders out to fight, as did the requirement of making out their wills. The **"division of spoils"** agreement indicates he had given his authorization for them to steal. The lying prophet was buying time, which is why he didn't send the booty back. He was trying to find a way to keep the money and maintain his dwindling prestige.

"When Allah's Messenger said this they were aghast and thought that they were doomed. The Muslims rebuked them severely for what they had done. They said, 'You have done what you were not commanded to do, and have fought in the sacred month.'" To salvage his reputation, and thus cling to his position of power, Muhammad made his men scapegoats. His letter confirmed his complicity, even that he had sent them out in Rajab, the idolaters' sacred month. The act made him an accessory to murder and a thief; the denial made him a pagan and a liar—something far more lethal to someone pretending to be a prophet.

Tabari VII:20/Ishaq:288 "The Quraysh said, 'Muhammad and his Companions have violated the sacred month, shed blood, seized property, and taken men captive.' The polytheists spread lying slander concerning him, saying, 'Muhammad claims that he is following obedience to Allah, yet he is the first to violate the holy month and to kill our companion in Rajab.'" The pagans knew that breaking treaties, murder, kidnapping, and thievery were wrong. It's a shame that Islam's lone prophet didn't.

I find it especially revealing that when the Meccans told the truth about what had just happened, they were called "lying slanderers." This has devastating implications for the totality of the Qur'an. Its second most repetitive theme is the never-ending argument. The Meccans said that Muhammad was a demon-possessed liar, not a prophet. They said that he had forged the Qur'an to serve his personal ambitions. They appeared to be right and yet Islam's dark spirit called them "lying slanderers." In this circumstance, the Meccans were absolutely right and yet Muhammad deployed the same strategy. At the very least, this suggests that the Hadith and Qur'an had the same speechwriter, the same agenda, and the same wanton disregard for truth. It also tells us that those who knew this "prophet" far better than we could possibly know him today, saw him as a terrorist raider, an immoral man, and as a liar.

Tabari VII:21 "The Muslims who were still in Mecca refuted this." It was embarrassing. It meant that they had placed their trust in a man unworthy of it. *Ishaq:288* "The Jews, seeing in this an omen unfavorable to Muhammad, said, 'Muslims killing Meccans means war is kindled.' There was much talk of this. However, Allah turned it to their disadvantage. When the Muslims repeated what the Jews had said, Allah revealed a Qur'an to His Messenger: 'They question you with regard to warfare in the sacred month. Say, "War therein is serious, but keeping people from Islam, from the sacred mosque, and driving them out is more serious with Allah."' [Qur'an 2:217] The Muslims now knew that seduction was worse than killing." Considering the facts, this was an inane excuse for violating treaties, kidnapping, theft, and murder. The Meccan merchants were minding their business. They weren't seducing anyone. And once again, the prophet behaves badly and it's the pagans' fault, not his own.

Ishaq:288 "When the Qur'an passage concerning this matter was revealed, and Allah relieved Muslims from their fear and anxiety, Muhammad took possession of the caravan and prisoners. The Quraysh sent him a ransom, but the Prophet said, 'We will not release them to you on payment of ransom until our companions (Sa'd and Utbah) get back, for we are afraid you may harm them. If you kill them, we will kill your friends.' They came back, however, and the Prophet released the prisoners on payment of ransom. When the Qur'an authorization came down to Muhammad, Abd Allah and his Companions were relieved and they became anxious for an additional reward. They said, 'Will this raid be counted as part of the reward promised to Muslim combatants?' So Allah sent down this Qur'an: 'Those who believe and have fought in Allah's Cause may receive Allah's mercy.' Allah made the booty permissible. He divided the loot, awarding four-fifths to the men He had allowed to take it. He gave one-fifth to His Apostle."

Mercy for murderers. Rewards for raiders. Loot for Muhammad. "Allah's Cause" has been defined for the first time, and it's directly linked to a terrorist raid—one in which Muslim militants attacked civilians. They committed capital murder, kidnapping, and armed robbery. Islam was not preached. Instead, Islam was used to motivate the bandits and reward the prophet. The "religion" *prompted* barbarism rather than discourage it.

This incident alone destroys Islam's religious credentials, Muhammad's authority, and Allah's credibility. The idea of god justifying violent criminal acts to satisfy a prophet's financial lust is unfathomable. If we are to believe Muhammad, Allah approved murder, terror, thievery, and kidnapping for ransom. Forget for a moment that this dark spirit was demented. This is immoral. An immoral god cannot be trusted. An immoral deity isn't worthy of a religion, devotion, sacrifice, or martyrdom.

The same is true for an immoral prophet. Muhammad had sent out armed brigades in search of Quraysh hoping to terrorize them and rob their caravans. When his militants succeeded, he betrayed his mercenaries to save his own hide, yet he still took the money. He threatened to kill his kin and then ransomed them back to his tribe. Then he claimed that his god approved this hellacious behavior, which was the biggest crime of all.

The only thing more devastating than a man professing situational scriptures to legitimize terror, murder, robbery, and kidnapping for ransom is to lure billions to their doom by implying these words were inspired by God. By doing so, Muhammad confirmed my theory. Islam was nothing more than the Profitable Prophet Plan. According to the Sira, Muhammad was a con man.

There have been millions of murderers, millions of kidnappers, millions of terrorists. There have been millions of sexual predators. Thieves are a dime a dozen. And there have been a score of men who have done these things while claiming to be anointed by God. Yet only one invented a "religion" and falsified "scripture" to satiate his demonic cravings. This is why Muhammad, Islam's lone prophet, qualifies as the most evil man to have ever lived.

14

THE ANTI-SEMITE

*"The bestial transformation occurred when
Allah turned Jews into apes."*

Let's move more deeply into the second year of the Islamic Era to see how Muhammad perpetrated his fraud. *Tabari VII:24* **"Allah changed the Muslim Qiblah from Jerusalem to the Ka'aba in the second year of residence in Medina. The people used to pray toward Jerusalem. He used to raise his head to see what he would be commanded. This was abrogated in favor of the Ka'aba,"** the true source of his inspiration.

When the prophet arrived in Yathrib he demeaned the Ka'aba, as this conversation with his new—real new—wife suggests: *Bukhari:V4B55N587* **"The Apostle said to Aisha: 'Don't you see that your folk did not built the Ka'aba on the foundations built by Abraham?' I said, 'O Apostle! Why don't we rebuild it on them?' He said, 'But for the fact your folk have recently given up infidelity.' Umar agreed. 'Aisha must have heard this from Allah's Apostle for he never touched the two corners facing Al-Hijr because the House had not been built on the right foundations.'"** Confession is good for the soul.

But this disdain could not last. Jerusalem was claimed by the God of the Jews and was in their land. For Muhammad to be important, for him to succeed in his quest, he needed something close at hand. Perhaps the Ka'aba could be buffed up a bit—legitimized by a little plagiarized and situational scripture. *Bukhari:V6B60N17/21* **"While some people were offering prayer a man came and said, 'Qur'anic Literature has been revealed to Allah's Apostle tonight. He is ordered to face the Ka'aba at Mecca, so you should turn your faces towards it.' At that moment they were facing Jerusalem so they turned to the Ka'aba."**

Allah was always so accommodating. *Bukhari:V6B60N13* **"The Prophet prayed facing Jerusalem but he *wished* that his Qiblah would be the Ka'aba at Mecca *so Allah Revealed* a Qur'an. A man who had prayed with him went out and said, 'I swear I have prayed with the Prophet facing Mecca.' Hearing that, they turned their faces to the Ka'aba while they were still bowing. Some men had died before the Qiblah was changed and we did not know what to say about them (whether their prayers toward Jerusalem were accepted or not)."** If the Islamic god was everywhere, all-powerful, ever-listening, always-watching, why would he care which direction a devotee turned in prayer? Why all the fuss? To quote a Meccan: "There must be some motive behind this."

Personally, I think it was to dump on the Jews: *Bukhari:V1B4N147* **"People say, 'Whenever you sit for answering the call of nature, you should not face the Qiblah of Jerusalem.' I told them. 'Once I went up the roof of our house and I saw Allah's Apostle answering the call of nature while sitting on two bricks facing Jerusalem."**

Since this is supposed to be a religion, let's review the first surah revealed in Medina to find a more inspired reason. The 2nd surah, the Qur'an's longest, is really its first surah, as the 1st is **"The Prologue,"** a sixty-word invocation. Its speaker isn't Allah. The 2nd surah, which was the ninetieth received, is called **"The Cow"** in reference to the golden calf cast by the Israelites during their Exodus nearly 2,000 years before Islam was invented. Muslim scholars acknowledge that the surah was handed down in pieces over the course of a decade.

Maududi, our esteemed scholar says: **"'The Cow' has been so named from the story of the golden calf associated with Moses. It has not, however, been used as a title to indicate the subject of the surah. It will, therefore, be as wrong to translate the name Al-Baqarah into 'The Cow' as to translate any English name, say Baker, Rice, or Wolf into their equivalents in other languages or vice versa, because this would imply that surah dealt with the subject of 'The Cow.'"** This argument is as irrational as it is telling. It goes to the very heart of Muhammad's deception. Names and words are different things. We can and should translate the word for the profession of baker but never the name of a person named Baker. Baqarah is the Arabic word for cow. It is not the *name* of a cow. Similarly, "il" and "ilah" are Arabic words for god, not the names *of* gods. Words for things must always be translated, while the personal names of deities and people should never be. Ar-Rahman, Allah, and Yahweh are the personal names of very different gods. Anyone who replaces the name "Allah" with the word "God" is guilty of deceiving their audience and of contradicting the Qur'an.

Maududi goes on to explain: **"The greater part of Al-Baqarah was revealed during the first two years of the Prophet's life at Medina. Some of it was revealed at a later period and has been included in this surah because its contents are closely related to those dealt with in this surah. For instance, the verses prohibiting interest were revealed during the last period of the Prophet's life. For the same reason, the last verses of this surah which were revealed in Mecca before the migration of the Prophet."** This argument is inconsistent with the Qur'an as a whole. If it were their god's plan to have like subjects grouped together, the never-ending argument and related depictions of hellish torments wouldn't be randomly strewn throughout the book. All things related to Moses would be brought together, not disseminated in two-dozen surahs. Further, the last verses are unrelated to the business discussion preceding them. They are therefore out of context and chronology.

A *perfect* book cannot by definition be disordered. Yet there is a larger problem. This surah contains the verse on abrogation which says: **"Whenever We cancel a message or throw it into oblivion, We replace it with a better one."** Without dismembering the entire Qur'an so that every line follows the revelation that immediately preceded it, the "cancel and replace" concept is futile. How is anyone to know which verses Allah "threw into oblivion?" Without context and chronology, the "cancel and replace" verse renders the entire Qur'an irrelevant. If one line encourages slavery and another condones it, which is to be believed? If one verse says that infidels are to be taxed to death and others order them *put* to death, what are Muslims to do?

The answer is obvious, but apparently not to Muslims (or those in our statehouses, media, and pulpits) who coddle Islam. A "god" who changes his mind repeatedly over a score of years and needs a verse to deal with his contradictions cannot be "God." A religion devoted to a false spirit isn't worth protecting—especially when it motivates men to murder.

Maududi wasn't finished incriminating his religion. **"At Mecca the Qur'an generally addressed the Quraysh who were ignorant of Islam. At Medina it was concerned with the Jews who were acquainted with the unity of Allah, Prophethood, Revelation, the Hereafter and angels. They also professed to believe in the law which was revealed by Allah to their Prophet Moses, and in principle, their way was the same Islam that was being taught by Prophet Muhammad."** Like all things Islam, the truth has been inverted. The reason both Jews and Muslims believed in prophets, revelation, and angels was because Muhammad stole these concepts, words, and names from them.

Further, Jews believed in the oneness of *Yahweh*—not in some pathetic pagan rock idol named Allah. They knew that the dark spirit of the Qur'an was Lucifer. It's obvious to anyone familiar with the Bible. Yahweh used his name 6,868 times in his scriptures. In addition, every seventieth Hebrew letter in the Torah's central book—Leviticus—forms YHWH, bringing the grand total to a perfect 7,000. Allah's name was never mentioned. The closest Hebrew word means "oak tree." The Jews had a word for god, too. It was "el," and they used it when describing pagan idols like the Islamic deity.

As for **"the Jewish way"** being **"the same Islam,"** that's ?*&%#!. Jewish prophets predicted the future and condemned immoral behavior. The Islamic prophet authorized immoral behavior and condemned the future. They are opposites.

Torah means "instructions" not "laws," but either way those guidelines were summarized in the Ten Commandments. Muhammad declared war on all of them, as did his god. They could not have been chiseled in stone by the rock idol who established a false doctrine promoting theft and murder.

I would like to give Maududi another chance, since this is the fulcrum surah of the Qur'an. More changed than just the Qiblah. He wrote, **"The Jews had strayed away from Islam during the centuries of degeneration and had adopted many un-Islamic creeds, rites, and customs of which there was no mention and for which there was no sanction in the Torah. Not only this: they had tampered with the Torah by inserting their own explanations and interpretations into its text. They had distorted even that part of the Word of God which had remained intact in their Scriptures and taken out of it the real spirit of true religion and were now clinging to a lifeless frame of rituals."** This is the very heart of the matter. It is the Qur'an's justification, its sole tenuous hope of authenticity. It is the reason for the change in Qiblah, and the impetus behind Islamic hatred and Muslim militancy.

If Islam were not so ruthless, so fixated upon submission for the benefit of cleric and king, this assertion would have killed it. The claim that the Torah was inspired by Allah and its characters were Muslims requires it to have been corrupted beyond recognition. The Septuagint and the Dead Sea Scrolls prove beyond any doubt that tampering did not occur. Since archeology has proven that the Jews did not distort the Torah, the Qur'an is a lie. Muhammad deceived men on behalf of a god no bigger than the rock he occupied.

However, it was not all as simple as that. The dark spirit that inspired Muhammad to make these preposterous claims was in a predicament himself. He (like his prophet) was covetous, so Lucifer wanted what belonged to Yahweh: the Jews and their Torah. It is no coincidence that a race representing a tiny fraction of one percent of the world's population became the victims of Islam's wrath. It should be no surprise that modern history's most famous occultist, Adolf Hitler, also wrapped himself in Bible symbols and picked the same enemy. They were both possessed by the same spirit. I dedicated the "Bad Boys" chapter in *Tea With Terrorists* to exposing the similarities between these men and their doctrines. I encourage you to read it if you haven't already.

Considering that Muhammad indulged in pedophilia, led a dozen terrorist raids, inspired thievery, kidnapping, and murder, and said that his "spirit" approved such things, Maududi's comments are astonishing: **"Consequently their [Jewish] beliefs, their morals and their conduct had gone to the lowest depths of degeneration. The pity is that they were not only satisfied with their condition but loved to cling to it. Besides this, they had no inclination to accept any kind of reform. So they became bitter enemies of those who came to teach them the Right Way and did their worst to defeat every effort. Though they were originally Muslims, they had swerved from real Islam and made alterations in it and had fallen victims to hair splitting. They had forgotten and forsaken Allah so much so that they had even given up their original name 'Muslim' and adopted the name 'Jew' instead. They made religion the sole monopoly of the Jews."** And I thought Muhammad was delusional. Islam is apparently contagious.

It's pathetic that Islamic clerics have to lie to make their prophet, scripture, god, and religion appear believable. These ideas are preposterous, wholly incongruous with history and reason. And while countless clerics have mumbled foolish things on behalf of their meal ticket, this is not Maududi's interpretation. This gross deception is proclaimed throughout the Qur'an.

I recognize that we have been over this material before, but it's essential that you appreciate the impossibility of Islam's position. For Yahweh to have been Allah, for Jerusalem to have been Mecca, for the Temple to have been the Ka'aba, for Judaism to have been Islam, for Jews to have been Muslims most every word on most every page of the Bible would have had to have been corrupted, as would world history. While there is no intersection of history and Islam prior to Muhammad's death, Judeo-Christianity lived in the crossroads of nations. Imagine millions of people not knowing *who* they were, *where* they were, *what* they were doing, or *why*. Imagine dismembering thousands of Torahs, Books of the Prophets, and Psalms in a massive conspiratorial fashion so that they would all be the exactly the same—so that they would all deny their name, their purpose, their city, their temple, their God. Not only would thousands of (at the time nonexistent) Islamic symbols, names, and places have had to have been edited out, the Jewish symbols, names and places would have had to have been surreptitiously and universally substituted. And for what—to foil a demon-possessed, dictatorial tyrant who wouldn't be born for 2000 years? But alas, it is no greater leap of faith to believe the impossible corruption occurred than to believe that Islam is divine.

The reason I encouraged you to read about Biblical archeology was so that you might have an appreciation for the magnitude of this deception. The 20th century brought an explosion of historically based Biblical verifications. Virtually every place, person, custom, and event depicted in the Bible has been shown to have been grounded in history. And every single archeological artifact, from Noah to Abraham, from Moses to Christ, is evidenced scripturally and dated to a time preceding Mecca's existence. Since the historically-verified people, places, and dates correspond perfectly to the Biblical account, things cannot be as the Qur'an protests. Islam is a lie.

One last dose of Maududi is in order: "A tiny Islamic State had been set up with the help of the Ansar (local supporters), so naturally the Qur'an had to turn its attention to the social, economic, political and legal matters. This accounts for the difference between the surahs revealed at Mecca and Medina. Half of this surah deals with regulations essential for the solidarity of a community." At least we agree on one thing: Islam was more about politics than religion—and we should treat it as such.

To understand the 2nd surah we must view it in the context of Yathrib, a town ten times the size of Mecca. It was principally a Jewish community. The Yathrib Jews were considerably more literate and prosperous than those who had mocked Muhammad's prophetic credentials in Mecca. Thin-skinned and insecure, the wannabe prophet chaffed at the verbal abuse. As he had with the Meccans, Muhammad unleashed his "god's" wrath on his tormentors.

Ibn Ishaq devotes forty pages, five percent of his Sira, to Muhammad's awkward transition from wanting to be the Jewish Messiah to being the Jews' mortal enemy. The prophet goes from being dependent upon the Jews for scriptural inspiration to condemning their scriptures. In the process he becomes a pathological liar. Everything he says of himself, his god, and his scriptures is not only false, the opposite is true.

The first 176 verses of the 2nd surah are devoted to Muhammad's new-found critics. Allah eagerly details the punishments that await Jews, putting the Qur'an in the untenable position of attacking the book, people, and religion that inspired it. Let's see why.

Ishaq:239 "About this time Jewish rabbis showed hostility to the Apostle in envy, hatred, and malice, because Allah had chosen His Apostle from the Arabs. The Jews considered the Prophet a liar and strove against Islam." Clearly, the Jews were not deceived.

"The Aus and Khazraj joined the Jews by obstinately clinging to their heathen religion. They were hypocrites. When Islam appeared and their people flocked to it, they were compelled to pretend to accept it to save their lives." This means that fundamental Islam, the Islam of the prophet Muhammad, was so immoral, intolerant, and violent, Arabs had to feign support to keep from getting killed. In that regard it was no different than Hitler's Germany or Stalin's Russia. And Islam hasn't changed one iota. Every Muslim in every Islamic nation is still "compelled to pretend to accept it to save their lives."

Ishaq:239 "Jewish rabbis used to annoy the Apostle with questions, introducing confusion." There was a reason neither prophet nor god tolerated questions. To know Muhammad, Allah, and Islam is to hate them. Their doctrine is a lie, their behavior is despicable, and the result is murderous.

"Qur'ans used to come down in reference to their questions." Ishaq lists the sixty Jewish inquisitors by name. Then: *Ishaq:240* "Labid bewitched Allah's Apostle so that he could not come at his wives [apparently he became as impotent as his god]. These Jewish rabbis opposed the apostle, they asked questions and stirred up trouble against Islam trying to extinguish it." They may have failed, but their legacy may help us today.

Alfred Guillaume, the scholar who translated Ibn Ishaq's *Life of Muhammad* into English, adds a worrisome footnote to the end of the "bewitched" allegation. He said, "The best Islamic scholars attest that this Tradition is sound. Other sources explain that the spell lasted for a year. But modernists reject the Tradition on the ground that prophets cannot be bewitched, otherwise they would sin and contradict Allah's Qur'an. They agree the Hadith is properly attested (i.e., its isnad or chain of transmitters is sound) but don't believe it is acceptable for prophets to be afflicted by sorcery."

Fortunately, there is a test to determine the influence of sorcery: Were the prophet's motivations caring or covetous; were his words truthful or deceitful; were his deeds just or immoral? You make the call.

As you ponder the source of Muhammad's inspiration, think about why spiritual inquiry would "stir up trouble" for a religion. Since a true prophet is called to reveal truth by answering questions, why would one object to them?

Ishaq tells us that one Jew was deceived, selling his soul for a buck. His name, according to Muhammad, was Abd Allah ibn Salam. But I find that hard to believe. The Arabic and Hebrew word for Jew is Yahuwdiy—as in the followers of Yahweh, not slaves-to-Allah. So this is just another Islamic deception. *Ishaq:240* "I concealed the matter from the Jews and then went to the Apostle and said, 'The Jews are a nation of liars and I want you to give me a house and hide me from them." The Jews were not a nation in the seventh century, which made at least one Jew a liar. "'If they learn I've become a Muslim, they'll utter slanderous lies against me.' So the prophet gave me a house, and when the Jews came, I emerged and said, 'O Jews, fear Allah and accept what He has sent you. For you know that he is the Apostle of Allah. You will find him described in your Torah and even named.' They accused me of lying and reviled me. I told Muhammad, 'The Jews are a treacherous, lying, and evil people.'"

Did "Abd Allah" betray God for a house? Here are some clues: "allah" means "oak tree" in Hebrew, so this man's name was "slave-to-a-tree." He said "your Torah" not *our* Torah. He claimed that Muhammad was "described" in it when in fact no prophet was ever described in scripture. The Jews didn't believe in "Apostles;" that was a Christian thing. "Apostle" comes from the Greek word "apostolos" which means "ambassador." Jews never evangelized. The name "Muhammad" does not appear anywhere in the Bible. Lastly, a learned Jew would quote the Torah reference, and none was mentioned.

Ishaq:241 "Mukhayriq was a learned rabbi owning much property in date palms. He recognized the Apostle by his description and felt a predilection for his religion. He violated the Sabbath to fight on behalf of Islam and was killed in battle. I am told the Prophet used to say, 'Mukhayriq is the best of the Jews [a dead one].' The Apostle took his property."

Ishaq:242 "Julas the Jew used to say, 'If Muhammad is right we are worse than donkeys.' Allah sent down concerning him: 'They swear that they did not say it, when they did say the words of unbelief.... Allah will afflict them with a painful punishment in this world and in the next.'" [Surah 9:75] "God" must have been a bit tardy with his condemnation as the 9th surah wouldn't be "handed down" for another nine years. *Ishaq:242* "The Apostle ordered Umar to kill him, but he escaped to Mecca."

This next Hadith sports a long and distinguished isnad. There must be a reason. *Ishaq:243* "I have heard the Apostle say: 'Whoever wants to see Satan should look at Nabtal!' He was a sturdy black man with long flowing hair, inflamed eyes, and dark ruddy cheeks. He used to come and talk with the Prophet and listen to him. He would carry what he had said to the hypocrites. Nabtal said, 'Muhammad is all ears. If anyone tells him something he believes it.' Allah sent down concerning him: 'To those who annoy the Prophet and say that he is all ears, say, 'Good ears for you.' For those who annoy the Apostle there is a painful punishment." [Surah 9:61] "Gabriel came to Muhammad and said, 'If a black man comes to you, his heart is more gross than a donkey's.'" The Islamic prophet was an equal-opportunity racist. It was so tolerant of him. I wonder if Louis Farrakhan ever preached from this Hadith?

The **"he is all ears"** line is telling. It's possible a Jew told Muhammad he was **"mentioned in their scriptures."** Not being a prophet, he believed it.

Ishaq:243 "Muhammad promised that we would enjoy the treasures of the Persians and Romans but it isn't safe for us to go to the privy!' So Allah revealed: 'The hypocrites and those with diseased hearts say Allah and His Apostle have promised nothing but delusion." [33:12] Privy or not, this stinks. Muhammad lured Muslims into Islam with promises of booty. It's another confirmation of the Profitable Prophet Plan.

Ishaq and Tabari disagree as to when this conversation occurred and when the charge was leveled. While I agree with the Historian's timing, the message is really all that matters so I'm going to cover these Hadith as they arise in both chronologies. *Ishaq:244* **"Hatib was a sturdy man steeped in paganism. Yazid, his son, was one of the best Muslims when he was disabled by wounds. At the point of death, Muslims said, 'Rejoice, son of Hatib, in the thought of Paradise!' Then his father's hypocrisy showed it self. He said, 'Humph! It is a Garden of Rue. You have sent my son to his death by *your deception.'* Concerning him, Allah said: 'Argue not on behalf of those who deceive themselves. Allah does not love a sinful deceiver.'"** [4:107] I am bereaved of words.

Muhammad was not. *Ishaq:245* **"The Apostle used to say, 'He belongs to the people of Hell.' Yet he had fought valiantly and killed many polytheists. So when he became severely wounded Muslims said, 'Cheer up, you have done gallantly and your sufferings have been for Allah's sake.' "Why should I cheer up? I fought to protect my people.' When the pain of his wounds became unbearable he took an arrow from his quiver, slit his wrist and committed suicide. He was suspected of hypocrisy and love of Jews. This poem was written of him: 'Who will tell him that by cutting his vein he won't be glorified in Islam? Do you love Jews and their religion, you liver-hearted ass, and not Muhammad? Their religion will never march with ours.'"** With each new line, Muhammad's heart grew darker and his spirit became more aligned with Lucifer's. His reaction to the boy's death and his father's suffering was perverse. And he was responsible. He had deceived him. And while that's bad, consider the damage done to Islam. The Torah and Qur'an were supposed to be the same. Islam was supposed to be uncorrupted Judaism; but now: **"Their religion will never march with ours."**

Ishaq:245 **"I have heard that Julas the Jew used to make false professions of Islam. So Allah sent down: 'Satan wishes to lead them astray.'"** [Surah 4:63] Yes, he does.

This is one of many verses Allah uses to coax young Muslim boys into becoming terrorists. *Ishaq:245* **"O Muhammad, give me permission to stay at home and don't tempt me to fight.' So Allah sent down: 'Of him who says, "Give me leave to stay home and tempt me not," surely it is into temptation they have fallen and Hell encompasses them.'"** [9:49] The Qur'an says that peaceful Muslims who refuse the temptation of booty for fighting jihad in Allah's Cause will be roasted in hell.

Ishaq:246 **"The surah of the Hypocrites came down because some men sent secret messages to the Nadir Jews when the Apostle besieged them. So Allah sent down, "Have you not considered the Hypocrites who say to their brethren, the People of the Book [Jews], 'We shall never obey anyone against you. If you are attacked [by the Muslims] and driven out we will help you. Allah bears witness that they are liars. Like Satan when he says to men, "Disbelieve."'** [59:11] This surah goes on to say: *059.014* **"They are a divided people devoid of sense. There is a grievous punishment awaiting them. Satan tells them not to believe so both of them will end up in Hell."** Other Hadith say this surah was handed down regarding the expulsion of the Qaynuqa Jews, and the confiscation of their property, rather than the Nadir.

The 59th surah, called **"Confrontation,"** was one of many anti-Semitic rants.

Highlights include: *059.002* "It was He [Allah] who drove the [Jewish] People of the Book from their [Medina] homes and into exile. They refused to believe. You did not think that they would go away. And they imagined that their settlement would protect them against Allah. But Allah's [actually Muhammad's] (torment) came at them from where they did not suspect and terrorized them. Their homes were destroyed. So learn a lesson O men who have eyes. This is My warning. Had Allah not decreed the expulsion of the Jews, banishing them into the desert, He would certainly have punished them in this world, and in the next they shall taste the torment of Hell Fire."

Why, you may wonder, were the Jews terrorized? Why were their homes stolen and destroyed? Why were Jewish families pushed into the desert to die? Why does Allah want to abuse them? *059.004* "That is because they resisted Allah and opposed His Messenger. If any one resists Allah, verily Allah is severe in Punishment, stern in reprisal." *059.006* "What Allah gave as booty to His Messenger He has taken away from them. For this you made no raid. Allah gives His Messenger Lordship over whomsoever He wills. Allah is Able to do all things. Whatever booty Allah has given to His Messenger and taken away from the [Jewish] people of the townships, belongs to Allah and to His Messenger.... So take what the Messenger assigns to you, and deny yourselves that which he withholds from you. Fear Allah; Allah is Severe in Punishment." Someone may have spoken more demented words than these but surely none ever attributed them to "God." To call Muhammad an anti-Semitic psychopath is too kind.

Three of Muhammad's greatest flaws were included in his racist rant. He was greedy. He wanted the entire spoil for himself. Muhammad had his god say that the Muslim militants who besieged the Jewish settlement weren't entitled to anything. A blockade, according to the dark spirit, was less deserving of booty than a terrorist raid. Muhammad was abusive. When the Jews wouldn't submit to *his* authority, and crown *him* Messiah, he starved a thousand families into submission. He stole their homes, property, businesses, and money. He threw them into the desert to die. Muhammad was also delusional. Having had his mercenaries blockade the township, the prophet said that it was really his *god* who had terrorized them. Then, he assuaged his guilt by saying that had he *not* cast the Jews out and stolen their homes his spirit buddy would have dealt them an even more vicious blow.

For emphasis, I edited the means to this madness out of the passage. Muhammad bribed his mercenaries. He stole to acquire and motivate raiders. He literally bought their loyalty. Check out what followed the ellipsis in the verse: "Whatever booty Allah has given to His Messenger and taken away from the people of the townships belongs to Allah and to His Messenger [....] for near relations (of Muhammad) [his family and wives], the orphans [himself and the children of his dead raiders], and the needy wayfarers [his Meccan loyalists]." In later Hadiths, Muhammad will admit using spoils to buy loyalty. While the mercenary nature of the first Muslims is strongly implied here, it will become blatantly obvious with time.

One last note before we return to Ishaq's narrative. What was Allah going to do with the stolen property? Did Muhammad throw booty toward the Ka'aba and ask Allah to grab whatever he wanted? Or was this all a ruse?

Ishaq attempts to prove that the profiteer was a prophet too. *Ishaq:246* "**Jewish rabbis who took refuge in Islam hypocritically, said one day after Muhammad's camel had wondered off, 'He alleges that revelations come to him from heaven yet he doesn't even know where his camel is.' When the Apostle heard what this enemy of Allah said, Allah told him where his camel was. 'It's in such-in-such a glen.' Surely it was in that very spot.**"

One day the wind blew: *Ishaq:246* "**The Prophet said, 'Don't be afraid; the wind is blowing because a great unbeliever is dead.' When he got back to Medina he found that a hypocrite had died the day the wind blew.**"

The prophet's preaching must have been as "inspired" as his scripture because: *Ishaq:246* "**These Hypocrites used to assemble in the mosque and listen to the stories of the Muslims and laugh and scoff at their religion. So Muhammad ordered that they should be ejected. They were thrown out with great violence. Abu went to Amr, who was a custodian of the gods. He took his foot and dragged him out of the mosque. Another Muslim slapped a man's face while dragging him forcefully. 'Keep out of the Apostle's mosque, you Hypocrite,' he said. Another was punched in the chest and knocked down. One was pulled violently by his hair. 'Don't come near the Apostle's mosque again for you are unclean.' The first hundred verses of the Cow surah came down in reference to these Jewish rabbis and Hypocrites.**" Fundamental Islam at its best.

The Hadith goes on to explain the purpose of the religion: *Ishaq:247* "**It is a guide for those who fear Allah's punishment. It is for those who believe in the unseen, perform prostrations, share what Allah provides with the Apostle, and pay the zakat tax expecting a reward.**" Then speaking of the Jews, Muhammad claims his "god" said: *Ishaq:248* "**Allah has sealed their hearts and their hearing, blinding them so that they will never find guidance. And that is because they have declared you a liar and they do not believe in what has come down from their Lord to you even though they believe in all that came down before you. For opposing you they will have an awful punishment.**" According to Muhammad, the reason the Jews rejected him had nothing to do with his hypocrisy, his acting like a pirate while pretending to be a prophet. It had nothing to do with the demented nature of his scripture. Their denial was a miracle from "god." How's that for delusional?

Healing the sick wasn't part of Allah's repertoire: *Ishaq:248* "**Allah increases their sickness. A tormented doom awaits the Jews.**" The terrorist spirit known as: "**Allah said, 'They are mischief makers. They are fools. The Jews deny the truth and contradict what the Apostle has brought.' Allah said, 'I will mock them and let them continue to wander blindly.'**" Muhammad was personally guilty of everything he falsely attributed to the Jews. As a terrorist raider, he was a "**mischief maker.**" He was a "**fool denying truth.**" And it was Muhammad who "**contradicted**" the Torah, twisting Hebrew scripture to serve his interests.

Arabs and Jews alike were openly doubting the prophet's preposterous claims: *Ishaq:249* "**The Apostle calls you to the truth about which there is no *doubt*. And if**" you are in *doubt* about what We have sent down to him or in *doubt* about what he says, then produce a surah like it and summon witnesses other than Allah. But you won't because you can't, for the truth is beyond *doubt.* Fear Hell, whose fuel is men and stones prepared for the infidels.'" Posturing, propaganda, and threats are standard rhetoric for despots everywhere. Most are more credible than Muhammad, however.

Inviting Jews to Islam, the prophet preached: *Ishaq:250* "Stand in awe of Me lest I bring down on you what I brought down on your fathers. The vengeance that you know of, the bestial transformation and the like." Turning Jews into apes and swine was Allah perverse rendition of bestiality.

"Believe in what I have sent down, confirming what you already have. Be not the first to disbelieve it." [Qur'an 2:41] The Jews weren't in a race. They were just in the wrong place at the wrong time. It's ironic in a way. Had the Jews not been in Yathrib, Islam would never have survived. Without the money Muhammad confiscated by stealing Jewish homes, property, and businesses, and selling Jewish women and children into slavery, he wouldn't have been able to bribe enough militants to conquer the merchants of Mecca, much less the whole Middle East. Without the scripture he bought from the Yathrib Jews, Muhammad wouldn't have had enough religious material to make the Qur'an appear believable. Void of bastardized Bible stories, Islam's holy book is little more than hellish threats, lewd enticements, racist rants, and a call to war.

Ishaq:250 "Fear Me and do not mingle truth with falsehood or hide the truth which you know. Do not conceal the knowledge which you have about My Messenger. You recognize what he has brought to you because you find it with you in the books that are in your hands. You are readers of scripture. Why do you forbid men to believe in the prophecy you have and in the covenant of the Torah. You must pronounce My Apostle to be true." [Qur'an 2:40] Give a dishonest man enough rope and he will eventually hang himself. Desperately trying to establish his own credibility, Muhammad destroyed the last bastion of Allah's. The line, "you will find it with you in the books that are in your hands," says that the Torah of the seventh century A.D. confirmed Muhammad's Islam. It contained "prophecy" pointing to him. Its "covenant" was what "he brought." According to Allah, the Torah proclaimed the "Apostle was true." But nothing could be further from true. The Masoretic text of Muhammad's day matches today's Torah—verbatim. Read it and weep. Sorry pal, you're dead.

To demonstrate just how feeble Muhammad's mental prowess really was, I present the Sira's next paragraph: *Ishaq:250* "Allah said to them, 'Enter the gate with prostrations and say, 'Hitta.' Say what I command you. But they changed that word making a mockery of His command. With regard to their changing that word, the Apostle said according to someone above suspicion: 'They entered the gate they were ordered to enter with prostrations in a crowd saying, 'Wheat is in the barley.'" Yep, the Torah that just anointed Messiahship on the Arab prophet was corrupt. The Jews had edited out the Arabic word "Hitta" from their scriptures, making a mockery of Allah's commands. Unfortunately, the Arabic word wouldn't come to have a written form for 2000 years. Yet we're told it was edited out of written scripture. If you're curious, "Hitta" means "unloading." It's nonsensical. And "barley and wheat" were associated with the Meccans and their idol Manat (Ishaq:39), not Yahweh and the Jews. Muhammad was as dumb as the rock he called "god." You can fix a lot of things but you can't fix stupid.

The paragraph goes on to report: *Ishaq:250* **"Allah raised the mountain above the Jews so that they might receive what was brought to them; and the bestial transformation occurred when Allah turned Jews into apes."** [Qur'an 2:65] A billion souls believe this beast of a man was a prophet. Sadly, they don't know his spirit was Satanic.

I am certain the Yathrib Jews told him that his Five Pillars conflicted with Yahweh's Ten Commandments. So the prophet who insisted his brand-new Islam confirmed the 2000-year-old Judaism said, *Ishaq:251* **"Moses commanded them to prostrate themselves and his Lord spoke to him and they heard His voice giving them commands and prohibitions so that they understood what they heard. But when Moses went back to the Jews a party of them changed the Commandments they had been given."** [Qur'an 2:75] As you might expect, Muhammad didn't bother explaining what the Commandments originally proclaimed, which of the ten the "party" changed, how they corrupted them, why they bothered, or even how they could have gotten away with the most monumental edit of all time.

Muhammad was certain his name and description were plastered throughout the Torah. He actually "believed" (if we can trust him) the "Covenant" between the Jews and Yahweh pertained to him. His arguments were equal parts delusional and egotistical. The following conversation allegedly occurred between Muhammad's "god" and the Yathrib Jews: *Ishaq:252* **"Have you no understanding? Why do you maintain that he is not a prophet since you know that Allah has made a Covenant with you that you should follow him? While he tells you that he is the prophet whom you are expecting, and that you will find him in Our book, you oppose him and do not recognize him. You reject his prophethood on mere opinion."** [Qur'an 2:77] If this is true; if Allah spoke to the Yathrib Jews, why didn't he speak to the Muslims? And since Allah alleges that he wrote the Torah, why didn't he tell the Jews where to look for descriptions of his Arab prophet? All this verse actually proves is that Muhammad claimed to be the Messiah.

The next Hadith explains how Muhammad came to speak about Yahweh's 7,000-year plan. *Ishaq:252* **"The Apostle came to Medina when the Jews were saying the world would last 7,000 years and that God would only punish men in hell one day for every thousand. Allah sent down: 'And they say, "The fire will not touch us except for a few days"'... so they became the people of hell where they will live forever.'"** [2:80] Like everything Muhammad stole from the Bible, he was right up to his point of departure. By putting Yahweh's prophetic calendar together, one discovers that seven distinct one thousand-year periods follow the fall of Adam. There is no reference to hellish days, however, and Muhammad misdated himself in the mix, wrongly predicting that the world would end in the year 1110 A.D. Since our current calendar is as pagan as Islam's, I cannot pinpoint where we are in this chronology, but there is considerable reason to believe that the sixth one thousand-year period will end during the Feast of the Tabernacles in 2033 A.D., following seven years of extreme tribulation at the hands of Satan and Islam.

Showing that Allah didn't know the difference between a covenant and a commandment, Muhammad claims he said: *Ishaq:252* **"We made a covenant with the Children of Israel, which is your covenant. Worship none but Allah, show kindness to parents, near relatives, and orphans. Speak kindly to men, establish obligatory prayer, and pay the zakat."** [2:80] The Bible speaks of seven Covenants. They are agreements, not commandments. Some are unilateral, including the one Islam claims to be modeled after—the Covenant with Abraham. In it, Yahweh made promises but asked for nothing in return. The New Covenant, first presented by Jeremiah and fulfilled by Yahshua, is also unilateral. Yahweh promises salvation, eternity with him; all we can do is accept his gift.

Islam's Five Pillars which are hinted at here, are commandments, not agreements. Allah makes no promises. Further, there was never a "worship none but Allah," "speak kindly," "prostration prayer," or "zakat" tax agreement, covenant, or commandment in the Bible.

Projecting his faults on his opponents, in this case the Jews—speaking unkindly of them and killing their parents—was something Muhammad did with great regularity. He would soon violate all of these commandments he had wrongly called covenants. Although we are still in the same paragraph, it appears that Allah is now speaking to the Jews: *Ishaq:253* **"When we made a covenant with you, saying 'Shed not your blood and do not turn people out of their dwellings,' you ratified it. Yet you take prisoners and ransom them and expel people although it is forbidden in your religion.... Allah cursed them for their unbelief. When a scripture comes to them from Allah confirming what they already have, they deny it. Allah's curse is on them."** [2:82] The Jews did none of these things. Muhammad did them all.

The following Hadith is one of many that show Muhammad tried to pass himself off as the Messiah. *Ishaq:254* **"In the pagan era the Jews were scripture folk and we were pagans. They used to say, 'Soon a prophet will be sent whom we shall follow.' When Allah sent his Apostle from the Quraysh and we followed him they denied him. Allah revealed, 'When there comes to him one they recognize, they deny him. They are wretched, so Allah cursed them, and He will give them a shameful punishment.' The double anger is His wrath because they have disregarded the Torah and anger because they disbelieved in this Prophet whom Allah has sent to them."** [2:89] The false prophet was as similar to the Anti-Christ, and as dissimilar to the Messiah as any man who has ever lived.

There is nothing Muhammad wanted more than for the Jews to proclaim that he was the Messiah. And when they didn't (for a thousand obvious reasons), he turned his wrath on them: *Ishaq:254* **"Long for death [Jews], if you are truthful. Pray that God will kill whichever one of us is the most false. The Jews refused the Prophet's dare."** This is not only childish, it's damning. The point of contention was whether Muhammad was the Messiah, or at least a prophet sent by God. The Jews (and the Bible) said, "No." Muhammad and his Qur'an said, "Yes." So he dared the Jews to have God kill the biggest liar.

"Allah said to His Prophet, 'They will never accept your dare because of their past deeds. But they recognize you from the knowledge they have. Yet they deny. Had they accepted your dare, not a single Jew would have remained alive on the earth." [2:94] Muhammad wanted the Jews to accept something he believed would have led to their annihilation. He wanted them wiped them out to the last—every Jew dead. So did his god. *008.007* "Allah wished to confirm the truth by His words, 'Wipe the Unbelievers out to the last.'" Genocide. The paragraph ends with: *Ishaq:254* "We will not remove a Jew from the punishment. The Jew knows the shameful thing that awaits him in the next life because he has wasted the knowledge he has." [2:96]

Tabari, Bukhari, and Ishaq all chronicle a variety of tests Jewish rabbis allegedly put Muhammad through to determine whether he was a prophet speaking on the authority of God as he claimed. They are dated to different times and include some repetitive material. While there is no chance these discussions occurred as they are reported, Muhammad's answers are revealing. *Ishaq:255* "Jewish rabbis came to the Apostle and asked him to answer four questions saying, 'If you do so we will follow you, testify to your truth, and believe in you.' They began, 'Why does a boy resemble his mother when the semen comes from the father?' Muhammad replied, 'Do you not know that a man's semen is white and thick and a woman's is yellow and thin? The likeness goes with that which comes to the top.' 'Agreed,' the rabbis proclaimed." First, only an imbecile would believe that Jewish rabbis, students of the Torah, would test a prophet's credentials in such a moronic fashion, much less concede he was right. Second, he was wrong. Third, this answer contradicts his earlier testimony in which he claimed that "likeness" was based upon who "discharged first."

Question: "Tell us about your sleep." Answer: "Do you not know that a sleep which you allege I do not have is when the eye sleeps but the heart is awake?" Question: "Tell us about what Israel [Jacob] voluntarily forbade himself." Answer: "Do you not know that the food he loved best was the flesh and milk of camels or perhaps two lobes of liver, kidneys, and fat?" Question: "Tell us about the spirit." Answer: "'Do you not know that it is Gabriel, he who comes to me?' 'Agreed,' the rabbis said. 'But Muhammad, your spirit is an enemy to us, an angel who comes only with violence and the shedding of blood, and were it not for that we would follow you." Anyone familiar with the Bible, and that would include these Jews, would have instantly recognized Muhammad's spirit as that of the fallen angel Lucifer. The description is a perfect fit.

Allah even speaks of Satan in the same paragraph. "So Allah sent down concerning them: 'When the Apostle comes to them from Allah confirming that which they have received in scripture, they put it behind their backs as if they did not know it. They follow that which Satan read concerning the kingdom of Solomon—sorcery.' One of the rabbis said, 'Don't you wonder at Muhammad? He alleges that Solomon was a prophet, and yet he was nothing but a sorcerer.' So Allah sent down, 'Solomon did not disbelieve but Satan did, practicing sorcery.'" [Qur'an 2:101] According to Muhammad and Allah, the Jews read scriptures dictated by Satan. Since Allah claims he dictated the Jewish scriptures, we have been formally introduced.

Ishaq:256 **"The Apostle wrote a letter to the Jews of Khaybar [before he annihilated them]. In the name of Allah, Ar-Rahman, Ar-Rahim from Muhammad the Apostle of Allah, friend and brother of Moses who confirms what Moses brought [the Torah]. Allah says to you, 'O Scripture folk, and you will find it in your scripture "Muhammad is the Apostle of Allah. Those with him are severe against the unbelievers. You see them bowing, falling prostrate, seeking bounty, and acceptance. The mark of their prostrations is on their foreheads." That is their likeness in the Torah and in the Gospels.'"** While the mark of the beast is in the Bible, it serves to prove that Islam is Satanic. As for finding "Muhammad is the Apostle of Allah. Those with him are severe against the unbelievers," written in the Torah and Gospels; I'll become a Muslim and worship Lucifer the moment someone shows me where.

The Hadith continues: *Ishaq:256* **"Do you find in what He has sent down to you that you should believe in Muhammad? If you do not find that in your scripture then there is no compulsion upon you. 'The right path has been plainly distinguished from error' [2:257] so I call you to Allah and His Prophet."** Somebody sold this sorry sack a bag of manure. But thankfully, since Muhammad cannot be found in my scripture, there is no compulsion for me, or anyone else, to serve Satan.

Ishaq:256 **"The Jews used to ask Muhammad questions which annoyed and confused him."** *Ishaq:257* **"Your situation seems obscure to us, Muhammad."** And it remains so.

But team Islam was undeterred. *Ishaq:257* **"'O Jews, fear Allah and submit, for you used to hope for the Messiah's help against the Arabs when we were pagans. You told us that he would be sent and then told us about him.' A Jew responded, 'Muhammad has not shown us anything we recognize as prophetic. He is not the one we spoke to you about.' So Allah revealed, 'We confirmed what they had, and We sent one they recognized, but they rejected him so We are cursing them.' The Jews replied, 'No Covenant was ever made with us about Muhammad.'"** Then turning to face their tormentor, the Medina Jews said, **"'Muhammad, you have not brought anything we recognize. And God has not sent down any sign or miracle suggesting that we should believe you.' So Allah said, 'We have sent down to you plain signs and only evildoers disbelieve them.'"** The truth hurts. Neither prophet nor god knew how to respond.

Ishaq:257 **"The Jews told Allah's Messenger, 'Bring us a book. Bring us something down from heaven that we might read it.'"** After all this whining and anti-Semitism, Muhammad still didn't have a book. Nothing had been written down, much less collated into scripture. Not only couldn't our boy find a prophecy pointing to himself, not only couldn't he perform a miracle, he couldn't even produce a book. But alas, he couldn't have read it if he had.

Ishaq:258 **"The Jews used to turn men away from Islam. So Allah said, 'Many of the Scripture folk wish to make you unbelievers after you have believed. They are envious. But be** indulgent until Allah gives you his orders [to rob them, rape them, sell them into slavery, and murder them.]" I'm not being unkind. That is precisely what he would order them to do. (Qur'an 33:25-27)

Muslims had this right, although not in the way they imagined: *Ishaq:262* "'To arms! To arms!' the Muslims said quarreling and boasting among themselves. When this reached the Prophet, he said, 'Muslims, will you act as pagans while I am with you?' They realized that their dissension was due to Satan and the guile of their enemy. Then they went off with the Apostle attentive and obedient."

Like Hitler after him, the anti-Semitic prophet wanted to be sure no one would befriend a Jew. He had plans for them. *Ishaq:262* "Some Muslims remained friends with the Jews, so Allah sent down a Qur'an forbidding them to take Jews as friends. From their mouths hatred has already shown itself and what they conceal is worse."

An enemy must be isolated and vilified to be conquered. So Muhammad said, "You believe in their Book [though you don't have a clue what it says] while they deny your book, so you have more right to hate them than they have to hate you."

Ishaq:263 "Abu Bakr went into a Jewish school [there is no mention of him ever going into a Muslim school] and found many pupils gathered around Finhas, a learned rabbi. Bakr told the Jews to fear Allah and submit. He told them that they would find that Muhammad was an Apostle written in the Torah and Gospels." Muhammad's lead general was so unaware he told *Jews* to look for prophetic confirmation of Muhammad in the *Christian* Gospels. These boys were dumb. "Finhas replied, 'We are rich compared to Allah. We do not humble ourselves to Allah [read Satan]. He humbles himself to us. We are independent of him, while he needs us. Why does your god ask us to lend him money as your master pretends.' Abu was enraged and hit Finhas hard in the face [for telling the truth]. Were it not for the treaty between us I would cut off your head, you enemy of Allah [Satan]. So Allah [Satan] said, 'They will taste Our punishment of burning.'" [Qur'an 2:7,11,24,27,39,81,85-90,96,104,114,119,126,162,165-7,174-5,196,201,206, 211,217,257, and 275]

Muhammad hated Jews. *Ishaq:264* "Allah revealed concerning Finhas and the other rabbis: 'Allah issued orders to those who had received the Book [Torah]: 'You are to make it clear to men and not conceal it, yet they cast the Torah behind their backs and sold it for a small price. Wretched was their exchange. They will therefore receive a painful punishment.'" While the Qur'an complains about the Jews selling Muhammad Bible stories a dozen times, this is the most direct confession in the Hadith.

Next, Muhammad puts the caravan before the camel: *Ishaq:264* "The Torah confirms what Muhammad brought." Then: "Rifa'a, a notable Jew, spoke to the Apostle, twisting his tongue: 'Give us your attention, Muhammad, so that we can make you understand.' Then he attacked Islam and reviled it. So Allah sent down, 'Allah knows about your enemies. Some of the Jews change words from their contexts and say: "We hear and disobey," twisting their tongues and attacking the religion. But Allah cursed them.'" [Qur'an 2:59 & 4:47] One has to be ignorant or oblivious not to condemn this stuff.

Ishaq:264 "The Jewish rabbis knew that Muhammad had brought them the truth, but they denied that they knew it. They were obstinate. So Allah revealed, 'People of the Book, believe in what we have sent down in confirmation of what you had been given before or We will efface your features and turn your face into your ass, cursing you.'" Allah was such a loving and nurturing god.

The Jews said: *Ishaq:269* "'Tell us when the Day of Doom will be, Muhammad, if you are a prophet as you say.' So Allah sent down, 'They will ask you about the hour when it will come to pass. Say, only my Lord knows of it. None but He will reveal it at its proper time. Say, 'Only Allah knows about it but most men do not know.'" In other words, neither Muhammad or Allah were prophets. And since the Mighty Mo claimed to be the last messenger, who was going to share Allah's big surprise? "'How can we follow you, Muhammad, when you have abandoned our Qiblah? And you do not allege that Uzayr [who knows?] is the son of God.' So Allah revealed, 'The Jews say that Uzayr is the son of God [no they don't] and the Christians say the Messiah is the son of God. That is what they say with their mouths, copying the speech of those who disbelieved in the earlier times. Allah fight them! How perverse are they?'" That's so stupid, I'm speechless.

Trying to reason with the man, the Jews said: *Ishaq:269* "'For our part we don't see how your Qur'an recitals are arranged anything like our Torah is.' [So Muhammad who couldn't read said,] 'you know quite well that the Qur'an is from Allah. You will find it written in the Torah which you have.'" Sorry, you won't find any mention of the Qur'an in any Torah. Not in the original from 1200 B.C., not from the Septuagint from 275 B.C., not in any of the Dead Sea Scrolls, dating from 250 B.C. to 70 A.D., not in the "Torah which they had" in 625 A.D., nor in one from 2003. Since the most important and oft repeated claim in Muhammad's prophetic career was false, Muhammad was a false prophet. It's as simple as that.

Yet the charlatans bragged: *Ishaq:269* "'If men and jinn [demons] came together to produce its like they could not.' Finhas said, 'Did men or jinn tell you this, Muhammad?' [The answer was yes to both, but he said,] 'You know full well that the Qur'an is from Allah and that I am the Apostle of Allah. You will find it written in the Torah you have.' The rabbi replied, 'When God sends a prophet, He provides for him, so bring us a book that is divinely inspired that we may read it and determine if you are telling the truth. We can produce *our* Book.'" Unable to produce so much as a single chapter, Muhammad and his god retreated to the state of denial, their most familiar territory. "So Allah revealed, concerning their words, 'Say, "Though men and jinn should meet to produce this Qur'an, they would not produce its like, even working together."'" Let's see if Allah is right.

The 2nd surah begins with a contradiction: *002.001* "Alif-Lam-Min. (These letters are a miracle of the Qur'an and only Allah knows what they mean.) This is the Book free of doubt, a guidance to those who ward off (evil), who believe in the Unknown, fulfill their devotional obligations, and pay (zakat) out of what We have provided." There is no doubt: these uninspired rantings have guided more evil than they have warded off.

Allah's "Book" is asking people to believe in the "Unknown." Unable to produce a miracle, prophecy, or even a sane depiction of God, Muhammad just gives up and says, "believe in the unknown." We're ninety-one surahs into the

Qur'an, and what little is known about this spirit is demonic. He spends his days torturing unbelievers in hell, and he spends his nights leading believers astray. He supports immorality when it serves his prophet's interests, and he doesn't want his true identity to be known.

But the dark spirit wants to be worshiped. The passage defines Muslims as those who **"fulfill their devotional obligations."** Although this may sound pious, it's wrong too. Devotion and obligation are incompatible, mutually exclusive concepts. Devotion—love—requires choice. The lack of choice is Islam's greatest deficiency, as the word "obligation" suggests.

That brings us to the zakat, the tax imposed on all Muslims; it's one of the Five Pillars. Islam gives monetary confiscation a politically correct veneer by calling it charity, the giving of alms. But Muhammad used it exactly like politicians use taxes. At swordpoint, he took money from productive people so that he could bribe his unproductive supporters. It made Muhammad powerful and Muslims dependant. It's no different from the tactics Saddam Hussein used to ensure Baath Party loyalty.

002.004 **"Whoever believes in (the Qur'an and Sunnah) which has been sent down to you (Muhammad) and in that which was sent to those before your time (the Torah and Gospel), have the assurance of the Hereafter."** Although there are a thousand reasons to discard the Qur'an, this is one of the best. Allah is taking credit for prior scripture, saying that it should also be believed. Since the Torah and Qur'an are irreconcilably different, the order is impossible. It's like telling someone to be a democratic capitalist and a totalitarian communist at the same time.

002.006 **"As for the disbelievers, it is the same whether you warn them or not; they will not believe. Allah has set a seal upon their hearts, upon their hearing, and a covering over their eyes. There is a great torment for them."** It's another Islamic first: a spirit so perverse, so evil, he precludes people from knowing him. And he does it so that he can torture them. The concept is demonic; the words are Satanic.

The next thirteen verses rekindle the never-ending argument; only this time the victims are Jews, not Arabs. *002.009* **"They deceive Allah and those who believe, but they only deceive themselves, and realize (it) not! In their hearts is a disease; and Allah has increased their disease. Grievous is the painful doom they (incur) because they (lie)."** Only in Islam could man deceive God. But that's child's play compared to a god who calls men diseased, and then, rather than curing them, makes them sicker. The Qur'an begins as badly as it ends.

002.011 **"When it is said to them: 'Make not mischief on the earth,' they say: 'We are peacemakers only.'"** Propagandists and political strategists know that the most effective deception is one that projects a doctrine's or a candidate's faults onto their rivals. That is precisely what is being done here. The "mischief makers" are Muslims, not Jews. As proof, the Jews were tending to their businesses while the Muslims were out pirating. But it is the last line that haunts us today. In the face of worldwide Islamic terror, Muslims say, **"We are peace-**

makers only." And we believe them. Shame on us.

Still attacking Jews, the Qur'an says: **"They are mischief-mongers, but they realize not. When it is said to them: 'Believe as the others believe:' They say: 'Shall we believe as the fools?' Nay, surely they are the fools, but they know not. When they meet the faithful, they say: 'We believe;' but when they are alone with the devils, they say: 'We are really with you: We (were) only mocking.'"** Obviously, it didn't take the Jews long to assess the merits of Islam. Knowing who God *is* helped them recognize who He was *not*. And therein lies our problem. We have lost sight of Yahweh, having separated ourselves from him. Most don't even know his name, much less his character and plan. Not knowing Yahweh makes Lucifer more deceptive.

For example, this is Lucifer speaking, not God: *002.015* **"Allah mocks them, paying them back, increasing their wrong-doing so they wander blindly."**

Then the Devil says: **"These are they who have bartered guidance for error, and have gained nothing from the deal."** Another translation reads: **"These are they who purchase error at the price of guidance, so their bargain shall bring no gain."** This is Allah's first attempt at condemning Jews for selling (not giving) their oral traditions to Muhammad. He is inferring that his bastardized accounts, the ones twisted to make his immoral behavior look divine, are true guidance while the originals are erroneous. Remember, people believed Hitler's lies too—lies that were indistinguishable from Islam. Working for the same master, they were equally seductive, racist, demonic, and destructive.

002.017 **"They are like one who kindled a fire; when it burned around him, Allah took away their light and left them in darkness so they could not see. They are deaf, dumb, and blind, so they return not. Or like a storm with darkness, thunder and lightning. They thrust their fingers in their ears for fear of death. But Allah surrounds the disbelievers. The lightning snatches away their eyes; when darkness covers them, they stand still; and if Allah pleased He would take away their hearing too."** Allah is harming men, not condemning doctrines. And the dark spirit is shown thwarting man's efforts to know him (which is probably a good thing).

After a series of "proofs" Allah says: *002.023* **"If you are in doubt of what We have revealed to Our Votary, then bring a surah like this, and call any witnesses apart from Allah. But you cannot, as indeed you cannot guard yourselves against the Hell Fire whose fuel is men and rocks, which has been prepared for the infidels."** Dr. Seuss writes better sonnets than this. They are original, instructive, nurturing, and chronological. So I call the Grinch to witness; he is no less real, and a lot less disturbed.

I am going to skip the debate between Allah, Adam, and Satan, as we have played the "can-you-name-the-animals" game before. It ends with a clever impersonation, however, with Adam playing Muhammad: *002.039* **"Those who reject and deny Our Signs will be inmates of the Hell Fire and will abide there forever."**

Proving that the Qur'an was as crazy as its god, the book that had just invested the better part of forty verses condemning Jews to hell, telling them that they were deaf, dumb, blind, diseased, and led astray, now says: *002.040* **"O**

Children of Israel, remember the favors I bestowed on you. So keep My Covenant so that I fulfil your covenant. Fear Me. And believe in what I sent down, confirming and verifying the Scripture which you possess already." This reconfirms that Islam is irrational. Q cannot verify or confirm B if Q condemns and contradicts B. Further, if B is true and Q opposes B, then Q must be false.

While an irrational god is a problem for Islam, there is a bigger issue. *002.041* "Be not the first to deny or sell My Verses for a small price; and fear Me, and Me alone." Another translation reads: "Part not with My Revelations for a trifling price (getting a small gain by selling My Verses)." The Qur'an just confirmed that Muhammad bought his "divine revelation" from the Jews. It wasn't "handed down," "deciphered from clanging bells," or "dictated by Gabriel." It was purchased in a business transaction. Islam is a fraud.

002.042 "Do not mix truth with falsehood, nor conceal the truth when you know." The truth is: all doctrines based upon fear and submission are bad. They are designed to empower the few so that they might fleece the many.

Almost three thousand years ago, the Jews substituted a powerful and nurturing relationship with Yahweh for a complex and stifling religion. The religion was good for cleric and king but devastating for the Jewish people, separating them from their land and God. The Catholic Church did the same thing, elevating rites and rituals above relationship. It was great for cleric and king but devastating for humankind. Likewise Islam offers nothing to men but the false hope of a twisted paradise. It uses fear to suppress and stupefy the masses, enriching and empowering imams and tyrants alike.

Islam, more than any doctrine conceived by man, uses mind-numbing ritual and senseless rites to manipulate and fleece the flock. Islamic prayer is not a conversation with God; it is a performance to be acted out. Islamic worship isn't heartfelt praise; it's mindless, obligatory, and repetitive. The Qur'an is not to be questioned or understood; it is to be obeyed. The Islamic "god" is "unknown" for a reason. He is repulsive.

Chairman Muhammad was ordering the Jews to capitulate to him. But they saw right through his act: *002.043* "Perform prayer; pay the zakat tax; bow down and prostrate yourself with Ar-Raki'un (the obedient bowers). You read, recite, and study the Scripture. Why don't you understand? [Why don't you capitulate?] Nay, seek [Islamic prostration] prayer: It is indeed hard, heavy, and exacting, except for those who obey in submission." In other words, "Become Muslims and subject yourselves to my obligations because I need to control you and I covet your money."

Allah, the god who said he turned Jews into "swine and apes," claims: *002.047* "Remember, Children of Israel, the favor which I bestowed on you, and made you exalted among the nations of the world, preferring you to men and jinn." But then: *002.059* "The [Jewish] transgressors changed and perverted the word from that which had been spoken to them to a word distorted; so We sent a plague upon them from heaven, for their evildoing." The god of "favors" "bestowed a plague from heaven." *Bukhari:V4B56N679* "Allah's

Apostle said, 'Plague was a means of torture sent on the Israelis.'" While we differ on plagues being heavenly, bigger questions remain: when, how, and why did the Bible get so distorted that it became the opposite of the Qur'an? The claim is the crux of Islam, yet no Muslim cleric, prophet, or god has ever provided a rational explanation. And without an answer, Islam is a counterfeit, a lousy job of plagiarizing, nothing more.

The Septuagint and Dead Sea Scrolls irrefutably prove that the Torah has remained unchanged since at least 250 B.C., a thousand years before the Qur'an was written. Since Islam claims otherwise, it's a fraud, not a religion.

Not only is there a mountain of historical evidence that refutes Muhammad's claim, reason alone will suffice. For the nation of Israel to have written Allah, Muhammad, Mecca, the Ka'aba, Arabic, Islam, Muslim, and the Five Pillars out of the Torah and Yahweh, the Messiah, Jerusalem, the Temple, Hebrew, Judaism, Jews, and the Ten Commandments in, requires a conspiracy infinitely beyond anything the world has ever known. A total suspension of rational thought is required to believe Allah. And then there is the little problem of motivation. Why would the nation of Israel collectively and comprehensively alter the totality of their scriptures and history in an attempt to foil a conman a thousand miles away and a thousand years distant?

The dark spirit of Islam has sent a "plague" from his abode and it has consumed men's minds. Hopefully there will be enough healthy neurons left for Muslims to make wise choices once they are exorcised from this pestilence.

002.061 **"Humiliation and wretchedness were stamped upon the Jews and they were visited with wrath from Allah. That was because they disbelieved Allah's Proofs, Signs and Verses and killed the prophets. They disobeyed and rebelled. Surely those who believe and Jews, and Nazareans [Christians], and the Sabaeans [Zoroastrians], whoever believes in Allah and in the Last Day, and whosoever does right, shall have his reward with his Lord and will neither have fear nor regret."** Muslims quote the last part of this verse to the media to demonstrate how tolerant Islam is. Yet they must take it out of context. The prior verse that says that Allah stamped the Jews with wretchedness and that his wrath was justified. Further, Muslims must mistranslate it, too, replacing the name "Allah" with the word "God." The passage actually says: tolerance is only extended if the Jews, Christians, and Zoroastrians believe in Allah and become Muslims. Convert: or fear and regret it.

Two verses later, the intolerant Allah is back on the warpath, acting like a racist. *002.064* **"But you [Jews] went back on your word and were lost losers. You know that you have broken the sanctity of the Sabbath, so We said: 'Become monkeys despised and hated.' We made this punishment an example and a warning for those who fear Allah."** Whether you choose to interpret this as god calling Jews despised apes or turning them into hated monkeys, it isn't godly. And if the Sabbath was sanctified by Allah, why do Muslims ignore the warning and worship on Friday?

The following Hadith was designed to answer that question: *Bukhari:V4B56N693*

"The Prophet said, 'We [Muslims] are the last (to come) but we will be the foremost. Nations were given the Scripture Book before us, and we were given the Holy Book after them. Friday is the day about which they differed. So the next day, Saturday, was pre-scribed for the Jews and the day after it, Sunday, for the Christians. It is incumbent on every Muslim to wash his head and body on Friday.'" I suppose it would be too much to ask for the prophet to explain how a "Friday dispute" could have arisen between Jews and Christians, considering it was chiseled in stone twelve cen-turies before the first Christian was born.

In the next fifteen verses, Allah bounces between arguing with Jews and regaling their history. Then he condemns them for overcharging Muhammad for "erroneous" Bible stories: *002.079* **"But woe to the Jews who fake the Scriptures and say, 'This is from God,' so that they might earn some profit thereby.' And woe to them for what their hands have written, and woe to them for what they earn from it.'"** What makes them "fake" is the Biblical accounts the Jews sold to Muhammad differed from the version the prophet twisted to serve his interests.

002.080 **"Yet they (Jews) say: 'The Fire will not touch us for more than a few days...but they are enclosed in error and are inmates of Hell."** Failing to scare them, Muhammad ordered Jews to: **"Pay the zakat tax on your wealth for the welfare of others [Muslims]. And remember we took your Covenant: shed not blood among us or turn people out of their homes; you promised and bear witness. But you kill one another, call people guilty, and use oppression. When captives are brought you ransom them, although it was forbidden."** The Yathrib Jews did none of these things. The Muslims did them all. They shed blood, murdering thousands. They forced thousands more from their homes. Their god condemned men, and his prophet founded the most oppres-sive regime ever conceived. During the month these situational scriptures were contrived, Muhammad personally took captives and ransomed them. Even if you don't see Muhammad as the Meccans and Jews saw him—as an insane, demon-possessed liar, forging scriptures for his own selfish gain—it's hard to miss the fact he was a hypocrite.

It's amazing how much difference a year and a few miles can make. In the last Meccan surah, Allah was congratulating the Jews for testifying to the truth of his Qur'an. Now they're going to roast in hell for not swallowing it whole. *002.085* **"Do you [Jews] believe a part of the Book and reject a part? There is no reward for them who so act but disgrace in the world, and on the Day of Doom, the severest of punishment...their torment will never decrease!"** The more one is exposed to Muhammad's poisonous brew, the worse it tastes.

As we move on, Jesus is brought into the fray, and we are told that the Gospels and Torah were divinely inspired. But then we learn that Allah has cursed Christians and Jews for their disbelief. Allah's anti-Christian, anti-Jew diatribe continues for 50 verses. The same Allah who refers to himself as "We" and "Our" claims that Jesus cannot be His son because He is "One."

Allah's racist rant includes the twentieth rendition of: *002.089* **"The [Qur'an]**

Book was sent to them (the Jews) by Allah verifying and confirming what had been revealed to them already (the Torah and Gospel). They used to pray for victory over the unbelievers— and even though they recognized it when it came to them, they renounced it. The curse of Allah be on those who deny!" By slipping out of first person to curse the Jews, Muhammad has lifted the veil and shown us who is really behind the curtain.

We are three quarters of the way through the Qur'an, and yet this is the first time Gabriel, the Messenger's messenger, is named. *002.097* "Say (Muhammad): Whoever is an enemy to Gabriel—for he brings it down to your heart by Allah's leave, a confirmation of what was (revealed) before, and guidance and glad tidings for those who believe. Whoever is an enemy to Allah, His angels, His Messengers, to Gabriel and Michael, Lo! Allah (Himself) is an enemy of the disbelievers." The spirit who terrorized Muhammad in the cave is now given a name, and wouldn't you know it, his name is from the Bible too. Allah seems to have a very limited imagination. And a limited range of emotions: the moment we meet the heavenly cast, they are off to war, condemning their enemies for rejecting their doctrine of submission. Every word of this reeks of Lucifer.

002.099 "We have sent down to you Manifest Signs; and none reject them but those who are perverse." How, pray tell, can a doctrine be tolerant when its spiritual leader says that all who reject his claims are perverse? And you'd think that if Allah was going to brag about all his "signs" he would perform one—one lousy miracle. (Making the blind lame or the deaf dumb doesn't count.) Muhammad and Allah simply promise and protest. They are more like Hitler and Goebbels than Prophet and God.

Once again: *002.101* "When there came a messenger from Allah confirming what was with them, a party of the people of the (Torah and Gospel) Scripture Book fling away the Book of Allah, tossing it behind their backs, as if they did not know!" You've probably noticed a pattern in the Qur'an. The things Muhammad and Allah protest *most*, they are most guilty of. They claim repeatedly that the Qur'an confirms the scripture it twists. Similar verbose assertions are: The Qur'an was a book, Allah created man, Allah showed his signs, Jews were Muslims, and Muhammad wasn't a demon-possessed madman.

002.102 "They follow what Satan chanted and gave out during the lifetime of Solomon. Though Solomon never disbelieved, the devils denied and taught sorcery to men, which they said had been revealed to the angels of Babylon, Harut, and Marut. However, these two (angels) never taught without saying: 'We have been sent to deceive you.'" Harut and Marut are Persian names not Hebrew or Arabic. And while the implication is that the Jewish King Solomon was a Muslim during the time the Jews were influenced by the Babylonians, Allah's timeline is errant by 400 years. While that's indicting, what's really incriminating is Allah's claim that the Torah was inspired by the Devil and yet his Qur'an verifies it's message. This, ever so appropriately, is followed by three repetitions of: "If only they had sense!"

Now that the Jews had been properly chastised it was time to get down to business. Muhammad had a tenuous grip on his fledgling community, and that just wouldn't do. Tyrants require unquestioned obedience, total submission. *002.104* **"You of [the Islamic] Faith, say not (to the Prophet) words of ambiguous import like 'Listen to us,' but words of respect; and obey (him): To those who don't submit there is a grievous punishment."** While there are countless verses that confirm Islam was invented to serve Muhammad, this is as effective as any.

This brings us to one of the Qur'an's biggest problems—Allah's contradictions. Muhammad wants us to believe that the creator of the universe, is capricious and unreliable, changing his mind by canceling prior truths and obliterating his divine revelations. *002.106* **"When we cancel a Verse or throw it into oblivion, We replace it with a better one."** Or: **"Whatever Revelation We abrogate or cause to be forgotten, We substitute something better."** In the context of God, this is senseless. But in the context of a forgetful man trying to counterfeit the written record of God to serve his agenda, it's perfect.

The religion of Islam failed in Mecca. Muhammad had to cast it into oblivion, to abrogate it, to move on with the doctrine of politics and submission. Allah replaces Ar-Rahman. Piracy replaces inheritance. Jews replace Meccans. Swords replace words. Muslims replace everybody. And Muhammad gets what he wants: money, women, and power.

The reason the "abrogation" verse is so important is that it wipes out Islam as a religion. The first ninety surahs are cast into oblivion. The prophet has a new Qiblah—and a political doctrine built upon submission and sword. But as bad as that sounds, you don't know the half of it yet. The last two-dozen surahs are by far the worst; they contain some of the most immoral, hateful, intolerant, and violent words ever uttered by men.

Returning to the second edition of the never-ending argument we are told that the non-prostelizing Jews were evangelizing: *002.109* **"Quite a number of the People of the Book wish they could turn you [Muslim] (people) back to infidelity after you have believed [submitted], through selfish envy, even after the Truth has become manifest to them. Indulge them until Allah issues his orders."** The first part is funny. The second is not. Jews, who were employed, prosperous, and literate, who possessed the longest surviving and best-documented monotheistic faith in the world were *jealous* of Muhammad's band of bandits? I don't think so. But what's sinister is Allah's ultimate order to exile and murder them. Within a mere six months Muhammad would perpetrate a horrible crime.

That said, it was back to business. Muhammad needed more rituals and taxes. They became his means of suppression and oppression. *002.110* **"Establish worship, ritual prayer, and pay the zakat tax; whatever good you send before for your souls, you will find with Allah; surely Allah sees what you do."** Pay now, receive later.

Then it was back to the never-ending argument. *002.111* **"They say: 'None shall enter Paradise unless he be a Jew or a Christian.' Those are their (vain) desires. Say: 'Produce your proof if you are truthful.' Nay [the tolerant religion said], whoever submits His** face to Allah and surrenders, he will get his reward; on such shall be no fear, nor shall they grieve. The Jews say: 'The Christians follow nothing; and the Christians say: 'the Jews follow nothing (true);' Yet they (profess to) recite the (same) Scripture Book. But Allah will judge between them in their quarrel." By the seventh century, Jews had long since stopped criticizing Christians. And Jews only read out of half the book. Moreover, Christians believe every word of the Hebrew scriptures. So, once again, Allah has his facts entirely wrong.

Finished with the Christians and Jews for the moment, it was time for Allah to take a swipe at the Meccans. *002.114* "And who is more unjust than he who forbids Allah's Name to be celebrated and mentioned in the sanctuary places (mosque) and strives for their ruin? It was not fitting that such should enter them except in fear. For them there is nothing but disgrace in this world, and in the next an exceeding torment, an awful doom." This is Muhammad's feeble attempt to justify his new career path as pirate, kidnapper, and murderer. "Terrorism is justified because the Meccans shooed me away from Allah's House." And while that's as lame as it is immoral, the verse is not without a pearl. If Allah's *name* should be celebrated then "Allah" *is* a name, not a word. In other words, Allah cannot be both the Arabic word *for* God and the name *of* its god at the same time. That would be like naming your pet dog "Dog." (Dog is god, backwards; so we may have stumbled onto something.)

Now that "dog" has bared his fangs at the Meccans, it's time to bite Christians. *002.116* "They say: 'Allah hath begotten a son: glory be to Him.' Nay, to Him belongs all that is in heavens and on earth: All are subservient and obedient to Him." It's all right to say Allah has daughters if there's a buck in it, but heaven forbid you should say Christ is the son of God. "To Him is due the primal origin of the heavens and earth: When He decrees a matter, He says to it: 'Be,' and it is." It's a good thing that contradictions are abrogated in the Qur'an or this would be a problem. Everything the Qur'an says Allah created, including the earth, Adam, and Jesus, were made in a manner other than saying "Be, and it is."

In an earlier chapter, the Islamic Abraham introduced us to the second surah, starting with the 118th verse. Allah lured Abraham out of Israel, the "land flowing with milk and honey," into the wastelands of Arabia to make the pagan Ka'aba appear monotheistic. The Qur'an, however, was not as daring as the Hadith. It made no attempt to explain how or why a hundred-year-old man crossed a thousand miles of desert with an illegitimate infant and a slave girl to reach a place that wouldn't be inhabited for twenty-five centuries.

In a long-winded speech, Allah said that Abraham and his Jewish kin were Muslims practicing Islam. *002.132* "And this was the legacy that Abraham left to his sons by Yah'qub (Jacob); 'Oh my sons! Allah has chosen the Faith for you—the true religion; then die not except in the faith of Islam as Muslims. He said to his sons: 'What will you worship after me?' They said: 'We shall worship your Ilah (God), the Ilah (God) of your fathers, of Abraham, Ishmael and Isaac, the one Ilah (God): To Him we submit in Islam.'"

It's a wonder such an important profession of faith eluded the Hebrew prophets. Nowhere in the Bible are the words "Muslim, Muhammad, Allah, or Islam" written. It's inconceivable that Abraham could have had such a fine religion and not even mentioned it or his pal Allah.

We also covered Allah's admission in the 138th verse that he was a Baptist. This was followed by Allah's delusional claim that he was Yahweh.

Starting at verse 142 Allah tells us that Muslims should no longer play with the Christians and Jews. They must now recognize the monotheistic holiness of Allah's pagan shrine, the rock pile in Mecca. The Ka'aba is called a sacred and holy mosque, even though the *only* actual mosque at this time served as Muhammad's brothel. (The mosque in Medina was an open court-yard. The buildings that surrounded it served as apartments for Muhammad's wives, sex slaves, and concubines.) And the shrine of which they spoke was still home to hundreds of rock idols, including Allah's Black Stone.

002.142 **"The fools among the people will say: What has turned them from their Qiblah which they had? Say: The East and the West belong only to Allah; He guides whom He likes to the right path. Thus We have appointed you a medium nation, that you may be witnesses against mankind, and that the Messenger may be a witness against you. And We appointed the Qiblah which you formerly observed only that We might know him who follows the messenger, from him who turns on his heels."** Muhammad had just arrived in Yathrib and his foolish spirit was already calling the townsfolk "fools." The one-time prophet turned profiteer had moved away from Allah's House in disgrace following the Satanic Verses. He had changed his Qiblah to Jerusalem opportunistically—naïvely thinking the Jews would accept him as their Messiah. When they rejected him for the fool he was, his "god" told his cocon-spirator: "The Jews have rejected our bogus claims, so we aren't going to play with them any more." Team Islam issued an about-face.

You probably noticed that the never-ending argument gained a larger antagonist. Muhammad and his dark spirit are now **"against mankind."** What you may not have noticed, however, was the admission of failure. Muham-mad needed a way to determine who was in lockstep with him, as he had been unable to seduce a sufficient quantity of the Ansar Helpers to go along with his new program. Not a single Ansar joined the pirates in any of the first dozen Muslim raids. Then when the last one prevailed, ending in murder, theft, and kidnapping for ransom, they cried foul, since the raid breached the "religious" covenants.

Maududi acknowledges Muhammad's problem in his commentary. **"Dur-ing this period a new type of Muslim, called munafiqin or hypocrite, began to appear.... They professed Islam but were not prepared to abide by the consequences.... There were some who had entered the Islamic fold merely to harm it from within. There were others who were surrounded by Muslims and, therefore, had become 'Muslims' to safeguard their worldly interests."** They knew "good" Muslims were terrorist thieves.

So Muhammad came up with a plan to separate the hypocrites from his raiders. He had his dog bark: **"We appointed the Qiblah which you formerly observed only that We might know him who follows the Messenger from him who turns on his heels [and doesn't submit]."** God knows all, so this cannot be god speaking. These words must therefore be Muhammad's. **"This was surely a hard test except for those whom Allah has guided; and Allah was not going to make your faith fruitless and go to waste; surely Allah is Merciful."** Since bowing south verses north isn't a test, we must read between the lines and assume Muhammad was testing Ansar and Emigrant obedience. He needed to know whom he could count on to raid, terrorize, and plunder his enemies.

002.144 **"We see the turning of your face: now shall We turn you to a Qiblah that shall please you. Turn then your face in the direction of the Sacred Mosque (at Mecca): Wherever you are, turn your faces in that direction. The People of the Book (Jews and Christians) know well that (the Ka'aba) is the truth from their Lord. Nor is Allah unmindful of what they do."** When "god" has to lie, there's a problem. If the Jews thought the Ka'aba was godly, why did they pray facing the site of their former Temple in Jerusalem? More importantly, why did Muhammad join them? Further, how could the Ka'aba be "sacred" when it was a pagan shrine?

Unable to perform miracles, the prophet dismissed their significance. *002.145* **"Even if you were to bring to the people of the Scripture Book all the Signs, they would not follow Your Qiblah; nor are you going to follow their Qiblah; nor indeed will they follow each other's Qiblah."** This is another Allah-Oops. Christians have never had a Qiblah for Yahweh's spirit resides in us. Since Allah claims to have inspired the Gospels, he ought to have known that. **"If you, after knowledge has reached you, were to follow their (vain) desires, then were you indeed (clearly) in the wrong."**

002.146 **"The People of the Book, unto whom We gave the Scripture, know/recognize this revelation/him as they know/recognize their own sons; But lo! a party of them knowingly conceals truth."** Like all things made of man, the deeper one digs into the Qur'an the more its flaws become apparent. Before we resolve the "know/recognize" and "this/him" controversy, ponder the impossibility of **"the People of the Book unto whom We gave the Scripture"** believing that every time the Bible referenced something happening in the land of Israel, the city of Jerusalem, on Mount Moriah, or in the magnificent Temple of Solomon, it was a purposeful deception. They would have to believe that it was possible for the thousands of events chronicled in the Bible to have actually occurred in Arabia, at a rock pile in a barren and deserted ravine that a thousand years later would become a motley collection of mud huts called Mecca. They would have to believe that tens of millions of people conspired together over the course of two millennia to write the Jewish Temple in and the Muslim Ka'aba out of thousands of pages of the most meticulously maintained, most broadly read and distributed scripture of all time. Then they would have to believe that Muhammad, the pirate of Medina, was actually talking with Yahweh, the God of the Bible, and telling the truth about what happened in another time and place. It's so preposterous it begs a question. Does *anyone* really believe Islam? Or, as Ishaq and Maududi suggest, are they all hypocrites, merely going along to keep from losing their possessions and their lives?

The translations that read **"recognize him (Muhammad)"** rather than "know this" are equally outrageous. Muhammad is suggesting that the Jews of Yathrib recognized him as their Messiah but were concealing the truth. Yet in truth, the Jews didn't even recognize Yahshua as their Messiah, and he ful-filled hundreds of exacting prophecies regarding his genealogy, birth, time, life, mission, death, and resurrection. Muhammad didn't fulfill one. So to say that the Jews recognized Muhammad's prophetic credentials as they recog-nized their own sons tells us a great deal about the mindset of the man. He was as delusional as he was egotistical.

The next five verses wallow in the new Qiblah. The most important line warns the raiders not to fear the hypocrites: *002.150* **"Do not fear them; fear Me."**

Motivating men to murder requires conditioning them to hate first. The intended victims must be dehumanized: *002.171* **"The semblance of the infidels is one who shouts to one who cannot hear. They are deaf, dumb, and blind. They make no sense."** *002.174* **"Those who conceal Allah's revelations in the [Bible] Scripture Book, and thus make a miserable profit thereby [selling it to Muhammad], swallow Fire into themselves; Allah will not address them. Grievous will be their doom."** Since they're destined for hell anyway, why not kill them? *002.175* **"They are the ones who bartered away guidance for error and Torment in place of Forgiveness. Ah, what boldness (they show) for the Fire! (Their doom is) because Allah sent down the Book in truth but those who seek causes of dispute in the Book are in a schism of great opposition."**

Although this was written in code (or maybe just written badly), it pro-vides the entire equation. It confirms that the Jews sold Muhammad the Bible stories he used to try to make himself look like a prophet. As we have discov-ered, Muhammad changed these to suit his agenda. Then, since the Qur'anic accounts were different, Muhammad accused his suppliers of selling him a faulty product. He said that B and Q were once identical but that the Jews corrupted B so that they could argue with him about Q.

002.177 **"It is not piety that you turn your faces east or west; but it is the quality of one who believes in Allah and the Last Day, the Angels, the Book, and Prophets; to spend your substance in spite of love for it, for [Muhammad's] kin, for orphans, for the wayfarer [Muhammad's mercenaries], for those who ask, and for the ransom of captives; to be steadfast in devotional obligations, and paying the zakat tax."** Although two of Islam's five pillars are based upon the new Qiblah, we are told here that it isn't pious. And, while it may be a detail, Allah should have a better sense of direc-tion. The old Qiblah was north of Medina and the new one was south; nei-ther were east or west. Further, as with the first attempts at "religion" in Mecca, the first try in Medina was centered on Muhammad. He was even the one with captives to be ransomed.

The Meccans who teased Muhammad and shooed him away from their pagan Moon God shrine must now pay for their hate speech. He begins conditioning his faithful to believe retribution is good. Muhammad claims that Allah has told him that the mocking he suffered at the hands of his clan was so egregious that heads must roll. By verse 191, Allah has his war paint on and continues to whoop it up through verse 210, commanding Muslims to attack and kill their brethren.

The next verse is Muhammad's first stab at instituting a law. It's as barbaric as his religion. *002.178* **"Retaliation is prescribed for you in the matter of the murdered; the free for free, slave for slave, and female for female. And for him who is pardoned somewhat by his (injured) brother, then prosecution should be according to payment of blood money. He who transgresses after this will have a painful doom."**

002.185 **"Ramadhan is the (month) the Qur'an was sent down as a guide to mankind, also clear Proof/Signs for guidance and the criterion. So every one of you who is present during that month must spend it fasting."** The only reason Muhammad wrestled with the cave demon during Ramadhan was because it was the pagan practice of his people to observe the *Tahannuth* rituals in Ramadhan. *Tahannuth* was based upon self-deprivation and fasting, thus the idolatrous practice and holy month were incorporated into Islam. The Ka'aba Inc. made a new pillar out of an old one. **"And you must magnify Allah (Say Allahu Akbar—Allah is Greater.)"**

Speaking of Islamic pillars being constructed from regurgitated paganism: *002.189* **"They ask you about the New Moons. Say: They are but signs to mark fixed seasons in (the affairs of) men, and for Hajj Pilgrimage."** The enlightened world had long since abandoned the lunar calendar for the solar one we use today. Rather than "fixing seasons," the lunar calendar Muhammad's god was prescribing caused dates to float around the year. But Allah was the Moon God, so Muslims were forever condemned to the lunacy of ignorance.

Muhammad was now ready to reveal the real reason behind his new Qiblah. He wanted his militants to fight for what he coveted. *002.190* **"Fight in Allah's Cause those who fight you, but do not transgress limits; for Allah like not the transgressors. (This is the first Verse revealed in connection with Jihad, it was supplemented by the 9ᵗʰ Surah.)"** Although this verse clearly orders Muslims to fight, the first of many such commands, Islamic apologists use this passage in the Western media to infer that Islamic fighting can only be defensive and moderate. Yet in context, that is not what it says. Just read the next verse: *002.191* **"And kill them wherever you find and catch them, and drive them out from where they have turned you out; for Al-Fitnah (polytheism, disbelief, oppression) is worse than slaughter."** Slaying them **"wherever you find and catch them"** is clearly offensive, not defensive. So the prior verse has already been abrogated. And there is no moderation when one says that a belief, or even verbal abuse, is worse than slaughter.

"Fight them not at the Sacred Mosque, until they fight you there; but if they fight you,

kill them. Such is the reward of those who are unbelievers." This is nonsensical. It is not possible for the Muslims of Medina to be defensive fighters if they have marched to Mecca with their fighting gear.

002.192 "But if they cease/desist, Allah is Forgiving, Merciful." That sounds nice until you realize what they must "cease" doing. One must desist from rebuking Muhammad's claims—in other words, they must *become a Muslim* to avoid slaughter. Remember, no one was fighting the Muslims when this was handed down. They were the hunters. The Meccans were the prey. To be "forgiven" and not "slaughtered," one had to bow in submission and pay the zakat.

002.193 "And fight them until there is no more Fitnah (disbelief) and religion is only for Allah. But if they cease/desist, let there be no hostility except against infidel disbelievers." Muslims have been ordered to fight until the *only* religion is Islam—world conquest. And even when they have overrun the world, there shall be no safe haven for "infidel disbelievers." This is as clear as a swastika.

002.194 "The prohibited month for the prohibited month, and so for all things prohibited, there is the law of retaliation. If any one transgresses the prohibition against you, transgress likewise against him. But fear Allah, and know that Allah is with the pious." That was verbal diarrhea, so let's try another translation: "The forbidden month for the forbidden month, and forbidden things in retaliation. And one who attacketh you, attack him in like manner as he attacked you. Observe your duty to Allah, and know that Allah is with those who ward off (evil)." That was worse—there was no hint of restraint. Maybe a third translation will clear up Islam's "Golden Rule." "The Sacred month for the sacred month and all sacred things are retaliation; whoever then acts aggressively against you, inflict injury on him according to the injury he has inflicted on you." The problem isn't with the translators.

Remember Muhammad's problem? His henchmen murdered, robbed, and kidnapped in the pagan sacred month of Rejab when violence and thievery were forbidden. Muhammad couldn't pocket the booty because the offense was so heinous. This handy situational scripture, garbled as it may have been, said, "The pagan month is important because I'm a pagan god but I'm granting Muhammad a special exemption because I('m) like him."

Now that the booty was safely pocketed, it was time to encourage more of the same. *002.195* "Spend your wealth in Allah's Cause [fighting infidels], and be not cast by your own hands to perdition; and do good. Lo! Allah loves the doers of good." The Qur'an finally speaks of love, and wouldn't you know it: Allah loves Jihadists who do good by slaughtering in his cause.

Now that fighting is good, Muslims needed a place to fight, so it was off to "Perform properly (according to the Prophet's Sunnah) the Hajj or Umrah, visiting Mecca for Allah. But if you are prevented then send such gifts as you can afford [i.e. if you can't go and fight, send money so that others can fight], and do not shave your heads until the offering reaches the place of sacrifice.... Fear Allah; He is severe in punishment."

Send money even if you *can* fight: *002.215* "They ask you what they should spend.

Say: Whatever they spend is good.... Allah is aware of it."

According to Allah peace is bad and fighting is good. *002.216* "Jihad (holy fighting in Allah's Cause) is ordained for you (Muslims), though you dislike it. But it is possible that you dislike a thing which is good for you, and like a thing which is bad for you. But Allah knows, and you know not." Another translation reads: "Warfare is ordained for you, though it is hateful unto you." This is an open-ended commandment to fight anyone and everyone who has not surrendered to Islam. How, pray tell, do the "Islam-is-a-peaceful-religion" folks explain…"Jihad is ordained for you?"

002.217 "They question you concerning fighting in the sacred month. Say: 'Fighting therein is a great/grave (matter); but to prevent access to Allah, to deny Him, to prevent access to the Sacred Mosque, to expel its members, and polytheism are worse than slaughter. Nor will they cease fighting you until they make you renegades from your religion. If any of you turn back and die in unbelief, your works will be lost and you will go to Hell. Surely those who believe and leave their homes to fight in Allah's Cause have the hope of Allah's Mercy." The Islamic god must be very small if access to him can be prevented by men. But that wasn't the purpose of this passage. Muhammad wanted the Ansar Helpers or Hypocrites to know it would get nasty if they didn't join the party. He wanted fighters, not pacifists. What's more, the last line suggests something that will be made abundantly clear in later surahs: "Fight in my cause and paradise will be yours."

Muhammad had to be certain the Ansar knew that his party was not fun and games, so he had his "god" say: *002.219* "They ask you about wine and gambling. Say: 'In them is great sin, and some profit, for men; but the sin is greater than the profit.'" But if you are willing to "gamble" your soul on Muhammad's scheme, you'll find rivers flowing with "wine."

After polishing his war manifesto and get rich scheme, Muhammad turned his attention to his next favorite subject—women. Qur'anic Laws were dictated that placed women in submissive roles to men just as men had been placed in submission to Muhammad. To enforce his laws, he said: "Big Brother is watching. You'll be punished if you don't obey me."

The dark spirit returned to the main theme of the surah: "Fight because our enemies have mocked us and we hate them." The infidels were called a series of childish names. Then Muhammad convoluted Bible stories to make his crusade appear religious. These twisted portrayals continued through verse 257. A delusional trip down Jewish memory lane followed. Muhammad's twisted story of Abraham was as different from the original account as it was vulgar and insulting. Next, Allah attempted rational religious thought. His stories were moral and Biblically inspired. But sadly, even the more rational passages focused on taxes, of which Muhammad was beneficiary. This led to a rant on interest and a discussion of business contracts starting in verse 275. The motivation: Muslims borrowed money from the Jews to survive. These sections were short on spirituality and long on pent-up rage.

002.244 **"Fight in Allah's Cause, and know that Allah hears and knows all."** *002.245* **"Who is he that will loan Allah a beautiful loan, which Allah will double to his credit and multiply many times?"** Allah's boy was broke and was begging for money.

All Muhammad had to do to justify his new behavior was bastardize Hebrew scripture. *002.246* **"Have you not considered the chiefs of the Jews after Moses? They said to a prophet of theirs: Raise up for us a king, (that) we may fight in Allah's Cause. He said: 'Would you refrain from fighting if fighting were prescribed for you?' They said: 'How could we refuse to fight in Allah's Cause, seeing that we were turned out of our homes?' But when they were commanded to fight, they turned back, except a small band."** According to Allah, peace is wrong.

Some of the most incriminating Qur'anic errors are those in which Muhammad transparently projects his words and situation into the mouths and times of Jewish leaders. The Islamic scriptures have a complete disregard for time. Saul wasn't a contemporary of Moses. Therefore, in the context of history, this conversation was impossible. As such, it means either that Allah was a nincompoop or that Muhammad was an incompetent prophet, or both. *002.247* **"Their Prophet said: 'Allah has appointed Talut [Saul] as king over you.' They said: 'How can he exercise authority over us when we are better fitted than he, and he is not gifted with wealth?' He said: 'Allah has chosen him above you in preference to you, and has gifted him with knowledge, physique, and stature: Allah grants His authority to whom He pleases.'"**

002.256 **"There is no compulsion in religion."** That would be tolerant if Allah didn't abrogate the verse by proclaiming: *004.090* **"If they turn back from Islam, becoming renegades, seize them and kill them wherever you find them."**

The second surah ends with Allah's lap dog telling his people what his master wanted to hear: *002.285* "**The Messenger believes in what has been sent down to him, (as do) the believers. Each believes in Allah, His Angels, His Books, and His Messengers. 'We make no distinction between His Messengers.' And they say: 'We hear and obey.'"** The only reason such foolishness survived was the Islamic code: **"We hear and obey."** Muslims don't think; they obey. They don't believe, they surrender.

Muslims, like Germans, were deceived by an anti-Semitic charlatan: *Bukhari: V7B71N662* **"Allah's Apostle said, 'Eloquent speech is as effective as magic.'"** *Bukhari:V9B87N127* **"The Prophet said, 'I have been given eloquent speech and have been awarded victory by terror so the treasures of the earth are mine.'"**

The former wannabe prophet, turned pedophile pirate, was a racist tyrant: *Bukhari: V9B89N256* **"Allah's Apostle said, 'You should listen to and obey your ruler even if he is a black African slave whose head looks like a raisin.'"** He required obedience, not faith: *Bukhari:V9B89N258* **"The Prophet said, 'A Muslim has to listen to and obey the order of his ruler whether he likes it or not.'"** Hitler and Muhammad were cut from the same cloth. Hitler was stopped, *Mein Kampf* was exposed, and Nazism was eradicated, as they could not coexist with a civilized world. Haven't Muhammad, the Qur'an, and Islam earned the same fate?

15

WAR MADE A PROFIT

*"Prepare against them whatever arms and cavalry you can muster,
that you may strike terror in the enemies of Allah."*
"Allah desires killing them to manifest the religion."

Coveting what belonged to others, Muhammad gave us another glimpse
into his soul. *Tabari VII:26* **"When the Prophet came to Yathrib he saw the Jews fasting on
Ashura day. He questioned them, and they told him that it was the day upon which God
drowned Pharaoh and saved Moses from the Egyptians. He said, 'We have a better right
to Moses than you do.' He fasted and ordered his fellow Muslims to fast with him. When
the fast of Ramadhan was prescribed, he made Ashura optional."**

The Bible's Messianic message—past, present, and future—revolves
around the Seven Festivals of Yahweh. When the pretend Messiah asked the
Jews why they were fasting, Muhammad proved he was a phony. What's
more, he got it wrong. There is only one fast on the Jewish religious calendar,
Yom Kippur—known as the Day of Atonement. But it's celebrated in the fall,
and it has nothing to do with Pharaoh. The spring Feast of Passover commemorates freedom from Egyptian bondage. And it took the Jews more like
six days, not six months, to elude his army. (As an interesting aside, in 1978
Ron Wyatt discovered Pharaoh's graveyard in the Gulf of Aqaba branch of
the Red Sea—proving once again that the Bible's chronology was accurate.)

When Muhammad said that he had a better right to Moses than did the
Jews, his counterfeit religion became as obvious as a pink six-dollar bill with
a turbaned president. Needing to corrupt all things Biblical to please his dark
spirit, Muhammad told his fellow terrorists that they should take a break
from raiding civilians. But it wouldn't last. Stealing a ritual was insufficient.
Muhammad needed to own *everything* the Jews possessed and held sacred.

In actuality, both Ashura and Ramadhan honor false gods. The spring fast
being erroneously observed was "Crying for Tammuz," a legacy of Jewish captivity. It honors the Babylonian sun god. Catholic Lent is derived from the same
rite. And Muhammad reestablished the pagan *Tahannuth* fasts of Ramadhan
saying that they commemorated his wrestling match with the cave spirit.

Returning to Muhammad's scheme: *Tabari VII:26* **"In this year Muhammad ordered
people to pay the zakat tax. It is said that the Prophet commanded them to do this."**

Allah and Muhammad spoke with one voice. Paying the zakat became an order and then a pillar. The political manifesto was ushered in with these words: *Ishaq:235* "When the Apostle was settled in Medina and his comrades were gathered to him, the affairs of the workers were arranged, and Islam became firmly established. Prayer was instituted [the prostration was the sign of his power], the zakat tax was prescribed [dictators thrive on money], legal punishments were fixed, as were all things permitted and forbidden [as a confirmation of the tyrant's supreme authority]."

A benevolent dictator, however, he was not. *Ishaq:280* "When Allah's Apostle came to Medina it was the most fever-infested place on earth. It smote Muslims to such a degree they could only pray sitting. Muhammad came out when they were praying thus and said, 'Know that the prostration of the sitter is only half as valuable as that of the stander.' The Muslims painfully struggled to their feet despite their weakness, seeking a blessing."

This is followed by: "Then the Apostle prepared for war in pursuance of Allah's command to fight his enemies and to fight the infidels who Allah commanded him to fight." Fighting was such an essential part of Islam's formation that Tabari devoted the next sixty pages to a single conflict—the Battle of Badr. It gets five times more attention than Abraham's pilgrimage to the Ka'aba—the establishment of Islam. It gets ten times more ink that the first revelation—Muhammad's call to prophethood. It garners twenty times more coverage than Muhammad's migration to Yathrib—the Hijrah that instigated the Islamic Era. How is it that a battle became the centerpiece of a religion?

The initial salvo of the battle to resurrect Islam nearly crucified it. We are told that Muhammad led his militants on a terrorist raid designed to rob another caravan in of all months, Ramadhan. *Tabari VII:26* "In this year the great battle of Badr took place between the Messenger of Allah and the Quraysh Unbelievers in the month of Ramadhan." Since fasting was required in the sacred month, since the observance of Ramadhan was a religious obligation, a pillar of Islam, why were the first Muslims and their prophet on the prowl during their most holy time? Do you suppose money was more important than piety?

At Badr, Muhammad was the aggressor, just as he was on seventy-three of his seventy-five raids. The prophet got to choose the time, place, and victim. So he elected to terrorize money-laden civilians during Ramadhan. Reason would thus dictate that the "prophet" had discarded his original calling and become a pirate.

As you contemplate what motivated Islam's bad boy, consider this: *Tabari VII.28* "Abd al-Rahman said, 'Muhammad celebrated the night of 17 Ramadhan. In the morning traces of sleeplessness would be on his face. He would say, "On this morning Allah distinguished between truth and falsehood, revealing the Qur'an. On this morning he made Islam mighty, humbling the leaders of unbelief at Badr."'" Submission was made mighty because the Quraysh were humbled. Allah distinguished between truth and falsehood by having Muslim militants murder Meccan merchants.

But violence isn't cheap. Like today's terrorists, the first Muslims needed money. *Tabari VII:29/Ishaq:289* **"The Apostle heard that Abu Sufyan [a Meccan merchant] was coming from Syria with a large Quraysh caravan containing their money and their merchandise. He was accompanied by only thirty men."** The Meccans were going about their lives, working to make a living, something Muslims were unwilling to do. So Islam was about to rob them.

"This was after fighting had broken out between them, and people had been killed and taken captive at Nakhlah." If you were reading this out of context you might assume that these parties were in a state of war, and that both were to blame for escalating hostilities. But you know better, because the Islamic Hadith has shown that only the Muslims were militants. They had set out on a dozen terrorist raids. They had ventured out as far as two hundred miles to rob Meccan civilians. They were the sole perpetrators, having killed the Meccan, Hadrami, in cold blood. They kidnapped his companions and held them for ransom.

Ever inclined to put the best possible spin on their violent beginnings, the first Muslims claimed: *Tabari VII:29* **"This incident had provoked a state of war between the Prophet and the Quraysh and was the beginning of the fighting in which they inflicted casualties upon one another."** In other words, before the Islamic raid, there was no fighting. Not a single Muslim had been killed. In fact there were no armies. The Muslims had raiders—terrorists, in our parlance. The Meccans had merchants—businessmen, in today's vernacular.

But if pirates are shady entrepreneurs, Muhammad was a businessman, *par excellence. Ishaq:288* **"Allah divided the booty stolen from the first caravan after he made spoils permissible. He gave four-fifths to those He had allowed to take it and one-fifth to His Apostle."** Not one to miss another opportunity: *Ishaq:289* **"Muhammad summoned the Muslims and said, 'This is the Quraysh caravan containing their property. Go out and attack it. Perhaps Allah will give it to us as prey."** These lines forever damn Islam's pretense of religiosity. They bear repeating: **"This is the Quraysh caravan containing their property. Go out and attack it. Perhaps Allah will give it to us as prey."**

The motivation was piracy—not religion. The historian reports: *Tabari VII:29* **"Abu Sufyan and the horsemen of the Quraysh were returning from Syria following the coastal road. When Allah's Apostle heard about them he called his companions together and told them of the wealth they had with them and the fewness of their numbers. The Muslims set out with no other object than Sufyan and the men with him. They did not think that this raid would be anything other than easy booty."** These armed raiders wanted to steal assets and kidnap people. Since the prophet's sole motivation was piracy, not piety, Islam cannot be a "religion."

The very fact the first adherents of this perverse doctrine recorded this stunning admission of guilt reminds me of the Nazis and the way they chronicled their atrocities in World War II. Immoral, hateful, and violent doctrines like Islam and Nazism corrode men's minds and consciences to the point they become unable to differentiate right from wrong. Ridding the world of those they view as inferior, stealing their possessions, becomes part of their mission and thus becomes good—deeds worthy of heroic lore and scripture.

As further proof that the Badr raid was an act of terrorism, another Hadith reports: *Bukhari:V5B59N702* "Allah did not admonish anyone who had not participated in the Ghazwa [raid] of Badr, for in fact, Allah's Apostle had only gone out in search of the Quraysh caravan so that he could rob it. But Allah arranged for the Muslims and their enemy to meet by surprise. I was at the Aqaba pledge with Allah's Apostle when we gave our lives in submission, but the Badr battle is more popular amongst the people. I was never stronger or wealthier than I was when I followed the Prophet on a Ghazwa.'" That pretty much sums up Islam.

Upon hearing that Muhammad was on the prowl, the Quraysh sent a delegation out to protect their people and business assets. This explains why the Qur'an said Muslims were contemplating a "choice" between taking "easy booty" and fighting for doctrinal supremacy. "They did not suppose that there would be a great battle. Concerning this Allah revealed a Qur'an: 'And you longed that other than the armed one might be yours.'" [Qur'an 8:7]

Before I comment, I would like you to have the benefit of the entire verse: *008.007* "Behold! Allah promised you that one of the two parties would be yours. You wished for the unarmed one, but Allah willed to justify His truth according to His words and to cut off the roots of the unbelievers." This means Muhammad was a pirate in the worst sense of the word. He was after money—booty. But it was worse than that. He led a gang of armed men to attack a defenseless civilian enterprise, one owned by his rival. As such, it was an act of terrorism. And there is no way to discount the source of this condemning scripture. It was covered in all three Hadith collections and in the Qur'an.

The Traditions report: *Ishaq:289* "The people answered the Prophet's summons; some eagerly, some reluctantly." *Tabari VII:29* "When Abu Sufyan heard that Muhammad's Companions were on their way to intercept his caravan, he sent a message to the Quraysh. 'Muhammad is going to intercept our caravan, so protect your merchandise.' When the Quraysh heard this, the people of Mecca hastened to defend their property and protect their men as they were told Muhammad was lying in wait for them."

The Sira suggests that they weren't quite so hasty: *Ishaq:290* "Some of the Meccans got up to circumambulate the Ka'aba…. Sitting around the mosque, they wondered why they had allowed this evil rascal to attack their men." The pagans were being religious, worshiping Allah in his mosque. The Muslims had abandoned religion, setting out on a terrorist raid in the holy month of Ramadhan.

Ishaq:292 "Setting out in Ramadhan, Muhammad was preceded by two black flags. His companions had seventy camels on which men rode in turns." It's interesting: the white battle flags of the Maghazi raids inspired by Muhammad turned black when the "prophet" personally led the parade. *Tabari VII:38* "I have been informed by authorities that Muhammad set out on 3 Ramadhan at the head of 310 of his companions. The Emigrants on the day of Badr were 77 men, and the Ansar were 236. The war banner of the Messenger was carried by Ali. The banner of the Ansar was carried by Sa'd."

Back in Ka'abaVille: *Tabari VII:30* **"A body of Meccan men was drawn from the clans. Neither the Prophet nor his Companions heard about this force until they reached Badr, which was on the coastal route the Quraysh caravan had taken from Syria."** These passages confirm that Muhammad was on the prowl. They reveal that the caravan was comprised of a poorly protected assemblage of businessmen. They suggest that when Abu sent for help, it came in the form of townsfolk. There was no standing army. Mecca was a tiny village of some five thousand traders eking out a humble living. They didn't have a police force much less a military. Before Muhammad and Islam, they hadn't needed one.

Ishaq:293 / Tabari VII:30 **"The prophet marched forward and spent the night near Badr with his Companions. They did not know that the Quraysh had come out against them. While the Prophet was standing in prayer [asking Allah to help him steal] some Quraysh water-carriers came to the well. Among these was a black slave. Muhammad's men seized him and brought him to the Messenger's bivouac. They ordered him to salute Allah's Apostle. Then they questioned him about Abu Sufyan, having no idea that he was not from the caravan. When the slave began to tell them about the protecting force, it was unwelcome news, for the only object of their raid was Abu Sufyan and [the booty from] his caravan."**

Picture this scene. The founder of a "religion" is out on a terrorist mission designed to raid a civilian business. He is praying, asking his spirit to help him kidnap innocent people and steal their possessions. His fellow militants capture a slave and torture him, trying to solicit information. *Tabari VII:30* **"Meanwhile the Prophet was praying, bowing and prostrating himself, and also seeing and hearing the treatment of the slave. When the slave told them that the Quraysh had come to meet them, they began to beat him and called him a liar. 'You are trying to conceal the whereabouts of Abu Sufyan and his caravan. They beat him severely and continued to interrogate him but they found that he had no knowledge of what they were looking for."**

I have said that Muhammad was the most vile and immoral man to have ever walked the earth. The first Muslims agree, although their hearts and minds have been so corroded by Islam they don't seem to care. They think that they are just describing a normal day at the prophetic office. For such immoral and barbaric acts to have been passed on as Traditions and linked to the Qur'an, Muslims must view these terrorist raids and the ensuing crimes favorably. They must see such ungodly behavior as a living witness of Allah's Cause—an example of how to be a good Muslim.

Tabari VII:31 **"When the slave said, 'I am from the Quraysh who have come out against you,' they beat him, but when he said, 'I am with Abu Sufyan,' they left him alone. When the Prophet saw what they were doing he stopped his prayer. He said, 'By Him in Whose hand my soul rests, you beat him when he tells the truth and leave him alone when he lies.'"** Muhammad wasn't bothered by Muslims beating the black slave, just by their inept interrogation technique.

And he was nervous. Mercenaries can be an unruly lot: *Ishaq:294* **"The Apostle was afraid the Ansar would not feel obliged to help him fight without the enemy being the** aggressor and attacking in Medina." This is further evidence Muhammad wasn't defending Muslims and Islam. As proof he wasn't a prophet, the Ansar surprised him: "Sa'd said, 'We hear and obey. We are experienced in war, trustworthy in combat. Allah will let us show you something that will bring you joy. The Apostle was delighted at Sa'd's words which greatly encouraged him. Muhammad shouted, 'It is as if I see the enemy lying prostrate.'" The founder of Islam was pleased by the prospect of war and encouraged by the thought of his foe bowing in submission. That's fine if you're Stalin, Mao, or Hitler. It's bad if you're Muhammad.

The Sira speaks of another interrogation. *Ishaq:295* "A young man was brought to the Apostle and beaten. When the Muslims were displeased with his answers they beat him soundly. Watching the interrogation while performing two prostrations, the Prophet interrupted the proceedings and said, 'Mecca has thrown us pieces of its liver!'"

But alas, the intended target escaped the raiders' grasp. *Ishaq:295* "Abu Sufyan changed the caravan's direction from the shore road, traveling as quickly as possible." *Ishaq:296* "When Abu saw that he had saved his caravan he sent word to the Quraysh. 'Since you came out to save your caravan, your men, and property, go back home.'" Some of the merchant militia left but, "Abu Jahl said, 'Badr was the site of an Arab fair. We are going to spend a few days, slaughter camels, feast, drink wine, and have some girls play for us.'" The non-partiers said, "'We came out to protect our property and defend our men. There is no point of staying to fight.' So they returned to Mecca."

On the Muslim front, we discover that Muhammad wasn't much of a general. We are told that a man named Hubab asked him, *Ishaq:297* "Did Allah order you to occupy this place so that we have no choice, or was this position chosen as a matter of opinion for military tactics?" When Muhammad said that Allah had not spoken to him about it the Ansar chief saved the day and ruined the world: "'This is not the proper place.' Hubab said, 'We should go to the well nearest the enemy, stop up all other wells, and deprive them of water.' Then Sa'd said, 'Prophet, let us build you a booth of palm fronds from which you can watch the battle safely.' The Apostle thanked and blessed them."

So let the battle begin: *Tabari VII:32* "When the Quraysh advanced, Muhammad threw dust in the direction of their faces, and Allah put them to flight.... The Meccan [merchant] force and the Prophet's [pirates] met and Allah gave victory to His Messenger, shamed the unbelievers, and satisfied the Muslims' thirst for revenge on them." To think that these delusional and immoral boys started a religion is beyond belief.

Ishaq:297 "When the Apostle saw them he cried, 'Allah, they called me a liar. Destroy them this morning.'" Jeremiah, he was not. The Meccans, however, were civilized: *Ishaq:298* "Utba rose to speak. 'Let us turn back and leave Muhammad to the rest of the Arabs. If we fall upon him, we will be haunted for having slain the son or brother of our kin.'"

Tabari VII:52 "The Prophet said to his companions, 'You are the same number as the people of Saul on the day he met Goliath." Actually, Saul and his men were far more numerous. Yet they refused to fight the Philistines, which is why David was given the opportunity to sling himself into immortality. Had Muhammad been a real prophet, he never would have quoted this story. Had he had any faith, he would have followed David's example.

Tabari VII:52/Ishaq:299 "Aswad, an ill-natured man, took the field, and Hamzah came out to meet him. In the encounter Hamzah cut off Aswad's foot and half his leg.... Hamzah pursued him and struck a blow, killing Aswad. After this, Utbah took the field and issued a challenge to single combat. Three young Ansar Muslims came forward to meet him." The Emigrants had cowered, so Muhammad commanded. "'Arise Ubaydah, Hamzah, and Ali.' It was no time before Hamzah had killed Shaybah and Ali had killed Walid. Ubaydah and Utbah each inflicted a blow upon his adversary. Hamzah and Ali then turned on Utbah with their swords and finished him off. They lifted up their companion Ubaydah to safety. His foot had been cut off and the marrow was flowing out. When they brought him to Muhammad, Ubaydah said, 'Am I not a martyr, O Messenger of Allah?' 'Yes indeed,' the Prophet replied." We have our first entrant into Islamic paradise. Can you imagine the surprise on his face when he discovered that it wasn't as Muhammad had described and that Allah was indeed waiting for him?

Tabari VII:54 "Muhammad turned toward his new Qiblah and said. 'Allah, if this band perishes today, you will be worshipped no more.'" Since Meccan Moon Gods were in sparse demand, he was probably right. "Abu Bakr picked up his cloak and put it on him, grasping him from behind. 'O Prophet whom I value more than my father and mother, this constant calling on your Lord is annoying.' Then Allah revealed, 'When you sought the help of your Lord he answered you saying, "I will help you with a thousand angels, rank on rank."'" [Qur'an 8:9] Sure, why not? Allah's angels are so feeble it takes a thousand of them to do battle with a few hundred intoxicated merchants. And lest we forget, the future Caliph found prayer annoying. He was there for the booty.

Muhammad cried out, *Bukhari:V5B59N330/Ishaq:300* "Here is Gabriel holding the rein of a horse and leading the charge. He is equipped with his weapons and ready for the battle. There is dust upon his front teeth." Why was Muhammad's spirit so eager to kill? And why was he a dirty fighter? *Bukhari:V5B59N327* "Gabriel came to the Prophet and said, 'How do you view the warriors of Badr?' The Prophet said, 'I see the fighters as the best Muslims.' On that, Gabriel said, 'And so are the Angels who are participating in the Badr battle.'" The "best" Muslims are warriors. And Allah's best angels are demons. Is this a great religion, or what?

Tabari VII:54 "The Prophet said when he was in his awning, 'Allah, keep your contract and your promise.'" The dark spirit's contract with his prophet traded submission to him for a founder's share in the Ka'aba Inc. His promise was to make Muhammad rich, powerful, and amply sexed. *Bukhari:V5B59N289* "Abu Bakr took his hand and said, 'This is enough, Prophet. You have tired your Lord with your pestering.'"

The next line distinguished Muhammad from the prophets he claimed were his peers. "Muhammad was wearing his coat of mail." Armor was something Noah, Abraham, Jonah, Moses, and Jesus seldom wore. Nor did they say, "They will be routed and will turn and flee. The hour of doom is their appointed tryst, and it will be more wretched and more bitter than this earthly failure." [54:45] In other words, "To hell with them."

Thus far, from a religious perspective, the battle of Badr has been a bust. But things were about to change: *Tabari VII:55* **"Mihaja, the mawla [slave] of Umar [the future Caliph] was struck by an arrow and killed. He was the first Muslim to die."**

Mihaja's death must have rattled the militants because Muhammad was forced to preach a sermon that would make him the Prophet of Doom: *Ishaq:300/ Tabari VII:55* **"Allah's Messenger went out to his men and incited them to fight. He promised, 'Every man may keep all the booty he takes.' Then Muhammad said, 'By Allah, if any man fights today and is killed fighting aggressively, going forward and not retreating, Allah will cause him to enter Paradise.'"** They were just words—sound waves that filtered through the air. Yet they have reverberated for 1400 years. They echo still.

"Umayr, who was holding some dates in his hand and eating them, said, 'Fine, fine. This is excellent! Nothing stands between me and my entering Paradise except to be killed by these people!' He threw down the dates, seized his sword, and fought until he was slain." The means behind the madness had finally materialized. Muhammad told his fellow militants that their reward was Allah's paradise. All they had to do to earn their prize was to die murdering others in pursuit of booty.

This Muslim militant, this disciple of Muhammad, this misguided youth who had gone off on a terrorist raid to kidnap defenseless civilians and steal their possessions, died shouting these words: *Ishaq:300* **"I am fighting in Allah's service. This is piety and a good deed. In Allah's war I do not fear as others should. For this fighting is righteous, true, and good."** Consider the number of times the Qur'an has spoken of "righteous, true, and good deeds." Now you know Allah's definition of "piety," and what a "good deed" actually represents. You also learned Muhammad's definition of a good Muslim.

In a way, Muhammad may have been right. If he was speaking on behalf of Lucifer, not Gabriel, as I suspect, "fighting aggressively" for "booty" would have earned a murdering thief direct admission into Satan's paradise. As for Muslim martyrs finding virgins—I wouldn't bet my life on it.

But Muslim lives were meaningless to Muhammad; just as Islamic clerics find suicide bombers expendable. In that light, Muhammad issued the "Suicide Bomber Creed" (not for himself, mind you): *Ishaq:300/ Tabari VII:56* **"'O Messenger of Allah, what makes the Lord [Lucifer] laugh with joy at his servant?' He replied, 'When he plunges his hand into the midst of an enemy without armor.' So Auf took off the coat of mail he was wearing and threw it away. Then he took his sword and fought the enemy until he was killed."** It was the seventh century version of today's boy bombs.

While that's clear, I am perplexed by what Muhammad said. It's odd that he didn't need an angelic revelation to know what made Allah **"laugh with joy."** And it sounds as if Allah likes to do the plunging and killing. Further, can you fathom a "religion" built around a spirit who prefers death to salvation?

Then in a tone as demented as the spirit guiding him: *Ishaq:301/Tabari VII:56* **"Muhammad picked up a handful of pebbles and faced the Quraysh. He shouted, 'May** their faces be deformed!' He threw the pebbles at them and ordered his companions to attack. The foe was routed. Allah killed Quraysh chiefs and caused many of their nobles to be taken captive. While the Muslims were taking prisoners, the Messenger was in his hut." Whether you are Biblically grounded and see Muhammad and his spirit as demonic, or just the personification of evil, there is no way to see them as *good*.

While it's subtle, there is a bit of psychological gamesmanship going on here. Allah was credited with the killing and kidnapping—it wasn't Muhammad or his militants. No. They weren't murdering thieves. Their god was.

Bukhari:V5B59N290 "The Prophet said, 'The believers who failed to join the Ghazwa of Badr and those who took part in it are not equal in reward." Muhammad loved murderers. He even loved their weapons: *Bukhari:V5B59N333* "Az-Zubair said, 'I attacked him with my spear and pierced his eye. I put my foot over his body to pull the weapon out, but even then I had to use great force. Later on Allah's Apostle asked me for that spear and I gave it to him.'" Show me your treasure and I will reveal your soul.

Ishaq:301/Tabari VII:56 "As the Muslims were laying their hands on as many prisoners as they could catch, the Prophet, I have been told, saw disapproval in the face of Sa'd. He said, 'Why are you upset by the taking of captives?' Sa'd replied, 'This was the first defeat inflicted by Allah on the infidels. Slaughtering the prisoners would have been more pleasing to me than sparing them.'" Remember these hateful words and who spoke them. We have not heard the last of Sa'd.

In a long Hadith from Abd Al-Rahman, one of the butchers of Nakhlah, we hear: *Ishaq:302/Tabari VII:60* "Umayyah [a merchant] was a friend of mine in Mecca. My name was Abd Amr, but when I became a Muslim I was called Abd al-Rahman." This militant was renamed after the first Islamic god. As such, this is a stinging repudiation of Islam's first pillar. "Umayyah used to meet me when we were in Mecca and would say, 'Abd Amr, do you dislike the name your father gave you?' I would reply, 'Yes.' Umayyah would then say, 'I do not recognize Ar-Rahman [as a god], so adopt a name that I can call you by when we meet.'"

After some chatter the friends turned enemies by Islam settled on a name. "'Well then, you are Abd al-Ilah [Slave-to-the-God].' I agreed." This line confirms the single most fatal charge that can be leveled against Islam. The Arabic word for god is "ilah" not "allah." Like Ar-Rahman, Allah was the personal name of a rock idol that became one of the Islamic gods. This simple conversation obliterates Muhammad's credibility, the Qur'an's authority, and Islam's legitimacy. Since Ar-Rahman and Allah are names of gods used throughout the Qur'an and Hadith, Islam's central claim is bogus. Neither Allah nor Ar-Rahman are Yahweh or Yahshua. And since the Islamic duo are incompatible by name and character with Yahweh and Yahshua, all Biblical references are just crass plagiarism—inspired by a man's lust for money, sex, and power.

The Tradition continues, giving us an up close and personal insight into what Islam did to a man's mind and soul. Fair warning, this isn't pretty: *Tabari VII:59/Ishaq:303* "On the day of Badr I passed Umayyah as he was standing with his son Ali, holding his hand. I had with me some coats of mail which I had taken as plunder. Umayyah said, 'Abd al-Ilah, would you like to take me as a prisoner? I will be more valuable to you as a captive to be ransomed than the coats of mail that you are carrying.' I said, 'Yes. Come here then.' I flung away the armor and bound Umayyah and his son Ali, taking them with me." According to Muhammad and his god, kidnapping for ransom was a legitimate religious practice—one more profitable than stealing armor.

And in case you're wondering, the Meccan surrendered because he didn't want the Muslim raiders to kill his son. But it didn't work out very well. "People [Muslim militants] encircled us [Abd al-Rahman and his captives]. Then they restrained us physically. One of the Muslims drew his sword and struck Ali in the leg, severing it so that he fell down. Umayyah gave a scream the like of which I have never heard. I said, 'Save yourself, for there is no escape for your son. By Allah, I cannot save him from these men.' Then the Muslims hacked Ali to pieces. Abd al-Rahman used to say, 'May Allah have mercy on Bial [a former slave turned Muslim marauder]! I lost my coats of mail, and he deprived me of my captives.'" In trying to hype the religion of war, the practitioners harpooned it. They not only demoted their gods to pagan status, they exposed their immoral motives. Islam was all about the money. And while that should have been enough to impugn the doctrine, the fatal blow was in the last paragraph. Muhammad so corrupted these men that they mutilated a child in front of his father. And there was no sense of guilt, no glimmer of humanity. Their only remorse was over lost booty.

Yes, Islam is an evil curse that must be dispelled: *Bukhari:V5B59N297* "The Prophet faced the Ka'aba and invoked evil on the Quraysh people specifically cursing: Shaiba, Utba, Walid and Abu Jahl. I bear witness, by Allah, that I saw them all dead, putrefied by the sun, as Badr was a very hot day." Lucifer and his demons must have been in paradise: evil curses were being invoked, people were dying, bodies were putrefied, and it was hot. Moreover, their favorite prophet was on duty: *Bukhari: V5B59N397* "Allah's Apostle raised his head after bowing the first Rak'a of the morning prayer. He said, 'O Allah! Curse so-and-so and so-and-so.' After he had invoked evil upon the Quraysh, Allah revealed: 'Your Lord will send thousands of angels riding upon chargers sweeping down as a form of good tidings to reassure you that victory comes from Him. He will cut off parts of the unbelievers, overthrow them, and turn them back in frustration. For Allah is forgiving and kind.'" [3:124] Islam was a team effort.

Ibn Ishaq tells us: *Tabari VII:60/Ishaq:303* "A cousin of mine and I mounted a hill from which we could overlook Badr and see who would be defeated, so that we could join in the plundering afterwards." "I was pursuing one of the Meccan polytheists in order to smite him, when his head suddenly fell off before my sword touched him. Then I knew that someone other than I had killed him." The implication is that one of Allah's angelic brigades did the dastardly deed. "My son, I saw Muslims on the day of Badr, and saw that one of us would wave his sword at a polytheist, and the man's head would fall from his body before the sword touched him." "The sign of the angels on the day of Badr was white turbans which trailed down their backs, and on the day of Hunayn it was red turbans.

The angels did not fight on any day except the battle of Badr; on the other days they were reinforcements, assistants, and helpers, but they struck no blows." It was another Islamic first: killer angels wielding swords. Either way Islam loses. If there were no angels, then Muhammad and his disciples were liars. If an angelic horde was out chopping off the heads of merchants so militants could rob them, they were demons.

For those familiar with the Bible, you may recall that over the course of 4,000 years, angels caused men to die on only two occasions. Both were in self defense and no one got rich. The Egyptians lost their first-born sons so that the Jewish slaves might be freed, and the Assyrians who were besieging Jerusalem were foiled.

Confirming that the Badr terrorist campaign was personal and political, not religious, we read: *Tabari VII:61/Ishaq:304* "When the Prophet had finished with his enemy, he gave orders that Abu Jahl should be found among the dead. He said, 'O Allah, do not let him escape!' The first man who encountered Abu Jahl yelled out and I made him my mark. When he was within my reach, I attacked him and struck him a blow which severed his foot and half his leg. By Allah, when it flew off I could only compare it to a date-stone which flies out of a crusher when it is struck. Then Abu's son hit me on the shoulder and cut off my arm. It dangled at my side from a piece of skin. The fighting prevented me from reaching him after that. I fought the whole day, dragging my arm behind me. When it began to hurt me, I put my foot on it and stood until I pulled it off.'" Consider the indoctrination and the motivation required to inspire such devotion. And contemplate how the same prophet and doctrine arouse the same hateful passions today—passions capable of toppling economies and nations.

"Then Mu'awwidh passed by Abu Jahl, who was now crippled and laying there helpless. He hit him until he could no longer move, leaving Jahl gasping for his last breath. But then Mu'awwidh was killed. Abd Allah bin Mas'ud passed by Jahl right when the Messenger ordered us to search for him among the corpses. The Prophet said, 'If you cannot identify him, look for the mark of a wound on his knee, for I jostled against him when we were boys. I pushed him so that he fell and scratched one of his knees.'" Translated: "I may be a cowardly slithering snake of a man now, but I wasn't always a weasel."

Ishaq:304 "Abd Allah bin Mas'ud said, 'I found Abu Jahl in the throws of death. I put my foot on his neck because he had grabbed me once at Mecca and had hurt me. Then I said, Has Allah disgraced you and put you to shame, O enemy of Allah?' 'In what way has he disgraced me?' he asked. 'Am I anything more important than a man whom you have killed? Tell me, to whom is the victory?' I said, 'To Allah and his Messenger.'" *Bukhari:V5B59N298* "Abu Jahl said, 'You should not be proud that you have killed me.'" It was the Muslims who had disgraced themselves. A few hundred militants had gone out to rob some merchants, yet god and prophet declared a glorious victory. Even the pagan Abu Jahl knew that it was a meaningless skirmish, an embarrassment.

Ishaq:304/Tabari VII:62 "I cut off Abu Jahl's head and brought it to the Messenger. I said, 'O Allah's Prophet, this is the head of the enemy of Allah, Abu Jahl.' Muhammad said, 'Is this so, by Allah, than whom there is no other deity?' This used to be the Messenger of Allah's oath. [The vengeful Muhammad was no more articulate than the inspired one.] I said, 'Yes.' Then I threw down his head before the Prophet's feet. He said, 'Praise be to Allah.'" God doesn't have enemies; only men and demons do.

Bukhari:V5B59N572 "O Muslims, take not My enemies as friends, offering them kindness when they reject Allah, the Prophet Muhammad, and his Qur'an. And whoever does that, then indeed he has gone (far) astray. You have come out to fight in My Cause, seeking My acceptance so do not be friendly with them, even in secret." [60:1]

It's hard to imagine men writing this down as if it were "religious." *Ishaq:305* "Ukkasha fought until he broke his sword. He came to the Apostle who gave him a wooden cudgel telling him to fight with that. He brandished it and it became a brilliant weapon. Allah gave him victory while he wielded it. He took that weapon with him to every raid he fought with Allah's Apostle until he was killed in the rebellion [the War of Compulsion]. These were his dying words: 'What do you think about when you kill people? Are these not men just because they are not Muslims?'" Sobering, isn't it?

According to Ibn Ishaq, Muhammad's quota on paradise was proclaimed at Badr. *Ishaq:306* "When the Allah's Apostle said, '70,000 of my followers shall enter Paradise like the full moon,' Ukkasha asked if he could be one of them. Then a lesser Ansari asked to be included, but the Prophet replied, 'Ukkasha beat you to it and my prayer is now cold.'" At this point in his "mission," Muhammad's vision was no greater than the conquest of Mecca and central Arabia. Inciting 70,000 fools to die for what he coveted seemed sufficient at the time. Little did he know that his scam would live on, infecting billions, and sending millions to their death. Second, the **"like a full moon"** was an acknowledgement of Allah's lunar genealogy. Third, to "earn" Allah's paradise one has to be a big-time murderer. And fourth, imagine risking your soul on a man who said: **"my prayer is cold."**

Yet both prophet and god loved nothing more than for men to sacrifice their lives satiating their lust for carnage. *Bukhari:V5B59N379* "When we wrote the Holy Qur'an, I missed one of the verses I used to hear Allah's Apostle reciting. Then we searched for it and found it. The verse was: 'Among the Believers are men who have been true to their Covenant with Allah. Of them, some have fulfilled their obligations to Allah (i.e. they have been killed in Allah's Cause), and some of them are (still) waiting to be killed.' (Surah 33.23) So we wrote this in its place in the Qur'an." According to the Qur'an, all *good* Muslims fall into one of two categories: those who *have* died killing infidels for Allah, and those who *will* die killing infidels for Allah.

The Badr raiders failed as pirates. The caravan they went out to plunder got away. Yet the skirmish that ensued between militants and merchants resurrected a dying doctrine and ultimately reshaped the world. The Islamic lore that emerged that spring morning in 623 from the blood-soaked sands near the eastern shore of the Red Sea, serves as the only report of what happened at Badr. Here are some of the most insightful lines spoken that day:

The Muslim Abdallah recited this poem: *Ishaq:315* "It was so criminal, men could hardly imagine it. Muhammad was ennobled because of the bloody fighting. I swear we shall never lack soldiers, nor army leaders. Driving before us infidels until we subdue them with a halter above their noses and a branding iron. We will drive them to the ends of the earth. We will pursue them on horse and on foot. We will never deviate from fighting in our cause. We will bring upon the infidels the fate of the Ad and Jurhum. Any people that disobey Muhammad will pay for it. If you do not surrender to Islam, then you will live to regret it. You will be shamed in Hell, forced to wear a garment of molten pitch forever!" Second only to the Qur'an, this may be the nastiest, meanest, most intolerant, violent, and sadistic poem ever recited.

Fulfilling prophecy, another Muslim said, speaking of the sons of Ishmael: *Ishaq:316* "In peace you are wild asses—rough and coarse. And in war you are like women wearing corsets. But I care not so long as my hand can grasp my trusty blade."

Ishaq:310 "A Meccan said, 'As soon as we were confronted by the raiding party, we turned our backs and they started killing and capturing us at their pleasure. Some of our men turned tail humiliated. Allah smote some of us with pustules from which we died.'" *Ishaq:311* "When the Quraysh began to bewail their dead, consumed in sorrow, one said, 'Do not do this for Muhammad and his companions will rejoice over our misfortune.'" These Hadith are eerily prophetic of the Islamic reaction to 9/11.

Hamzah recited: *Ishaq:340* "Surely Badr was one of the world's great wonders. The roads to death are plain to see. Disobedience causes a people to perish. They became death's pawns. We had sought their caravan, nothing else. But they came to us and there was no way out. So we thrust our shafts and swung our swords severing their heads. Our swords glittered as they killed. The banner of error was held by Satan. He betrayed the evil ones, those prone to treachery. He led them to death crying, 'Fear Allah. He is invincible!' Satan knew what they could not see. On that day a thousand spirits were mustered on excited white stallions. Allah's army fought with us. Under our banner, Gabriel attacked and killed them." I agree; Satan was there.

Ali recited: *Ishaq:341* "Have you seen how Allah favored His Apostle and how He humiliated the unbelievers? They were put to shame in captivity and death. The Apostle's victory was glorious. Its message is plain for all to see. The Lord brought repeated calamities upon the pagans, bringing them under the Apostle's power. Allah's angry army smote them with their trusty swords. Many a lusty youngster left the enemy lying prone. Their women wept with burning throats for the dead were lying everywhere. But now they are all in Hell." It's hard to believe. Violence and pain begat a religion.

One of the Meccan merchants said in response: *Ishaq:342* "I wonder at foolish men like these who sing frivolously and vainly of the slain at Badr. This was nothing more than an impious and odious crime. Men fought against their brothers, fathers, and sons. Any with discernment and understanding recognize the wrong that was done here." Al-Harith was right. I find his words rational and sobering—foreboding.

Ka'b, a Muslim commander, recited: *Ishaq:344* "I wonder at Allah's deed. None can defeat Him. Evil ever leads to death. We unsheathed our swords and testified to the unity of Allah, and we proved that His Apostle brought truth. We smote them and they scattered. The impious met death. They became fuel for Hell. All who aren't Muslims must go there. It will consume them while the Stoker [Allah] increases the heat. They had called Allah's Apostle a liar. They claimed, 'You are nothing but a sorcerer.' So Allah destroyed them."

As you read these words, remember, this day *made* Islam. On it, Hassan proclaimed: *Ishaq:348* "They retreated in all directions. They rejected the Qur'an and called Muhammad a liar. But Allah cursed them to make his religion and Apostle victorious. They lay still in death. Their throats were severed. Their foreheads embraced the dust. Their nostrils were defiled with filth. Many a noble, generous man we slew this day. We left them as meat for the hyenas. And later, they shall burn in the fires of Hell." A terrorist raid designed to loot a caravan had become a noble crusade. These men who had come to protect their property and family were butchered. Their only crime was calling a sorcerer a liar.

Pirates and mercenaries fight for booty, not piety. Ubayda was no exception: *Ishaq:349* "The battle will tell the world about us. Distant men will heed our warning. The infidels may cut off my leg, yet I am a Muslim. I will exchange my life for one with virgins fashioned like the most beautiful statues."

A Muslim recited these lines: *Ishaq:357* "Their leaders were left prostrate. Their heads were sliced off like melons. Many an adversary have I left on the ground to rise in pain, broken and plucked. When the battle was joined I dealt them a vicious blow. Their arteries cried aloud, their blood flowed. That is what I did on the day of Badr."

At the end of the fighting: *Ishaq:306/Tabari VII:62* "Allah's Apostle ordered the dead to be thrown into a pit. All were thrown in except Umayyah. He had swollen up in his coat of mail and filled it. They went to move him, but he fell apart, so they left him where he was and flung some rocks over him. As the dead were being thrown in, Muhammad stood over them and said, 'O people of the pit, have you found what your Lord promised you to be true? For I have found what my Lord promised me to be true.' The Muslims said to him. 'O Allah's Messenger, are you speaking to dead people who have been putrefied?' He replied, 'They know what I promised them is the truth.' You hear what I say no better than they, but they cannot answer me." This is almost as sick as the Islamic god gloating over the new arrivals to hell. It's almost as if Muhammad's warped character rubbed off on Allah. (Did I say *almost?*) They became twins. Muhammad was the first prophet to promise his people slaughter rather than salvation. It was one prophecy he got right.

Bukhari:V5B58N193 "The Prophet cursed those that had teased him. He said, 'O Allah! Destroy the chiefs of Quraysh, Abu Jahl, Utba, Shaba, Umaiya, and Ubai.' I saw these people killed on the day of Badr battle and thrown in the pit except Ubai whose body parts were mutilated." He was putrid, possessed, and pathetic, not prophetic.

While some of this material is redundant, it's important to see how the four prime Islamic sources work together to provide us with a portrait of this man, his spirit, and religion. Every word devastates Muhammad's character; every stroke reveals his motives. The battle of Badr resurrected the fledgling political doctrine of Islam. Yet the motive was greed. The means was terror. The reason was Muhammad. He had come full circle. The abused child was now an empowered, demented, and vicious abuser.

This Hadith is telling: *Bukhari:V5B59N314-7* **"At Badr, the Prophet ordered the corpses of twenty-four Quraysh leaders to be thrown into a pit. It was a habit of the Prophet that whenever he conquered some people, he used to stay at the battlefield for three nights [to gloat]. So, on the third day he ordered that his she-camel be saddled and he set out. His Companions followed, saying: 'The Prophet is proceeding for some great purpose.' When he halted at the edge of the pit, he addressed the corpses of the Quraysh infidels by their names, 'O so-and-so, son of so-and-so! Why didn't you obey Allah's Apostle? I have found true what my Lord [Lucifer] promised me. Have you found true what your Lord promised you?' Umar said, 'O Apostle! You are speaking to the dead!' Muhammad said, 'Allah brought them to life (again) to let them hear me, to reprimand them, to slight them, and so that I might take my revenge over them.' Then he quoted the Holy Verse out of the Qur'an: 'You cannot make the dead listen or the deaf hear your call...until they believe Our Signs and come into submission."** [30:52] Both prophet and his spirit needed men to obey; they required full and unquestioned submission. That, in a nutshell, was what Islam was all about.

The first Muslim historian covers the despicable dialog in a manner that nails Muhammad's motives: *Tabari VII:63* **"The Messenger uttered these words: 'O people of the pit, you were evil fellow tribesmen to your Prophet! You disbelieved me when other people believed me. You drove me out when other people gave me shelter. You fought me when other people came to my aid.'"**

This sorry excuse for a man wasn't finished gloating. *Ishaq:306* **"The Apostle's Companions heard him get up in the middle of the night. He went to the pit and said, 'O people of the pit,' enumerating all who had be thrown into the dirty well. 'I have found what my Lord promised me to be true.'"** Normal men would have been repulsed by the sight and smell of rotting corpses. But not this man, he was inspired. So was his spirit, the Lord of the Pit.

This next vignette is equally disturbing. The foolishness of Islam is behind us. All that remains is tragic. *Tabari VII:63/Ishaq:307* **"Utbah was dragged to the well. Muhammad looked into the face of his son Abu, who was dejected. 'I fear perhaps some sadness has entered you on account of your father.' 'No, by Allah, O Prophet of Allah,' Abu replied. 'I had no misgivings about my father, nor about his death. But I knew my father to be a judicious, wise, forbearing, cultured, and virtuous man. I used to hope that these qualities would lead him to Islam.'"** No. These qualities kept him from Islam.

The skirmish over, it was time to divvy up the spoils. The next section of al-Tabari begins under the headline: **"The Division of the Booty."** *Tabari VII:64/Ishaq:307* **"The Messenger of Allah gave orders concerning the contents of the camp which the people had collected, and it was all brought together. Among the Muslims, however, there was a** difference of opinion concerning it. Those who had collected it said, 'It is ours. Muham-mad promised every man that he could keep the booty he took.' Those who were fighting said, 'If it had not been for us, you would not have taken it. We distracted the enemy from you so that you could take what you took.' Those who were guarding the Prophet for fear the enemy would attack him said, 'By Allah, you have no better right to it than we have. We wanted to kill the enemy when Allah gave us the opportunity and made them turn their backs, and we wanted to take property when there was no one to protect it; but we were afraid that the Meccans might attack the Prophet. We protected him so you have no bet-ter right to it than we have.'" These covetous and militant marauders were the antithesis of Christ's disciples.

According to Muhammad's gospel: it's good to kill for money, but it's bad to argue about it later. "When we quarreled about the booty we became very bad tem-pered. So Allah removed it from our hands and handed it over to His Messenger. He divided it equally among the Muslims. In this matter there can be seen fear of Allah, obedience to his Messenger, and the settling of differences." This was the proposition and the conclusion. Islam was about money. Islam made men mad. Muhammad and Allah were partners. Muhammad was to be obeyed. Allah was to be feared.

Muslims were enticed into submission: *Bukhari:V5B59N360* "The total number of Muslim fighters from Mecca who fought at Badr and were given a share of the booty, were 81. When their shares were distributed, their number was 101. But Allah knows it better."

And the great deceiver was ever ready to help his pal pile up the booty. *Ishaq:307* "The 'Spoils of War' Surah came down from Allah to His Prophet concerning the distribution of the booty when the Muslims showed their evil nature. Allah took it out of their hands and gave it to the Apostle."

Tabari VII:65 "Allah's Messenger came back to Medina, bringing with him the booty which had been taken from the polytheists.... There were forty-four captives in the Messenger of Allah's possession. There was a similar number of dead."

Ishaq:308 "Muhammad halted on a sandhill and divided the booty Allah had given him equally. Then Muslims from Medina met him at Rauha. They congratulated him on the vic-tory Allah had granted. But one of the warriors replied, 'What are you congratulating us about? We only met some bald old women like the sacrificial camels who are hobbled, and we slaughtered them!' The Apostle smiled because he knew that description fit ." By any historical or rational criterion, the battle of Badr was meaningless—a tus-sle between militants and merchants. And yet Muhammad turned it into a miracle from Allah. And he used it to resurrect his dying doctrine.

The prophet's blood lust led to these chilling lines... *Ishaq:308/Tabari VII:65* "When the Apostle was in Safra, Nadr was assassinated. When Muhammad reached Irq al-Zabyah he killed Uqbah. When the Holy Prophet ordered him to be killed, Uqbah said, 'Who will look after my children, Muhammad?' 'Hellfire,' the Apostle replied, and he was killed." No Geneva Convention here.

Ishaq:312 "Umar said to the Apostle, 'Let me pull out Suhayl's two front teeth. That way his tongue will stick out and he will never be able to speak against you again.'"

Tabari VII:66/Ishaq:309 "Sawdah [the prophet's second wife] said: 'I went to my house, and the Messenger was there with Abu Yazid [a Meccan prisoner]. His hands were tied to his neck. I could not restrain myself when I saw Abu like that and I shouted out to him. So Muhammad asked, "Sawdah, are you trying to stir up trouble against Allah's Messenger?" This brought me back to my senses.'"

Ishaq:309 "'Bind Abu Aziz tight for his mother is rich and she may ransom him for a great deal of money,'" Allah's Profit proclaimed.

Confirming that Islam was all about the money: *Tabari VII:71/Ishaq:311* "Among the captives was Abu Wada. Muhammad said, 'He has a son who is a shrewd merchant with much money." The son "slipped away at night, went to Medina, ransomed his father for 4,000 dirhams." There was no preaching, no Qur'an recitals, no message of salvation. Just: "Gimme da money."

Tabari VII:71/Ishaq:312 "The Prophet said, 'Abbas, you must ransom yourself, your two nephews, Aqil and Nawfal, and your confederate, Utbah, for you are a wealthy man.' 'Muhammad,' Abbas said, 'I was a Muslim, but the people compelled me to fight against my will.' Allah knows best concerning your Islam,' Muhammad said. 'If what you say is true, Allah will reward you for it. As for your outward appearance, you have been against us, so pay to ransom yourself.' The Messenger had previously taken [stolen] twenty ounces of gold from him following the battle. So Abbas said, 'Credit me with this amount towards my ransom.' 'No,' Muhammad replied. 'That money Allah has already taken from you and given to us.'" Islam equals money, not souls. The Hadith remains transparent.

Ishaq:313 "The Muslims told Abu Sufyan to pay them a ransom to free his son, Amr. He replied, 'Am I to suffer the double loss of my blood and my money? After you have killed my son Hanzala, you want me to pay you a ransom to save Amr?'" How on earth do Muslims see this behavior as "religious," or even "good?"

Bukhari:V5B59N357 "The Badr warriors were given five thousand dirhams each, yearly. Umar [the future Caliph] said, 'I will always give them more than what I will give to others.'" And while money was good, Muhammad craved more... *Bukhari:V5B59N342* "Umar said, 'When my daughter Hafsa lost her husband in the battle of Badr, Allah's Apostle demanded her hand in marriage and I married her to him.'"

The battle over, the booty collected, the ransoms negotiated, it was time for some situational scriptures. Most religions considered murder, piracy, kidnapping, and terrorism bad, so Muhammad needed a special dispensation.

As before, I will weave the Hadith into the fabric of the Qur'an to give Allah's scriptures the context of time, circumstance, and place they otherwise lack. *Tabari VII:80* "When the events of Badr were over, Allah revealed the 8th surah, 'The Spoils of War,' in its entirety. The two armies met [there were no armies—just merchants and militants] and Allah defeated the Meccans [with Muslim swords]. Seventy of them were killed, and seventy were taken captive." The previous death toll was forty-four killed and an equal number brought back for ransom. The lower number is also in line with Ishaq's meticulously documented total of fifty dead, and forty-three taken hostage. **"Abu Bakr said, 'O Prophet of Allah, these are your people, your family; they are your cousins, fellow clansmen, and nephews. I think that you should accept ransoms for them so that what we take from them will strengthen us.'"** Yes, it's true: Islam was financed by kidnapping ransom. The wealth of pagans was forged into the sword of Islam. And Abu Bakr, Muhammad's bloodsucking promoter, was only interested in the money—never religion.

Tabari VII:81 **"'What do you think Khattab?' Muhammad asked. 'I say you should hand them over to me so that I can cut off their heads. Hand Hamzah's brother over to him so that he can cut off his head. Hand over Aqil to Ali so that he can cut off his brother's head. Thus Allah will know that there is no leniency in our hearts toward the unbelievers.' The Messenger liked what Abu Bakr said and did not like what I said, and accepted ransoms for the captives."** Bloodshed was good; money was better.

This Tradition continues to pull back the veil on Islam. It was a performance, one in which a pagan god played a staring role. *Tabari VII:81* **"The next day I went to the Prophet in the morning. He was sitting with Abu Bakr, and they were weeping. I said, 'O Messenger of Allah, tell me, what has made you and your companion weep? If I find cause to weep, I will weep with you, and if not, I will pretend to weep because you are weeping.' The Prophet said, 'It is because of the taking of ransoms which has been laid before your companions. It was laid before me that I should punish them instead.' Allah revealed: 'It is not for any Prophet to have captives until he has made slaughter in the land.' After that Allah made booty lawful for them."** Because money enabled slaughter, Muhammad would have both.

Ishaq:316 **"Following Badr, Muhammad sent a number of raiders with orders to capture some of the Meccans and burn them alive. But on the following day he sent word to us, 'I told you to burn these men if you got hold of them. But I decided that none has the right to punish by fire save Allah. So if you capture them, kill them.'"**

The Hadith report on the battle of Badr ends with these words: **"On the Badr expedition, the Messenger took the sword of Dhu al-Faqar as booty. It had belonged to Munabbih. On that day he also took Abu Jahl's camel as booty. It was a Mahri dromedary on which he used to go on raids."** Nothing but the best for Muhammad—after all, he was a prophet. **"It is said that he wrote 'Ma'aqil' [Blood-Money] on his sword."**

Blood still dripping from the implements of war, the dark spirit of Islam revealed a surah that made killing a religious duty and thievery a sacred rite: **"The Spoils of War."** *008.001* **"They question you about (windfalls taken as) spoils of war. Say: 'Booty is at the disposal of Allah and the Messenger; they belong to Us and are for Our benefit. So fear Allah, and adjust your way of thinking in this matter. Obey Allah and His Messenger.'"** How convenient. But this was crass, even for Muhammad. His propensity to steal was obviously being questioned. So he claimed that his god said: "The booty is ours—it belongs to us." And I suppose Muhammad threw their share up in the air and told his Allah to grab whatever he wanted.

Some might think being a pirate would be a great gig if you could get "god" to sponsor your raids. But for Muhammad, that wasn't enough. He was after more than money. He coveted power, too. So he had his god say: **"Obey Allah and the Messenger."** Then, for those who were squabbling over the prophet's new career path, he professed: **"Adjust your way of thinking and fear me."** The Communists used to call it "re-education." But no matter how you interpret this, it isn't religious. It's disgusting.

Muhammad's Companions agree with my assessment: *Ishaq:321* **"The Spoils of War surah was handed down because we quarreled about the booty. So Allah took it away from us and gave it to His Apostle. When He did, we learned to fear Allah and obey his Messenger."** The Hadith goes on to report: **"For in truth, our army had gone out with the Prophet seeking the caravan because we wanted its booty."**

The Qur'an's attempts at religion were overt efforts to control people through fear, ritual, indoctrination, and taxation: *008.002* **"The only believers are those who feel fear and terror when Allah is mentioned. When His [Qur'an] revelations [like this one focused on killing and stealing] are recited to them it increases their faith. Muslims establish regular prayers and pay out of the booty We have given them."** Muslims who fear will obey—and they will pay.

Conditioning men to be submissive through the implementation of religious rituals was good; motivating them to loot was better. *008.004* **"These are true Muslims. For them are exalted grades (of honor) with their Lord, and pardon, and a bountiful provision."** Who gets the exalted grades of honor, the bountiful provision, you ask? Muslim militants who leave their homes to rob caravans and murder their kin, that's who! *008.005* **"Your Lord ordered and caused you [the good Muslims] out of your homes to fight for the true cause, even though some Muslims disliked it, and were averse (to fighting). They argued with you concerning this matter [of piracy] even after it was made clear to them. It was as if they were being driven to their death."** This verse is speaking to the rift between the "good," warlike, Muslims and the "bad," peaceful ones. Good Muslims were ready, willing, and able to plunder and kill—just as they are today. The bad, peaceful Muslims just wanted to live and let live. But peace was something Allah couldn't tolerate.

008.007 **"Behold! Allah promised that one of the two parties would fall and become yours. You (Muhammad) coveted (the caravan,) the one which was not armed."** This verse confirms that Muhammad was a pirate, not a general or a prophet. It devastates Islam's credibility. Yet it is often missed because the passage goes on to proclaim the most fearsome words every spoken: **"Allah wished to confirm and justify the truth by His words. Wipe the infidels out to the last."**

The confirmation is clear. It is the justification that's muddled. Muhammad left Medina with his militants for the express purpose of robbing an unarmed caravan. He wanted money. His god wanted war. The dark spirit of Islam wanted to slaughter and humiliate all those who didn't bow to his authority.

Lucifer enticed men to do his bidding. His goal was to cloud men's minds so that they would no longer recognize truth. *008.008* **"That He might justify Truth and prove Falsehood false, distasteful though it be to the disbelievers who oppose."** The writing quality is dreadful so let me translate this for you. The verse says: the people whose conscience had not yet been eroded opposed terror. That made them "guilty." From Lucifer's perspective, truth could only be justified by killing men with a conscience—men with the ability to discern right from wrong. You are witnessing spiritual warfare of the highest order. And the stakes in this game are men's souls.

Muhammad made a deal with the Devil: *008.009* **"(Remember,) you implored the assistance of your Lord, and He heard what you requested: 'I will assist you with 1,000 angels, ranks on ranks.'"** If ever a verse proved that the Qur'an was as false as its deity, this is it. It is beyond comprehension that the creator of the universe would send his angels to help a pirate. Moreover, can you imagine angels so impotent it takes 1,000 of them to kill fifty merchants?

There is more to this demonic assistance than I have shared thus far. According to both the Hadith and Qur'an, Allah used rain and wind to foil the merchants. Rain was said to have secured the gravel under the militants and undermined the sandy slopes beneath the merchants' feet. And a wind from behind the militants' backs blew coarse sand in the merchants' faces, impairing their vision. The Bible calls Lucifer "the prince of the power of the air." He was given control over weather. In the book of Job, Satan uses wind and a thunderstorm to try and lure a man of God away from the truth. He also incites men to kill and steal on his behalf. That is precisely what happened at Badr and for the same reasons. Is it a coincidence or not?

The Hadith and Qur'an reveal something more sinister than just a bad man who craved power, sex, and money. To understand what was at stake, we need to expose the spirit that inspired Islam. And to accomplish this, we must turn to the same place Muhammad turned for enlightenment—the Hebrew Bible. By lifting the majority of the Qur'an from its pages, he left the honest searcher with no option but to compare where they agree and where they conflict. And what we find is that spirit of Islam is identical to that of a fallen angel, Lucifer, or Satan. Allah's nature, character, motivations, means, and limitations are a carbon copy of the Devil's. He deceives men and leads them astray. He enjoys torment, killing, and death. He entices lost souls.

For the purpose of this book, it matters not if you view the Bible as inspired or Satan as real. If you do, you will see Allah more nearly and understand the significance of the problem currently facing our world. If not, it is sufficient that you see Muhammad's words and behavior as deceitful and demented. Either way, the greatest service we can render Muslims is to free them from Islam. In so doing we will free ourselves from the terror this man, his spirit, and doctrine inspire.

Reading on we discover that Muhammad was no better at piracy than he was at prophecy. *008.010* "Allah made the victory [killing, kidnapping, and stealing] but a message of hope, a glad tiding, to reassure you. Victory [of this kind] comes only from Allah [Lucifer]. Lo! Allah is Almighty. (Remember) He covered you with slumber, as a security from Him. He sent down rain to clean you of the plague of evil suggestions of Satan, that you might plant your feet firmly." Satan's plague was being cast out of heaven for disobedience. His cure was to bring mankind down to his level.

A Hadith says: *Ishaq:321* "Allah sent down water from the sky at night and it prevented the polytheists from getting to the well before us." This Tradition is followed by a hellish one, suggesting the source of the inclement nocturnal weather. *Ishaq:322* "I will cast terror into the hearts of those who reject Me. So strike off their heads and cut off their fingers. All who oppose Me and My Prophet shall be punished severely."

Then from the Qur'an: *008.012* "Your Lord inspired the angels [fellow demons] with the message: 'I am with you. Go and give firmness to the Believers. I will terrorize the unbelievers. Therefore smite them on their necks and every joint and incapacitate them. Strike off their heads and cut off each of their fingers and toes." Allah is calling himself a terrorist. He is ordering his fellow demons to decapitate and mutilate men so that their fathers, sons, and brothers might rob them. Islam has sunk to a new low.

Ah, but it was justified, according to the spirit of Islam: *008.013* "This because they rejected Allah [The Meccans invented Allah; they never rejected him. So this was all about:] and defied His Messenger. If anyone opposes Allah and His Messenger, Allah shall be severe in punishment. That is the torment: 'So taste the punishment. For those infidels who resist there is the torment of Hell.'" While Allah's command to fight is new, as is his bribe of booty, his character hasn't changed. He is the same ol' demented fellow we grew to despise in Mecca. Surrender and obey, or die.

008.015 "Believers, [Muslims] when you meet unbelieving infidels in battle while you are marching for war, never turn your backs to them. If any turns his back on such a day, unless it be in a stratagem of war, a maneuver to rally his side, he draws on himself the wrath of Allah, and his abode is Hell, an evil refuge!" This is like the pseudo-religious Teutonic Oath of the Nazi S.S. It's identical to the mindset of the Kamikaze Divine Wind. Not only are Muslims ordered to attack, they are condemned if they retreat. Islam is a fight to the death.

And lest we forget: Allah hates peaceful Muslims. If you know one, you ought to share this verse with them. They could do better than to follow a god who hates them for doing the right thing.

The following verse is one of many that is meaningless outside of the context the Hadith provides. As you recall, Muslims claimed that Allah's angels severed men's heads before their swords reached them. And we learn: *Ishaq:322* "Allah said concerning the pebbles thrown by the Apostle, 'I threw them not you. Your tossing them would have had no effect without My help. But working together, We terrorized the enemy and put them to flight." In that context, I present the Qur'an: *008.017* "It is not you [Muslims] who slew them; it was Allah who killed them. It was not you (Muhammad) who threw (a handful of dust), it was not your act, but it was Allah who threw (the sand into the eyes of the enemy at Badr) in order that He might test the [Muslim] Believers by doing them a gracious favor of His Own: for Allah is He Who hears and knows."

By adding the words inside the parenthesis, the Islamic scholars who translated the Qur'an have admitted two things: the Qur'an is senseless without the Sira, and the Sira is scripture. Furthermore, the passage is worse in context, not better. Allah is confessing to a crime. The men that he claimed he killed were neither warriors nor criminals. They were businessmen trying to keep Muslims from stealing their wares. By any sane definition, when he pursued and killed these men he committed an act of first-degree murder—a capital offense. In all civilized societies, murderers are either put to death or separated for life. Shouldn't Allah receive the same sentence?

And as is often the case, the murdering spirit is insane. He said that his rage was a "a gracious favor." So why would Allah confess to such a heinous crime and why did he elect to gloat about his outing with the pirates? The reasons are threefold. First, Lucifer had done all he could. He had manipulated the weather and induced men to behave badly. He was proud of himself—the failing that got him into trouble in the first place. Second, Muhammad was a coward in battle. He hunkered down in his palm-frond hut a safe distance behind the battle lines. He needed to revise history so that his militants would believe that by tossing pebbles he was actually fighting with god. Third, Muhammad took twenty percent of the spoils, a hundred times larger share than any of the combatants. If Allah was the most vicious and prolific killer rather than the pirates, he deserved the largest share.

008.018 "This and surely; Allah weakens the deceitful plots of unbelieving infidels." In order to justify this excrement, Muhammad and Allah had to stupefy their militants first. Good must be made to appear bad, and bad must become good. The "unbelieving infidels" were at Badr to defend their people and protect their property from the bad militants, and yet this good motive is twisted into a "deceitful plot." It's but another Qur'anic lie.

008.019 "(Quraysh Unbelievers!) You asked for a judgment so the judgment came to you. If you desist, it will be best for you. If you return (to the attack), so shall We. And your forces, no matter how large, will fail. For verily Allah is with those who believe Him!" Unable to deliver the threatened Day of Doom, Allah is suggesting that this sandlot skirmish is its equivalent. It is also interesting that this spirit's "judgment" renders booty to criminals. Further, the defensive tactics of the merchants were wrongly twisted into looking like an attack by the delusional spirit. Yet the Meccans were merely safeguarding their wares. The Muslims were on the prowl trying to steal them. This convoluted reasoning is the same strategy modern Muslims foist on an ignorant media. Thus when the Israelis defend themselves from Islamic terror they are recast as the aggressors.

With situational scriptures issued and history twisted, it was time to reinforce the purpose of Islam: 008.020 "O you who believe! Obey Allah and His Messenger. Do not turn away from *him* when you hear *him* speak. Do not be like those who say, 'We hear,' but do not listen. Those who do not *obey* are the worst of beasts, the vilest of animals in the sight of Allah. They are deaf and dumb. Those who do not understand are senseless. If Allah had seen any good in them, He would have made them listen. And even if He had made them listen, they would but have turned away and declined submission." When you consider the audience and the circumstance, this is as transparent. Muhammad was lashing out against the good people of Medina and calling them bad Muslims for not following *his* orders to fight. The bad Muslims still knew right from wrong. Their consciences told them that piracy, terrorism, murder, kidnapping, ransom, and thievery were evil. As such, they were "good" people. When the "prophet" spoke to them, commanding them to become pirates, they turned away and did not listen to him.

The good Muslims, however, like their counterparts today, had been corrupted by Islam. They could no longer distinguish between right and wrong so they zealously followed the profiteer on raids to pillage and plunder.

While it is obvious that this demented doctrine needs to be exposed and exterminated—sentenced to die for its crimes—bad Muslims should be leading the parade. Their faux deity just called them the vilest of creatures. Yes, any Muslim who does not follow Muhammad's orders to murder infidels, to pillage and plunder them is deaf and dumb, senseless, the worst of beasts. Allah hates, above all else, peace-loving Muslims (even more than he hates Jews).

I beg any Muslim reading these words to let them sink in. Your god condemns you if you to not lash out in Jihad, if you do not fight to the death for his demented cause. If the Qur'an is true, if Allah is God, if Muhammad was a prophet—and you are a peaceful, loving Muslim—you are destined for a hell even more torturous than that prepared for the hospitality of the infidels. It's a lose-lose game, with your soul at stake. If Islam is true, you're toast. If Islam is a lie, you live in the poverty of a delusional doctrine and will spend eternity separated from Yahweh, your creator. It doesn't have to be that way.

Before we leave this stunning indictment of Islam, I'd like to address the opening salvo of the 20th verse. Muhammad said that any time he speaks he must be believed, followed, and obeyed. Not Allah, *him*. Even Ishaq agrees: *Ishaq:322* **"Allah said, 'Do not turn away from Muhammad when he is speaking to you. Do not contradict his orders. And do not be a hypocrite, one who pretends to be obedient to him and then disobeys him. Those who do so will receive My vengeance. You must respond to the Apostle when he summons you to war."** Technically, one cannot be a bad Muslim. A peaceful, loving person is either a non-Muslim or a hypocrite. Therefore, all true Muslims obey Islam's dictates and become bad people!

Muhammad's summons was to raid civilians and steal their property. This wasn't holy war; it was terrorism. Also, to follow Muhammad's orders, as Allah is compelling, one must understand the Sunnah and comply with its Hadith. That is the only place the prophet's commands and terrorist example can be found. (Unless you see Muhammad as Allah and in that case the Qur'an is just a redundant Sunnah.) Either way, from this point forward Islam is a terrorist manifesto. Its creed is: obey Muhammad, fight for Muhammad, and pay Muhammad.

Since the last Qur'anic pronouncement was too transparent even for Islam's prophet, the megalomaniac stepped aside momentarily and placed himself back on equal footing with his god: *008.024* **"O Believers! Answer Allah and (His) Messenger when he calls you to that which will give you life [martyrdom]. And know that Allah comes in between a man and his heart. To Him you shall be gathered. Fear the affliction and trial that awaits those who do not obey. Allah is severe."** Yes, all Muslims will meet Allah, the demonic spirit of Islam. Their affliction at his hands will be severe.

Ever deceitful, Muhammad and Allah are calling Muslims to fight to the death for their benefit, yet they say they are being called to life. This reminds me of Satan's temptation in the Garden. The apple represented death yet Lucifer called that choice immortality—life.

008.026 **"And remember, when you were a small band [i.e., bandits] and reckoned feeble and despised in the land, and were afraid that men might despoil and kidnap you, carrying you off by force, how He provided a safe asylum for you, strengthened you with His aid. He gave you refuge, and gave you the good [stolen] things, that haply you might be thankful. O you that believe, don't betray Allah and the Messenger, nor misappropriate things entrusted to you."** Gloating is unseemly. Muhammad's militants had won a skirmish against some poorly equipped and out-of-shape businessmen. The Muslims were a small band of bandits, feeble and despised before Badr, and they remained so after the battle. No Muslim was carried off by force. *They* were the kidnappers. As for an asylum, I would be happy to recommend one.

008.028 **"And know that your property and your children are just a temptation, and that Allah has the best rewards."** The idea that **"children are just a temptation"** is telling. Is Muhammad suggesting that men might be tempted to abuse their sons as he himself was abused as a child? Or is he asking parents to sacrifice their children and their money on Jihad's altar, as so many Muslims do today? While perverse, neither is as twisted as the notion that god's "best reward" is an inebriated stay in his whorehouse. Nor are they any more evil than an Islamic imam seducing mercenary militants to murder innocents to gain entry.

008.029 **"O you who believe! If you obey and fear Allah, He will grant you a criterion to judge between right and wrong, or a way to overlook your evil thoughts and deeds."** If you are a good Muslim and obey out of fear, Allah will grant you a new **"criterion to judge between right and wrong."** And that is because all *other* religions, moral codes, and societal mores define piracy, murder, plunder, terrorism, kidnapping, thievery, and ransom as evil. But not to worry, O Islamic terrorist, because Allah will forgive your crimes, corrode your mind, and rid you of the pangs of conscience.

008.030 **"Remember how the unbelievers [Meccan merchants] plotted against you (O**

Muhammad), to keep you in bonds, or slay you, or get you out (of your home). They plot-ted, and Allah too had arranged a plot; but Allah is the best schemer." Because you have read the Hadith and studied the Qur'an in context, you know that Muhammad claimed he "received" this verse two years earlier. And you know that the kidnappers and the slayers were Muslims. As for Allah being the best plotter, a world-class schemer, I couldn't agree more. He is the best in the world at what he does.

Prince Charming says: *Ishaq:323* **"I am the best of plotters. I deceived them with My guile so that I delivered you from them."** Webster defines "guile" the way the Bible defines Satan: "insidious and cunning, a crafty or artful deception, duplicity."

008.031 **"When Our Verses are rehearsed to them, they say: 'We have heard this (before) [i.e., it's plagiarized]. If we wished, we could say (words) like these [i.e., it's poorly written (or spoken)]. These are nothing but stories of the ancients.'"** The reason the local Arab population in Yathrib was questioning the prophet's credentials was that he had already trotted out the 2nd surah. It was filled with convoluted stories lifted from the pages of the Torah. This verse confirms that bad Muslims were smart enough to recognize a false prophet.

In the next passage we find Muhammad sidestepping the "no miracles-no prophet" and "no signs-no god" criticisms. It's as feeble as ever. *008.032* **"Remember how they said: 'O Allah, if this (Qur'an) is indeed the Truth (revealed) from You, rain down on us a shower of stones from the sky, or send us a painful doom!' But Allah was not going to send them a penalty while you (Muhammad) were among them. But what plea have they that Allah should not punish them; what makes them so special? They obstructed (men) from the Holy Mosque, though they were not its fitting and appointed guardians? Its custodian can only be one who keeps his duty to Allah. Their prayer and worship at the House of Allah (the Ka'aba) is nothing but whistling and clapping of hands. They will have to taste the punishment because they disbelieved.'"** This passage says that pagans believed Allah was God; they prayed to him and worshiped at his House. As such, it destroys Muhammad's justification for killing them.

These verses also contain lies and a confession. The Meccans never restricted access to the mosque. The Ka'aba was the centerpiece of Qusayy's religious scam. It was their meal ticket. The more pilgrims the better. It was Muhammad and his Muslims who were intolerant. They would ultimately restrict access, prohibiting all non-Muslim from entering Mecca. The confession provides additional support for the Profitable Prophet Plan. Muhammad was claiming ownership of the Ka'aba Inc. because he deemed himself more deserving than the rightful owners. He had made a deal with the Devil. Custodianship of Allah's House was to be his reward.

008.036 **"The unbelievers spend their wealth to hinder (man) from the Way of Allah, and so will they continue to spend; but in the end they will have intense regrets and sighs. It will become an anguish for them, then they will be subdued. The unbelievers shall be driven into hell in order that Allah may distinguish the bad from the good and separate** them. Allah wants to heap the wicked one over the other and cast them into Hell. They are the losers." The Meccan merchants promoted the "way of Allah." Allah's House was all the Quraysh had going for them. But that lie isn't the problem with this verse. Muhammad, on behalf of his spirit, is telling non-Muslims that anguish awaits them, that they will be subdued, forced into submission and then driven into hell. Terror, a living hell, is the legacy of Muhammad.

Even Ishaq sees Allah as demonic: *Ishaq:324* "**Allah said, 'Leave Me to deal with the liars. I have fetters and fire and food which chokes. I will smote the Quraysh at Badr."**

The hateful and violent message of the Qur'an is as clear as *Mein Kampf.* *008.039* "**So fight them until there is no more Fitnah (disbelief [non-Muslims]) and all submit to the religion of Allah alone (in the whole world). But if they cease, Allah is Seer of what they do.**" In or out of context, this is unequivocal. The Islamic war machine must continue to roll until every soul on earth "**submits to the religion of Allah.**" There will be no understandings, no appeasements, no compromises, no treaties. It is surrender or die. And this verse cannot be misinterpreted, corrupted, or dismissed. The order is clear: "**Fight until the whole world is in submission to Islam.**"

But should you want confirmation, Ishaq, the first imam to record the message of fundamental Islam interprets the verse this way: *Ishaq:324* "**He said, Fight them so that there is no more rebellion, and religion, all of it, is for Allah only. Allah must have no rivals.**" This verse should be hung in every church, in every synagogue, in every school, and statehouse. It ought to be plastered on the front door of the State Department, Pentagon, Capitol, and White House.

Incidentally, there are two wars being announced here, not one. The first is religious; the second is spiritual. Submission to the religion of Islam is entirely political, a war designed to suppress and plunder. That battle is being fought with swords, guns, and bombs. It destroys physical things including the flesh. The spiritual war is being waged for souls. Allah, as Satan, will not tolerate a rival. *"Allahu Akbar,"* (Allah is Greater) is the battle cry. Lucifer wants us to worship him. Islam is simply his most effective and deadly scheme.

Unfortunately, the Qur'an's dark spirit knew how to motivate a merciless band of religious fanatics. *Ishaq:324* "**Allah taught them how to divide the spoil. He made it lawful and said, 'A fifth of the booty belongs to the Apostle.'** This is confirmed in the surah: *008.040* "**If people are obstinate, and refuse to surrender, know that Allah is your Supporter. And know that one fifth of all the booty you take belongs to Allah, and to the Messenger, and for the near relatives (of the Messenger), orphans, and the needy wayfarer [we've heard this before]. Believe in Allah and in what We sent down to Our slave on the Day of victory over the infidels when the two armies clashed. And Allah has the power to do all things.**" Fortunately, all Allah/Satan can do is play with the weather and tempt men to do his bidding. Unfortunately, all too many are willing. The temptation in this case was money. Muslim militants got rich [by Arab standards] robbing Muhammad's enemies. Of course, they had to give the prophet a fifth of the spoil, yet that was no more onerous than what Black

Beard required. But since Badr was only a ragtag mob of mercenary misfits against a bunch of camel-driving merchants, you have to wonder about the inadequacy of a spirit who called them "armies" and required a thousand demonic angels to carry the day. I wouldn't bet my life on Team Islam.

You may have picked up on it already, but if not, Muhammad had a little problem. He and his raiders had gone after a merchandise-laden caravan. The money they sought eluded them. So while they stole some swords and coats of mail, and kidnapped some men for ransom, the expedition was a bust. The caravan got away. *008.042* "(Remember) you were on the hither side of the valley, and they were on yonder bank. The caravan was on lower ground still (by the coast). Even if you had made a mutual appointment to meet, you would certainly have declined to fight and failed to achieve your goal because Allah needed to accomplish a different matter. Those who were destroyed had to perish as a clear demonstration [of Allah's seductive control]. And those who lived survived as a positive proof (of His authority). Allah is He Who hears and knows." In other words, Allah won the coin toss. His lust for murder took precedence over Muhammad's yearning for money. As for the dark spirit of Islam hearing and knowing; it's true. Lucifer is able to maneuver in time and travel unseen. He listens and learns how to best tempt his stooges. Everyone has a soft spot, a longing, a desire, something that they crave.

008.045 "O believers! When you meet an army, be firm, and think of Allah's Name much; that you may prosper." It was a hellish bargain they made for money. "Obey Allah and His Messenger; and do not dispute [with them], lest you lose courage and your power departs; persevere!" The Hadith says: *Ishaq:325* "Muslims, fight in Allah's Cause. Stand firm and you will prosper. Help the Prophet, obey him, give him your allegiance, and your religion will be victorious."

But not everyone had joined the party. So the bad Muslims had to be rebuked. There was no room in Islam for a second leader or for peace: *008.047* "Be not as those who came from their homes full of their own importance, trying to turn men away from [fighting] in Allah's Cause. Allah is encircling them. Satan made their acts seem alluring to them, and said: 'No one can conquer you this day, while I am near you.' But when the two armies came in sight of each other, he turned on his heels, and said: 'Lo! I am not with you. I see what you cannot. Verily, I fear Allah: for Allah is severe in punishment.'" Ishaq tells us: "Umayr saw Satan at Badr. When the Devil turned, a surah was handed down concerning him." Then describing Allah, Umayr says: *Ishaq:319* "Satan made their deeds seem good to them and said that they would be victorious because he was their protector. But the Devil deceived them." And he continues to do so.

Following the Satanic interlude, Allah calls bad Muslims "diseased." Their peaceful nature evidently irked the spirit of war. *008.049* "When the hypocrites [bad Muslims] and those in whose hearts is a disease said: 'The religion has deceived and misled them.'" Bad Muslims could be good people, discerning people. They recognized that fundamental Islam was deceitful. And they knew Islam, Muhammad, and Allah better than anyone.

If this is "God" speaking, I move that we elect a new one. *008.050* "**If you could have seen the infidels when the angels drew away their souls, striking their faces and smiting their backs. The angels said: 'Taste the penalty of the blazing Fire.'**"

008.052 "**They [Meccans] brought this on themselves. Their case is like that of Pharaoh and of those before them. They denied and rejected the revelations of Allah, and Allah destroyed them, punishing them for their crimes: for Allah is strict, severe in punishment.**" And what bears saying bears repeating…*008.054* "**This was the case with Pharaoh and those before them: They denied and rejected the revelations of their Lord: so We destroyed them.**" This wasn't a second translation; it was a "senior moment."

The war surah marches on with these lovely words: *008.055* "**Verily the worst of creatures, the vilest of beasts in the sight of Allah are those who reject Him and will not believe. They are those with whom you make an agreement, but they break their covenant every time, and they keep not their duty [to fight].**" The bad Muslims are being hammered again. Muhammad is miffed that they reneged on the Pledge of Aqabah. Muslims agreed to protect the prophet like they did their women and to fight whomever he fought. They didn't figure on that including terrorism and piracy, so they bailed on him. As a consequence, the bad peace-loving Muslims were labeled the "**worst of creatures.**"

Enough Mr. Nice Guy. It was time to go back on the warpath. These are some of the most chilling words ever uttered in the name of god: *008.057* "**If you gain mastery over them in battle, inflict such a defeat as would terrorize them, so that they would learn a lesson and be warned.**" It's pretty hard to reconcile these words with the Islam-is-a-peace-loving-religion myth. This sounds like one of al-Qaeda's speeches to me. The Sira presents the "Terror Manifesto" this way: *Ishaq:326* "**If you come upon them, deal with them so forcibly as to terrify those who would follow them that they may be warned. Make a severe example of them by terrorizing Allah's enemies.**"

Before anyone puts their trust in the "peace process" or supports a treaty with an Islamic organization or nation, they should consider Allah's admonition: *008.058* "**If you apprehend treachery from any group on the part of a people (with whom you have a treaty), retaliate by breaking off (relations) with them: for Allah loves not the treacherous. The infidels should not think that they can bypass (the law or punishment of Allah). Surely they cannot get away.**" A second translation reads: "**The unbelieving infidels should not think that they can bypass Islam; surely they cannot escape.**"

Now that Islam has our undivided attention, it's time for Allah to scare us to death. *008.060* "**Prepare against them whatever arms and cavalry you can muster that you may strike terror in the enemies of Allah, and others besides them not known to you.**" This is a call for all good Muslims to amass their weapons of mass destruction. The Noble Qur'an even adds "**tanks, planes, missiles, and artillery**" to the text. Allah is ordering Muslims to terrorize his enemies, their enemies, and enemies yet unknown. This is as purposeful as a panzer tank, as unyielding as a kamikaze. It explains why Muslims are terrorists. And it foretells our future if we fail to expose this doctrine, if we fail to annihilate it before it annihilates us.

This is a matter of life and death, so I want to give you the benefit of another translation: "Against them make ready your strength to the utmost of your power, including steeds of war, to strike terror into the enemies of Allah and your enemies, and others besides, whom you may not know. Whatever you spend in Allah's Cause will be repaid in full, and no wrong will be done to you [for killing others]."

If you were ignorant of verses 57 through 60, you might be suckered by the 61st. *008.061* "But if the enemy inclines toward peace, do you (also) incline to peace, and trust in Allah." However…"Should they intend to deceive or cheat you, verily Allah suffices: He strengthened you with His aid and with the Believers." The small print here is real important. "Should they intend to deceive or cheat" is an open invitation to invoke 8:57 to 60. It presupposes a hypothetical before anything occurs. And Muhammad knew it. Within days he would claim that he "feared" the Jewish Qaynuqa. He broke the treaty he had formed with them, besieged them, exiled them, and stole their homes, property, and businesses.

The first to interpret this surah said: *Ishaq:326* "If they ask you for peace on the basis of Islam (submission), make peace on that basis. Be of one mind by His religion."

The next two verses, which speak of cementing love in the midst of a killing spree, are incomprehensible. This odd segue brings us to one of Allah's most ominous lines. *008.065* "O Prophet, urge the Believers to the fight. If there are twenty among you with determination they will vanquish two hundred. If a hundred, they will slaughter a thousand of the unbelieving infidels: for these are a people devoid of understanding." This is the math of terror. On September 11th nineteen "good" Muslims followed Allah's instructions and murdered 3,000 innocent men, women, and children, fathers and mothers, sons and daughters, brothers and sisters. They snuffed out their lives because we were a people devoid of understanding.

I know that the temptation is to read on. But please, before you do, ponder the implications of this surah. This is the spirit of Islam speaking directly to Muslims. It is why they are terrorists.

The Sira proclaims: *Ishaq:326* "O Prophet exhort the believers to fight. If there are twenty good fighters they will defeat two hundred for they are a senseless people. They do not fight with good intentions nor for truth." Such could be said for America. The U.S. State Department has managed to lose the peace because they are ignorant of the truth. Believing that the "enemy of my enemy is my friend," we fight with less than ideal intentions. As a nation we have partnered with the wrong people and thereby created our next foe. We liberated China and they slaughtered us in Korea. We supported Stalin and it killed us in Vietnam. We funded the Mujahidun and they became al-Qaeda. We furnished biological weapons to Saddam and Americans died to keep him from using them. Not to be outdone, we have formed alliances with Saudi Arabia, Egypt, and Syria against Israel so that our friend might be victimized.

Allah wasn't finished motivating his terrorists to attack us. *008.066* "Now Allah has lightened your (task), for He knows that there is a weak spot in you [which is precisely what he is exploiting]. So if there are a hundred of you with determination they will van-quish two hundred, and if a thousand, they will kill two thousand by the will of Allah. For Allah is with those who are determined." It's true. Letters taken from the cars the suicide bombers of 9/11 left behind included prayers to Allah. The Muslims were singing *Allahu Akbar* as they slit the stewardess' throats and pointed the planes at our buildings. This is the price we pay for our blindness, for seeing Islam as a religion rather than a terrorist dogma. We allow mosques to preach the hatred and violence of the 8th surah right next door to our businesses, our schools, and our homes. The crater that was the World Trade Center stands as a memorial to our ignorance. The destruction of New York will be the legacy of our inaction.

Ishaq:326 "Abdallah told me that when this verse came down it was a shock to the Mus-lims who took it hard. They were afraid, as the odds were too great. So Allah relieved them and cancelled the verse with another: 'Now has Allah relieved you and He knows that there is a weakness among you, so if there are 100 [rather than 20] they shall vanquish 200.'"

Now that he had calmed the nerves of his squeamish militants, the war god of Islam was ready to approve kidnapping for ransom. He knew that ter-rorists craved money as much as they enjoyed murder. *008.067* "It is not fitting for any prophet to have prisoners until he has made a great slaughtered in the land. You desire the lure of the frail goods of this world while Allah desires the Hereafter, and Allah is Mighty." Another translation begins: "No apostle should take captives until he has battled and subdued a nation." This is a dual confession. Muhammad lusted for the ransom captives would bring, but his Allah persona was unwilling to enrich the prophet until he became a psychopathic killer. That's because Allah was entertained by torturing men in the fires of hell. And if you're unsure whether calling Muhammad a psychopath is fair, go back and read his conversation with the mutilated bodies in the pit.

Every word of this is so unbelievable, so maniacal, I have tried to buttress the Qur'anic presentation with an ample dose of Ishaq's insights. *Ishaq:326* "Allah said, 'No Prophet before Muhammad took booty from his enemy nor prisoners for ran-som.' Muhammad said, 'I was made victorious with terror. The earth was made a place for me to clean. I was given the most powerful words. Booty was made lawful for me. I was given the power to intercede. These five privileges were awarded to no prophet before me.'" There is no denying that Muhammad was unlike all other prophets.

The Sira continues to interpret the Qur'an: *Ishaq:327* "Allah said, 'A prophet must slaughter before collecting captives. A slaughtered enemy is driven from the land. Muham-mad, you craved the desires of this world, its goods and the ransom captives would bring. But Allah desires killing them to manifest the religion.'" This is so ungodly, so demonic, I don't even know what to say. "Allah desires killing them to manifest the religion.'"

008.068 "Had it not been for a previous agreement from Allah, a severe penalty would have reached you for the (ransom) that you took as booty." In other words, the prophet was given a special dispensation. Since he had shown himself worthy and been willing to slaughter his kin, ransom was his just reward. Imagine that.

But since you're my boy, revel in the loot, celebrate the butchering of your kin, turn your murderers into martyrs...*008.069* "**So enjoy what you took as booty; the spoils are lawful and good.**" Once again, this is demonic. Lucifer is the only spirit capable of not only authorizing thievery, but actually calling it good. And it was "good" from his perspective, because it seduced men to act badly.

The Hadith agrees: *Ishaq:327* "**Allah made booty lawful and good. He used it to incite the Muslims to unity of purpose. So enjoy what you have captured.**"

The following is hideously out of character for the author of this surah. As such, it's all part of the deception: "**Fear Allah: for Allah is Forgiving, Merciful.**"

008.070 "**O Prophet, tell the captives in your hands: 'If Allah knows or finds any good in you, He will give you something better than what has been taken from you.'**" What is the Black Stone supposed to do when it finds something good? Roll over? Jump for joy? And by the way, why do the captives who lost their sons and brothers trying to protect their belongings need forgiveness? They were victims, not villains. But that wasn't the purpose of this verse. It was designed to lure Meccans into Muhammad's service. If they joined him they too would be able to steal and kidnap with "god's" blessing.

Only the illiterate messenger of a rock idol would recite something this foolish: *008.071* "**If they try to deceive you, remember they have deceived Allah before. So he gave you mastery over them.**" Fortunately, Allah is dumb enough to be deceived by man. We *can* prevail against Lucifer and his Islam.

But first we must break the curse. We must free Muslims to think for themselves. For until we do, they will continue to pit good Muslims against bad Muslims. *008.072* "**Those who accepted Islam, left their homes, and fought with their property and lives in Allah's Cause, as well as those who gave (them) asylum, aid, and shelter, those who harbored them—these are allies of one another.**" According to Allah: a good Muslim kills and aids or abets killers. That explains the Taliban. What's more, a good Muslim is a suicide bomber. They sacrifice their life and property in Allah's Cause.

To define bad Muslims, the verse says: "**You are not responsible for protecting those who embraced Islam but did not leave their homes [to fight] until they do so.**" And so that there would be no doubt, Muhammad once again helped his god characterize the nature and deeds of "good" Muslims: *008.073* "**The unbelieving infidels are allies. Unless you (Muslims of the whole world unite and) aid each other (fighting as allies, as one united block under one Caliph to make Allah's religion victorious), there will be confusion, anarchy, and discord on earth, great mischief and corruption. Those [good Muslims] who accepted Islam, left their homes to fight in Allah's Cause (al-Jihad), as well as those who give them asylum, shelter, and aid—these are (all) [good Muslim] Believers: for them is pardon and bountiful provision (in Paradise).**" By definition: all good Muslims are bad people. Islam makes them that way.

We have seen Islam in action. God and prophet have revealed their true identities, their motivations, and their rage. There is no retreat from the battle-fields of Badr. As with the Nazis documenting their barbaric behavior in Poland, Islam chronicled its deeds. The doctrine cannot escape the damage that it did to itself in the month of Ramadhan A.H. 2 (March, 624 A.D.). The books of Ishaq, Tabari, Bukhari, Muslim, and Allah agree. The verdict is unanimous: Islam is a violent and inept political doctrine, not a religion. Its founder was a pirate, not a prophet. We know this because they told us.

I'd like to leave Badr by sharing some Hadith that expose the nature of the egotistical monster Muhammad had become. *Bukhari:V1B3N65* **"The Prophet got a silver ring made with 'Muhammad Allah's Apostle' engraved on it. The ring glittered on his hand."** *Bukhari:V4B56N732* **"Allah's Apostle said, 'I have five names: I am Muhammad and Ahmad, the praised one; I am al-Mahi through whom Allah will eliminate infidelity [by killing every infidel]; I am al-Hashir who will be the first to be resurrected [beating Jesus]; and I am also al-Aqib, because there will be no prophet after me.'"**

Muhammad "succeeded" in Medina because the heathen Arabs were led to believe that he was the Messiah, a title this "prophet" was all too willing to accept: *Bukhari:V4B55N651-2* **"I heard Allah's Apostle saying, 'I am the nearest of all the people to Jesus. All the prophets are paternal brothers—their mothers are different, but their religion is one. There has been no prophet between me and Jesus.'"** No behavior in human history, no message in all of time was more counter to Yahshua's than that which flowed from this ignorant and immoral beast.

And this "scripture" we've been reading was Muhammad's lone "miracle." *Bukhari:V6B61N504* **"Allah's Apostle said, 'Every Prophet was given miracles because of which people believed, but what I have been given is Divine Inspiration which Allah has revealed to me. So I hope that my followers will outnumber the followers of the other Prophets.'"** But even *he* had a low regard for his **"Divine Inspiration."** *Bukhari:V1B3N68* **"The Prophet preached at a suitable time so that we might not get bored. He abstained from pestering us with sermons and knowledge.'"** That's because Islam was a scam; it was neither enlightenment nor religion. It was about *a man*: *Bukhari:V9B92N384* **"Allah's Apostle said, 'Whoever obeys me will enter Paradise, and whoever disobeys me will not enter it.'"**

Muhammad and Islam were poison. This is what happened to those who were exposed: *Bukhari:V4B52N260* **"Ali burnt some [former Muslims alive] and this news reached Ibn Abbas, who said, 'Had I been in his place I would not have burnt them, as the Prophet said, "Don't punish (anybody) with Allah's Punishment." No doubt, I would have killed them, for the Prophet said, "If a Muslim discards his Islamic religion, kill him."'"**

So, now you know who the enemy really is. You know why they kill. You know that the civilized world will continue to be terrorized as long as we tolerate Islam. It will continue to destroy men's souls, seducing them to murder and mayhem. Only one question remains: what will you do about it?

16

MEIN KAMPF

"Kill every Jew."

Passions inflamed by the atrocities perpetrated at Badr, Muhammad and his henchmen immediately turned a covetous eye toward the Yathrib Jews. The prophet besieged them and established the Nazi mindset of Islam.

Hitler behaved the same way. After using violence and deceit to disrupt the German political system, he schemed himself into power, opening the first concentration camp—Dachau—within weeks of his appointment as Chancellor. The implements of his pathological rage were Storm Troopers. Steeped in the hatemongering rhetoric of *Mein Kampf* they mercilessly besieged the Jews for political and economic gain, offering them a one-way ticket to hell.

I believe that Adolf Hitler was influenced by Islam and inspired by the same spirit that possessed *der prophet*. Their doctrines were indistinguishable, as were their deeds. *Tabari VII:85* "**After Muhammad killed many Quraysh polytheists at Badr, the Jews were envious and behaved badly toward him, saying, 'Muhammad has not met anyone who is good at fighting. Had he met us, he would have had a real battle.' They also infringed the treaty in various ways.**" Since the Jews *never defended* themselves against Muhammad, it is inconceivable that they picked a fight. As for Jews being envious of a pirate, now terrorist, I don't think so. But Muhammad needed an excuse. It's hard to square genocidal rage with being God's messenger.

According to Ishaq, the treaty: *Ishaq:231* "**established the Jews in their religion and gave them rights to their property.**" Consider the arrogance and ignorance of these words. An anti-Semite claimed to have "**established the Jews in their religion.**" Not only was he 1,800 years late, his "religion" was the antithesis of their Covenant. As for *him* granting *their* property rights: the Jews had lived in Yathrib for a thousand years—they built the town into a thriving community. Muhammad had just slithered in.

Ishaq:231 "**The document stated reciprocal obligations: 'In the name of Allah, Ar-Rahman, and Ar-Rahim. This is a treaty from Muhammad the Prophet governing relations between Muslims. They are one ummah (community) to the exclusion of all men.**" Chairman Mo had formed his commune and named himself dictator. He told his comrades:

"Believers are friends of one another to the exclusion of all outsiders. No separate peace shall be made when Muslims are fighting in Allah's Cause and Muslims must avenge bloodshed in Allah's Cause." So far it's intolerant, violent, and dictatorial..."Whenever you differ about a matter it must be referred to Allah and Muhammad." But since Allah never spoke, obeying the latter sufficed.

Ishaq:232 "The Jews shall contribute to the cost of war so long as they are fighting alongside the believers. The Jews have their religion, the Muslims have theirs." Holy camel wreck, don't these boys think? Allah and Muhammad have told us a hundred times that Judaism was Islam. The Torah was said to have been Islamic scripture foretelling the blessed arrival of the Arab prophet.

But not to worry about these little religious misunderstandings, Muhammad had become a warlord. "None of them shall go out to war unless they have Muhammad's permission. The Jews must pay, however, for as long as the war lasts. If any dispute or controversy should arise it must be referred to Allah and Muhammad, His Apostle. If the Jews are called to make peace they must, except in the case of Holy War. Allah approves of this document. Fear Allah, and Muhammad is the Apostle of Allah." The manifesto was signed with these egotistical words: *Ishaq:233* "Allah's Apostle, the Lord of the Muslims, Leader of the Allah Fearing, Messenger of the Lord of the Worlds, the Peerless and Unequalled." The egotistical Hitler had nothing on this guy.

The political treaty was allegedly drawn up after Muhammad's fifty "Emigrants" invaded Yathrib, a town of some forty thousand inhabitants. Muslims claim that the Jews, who were craftsmen, merchants, and farmers, not warriors, signed the quasi-military accord. Further, they attest that the Jews agreed to acquiesce to Muhammad's supreme authority on all matters. But since the 2nd surah said that the Jews had mocked Muhammad's every word, a total suspension of reason is required to trust this absurd position.

And let's be clear. By the seventh century the Jews had been pummeled by the best and sent into diaspora, away from their land. They had no army, and it had been 900 years since they had last scored a military victory. So the reason the first Muslims tried so hard to establish this impossible scenario was that Muhammad's behavior toward the Jews was impossible to justify without it. And the prophet's wanton behavior must be excused, or at least explained, or he couldn't have been a prophet.

The real motivation for what was about to occur was directly related to the failure of Badr. The caravan got away. Muhammad needed money. The 8th surah was named "The Spoils of War" because Islam was being established through piracy. The sword had replaced words. And once a mercenary machine is built, it must be fed. Its ravenous appetite requires ever larger and more frequent fixes.

And the Jews were right in a way. Badr was an over-hyped temper tantrum in a man-sized sandbox. It was a clash of misfits and merchants, not titans. Muhammad, in an effort to establish his authority, oversold the whole bloody affair. A thousand angels in white turbans decapitating out-of-shape businessmen was a little hard to swallow.

Ishaq reports: *Tabari VII:85/Ishaq:363* **"What happened to the Banu Qaynuqa [the wealthiest Jewish tribe in Yathrib] was that Muhammad assembled them in their Marketplace and said, 'Jews, beware lest Allah brings on you the kind of vengeance which He brought on the Quraysh. Accept Islam [submit] and become Muslims [surrender]. You know that I am a Prophet. You will find me in your Scriptures and in Allah's Covenant with you.'"** Muhammad was proclaiming himself to be the Messiah, once again. Yet in actuality, he had become the seventh-century embodiment of the Anti-Christ.

Let's compare Muhammad and Yahshua to see who better reflected the nature of the Biblical God, and thus had Messianic qualities. Based upon the Scriptures, Yahshua was the perfect reflection of Yahweh. He was loving, rational, miraculous, prophetic, truthful, sacrificial, and wise. Everything he said and did was in perfect harmony with the Torah, Psalms, and Prophets. He neither abused, attacked, enslaved, nor robbed anyone. Anger was demonstrated only when it was justified—and even then it was directed against religious institutions, not men. He hated false doctrines, false gods, and false prophets to be sure. These things separated men from him. Yahshua was like Yahweh because he *is* Yahweh.

Muhammad, in contrast, was the perfect reflection of Allah. Like his spirit, he was lustful and hateful; he couldn't perform a miracle. Nor could he conceive or fulfill a prophecy. He was irrational, deceitful, self-serving, violent, and foolish. Everything he said was a gross corruption of the Bible or a regurgitated version of his pagan past. Anger was his trademark, and he despised anyone who challenged him. He led billions away from Yahweh. He abused tens-of-thousands—stealing property, raping women, selling children into slavery, and massacring men. Muhammad was like Allah because he *was* Allah.

Recognizing this, *Tabari VII:85/Ishaq:363* **"The Jews of the Banu Qaynuqa replied, 'Muhammad, do you think that we are like your people? Do not be deluded by the fact that you met a people with no knowledge and you made good use of your opportunity.'"** The Jews knew right from wrong because they were literate and schooled in their Scriptures. They knew that Muhammad was a charlatan, a false prophet pursuing his own ambition. Pirate and terrorist didn't mesh with the Biblical profile of a prophet, much less the Messiah.

But as with all insecure liars, Muhammad attacked those who had the will and sense to expose him. *Ishaq:363* **"Say to those who do not believe you: 'You will be vanquished and gathered into Hell, an evil resting place. You have already had a sign by way of the two forces which met, the Apostle's Companions and the Quraysh. One side fought in Allah's Cause. Verily that was an example for the discerning.'"** Indeed it was. And that's why understanding Badr is essential if we are to discern the truth about Muhammad and thereby predict how Muslims will respond today.

Although we are never told how or why, Islamic apologists insist: *Tabari VII:85/*

Ishaq363 "The Banu Qaynuqa were the first Jews to infringe the agreement between them and the Messenger." "The campaign of the Prophet against the Banu Qaynuqa was in Shawwal (March 27, 624) in the second year of the Hijrah [migration from Mecca]."

Demonstrating the pattern that would be followed for all time by Muslim statesmen, Muhammad unilaterally reneged on the treaty he claimed governed the affairs of Yathrib. As you read these words consider the wisdom of forcing Israel to sign a land-for-peace accord with its Muslim neighbors. *Tabari VII:86* "Gabriel [Lucifer] brought down the following verse to the Messenger: 'If you apprehend treachery from any people (with whom you have a treaty), retaliate by breaking off (relations) with them.' [Qur'an 8:58] When Gabriel had finished delivering this verse, the Prophet said, 'I fear the Banu Qaynuqa.' It was on the basis of this verse that Muhammad advanced upon them." The Qur'an from this point forward is simply a series of situational scriptures. Allah stands ever ready to endorse whatever his prophet desires. Further, Muhammad just confirmed that my interpretation of the "breaking treaties" verse was accurate. In Islam, treaties are used to lure nations into a false sense of peace so that they become easy prey.

Tabari VII:86/Ishaq:363 "Allah's Apostle besieged the Banu Qaynuqa until they surrendered at his discretion unconditionally." These are just words; they look so benign on the page. Yet consider what lies beneath them. The Qaynuqa township was comprised of several thousand families, maybe more. These Jews had lived among Arabs without incident for a thousand years. They had built a life worth living. Then one day a bloodthirsty thug returned from a terrorist raid and knocked on their door. He ordered them to surrender their lives, their property, and their souls to him.

When they said no, Muhammad had his militants surround their homes. The Muslims deprived the Jews of water and food. We can appreciate their suffering because this is exactly what der fuhrer did to Jews in the Warsaw Ghettos. *Tabari VII:86/Ishaq:363* "Abd Allah [a Yathrib chief] rose up when Allah had put them in his power, and said, 'Muhammad, treat my ally well, for the Qaynuqa are a confederate of the Khazraj.' The Prophet ignored him, so Abd Allah repeated his request."

For the centuries before Muhammad's arrival, tribal alliances had formed the foundation of peace in the Arab world. There were no policemen or courts, as none were needed. Caravans traveled safely and people lived in harmony because they had established a means to work together and to work things out. But Muhammad was a breath away from destroying all of that and transforming the Arab word into a killing machine poised to plunder Arabia and then the rest of the world. *Ishaq:363* "The Prophet turned away from him so Abd Allah put his hand on the collar of the Messenger's robe. Muhammad said, 'Let go of me!' He was so angry his face turned black. Then he said, 'Damn you, let me go!' Abd Allah replied, 'No, by God, I will not let you go until you treat my ally humanely. There are seven hundred men among them, some with mail, who defended me from my foes when I needed their help. And now, you would mow them down in a single morning? By God I do not feel safe around here any more. I am afraid of what the future may have in store.' So the Messenger said, 'You can have them.'" Muhammad would not tolerate any affront to his supreme authority, which is why he turned black with anger. And make no mistake; he was ready, willing, and able to mow the Jews down.

There is a subtlety in the unabridged version of this dialog that I would like to bring to your attention. The Jews were described as having armor and coats of mail but not swords. And that is because the Qaynuqa were gold and metal smiths. They made jewelry for their wives and armor for the Arabs. And that's why Muhammad targeted them first. They had what he coveted—money and the implements of war.

When trying to understand or predict Muhammad's behavior, always keep the Quraysh Bargain and Satanic Verses in mind. Muhammad's kin knew him better than we do. They successfully tempted him with money, power, and women. The "holy" prophet was even willing to renounce his god and his prophetic authority to acquire these things.

If you doubt the veracity of the Quraysh assessment, listen to what happened next: *Tabari VII:87* "The Prophet said, 'Let them go; may Allah curse them, and may he curse Abd Allah with them.' So the Muslims let them go. Then Muhammad [went back on his word and] gave orders to expel the Jews. Allah gave their property as booty to his Messenger. The Qaynuqa did not have any farmland, as they were goldsmiths. The Prophet took many weapons belonging to them and the tools of their trade. The person who took charge of their expulsion from Yathrib along with their children was Ubadah. He accompanied them as far as Dhubab, saying: 'The farther you go the better.'"

Bukhari:V5B59N362 "He exiled all the Qaynuqa Jews from Medina." For good measure, Muhammad claimed Allah revealed this Hitlerish warning to leaders like Abd Allah: *Ishaq:364* "Muslims, take not Jews and Christians as friends. Whoever protects them becomes one of them, they become diseased, and will earn a similar fate." In reply, Abd Allah said: *Ishaq:364* "'I fear this change of circumstance may end up overtaking us.' So Allah replied, 'He will be sorry for his thoughts. True believers perform prostrations, they pay the tax, they bow in homage, and renounce their agreements with the Jews. They are Hezbollah—Allah's Party.'" Yes, it's true: the terrorist organization "Hezbollah" is "Allah's Party." Surely, you are not surprised.

It's a simple story with haunting repercussions. A self-proclaimed prophet fled his flea-infested mud hut of a town in shame and shuffled into a city filled with literate, moral, and prosperous Jews. The profiteer convoluted their scriptures, proclaimed himself their Messiah, and commanded them to submit to his authority. Then he besieged them, forcing them, men, women and children, into the desert to die. He stole their treasure, dividing their homes among his militants. Islam had hit a new low. But rest assured, this would not be its darkest hour.

Tabari VII:88 "Some say there were three Ghazwa [Muslim raids] led by the Messenger himself and one Maghazi raiding party which he dispatched between his expedition to

Badr and the campaign against the Qaynuqa." Others say: one event followed the other. I share this so that you might know that I have not jumped from the viciousness of Badr to the wanton immorality of the Qaynuqa siege, skipping over a sea of pious religious activity. There was none. One "battle" followed the next. Muhammad dropped all pretenses of religious trappings. He became a pirate pursuing plunder, a terrorist—nothing more.

Before we leave this troubled time, let's return to the surah that "approved" exiling Jews. In this passage, Allah takes "credit" for Muhammad's actions—something that is both bizarre and sinister. *059.002* **"It was Allah who drove the (Jewish) People from their [Yathrib] homes and into exile. They refused to believe. You did not think that they would go away. And they imagined that their strongholds would protect them against Allah. But Allah's Torment came at them from where they did not suspect. He terrorized them. Their homes were destroyed. So learn a lesson, men who have eyes. This is My warning. Had I not decreed the expulsion of the Jews, banishing them into the desert, I would have punished them in this world, and in the next they shall taste the punishment of Hell Fire."** *059.004* **"That is because they resisted Allah and His Messenger. If any one resists Allah, verily Allah is severe in Punishment, stern in reprisal."** Their only crime was "resisting Islam." By that logic all non-Muslims are fair game.

The obviously powerless, and thus delusional Islamic spirit said: *059.006* **"What Allah gave as booty to His Messenger, He has taken away from the Jews. For this you made no raid. Allah gives His Messenger Lordship over whom He will. Whatever booty Allah has given to Muhammad and taken away from the (Jewish) people of the townships, belongs to Allah and to His Apostle.... So take what the Messenger assigns to you, and deny yourselves that which he withholds. And fear Allah, for He is severe in Punishment."**

This all-in-one Islamic verse is the reason the "religion" cannot be fixed. It features: racism, violent hostility, banishment, destruction, thievery, wrath, terror, forced exile, severe punishment, and threats for those who resist. A doctrine this perverse will continue to fester and grow. It will infect men's minds and souls until the whole world is consumed in war.

Year three of the Islamic Era opens with a story. The headline reads: **"The Murder of Ka'b bin Ashraf, The Evil Genius of the Jews."** The drama begins with some boasting: *Tabari VII:94* **"The Prophet sent messengers to the people of Medina announcing the good news of the victory granted to him by Allah at Badr. They listed the names of the polytheists they had killed."** Only a sick man gloats over the death of others.

I recognize that you have been overwhelmed with a steady diet of revolting stories. But I want to remind you that I am not avoiding "religious" stuff to prove Muhammad was a terrorist. There hasn't been a single nurturing, loving, positive, tolerant, or even remotely religious thought presented in the Islamic Hadith since we arrived in Yathrib/Medina.

While there is no message of salvation in Islam, there is an overwhelming need for one. Simply stated: Muhammad was unable to give Muslims a reason to live so he gave them a reason to kill. *Ishaq:365* **"Ka'b bin Ashraf was from the Jewish clan of Banu Nadir. When he heard the news, he said, 'Can this be true? Did Muhammad actually kill these people? These were fine men. If Muhammad has slain them, then the belly of the earth is a better place for us than its surface!'"** Ka'b understood the danger of mixing false religion, booty, and swords. The future looked ominous. For Muhammad, the only good non-Muslim was a dead one.

Ishaq:365 **"When the enemy of Allah became convinced the report was true, he set out for Mecca. He began to arouse people against Muhammad [i.e., he exposed him]. He recited verses in sympathy for the Quraysh men Muhammad had cast into the pit. Ka'b Ashraf composed the following poetic lines: 'The blood spilled at Badr calls to its people. They cry and weep. The best men were slain and thrown into a pit.'"** Poets were the journalists of Muhammad's day. Apart from the Jews, most Arabians were illiterate, so poetry became the most effective means of disseminating a message. The poem Ka'b wrote on this occasion was seven lines long, and there wasn't a violent word among them. Ka'b urged the good people of Yathrib to: *Ishaq:365* **"Drive off that fool of yours so that you might be safe from talk that makes no sense. Why do you taunt those who mourn over their dead? They lived good lives, and as such we must remember them. But now you have become like jackals."** Astute, concise, and accurate.

Tabari VII:94 **"Then Ka'b composed poetry about some Muslim women."** As we have learned, chivalry had no place in Islam, so this made the prophet angry. If Ka'b had written of lust, pedophilia, and incest, I'm certain Muhammad would have been more understanding.

With these next words, Muhammad ordered his first assassination. While only two men were slain, the nature of his crime has far-reaching implications. Every detail haunts us today. *Tabari VII:94* **"The Prophet said, 'Who will rid me of Ashraf?' Muhammad bin Maslamah, said, 'I will rid you of him, Messenger of Allah. I will kill him.' 'Do it then,' he said, 'if you can.'"** One of the things that makes Islam lethal is that men are ever ready to kill on the prophet's command.

Ordering the assassination of a journalist for exposing a false prophet, a pirate, and a terrorist, is serious business. Let's check another source to make sure we have this right. *Bukhari:V4B52N270* **"The Prophet said, 'Who is ready to kill Ka'b bin Ashraf who has really hurt Allah and His Apostle?' Muhammad bin Maslama said, 'O Allah's Apostle! Do you want me to kill him?' He replied in the affirmative."**

That wasn't any better. Let's see what the earliest source has to say: *Ishaq:365* **"'Who will rid me of Ashraf?' Maslama said, 'I will deal with him for you. O Apostle, I will kill him.' Muhammad said, 'Do so if you can.'"**

Returning to Tabari: *Tabari VII:94* **"Muhammad bin Maslamah was quiet for three days, neither eating nor drinking more than would keep him alive. The Prophet summoned him and said, 'Why have you given up food and drink?' 'O Prophet, I said something and do not know if I can fulfill it.' 'All that is incumbent on you is to try,' Muhammad replied."**

This response is chilling when you consider the subject was assassination.

Ishaq:365/Tabari VII:94 **"Muhammad bin Maslamah said, 'O Messenger, we shall have to tell lies.' 'Say what you like,' Muhammad replied. 'You are absolved, free to say whatever you must.'"** The moment this man walked out of the room, Muhammad must have doubled over laughing. The stooge was willing to commit murder yet he was concerned about lying. And while that's hilarious in a macabre sort of way, consider the value of Muhammad's absolution. Since he had just approved lying, it couldn't have been worth the air it took to offer it. But Muhammad's assassin believed him. And that is why false prophets and corrupt doctrines are so diabolical. Muslim militants still believe him.

While the circumstances are as bizarre as the orders are vile, we do have another first. Islam was the first "religion" to command its faithful to murder and deceive. But since that's a serious charge, let's triple-check our sources. *Bukhari:V5B59N369* **"Allah's Apostle said, 'Who is willing to kill Ka'b bin Ashraf who has hurt Allah and His Apostle?' Thereupon Muhammad bin Maslamah got up saying, 'O Allah's Apostle! Would you like me to kill him?' The Prophet said, 'Yes,' Maslamah said, 'Then allow me to say false things in order to deceive him.' The Prophet said, 'You may say such things.'"**

Returning to Tabari, we are told that Maslamah **"made a plan to kill Ka'b, the enemy of Allah. Before they went to him, they sent Abu ahead. When he arrived, they spoke together for a while. They recited verses to one another, for Abu was something of a poet."** Consider the depth of the corruption necessary for a man to lure another to his death by reciting poetry. And as you read on, think of how the Palestinians use their "we are suffering under Israeli oppression" tale of woe to deceive us today, drawing us ever closer to war. *Tabari VII:94/Ishaq:367* **"Then Abu said, 'Ka'b, I have come to you about a matter which I want you to keep secret.' 'Go ahead,' he replied. 'The arrival of the Prophet Muhammad has been an affliction for us.' Abu said, 'Most Arabs are now hostile to us. We cannot travel along the roads, and the result is that our families are facing ruin. We are all suffering.' Ka'b replied, 'I warned you, Abu, that things would turn out like this.' Abu said, 'I would like you to sell us some food. We will give you some collateral and make a firm contract. Please treat us generously.'"** The Arabs who call themselves Palestinians delivered this same message to Bill Clinton during the Oslo negotiations and he gave them the guns they now use to kill Jewish women and children. Bush is following in his footsteps. Lies remain seductive.

Returning to al-Bukhari, we find Maslama having a similar chat with Ka'b. *Bukhari:V5B59N369* **"Muhammad bin Maslama went to Ka'b and said, 'The Prophet Muhammad demands payment of the zakat tax from us, and he has brought us nothing but trouble. I have come to borrow something from you.' On that, Ka'b said, 'I knew you would tire of him!' Maslama said, 'But since we have followed him, we do not want to leave until we see how all of this is going to turn out.'"**

Although, Ka'b Ashraf was but one man, the circumstances surrounding his assassination provide us with an unparalleled window into the Islamic mindset—their means and motives. The deception that is being presented by

Abu and Maslamah on behalf of Muhammad should be a warning to us today. When Muslim spokespeople deceive our media, they are following their prophet's orders and relying on his absolution.

Now, as then, economic interests cloud our judgment. *Tabari VII:95* "**Abu said, 'I have some companions with me who think the same way I do. I would like to bring them to you so that you can do business with them as well. We will deposit sufficient weapons with you to guarantee the payment of our debt.' Abu wanted to fool the Jew so that he would not be suspicious about the weapons when they came bearing them. Ka'b replied, 'Your weapons will be a satisfactory guarantee.' Abu went back to his companions, informed them of what had happened. He told them to grab their swords and join him. Before leaving, they went to the house of the Messenger. Muhammad walked with them as far as Baqi al-Gharqad. Then he sent them off, saying, 'Go in Allah's name; O Allah, help them [assassinate the outspoken Jew]!' Then the Prophet went back home. It was a moonlit night, and they went forward until they reached Ka'b's house.**" I believe we will see Muslims use this same strategy to kill millions of Jews. They will bring American, Russian, Saudi, Syrian, Iranian, and Egyptian weapons into the West Bank under the ruse of "guaranteeing" to protect Jews from Islamic terrorists. Yet they will be used by the Islamic terrorists to slaughter Jews. It is why the "land-for-peace process" is the most direct path to World War.

Before we go on, recognize what Ashraf represented. Ka'b was a poet, a journalist. The reason Muhammad singled him out for assassination was to control the public debate. This murder was about politics, not religion. It was about power and control—nothing else. The model Muhammad established still performs as intended. Virtually every member of the American media is afraid to do what Ashraf did; they are afraid to expose Islam. They know that Muslims assassinate men and women with the courage to denounce their doctrine. As a result, true Islam remains a well-guarded secret.

Ishaq:368 "**Then Abu called out to him. He had recently married, and he leapt up in his bed. His wife took hold of the sheets, and said to the strange voice, 'You are a fighting man; as only a man of war leaves his house at an hour like this.'**" Ignoring his bride's advice, Ka'b got out of bed with all the best intentions. He walked into a trap. *Bukhari:V5B59N369* "**His wife asked him, 'Where are you going?' Ka'b replied, 'Out with Muhammad bin Maslamah and my brother Abu.' His wife said, 'I hear evil in his voice as if his words are dripping blood.' Ka'b said. 'They are my brother and my foster brother. A generous man should respond to a call at night even if invited to be killed.'**" Islam is so corrosive, Muslims think nothing of murdering their kin.

Under the cover of darkness...*Muslim:B19N4436* "**Muhammad said to his companions: 'As he comes down, I will extend my hands towards his head, I will touch his hair and smell it. When you see that I have got hold of his head, strip him. When I hold him fast, you do your job.' Ka'b bin Ashraf came down wrapped in his clothes.**" *Tabari VII:97* "**He spoke with them for a while. Then they said, 'Would you like to walk with us, Ka'b, so that we can talk?'**" *Bukhari:V5B59N369* "**Muhammad said. 'I have never smelt a better perfume than this,'**" so that Ka'b would relax his guard. 'Will you allow me to smell your head?' Then Abu thrust his hand into the hair near his temple. When Muhammad got a strong hold of him, he said, 'Strike the enemy of Allah!' So they smote him."

Ishaq:368 "Their swords rained blows upon him, but to no avail. Muhammad bin Maslamah said, 'When I saw that they were ineffective, I remembered a long, thin dagger which I had in my scabbard. I took hold of it. By this time the enemy of Allah had shouted so loudly lamps had been lit in the homes around us. I plunged the dagger into his breast and pressed upon it so heavily that it reached his pubic region. Allah's enemy fell to the ground.'"

But dead was not enough. *Tabari VII:97/Ishaq:368* "We carried Ka'b's head and brought it to Muhammad during the night. We saluted him as he stood praying and told him that we had slain Allah's enemy. When he came out to us we cast Ashraf's head before his feet. The Prophet praised Allah that the poet had been assassinated and complimented us on the good work we had done in Allah's Cause. Then he spat upon our comrade's wounds and we returned to our families. Our attack upon Allah's enemy cast terror among the Jews, and there was no Jew in Medina who did not fear for his life.'" The last line is especially repugnant. It is not enough to murder Jews; Muslims must terrorize them as well.

The assassins recited these lines: *Ishaq:368* "Ka'b's body was left prostrate [humbled in submission]. After his fall, all of the Nadir Jews were brought low. Sword in hand we cut him down. By Muhammad's order we were sent secretly by night. Brother killing brother. We lured him to his death with guile [guile is cunning, craftiness, or deviousness]. Traveling by night, bold as lions, we went into his home. We made him taste death with our deadly swords. We sought victory for the religion of the Prophet." The guile of Islam is so evil it takes your breath away.

Only two men in human history have spoken and then implemented the words you are going to read next: der fuhrer and der prophet. *Tabari VII:97/Ishaq:369* "The next morning, the Jews were in a state of fear on account of our attack upon the enemy of Allah. After the assassination, the Prophet declared, 'Kill every Jew.'" It's hard to imagine the lone prophet of a billion people uttering such words. But recognizing he did may serve to save us from the men "his religion" has poisoned. Exposing Muhammad is the surest way to protect the world from his legacy.

Along these lines we find another blunt reminder of Islam's violent hatred. *Bukhari:V1B1N6* "Just issue orders to kill every Jew in the country."

Tabari VII:97/Ishaq:369 "Thereupon Mas'ud leapt upon Sunayna, one of the Jewish merchants with whom his family had social and commercial relations and killed him. The Muslim's brother complained, saying, 'Why did you kill him? You have much fat in you belly from his charity.' Mas'ud answered, 'By Allah, had Muhammad ordered me to murder you, my brother, I would have cut off your head.' Wherein the brother said, 'Any religion that can bring you to this is indeed wonderful!' And he accepted Islam."

Over the course of these pages we have progressed from silly creation accounts to devilish encounters with rascally spirits, from laughable corruptions of Biblical stories to lustful renditions of a perverse paradise. But we have left all that now. Muhammad has been empowered to implement Islam, and his method of choice is murder. Yet there is something far more sinister lurking behind every word. Throughout the Islamic depiction of these hell-bent activities, Team Islam consistently championed behavior we would expect from Satan. The Gospel of Christ, this is not.

I realize that Muhammad's demonic nature has become oppressive. So I'm going to switch gears and see what Allah has to say for himself. Five relatively short surahs were revealed during this hellish time. Let's begin by reviewing the passages I previously omitted from **"The Confrontation."**

By way of introduction, in the first six verses Allah confessed to being a terrorist and pirate. He claimed responsibility for exiling the Jews, and he gave his apostle the booty. Then in the 8th verse, Allah played favorites. The Emigrants were preferred over the Ansar. Having been Muslims longer, they were better terrorists. *059.008* **"The spoils are for the Emigrants who were expelled from their homes and from their belongings while seeking the bounty of Allah, and aiding His Messenger: such are the sincere ones. They are loyal."** Mercenaries are motivated by money. When it comes to killers, you get what you pay for. Whether in business or piracy, war or terror the principle holds true today. Understand this and you will see suicide bombing not as a sacrifice, but as a selfish act. The bomber is expecting dual rewards: his family will be enriched monetarily and he will be given a lifetime pass into Allah's brothel. The first Muslim militants didn't rob Jews and Arabs for Islam; they did it for the money.

When you come to understand the nature of the relationship between warlord and mercenary, all of Islam becomes clear. Muhammad was ensnared by the monster he had created. He lured disgruntled and covetous thugs into his lair by promising booty. Terror became a job—one that required ever more revenue. Mercenaries sell their souls for money. It's as simple as that. The most loyal killers are the highest paid and the most corrupt. But when revenues run dry, as they did when the militants missed the merchants at Badr and were forced to fight the warlord became desperate. A poor tyrant is a dead one. So the Jews were robbed in lieu of the caravan. And the most loyal mercenaries received the lion's share.

Hitler played the same game, as do all dictators. The only difference is that with early Islam, the justification was attributed to God. And that is what makes Islam more lethal than any other doctrine.

Reminding us that a peaceful Muslim is a hypocrite, Allah says that they are no better than the Jews: *059.011* **"Have you not observed the Hypocrites saying to their unbelieving brethren among the People of the Book, 'If you are expelled [from your homes by the Muslims], we will go with you? We will never listen to anyone who acts to** harm you; and if you are attacked we will help you.' But Allah is witness that they are liars. If the Jews are expelled, never will the Hypocrites go with them; if they are attacked, they will not help them defend themselves. In truth you [good jihadist Muslims] are more fearful and awful (than they) because they are afraid of you. This is a result of the terror (sent) by Allah. They are men devoid of understanding." Good Muslims are to be feared. They are awful terrorists—their scriptures say so.

Occasionally, I find myself checking the cover of the book just to make sure I haven't replaced the Qur'an with Mein Kampf. *059.014* "The Jews will not unite and fight against you except from behind walls. They hate themselves. You would think they were united, but their hearts are divided. That is because these [Jews] are a people devoid of sense. Like those who recently preceded them [the Meccans at Badr], they [the Jews who were just sent into the desert to die] have tasted the evil result of their conduct. And (in the Hereafter there is) for them a grievous punishment." Replace ghettoes with townships, Poles for Meccans, and the evil result of exile with a concentration camp and this could easily have been one of Hitler's rousing recitals. Makes you wonder if they had the same speechwriter.

This next verse perplexed me until I came to know the nature of the spirit named "Lucifer" and his derogatory title "Satan." *059.016* "They [the Jews] are like Satan when he tells man, 'Not to believe,' When (man) denies, Satan says, 'I have nothing to do with you. I fear Allah, the Lord of men and jinn!'" While it's fascinating that Satan "fears Allah" and sees him as the "Lord," this isn't the most important insight. *059.017* "Both [Jews and Satan] will go into the Fire of Hell, dwelling therein forever. Such is the reward of the Zalimun (disbelievers and polytheists)." At first blush, this is a house divided. We have seen time and again that the only spirit dark enough to have inspired Islam is Lucifer. But this verse condemns Satan to hell. How is that possible if they are one in the same?

For the answer to that question, let's turn to the book that introduced the world to this demonic spirit. The name Lucifer is only mentioned once in the entire Bible. In the midst of his prophecy on World War III—the all Islamic war to be launched against Israel in the last days—Isaiah says this about Islam and its dark spirit: "The rule of the oppressor [*nagras*: one who uses tyranny to harass, tax, and oppress, i.e., Islam] will come to an end. Those who smote [*nakah*: to strike, exile, murder, punish, or slaughter] the Jews in rage and anger with unceasing blows, and in fury subdued [terrorized] the nations with relentless aggression, will be prosecuted. Hell itself will be moved. The pompous gloating leaders, arrogantly swelling with pride and boastful speech will be brought from their graves like maggots spread out. How you have fallen, cast out of heaven, O Lucifer, the one with the brightness of the morning star. You have been cast down to the earth and diminished. You used prostration to weaken the Gentile nations. You boasted 'I will ascend to heaven; I will exalt my throne above God. I will abide in the meeting place on the most sacred Mount [Moriah—home of Lucifer's most flamboyant shrine: the Dome of the Rock]. You said, 'I will make myself like the Most High.' But you are brought down to the grave, to the depths of the pit.... The offspring of the wicked will not rise up to inherit the land [Israel] or rule over the earth." (Isaiah 14 amplified from the original Hebrew.)

The prophet Isaiah connected many of the dots for us. He reveals that Lucifer was a fallen angel and that pride led to his ruin. He is destructive, leading men to their doom. And he wants to be worshiped in place of Yahweh. Further, he connects Lucifer to Islam by saying that he is the inspiration of those who oppress the Jews and covet their land. The fact he uses "prostration" to weaken the Gentile nations is quite a clue.

"Satan" is Lucifer's title. It means "The Adversary." John, in Revelation, writes: "I saw an angel coming down from heaven, having the key to the bottomless pit and a great chain in his hand. He laid hold of the dragon, that old serpent, which is the Devil, or Satan. He bound him for a thousand years. He shut him up so that he could no longer deceive the nations." (Revelation 20) Satan is a derogatory title for Lucifer—a spirit who deceives and leads men astray. Lucifer, of course, detests "The Adversary" title, as he wants to be God, not God's opponent. Adverse means unfavorable, unpleasant, poor, or undesirable. It's not the kind of image a spirit who wants to be worshiped would be fond of having hung around his neck.

Understanding Lucifer and his disdain for the Adversary, or Satanic title, is central to understanding the spirit that underlies Islam, the spirit that enticed and inspired Muhammad to such egregious behavior. Paul, speaking to the Corinthians of the false doctrine and prophet to come said: "I am concerned that just as Eve was deceived and beguiled by the serpent's cunning, your minds may someday be corrupted. For if someone comes and preaches another Yahshua who is different, if you receive another spirit, or hear a different Gospel, you may be susceptible. I may not possess eloquent speech or be an Apostle who requires your obedience, but I know what is true and have manifest it to you.... The truth of Christ is in me. And I will continue doing this in order to cut the ground from under those who would seize the opportunity to boast about. For such men are false prophets, deceitful teachers, masquerading as messengers of God. And no wonder, for Satan transfigures and disguises himself into an angel of light [i.e., Lucifer pretends to be Gabriel]." (2 Corinthians 11 amplified from the original Greek.)

Paul is saying that Lucifer will transform himself into the image of an angel and deceive men using a false prophet. The messenger will be boastful, yet speak eloquently; he will be deceitful, yet require obedience. He will come with a new Gospel. He is speaking of Muhammad and his Qur'an.

By putting these things together we discover that Lucifer, as presented in the Bible, is a perfect match for Allah, the demented and deceitful spirit of the Qur'an. And we know that Lucifer hates the Satanic title. So now, the only

pieces of the puzzle that remain are why Lucifer chose to disguise himself as
Gabriel and why he chose Muhammad to be his prophet.

The Hebrew word for "angel" means "messenger." And the angel named
Gabriel was only called to deliver three messages. The first is to Daniel. He
told the prophet the exact day the Messiah would enter Jerusalem, five hun-
dred years in advance of the occasion. He spoke of the destruction of the
Temple, which followed Christ's crucifixion and resurrection. Then Gabriel
told Daniel that Satan would cause great devastation that he would defile·
Mount Moriah in the last days. The second and then final time we hear from
Gabriel is in the second chapter of the Gospel of Luke. Gabriel relays a message heralding the birth of John the Baptist—the one who announced the
Messiah's arrival. And he told Mary she would give birth to Yahshua, the Son
of Yahweh. In other words, Gabriel had only one job: announce the arrival
of the Messiah. Lucifer chose to impersonate him because his Muhammad
was the counterfeit Messiah. So now we know who the players are and why
they are acting so devilishly.

Returning to the Qur'an we learn that even the mountains fear Allah.
059.021 **"Had We sent down this Qur'an on a mountain, verily, you would have seen it humble
itself, turn desolate and cleave asunder, splitting in two for fear of Allah. Such are these
parables which We propound to men, that they may reflect."** Sounds like Yahweh on
Sinai; so Allah whines, "Me too!"

The **"Confrontation"** ends with a self-indulgent love fest. Since the Qur'an is
supposed to be Allah speaking, he sure seems to have a lofty view of himself.
It's no wonder pride was Lucifer's undoing. *059.022* **"Allah is He, no other Ilah may
be worshiped; Who knows both secret and open; He, Most Gracious, Most Merciful. He is
Allah, Whom there is no other Ilah; the Sovereign, the Holy One, the Source of Security, the
Guardian of Faith, the Majestic, the Irresistible, the Superb, the Compeller: Glory to Allah!
He is Allah, the Creator, the Evolver, the Bestower of Forms (or Colors). To Him belong the
Best Names: whatever is in the heavens and on earth declares His Praises and Glory: and
He is the Mighty, the Wise."** Pretty flowery language for a demon impersonating
a rock idol. And it's a wholly deceptive, even beguiling, description of the
author of the opening salvo of this very surah. As I recall, Allah confessed to
being a racist, terrorist thief. In fact, he was proud of it.

Moving on, we find that the 61st surah is equally violent and delusional.
Its opening salvo blasts away at the prophet's favorite subject, "fighting." *061.002*
**"O Muslims, why say one thing and do another? Grievously odious and hateful is it in the
sight of Allah that you say that which you do not. Truly Allah loves those who fight in His
Cause in a battle array, as if they were a solid cemented structure."** While that might
explain why there were so many concrete statues of Saddam Hussein, **"Allah
"loving those who fight"** destroys the myth that Islam is a religion.

Coveting that which is Yahweh's, Allah claimed that Moses was really
Muhammad, practicing Islam, in an earlier life. *061.005* **"And (remember), Moses**

said: 'O my people, why do you annoy and insult me, when you well know that I am Allah's Messenger?' Then when they turned away, Allah caused them to be deceived."

According to Allah, even Jesus was converted to Islam…_061.006_ **"And Jesus, the son of Mary, said: 'Children of Israel, I am the Messenger of Allah (sent) to you, confirming that (which was revealed) before me in the Torah, and giving Glad Tidings of a Messenger to come after me, whose name shall be Ahmad, the Praised One.' But when he came to them with Clear Signs, they said, 'this is sorcery!'"** Search as I might, I can't find this in my Bible. But it sure makes Paul's warning ring true.

_061.007_ **"Who does greater wrong than one who invents falsehood against Allah, even as he is being summoned to Islam? And Allah guides not the disbelievers. Their intention is to extinguish Allah's Light (by blowing) with their mouths: But Allah will complete His Light, even though the Unbelievers detest (it). It is He Who has sent His Messenger with Guidance and the Religion of Truth (Islam), that he may make it conquer all religion, even though the disbelievers hate (it)."** The phrase **"conquer all religion"** should be fair warning to the ecumenical movement, those who say all faiths present different paths to the same God, and should therefore be approached with respect and tolerance. Further, in light of what we just read in Isaiah, this pronouncement is a dead ringer for Lucifer.

It's time to make a deal. Sell your soul to this devil and he will escort you into the gardens of delight. _061.010_ **"Believers, shall I lead you to a bargain or trade that will save you from a painful torment? That you believe in Allah and His Messenger (Muhammad), and that you strive and fight in the Cause of Allah with your property and your lives: That will be best for you, if you but knew!"** Since Allah's Cause is defined as fighting or jihad, this is a call to martyrdom—it's the anthem of suicide bombers. _061.012_ **"He will forgive you your sins, and admit you to Gardens under which rivers flow, and to beautiful mansions in Eden: that is indeed the Supreme Achievement. And another (favor) which you love: help from Allah for a speedy victory over your enemies."** Yes, Muslim militants love a speedy victory. Time is money.

_061.014_ **"O Muslims! Be helpers of Allah: As Jesus the son of Mary said to the Disciples, 'Who will be my helpers (in the Cause) of Allah?' Said the disciples, 'We are Allah's helpers!' Then a portion of the Children of Israel believed, and a portion disbelieved: But We gave power to those who believed against their enemies, and they became the victorious."** Allah is saying, "Fight for me and I will give you the power to kill my enemies—the Children of Israel."

So that we might know why the Qur'an was so poorly written, Allah began the 62nd surah proclaiming: _062.002_ **"It is He Who has sent to the unlettered ones a Messenger from among them, to rehearse and recite to them His Verses, to purify them, and to instruct them in the Book and Sunnah (of Muhammad); they had been in manifest error."** The Qur'an is an illiterate rehearsing scripture to the unlettered. Perfect.

This next verse is vintage Muhammad. It's proof he and his wannabe god were racists. _062.005_ **"The likeness of those who are entrusted with the Taurat (Torah), who subsequently failed in those (obligations), is that of an _ass_ which carries huge books (but** understands them not). Wretched is the likeness of folk who deny the Verses of Allah. And Allah guides not disbelievers." Not that it's important, but we have a contradiction here. Earlier, Allah said that Jews were swine and monkeys, not asses. Make up your mind. But maybe he has lost his. You see, Allah just had his *illiterate* prophet call the *literate* Jews "asses" for carrying books they did not understand. Astonishing.

For a "book" so fixated on the Jews and their scripture, Allah and his unlettered pen pal sure don't seem to like them very much. 062.006 "Say: 'You Jews! If you think that you are friends to Allah, to the exclusion of (other) men, then desire death, if you are truthful!' But never will they long (for death), because of what their hands have done before them! Allah knows well the polytheists! Say: 'The Death from which you flee will truly overtake you. Then will you be sent back to the Knower of things secret and open, and He will tell you the things that you did!'" How's that for a bottom line? Desire death if you are truthful.

Now that Allah has helped his prophet condemn Jews, it's time to turn on the "bad" Muslims—those nasty hypocrites. In a surah named in their honor, we read: 063.001 "When the Hypocrites come to you they say, 'We bear witness that you are indeed the Messenger of Allah.' Allah knows you are His Messenger, and Allah bears witness the Hypocrites are indeed liars." Which means they were liars when they: "bore witness that Muhammad was the Messenger of Allah."

063.002 "They have made their oaths a screen, thus they obstruct (men) from the Path of Allah: truly evil are their deeds. That is because they believed, then they rejected Faith: So a seal was set on their hearts: therefore they understand not." I'm curious. If Muhammad was so wonderful, how could so many of those who lived in his presence have rejected him and his religion? This avalanche of abandonment was clearly the reason Muhammad had to tell his militants: Bukhari:V4B52N260 "If a Muslim discards his faith, kill him." Islam must be forced on people. No one in their right mind chooses it. And once in, no one leaves this club alive.

063.004 "When you look at them, their bodies please you; and when they speak, you listen to their words. They are pieces of wood propped up. They think every cry is against them. They are the enemies; so beware of them. The curse of Allah is on them! Allah will destroy them. How are they deluded and perverted?" Since Allah repeatedly defines "bad" Muslim hypocrites as those unwilling to leave their homes to fight, peaceful Muslims ought to know that their god has "cursed" them, that they are his "enemy," and that he wants to "destroy" them because they're "perverted."

So how does all of this square with predestination? 063.006 "It is equal to them whether you ask forgiveness or not. Allah will never forgive them. Allah does not forgive the transgressing people." Then whom, might I ask, does he forgive? Perfect people like Muhammad? Think about the absurdity of this statement. Only transgressors need forgiveness, yet they will receive none. So only those who don't need to be forgiven will be forgiven for what they didn't need to be forgiven for. No one is going to accuse Allah of being smart.

This makes it sound like Muhammad and his clan of misfits had over-stayed their welcome: *063.007* **"They are the ones who say, 'Spend nothing on those who are with Allah's Messenger so that they will desert him.' But to Allah belong the treasures of the earth; but the Hypocrites understand not. They say, 'If we return to Medina, surely the more honorable (element) will expel the meaner (i.e., Muhammad).' But honor, power and glory belong to Allah and His Messenger."** It's interesting that the first Muslims considered Muhammad "mean." They also recognized that his parasites, or mercenaries, were only hanging around for the money. And why, if the "treasures of the earth" belonged to Allah, did Abu Bakr prowl the streets begging Jews to "give Allah a good loan?"

Since the established families of Yathrib were unwilling to finance the prophet's piracy, Allah repeatedly ordered Muslims to pay the zakat, a tax of which Muhammad was beneficiary. *063.010* **"Spend out of the substance [booty] which We gave you before death comes and you say, 'My Lord, why didn't You give me respite for a little while? I wish I had given (more).'"** Financing the prophet's terrorist campaigns was now on Allah's list of "good deeds."

The Noble Qur'an footnotes a Bukhari Hadith to explain this verse. **"The Prophet said, 'Everyday two angels come down from heaven. One says, "O Allah, reward every person who spends in Your Cause." The other says, "O Allah, destroy every miser.""'**

Moving on to the 64th surah, we discover that the prophet is losing believers in droves. He remains focused on those who are rejecting of Islam: *064.005* **"Has not the story reached you of those who disbelieved before? They tasted the ill effects of their unbelief. They tasted a painful torment because there came to them messengers with Clear Proofs, but they said: 'Shall (mere) human beings direct us?' So they rejected and turned away. But Allah can do without (them): Allah is Rich, the Owner of Praise. Those who reject Faith and treat Our Signs as falsehoods, they will be Companions of the Fire, to dwell therein forever: an evil resort."** If Allah is indeed Satan, he can't do without man. He needs men to doing his bidding.

The following verse establishes Allah as the lord of disasters, pain, and suffering, of disease, failure, and heartache. *064.011* **"No calamity occurs, no affliction comes, except by the decision and preordainment of Allah."** *064.012* **"So obey Allah, and obey His Messenger (Muhammad): but if you turn back, the duty of Our Messenger devolves only to convey. Allah! There is no ilah but He."**

Returning to the hypocrites, we are told that they are lurking everywhere. *064.014* **"Believers, truly, among your wives and your children there are enemies for you: so beware of them! ... Your wealth and your children are only a trial."** Islam is twisted and inverted. Wives and children are a blessing, not enemies—a joy, not a trial.

Ever eager to fleece his flock, the profiteer recited: *064.016* **"Fear Allah as much as you can; listen and obey. Pay the zakat. Those saved from covetousness prosper. If you loan to Allah a beautiful loan, He will double it. He will grant Forgiveness: for Allah is most ready to appreciate."** Just think of what this guy could have done with cable TV. "Step right up and buy your forgiveness here."

✡ ✝ ☪ 💣

Against this backdrop of money-grubbing scriptures, the terrorist raids continued. *Tabari VII:98* "The Messenger ordered Zayd [the prophet's former slave turned adoptive son] out on a raid in which he captured a Quraysh caravan led by Abu Sufyan at a watering place in Najd." Proving that they were civilian businessmen, and thus a terrorist target…"A number of their merchants set out with a large amount of silver since this was the main part of their merchandise. They hired a man to guide them along this route. Zayd captured the caravan and its goods but was unable to capture the men. He brought the caravan to the Prophet." If this isn't piracy and terror the words need to be redefined.

Tabari VII:98 "The reason for this expedition was that the Quraysh said, 'Muhammad has damaged our trade, and sits astride our road. If we stay in Mecca we will consume our capital.' …The news of the caravan reached the Prophet, as did the information that it contained much wealth and silver vessels. Zayd therefore intercepted it and made himself master of their caravan. The fifth (khums) was twenty thousand dirhams; Allah's Apostle took it and divided the other four fifths among the members of the raiding party. Furat was taken captive. They said to him. 'If you accept Islam the Messenger will not kill you.'" Submit or die has been the *modus operandi* of Islam ever since. It is a most interesting form of evangelism.

Another terrorist raid under their belts, it was time for murder. "The Killing of Abu Rafi the Jew" is the next Hadith. *Tabari VII:99* "In this year, it is said, the killing of Abu Rafi the Jew took place. The reason for his being killed was, it is said, that he used to take the part of Ka'b bin Ashraf against the Messenger. The Prophet is said to have sent Abd Allah bin Atik against him in the middle of Jumada (November, 624)." Muhammad had a rougher time controlling the media than today's terrorists do. Now Muslims just lie, and the press laps it up. There aren't five journalists in the Free World with the will and wisdom to expose Islam.

"The Messenger sent some Ansar under the command of Abd Allah and Abd Allah against Abu the Jew. Abu Rafi used to injure and wrong the Prophet." *Bukhari:V4B52N264* "One of them set out and entered their fort. He said, 'I hid myself in a stable for their animals. They closed the gate. Later they lost a donkey. I went out with them, pretending to look for it. They found the donkey and went home. I went with them." It appears we have a pair of donkeys. And I don't say that to be unkind. I love Muslims and animals.

Tabari provides a slightly different twist, one more in keeping with today's jackasses: "Abd Allah said to the others, 'Stay where you are, and I will go and ingratiate myself with the doorkeeper to gain entrance.' When he was close to the door, he wrapped himself in his cloak as though he were relieving himself. The doorkeeper called, 'You there, if you want in, come now because I want to shut the gate.' I went in and hid myself in the donkey pen."

Returning to Bukhari: "They closed the gate at night, and kept its keys in a small window where I could see them. When the people slept, I took the keys and opened the door. Abu Rafi had company that night but when they left I went to him." Then, revealing the reason that Islam must be exposed, Tabari reports: *Tabari VII:100* "**Every time I opened a door, I shut it behind me from the inside, saying to myself, 'If they become aware, they will not have time to stop me from killing him.' When I reached Abu he was in a dark room with his family. As I did not know where he was in the room, I said, 'O Abu Rafi.' When he replied, I proceeded toward the voice and gave him a blow with my sword. He shouted and I came back, pretending to be a helper. I said, 'O Abu,' changing the tone of my voice. He asked me, 'I don't know who came to strike me with his sword.' Then I drove my sword into his belly and pushed it forcibly till it touched the bone. I hit him again and covered him with wounds, but I could not kill him, so I thrust the point of my sword into his stomach until it came out through his back. At that, I knew that I had killed him [in front of his wife and children]."**

"**I came out, filled with puzzlement, and went towards a ladder in order to get down but I fell into a moonlit night and sprained my foot. I bound it with my turban and moved on. I came to my companions and said, 'By Allah, I will not leave till I hear the wailing of their women.' So, I did not move till I heard them crying for Abu, the Jewish merchant. I said, 'Deliverance! Allah has killed Abu Rafi.' I got up, feeling no ailment, and proceeded till we came upon the Prophet and informed him.**" Each time Muslims kill they absolve themselves of the crime and blame their "god." While calling Allah an assassin seems odd, it proves my theory. Allah needs men to do his bidding. Satan is helpless without stooges.

And, lest we forget, Muhammad had now become a serial killer. Usually such men are condemned, locked up, and repudiated. This one was followed.

The next Hadith turns murder into a contest. *Tabari VII:101* "**Abu Rafi was one of those who had mustered ahzab against the Prophet. The Aws had killed Ka'b Ashraf on account of his enmity to the Messenger and his inciting people against him, so the Khazraj asked the Prophet for permission to kill Sallam Huqayq, who was in Khaybar. He granted this.**" The Ansar were comprised of Aws and Khazraj. They were vying for the prophet's attention by killing Jewish poets. It was an ungodly game.

Tabari VII:101/Ishaq:482 "**One of the favors which Allah conferred upon his Prophet was that these two tribes of the Ansar, the Aws and the Khazraj, used to vie with one another like stallions to carry out the will of Muhammad. The Aws did not do anything which benefited him without the Khazraj saying, 'By Allah they will not gain superiority over us in Islam in the eyes of the Messenger by doing this.' And they would not cease until they had done something similar. Thus when the Aws killed Ka'b Ashraf on account of his hostility to Muhammad, the Khazraj conferred to find a man comparable to Ka'b in hostility and called to mind Sallam Huqayq in Khaybar. They asked the Prophet for permission to kill him, and it was granted.**" Proving, once again, that the best Muslims are killers.

Deception was a hallmark of this assassination as had been in the others. So was cowardice. *Tabari VII:101/Ishaq:483* "**His wife came out and we told her that we were Arabs in search of supplies. When we entered, we bolted the door on her so she gave a shout to warn him of our presence. We rushed upon him with our swords as he lay in his** bed. He took his pillow and tried to fend us off. Abd Allah thrust his sword into his stomach and transfixed him while he was shouting, 'Enough! Enough!' At once we went out but Abd Allah had bad eyesight, and he fell off the stairway, bruising his leg or arm. 'How shall we know that the enemy of Allah is dead?' one of us asked. 'I will go and look,' one replied. He set off and mingled with the people. He said, 'I found him with the men of the Jews, and with his wife, who had a lamp in her hand, peering into his face. She said, 'By the God of the Jews, he is dead.' I never heard any more pleasing words than these. We went to the Messenger of Allah and told him that we had killed the enemy of Allah. We disagreed in his presence about the killing of Sallam, each of us claiming to have done it. The Prophet said, 'Bring me your swords.' We did and he looked at them. He said, 'This sword of Abd Allah killed him. I can see the marks left by bones on it.'"

There are no words more pleasing to a good Muslim than "a Jew is dead." The first followers of this perverse doctrine, Muhammad's Disciples, had been so corrupted by Islam they believed they were doing "god" a service by eliminating Jews. They fought over who should be given "credit" for the kill. It is why Christ warned his disciples: "A time is coming when everyone who kills you will think that he is offering service to God." (John 16:2)

To celebrate Sallam's murder, Muslim militants sang the following chorus: *Ishaq:483* "Allah, what a fine band you have, one willing to kill Sallam and Ashraf! We went with sharp swords, like fighting lions. We came upon their homes and made them drink death with our swift-slaying swords. Looking for the victory of our Prophet's religion, we ignored every risk."

The "poligious" doctrine of Islam—that caustic blend of politics and religion—was the motivation behind the forced banishment of the Qaynuqa, a Jewish township larger than Mecca. It enabled Muhammad to instigate the murder of two Jewish journalists. It inspired the grotesque slaying of a Jewish merchant. Muhammad, in cahoots with his demonic spirit, lured men into hellish duty with the dual enticements of worldly booty and heavenly lust. Islam corroded minds and corrupted souls beyond salvation. The Islamic economy and governance was based upon piracy and militancy. Muslim mercenaries could no longer distinguish right from wrong, truth from deceit. Their "religotic" (politicized religion) created the culture needed to motivate men to madness and murder. It still does.

Hopefully, you have not felt the sting of Islamic terror personally. As such, you may be able to compartmentalize the horror of these events. And that's understandable. We do not know how many Qaynuqa women and children died after being thrown into the desert. We can only imagine how they suffered. And up to this point, Muhammad's militants had slaughtered barely a hundred innocent souls. By the close of the second year of the Islamic Era, the first Muslim marauders were still small-time tyrants. Close your eyes, set down the book, and they'll all just fade away...

Sorry. It won't work that way. We ignore Islam at our peril. Undiagnosed and untreated, evil festers and grows. Like a cancer, it leaves nothing but death and destruction in its wake. Whether you view the world through the prism of the Islamic scriptures, the Bible, or history, the inevitable consequence of our present course will lead to World War III. I believe over a billion people will die in the first third of the twenty-first century as a result of our ignorance and our tolerance of Islam. Biological and nuclear weapons will be unleashed in a war started by Muslims in pursuit of Jews. It will create hell on earth and destroy the world as we know it.

The Qur'an and Hadith serve as proof that Islam is destructive. With every page, this is made abundantly clear. Left to its own devices it's obvious where Islam will lead. Muhammad's legacy is terror. From the Biblical perspective, the prophecies pertaining to World War III are laid out in the last chapter, so for now, let's focus on the historical justification for my rather dire prediction. To stress the consequence of tolerating Islam, I'm going to share some quotations from the "gospel" of the twentieth century's most famous poligious doctrine. The prophet's name was Adolf Hitler. His book was *Mein Kampf*. His religotic was Nazism. The consequence was World War II.

Even in the tolerant realm of political correctness, Nazism is rebuked. So, if I can demonstrate that apart from time and place, Nazism is virtually identical to Islam, I will have removed the veil of religiosity that protects Islam from scrutiny. Even pacifists understand the consequence of ignoring Hitler. By showing that Mein Kampf and the Qur'an were authored by the same spirit, and that their motives, mission, and means were indistinguishable, I will have made exposing and rebuking Islam relevant, as *Mein Kampf* led to the Holocaust and the brutal death of 55 million people. By proving that Nazism was founded as a religion, as a tool a covetous man used to satiate his personal craving for power, sex, and money, I will have awakened an unquenchable desire to eradicate the poligious dogma that inspired it— Islam—before it obliterates all mankind. In that light, I beg your indulgence.

Mein Kampf is a 1000-page rant. I will be revealing passages (edited of verbosity) found in the 1939 English translation I urge you to read: Reynal & Hitchcock, by Houghton Mifflin. We have already reviewed the introduction, one written immediately after the "land for peace" treaty severed Czechoslovakia, starting World War II. The translators warned that ignoring the "Nazi Gospel" would have catastrophic consequences. They were right. To discover why they came to that conclusion and to see why I believe ignoring the "Islamic Gospel" will lead to World War III, let's dive into the words, world, and mind of Adolf Hitler and compare them to Muhammad's.

Mein Kampf was written from Landsberg on the Lech prison in 1924, precisely 1300 years after the Qaynuqa Jews were abused so horrifically in 624 A.D.

It was dedicated to sixteen martyrs, men Hitler praised as: *Mein Kampf:Dedication* *"Dead heroes, blood witnesses who continue to serve as brilliant examples for the followers of our movement. They were steadfast in their belief in the resurrection of their people."* The Muslim martyrs at Badr served Muhammad just as aptly. And I'm sure you noticed Hitler's predilection for religious terms. In his opening salvo he unleashed: *"witnesses," "serve," "examples," "followers," "movement," "steadfast," "belief,"* and *"resurrection."* It wasn't by chance.

Although better written and more insightful, the object and style of Mein Kampf is identical to the Qur'an and Hadith. *Mein Kampf:Preface "I resolved to set forth, in two volumes, the object of our movement and to draw a picture of its development. From this more can be learned than from any purely doctrinary treatise."* Mein Kampf, like the Qur'an, was written in first person. The royal "our" in the preceding quote was collective because Hitler saw himself as being spiritually guided. Although much of Mein Kampf was plagiarized, its formulation and proclamation, like Islam, was the work of a solitary man—one inspired by a dark, deceitful, hateful, and violent spirit.

The Qur'an and Hadith were never meant for non-Muslims to read. *Mein Kampf:Preface "With this work I do not address myself to strangers, but to those adherents of the movement who belong to it with their hearts and whose reason now seeks a more intimate enlightenment."* Muhammad ordered Muslims not to take the Qur'an with them when they conquered new lands. *Bukhari:V4B52N233* **"Allah's Apostle forbade the people to travel to a hostile country carrying copies of the Qur'an."** He said: **"Unbelievers will never understand our signs and revelations."**

Muhammad also claimed that nothing should be written if it could be spoken. He believed that eloquent speech had been the magic that had enabled his destiny. His Qur'an was, after all, an oral recital. The Hadith remains nothing more than an oral report. Hitler tells us why: *Mein Kampf:Preface "I know that one is able to win people far more by the spoken word than by the written word. Every great movement on this globe owes its rise to great speakers and not to writers."* Muslims and Nazis alike report that men swooned in their founder's presence as he so passionately called them to his cause. But I must say in Hitler's defense, he was a much more coherent writer than was Allah.

But alas: *Mein Kampf:Preface "Nevertheless, the basic elements of a doctrine must be set down in permanent form in order that it may be represented in the same way and in unity."* In other words: "I want my prophetic words to survive me." And that's because both men wanted to outlive those who tormented, mocked, and rejected them. *Mein Kampf:Preface "Mein Kampf will serve to destroy the evil legends created about my person by the Jewish press."*

Muhammad and Hitler saw themselves and their followers as a nation in distress, one that could, should, and would righteously steal what belonged to others. Hitler said: *Mein Kampf:1 "The distress of the nation gives us the moral right to acquire foreign soil and territory. The sword is then the plow. From the tears of war there grows the daily bread for generations to come.*" Muhammad said: *013.041* **"Do they not see Us advancing from all sides into the land (of the disbelievers), reducing its borders (by giving it to believers in war victories)?"** Inspiring militants to become plundering pirates, both religotics turned their adherents into parasites. Their economies became dependent upon booty. Honest labor was confined to fighting.

Mein Kampf:Preface "*That also gave me the opportunity to describe my own development as far as it is necessary to understand these volumes.*" The Qur'an screams out to us today, testifying that Muhammad was an abused child, hating all who withheld the power and wealth he craved. Mein Kampf is more direct. Hitler admits to being abused, orphaned, and poor. He tells us how this led him to create his new religion, and how he would use it to attack both his powerful peers and the defenseless Jews. As such, reading Mein Kampf is like having a conversation with Muhammad.

Hitler and Muhammad rose from tiny towns they ultimately attacked. *Mein Kampf:1* "*Today I consider it my good fortune that Fate designated the small town of Braunau as the place of my birth.*" Der fuhrer called his guiding spirit "Fate" and "Nature." Both were always capitalized as if divine and used interchangeably with "Lord" and "God." These words are found throughout English translations of the Bible and Qur'an. Both have pagan origins. "Lord" was the title of "Baal," the Canaanite god. The English "God" is derived from the Germanic "Gott." Pagan Aryans coined the term in reference to the dark spirits they worshiped. Lucifer would be honored with either moniker.

Like Muhammad, Hitler was orphaned and abused. He described his youth in these terms: *Mein Kampf:6* "*endless poverty, misery and hardship, want and sorrow.*" *Mein Kampf:7* "*I was a quarrelsome boy.*" *Mein Kampf:29* "*Hunger was my faithful guard, the only friend who never left me.*" *Mein Kampf:33* "*I have felt poverty's grip, a murderous viper with poisonous fangs.*" *Mein Kampf:32* "*The relentless struggle killed all pity. My painful existence suffocated any feeling of sympathy.*" Remember these words.

Hitler described his torment: *Mein Kampf:43* "*I was familiar with nothing but filth and despised all authority.*" *Mein Kampf:39* "*What grew out of this unhappiness and misery, of this filth and decay, was no longer a human being. I possessed a ruthless resolution to destroy the incurable social tumors.*" I believe that this is how Muhammad felt as he endured the anguish of poverty and the unrelenting harshness of the Arabian desert. He came to despise all authority except his own.

Understanding Hitler's motivation is important because ultimately the two most diabolical doctrines ever conceived by man were the direct result of an abused childhood. A festering rage caused both founders to covet what they were denied and hate those they viewed responsible for their torment.

Speaking of his abusive father, Hitler said, *Mein Kampf:14* "*The old man became embittered. I got the worst of it as he relentlessly began to enforce his authority.*" *Mein Kampf:38* "*He became familiar with alcohol, coming home drunk and brutal. God have mercy on the scenes which followed. I witnessed it all personally, hundreds of times with disgust and indignation. Even now I shudder when I think of those pitiful times. The pictures are haunting. But Fate will take its revenge."* The most telling line is: *"Fate will take its revenge."* Hitler, like Muhammad was fatalistic. Der fuhrer named his guiding spirit "Fate" while the prophet usurped every characteristic of Manat, the Arab goddess of fate. Both believed that their "god" would help them avenge their tormented youth. They preached predestination.

Being abandoned shaped the boys who would become tyrants: *Mein Kampf:24 "When I was thirteen my father died quite suddenly. Mein Kampf:25 "Two years later my mother's death put a sudden end to all my plans. Her illness exhausted our meager funds. The orphan's pension I received was not nearly enough for me to live on. I hoped to wrest from Fate some success; I needed to become something."* This was Muhammad's motivation. It resonates throughout the Qur'an and Hadith. He was insecure and needed to prove to the world that he was somebody.

Although he was disgusting and immoral, der fuhrer, like der prophet, saw himself as a bastion of virtue. *Mein Kampf:41 "I was shocked by the ethical and moral crudity of my comrades, and by their low level of spiritual development." Mein Kampf:41 "Not a shred of humanity is left, not a single institution is unattacked, from teacher to head of state, from religion to morality. Everything is abused, pulled down in the nastiest manner into filth and depravity."*

Muhammad saw Arabs as either good fighters in his cause, useless hypocrites, or enemy infidels. Hitler's view was no different. *Mein Kampf:16 "I saw the world in three groups: the fighters, the lukewarm, and the traitors."* Both doctrines were uncompromising, intolerant, born in blood, and propelled by sword.

The means to Hitler's madness was his corruption of history and his wanton disregard for facts and chronology. This was identical to Muhammad's dimwitted rape of the Bible. *Mein Kampf:18 "I learned how to forecast the future by recalling the past.... The chronology of history does not matter. It is the search for forces which cause effects.... Remember that which is important and forget the rest."*

The Aryan dictator twisted the past to serve his future, just like the Arab pirate before him. *Mein Kampf:47 "Content is registered in the mind, not according to the sequence it happened or the sequence in which the books were read, but just as small pieces of a mosaic that must be put into place."* While Muhammad wasn't this articulate or philosophical, he did have a penchant for taking unrelated pieces of Jewish history and rearranging them to his liking.

Mein Kampf and the Qur'an were comprised of the same raw material and crafted in the same fashion. *Mein Kampf:49 "As soon as the knowledge is gained it finds its due place in the picture the imagination has created. It acts as a supplement, enhancing truth and clarity."* Both men used their twisted histories to befuddle their assailants. *Mein Kampf:49 "A public speaker will never convincingly confront a contradiction without such information. A knowledge of history can be used to confound an adversary."* And they used the Bible to make the ungodly sound religious. *Mein Kampf:51 "The more the linguistic tohuwabohu (Hebrew, Genesis 1:2—meaning chaos, confusion, and hubbub) ate into the existing government, the faster they her-alded a day of doom for their Babylonian realm."* Muhammad's favorite predic-tion was of the Day of Doom. And it was in the Babylonian realm that Islam was molded into a poligious doctrine capable of seducing a billion souls.

Hitler's next line provides a wonderful insight into the mindset of Muhammad as his demonic spirit welled up inside him, causing him to chafe at the Hebrew Scriptures. *Mein Kampf:55 "An inner voice now urged me on…the effect was like a spiritual vitriol [anger, wrath, fury, rage, ire]. I had to fight down the rage rising in me. The enemy's wretched papers comprised a concentrated solution of lies."*

Hitler said of the Jewish inspired Socialist doctrine he would both emu-late and hate: *Mein Kampf:56 "Everything was written with an iron-faced prophetic cer-tainty. Contained in the literature was a doctrine of salvation for a new mankind. Yet they operated in the most base manner with brutal forces of calumny [slander and defamation]."* The master of propaganda said, *"They possess a virtuosity for lying that is outrageous!"* Der fuhrer must have shared der prophet's speechwriter.

While the populations of Austria and Germany were ten thousand times larger than Muhammad's Mecca, der fuhrer despised his rulers as much as der prophet disdained his chiefs. The empowered held what these men cov-eted. *Mein Kampf:20 "I have become an enemy of the ruling dynasty which has so disas-trously influenced the state. The imperials have betrayed the cause of the people for their own ignominious ends."* Mein Kampf's never-ending argument rivaled the Qur'an's. *Mein Kampf:21 "The hypocrisy of the Habsburgs [Quraysh] fanned the flames of hatred, indignation and contempt." Mein Kampf:42 "The rats of political poisoning gnaw away at the masses."*

Hitler and Muhammad stole the preponderance of their "new" poligious doctrines from established sources. Hitler borrowed from Islam and then usurped the writings of Nietzsche and Marx (both funded, interestingly enough, by the Illuminati—a religotic founded to serve and worship Lucifer). He was dependent upon Muhammad for his intolerance and terror, Nietzsche for his philosophy, and Marx for his politics. Yet der fuhrer, like his mentor, wasn't into sharing power or praise with anyone—especially a Jew. Muham-mad plagiarized the style of Zyad and the stories of Moses. Then, in identical fashion, both demagogues turned on the sources of their inspiration. And, as a not-so- coincidental aside, Yahweh's chosen people, the Jews, played a sig-nificant role in both men's revelation and rage.

The National Socialist German Workers Party, better known as Nazis, cloaked themselves in Marxist jargon. *Mein Kampf:51 "When I was young, Marxism, Social Democracy, and Socialism were identical ideas to me. But here, too, the hand of Fate opened my eyes to this betrayal of the people. I learned about the Social Democra-tic Party from a spectator's point of view without having the slightest insight into the meaning of their doctrine. But suddenly I came into contact with their view of life and realized that it was a pestilential whore masked in social virtue. I knew that I must rid the world of her."* Hitler's Reich was more controlling than Lenin's Russia. Labor, production, and all things economic were socialized, making his attack on Marxism as hollow as Muhammad's swipes at paganism and Judaism. And in like fashion, Muhammad initially saw no difference between his pagan past, Judaism, Christianity, and Islam. The Qur'an says, **"We make no distinction between them."** But then, when they wouldn't surrender, Muhammad became enraged. His final surahs proclaim: **"Wipe the Infidels out to the last."**

Hitler blamed the Jewish Marx for having turned unions into his personal playground just as Muhammad attacked the Quraysh for hoarding the Ka'aba Inc. *Mein Kampf:52 "When I was told to join a union, I refused and was thrown out immediately…. At first I was annoyed. I drank my bottle of milk and ate my piece of bread pondering my miserable fate. It annoyed me extremely. The Marxists were exploiting workers, suppressing the proletariat. The institution raised slaves for the new slave drivers. Religion was a means of doping the people destined for exploitation. It dragged people down into the dirt and filth of the lowest depths."* Nazism, like the religion named submission, was designed to exploit and suppress slaves on behalf of their new master, doping people by way of religion into submission. As such both condemnations were hypocritical. The perpetrators were worse than those they were assailing. If I were to compress Islam into a single sentence, it would be: *"Religion was a means of doping the people destined for exploitation."*

The tactics of the three religotics—Islam, Communism, and Nazism—become indistinguishable: *Mein Kampf:53 "I argued till finally one day they [the Marxist union] applied the one means that wins the easiest victory over reason: terror and force. The leaders gave me the choice of either leaving the job or being thrown from the scaffold. I was alone and resistance seemed hopeless."* This is Islam in its purest form. Terror and force compel the hopeless to forfeit their money or life. Like Muhammad, Hitler would build his religotic on this formula. *Qur'an 009.029* **"Fight those who do not submit to Islam until they pay the tribute tax in abject humility."**

While Hitler was trying to condemn Marxism with this next slogan, the line works equally well for the victims of Nazism or Islam. *Mein Kampf:55 "Aware of the terrible working of this poison, only a fool would condemn the victim."* This reminds me of the quote from Renan, the Islamic scholar, who wrote: "Muslims were the first victims of Islam. Many times I have observed in my travels that fanaticism comes from a small number of dangerous men who maintain others in the practice of this religion by terror. To liberate the Muslim from his religion is the best service that one can render him."

The Qur'an, like Mein Kampf, acknowledges the source of its inspiration. *Mein Kampf:55 "My eyes were opened to the inner causes of Social Democratic successes. I understood the brutal demand to subscribe, to only read red newspapers, red books, and to exclusively attend red meetings. Marxism was a doctrine of intolerance."* This is no different than the Qur'an's command for Muslims to shun contact with the Christians and Jews who had provided Muhammad's scripture.

Having studied Islam, Hitler explained the strategy that propelled Muham-mad's rise. *Mein Kampf:56* "*Like women, men will submit to a strong man. They are far more satisfied with a doctrine which tolerates no rival. With freedom, men feel at a loss as what to do with it. They feel deserted, spiritually terrorized. They will not recognize the outrageous curtailment of their human liberties, for in no way does the delusion of an intolerant doctrine dawn on them. They see force, brutality, and the aim of the doc-trine to which they finally and always submit.*" Once again, we see that Islam and Nazism are cut from the same cloth. Force and brutality are the tools of sub-mission. Terror and the outrageous curtailment of human liberties lie at the heart of both doctrines. Neither tolerates a rival. *Qur'an 008.039* **"Fight them until all religion is for Allah alone."**

The tyrants' methods were identical, as were their means: *Mein Kampf:56* "*If Social Democracy [Marxism] is confronted by a doctrine of greater truthfulness, carried out with the same brutality, then the latter will be victorious.*" Truth is not relative, thus "greater truth" only means: "My way is better (for me) than yours." This statement, which coincides entirely with Islam, means that the tyrant's way will be imposed on any conflicting doctrine by brutal force. Since Nazism wasn't "greater truth," it failed, but it took 55 million souls down with it. And since Islam isn't "greater truth" either, it will also fail, but the price will be higher still. *Bukhari:V4B53N386* **"Our Prophet ordered us to fight you till you worship Allah Alone or pay us the Jizyah tax in submission. Our Prophet informed us that our Lord says: 'Whoever amongst us is killed as a martyr shall go to Paradise to lead a luxurious life, and whoever survives shall become your master.'"**

Speaking of the Socialist doctrine he emulated, Hitler announced what he would do what Muhammad did: *Mein Kampf:56* "*The technical tools of Social Democ-racy became clear to me. I understood the infamous mental terror which this movement exercised on the population which could neither morally nor psychically resist such attacks. There was a bombardment of lies and calumnies toward the adversary who seemed most dangerous [threatening to the doctrine], till finally the nerves of those who had been attacked gave out and they, for the sake of peace, bowed down to the hated enemy. But these fools will not find peace after all.*" Unless I'm mistaken, this sounds similar: *Ishaq:461* **"Muhammad besieged them for twenty-five nights. When the siege became too severe for them, Allah terrorized them. Then they were told to submit to the judgment of Allah's Messenger."** *Bukhari:V5B59N448* **"They surrendered to the Prophet. 'I give my judgment that their men should be killed, their women and children should be taken as captives, and their properties distributed.'"** Muhammad, Hitler, Lenin, and Mao, poligious prophets all, deployed the same tactics to suppress their peo-ple and terrorize the world.

Mein Kampf foreshadows the future that awaits those who tolerate evil, for those who seek peace with terrorists: *Mein Kampf:57* "*The play begins again and is so often repeated the fear of the mad dog paralyzes suggestion. The Social Democrat [read Muslim or Nazi] knows from his own experience the value of strength. The doctrine praises every pacifist. Marxism is only afraid of strength."*

Hitler said that tyrannical regimes thrive on ignorance. *Mein Kampf:57* *"Most of all it recommends those who are weaklings in mind and power. Social Democracy knows how to create the appearance that it is the only way in which peace can be maintained, yet relentlessly it conquers."* Yes, even today, those who promote peace with Islam simply facilitate their conquests.

Hitler, as we shall see, linked Judaism to Marxism. With that in mind consider these prophetic words: *Mein Kampf:58* *"These [terror] tactics are based on an exact calculation of all human weaknesses. They will lead to success with mathematical certainty unless the other side learns to fight poison gas with poison gas."*

As with Muhammad and Islam, terror was the central ingredient in Hitler's Nazi religotic: *Mein Kampf:58* *"The importance of physical terror against the individual and the masses also became clear to me."* Muhammad agreed: *Bukhari: V4B52N220* **"Allah's Apostle said, 'I have been sent with the shortest expressions bearing the widest meanings, and I have been made victorious with terror.'"**

Der fuhrer emulated his mentor: *Mein Kampf:58* *"Here, too, we find exact calculations of the psychological effect. Terror in the workplace, in the factory, in the assembly hall, and on occasion in the mass demonstration, will always be accompanied by success as long as it is not met by an equally great force of terror."* I find it stunning that America sent emissaries to work with this man throughout the 1930s. I find it stunning that Great Britain capitulated to his will. It's as if they had never read his manifesto. It's as if they were ignorant of his motives and means. But it's understandable: it's directly analogous to Americans negotiating with Saudis, Egyptians, Iranians, and the so-called Palestinians without having read the Qur'an or Hadith.

Seventy-five years ago America's best and brightest ignored the words on these pages; in fact, they denied them, as did the nation's media. And this allowed a demented, violent, and hateful poligious cancer to fester. Rather than expose and eliminate it when it was weak, we allowed it to garner money, arms, and men. Nazis used them to kill us. And while that's inexcusable, there is something far more disturbing, immoral, and foreboding here. We are doing it all over again.

We are just fifty-eight pages into Mein Kampf, and yet we know what Hitler is going to do and how he is going to do it. You wouldn't think that it would have been too much to ask our leaders to have read fifty-eight pages and thereby saved the lives of fifty-five million people. Yet they didn't, and he lashed out as promised. And this is not just a lesson in comparative history—Nazism to Islam—for our leaders haven't cracked the covers of the terrorist manifesto that is motivating killers today. I can only hope and pray that this comparison between Hitler and Muhammad, Mein Kampf and the Qur'an, will awaken free peoples before terror succeeds once again.

Some may protest that Hitler was more ruthless, and thus a comparison is unfair. But one man's comparative "success" was merely a function of time and place, not doctrinal depravity. With swords and spears rather than tanks and planes, Muhammad was forced to be considerably more deliberate and homespun in his application of terror. Working with freedom-loving and peaceful Arabs rather than disciplined and warlike Aryans, early Islam was a less efficient killer. Without the population density of Europe in the twentieth century, the first Muslim militants were less murderous, as well. But transfer a billion dollars a day to the Islamic cause, give them time to develop nuclear and biological weapons and time to indoctrinate millions of martyrs to use them, and see what happens in a world of six billion souls.

The Bible says a quarter of the earth's population will die in the ensuing war, a third of the planet's surface will be scorched, and pestilence will render even more uninhabitable. Knowing what you know now, do you want to bet against it, risk your freedom and your life on the off chance that Muslims will not act like Muhammad?

Hitler said, speaking of the terror he wished to impose on Marxists (who like the Jews were both his inspiration and his rival): *Mein Kampf:58* *"Then, of course, the Marxists will cry havoc; scornful of the state [for not protecting them]. With the resulting disorder they will reach their goal of finding some idiot official who in the stupid hope of gaining something for himself, a favor from the dreaded enemy, will help break the adversary of this dreaded plague."* Hitler is implying that confronted with a terrorist doctrine like Islam, a nation like America is likely to comfort the terrorists and attack those with the courage to thwart them. He's right.

Just as Muhammad taught his militants to attack Judeo-Christianity, the doctrine that inspired him, Hitler said: *Mein Kampf:58* *"Only those who know the soul of a people, not from books but from life [his abused youth], can understand the impression such success [terrorism] makes on the sensibilities of adherents and adversaries. In the ranks of their adherents the victory gained is looked upon as the triumph of the righteousness of the cause. While the beaten adversary despairs entirely, viewing all further resistance futile."* As we have discovered in the Hadith and Qur'an, the terrorist raids perpetrated by militants against merchants, and by Muslims against Jews, had this very effect on both ally and adversary. *Qur'an 033.022* **"When the faithful saw the retreating allied armies this enhanced their faith and obedience...Allah drove the infidels back in their fury so that their resistance was futile."**

Mein Kampf:59 *"The more I became acquainted with the methods of physical terror, the more I asked forgiveness from the hundreds of thousands who succumbed to it."* They say that confession is good for the soul. Of course you need to have one for it to work. Then speaking of the abuse that gave rise to Islam and Nazism, der fuhrer proclaimed: *Mein Kampf:59* *"I owe [my inspiration] to that period of suffering because I learned to distinguish between victims and seducers."* Like Muhammad, Hitler, having been a victim, became a seducer so that he might victimize.

Both tyrants personified evil. Yet in their twisted minds, it was their enemies who: *Mein Kampf:60* *"sowed the seeds of hatred, creating the justification for their actions…. Fate gave me these lessons." Mein Kampf:62 "The battle against them has to be fought with weapons to have any hope of success…. The struggle for the abolition of evil will be decided in favor of the stronger force."* Muhammad and Hitler justified their actions by redefining good and evil. Fighting was good; pacifists were evil. Anything that served to satiate their cravings for power, sex, and money was good; anything that precluded them from taking these things was bad.

This next line explains how Muhammad enticed his mercenaries, building an economy based upon piracy and plunder. It's why everyone in Islam's path ultimately submitted. *Mein Kampf:63 "In politics, the application of economic means of pressure permits extortion so long as the doctrine is reckless and the people are stupid and sheepish."* Muhammad promoted similarly reckless odds by inferring that all non-Muslims were stupid. *Qur'an 008.065* **"O Prophet, urge the Believers to fight. If there are twenty among you with determination they will vanquish two hundred. If a hundred, they will slaughter a thousand infidels: for these are a people devoid of understanding."**

Mein Kampf:64 "So great was the fear [of terror] that people dreaded war. So the doctrine can ratchet up demands higher and higher. It's a devilish attempt to weaken or even paralyze the victim's holiest claims. Considering the limited thinking power of the masses, the success of this strategy is not surprising." This is precisely what we have been reading about. Fighting on behalf of the devil, the first Muslims used terror to paralyze everyone within their reach. *Qur'an 059.002* **"It was Allah who drove the People from their homes and into exile. They refused to believe. You did not think that they would go away. And they imagined that their strongholds would protect them. But Allah came at them from where they did not suspect, and terrorized them. Their homes were destroyed. So learn a lesson, men who have eyes. This is My warning.**

Hitler said this of Communism, but it is equally true of Islam: *Mein Kampf:64 "They fear actually lifting people from the depths of their present cultural and social misery because it would wrench from them their base of power."* So long as the militancy of disgruntled men can be channeled at an external enemy, tyrants retain power. Claiming to liberate men, Nazism and Islam: *Mein Kampf:65 "profane liberty with these words, 'If you don't join with us, we will crack your skull!'"* In the Hadith, we find: *Ishaq:470* **"We attacked them fully armed, sharp swords in our hand, cutting through heads and skulls."** *Ishaq:471* **"We were steadfast trusting in Him. We have a Prophet by whom we will conquer all men."**

Der fuhrer was as fixated on Marxism as the prophet was on Judaism. *Mein Kampf:65 "I had a longing to penetrate the nucleus of this doctrine, but the official literature was of little use, for it lies."* Muhammad falsely condemned the Jews for lying too. *Ishaq:240* **"The Jews are a treacherous, lying, and evil people."**

Sounding like Muhammad and his never-ending argument, Hitler protested like a schoolyard bully: *"I was disgusted by their pettifogging methods and writing. Words with unclear content or unintelligible meaning were piled up ingeniously and meaninglessly. It is a dung heap of literary Dadaism. Theoretical*

untruth and nonsense, combined with sad, foreboding, and depressing fear form a doc-
trine comprised of egoism and hatred. It could bring about the end of mankind. It is
a doctrine of destruction." This is an exacting description of the Qur'an. *002.059*
"The [Jewish] transgressors changed and perverted the word from that which had been
spoken to them to a word distorted; so We sent a plague upon them from heaven, for their
evil-doing." Muhammad and Hitler epitomized what they protested.

While I do not understand the connection or transition, that rant was followed by: *Mein Kampf:66* *"Understanding Jewry alone is the key to comprehending the*
real intention of Social Democracy. He who knows race will raise the veil of false con-
ceptions, and out of the mist and fog of empty phrases, there rises the grinning, ugly
face of Marxism." Why do you suppose these men chose to annihilate Yahweh's chosen people? Coincidence? Jews had neither army nor country. They
represented a tiny fraction of one percent of the earth's population. Yet one
of these men ordered his followers to kill every Jew. The other nearly *did.*

Hitler said: *Mein Kampf:66* *"When I came upon the word 'Jew' I felt a slight dislike*
and could not ward off a disagreeable sensation which seized me whenever they were
in my presence. Their external appearance had become human, but they had a strange
religion." Hitler would call them: *"halfwits, nags, malicious, envious annoyances,"*
and *"dangerous disgusting liars"* whose *"smell makes me ill."* *Mein Kampf:75* *"The phys-*
ical uncleanliness of the chosen people was as repelling as their moral blemishes."

Muhammad said Allah committed "bestiality, turning Jews into apes and
swine." He said that the Jews were "deaf, dumb, and blind." And referring to the
People of the Book he said, "They are a people in whose hearts is a disease." Hitler
said, *Mein Kampf:75* *"The little Jew, blinded by the sudden light, was like a maggot in a*
rotting corpse." *Mein Kampf:76* *"Jews are a spiritual pestilence—infected with a disease*
worse than the Black Plague. They are spiritual and moral poison, the carriers of the
worst sort of germs, infecting the minds of the world." *Bukhari:V4B56N679* "Allah's Apostle
said, 'Plague is a means of torturing the Israelis.'"

Muhammad's "Allah" and Hitler's "Fate" hated Yahweh's chosen. It's as
if they thought they could hurt him by hurting them. *Mein Kampf:79* *"Jews were*
cursed by Fate. They were hit so hard by Fate they have no understanding.... Their
boundless hate for themselves soiled their history and abused their heroes." *Ishaq:264* "The
Jews denied what they knew. They were obstinate. So Allah revealed, 'People of the Book,
believe in what we have sent down or We will efface your features, turning your face into
your ass, cursing you.'"

Der fuhrer justified his racism by suggesting that the Jews controlled the
world press and Marxism. Muhammad simply sent out assassins to murder
Jewish poets. *Mein Kampf:80* *"I traced the names of the authors of Marxist papers and*
they were all Jews. I became acquainted with their doctrine and used it as a weapon in
the battle for my own internal conviction." With every word, Hitler became more
like Muhammad. *Mein Kampf:81* *"It isn't possible to free a Jew from his convictions. I*
naively tried to make clear to them the madness of their ideas. I talked until my tongue

was weary but it only served to strengthen their determination. They refused to understand.... Their glibness of tongue and skill for lying caused me to hate them."

The Qur'an also claimed that the Jews would never believe. *Ishaq:248* **"Allah has sealed their hearts and their hearing, blinding them so that they will never find guidance. And that is because they have declared you a liar and they do not believe in what has come down from their Lord. For opposing you they will have an awful punishment."**

Islam and Nazism were fixated on dehumanizing Jews. *Mein Kampf:82* *"They are seducers who condemned truth and denied the word. They are not to be pitied, but to be given their due—to smash the seducer and corrupter against the wall."* This is the central message of the Medina surahs. *Ishaq:248* **"Allah increases their sickness. A tormented doom awaits the Jews. Allah said, 'They are mischief makers. They are fools. The Jews deny the truth and contradict what the Apostle has brought. I will mock them and let them continue to wander blindly.'"**

Mein Kampf and the Qur'an spew similar venom. *Mein Kampf:82* *"Jews are victims of error, instigators of illness, led by devils incarnate, with the brains of a monster. They would destroy the world if not for the salvation of a fight with all the weapons at our disposal. They veil their thoughts and conceal their intentions."*

Muhammad changed his Qiblah from Jerusalem to Mecca, from pretending to be a Jewish prophet to being their most ardent enemy. Hitler said: *Mein Kampf:83* *"This was the greatest change I was ever to experience inside me. I had turned into a fanatical anti-Semite.... Destiny itself gave me the answer. The Jewish doctrine of Marxism is chaos. If the Jew is allowed to conquer humanity, his crown will be man's funeral wreath."* For der fuhrer and der prophet, the elimination of the Jewish race was inspired: *Mein Kampf:80* *"Eternal Nature inexorably revenges the transgressors of her laws. I am acting on behalf of the Almighty Creator. By warding off the Jews I am fighting for the Lord's work."* This leaves us with a rather unpleasant choice. Either there are two "Lords" who despise Jews or the Nazi and Islamic god is the same spirit.

Hitler, like Muhammad, hated choice as much as he despised freedom: *Mein Kampf:99* *"Democracy is a universal plague. It creates a monstrosity of filth and fire. Fate showed me how ridiculous a parliament is as an institution."* *Mein Kampf:104* *"The invention of democracy is a crying shame.... A majority can never replace the Man."* Never forget: Nazism, like Islam, was created to serve one man. *Mein Kampf:106* *"The one true leader, provided by Fate, is to be placed in that position."* Muhammad said on behalf of his god: *002.104* **"You of [the Islamic] Faith, say not (to the Prophet) words of ambiguous import like 'Listen to us,' but words of respect; and obey (him): To those who don't submit there is a grievous punishment."** The core message of the Medina surahs is: submit and obey, fight and pay.

Muhammad and Hitler thought that they were superior to the people they controlled. The prophet called his people every derogatory word he knew. Hitler was slightly more refined. *Mein Kampf:107* *"The mass of people are not sufficiently developed to arrive at a political opinion by themselves and thus are not suited* to select the leader." *Mein Kampf:113* "It is easier for a camel to go through the eye of a needle than it is for a great man to be discovered in an election." *Mein Kampf:116* "Democracy shuns sunlight. Only a Jew could praise such a dirty and false institution."

Muhammad chose the grandiose titles of prophet and apostle. Hitler followed suit, suggesting that he was called to be the oracle or messenger of God. *Mein Kampf:117* "The word "fuhrer" (leader) has a very special connotation. Der Fuhrer is a man who gives expression to the divinity enshrined in his people. Der Fuhrer speaks as the Oracle or Messenger of his dreams. Der Fuhrer must have a feeling of certainty. He must not shrink from bloodshed or even war in pursuit of his goal. Der Fuhrer is the German Messiah whose kingdom is to last a thousands years. He is like Christ. He must allow Fate to dictate the course he is to pursue.... Any German who resists Der Fuhrer is a pariah, a blasphemer against Providence."* Muhammad wasn't the only tyrant with a messiah complex.

Muhammad wasn't the only dictator to found a religion. *Mein Kampf:120* "By using religious forces for political purposes, Der Fuhrer awakens a spirit most would not have believed possible." *Mein Kampf:123* "But once it is in danger of being oppressed, it is justified in fighting with all available weapons.... For any man who is not willing to fight, righteous Providence has already decreed his doom. The world is not intended for the cowardly."* Good Nazis, like good Muslims, fight. *Qur'an 002.191* **"Oppression is worse than killing."** *Qur'an 008.060* **"Prepare against them whatever arms and weaponry you can muster that you may terrorize Allah's enemies."**

Hitler, like someone else we know, possessed a delusional self image. *Mein Kampf:134* "Only the best and the most courageous characters are suited to act as leaders. If the fight for the new view of life [religotic] is not led by heroes then death-defying fighters will not be found."* Both men had a rather nasty habit of over-hyping themselves and their causes in hopes of attracting warriors. *Mein Kampf:135* "The mission of a successful movement is to gain leaders and fighters. It must embrace its destiny with force, defiance, and martyrdom. It must fight, not negotiate." *Qur'an 008.057* **"Inflict on them such a defeat as would be a lesson for others that they may be warned. If you apprehend treachery from a people with whom you have a treaty, retaliate by breaking it off."**

Continuing to connect fighting to religion, Hitler proclaimed: *Mein Kampf:127* "With religious conviction...the bearers of the new doctrine must declare themselves ready and willing to fight." *Mein Kampf:128* "The will to fight using all instruments of power gains favor and draws the greatest possible advantage to the movement." *Mein Kampf:132* "Greatness wins new fighters for the cause and they are rewarded with success." *Qur'an 008.065* **"O Prophet, urge the faithful to fight."** *Qur'an 009.005* **"Slay the infidels wherever you find them. Take them captive and besiege them."** *Qur'an 008.069* **"Know that the use of spoils is lawful and good."**

Suggestive and impassioned speech served both men. Their lives became a performance in which they played the staring role. *Mein Kampf:136* "The masses will always succumb to the force of the spoken word. They need volcanic eruptions of passion and spiritual sensations stirred by the cruel God of Misery and the fiery word."

Hitler's words, like Muhammad's before him, served as a confession. The *"cruel God of Misery"* was Lucifer. He seduced men with fiery-tongued accomplices.

Passions bubbled to the surface and men succumbed to their own desires. *Mein Kampf:137 "Only a storm of burning passion can turn people's destinies. Only he who harbors passion in himself can arouse passion [cravings]. Passion will be given to him by the cruel God of Misery. He will choose him, and will give him the words that beat like a hammer—words that will open the hearts of men. The passionate speaker has been chosen by Heaven as a prophet to do his will."* Hitler saw himself as a *"prophet chosen by the cruel God of Misery,"* one called to recite the Heavenly revelations of a *"new view of life,"* one called to incite violent passions so that men would fight for his cause. As such, he was the very reincarnation of Muhammad.

Hitler could have saved himself a lot of trouble. Had he dusted off the Qur'an's War surahs, he could have dispensed with Mein Kampf. Replace Arabs with Aryans, Mecca with Munich, and prophet with fuhrer, and the rest remains the same. The "cruel God of Misery" is a more fitting title for Allah's tormented spirit, anyway. Fear, submission, and obedience take their rightful place in both men's quest to gratify their flesh. The Qur'an and Mein Kampf were inspired by the same spirit and for the same purpose. They are equally false, intolerant, racist, hateful, and violent. While the original disciples of both men conquered much of the world, one poligious doctrine lives on. It continues to inflame terrorists everywhere.

As the beneficiary of the largest transfer of wealth in history—a billion dollars a day—Islam is on the verge of acquiring the weapons of mass destruction it needs to fulfill its destiny. Hitler, Mein Kampf, and Nazism gave us a taste of what awaits us. Unless we come to see Muhammad, the Qur'an, and Islam in the same light and eliminate their influence, the world will erupt in a war more hellish than we can imagine.

17

GOOD MUSLIMS KILL

*"The Messenger in your rear is calling you
from your rear, urging you to fight."*

Alas, Islam was not all murder, plunder, and lust. There was war. *Tabari VII:105* **"In this year there was the expedition of the Messenger to Uhud. In year three of the Islamic Era (March, 625) the Quraysh were provoked against the Messenger because he had killed their nobles and chiefs at Badr."**

The Meccans had witnessed the prophet's demented behavior at the pit. **"Muhammad has bereaved us and killed our best men. So help us defend ourselves against him and perhaps we will obtain vengeance for those he has slain."** They wanted to prevent the onslaught from continuing. Yet today, Muslims raise shrill voices protesting that Uhud was proof that the Meccans were the aggressors and that Muhammad was forced into defending his flock. But their own scriptures say otherwise, putting Islam in a difficult position. If these Hadiths are accurate, their prophet was a warmongering terrorist and a ruthless pirate. But if these Traditions are not true, they have no prophet and thus no religion—for nothing else is known about him or of Islam's beginnings.

While we are on the subject, I'd like to bring your attention to the format I have been using to present the events that comprise the Islamic Era. I have woven the Hadiths of Ishaq, Tabari, and Bukhari together with the Qur'an because I want you to appreciate the similarities between the four sources. Although there are some subtle differences, all four paint the same portrait, and it's the only picture of Muhammad and his Companions that can be drawn. Nothing predates these books. Any statement about Muhammad or Islam that contradicts what you are reading is opinion—either wishful thinking or purposeful deception.

That said, occasionally some positive words are sprinkled in amidst the horror; although they are few and far apart. For example: *Tabari VII:106* **"Abd Allah al-Jumahi had been treated kindly by the Messenger on the day of Badr, being a poor man with daughters. He was among the captives, and said, 'Muhammad, I am a poor family man with needs of which you are aware; so treat me well.' The Prophet treated him kindly."** I suppose that it bears mentioning that he was a pagan named Slave-to-Allah.

Being poor, he was of no value to the "profit." And the only reason he was a prisoner in Medina was because he was kidnapped during a Muslim raid.

The following chat allegedly took place between a militant and his victim. *Tabari VII:106* "Abu Azzah, you are a poet, so aid us with your tongue. Join our expedition and I swear before Allah I will make you a rich man.'" That was all there is to Islam. The first Muslims were mercenaries.

According to the Sira: *Ishaq:372* "The opinion of Abd Allah bin Ubayy was the same as the Prophet. He should not go out to meet the Meccans camped near Uhud. Yet some [the soon-to-be dead] Muslims whom Allah ennobled with martyrdom on the day of Uhud and others who had missed Badr jumped at the chance to fight. Yet Abd Allah said, 'We have never gone out of Medina to meet an enemy but that they have inflicted severe losses on us; and no enemy has ever entered Medina but that we inflicted severe losses on them. Leave them alone.'" Abd Allah laid out the perils of invading a city. "If they enter Medina, the men will fight them face to face, and the women and boys will hurl stones at them from above. They will retreat, wishing they had not come."

But unfortunately, Muhammad had oversold his ability to command angelic help as well as the value of martyrdom. The newly minted Muslims roared: "O Messenger of Allah, do not deprive us of Paradise!" *Bukhari:V4B52N61* "My uncle Anas said, 'Allah's Apostle! We were absent from the first battle you fought against the pagans. If Allah gives us a chance to do battle, no doubt, He will see how bravely we fight.'"

Unable to give Muslims a reason to live, Muhammad gave them a reason to die. *Bukhari:V4B52N72* "The Prophet said, 'Nobody who enters Paradise likes to go back to the world even if he got everything on the earth, except a Mujahid [Islamic fighter] who wishes to return so that he may be martyred ten times because of the dignity he receives.' Our Prophet told us about the message of Allah: 'Whoever among us is killed will go to Paradise.' Umar asked the Prophet, 'Is it not true that our men who are killed will go to Paradise and those of the Pagan's will go to Hell?' The Prophet said, 'Yes.'" *Bukhari:V4B52N73* "Allah's Apostle said, 'Know that Paradise is under the shade of swords.'"

The prophet, like der fuhrer, seduced militants to kill for him. His Hadith prioritizes Jihad over all else. In fundamental Islam, fighting is the ultimate "good" deed: *Bukhari:V4B52N85* "Allah's Apostle dictated the Divine Verse: 'Not equal are those believers who sit at home and those who strive hard, fighting in the Cause of Allah with their wealth and lives.' [Qur'an 4:95] Zaid said, 'Maktum came to the Prophet while he was reciting that verse. "O Allah's Apostle! If I had power, I would take part in Jihad." He was a blind man. So Allah sent down revelation to His Apostle while his thigh was on mine. [That's not a pleasant picture.] It became so heavy I feared he would break my leg before Allah revealed: "Except those who are disabled by injury or are blind or lame."'" If "jihad" were a "spiritual struggle" as the Islamic apologists claim, why would Allah have to give the physically disabled an exemption?

Fact is, jihad is always linked to fighting in the Qur'an and Hadith. It means to fight holy war for Allah without retreating, sacrificing one's life and resources. Any other definition makes Allah and Muhammad liars.

Since Qur'an 4:94-5 confirms the Mein Kampf nature of Islam from Allah's perspective, let's nail the coffin shut before we move on. *004.094* **"Believers, when you go abroad to fight wars in the Cause of Allah, investigate carefully, and say not to any one who offers you peace: 'You are not a believer,' seeking and coveting the chance profits of this life (so that you may despoil them). With Allah are abundant profits, plentiful spoils and booty."** Lucifer is announcing by way of his prophet: "Muslims, when you leave Arabia to fight and rob those who don't worship me, don't accept a peace offering and leave a potential victim alone. Rather, conquer them, for therein lies the greatest potential for profit. And always remember, you are a mercenary and that I have seduced you."

004.095 **"Not equal are those believers who sit at home and receive no injurious hurt, and those who strive hard [Jihad], fighting in the Cause of Allah with their wealth and lives. Allah has granted a rank higher to those who strive hard [Jihad], fighting with their wealth and bodies to those who sit (at home). Unto each has Allah promised good, but He prefers those [Jihadists] who strive hard and fight above those [pacifists] who sit home. He has distinguished his fighters with a huge reward."** The Qur'an confirms that **"Allah's Cause," "Jihad," "striving hard,"** and **"fighting"** are synonymous. The reference to **"leaving home," "injurious hurt," "life,"** and **"bodies"** confirms that there is nothing "spiritual" about jihad or Allah's Cause. The promises of **"inequality," "a higher rank," "preference,"** and **"a huge reward"** for jihadists are nails in Islam's "peace-loving" coffin. The crescent moon is as tolerant as the swastika. The Qur'an is as warlike as *Mein Kampf*. Peace in Islam is as Hitler defined it: *"There will be peace when Aryans alone rule the world."*

The 96th verse begins by confirming Allah's preference for warriors. It ends in contradictory fashion. Some would call it camouflage. *004.096* **"Ranks and higher grades are specially bestowed by Him. He is Forgiving and Merciful."** The god who prefers fighters to lovers, warriors to pacifists, is "merciful." No wonder Muslims say the Qur'an cannot be translated; the words don't make any sense.

The next verse is an example. Souls are taken *before* judgment. Further, in Islam, flesh is roasted in hell and gratified in paradise so the separation conflicts with the central pillar of the doctrine. Nonetheless, here it is: *004.097* **"Verily, when angels take the souls of those who die wronging themselves (by staying home), they say: 'In what (plight or engagement) were you?' They reply: 'Weak on the earth.' They say: 'Was not the earth spacious enough for you to move?' Such men will find their abode in Hell, an evil resort!"** Allah's communication skills are so poor I almost miss Hitler. Who knows what this actually means? But it takes us to: *004.098* **"Except those who are feeble—men, women and children—who cannot devise a plan nor do they have the means, power or (a guide-post) to their way. These are those whom Allah is likely to forgive."** The moral is: only the feeble of mind and body don't have to fight.

Returning to Muhammad's Sunnah we learn: *Tabari VII:109/Ishaq:372* **"The Messenger called for his coat of armor and put it on. When they saw this they repented, 'What an evil deed we have done. We have given him advice when inspiration comes to him!'**

Muhammad replied, 'It is not fitting for a prophet to put on his coat of mail and take it off before fighting.' So the Prophet went out to Uhud at the head of a thousand of his Companions, having promised them victory." That didn't make him much of a prophet; the Muslims were routed.

Ishaq:372 ""When he went out, Abd Allah bin Ubayy [the man who had advised against leaving town] came back with 300 men, saying, 'We do not know why we should get ourselves killed here.' So he went back to Medina with the Hypocrites [peaceful Muslims] and doubters who followed him. Abd Allah bin Amr said, 'Allah curse you, enemies of Allah. Allah will let us manage without you.'" A "peaceful" Muslim is such a "bad" person, he is considered Allah's enemy.

Ishaq and Tabari reveal that a Jew had to be abused before the battle could be joined against the Arabs. The troops were hungry so Muhammad led his militants through the fields of a blind Jew named Mirba. *Tabari VII:112/Ishaq:372* "When he became aware of the presence of the Messenger and the Muslims he rose and threw dust in their faces, saying, 'Even if you are a prophet, I will not allow you into my garden!' I was told that he took a handful of dirt and said, 'If only I knew that I would not hit anyone else, Muhammad, I would throw it in your face.' The people rushed up to kill him, but the Prophet said, 'Do not do so, for this man is blind of sight and blind of heart.' But [then the heartless] Sa'd rushed in before the Messenger had forbidden this and hit him on the head with his bow and split the Jew's head open." Sa'd murdered a blind and defenseless man for trying to protect his land with a handful of dust. He did it "before the Messenger had forbidden" it so the prohibition was disingenuous.

With their usual flair for exaggeration intact, a three-hundred-year old oral Tradition claims: *Tabari VII:112* "The polytheists numbered three thousand and their cavalry numbered two hundred. Their womenfolk numbered fifteen. Among the polytheists there were seven hundred men wearing coats of mail, while among the Muslims there were only one hundred. The Muslims had no cavalry."

If the prophet looked, he would have seen a rude and disorderly band of militants milling about in a dusty date plantation. The bloodstained face of a dead Jew lay at his feet. Mount Uhud loomed nearby, barely three miles from Medina. At its foot was a wadi, its course marked by sand and scattered stones.

At dawn, with the Meccan merchants in sight, Muhammad and his turbaned marauders, swords at the ready, prostrated themselves to Allah. Across the way, the businessmen, showing a complete ignorance of military strategy, huddled in the lowlands. They left the heights open to the Muslim archers. If the Muslims stood their ground, victory was assured. Muhammad put on a second coat of mail and waited. Holding the superior position, the militants appeared ready to halt the merchants' advance.

Ishaq:373 "The Apostle, wearing two coats of mail, drew up his troops for battle, about 700 men. There were 50 archers. Muhammad said, 'Keep their cavalry away with your arrows.' Then he asked, 'Who will take my sword with its right and use it as it deserves to be used?' Abu Dujana asked, 'What is its right, Apostle?' 'That you should smite the enemy with it until it bends.'" It was so religious of him. "When Abu took the sword from the Apostle's hand he walked toward the fight reciting: 'I'm the man who took the sword when "Use it right" was the Prophet's word for the sake of Allah.' When Muhammad saw Abu strutting, he said, 'This is a gait which Allah hates except on an occasion like this.'"

Muslim:B20N4678 "Before the battle of Uhud a Muslim asked, 'Messenger, where shall I be if I am killed?' He replied: 'In Paradise.' The man fought until he was killed." And if you think that he is cavorting with virgins, you might believe this: *Muslim:B30N5713* "Sa'd reported. 'On the Day of Uhud, I saw two persons dressed in white clothes whom I had not seen before or after at the side of Allah's Messenger (may peace be upon him). They were [the angels] Gabriel and Michael.'" Another Hadith proclaims: *Bukhari:V4B52N63* "A man whose face was covered with an iron mask came to the Prophet and said, 'Shall I fight or embrace Islam first?' The Prophet said, 'Embrace Islam and then fight.' He became a Muslim and was martyred. The Prophet said, 'A little work, but a great reward."

Muhammad's kin brought their slaves to do their bidding. *Ishaq:374* "The black troops and slaves of the Meccans cried out and the Muslims replied, 'Allah destroy your sight, you impious rascals.'" The merchants brought their womenfolk, too. *Ishaq:375* "Abu Dujana said, 'I saw a person inciting the enemy, shouting violently. When I made for him, I lifted my sword and he shrieked, and lo, it was a woman. I respected the Prophet's sword too much to use it on a girl.'" *Ishaq:380* "We attacked them thrusting, slaying, chastising, and driving them before us with blows on every side. Had not women seized their war banner they would have been sold in the markets like chattel." As we have discovered, and will continue to witness, Islam was financed by the slave trade. Muslims fought to capture women and children so they could sell them into bondage.

The Islamic scriptures are in conflict as to what happened at Uhud. Some verses proclaim that Allah sent his demonic angels to fight as promised. Others say that Allah abandoned his militants so that he could "harvest martyrs." *Ishaq:379* "Then Allah sent down His help to the Muslims and fulfilled His promise. They slew the enemy with the sword until they cut them off from their camp and there was an obvious rout." Then: *Ishaq:380* "The Muslims were put to the fight and the Meccans slew many of them. It was a day of trial and testing in which Allah honored several with martyrdom."

Hamza, Muhammad's most brutal militant, shouted: *Ishaq:375* "'Come here you son of a female circumciser.' His mother was Umm Anmar, a female circumciser in Mecca. Hamza smote and killed him." Virtually every Islamic ritual had a pagan origin. Female circumcision was no exception. It is still practiced throughout the Islamic world and is designed to assure that men alone are pleasured by sex.

The militants began to act like the pirates they had become. They rushed to plunder the merchants, rummaging through their baggage. The archers, seeing this, could not resist the temptation. They abandoned the high ground and hurried to the spoil. With the militants' flank and rear exposed, the merchants galloped in. The charge was devastating; the battle was over in minutes. Greed, the sole motivation for Islam, proved fatal. *Bukhari:V4B52N276* "By Allah, we saw the Meccan women running, revealing their leg-bangles. So, we cried out,

'The booty! O Muslims, the booty! Our Companions have become victorious. What are we waiting for? By Allah! We will go to the pagans and collect our share of the war booty.'"

This next Hadith is told from the perspective of one of the African slaves who fought at Uhud. *Tabari VII:121/Ishaq:375* "I saw Hamzah cutting down men with his sword, sparing no one. He yelled out to us, 'Come here, you son of a cutter-off of clitorises.' He hit Siba so swiftly, his sword could not be seen striking his head. So I balanced my javelin until I was satisfied. Then I hurled it at Hamzah. It struck him in the lower part of the belly with such force it came out between his legs. He came toward me, but was overcome and fell. I waited until he was dead and recovered my javelin. I returned to the camp since there was nothing else I wanted." Unlike the Muslims, the Africans were civil.

With the Muslim ranks broken and his militants either money-grubbing or in full retreat, Muhammad tried to avert disaster and save his sorry soul. He cried: *Wackidi:107* "Don't run away! Come back! I am Allah's Apostle! Return!" Muhammad didn't bother calling upon Allah or his demonic angels. Apart from rain and wind, they were useless, and it was a little late to be saved by bad weather. Muhammad was learning that being a pirate is a bloody, rough business. On this day his unruly mercenaries were whipped by some pudgy salesmen.

The prophet's call was unheeded; the retreat went unchecked. Rocks and arrows flew around Islam's bad boy. A stone, we are told, wounded the stone worshiper in the under lip, chipping a tooth. Another dented his helmet. Presuming Muhammad was dead and that the terrorists were defeated, the Meccan merchants collected their belongings and went home. The scene was reminiscent of Desert Storm, although the weapons were not so high tech. *Ishaq:380* "The enemy got at the Apostle who was hit with a stone so that he fell on his side and one of his teeth was smashed, his face scored, and his lip injured." *Tabari VII:124* "Abd Manat came and threw a stone at Muhammad, breaking his nose and his lateral incisor, splitting his face open, and stunning him. His Companions dispersed and abandoned him, some of them going to Medina and some climbing up Uhud and standing there. The Messenger cried out to his men, 'To me. To me.'" Caught up in the moment, Muhammad confessed. "It's all about *me*."

Ever willing to lure his pirates to their doom with bribes of booty and never-ending sex, we find the pathetic prophet promising that which he could not deliver. Well over a million souls have succumbed to this temptation: *Muslim:B19N4413* "When the enemy got the upper hand at Uhud, the Messenger was left with only seven Ansar and two Emigrants. When the enemy advanced towards him and overwhelmed him, he said: 'Whoso turns them away will be my companion in Paradise.' An Ansar man came forward and fought until he was killed. The enemy advanced and overwhelmed them again so Muhammad repeated: 'Whoever turns them away will attain Paradise.' Another Ansar fought until he was slain. This state continued until all seven Ansari were killed, one after the other. The Prophet (peace be upon him) said to the Muslims: We have not done justice to them." That was true enough.

Ishaq reports: *Ishaq:380* "When the enemy hemmed him in, the Apostle said, 'Who will sell his life for me.' Five Ansar arose. All were killed. Abu Dujana made his body into a shield for the Apostle. Arrows were falling and sticking in his back as he leaned over him." Men sacrificing their lives for this con man is enough to make you sick.

Stress brings out the best in good people and the worst in others. Let's review this revolting episode from the historian's perspective. *Tabari VII:120* **"When the enemy overwhelmed the Holy Prophet he said to the Ansar, 'Who will sell his life for me?'"** *Muslim:B19N4420* **"The Prophet said: 'Great is the wrath of Allah upon a people who have done this to the Messenger.' At that time he was pointing to his front teeth. The Apostle said: 'Great is the wrath of Allah upon a person who has been killed by me in Allah's Cause.'"** *Ishaq:380* **"Muhammad cried out, 'How can a people prosper who have stained their Prophet's face with blood while he summoned them to their Lord?'"**

Next we discover: *Tabari VII:126/Ishaq:383* **"The Prophet went up the mountain. He had become stout and heavy with age. He was wearing two coats of mail. When he tried to climb up, he could not manage on his own. Talba Ubaydullah squatted beneath him and lifted him up until he settled comfortably on a rock."**

As soon as the salesmen cleared the field, Muhammad and his fellow Muslims surveyed the extent of their ignominious defeat. Seventy-four corpses were strewn upon the plain; four were Emigrants, seventy were Ansari. The Meccans lost fewer than twenty. (They probably died laughing.) The battle of the Bulge this was not. If it weren't for the propensity of Islam to corrupt men's minds, this would have been an insignificant skirmish, a meaningless tussle between misfits. *Bukhari:V4B52N70* **"Some people drank alcohol in the morning of the day of the battle of Uhud and were martyred on the same day."** As a result, there was dissention in the ranks. *Bukhari:V4B52N147* **"Allah's Apostle and the pagans faced each other and started fighting. When the Apostle returned to his camp somebody talked about Quzman, a Muslim who had killed many pagans. The Apostle said of him, 'Nobody did his job of fighting as well as that man. Indeed, he is amongst the people of the Hell Fire."** So why did Muhammad condemn his most valiant militant to hell?

Sore loser, perhaps: *Tabari VII:136/Ishaq:383* **"During Uhud, Quzman fought hard and killed seven to nine polytheists with his own hands, being brave, bold, and strong. But he got wounded so seriously, he had to be carried off by his comrades. They said, 'Rejoice, you fought valiantly.' He replied, 'For what have I fought?' When the pain of his wounds became too severe he decided to bring about his death more quickly."** *Bukhari:V4B52N147* **"He planted the blade of the sword in the ground directing its sharp end towards his chest. Then he leaned on the sword and killed himself. A Muslim in Muhammad's presence said, 'The man whom you described as one of the people of the Hell Fire got severely wounded, and hastening to die, he eased on his sword and killed himself.'"** *Tabari VII:136/Ishaq:384* **"Upon hearing this, Muhammad proclaimed, 'I testify that I am truly the Messenger of God, Allah's Apostle.'"** The moral of the story is: Don't die trusting a false prophet.

Then, in a single sentence, Muhammad defined the nature of Islam and the terror it inspires: *Bukhari:V4B52N147* **"Allah's Apostle said, 'A man may seem as if he were practicing the deeds of Paradise while in fact he is from the people of Hell.'"**

Remember Talha, the man who lifted the prophet's fat behind up on a rock? *Ishaq:383* **"That day I heard the Prophet saying, 'Talha earned paradise when he did what he did for the Apostle.'"** It's hard to imagine a more self-centered scumbag. The battle lost, Muhammad wanted his Companions to know that the dead had failed to serve his interests and thus they were unworthy of paradise.

Upon hearing this, two of Muhammad's militants got up and said, *Ishaq:383* **"Perhaps Allah will grant us martyrdom.' So they took their swords and sallied out until they mingled with the [retreating] army. One was killed by the Meccans, the other by his fellow Muslims who failed to recognize him. One of the young men's fathers confronted Muhammad and said, 'You have robbed my son of his life by your deception and brought great sorrow to me.'"** His tear-filled eyes saw more clearly than do ours today.

Yet others believed the deception and forfeited their lives for booty. *Ishaq:385* **"Amr Jamuh was a very lame man. He had four lion-like sons who were present at the Apostle's battles. At Uhud he came to the Prophet and told him that his sons wanted to keep him back and prevent his joining the army. 'Yet, by Allah, I hope to tread in the Heavenly Garden of Paradise despite my lameness. The Apostle said, 'Allah has excused you, and Jihad is not incumbent on you.' Then Muhammad turned to his sons and said, 'You need not prevent him. Perhaps Allah will favor him with martyrdom.' So the lame old man went into battle and was killed."** This Hadith, like the Qur'an, makes Jihad "incumbent" on all Muslims who are not lame. And it proclaims that martyrdom is rewarded. It is one of a thousand reasons Islam must be repudiated.

Bukhari:V4B52N276 **"Abu Sufyan [the Quraysh leader] shouted, 'Our victory today is a counterbalance to yours at Badr. Fighting is always undecided and is shared in turns by the belligerents. You will find some of your men mutilated. I did not urge my men to do so, yet I do not feel sorry for their deed.' After that he started reciting cheerfully, 'O Hubal [a high-ranking Meccan idol worshiped in the Ka'aba], be high!' On that the Prophet said to his companions, 'Why don't you answer him back?' They said, 'O Allah's Apostle, what shall we say?'"** They were bewildered. The militants hadn't gone out on a religious crusade. They were there for the booty. They didn't know how to respond. **"Muhammad said, 'Say, Allah is Higher and more Sublime.' Then Abu Sufyan said, 'We have Al-Uzza, and you have no Uzza.' The Prophet said to his companions, 'Why don't you answer him back?' They asked, 'O Allah's Apostle! What shall we say?' He said, 'Say Allah is our Helper and you have no helper.'"** This drama is being played out at the level of a grade-school tussle between pre-adolescent bullies. To think a billion people submit to this foolishness is mind boggling.

Beyond foolish, the previous admission is devastating to Islam. The first Muslims, Muhammad's disciples, were unaware of the most fundamental claim of their religion.

Tabari VII:126 **"Allah spoke of Abu Sufyan's approaching them and said, 'Therefore, He rewarded you with grief upon grief that you not sorrow for that which you missed or for that which befell you.' [3:153] The first grief was the victory and booty that eluded them. The second grief was the enemy's approaching them. They were not to grieve for the booty or** the men they had lost. Abu Sufyan distracted them from this." The words of a pagan bothered them more than the death of their comrades.

A couple of hundred years after the blood had dried at Uhud, some Islamic sage must have been ordered to make all of this sound a little more "religious." So he pored over the only real scriptures available to him and read what Yahshua, the Messiah, said while he was being nailed to a cross to save mankind. *Muslim:B19N4418* **"It has been narrated on the authority of Abdullah who said: 'It appeared to me as if I saw the Messenger relate the story of a Prophet who had been beaten by his people, wiping the blood from his face, saying. "My Lord, forgive my people, for they do not know [what they do]."'"**

The sage who chronicled the next Tradition recorded what Muhammad probably said: *Bukhari:V4B52N69* **"For thirty days Allah's Apostle invoked Allah to curse those who had killed his companions. He invoked evil upon the [Ansari] tribes who disobeyed Allah and His Apostle. There was revealed about those who were killed a Qur'anic Verse we used to recite, but it was cancelled later on. The Verse was: 'Inform our people that we have met our Lord. He is pleased with us and He has made us pleased.'"** The real Messiah and the wannabe messiah were opposites. On the cross Christ forgave those who were terrorizing him. On the field of battle Muhammad evoked a curse on those whom he was terrorizing.

Although the battle had been lost because greed overwhelmed military discipline, Muhammad, the grand pontiff of greed, failed to comprehend the obvious. Rather than admit that his "dogma" was flawed beyond redemption, he decided he needed more firepower, urging his militants to acquire a cavalry. *Bukhari:V4B52N104* **"The Prophet said, 'Good will remain in the foreheads of horses for Jihad till the Day of Resurrection, for they bring about either a reward in the Hereafter or booty in this world.' Allah's Apostle fixed two shares for the horse and one share for its rider from the war booty."** *Bukhari:V4B52N105* **"The Prophet said, 'If somebody keeps a horse in Allah's Cause motivated by his faith in Allah and his belief in His Promise, then he will be rewarded for what the horse has eaten or drunk and for its dung and urine.'"** I can only wonder what goes through the minds of Muslims as they read this garbage. Its bad enough that the wannabe prophet promised paradise to those who turned beasts of burden into an implements of war, to those who turned plowshares into swords, but to suggest that there was a heavenly dung and urine quotient is beyond the pale. I do not know if it's desperate, pathetic, or simply perverse. But clearly, it isn't true.

Some thinking person must have challenged Muhammad's sanity, so by way of explanation, this spilled from the lips of the most dimwitted prophet of all time: *Bukhari:V4B52N112* **"Allah's Apostle said, 'Horses are kept for one of three purposes. For some people they are a source of reward, for some they are a means of shelter, and for some they are a source of sins. The one for whom they are a source of reward is he who keeps a horse for Jihad in Allah's Cause. He ties it with a long tether in a meadow or in a garden with the result that whatever it eats from the area of the meadow or garden will** be counted as good deeds for his benefit, and if it should break its rope and jump over one or two hillocks then all its dung and its foot marks will be written as good deeds for him. And if it passes by a river and drinks water from it even though he had no intention of watering it, he will get the reward for its drinking. As for the man for whom horses are a source of sins, he is the one who keeps a horse for the sake of pretense, showing enmity for Muslims.' When Allah's Apostle was asked about donkeys, he replied, 'Nothing has been revealed to me about them except this unique, comprehensive Verse: "Then anyone who does a small ant's weight of good shall see it; And anyone who does a small ant's weight of evil, shall see it."'" [101:7]

In the passage, Muhammad defined "Allah's Cause" as "Jihad." Previously he defined Jihad as fighting or holy war. And while I recognize that many of history's pagans worshiped "war gods," no one takes them seriously today. Islam is the only surviving religotic in which the central *purpose* is to fight. It's so bad, a man who doesn't turn a productive asset (a beast of burden) into a destructive one (a cavalry mount) is called a sinner. Further, by establishing this Hadith, Muhammad brought Allah down to his level. He said that this inane answer was divinely inspired, something that would be lethal to Islam if Muslims were only given the opportunity to think.

One of the few Ansari who actually had a horse didn't measure up. *Bukhari:V4B52N137* "The Prophet said, 'Let the negro slave of Dinar perish. And if he is pierced with a thorn, let him not find anyone to take it out for him. Paradise is for him who holds the reins of his horse to strive in Allah's Cause with his hair unkempt and feet covered with dust. If he is appointed in the vanguard, he is perfectly satisfied with his post of guarding, and if he is appointed in the rearward, he accepts his post with satisfaction. If he [the black slave] asks for anything it shall not be granted, and if he needs intercession [to get into paradise], his intercession will be denied.'" Allah is "Forgiving, Kind."

During the skirmish, Islam's lone troubadour cried: *Tabari VII:120* "May Allah's anger be intense against those who have bloodied the face of His Prophet." And: "By Allah, I never thirsted to kill anyone as I thirst to kill a Meccan." This "prophet" was one sick puppy.

Tabari VII:127 "The Messenger said, 'Hamzah is being cleansed by the angels. He went into battle in a state of ritual impurity when he heard the call to arms. That is why the angels are cleansing him.'" Does that mean Allah loves or hates dirty fighters?

Abu Sufyan, the Meccan leader, explained why he and his men had traveled north. *Tabari VII:129* "If you had seen what they did at the pit of Badr you would have been terror struck for as long as you lived. Our mourning women have called us to grieve. I requited Badr with its like." The pagan Sufyan continues to be the Hadith's only sane voice. Umar replied: *Ishaq:386* "Our dead are in Paradise; your dead are in Hell."

Tabari VII:129/Ishaq:385 "Hind [a Meccan woman who had lost her father, husband, son, and brother to Muhammad's raiders at Badr] stopped to mutilate the Muslim dead, cutting off their ears and noses until she was able to make anklets and necklaces of them. Then she ripped open Hamzah's body for his liver and chewed it, but she was not able to swallow it and spat it out. Then she climbed a high rock and screamed rajaz poetry at the top of her voice, taunting us. 'We have paid you back for Badr. A war that follows a war is always violent. I could not bear the loss of Utba nor my brother, his uncle, or my first-born son. I have slaked my vengeance and fulfilled my vow.'"

"Umar [the future leader of the Islamic world] recited these verses back to her: 'The vile woman was insolent, and she was habitually base with disbelief. May Allah curse Hind, she with the large clitoris. ...Her backside and her genitals are covered with ulcers as a result of spending too much time in the saddle. Did you set out seeking to avenge our killing of your father and your son at Badr? And for your husband, who was wounded in the backside, lying in his blood, and your brother, all of them coated in the grime of the pit. What a foul deed you committed. Woe to you Hind, the shame of the age.'" Hind was called "foul" by the founder of a religion because she was upset with Muhammad's thugs for butchering her family. It's enough to make you want to scream, vomit, and cry, all at the same time.

Muhammad was more like Hitler than Christ. Islam was more like Nazism than Judaism. *Tabari VII:133/Ishaq:387* "When Muhammad saw Hamzah he said, 'If Allah gives me victory over the Quraysh at any time, I shall mutilate thirty of their men!' When the Muslims saw the rage of the Prophet they said, 'By Allah, if we are victorious over them, we shall mutilate them in a way which no Arab has ever mutilated anybody." And they did.

While hardly religious, this is a testament to the power of Islam. It is the reason the doctrine must be exposed—and then banished. The religotic is so corrosive, these men were unable to see their own hypocrisy. Hind's behavior, while despicable, was understandable. Islamic terrorists had victimized all of the men in her family. Maniacal militants had mutilated her father, brother, husband, and son in search of booty. Their leader had tossed their lifeless bodies into a pit and then gloated over their mangled and rotting corpses, condemning them to hell. She had every right to be out of her mind, tormented with anguish. The first Muslims, however, were without excuse.

The demonic spirit of Islam was equally perverse, offering this situational scripture in the 3rd surah: *Tabari VII:133/Ishaq:387* "Allah revealed concerning this threat made by His Messenger: 'If you have to retaliate and punish them, do so to the extent you have been injured." It's okay with Allah to mutilate so long as your terrorist raids have enraged your foe sufficiently for them to mutilate you.

Ishaq:388 "Some Muslims wanted to bury their dead in Medina. The Apostle forbade this and told them to bury them where they lay." Anything that didn't serve Muhammad's interests didn't get done. He didn't want seventy-four reminders in Medina of his failure. So Islam's lone prophet lied to his comrades. *Ishaq:388* "Abu Qasim [Muhammad] said, 'I testify concerning these that all wounded for Allah's sake will be raised with his wounds bleeding, the color of blood, the smell of musk. Look for the one who has remembered the most surahs and put him in front of his Companions in one mass grave.'"

Hunkered back in Medina and licking his wounds, *Ishaq:389* "The Apostle passed by one of the Ansar settlements and heard the sound of weeping and wailing over the dead. The Apostle's eyes filled with tears. He wept and said, 'There are no weeping women for Hamza.'" Bravo. It was a masterful performance. *Ishaq:389* "When the Apostle came home he handed his sword to his daughter Fatima, saying, 'Wash the blood from this, daughter, for by Allah it has served me well today.'"

Tabari VII:139/Ishaq:389 "The battle was fought on the Sabbath. On the following day, Sunday, 16 Shawwal (March 24, 625) the Messenger of Allah's crier called out to the people to go in pursuit of the enemy. His only purpose was to lower the morale of the Quraysh; by going in pursuit of them, he wanted to give the impression that his strength [not his god's or his faith's] was unimpaired, and that the Muslim casualties had not weakened their ability [...to be religious? ...to be faithful to their god? Alas, no...] to engage in fighting."

The beguiling maneuver was blended with a little deceit. Muhammad sent Ma'bad, a polytheist, out to fool the Meccans. He arrived as Abu Sufyan was speaking to his fellow merchants: *Ishaq:390* "'We have killed the best of Muhammad's companions. Shall we go back and exterminate the rest of them?' Ma'bad said, 'Muhammad has come out with his Companions to pursue you with an army whose like I have never seen. They are burning with anger against you. You'd better go home before his cavalry gallops upon you.'"

Abd Allah Ubayy, the Ansar leader who had retreated with a third of the Muslim force before the battle began, tried to make amends at the mosque. He knew Muhammad played rough. *Ishaq:391* "O people, Allah's Apostle is among you. Allah has honored and exalted you by him. So help him and strengthen him. Listen to his commands and obey them.' But the Muslims in attendance took hold of his garments and said, 'Sit down, you enemy of Allah. You are not worthy of that, having behaved as you did.'" Peace is not to be tolerated in Islam. It is an unforgivable sin.

Ishaq:391 "The day of Uhud was a day of trial, calamity, and heart-searching on which Allah tested the believers. He put the hypocrites [peaceful Muslims] on trial, those who professed faith with their tongue and hid unbelief in their hearts. And it was a day in which Allah honored with martyrdom those whom He willed." With the induction of martyrs behind us, year three of the Islamic Era came to an ignominious close.

Before we move on, I'd like to bring your attention to the small print. All of the Islamic scriptures cry out with a unified voice. The ugliness of Uhud has been brought to you by Tabari, Ishaq, Muslim, and Bukhari. And soon you will discover that the Qur'an's second longest surah was revealed expressly to address the Uhud disaster. What's more, the context provided by the Hadith is missing from the Qur'an, information that is required for one to understand Allah's word. The books of Tabari, Ishaq, Muslim, and Bukhari are like four fingers inside the glove of Islam, with the Qur'an being the sore thumb. Together they give the perverted doctrine shape, purpose, and power. And they cause the sword of Islam to be wielded against the world.

✡ ✟ ☾ ☪

According to the Hadith, the 3rd surah was the lone revelation handed down during the third year of the Islamic Era. At half the length of the 2nd surah, it is still too long and convoluted to review in its entirety here. It begins by listing some Arabic letters. The Noble Qur'an explains: *003.001* **"Alif-Lam-Mim. (These letters are one of the miracles of the Qur'an but only Allah knows their meaning.)"** How's that for desperate? If you can't perform a miracle and can't compose intelligent scripture, claim that the incomprehensiblity itself is a miracle.

Along that same line, Allah declares the impossible: *003.003* **"He has verily revealed to you this Book, in truth and confirmation of the Books revealed before, as indeed He had revealed the Taurat (Torah) and the Injeel (Gospel)."** Although we have covered this before, it bears repeating. The Dead Sea Scrolls and the Septuagint prove that the words of the Torah, Psalms, and Prophets did not change during the thousand years preceding Islam—or in the fourteen hundred years since. And twenty-five thousand New Testament fragments and scrolls dating to more than five hundred years before the earliest surviving Qur'an testify that the Gospels remain unaltered. Allah's claim that his Qur'an confirms books that differ in every way and on every page is ludicrous to the point of lunacy. Further, the magnitude of the supposed conspiracy to write Yahweh, Jews, Judaism, Israel, Jerusalem, the Temple, the Messiah, love, relationship, and peace into the Scriptures—and Allah, Arabs, Islam, Arabia, Mecca, the Ka'aba, Muhammad, hate, punishment, and war out—is beyond comprehension. The odds are beyond impossible. Islam is therefore based upon a false proclamation, a false god, and a false prophet.

Moving on, Allah confirms that he is still demented and dimwitted. *003.004* **"As a guidance to mankind, He sent down the criterion (to judge between right and wrong). Truly, for those who deny the proofs, signs, and lessons of Allah, the torture will be severe; Allah is powerful, the Lord of Retribution."** While there have been no signs or proofs, there has been a lesson. Islam has redefined right and wrong. Its tortured and vindictive spirit has spit upon the Ten Commandments.

The seventh verse says the unclear parts of the Qur'an are for the perverse. The verse warns us not interpret the Qur'an. We're not to look for hidden meanings because searching will bring discord. Then, contradicting the concept of a "revelation," Allah says that he alone knows the meaning. To add insult to injury, we're told that good Muslims believe it all, even the parts written for the perverse. Then to rub salt into the wound, the passage squelches honest inquiry by saying that anyone who doesn't grasp it all lacks understanding.

003.007 **"He it is Who has sent down to you the Book. In it are entirely clear verses, decisive, or fundamental (with established meaning); they are the foundation of the Book: others are unclear or allegorical. As for those who are perverse, they follow the part that is not entirely clear, trying (to cause) dissension by seeking to explain it and searching for hidden meanings. But no one knows its explanation or meaning except Allah. And those who are firmly grounded in knowledge say: 'We believe in the Book; the whole of it (clear and**

unclear) is from our Lord.' None will grasp the Message except men of understanding."
This is about as dumb as dumb ever gets.

003.010 "As for those who deny [Islam], neither their wealth nor their children will help
them in the least against Allah. They shall be faggots for the fire of Hell." This must be
one of the clear verses, as in clearly demonic! *003.011* "The punishment of Allah is
severe. So tell the unbelieving infidels: 'You will surely be vanquished, seized by Allah, and
driven to Hell. How bad a preparation.'" Fire and brimstone preachers of days long
past used to stand in their pulpits and speak of hell in order to draw people
to salvation. But that isn't what is happening here. Allah is not calling people
to deliverance; he is not warning them. He is announcing his condemnation—preparation H. This is as perverse as calling men the firewood of hell.
The creator of the universe cannot be this demented. Allah cannot be God.

In the next verse, the dark spirit of Islam confirms that the terrorist raids
leading to Badr were "in Allah's Cause," and that the militants' victory over
the merchants was a miraculous sign. *003.013* "There has already been for you a Sign
in the two armies that met (in combat at Badr): One was fighting in Allah's Cause, the other
resisting Allah; these saw with their own eyes twice their number. But Allah supports whom
He pleases. In this is a warning for such as have eyes to see." Badr occurred because
Muhammad was out on a terrorist raid trying to loot a caravan. By saying
that this behavior was in "Allah's Cause," Islam has officially become the "religion of pirates and terrorists."

Now, speaking of the covetous behavior that founded the religotic of submission, Allah says: *003.014* "Beautified for men is the love of the things they covet,
desiring women, hoards of gold and silver, attractive horses, cattle and well-tilled land.
These are the pleasures of this world's life. But Allah has a more excellent abode." Since
the only guaranteed entrance into the "excellent abode" is to die a martyr
murdering infidels, Allah is telling Muslims that fighting to the death for
Muhammad is better than "earning" the survivor's booty—beautiful women,
gold and silver, horses, cattle, and productive farmland. And make no mistake,
Allah isn't against Muslims stealing these things. In fact, he think it's "beautiful" men covet them. He just wants them to believe his stash is better.

Allah goes on to describe paradise. However, something has changed.
Now that Muhammad has four wives, two of whom are little girls, he no
longer brags about virgins. Then in six words, Allah summarizes the con that
became Islam: *003.019* "Lo! religion with Allah (is) Surrender."

Jumbled as ever, the passage demeans Christians and Jews next. "Nor did
the People of the Book differ except out of envy after knowledge had come to them. But if
any deny the proofs, signs and lessons of Allah, Allah is swift in reckoning." A second
translation reads: "Surely the religion with Allah is Islam, and those to whom the Book
had been given did not show opposition but after knowledge had come to them, out of
envy among themselves; and whoever disbelieves in the communications of Allah then
surely Allah is quick in reckoning." No matter how one goes about interpreting this

verse, it's nonsense. Jews and Christians don't envy each other—not then, not now, not ever. And it's for certain they never envied Satan's sadistic scriptures. Further, Christ was an observant Jewish rabbi. Pure Christianity embraces all things Jewish: festivals, scriptures, and God. So what I think Allah is trying to say is: Judaism was Islam until Christianity. Christianity was Islam until Islam. Then Islam caused Judeo-Christianity to differ, envying Islam.

In verse 20, Lucifer tells his prophet: "**If they argue with you, (Muhammad), say: 'I have surrendered to Allah (in Islam) and those who follow me.' And say to those who were given the Scripture (Jews and Christians) and to the illiterates (Arabs): 'Do you also submit? If they surrender, then they are rightly guided, and if they turn away, then it is your duty only to convey the message.'**" Predestination renders this verse as absurd as the rest of the surah. Why deliver a message if it makes no difference? Why have a religion if all men are predestined to either brothels or fires? And why have a book if the intended audience can't read?

Just in case Muhammad failed sweet talking his brethren into submission, he warned… *003.021* "**Verily, to those who deny the signs, verses, and proofs of Allah, and slay the prophets [like Muhammad], and kill the upholders of justice [Muslim militants], give the news of painful torments [a.k.a. terrorism].**" This ungodly chat goes on to say that the Christians and Jews "**who have received a part of Revelation**" will claim that "**the fires of hell will not touch us for more than a few days.**" Within this short passage there are two poison pills. If the Bible is part of the revelation why is the Qur'an opposed to its every doctrine? And why isn't a single verse from the New Testament included in the Qur'an? Second, what are the odds that lettered people would say "the fires of hell will only burn us for a few days?" There is no indication in the Bible that hell is temporary.

This is what Islam does to Muslims: *003.024* "**They have been deceived by the lies they have themselves fabricated; their religion has deceived them.**" Allah is trying to dress down Christians and Jews. But if "They" were replaced by "Muslims" this would be the Qur'an's most accurate verse. If Allah and his pal wanted to find a "fabricated deceitful religion," they wouldn't have to look very far.

In the 26th verse we learn, "**You [Allah, second person] exalt whom You please and debase and humiliate whom You will.**" That leads to another confirmation of Islam's intolerance. "**Those who believe should not take unbelievers as their friends…guard yourselves from them.**" And…"**Allah commands you to beware of Him.**"

Returning to the purpose of Islam: *003.032* "**Say: 'Obey Allah and His Messenger;' If they refuse, remember Allah [third person] does not like unbelieving infidels.**" This is the inverse of the Bible. Yahweh loves everyone, including unbelievers.

Then in the "he-is-too-dumb-to-be-god" category we find: *003.033* "**Allah chose Adam and Nuh (Noah) and the families of Ibrahim (Abraham) and Imran in preference to others.**" Adam couldn't have been chosen in preference to others as he was the only man. Further, Noah was saved and Abraham was blessed because they chose Yahweh, not the other way around. Sadly for Muslims, the fine line between a stupid god and no god has been crossed.

According to Allah, Imran was Mary's father, and that's a problem. The Bible says Mary's father was Heli in Luke 3:24. Imran isn't a Hebrew name, but Amram is. Numbers 26:59 identifies him as the father of Moses, Aaron, and Miriam. This misunderstanding may be why Allah, in surah 19:28, calls Mary "Miriam, the sister of Aaron." As such she would have been over 1,200 years old when Christ was born. And while that's bad, the verse begins with "remember," yet there was no prior "Imran" revelation. *003.035* "Remember, when the wife of Imran prayed: 'Lord, I offer what I carry in my womb in dedication to Your service, accept it, for You are the Hearer, the Knower.' And when she had given birth, she said: 'O my Lord I have delivered but a girl, a female child.' [Remember: girls are worthless in Islam apart from luring boys to their doom.] But Allah knew better what she had delivered: 'The male is not like the female, and I have named her Mariam (Mary).'"

Allah is very confused, demonstrating an embarrassing lack of knowledge for the scriptures he claims to have inspired. Yahweh sent Gabriel to talk to Zechariah about his wife Elizabeth having a baby who would preach with the power of the Holy Spirit, like Elijah of old. So as to try to unmuddle the mess, Allah has Zechariah adopting Mary, as well as fathering John the Baptist. *003.037* "Mariam was given into the care of Zacharyah. Whenever he came to see her in her chamber he found her provided with food, and he asked, 'Where has this come from Mary?' She said, 'From Allah who gives in abundance to whomsoever He will. Zacharyah prayed, 'Bestow on me offspring that is good [i.e., not a girl]. As he stood in the chamber the angels said, 'Allah sends you tidings of Yahya (John) who will confirm a thing from Allah (the creation of Isa (Jesus), the Word of Allah) and be a noble prophet, one who is upright and does good [a Muslim]." In trying to dig himself out, Allah fell deeper into his pit. Magical food for Yahshua's mother doesn't square with Muhammad's mother's misfortune, especially if Muhammad is to be believed over "Jesus." And John proclaimed that Yahshua was from Yahweh, not Allah.

And yet they were so close. The Arabic name for John identified the name of his God YAHya, as did ZacharYAH's. Even the Arabic word for Jew used throughout the Qur'an is YAHdodi. Biblical names acknowledge Yahweh: YAHshua (Joshua and Jesus), YAHayahu (Isaiah), YirmeYAHu (Jeremiah) YAHezqel (Ezekiel), NehemYAH (Nehemiah), MattihYAHu (Matthew), YAHaqob (Jacob and James). There wasn't an Allah in the batch.

As misguided as this twisted account is, it gets worse in a hurry. *003.042* "Behold! the angels said: 'Marlam! Allah has chosen you and purified you above the women of all nations and creation (including jinn)." That's also a problem for Islam. How can Mary be the best if Yahshua is a second-rate "prophet?" In Islam, Adam, Noah, Abraham, Moses, Qusayy, and Muhammad are more important than the Messiah. If Muhammad is *numero uno*, why wasn't his mom mentioned in the Qur'an?

The answer is simple. Amina, Muhammad's mother, abandoned her son at birth and was a source of rage, not praise. The abuse he suffered as a child gave rise to his religion. And for the "Religion of Submission" to be credible, Yahshua and Mary had to be converted into Muslims…**"Mary! submit with obedience to your Lord (Allah). Prostrate yourself, and bow down with those [Muslims] who bow down."** In 2 B.C. there were no Muslims with which Mary could have prostrated herself. Gabriel would never have referred to Yahweh using the pagan "Lord." Islam's Black Stone wouldn't come to be named "Allah" for another five hundred years. And why, pray tell, would the Islamic god visit Mary in Israel if Mecca and the Ka'aba were his sacred territory and house? Further, why is there no mention in all of the Qur'an and Hadith of the Messiah visiting Allah at his "House?" After all, the big Mo made the Night's Journey to the Jewish Temple. The answers are: there was no Ka'aba, no Mecca, no Allah, and there were no Muslims back when Yahshua was born. And that makes the primary premise of Islam—that it was the religion of Adam, Noah, Abraham, Moses, David, Solomon, and the Messiah—a bold-faced lie. Islam's premise is as rotten as its prophet, as false as its god.

Next we learn why this impossible—and thus untrue—scenario was revealed only to Muhammad… *003.044* **"This is part of the tidings of the things unseen, which you have no knowledge and We reveal unto you (O Messenger!) by inspiration. You were not with them when they cast lots with arrows, as to which of them should be charged with the care of Mariam. Nor were you with them when they disputed."** Casting arrows was an occult rite performed around the Ka'aba. Abu Muttalib did this very thing to spare the life of Abd-Allah—Muhammad's father—after consulting with sorcerers. Jews never did such a thing—ever. And while that makes Allah a liar, it's worse than that. Ascribing a demonic gambling game designed to elicit the oracle of manmade idols to Mary **"the pure, the chosen above all creation"** means that Allah is unable to distinguish sorcery from truth. This verse proves that Allah isn't God, no matter how badly he wants to be.

While I don't mean to kick a dead camel, Allah is insistent on dying a hundred ugly deaths. *003.045* **"Behold, the angels said: 'O Mariam! Allah gives you glad tidings of a Word from Him: his name will be the Messiah, Isa (Jesus), the son of Mariam, held in honor in this world and the Hereafter and of those nearest to Allah."** By saying that "Jesus" was the "Messiah," Allah fractured his stone. If Jesus was the Messiah, he is God and Allah isn't. Oops.

The verse is fatal to Islam, so let's try another translation. **"(And remember) when the angels said: Mary! Lo! Allah gives you glad tidings of a word from him, whose name is Christ Jesus, the Messiah, son of Mary, illustrious in the world and the hereafter."** The problem isn't the translation; it's the inspiration. The instant Allah admitted that Jesus was the Messiah, Islam was finished—at least for anyone who knows anything about "Allah's" divinely inspired Bible.

But it's a great trick if you can pull it off. So in the 4th surah Allah bares all: *004.171* **"O people of the Book (Christians), do not be fanatical in your faith, and say** nothing but the truth about Allah [Lucifer]. The Messiah who is Isa (Jesus), son of Mariam, was only a messenger of Allah, nothing more. He bestowed His Word on Mariam and His Spirit. So believe in Allah and say not Trinity for Allah is one Ilah (God)...far be it from His Glory to beget a son." The "Messiah" is Yahweh's "Anointed." There are over 500 prophecies proclaiming His arrival, all of which Yahshua fulfilled (or will fulfill in his second coming). The prophet Isaiah wrote these words about him in chapter 9 of his book: "For unto us a child will be born...and His name will be Wonderful Counselor, Mighty God, Eternal Father." In the 53rd chapter, Isaiah, speaking of the salvation the Messiah would bring to mankind from his cross, said: "He will be wounded for our transgressions.... We are like sheep, gone astray, so He will lay on Him the iniquity of us all.... The Righteous One shall bear the sins of many." If Allah was right, and "Jesus" is the Messiah, he is Mighty God. If he is God, the Allah/Lucifer combo aren't.

So that there is no misunderstanding here, you should know that the Messiah is central to the Bible, the fulcrum upon which the entire story pivots. His coming was proclaimed throughout the Scriptures. And there isn't the slightest possibility of revisionist history. The Biblical prophecies were written 400 to 1200 years before Yahweh entered our world as a man to show us what he was like, building a bridge from our polluted world to his perfect realm. The oldest Dead Sea Scroll fragments date to 250 B.C., a thousand years before the earliest surviving Qur'an. The Isaiah scroll is preserved in one piece, unaltered. It still proclaims the truth more than 2700 years after it was inspired and 2000 years after a scribe copied Isaiah's predictions onto the scroll that was discovered in Qumran.

The combination of that scroll and these verses render an undeniable verdict: Islam is a complete fraud. It provides irrefutable proof that Allah was no more divine than an average garden rock. Lucifer, the wannabe god, and Muhammad, the wannabe prophet, were a pair of cons—just common crooks. Ill-mannered and moronic, they tried to play in Yahweh's league. Moreover, they tried to steal Yahweh's league—our souls. It's little wonder Allah says, "Booty is lawful and good," that he admits to being a deceptive schemer, or that he is fixated on hell.

Continuing to speak of Yahshua, the Qur'an proclaims: 003.046 **"And he shall speak to the people when in the cradle and when of old age, and shall be one of the good ones."** By claiming that he spoke while in swaddling clothes, Allah is conferring supernatural status on Christ—a status Muhammad did not enjoy. As for speaking in old age, that's impossible. There are ossuaries from mid first-century tombs with crosses carved into them and the words "Yahshua Saves." Since the Messiah was born around 2 B.C., and the sarcophaguses memorializing his crucifixion are dated to as early as 50 A.D., he couldn't have been old. Further, the Gospels detail his life in the context of history and they say that he was in his mid-thirties when he entered Jerusalem, died for our sins, and was resurrected.

Muhammad continued to impugn his own credibility with the following Hadith. He forgot that he had told Muslims that the Islamicized Abraham spoke in the cradle, too. *Bukhari:V4B55N645* **"The Prophet said, 'None spoke in cradle but three: The first was Jesus, the second was an Israeli called Juraij. While he was offering his prayers, his mother called him. He said, "Shall I answer her or keep on praying?" He went on praying and did not answer her. His mother said, "O Allah! Do not let him die till he sees the faces of prostitutes."** The story goes downhill from there, but you get the picture. And speaking of pictures, in the very next Hadith, the man who claimed to know more about Yahshua than Christ's Disciples, said: *Bukhari:V4B55N646* **"The Prophet shared, 'I met Jesus.' The Prophet described him saying, 'He was one of moderate height and was red-faced as if he had just come out of a bathroom.'"**

003.047 **"Mary said: 'O my Lord! How shall I have a son when no man has touched me?' He said: 'Even so: Allah creates what He wills: When He has decreed a plan, He but says to it, 'Be,' and it is!"** If Yahshua was virgin born, if he was created as a result of a Godly order, then he is unique among all creation. While it's true, it makes Islam false. According to the Qur'an, Allah made Adam and then from Adam came all men including Muhammad. But not "Jesus." So how can Christ be born of a virgin and not be divine? Ask yourself this: if Muhammad was conceived the old-fashioned way, and "Jesus" was formed by a direct order from God, whom should we trust to tell us the way to God?

Islam's prophet covers this same material in his Hadith. The Noble Qur'an refers to: *Bukhari:V4B55N657* **"Allah's Messenger said, 'Isa (Jesus), the son of Mariam, will shortly descend amongst you Muslims and will judge mankind by the law of the Qur'an. He will break the cross and kill the swine [Jews] and there will be no Jizyah tax taken from non-Muslims. Money will be so abundant no one will accept it. So you may recite this Holy Verse: "Isa (Jesus) was just a human being before his death. On the Day of Resurrection he (Jesus) will be a witness against the Christians."'"** I wonder if the Pope read this before he kissed the Qur'an and praised Islam?

On a roll, the false prophet proclaimed: *Bukhari:V4B55N658* **"Allah's Apostle said 'How will you be when the son of Mary (i.e. Jesus) descends amongst you and he will judge people by the Law of the Qur'an and not by the law of Gospel.'"** First, there are no laws in the Gospels. Christ's sacrifice on the cross provided a reprieve from the Old Covenant laws. Second, if the Qur'an existed before "Jesus" was born, and if the Gospels are of no value, why did Allah bother revealing them?

Before we leave this section of Bukhari, I'd like to reiterate Muhammad's greatest lie: *Bukhari:V4B55N651-2* **"I heard Allah's Apostle saying, 'I am the nearest of all the people to Jesus. There has been no prophet between me and Jesus. All the prophets are paternal brothers; their mothers are different, but their religion is one.'"** No, no, no, and especially no. But it's interesting: Muhammad is either claiming that God begot many sons, in total conflict with the Qur'an, or that he is a Jew.

Returning to the Qur'an: *003.048* **"And Allah will teach him the Scripture Book and**

Wisdom, the Torah and the Gospel, and appoint him a messenger to the Children of Israel, with this message: 'Lo! I come unto you with a Sign from your Lord. Lo! I fashion for you out of clay the likeness of a bird, and I breathe into it and it is a bird, by Allah's leave. I heal him who was born blind, and the leper, and I raise the dead, by Allah's leave." Since the Gospels record the words and deeds of Christ—past tense—saying that Allah taught him his history and life makes absolutely no sense. And if the Gospels were so important, why aren't any of its teachings found in the Qur'an?

Further, if Yahshua was the Messiah, he "authored" the Torah. Christ came to save all mankind, not just the Jews. The story of the clay bird comes from an apocryphal work attributed to Thomas. Not only didn't it occur, think for a moment about the absurdity of singling out something that trivial from a laundry list that includes: returning sight to men born blind, curing leprosy, and bringing the dead back to life. What's more, this is one of those things that is so right, it makes Islam wrong. Yes, Allah's right—Yahshua did heal the blind, the lepers, and he brought the dead back to life. So how did he do that if he wasn't God? And equally important, since Muhammad didn't do a single miracle, why would anyone believe him over the Messiah?

As if reading a different Arabic text, the Ali translation says: *003.048* **"He will teach him the Law and the Judgment, the Torah and the Gospel, and he will be Apostle to the children of Israel, (saying) 'I have come to you with a prodigy from your Lord that I will fashion the state of destiny out of the mire for you and breathe (a new spirit) into it, and (you) will rise by the will of Allah.'"** Again, Allah is confused. The Torah is the Law (actually the instructions). There is no book of "Judgment" in Judaism. In Christianity, the Good News of the Gospel is that judgment has been eliminated. Since the central message of the Gospels is not laws and judgment, but a reprieve from them, why would Allah bother to teach Jesus such things? And why would Allah say that Jesus was going to fashion a state of destiny out of the mire for Israel, and breathe new life into it, when in fact, as predicted in the Bible, Israel was destroyed shortly after Yahshua was crucified, and the Jews were dispersed for nearly 2,000 years? I recognize that Mecca is a long way from civilization, but Allah ought to be smarter than this. Yahshua correctly predicted the future; Allah couldn't even get the past right.

Allah, speaking as if he were Yahshua, continues to flail blindly. *003.050* **"(I have come to you) to attest the Torah which was before me. And to make lawful to you part of what was forbidden; I have come to you with a Sign from your Lord."** That's interesting: Muhammad said countless times that Allah had brought signs during his life, yet there were none. So why is it then that Yahshua was able to perform them? **"So fear Allah, and obey me. Lo! Allah is my Lord and your Lord, so worship Him. That is a straight path."** Yahshua came to fulfill the Scriptures, not eradicate them. Said another way, he made nothing that was "forbidden" lawful. He established the mechanism of forgiveness so we might be saved from judgment. Further, he knows who he is. The Messiah's name is Yahshua, which means "Yahweh

Saves." He commanded us to love Yahweh, not fear Allah. And he said, "Follow me." Muhammad's ignorance is appalling.

But Islam wouldn't be Islam if it didn't expose itself. *Bukhari:V4B56N814* **"There was a Christian who embraced Islam and he used to write the revelations for the Prophet. Later on he returned to Christianity again he used to say: 'Muhammad knows nothing but what I have written for him.'"** This Hadith impugns Islam coming and going. A literate man **"who used to write the revelations *for* the Prophet"** rejected Islam. A man Muhammad trusted enough to **"write the revelations for"** him said that **"Muhammad knows nothing but what I have written for him."** And that's the bottom line. The Qur'an is little more than a racist and violent rant sandwiched between a pathetic job of plagiarism. Islam's prophet knew so little about the Gospels, and Christ in particular, everything he professed was wrong.

003.052 **"But when Jesus became conscious of their disbelief, he cried: 'Who will be my helpers in the Allah's Cause? The disciples said: We will be Allah's helpers. We believe in Allah, and do you bear witness that we are Muslims."** The very idea of an ignorant and perverted terrorist thug and his demonic partner proclaiming in the sand dunes of Arabia that the Messiah believed in a pagan moon rock and called men to be Muslims is as preposterous as it is factually and historically impossible. So why did these buffoons so thoroughly trash their own credibility? Why didn't the Muhammad-Lucifer team simply ignore Christ in their Qur'an rather than falsely converting the Messiah to Islam? Sure, for the wannabe Messiah it was one-upmanship, but what was Lucifer's excuse? The answer is shocking. By deceiving mankind, by corrupting the Messiah's message, demoting him by artificially removing his divinity, sacrifice, and resurrection, Lucifer removed the only means of salvation. He damned billions. In Islam, Jihad saves but Jesus doesn't. Never forget, there is nothing Lucifer covets more than deceit, death, and damnation.

Speaking of Christ's disciples, the Qur'an reports: *003.054* **"And they (the disciples from the previous verse) schemed, and Allah schemed and plotted (against them): and Allah is the best of schemers."** While that's true, a good schemer does not a good god make. I appreciate the confession, though. It makes the job of exposing Islam easier. Another translation reads: *003:054* **"'Lord, we believe in Your revelations [the Torah and Gospels] and follow this Apostle [Jesus]. Enroll us among the witnesses.' But the Christians contrived a plot and Allah did the same; but Allah's plot was the best."** That's the premise of this book. Islam is a plot.

A third translation says that "they" refers to "disbelievers," not the disciples and they plotted to kill Jesus. **"And they (disbelievers) plotted (to kill Isa [Jesus]) and Allah plotted too."** In this case, Allah's plot is the denial of Christ's crucifixion.

In the next verse Lucifer divulged the nature of his scheme. *003:055* **"Allah said, 'Jesus, I will take you and raise you to Myself and rid you of the infidels (who have forged the lie that you are My son).... Those who are infidels will surely receive severe torment both in this world and the next; and none will they have as a savior for them."** As you recall, Allah defines "infidels" in surah 5:72: **"They are surely infidels who say; 'God is the Christ, the Messiah, the son of Mary."**

Mecca, I think we have a problem. "Christ" is the Greek word for the Hebrew "Messiah." So those who *agree* with Allah and say that Jesus is the Messiah, the Christ, are infidels, and they are going to receive a severe punishment in this world and the next. Those who trust Jesus to be their savior—the good news for which the Gospels are named—will find no savior, according to Allah. This is some plot.

Said another way: If you say that Jesus is the Christ, the Messiah, you are acknowledging his divinity. But if you say that God (divinity) is the Christ, you are an unbelieving infidel. It's little wonder Muhammad claimed that anyone who questioned the Qur'an would reject Islam. JC=M=G. Yet G does not = JC, even though according to Allah, JC=M. Muslims must practice a new form of logic.

After defining Jesus as the virgin born, miracle working, divinely inspired, and resurrected Messiah, the Qur'an claims Christ was just kidding about dying on the cross as our savior and calling himself God. Yet it professes to confirm the Torah and Gospels—books that predict and proclaim the truth it denies. Methinks this invites comparison, and even Allah seems to agree. *004:082* **"Do they not ponder over the Qur'an? Had it been the word of any other but Allah they would surely have found a good deal of variation in it."** Continuing, he says: **"...those who check and scrutinize will know it."** This sounds like an invitation, even a dare, to do exactly as we are doing. And what we have found by **"scrutinizing it"** is **"a good deal of variation."**

If Muhammad had ignored the Bible, Adam, Satan, Noah, Abraham, Lot, Moses, and especially Christ, I would have judged Islam independently, based solely upon its own merits. But he wasn't that smart, and his dark spirit was a liability, having his own agenda.

In case you were wondering, the scheme or plot the disciples concocted according to Allah was the Gospel account of Christ—the one in which Yahshua claimed to be God in the flesh. The one in which the Messiah taught us what he's like so that we might know Yahweh and form an eternal relationship with our creator. The one in which he allowed the Romans to crucify him for proclaiming that he was divine. The one in which he rose from the dead so that his sacrifice would enable us to live forever in his presence. It was the plot of the greatest story ever told.

Muhammad's dark spirit acknowledged the single most important event in history—the resurrection of Yahshua. But then, knowing that his religion of submission didn't mesh with Yahshua's Gospel of freedom, Lucifer called the God's plan of salvation blasphemy. He said the disciples' account recorded in the Gospels was false—a reason for dispute—even though he claimed he inspired them. *003:055* **"Behold! Allah said: 'O Jesus! I will take you and raise you to**

Myself and clear you (of the falsehoods) of those who blaspheme; I will make those who follow you superior to those who reject faith, to the Day of Resurrection: Then shall you all return unto me, and I will judge between you on the matters wherein you dispute."

If Yahshua was raised unto God, if he cheated death by way of divine order, he was the Messiah—and thus he was the creator of the universe. Therefore, Muhammad must be condemned, the Qur'an burned, and Islam repudiated. Nothing bothers Yahweh more than false prophets, false doctrines, and false gods. So let's review another translation to make certain we have this right. "(Remember) when Allah said: 'Jesus! Lo! I am gathering you and causing you to ascend unto Me. I am cleansing you of those who disbelieve.'"

A third reads: "When Allah said: 'Jesus, I am going to terminate the period of your stay (on earth) and cause you to ascend unto Me and purify you of those who disbelieve.... I will decide between you concerning that which you differed.'" While meaningless in the context of the greater whole, if Christ's life was cut short, he couldn't have talked while he was old, as an earlier verse alleged. But the overall message is clear: according to the Qur'an, Christ was an ordinary man and a Muslim to boot. His Gospel message of salvation wasn't true, even though Allah revealed it. He didn't die on a cross, and yet he was resurrected. And most importantly, those who believe he is God have no savior and will roast in hell.

Speaking of Christians, Allah proclaims: *003.056* "As for those disbelieving infidels, I will punish them with a terrible agony in this world and the next. They have no one to help or save them." It's Satan's ultimate fantasy.

Continuing on, we are told that this lunacy is a rehearsal directly from god: *003.058* "This is what We rehearse to you of the Signs and Message, a wise reminder. The similitude (likeness) of Jesus before Allah is as that of Adam; He created him from dust, then said to him: 'Be.' And he was." Allah was digging himself in deeper. Now he claims that "Jesus" was created miraculously like Adam. While that's not exactly true, if it were, it would render Muhammad meaningless.

Despite all evidence to the contrary: *003.060* "The Truth (comes) from Allah alone." That would mean that all scientific discoveries are erroneous. Math is without merit and courts are folly. "So be not of those who doubt, waver or dispute. If any one disputes in this matter with you, now after knowledge has come to you, say: 'Come! Let us gather together our sons and women among ourselves. Then let us earnestly pray, and invoke the curse of Allah on those who lie!'" So if someone tells a Muslim that Allah's book proves he's a phony, they're told to gather their sons and women and leave. They are not to look into the merits of the allegation. They aren't to even try and refute the charge. There is to be no discussion, no investigation, no evangelism, no thinking. None of that is in Satan's interest. Lucifer wants Muslims to pray that he will invoke a curse on those who expose him.

By the way, the Noble Qur'an says *003.061* "If anyone disputes with you about Jesus being divine, flee them and pray that Allah will curse them." (Not save them.)

Rather than provide any proof that his view isn't a hoax, Allah simply protests: "The Qur'an is true because I said so." *003.062* **"This is the true account, the true narrative, the true explanation: There is no ilah except Allah; and Allah—He is the Mighty, the Wise. And if they turn away, then lo! Allah is aware of the corrupters, the mischief-makers. Say: 'O People of the Book, come to common terms as an agreement between us and you: That we all shall worship none but Allah; that we associate no partners with him; and that none of us shall take others for lords beside Allah.' If then they turn back, say you: 'Bear witness that we (at least) are Muslims surrendered.'"** Such a deal. Everybody needs to come together and surrender to this demented, delusional, and dimwitted doctrine. What a wonderful world it would be. Or would it? Think about where terrorists are bred. Think about where the most impoverished people on earth live—those with the least freedoms. That is the world that accepted this invitation (or more correctly—the one that had it thrust upon them). Just like Hitler, Allah promises that there will be peace just as soon as he controls every soul. And even then, he's lying.

There was a phrase in the last verse I feel compelled to bring to your attention. If you **"turn away"** from Islam you are accused of being a **"mischief-maker."** In Allah's farewell address, this is what he had to done to them: *005.033* **"The recompense for those who fight against Allah and His Messenger and are mischief-makers in the land is only that they shall be killed or crucified or their hands and their feet be cut off from opposite sides, or be exiled from the land. That is their disgrace in this world, and a great torment is theirs in Hell."** It's little wonder Islamic terrorists are so brutal.

Next, the spirit who knows just enough about the Bible to make a fool of himself says to the people who know it by heart: *003.065* **"You People of the Book! Why dispute you about Abraham, when the Law and the Gospel were not revealed till after him? Have you no understanding? Ah! You are those who fell to disputing (even) in matters of which you had some knowledge! But why dispute in matters of which you have no knowledge? It is Allah Who knows, and you who know not!"** According to Allah, Abraham was supposed to have scrolls. So were Adam, Noah and others. So why is Allah only aware of the revelations that started with Moses?

003.067 **"Abraham was not a Jew nor yet a Christian; but he was a true Muslim, surrendered to Allah (which is Islam), and he joined not gods with Allah."** The line: "Nor yet a Christian" means that according to Muhammad's Allah, Abraham was a Muslim who became a Christian. I don't think so.

003.069 **"It is the wish of the followers of the People of the Book to lead you astray."** That's true if the "Book" is the "Qur'an" and the "people" are "Muslims." **"But they make none to go astray except themselves, but they perceive not. You People of the Book! Why reject you the signs, proofs, and verses of Allah, of which you are witnesses?"** This is also true. The witnesses to the "signs of Allah"—terrorism and piracy—rejected Islam. The Qur'an is full of their protestations.

"You People of the Book! Why do you clothe Truth with falsehood, and conceal the Truth?" The anti-Jew version of the never-ending argument is as lame as the anti-Meccan rant. If everyone Muhammad couldn't bribe with booty and babes was calling him, his Qur'an, and his religion a lie, maybe it was.

Team Islam, still miffed that they had to buy Bible stories from the Jews in order to sound prophetic, gave the "People of the Book" another shot. *003.077* **"As for those who sell for a small price the covenant and faith they owe to Allah and their own plighted word for a small price, they shall have no portion in the Hereafter. Nor will Allah speak to them or look at them on the Day of Judgment, nor will He cleanse them: They shall have a grievous torment, a painful doom."**

Then Allah says that the Jews sold Muhammad damaged goods. **"There is among them a section who distort the Book with their tongues. (As they read) you would think it is from the Book, but it is not from the Book; and they say, 'That is from God,' but it is not from Allah: It is they who tell a lie against Allah, and (well) they know it!"**

This is the boldest confession yet. The Qur'an is confirming that Jews sold Bible stories to Muhammad for some paltry price. For doing so, they're going to hell. Then we learn that they distorted the Scriptures as they *read* them— causing the "messenger" to *believe* that they were reading it accurately. In other words, the actual Scriptures weren't corrupted. The only thing that was perverted was the "version" the Jews *recited* to the wannabe-prophet. What you'll discover in the "Source Material" appendix is that many of Muhammad's twisted variants were pilfered verbatim from the Talmud—Jewish *oral* traditions and folklore. They became the "revelations" that formed the Qur'an. Further, the Jews were honest with Islam's prophet. They told him the Bible wasn't from Allah. Able to read it, they knew that Yahweh's name was revealed as the source 7,000 times. Allah's name was never mentioned.

This is odd enough to expose but too weird to analyze. *003.083* **"Do they seek for other than the Religion of Allah while all creatures in the heavens and on earth have, willing or unwilling, submitted, bowing to His Will (accepting Islam)?"**

There is something about megalomaniacs. It's as if they believe that a big lie told often becomes true. *003.084* **"Say (O Muhammad): 'We believe in Allah and that which is revealed to us and that which was revealed unto Abraham and Ishmael and Isaac and Jacob and the tribes [of Israel], and in (the Books) given to Moses, Jesus, and the prophets, from their Lord. We make no distinction between any of them, and unto Him we have surrendered, bowing our will (in Islam).'"** Then after proclaiming that Muslims are unable to distinguish between truth and a sloppy counterfeit, we're told: *003.085* **"If anyone desires a religion other than Islam (Surrender), never will it be accepted of him; and in the Hereafter He will be in the ranks of those who are losers."** *003.087* **"Of such the reward is that on them (rests) the curse of Allah, of His angels, and of all men, all together. In that will they dwell; nor will their penalty of doom be lightened, nor respite be (their lot)."** That pretty much blows the tolerance myth to smithereens.

Then proving that he didn't even understand his own religion, the illiterate prophet proclaimed: *003.089* **"Except for those that repent after that, and make amends; for verily Allah is Forgiving, Merciful."** Since men are predestined to their fate, repentance is folly.

Speaking of folly, the Qur'an orders Muslims to the Ka'aba, claiming that Abraham stood there. *003.097* "**Wherein are plain memorials; the place where Abraham stood up to pray; and whosoever enters it is safe. And pilgrimage to the House is a duty unto Allah for mankind, for him who can find a way thither. As for him who denies [Islamic] faith, Allah is self-sufficient, standing not in need, independent of any of His creatures.**" If Allah is independent of us, then why did he create mankind? Perhaps it was for the entertainment value—the enjoyment he would get from personally torturing 99.9 percent of us in his hell. And why, if Allah has no needs, does he beg for money and seduce Muslim militants to fight, rob, and terrorize for him?

If nothing else, Allah seems to need us to fear him: *003.102* "**You who believe! Fear Allah as He should be feared, and die not except in a state of Islam [submission].**"

Muhammad was the world's most vulgar hypocrite. The Qur'an orders Muslims not to be "intimate" with non-Muslims, and yet the perverted prophet took Jewish, Christian, and pagan concubines, sex slaves, and wives into his harem. So is Islam do as I do, or do as I say? Are Muslims to emulate the prophet's example, or Sunnah, as detailed in the Hadith or follow Allah's commands as presented by Muhammad in his Qur'an recitals? Or better question yet: if this stuff was such good advice, why didn't Muhammad follow it? *003.118* "**O you who believe! Take not into your intimacy those outside your religion (pagans, Jews, and Christians). They will not fail to corrupt you. They only desire your ruin. Rank hatred has already appeared from their mouths. What their hearts conceal is far worse.**" It's hard to imagine a more intolerant decree. "**When they are alone, they bite off the very tips of their fingers at you in their rage. Say unto them: 'Perish in your rage.'**" The verse makes *Mein Kampf* seem genteel by comparison.

Two-thirds of the way through the second longest surah, Muhammad's and Allah's hatred for Christians and Jews finally subsides long enough for the Islamic duo to attack their latest prey: peace-loving Muslims. *003.121* "**Remember that morning [of Uhud]? You left your home to post the faithful at their stations for battle at the encampments for war. Remember two of your parties were determined to show cowardice and fell away. Allah had helped you at Badr, when you were a contemptible little force.**" A contemptible *farce* would be more accurate.

Unable to count—or worse, unable to remember—the fighting angels have been increased by two thousand. As such, it took forty of them to kill each merchant. *003.124* "**Remember you (Muhammad) said to the faithful: 'Is it not enough for you that Allah should help you with three thousand angels (specially) sent down? Yea, if you remain firm, and act aright, even if the enemy should rush here on you in hot haste, your Lord would help you with five thousand havoc-making angels for a terrific onslaught.**" Another Islamic first: havoc-making angels ready for terrific onslaughts. Allah's angels and Lucifer's demons have a lot in common.

Ibn Ishaq, Muhammad's first biographer, felt that it was important to comment on this verse. *Ishaq:392* "**Allah helped you at Badr when you were contemptible, so fear Allah. Fear Me, for that is gratitude for My kindness. Is it not enough that your Lord** reinforced you with three thousand angels? Nay, if you are steadfast against My enemies, and obey My commands, fearing Me, I will send five thousand angels clearly marked. Allah did this as good news for you that your hearts might be at rest. The armies of My angels are good for you because I know your weakness. Victory comes only from Me because of My sovereignty and power for the reason that power and authority belong to Me, not to any one of my creatures." If Lucifer wants to convince us that he is God, he's got to be less transparent than this.

Assisting terrorists is hardly hopeful: 003.126 "Allah made it but a message of hope, and an assurance to you, a message of good cheer, that your hearts might be at rest. Victory comes only from Allah that He might cut off a fringe of the unbelievers, exposing them to infamy. They should then be turned back overwhelmed so that they retire frustrated."

The reason Allah was stingy with his killer angels at Uhud was that Muslims didn't... 003.131 "Fear the Fire, which is prepared for those who reject Faith: and obey Allah and the Messenger." So Allah decided to harvest some martyrs. 003.140 "If you have received a blow (at Uhud) and have been wounded, be sure a similar wound has hurt others. Such days (of varying fortunes) We give to men and men by turns: that Allah may know those who believe, and that He may take to Himself from your ranks Martyrs." While harvesting martyrs is a shoddy reason for fighting, it isn't as lame as god saying that battles are needed so that he can figure out who believes.

I find it interesting that Ishaq's rendering of the Qur'an is so much more vivid, even incriminating, than the modern translations. And considering that he was the foremost authority on Muhammad, and wrote a thousand years before the first English translation, his interpretations are worthy of our consideration. Ishaq:394 "Allah said, 'I let them get the better of you to test you. So fear Me and obey Me. If you had believed in what My Prophet brought from Me you would not have received a shock from the Meccan army. But We cause days like this so that Allah may know those who believe and may choose martyrs from among you. Allah must distinguish between believers and hypocrites so that He can honor the faithful with martyrdom.'" So, let me get this straight: Allah kills the good, loyal Muslims as his way of bestowing honor on them? Islam continues to be a dogma to die for.

The Qur'an is as unambiguous: good Muslims kill. Ishaq:394 "Did you think that you would enter Paradise and receive My reward before I tested you so that I might know who is loyal? You used to wish for martyrdom [and entry into my brothel] before you met the enemy. You wished for death before you met it. Now that you have seen with your own eyes the death of swords...will you go back on your religion, Allah's Book, and His Prophet as disbelievers, abandoning the fight with your enemy? He who turns back [from fighting] in his religion will not harm Allah. He will not diminish His glory, kingdom, sovereignty and power.'" The greatest sin a Muslim can commit is to refrain from fighting.

003.141 "This is so that Allah may test the faithful and destroy the unbelieving infidels." Another translation proclaims: "Allah's object is to purge those that are true in Faith and blight the disbelievers." A good Muslim kills; a bad Muslim is blighted for being peaceful. "Did you think that you would enter Paradise while Allah does not know those of you who really fights hard (in His Cause) and remains steadfast? You wished for death before you met it (in the field of battle). Now [that] you have seen it with your own eyes, (you flinch!)" This passage is pretty tough to reconcile with the "peace-loving" myth. And it's even harder to square with a god who claims to know everything Muslims think, say, and do.

Another translation reads: "Did you think you would enter Paradise without Allah testing those of you who fight in His Cause?" To pass Allah's test, Muslims must fight.

The Sira says: *Ishaq:392* "It is not your affair whether Allah changes His attitude to them or punishes them, for they are evildoers. You are not to be bothered with My judgment of My slaves except in so far as I give you orders concerning them [i.e., to kill or rob them]. I may change My mind toward them. Punishing them is my prerogative. They deserve this for their disobedience to Me.'" Muhammad was in a pickle, and Satan knew it. The Medina Muslims were in revolt. If Muhammad lashed out at them too forcefully they would exterminate him. If he were too lenient, they would ignore him. Muhammad had to woo them back into the fold with carrot and stick.

As proof, I offer this evidence: *Ishaq:393* "Fear Allah that you may be prosperous. Obey Allah and perhaps you may escape from His punishment of which He has warned you and attain His reward which He has made you desire. And fear the fire which He has prepared for the disbelievers, a resort for those who disbelieve Me." Satan knows what men desire and seduces them with whatever they covet most. He knows what men fear and threatens them with it. It's so considerate of Ishaq to expose the spirit behind Islam. *Ishaq:393* "Then Allah said: 'Obey Allah and the Apostle and maybe you will attain mercy.' Reproaching those who disobeyed the Apostle in the orders he gave them that day [to fight] He said, 'Vie with one another for forgiveness from your Lord and for the Garden of Bliss prepared for those who fear, a dwelling for those who obey Me and obey My Apostle.... They have wronged themselves by disobedience. But they must not continue disobeying Me for I have prohibited the worship of any but Myself.'"

Satan needed his militants back under his control, so he said: *Ishaq:396* "Allah pardoned the great sin in that He did not destroy you for having disobeyed your Prophet. I did not exterminate all for the debt you owed Me. You have suffered for disobeying Me." Then he added: *Ishaq:397* "It was by the mercy of Allah that you (Muhammad) were lenient to them. Had you been stern and rough they would have dispersed and been no longer around you. They would have left you. So overlook their offence and ask pardon for them and consult with them about the matter." In other words: beg them to come back because Islam is useless to us without stooges. "They have the duty to obey their prophet." *Ishaq:398* "Show them that you listen to them and ask them for their help. Thereby make the religion of Islam agreeable to them. And when you are resolved in the matter of religion concerning fighting your enemy you will have the advantage." The Hadith says that the prophet eased up on the religious stuff as a result. *Bukhari:V1B3N68* "Muhammad used to take care of us in preaching by selecting a suitable time, so that we might not get bored. He abstained from pestering us with sermons and knowledge."

Ishaq:397 "Then Allah said, 'It is not for any prophet to deceive." Since Islam is about war and since Muhammad said, "War is deceit," I think I smell a contradiction.

Returning to the Qur'an, the next line is in reference to the humiliating retreat at Uhud. *003.144* "And Muhammad is no more than a Messenger. Messengers have passed away before him. If then he dies or is killed will you turn back upon your heels? And whoever turns back upon his heels, he will by no means do harm to Allah in the least and Allah will reward the grateful. No person can ever die except by the permission of Allah, the term being fixed as by writing. If any do desire a reward in this life, We shall give it to him," so long as he doesn't retreat from fighting in Allah's Cause. Allah needs to seduce men to do his bidding. He is otherwise impotent. Further, this Qur'anic passage confirms Islam's predestination problem. Everything is fixed by Allah; the religion can't save men.

Speaking of this verse, the first to interpret the Qur'an, said, *Ishaq:395* "No soul can die but by Allah's permission in a term that is written." While predestination is incompatible with all rational thought, I can only wonder why a spirit would write the details of every life on a tablet and then provide his Qur'an orally. But that wasn't the point of the message. Muhammad wanted Muslims to know that Allah was going to kill them whether they fought or not so they might as well fight for babes and booty.

003.146 "How many of the prophets fought in Allah's Cause? With them (fought) myriads of godly men who were slain. They never lost heart if they met with disaster in Allah's way, nor did they weaken nor give in. Allah loves those who are firm and steadfast [warriors]." It's the doctrine of Jihad. But Allah only loves Muslims who die fighting. Fighting alone isn't good enough—you have to die.

Ishaq:393 "Allah loves the steadfast [fighters]. How many a prophet has death in battle befallen and how many multitudes with him? They did not show weakness toward their enemies and were not humiliated when they suffered in the fight for Allah and their religion. That is steadfastness, and Allah loves the steadfast." Ishaq's interpretation of the Qur'an is identical to my own. Islam and fighting are inseparable.

Ishaq:395 "Practice your religion as they did, and be not renegades, turning back on your heels, retreating. Those who retreat and turn away from the battle are losers in this world and in the next." According to history's foremost expert on Islam, the best way to "practice the religion" is to fight to the death. Further, the only Islamic term more vile than "hypocrite" (which stands for peaceful Muslim) is "renegade" (which stand for retreating Muslim in this context and one who abandons Islam in others). Being a renegade is unforgivable. It's a death sentence.

Muhammad may have lost the skirmish with merchants, but rest assured, his Allah was still the best terrorist. *003.150* "Nay! Allah is your Patron and He is the best of the helpers. Soon We shall strike terror into the hearts of the Infidels, for that they joined companions with Allah, for which He had sent no authority: their abode will be in the Fire. And evil is the home of the wrong-doers!" The next time you hear Muslims say that Islam is a peace-loving and tolerant religion, you will know that one of two things must be true: they are either bad Muslims, unwilling to fight, or they are good Muslims, eager to fight but willing to deceive on Muhammad's orders to facilitate the battle. As their prophet said: **"War is deceit."**

Interpreting this passage, Ishaq claims Muhammad equates battlefield advances with the religion of Islam. *Ishaq:395* **"Muslims, if you listen to the unbelievers you will retreat from the enemy and become losers. Ask Allah for victory and do not retreat, withdrawing from His religion. 'We will terrorize those who disbelieve. In that way I will help you against them.'"** By his own admission, Allah was a terrorist, and Islam exists to fight.

This next verse is chilling. *003.152* **"Allah did indeed fulfill His promise to you when you, with His permission were about to annihilate your enemy, until you flinched and fell to disputing about the order, and disobeyed it after He brought you in sight (of the booty) which you covet. Among you are some that hanker after this world and some that desire the Hereafter."** This is the essence of Islam—the motivation for terror.

Ishaq agrees: *Ishaq:396* **"I promise to give you victory over your enemy. You routed them with the sword, killing them by My permission. Then you deserted Me and disobeyed My order and disputed about the order of My Prophet. He told the archers to stay put. But after I showed you what you were desiring, the Meccan wives and property, you desired the spoil and abandoned the order to fight."** These words are as biting as their swords. **"Only those who fought for religion did not transgress in going after the booty. Allah reproached the hypocrites for running away from their Prophet and paying no heed when he called to them."** According to Islam, if you're a religious fighter it's okay to kill unbelievers, possess their wives and steal their property.

And keep in mind why the Muslims were confronted at Uhud. They had terrorized dozens of Quraysh caravans. They had gone out as pirates in pursuit of booty. They had looted, murdered, kidnapped, ransomed, and gloated. The Meccans simply wanted to stop the terror. That's why they went home after having thought they had eliminated the nuisance. Unlike Muslims, the Meccans collected no spoils and took no prisoners. Yet we're told that the militants were fighting in Allah's Cause and that the pirates will be rewarded.

Back on the battlefield, with the Muslims in full retreat, Muhammad cried, **"Come back to me. Don't run away for I am the Messenger of God."** *003.153* **"Behold! You ran off precipitately, climbing up the high hill without even casting a side glance at anyone, while the Messenger in your rear is calling you from your rear, urging you to fight. [That's quite a picture.] Allah gave you one distress after another by way of requital, to teach you not to grieve for the booty that had escaped you and for (the ill) that had befallen you."** Only mercenaries would grieve over lost booty.

There is an interesting line in the next verse that underscores the problem of predestination. *003.154* **"Say: 'Even if you had remained in your houses, those ordained to be slaughtered would have gone forth to the places where they were to slain.'"** Men are condemned to die and go to hell without choice. Even if a Muslim wants to be peaceful, Allah will drag him to his death. So why bother with a religion, a prophet, or acts of terror? It's all meaningless.

Next we learn that Satan inspires peaceful Muslims who refrain from fighting. *003.155* "Those who turned back the day the two armies clashed, Satan caused them to backslide, fail in their duty, and run away from the battlefield." In plain English: Satan is to blame for their failings, but they will roast in hell anyway.

Ever willing to define good Muslims as "fighters" and bad Muslims as "peacemakers," we hear this from the god of war: *003.156* "O you who believe! Be not like the Unbelievers, who say of their brethren when they are traveling through the land engaged in raids and fighting: 'If they had stayed with us, they would not have died or been slain.' This is that Allah may make it anguish, a cause of sighs and regrets in their hearts. It is Allah that gives Life and causes Death by His power, as He wishes. And if you are slain, or die, in Allah's Cause [as a martyr], pardon from Allah and mercy are far better than all they could amass." Allah issues his terrorists a pardon. And to make sure no Muslim would miss the message, Ishaq reports: *Ishaq:397* "There is no escape from death, so death for Allah's sake in battle is better than all one can amass in life while holding back from fighting in fear of death. Let not the world deceive you and be not deceived by it. Let fighting and the reward which Allah holds out to you be the most important thing." Good Muslims are mercenaries, not missionaries.

Ishaq:398 "Allah says, 'Is one who obeys Me like one who has incurred Allah's anger and deserves His anger, whose home is hell? So know that there are degrees with Allah and Allah is a seer of what you do and of all the degrees of what they do in Paradise and Hell. Allah knows those who obey and those who disobey Him.'" If all is "a seer" of what men do, why does he need a test to determine who believes him?

In the upside down world of Islam where the good are bad and the bad are good we discover: *Ishaq:398* "Allah sent you an Apostle of your own, reciting to you His verses concerning what you did, and teaching you good and evil that you might know what is good and do it, and know what is bad and refrain from it, and so that you might gain much from obeying Him and avoid His wrath proceeding from disobedience and thereby escape His vengeance and obtain the reward of His Garden of Bliss." If you were reading this out of context, it would sound rational and religious. Yet in context it is neither. Allah and Muhammad have made a career out of defining "bad" as "not fighting" and "good" as "killing infidels."

Since Muhammad had orchestrated two-dozen terrorist raids to fund his fledging "religion," and his god had said "booty is lawful and good," this is a quite a contradiction: *003.161* "It is not for any prophet to embezzle. Whoever embezzles will bring what he embezzled with him on the Day of Doom. Then every soul will be paid in full what it hath earned." Stealing booty at swordpoint (a.k.a. armed robbery) in the name of Islam is an honest day's work but embezzling is bad. Okay.

003.162 "Is the man who follows the good pleasure of Allah like the man who draws on himself the wrathful condemnation of Allah, and whose abode is in the Hell Fire? A woeful destination!" This is supposed to be a rhetorical question. But think about it.

Back to war: *003.165* "What! When a single disaster smites you, although you smote with one twice as great, do you say: 'Whence is this?' Say: 'It is from yourselves.'" 'Cause it couldn't be the *prophet's* fault. **"What you suffered on the day the armies clashed was by permission of Allah; that He might know the true believers."** If it's dumb to say once, it's dumber to repeat.

Muhammad's favorite epithet for a bad, peace-loving Muslim was "Hypocrite." Let's listen in as he condemns them (again) for not fighting: *003.167* **"And that He might know the Hypocrites, unto whom it was said: 'Come, fight in Allah's Cause, or (at least) drive (the foe from your city).' They said: 'Had we known how to fight, we should certainly have followed you.' They were that day nearer to Unbelief than to Faith, saying with their lips what was not in their hearts but Allah hath full knowledge of all they conceal."** That wasn't the least bit ambiguous, or peaceful. Hypocritical "bad" Muslims don't even know how to fight. Good Muslims on the other hand are expert jihadists, "fighters in Allah's Cause."

Allah despises pacifists. *003.168* **"Those who, while they sat at home, said (of their brethren slain fighting for the cause of Allah), while they themselves sit (at home at ease): 'If only they had listened to us [and been bad Muslims] they would not have been killed.' Say: 'Avert death from your own selves, if you speak the truth.'"**

Ah, but there is a reward for militants: *003.169* **"Think not of those who are slain in Allah's Cause as dead. Nay, they live, finding their provision from their Lord."** All good Muslims go to heaven (well, the first 70,000, anyway). Unfortunately, you have to be a bad person to get there. **"Jubilant in the bounty provided by Allah: and with regard to those left behind, who have not yet joined them (in their bliss), the Martyrs glory in the fact that on them is no fear, nor have they cause to grieve. Allah will not waste the reward of the believers."** This is one of the many Qur'an verses Muslim suicide bombers read on videotape prior to slaughtering innocent women and children. It's so religious of them.

Islam in its original, uncorrupted, and most fundamental form manufactures terrorists. If bad men misinterpreted Allah's words in the Qur'an, or Muhammad's example in the Hadith, to justify their criminal behavior, then it would be different. But that is not the case. Anyone who acts like Muhammad will be a sexual pervert, a vicious thief, and a genocidal terrorist. Anyone who obeys the Qur'an will be a mercenary—a killer motivated by greed.

Ishaq:399 **"You had smitten your enemy with a double dose of torment at Badr, slaying them and taking prisoners. Yet you disobeyed your Prophet's orders and brought the defeat of Uhud on yourselves. And it was said to them: 'Come, fight for Allah's sake.' The hypocrites stopped fighting for Allah's sake, eager to survive, fleeing death. So Allah said to His Prophet to make the Muslims wish to fight and to desire battle: 'And do not think that those who were killed for Allah's sake are dead. Nay, they are alive with their Lord being nourished, glad with the bounty Allah has brought them and rejoicing for those who have not yet joined them that they have nothing to fear or grieve over.'"** It's a confession. Muslims must be seduced to the point they **"wish to fight and desire battle."** Allah just said, "Murder for Muhammad and heaven is yours."

And then this newsflash from the Islamic paradise, the retirement home for Muslim martyrs: *Ishaq:400* **"'If our fellow Muslims knew what Allah has done for us they would not dislike fighting or shrink from war!' And Allah said, 'I will tell them of you,' so He sent down to His Apostle these verses."**

Evidently some of Muhammad's comrades were a little suspicious of the authenticity of the martyrs' message. So... *Ishaq:400* **"One whom I do not suspect told me that he was asked about these verses and he said, 'We asked Muhammad about them and we were told that when our brethren were slain at Uhud Allah put their spirits in the crops of green birds which come down to the rivers of the Garden and eat of its fruits. In the shade of the Throne of Allah [that would be the same Throne that made the sun] the Lord takes one look at them and says three times: 'O My slaves, what do you wish that I should give you more?' They say, "We should like our spirits to return to our bodies and then return to the earth and fight for You until we are killed again.'"** This is so dimwitted and demented, so obviously false, I don't understand why anyone believes it.

Or for that matter, believes Muhammad: *Ishaq:400* **"The Apostle swore that there was no believer who had parted from the world and wanted to return to it for a single hour even if he could possess it with all it has except the martyr who would like to return and fight for Allah and be killed a second time."**

003.172 **"Of those who answered the call of Allah and the Messenger (at Uhud), even after being wounded (in the fight), those who do right and ward off have a great reward."** Allah rewards those who kill for him. Terrorists go straight to him (wherever that might be): **"And they returned with grace and bounty from Allah: no harm ever touched them: For they followed the good pleasure of Allah: Allah is of Infinite Bounty."**

During debates with Islamic imams, I'm told that these war surahs aren't relevant and that Allah's command to fight was only for Muhammad's Companions. Yet the Qur'an didn't become a book until after Muhammad's death, so that makes no sense. Further, Allah identifies the enemy "infidels" as Christians. He orders Muslims to fight, murder, enslave, and mutilate them until every soul has surrendered to Islam. The order to kill is clear and open ended.

By suggesting that the Medina surahs don't speak to people today, most of Islam becomes irrelevant, which has been my point all along. At its best, the Qur'an is little more than an elongated rant—a series of situational scriptures designed to serve Muhammad. Islam was a vicious con, little more than the Profitable Profit Plan gone awry. At its worst, it is a terrorist manifesto—a religotic that manufactures murderers and seeks world domination.

Trying to shed his Satanic "Adversary" designation, Lucifer besmirches the character of his alter ego (while demonstrating his duplicitous nature): *003.175* **"It is the Devil who would make (men) fear his messengers and frighten you. Fear them not; fear Me [first person], if you are true believers. And let not those grieve you who fall into unbelief hastily; surely they can do no harm to Allah [third person]; they cannot injure Him [second person]; Allah intends that He should not give them any portion in the hereafter, and they shall have a grievous punishment."**

The next verse borders on pathetic: *003.181* **"Verily Allah heard the taunt of those** who said, (when asked for contributions to the war): 'Allah is poor, and we are rich!' We shall record their saying and We shall say: Taste you the penalty of the Scorching Fire!" If Allah is independent of men, why does he need their money?

According to Allah, those who knew the miracleless, prophetless, scriptureless messenger best rejected him. *003.184* "Then if they reject you (Muhammad), so were rejected messengers before you, who came with miracles and with the prophetic Psalms and with the Scripture giving light." Since Muhammad performed no miracles, made no prophecies, and delivered the darkest recitals of all time, rejecting him would seem to be the most enlightened course.

Ibn Ishaq commemorates Uhud with twenty-four pages of poetry. I would be remiss if I didn't share the most disturbed lines. Let's start with a murder confession: *Ishaq:403* "Allah killed twenty-two polytheists at Uhud."

Then: *Ishaq:404* "War has distracted me, but blame me not, 'tis my habit. Struggling with the burdens it imposes, I bear arms bestride my horse at a cavalry's gallop. Running like a wild ass in the desert I am pursued by hunters."

And...*Ishaq:405* "It is your folly to fight the Apostle, for Allah's army is bound to disgrace you. We brought them to the pit. Hell was their meeting place. We collected them there, black slaves, men of no descent. Leaders of the infidels, why did you not learn from those thrown into Badr's pit?" I beg to differ. The Meccans *did* learn the lesson of Badr's pit. They knew that a disease as vile as Islam, one that would cause terrorists to gloat over the mangled bodies of their slain victims, must be stopped at any cost. That's why they came to Uhud.

The doctrine of the sword will prevail by the sword if unchecked. *Ishaq:406* "Among us was Allah's Apostle whose command we obey. When he gives an order we do not examine it. The spirit descends on him from his Lord [and possesses him]. We tell him about our wishes and our desires which is to obey him in all that he wants. Cast off fear of death and desire it. Be the one who barters his life. Take your swords and trust Allah. With a compact force holding lances and spears we plunged into a sea of men....and all were made to get their fill of evil. We are men who see no blame in him who kills."

While bad Muslims can and should be saved from Islam, I believe the good ones are beyond hope. They are so corrupted; their continued presence will only serve to condemn others. *Ishaq:414* "If you kill us, the true religion is ours. And to be killed for the truth is to find favor with Allah. If you think that we are fools, know that the opinion of those who oppose Islam is misleading. We are men of war who get the utmost from it. We inflict painful punishment on those who oppose us.... If you insult Allah's Apostle, Allah will slay you. You are a cursed, rude fellow! You utter filth, and then throw it at the clean-robed, godly, and faithful One." It's a rotten job, but someone has to do it.

18

LUSTFUL LIBERTINE

*"The Prophet has a greater claim on the faithful
than they have on themselves."*

The fourth year of the Islamic Era begins oddly. *Ishaq:426* **"After Uhud, a group of men from Adal and Qarah came to the Messenger of Allah and said, 'O Prophet, we are good Muslims and have accepted Islam. Please send us some of your Companions to instruct us in the religion. Teach us to recite the Qur'an, and teach us the laws of Islam.'"** If they were unaware of the faith, the Qur'an, and Islamic law, how could they have been "good" Muslims? Tabari gives us the answer. *Tabari VII:145* **"The tribe of Lihyan was seeking vengeance for the killing of their chief, and they paid these men to ask for instructors."** They were "good" Muslims because they wanted to become better militants. At least Islam is consistent.

Tabari VII:145 **"Other authorities have a different account of this expedition. One variant says: 'The Messenger sent out a group of ten men, putting Asim in command. When they arrived someone told the Lihyans about them. They sent a hundred archers against the Muslims."** Why do you suppose they would do that? Weren't these men on a religious mission? No, not hardly. Not only were they armed to the teeth, the mission itself was called a raid. Furthermore, most of Muhammad's terrorist attacks hadn't been against the Quraysh, but instead against neighboring tribes. The bad boys of Medina had developed a reputation. Today, our politicians and media would say that they had ties to al-Qaeda.

Tabari VII:144/Ishaq:426 **"The Muslims bivouacked for the night and were taken by surprise. So the Muslims took up their swords [not Qur'ans] to fight them, but the Lihyans said, 'We do not want to kill you. We only want to get some money by selling you to the Meccans. We swear by Allah's Covenant that we will not kill you.' 'By Allah,' Asim said, 'we will never accept an agreement from an unbelieving infidel.' They fought until they were killed."** Both pagan and Muslim swore by the same god. What's more, the pagans referenced "Allah's Covenant,"—Qusayy's scheme—the foundation of Islam.

Later, we are told, *Tabari VII:145* **"Khubayb gave himself up" and became a prisoner. "They took him to Mecca and handed him over to the sons of al-Harith, as Khubayb had killed their father at Uhud.... They took Khubayb out of the Haram (sacred area around Mecca) to kill him. He asked to pray two rak'ahs, and he made two prostrations. After that,** it became the Sunnah [example] for those about to be executed to pray two rak'ahs. Khubayb said, 'My death is for Allah...he will bless the limbs of my mangled corpse.'" This is what the suicide bombers who destroyed the World Trade Center said between shouts of "Allahu Akbar!" "They took him out and beheaded him."

Next we discover that Khubayb was crucified, not beheaded: *Tabari VII:146* "The Messenger sent Amr to the Quraysh as a spy. He said, 'I came to the cross on which Khubayb was bound and untied him. He fell to the ground, and I withdrew a short distance. When I turned round, I could not see a trace of Khubayb—the earth had swallowed him up." While Muslim militants are granted a stay in Allah's brothel, Khubayb, appears to have gone down, not up.

Moving on, it's time for another assassination. *Tabari VII:147* "Amr was sent by Muhammad to kill Abu Sufyan [the Quraysh leader and merchant]. The Prophet said, 'Go to Abu Sufyan and kill him.' ...When I entered Mecca I had a dagger ready to slay anybody who laid hold of me. My Ansar companion asked, 'Should we start by circumambulating the Ka'aba seven times and praying two rak'ahs?' I said, 'I know the Meccans better than you do.' But he kept pestering me until in the end we went to the Ka'aba, circumambulated it seven times, and prayed." A good Muslim is a religious assassin.

The Quraysh understood the corrosive influence of Islam better than we do. *Tabari VII:148* "One of the Meccans recognized me and shouted, 'That is Amr!' They rushed after us, saying, 'By Allah, Amr has not come here for any good purpose! He has come for some evil reason.' Amr had been a cutthroat and a desperado before accepting Islam." So naturally, he was attracted to Muhammad and inspired by Islam.

"The Meccans set out in pursuit so I said, 'Let's get out of here! This is what I was afraid of! We will never reach Abu Sufyan now, so save your own skin.' We left at full speed, took to the hills, hiding in a cave. In this way we gave them the slip." A life was spared because the Quraysh understood the nature of Islam. They recognized their enemy and correctly profiled their behavior.

While not all Muslims are terrorists, virtually all terrorists are Muslims. This should tell us something about Islam. According to independent surveys, eighty-five percent of terrorist acts worldwide are directly attributable to the Islamic faith. Yet Muslims represent less than twenty percent of the world's population. Since the militants are called "a radical minority" let's say that only twenty percent of Muslims are "good" ones—jihad fighters in Allah's Cause. If that's true, four percent of the world's population takes Islam seriously. One out of twenty-five humans emulate Muhammad and follow Allah's orders as revealed in the Qur'an and Hadith. These men and women are 2,000% more lethal than the rest of us.

Tabari VII:148 "Amr said, 'Let's wait here until the cry has died down. They are sure to hunt for us tonight and tomorrow." In shades of Mogadishu, the Meccans sent too few men into harm's way. "I was still in the cave when Uthman bin Malik came riding proudly on his horse. He reached the entrance to our cave and I said to my Ansar companion, 'If he sees us, he will tell everyone in Mecca.' So I went out and stabbed him with my dagger. He gave a shout and the Meccans came to him while I went back to my hiding place. Finding him at the point of death, they said, 'By Allah we knew that Amr came for no good purpose.' The death of their companion impeded their search for us, for they carried him away." Murder number one.

"We remained in the cave for two days until the pursuit had died down and then went out to Khubayb's cross. My companion said, 'Shall we take Khubayb down from his cross?' I went to the cross and untied Khubayb [again]. I carried him on my back and had gone about forty paces when a guard spotted me. I threw Khubayb down, and will never forget the sound his body made when it fell. I managed to throw the guard off, ran to my companion, mounted his camel, and went to the Prophet to tell him what had happened."

A foiled assassination attempt and an isolated murder may seem unworthy of the attention I'm affording them. But they were important to Muhammad, Ishaq, and Tabari, and thus to fundamental Islam. And by sharing every episode recorded by Islam's first biographer and historian, leaving nothing of consequence out, I am confirming a profound truth. Islam, as it was taught and lived by Muhammad, was a terrorist dogma.

Tabari VII:149 "On the way I went into a cave with my bow and arrows. While I was in it a one-eyed man from the Banu Bakr came in driving some sheep. He said, 'Who's there?' I said [lied], 'I'm a Banu Bakr.' 'So am I.' Then he laid down next to me, and raised his voice in song: 'I will not be a Muslim and will not believe in the faith of the Muslims.' I said, 'You will soon see!' Before long the Bedouin went to sleep and started snoring. So I killed him in the most dreadful way that anybody has ever killed. I leant over him, struck the end of my bow into his good eye, and thrust it down until it came out the back of his neck. After that I rushed out like a wild beast and took flight." Murder number two.

"I came to the village of Naqi and recognized two Meccan spies. I called for them to surrender. They said no so I shot and arrow and killed one, and then I tied the other up and took him to Muhammad." Murder number three. Kidnapping number one. The Muslims were having fun. *Tabari VII:150* "I had tied my prisoner's thumbs together with my bowstring. The Messenger of Allah looked at him and laughed so that his back teeth could be seen. Then he questioned me and I told him what had happened. 'Well done!' he said, and prayed for me to be blessed." These are the ominous words of the Islamic Hadith, the only words written about this man and his religion within centuries of his death. And they are perverse. Three cold-blooded murders and a hostage taking earned a jovial laugh and a hearty, "Well done!"

Although I have shared this with you before, it bears repeating. While some Hadith may be exaggerated and some may be untrue, it doesn't matter. All that counts is that this is the sum total of what is known about the Muhammad of Islam. I have reported every significant event recorded by Tabari and Ishaq—the earliest, most respected, and comprehensive chroniclers of the Islamic faith. Therefore, what you have been reading is all Muslims know about their prophet. And that, I dare say, explains their behavior.

Tabari VII:150 "In the month of Ramadhan (February 626), the Messenger married Zaynab bt. Khuzaymah. She had been married to Tufayl, who had divorced her." I believe that makes her the fifth member of the prophet's collection.

Tabari VII:151/Ishaq:433 "**In this year there occurred the disaster of the expedition sent out by the Messenger to Bi'r Ma'unah. The polytheists had charge of the pilgrimage that year [confirming that the Hajj was pagan]. Abu Bara (One-Who-Plays-With-Spears), the chief of the Banu Amir, came to the Prophet and presented a gift. Muhammad said, 'I do not accept presents from pagans, so become a Muslim if you want me to accept it.'**" He was willing to steal from any Abu, Tufayl, or Harith, but would not accept diplomatic gifts. Further, there is no empirical evidence that shows men behave better who worship one false god rather than many of them.

"**Muhammad expounded Islam to Abu Bara and invited him to accept it. He explained its advantages for him and Allah's promises to believers. He recited the Qur'an. Abu did not accept Islam. He said, Muhammad, this affair of yours is most excellent. If you were to send some of your Companions to my people to call them to your religious affair, I would hope that they would respond.'**" This is great stuff. Muhammad presented the "advantages for *him*" to convert his *subjects* to Islam: "It's the perfect tool for a chief like you," der prophet undoubtedly said. Muhammad's religotic was designed to empower dictators. This is why the poligious doctrine survives after fourteen centuries. Islam wasn't called submission for nothing. Religion is an effective tool in the wrong hands.

Allah's prophet reviewed the dark spirit's "promises:" booty for fighters, loot for the living and virgins for the victims; what's not to like? But, Chief Abu wouldn't accept Islam. Instead, he wanted his people converted. And that is the essence of the doctrine of submission. Even today, the tyrannical despots who rule the Islamic world aren't Muslims—their people are. The "religion" is used to control the masses, to fleece them for benefit of cleric and king. Chief Abu knew that Islam would only be to his advantage if his people were coerced into submission.

Tabari VII:152/Ishaq:434 "**The Apostle was afraid to send his people to Abu's tribe for fear they would kill them. But Chief Abu gave Muhammad a surety [collateral guarantee] so the he sent Mundhir (The-Quick-to-Seek-Death) with forty to seventy riders. After halting at Bi'r Ma'unah, they sent Haram to Amir Tufayl with a letter from Muhammad. When Haram arrived, Amir killed him. Then he set out and took the Muslims by surprise, surrounding them while they were encamped. On seeing them, the Muslims snatched up their swords and fought until they were all killed except Ka'b. The enemy left him at the point of death.**" Remember, this is after Allah had revealed the 8th and 3rd surahs, so the Muslims believed that they had to fight to the death.

As we pick up the story, word gets back to the prophet. *Ishaq:434* "**Amr and an Ansari were out grazing camels and saw vultures circling around the camp. They went to investigate and saw their Companions lying in their blood. The Ansari said, 'What do you think we should do?' Amr answered, 'Go tell the prophet.'**" But they were spotted and the Ansari was killed. Amr was taken prisoner. He lied, we're told, "**taking an** oath on his mother's life," so they set him free. Amr hightailed it "towards Medina, until, when he was at Qarqarah, two Banu Amir men halted near him in the shade. They had a compact of protection with Allah's Messenger which Amr knew nothing. Amr waited until they were asleep. Then he killed them, thinking that he had taken vengeance for the Muslims who had been slain. When he came to the Messenger, he told him what had happened. The Prophet said, 'You have killed men for whom I shall have to pay blood-money.'"

Muhammad's soul wasn't troubled by the news that innocent men had been murdered. His only worry was that coin was going to slip from his pockets. Islam was never about saving souls; it was about stealing money.

In the midst of these Islamic terrorist raids, assassinations, murders, and kidnappings for ransom, the next headline appears somewhat benign. It reads: "Expulsion of the Banu Nadir." *Tabari VII:156/Ishaq:437* "In the fourth year of the Islamic Era the Prophet expelled the Banu Nadir [a large Jewish community in Yathrib] from their homes. The cause of this was that Amr killed two men to whom had been given a promise of protection by the Apostle. Their chief wrote Muhammad asking him for blood-money. So the Prophet turned towards the Nadir [Jews] to seek their help in the payment of the blood money. With him were Bakr, Umar, and Ali." The Muslims had raided a caravan just north of Mecca. Muhammad's adoptive son grabbed another east of Medina. They allegedly "earned" huge ransoms "selling" the Badr captives back to their families. They had plundered the Qaynuqa Jews, stealing their gold, armor, businesses, and homes. So, how could the pirate chest be bare?

The answer is as old as time. Those who steal don't value anything. They go on binges and need ever-larger fixes. Easy come; easy go. So turban in hand, Muhammad had to go begging, this time to the kin of those he had previously plundered. Wouldn't you like to have been a fly on the wall? *Tabari VII:157/Ishaq:437* "When the Prophet came to ask for their help in the payment of the blood-money, the Jews said, 'Yes, Abu al-Qasim [Muhammad]. Of course, we will give you the help you want in the way you want it.' Then they spoke privately with one another... [Before we listen to what Islam wants us to believe the Jews said in "private," ask yourself, how did the Muslims know? And since they couldn't have known, what were they trying to accomplish by *pretending* to know?] Muhammad had gone outside and was sitting by a house wall. The Jews said, 'Who will go on the roof of this house and drop a stone, relieving us of him?'" The Muslim sages were trying to justify the exceedingly hostile behavior their prophet was about to exhibit.

I do not doubt that the Jews might have wanted the prophet dead. I would have wanted him dead. He was a menace to society—a violent terrorist and common criminal. However, this plot is absurd. There is no chance Allah's guy, the grand pontiff of Medina, was sitting in the dirt against the wall of a Jewish home. And there was no chance someone had a stone big enough to kill a man sitting on a thatched (and thus pitched) roof. Further, the Nadir were prosperous farmers. If they wanted to execute Muhammad they would have used an implement more lethal than a stone.

Ishaq:437 **"Amr Jihash, who was one of the Jews, came forward and said, 'I am your man.'
He went up to the roof to drop the stone as arranged. Muhammad was with Bakr, Umar,
and Ali [future Caliphs all], and the news of what the people intended came to him from
Heaven. He got up and said, 'Do not leave until I come to you.'"** This is Ali's second run
as stooge. A few years earlier he had been asked to wear the prophet's pajamas, laying in wait for assassins wielding swords.

Guillaume in his translation of Ishaq's *Sirat Rasul Allah*, said: "It is clear
that a later story has been attached to this incident. Obviously, if the prophet
had overheard their designs there was no need of a supernatural communication from heaven." In other words: the godly inspiration was a hoax.

While this account has more holes than a leaky roof, Tabari shares another
take on Islam's excuse, I mean, "inspiration." *Tabari VII:157* **"Amr went up to the roof
to roll the stone. News of this came to the Prophet from Heaven, and he got up as though
he wished to relieve himself. His companions waited for him but he was gone for a long
time. The Jews began to say, 'What has delayed Abu al-Qasim?' Muhammad's Companions left and Kinanah said, 'News of what you intended has reached him.'"**

This justification is essential for Islam. It serves to excuse grotesque barbarism, grand larceny, and ultimately, genocide. Yet Muhammad had to come
to the Nadir to beg for blood money to excuse a double homicide. That does
not bode well for their credibility. *Ishaq:437* **"The Prophet went back to his home. When
his Companions thought that he had been gone a long time they got up to look for him. On
the way they told a man the story of the treachery intended by the Jews and ordered them
to get ready to fight them and march against them."** Since Muhammad had run
away without telling his gang anything, how did they know?

Tabari VII:158 **"When the Messenger's Companions returned they found him sitting in the
mosque. They said, 'O Prophet, we waited for you but you did not come back.' 'The Jews
intended to kill me,' he replied, 'and Allah informed me of it. [One rock to another, I suppose.] Call Muhammad bin Maslamah to me.' When Muhammad came, he was told to go
to the Jews and say, 'Leave my country. You have intended treachery.' He went and said,
'The Messenger orders you to depart from his country.' They replied, 'We never thought
that an Aws would come with such a message.' 'Hearts have changed,' Muhammad said.
'Islam has wiped out our old covenants.'"**

This is a stinging indictment. First, these Hadiths are contradictory. While
conflicting scripture is common for Islam, this time it's being used to justify
a hideously immoral act. Second, Muhammad, the bad boy who had been
banished from Mecca for reneging on the Quraysh Bargain and for threatening
to slaughter his kin, was now claiming that Yathrib was *his* country. It wasn't
Allah's; it wasn't Islam's. It was his. Third, without any actual provocation,
he ordered established families, thousands of them, from their homes because
he wanted their money.

The most incriminating lines were saved for last: **"Hearts have changed. Islam
has wiped out our old covenants."** Muhammad's poligious doctrine was corrosive

—more dangerous than *Mein Kampf*. Anyone who trusts it is ruined—as is everyone around them. Today's terrorists have not corrupted their religion; Islam has corrupted them. There will be no peace until this false, intolerant, and violent doctrine is expunged from the earth.

Tabari VII:158/Ishaq:437 **"After telling his Companions about the treachery which the Jews had meditated against him, the Apostle ordered them to prepare for war and to march against them."** To "meditate" is to quietly engage in thought or contemplation. If this is true, the Jews said nothing and did nothing. If it's not true, Islam's prophet is a liar. Either way, Muhammad was totally unjustified in ordering his militants to attack. The siege of the Nadir was an act of terrorism and piracy, proving that the sole founder of Islam was a vicious criminal.

Tabari VII:158/Ishaq:437 **"Muhammad personally led his men against the Nadir and halted in their quarter. The Jews took refuge against him in their homes, so he ordered their date palms to be cut down and burnt. They shouted, 'Muhammad, you have forbidden wonton destruction of property and have blamed those who perpetrated it. Why are you doing this?'"** Muhammad didn't answer the question directly. He delegated the excuse to his god. A situational scripture authorizing destruction was "handed down." *059.005* **"The palm trees you cut down or left standing intact was by Allah's dispensation so that He might disgrace the transgressors."** I'll let you decide if the creator of the universe etched this line on an eternal tablet before the world was created or if Muhammad just made it up. But you should know that the 59th surah was revealed following the banishment of the Qaynuqa Jews the prior year, and yet the verse's authorization was recited in past tense. Also, the obliteration of the date farm "disgraced the transgressors" only in the sense that Muhammad was the transgressor. Muslims confiscated the groves.

Wackidi writes: *Tabari VII:158/Ishaq:437* **"Abd Allah bin Ubayy sent a message to the Nadir saying, 'Stand firm. I have two thousand Bedouin men who are united around me. Stay, and they will battle with you as will the Qurayza.' However, Sallam, a Qurayza Jew said, 'We shall not break our compact as long as I am alive. We are eminent among the Jewish people by virtue of our wealth.' Continuing to speak to the Nadir Jews the Qurayza leader said, 'Accept what Muhammad has proposed before you have to accept what is worse.' 'What could be worse?' Huyayy, the Nadir chief asked. 'The seizure of your wealth, the enslavement of your children, and the killing of your men,' the Qurayza Jew replied. Huyayy refused to accept his advice. He told a Muslim courier, 'We will not leave our homes and farms; so do what you see fit.'"**

How bizarre, a man named Slave-to-Allah rallied to aid the Jews against the Muslims. But it's the Qurayza response that is foreboding. They were the largest community in Yathrib. By capitulating to the tyrant, by sacrificing their brethren, they doomed themselves to the very fate they feared. They were soon plundered, raped, sold into slavery, and murdered. This should be a haunting warning to the West, and particularly to the Israelis. Divided as they are now, with many willing to appease Islamic tyrants and trade land in hopes of retaining their treasure, they will lose everything.

As we continue with this horrific tale, consider the implications of the following Hadith in the context of Allah being either a pagan idol or Lucifer. **"The Messenger magnified Allah and the Muslims magnified Allah with him."** This means they yelled, "Allahu Akbar!"—"Allah is Greatest!" *Ishaq:437* **"So Allah cast terror into the hearts of the Jews. Then the Prophet said, 'The Jews have declared war.'"** According to the Islamic scriptures, there was no declaration of war.

Tabari VII:158 **"Judayy went to Abd Allah Ibn Ubayy to ask for support. He said, 'I found him sitting among a number of his companions while the Prophet's crier was calling men to arms. He said, 'This is a clever trick of Muhammad's.'"** Yes, indeed. The Profitable Profit Plan was about to benefit from another **"clever trick."** If mugging a jogger in Central Park is "clever," this was downright brilliant.

"The Messenger of Allah besieged the Nadir Jews for fifteen days. In the end they made peace with him on the condition that the Prophet would not kill them and that their property and their coats of mail would be his." According to the lying prophet, the Jews had "declared war," yet they never wielded a sword or shot an arrow. They were simply "besieged"—starved into submission. Then they were forced to make "peace," Islamic style. The false prophet said: "You give me your property and I will allow you to live." But of course, our profiteer acted with Allah's blessing, making him an Apostle.

If, after reading these words, you believe that Muhammad, the instigator and perpetrator of this heinous crime, was a conduit to God, you are as lost as he was. If you believe that Islam was conceived as a tolerant and peaceful religion to save men's souls, you are sadly mistaken.

For non-Muslims, I trust you find these words sobering. The negative implications associated with our continued ignorance of Islam are staggering. This is not merely a history lesson. Muhammad claimed that he had "spiritual authority" for his barbarism. He started a "religion" to justify his atrocities and to perpetrate others. That makes Islam the most evil dogma ever conceived—and the most dangerous.

What's more, the first Muslims were proud of themselves. They conceived many Hadith to express their *joy*. The first is rather blunt: *Tabari VII:159* **"The Messenger of Allah besieged the Banu Nadir for fifteen days until he had reduced them to a state of utter exhaustion, so that they would give him what he wanted. The terms in which the Prophet made peace with the Jews were: he would not shed their blood, he would expel them from their lands and settlements, providing for every three of them a camel and a water-skin."** It's getting harder to write polite commentary on this %#$@&! behavior. With Islam, the price of peace has been defined: your home, your property, your business, your country, your everything.

Tabari VII:159 **"The Prophet fought them until he made peace with them on condition that they evacuate Yathrib. He expelled them to Syria but allowed them to keep what their camels could carry, except for their coats of mail and weapons."** Imagine what it was like to record this Hadith. What must the Islamic sage have thought? Imagine being a Muslim today and stumbling upon this. What are your options? If you reject these Hadith Collections, there is no record of the prophet and thus there is no Islam, as he was the *lone* messenger. Apart from the Sira and Sunnah, nothing is known about Muhammad or Islam's formation. Without his example, the Five Pillars all vanish. Without context and chronology, the Qur'an becomes a meaningless and disjointed rant.

It's a lose-lose proposition. If you *accept* the Hadith as true, as the path to God, the model of morality, you are destined to become a like-minded terrorist. But if you *reject* them, you lose everything: your culture, political system, religion, prophet, and god. Further, the faithful will kill you.

In context, the siege and banishment of the Nadir was outrageous. The people who had built Yathrib, who had lived there peacefully for a *thousand years*, were forced out of their homes and from their farms by men who had just barely arrived. Less than seventy Muslims had invaded their town, yet, burning with hatred and uncontrollable greed, they plundered it.

Ishaq:438 **"The Jews loaded their camels with their wives, children, and property. There were tambourines, pipes and singing. They went to Khaybar with such splendor as had never been seen from any tribe."** The Jews were giving the Muslims an important message. Even deprived of their worldly possessions, Yahweh's chosen possessed something better than Allah's chosen would ever know.

Ishaq:438 **"The Nadir left their property to Muhammad and it became his personal possession, to do with it as he wished. He divided it among the Emigrants, to the exclusion of the Ansar."** But gone was not forgotten. Before we leave this dreadful example of what fundamental Islam did to men's minds and souls, you must know that the Nadir will be hunted again. The next time it won't be so pleasant.

Muhammad's biographer claims Allah revealed these Qur'an verses to his prophet to celebrate the occasion: *Ishaq:438* **"Allah wreaked His vengeance on the Jews and gave His Apostle power over them and control to deal with them as he wished. Allah said, 'I turned out those who disbelieved of the Scripture People from their homes. You did not think that they would go but I came upon them and terrorized them. And in the next world I will torment them again with a painful punishment in Hell. The palm trees you cut down were by Allah's permission; they were uprooted on My order. It was not destruction but it was vengeance from Allah to humble the evildoers. The spoil which Allah gave the Apostle from the Nadir belongs to him."** Ishaq is suggesting that the 59th surah was handed down regarding the Nadir siege rather than the Qaynuqa raid. But that can't be, since the rest of the surah deals with the defeat at Uhud that prompted the Qaynuqa attack.

Muhammad dropped a string of prophetic pearls, all dutifully collected by al-Bukhari, so that Muslims would not miss his message of racial hatred, terrorism, oppression, and greed: *Bukhari:V4B52N153* **"The properties of Banu Nadir which Allah had transferred to His Apostle as Fair Booty were not gained by the Muslims with** their horses and camels. The properties therefore, belonged especially to Allah's Apostle who used to give his family their yearly expenditure and spend what remained thereof on arms and horses to be used in Allah's Cause." Since the dastardly deed was Muhammad's scheme start to finish, the booty was all his. And, in direct contradiction with the Qur'an, Muhammad didn't use his ill-gotten gain to bribe his mercenaries. He used it to buy the affection of his wives and to acquire more weapons of war. Saintly behavior, it was not.

Muhammad was not the first tyrant to besiege and plunder, to terrorize, a defenseless community. He was not the first warlord to lure mercenaries into his ranks by sharing some of the property he had stolen. Allah's messenger wasn't the first pervert to buy love following a conquest. And Islam's prophet wasn't the first psychopath to trade booty for weapons so that he could continue plundering. But he was the first do do so while perpetrating a religious scam.

Bukhari:V4B52N176 "Allah's Apostle said, 'You Muslims will fight the Jews till some of them hide behind stones. The stones will betray them saying, "O Abdullah (slave of Allah)! There is a Jew hiding behind me; so kill him."'" This must have been a real crowd pleaser because there is a second variation. *Bukhari:V4B52N177* "Allah's Apostle said, 'The Hour will not be established until you fight with the Jews, and the stone behind which a Jew will be hiding will say. "O Muslim! There is a Jew hiding behind me, so kill him."'" By this time, the talking Black Stone had delivered ninety percent of the Qur'an, so Muhammad was familiar with interpreting their special form of communication.

The next Hadith is among the most telling in Islam. *Bukhari:V4B52N220* "Allah's Apostle said, 'I have been sent with the shortest expressions bearing the widest meanings, and I have been made victorious with terror. While I was sleeping [besieging], the keys to the treasures of the world were brought to me and put in my hand.'" He started with his own family, the Quraysh, and then moved on to Yahweh's family, the Jews.

Some of the poetic highlights associated with this abusive behavior include: *Ishaq:440* "Helped by the Holy Spirit we smited Muhammad's foes. He is a true Messenger from the Compassionate, an Apostle reciting Allah's Book. He became honored in rank and station. So the Apostle sent a message to them with a sharp cutting sword." The "Holy Spirit" is another concept stolen from the Bible. It is grossly misapplied here. I cover the Holy Spirit's actual nature on page 608 in response to another bogus claim. But there was some Islamic truth revealed here. "The Apostle sent a message with a sharp cutting sword."

Ishaq:441 "A man who had neither shown treachery nor bad faith haply had a change of fortune and took revenge, cutting down their palm trees and killing the Nadir. A sharp sword in the hand of a brave man kills his adversary. The rabbis were disgraced for they denied mighty Lord Allah." *Ishaq:442* "Sword in hand we brought down the Nadir. By Muhammad's order we beguiled them." Actually it was the Muslims who were "beguiled."

Moving on, we find that it didn't take long before the Muslim militants needed another fix: *Tabari VII:162/Ishaq:445* "There is a difference of opinion as to which of his expeditions [terrorist raids] took place after the one against the Banu Nadir. Some say

Muhammad remained in Yathrib for two months before leading a raid on Najd, directed against the Banu Muharib and Tha'labah. As the armies approached one another, no fighting took place, because our army was afraid of theirs." Allah's killer angels must have been preoccupied. This also suggests that the Nadir Jews were unarmed.

The Sira and Sunnah say: *Tabari VII:162/Ishaq:445* "The rules of the Prayer of Fear were revealed during this raid. [And confirmed in surah 4:102] The Messenger of Allah divided the Companions into two groups; one stood facing the enemy while the other stood behind the Prophet. He magnified Allah by shouting 'Allahu Akbar.' Then he and those behind him performed a rak'ah and prostrated themselves." Magnifying Allah is "The Prayer of Fear"—how appropriate for a terrorist dogma. According to the Hadith, "The Prayer of Fear" is comprised of shouting: "Allahu Akbar!"—"Allah is Greatest!"

Greater than whom is the obvious question. Greater than Ar-Rahman? Greater than Hubal, Al-Lat, Al-Uzza, or Manat? Or does Allah want to be greater than Yahweh? And while you might think that I'm poking fun, I'm not. This is a lose-lose game for Islam. If Allah is claiming to be the greatest pagan god, Islam is a farce. And Allah cannot be greater than Yahweh because he claimed to be the Ilah of Abraham and the author of the Torah and Gospels.

"Allahu Akbar!" is the war chant of Islamic terrorists everywhere, even today. The fact it's called "The Prayer of Fear" reveals the doctrine's purpose.

Islamic dictionaries translate "Allahu Akbar" as "Allah is Greater, Greatest, or Most Great." Yet contemporary Muslim apologists would prefer you to believe that it means "God is Great." Those who profit from imposing Islam recognize that exposing such truth would devastate their power base. So they willfully and knowingly contradict Allah and Muhammad, the Qur'an and Sunnah, to protect what they covet. Since so much is at stake, let's examine Islam's most telling and most frequently quoted slogan in context. While out on a terrorist raid: "The Prophet *magnified* Allah by shouting 'Allahu Akbar.'" To "magnify" is to make bigger or greater. Yet God is infinate. Yahweh cannot be magnified or be made greater. But a *man* can be magnified, and so can Satan.

The only scenario in which Islam's most important slogan makes sense is as follows: Muhammad created Allah's persona. A rock idol became his alter ego. But it was worse than that. Muhammad was possessed, selling his soul to the Devil. He spoke on Lucifer's behalf. The fallen angel masqueraded as Gabriel and inspired much of the Qur'an. Insecure and insignificant, deceitful, evil, and covetous, they needed to be feared and to be magnified.

In the overall scope of things, this next Tradition is of little consequence. Yet, in its own way, it helps establish the relationship between the true nature of Islam and the behavior of Muslims. *Tabari VII:164* "We went out with the Messenger on a raid to Dhat Riqa in the neighborhood of Nakhl. At one point, a Muslim killed a polytheist woman. When Muhammad was on his way back to Yathrib, her husband swore he would not rest until he had wrought bloodshed among the Prophet's Companions. He followed our tracks. Muhammad set up guards at night, an Ansar and an Emigrant.... The woman's husband saw them and shot an arrow. The Ansari pulled it out, put it down, and remained standing in prayer. The man shot a second and third arrow at him, but exactly the same thing happened. Finally the Ansari, after bowing and prostrating himself, woke his companion. 'Sit up. I have been wounded.' The Emigrant leapt to his feet. When the woman's husband saw the two of them there, he fled. Then the Emigrant, seeing the Ansari's bloodstained condition, exclaimed, 'Allah Almighty! Why didn't you wake me the first time he shot you?' 'I was in the middle of reciting a Surah and I did not want to stop without finishing it.'" Islam precludes rational thought and behavior.

After murdering one man's wife, Muhammad added a sixth to his harem. *Tabari VII:167* "The Messenger married Umm Salamah. In this year also, the Prophet commanded Zayd bin Thabit to study the Book of the Jews, saying, 'I fear that they may change my Book.' In this year the polytheists were in charge of the Meccan Pilgrimage." These three sentences end year four of the Islamic Era. An overly-sexed prophet comes within one of having a different girl for every night of the week. Then the prophetic imposter called the Bible his book, rather than Allah's, and said that he was afraid the Jews would change it. Muhammad may, therefore, have been so delusional that he thought these local Jews would alter Scripture to foil him. Or he was so deviously deceitful, he needed more scripture than the Jews were willing to sell. So he asked Zayd to study the "Book" as a source of future Qur'an revelations. And finally, proving that Islam was just regurgitated paganism, the Pilgrimage, or Hajj, was in the hands of the polytheists.

Opening Volume VIII of Tabari's History, *The Victory of Islam,* we are confronted by an editor's note. Rather somber in tone, it reveals that years five through eight of the Islamic Era were ugly. We discover: "The religion embodied in the Qur'an changed dramatically. Mecca capitulated. Medina became a purely Muslim polity. The last remaining Jewish tribe was annihilated. Internal Arab opposition from the 'hypocrites,' disintegrated. In short, although Muhammad had begun the period as a local phenomenon, by the end he was 'King of Arabia.'"

But some things remained the same. If six wives were good, seven were better. *Tabari VIII:1* "In this year the Messenger married Zaynab bt. Jahsh [a first cousin]." But it wasn't as simple as all of that. The story that follows may be more shocking than pedophilia—and that's because Allah wallows in it.

It begins with our hero stumbling into the home of his adopted son Zyad. "Allah's Messenger came to the house of Zayd bin [son of] Muhammad. Perhaps the Messenger missed him at that moment. Zaynab, Zayd's wife, rose to meet him. Because she was dressed only in a shift, the Holy Prophet turned away from her. She said: 'He is not here. Come in, you are as dear to me as my father and mother!' Muhammad refused to enter. Zaynab had dressed in haste when she heard that the Prophet was at her door. She jumped up eagerly and excited the admiration of Allah's Messenger, so that he turned away murmuring something that could scarcely be understood. However, he did say overtly, 'Glory be to Allah Almighty, who causes hearts to turn!'" (That, of course, would make Allah the god of lust, better known as Lucifer.)

Since the Islamic Era dawned with pedophilia, it should be no surprise that our lustful libertine has migrated to the verge of incest. The same man who asked his son Ali to serve as bait for Arab swordsmen in Mecca and a Jewish rock roller in Medina now sends his other son, Zayd, off on a terrorist raid so that he might excitedly admire his daughter-in-law. Glory be.

Tabari VIII:2 "When Zayd came home Zaynab told him that Muhammad had come. Zayd said, 'Why didn't you ask him to come in?' Zaynab replied, 'I asked him but he refused.' 'Did he say anything?' 'Glory be to Allah Almighty, who causes hearts to turn!' So Zayd went to Muhammad. 'Prophet, I have heard that you came to my house. Why didn't you go in? [Dad,] Perhaps Zaynab has excited your admiration, so I will leave her.'"

Tabari VIII:3 "Zayd left her, and she became free. While the Messenger of Allah was talking with Aisha, a fainting overcame him. When he was released from it, he smiled and said, 'Who will go to Zaynab to tell her the good news? Allah has married her to me.'" Gods like that can only be found buried in Arabian rock piles. "Then the Holy Prophet recited [Qur'an 33] to the end of the passage. Aisha said, 'I became very uneasy because of what we heard about her beauty and another thing, the loftiest of matters—what Allah had done for her by personally giving her to him in marriage. I said that she would boast of it over us.'" The victim of prophetic pedophilia had become so insecure, she was jealous of the object of inspired incest. This isn't a very attractive picture.

Before we peek into the 33rd surah to see why the god of Islam authorized his lone prophet to indulge in this kind of immorality, let's examine a second Hadith. Incest is a serious offense. If Allah's lone conduit was guilty of such a crime, he became worthy of condemnation, not admiration. *Tabari VIII:4* "One day Muhammad went out looking for Zayd. Now there was a covering of haircloth over the doorway, but the wind had lifted the covering so that the doorway was uncovered. Zaynab was in her chamber, undressed, and admiration for her entered the heart of the Prophet. After that Allah made her unattractive to Zayd.'"

Now that we have exposed Zaynab and confirmed that the motive was lust, it's time to expose Allah and the nature of Muhammad's situational scriptures. While the 33rd surah, called **"The Confederates,"** isn't the Qur'an's most lethal, it is the most vulgar. *033.001* **"Prophet (Muhammad)! Fear Allah, and do not obey the Disbelievers and Hypocrites: Lo! Allah is Knower, Wise."** A second translation says: **"Prophet! Be careful of Allah and do not comply with the unbelievers and hypocrites."** Allah is condemning "hypocrites,"—the same people Muhammad has been assailing for being peaceful and disobedient Muslims. But in the context of this story on incest, it's lunacy for him to do so. Our boy was committing pedophilia while lusting for incest and Allah had the nerve to call his critics hypocrites! The greatest hypocrite who ever lived prevailed by projecting his own faults on those with the good sense to question his scandalous lifestyle.

033.002 **"Follow that which comes to you by inspiration from your Lord: for Allah is well acquainted with (all) that you do."** The last Hadith said that while engaged in pedophilia with Aisha, the prophet was inspired to commit incest with Zaynab. If you were wavering on whether the Qur'an was divine revelation or simply situational scriptures, you have just been given a rather profound clue. Imagine the preposterousness of God jotting down and then endorsing a specific incident of prophet immorality before creating the universe and then handing such rubbish down to a pirate as his final revelation to mankind. Yet that is precisely what must have happened if Islam is to be believed.

033.003 **"And put your trust in Allah; enough is Allah as a disposer of affairs. [A garbage disposal is more like it.] Allah has not made for any man two hearts in his body: nor has He made your wives whom you divorce your mothers: nor has He made your adopted sons your sons. Such is (only) your (manner of) speech by your mouths. But Allah tells the Truth, and He shows the (right) Way."** Endorsing incest is sticky business. So that we aren't too rash in our condemnation, let's give the Islamic god another chance: **"Allah hath not assigned unto any man two hearts within his body, nor hath He made your wives whom ye declare your mothers, nor hath He made those whom ye claim (to be your sons) your sons. This is but a saying of your mouths. But Allah saith the truth and He showeth the way."** That translation wasn't any better.

A third and fourth translation serve to confirm my original theory of child abuse stemming from Muhammad's mother having abandoned him. If this occurred it would explain why he craved women, why he mistreated them, and why he saw them fulfilling maternal roles. **"Allah has not made for any man two hearts within him; nor has He made your wives who you liken to your mother, nor has He made those whom you assert to be your sons your real sons..."** And: **"...your wives whom you declare to be like your mother, your real mother..."**

Next, Lucifer demeans adoption to satiate Muhammad's cravings. *033.005* **"Call them by (the names of) their fathers: that is juster in the sight of Allah. But if ye know not their father's (names, call them) your brothers in faith, or your slaves. But there is no blame on you if ye make a mistake therein. (What counts is) the intention of your heart: and Allah is Oft-Returning, Most Merciful."**

This pathetic pretence of scripture continues to wallow in the muck of Muhammad's troubled mind. *033.006* **"The Prophet has a greater claim on the faithful than they have on themselves, and his wives are their mothers. And the possessors of relationship have the better claim in the ordinance of Allah to inheritance, one with respect to another, than (other) believers, and (than) those who have fled: nevertheless do what is just to your closest friends: This is written in the Book."** Let me take a whack at interpreting this for you. A fifty-seven year-old man in bed with a twelve year-old girl just told us that his god, a pagan rock idol, inspired him to say that he has first dibs on anyone and anything he covets. "Themselves" refers to people and "inheritance" refers to money. Then to assure that his fellow Muslims would support him, he says that they are next in line to be abused. And what makes this so damning is that the justification is alleged to be scriptural. It's the heavenly endorsement of the Profitable Prophet Plan—the means to steal power, sex, and money.

Islam is a paper-thin scam. It was perpetrated to satisfy Muhammad's insecurity. *Bukhari:V8B78N628* **"The Prophet was holding Umar's hand. 'O Allah's Apostle! You are dearer to me than everything except my own self.' The Prophet said, 'No, by Him in Whose Hand my soul is, you will not have faith till I am dearer to you than your own self.' Then Umar said, 'However, now, by Allah, you are dearer to me than my own self.' The Prophet said, 'Now, Umar, you are a believer.'"** That was all there was to Islam.

But so that it wouldn't be obvious to the unthinking, Muhammad confounded them with garbage like: *033.007* **"And remember We took from the prophets their covenant: As from thee: from Noah, Abraham, Moses, and Jesus: We took from them a solemn covenant: That (Allah) may question the (custodians) of Truth concerning the Truth they (were charged with): And He has prepared for the Unbelievers a grievous Penalty."** A second translation reads: **"That He may ask the loyal of their loyalty. And He hath prepared a painful doom for the unbelievers."** Even with the parenthetical explanations added by the translators, it's senseless. "Covenants" are reciprocal agreements; they can't be taken. And what's up with "the loyal of their loyalty." Moreover, why lash out at unbelievers? What have they done?

If I'm right, what's really happening here is that Muhammad made a deal with the Devil. Satan promised him power, sex, and money. But Lucifer wanted something in return—Islam—a doctrine founded on deceit, death, and damnation. He wanted to be worshiped as God. (Not loved, by the way, which is why Islamic "worship" is comprised entirely of obligatory duties and prostrations.) And knowing that there was a real God, Lucifer wanted Yahweh's chosen people abused and their scriptures assailed. Then he wanted Muhammad to attack Christ, revealing scripture that placed the Messiah beneath him. And from what I can tell, they both got what they bargained for.

But the Demonic Covenant, the Religion of fools, by fools, and for fools, was too foolish to remember what had happened one battle to the next. So now we're told that the Badr victory was due to a hurricane. *033.009* **"O ye who believe! Remember the Grace of Allah on you when there came down an army. But We sent against them a hurricane and forces that ye saw not: but Allah sees all that ye do. Behold! They came on from above and from below you, and eyes became dim and hearts gaped up to the throats, stupefied with terror, and ye imagined various vain thoughts about Allah!"** The deceitful duo is protesting: "I know you couldn't see the angels, and a hurricane in Arabia is pushing it, but trust me on this, they were there all the same. Sure, it seems laughable, causing you to think various vain thoughts about Allah, but you just gotta believe us. Otherwise, how am I going to justify stealing your money, mind, soul, and freedom?"

In a related Hadith: *Bukhari:V8B75N417* **"Allah's Messenger said, 'Allah has some** angels who look for those who think about Allah while they're out [fighting] and they encircle them with their wings. Allah [who hears all] asks these angels, 'What do my slaves say?' The angels reply, 'Allahu Akbar!' Allah [who sees all] asks, 'Can they see Me?' The angels answer, 'No. They can't see you.' Allah [who knows all] says, 'How would it have been if they had seen Me?' 'If they had seen You [one spirit said to another] they would have worshiped you more.' Allah [who created the largest brothel] asks, 'What do they desire?' 'They ask for your Paradise.' 'Have they seen it?' 'No. But if they had they would covet it all the more.' 'What do they fear?' 'Hell Fire.' 'Have they seen it?' 'No. If they had seen it they would flee it with extreme fear.' Allah said, 'I will not reduce every Companion to misery.'" Lucifer knows that fear is more compelling than lust. That is why his brothel is described in five surahs and hell's torments are threatened 1,000 times.

Moving on with our romp through Muhammad's personal scriptures, we learn that even the militants were aghast. *033.011* **"In that situation the Believers were sorely tried and shaken as by a tremendous shaking. And behold! The Hypocrites and those in whose hearts is a disease said: 'Allah and His Messenger promised us nothing but delusion!' Or… "Allah and His Messenger promised only to deceive us."** The bad Muslims, or hypocrites, are now "diseased" because they had the common sense and courage to say that Muhammad's mutterings were deceptive. In Islam, morality is a sickness. Sanity is a disease.

Awkwardly transitioning to Uhud, the prophet reveals: *033.013* **"Behold! A party among them said: 'Men of Yathrib! You cannot stand (the attack); therefore go back!' And a band of them asked for leave of the Prophet, saying, 'Our houses are bare and exposed,' though they were not exposed. They intended nothing but to run away. If the enemy [Meccan merchants] had entered from all sides [of Yathrib] and had they been exhorted to treachery, they would have committed it, and they would not have hesitated."** In Islam, peace is treachery. Everything is upside down.

Next, our tattered hero uses the Pledge of Aqabah, the oath of war that preceded the Hijrah, to condemn peaceful Muslims: *033.014* **"And yet they had already covenanted with Allah not to turn their backs, and a covenant with Allah must be answered."** At the Pledge of Aqabah, allegiance was sworn to Muhammad, not Allah. The first Muslims said it was an **"oath to wage war against all mankind."**

In a second translation: **"And verily they had already sworn to Allah that they would not turn their backs (to a foe). An oath to Allah must be adhered to. Say: 'Running away will not profit you if you are running away from death or slaughter; and even if (you escape), no more than a brief (respite) will you be allowed!'"** This verse is so devastating to the "peaceful myth" of Islam, it deserves a third look: **"Say: Flight will not avail you if you flee from death, killing, or slaughter. In that case you will not be allowed to enjoy yourselves but a little while. Say, 'Who will screen you, saving you from Allah if he intends to harm and injure you?'"**

This sounds like Stalin's command at the battle of Stalingrad. He ordered his comrades to eliminate any Russian who fled from death, killing, or slaughter. There were as many guns pointed at their backs as there were in their faces. Muhammad and Allah are saying the same thing to their comrades. "If you don't fight to the death for us, we will kill you ourselves." And throughout time good Muslims have done just that. They have slaughtered millions more bad Muslims than they have good infidels.

Pacifists really annoyed Islam's war god. *033.018* **"Verily Allah already knows those among you who keep back and those who say to their brethren, 'Come along to us,' but come not to the fight in the stress of battle except for just a little while. Being covetous and niggardly with respect to you; but when fear comes, you will see them looking to you, their eyes rolling like one swooning because of death. But when the fear is gone they smite you with sharp tongues, covetous of goods, in their greed for wealth (from the spoil). Such men have no faith, and so Allah has made their deeds of none effect: and that is easy for Allah."** Bad Muslims pretend to go along with the program but when the going gets tough, they don't fight; they faint. They only want the booty. So Allah will nullify their deeds sending every peaceful Muslim to hell.

The devilish duet consistently defines "bad Muslims" as nonviolent. *033.020* **"They...wish the allied clans were (wandering) in the desert among the Bedouins. But if they were in your midst, they would only battle or fight with them for moment."**

The next verse is among the most important in Islam. It makes every word in the Hadith relevant. *033.021* **"You have in (Muhammad) the Messenger of Allah a beautiful pattern of conduct for any one to follow."** Islamic terrorists the world over are doing just that. They are following the **"beautiful pattern of conduct"** established by Muhammad. They are simply following his example, heeding Allah's advice.

Other translations read: *033.021* **"Verily in the Messenger of Allah you have a good example for him who looks unto Allah and the Last Day."** Or: **"Certainly you have in the Messenger of Allah an excellent prototype..."** And: **"You have indeed a noble paradigm [archetype, exemplar, standard, model, or pattern] to follow in Allah's Apostle."** The Hadith agrees with Allah's assessment. *BukhariV7B63N1891* **"Indeed in the Apostle of Allah you have a good example to follow."**

Reading the Ishaq, Tabari, Bukhari, and Muslim Hadith Collections is essential because Allah told Muslims to follow Muhammad's example. Yet the behavior recorded in these books is criminal. They say that Muhammad was incestuous, a pedophile, pirate, liar, thief, sexual libertine, rapist, sadist, sexist, assassin, kidnapper, slave trader, racist and war-mongering terrorist. He got his jollies slaughtering all who didn't capitulate. So following his example would make one a very bad person.

If you think the world needs more people like Muhammad, then let's let Muslims build more mosques. And while we're at it, let's continue to transfer a billion dollars a day into the coffers of those who manufacture men in the mold of Muhammad. Just think of what a wonderful world it would be.

I'm going to skip over the next seven verses of the 33rd surah, called the **"Allied Troops."** They speak of atrocities yet to come. Another battle must be fought with the Arabs and another Jewish settlement must be annihilated before we are ready to hear Allah's justification.

But you need to know that the transition I have omitted (for now) is the worst in the Qur'an. Satan segues from genocide to lust without a single intervening verse. It's proof that the Qur'an was composed by a lesser life form. While we will review these passages later, the 26th and 27th verses of the 33rd surah are the most heinous in the Qur'an. They speak of horrific terror, Holocaust style genocide, grand larceny, and selling women and children into slavery. Then without missing a beat, Allah speaks to Muhammad about his playthings, his wives and consorts, and their glittering adornments: *033.028* "**O Prophet, say to your wives and consorts: 'If you desire this world's life and its glittering adornment, then come! I will provide them for your enjoyment and set you free in a handsome manner. And if you desire Allah and His Messenger and the latter abode, then lo! Allah hath prepared for the good-doers an immense reward.**" It's hard to tell if the prophet wasn't desirable and was thus trying to buy sex or if he wanted to bribe his consorts into leaving so that he could collect a fresh batch.

Aisha explains: *BukhariV7B63N188* "**The Prophet gave us the option (to remain with him or to be divorced) and we selected Allah and His Apostle.**" Even when it came to sex, Allah and his Apostle were inseparable. It's another important clue.

The addition of Zaynab and her exotic charms to the prophet's lair stirred up a hornet's nest and caused dissention in the ranks. So the unbridled pervert had his "god" warn the remainder of his sex toys: *033.030* "**O Consorts of the Prophet! If any of you are guilty of unseemly conduct, shamelessness, or lewdness, the punishment will be doubled, and that is easy for Allah. But any of you that is devout, obedient, and submissive in the service to Allah and His Messenger, and does good, to her shall We grant her reward twice. We have prepared for her a generously rich provision.**"

When situational scriptures focus on murdering neighbors, stealing property, and sexual submissiveness, we have a problem. Good and bad Muslims alike have read these "scriptures" for 1400 years, and yet they seem oblivious to the fact they are ungodly. Therefore, one of only two conclusions can be drawn. Either Islam has corrupted souls and corroded minds to the point that Muslims can no longer reason, or the sword of Islam has prevented them from acting rationally. But either way, unless we free Muslims from Islam and establish in its stead a credible educational curriculum, there is no hope. Tyranny and terror will march on for benefit of cleric and king.

Under the pretense of Qur'an revelation, Muhammad lectured his wives and put down the revolt that emanated from his incestuous act. *033.032* "**O Consorts of the Prophet! You are not like any of the (other) women. Fear and keep your duty, lest one in whose heart is a disease should be moved with desire. Stay quietly in your apartment. Make not a dazzling display like that of the former times of Ignorance. Perform the devotion, pay the zakat; and obey Allah and His Messenger. And Allah wishes to cleanse you with a thorough cleansing. And bear in mind that which is recited in your** houses of the revelations of Allah and the wisdom." It's hard to believe that anyone thinks these self-serving words are scripture.

His harem in check, we find Muhammad confirming the central message of Islam: surrender, submit, obey, and pay. *033.035* "Lo! Men who surrender, and women who submit, and who believe and obey...who are humble, and pay the tax, and men who fast and guard their modesty and private parts—Allah hath prepared for them forgiveness and a vast reward." While forgiveness sounds religious, contemplate what one would be forgiven for—Allah has condoned every perverse act known to man. And while we're poking holes, ponder why a doctrine built on predestination rather than choice would even bother with forgiveness.

By way of example: *033.036* "It is not fitting for a Muslim man or woman to have any choice in their affairs when a matter has been decided for them by Allah and His Messenger. They have no option. If any one disobeys Allah and His Messenger, he is indeed on a wrong Path." That was a wonderful explanation of Muhammad's motivation for implementing Islam. And it coincides perfectly with Hitler's motivation for implementing Nazism.

Now that Allah has reconfirmed that Islam is devoid of choice, merely a doctrine of submission, it's time for another situational scripture condoning incest—the marriage of a father to his daughter-in-law. Muhammad's Muslims knew it was wrong, and they were assailing their dictator. So the tyrant said his spirit friend revealed a verse which I'm going to leave in "King James" English so that you might appreciate its religious flair. (As an interesting aside, I was curious as to how long ago the "thee and thou" translation was made so as to determine if using 400-year-old English was reasonable or just another Islamic deception. The first Qur'an I opened said that it was completed courtesy of a 1419 A.H. endowment. That's the year 2041 A.D.) *033.037* "Behold! Thou didst say to one who had received the grace of Allah and thy favor: 'Retain thou thy wife, and fear Allah.' But thou didst hide in thy mind and thy heart that which Allah was about to make manifest: thou didst fear the people, but it is more fitting that thou shouldst fear Allah. Then when Zayd had dissolved (his marriage) with her, with the necessary (formality), We gave her to thee, joining her in marriage to thee: in order that there may be no difficulty or sin for the Believers in the wives of their adopted sons, when the latter have dissolved with the necessary (formality) (their marriage) with them. And Allah's command must be fulfilled." The odds against our Creator approving incest are incalculable.

Not finished indicting himself, Satan now claims that incest is an ordained *duty*, that all messengers are scumbags, and that old societal values are passé. *033.038* "There can be no difficulty, harm, or reproach to the Prophet in doing what Allah has ordained to him as a duty. It was the practice (approved) of Allah amongst those of old that have passed away. And the commandment of Allah is a decree determined. (It is the practice of those) who deliver the Messages of Allah, and fear Him. Allah keeps good account. Muhammad is not the father of any of your men, but (he is) the Messenger of Allah, and the Last of the Prophets with the Seal: and Allah has full knowledge of all things." The hairy mole "seal" on his back was as phony as his pretending to be a prophet. And no prophet was ever commanded to be immoral.

In the next series of verses the god of incest wallows in self promotion. He bribes Muslims with promises of generous rewards, and says that his overly sexed messenger is "a lamp spreading light." This is followed by another attack on the "bad" Muslims—the Hypocrites—who were obviously troubled by the "prophet's" immorality. *033.048* "And obey not (the behests) of the Unbelievers and the Hypocrites. Disregard their noxious talk and heed not their annoyances, but put thy trust in Allah. For enough is Allah as a Disposer of affairs."

No sane person would even contemplate uttering the following words. Muhammad's willingness to satiate his carnal desires by attributing them to God takes us beyond depravity. The Qur'an claims that Muhammad can have as many wives as he wants. He can have sex with prisoners, cousins, nieces, and captives. *033.050* "O Prophet! We have made lawful to you all the wives to whom you have paid dowers [with stolen property]; and those whom your hands possess out of the prisoners of war spoils whom Allah has assigned to you; and daughters of your paternal uncles and aunts, and daughters of your maternal uncles and aunts, who migrated with you; and any believing woman who dedicates her soul to the Prophet if the Prophet wishes her; this is a privilege for you only, and not for the rest of the Believers; We know what We have appointed for them as to their wives and the captives whom they possess; in order that there should be no difficulty for you and that you should be free from blame."

Sex with a prisoner is rape—a crime Muhammad would commit countless times with his god's approval. Sex with family members is incest. Sex with youngsters is pedophilia. Sex with many wives is polygamy. Sex with anyone you wish is either fornication or prostitution, depending on whether money changes hands. And offering fellow militants sex with "the captives they possess" is bribery. There is only one spirit demented enough to approve such a lurid laundry list of offenses—Satan. And frankly, some of this is beneath *him*.

Now that Allah had approved pedophilia, rape, incest, fornication, prostitution, bribery, and polygamy, it's time to ordain an orgy. *033.051* "You may put off whom you please, and you may take to you whomever you desire. You may defer any of them you please, and you may have whomever you desire; there is no blame on you if you invite one who you had set aside. It is no sin. They should all be pleased with whatever you give them. Allah knows what is in your heart." Wow! Speaking of sex, Allah said: "You may have whomever you desire. There is no blame." This is so blatantly devoid of morality, it's a disgrace to call Islam a religion. Even Hitler was better than this.

Now that we've got an orgy going, how about gluttony? And with all this hedonism, Allah wants Muslims to give Muhammad the time he needs to enjoy his brothel (which, by the way, is his mosque—they were literally one in the same). *033.053* "O ye who believe! Enter not the Prophet's apartments until leave is given you for a meal. (And then) not (so early as) to wait for its preparation. But when you are invited, enter; and, when your meal is ended, then disperse. Linger not for conversation. Lo! that would cause annoyance to the Prophet. Such (behavior) bothers him. He is ashamed to dismiss you, but Allah is not ashamed (to tell you) the truth. And when ye ask (his ladies) for anything, ask them from behind a screen: that makes for greater purity for your hearts and for theirs. Nor is it right for you that you should annoy Allah's Messenger, or that you should marry his widows after him at any time. Truly such a thing is in Allah's sight an enormous offense." This is stunning. Conversation with a "messenger" is an "annoyance." People "bother" an "apostle." A "prophet" is "ashamed" to "tell the truth." After all the evil Allah has drenched us in throughout this surah, this is unconscionable. If conversation is an annoyance, if people are a bother, and if truth is shameful, then there was obviously an ulterior motive for Islam—for it's for damn sure (literally) it has got nothing to do with revealing truth or saving souls.

No! Islam is about an insecure man coveting power, sex, and money. Period. The last line is proof. Only an insanely insecure man would fear his widows having sex with another man after he was gone.

I find it laughable that Muhammad purports the Qur'an to be eternal, a perfect book, written by the pen before time began, when so much of it is preoccupied with his temporal situation and carnal desires. Methinks Muhammad was simply making it up as he went along to achieve whatever he craved. *033.054* "Whether you divulge anything or conceal it, verily Allah has full knowledge of all things." *033.056* "Allah and His angels shower blessings on the Prophet. So O ye who believe! Send your blessings on him, and salute him with all respect—a worthy salutation." *Heil Hitler!* "Those who annoy Allah and His Messenger and speak evil things of them—Allah has cursed them in this World and in the Hereafter, and has prepared for them a humiliating Punishment—the doom of torment for the disdained." It's not hard to see where der fuhrer got his ideas. *033.058* "And those who annoy or malign Muslims bear (on themselves) a crime of calumny [Hitler's favorite word] and a glaring sin."

Now that we have made Muhammad's sex toys subservient to their master, and Muslims subservient to Muhammad, it's time to institute one of the most demeaning religious doctrines of all time—the veiling of Islamic women. *033.059* "Prophet! Tell your wives and daughters and all Muslim women to draw cloaks and veils all over their bodies (screening themselves completely except for one or two eyes to see the way). That will be better. They will not be annoyed and molested." Actually, by degrading women this way, they *are* "annoyed and molested."

With women subdued, Allah wants Muslims to know that those who speak out against his immorality and violence will be terrorized—literally. *033.060* "Truly, if the Hypocrites, those in whose hearts is a disease, those who stir up sedition, the agitators in the City, do not desist, We shall urge you (Muhammad) to go against them and set you over them. Then they will not be able to stay as your neighbor for any length of time. They shall have a curse on them. Whenever they are found, they shall be seized and slain without mercy—a fierce slaughter—murdered, a horrible murdering. (Such was) the practice (approved) of Allah among those who lived before. No change wilt thou find in the practice of Allah." Allah is a confessed murderer. He is a savage and merciless terrorist. According to this surah, he is insatiable. And keep in mind, the crime that earned Allah's wrath—the godly seizure and torment— was sedition and agitation. If you speak out against Islam's demonic teachings you will be demonized.

Islam isn't the only doctrine that terrorizes those it cannot subdue. Hitler's Nazism, Lenin's Communism, and the Pope's Catholicism all did the same thing. Three of the four even claimed to have divine authority for inflicting terror. But since we don't tolerate such behavior any more, why do we tolerate Islam? The Qur'an just ordered Muslims to seize, terrorize, and brutally murder anyone who disagrees with them. **"The agitators...have a curse on them. When they are found they will be seized and slain without mercy."** That's an unconscionable position—one completely incompatible with peace or civility.

Before we move on, I'd like to make an important distinction. The inspiration for the intolerance and brutality of Islam, Nazism, and Communism is markedly different than that of Catholicism. With Islam, Nazism, and Communism, the founders themselves were the problem. Their religotics were born ugly. Muhammad, Hitler, and Lenin were disgusting, demented, deceitful, power-hungry demagogues. The Catholic clergy had to corrupt Christ's message to justify their brutality. In fact, they had to hide Christ's message—outlawing Bibles and sermons in the common tongue—to perpetrate their ill-advised schemes.

However, if one sees Constantine, not Christ, as Catholicism's founder, all four religotics are identical. This may be why Pope John Paul II bowed to and kissed a Qur'an publicly, acknowledging his respect for it in front of cameras. It is why item #841 of the Catechism says: "The Church's relationship with Muslims: The plan of salvation also includes those who acknowledge the Creator. In the *first* place amongst whom are the *Muslims*. They profess to hold the faith of Abraham, and together with us adore the one, merciful God, mankind's judge on the last day."

Marching ever toward hell, the Qur'an proclaims: *033.064* **"Verily Allah has cursed the Unbelievers [whom he defines as Christians in the 5th surah] and has prepared for them a Blazing Fire to dwell in forever. No protector will they find, nor savior. That Day their faces will be turned upside down in the Fire. They will say: 'Woe to us! We should have obeyed Allah and obeyed the Messenger!' 'Our Lord! Give them double torment and curse them with a very great Curse!'"** That's quite a picture. Allah is threatening to turn us upside down and rub our faces in the fire while Muhammad screams: **"Give them a double dose of torment! Curse them!"** Something tells me that this really isn't God speaking and Muhammad isn't a prophet. But hey, all I've got to go by are their scriptures.

The next verse requires some explanation. Allah said, *033.069* **"Believers, be** not like those who annoyed Moses. Allah proved his innocence of that which they alleged." The allegation isn't presented in the Qur'an. Allah simply moves on. So I'd like to share a moment of levity. Had Allah really been Yahweh, this is what you would have read in the Torah: *Bukhari:V4B55N616* **"Allah's Apostle said, 'The Prophet Moses was a shy person and used to cover his body. An Israeli insulted him, saying, "He covers it because of some defect like leprosy or scrotal hernia." Allah wished to clear Moses of this allegation, so one day he took off his clothes, put them on a stone and started taking a bath. When he moved towards his clothes the stone took them and fled. Moses picked up his staff and ran after the stone saying, "O stone! Give me back my clothes!" He reached some Israelis who saw him naked, and found him to be the best of what Allah had created. The stone stopped there and Moses took his garments and started hitting the stone with his stick. By Allah, the stone still has some traces of the hitting, three, four or five marks. This was what Allah meant when he revealed the surah saying: "O you who believe! Be you not like those who annoyed Moses. Allah proved his innocence of that which they alleged."'"** I vote we keep the Ten Commandments in the Bible instead.

The **"Allied Troops"** surah ends with Allah proclaiming that men were his fourth choice, and that we are foolish and ignorant tyrants. *033.072* **"We did indeed offer the opportunity to the Heavens, the Earth, the Mountains, but they refused to take it, being afraid (of Allah's torment). But man undertook it. He was unjust and foolish. Lo, he has proved a tyrant and fool, ignorant. Allah has to punish the Hypocrites, men and women, and the Unbelievers."** The 33rd surah is sufficient to prove that Islam is a fraud, an intolerant, immoral, and vicious scheme that must be condemned.

Returning to the Hadith, we find Muhammad out terrorizing his neighbors. Evil is as evil does. *Tabari VIII:4/Ishaq:449* **"In the fourth year of the Islamic Era the Prophet led a raid against Dumat Jandah because word had reached him that they had approached his territories."**

This brings us to the Battle of the Trench. *Tabari VIII:6* **"What brought on the battle, according to what has been reported, was related to the expulsion of the Banu Nadir from their settlements by Allah's Apostle."**

Ishaq:450 **"The account of the trench is as follows. A group of Jews were the ones who assembled parties against the Messenger. They went to the Quraysh in Mecca and invited them to rid themselves of Muhammad. They said, 'We will be with you against him until we root him out.'"** While it is easy to understand why the Jews who had been harassed, besieged, cast out of their ancestral homes, and looted might have been miffed at our illustrious Profit, their offer couldn't have been credible to the Quraysh. Since they hadn't lifted a finger to defend themselves against Muhammad's aggression, how were they going to assist others?

Tabari VIII:7 **"The Quraysh said: 'Jews, you are the people of the first Scripture, and you have knowledge about the subject on which we and Muhammad have come to differ. Is our** religion better or his?' 'Your religion is better,' they said. 'You are closer to the truth than he.'" Based upon what we have read in the Hadith and Qur'an, that wasn't saying much. *Voodoo* is closer to the truth than Islam.

Ishaq:450 "They are the ones concerning whom Allah revealed: 'Have you not seen those to whom a portion of the Scripture has been given? They believe in idols and false deities. They say, "These are more rightly guided than those who believe?"—until the words, "Hell is sufficient for their burning. They are jealous and Allah has cursed them."'" [Qur'an 4:51] The 4th surah is as packed with perversity and is as delirious as the 33rd. Attributing idols and false deities to the Jews was one of the many incoherent thoughts mumbled by the rock idol who claimed to be the Jewish God.

Tabari VIII:8/Ishaq:450 "When Muhammad received word of them and what they had determined to do, he laid out a trench to protect Medina. He encouraged the Muslims to dig it with promises of a Heavenly reward. The person who advised him about the trench was Salman. He said, 'In Persia, whenever we were surrounded, we would dig a trench to protect ourselves.' Certain men of the hypocrites slacked off and disobeyed the Messenger. They pretended to be too weak to work, slipping away to their families without the knowledge or permission of the Prophet." As we learned in the 33rd surah, Muhammad considered Muslims to be his personal property.

Composing scripture in Baghdad three hundred years after the fact, the sages attributed these words to their prophet: *Tabari VIII:12/Ishaq:451* "I have heard some stories about the digging of the trench in which there is an example of Allah justifying His Apostle and confirming his prophetic office. For example, Muhammad spat on a rock, sprinkled water on it, and it crumbled. Then the Apostle said, 'I struck the first blow and what you saw flash out was Iraq and Persia would see dog's teeth. Gabriel informed me that my nation would be victorious over them. Then I struck my second blow, and what flashed out was for the pale men in the land of the Byzantines to be bitten by the dog's teeth. Gabriel informed me that my nation would be victorious over them. Then I struck my third blow and Gabriel told me that my nation would be victorious over Yemen. Rejoice, victory shall come. Praise be to Allah. He has promised us victory after tribulation. And this increased the Muslims faith and submission." With divine approval to make war: *Tabari VIII:13* "These cities were conquered in the time of Umar, Uthman, and others, Muslims used to say, 'Conquer for yourselves whatever seems good to you; for by Allah you have conquered no city but that Muhammad was given its keys beforehand.'"

Back in the pit: *Tabari VIII:13* "When Allah's Apostle finished the trench, the Quraysh came and encamped near streams with 10,000 men from many tribes. The Messenger went out with 3,000 Muslims. The enemy of Allah, Huyayy bin Akhtab, came to Ka'b bin Asad, who had formed a treaty with the Qurayza [the only remaining Jewish settlement in Yathrib]. Ka'b made a truce with Muhammad on behalf of his people. When Ka'b heard Huyayy, he shut the door in his face. Huyayy asked to be allowed in, but Ka'b refused. 'Woe to you, Huyayy,' answered Ka'b. 'You are a man who brings bad luck. I have made a treaty with Muhammad and will not break the pact. I have seen nothing but faithfulness and truth on his part.'" It's hard to imagine less believable dialog. The Qurayza, after all, had seen the Qaynuqa and Nadir settlements besieged my Muhammad. They had witnessed his deceit, violence, thievery, and barbarism.

Tabari VIII:15 "Ka'b said, 'Leave me alone to deal with Muhammad.' But Huyayy kept wheedling and twisting until Ka'b yielded. Huyayy promised, 'If the Quraysh and Ghatafan retreat without having killed Muhammad, I will enter your fortress so that whatever happens to you shall happen to me.' So Ka'b broke his treaty and renounced the bond." The Muslims, who can't keep their own story straight, cannot be believed when it comes to private conversations between opposing parties.

Tabari VIII:15 "When the news reached Muhammad, he sent Sa'd, chief of the Aws to Ka'b. 'If it is true, speak to me in words that we can understand but that will be unintelligible to others. So he went out and found them engaged in the worst of what had been reported. They slandered the Messenger and said, 'There is no treaty between us.' Sa'd reviled them, and they reviled him. Sa'd was a man with a sharp temper. He told the Jews, 'Stop reviling him for the disagreement between us is too serious for an exchange of taunts.'" Since Sa'd was easily the most enraged anti-Semite in Medina, the Jews would never have granted him an audience. And once given, they would never taunt him—proclaiming their vulnerability. So why did the Islamic sages go to the trouble of writing such irrational dialog? Might Muhammad have already turned on the Qurayza and needed an excuse to justify his rage? Stay tuned.

Returning to the siege of the Quraysh we find more evidence that Islam was all about money. *Tabari VIII:16/Ishaq:454* "Soon the trial became great for the Muslims and fear intensified. Their foe came at them from above and below, so that the believers were beset with fear. The hypocrisy of the hypocrites became evident. One said, 'Muhammad was promising us that we should eat up the treasures of Chosroes [the Persians] and Caesar [the Byzantines], and now none of us even can go out to relieve himself!'" We were told way back in Mecca that Muhammad lured Muslims into Islam by promising them that they would steal the treasures of the Persians and Byzantines by conquest. It must have been an effective ploy because even now the Medina Muslims were repeating it.

Unfortunately for the victims of Islamic terror, the Persian trench prevailed. The merchants of Mecca were unable to traverse the crude defense. *Tabari VIII:17* "The Muslims and the polytheists stayed in their positions for twenty nights with no fighting except for the shooting of arrows and the siege. When the trial became great for the people, the Messenger sent for the leaders of the Ghatafan [Meccan comrades]. He offered them a third of the date harvest of Medina on condition that they leave. [The bribe is interesting, as the dates being offered didn't belong to Muhammad.] The truce between the sides progressed to the point of drawing up a written document, but there was no witnessing or firm determination to make peace; it was only a matter of maneuvering." The prophet was a shifty fellow. But what I don't get is Muslims. Since Muhammad was so obviously willing to deceive, cheat, bribe, rape, kidnap, or kill anyone he met, why do they trust him with their soul?

The date farmers, having been corrupted by Islam, said, *Ishaq:454* "Now that

Allah has conferred Islam on us, and made us famous, shall we give them our property? By Allah, we will offer them only the sword until Allah judges between us.' 'As you wish,' said Allah's Messenger."

Tabari VIII:18 "The Quraysh rode out on their horses and said, 'Get ready for warfare. Today you shall know the real horsemen.' Then they advanced toward the trench [which they had been staring at for a month] and halted by it. When they saw it, they said, 'By Allah, this is a stratagem that the Arabs have never employed.'" How is it possible that these men could have been so dense that they didn't simply go to one of the many piles of dirt that had been taken out of the trench and push it back in?

They didn't, so we're told that Ali, the darling of the Shi'ites in Baghdad, challenged Amr to a duel: *Tabari VIII:18/Ishaq:455* "'I summon you to Allah, to His Messenger, and to Islam.' Amr replied, 'I have no use for these.' So Ali said, 'Then I summon you to fight.' Amr replied, 'Why, son of my brother? By Allah, I do not want to kill you.' Ali shouted, 'But I, by Allah, want to kill you.'" Islam is so poisonous men actually *want* to kill family members. "Amr jumped from his horse and advanced toward Ali. The two fought until Ali killed Amr. He shouted, 'Allahu Akbar!'" *Ishaq:456* "As he returned to the Apostle smiling with joy [for having killed his uncle] Jumar asked him if he had stripped Amr of his armor. 'No,' Ali answered. 'I saw his private parts and was ashamed.'"

Tabari VIII:19 "Nawfal plunged into the trench and became trapped in it. The Muslims pelted him with stones. He said, 'Arabs, a slaying is better than this.' So Ali went down and killed him. The Muslims took his corpse. They asked the Messenger to sell them his body. The Prophet said, 'We have no need for his body or its price. Do with it as you like.'" Just then, our favorite anti-Semite entered the fray. *Tabari VIII:20* "His mother said, 'Hurry up, son; you are late!' Aisha replied, 'I wish Sa'd's coat of mail were ampler. I fear for him.'"

Ishaq:457 "Sa'd was hit by an Arab arrow and the median vein of his arm was cut. He said, 'Allah make your face sweat in the hellfire, grant me martyrdom, and do not let me die until I see my desire done to the Qurayza.'" This is an odd request, even for an embittered racist. The arrow that had pierced him was from an Arab, not a Jew.

Speaking of Jews, this next Hadith provides an excellent look into Muslim minds. *Tabari VIII:22/Ishaq:458* "Hassan was with the women and children. A Jew passed by and began to walk around his settlement. There was no one to protect them while the Apostle and his Companions were at the Meccans' throats. So I said: 'Hassan, this Jew is walking around. I fear he will point out our weakness while the Muslims are too busy to attend to us. So go down to him and kill him." All this poor Jewish man did was take a walk. Yet in the paranoid mind of a Muslim woman, he was at war.

Tabari VIII:22/Ishaq:458 "'Allah forgive you, daughter of Abd al-Muttalib,' Hassan said. 'You know that I am not the man to do it.'" Muslim sages reject this Tradition because they are embarrassed by Hassan's cowardice. They aren't however, troubled by what happened next…"When he said that to me I saw that nothing could be expected from him. I girded myself, took a club, and, having gone down from the fortress to the man, I struck him with the club until I killed him. When I had finished with him, I returned to the fortress and said, 'Hassan, go down to him and strip him—only his being a man kept me from taking his clothes.' Hassan replied, 'I have no need for his spoils.'" The Jewish man was so menacing, a Muslim woman beat him to death with a club. And Islam was so corrosive, all the Muslim murderer could think about was stealing his possessions. Fundamental Islam did terrible things to people. This woman was so morally disoriented, she had no qualms about clubbing an unarmed man to death, but was too modest to strip him.

In a Hadith that haunts us today, Muhammad told his fellow militants that deception was an authorized Islamic strategy. *Tabari VIII:23/Ishaq:458* "**The Messenger and his Companions continued in the fear and distress that Allah has described in the Qur'an. Then Nu'aym came to the Prophet and said, 'I have become a Muslim, but my tribe does not know of my Islam; so command me whatever you will.' Muhammad said, 'Make them abandon each other if you can so that they will leave us; for war is deception.'**"

With prophetic encouragement, our neophyte Muslim went out to mislead non-Muslims. *Tabari VIII:23/Ishaq:458* "**Nu'aym went to the Qurayza. He had been their drinking companion in the Time of Ignorance. He said, 'You know my affection for you and the special ties between us.' 'Yes,' they said. 'You are not a person whom we doubt.'** [If he was honest before Islam and a liar now, what changed him?] "**Nu'aym said, 'The Quraysh and Ghatafan have come to make war on Muhammad, and you have aided them against him.'**" By saying this, Nu'aym tied himself directly to Sa'd and Muhammad, and thus identified himself as a Muslim. Therefore, this dialog isn't believable.

Nu'aym continued: *Tabari VIII:23/Ishaq:458* "'**The position of the Quraysh is not like yours. This land is your land. Your wealth, your children, and your women are in it. You can't move. The Quraysh live elsewhere. If they see an opportunity and booty, they will take it. If it turns out otherwise, they will return home and leave you exposed to Muhammad. You will lose if you have to deal with him alone. So don't support the Quraysh until you take hostages from them as assurance they'll stay.' They said, 'You have given good advice.'**"

Long story short, Nu'aym manages to cross the impenetrable trench and scampers off to chat with the Quraysh. *Tabari VIII:24* "**You know my affection for you and how I have separated from Muhammad. Word has come to me of something that I consider my duty to pass on as a matter of sincere advice. But keep it to yourselves what I say.**" Again, this is ridiculous. Nu'aym volunteered for this mission because no one knew that he *was* a Muslim. If that were so, why would he begin by saying that he had separated from Muhammad? And while we're pondering that, consider what other things Muslims might be willing to lie about if they are willing to renounce their religious affiliation? Peace? Tolerance?

Ishaq:459 "'**Then know,' Nu'aym said, 'the Jews regret what they did regarding relations with Muhammad. They told him, "Will you forgive us if we take nobles from the Quraysh and give them to you, so that you can behead them?" If the Jews ask for hostages, don't comply.'**" So, with the Meccans duped, the Qurayza Jews crossed the impenetrable trench and told them: *Tabari VIII:25* "**We will not fight on your side until you give us hostages for we fear that war tests your mettle. When fighting becomes difficult you will go to Mecca, leaving us alone with this man. We do not have the strength to fight with**

Muhammad." The ruse worked and the multinational alliance fell apart.

Then doing what he did best, Lucifer whipped up some nasty weather. *Ishaq:459* **"Allah sent against them bitter cold winter nights and a wind that overturned their cooking pots, blowing away their tents. This combined with the disagreement and how Allah had disrupted their unity sowed distrust."** So…**"Muhammad began to wonder what they were doing."** *Tabari VIII:26* **"The Prophet asked, 'Who will go and spy on the enemy?' The Messenger stipulated that should he come back, Allah would cause him to enter paradise. But no one stood up. The Prophet prayed and then uttered the same words, but no one volunteered. Again he asked, 'Whoever goes may be my companion in paradise.' Yet none stood, so intense was the fear, hunger, and cold."** No one believed Muhammad. The first Muslim militants were obviously in it for the money, for the spoils of piracy and the thrill of terror, not the promises of paradise. If only today's martyrs understood the implications of this Hadith—one directly from those who fought alongside Islam's lone Profiteer.

Cold, hungry, frustrated, duped, and windblown, the merchants of Mecca simply gave up and went home. As a result, they were about to learn a harsh lesson—a lesson America has failed to heed. The consequence of attacking Islam and then departing, allowing it to fester, is fatal.

Tabari VIII:27 **"The next morning, the Prophet left the trench and went back to Medina with the Muslims, and they laid down their weapons."** But not for long: the most disgusting tale in the sorry history of Islam was about to unfold.

Before we turn the page and deal with the Islamic Holocaust, lets close the book of the Trench. Speaking of it, the 33rd surah says: *033.022* **"When the Believers saw the clan's forces, they said: 'This is what Allah and his Messenger promised us.' It added to their faith, obedience, and submission. Among the Believers are men who have been true to their covenant with Allah (and have gone out for Jihad (holy fighting)). Some have completed their vow to extreme (and have been martyred) fighting and dying in His Cause, and some are waiting, prepared for death in battle."** This is about as chilling as anything we have read thus far. Good Muslims can't wait to die killing infidels for Allah. One translation says that they are: **"waiting and prepared to die."** It's the suicide bomber's oath.

19

ISLAM'S HOLOCAUST

"I pass judgment on them that their men shall be killed, their women and children made captives, and their property divided."

Darkness was about to descend upon Islam. *Ishaq:461* "**Just before the noon prayers, Gabriel came to the Apostle wearing a gold turban. He was riding a mule. He said, 'Have you laid down your weapons and stopped fighting, Muhammad?' 'Yes,' he replied. Gabriel said, 'The angels have not laid down their arms! I've just returned from pursuing the enemy. Allah commands you to march to the Qurayza. I, too, will attack the Jews and shake them out of their homes.'**" Angels in turbans, lumbering on donkeys, wielding swords, commanding Arabs to slaughter Jews—it's quite a picture.

Aisha, the prophet's child wife, put down her dolls long enough to give us this report: *Tabari VIII:29* "**Muhammad pitched a round tent over Sa'd [the wounded anti-Semite] in the mosque. He laid down his sword, having just returned from the Trench. Then Gabriel came to him and said: 'Have you abandoned the fight? By Allah, the angels have not yet put down their weapons! Go out and fight the Jews!' So he called for his breastplate and put it back on. Then he went out and the Muslims followed him.**"

I would be remiss if I did not share Bukhari's theory on the arrival of the angelic tormentors: *Bukhari:V5B59N443-8* "**When the Prophet returned from the Trench, laid down his arms and took a bath, Gabriel came to him covered in dust. "Why have you laid down your sword? We angels have not set them down yet. It's time to go out against them.' The Prophet said, 'Where to go?' Gabriel said, 'This way,' pointing towards the Qurayza. So the Prophet went out to besiege them.**" And: *Bukhari:V5B59N444* "**The dust rose in the streets of Medina as Gabriel's regiment marched through. The angels joined Allah's Apostle in attacking the Qurayza Jews.**"

Putting terror and piracy ahead of teaching and prophecy: *Ishaq:461 / Tabari VIII:28* "**The Messenger commanded a crier to announce that all should heed and obey. He ordered that none should perform the afternoon prayer until after they reached the Qurayza settlement. The Prophet sent Ali ahead with his war banner against the Jews, and the Muslims hastened to it. Ali advanced toward their homes and heard insulting language from the Jews about Allah's Messenger. Ali ran back and told the Prophet that the Jews were rascals and that there was no need for him to go near those wicked men. 'Why?' Muhammad asked. 'Have you heard them insult me?' 'Yes,' Ali answered. 'Had they seen** me,' Allah's Apostle replied, 'they would not have said anything of the sort.'"

This next passage is illuminating. The Bible suggests that Lucifer was beautiful. Islam agrees. *Ishaq:461 / Tabari VIII:28* **"Before reaching the Qurayza, Muhammad greeted his Companions. 'Has anyone passed you?' he asked. 'Yes, Prophet,' they replied. 'Dihyah ibn Khalifah passed us on a white mule with a brocade covered saddle.'"** The translators of Tabari's History confirm: "Dihyah was a rich merchant of such beauty, the angel Gabriel is said to have assumed his features. When he arrived in Medina, every woman came out to look at him." **"Allah's Apostle said, 'That was Gabriel. He was sent to the Qurayza to shake their homes and terrorize them.'"** Billions have been conned into believing that a dust-covered, sword-wielding terrorist was God's messenger to mankind.

War was more important than prayer to Islam's dark spirit: *Tabari VIII:29* **"The Holy Prophet (peace be unto him) said, 'No one should pray the afternoon prayer until they are in the territory of the Qurayza because warfare against the Jews is incumbent upon Muslims.'"** *Ishaq:461* **"The Muslims had been totally occupied with warlike preparations. They refused to pray until they had come upon the Jews in accordance with Muhammad's order. Allah did not find fault with them in His Book, nor did the Messenger reprimand them for it."** Postponing a prayer so that they could besiege innocent families was so religious of them. They were setting a fine example for terrorists everywhere. And it's pretty hard to misinterpret this prophetic decree: **"War-fare against the Jews is incumbent upon Muslims."**

Demonstrating his deep-seated racial hatred, Muhammad unleashed what we would call hate speech: *Tabari VIII:28* **"When the Messenger approached the Jews, he said, 'You brothers of apes! Allah shamed you and cursed you.'"** Muhammad's mouth was as foul as him manners. *Bukhari:V5B59N449* **"On the day of the Qurayza siege, Allah's Apostle said to Hassan, 'Abuse them with your poems, for Gabriel is with you.'"** When it came to racial hatred, Islam's prophet was a full service provider.

Demonstrating the lack of objectivity Islam inspires, those who recorded this Hadith said that the Jews responded sarcastically to Muhammad's slur. **"They said, 'Abu al-Qasim, you have never been one to act impetuously or violently.'"**

Ishaq:461 / Tabari VIII:29 **"Muhammad besieged them for twenty-five nights. When the siege became too severe, Allah terrorized them. Then they were told to submit to the judgment of Allah's Messenger."** Muhammad and Allah had become indistinguishable. And that's because, together with Lucifer, they were now Islam's Unholy Trinity—a false god, a false prophet, and a demonic spirit. Their personas were one.

Tabari's Hadith says: **"Abu gave a sign that it would mean slaughter. So they said, 'We will submit to the judgment of Sa'd.'"** Since Sa'd's dying wish was to see the Jews massacred, and since he was the most fervent Jew hater in the land, I find this request less than credible.

"The Holy Prophet said, 'Submit to his judgment.' So they submitted. The Messenger of Allah sent a donkey with a saddle padded with palm fiber, and he was mounted on it."

That's obviously not how it happened, so let's check the Sira: *Ishaq:461* **"After** the siege exhausted and terrorized them, the Jews felt certain that the Apostle would not leave them until he had exterminated them. So they decided to talk to Ka'b Asad. He said, 'People of the Jews, you see what has befallen you. I shall propose three alternatives. Take whichever one you please.' He said, 'Swear allegiance to this man and accept him; for, by Allah, it has become clear to you that he is a prophet sent from Allah. It is he that you used to find mentioned in your scripture book. Then you will be secure in your lives, your property, your children, and your wives.'" Getting one out of three right wasn't bad for a Muslim: Muhammad *was* Allah's prophet.

However, there is no mention of an Arab prophet in the Hebrew Scriptures, much less of a coming terrorist thug. But consider the gall it took to suggest this delusional alternative to the besieged Jews—especially after what they had endured at the hands of the wannabe "messiah." And even the Qur'an admits that the Jews had repeatedly rejected Muhammad's assertions as being preposterous. They had disclaimed his bastardization of their Torah, and they had been repulsed by his warmongering nature and grotesque immorality. Just imagine swearing an oath to a "religious prophet" so that he would not kill you, steal your property, enslave your children, and rape your women. Sure, a Muslim would do it; they're trained to lie, but not a Jew.

Ishaq:462/Tabari VIII:30 "The Jews said, 'We will never abandon the Torah or exchange it for the Qur'an.' Asad said, 'Since you reject this proposal of mine, then kill your children and your wives and go out to Muhammad and his Companions as men who brandish swords, leaving behind no impediments to worry you. If you die, you shall have left nothing behind; if you win you shall find other women and children.' The Jews replied, 'Why would we kill these poor ones? What would be the good of living after them?'" While I don't believe a word of this, it does provide a window into the depraved character of the first Muslims as well as to the godly nature of these Jews.

In the third alternative, Asad asked the Jews to violate their Sabbath and attack Muhammad by surprise. It was another ploy. Muslims like to call infidels ungodly when they fight on holy days or in sacred months, yet they do so with glee. And if memory serves me right, in their last major offensive against the Jews in 1974, Muslims launched a surprise attack on Yom Kippur. *Tabari VIII:30* "The Jews said, 'We will not profane our Sabbath.'"

Ishaq:462 "Then the Jews asked Muhammad, 'Send us Abu Lubaba, one of the Aws,' for they were confederates, 'so that we can ask his advice.' The Prophet complied and the Jews grabbed hold of him. The women and children were crying, so he felt pity for them. They said, 'Abu, do you think we should submit to Muhammad's judgment?' 'Yes,' Abu said. But he pointed with his hand to his throat, indicating that it would be slaughter. Abu later said, 'As soon as my feet moved, I knew that I had betrayed Allah's Apostle. Abu rushed away and tied himself to a pillar in the mosque. He cried, 'I will not leave this spot until Allah forgives me for what I've done. I betrayed His Apostle.'" This confirms Muhammad had intended to slaughter the Jews from the very beginning. There would be no Islamic peace this time—no surrendering, no being looted and then exiled.

Ishaq:462/Tabari VIII:32 **"I heard Allah's Apostle laughing at daybreak; so I said, 'Why are you laughing, Prophet? May Allah make you laugh heartily!' He replied, 'Abu has been forgiven.'"** Consider the character of a man who would laugh at such a time. This reminds me of Hitler, who in *Mein Kampf* said, *"I have become incapable of pity."* And the similarities don't end there. Hitler turned his command posts into mini brothels from which he orchestrated the extermination of 6 million Jews. This last conversation took place in one of the many apartments that comprised Muhammad's mosque—his command center. When Umm Salama, the wife with whom der prophet was being intimate, heard that Abu had been forgiven, she asked, **"'Can I give him the good news?' He said yes, so she went and stood at the door of her room and said, 'O Abu, rejoice, for Allah has forgiven you.'"**

Another treasure from this dark dawn also smacks of Hitler and his Nazi goons. Muhammad had personal guards like der fuhrer's Storm Troopers and S.S. *Ishaq:463* **"Amr went passed the Apostle's guards who were commanded that night by Maslama. He challenged him."** Last time I checked, the founders of Christianity and Judaism, Yahshua and Moses, didn't have guards. Muhammad not only had them, Maslama, his senior guard, was none other than the assassin who had murdered the first Jewish journalist. Remember: **"I will kill him for you."**

The Islamic world appears to have used Gestapo tactics. After Maslama interrogated Amr at the door of Muhammad's mosque: *Ishaq:463* **"Amr vanished into the night. It is not known to this day what happened to him. Some allege that he was bound with a rotten rope and cast away."**

Ishaq:463/Tabari VIII:33 **"In the morning, the Jews submitted to the judgment of Allah's Messenger. The Aws leapt up and said, 'Muhammad, they are our allies. You know what you did the other day with the allies of the Khazraj! (Before besieging the Qurayza, the Messenger had besieged the Qaynuqa, who were the confederates of the Khazraj. They had submitted to his judgment and were banished.) Therefore, when the Aws spoke to him, the Messenger said, 'People of the Aws, will you not be satisfied if one of your own men passes judgment on them?' Yes,' they proclaimed. So the Prophet said, 'It shall be entrusted to Sa'd [the Jew-Hater] Mu'adh.'"** Sa'd had been so fat his armor failed to protect his extremities. He had been shot with an Arab arrow during the battle of the Trench. To say he was a militant would be too kind. *Bukhari:V5B59N448* **"Sa'd said, 'O Allah! You know that there is nothing more beloved to me than to fight in Your Cause against those who disbelieve Your Apostle. O Allah! I think you have put to an end the fight between us and the infidels. But if there still remains any fight with the infidels, then keep me alive till I fight against them for Your sake.'"** Sa'd was hardly a saint.

Ishaq:463/Tabari VIII:33 **"The Prophet had placed Sa'd in the tent of a Muslim woman in his mosque. She nursed his wound and earned merit for herself by serving Muslims. When Sa'd was struck by the arrow, Muhammad said, 'Put him in Rufaydah's tent, so that I can visit him from nearby.' Then the Prophet appointed him judge over the Qurayza Jews. His tribesmen lifted him onto a donkey on which they had put a leather cushion, for he was a** stout, corpulent man. En route to Muhammad, the Aws said, 'Treat our client well for the Prophet has put you in charge of this matter. After many requests, Sa'd said, 'The time has come for Sa'd, in the Cause of Allah, not to be influenced by anyone's reproach.' Some of the people who heard him, announced the impending death of the Qurayza before Sa'd Mu'adh reached them because of the words he had said." Satan, I mean Allah, had it in for the Jews. For Sa'd to gain entry into the Islamic brothel he would have to support his master's agenda.

Ishaq:463/Tabari VIII:34 "When Sa'd reached the Messenger of Allah and the Muslims, the Prophet said, 'Arise and go to your master and help him dismount.' Then Muhammad said, 'Pass judgment on them.' Sa'd replied, 'I pass judgment that their men shall be killed, their women and children made captives, and their property divided.' Allah's Apostle proclaimed, 'You have passed judgment on the Jews with the judgment of Allah and the judgment of His Messenger.'" The Unholy Trinity was pleased.

It's important for you to know that I have reported every Hadith collected by Tabari, Ishaq, and Bukhari regarding the assault on the Jews. There wasn't a single word written about Jewish combatants. Three settlements, three sieges, and yet the Jews never struck a blow—not one. There was no excuse. There was no claim of self defense. This was a grotesque act of racially inspired genocide. And the motivation was greed. The Jews embodied everything the Muslims had failed to achieve. They were productive, prosperous, moral, literate, peaceful, honest, discerning, and religious.

Bukhari collected a series of Hadith that spoke about this diabolical verdict: *Bukhari:V5B58N148-B59N447* "Sa'd came riding a donkey, and when he approached the mosque, the Prophet said, 'Get up for the best amongst you.' Then the Apostle said, 'O Sa'd! These people have agreed to accept your verdict.' Sa'd said, 'I judge that their men should be killed and their offspring and women should be taken as captives.' The Prophet said, 'You have given a judgment similar to Allah the King's Judgment.'" A second reveals: *Bukhari:V5B59N448* "They then surrendered to the Prophet's judgment but he directed them to Sa'd to give the verdict. Sad said, 'I give my judgment that their men should be killed, their women and children should be taken as captives, and their properties distributed.'" A third proclaims: *Bukhari:V5B59N362* "The Nadir and Qurayza violated their peace treaty, so the Prophet exiled the Nadir and then he killed the Qurayza men. He distributed their women, children and property among the Muslims." And what do you suppose the Muslim militants did to their women? The Qur'an says that they forced them into prostitution. The Hadith says that they raped them. *Bukhari:V5B59N459* "I entered the Mosque, saw Abu, sat beside him and asked about sex. Abu Said said, 'We went out with Allah's Apostle and we received female slaves from among the captives. We desired women and we loved to do coitus interruptus.'" (Yes, that's what it says.)

Another Bukhari Hadith goes on to report that Muhammad never grew weary of tormenting Jews: "He exiled all the Jews from Medina. They were the Jews of the Qaynuqa and the Jews of the Haritha and all the other Jews from their homes."

With something this morally crippled, it's important to know that there are many confirmations—each destroying the myth Muhammad was a prophet. His Islam was a terrorist manifesto. It was conceived for rape and plunder. And on this day it was doing what it did best. *Tabari VIII:34* **"Sa'd turned away from the Messenger out of respect. He said, 'I pass judgment that the men shall be killed, the property divided, and the children and women made slaves.' Muhammad replied, 'You have passed judgment on them with the judgment of Allah from above seven heavens.'"**

The chorus continues with this refrain: *Tabari VIII:39* **"After the affair of the Qurayza ended, the wound of Sa'd broke open. Aisha reports: He passed judgment on the Jews and prayed saying, 'O Allah, You know that there are no men whom I would rather fight and strive to kill than men who called Your Messenger a liar.'"**

Before we review what happened next, I want to share the verses I omitted earlier from the 33rd surah: the model for the Holocaust: *033.026* **"Allah took down the People of the Scripture Book. He cast terror into their hearts. Some you slew, and some you made prisoners. And He made you heirs of their lands, their houses, and their goods, giving you a land which you had not traversed before. And Allah has power over all things."** Version two: **"And He drove the People of the Scripture down from their homes and cast panic into their hearts. Some you killed, and you made some captive. And He caused you to inherit their farms, houses, wealth, and land you have not trodden. Allah is ever Able to do all things."** This Qur'anic verse is among Islam's most stinging indictments. It confirms its most barbaric act.

But it's worse than it appears on the surface. Since it was Muhammad who actually perpetrated these crimes, it confirms that Muhammad was Allah. Allah was never anything more than a rock idol, the Black Stone stuck in the wall of the Ka'aba. Muhammad created his persona and his revelations. And that is why Muhammad's personality, character, behavior, and words are identical to Allah's. But Muhammad had help. Lucifer, just as Paul had warned, transformed himself into an angel of light. Pretending to be Gabriel, he struck a bargain with the insecure and covetous Arab. In the exchange, Muhammad was possessed by Lucifer's most able demon. Working together, the Unholy Trinity established the religion of deceit, death, and damnation.

Muhammad's behavior was covetous, ruthless, and murderous to be sure. Yet attributing this debauchery to deity was his most vile act. Men have plundered before. Men have robbed before. Men have murdered before. But no "god" has ever said: **"'God' drove the unbelievers back in fury, and they gained no advantage. Allah was sufficient to help the believers in battle. He made the People of the Book descend from their homes, and He terrorized them, so that you killed some and made many captive. And He made you inherit their property, homes, wealth, and a country you had not trodden under foot before."**

In the first chapter I included a speech from the Islamic world's leading imam. Al-Buraik, the Saudi ruling family's favorite sheik, spoke at a telethon the Fahd family dictators hosted to enrich the families of Palestinian suicide bombers. This esteemed Islamic cleric said, "O, Muslims, don't take Jews and

Christians as allies. Muslim brothers in Palestine do not have any mercy or compassion on the Jews, their blood, their money, or their flesh. Their women are yours to take, legitimately. Allah made them yours. Why don't you enslave their women? Why don't you wage jihad? Why don't you pillage them?" Now you know where he got his material.

And this was the result: *Tabari VIII:35/Ishaq:464* "The Jews were made to come down, and Allah's Messenger imprisoned them. Then the Prophet went out into the marketplace of Medina (it is still its marketplace today), and he had trenches dug in it. He sent for the Jewish men and had them beheaded in those trenches. They were brought out to him in batches. They numbered 800 to 900 boys and men." The lone prophet of the Islamic religion had the imprisoned Jews brought to *him* so that *he* might enjoy the ghoulish spectacle. Even Hitler was too ashamed to visit Auschwitz.

Then in words hauntingly similar to what Jews must have asked as Nazi trains hauled their families off to concentration camps: "As they were being taken in small groups to the Prophet, they said to one another, 'What do you think will be done to us?' Someone said, 'Do you not understand. On each occasion do you not see that the summoner never stops? He does not discharge anyone. And that those who are taken away do not come back. By God, it is death!' The affair continued until the Messenger of Allah had finished with them all." If 900 men and boys were dragged out of their imprisonment in "batches" and led into the central market square of Medina to be beheaded in front of Muhammad, the "affair" would have lasted eight to ten hours. Imagine a "prophet" perverted enough to watch until he had "finished with them all." It's enough to make you vomit.

Surely, he could not have been this twisted. *Tabari VIII:40* "The Messenger of God commanded that furrows should be dug in the ground for the Qurayza. Then he sat down. Ali and Zubayr began cutting off their heads in his presence." Muhammad was a prophet of a different color.

Tabari VIII:35/Ishaq:464 "Huyayy, the enemy of Allah, was brought out. He was wearing a rose-colored suit of clothes that he had torn all over with fingertip-sized holes so that it would not be taken as booty. His hands were bound to his neck with a rope. When he looked at Muhammad he said, 'I do not regret opposing you. Whoever forsakes God will be damned.' He sat down and was beheaded." The rabbi synthesized the Bible into a single sentence, "Whoever forsakes (separates) himself from Yahweh will be damned (separated) from him." In the Scriptures, forsaken, damned, and separated are synonymous. This fine man chose not to separate himself from Yahweh and worship his adversary Satan, so he lost his life but saved his soul. Huyayy is now living eternally with his Creator. Muhammad, the recipient of this message forsook Yahweh and damned himself—choosing instead to form an alliance with Lucifer. Today Muhammad's soul is eternally damned in the place of separation, called hell—Satan's paradise.

Ishaq:464/Tabari VIII:36 "According to Aisha, one Jewish woman was killed. By Allah, she was by my side, talking with me and laughing while Allah's Messenger was killing her men

in the marketplace." Psychologists call this a "gallows laugh." It's a common manifestation of extreme stress. So while the reaction of the Jewish woman was excused, the behavior of the Muslim men is not. They were forcing Qurayza women to watch as they severed the heads of their fathers, husbands, brothers, and sons. The level of human depravity depicted here wouldn't replayed again for 1300 years. Muhammad's apprentice, Adolf Hitler, forced Jews to remove their kin from cyanide showers, only to place them in the roaring fires of his crematorium. Doctrines demented enough to compel such behavior cannot be tolerated. While the Pope may wish to kiss the Qur'an, I'd prefer to spit on it. But then again, the Pope was wrong about Hitler, too.

Ishaq:464/Tabari VIII:36 **"Suddenly an unseen voice called out her name. It said, 'Where is so and so?' She said, 'Here I am.' 'Good heavens,' I cried, 'what is wrong?' She said, 'I am going to be killed because of something I did.' She was taken away and beheaded. Aisha used to say, 'I shall never forget my wonder at her good spirits, even when she knew she would be killed.'"** The witness of Jews continues to be remarkable.

Tabari VIII:37 **"Thabit said, 'O Allah's Messenger, Zabir, who was Abu Ar-Rahman, did me a favor, sparing my life, and I owe him a debt of gratitude. I wish to repay him for it. Grant me his life.' The Prophet said, 'It is yours.'"** The source of this Hadith wants to make sure Muslims didn't equate this act of "mercy" with the "prophet" being soft on Jews. That is why he said that this man's real name was "Slave-to-Muhammad's-First-God-Ar-Rahman." *Ishaq:465* **"So Thabit went to him and Zabir said, 'Why do this? I'll be an old man without family and children.' Thabit asked Muhammad for his family and he said, 'His wife and children are yours.' But Zabir said, 'Without my property, how will we survive?"** So Thabit asked the Prophet for Zabir's wealth and it was given to him. Thabit went to Zabir and announced that he had been given all of his property. Zabir said, 'Thabit, you are two-faced. What has happened to Asad?' 'He has been beheaded.' 'How about Huyayy?' 'He has been killed.' And how fares Azzal?' 'He has been slain.' 'How about the rest of the Qurayza men?' Thabit said, 'They have all gone to their death.' Zabir said, 'Then for the sake of the favor I once did for you, there is no good in living anymore. So Thabit brought him forward, and they struck off his head. When what he said was reported to Abu Bakr, he replied, 'He will soon meet his dear ones in the fires of Hell, and there they will dwell forever.'"**

In the most tortured words ever uttered in the name of religion: *Tabari VIII:38* **"The Messenger of Allah commanded that all of the Jewish men and boys who had reached puberty should be beheaded. Then the Prophet divided the wealth, wives, and children of the Banu Qurayza Jews among the Muslims."** *Ishaq:465* **"When their wrists were bound with cords, the Apostle was a sea of generosity to us."** It's hard to imagine evil this dark.

Further confirming that he was a terrorist and pirate, not a messenger or prophet, Muhammad's first biographer said: *Ishaq:465* **"Then the Apostle divided the property, wives, and children of the Qurayza among the Muslims. Allah's Messenger took his fifth of the booty. He made known on that day the extra shares for horses and their riders —giving the horse two shares and the rider one. A Muslim without a horse got one share of** the spoil. It was the first booty in which lots were cast." Why lots, you may be wondering? Casting lots is a gambling game, one expressly forbidden by Islam. The reason is two fold. First, the religion of Islam was a joke to these fellows. They simply used it as a tool to justify their disgusting behavior. The first Muslims were less religious than Hitler's S.S. Second, the mercenaries needed a picking order in which to draft Jewish homes, property, businesses, women, and children. Muhammad didn't want them squabbling. Some sex slaves were prettier than others.

In the name of full disclosure, here is the report of Islam's first historian: *Tabari VIII:38* **"On that day Muhammad made known the shares of the horsemen and shares of the foot soldiers, and he deducted from these shares his fifth. A horseman received three shares: two shares for the horse and one for its rider. A foot soldier received one share. The cavalry at the battle with the Qurayza numbered thirty-six horses. It was the first booty in which shares were allotted to them. According to this example (Sunnah), the procedure of the Messenger of Allah in the divisions of booty became a precedent which was followed in subsequent raids."** Every Islamic apologist could cry out for a thousand years and not undo the damage done by Muhammad and his militants. We put ourselves, our men, women, and children, into harm's way when we allow Islam to masquerade as a legitimate religion. Fundamental Islam is no different than fundamental Nazism. These crimes must not go unpunished.

As further evidence that militant Islam is fundamental Islam, and that the Islam of Muhammad was built upon the slave trade, we find: *Tabari VIII:39* **"Then the Messenger of Allah sent Sa'd bin Zayd with some of the Qurayza captives to Najd, and in exchange for them he purchased horses and arms."** Nothing could be more clear. Hitler financed his war machine on booty he stole from the Jews. In slave labor camps he forced Jews to work without pay building planes, tanks, and bombs. Muhammad set the precedent, funding his war effort on the flesh and property of Jews. These men and their methods were identical. And one day, in the not too distant future, this misguided doctrine will be unleashed on a world comprised of six billion souls. Replete with nuclear and biological weapons, a billion five hundred million of them will perish.

The reason Allah approved rape, involuntary sex with prisoners, in the 33rd surah was because Muhammad was about to indulge. *Tabari VIII:38* **"The Prophet selected for himself from among the Jewish women of the Qurayza, Rayhanah bt. Amr. She became his concubine. When he predeceased her, she was still in his possession. When the Messenger of Allah took her as a captive, she showed herself averse to Islam and insisted on Judaism."** Imagine the horror of being the sex slave of the man who had murdered your father and your brothers. Imagine being forced to have sex with a man who had given your mother up to be raped and had sold your sisters into slavery to buy swords so that he could torment others. It's chilling—perversity on an unimaginable scale. Muhammad may well have been the most vile human to have ever lived.

The first to chronicle the prophet's revolting life explains: *Ishaq:466* "**The Apostle [taking first dibs] chose one of the Jewish women for himself. Her name was Rayhana. She remained with him until she died, in his power. The Apostle proposed to marry her and put the veil on her but she said, 'Leave me under your power, for that will be easier. She showed a repugnance towards Islam when she was captured.**" Muhammad raped Rayhana after killing, enslaving, and plundering her family. If you want to understand the doctrine of submission, put yourself in her sandals and gaze deeply into the eyes of the man who is abusing you.

Ishaq:466 "**Allah sent down [a Qur'an surah] concerning the Trench and Qurayza raid. The account is found in the Confederates or Allied Troops. In it He mentions their trial and His kindness to the Muslims. 'Remember We sent a wind against the armies and they could not see. Allah sent this wind with his angels. Allah said, When they came at you from above and below, and when eyes grew wild and hearts reached your throats, you harbored doubts about Allah. Those in whose hearts is a disease said, 'What Allah and His Messenger has promised us is nothing but delusion.'**"

Before I comment, let's read on: *Ishaq:467* "**Allah addressed the believers and said, 'In Allah's Apostle you have a fine example for anyone who hopes to be in the place where Allah is.'**" *Ishaq:468* "**Then Allah said, 'Some of you have fulfilled your vow to Me by dying; you have finished your work and returned to Me like those who sought martyrdom in prior battles. And some of you are still waiting to capitalize on Allah's promise of martyrdom. You do not hesitate in your religion and never doubt.'**" *Ishaq:468* "**Allah brought down the People of the Scripture Book. I forced the Qurayza from their homes and cast terror into their hearts. Some you slew, and some you took captive. You killed their men and enslaved their women and children. And I caused you to inherit their land, their dwellings, and their property. Allah can do all things.'**"

While I recognize that we have reviewed Allah's endorsement of genocide in the 33rd surah, Ishaq's review of the Qur'an ties the Islamic god irrevocably to the event. And there is no question that Ishaq's interpretation of the surah —as the earliest and best researched—is the most credible in Islam. Moreover, when Allah told Muslims to follow Muhammad's example he was specifically encouraging terrorism, mass murder, piracy, the slave trade, and rape.

The Qur'an said that its dark spirit deployed killer angels. The first Muslims harbored doubts about Allah. They believed that Muhammad's message was delusional. Good Muslims vowed to die as martyrs killing infidels. They were mercenaries, as they expected a reward. Allah was presented as an anti-Semite and a terrorist. Islam's "god" approved genocide and the enslavement of women and children. He even confessed to being a pirate, claiming to have caused Muslims to inherit stolen land, possessions, and homes.

There is no other way to interpret these confessions or to explain them away. The dark spirit, demented prophet, and delusional doctrine that seduced men into perpetrating these heinous acts must be exposed, repudiated, and then banished from the earth. Or tomorrow, men following Muhammad's example will terrorize *you*, forcing *you* into submission. They will rape, rob, enslave, and kill your family. And while the Islamic terrorists will earn their just reward for following Muhammad's example—"going to the place where Allah is"—the pain they will inflict cannot be undone.

The first Muslims were proud of themselves. *Ishaq:468* **"Gabriel came to the Apostle when Sa'd was taken. He visited him in the middle of the night wearing an embroidered turban and said, 'O Muhammad, who is this dead man for whom the doors of heaven have been opened and at whom the throne shook?'"** Since Gabriel is "credited" with revealing the Qur'an to Muhammad, it's odd that he would need to ask the "messenger" about something that happened in heaven. And Sa'd was a thug, a man who loved to kill. He was a racist and a thief. If these behaviors rock Allah's throne, the Islamic god is a rather nasty fellow.

Ishaq:468 **"Sa'd was a fat man but those who carried his funeral bier said that they had never carried a lighter one. Muhammad said, 'He had angelic pallbearers because the angels rejoiced when Sa'd's spirit shook Allah's throne.'"** *Ishaq:469* **"An Ansar recited this poem: 'The throne of Allah shook for only one man: Sa'd the brave and bold, a glorious leader, a knight ever ready. Stepping into the battle, he cut heads to pieces."** Saint Sa'd, a genuine Muslim hero. *Ishaq:469* **"The Apostle said, 'Every wailing woman lies except those who wept for Sa'd.'"** *Tabari VIII:40* **"Aisha, the Mother of the Faithful, was asked, 'How did the Messenger of God behave?' She replied, 'His eye did not weep for anyone.'"** Der prophet and der fuhrer were cut from the same cloth.

Ishaq:469 **"On the day the Qurayza were slain, one Muslim was martyred. A stone was thrown on him and it inflicted a shattering wound. The Apostle said, 'He will have the reward of two martyrs.'"** In Islam you get bonus points for killing, robbing, and enslaving Jews.

Theses poetic lines were recited during the Islamic Holocaust: *Ishaq:470* **"We attacked them fully armed, sharp swords in hand, cutting through heads and skulls."** *Ishaq:471* **"We were steadfast trusting in Him. We have a Prophet by whom we will conquer all men."** All means all, that's all all means. So this could serve as Islam's byline: **"We have a Prophet by whom we will conquer all men."**

Ishaq:472 **"Muhammad's Companions are the best in war."** *Ishaq:473* **"Muhammad and his Companions humiliated every doubter."** *Ishaq:475* **"Allah commanded that horses should be kept for His enemy in the fight so they might vex them. We obeyed our Prophet's orders when he called us to war. When he called for violent efforts we made them. The Prophet's command is obeyed for he is truly believed. He will give us victory, glory, and a life of ease. Those who call Muhammad a liar disbelieve and go astray. They attacked our religion and would not submit."** The last was a full service sonnet. It contained an incentive to amass weapons and incentive to use them, a command to annoy the enemy and a command to fight them. It encouraged and acknowledged violence. It even admitted that violence was perpetrated for money—to gain a life of ease.

Ishaq:479 **"Slain in Allah's religion, Sa'd inherits Paradise with the martyrs. His was a noble testimony. When he pronounced his verdict on the Qurayza, he did not judge on his** own volition. His judgment and Allah's were one. Sa'd is among those who sold his life for the Garden of Bliss." Considering the verdict called for genocide, larceny, and enslavement, Allah's complicity in these crimes is bothersome.

This, too, is hideous: *Ishaq:481* "The Apostle slew them in their own town. With our troops he surrounded their homes. We shouted out cries in the heat of battle. The Jews were given the Scripture and wasted it. Being blind, [the illiterate man said] they strayed from the Torah. You Jews disbelieved the Qur'an and yet you have tasted the confirmation of what it said. May Allah make our raid on them immortal. May fire burn in their quarter. They will no longer ruin our lands. You [Jews] have no place here, so be off!"

I saved the worst for last...*Ishaq:480* "The Qurayza met their misfortune [now there's an understated word]. In humiliation they found no helper. A calamity worse than that which fell upon the Nadir befell them. On that day Allah's Apostle came to them like a brilliant moon. We left them with blood upon them like a pool. They lay prostrate with the vultures circling round."

I am going to dedicate the remainder of this chapter to the similarities between *Mein Kampf* and the Qur'an because I do not want the world to endure a third Holocaust. The veil of religiosity must be removed from Islam so that we might defend ourselves from its racial hatred and intolerance—its command to wipe infidels out to the last. I know of no better way to accomplish this goal than to expose the similarities between Muhammad and Hitler, Islam and Nazism, the Islamic scriptures and *Mein Kampf.*

Before we dive back into the Nazi Gospel, which I believe is simply an updated and a more intelligible version of the Qur'an, consider these Nazi proclamations. The first was penned by Dr. Paul Joseph Goebbels in 1929. He confirmed that Hitler, like Muhammad, was a messianic figure, and that Nazism, like Islam, was intentionally veiled in religiosity. *"We believe that Fate has chosen him to show the way to his people. Therefore we greet him in devotion and reverence, and can only wish that he may be preserved for us until his work is completed. Der Fuhrer works the miracle of faith, enlightening our people like a meteor before their astonished eyes, instilling in us a belief that eliminates despair."*

These stirring words are from Sontheimer in Munich, although they sound more like Muslims in Medina. *"Salvation can only come about through a leader selected and blessed by Providence, who can rescue his people from their plight, restore them, make them honest, and serve as the embodiment of their longing, the bearer of Godly power and Destiny; an organ of a Power transcending him."*

As with the Islamic Pledge of Aqaba, Nazis pledged their loyalty: *"Friends, raise your right arm and cry out with me proudly, eager for the struggle, and loyal unto death, 'Heil Hitler!'"* Then with religious symbolism oozing out of every pore, Goebbels introduced his Apostle: *"The Leader of a new, young Germany, der Fuhrer, the Prophet, the Fighter...the last hope of the masses."*

Rudolf Heb embodied the spirit of both movements when he wrote: *"The Leader must be absolute in his propaganda, in his speeches, and words. He must not weigh the pros and cons like an academic, he must never leave his listeners the freedom to think.... The great popular Leader is similar to the great founder of a religion. He must communicate to his listeners an apodictic faith. Only then can the masses be led where they should be led. They will then also follow the Leader if setbacks are encountered; but only if he has communicated an unconditional belief in the absolute rightness of his cause."* He was saying that Hitler was just like Muhammad.

And Heb's claims on behalf of his fuhrer were similar to Allah's on behalf of his prophet. *Ishaq:249/Qur'an:2.23* **"The Apostle calls you to the truth about which there is no doubt. And if you are in doubt about what We have sent down to him or in doubt about what he says, then produce a surah like it and summon witnesses other than Allah. But you will not because you cannot for the truth is beyond doubt."**

Apart from time and place there is no appreciable difference between the founder of Islam and Nazism. Their "poligious" doctrines and their holy books are indistinguishable. They cannot coexist in a civilized world because neither tolerates a rival. *Mein Kampf:137* *"The movement has to avoid everything that could diminish or even weaken its ability to influence the masses; perhaps not for demagogic reasons, but because without the enormous power of the masses no great idea, no matter how lofty it may appear, is realizable."* Islam says: *Qur'an 009.029* **"Fight the People of the Book [Christians and Jews], and those who do not believe in Allah [everybody else] until all of them pay the jizyah protection tax in submission."** *Qur'an 009.123* **"O believers, fight the unbelievers around you, and make them realize that you are unrelenting."**

Like Muhammad, Hitler was an equal opportunity hater. While his favorite enemy was Jews, he despised those who held the political power he craved as well as those whose "view of life" conflicted his own—those pesky Christians. *Mein Kampf:139* *"The Catholic clergy brutally infringes German rights. They side with the enemy because the head of the Catholic Church is not in Germany, a fact which contributes to their hostility."* *Mein Kampf:140* *"Germany would gain enormously by a victory against the Church."*

Of Protestantism and Catholicism, der fuhrer wrote: *Mein Kampf:141* *"Both religions take an attitude toward the Jews that is counter to the concerns of the nation and the real needs of religion."* Hitler didn't bother demeaning Islam, the next largest religion, because he recognized that the Qur'an shared his demented view. It says: *Qur'an 005.051* **"Believers, do not accept Jews and Christians as allies. They are allies of one another. Any one of you who befriends them is surely one of them."** *Ishaq:369* **"The Jews were in a state of fear on account of our attack upon them. The Prophet declared, 'Kill every Jew who falls into your hands.'"** *Mein Kampf:414* *"Witness the 'Juda verrecke' (May Jews die) outcry in which our youth organizations have taken up."*

Projecting his faults on his enemy, Hitler impersonated Muhammad. *Mein Kampf:415* *"Jews are a pack of wolves whose appetite for booty only dissolves when the pack's hunger abates. They are united only by common booty or a common enemy.*

Otherwise they are a horde of rats, fighting bloodily among themselves. If the Jews were left alone, they would suffocate in their own dirt and filth. Jews have a shame culture in which everything they possess is really the property of other peoples and it is spoiled in their hands." Speaking of the same people, the Qur'an says: Qur'an 059.014 **"They are a divided people devoid of sense.** Qur'an 004.055 **"Sufficient for them is Hell and the Flaming Fire! Those [Jews] who disbelieve Our Revelations shall be cast into Hell. When their skin is burnt up and singed, We shall give them a new coat that they may go on tasting the agony of punishment."** Alas, Hitler could only burn them once.

These men recognized that the easiest way to defame the race was to lie about them. Mein Kampf:418 *"The Jew never possessed a state with a territorial boundary." Mein Kampf:420 "Jews live in other states as parasites, disguised under the name of religion. The Jew is a master of lying…. Everything they have is purloined or stolen. The Jew cannot be religious because he lacks idealism and he does not believe in the Hereafter."*

Remember what Maududi said in his commentary on the anti-Semite surah: **"Consequently their [Jewish] beliefs, morals and conduct has gone to the lowest depths of degeneration. The pity is that they were not only satisfied with their condition but loved to cling to it."**

Der fuhrer explained why der prophet turned three distinctly different enemies into one, hating Meccans, then Jews and Christians. He called them all pagans, unbelievers, infidels, and even friends of one another. Here's why: Mein Kampf:152 *"The efficiency of the true national leader consists primarily in preventing the division of the attention of a people, always concentrating it on a single enemy. The fighting will be more uniform, the force will be greater, the cause more magnetic, and the blow more powerful. It is part of the genius of a great leader to make adversaries in different fields appear as always belonging to one category. People are weak and unstable characters and thus various enemies will lead to incipient doubts as to their own cause. As soon as the masses waver, due to confronting too many enemies, objectivity steps in, and the question is raised whether all others are wrong and their movement alone is right."* This provides a brilliant insight into Muhammad's tactics.

Allah's Apostle said that the Jews were aiding the Meccans so they were really the same enemy. But once Muslims had robbed every Jew of every possession and plundered every Arab, Muhammad needed a bigger target. So the prophet claimed that the Christians were allies of Allah's enemy. As a result, his Companions plundered the Byzantine world for booty. Bukhari:V4B52N267 **"The Prophet said, 'Khosrau will be ruined. There won't be a Persian King after him. Caesar will be ruined. There will be no Caesar after him. You will spend their treasures in Allah's Cause.'"** Then speaking of a single enemy: Qur'an 008.073 **"Those who are infidels aid one another. Unless you do the same there will be discord in the land. Those who accepted Islam and left their home to fight in Allah's Cause and those who gave them shelter and assistance are the true believers."**

Hitler sang from the same hymnal. He said Germany's leaders were supported by Jews and said the Church was protecting them. Thus the political leaders, the Jews, and Church were actually the same enemy. But once he had subdued and raped them, he needed a bigger target. So he said that the Jews and the Church were in cahoots with governments on the left and right promoting Marxism and Democracy. They became an enemy that needed to be conquered so that Nazi Aryans might rule the world uncontested.

According to der fuhrer, you were either a Nazi or an enemy. Today you are either a Muslim or an enemy of Islam. Der prophet saw the world in two pieces: the "House of Islam" or the "House of War." This fundamental agreement between Islam and Nazism is why we must come to terms with Muhammad's legacy. For the only difference between Mein Kampf and the Qur'an is that Hitler was a more inspired writer than Allah.

Mein Kampf:153 "*Therefore, a number of essentially different enemies must always be regarded as one in such a way that in the opinion of one's own adherents the war is being waged against one enemy alone. This strengthens the belief in one's own cause and increased one's bitterness.*" We have seen how Muhammad's militants have become increasingly bitter. The poems they recited as they beheaded, enslaved, plundered, and raped the Qurayza Jews serve as proof.

Mein Kampf:144 "*Protestantism will fight every attempt at saving the nation from the grip of its most deadly enemy as its attitude towards Judaism is fixed by dogma.*" A translator's note says: "When Hitler came to power, he immediately tried to place the governance of the Lutheran Church in the hands of men who were willing to alter its teachings. Pastor Ludwig Muller was named Archbishop, but most clerics refused to accept Hitler's tampering. The most outspoken was Pastor Martin Niemoller. He was imprisoned on Hitler's command and held in solitary confinement. More than 1,200 pastors were jailed or slain."

Islam agrees with Hitler's assessment. In the last fifteen years the fundamental Islamic government of Sudan has murdered and mutilated two million Christians. The Qur'an is the reason why. *Qur'an 005.033* **"The punishment for those who oppose Allah and His Prophet, making mischief in the land, is to kill them or crucify them. Or to have a hand on one side and a foot on the other cut off. Or to banish them from the land. Such is their disgrace in this world and in the hereafter, their doom will be dreadful.... The unbelievers' [Jews and Christians] punishment will surely be painful. They will not be able to escape the Fire."** Allah said in the same surah: *Qur'an 005.073* **"Unbelievers are surely those who say God is the third of the Trinity."**

Chancellor Hitler spoke these words: *Mein Kampf:148* "*If the clerical caste does not disappear voluntarily, I will direct propaganda against the Church until people will be unable to hide their disgust when the word "church" is mentioned. I will have movies made to show how the clergy has exploited people, lived off them, and how they sucked money out of the country. I will show how they worked with Jews, how they practiced immoral vice, and how they spread lies. I will make the clergy look ridiculous—a tangled mass of corruption, selfishness, and deceit. Let them complain for I will have youth and the masses on my side. If I set my mind to it I will destroy the Church. The whole institution is just a hollow shell. One good kick and it will tumble together in a heap."* It wasn't a coincidence that the dark spirit of Nazism focused on Islam's enemies. It merely tells the discerning who their "god" really was. Rebuking the same enemy—Christians and Jews—Islam's "god" cried: Qur'an 009.030 **"The Jews and the Christians...are damned by Allah. How perverse are they!"**

Hitler was a prophet engaged in spiritual warfare. He had to destroy Judeo-Christianity in order to establish his own religion. Mein Kampf:148 *"One cannot serve two masters [Lucifer and Yahweh]. In this I consider the foundation and the destruction of religion more important than the foundation and destruction of a state, let alone a party."* Yes, Nazism was founded as a religion—one designed to attack and destroy other religions. This revelation is stunning because it makes Nazism and Islam identical. Both tyrants rebuked Judeo-Christianity so that they could build their own religious dogma in its place. Mein Kampf and the Qur'an gave Hitler and Muhammad the ultimate weapon.

Here's how he used it: Mein Kampf:148 *"It is certain that at all times unscrupulous men did not shrink from making religion a tool for their political business affairs—for this is always the object. Scoundrels abuse it to serve their base instincts."* Hitler is right. Throughout time men have used religion to control and fleece the masses and thereby satiate their personal cravings. But he was also wrong, for the ultimate maestros of religious malfeasance were der fuhrer, and der prophet.

Muhammad's situational Qur'an revelations justified thievery, kidnapping, terrorism, and murder as Islamic necessities. Recognizing the reason and the benefit, Hitler explained: Mein Kampf:149 *"As soon as a religion's wickedness is attacked, the mendacious clerics will claim that their actions were justified. The leader will say that the salvation of the religion and the church is due to him and his eloquence alone. And since the citizens are as stupid as they are forgetful, they will not see past the great noise he makes. As such, the scoundrel achieves his goal."* Like Muhammad, Hitler became what he condemned. *"But the sly fox of a cleric knows only too well that this has nothing to do with religion, and thus he laughs up his sleeve."* Allah said, Qur'an 008.001 **"They ask you [Muhammad] of the benefits of accruing spoils of war. Tell them that the booty belongs to Allah and His Messenger. So fulfill your duty and obey Allah and the Prophet."** Both tyrants ultimately claimed that the most immoral means were justified by the end result.

Mein Kampf:149 *"Among the priests are those whom their office is only an instrument for the gratification of their political ambition. Rather than uphold truth they promote lies and calumnies. An honest pastor devoted to his mission is an island in a communal swamp. I condemn the Church as such...and long for the hour when at last Heaven will smile on us again."* Allah said: Qur'an 005.077 **"People of the Book, do not overstep the bounds in your religion, or follow the people who erred and led many astray. Cursed are the unbelievers among the Children of Israel by David and Jesus.... They do vile things, allying themselves with the infidels so that Allah's indignation is upon them and in torment they will suffer for all eternity."**

This next passage was designed to clear the field for der fuhrer's ambition: *Mein Kampf:150* *"If you believe yourself to be chosen by Destiny to announce the truth, then do so, but then have the courage to do so not by way of politics."* In other words: "If you have been chosen by the Devil you must destroy other religions and start your own."

Working for Lucifer, like his mentor Muhammad, Hitler had to keep the heat on the Jews and keep folks focused on the flesh, not the spirit. *Mein Kampf:154* *"I had found a slogan against Judaism on a religious basis, overshadowing all racial differences."* *Mein Kampf:160* *"I detested the conglomerate of races like the eternal fission of fungus—Jews and more Jews—the personification of incest."* Allah said: *Qur'an 005.082* **"You will find the Jews and idolaters the most excessive in their hatred of Muslims."** *Ishaq:250/Qur'an:2.65* **"Allah brought the bestial transformation, turning Jews into apes despised."** *Ishaq:254/Qur'an:2.89* **"Allah revealed, 'The Jews deny him. They are wretched, so Allah cursed them and He will give them a shameful punishment.'"**

Hitler believed that he was Fate's messenger, the final prophet, the man called by God to plunder the world and establish an uncontested religion. *Mein Kampf:161* *"Fate bestowed upon me that I should devote my honest services to the nation. Most will not be able to understand the intensity of such a longing [craving for power]. By the will of Fate we will fight for the holy treasure." "This longing tortures those it has seized and denies them contentedness and happiness until the doors of the house are open and our blood finds peace in one Reich."* We've heard this before: *Qur'an 033.038* **"There can be no difficulty or reproach to the Prophet in doing what Allah has ordained to him as a duty. It was the practice approved of Allah, a decree determined for those who deliver His Messages; fear Him. Muhammad is the Messenger of Allah, and the Last of the Prophets with the Seal."** *Qur'an 008.039* **"Fight them until all opposition ends and all religion is for Allah alone."** And...*Bukhari:V4B52N220* **"The treasures of the world were brought to me and put in my hand."** Sure sounds like the same mission to me.

The next *Mein Kampf* taunt reminds us of the Hadith's first attempt to explain why Islam was created. *Tabari VI:82* **"'Muhammad claims that Allah has sent him as His Messenger with this religion and that the treasures of Chusroes and Caesar will be given to him by conquest.'"** *Mein Kampf:174* *"Nature [as in 'God'] does not know political frontiers. She puts people on the globe and watches the game. He who is the strongest becomes Her favorite child, the right to be the master of existence."* *Mein Kampf:175* *"The more brutal the people the greater their living area. In other words, the world will some day come into the hands of the superior people. And one should know that this world will be subject to the fiercest fights in mankind's existence. Man grows strong in struggles but perishes through peace."* Allah said, *Qur'an 061.004* **"Surely Allah loves those who fight in His Cause."** *Qur'an 061.011* **"Come to believe in Allah and His Apostle and struggle in the Cause of Allah with your wealth and person. This will be good for you.... Allah will give you an early victory."**

Hitler got Germans to kill the same way Muhammad did, by convincing them that they would live forever. *Mein Kampf:422* *"One cannot conceive of a religion which lacks the conviction of the continuation of life after death in some form."* The Qur'an proclaimed: *Qur'an 004.074* **"Those who barter their life in this world for the next should fight in Allah's Cause. We shall bestow on him who fights in Allah's Cause, whether he is killed or victorious, a glorious reward."** *Qur'an 003.169* **"Never think that those who are killed in Allah's Cause are dead. They are alive, getting rewards from their Lord."**

As with Islam, the quest for booty was violent. *Mein Kampf:188* *"The talk of 'peaceful economic conquest' of the world is the greatest folly that has ever been perpetrated. It is nonsense…. Weapons are required for success. Mercenaries can be used but a nation must dip into its most valuable blood and make sacrifices to bring about victory. The determination to fight and the tenacity of unflinching conduct is required."* The Qur'an says: *Qur'an 003.146* **"Many have fought in Allah's Cause…against unbelieving people. So Allah rewarded them."** *Qur'an 008.060* **"Prepare against them whatever arms and cavalry you can muster, that you may terrorize Allah's enemies as well as your own."**

Mein Kampf:196 *"Jews always form States within other States using one of the most ingenious tricks ever invented. They sail under the flag of religion, securing tolerance for themselves. But actually the Mosaic religion is nothing but a doctrine of the preservation of the Jewish race."* Alfred Rosenberg, who crafted the Nazi's position papers on Judeo-Christianity, said, *"As a book of religion, the Old Testament must be done away with once and for all…. By comparison, the Germanic legends and the German mystics [pagans] teach heroism, soldierly conduct, and purity."* The Nazis were no different than the Muslims. They resurrected pagan mystical rituals to mold the masses into unflinching warriors.

And, of course, they attacked the Jews. *Ishaq:239* **"Jewish rabbis showed hostility to the Apostle in envy, hatred, and malice, because Allah had chosen His Apostle from the Arabs. The Jews considered the Prophet a liar and strove against Islam."** Here's what the dark spirit of Islam has to say about the corruption of the Torah: *Qur'an 004.044* **"Have you not seen the [Jewish] people who were given a share of the Book, but who purchased only error, and wish to lead you astray? Allah knows your [Jewish] enemies well. Some of the Jews distort the words out of context…they twist their tongues, reviling your faith…. But Allah has disgraced them. O People of the Book, believe [in Islam] before we disfigure your visages, turning your face into your ass and curse you."**

Hitler and Muhammad were happiest when people were dying for them. *Mein Kampf:198* *"Unless you stake your life, never will life be won. The sacrifice of one's existence is the most essential supposition for the formation and preservation of a State with the necessary feeling of homogeneity. The readiness to risk one's life for this with all means possible, is something that will lead to the creation of heroic virtues."* Allah said: *Qur'an 003.195* **"For those who fought and were killed in My Cause, I shall blot out their sins and admit them indeed to Paradise."** *Ishaq:294* **"Sa'd said, 'We hear and obey. We are experienced in war, trustworthy in combat. Allah will let us show you something that will bring you joy. The Apostle was delighted at Sa'd's words which greatly encouraged him. Muhammad shouted, 'It is as if I see the enemy lying prostrate.'"**

Mein Kampf:200 *"One does not die for business, but for ideals…. When a man fights for economic gain he tries to avoid death, as this would rob him of the enjoyment of the reward of his fighting. Only the fight for the preservation of the Aryan species will drive men towards the spears of the enemy."* The Islamic version says: Bukhari:V4B52N65 "A man came to the Prophet and asked, 'A man fights for war booty; another fights for fame and a third fights for showing off; which of them fights in Allah's Cause?' The Prophet said, 'He who fights that Allah's Word, Islam, should be superior, fights in Allah's Cause.'"

Speaking as if he were Muhammad bragging about Sa'd's wounding at the battle of the Trench, Hitler said, *Mein Kampf:220 "If the best men were killed on the front, then one should at least destroy the vermin [Jews] at home."*

Touting the power of religion and sword, der fuhrer set the stage for holy war: *Mein Kampf:220 "Can spiritual ideas be extinguished by the sword? Can one fight 'views of life' by applying brute force? When contemplating history from a religious perspective, the following fundamental realization came upon me: Movements with a certain spiritual foundation, may they be right or wrong, can only be broken early in their development with power, and only then if physical weapons are at the same time supported by a new idea, or view of life. The use of force alone, without the driving force of a spiritual idea, can never lead to the destruction of a movement and its spreading, unless the new spiritual idea combines a thorough repudiation of the last tradition. This requires a sacrifice of blood and a spiritual presupposition."* Hitler, like Muhammad, couldn't destroy Judeo-Christianity with force alone. Both men needed a "new view of life"—a religion—combined with force to accomplish their agenda. Their new "spiritual idea," or "view of life," was called Nazism and Islam.

Hitler explained Muhammad's rationale for clothing a militant doctrine in religious garb. These are some of the most insightful words every written by an evil man: *Mein Kampf:222 "All attempts at the extinction of a doctrine and its effects by force without a spiritual foundation lead to failure. Only in the eternal and regular use of force lies the preliminary condition for success. This perseverance is only and always the result of a certain spiritual conviction. All force which does not spring from a firm spiritual foundation will be hesitating and uncertain. It will lack the stability which can only result from a fanatical view of life, giving it a brutal determination."* If the Hitler is right, this passage has foreboding implications for America.

Allah echoed similar sentiments: Qur'an 004.084 "So fight on in the Way of Allah... urge the believers to fight the infidels." Qur'an 004.090 "They will grow weary of fighting you."

Back when Muhammad and Allah were bragging that Islam was the "religion of Abraham," I shared something that I hope you found shocking: the word "religion" does not exist in the Old Testament. It appears three times in the New Testament, but each reference is derogatory. Judeo-Christianity is not a religion—it's a relationship. All religions, including Nazism and Islam, are man made constructs. They are all specifically designed to control and rob people, motivating men to fight for the benefit of cleric and king.

Mein Kampf:222 "Every view of life [religion], be it more of a political or a religious nature (sometimes the borderline between them can only be ascertained with difficulty), fights less for the negative destruction of the adversary's world of ideas, and more for the positive carrying out of its own doctrine. Therefore, its fight is less a defense than an attack. The goal represents the victory of its own idea and the destruction of the enemy's doctrine. The attack on a view of life will be more carefully planned and more powerful than the defense of a doctrine. But the fight against a spiritual power by means of force is only a defense as long as the sword itself does not appear as the supporter, propagator, and announcer of a new spiritual doctrine." This is why I coined the word "religotic" to describe doctrines like Nazism and Islam that were as political as they were religious. This "poligious" view of life is easily the most menacing force on earth. It breeds tyranny, intolerance, deceit, death, thievery, and terror. And not so coincidentally, these are the hallmarks of Islam.

Mein Kampf:222 "Every attempt at fighting a view of life by means of force will fail, unless the fight against it is for the sake of a new spiritual direction. Only in the struggle of two views of life with each other can the weapon of brute force, used continuously and ruthlessly, bring about the decision in favor of the side it supports…. One needs a spiritual impetus for a struggle for life and death." Touting the same party line, the Qur'an preaches: Qur'an 008.059 **"The infidels should not think that they can bypass Islam. Surely they cannot get away."**

The only difference between Islam and Nazism is that the former was sneaky. Der fuhrer told the "sheeple" exactly what he was going to do to them. *Mein Kampf:232 "Propaganda has to be popular and it has to adapt its spiritual level to the perception of the least intelligent of those towards whom it intends to influence."* After enduring Allah's dimwitted creation accounts and shameless bastardizations of the Torah, you know that Islam was designed for unthinking people, too.

Mein Kampf:233 "The more modest the spiritual assumptions and scientific ballast, the more it exclusively considers the feelings of the masses, the more striking will be its success." From Hitler's perspective, Islam was the perfect religion. It was dumbeddown to the lowest common denominator.

Speaking of how Hitler conditioned his faithful to hate, Goebbels said: *"When the we drove dissenters from our meetings with cudgels, the audiences grew larger. Few people originally felt anti-Semitic, but the joy large numbers felt in the promise of blood-curdling treatment to be meted out to the helpless minority made them responsive to our suggestions. Smashing windows and street fighting were relied upon to win the crowd. We shall reach our goal when we have the courage to laugh as we destroy, as we smash, whatever was sacred to us as tradition, as education, as friendship and as human affection. The people express a strange delight in the sufferings visited upon the Jews."* Muhammad's laughter in the midst of the Jewish Qurayza massacre, the gloating poetry of his mercenaries following the slaughter, testify to the similarity between Nazi and Islamic methods.

Neither Muhammad nor Hitler viewed those whom they seduced favorably. *Mein Kampf:234 "The receptive ability of the masses is very limited, their understanding is small, but their forgetfulness is great. All effective propaganda has to limit itself to a very few points and to use them like slogans until even the very last man is able to imagine what is intended by such a word.*" In Islam, these slogans were: "submit and obey or burn," "booty for fighters" and "paradise for martyrs."

Explaining why the Qur'an was so repetitive and mind-numbing, der fuhrer said, *Mein Kampf:239 "Looking for new stimulants, the people tire of everything after a short time…. Thus the slogan has to be illuminated from various sides. Success comes from continual, regular, and consistent emphasis. Propaganda must be limited to a few points of view, calculated exclusively for the masses, and carried out with untiring persistency.*" Allah repeated his "painful punishment" theme a thousand times in the Qur'an. The never-ending argument, which was designed to terrorize those who rejected Islam, was replayed four hundred times. The last twenty surahs focus on a trio of commands: submit, pay, and fight.

Ernst Bohle, the manager of the *Nazi Journal* said: "*Our most important weapons are: the contention that Hitler is the bulwark of civilization against the Marxists, and that the doctrine of Jewry is the root of all evil. There are many who fear Communists and many more who can be persuaded to dislike Jews. When violent nationalism is in ascendancy, as is the case at present, both Jew and Christian necessarily suffer.*" Hitler shared, *Mein Kampf:673 "If the Jews continue unrestricted, they will ultimately fulfill their prophecy—the Jew would actually devour the nations of the world, he would become their master.*" We have arrived at the kernel of what the Satanic schemes called Islam and Nazism were all about.

Likewise: *Ishaq:245* **"The Apostle used to say, 'Do you love Jews and their religion, you liver-hearted ass, and not Muhammad? Their religion will never march with ours.'"** *Ishaq:239* **"Jewish rabbis used to annoy the Apostle with questions and introduce confusion."** *Ishaq:240* **"I went to the Apostle and said, 'The Jews are a nation of liars…a treacherous and evil people.'"** *Ishaq:248* **"Allah increases their sickness. A tormented doom awaits the Jews."** *Mein Kampf:252 "The Jew robbed the entire nation…and was bound to hurl us hopelessly into the abyss." Mein Kampf:268 "Wretched and miserable criminals. In those nights my hatred arose against the instigators…. With Jews there is no bargaining, but only the hard either-or. [Islam's 'Your money or your life.']*" Allah was in lock step: *Qur'an 059.014* **"They are a divided people devoid of sense. There is a grievous punishment awaiting them."** *Qur'an 059.004* **"That is because they resisted Allah and His Messenger. If any one resists Allah, verily Allah is severe in Punishment, stern in reprisal."**

Mein Kampf:244 "I often felt fury and indignation rise in me. I was tormented by the thought of Destiny putting me in the place of the incapable, criminal, incompetent scamps of rulers." In the first Qur'an revelations, Allah had to threaten a nearly suicidal Muhammad to get him to crawl out of his bed and accept his prophetic duty. *Qur'an 074.001* **"O you enwrapped in you blanket, arise and warn."**

Hitler considered himself the "program-maker" or founder of the religion of Nazism. In this next passage he makes it clear, as did Muhammad, that the ends justify the means. *Mein Kampf:283 "The task of a program-maker is not to state the various degrees of a matter's realizability, but to demonstrate the matter as such. That means he has to care less for the way, but more for the goal."* The means to Muhammad's end was thievery and the slave trade. His god said that the ends justified the means when he proclaimed: *Qur'an 008.069* **"But now the use of spoils, the booty you took, is lawful and good."** The following Hadith demonstrates how Islam used criminal behavior to accomplish its goals: *Bukhari:V4B52N153* **"The properties of Banu Nadir which Allah transferred to His Apostle as Booty were...used to buy arms and horses to be used in Allah's Cause."**

Giving Muhammad a complement, Hitler said, *Mein Kampf:285 "The founders of religions are among the greatest men on earth."* He considered himself foremost among them—a fellow prophet. *Mein Kampf:286 "The program-maker may be counted among those of whom it is said that the gods like them only if they ask for, and desire, the impossible. They will always renounce the present. He will harvest the fame of posterity provided his ideas are immortal. His life is torn between love and hate."* *Mein Kampf:287 "Their life and work is followed in touchingly grateful admiration, and especially in gloomy days, it will be able to uplift broken hearts and despairing souls."* *Mein Kampf:289 "What we have to fight for is the security and existence of our race...for the fulfillment of the mission which the Creator of the universe has allotted."*

Muhammad was also a demagogue. As we learned in the 33rd surah, Allah said that he was the ultimate example—the perfect paradigm—the prototype of perfection. *Qur'an 033.021* **"You have indeed a noble paradigm in the Apostle of Allah."**

Mein Kampf:297 "I had no intention of joining a ready-made party, but wished to found a party of my own." This too is like Muhammad. Rather than starting a religious scam of his own he stole Qusayy's from its rightful heirs. He incorporated every existing pagan ritual into Islam. Then he stole Judaism from the Jews, joined their prophetic club, and then paid them a pittance for their scripture.

Neither Hitler nor Muhammad liked journalists very much. *Mein Kampf:335 "Freedom of the press is a nuisance that allows unpunishable lies to poison the people."* Der fuhrer and der prophet had their goons assassinate all who assailed the horror of their regimes. *Bukhari:V4B52N270* **"Allah's Messenger said, 'Who is ready to kill Ashraf? He has said injurious things about Allah and His Apostle.' Maslama got up saying, 'Would you like me to kill him?' The Prophet proclaimed, 'Yes.'"** He was but the first of many who would pay the ultimate price for the courage to speak candidly.

Der fuhrer believed: *Mein Kampf:335 "An institution which is not determined to defend itself with all weapons practically gives itself up."* *Mein Kampf:336 "A 30cm. shell has always hissed more than a thousand Jewish newspaper vipers; therefore let them hiss."* Not having cannons, Muhammad was forced to use swords. Both men, however, were always ready to threaten god's wrath. *Mein Kampf:338 "In pious disgust towards this vicious disease, God will rain fire and brimstone upon this Sodom and Gomorrah to make an example out of this disgrace to mankind."* Unable to get their "god" to help, the tyrants abused Jews for him. *Bukhari:V4B52N280* **"I give the judgment that their men should be killed and their children and women should become slaves."**

Both tyrants were hypocrites. They were guilty of pedophilia, incest, polygamy, and rape, yet they condemned such behavior in others. *Mein Kampf:346* *"There is no liberty to sin.... Our entire public life today resembles a hothouse of sexual stimulants."* There may have been a method to their madness. An editor's note says: "Communism was hedonistic at its core. A good many sound Germans turned to Hitlerism because they could not stomach Communist approval of free contraceptives, aid to unmarried lovers, and unrestricted sex." *Mein Kampf:348* *"Our culture must be cleaned up...and we must fight against these evils...or we will lose sight of God and insult the All Highest."*

Muhammad incorporated Qusayy's pagan rituals into Islam. *Ishaq:53* **"Qusayy's authority among the Quraysh was like a religion which the people followed and which could not be infringed; they acted in accordance with its laws. He took for himself the mosque (place of prostration) of the Ka'aba."** Hitler agreed with his strategy: *Mein Kampf:356* *"The more wretched and miserable a new institution is, the more it will endeavor to extinguish the last traces of past times, whereas a really valuable renovation must include the good achievements of past generations."* *Mein Kampf:357* *"Superior revolutionary movements will embrace the old forms [of ritual and dogma]. Only when the rays of the sun are gone is the moon able to shine. [Satan is consistent if nothing else.] Any new idea, new doctrine, or new view of life which tries to deny the past or wants to deride it, making it valueless and untrustworthy will fail."* *Ishaq:57* **"Allah's Apostle said, 'Whatever deal there was in the days of ignorance, Islam strengthens it.'"**

The first Muslims were comfortable with Islam, trusting it because in practice it was no different than Qusayy's mystic scheme. *Tabari VI:25* **"Qusayy's commands were never disobeyed." "As regards the hajj, he confirmed the right of Arabs to continue their previous customs. He considered these to be a religious duty which should not change."** *Mein Kampf:358* *"The reason men hate new moons is either their inferiority or evil intent. A genuinely blissful renovation builds upon the place the last foundation ends. It isn't ashamed to use existing truths. The new building stones should not wreck the old building, but rather take away unsuitable stuff which was badly fitted and then add on to that spot."* Muhammad's "three batches of builders—Jews, Christians, and Muslims" comes to mind. Islam is the perfect embodiment of Hitler's mantra. It was built on Judeo-Christian foundations for the reason der fuhrer specifies: to make it appear "trustworthy."

Hitler explains why Muhammad had to change his Qiblah to the Ka'aba. *Mein Kampf:364* *"Our cities lack the outstanding symbol of national community. The lack of such a symbol leads to spiritual dullness which manifests itself in indifference."* Der prophet coveted the revenue streams that flowed from the Ka'aba Inc. In the 2nd surah he used the pagan shrine to justify mass murder and kidnapping for ransom. He used it to transform his people's spiritual dullness and indifference into violent rage. *Qur'an 002.217* **"They ask you about war and fighting but a greater sin is to hinder people from Allah's Cause and to bar access to the Holy Mosque [Ka'aba], and to turn people out of its precincts. Oppression is worse than killing."**

Despots require uniformity of purpose. *Mein Kampf:364* *"The symptoms of decay include the lack of a commonly acknowledged view of life and uncertainty in the judgment and definition of an attitude towards the various great questions."* You'll note that Hitler is not suggesting that Nazis ask questions, but rather that they all agree with his answers. *"Therefore, everything beginning with education is half-hearted and wavering, shuns responsibility and ends thus in cowardly tolerance of recognized evils."* This synthesizes the 3rd and 33rd surahs. The recognized evil was Jews. Muslims were taught to hate them. They were told that anyone who didn't agree with Muhammad's interpretation couldn't be tolerated. Anyone who accommodated Jews, and lived peaceably with them, was a hypocrite.

Muhammad, during the battles of Uhud and the Trench, was afraid that his world was about to implode. His followers were beginning to think for themselves. They were questioning the righteousness of a religion based upon terror and booty—**"They were thinking vain thoughts about Allah."** So the Medina surahs established what der fuhrer suggested: *Mein Kampf:364* *"Uniform religious convictions through a view of life are required."* Hitler even acknowledged the superiority of Islam in this regard. *Mein Kampf:365* *"While the Catholic and Protestant denominations build missions abroad in order to lead new followers to the doctrine (an activity, which compared with the advance of Muhammad's faith, can show only very modest successes), in Europe they lose millions of adherents who now face religious life on their own. The consequence is unfavorable."* Hitler recognized that Muhammad didn't tolerate renegades and that the sword of Islam was wielded above the necks of those who contemplated independence or freedom. Der fuhrer and der prophet saw religion as their ultimate weapon—without it there was no possible way to acquire the power, wealth, and praise they craved.

Hitler warned that religotic founders had to be careful not to completely destroy what they are attacking: *Mein Kampf:365* *"The violent fight against the dogmatic fundamentals of the various churches must recognize that without them the practical existence of a religious faith is unthinkable to man. The masses of people do not consist of philosophers, and faith for them is their sole basis for a moral view of life. The various substitutes have not proved useful in exchange for former religious creeds."* So in Hitler's twisted mind a new creed was necessary—his creed. Without it he knew that there would be chaos in the wake of his attack on Christianity. And while chaos abroad was supported by both Islam and Nazism, it's untidy at home. *"But if religious doctrine and faith are really meant to seize the great masses, then the absolute authority of the contents of this faith must become the basis of all effectiveness…. The dogma of the religion, or the spiritual idea, must be limited and brought into shape without wavering or it will never become a faith."* Hitler is explaining that the purpose of the religotics derived from *Mein Kampf* and the Qur'an/Sunnah was to establish absolute authority. Allah says: *Qur'an 059.006* **"Allah gives authority to His Apostle over whoever He pleases."**

This Hadith established Islam's absolute authority (and explains why the poligious doctrine was allergic to democracy): *Bukhari:V4B52N203* **"I heard Allah's Apostle saying, 'We are the last but will be the foremost to enter Paradise.' The Prophet added, 'He who obeys me, obeys Allah, and he who disobeys me, disobeys Allah. He who obeys the chief, obeys me, and he who disobeys the chief, disobeys me. The Imam is like a shelter for whose safety Muslims should fight and seek protection.'"** George Bush should have read this Hadith before he spilled American blood in pursuit of an impossible goal—establishing a democracy in Iraq without dealing with Islam first. When our politicians are ignorant and act impulsively without thinking, bad things happen.

Mein Kampf says that if an old religion doesn't concentrate authority on a single man, then a new religion is needed. *Mein Kampf:366 "The value of an existing religion to a politician must be decided less by its deficiencies than by the presence of a visibly better substitute. As long as there is no apparent substitute, the existing religion can be demolished only by fools or by criminals."* Muhammad and Hitler attacked Judeo-Christianity because they believed their religion was a superior substitute, in that it was designed to empower their personal ambitions. Their religotics were control mechanisms. "Submit and obey" is hardly a vague command. The translators of *Mein Kampf* said, "Hitler attempted to make himself the 'prophet of the new German religion.... He believed that if a new 'myth' could be created and propagated as stubbornly, it would give Germans a new faith which the masses would cherish as tenaciously as they previously followed Christianity." Like Islam, Nazism was a replacement or substitute religion. These doctrines are different sides of the same coin.

Der fuhrer, like der prophet, had to condemn those who stood in his way. Although both dictators became what they denounced, they had to clear the world of rivals. *Mein Kampf:367 "Worst of all are those who abuse religious convictions for political purposes. One cannot proceed too aggressively against those wretched profiteers who like to see in religion an instrument which may render them political or commercial service. These impudent liars shout their creed into the world with a stentorian voice in order that others might die for it so that they might live better. The entire faith is for sale. For the seat of power they would certainly marry the Devil."* This is as clear a definition of the *modus operandi* behind Islam as was ever written.

Muhammad and Allah were simply more crude. *Qur'an 059.007* **"Whatever booty Allah gives to His Apostle is for Allah and His Apostle. Accept what the Apostle gives you and refrain from what he forbids."** *Bukhari:V9B84N59* **"Abu Bakr said, 'By Allah! I will fight whoever differentiates between prayers and the zakat tax, as the zakat is rightfully taken from property according to Allah's Orders. If they refused to pay me even so little as a kid they used to pay to Allah's Apostle, I will fight with them for withholding it.'"** *Bukhari:V4B53N386* **"Umar sent Muslims to great countries to fight pagans. He said, 'I intend to invade Persia and Rome.' When we reached the enemy, we said, 'We are Arabs. Our Prophet, the Messenger of our Lord, ordered us to fight you till you serve Allah Alone or pay us the Jizyah tribute tax in submission. Our Prophet has informed us that our Lord says: 'Whoever** amongst us is killed as a martyr shall go to Paradise to lead a luxurious life, and whoever survives shall become your master.'"

There are three reasons I believe this review of *Mein Kampf* is important. First, the religotics of Nazism and Islam are so similar, the world will gain a new appreciation of how poligious doctrines teach men to hate, seduce them to plunder, and compel them to murder. The veil of religiosity will be removed from Islam and with it the unwarranted protection it is granted *vis-à-vis* its religious status.

Second, the consequence of the world's ignorance and tolerance of *Mein Kampf* was devastating. The synthesis of Nazism and modern technology stole millions of lives. Imagine what a similar doctrine would do with unlimited financial resources, nuclear, and biological weapons.

Third, *Mein Kampf* is an insightful book, albeit in a sinister way. It's like having the author's notes to the Qur'an. It's like having an unguarded conversation with Muhammad. Hitler gives us the methodology behind the madness.

Consider this insight: *Mein Kampf:379* *"With the clever and persistent application of propaganda even heaven can be palmed off on a people as hell, and the other way around. The most wretched life can be presented as paradise."* In all of human history, no one was better at this than Allah's Messenger.

At their core, both Islam and Nazism were war manifestos. In their hearts, both Muhammad and Hitler were terrorists. Of the seventy-five raids chronicled in the Qur'an and Hadith during the first decade of the Islamic Era, only two were defensive. The Muslims lost one (Uhud) and barely escaped from the other (Trench). The Islamic terrorists quickly learned how to be offensive. Having studied them, der fuhrer agreed. *Mein Kampf:376* *"The goal must be to achieve a superior fighting power…. Success lies only in the offensive."* *Mein Kampf:384* *"What the German people owe the army may be summed up in a single word: everything…. The army taught personal courage [martyrdom] in a time when cowardice [peace] threatened to become a spreading disease, and when the willingness to sacrifice, to stand up for the general welfare, was looked upon as stupidity."* Much of this Hitler copied from the Medina surahs.

The translators of *Mein Kampf* protest: "Not to have foreseen what was to come was the tragic blunder of Woodrow Wilson—a blunder which was worse than any crime." I suppose these men would also view George Bush as a criminal, as he ignored even better tools from which to foresee the future. The Qur'an and Sunnah are no less coy.

Der fuhrer viewed the army as favorably as did his mentor. *Mein Kampf:386* *"The army teaches young men obedience. The German army is the most powerful weapon in the service of freedom."* *Qur'an 061.004* **"Surely Allah loves those who fight in His cause as an army in full formations as though they were a compact wall."**

Mein Kampf:234 *"To condition the soldier for the terrors of war the enemy must be introduced as a barbarian."* Muhammad wanted to annihilate Jews so that they wouldn't continue to expose him as a fraud. After all, they held the receipts. They knew that he had purchased his scripture. Hitler, likewise, had stolen the dogmas of National Socialism from the Jewish Marxists. If he killed them all, no one would ever know. It was his "final solution." *Mein Kampf:392* "*Historical experience offers countless proofs of this. [We've heard this before.] It shows with terrible clarity that with any mixing of blood of the Aryan with lower races [Jews] the result is the destruction of culture.... It is nothing less than sinning against the will of the Eternal Creator. By trying to resist this logic of Nature [the dark spirit of Nazism], man becomes entangled in a fight against his own existence, an attack that will lead to his doom. So the stupid and impudent Jew objects along with the modern pacifist, by saying, 'Man conquers Nature!' Millions mechanically and thoughtlessly repeat this Jewish nonsense. They have no weapons at their disposal except this wretched idea.*"

As if goose-stepping to the same drumbeat, Allah proclaims: *Qur'an 003.069* **"The People of the Book wish to lead you astray yet they lead none astray but themselves."** *Qur'an 003.111* **"The People of the Book will do you no harm but only annoy you, as they will turn their backs rather than fight. They are degraded and have earned the anger of Allah. Misery overhangs them."** *Qur'an 003.118* **"They desire your annihilation. Hate is on their tongues. And they hide disease in their hearts. Say, 'Die in your rage.' They are vexed but their cunning will do you no harm."**

Mein Kampf:422 "*The Jewish religious doctrine is primarily a tool for preserving the purity of Jewish blood...and regulating intercourse.*" *Mein Kampf:448* "*The black-haired Jew boy, diabolic joy in his face, waits in ambush for the unsuspecting girl whom he defiles with his blood and thus robs her from her people.*" Suggesting that a veil might protect women from defilement, Hitler says: *Mein Kampf:619* "*If today physical beauty of the Aryan girl were not pushed into the background by our dandified fashion, the seduction of hundreds of thousand of girls by bow-legged, disgusting Jewish bastards would never be possible. It is in the interests of the nation that the most beautiful bodies find one another,*" and produce the Nazi Paradise. *Mein Kampf:406* "*Without purity of blood, the Aryan looses the Paradise which he has created for himself.*" *Mein Kampf:413* "*The Jews are neither a race nor a people... They are an example of a purely parasitic product of decay.*"

Mein Kampf:450 "*The most terrible example of the Jew's desire to become a tyrant, to enslave others, and for permanent subjugation is offered by Russia where Jews killed or starved thirty million people with a truly diabolic ferocity and inhuman torture. Now Jewish scribblers and robbers rule over a great people. Jews are vampires who must die sooner or later.*" While Lenin was a Jew, as was Marx, the other founders of Communism, Engels and Hegel, were Aryan. Further, Lenin was a piker when it came to killing Russians. Hitler slaughtered 10 million and Stalin, 20.

Hitler's "god" loved killing Jews as much as Muhammad's did. *Mein Kampf:452* "*Peoples who bastardize themselves, or permit themselves to be bastardized, sin against the will of eternal Providence, and their ruin by the hand of a stronger nation is consequently not an injustice, but only the restoration of right. Nature proclaims that they*

have no right to complain about the loss of their worldly existence." Mein Kampf:454
*"Determined to fight to the extreme with the poison of Marxist ideas, the Jew and his
star of David rose higher as our people's will to live vanished…. Just when resistance
appeared vain, Providence gave the reward; victorious by the sword, it followed the law
of eternal revenge."* Mein Kampf:489 *"Woe to the people that is shamed of seizing the Jews!"*

Trying to pit Christians against Jews, Hitler said of Christ: Mein Kampf:423
*"The Sublime Founder of the new doctrine made no secret of His disposition towards
the Jewish people. He even took to the whip to drive them out of the Lord's temple. For
this Christ was crucified."* Not only *was* Christ a Jew, he loved Jews so much he
surrendered his life to save them. What Christ didn't like was the Jewish religotic—the manmade and political departure from a simple and powerful relationship to a complex and emasculated religion.

I am often confronted with racist Muslims condemning Jews based upon
a book called the *Protocols of the Wise Men of Zion*. In that light, I find the next
entry in *Mein Kampf* incriminating. Mein Kampf:423 *"The entire existence of the Jews
is based upon a continuous lie, one shown in an incomparable manner and certainty
in the Protocols of the Wise Men of Zion. The Jews say that they are a forgery which
is the best proof that they are genuine after all."*

The scholars who translated *Mein Kampf* wrote: "The *Protocols of the Wise
Men of Zion* were first circulated in Russia during the early years of the twentieth century. The tract purports to be an account of a meeting between Jewish leaders in the fall of 1897, the year of the first Zionist Congress. It became
effective propaganda as it contains a horrible plot to undermine society, overthrow governments, and destroy Christianity. However, the 'minutes' of the
meeting are copied verbatim from *A Dialogue in Hades Between Machiavelli and
Montesquiou*, in an attack on the *Masons and the Bonapartists* written in French
by Maurice Joly in 1868. The *Protocols* merely substituted the word 'Jew' for
'Devils.' Further, the anti-Christian plot was stolen from a novel published by
John Retcliff in 1868. He depicts a fictional scene in which an imaginary
annual meeting of the 'twelve Tribes of Israel' occurs in Prague's Jewish
cemetery. They discuss measures calculated to destroy Christians. So, even
though the *Protocols* are a farce, editions edited by the Nazis were widely circulated in Europe."

This is reminiscent of Muhammad's attack on Judeo-Christianity based
upon his bogus versions of the Torah and Gospels. Holocaust cannot be justified without lies.

Muhammad and Hitler, the Qur'an and *Mein Kampf*, Islam and Nazism
are indistinguishable—couplets apart from time and place. Deceit was their
common currency. The blood of Jews was their common goal. Fighting was
justified, even glorified. And millions have been sacrificed at the altar of our
ignorance.

20

THE TORMENTED TERRORIST

"As often as their skin is burnt and singed, roasted through, We shall change it for fresh skin, so that they may go on tasting the torment."

Islam's sixth year dawned like all others. Muhammad scurried off on yet another terrorist raid. *Tabari VIII:42* **"Allah's Messenger set out six months after the conquest of the Qurayza. He went to Lihyan, seeking vengeance for the men betrayed at Faji. To take the enemy by surprise, he pretended to go north. Then he veered to the left and, having passed Yayn, his route led him directly by the main road of Mecca."**

But the bad boy had earned a bad reputation so... *Ishaq:485* **"Muhammad found that the Lihyan had been warned. They had taken secure positions on the mountaintops. After he failed to take them by surprise as he intended, he said, 'If we go down to Usfan, the Meccans will think we have come to [terrorize] them.' So he set out with two hundred Muslim riders before halting at Usfan, and then he returned to Medina."** Crime evidently pays. A few months earlier, Muhammad and his fellow militants could only muster thirty-six horsemen against the Jews. But now, after having sold their children into slavery, they are two hundred strong.

While the raid failed, the militants recorded this little ditty: *Ishaq:486* **"If the Lihyan had remained in their homes they would have met bands of fine fighters, audacious warriors who terrorize. They would have confronted an irresistible force glittering like stars. But they were weasels, sticking to the clefts of rocks instead."**

The next Hadith chronicles another failed raid. We learn that a man named after the Qur'an's first god, Abd-Rahman, raided the prophet's camels, driving them off and killing a herdsman. *Tabari VIII:44* **"Salamah said, 'Tell the Messenger that the polytheists have raided his camels.' Standing on a hill, I faced Medina and shouted, 'A raid!' Then I set out after the enemy, shooting arrows and saying rajaz verses: 'Today the mean ones will receive destruction.'"** Since all of Muhammad's camels were either stolen outright, or purchased with stolen booty, the moral of the story is: stealing what's stolen is bad. The Islamic cavalry was sent in hot pursuit. *Tabari VIII:46* **"If you believe in Allah and know that Paradise is real and that the Fire is real, do not stand between me and martyrdom!' But Abd-Rahman dismounted and thrust his spear into Akhram. So I shot Abd-Rahman with an arrow, and said, 'Take that!'"**

Muhammad's marauding horde failed to recapture the twice-stolen booty, but they managed to recite some revealing poetry: *Ishaq:489* **"War is kindled by passing winds. Our swords glitter, cutting through pugnacious heads. Allah puts obstacles in our victims' way to protect His sacred property and our dignity."** The man who kindled the winds of war was: **"Allah's Apostle, our amir, a man whose message we believe; he is a Prophet who recites a luminous light-bringing Book."**

As you read this next angry diatribe, consider the message and style. This is the same rajaz poetry in which the surahs were revealed. And it is the same message, making it synonymous with Allah's voice. *Ishaq:489* **"Do the bastards think that we are not their equal in fighting? We are men who believe there is no shame in killing. We don't turn from piercing lances. We smite the heads of the haughty with blows that quash the zeal of the unyielding [non-Muslims]. We're heroes, protecting our war banner. We are a noble force, as fierce as wolves. We preserve our honor and protect our property by smashing heads."** It's little wonder Hitler modeled Nazism after Islam.

Turning the page, we are confronted with childish tales of braggadocios bullies vying for the prophet's attention. One concludes with: *Tabari VIII:48* **"Then he set out at full speed after the enemy—he was like a beast of prey."** Fixated on raiding civilians, a series of Traditions praise Muslims who could shoot and shout at the same time. Muhammad assigns commanders, reviews his ranks, judges his companions' killing prowess, and sends everyone out against his enemies. Then: *Ishaq:490/Tabari VIII:51* **"When Allah's Messenger heard about the Mustaliq gathering against him he set out and met them at one of their watering holes near the coast. The people advanced and fought fiercely. Allah caused the Mustaliq to fight and killed some of them. Allah gave the Apostle their children, women, and property as booty."**

When the Muslim militants went after the Meccan caravan and ended up fighting merchants at Badr, Allah said in the 8th surah that it was he, not them, who wielded the sword. When the Qaynuqa, Nadir, and Qurayza Jews were terrorized, Allah again claimed credit in the 33rd and 59th surahs. On this day, Muhammad sets off with an army, they fight, and yet Allah says that he was the killer, the thief, and the slave trader. Believe what you will about "god" being an immoral thug; the creator of the universe cannot be so impotent and delusional he has to usurp credit for acts clearly performed by others.

What's really happening here is the essence of Islam. Muhammad needed a spiritual endorsement to make his vulgar deeds—piracy, the slave trade, and terrorism—seem godly. By alleging that Allah perpetrated the crimes, Muhammad obfuscated personal responsibility for his heinous behavior.

Islam's founder was a rather simple character. Abused as a child, he craved revenge. The Meccan leaders became his enemy as they withheld the sustenance that flowed from the Ka'aba Inc. Muhammad sold his soul to the Devil to take it away from them. As insecure as Hitler, he craved the things he thought would make him *feel* worthy: sex, power, and money. The motivation behind each of his terrorist raids was money. Allah's alleged endorsement of his dictatorship gave him power. But let us not forget sex. The king of the

Banu Mustaliq sired Juwayriyah, the most beautiful woman in the land. She was taken by the prophet.

Placed into the context of these historical Hadith, the following Tradition from Muslim is untrue. An invitation to surrender was not part of Muhammad's battle plan. *Muslim:B19N4292* **"Aun inquired whether it was necessary to extend (to the infidels) an invitation to submit to Islam before murdering them in the fight. Nafi told me that it was necessary in the early days of Islam. The Messenger (may peace be upon him) made a raid upon Mustaliq while they were unaware and their cattle were having a drink at the water. He killed those who fought and imprisoned others. On that very day, he captured Juwayriyah. Nafi said that this Tradition was related to him by Abdallah Umar who was among the raiding troops."** The first Muslims admitted that they were raiders who launched surprise attacks on unsuspecting civilians. This is textbook terrorism. They confessed to murder and to taking captives whom they sold into slavery. They even confirmed Muhammad's personal involvement, acknowledging that "he killed," "imprisoned," and "captured Juwayriyah," the chief's daughter. This is a very unappealing picture—one completely inconsistent with a religion worthy of human souls.

What's more, the premise of the Hadith was rejected by the body of the Tradition. There was no invitation to Islam. This was a surprise attack by armed raiders on defenseless and unsuspecting civilians. The stated purpose was to assert Muhammad's power over the Arabs, to steal their possessions and their lives, turning them into slaves. In a way, it was Islam.

Returning to the rape and plunder of the Mustaliq Arabs: *Tabari VIII:56/Ishaq:493* **"According to Aisha: 'A great number of Mustaliq were wounded. The Messenger took many captives, and they were divided among all the Muslims. Juwayriyah was one of the slaves. When the Prophet divided the captives by lot [a gambling game], Juwayriyah fell to the share of Thabit, Muhammad's cousin. She gave him a deed for her freedom which he did not accept. Juwayriyah was the most beautiful woman and she captivated anyone who looked at her. She came to the Apostle seeking his help. As soon as I saw her at the door of my chamber, I took a dislike to her, and I knew that he would see in her what I saw.'"**

Aisha was right... *Tabari VIII:57* **"Muhammad said, 'Would you like something better than that? I will discharge your debt [ransom payment] and marry you.'"** The story is that she agreed. The reason: **"A hundred families of the Mustaliq were freed as a result of the marriage. I know of no woman who was a greater blessing to her people than she."** Juwayriyah was a real martyr.

The Emigrant Muslims from Mecca and the converted ones from Medina were often hostile, even with one another. Such was the case on this day: *Tabari VIII:52/Ishaq:491* **"Jahjah and Juhani began crowding each other at the watering place and fought. Juhani shouted, 'People of the Ansar [Medina Muslims].' Jahjah shouted, 'People of the Emigrants [Meccan Muslims].' Abdallah bin Ubayy [the leader of the Ansar] became enraged and said, 'Why are they doing this? Are they trying to outrank us and outnumber us in our own land? The proverb "Feed a dog and it will devour you" fits these Quraysh** vagabonds. When we go back to Medina, those who are stronger will drive out the weaker. Then he turned to his tribe and said, 'This is what you have done to yourselves! You have allowed them [the Meccan Muslims] to settle in your land [Yathrib] and divide your wealth. Had you kept from them what you had, they would have moved to another place.'" The first Muslims were at each other's throats.

Back in Medina, and in the presence of the prophet, the Emigrants weren't ready to let Abdallah Ubayy's outburst drop. They wanted blood. *Tabari VIII:53* "Abdallah said, 'Those who are stronger will drive out the weaker from Medina.' But you, O Messenger of Allah, will drive him out if you wish. He is the weak one, and you are the strong one. Allah caused you to arrive at the moment when his people were stringing precious stones to make him a crown; he thinks that you deprived him of a kingdom.'" *Ishaq:491* "Umar said, 'Tell someone to go kill him.' The Apostle answered, 'But what will men say about me if I start killing Muslims?'"

A young recruit must have rushed in: *Tabari VIII:55/Ishaq:492* "'Messenger of Allah, I have been told that you want to kill Abdallah bin Ubayy. If you are going to do it; command me and I will bring you his head. I will kill a believer to avenge an unbeliever, and thereby enter the Fire of Hell.' The Prophet said, 'No.' Thus after that day it was his own tribesmen who censured him and threatened him. When word of how they were behaving reached Muhammad, he said to Umar, 'What do you think, Umar? Had I killed him the day you ordered me to, prominent men would have been upset, who, if I ordered them today to kill him, would do so.'" Muhammad was evil, not stupid.

Other than prostrating oneself in submission, paying the zakat, and fighting Jihad, Muslims have never had a way to determine who really was one. Even Muhammad couldn't tell. *Tabari VIII:55* "Miqyas came from Mecca, pretending to have become a Muslim, and said, 'Muhammad, I have come to you as a Muslim to seek blood money for my brother who was killed by mistake.' The Prophet ordered him to be paid blood money for his brother and he stayed briefly with Muhammad. Then he attacked his brother's slayer, killing him. He left for Mecca as an apostate." According to Lucifer's Islam, an apostate endures hell's hottest flames. So it's okay to kill and good to accept booty for killing, but only if Allah is credited with the murder.

This Hadith is especially revealing: *Ishaq:485* "'O Apostle, I will accept Islam and give you my allegiance on the condition that my past faults are forgiven and no mention is made of what has gone before.' Allah's Messenger said, 'Give your allegiance, for Islam does away with all that preceded it, as does the Hijrah [Muhammad's shameful flight from Mecca].'" Muhammad proudly announced, and Ishaq dutifully recorded, words that should send shivers up the spine of every non-Muslim. The "religion" of Islam, the feeble and demented doctrine that emerged before the terrorist raids, before piracy, kidnapping, the slave trade, and mass murder, was no more. All that preceded the Hijrah had been abrogated. All that remained of the poligious doctrine now was vice, villainy, and violence.

It's apparent that Aisha got her pigtails bent out of shape with the addition of the seductive Juwayriyah to the harem. The next six pages in both

Tabari and Ishaq are dedicated to what is called, "The Account of the Lie that Was Uttered." Ishaq says, with great trepidation: *Tabari VIII:58/Ishaq:493* "According to a man I do not suspect, and others who contributed parts of the story, a report has been assembled for you based upon what people have told me in regards to the account of Aisha's story about herself, when the authors of the lie said about her what they said." Muhammad's fellow Muslims accused Aisha of infidelity—cheating on the prophet. It's hard to believe that she would act so immaturely at fourteen. It's hard to imagine why she would want to be loved by someone within forty years of her age. Yet apparently after becoming just one of a score of sex toys in the prophet's collection, there was some unauthorized fornication.

Afraid to demean Muhammad's excuse and contradict the Qur'an, Tabari treads lightly, as well. *Tabari VIII:58* "Each contributed to her account. Some related what others did not. Each was a reliable informant concerning her, and each related about her what he had heard. The whole of her story rests on these men." Neither Tabari nor Ishaq batted an eye when they told us that Muhammad had spoken for the Devil, that Allah had approved booty, rape, and the slave trade. They reported the annihilation of the Jews like true soldiers. But, now they have made a dozen excuses so as to say: "If you don't like this report, don't blame me."

Tabari VIII:58/Ishaq:494 "Aisha said, 'When the raid on the Mustaliq took place, Muhammad had his wives draw lots as he used to do to see who would accompany him. My lot came out over theirs, and he took me along. Women in those days used to eat only enough to stay alive; they were not bloated with meat so as to become heavy. While my camel was being saddled, I would sit in my litter; then the men who were to bind my litter onto my camel would come and place my howdah on the camel. They would take hold of the camel and walk alongside." This provides an interesting insight into Muhammad's priorities. Setting off on a terrorist raid he used men and a camel to carry a girl so that he might not be deprived of sex. As such, believing that this man was a prophet speaking on behalf of God requires one to be deprived of a brain.

Ishaq:494 "When the people had mounted, I went out to attend to a need of mine (to relieve myself). I had a necklace with onyx beads. When I was finished it came undone without my noticing. I retraced my steps to the place where I had gone looking until I found it. But while I was away, the men who saddled the camel for me assumed that I was in the litter and lifted it up. When I returned to the camp, not a soul was there. I wrapped myself in my jilbab and lay down in the place where I had gone. I thought they would return."

The continuing saga is so peppered with innuendo, it's embarrassing: *Tabari VIII:58/Ishaq:494* "I had just lain down when Safwan al-Sulami passed by. He had lagged behind attending to a need of his. He had not spent the night with the troops. When he saw my form, he approached me and stood over me. He used to look at me before the veil and hijab was imposed on us. When he saw me, he exclaimed in astonishment, 'The Apostle's wife!' He asked why I was alone, but I did not speak. Then he brought his camel near and said, 'Mount! I mounted and he came. He took hold of the camel's head and set out with me, hastening in pursuit of the party. He told me to ride it while he kept behind. So I rode it."

To cut to the chase, the rumors of their party were vicious. Aisha said, *Tabari VIII:60* "**The story reached the Prophet and I missed the attention he once showed me.... He would come to see me while my mother was nursing me, and say 'How is she?' and nothing more. We were Arab folk. We did not have these privies in our houses that the foreigners have; we loathed such things. Instead, we would go out into the fields of Medina. One day while I was out with the girls. One said, 'Daughter, take it lightly. Whenever a beautiful woman married to a man has rival wives, they always gossip about her, and people do the same.' I showed my astonishment.**"

So Muhammad used his mosque to attack those who had defamed his favorite toy. When he finished, Usayd said, "**Even if they are brothers, give the command. I will rid you of them because they deserve to have their heads cut off!**" A squabble ensued. *Ishaq:496* "'**By Allah you lie,' one said to another. 'Liar yourself!' 'You are a disaffected person arguing on behalf of the diseased,**" another shouted, providing fodder for the fourth surah. "**Over this affair, fighting almost broke out between the Muslim clans.**"

Yet some men were simply rude rather than rash. *Tabari VIII:62/Ishaq:496* "**Ali [Muhammad's adopted son, son-in-law, and future Caliph] said, 'Prophet, women are plentiful. You can get a replacement, easily changing one for another.'**" Studying the formation of Islam is like wallowing in the mud with pigs. It stinks to high heaven and there are swine everywhere.

But this little pig wasn't finished. He huffed: "**Ask the slave girl; she will tell you the truth.' So the Apostle called Burayra to ask her. Ali got up and gave her a violent beating first, saying, 'Tell the Apostle the truth.'**" Caught between a sexist and a sadist, the slave was of no value to either man. Ali couldn't force her to speak badly of Aisha and Muhammad chose not to listen. All we know is that the founders of Islam captured and owned slaves, and they beat them without remorse.

In a related Hadith: *Muslim:B40N6837* "**Allah's Messenger delivered an address, mentioning a camel and a bad person who cut off its hind legs, reciting: 'When the basest of them broke forth with mischief.' He then delivered instruction saying: 'There are amongst you those who beat their women. They flog them like slave girls. Then after flogging them like slaves they comfort them in their beds as a result at the end of the day.' He then advised in regard to people laughing at the breaking of wind and said: 'You laugh at that which you yourself do.'**" It may have been the world's worst sermon.

While this is a story about Aisha's infidelity, we are learning a great deal about the nature of Islam and the character of Muhammad and his cronies. For example, Bakr wasn't much of a father. *Tabari VIII:63/Ishaq:496* "**When Muhammad came into my room, my parents were with me. I was crying. I waited for my mother and father to reply to the Apostle, but they did not speak. I asked my parents why they were afraid to defend me, but they said nothing. My weeping broke out afresh. I swear, I considered myself too lowly and unimportant for Allah to reveal a Qur'an about me to be recited in mosques and used in worship. But I was hoping that the Prophet would see something in a dream from Allah which would clear me of this.**"

Aisha was young and cute, so what do you suppose the over-hormoned profiteer did next? Muhammad contrived another Allahism to satiate his cravings. He was as predictable as a mosquito at a nudist colony. *Tabari VIII:63/Ishaq:497* "Before Allah's Messenger left the place where he was sitting, there came over him from Allah what used to come over him. They covered him with his garment and set a leather cushion under his head. Then he recovered and sat up; drops of sweat fell from him like silver beads. He began wiping the perspiration from his brow and said, 'Good news, Aisha! Allah has sent down word about your innocence.' I said, 'To Allah's praise and your blame!' Then he went out to the people and preached to them. He recited the Qur'an Allah had revealed concerning me and gave orders concerning Mistah, Hassan, and Hamnah who were the most explicit in their slander. They received their prescribed flogging of eighty lashes. They were beaten to the boundary of death for their crime against the religion of Islam." This equates "the religion of Islam" with "making Muhammad feel good."

Islam's founder routinely made up Qur'an scripture to suit his agenda. However, there was a glimmer of light in this story. Aisha knew better. That's why she condemned Muhammad the moment he revealed the 24th surah, a "divine" revelation inspired by infidelity. It's called "The Criterion." *024.001* "(This is) a surah which We have revealed and made obligatory and in which We have revealed clear communications that you may be mindful. For the woman and the man guilty of adultery or fornication, flog each of them with a hundred stripes. Let not compassion move you in their case, in a matter prescribed by Allah. And let a party of the Believers witness their punishment." For Muhammad to avoid having the lash applied to him, he had to have his god condone polygamy (which is adultery in all sane religions and societies), as well as pedophilia (which is what is being approved here), incest (approved earlier in the 33rd surah), unwed sex with concubines (which is fornication) and sex with slaves (which is rape). In other words, Muhammad was a hypocrite—the embodiment of the condition he condemned.

That said, it was time for a situational scripture. Muhammad's plaything had been accused of adultery, but in order that her services might continue to arouse him, this Qur'anic surah was conveniently revealed. *024.004* "And those who launch a charge against chaste women, and produce not four witnesses (to support their allegations), flog them with eighty stripes; and reject their evidence ever after: for such men are wicked transgressors." Aisha had but three accusers. How fortuitous.

Now that the witnesses have been punished and the perpetrators exonerated, Muhammad put Muslim women in their place—in submission to men. *024.006* "And for those who launch a charge against their wives, accusing them, but have no witnesses or evidence, except themselves; let the testimony of one of them be four testimonies, (swearing four times) by Allah that he is the one speaking the truth. And the fifth (oath) that they solemnly invoke the curse of Allah on themselves if they tell a lie." That pretty much sums up the plight of Islamic women. If their husbands say that they are bad four times, they are as good as dead. Men don't need evidence.

In the Islamic world, women can't speak or even leave home without their husbands' permission. So this next verse is rendered moot. *024.008* "But it would avert the punishment from the wife (of being stoned to death), if she bears witness four times by Allah, that (her husband) is telling a lie. And the fifth (oath) should be that she solemnly invokes the wrath of Allah on herself if (her accuser) is telling the truth."

Returning to Muhammad's predicament, we find another series of verses that are senseless without the context of the Hadith. And within their context, they are petty and vengeful, focused on the desires of the Qur'an's author. The sheer volume of these verses should tell you all you need to know about his priorities. *024.011* "Those who brought forward the lie are a body among you: but think it not an evil to you; on the contrary, it is good for you: to every man among them (will come the punishment) of the sin he earned, and for him who took the lead in the slander, his will be an awful doom. Why did not the believers, when you heard of the affair, put the best construction on it in their minds and say, 'This is an obvious lie?' Why did they not bring four witnesses to prove it? Since they produce not witnesses, they are liars in the sight of Allah. Were it not for His mercy a grievous penalty would have seized you in that you rushed glibly into this affair. You received it on your tongues, and said out of your mouths things of which you had no knowledge; and you thought it to be a light matter, while it was most serious in the sight of Allah, a grave offense. And why did you not, when you heard it, say? 'It is not right of us to speak of this: this is a most serious slander, an awful calumny!' Allah does admonish you, that you may never repeat such, if you are Believers. And Allah makes clear the communications. Allah is the Knower, Wise. Those who love scandal to be broadcast among the Believers will have a painful punishment in this life and the hereafter."

How is it possible that a book allegedly written before the world began could focus so intently on a child accused of fornication and yet say nothing about the indiscretion that prompted the infidelity? Aisha was upset because Muhammad purchased—with money he "earned" selling children into slavery —sex with an alluring slave. It's obvious Ibn Ishaq, the prophet's earliest and most trusted biographer, and Tabari, the first Islamic historian, were bothered too. And that's why they said: *Ishaq:493* "According to a man I do not suspect, and others who contributed parts of the story, a report has been assembled for you based upon what people have told me in regards to the account of Aisha's story about herself, when the authors of the lie said about her what they said." In other words, the same sources who have brought us the Hadith and Qur'an were witnesses against Aisha and thus witnesses against Muhammad and the Qur'an.

Speaking of hypocrites, the man who admitted to reciting a surah dictated by Satan now tells others: *024.021* "Believers, follow not Satan's footsteps: if any will follow Satan, he will command what is shameful, filthy, and wrong." Since every deed Muhammad has perpetrated since the Hijrah has been shameful, filthy, and wrong, he has revealed who commanded him.

The demon-possessed prophet wasn't done attacking those who had tried to deprive him (a nearly sixty-year-old man) of the pleasures of possessing a fourteen-year-old child. *024.023* "Those who slander chaste women, indiscreet and careless but believing, are cursed in this life and in the hereafter: for them is an awful doom.

On the Day when their tongues, their hands, and their feet will bear witness against them as to what they did. On that Day Allah will pay them back their just reward."

Considering Muhammad's collection of concubines and sex slaves were from all races and religions, this next verse would make him impure. *024.026* "Women impure are for men impure, and men impure for women impure..."

Moving on, we find the Muhammad/Allah team treating women differently, and less favorably, than men. *024.031* "And say to the believing women that they should lower their gaze and guard their modesty; that they should not display their beauty except what (must) appear; that they should draw their veils over their bosoms and not display them except to their husbands, their fathers, their husband's fathers, their sons, their husbands' sons, their brothers or their brothers' sons, or their women, or the slaves whom they possess, or male servants free of physical needs, or small children who have no sense of the shame of sex; and that they should not strike their feet in order to draw attention to their hidden ornaments." To this prophet, women were objects, not people.

Since Muhammad financed his war machine on the slave trade, and satiated his libido by the admission of slaves into his harem, we shouldn't be surprised by: *024.032* "And marry such as are your slaves and maid-servants [female slaves]. If they be poor, Allah will enrich them of His bounty." It was another form of booty.

This next verse confirms what I surmised from the Hadith. When enslaved women were given to Muhammad's militants as booty, they were forced into prostitution. *024.034* "Force not your slave-girls to whoredom (prostitution) if they desire chastity, that you may seek enjoyment of this life. [And here's the freedom-to-pimp card:] But if anyone forces them, then after such compulsion, Allah is oft-forgiving." These guys weren't qualified to open a brothel, much less start a religion.

If we didn't know Muhammad better, this symbolism might appear inspired (that is, if it weren't so poorly written): *024.035* "Allah is the Light of the heavens and the earth. The Parable of His Light is a niche and within a lamp: the lamp is in a glass: the glass as it were a shining star kindled from a blessed tree, an olive, neither of the east nor west, whose oil is nigh luminous though fire scarce touched it. Light upon light! Allah does guide whom He will to His light: Allah sets forth parables for men: and knows all things."

Confirming that Allah was the name of a pagan idol, not the word for God, we discover: *024.036* "(Lit is such a light) in houses which Allah has permitted to be exalted that His name shall be remembered, for the celebration of His name."

Leaving dimwitted we return to demented. Business is a distraction for those trapped in the terrorist creed but paying taxes is good. *024.037* "Men who do not let business devert them from prayers and paying the zakat fear a day when eyes will roll back (in horror of the Day of Doom)." And once again, we find Allah in hell. *024.039* "For those who disbelieve, their deeds are like a mirage in the desert. There is no water for the thirsty. He only finds Allah, who will pay him his due in Hell."

Muhammad said that Allah sent 999 out of every 1000 people to hell (*Bukhari:V8B76N537*), predestining them to be abused. *024.040* "Their fate is like the depths of darkness in the abysmal sea, overwhelmed with dark clouds: layers of darkness. If a man stretches out his hands, he can hardly see it. For he whom Allah has not appointed light, for him there is no light." The matching verse from the previous surah adds: *023.040* "Soon they will regret. Torment and an awful cry will overtake them. We have made such men rubbish, like rotting plants. So away with the people." Being sent to hell to be tortured without being given a choice is sadistic. Being called rotting rubbish is demented. Only Satan would call this scripture.

Next we move from demented to delusional. Unable to perform a miracle or produce a prophecy, Muhammad tells us that rain was proof that his spirit was divine. *024.043* "Do you not see that Allah drives along the clouds, then gathers them together, then piles them up so you see the rain coming forth from their midst? And He sends down hail like mountains, striking and afflicting whom He wills and turning it away from whom He pleases. The flash of His lightning almost takes away the sight. It is Allah Who alternates the Night and the Day. In these things is an instructive example for those who have vision!" These aren't poetic metaphors; they are pathetic proofs.

The next creation account is the twenty-fifth variant. After suggesting that we were made from a blood clot in the first surah, then sperm, base fluid, stinking slime, and clay, we learn: *024.045* "Allah has created every animal from water: of them there are some that creep on their bellies; some that walk on two legs; and some that walk on four." *024.046* "We have indeed sent down proofs and signs that make things manifest, [and sent] revelations and explained them."

It was time for Muhammad's rock idol to denounce his critics—the bad Muslims who were abandoning him in droves. *024.047* "They say, 'We believe in Allah and in the Messenger, and we obey,' but even after that, some of them turn away: they are not (really) Believers. When they are summoned to Allah and His Messenger, in order that He may judge between them, behold some of them decline (to come) and are averse; But if right is on their side, they come quickly to him in submission, obedient." Sometimes the smallest details reveal the biggest flaws. The letter "h" in "him" wasn't capitalized, which means "him" was Muhammad. Therefore, the doctrine of submission was all about obedience to a man.

024.050 "Is there a disease in their hearts, do they have doubts? Do they in fear that Allah and His Messenger will deal unjustly, acting wrongfully toward them?" Now what would give the citizens of Medina that impression? Just because Muhammad had assassinated journalists, led scores of terrorist raids, motivated militants with booty, murdered thousands in cold blood, raped women, stole property, and sold children into slavery, doesn't mean that he couldn't be trusted, did it?

Muhammad devised a test, a way of distinguishing between the good and bad Muslims. *024.051* "The only response of the (true) Believers when summoned to Allah and His Messenger in order to judge between them, is no other than this: they say, 'We hear and we obey.' Such are successful. Those who obey Allah and His Messenger, fear Allah and do right, such are the victorious. Whoever obeys Allah and His Messenger fears Allah and keeps his duty." Since there isn't a single verse that suggests Allah ever spoke to his "believers," Muslims must "hear and obey" Muhammad. Thus, a good Muslim is one who obeys his commands to: conduct terrorist raids, engage in fighting and genocide, prosper using the slave trade, steal what belongs to others through conquest, always giving the prophet his fifth. Such behavior makes men good Muslims and bad people. I recognize that this is unflattering, but it's Islam's definition, not mine.

And lest we forget, we have been given a slightly expanded version of the dictatorial dogma first preached in Mecca: **"He who fears will mind."** This time it's: **"Whoever obeys Allah and His Messenger fears Allah and keeps his duty."**

Muhammad, frustrated by the peaceful Muslims who were unwilling to leave their homes to fight for him, said: *024.053* **"They swear their strongest oaths saying that if only you would command them."** In other words, what Muhammad wanted was for them to go out fighting while *he* stayed home! **"They would leave their homes (and go forth fighting in Allah's Cause). Say: 'Swear not; Obedience is (more) reasonable.' Say: 'Obey Allah, and obey the Messenger."** Obedience is, once again, to Muhammad and the required behavior is Jihad.

Muhammad now says on behalf of Allah that if you follow him into battle, the earth and its people will be yours. There is nothing like a good bribe to motivate mercenaries. Allah promised to make Muslims **"rulers of the earth."** *024.055* **"Allah has promised to those among you who believe and do good work that He will make them rulers of the earth as He granted it to those before them. He will establish in authority their religion—the one which He has chosen for them..."** There *is* choice in Islam, only it doesn't belong to people.

To be a Muslim, all you have to do is perform rituals, pay taxes, and obey Muhammad. *024.056* **"Perform prayer, pay the zakat and obey the Messenger."** In this verse, Muhammad dispensed with Allah because all he wanted was obedience and money. *024.057* **"Never think that the unbelievers can escape in the land. Their abode is Fire!"** There is no escaping Islam, which is why it must be exterminated.

The prophet's desire to nap nude with his harem is the only possible rationale for this being in the Qur'an: *024.058* **"Believers, let your slave girls, and those who have not come to puberty, ask permission (before they come in your presence) on three occasions: before dawn, while you take off your clothes at midday, and after the night prayer. These are your times of undress—times of privacy for you. Outside those times it is not wrong for them to move about: Thus does Allah make clear the Signs."**

Returning to the theme of "submit and obey:" *024.062* **"Only those are believers in Allah and His Messenger who, when they are with him on a matter requiring collective action [like fighting], do not depart until they have asked for his permission. Deem not the summons of the Messenger like the summons of one of you. Allah knows those who slip away, making excuses. Beware of rejecting the Messenger's orders lest a grievous penalty be inflicted."** Since Muhammad was dead before the Qur'an became a book, why was this verse included? It ceased to be relevant the moment he died.

✡ ✝ ☾ ☀

Muslims could dish it out, but they couldn't take it. One was overcome with rage after being satirized in a poem. *Ishaq:498* **"Safwan smote Hassan with his sword and tied his hands to his neck."** When Muhammad asked why, he explained: **"'He insulted and satirized me and I became enraged. So I smote him.' The Apostle said, 'Hassan, did you look on my people with an evil eye because Allah has guided them to Islam?'"** Without benefit of an answer, the prophet told the shackled and beaten pagan to forget what the Muslim had done. Then we're told that he offered him a bribe. *Ishaq:499* **"The Apostle provided some compensation that included a castle, some property, a portion of the zakat tax, and a Copt slave girl."**

This leads us to the haunting betrayal of Hudaybiyah. *Tabari VIII:67/Ishaq:499* **"The Prophet set out to make the lesser pilgrimage, not intending to make war. He had asked the Arabs and Bedouin desert dwellers who were around him to help by setting out with him, for he feared [for some reason] that the Quraysh would oppose him with fighting or turn him away from Allah's House [Ka'aba]. Many Bedouins were slow in coming to him. So the Messenger set out with the Emigrants and Ansar. He took sacrificial animals with him and put on the pilgrim garb."** The Qur'an hasn't bothered to describe the pilgrimage, the use of sacrificial animals, or special garb. And that's because Arabs already knew about these things. They were part of their prior pagan lore. Islam simply incorporated old rites into its new dogma.

We are told that there were 700 men, 1400 men, 1300 men, or 1900 men, depending on who is telling the story. *Tabari VIII:71* **"Umar said, 'Messenger, will you without arms or horses enter the territory of people who are at war with you?' So the Prophet sent men back to Medina and they gathered all of the horses and weapons they could find. When they approached Mecca, they prohibited him from entering, so they marched to Mina. Muhammad's spy brought him word that Ikrimah was coming out with five hundred men. Muhammad said, 'Khalid, your paternal uncle's son is coming against you.' Khalid replied, 'I am the sword of Allah and the sword of His Messenger! Direct me to whatever you wish!' Muhammad sent him in command of horsemen, and he met Ikrimah in the canyon and routed him—driving him back into Mecca. Khalid then routed him twice more. Regarding him, Allah revealed: 'It is he who restrained their hands from you, and your hands from them in the hallow of Mecca, after he made you victors over them'—until the words—'painful punishment.'"** [Qur'an 48:24]

Ishaq:500 **"The Messenger said, 'Woe to the Quraysh! War has devoured them! What harm would they suffer if they left me to deal with the rest of the Arabs? [Besides having their property seized and their people terrorized and killed?] If the Arabs defeat me, that will be what they want. If Allah makes me prevail over the Arabs [not save them], the Quraysh can enter Islam [surrender] en masse. Or they can fight. By Allah, I shall not cease to fight against them for the mission which Allah has entrusted me until Allah makes me victorious or I perish."** For Muhammad, it was a never-ending war. Salvation never entered the picture.

After making his "give me victory or give me death" speech, the weasel whispered: *Ishaq:500* **"Who will take us out by a way in which we will avoid the Quraysh?"**

Suggesting that the pilgrims were really an army, *Tabari VIII:73/ Ishaq:500* **"The Messenger gave orders to the force, saying, 'Turn right, amid the saltbush on a path that will bring the army out over Murar Pass to the descent of Hudaybiyah below Mecca.' So the army traveled that path. When the horsemen of the Quraysh saw the dust of the army and that the Messenger had turned away from their path, they galloped back to Mecca."**

The Hadith continues by disclosing the source of the prophet's guidance. **"When Muhammad's camel entered the pass, she kneeled down. "She has not balked,' the Prophet said. 'The One who restrained the elephant restrained her. I will grant the Quraysh any wish today.'"** The reference is to Abraha's elephant who prostrated herself to the Ka'aba rather than enter Mecca. Allah was so proud of the way he killed the Yemeni, he revealed the 105th surah in his honor.

Tabari VIII:75 **"The Prophet said, [after returning to Medina for his weapons and routing the Meccans three times with his cavalry] 'We have not come to fight anyone; we have come to make the lesser pilgrimage. War has exhausted and harmed the Quraysh. [And whose fault might that be?] If they wish, we will grant them a delay [in killing them] and they can leave me alone to deal with the Arabs. If they refuse the delay, I shall fight them for the sake of this affair of mine as long as I live.'"** It's another confession. Muhammad was terrorizing his people **"for the sake of this affair of mine."**

Tabari VIII:76 **"Urwah went to the Prophet. 'Muhammad, tell me, if you exterminate your tribesmen—have you ever heard of any of the Arabs who has destroyed his own race before you?'"** Good question—one without an answer. Muhammad was the first to terrorize, enslave, and murder Arabs *en masse*. *Ishaq:502* **"Muhammad, you have collected a mixed group of people and brought them to your kin to destroy them. By Allah, I see both prominent people and rabble who are likely to flee, deserting you tomorrow.' Now Abu Bakr who was standing behind the Apostle, said, 'Go suck the clitoris of Al-Lat!'"** The future Caliph was a master linguist and skilled in the snappy comeback.

Urwah had spoken truthfully, placing Muhammad's barbaric deeds in the context of history and reason. But the Muslim brain trust couldn't handle the truth, so they slandered him. Even today, when I engage Islamic clerics in debate, they attack the me rather than defend their scriptures.

Urwah rose above the insult. *Tabari VIII:76/Ishaq:502* **"He began speaking to the Prophet again, stroking his beard. Mughira, clad in mail, was standing next to him with his sword. Whenever Urwah extended his hand toward the Prophet's beard, Mughira struck his hand with the lower end of the scabbard and said, 'Take your hand away from his beard before you lose it!' Urwah raised his head and asked, 'Who is this?' They said, 'Mughira.' Urwah said, 'Rude man, I am trying to rectify your act of treachery.' During the Time of Ignorance [pre-Islam] Mughira had accompanied some men and killed them, taking their money."** Nothing has changed. **"The Apostle just smiled."**

Tabari VIII:77 **"Urwah began looking at the Companions of the Prophet. He said, 'If Muhammad coughs up a bit of phlegm and it falls onto the hand of one of them, he rubs his face in it. If he gives them an order, they vie with each other to carry it out."**

The next four pages of Tabari's History wallow in the dust-filled ravines surrounding Mecca as Quraysh and Muslims jockey for position. Then they get down to business. *Tabari VIII:82* **"Allah's Messenger summoned Uthman and sent him to Abu Sufyan and the dignitaries of the Quraysh to inform them that he had come not for war but merely to visit the House [of pagan idols] and venerate its sanctity. When Uthman delivered the message, the Quraysh said, 'If you wish to circumambulate the Temple, do so.' He replied, 'I will not do it until the Messenger does.' So the Quraysh imprisoned him."**

But Islamic intelligence wasn't very good so the chief Muslim became enraged. *Ishaq:503/Tabari VIII:82* **"When Muhammad received a report that Uthman had been killed, he said, 'We will not leave until we fight it out with the enemy.' He summoned the people to swear allegiance. The Prophet's crier announced: People, an oath of allegiance! The Holy Spirit has descended!"** These folks were so deceived they thought that the "Holy Spirit" was an oath of war.

Ishaq:503/Tabari VIII:83 **"On the day of Hudaybiyah we swore allegiance to the Messenger while Umar was holding his hand under the acacia tree. It was a pledge unto death."** The *Kum-ba-yah* handholding around the tree was sweet and all but I'm sure you noticed that the oath of allegiance was sworn to Muhammad, not Allah. The Qur'an agrees: *048.010* **"Those who swear allegiance to you (Muhammad) indeed swear allegiance to Allah."** They were, after all, one in the same.

Having assembled his biography from oral traditions a century after these events unfolded, Ibn Ishaq knew what would ultimately unfold in the dry and barren lands of the Arabian Desert. So he wrote: *Ishaq:503* **"Allah saw what was in their hearts [what they coveted] so he rewarded them with victory and with as much spoil as they could take. Allah promised that they would soon capture a great deal of booty."**

Ishaq:504/Tabari VIII:85 **"The Quraysh intended peace when they sent Suhayl to Muhammad. He spoke for some time and they negotiated with each other. When the matter had been arranged and only the writing of the document remained, Umar jumped up and went to Abu Bakr and said, 'Isn't he the Messenger of Allah?' 'Yes' Bakr replied. 'And are we not Muslims?' Umar asked. 'Yes,' answered Abu Bakr. 'And are they not the polytheists?' he asked. 'Yes.' "Then why,' asked Umar, 'should we grant what is demeaning to our religion?"** So, what's up? What could have been so awful that Umar, the future Caliph, was questioning the credentials of the man who had murdered, looted, and terrorized his way to immortality?

It was no big deal really. All Muhammad did was abandon Ar-Rahman and Ar-Rahim and then renounce his claim to being Allah's Messenger. But not to worry, Muslim brothers, he did it for the right reason: to acquire what he coveted most—the keys to the Ka'aba Inc.

Not satisfied with Abu Bakr's response: *Ishaq:504* **"Umar jumped up and went to the Prophet. 'Are you not the Messenger of Allah?' 'Yes,' Muhammad replied. 'Are we not Muslims?' Umar asked the Prophet. 'Yes.' 'Are they not polytheists?' Umar questioned. 'Yes,' Muhammad said. 'Then why should we grant what is detrimental to our religion?' He replied, 'I am Allah's Messenger. I will not disobey and He will not allow me to perish.'"** Muhammad was working for the wrong boss. Within two years the terrible tyrant would be worm food. Allah couldn't, and therefore didn't, save him.

But on this day, Islam's pirate was just a common weasel. Those words still lingering on his lips, Allah's boy denied his gods and his calling: *Ishaq:504/ Tabari VIII:85* **"The Prophet summoned me and said, 'Write: "In the name of Allah, Ar-Rahman and Ar-Rahim."' Suhayl said, 'I do not know Ar-Rahman or Ar-Rahim. Should I write rather, "In Thy name, O Allah."' So Muhammad said, 'Write: "In Thy name, O Allah."' And I wrote it."** It's interesting that the pagan recognized the idol "Allah," since he was the head of the Meccan pantheon. But he did not know Muhammad's initial two deities because the prophet had borrowed Ar-Rahman and Ar-Rahim from the Yemeni Hanifs. It's also interesting to note how quickly Muhammad was willing to abandon his first "gods." Just a decade earlier, he had recited a Qur'an surah named in Ar-Rahman's honor. It began: *055.001* **"Ar-Rahman bestowed the Qur'an, He created man, and He taught him speech and intelligence."** Apparently, the lesson was lost on Muhammad. Easy come, easy go.

Having abandoned his gods, the prophet was a breath away from disavowing his ministry. *Ishaq:504/ Tabari VIII:85* **"He said, 'Write: "Muhammad, the Messenger of Allah, has made peace with Suhayl."' Suhayl said, 'If I testified that you were the Messenger of Allah, I wouldn't fight you. Why not write your name and the name of your father.' So Muhammad said, 'Write: "Muhammad bin Abdallah has made peace with Suhayl."**

This Hadith also confirms Muhammad's capitulation: *Bukhari:V4B53N408* **"When the Prophet wanted to perform the Umrah, the Quraysh stipulated that he could not preach (Islam). So Ali started writing a treaty. 'This is what Muhammad, Apostle of Allah, has agreed to.' The (Meccans) said, 'If we believed that you were the Apostle of Allah we would have followed you. So write, 'This is what Muhammad bin Abdallah has agreed to.' The Apostle could not write, so he asked Ali to erase the expression: 'Apostle of Allah.' On that Ali said, 'I will never erase it.' Muhammad said, 'Let me see the paper.' The Prophet erased the expression with his own hand."** There was nothing Muhammad wouldn't forsake if the price was right. Nothing was sacred. And knowing that Allah's lone messenger renounced his god and his witness, why does anyone trust him? Why believe anything he said—including the Qur'an?

Adding injury to insult, the former **"Messenger of God"** proceeded to renounce his methods. *Tabari VIII:86* **"They agreed to terms: warfare shall be laid aside for ten years, during which men can be safe and refrain from hostilities."** What are the odds that Muhammad could endure ten days, much less ten years without terrorizing, robbing, or raping someone? I'd wager 1.2 billion souls to one.

The Hudaybiyah Armistice went on to say: **"During this time whoever comes to Muhammad from the Quraysh without the permission of his guardian, Muhammad shall return him to them; and whoever shall come to the Quraysh from those who are with Muhammad, they shall not return him to Muhammad. There shall be neither clandestine theft nor betrayal."** The warrior committed to lay down his weapons—which was all the Quraysh wanted. There would be no more attacks on their caravans. Anyone fleeing Mecca for Medina would be returned to their families.

Yet the Quraysh were not similarly obliged. And betrayal, the principle tool of terror, was being abandoned—or so Muhammad said. The question is: could this prophet be trusted?

After completing the treaty of Hudaybiyah, Suhayl, the Quraysh scribe and negotiator, rose and said: *Ishaq:504* **"You shall go back, leaving us this year and not enter Mecca. When the next year comes, we will go out, and you shall enter Mecca with your companions and stay for three nights. Your swords must remain in scabbards. You shall not enter with other weapons."** And so it would be. The pilgrimage of a thousand was jilted at the altar.

Thus the warlord abdicated his authority. He turned away from the dilapidated rock shrine that had been the inspiration for this whole sorry affair. It wasn't Islam's proudest moment. Although, I don't know what was…

Ignorant, brutal, and bewildered, the Muslim militants crowded around Muhammad. They knew that their leader had sold himself out—and them along with him. They had come to conquer and plunder. *Tabari VIII:87/Ishaq:505* **"The Companions of the Prophet had set out not doubting that they would conquer, because of a vision Muhammad had seen. Therefore, when they saw the negotiations for peace, the retreat, and the obligations the Messenger agreed to—the Muslims felt so grieved about it that they were close to despair. Some were depressed to the point of death."** There is nothing a terrorist hates more than peace negotiations.

The harsh reality of what he had done soon came to haunt the Muslims. *Tabari VIII:87* **"While the Prophet was writing the document, Abu Jandal, the son of Suhayl, came in shackles. He had escaped to the Muslims. When Suhayl saw Jandal, he struck him and grabbed his garment. 'Muhammad,' he said, 'the pact was ratified between me and you before he came to you.' 'You are right,' he replied. Suhayl began dragging his son by his robe. Jandal began screaming at the top of his voice, 'Muslims, shall I be returned to the polytheists so that they can entice me from my religion?' This made the people feel even worse. The Messenger said, 'Abu Jandal, count on a reward, for Allah will give you a way out. We have made a treaty, and we will not act treacherously toward them.'"**

The terrorists were chafing at the bit. *Ishaq:505* **"Umar jumped up, walking beside Jandal, and saying, 'Be patient. They are only pagans, and the blood of any of them is no more than the blood of a dog!' Umar held the hilt of his sword close to him. He said, 'I hoped he would take the sword and kill his father with it.' But Jandal was too attached to his father to kill him."** They had just signed a peace treaty, and the future Caliph wanted one his young recruits to murder his father.

Tabari VIII:89 **"When the Messenger had finished his pact, he said to his Companions, 'Arise, sacrifice, and shave.' Not a man stood even after he had said it three times. When no one stood up, went into Umm's tent and told her what he had encountered from the Muslims. She said, 'Do you approve of this? Go out, and speak not a word to any of them until you have slaughtered your fattened camel and summoned your shaver to shave you.'"** He did as she said. **"When they saw this, they rose, slaughtered, and shaved until they almost killed each other in grief."** If these boys didn't get a terrorist fix in a hurry, there would be hell to pay.

Tabari VIII:90 **"Abu Basir was a Muslims confined in Mecca. He escaped and headed to Medina. There, the Prophet told Basir, 'We have given these people our word. Breaking a promise is not right in our religion.'"** But the Qur'an says: *066.001* **"Allah has already sanctioned for you the dissolution of your vows."** Who was lying: prophet or god?

Muhammad didn't return Abu in accordance with the treaty. *Tabari VIII:90* **"Abu Basir went out with his companions. When they stopped to rest he asked one of them, 'Is this sword of yours sharp?' 'Yes,' he replied. 'May I look at it?' Basir asked. 'If you wish.' Basir unsheathed the sword, attacked the man, and killed him. The other Muslim ran back to the Messenger, saying, 'Your Companion has killed my friend.' While the man was still there, Abu Basir appeared girded with the sword. He halted before Muhammad and said, 'Messenger, your obligation has been discharged.' The Prophet said, 'Woe to his mother—the kindler of war's fire.'"** Not returning Abu Basir to Mecca was Muhammad's first violation of the Hudaybiyah treaty. Not condemning the murder and paying restitution was the second breach.

Ishaq:508 / Tabari VIII:91 **"Abu Jandal, Suhayl's son, escaped and joined Abu Basir. Nearly seventy Muslim men gathered around them and they harassed the Quraysh. Whenever they heard of a Meccan caravan setting out for Syria, they intercepted it, and killed everyone they could get a hold of. They tore every caravan to pieces and took the goods. The Quraysh, therefore, sent to the Prophet, imploring him for the sake of Allah and the bond of kinship to send word to them."** Not returning Suhayl's son was the third Muslim violation. Harassing the Quraysh was the fourth; raiding caravans was fifth; killing and stealing were the sixth and seventh.

Tabari VIII:91 **"When word of how Abu Basir had killed his companion reached Suhayl, he leaned his back against the Ka'aba and said, 'I will not move until they pay blood money for this man.' By Allah,' a Quraysh man said, 'they will never pay.'"**

Tabari VIII:92 **"On that day Umar divorced two women who had been his wives in polytheism. Thus, he forbade them to send the women back, but commanded them to return the bride price. Then Mu'ayt emigrated to the Messenger. Her brother went to the Prophet and asked him to return her to them according to the treaty of Hudaybiyah. But he did not do so. Allah rejected it."** Not only were these the eighth and ninth Muslim violations, there hadn't been a single breach attributed to the Meccans. So we must ask ourselves, why were these abuses chronicled in the Hadith? Did the Muslims sages believe that their prophet condoned deception, treachery, murder, thievery, and terror? Did they record these things so that young Muslims today might behave in like manner?

With the natives restless, Muhammad breached the treaty a tenth time. *Tabari VIII:93* **"According to Waqidi, in this month, the Messenger sent out Ukkashah with forty men to raid Ghamr. He traveled quickly, but the enemy became aware and fled. He sent out scouts and they captured a spy who guided them to some of their cattle. They took two hundred head back to Medina."** Once a pirate, always a pirate. If you bet in favor of Muhammad abstaining from terror for ten days, you lost—as did the world.

Earning a living, and actually producing something of value, was beyond the first Muslims. They stole everything and produced nothing. Muhammad and his Companions became bloodsucking parasites.

However, they weren't particularly good parasites. *Tabari VIII:93* "The Messenger sent out Muhammad Maslamah with ten men. The enemy lay in wait for them until he and his companions went to sleep. Before they suspected anything, the Muslims were killed; Muhammad escaped, wounded."

Tabari VIII:93 "In this year, according to Waqidi, the Messenger dispatched the raiding party of Abu Ubaydah with forty men. They traveled through the night on foot and reached Qassah just before dawn. They raided the inhabitants, who escaped them by fleeing to the mountains. They took cattle, old clothes, and a man." Muhammad's hit men were a less civil version of Hitler's S.S.

Moving on to the next Hadith in this "religious" book: *Tabari VIII:93* "In this year a raiding party led by Zayd went to Jamum. He captured a Muzaynah woman named Halimah. She guided them to an encampment of the Banu Sulaym where they captured cattle, sheep, and prisoners. Among the captives was Halimah's husband. When Zayd brought back what he had taken, the Prophet granted the woman and her husband their freedom." This wasn't compassionate terrorism. Muhammad liked her because she, like he, had betrayed and plundered her kin.

Tabari VIII:94 "In this year a raiding party led by Zayd went to al-Is. During it, Abu As'b's property was taken." *Tabari VIII:94* "A fifteen-man raiding party led by Zayd went to Taraf against the Banu Thalabah. The Bedouins fled, fearing that Allah's Messenger had set out against them. Zayd took twenty camels from their herds. He was away four nights."

In the midst of all of this fundamental Islamic terrorism, I want to insert a friendly reminder. I have not taken these raids out of context. I have not skipped over the "religious" references in an effort to slander Muhammad or disgrace Islam. There has been nothing religious—not a word. Islam as chronicled in the Islamic Hadith is a terrorist manifesto. Nothing more.

Tabari VIII:94 "In this year Umar married Jamilah. She bore him Asim; then Umar divorced her. Yazid married her after him, and she bore him Abd al-Rahman [a son named after the first pagan god of the Qur'an]." Perhaps *that's* religious.

Tabari VIII:95 "In this year a raiding party led by Abd al-Rahman bin Awf went to Dumat. The Messenger said to him, 'If they obey you, marry the king's daughter.'"

Tabari VIII:95 "In this year a raiding party led by Ali went to Fadak with a hundred men against a clan of the Banu Sa'd. This was because the Prophet had received information that a force of theirs intended to aid the Jews of Khaybar. Ali traveled toward them by night and lay in wait during the day. He captured a spy, who confessed to them that he had been sent to Khaybar to offer the people aid on condition that they would give them the date harvest of Khaybar." This is the seventeenth Muslim violation of the treaty.

In each raid Muhammad's militants were the aggressors. They have not been depicted defending themselves as Islamic apologists claim. They were heartless thugs doing what lost souls do—murdering and plundering. Even now, this township's only crime was trying to offer aid to the Jewish families the Muslims had banished from their homes in Yathrib.

Tabari VIII:96 "**A raiding party led by Zayd set out against Umm in the [supposedly holy] month of Ramadan. During it, Umm suffered a cruel death. Zyad tied her legs with rope and then tied her between two camels until they split her in two. She was a very old woman.**" If Islam gets any more peaceful, this book is going to start bleeding.

Tabari VIII:96 "**Umm's story is as follows. Allah's Messenger sent Zayd to Wadi Qura, where he encountered the Banu Fazarah. Some of his Companions were killed there, and Zayd was carried away wounded. One of those killed was Ward. He was slain by the Banu Badr. When Zayd returned, he vowed that no washing should touch his head until he had raided the Fazarah. After he recovered, Muhammad sent him with an army against the Fazarah settlement. He met them in Qura and inflicted casualties on them and took Umm Qirfah prisoner. He also took one of Umm's daughters and Abdallah bin Mas'adah prisoner.**" A pagan couldn't be named "Slave-to-Allah" if Allah weren't the name of a pagan god. And the reason I continue to harp on this point, is that if Allah was a Meccan rock idol, Muhammad was a liar, Islam is without merit, the Qur'an is rubbish, and jihad terrorism is nothing more than murder—an express ticket to hell.

Tabari VIII:96 "**Zyad bin Harithah ordered Qays to kill Umm, and he killed her cruelly. He tied each of her legs with a rope and tied the ropes to two camels, and they split her in two. Then they brought Umm's daughter and Abdallah to the Messenger. Umm's daughter belonged to Salamah who had captured her. Muhammad asked Salamah for her, and Salamah gave her to him.**" This is tragic to the point of agony.

Yet the first Muslims enjoyed this story so much they want to share another Hadith. Let's pray it's less sadistic. *Tabari VIII:97* "**The Messenger appointed Abu Bakr as our commander, and we raided some of the Banu Fazarah. When we came near the watering place, Bakr ordered us to rest. After we prayed the dawn prayer [Terrorists that pray together stay together.], Abu ordered us to launch the raid against them. We went down to the watering hole and there we killed some people. I saw women and children among them, who had almost outstripped us; so I sent an arrow between them and the mountain. When they saw the arrow they stopped, and I led them back to Abu Bakr. Among them was a woman of the Banu Fazarah. She was wearing a worn-out piece of leather. With her was her daughter, among the fairest of the Arabs. Abu Bakr gave me her daughter as booty.**" Remember, this was Umm's daughter, a woman whom the Muslims had brutally tortured and mutilated.

Tabari VIII:97 "**When I returned to Medina, the Prophet met me in the market and said, 'Salamah—how excellent the father who begot you! Give me the woman.' I said, 'Holy Prophet of Allah, I like her, and I have not uncovered her garment.' Muhammad said nothing to me until the next day. He again met me in the market and said, 'Salamah, give me the woman.' I said, 'Prophet, I have not uncovered her garment but she is yours.' Muhammad sent her to Mecca, and with her he ransomed some Muslim captives who were in the hands of the Quraysh.**" The first Muslims had terrorized her town. Her property was stolen, her people were killed, her mother was mutilated, and now she was being traded as a piece of meat by the regime's founder and prophet.

Tabari VIII:98 "**In this year a raiding party led by Kurz set out against the members of the Banu Uraynah with twenty horsemen.**" I wonder if there was any village within reach of Muhammad's Muslim militants that they did not plunder?

We close out the violent sixth year of the Islamic Era with some extraordinarily delusional diplomacy. *Tabari VIII:98* "**Between the truce of Hudaybiyah and his death, the Messenger dispersed some of his Companions to the kings of the Arabs and the foreigners to call them to Allah. He sent a letter to Ibn Shihab. The letter stated: 'I have been sent as a mercy and for all. Therefore, convey the message from me, and Allah shall have mercy on you. Do not become disobedient to me as the Disciples became disobedient to Jesus. He called them to the like of what I called you to. Those whom he sent close by were pleased and accepted; those whom he sent far off were refused. Jesus complained of their behavior to Allah, and when they awoke the next morning, each could speak the language of the people to whom he had been sent. Then Jesus said, 'This is an affair that Allah has determined for you; so go forth!'**"

Muhammad has so utterly disgraced himself, there is little he can do or say that gets my goat...but calling Yahweh "Allah" and putting foolish words into Christ's mouth is not something I can let slide without comment. The disciples who experienced Yahshua's resurrection were as true to their calling as any men have ever been. They had no language barrier. Unlike Muhammad, they were literate. They read, wrote, and spoke the dominant and enlightened languages of their day—Greek and Aramaic. They were not called to deceit, plunder, or terror. They were called to demonstrate sacrificial love. And Yahshua never complained about them to Yahweh or anybody else. Instead he gave them his spirit, the Holy Spirit, to comfort, teach, and empower them, making them the most influential men who ever lived. Now that I have that off my chest, let's return to the perverse story of Islam.

Tabari VIII:100 "**The Messenger sent Hatib to Muqawqis, the ruler of Alexandria. Hatib delivered the letter of the Prophet, and Muqawqis gave Allah's Apostle four slave girls. The Messenger sent Dihyah to Caesar who was Heraclius, the king of the Romans. When Dihyah brought him the letter, he looked into it and then placed it between his thighs and his flanks.**" There were no Caesars in the seventh century; the "Romans" were Byzantines. "Prophets" don't take "slave girls." I am surprised these fools managed to fool so many fools. They didn't get anything right.

Back in Mecca: *Tabari VIII:100* "**Abu Sufyan said, 'We were merchants but the fighting between us and Muhammad has prevented us from journeying, so our wealth is depleted. [This is the purpose of terrorism.] Even after the truce with the Muslims, we fear that we still are not safe. [Muslims had continued to plunder Meccan caravans and had violated the** treaty twenty times.] Nevertheless, I shall set out with a group of merchants for Gaza.'"

"Sufyan said, 'We arrived at the time of Heraclius' victory over the Persians who were in his land. He expelled them and regained his Great Cross, which they had carried off. Having accomplished this and having received word that his Cross had been rescued he set out on foot to pray in Jerusalem. Carpets were spread before him and fragrant herbs were strewn in his path. When he arrived in Jerusalem, he performed his worship." Heraclius and the Byzantines did attack the Persians in 627, but near Nineveh, in today's Iraq, not Gaza. There was no "Great Cross" to be claimed. Further, the road from Constantinople to Jerusalem was not restored until 630. I share these historical facts so that you might recognize the fictitious nature of Islam.

Since the story was not true, there must have been an ulterior motive for sending the pagan Quraysh leader on this mission. And so there was. In a long Tradition with a distinguished isnad, we find fanciful stories proclaiming Muhammad's importance. While fictitious, they are entertaining. *Tabari VIII:101* "**King Heraclius arose troubled as he was shown in a dream that the kingdom of circumcision would be victorious. 'O King,' his Roman commanders said, 'the only nation that practices circumcision is the Jews [wrong again, on both counts], and they are under your authority. Send orders to have every Jew beheaded and be rid of this care.' As they were debating this proposal, a messenger from the ruler of Busra [a tribal kingdom in Bostra, Syria] arrived with an Arab. 'O King, an Arab man from the people of sheep and camels reported something marvelous that has happened in his land.' The Arab said, 'A man has appeared among us claiming to be a prophet. Some believe him and follow him and some oppose him. There have been bloody battles in many places.' Heraclius listened to his report and said, 'Strip him!' And behold, he was circumcised.**"

Heraclius continued his interrogation. *Tabari VIII:102* "**Tell me about this man and his claims.**'" Since the Hadith began in first person with Abu Sufyan speaking, I assume he is the one answering. "**I began minimizing his importance to him and disparaging him. 'O king, don't worry about him. He's too small to bother you.' The king asked, 'What is his lineage?' I said, 'Pure—the best of us in lineage.' [Mind you, they were clueless. Illiterate people can't maintain genealogies back more than a handful of generations.] He asked, 'Has anyone from his family ever said the like of what he says, so that he would be imitating him?' 'No,' I said.**" Fortunately, we know better. Muhammad started by parroting the dogma Qusayy had established. Then he plagiarized Zayd, the Hanif poet, before he stole Moses' material from the Torah.

"**King Heraclius asked, 'Did he have authority among you, of which you then stripped him, so that he brought this discourse in order that you might restore his authority?' 'No,' I said.**" Actually, that query hit pretty close to home. Muhammad believed the "authority" of the Ka'aba had been "stripped" from him at birth and this whole "discourse" has been about getting it back. "**The king asked, 'Tell me about his followers.' I said, 'The weak, poor, young boys, and women. As for those of his people who have years and honor, none has followed him.'**" While that's a lie, it is interesting. Abu Bakr was rich and powerful, as were Umar and Uthman. However, "poor, young boys" continue to find the promise of booty and lust alluring.

"'Do his followers love him?' Heraclius asked. 'No man has followed him and then abandoned him.'" Whoever wrote this Tradition ought to have read the Qur'an before scribbling such nonsense. The last ten surahs have been fixated on bad Muslims—hypocrites—abandoning the prophet and Islam in droves. "'Tell me,' the king said, 'how the war between you and him is going.' I replied, 'Sometimes it's his luck to prevail against us, and sometimes our luck to prevail against him.' 'Does he act treacherously?' I found nothing in what he asked me about him in which I could impugn Muhammad's character except to say, 'No. We are in a state of truce with him, and yet we fear he may act treacherously.'" I suppose the fifty terrorists raids the prophet had instigated thus far were all in good fun.

Tabari VIII:103 "Heraclius said, 'If you have told me the truth then he shall surely wrest this very ground from under me. I only wish I were with him so that I could wash his feet.'" Having this "Christian" king say that he wanted to serve Muhammad by "washing his feet" is reminiscent of the monk confirming his prophetic calling forty years earlier. Being a fraud, the only means Muhammad had to authenticate his god and his calling was to fabricate fictitious endorsements.

Tabari VIII:104 "Heraclius received the following letter from the Messenger. 'In the name of Allah, Ar-Rahman, Ar-Rahim. From Muhammad, the Messenger of Allah, to Heraclius, the ruler of the Romans. Peace to whoever follows the right guidance! To proceed; Submit yourself, and you shall be safe.'" Muhammad's idea of "peace" is the same as the Islamic world's today: "Surrender and become a Muslim and we will tax, deceive, and oppress you, but not kill you. Obey and you will have peace. Otherwise, we'll hurry you off to Allah so he can torture you in hell."

Ever desperate for confirmation, the Muslim sages bring us this: *Tabari VIII:105* "Al-Zuhri said, 'A Christian bishop whom I met in the time of Abd al-Milik [a Umayyad Caliph who ruled from 685 to 705] told me that he was acquainted with an affair involving the Messenger, Heraclius and his intelligence. According to the bishop, when Heraclius received the letter from Muhammad, he wrote to a man in Rome who used to read from the Hebrew what they use to read, mentioning the affair of the man, describing him, and informing him of what he had received from him. The ruler of Rome wrote back to him; "He is indeed the prophet we have been awaiting. There is no doubt about it. Follow him, and believe him."'" The Old Testament had been translated into Greek in Alexandria in 275 B.C. It was then translated into Latin in the fourth century. A Roman would have read the Latin Vulgate. Further, Muhammad wasn't foretold in the Bible. And the only thing Christians await is the Messiah's return. So, why are the Muslims lying—again? And why are they such bad liars?

Tabari VIII:105 "Heraclius then gave orders to gather the commanders of the Romans for him in a palatial building and ordered its doors to be closed on them. He looked down on them from an upper chamber because he was mortally afraid of them. He said, 'People of the Romans, I have received this man's letter calling me to his religion. By Allah, he is indeed the prophet whom we have been awaiting and whom we find in our Books. Come, let us follow him and believe him, that our life in this world and the next may be secure.' Without exception, they snorted angrily at him and hastened to the doors of the building." Somewhere, sometime, someone may have contrived a more fictitious and lame endorsement, but by Allah, it's hard to imagine.

This feeble attempt at legitimizing Muhammad's claim to have been foretold in the Bible continues with the Christian bishop and Byzantine king saying that he was mentioned by name and described in detail. They don't say where, of course, because it isn't there. And with 25,000 ancient Bible fragments and copious Roman books, not a word can be found anywhere to corroborate anything in this preposterous tale. The "Muhammad-was-foretold-and-described proof" is repeated a hundred times in the Qur'an and Sunnah. Yet neither Muhammad, Allah, nor their contemporaries ever identified a single supportive verse. Centuries later Muslim apologists claimed these verses were in Deuteronomy and John. I deal with those lies on page 608.

The never-ending Tradition goes on to say: *Tabari VIII:107* **"'Shall we be under the hands of the Arabs when we are mankind's greatest kingdom, most numerous nation, and best land?' Heraclius said, 'Then let me give him tribute each year so that I can avert his vehemence and find rest from his warfare by means of money that I give to him.' The Romans said, 'Shall we concede to the Arabs our own humiliation and abasement by a tax that they take from us?' The king said, 'Then let me make peace with him on condition that I give him the land of Syria [Israel, Jordan, and Lebanon,] and that he leave me with the land of al-Sha'm.' They replied, 'Shall we give him Syria when we know it to be the navel?' Having refused him, Heraclius said, 'You will be defeated.' He offered a farewell salutation and galloped to Constantinople."** This is as desperate as it is fictitious.

Muhammad's letter to Amr in Negus serves as further confirmation that the prophet was as dumb as the Stone for whom he spoke. *Tabari VIII:108* **"In the name of Allah, Ar-Rahman, Ar-Rahim. From Muhammad, the Messenger of Allah, to the Negus, king of the Ethiopians. May you be at peace. I praise you to Allah, the King, the Most Holy, the Peace, the Watcher, and I bear witness that Jesus the son of Mary is the Spirit and Word of Allah, which He cast into the goodly and chaste Virgin Mary, so that she conceived Jesus; whom Allah created from His Spirit and breathed into him, even as He created Adam by His hand and breathed into him, I call you to Allah alone, Who has no partner, to continued obedience to Him, and that you follow me and believe in what has come to me; for I am the Messenger of Allah. I call you and your armies to Allah."**

The Ethiopians laughed themselves silly. Since the Bible claims God's name is "Yahweh" 7000 times, it can't be "Allah." Christ cannot be God's Word—virgin born, created from His Spirit, with life personally breathed into him from God, and created like Adam by God's hand—and not be God, or at least God's *partner*. And how does one transition from Christ being a special creation to following Muhammad and surrendering an army to him?

Confirming that he was the antithesis of Christ, Muhammad told the Ethiopians to send him a slave girl as a gift. *Tabari VIII:110* **"When Abu Sufyan learned** that the Prophet had married her, he said, 'That stallion's nose is not to be restrained!'"

There are other nonexistent letters to Persia, Iran, and Iraq but they're repetitive. I'm going to skip them and return to the Qur'an to see how Muhammad is using Allah. Let's begin by reviewing the 4ᵗʰ surah, which the "stallion" named after the women he craved. It opens with yet another version of creation: *004.001* "People! Be careful of your Lord, Who created you from a single being and created its mate of the same (kind) and spread from these two, many men and women."

Returning to his favorite Meccan theme, the orphan wants his property returned. *004.002* "To orphans restore their property...and devour not their substance (by mixing it up) with your own. For this is a great sin." Muhammad was worried that the Meccans were devouring the assets of the Ka'aba Inc. After all, he had raided their caravans, destroying their only other source of income. And being the world's biggest hypocrite, the prophet never returned the property of the orphans he had created by killing their parents and selling them into slavery.

Since this surah was named "Women," it's only fair that men have more than one. *004.003* "If you fear that you shall not be able to deal justly with orphans, marry women of your choice who seem good to you, two or three or four; but if you fear that you shall not be able to do justice (to so many), then only one, or (a slave) that you possess, that will be more suitable. And give the women their dower as a free gift; but if they, of their own good pleasure, remit any part of it to you, eat it with enjoyment, take it with right good cheer and absorb it (in your wealth)." According to Muhammad, it's even okay to beat them until they "remit the dower of their own good pleasure."

Returning to what Muhammad craved: *004.010* "Those who unjustly eat up the property of orphans, eat up a Fire into their bodies: They will soon endure a Blazing Fire!"

Next we learn that Allah thinks that men are twice as valuable as women. *004.011* "Allah directs you in regard of your Children's (inheritance): to the male, a portion equal to that of two females.... These are settled portions ordained by Allah." *004.013* "Those are limits imposed by Allah." In future surahs and Hadiths, Team Islam would call women "half wits," too.

Muhammad was itching for a "submit and obey" verse, so...*004.012* "Those who obey Allah and His Messenger will be admitted to Gardens to abide therein and that will be the supreme achievement. But those who disobey Allah and His Messenger and transgress His limits will be admitted to a Fire, to abide therein: And they shall have a humiliating punishment." In other words, if you treat women as equals, you'll burn in hell. *004.015* "If any of your women are guilty of lewdness, take the evidence of four witnesses from amongst you against them; if they testify, confine them to houses until death [by starvation] claims them. If two men among you are guilty of lewdness, punish them both. If they repent and improve, leave them alone; for Allah is Oft-Returning."

The following words, coming as they do from the most perverted sexual libertine to have ever claimed prophetic status, are hilarious: *004.023* "Prohibited to you are: your mothers, daughters, sisters; father's sisters, mother's sisters; brother's daughters, sister's daughters; foster-mothers (who gave you suck), foster-sisters; your wives' mothers; your step-daughters born of your wives to whom you have gone in, no pro-hibition if you have not gone in; (those who have been) wives of your sons proceeding from your loins [leaving wives of adopted sons—like his Zayd—fair game]; and two sisters in wedlock at one and the same time, except for what is past; for Allah is Oft-Forgiving. Also (prohibited are) women already married, except slaves who are captives (of war)." Rape is still okay with Rocky.

Since Muhammad's harem included countless concubines and sex slaves, this too is laughable. *004.027* "Allah likes to turn you, but those lost in the lusts of the flesh wish to turn away—far, far away. Allah does wish to lighten your (difficulties): For man was created weak [and he should know]. Believers, you should not usurp unjustly the wealth of others, except it be a trade by mutual consent, and kill not one another. If any do that in rancor and injustice, soon shall We cast them into the Fire: And easy it is for Allah." This admonition is obviously meant to prevent the growing Muslim horde from turning on itself when infidel targets become harder to find. "Plunder and kill anyone you like, except fellow pirates," the chief hypocrite said.

Some verses later, we are reminded that Muhammad was *against* people and that his god was mean-spirited. *004.041* "We brought from each people a witness, and We brought you (O Muhammad) as a witness against these people! On that day will those who disbelieve and disobey the Messenger desire that the earth were leveled with them in it, but they shall not be able hide from Allah." "Obey me or my god'll get ya."

For a religion fixated on mindless ritual and against honest inquiry, this makes no sense: *004.043* "Believers, approach not prayers with a mind befogged or intox-icated until you understand what you utter. Nor when you are polluted, until after you have bathed. If you are ill, or on a journey, or come from answering the call of nature, or you have touched a woman, and you find no water, then take for yourselves clean dirt, and rub your faces and hands. Lo! Allah is Benign, Forgiving." While this is too weird for words, it's troubling that the Qur'an claims women are unclean and polluted—worse than dirt. It's yet another sign suggesting that Muhammad was abused.

Like so much of the Qur'an, there is no intelligent transition from the dirt bath to this attack on Jews. The entire book is random and chaotic; it is the product of a cluttered and tormented mind. *004.044* "Have you not considered those to whom a portion of the Book has been given? They traffic in error and desire that you should go astray. But Allah has full knowledge of your enemies. Of the Jews there are those who displace words from their (right) places, saying, 'We hear and we disobey' with a twist of their tongues they slander Faith.... Allah has cursed them for disbelief." O great Mus-lim scholars, if the Jews altered their scriptures to slander Islam as Allah claims, where is the evidence, the proof? What books did they alter? How did they change them? When? And why is there overwhelming evidence that they have not been changed in 2,300 years? The foundation of Islam is a lie.

004.047 "O you People of the Book to whom the Scripture has been given, believe in what We have (now) revealed, confirming and verifying what was possessed by you, before We destroy your faces beyond all recognition, turning you on your backs, and curse you as We

cursed the Sabbath-breakers, for the decision of Allah Must be executed." Let me see if
I understand this. The Jews were given the Scripture Book by Allah, and the
Qur'an is new. But it confirms what it condemns. So the Islamic god is going
to turn the Jews on their backs and disfigure their faces while cursing them.
Forget for a moment that Allah was a rock, and a dumb one at that, and that
Muhammad was a sexual pervert, bloodthirsty terrorist, and a pirate; this just
isn't up to the level of scripture. I'd be embarrassed if I were Satan.

Having slimed the Jews, it was time for the dark spirit of Islam to attack
Christians. *004.048* "Allah forgives not that partners should be set up with Him; but He forgives anything else, to whom He please; to set up partners with Allah is to devise a sin
most heinous." If that's true, Muhammad is toast. Remember the Quraysh Bargain and the Satanic Verses? By setting up Al-Lat, Al-Uzza, and Manat as
partners with Allah, his sin was heinous and *unforgivable*. *004.050* "Behold! how
they invent lies against Allah! That is flagrant sin." Therefore, Muhammad is in hell.

Continuing to assault Christians, Allah says: *004.051* "Have you not seen those
to whom a portion of the Book has been given? They believe in sorcery and false deities
and say of those who disbelieve: these are better guided than those who believe. They are
(men) whom Allah has cursed: And those whom Allah has cursed, you will find that they
have no savior." The sorcery and false deities accusation is suicidal. Allah
claims to be the God of the Bible so he's condemning himself.

Ever delusional, Muhammad's demonic sidekick is alleged to have said
that Christians are envious of Muslims because of the spoils Allah had given
his jihad fighters. *004.054* "Are they jealous and envious what Allah has given them of his
bounty? But We had already given the house of Abraham the Book, and conferred upon
them a grand kingdom. Some of them believed, and some of them averted their faces from
him. And Hell is sufficient for their burning. Those who reject our Signs, We shall soon cast
into the Fire. As often as their skin is burnt and singed, roasted through, We shall change
it for fresh skin, so that they may go on tasting the torment." Once again, we find
Allah in Hell. This time he is exchanging the skin of his Christian victims so
that their torture can be extended. With every word, Allah grows more
Satanic. The veil that once kept us from seeing Lucifer behind these words
has been singed. We are now peering directly at Satan, the Prince of Darkness,
the Whore of Babylon.

For those in churches, the media, and politics eager to embrace Islam,
beware. You are dealing with the Devil, and he will kill you. It isn't by chance
that hell and punishment are the Qur'an's most repeated and vivid themes. It
isn't a coincidence that Allah loves death and awaits the Day of Doom. Nor
is it an accident that surest path to Allah's Whore House is martyrdom—
death killing Christians and Jews. There is a reason the Qur'an obliterates
love, trust, peace, freedom, choice and rational inquery, imposing in their
place hate, fear, war, submission, obedience, and deception.

Since the rivers in Allah's paradise flow with wine, and the entertainment is virgins, Islamic heaven as demented as Islamic hell. *004.057* **"But those who believe and do good deeds, We shall soon admit to Gardens, with rivers flowing, their eternal home: Therein shall they have pure companions."**

For another a reminder as to why Islam—the religion of submission—is incompatible with freedom and democracy, consider this: *004.059* **"Believers, obey Allah, and obey the Messenger, and those charged with authority. If you dispute any matter, refer it to Allah and His Messenger. That is best, and most suitable for final determination."** There is no freedom of choice in "submit and obey." And the Hadith and Qur'an speak with one voice as it relates to the central mission of the poligious doctrine. *Bukhari:V4B52N203* **"I heard Allah's Apostle saying, 'He who obeys me, obeys Allah, and he who disobeys me, disobeys Allah. He who obeys the chief, obeys me, and he who disobeys the chief, disobeys me.'"** Without choice there can be no democracy. There can't be a religion either, but that's another matter.

Continuing to focus on the prophet's favorite theme: *004.064* **"We sent not a messenger but to be obeyed, in accordance with the will of Allah."** *004.065* **"But no, by the Lord, they can have no Faith until they make you (Muhammad) judge in all disputes, and find in their souls no resistance against Your decisions, and accept them with complete submission."** *004.066* **"If We had ordered them to sacrifice their lives or to leave their homes [to fight], very few of them would have done it: But if they had done what they were told, it would have been best for them, and would have strengthened their (faith)."** *004.069* **"All who obey Allah and the Messenger are the ones whom Allah has bestowed favors [war booty]."**

Each time I read these passages I close my eyes in horror. The fact that the president of the United States sent America's finest men and women into harm's way to accomplish the impossible is unforgivable. There will never be freedom or democracy in any Islamic state. Sixty percent of Iraqis are Shi'ite Muslims, from which Hezbollah—Allah's Party—is formed. Thirty-five percent are Sunni Muslims. Enough will follow their prophet's and god's orders to assure two things: American's will die and we will fail.

I am also horrified that so few people see through this demented hoax. Islam wasn't created to lead men to a god. It was perpetrated to empower *a man*.

Moving on to war we learn: *004.071* **"Believers, take your precautions, and advance in detachments or go (on expeditions) together in one troop. There are among your men who would tarry behind (not fighting in Allah's Cause). If a misfortune befalls you, they say: 'Allah favored us in that we were not present among them.'"** *004.074* **"Let those who fight in Allah's Cause sell the life of this world for the hereafter. To him who fights in the Cause of Allah, whether he is slain or gets victory—We shall give him a great reward."** Jihad is all about greed. The Muslim god promises booty for those who live and paradise for those who die. It's little wonder there are so many suicide bombers selling this life for the hereafter. Sadly, they lose both.

Muhammad spoke as if he were Allah. *Bukhari:V4B52N44* **"A man came to Allah's Apostle and said, 'Instruct me as to such a deed as equals Jihad in reward.' He replied, 'I do not find such a deed.'"** If the best thing a Muslim can do is fight Jihad in

Allah's Cause then Islam is a call to war. *Bukhari:V4B52N50* **"The Prophet said, 'A single endeavor of fighting in Allah's Cause in the forenoon or in the afternoon is better than the world and whatever is in it.'"** Jihad is, therefore, more important than all of the Five Pillars of Islam combined. *Bukhari:V4B52N46* **"I heard Allah's Apostle saying, 'Allah guarantees that He will admit the Mujahid [Muslim fighter] in His Cause into Paradise if he is killed, otherwise He will return him to his home safely with rewards and war booty.'"** If you die, you get heavenly booty. If you live, you get earthly booty.

Islam is a religion to die for: *Bukhari:V4B52N53* **"The Prophet said, 'Nobody who dies and finds Paradise would wish to come back to this life even if he were given the whole world and whatever is in it, except the martyr who, on seeing the superiority of martyrdom, would like to come back to get killed again in Allah's Cause.'"** "Martyrdom," "fighting," "Allah's Cause," and "Jihad" are synonymous. *Bukhari:V4B52N54* **"The Prophet said, 'By Him in Whose Hands my life is! Were it not for the believers who do not want me to leave them, I would certainly and always go forth in army-units setting out for Jihad. I would love to be martyred in Allah's Cause and then get resurrected and get martyred again only to be resurrected so that I could get martyred once more.'"** But like Imams today, Allah's prophet preferred to send boys out to do his dirty work.

Returning to the Qur'an, we don't miss a beat. *004.075* **"What reason have you that you should not fight in Allah's Cause?"** Another translation says: **"What is wrong with you that you do not fight for Allah?"** *004.076* **"Those who believe fight in the Cause of Allah, and those who disbelieve fight in the cause of idols: So fight the allies of Satan: feeble indeed is the plot of Satan."** This is why the Islamic world refers to America as the "Great Satan." And now that you know the root from which Satan was derived—Adversary—it all makes sense. America is perceived to be a nation comprised of Christians and Jews. We are Lucifer's, and thus Islam's, adversary. Islam is ugly, not complicated.

Speaking for the dark spirit of Islam, Muhammad reminds us how much he despises peaceful Muslims. He also confirms that "fear" in the Islamic sense does not mean reverence, but fright. *004.077* **"Have you not seen those to whom it was said: Withhold your hands from fighting, perform the prayer and pay the zakat. But when orders for fighting were issued, a party of them feared men as they ought to have feared Allah. They say: 'Our Lord, why have You ordained fighting for us, why have You made war compulsory?'"** The Qur'an ordains Muslims to fight, whether they like it or not. War is compulsory. The enemy is all non-Muslims. The timeline is forever.

Allah is going to kill the pacifists, so they might as well fight. *004.078* **"Wherever you are, death will find you, even if you are in towers built up strong and high! If some good befalls, they say, 'This is from Allah;' but if evil, they say, 'This is from you (Muhammad).' Say: 'All things are from Allah.' So what is wrong with these people, that they fail to understand these simple words?"** Arabs recognized that evil flowed directly from Muhammad and his dark spirit. What's more, the Qur'an agrees.

The man who folded while negotiating with a Meccan merchant claims he's Allah's messenger to all mankind. But first, Allah must contradict himself.

004.079 "Whatever good happens to you is from Allah; but whatever evil happens to you is from yourself. We have sent (Muhammad) as a Messenger to (instruct) mankind. And enough is Allah for a witness." How, pray tell, is Allah a sufficient witness? The Black Stone never spoke, performed a miracle, or issued a prophecy. This feeble attempt at scripture deserves an "F." The subject matter is ugly—overly focused on demented torments, violence, and war. The message is immoral—approving thievery, murder, kidnapping, the slave trade, rape, incest, and even genocide. The book is plagiarized, and poorly, I might add. And it's jumbled together without context or chronology. It is only a witness in that it exposes the fraudulent nature of Muhammad, Allah, and Islam.

004.080 "He who obeys the Messenger obeys Allah." If it weren't for Muhammad, Allah would be unknown today. He was merely a stone to be thrown.

Next, we are reminded that prophet and pal were losing their grip. Muslims were beginning to think for themselves. *004.081* "They have obedience on their lips; but when they leave you (Muhammad), a section of them plots things that are very different from what you commanded them. So keep clear of them." The reason the first Muslims feigned support was obvious. It's the same reason the vast majority of Germans and Russians pretended to be Nazis and Communists. Dissent was met with imprisonment and death. And this is why we must care enough about "bad" Muslims to free them from "good" ones.

004.082 "Do they not consider and ponder the Qur'an? Had it been from other than Allah, they would surely have found therein much discrepancy and incongruity." The 78th verse says: "All things are from Allah." The 79th contradicts it saying: "Whatever good happens to you is from Allah; but whatever evil happens to you is from yourself." The Qur'an is so rife with contradictions, it has a verse explaining how to deal with them. "Whenever We cancel a verse or throw it into oblivion, We bring one which is better." That's why the "book" warns: "Do not question the Qur'an. There was a party of you who questioned it and as a result, they lost their faith."

Much of the Qur'an was anachronistic—only pertaining to Muhammad, focusing on his critics, his sexual indulgences, his financial appetite, and lust for power. Muslims are ordered to submit and obey a dead man. Which means the Qur'an only served Muhammad; it was "revealed" for his benefit. This next verse is one of a thousand examples. *004.083* "When there comes to them some matter regarding war, they discuss it. If only they had referred it to the Messenger, or to those charged with authority, the proper investigators would have understood it. Were it not for the grace of Allah, most of you would have fallen into Satan's clutches." Along these lines the Noble Qur'an references this Hadith: *Bukhari:V9B92N384* "Allah's Apostle said, 'Whoever obeys me will enter Paradise, and whoever disobeys me will not.'"

Muhammad's never-ending war marched on. *004.084* "Then fight (O Muhammad) in Allah's Cause—you are only responsible for yourself. Incite the believers to fight along with you." How can there be no contradictions in the Qur'an if five verses earlier we read: "We have sent (Muhammad) as a Messenger to mankind," and now he's **"only responsible for himself?"** And how can Islam be peaceful if its scripture says: **"Incite the believers to fight along with you?"**

The pacifist uprising became so severe, the peaceful Muslims had to be kicked out of the way. *004.088* **"What is the matter with you that you are divided about the Hypocrites? Allah has cast them back (causing their disbelief). Would you guide those whom Allah has thrown out of the Way? For those whom Allah has thrown aside and led astray, never shall they find the Way."** Once again, we see Allah imitating Satan.

004.089 **"They wish that you would reject Faith, as they have, and thus be on the same footing: Do not be friends with them until they leave their homes in Allah's Cause. But [and this is a hell of a but...] if they turn back from Islam, becoming renegades, seize them and kill them wherever you find them."** The book that preached: *002.256* **"There should be no compulsion in religion,"** just said **"if they turn back from Islam, becoming renegades, seize them and kill them wherever you find them."** If that isn't a contradiction, the word needs to be redefined.

This verse is among the most heinous ever attributed to god. It is the reason Islam has managed to enslave a billion people. If a Muslim rejects Islam, he is labeled a renegade, and must be seized and killed on direct orders from Allah. It's hard to imagine a dogma—religious or political—so *unappealing* it has to murder those who leave, just to keep others in line.

Moving on we find Muhammad attempting to justify his cowardice, capitulation, and abdication at Hudaybiyah. Allah says the treaty was an interim strategy designed to deceive the enemy—to lull them into a false sense of peace. *004.090* **"Except those who join a group between you and whom there is a treaty, or (those who become) weary of fighting you. If Allah had willed, He could have given them power over you, and they would have fought you. Therefore if they withdraw from you and wage not war, and send you (guarantees of) peace, then Allah has not given you a way (to war) against them."** The purpose of terror is to cause people to become so "weary of fighting" they surrender. That's what is happening in Israel today.

But if a people desiring peace are *perceived* to be mischievous, Allah commands his militants to kill them. *004.091* **"You will find others who, while wishing to live in peace and being safe from you to gain the confidence of their people; thrown back to mischief headlong; therefore if they do not withdraw from you, and offer you peace besides restraining their hands, then seize them and kill them wherever you find them; and against these We have given you a clear sanction and authority."** So if you wish to live in peace, but are *perceived* as being mischievous (i.e., non-Muslim), Allah has given his Jihad warriors **"a clear sanction and authority to seize and kill"** you.

Islam is an equal opportunity hater. Even today, "good" Muslims fight and kill more "bad" Muslims than they do infidels. As such, they must be either accident prone or mistaken. *004.092* **"Never should a believer kill a believer unless (it be) by mistake."** *004.093* **"If a man kills a believer intentionally, he will be cast into Hell, to abide therein. The wrath, damnation, and curse of Allah are upon him, and a dreadful penalty is prepared for him."**

For the hundredth time we are reminded that "Allah's Cause" is "Holy War," better known as "Jihad." *004.094* **"Believers, when you go abroad to fight wars in the Cause of Allah, investigate carefully, and say not to anyone who greets you: 'You are not a believer!' Coveting the chance profits of this life (so that you may despoil him). With Allah are plenteous spoils and booty."** Muhammad has bribed his mercenaries to fight for booty. He has demonstrated how easy it is to rob unarmed civilians. So now he is afraid that Muslims will loot everyone they meet. While loot is fine, according to Allah, there is more to destroying a man than just plundering his possessions. Muhammad and Allah were looking at the bigger picture. A world submissive to them was a far greater prize.

"Good" Muslims fight. *004.095* **"Not equal are believers who sit home and receive no hurt and those who fight in Allah's Cause with their wealth and lives. Allah has granted a grade higher to those who fight with their possessions and bodies to those who sit home. Those who fight He has distinguished with a special reward."** A Muslim Hadith explains the verse: *Muslim:C40B20N4676* **"Believers who sit home and those who go out for Jihad in Allah's Cause are not equal."** Fundamental Islam, the Islam of Allah, Muhammad, and the Qur'an preaches Jihad. Islam was born violent and weaned on blood.

Muhammad may have felt a momentary twinge of guilt for having banished the Jews. So he had his god say that that the earth was big and the Jews ought to have migrated out of Medina on their own. But since they didn't, they're off to hell. *004.097* **"Surely those whom the angels cause to die while they are wrong, shall say: 'In what plight were you?' They say: 'We were weak in the earth.' 'Was not Allah's earth spacious, so that you should have migrated?' So their abode is hell, an evil resort."** The prophet's last words were: **"Banish the Jews from Arabia."**

Allah wants Jihadists to live off the land. *004.100* **"He who leaves his home in Allah's Cause finds abundant resources and many a refuge. Should he die as a refugee for Allah and His Messenger his reward becomes due and sure with Allah. When you travel through the earth there is no blame on you if you curtail your worship for fear unbelievers may attack you. In truth the disbelievers are your enemy."** Either fighting is more important than religion or this religion is *about* fighting. But either way, that's disconcerting because Muslims see all non-Muslims as their enemy.

In Islam, religion and war are inseparable. *004.102* **"When you (Prophet) lead them in prayer, let some stand with you, taking their arms with them. When they finish their prostrations, let them take positions in the rear. And let others who have not yet prayed come—taking all precaution, and bearing arms. The Infidels wish, if you were negligent of your arms, to assault you in a rush. But there is no blame on you if you put away your arms because of the inconvenience of rain or because you are ill; but take (every) precaution. For the Unbelieving Infidels Allah hath prepared a humiliating punishment."** Translated: Thugs who murder for god and booty need to watch their backs. After a while, such thugs become known as terrorists—and people start disliking them.

Islam's war is never-ending. *004.104* **"And do not relent in pursuing the enemy. If you are suffering hardships, they are suffering similar hardships; but you have hope from**

Allah, while they have none." So long as Islam exists they will never relent.

Religions empower men, giving them authority over others. *004.115* **"If anyone contradicts or opposes the Messenger [not Allah] after guidance has been conveyed to him, and follows a path other than the way [of Muhammad], We shall burn him in Hell!"**

Trying to make amends for the Satanic Verses, Muhammad recited: *004.116* **"Surely Allah does not forgive setting up partners with Him; and whoever associates any-thing with Allah, he indeed strays off into remote error. They call but upon female deities. They call but upon Satan, the persistent rebel!"** Muhammad admitted to having been duped by Satan. His crime was associating "female deities" with Allah. Since such sins are unforgivable, I wonder if he's enjoying hell as much as Allah seems to? And while this is a fatal problem for Islam, Muhammad did-n't learn his lesson. Rather than calling Allah's daughters "idols" or "false gods," he just called them "deities" again.

Allah is the spirit of deceit. *004.118* **"Allah did curse him. He said: 'I will mislead them, and I will create in them false desires; I will order them to slit the ears of cattle, and to deface the (fair) nature created by Allah.' Whoever, forsaking Allah, takes Satan for a patron, they are a loser. Satan makes them promises, and creates in them false desires; but Satan's promises are nothing but deception. (His dupes) will have their dwelling in Hell, and from it they will find no way of escape."** Satan doesn't create false desires; he preys on carnal and vain desires. He defaces mankind, not cattle. But since Islam is war and war is deception, how are Muslims to differentiate between Allah and Satan?

In a line that would feel equally at home in the *Communist Manifesto*, *Mao's Little Red Book*, or *Mein Kampf*, Allah instructs Muslims to rat on their parents. *004.135* **"Believers, stand out for justice as witnesses for Allah even against yourselves, your parents, your family, and relatives whether it be against rich or poor.... Allah is aware of what you do."** This verse serves godless tyrants and their regimes. It's neither civil nor religious. But it helps us understand why Islam and Nazism embraced and why Muslims later aligned themselves with the Communists.

Putting himself on par with the god he created, Muhammad tells Muslims to believe in *him*. *004.136* **"O Believers! Believe in Allah and His Messenger, and the Scripture which He has sent to His Messenger, and the Scripture which He revealed to those before. Any who denies Allah, His angels, His Books, His Messengers, and the Day of Judgment, hath gone far astray."** Setting aside for a moment that he was a per-vert and a terrorist, how are Muslims to believe in the **"scripture revealed before"** if it is the antithesis of the **"scripture revealed to Muhammad?"** And if there was an "uncorrupted" version of the Torah, Psalms, and Gospels, why didn't the Allah/Muhammad brain trust provide Muslims with a copy?

It's evident that Muhammad lost his grip on the Medina Muslims. Many came to think as little of him as the Meccans had before. *004.137* **"Those who believe, then reject faith, then believe and reject faith, and go on increasing in unbelief, Allah will never pardon them, nor guide them. To the Hypocrites give the glad tidings that** there is for them a grievous penalty, a painful doom." The "glad tidings" line is especially perverted. It reveals Muhammad's deeply disturbed character.

004.140 "You have been commanded in the Book that whenever you hear Verses of Allah denied, derided, ridiculed, or mocked [as is the only reasoned response], do not sit with them and engage them in this talk or you will be no different from them. Indeed, Allah will collect the Hypocrites and Infidels together and put them all in Hell." Those who heard Muhammad's feeble, immoral, and violent "scriptures" directly from his lips denied, derided, ridiculed, and mocked them. So Muhammad banned debate. Even to this day, any Muslim who criticizes Islam is imprisoned or murdered.

If Islam were open to scrutiny there would be no Muslims. To survive, the poligious doctrine requires its tyrannical dictators to use draconian measures to repress freedom of thought, debate, speech, press, and religion. It's why Islam is wholly incompatible with freedom and democracy. It is why Islamic governments are the most repressive regimes on earth. Islam thrives in submission and ignorance. Therefore, we must defy this ungodly ban and free Muslims from Islam if we hope to free ourselves from the terror it breeds. And the best way to free billions from this lie is to expose it. Truth is lethal to Islam. William Muir, a man considered to be one of Islam's foremost scholars, agrees: "The Qur'an is the most stubborn enemy of Civilization, Liberty, and Truth which the world has yet known."

Those who knew Muhammad best rejected him. They only feigned belief in order to avoid being killed by his goons. *004.142* "The Hypocrites try to deceive Allah, but it is He Who deceives them. When they stand up performing the prayer, they stand sluggishly, to be seen, but they are mindful of Allah but little. (They are) distracted in mind even in the midst of it, swaying between this and that, one group or the another. Those who Allah causes to go astray and err will not find a way. Believers, take not for friends unbelieving infidels rather than believers [because rational thought is contagious]. Do you want to offer Allah an open proof against you? The Hypocrites will be in the lowest depths of the Fire." There's a lot of bad stuff in this passage. First, "Allah deceives." "Those who Allah causes to go astray and err will not find a way." We've been bombarded with this concept so often we've become callous to its implications. God by his very nature is incapable of deceit. The moment he becomes dishonest, he ceases to be good. If God is not true, there is no value in knowing him. And since the Islamic god deceives and leads men astray he can never be trusted, as there is no way of knowing when he is lying.

Second, dogmas that require their subjects to feign support in order to avoid death and imprisonment are acknowledging defeat. They are admitting that given the freedom to choose, people would opt out of their repressive regime.

Third, hypocrites are defined as Muslims who don't obey the messenger's orders to leave their homes to fight in Allah's Cause. In this verse the pacifists have descended a notch. They have gone from being "the most vile of animals," to "the lowest depths of the fire." If you are a "peace-loving" Muslim, you may want to find a new religion. You're in a lose-lose situation. If Islam is true, you're going to hell. If Islam isn't true, you're being deceived.

Lastly, truth is so devastating to Islam, association with non-Muslims must be prohibited and condemned. Violating this restrictive order provides "open proof" that Muslims are not sufficiently submissive.

This next verse has an odd beginning. *004.147* **"What can Allah gain by your punishment..."** I don't know, and the verse doesn't say. But it's a good question.

The Islamic world seems to have ignored this one: *004.148* **"Allah does not love the public utterance of hurtful, harsh speech unless (it be) by one to whom injustice has been done."** I guess every Muslim in every Islamic hate parade feels that he or she has been injured. Fact is, they have: but only by Muhammad and Islam.

Returning to those pesky "bad" Muslims...*004.150* **"Those who deny Allah and His Messengers, and (those who) wish to separate Allah from His Messengers, saying: 'We believe in some but reject others:' And (those who) wish to take a course in between; They are the real unbelievers; and we have prepared for unbelievers a humiliating punishment, a shameful doom."** Methinks our boy doth protest too much. He's losing control, and it shows. The first Muslims, those who had the "benefit" of Muhammad's preaching, had to be threatened to swallow the bitter hatred, violence, and immorality of Islam. They knew that there was something very, very wrong with the medicine he was dispensing.

It appears that the fine folks of Medina asked for a little proof, a miracle perhaps, to show that these situational "scriptures" were from God, not merely Muhammad. *004.153* **"The people of the Book ask you to cause (an actual) book to descend to them from heaven. Indeed they asked Moses for an even greater (miracle), for they said: 'Show us Allah in public,' but they were dazed for their presumption. Allah's storm of thunder and lightning seized them for their wickedness."** In other words, "No miracles for you. And if you ask again, my god is going to frighten you with a thunderstorm like Moses' God did on Mt. Sinai."

As an aside, the request for an actual book was astute. Not a word of the Qur'an had been scribed on a scroll. The Qur'an was little more than a stream of situational recitals thinly disguised to serve Muhammad's agenda.

The next series of verses attacks Jews and assails Christ's mission. In the 154th verse the Covenant was described as **"the raising of the Mount over the Jews,"** and them becoming Muslims by **"prostrating themselves in submission."** In the 155th verse Jews were condemned for **"killing the Prophets unjustly."** Then in the next they were berated for **"uttering a grave false charge of illegal sexual intercourse against Mary."** Yet in the 157th Allah contradicted himself by having Jews say: **"'We killed the Messiah, Jesus, son of Mary,' but they killed him not, nor crucified him. But it appeared so to them (as the resemblance of Jesus was put over another man and they killed that man). Nay, Allah raised him up unto Himself. Those who differ with this version are full of doubts. They have no knowledge and follow nothing but conjecture. For surely they killed him not."**

As we ponder why Muhammad would lie about such a thing, we must deal with the preposterousness of the allegation. Six hundred years after the single most life- and civilization-altering event in human history, an illiterate and immoral Arab terrorist said it didn't happen and that any who differ have no knowledge. That's like the Soviets saying that Americans didn't walk on the moon simply because the truth didn't fit their agenda. The evidence for Christ's crucifixion is overwhelming. You can argue that he wasn't divine or that he wasn't resurrected but not that he didn't die on a cross believing that he was sacrificing himself for our sins. For that matter, you can't say that "Jesus" was a prophet, or even a great moral teacher, but wasn't God, because he claimed to be God. If he wasn't God, he was a fool at best and more likely a lunatic and charlatan. Moreover, the Jews never claimed to have "crucified the Messiah" because: (a) the Romans crucified him, and (b) the Jewish clerics who wanted him dead didn't recognize him as the Messiah. Simply stated, the Qur'an's position is impossible, and thus it is untrue.

Muhammad's motivation, however, was transparent. If Christ's sacrifice on the cross reconciled man with God, the Arab prophet was irrelevant. If even one percent of the Gospel account was accurate, Muhammad was a complete fraud, the most vile liar to have ever lived. And then there was Muhammad's boss, Lucifer. If Christ was not crucified, he killed two birds with one stone. Judaism and Christianity were destroyed. Psalm 22 begins with the Messiah's last words on the cross. It then describes the torment of crucifixion in excruciating detail, five hundred years before the Assyrians invented it. Yet we are told that the Messiah's sacrifice was for all time, applying to those who were yet unborn. It says that all would eventually come to serve him as God.

Isaiah 53 is equally specific. Speaking of the importance of the Messiah's sacrifice, the prophet proclaimed: "He was pierced for our transgressions, crushed for our iniquities, and chastised for our well being. By his scourging we are healed. All of us like sheep have gone astray, each of us has turned to his own way; but Yahweh has caused the iniquity of us all to fall upon him." If that didn't happen as predicted outside the walls of Jerusalem on Passover, Yahweh is a liar and there is no savior. Since God cannot lie, Yahweh would not be God and the Messiah would be irrelevant. It's Satan's ultimate fantasy. By deceiving us he achieves his agenda, which is our damnation.

Skipping ahead, we rediscover Allah's dependence on Jews for meaningful Qur'anic content. *004.163* **"We have sent you inspiration, as We sent it to Noah and the Messengers after him. We sent inspiration to Abraham, Ishmael, Isaac, Jacob and the [twelve Jewish] Tribes, to Jesus, Job, Jonah, Aaron, and Solomon, and to David We gave the Psalms. Of some messengers We have already told you the story; of others We have not; and to Moses Allah spoke directly."** Funny thing, though; Moses didn't mention Allah. Nor did any of the other "messengers." I wonder why?

Then, demonstrating his disdain for those he plagiarized, Muhammad said on behalf of Allah: *004.168* **"Those who reject [Islamic] Faith and deal in wrong, Allah will not forgive them nor guide them to any path except the way to Hell, to dwell therein forever. And this to Allah is easy."** Regurgitating Lucifer's hatred for Jews and Christians was the easiest thing Allah ever did. Leading mankind astray and directing us to hell was all in a day's work for the demented spirit of Islam.

Then the terrorist pirate and immoral libertine said: *004.171* **"O People of the Book! Do not exaggerate in your religion; nor speak lies of Allah. The Messiah, Christ Jesus, the son of Mary was (no more than) a messenger of Allah, and His Word, which He bestowed on Mary, and a Spirit proceeding from Him. So believe in Allah and His messengers. Say not 'Trinity.' Cease and Desist: (it is) better for you: for Allah is one Ilah (God). (Far it is removed from him of) having a son. To Him belong all things in the heavens and on earth. And enough is Allah as a Disposer of affairs. The Messiah is proud to be a slave of Allah, as are the angels, those nearest. Those who disdain His worship and are arrogant. He will gather them all together unto Himself to (answer).... He will punish with a painful doom; Nor will they find, besides Allah, any to protect or save them."** Wow! That was ugly. Not only does Allah demote Christ and rebuke the Trinity, he claims to be the lone God of Creation. The only thing needed to make Satan's wish list complete was to gather Christians and Jews together and roast them in hell.

The word's most heinous hater of Jews and Christians went on to say that the Messiah will condemn them: *004.159* **"And there is none of the People of the Book but will believe in him (Jesus as only a messenger of Allah and a human being) before his (Jesus') death. He will be a witness against them."**

004.160 **"For the iniquity of the Jews We made unlawful for them certain (foods) in that they hindered many from Allah's Way, that they took usury, though they were forbidden, and that they devoured men's wealth on false pretenses, We have prepared for those among them who reject [Islamic] Faith a painful doom."** Stunning! The Jews are being condemned to hell for charging interest on loans they made to the Muslims in Medina. Yet the Muslims who stole their homes, robbed their businesses, confiscated their land, slaughtered their men, raped their women, and sold their children into slavery are in paradise conquering virgins.

Based upon this I think it's fair to say that Islam is without peer. It's the most dimwitted, deceitful, demonic, intolerant, immoral, and violent dogma ever perpetrated on mankind.

21

BLOOD & BOOTY

"We ask Thee for the booty of this town and its people."

Year seven of the Islamic Era got off to a horrendous start. The prophet, without provocation, led a terrorist raid to torment another Jewish community. *Tabari VIII:116/Ishaq:510* **"After his return from Hudaybiyah, Allah's Messenger marched against Khaybar. He halted with his army in a valley between the people of Khaybar and the Ghatafan tribe to prevent the latter from assisting the Jews."** The motivation for the attack was obvious. Muhammad's militant and mercenary horde was up in arms over his capitulation at Hudaybiyah. Out of control, they would have turned against their warlord if he hadn't found a way to satiate their growing lust for blood, babes, and booty.

For those who think this conclusion is unfair and overly cynical, consider the facts. When the Muslims failed to capture the Meccan caravan at Badr, the prophet stole property and possessions of the Qaynuqa Jews. Following the Uhud defeat, he immediately plundered the Nadir Jews. The siege of the Trench was not only the third in a series of four battles without booty; it was also bloodless. So Islam's demented dictator provided slaughter, sex, and spoil by murdering, enslaving, and robbing the Qurayza. The Jews had become easy prey. So following the bootyless and bloodless "peace" of Hudaybiyah, Muhammad set out to terrorize the only Jewish community within reach that he hadn't previously sacked and plundered—Khaybar. It was their turn to feel the wrath of Islam.

Incidentally, neither Allah, Muhammad, Ishaq, Tabari, Bukhari, nor Muslim made an attempt to justify Islam's ruthless assault on the Khaybar Jews. They knew the truth and didn't try to disguise it. Islam was no longer a religion; it was a terrorist dogma. The first Muslims weren't disciples; they were mercenaries. Muhammad wasn't a prophet; he was a pirate. Allah wasn't a god; he was the Devil incarnate. And together, they were about to prove that they were a blight on humankind.

As transparent as ever, these words, directly from Muhammad's lips, demonstrate that he was working for the Prince and the Power of the Air, the

Lord of Devils, the Prince of Darkness, the Great Deceiver, the Adversary— Satan. *Ishaq:510* "When the Apostle looked down on Khaybar he told his Companions, 'O Allah, Lord of the heavens and what they overshadow, and Lord of the Devils and what into error they throw, and Lord of the winds and what they winnow, we ask Thee for the booty of this town and its people. We take refuge in Thee from its evil and the evil of its people. Forward in the name of Allah.' He used to say this of every town he raided."

Serving Lucifer was no easy task. Good and evil had to be redefined so that the good people of Khaybar, who were just going about their lives trying to make an honest living, had to be called "evil." And the bad terrorist thugs lurking in the hills above them, armed to the teeth and ready to pounce on the on the unsuspecting village, murdering, enslaving, robbing, and raping, had to be called "good."

Ishaq:511 "When the Apostle raided a people he waited until morning, and then he attacked. We came to Khaybar by night. When morning came and he did not hear the call to prayer, he rode and we rode with him. We met the workers of Khaybar coming out in the morning with their spades and baskets. When they saw the Prophet and our army they cried, 'Muhammad with his force.' They turned tail and fled. The Apostle yelled, 'Allahu Akbar! Khaybar is destroyed.' When we arrive at a people's square, it is a bad morning for them."

All of the deceptions, justifications, and apologies ever spoken would be insufficient to make this horrible day appear religious. And it does not stand alone. Khaybar was but one of seventy-five merciless raids instigated by the first Muslims. Armed raiders attacked civilians for no other reason than to seize their possessions. "Allahu Akbar!" was the terrorists' "Prayer of Fear."

Ibn Ishaq's compilation of Islamic scripture—the inspired Sira, or biography of the prophet—is the earliest and most accurate accounting of Muhammad's life and of the formation of Islam. It was compiled a century before Tabari, Muslim, and Bukhari. But for those who might want to dismiss the Hadith report on the basis that it sounds too condemning of the prophet, consider these confirming words from imam Bukhari. Of his collection, Islamic sages wrote: "Second only to the Qur'an, Bukhari's Hadith is the most important book in Islam." He claims: *Bukhari:V5B59N510* "Allah's Apostle reached Khaybar at night. It was his habit that, whenever he reached an enemy at night, he would not attack them till it was morning. When morning came, the Jews came out with their spades and baskets. When they saw the Prophet, they said, 'Muhammad! O dear God! It's Muhammad and his army!' The Prophet shouted, 'Allahu-Akbar! Khaybar is destroyed, for whenever we approach a nation, evil will be the morning for those who have been warned.'"

The more you know, the worse it gets. This is why Islamic leaders must keep good people from reading these words. It is why they lie to themselves, to our citizens, the media, and politicians alike. Islam is self destructive, mutilating its own credibility.

The Hadith said Muhammad made a "habit" of this perverse behavior. The Jews were his enemy, although none had lifted a finger in violence towards him. The Jews were farmers, going to work with gardening tools, and yet Muhammad led a surprise "attack" against them with his "army." He professed "destruction," not salvation. But it's his last line that's especially haunting. With Islam, the nations of the world are approached by "evil."

Muhammad's ruthless terror campaign against the townships of Qurayza and Khaybar was worse than Osama bin Laden's assault on New York and Washington. The first Islamic terrorist was more destructive, savage, and sadistic than his later-day incarnations in the Taliban, Hezbollah, Hamas, the Muslim Brotherhood, Black September, Jemaah Islamiyah, al-Aqsa Martyrs' Brigade, al-Qaeda, and Islamic Jihad. And Muslims know it. In their media, in their mosques, and in their madrassa, they compel young boys and girls to follow Muhammad's example. When they bomb our buildings, blow holes in our ships, hijack or planes, and kidnap our people, they doing what they have been commanded to do. Islam cannot be fixed; it cannot be reformed. Islam cannot coexist with civilized people. It is a terrible disease. Through indoctrination Islam destroys Muslim minds, corroding them. By way of its grotesque immorality and criminal nature it attacks Muslim hearts, corrupting them. Worst of all, by way of deceit and deception Islam beguiles Muslim souls, damning them forever. That is the crime of Islam.

To add insult to injury, Bukhari noted: *Bukhari:V5B59N512* **"The Prophet offered the Fajr Prayer [the Prayer of Fear] near Khaybar when it was still dark. He said, 'Allahu-Akbar!' [Allah is Greatest] Khaybar is destroyed, for whenever we approach a hostile nation to fight, then evil will be the morning for those who have been warned.' Then the inhabitants of Khaybar came out running on their roads. The Prophet had their men killed; their children and woman were taken as captives."** Calling the Jews a hostile nation is a farce. Muhammad and the Muslim militants, according to their own accounting, had either murdered, terrorized, enslaved, or raped tens-of-thousands of Jews yet the Jews had killed but one Muslim. Even that was self defense, allegedly occurring during the Islamic siege of the Qurayza.

The warning these Jews were given before evil befell them was no different than Muslims provide today. The 9/11 terrorists shouted "Allahu Akbar" before they slaughtered thousands. By proclaiming the Prayer of Fear, Islamic terrorists tell us who they are, what they believe, who they serve, and why they kill.

There is nothing Islam could do to make their terrorist nature more obvious. *Bukhari:V5B59N516* **"When Allah's Apostle fought the battle of Khaybar, or when he raided any other people, we raised their voices crying, 'Allahu-Akbar! Allahu-Akbar! None has the right to be worshipped except Allah.' [Muslims will continue to terrorize until every soul submits to Islam.] On that Allah's Apostle said, 'Lower your voices, for you are not calling a deaf or an absent one, but a Hearer Who is with you.' On that he said to me, 'O Abdallah, shall I tell you a sentence which is one of the treasures of Paradise?' I said, 'Yes, O Allah's Apostle! Let my father and mother be sacrificed for your sake. [What an utterly perverse**

and odd thing to say.]' He said, 'It is: There is neither might nor power but with Allah.'"
Then why, pray tell, did he require militants to kill and pillage for him?

Tabari VIII:116/Ishaq:511 **"So Muhammad began seizing their herds and their property bit by bit. He conquered Khaybar home by home. The first stronghold defeated was Naim. Next was Qamus, the community of Abi Huqayq. The Messenger took some of its people captive, including Safiyah bt. Huyayy, the wife of Kinanah and her two cousins. The Prophet chose Safiyah for himself."** Perverted is too kind a word for this man. He became the first serial rapist to call himself a prophet. And make no mistake; having sex with a captive is rape.

Tabari VIII:117 **"Dihyah had asked the Messenger for Safiyah when the Prophet chose her for himself. Muhammad gave Dihyah her two cousins instead."** It was a two for one deal. The prophet could be so considerate. *Ishaq:511* **"When Dihyah protested, wanting to keep Safiyah for himself, the Apostle traded for Safiyah by giving Dihyah her two cousins. The women of Khaybar were distributed among the Muslims."** Wow! Muhammad had men killed so that he could have sex with their wives and daughters. He traded human beings. And the "prophet" rewarded his Muslim militants by distributing the remaining women among them. Good Grief!

Faced with a problem, Muhammad used some magic to turn rape into an approved Islamic act. The slight of hand was called "the Mut'a." It was a three-day "marriage" giving he and his militants a license to do with their prisoners whatever they pleased. But on this day, only the prophet's indiscretion was "approved." *Bukhari:V5B59N527* **"On the day of Khaybar, Allah's Apostle forbade the Mut'a or temporary marriage."**

Bukhari:V5B59N512 **"The Prophet had their men killed, their children and woman taken as captives. Safiyah was amongst the captives, She first came in the share of Dihyah but later on she came to belong to the Prophet. Muhammad made her manumission [Webster: "a Medieval word signifying the authority of a master to release one from slavery"] as her 'Mahr [wedding gift].'"** Translated into common English, Muhammad performed some Islamic hocus pocus to make nonconsensual sex seem moral. And that's all Islam was really. It was just an act—an Oscar winning performance by one of the great con artists of all time. The Bukhari Tradition winds down with these words: **"The captives of Khaybar were divided among the Muslims. Then the Messenger began taking the homes and property that were closest to him."**

The prophet was busy establishing Islamic Sunnah, or custom, on this day. *Ishaq:512* **"The Apostle prohibited four things the morning of the Khaybar raid: carnal intercourse with pregnant women who were captured, mingling his seed with another man's [which means the Muslims were free to rape those who weren't pregnant]; nor it is lawful for him to take [rape] her until she is in a state of cleanness [not menstruating]; nor can a Muslim eat the flesh of donkeys; nor eat any carnivorous animal; nor sell any booty before it has been duly allotted."** That's because the prophet took his cut off the top and didn't want it diminished. The Tradition continues to lay down the law: **"Nor is it lawful for a Muslim to ride an animal belonging to the booty with the intention of** returning it to the pool when he has worn it out; nor is it lawful for him to wear a garment belonging to the booty of the Muslims with the intention of returning it to the pool [of stolen goods] when he has reduced it to rags." If you desire to be a pirate, I suppose that these might be words to live by.

Ishaq:512 "On the day of Khaybar, the Apostle forbade us to by or sell gold ore for gold coin or silver ore for silver coin." He who controls the bank, the means of commerce and trade, controls men by way of their purse strings.

Before we leave this rather dismal attempt to establish Islamic law, I want to solve the perplexing donkey conundrum. It's no small matter to Muslims. There are no fewer than a dozen Bukhari Hadiths from this day alone were focused on the lowly ass. Let's see if we can figure out why. *Bukhari:V5B59N526* "On the day of Khaybar Allah's Apostle forbade the eating of garlic and the meat of donkeys." That wasn't much help; all it did was demonstrate that Muhammad was a fool. Garlic is nature's best antibiotic and thus should be consumed. But Muhammad wasn't much of a medicine man.

This trio of prescriptions should tell the tale: *Bukhari:V7B71N590* "The climate of Medina did not suit some people so the Prophet ordered them to drink camel urine as a medicine." And when that made them even sicker, *Bukhari:V7B71N592* "I heard Allah's Apostle saying, 'There is healing in black cumin for all diseases except death.'" And lest we forget: *Bukhari:V7B71N673* "Allah's Apostle said, 'If a fly falls in your drink, dip all of it into the cup and then throw it away, for in one of its wings there is a disease and in the other there is healing, an antidote or treatment for that disease.'"

But foolish did not make him frivolous. The next Tradition provides a clue as to why he was upset. *Bukhari:V5B59N511* "Someone came to Allah's Apostle and said, 'Donkeys have been eaten by Muslims.' The Prophet kept quiet. The man again and said, 'Their donkeys have been eaten.' The Prophet kept quiet. After the third time the Prophet ordered his caller to announce, 'Allah and His Apostle forbid you to eat the meat of donkeys.' Then the cooking pots were overturned while the meat was still boiling in them."

I discovered the clue when I read this: *Bukhari:V5B59N531* "We were afflicted with severe hunger the day we raided Khaybar. While the cooking pots were boiling and the food was ready to eat, the announcer of the Prophet said, 'Do not eat anything, especially the donkey-meat. Turn your cooking pots upside down and throw it away.' We realized that the Prophet had prohibited such food because the Khumus had not been taken out of it." The "Khumus" or "Kumis" is the prophet's share of all booty seized by Muslim militants. The donkeys belonged to the Jews. They were beasts of burden used to till fields and carry crops to market. Thus they were a spoil to be divided, with Muhammad getting the largest share. And he would rather see his people starve than renounce his claim to stolen property.

The first Islamic historian and biographer each report a Hadith along the same lines: *Tabari VIII:117/Ishaq:512* "The Banu Sahm of Aslam [newly recruited Muslim militants] came to the Messenger and complained, 'Muhammad, we have been hurt by drought and possess nothing.' Although they had fought for the Prophet they found he had nothing [he was willing] to give them. The Apostle said, 'O Allah, You know their condition— I have no strength and nothing [I want] to give them [from the booty I have stolen]. So conquer for them the wealthiest of the Khaybar homes, the ones with the most food and fat meat.'" In other words, "Steal your own damn booty. You'll starve before I share any of my confiscated wealth with you."

Then, proving that Allah was a wannabe terrorist too: *Tabari VIII:117* **"The next morning Allah opened the township of Sa'b bin Mu'adh for them to conquer. There was no stronghold in Khaybar more abounding in food. After the Prophet had defeated some of their settlements and taken their property, they reached the communities of Watib and Sulalim, which were the last of the Khaybar neighborhoods to be conquered. Muhammad besieged the inhabitants between thirteen and nineteen nights."** Calling Islam "peaceful" ranks as one of the most egregious lies of all time. This wasn't even war. The Muslims weren't out defending themselves or their religion. This was nothing more than a terrorist raid with a racist bent.

While Islam has always been violent, Muslims have seldom been good at it. *Ishaq:514/Tabari VIII:119* **"Encamped at their fortress, Muhammad presented his war banner to Abu Bakr and sent him against the Jews. He fought but he retreated, suffering losses. The following morning the same thing happened to Umar. When they returned to Muhammad, Umar's companions accused him of cowardice, and he accused them of the same. The Messenger said, 'Tomorrow I shall give the banner to a man who loves Allah and His Messenger. Allah will conquer it by his means.' The next day Bakr and Umar vied for the war banner, but the Prophet called Ali, who was suffering from inflamed eyes, and, having spat on his eyes, gave him the banner. Ali advanced upon the people of Khaybar. In the fight he lost his shield so he laid hold of the fort door and used it as a shield. He kept it in his hand as he fought until Allah gave Muslims the victory. When the siege was over eight of us tried to lift he door but we couldn't even turn it over."** Either the skinny-legged fat boy of Mecca got a personal trainer or he found a hell of a propagandist.

A Bukhari Hadith starts off the same way but ends oddly. *Bukhari:V5B59N521* **"On the day of Khaybar, Allah's Apostle said, 'Tomorrow I will give this flag to a man through whose hands Allah will give us victory.... Ali said, 'O Allah's Apostle! I will fight them till they become like us.' [Cruel? Demonic? Mercenaries? Terrorists?] Allah's Apostle said, 'Proceed, and when you enter their town, call them to embrace Islam and inform them of Allah's Rights which they should observe, for if a single man is led on the right path (of Islam) by Allah through you, then that will be better for you than nice red camels.'"** I don't know what is more perverse: suggesting that the victims of a terrorist raid should be called to Islam before they are slaughtered, robbed, enslaved, and raped, or suggesting that a man's soul is better than **"nice red camels?"**

Moving on, the Sunnis wanted us to know that Abu Bakr and Umar were no less brutal. *Tabari VIII:119* **"The Messenger often had migraines and would remain a day or two without coming out. When Muhammad encamped at Khaybar, he came down with a migraine and did not come out. Bakr took the Prophet's war banner and fought vigorously. Next Umar took it, fought with even more ferociously than the first fighting."**

Then, in some of the most despicable words ever scribed in the name of religion: *Tabari VIII:121/Ishaq:515* "Ali struck the Jew with a swift blow that split his helmet, neck protector, and head, landing in his rear teeth. And the Muslims entered the city. Muhammad conquered Qamus, the [Jewish] neighborhood of Abi Huqayq. Safiyah bt. Huyayy was brought to him, and another woman with her. Bilal led them past some of the Jews we had slain including the woman's dead husband. When she saw them, the woman with Safiyah cried out, slapped her face, and poured dust on her head. When Allah's Prophet saw her, he said, 'Take this she-devil away from me!'" Grieving for those who had been butchered as a result of Islam was beyond Muhammad. This woman cried as she was dragged past the mutilated corpses of her family and friends. Yet the man who had led the terrorist raid so that he could steal their possessions called the victim a "devil."

I dare say that when you began this journey you did not expect Islam to be this bad. This is a special kind of evil. Muhammad terrorized, plundered, and murdered while professing to be God's Messenger. That, in my opinion, made him the most wretched man to have ever lived.

Yes, I know that the Crusades and Inquisition were brutal, and that Protestantism was born out of a lust for power, sex, and money, but it's not the same—not even remotely. The clerics and kings that conspired together to control their subjects, hid the Bible and perverted its message. They were misguided hypocrites who used religion to satiate their own cravings. Muhammad, by contrast, claimed to speak for God. He didn't corrupt Islam—he made Islam as perverted as the spirit that possessed him.

Therefore, Muhammad's legacy haunts us today. It pains me beyond words to look into the eyes of a Muslim woman or child trapped in Islam. There is almost no way to reach them. And if this tortures my soul, what must it do to our Creator? Islam, the curse of Muhammad, has damned over two billion men and women. It has left nothing but death and destruction, poverty and despair, persecution and indoctrination, terror and deceit in its wake. Muhammad was the Prophet of Doom.

This beast of a man was now totally out of control. *Tabari VIII:122/Ishaq:515* "Muhammad commanded that Safiyah should be kept behind him and he threw his cloak over her. Thus the Muslims knew that he had chosen her for himself."

Moving on with the saga of the only "religion" to be born in a milieu of grotesque immorality, piracy, and terror we are about to add torture to its list of hate crimes. *Tabari VIII:122/Ishaq:515* "Abi Huqayq [Safiyah's father] held the treasure of the Nadir [the second Jewish tribe Muhammad exiled from Yathrib]. He was brought to Allah's Messenger, and he questioned him. But Huqayq denied knowing where it was. So the Prophet questioned other Jews. One said, 'I have seen Kinanah [Safiyah's husband] walk around a ruin.' Muhammad had Kinanah brought to him and said, 'Do you know that if we find it, I shall kill you.' 'Yes,' Kinanah answered." This was Muhammad's second assault on the Nadir. He had stolen their homes, businesses, and land the year after he banished the Qaynuqa, a year before he slaughtered the Qurayza. All the Nadir had left was what they had been able to carry on their backs.

And remember, this accounting of events is from the Islamic Hadith. There is no other source of information from which a different impression may be drawn. Not a word concerning this man's life or deeds was chronicled within three hundred years of his death apart from these books. Therefore, the Muhammad of Islam, the first Muslims, and the formation of the religion are just as you are seeing them here. Alternate theories have nothing to stand on.

With each act of violence, Islam's lone prophet became more gluttonous, callous, heinous, and ultimately, insane. *Tabari VIII:122/Ishaq:515* **"The Prophet commanded that the ruin should be dug up. Some treasure was extracted from it. Then Muhammad asked Kinanah for the rest. He refused to surrender it; so Allah's Messenger gave orders concerning him to Zubayr, saying, 'Torture him until you root out and extract what he has. So Zubayr kindled a fire on Kinanah's chest, twirling it with his firestick until Kinanah was near death. Then the Messenger gave him to Maslamah, who beheaded him."**

Torturing a man whose home and property he had stolen twice, and whose wife he was about to rape, demoted Muhammad from a bloodthirsty terrorist and pirate to a demonic sadist. Anyone who promotes Muhammad's verbal diarrhea as scripture, Muhammad's life as exemplary, or Muhammad's war manifesto as a peaceful religion, is no better than the degenerate who began it all simply to satiate his cravings.

It's time we shed our ignorance, and admit the truth about Islam. Three score and three years ago, Pearl Harbor was a wakeup call. America correctly identified the enemy and declared war on Imperial Japan and Nazi Germany. Had the nation, in the aftermath of the September 11th bombings of New York and Washington, protected its citizens by declaring war on fundamental Islam for having perpetrated that attack, the world would have been safer today. By defending ourselves intelligently against those who attacked us, the legal context for rebuking the hateful and violent religotic of Islam would have been established, as well as the ability to legally silence the deadly doctrine's most vocal advocates.

Under those circumstances, anyone guilty of seducing lost souls, be it in the media, madras or mosque, into the clutches of this poligious dogma could have been identified and punished. Ignoring Islam and going after al-Qaeda is akin to targeting Hitler's S.S. instead of Nazism or Kamikazes instead of the belief system that turned them into suicidal killing machines. If we continue to fight the symptoms of this disease, like the fascist Baath party in Iraq and organizations like al-Qaeda, the real villain—Islam—will manufacturer more terrorists than the world can endure. And while I do not advocate murder, killing in the context of a justifiable defensive war against a force whose leaders will send thousands, if not millions, to their doom is compassionate.

Tabari VIII:123/Ishaq:515 **"Allah's Apostle besieged the final [Jewish] community of Khaybar**

until they could hold out no longer. Finally, when they were certain that they would perish, they asked Muhammad to banish them and spare their lives, which he did. The Prophet took possession of all their property." Before you look at this as an act of mercy, allowing people to live that he had nearly starved to death, you should know it was really economics. By getting the Jews to surrender, Muhammad claimed the entire spoil for himself.

Ishaq:515 **"When the people of Fadak heard of what had happened, they sent word to the Messenger, asking him to banish them and spare their lives, saying they too would leave him their property. When the people of Khaybar surrendered on these conditions, the survivors asked Muhammad to employ them on their farms for a half share of whatever they produced. They said, 'We know more about farming [seeing that you are terrorists and all].' So Muhammad made peace with them for a half share, provided that: 'If we want to expel you, we may.' He made a similar arrangement with Fadak. So Khaybar became the prey of the Muslims, while Fadak belonged exclusively to the Messenger of Allah, becoming his personal property, because the Muslims had not attacked its people with cavalry."** "Prey" is an apt description of what the Jews were to the first Muslims.

And it was to be a never-ending assault. *Bukhari:V4B53N380* **"Umar expelled all the Jews and Christians from Arabia. Allah's Apostle after conquering Khaybar thought of expelling the Jews from the land which, after he conquered it, belonged to Allah, Allah's Apostle and the Muslims. But the Jews requested Allah's Apostle to leave them there on the condition that they would do the labor and get half of the fruits (the land would yield). Allah's Apostle said, 'We shall keep you on these terms as long as we wish.' Thus they stayed till the time of Umar's Caliphate when he expelled them."**

I recognize that this is hard to believe. It's so inconsistent with our popular view of prophets and religions. Yet the bloodied and broken bodies of the Khaybar Jews, like the Qurayza before them, reveal what Islam does to men. Pure, fundamental, original, and uncorrupted Islam turned men into terrorists. They became as immoral as the beast who seduced them.

As additional proof, I offer one of the most startling Hadiths in Islam: *Bukhari:V4B52N143* **"The Prophet told an Ansar, 'Choose one of your slave boys to serve me in my expedition to Khaybar.' So, he chose me, even though I was just nearing puberty. I served Muhammad when he stopped to rest. I heard him saying repeatedly, 'Allah! I seek refuge with you from distress and sorrow, from helplessness and laziness, from miserliness and cowardice, from being heavily in debt and from being overcome by men.'"** This was how Muhammad saw himself, and in fact, it was what he had become.

Muhammad was stressed-out, helpless, and lazy. He was a miser. Never having actually earned a dime in his life, Muhammad had no way to value capital or labor. He was always in debt, no matter how much he stole. The economic plight of the Islamic world is a direct result of Muhammad's unwillingness to engage in honest work. It is why the Islamic nations remain the world's least productive. In fact, Muslims as a whole are destructive economically, stifling far more commerce than they inspire.

And that's because their leader was a pirate. Islam was financed by stolen booty and the slave trade. As parasites, they survived by sucking every productive host within a camel's ride dry. The Bedouins of Arabia were poor, and while the Jews were a tasty treat, Islam would soon sink its fangs into a more plentiful prey. Within a year, Muhammad would attack the Byzantines. Within three, his Companions would subdue Arabia in the War of Compulsion, taxing everyone. Within a decade the first Muslims would conquer Yemen, Persia, Egypt, Syria, and Judea. Within a century, the sword of Islam would be wielded above the necks of millions. And it was all for money. They plundered and raped to be sure, but their principle tools were the zakat and jizyah taxes, which they imposed on all people rich and poor.

But most of all, Muhammad was coward, as are all Islamic imams today. They are ever ready to send others to their death, but never willing to fight themselves. They corrupt boys with promises of virginal rewards while they remain in the comfort and safety of mosque and madrasa. Like most loud-mouthed bullies, Muhammad, and those who followed him, found pleasure in tormenting the defenseless.

And with each passing day it became evident that Muhammad had lost control of himself and that he was "overcome by men." The Medina surahs have been fixated on attacking deserters. Orders to submit and obey dominate his final revelations. As men sought freedom and peace, Muhammad reacted by becoming more dictatorial and warlike. As a result, Islamic nations are the least-free places on earth. In the land of submission there are no true democracies, no freedom of religion, of the press, of speech, or travel. One billion Muslims struggle to survive in countries brutalized by tyrants and dictators. And it's not hard to see why. The first Muslims emulated their warlord, becoming increasingly belligerent, callous, and brutal.

So, that leads us to a very unattractive place. As a direct result of Muhammad's personal failings the Islamic world is devoid of everything civilized people hold dear. Muslims wallow in poverty. Life isn't worth living. They have no freedom of speech or religion. With the educational process focused on Qur'anic studies, Muslims are among the most poorly educated and most indoctrinated people on earth. Following the example of a perverted sexist, Muslim men abuse women. And they are violent. Twenty percent of the world's population is responsible for ninety percent of the planet's upheaval— terror and war. If only twenty percent of Muslims are "good" ones, then Islam makes them 2000% more violent than the rest of us. Frankly, I don't see any benefit to any of this. Islam is a liability the world could easily do without.

In the Prologue I shared a pair of quotes from Islamic scholars. This might be a good time to review them in context of what we have learned. What may have once seemed extreme will now appear understated. Here is what Dr. D.S. Margoliouth had to say: "The character attributed to Muhammad in the biography of Ibn Ishaq is exceedingly unfavorable. In order to gain his ends Muhammad recoils from no expedient, and he approves of similar unscrupulousness on the part of his adherents, when exercised in his interest… He organizes assassinations and wholesale massacres. His career as the tyrant of Medina is that of a robber chief whose political economy consists of securing and dividing plunder…. He is himself an unbridled libertine [morally and sexually unrestrained] and encourages the same passion in his followers. For whatever he does he is prepared to plead the express authorization of his deity. It is, however, impossible to find any Islamic religious doctrine which he is not prepared to abandon in order to secure a political end. At different points in his career he abandons the unity of God and his claim to the title of Prophet. This is a disagreeable picture for the founder of a religion, and it cannot be pleaded that it is a picture drawn by an enemy."

Renan wrote: "Muslims were the first victims of Islam. Many times I have observed that fanaticism comes from a small number of dangerous men who maintain others in the practice of this religion by terror. To liberate the Muslim from his religion is the best service that one can render him."

Considering the nature of their prophet, it should be no surprise that the Islamic world is such a mess. *Bukhari:V4B52N143 /V5B59N523* **"When we reached Khaybar, Muhammad said that Allah had enabled him to conquer them. It was then that the beauty of Safiyah was described to him. Her husband had been killed, so Allah's Apostle selected her for himself. He took her along with him till we reached a place called Sad where her menses were over and he took her for his wife, consummating his marriage to her, and forcing her to wear the veil.'"**

Bukhari:V5B59N524 **"The Muslims said among themselves, 'Will Safiyah be one of the Prophet's wives or just a lady captive and one of his possessions?'"** Muhammad was guilty of every sex crime known to man: pedophilia, incest, rape, polygamy, adultery, womanizing, fornication, sexism, and abetting prostitution. Worst of all, he rewarded his mercenaries by dividing captured young girls among them. It's little wonder the Qur'anic paradise was so perverted.

The Sira reports: *Ishaq:517* **"When the Apostle married [using a word designed to convey the nature of a moral and loving relationship to this situation is repulsive] Safiyah on his way out of town, she was beautified and combed, putting her in a fitting state for the Messenger. The Apostle passed the night with her in his tent. Abu Ayyub, girt with his sword, guarded the Apostle, going round the tent until he saw him emerge in the morning. Abu said, 'I was afraid for you with this woman for you have killed her father, her husband, and her people."** As an interesting aside, Safiyah, like the Jewish Juwayriyah (the sex slave before her), bore the identity of her God in her name.

Imagine for a moment, being Safiyah. You awaken one morning to find a gang of godless pirates prowling the outskirts of your town. After rattling their sabers, you witness thousands of them performing a prostration "prayer." You recognize them, for they are the same men who threw you out of your home in Yathrib. Their bone-chilling shouts of "Allahu Akbar" pierce your soul. Before you can run, the mercenaries swarm at you from every direction. They continue to howl as one thrusts a sword into your father's flesh; they torture your husband, building a fire on his chest, ultimately decapitating him. They murder your brothers. Then they shackle your cousins, hauling them away to become sex slaves. They ransack your home and strip the clothes off your family as they lay dying, all in a frenzied quest for booty.

Hiding behind a door, you're terrified. Then it happens. One of the Muslims spots you; a crazed demonic lust explodes on his face. He knocks you down, pressing his knee against your back while he ties your hands to your neck. You can hardly breathe. It's the worst moment of your life. The filthy and sweaty militant fondles you, dragging you past the bloodied bodies of your neighbors; you want to cry, to scream, but nothing comes out.

Then you see Muhammad, the man you've grown to hate, the repulsive sixty-year-old animal responsible for this horror. He claims you as his "prize," tossing his cloak over your head. His words, his very presence, make your skin crawl. But as his slave you are helpless. He strips you of whatever little dignity you have left. Then he conquers your body just as he ravaged your town.

Now, consider the insanity of a man who claimed to be "the Messenger of God" raping a woman whose town he had terrorized, savaged, plundered, and enslaved. How could a man claim to be a "prophet" and yet be so demonic and sadistic, he would force a woman to have sex with him whose husband he had tortured and then beheaded, whose father he had assassinated, and whose cousins he had "given in trade" to one of his militants so that he might possess her?

The problem with Muhammad isn't that he was the most vile man who ever lived; it's his legacy. He perpetrated these heinous crimes while claiming to be "the best example," "the ideal role model," an Apostle speaking on behalf of God. This demented criminal established a new religion that has damned the souls of over two billion people; he inspired terrorism, and his legacy has led the world to the brink of global war.

I do not know if any part of the following is accurate. However, if there is an element of truth, it was too little, too late. Every Jewish settlement within Muhammad's reach had already been terrorized and plundered. *Bukhari:V5B59N551* "When Khaybar was conquered, a sheep containing poison, was given as a present to Allah's Apostle" *Tabari VIII:123/Ishaq:516* "When the Messenger rested from his labor [which says that terrorism and piracy were his chosen occupation], Zaynab, the wife of Sallam, served him a roast sheep. She had asked what part Muhammad liked best and was told that it was the shoulder and foreleg. So she loaded it with poison, also poisoning the rest.

Then she placed it before him. He took the foreleg and chewed it, but he did not swallow. With him was Bishr, who, like the Prophet, took some, but he swallowed it. The Prophet spat out the lamb saying, 'This bone informs me that it has been poisoned.'"

Talking bones and a gluttonous man spitting out his favorite celebratory meal are a little farfetched. But there was a reason for including the story. The cook was a Jew. The tale was concocted to infer that Khaybar deserved to be sacked. No one had bothered to provide any justification for the initial attack.

"Muhammad summoned the woman, and she confessed. He asked, 'What led you to do this?'" This goon claimed he was a prophet, and yet he couldn't figure this one out. Good grief. It's like Hitler asking a Polish Jew why he wanted him dead. **"She said, 'You know full well what you have done to my people.'"** It was as if Muhammad was surprised when folks were upset with his terrorist tactics. Caught up in his make-believe world, he had lost all sense of reality.

This next Hadith is mindless propaganda. *Tabari VIII:124/Ishaq:516* **"The Messenger, during the illness from which he died, said to the mother of Bishr who had come in to visit him, 'Umm, at this very moment I feel my aorta being severed because of the food I ate with your son at Khaybar.'"** Sure, that makes perfect sense. The poison he spit out years before killed him. **"The Muslims believed that in addition to the honor of prophethood, the Messenger died a martyr.'"** Well, at least we know the reason for this sorry tale of woe. Muslims who don't die martyrs have no chance of making it into paradise. The cowardly terrorist needed to miscast his personal history to die a worthy death.

Tabari VIII:124/Ishaq:516/Bukhari:V5B59N541 **"Having finished with Khaybar, the Apostle went to Wadi Qura and besieged its people for a while. Then we headed back to Medina, halting at Qura toward sunset. With Muhammad was a slave lad of his whom Rifa'ah had given him. Suddenly, as we were setting down the saddle of the Prophet, a stray arrow came and hit the slave boy, killing him. We congratulated him, saying, 'May he enjoy Paradise!' But Allah's Apostle said, 'Certainly not! The sheet of cloth on his back is now being burnt on him in the Hell Fire!' He pilfered it from the booty of the Muslims following the Khaybar raid before it was duly distributed."** You apparently aren't allowed to steal anything that's already been stolen.

And there's a significant conflict between Muhammad's personal example and the rallying cry of the Nation of Islam as they lure African Americans into their ranks. Muhammad not only enslaved people and built Islam on money "earned" selling them into bondage, he himself owned slaves. Boys were personal servants and girls were for personal services.

A poem recited this day proclaims: *Ishaq:517* **"Khaybar was stormed by the Apostle's squadron, fully armed, powerful, and strong. It brought certain humiliation with Muslim men in its midst. We attacked and they met their doom. Muhammad conquered the Jews in fighting that day as they opened their eyes to our dust."** It's hardly sermon material.

But sadly, imams have been preaching the following message for far too long: *Ishaq:518* **"Masud was one of those who found martyrdom at Khaybar. Muhammad** said, 'He has with him now his two dark-eyed virgins. When a martyr is slain, his two virgins pet him, wiping the dust from his face. They say, "May Allah throw dust on the face of the man who did this to you, and slay him who slew you!"'" It's the antithesis of Christ's: "Love your enemies."

In the next installment of Islamic scripture, a Muslim deceives the Quraysh to collect his belongings. What's interesting is that Muhammad gave him permission to lie and disavow Islam for money. *Ishaq:519* "**Hajjaj said to the Apostle, 'I have money scattered among the Meccan merchants, so give me permission to go and get it.' Having got Muhammad's permission, he said, 'I must tell lies.' The Apostle said, 'Tell them.'**" Muhammad didn't heed Yahweh's command not to bear false witness. This prophet spit on the Ten Commandments. As a result, the Islamic world cannot build a productive economy or develop a stable democracy. The currency for both is trust. The spirit of deceit still haunts Muslims.

The division of the "Spoils of Khaybar" was so important to the formation of Islam that both Ishaq and Tabari dedicate entire sections to it. One line in particular reveals Muhammad's motivation for attacking the Jews. *Tabari VIII:128* "**Khaybar was divided among the people who had been at Hudaybiyah.**" Each time Muhammad's mercenaries got down on him, he plundered Jews. This was no exception. The prophet redeemed himself for having been disgraced at Hudaybiyah; he quieted his critics by sharing the booty from an easy kill. *Ishaq:521* "**Khaybar was apportioned among the men of Hudaybiyah without regard to whether they were present at Khaybar or not. The spoil was divided into 1,800 shares.**"

This Ishaq Hadith reveals where the booty went. *Ishaq:521* "**When the spoil of Khaybar was apportioned, the settlements of Shaqq and Nata were given to the Muslims while Katiba was divided into five sections: Allah's fifth [which Muhammad was custodian]; the Prophet's fifth; the share to the kindred [Muhammad's kin]; maintenance of the Prophet's wives [now there's an honest report]; and payment to the men who acted as intermediaries in the peace negotiation with Fadak [which enabled the Profit to confiscate the entire spoil].**" Instead of a religious awakening, it was a repulsive accounting.

Ishaq:522 "**Then the Apostle distributed the booty between his relatives, his wives, and to other men and women. He gave his daughter Fatima 200 shares, Ali 100, Usama 250, Aisha 200, Bakr 100, Aqil ibn Abu Talib 140.... In the name of Allah, Ar-Rahman, Ar-Rahim—this is a memorandum of what Muhammad the Apostle of Allah gave his wives from the dates and wheat of Khaybar: 180 loads.**" The Hadith lists additional special favors and bequeaths but I'll spare you the gory details.

The first Islamic historian said, *Tabari VIII:130* "**The Prophet conquered Khaybar by force after fighting. Khaybar was something that Allah gave as booty to His Messenger. He took one-fifth of it and divided the remainder among the Muslims. The inhabitants who surrendered did so on condition that they should be expelled.**" *Tabari VIII:129* "**After the Messenger had finished with the Khaybar Jews, Allah cast terror into the hearts of the Jews in Fadak when they received news of what Allah had brought upon Khaybar. So they sent to Muhammad to make peace with him for a half share of Fadak's produce. Fadak became** the exclusive property of Allah's Messenger." Peace Islamic style means surrender. And surrender means giving Muhammad everything.

Continuing to impugn its claim of tolerance, the Islamic scripture reveals: *Tabari VIII:130* "The Messenger said during his final illness, 'Two religions cannot coexist in the Arabian Peninsula.' Umar investigated the matter, then sent to the Jews, saying: 'Allah has given permission for you to be expelled; for I have received word that the Prophet said that two religions cannot coexist in Arabia." *Ishaq:524* "We cannot accept the oaths of Jews. Their infidelity is so great they swear falsely."

Bukhari also chronicled the dispensation of stolen property. Here is a sampling: *Bukhari:V5B59N525* "While we were besieging Khaybar a person threw a leather container containing some fat and I ran to take it. Suddenly I looked behind, and behold! The Prophet was there. So I felt shy (to take it then)." *Bukhari:V5B59N537* "On the day of Khaybar, Allah's Apostle divided the war booty with the ratio of two shares for the horse and one-share for the foot soldier." *Bukhari:V5B59N541* "When we conquered Khaybar, we gained neither gold nor silver as booty, but we gained cows, camels, goods and gardens." *Bukhari:V5B59N544* "Abu Huraira came to the Prophet and asked him for a share from the Khaybar booty. 'O Allah's Apostle! Do not give it to him. He is a strange guinea pig from Qadum Ad-Dan!' On that the Prophet said, 'O sit down!' and did not give him a share." *Bukhari:V5B59N547* "When Khaybar was conquered, we said, 'Now we will eat our fill of dates!'" There are many more, but you get the picture. Islam was a "religion" only in the sense that it became one man's license to steal from many.

Swimming in the blood and plunder of Khaybar didn't satisfy the sharks. Instead, Muhammad's militants went off on a feeding frenzy. *Tabari VIII:131* "Allah's Apostle sent Umar with thirty men against the rear of Hawazin. They traveled by night and hid by day. However, word reached Hawazin and they fled." *Tabari VIII:132* "According to Waqidi, a thirty-man raiding party led by Bahir went to the Banu Murrah. His companions were killed and he was carried away wounded with the dead. They returned to Medina." So... "The Messenger sent Abdallah al-Kalbi to the land of the Murrah. During the raid, Usamah and one of the Ansar killed Mirdas. When they overcame him, Usamah said, 'I testify that there is no god but Allah,' but we killed him anyway."

Tabari VIII:133 "The raiding party led by Ghalib went to Abd Tha'labah. One of Muhammad's slaves, said, 'Prophet, I know where the Abd can be taken by surprise.' So Muhammad sent him with Ghalib and 130 men. They raided Abd, and drove off camels and sheep, bringing them back to Medina." Stealing sheep does not make one a shepherd.

Then: *Tabari VIII:133* "A raiding party led by Bahir went to Yumn. What prompted this raiding party was that Hussayl had been the guide of Muhammad at Khaybar, and he came before the Prophet. He claimed that the Ghatafan had been summoned to march against him. The Muslims went out and captured camels and sheep. A slave belonging to Uyaynah met them, and they killed him. Then they encountered Uyaynah's army which retreated."

So Muhammad returned to Mecca. *Tabari VIII:135/Ishaq:530* "When the Apostle returned from Khaybar he sent out raiding parties and expeditions before he made the hajj. When the Meccans heard of it they got out of the Muslims' way. Gathering at the door of the assembly house to look at them, they said, 'Muhammad and his Companions are in poverty and misery; they are covetous and miserly.'" From the very beginning the Meccans understood Muhammad and Islam.

The warlord made a beeline for Allah's House. *Ishaq:530* **"The Prophet stroked and kissed the Black Stone. Then he went out trotting around the Ka'aba as did his Companions. When the Temple concealed Muhammad from the Meccans and he had "istalama" (which means to embrace, stroke, and kiss) the southern corner of the Ka'aba, he walked to "istalama" the Black Stone a second time. Then he "harwala" (which means to trot or prance swinging the shoulders side to side in a gloating manner) similarly for three circumambulations. He walked the remainder of them. The Apostle only did this to show off in front of the Quraysh."** It was so pagan and childish of him.

Muhammad not only kissed, fondled, and trotted around a Black Stone wedged into the wall of a pagan rock shrine replete with 360 other idols, he claimed this exhibition was Islamic "Sunnah." As such, the practice became obligatory Islamic ritual with the binding power of law. *Ishaq:531* **"When the Prophet made his farewell pilgrimage he adhered to the practice making it required Sunnah to be carried out forever."** While Muhammad had not yet stolen their town, he had stolen their idol and their religion—the pagan religious scam founded by Qusayy—the Ka'aba Inc.

A poem from that black day says: *Ishaq:530* **"Get out of his way you infidel unbelievers. Every good thing goes with His Apostle. O Lord I believe in his word. We will fight you about its interpretations as we have fought you about its revelation with strokes that will remove heads from shoulders. And we will make enemies of friends."** The Meccans were being told to get out of Muhammad's way and yet it was their town, their god, their shrine, and their religious scam. Muhammad's example, as communicated through the Hadith, is being called "good." That means terrorist raids, piracy, the slave trade, torture, assassinations, mass murder, deception, and rape are all "good things" in Islam.

The line, "I believe in his word" can only be interpreted two ways, and both are bad. Either the Qur'an was comprised of Muhammad's words, as "his" isn't capitalized and follows a reference to the Apostle, or these Hadiths are being acknowledged as "scripture"—words to be "believed."

The *means* Muslims said they would use to win the debate over Muhammad's interpretation of Qusayy's scam and his claim to have received Allah's revelations would be *swords*, not words. Islam was too foolish, and the first Muslims were too ruthless, to impose the doctrine any other way. Islam, properly deployed, severs heads and turns friends into enemies.

Tabari VIII:138 **"According to Waqidi, Muhammad carried arms, helmets, and spears. He led a hundred horses, appointing Bahir to be in charge of the weapons and Maslamah to be in charge of the horses. When the Quraysh received word of this, it frightened them. The Prophet said, 'Young or old, I have never been known but for keeping a promise. I do not want to bring in weapons against you, but the weapons will be close to me.'"** So, which story is untrue? This Hadith says Muhammad never went back on a promise, but the Qur'an says: *009.003* **"And an announcement from Allah and His Messenger to the people on the day of the Great Pilgrimage is that Allah and His Messenger dissolve treaty obligations with the Pagans."** So who was lying, prophet or god?

I have saved the third installment of *Mien Kampf* for after the Khaybar raid because with it, Muhammad became Hitler's equal. He had now murdered and enslaved the majority of Arabian Jews, just as Hitler had murdered and enslaved the preponderance of European Jews. Following a peace treaty, Muhammad used negotiation and his war machine to turn Fadak and Khaybar into his own personal fiefdoms. In like fashion, Hitler parlayed the Munich treaty with Neville Chamberlain into the acquisition of Czechoslovakia and then to the rout of Poland.

But Muhammad and Hitler had more in common than just a demonstrated hatred for Jews and the willingness to use deceit and unprovoked violence. They are among a handful of men who founded their own religions. Hinduism didn't have a founder. And Buddha conceived a more enlightened way of life; *men* turned it into a religion. Abraham didn't have a religion, and Moses simply documented the Covenant between Yahweh and the Jewish people. As you know, the word "religion" doesn't even appear in the Hebrew Scriptures. Yahshua, the "founder" of Christianity, was *anti*-religious—saving his most heated words for the clerics of his day. So that leaves der prophet and der fuhrer. They established religions to serve their personal agendas. Their scriptures were little more than reflections of their flawed characters.

Prophet of Doom is dedicated to exposing Islam. Yet peering into Hitler's mind by examining *Mein Kampf,* enables us to understand Muhammad and Islam in ways that would otherwise not be possible. While their motives and characters were identical, Hitler had a vastly superior intellect and was a much better writer than was either Muhammad or his god. He was also more direct and honest, baring his soul and scheme for all to see. Furthermore, we know the consequence of ignoring *Mein Kampf.* By equating the poligious doctrines it is my hope that the world will not suffer similarly for its ignorance of Islam.

Diving back in where we left off we discover that der fuhrer and der prophet were equally fixated on money—other peoples' money. They condemned financial transactions involving Jews. *Mein Kampf:426* *"The Jew considers all money transactions as his own privilege, which he exploits ruthlessly. Manipulating money has become his monopoly—especially his usurious rates of interest.... It's a sign of open hatred, of his blood-sucking tyranny...a scourge of God."* Allah agrees: *Qur'an 004.160* **"For the iniquity of the Jews We made unlawful for them certain things in that they** hindered many from Allah's Way. They took usury, though they were forbidden; and they devoured men's wealth on false pretenses."

Insecure men like Muhammad and Hitler crave praise as much as they do power, sex, and money. They attack anyone they perceive as successful, bringing them down to their level, as they are inwardly threatened by them. The Jews were productive, and thus had money. Empowered, the dictators simply took it from them, justifying their attacks by calling the Jews evil. Further, der fuhrer and der prophet were possessed by the same demonic spirit—a spirit that needed to silence the voice of Yahweh's chosen people.

My first book, *In the Company of Good and Evil,* was a treatise on insecurity. It demonstrated in a corporate setting, what this cancer does to men, organizations, and even nations, and why insecure men are the Devil's easiest prey. Muhammad's nature, his character, motives, deeds, and scripture can best be understood when we see how the abuse he suffered as a child caused this emotional vacuum. For ultimately, the reason Hitler's and Muhammad's lives and mantras were so similar is that they suffered from the same affliction.

Insecurity causes men to say things like: *Mein Kampf:427 "No persecution can deter Jews from exploiting mankind. Even if you expel a Jew he comes back again after a short time. So to prevent the Jew from this one must take the soil out of his usurious hand, making it illegal for him to own it."* And if that doesn't suffice, you can always march them into the marketplace of Medina and cut off their heads or into concentration camps and shower them with cyanide. The only "human" (and I use that term loosely), that rivaled Hitler in the theft of Jewish land, property, and lives was his mentor, Muhammad.

Insecure men are particularly adept at stealing what belongs to others. And they always give their dastardly deeds a religious or moral spin so that their victims are verbally abused as they are robbed. The dark spirit of Islam reports: *Qur'an 033.026* **"Allah made the Jews leave their homes by terrorizing them so that you killed some and made many captive. And He made you inherit their lands, their homes, and their wealth. He gave you a country you had not traversed before."** Then, speaking of the Jews, der fuhrer stole a page from the Qur'an: *Mein Kampf:428 "They are God's chastisement. The Jews have only received a thousandth the reward they deserve for the sins they have committed. They sold themselves to the Devil and landed in his domain. They are monsters who torture the beloved people to the point of despair. The Jew will be punished by Heaven." Qur'an 059.014* **"The Jews are devoid of sense. There is a grievous punishment awaiting them. Satan tells them not to believe so they will end up in Hell."** *Ishaq:254/Qur'an 2:96* **"We will not remove a Jew from the punishment. They know the shameful thing that awaits them."** *Qur'an 004.055* **"Sufficient for the Jew is the Flaming Fire!"**

Jews represented less than one percent of the population of Arabia and of Germany, yet both men were fixated on punishing them, robbing them, annihilating them. The odds against the most prominent men to have established religions singling out *one* race for retribution are astronomical. The odds that it would be the same race, a pacifist people without an army or country, are incalculable. There must have been a reason.

Jews are distinguished from other races by only one thing: their covenant with Yahweh. It's the relationship that brought us the Bible and the Messiah. Therefore, if we are looking behind the anti-Semite veil to see who is lurking there, we must search for a spirit who has something to lose from mankind having access to the truth about God and salvation. There is one such a spirit. Lucifer is the inspiration for everything we have witnessed in Islam and Nazism. Jews were silenced and their scriptures were repudiated. Christians were terrorized and rendered impotent. Both religions deceived mankind— reshaping the definition of good and evil.

Mein Kampf:432 "Jews twist things to make it appear as though others had wronged them, not vice versa. Those who are especially stupid believe them and grant them unwarranted sympathy." Ishaq:264 **"A notable Jew spoke to the Apostle, twisting his tongue. He attacked Islam and reviled it, so Allah sent down, 'Allah knows best about your enemies. Some of the Jews change words from their contexts and say: "We hear and disobey," twisting their tongues and attacking the religion so Allah cursed them.'"**

The similarity between this next Hitlerism and Muhammad's terrorist campaign against the Jews is chilling: *Mein Kampf:445 "The Jewish allure is broken only by terror. The success of such activity is enormous."* Qur'an 059.002 **"It was Allah who drove the [Jewish] People of the Book from their homes and into exile. They refused to believe and imagined that their strongholds would protect them against Allah. But Allah came at them from where they did not suspect, and filled their hearts with terror. Their homes were destroyed. So learn a lesson, O men who have eyes. This is My warning...they shall taste the torment of Fire."** Hitler called them "crematoriums."

But since Jews were pacifists, they had to be demonized. *Mein Kampf:446 "The Jew is not the one who is attacked, but the attacker. But he will not stand for an honest fight and must use lies and calumny. They become the personification of the Devil, the symbol of all evil."* Ishaq:240 **"The Jews are a nation of liars.... The Jews are a treacherous, lying, and evil people."** Qur'an 059.014 **"They will not fight against you save in fortified townships, or from behind walls. Their hostility and hatred amongst themselves is strong: you would think they were united, but their hearts they are divided. That is because these [Jews] are a people devoid of sense."**

In shrill voices, the anti-Semite duet bellowed: *Mein Kampf:447 "The Jews slyly dupe the stupid goyim into creating a Palestinian State. But they have no intention of building a Jewish state, so that they might inhabit it. They only want a refuge for convicted rascals, international cheating, and a high school for future rogues."* Ishaq:245 **"Do you love Jews and their religion, you liver-hearted ass, and not Muhammad? Their religion will never march with ours.... Jews make false professions about Islam. So Allah sent down: 'Satan wishes to lead them astray."** Ishaq:248 **"Allah increases their sickness. A tormented doom awaits the Jews. Allah said, 'They are mischief makers. They are fools. The Jews deny the truth and contradict what the Apostle has brought. I will mock them and let** them continue to wander blindly.'" It's not a very pretty tune.

In Nazism, like Islam, to be a pacifist was nearly as bad as being Jewish. Pacifists didn't kill enough people to satisfy the boss or his spirit. *Mein Kampf:394* *"One would have to wage war in order to arrive at pacifism. The victory of the pacifistic idea requires the conquest of the world by Germans—making him the master of the globe."* Allah shouted: *Qur'an 009.038* **"Believers, what is the matter with you, that when you are asked to go forth and fight in Allah's Cause you cling to the earth? Do you prefer the life of this world to the Hereafter? Unless you go forth, He will afflict and punish you with a painful doom, and put others in your place."**

The next *Mein Kampf* passage begins where the Qur'an left off. *Mein Kampf:393* *"Man has never conquered Nature [Lucifer] in any affair. At most he tries to lift a flap on Her enormous veil of eternal riddles and secrets. He cannot dominate Nature in any way. But knowledge of the secrets of Nature [Satan] will enable him to rise to the position of master over all living beings. But apart from this knowledge, an idea cannot conquer."* Allah roars: *Qur'an 003.175* **"It is only the devil who would make (men) fear his messengers and frighten you. Fear them not; fear Me, if you are true believers. And let not those grieve you who fall into unbelief hastily; surely they can do no harm to Allah; they cannot injure Him."** "I am god, I am invincible." Pathetic is more like it. But just the same, if you want to conquer men and become their master, nothing beats using Satan's secrets to create a violent and carnal religion.

Such was the lesson of both Nazism and Islam. *Bukhari:V4B53N386* **"Our Prophet, the Messenger of our Lord, ordered us to fight you till you worship Allah alone or pay us the Jizyah tribute tax in submission. Our Prophet has informed us that our Lord says: 'Whoever amongst us is killed as a martyr shall go to Paradise to lead such a luxurious life as he has never seen, and whoever survives shall become your master.'"**

Once Hitler exposed the nature of his spirit, Biblically grounded Christians immediately recognized that his "god" was Satan. German pastors wrote Hitler a letter: "When blood, race, creed and nationality are raised to the rank of qualities that guarantee eternity, the Christian is bound by the First Commandment to reject the assumption." And we must come to the same conclusion about Islam, for the Qur'an's dark spirit says that killing guarantees paradise. His creed calls for blood, race war, and the Islamic domination of the world.

Turning the page we discover that religions are established by evil men because they put such men in control. The individual loses his individuality, sacrificing choice at the altar of obedience. *Mein Kampf:411* *"True idealism [religion] is nothing but subjecting the individual's life and interests to the community. The ultimate will of Nature leads men to acknowledge the privilege of force and strength…. Here the instinct is to unconsciously obey."* "Obey." It was Muhammad's favorite word. *Qur'an 047.021* **"Were they to obey, showing their obedience in modest speech after a matter had been determined for them, it would have been better."**

There are a limited number of ways to control people. Authority can be earned; it can be militaristic, seductive, coercive, or religious. Behaving in the manner necessary to "earn" authority was beyond men like Muhammad and Hitler. Militaristic authority was something that they craved, as such regimen bans choice, and orders must be obeyed by unthinking servants. Although both men ended up as dictatorial warlords, they couldn't start out that way. So they turned to seduction, the first tool of the pirate and profiteer. Muhammad enticed the unsuspecting into his lair with promises of booty and babes. Once these men had seduced sufficient militants into their ranks they used them to terrorize others into submission. Terror is the principle tool of the coercive manipulator.

But nothing beats religion. It provides an individual with ultimate authority, and it's the perfect platform for raping the world. *Mein Kampf:456 "For with all great reforms the remarkable thing is that at first they have only a single individual champion. The goal lays dormant until one man stands up as the proclaimer and flag bearer of an old longing. And he helps it to victory in the form of a new idea,"* so sayeth der fuhrer. And the reason is: *Mein Kampf:460 "We must produce that spirit which enables a people to bear arms."* And that's because when it comes to wars, Holy Wars are the most vicious. *Mein Kampf:467 "The movement intends to nationalize the masses by a ruthless and fanatically one-sided orientation."* Muhammad said: *Tabari VIII:12* **"'Rejoice, Allah has promised us victory after tribulation.' This increased the Muslims faith and submission." "When cities were conquered Muslims used to say, 'Conquer for yourselves whatever seems good to you because all treasures were given to Muhammad."**

Islam and Nazism concentrate power in the hands of an uncontested dictator. *Mein Kampf:478 "The movement in all things represents the absolute authority of the Leader.... The Leader bears the highest unrestricted authority. Only the Hero is chosen for this." Ishaq:471* **"We were steadfast trusting in Him. We have a Prophet by whom we will conquer all men."** *Bukhari:V4B52N203* **"I heard Allah's Apostle saying, 'He who obeys me, obeys Allah, and he who disobeys me, disobeys Allah. He who obeys the chief, obeys me, and he who disobeys the chief, disobeys me.'"** It's a simple yet sinister formula.

Next, Hitler explains why Muhammad focused on gratifying men's flesh and why he needed to attack Judeo-Christianity during the formation of Islam. *Mein Kampf:468 "He who would win the masses must know the key which opens the door to their hearts [sex, power, and money—and failing that, the promise of babes in paradise]. Its name is not objectivity, which is weakness, but willpower and strength. One can only succeed in winning the souls of people if in addition to fighting for one's own aims, one also destroys at the same time the supporters of the contrary. In the ruthless attack upon an adversary, the people see proof of their own right. They want victory of the stronger and annihilation or unconditional surrender of the weaker."* Islam means unconditional surrender. It achieves victory by annihilating all who oppose it. Allah said: *Qur'an 009.029* **"Fight those who do not believe until they all surrender, paying the protective tax in submission."**

Hitler was the prophet and messenger of Nazism, a religion he conceived to serve his interests. As you read these words, think of Muhammad. *Mein Kampf:481*

"An ingenious idea originates in the brains of a man who feels himself called upon to transmit his knowledge to the rest of mankind. He now preaches his views and gradually he gains a certain circle of followers. The direct and personal transmittal of the ideas of a man to rest of the world is the most ideal thing for the new doctrine." Mein Kampf:481 *"The community grows and the doctrine retains its uniformity when the authority of the spiritual founder is recognized."* This mirrors Islam's beginnings.

Hitler's quote regarding the importance of having a Qiblah like the Ka'aba is so similar to Islam; he calls it Mecca. Mein Kampf:481 *"The geo-political importance of a center of a movement cannot be overrated. Only the presence of such a center and place, bathed in the magic of a Mecca, can give a movement a force rooted in inner unity."* This is why Muhammad changed his Qiblah to Mecca in the 2nd surah.

For der fuhrer and der prophet, victory was achieved by violently forcing their religion upon others. Mein Kampf:486 *"The greatness of a movement is exclusively guaranteed by the unrestricted development of its inner strength to achieve final victory over all competitors. The justification…for fighting to achieve complete victory…is caused by absolute intolerance."* Muslim:C9B1N31 **"I have been commanded to fight against people till they testify to the fact that there is no god but Allah, and believe in me (that) I am the messenger and in all that I have brought."** Qur'an 009.123 **"Fight the unbelievers around you, and let them find harshness in you."**

Not only were Islam and Nazism founded as religions, both were fanatical, forcing themselves on the world. Mein Kampf:486 *"The greatness of every powerful organization or idea is rooted in the religious fanaticism with which it intolerably enforces itself against everything else, fanatically convinced of its own right."* In his final surah, Allah was as intolerant and fanatical as words allow. Qur'an 005.033 **"The punishment for those who wage war against Allah and His Prophet and make mischief in the land, is to murder them, crucify them, or cut off a hand and foot on opposite sides…their doom is dreadful. They will not escape the fire, suffering constantly."**

Muhammad focused on a few principles and repeated them. Hitler explains why: Mein Kampf:506 *"I carried out the proclamation of propaganda ruthlessly. Good propaganda influences the masses, it concentrates on a few points, and is continuously repetitious, self-assured and confident. It uses an apodictic assertion and great persistency."* Mein Kampf:512 *"I took up the word, and began to interpret the program [religotic] for the first time. The hall was filled with a people united by a new conviction, a new faith, a new will."* Muhammad's laundry list of requirements was shorter than Hitler's. He required obedience, fighting and money.

Sounding like a commentary on Islam, the manifesto of the twentieth century's most notorious terrorist says: Mein Kampf:570 *"One needs the great magnetic attraction which the masses follow under the forceful impression of convincing force and unconditional beliefs coupled with fanatical fighting courage. As one side, armed with all the weapons sets out to storm an existing order, it will succeed only if the resistance is clad in the form of a new faith and if it exchanges weak slogans and cowardly defense for the battle cry of a courageous and brutal attack."* Ishaq:204 **"'Men, do you know** what you are pledging yourselves to in swearing allegiance to this man?' 'Yes. In swearing allegiance to him we are pledging ourselves to wage war against all mankind.'"

Hitler confirms the importance of forming a "people oriented" religion. *Mein Kampf:573* *"The word 'folkish' [from the German word "volk," meaning people] was conceived to allow the formation of a close fighting community. The conception of 'folkish' can be defined as unlimited in its practical application as the word 'religious.' It is a very nice and cheap way to describe man as fundamentally religious."* *Mein Kampf:575* *"The designation 'folkish' presents a similar situation to that of the conception 'religious.'"* Nazism, like Islam, was founded as a religion for the purpose of controlling men and inspiring them to fight.

Hitler recognized that religion was a tool he could use to achieve his agenda. And like Muhammad, he hammered his point home. *Mein Kampf:574* *"A religious idea will free the individual of individual thinking and acting. Forming the new faith is not an end in itself, but a means to an end. It is an unavoidable necessity. Its purpose is not just to create an ideal but to form an eminently practical expedient."* It has always been this way. Religion is a tool, an expedient wielded ruthlessly above the masses. Religion isn't the opiate of the people; it is their poison.

Hitler explains why Muhammad created Islam and bribed his men to become militants. *Mein Kampf:575* *"For the materialization of the ideals of a view of life and the postulates derived from them takes place through pure feeling [seductions of the flesh] in the inner will of men.... These ideals can be used to form military power, and the fighting organization can inspire people to a glorious realization. Every view of life [religion], though it may be right, will remain without importance for the practical working out in detail of a nation's life, unless its principles have become the banner of a fighting movement which, in turn, will be a party until its effects have fulfilled themselves in the victory of its ideas. The dogmas now form the new basic principles of the people's community."* This was the recipe for Islam. Form a religion to create a force of men; then use that force to force the religion on men.

For Muhammad it was the amalgamation of his political Sunnah with his religious Qur'an that enabled him to guide inadequate men to their doom. *Mein Kampf:576* *"The correct spiritual conception which the program-maker has to preach must be accompanied by the practical knowledge of the politician. Thus an ideal, as the guiding star of mankind, must unfortunately resign itself to taking into consideration the weaknesses of mankind if it wants to avoid failing from the very beginning, in consequence of general human inadequacy."*

Mein Kampf:577 *"The transformation of an ideal view of life into a tightly organized political community of believers and fighters, uniform in spirit and willpower, is the most significant achievement."* Muhammad's ummah, or political community of unified fighters, was the model for *Mein Kampf.* 033.060 **"Truly, if the Hypocrites stir up sedition, if the agitators in the City do not desist, We shall urge you to go against them and set you over them. Then they will not be able to stay as your neighbor for any length of time. They shall have a curse on them. Whenever they are found, they shall be seized and** slain without mercy—a fierce slaughter—murdered, a horrible murdering."

Now for the clincher, the motivation for Nazism as well as for Islam: *Mein Kampf:577* *"Therefore, out of the host of millions of people, One Man must step forward in order to form, with apodictic force, out of the wavering world of imagination of the masses, granite principles, and to take up the fight for their sole correctness, until out of the waves of a free world a brazen rock of uniform combination of form and will arises."* Freedom is so untidy in the hands of others. *Ishaq:391* **"O people, this is Allah's Apostle among you. Allah has honored and exalted you by him. So help him and strengthen him. Listen to his commands and obey them."** *Tabari VIII:182* **"The people assembled in Mecca to swear allegiance to the Messenger in submission. He received from them the oath of allegiance to Muhammad, to heed and obey."**

Der fuhrer, like der prophet before him, saw himself as the final apostle in the line of Jewish prophets. He saw his role as correcting the errors of the prior religion, taking it away from the originators, and giving it to his people for the purpose of suppression—the total eradication of freedom. *Mein Kampf:579* *"The Jew Karl Marx was really the only one among millions who, in the swamp of a decomposing world, recognized, with the keen eye of the prophet, the most essential poison elements, took them out, in order to render them, like a magician of the black arts [Satan worshiper or Occultist], into a concentrated solution for the quicker destruction of the independent existence of the free nations of this earth. But this was all in the service of his race—the Jews. The Marxist doctrine is the brief spiritual extract of the view of life [religion] that is generally valid today…but it plans to transmit the world systematically into the hands of Jewry."* Hitler, hating the Jews, devised a Marxist derivative so that he could kill them with their own medicine. This, in essence, was also the purpose of Muhammad's early Medina surahs.

The exactitude to which Hitler followed Muhammad's program continues: *Mein Kampf:580* *"Eternal Will dominates this universe to promote the victory of the better and stronger, and to demand the submission of the worse and weaker. The program not only values men differently, but also values the differences between individual men. Out of the masses emerges the importance of The Person."* Muhammad viewed non-Muslims as unclean infidels who should be enslaved and then slain as they were merely fodder for hell's fires.

Compare Hitler's view: *Mein Kampf:580* *"I believe in the necessity of idealizing mankind. In the negrified world of opposing ideas my new culture is bound up with the Aryan. One who dares lay a hand upon the highest image of the Lord sins against the benevolent Creator of this miracle and helps in the expulsion from Paradise. When this religious view of life corresponds to the innermost will of Nature, Nature restores the forces which bind and lead the best of mankind to acquire the earth's possessions. For the conquest of the entire globe, only the highest race, as the master nation, will be called upon,"* to Muhammad's: *Tabari IX:69* **"Arabs are the most noble people in lineage, the most prominent, and the best in deeds. We were the first to respond to the call of the Prophet. We are Allah's helpers and the viziers of His Messenger. We fight people until** they believe in Allah. He who believes in Allah and His Messenger has protected his life and possessions from us. As for one who disbelieves, we will fight him forever in the Cause of Allah. Killing him is a small matter to us."

The scholars who translated *Mein Kampf* said, "This begs the question: Why should the superiority of the Aryan race be so important? Hitler gives the answer in this vitally significant passage: *'The race must be maintained in a position of superiority because it is the only foundation on which superiority can be conceded to the leader and exemplar of that race. Men are divided into rulers and ruled for racial aggrandizement. Those to whom guardianship is entrusted cannot tolerate any other ethical idea.'"* Unlike Muhammad, Hitler was an *honest* false prophet. He told us: "I'm doing this for me." *Qur'an 033.036* **"It is not for the true believers to order their own affairs if Allah and His apostle decree otherwise."**

Muhammad had to invent a persona for the imaginary spirit enshrined in the Black Stone. Allah served to justify Muhammad's superiority, his aggrandizement, his claim to power and money. While Allah never spoke, never so much as even rolled over, the Qur'an repeats the message: **"Obey Allah and His Apostle."** Hitler simply replaced "Allah" with "Aryan." It became: "Obey the Aryans and their Apostle." Muhammad was a bit sneakier. *Muslim:C22B20N4604* **"We pledged an oath to the Messenger of Allah that we would listen to and obey his orders."** *Qur'an 033.057* **"Those who speak negatively of Allah and His Apostle shall be cursed."**

The prophet of Nazism preached: *Mein Kampf:583 "Therefore, I saw my own task as extracting a general view of life [religion] and in molding it into a dogmatic form: the clear demarcation of ideas suitable for bringing together those people who will pledge their allegiance to this…. And through the organizational integration of humans, to create the presumption for victorious fighting for this view of life [religion]."* The Qur'an shouts the same mantra: *033.022* **"The Believers said: 'This is what Allah and his Messenger promised us.' It added to their faith, obedience, and submission. Among the Believers are men who have been true to their covenant with Allah and have gone out for Jihad (holy fighting). Some have completed their vow to extreme (and have been martyred) fighting and dying in His Cause, and some are waiting, prepared for death in battle."**

Muhammad used the words truly, verily, surely, and indeed, to fallaciously imply that his muddled message was clear. *Mein Kampf:592 "Therefore, the first obligation of a new [religotic] movement which is based upon the foundation of a folkish view of life is to see to it that the conception is clear…. For if the leader lacks a specific spiritual force he will fail to find the necessary weapons for his self-preservation."* Surrounded by his weapons, Muhammad was also fixated on his own self-preservation when he said, *Ishaq:504* **"He will not allow me to perish."**

Both poligious doctrines were built upon the pagan practices of their ancestors. Der fuhrer proclaimed: *Mein Kampf:594 "Therefore it is an unbelievable offense to portray the Germans of the pre-Christian era as cultureless barbarians. This they never were."* Hitler said this because he usurped their idolatrous rites, festivals, symbols and deities. It's reminiscent of Muhammad and Qusayy.

Hitler forewarned us that his methods, like Muhammad's, would be brutal and that the ends would justify the means. *Mein Kampf:596* *"Our determination must not be based upon the rejection or applause of our time, but by the binding obligation to a truth which we have realized, ennobling our methods today."* Hitler's torch burned brighter but not as long as Muhammad's. Yet the tyrants' lives were stunningly similar. Both came to see themselves as prophets when they were around forty, after having failed at other activities. They stumbled in the early years, recruiting an unimpressive number of adherents. Each composed scripture and eloquently recited racist drivel that most ignored. Only the dregs of society were enticed by their decadent promises. But in the last decade of each man's life they had seduced and deceived enough like-minded men to become plundering pirates. So they sent armed marauders off to terrorize and conquer in their name. Modern technology enabled Hitler's goons to "accomplish" more, faster. In five years the Nazis savaged a landmass equal to the size of Islam's one hundred year conquest.

Hitler's definition of peace was identical to Muhammad's. Peace meant surrender. *Mein Kampf:599* *"Our peace is not supported by the palm branches of a tearful pacifist and professional female mourner, but is founded by the victorious sword of a people of overlords which put the world into the service of a higher culture."* Somehow I don't think Neville Chamberlain read these words before he put Czechoslovakia into the service of the Nazis. Similarly, George Bush failed to heed Allah's words before he endeavored to sell his roadmap to destruction. *Qur'an 047.033* **"Believers, obey Allah, and obey the Messenger. Do not falter; become faint-hearted, or weak-kneed, crying for peace."** *Qur'an 009.003* **"Allah is not bound by any contract or treaty with idolaters, nor is His Apostle."**

Muhammad viewed surrender, submission, obedience, the payment of taxes, and the forfeiture of property as "peace." *Tabari VIII:104* **"Peace to whoever follows the right guidance! To proceed; Submit yourself, and you shall be safe.'"** *Tabari VII:158* **"The Messenger of Allah besieged the Nadir Jews for fifteen days. In the end they made peace with him on the condition that the Prophet would not shed their blood and that their property and possessions would be his."**

Replace the "Third Reich" with the "Nation of Islam," "German" with "Arab," and this passage could have been Qur'anic. *Mein Kampf:600* *"We have a solemn duty to act as God's viceroy on earth and to be His partner in the Divine government of men. The Third Reich's energies are expended on a noble endeavor, the aggrandizement of the chosen German race."* *Mein Kampf:601* *"Our high mission is by the benevolence of the Almighty. The German Reich…must lead to a dominating position."* If you were to distill the Medina surahs and Sunnah down to a singular idea, this would be it. Who would have thought that we would find the central message of Islam summarized in Hitler's *Mein Kampf?* *Qur'an 008.059* **"The infidels should not think that they can bypass Allah's law. Surely they cannot get away."** *Qur'an 008.088* **"Fight them until all opposition ends and all submit to Allah."**

Mein Kampf:602 "*The fight must be carried out with unshakable persistency. We must be compelled to fight for the Coming One. For the fighter's lives belong to the State.*" Hitler was saying, "I am the Messiah. You belong to me. And you must fight to make my dreams a reality." He was explaining Islam. Muhammad said it this way: *Qur'an 009.111* **"Allah has purchased the believers, their lives and their goods. For them (in return) is the Garden (of Paradise). They fight in Allah's Cause, they slay and are slain, they kill and are killed."** *Bukhari:V4B52N196* **"Allah's Apostle said, 'I have been ordered to fight with the people till they say, "None has the right to be worshipped but Allah."'"**

Clarifying the religotic of Submission, der fuhrer shared, *Mein Kampf:602* "*Authority is an end in itself, a powerful weapon in the service of the great struggle, a weapon to which everybody has to submit.*" Hitler, the twentieth century's most evil criminal, told us that "authority," Islam's "submit and obey," was the purpose of his crusade. He told us that the poligious doctrine of *Mein Kampf* was a "weapon" and that the ultimate goal was *Islam*—submission. Because we did not listen then, the world was covered in blood.

Mein Kampf:602 "*Therefore, in the fight for the new conception [poligious doctrine] which corresponds to the primal meaning of things [the pure religion of man], we will find fighting comrades.*" *Mein Kampf:603* "*If an active force appears united toward one goal, this minority will rise to become the master of the whole. World history is made by determined minorities. In the presumption of our victory the best fighters will be found.*" This is among the most important passages in *Mein Kampf*. It explains what happened in Mecca, Munich, and Moscow—and what will happen in America. Religiously inspired fighters impose their poligious doctrines on the majority. The presumption of victory justifies their ruthless tactics.

Muslims represented less than three percent of the Meccan population during Muhammad's day and yet they conquered the Quraysh, stealing their liberties. Only three percent of Germans were Nazis in the late 1920s when Hitler rose to power, yet they destroyed their nation and much of the world. Barely three percent of Russians were Communists during Lenin's revolution yet they managed to enslave and impoverish nearly a billion people for eighty years. Three percent of Americans today call themselves Muslims.

Speaking of Jewish children, der fuhrer plagiarizes Allah. *Mein Kampf:606* "*In the folkish state we will lift marriage out of race degradation in order to consecrate the image of the Lord and not the deformities of men who are half ape.*" And we wouldn't want to educate the apes: *Mein Kampf:640* "*It would be a criminal absurdity to train a half-ape to become a lawyer against the will of the Eternal Creator. The most talented beings degenerate in the proletarian swamp while Negroes are trained for intellectual vocations.*" *Qur'an 002.064* **"But you [Jews] went back on your word and were lost losers. So become apes, despised and hated. We made an example out of you."**

Then, like Allah before him, Hitler attacked the church while he focused his doctrine on the flesh rather than the spirit. *Mein Kampf:607* "*By not endeavoring to breed the best for posterity, churches sin against the image of the Lord. They speak to the spiritual and let the [flesh or] bearer, man, degenerate to depravity. The terrible ungodliness of the Christian faith in regard to the physically botched miserable lot, requires compensation."* According to the author of Mein Kampf, the Nazis were justified when they imprisoned pastors and stole their churches.

Ever the bigot, Hitler combined his disgust for blacks with his disdain for Christianity. *"European peoples fall into a state of physical and moral leprosy as the missionary wanders into Africa and establishes Negro missions while our higher culture turns primitive and inferior human children into a foul breed of bastards."*

As we discovered in "The Anti-Semite" chapter, Muhammad was also a complete racist. *Ishaq:243* **"I heard the Apostle say: 'Whoever wants to see Satan should look at Nabtal!' He was a black man with long flowing hair, inflamed eyes, and dark ruddy cheeks.... Allah sent down concerning him: 'To those who annoy the Prophet there is a painful punishment." [Surah 9:61] "Gabriel came to Muhammad and said, 'If a black man comes to you his heart is more gross than a donkey's.'"**

While there is no evidence that Hitler slaughtered and enslaved blacks like his mentor Muhammad, it's obvious he didn't like them very much. *Mein Kampf:608 "Christian churches, instead of annoying the Negroes with missions which they neither wish nor understand, should teach Europeans to take pity on the poor little orphan in order to give him a father and mother, rather than putting a sick child into the world which will bring itself and the rest of the world only misfortune and suffering."* Reading these words is like having a conversation with Muhammad. Hitler is miffed at the church for abandoning him in his time of need, when he was a poor orphan boy. For allowing him to suffer, he will take his revenge. The religious establishment in Mecca was Qusayy's Ka'aba Inc. When its clerics failed to comfort the now-famous orphan, there was hell to pay.

Both men dedicated their lives to seeking revenge. And for insecure souls, vengeance is defined as forcing all foes to submit in abject humility. Such men feel lifted up when others are torn down. With this line, der fuhrer defined Islam: *Mein Kampf:608 "The individual is nothing and has to submit."* *Qur'an 004.065* **"They can have no (real) Faith, until they make you (Muhammad) judge in all disputes, and find in their souls no resistance against Your decisions, accepting them with complete submission."**

In this pithy quote Hitler renounces Christianity while at the same time garnering a divine ordinance to wage genocide against Jews. *Mein Kampf:610 "The renunciation of the Church can help put an end to the original sin of race poisoning and to give the Almighty Creator a being as He Himself created them."* The spirit that possessed both these men hated Jews. *Qur'an 002.061* **"Humiliation and wretchedness were stamped upon the Jews and they were visited with Allah's wrath."**

Der fuhrer dedicated twenty pages to the process he intended to deploy to manufacture the perfect terrorist. *Mein Kampf:618 "His entire education and development has to be directed at giving him the conviction of being absolutely superior to others. With his physical force and skill he has to win the belief in the invincibility of his race. Confidence in the leader will lead the German army to victory."* And while he tried, he was not as adroit in this endeavor as his mentor was.

This next excerpt reads like a segue from the Sunnah. It's a declaration of war Islam style: *Mein Kampf:618 "He who believes in our work of educating our people for peace and order [a.k.a., the submission, enslavement, and plunder of all non-Nazis], will receive the force to break free of our present doom, to throw the shackles of slavery into the faces of our enemies." Qur'an 008.058* **"If you apprehend treachery from a people with whom you have a treaty, retaliate by breaking off relations with them."**

Throughout the Islamic world, everyone is schooled in the Qur'an and Sunnah. They are taught its message of hate and unrelenting Jihad. The chief Nazi saw merit in the Muslim solution. *Mein Kampf:620 "Education prepares men for future service in the army. It has to turn young men into soldiers…. Men must be trained to use arms, and they must learn to obey." Mein Kampf:621 "Seized by confidence in his own force, a commonly experienced esprit de corps gives the conviction of invincibility."* Muhammad preached: *Qur'an 008.065* **"O Prophet, urge the faithful to fight. If there are twenty among you with determination they will vanquish two hundred; if there are a hundred then they will slaughter a thousand unbelievers, for they are a people devoid of understanding."** Islamic clerics continue to plague the world by indoctrinating Muslims with a false sense of invincibility.

Neither Muhammad nor Hitler valued women for anything more than their bodies: *Mein Kampf:621 "The goal of female education is invariably to teach motherhood." Mein Kampf:659 "The German girl is a subject of the State."* In his farewell sermon the prophet equated women to cattle. *Tabari IX:113* **"Allah permits you to shut them in separate rooms and to beat them, but not severely. If they abstain, they have the right to food and clothing. Treat women well for they are like domestic animals and they possess nothing themselves. Allah has made the enjoyment of their bodies lawful in his Qur'an."**

About ten percent of America's population was enslaved when Abraham Lincoln became president and yet he righteously committed the nation to a war that freed them. In what was Rhodesia and the Republic of South Africa the percentages were different, but so were the conditions. A racial group had their rights infringed. The world protested so vehemently, apartheid was ended. Yet for fourteen centuries, a block of nations stretching from Western Africa across the Middle East and to the doorstep of Asia have treated women as if they were "domestic animals" who "possess nothing themselves." But rather than free them we call the nations that hold them in bondage our allies. Rather than speak out against the doctrine that enslaves women, we parade their spokesmen on national television. So the question is: have we lost our mind, or only our character? Or have we simply lost sight of our God?

Throughout the Islamic world, cleric and king maintain control by feeding the masses a continual diet of poison. Hitler knew all about such things. *Mein Kampf:623 "Loyalty, willingness to sacrifice, and silence are virtues which a great people urgently need, and their indoctrination by way of education is more important than the things that now fill the curriculum…. Our people need less knowledge and more self-restraint."* And that's because: Mein Kampf:634 *"The folkish State will have to fight for its existence…with a fanatical national enthusiasm."* Nazism had to manufacture martyrs to survive: Mein Kampf:635 *"He who loves his people proves this solely by the sacrifices which he is ready to make for them."*

The translators of *Mein Kampf* said, "The leaders of the S.S. and Hitler Youth Organizations have instituted ritualistic exercises derived from a composite Germanic religion. Pagan ceremonies in honor of birth, death, marriage, and other phenomena use Hitler's picture on the altars." Speaking of Qusayy and the pagan religious scam Muhammad inherited: Tabari VI:24/Ishaq:53 **"His authority among the Quraysh was like a religion which the people followed and which could not be infringed; they always acted in accordance with its laws. They regarded it as filled with good omens and recognized his superiority and nobility."** A new religion is easier to sell when it's based on an old one.

A footnote in Mein Kampf reads like the Qur'an: "Religious instruction degenerated into the exposition of anti-Semitic racial doctrine, and apotheosis of the Fuhrer. History is taught in accordance with the spirit of Mein Kampf. German children now recite: *'About thee stand thy people, oh my Fuhrer. In kindness and in wrath thou speakest. Thou are, by God's decree, the voice of the people. In thee do they form and believe. Thou are the law in them. In thee vast planning and pure dreams are made to come true.'"*

Bringing everything into focus, Hitler proclaimed: Mein Kampf:650 *"Our belief in bringing about a faultless era does not relieve us of the obligation of fighting."* This is reminiscent of Muhammad's obligatory fighting to bring an end to the "Period of Ignorance," and usher in the "Islamic Era." Qur'an 004.077 **"When the order for fighting is issued, a party of them feared men as they ought to have feared Allah. They say: 'Our Lord, why have You ordained fighting for us, why have You made war compulsory?'"**

Apart from place and time, Muhammad and Hitler, Islam and Nazism, My Recital and My Struggle are the same. These men created their religions for their own benefit. They corrupted everything, making good look bad and bad look good. They spewed hatred for their enemies: Jews and Christians. And they enticed men to fight for their cause to satiate their cravings. It's as simple and as frightening as that.

The *Mein Kampf* translators said Nazism was not an economic doctrine *vis-a-vis* Communism, Capitalism, or Fascism, as is commonly thought. Back when the religotic was conceived and its Gospel, *Mein Kampf,* was written, Nazis were unfamiliar with Fascism. It wasn't until Hermann Goering returned from exile in Italy that they became informed. "Hitler refused to be tied to any program of economic or fiscal policy. He was simply fixated on change. It would be some time before the Reichswehr program would manifest the doctrines of State control over domestic and export markets, the regimentation of industry, of labor, and capital, its control of the money supply, and its increased government expenditures." In this regard, Nazism was identical to

Islam. Founded as a religious tool to empower a single individual, it failed all others by failing to establish any non-parasitic industry. Economically, Nazi Germany was as bankrupt as the Nation of Islam.

From this perspective, Muslims, like Nazis, lose in every way. Muslims lose their soul, as the message is demonic. They lose their freedom, as the religotic requires submission. Muslims live in poverty since the only worthy endeavor is fighting. And too many forfeit their lives, dying as martyrs for a lost cause. There is no benefit, no reason, no justification to tolerate Islam.

Hitler was as self centered as Muhammad. *Mein Kampf:661 "A view of life must reject democracy and instead give the world the best people, the Superior Man, who must be obeyed...as The Personality, the dictator...the One Individual."* Qur'an 033.21 **"You have indeed a noble paradigm in the Apostle of Allah."** Qur'an 033.036 **"No Muslim has any choice after Allah and His Apostle have decided a matter."** Picking up where Allah left off, der fuhrer proclaimed: *Mein Kampf:665 "The inspired leader whom Nature has endowed with special gifts must be selected."* Qur'an 033.056 **"Allah and His angels shower blessings on the Prophet. So believers, send your blessings on him, and salute him with all respect—a worthy salutation. Those who annoy Allah and His Messenger and speak evil things of them—Allah has cursed them and prepared a humiliating torment."**

There were two reasons that Muhammad and Hitler established militaristic states. Militants were better equipped to steal what the dictators coveted. And military authority is unquestioned and absolute. The translators of *Mein Kampf* said, "Inside an army, soldiers do not ask questions, inquire about their rights, or insist upon privileges. They obey the leader." *Mein Kampf:793 "Army service secures absolute power of command, compelling obedience."*

While goose-stepping to the same beat, der fuhrer and der prophet sang the same tune: *Mein Kampf:669 "There must be no decisions by the majority. The Reich must be built upon the principle of personality [dictatorship]. One Man decides. He has absolute authority."* Qur'an 004.114 **"He who disobeys the Apostle after guidance has been revealed will burn in Hell."**

Hitler was a honest psychopath. He told us that he had established the religion of Nazism to compel men to obliterate all other doctrines. *Mein Kampf:674 "The fighter for our new ideal is compelled into battle to fight to abolish existing doctrines."* *Mein Kampf:675 "The view of life is intolerant. It cannot be content to share power. It demands dictatorial exclusivity. All must be completely readjusted according to its views. Therefore, exactly like a religion, it cannot tolerate the simultaneous existence of a prior doctrine. It must destroy all other altars."*

Muhammad said such things too, as did his god. Each of the following quotes is from the **"Spoils of War"** surah. It explains why Muslims are willing to kill to achieve their monopoly. Qur'an 008.001 **"They ask you about the benefits of capturing the spoils of war. Tell them: 'The benefits belong to Allah and to His Messenger.' So fulfill your duty to Allah and the Prophet."** 008.005 **"Your Lord sent you from your homes to fight for the true cause."** 008.007 **"Allah wished to confirm the truth by His words: 'Wipe** the infidels out to the last.'" *008.012* "I shall terrorize the infidels. So wound their bodies and incapacitate them because they oppose Allah and His Apostle. *008.015* "Believers, when you meet the unbelievers in battle, do not turn your back on them for any Muslim who retreats will bring the wrath of Allah on himself and will abide in Hell." *008.072* "Those who accepted Islam *and* left their homes to fight in Allah's Cause with their possessions and persons, and those who gave them shelter and aided them are your allies. You are only called to protect Muslims who fight." *008.073* "The infidels aid one another. Unless you do the same there will be anarchy in the land. Those who accepted Islam *and* left their homes to fight in Allah's Cause are good Muslims." *008.057* "If you meet them in battle, inflict on them such a defeat as would be a lesson for those who come after them, that they may be warned." *008.059* "The infidels should not think that they can get away from us. Prepare against them whatever arms and weaponry you can muster so that you may terrorize them. They are your enemy and Allah's enemy." *008.071* "He will give you mastery over them." *008.039* "So, fight them till all opposition ends and the only religion is Islam."

The Bible's tacit prediction that Islam will be responsible for the last World War appears probable in this context. But it's a shame that 1.5 billion people, a quarter of the earth's population, will die simply because we were willing to tolerate something this fixated on violent world conquest.

As a footnote to these verses calling all Muslims to global war, the Noble Qur'an explains that Tabari wrote the earliest commentary on the Qur'an. In it, he explained Muhammad's world view. The Nation of Islam must be united in war against all non-Islamic peoples. The infidel killing fields were called "Dar al-Harb," the Place of War. Muhammad envisioned Muslim militants rising up as a single nation under the rule of a dictatorial fuhrer. "The best interpretation of the Verse: 'Those who disbelieve are allies of one another, and if Muslims of the whole world collectively do not do so, and become allies, as one united block,' is Muslims must do what Allah has ordered. We must unite as one nation to make Allah's religion of Islam victorious. For there will be great wars, many battles, and much killing. There will be robbing, great mischief, corruption, and oppression. So to achieve victory, Muslims must unite under one Muslim leader [called Gog in Ezekiel's prophecy]. Muhammad said, 'If the Muslim world gives a pledge to two chiefs, the second one must be killed.' So it is an obligation, as proved by the Qur'an and the Prophet's Hadith, that there must be only one Muslim chief for the whole Muslim world and that all Muslims must unify around him." And when he prevails, (and he will) all hell will break loose.

While the Bible indicates that this leader will come from Iran, the Saudi ruling family's favorite imam, al Buraik, sounds like the perfect candidate. The esteemed Islamic cleric said, "I am against America. She is the root of all evils and wickedness on earth. Muslims, don't take Jews and Christians as allies. Muslim brothers, do not have any mercy or compassion on them, their blood, their money, or their flesh. Their women are yours to take, legitimately. Allah made them yours. Why don't you enslave their women? Why don't you wage jihad? Why don't you pillage them?"

22

LEGACY OF TERROR

*"The battle cry of the Companions of the Messenger of Allah
that night was: 'Kill! Kill! Kill!'"*

Let's return to the Qur'an and check in on the Black Stone. Now that Allah has been kissed and fondled by his perverted prophet I'm sure he's feeling frisky. It should be no surprise that we find Muhammad's alter ego frolicking in his brothel. The surah is called the **"Apartments."**

In order to provide the proper context for this divine revelation we need to understand the nature of Muhammad's mosque. First, it was *his* mosque, never Allah's. Second, it was symbolic of his mission. By building the Medina mosque, Muslims turned a productive farm into a command center for terrorist raids. (Some things never change.) The site had had also been a graveyard, so in a very real sense Islam was built on the backs of dead infidels. Third, the design reflected Muhammad's cravings. The place of prostration was an open and dusty courtyard. The only thing that gave it shape was the two-dozen interconnected apartments, or bedrooms, that had been built for his wives, concubines, and sex slaves.

The **"Apartments"** surah begins by putting Muslims in their place, although by doing so, Muhammad reveals that he's Allah. *049.001* **"Believers, be not forward in the presence of Allah and His Messenger, and fear Allah. Raise not your voices above the voice of the Prophet, nor speak loudly around him, as you speak to one another, lest your deeds become nullified unconsciously. Those that lower their voices in the presence of the Messenger have their hearts tested by Allah. Theirs will be an immense reward."** Allah was always around Muhammad because the prophet created his god's persona. And because Islam's founder was a tyrant, his god was feared. There was nothing new in those lines, but what followed was bizarre. After dedicating a score of surahs to defining fighting as the ultimate good deed, and to using the heavenly brothel deception to lure men to martyrdom, we're told that whispering is a test that earns an immense reward. Allah says that speaking loudly around Muhammad nullifies good deeds like piracy and terrorism. Islam is getting weirder by the minute.

049.004 **"Those who shout out to you from behind the private apartments have no sense."**

With so many women, Muhammad didn't want to be distracted from his duties; it's tough being a stallion. Yet, the notion that a godly revelation would focus on the temporal and vain desires of a sexoholic is beyond belief. *049.005* "If they had waited for you to come out, it would be best for them."

While I don't understand the connection between being silent and demure around the prophet and perpetrating an ignorant attack, that's where the next verse takes us. Muhammad pleads: *049.006* "O ye who believe! If a wicked person comes to you with any news, verify it first, lest you attack ignorantly, and later regret what you have done." Perhaps Muhammad wanted to spend his booty in his boudoir rather than forking over blood money to nullify hasty killings.

The remainder of this verse, like the surah's opening stanza, is useless to anyone reading the Qur'an today, for there is no way to indulge a dead prophet. Allah says: *049.007* "And know that among you is Allah's Messenger: were he to follow your (wishes), you would fall into misfortune...." There is no moral lesson that can be gleaned from being quiet around Muhammad or from respecting his "private time." The Qur'an's laundry list of godly indulgences for libertine behavior served but one man—not so coincidentally, the man who claimed that they were divine. This fraud is so transparent, it's clear why Muslims are told not to question their prophet or his Qur'an. If they did, they wouldn't be Muslims.

This doesn't square with Allah's command not to kill other Muslims but... *049.009* "If two parties among the Believers fall into fighting, make peace: but if one becomes aggressive, then fight against the one that transgresses until it complies with the command of Allah." With the exception of Islam's first century, good Muslims have killed far more bad Muslims than infidels. This verse might explain why.

Muhammad hated being mocked and called names so: *049.011* "Believers! Let not some men among you laugh at others, deriding folk that are better than they are. Nor defame nor be sarcastic, nor call each other by nicknames: Ill-seeming is a name connoting wickedness." Of course, it's okay to call Jews "apes and pigs."

Then the hypocrite who had issued countless orders to spy said: *049.012* "Believers, avoid suspicion as much (as possible): for suspicion in some cases is a sin: And spy not behind the backs of others." In other words, don't look too closely at Muhammad's personal life. "Would any of you like to eat the flesh of his dead brother? Nay, you would abhor it...But fear Allah." I'm sure glad Allah answered that probing question for the sake of the would-be cannibals out there.

Returning to his favorite theme, Muhammad orders Muslims to obey *him* and believe *in him*: *049.014* "The desert Arabs say, 'We believe.' Say: 'You have no faith; but you (only) say, "We submit." For not yet has Faith entered you. But if you obey Allah and His Messenger, He will not belittle your deeds.' Only those are Believers who have believed in Allah and His Messenger, and have never since doubted, and have striven with their belongings and lives in the Cause of Allah." Muslims must submit to Muhammad, relinquish their possessions to him, fight and die for him, never doubt him.

And don't be talking to Allah about this religious stuff, because he can't be bothered. *049.016* "Say: 'What! Will you instruct Allah about your religion?' Allah has full knowledge of things." Then: *049.017* "They impress onto you (Muhammad) that they have Surrendered (embraced Islam). Say, 'Count not your Surrender as a favor to me: Nay, Allah lays you under an obligation by guiding you to the Faith." Faith, by definition, cannot be obligatory. But that aside, the "**Apartments**" surah clearly explains why Muhammad conceived Islam. It covers all the bases: submission and obedience, Muhammad's perceived superiority, quality time for sex, and the prophet's lust for praise, power, money, and fighting.

The 66th surah was also revealed around this time. It's called "**Prohibition**." Incredibly, it too was focused on Muhammad's sexual indulgences. The only thing it "prohibited" was criticism of the prophet's decadent lifestyle. *066.001* "**O Prophet! Why forbid yourself that which Allah has made lawful to you? You seek to please your consorts. And Allah is Forgiving, Most Kind. Allah has already sanctioned for you the dissolution of your vows.**" Here's the rub. Earlier, Muhammad said that his god approved a maximum of four wives, inclusive of sex slaves. But he woke up one morning and had at least six times that number. He needed to prune his harem or get his god to amend the Qur'an—to cut his favorite prophet a deal. He chose the latter. In doing so, he made a mockery of his scripture. But not to worry; he banned mocking in the previous surah.

The passage contained a fatal line for a prophet: "**Allah has sanctioned the dissolution of your vows.**" A "sanction" is permission or approval. It authorizes or ratifies something. In this context "dissolution" means to abrogate, dissolve, or break. A "vow" is a solemn promise, a pledge or an earnest declaration. Muhammad's principal vows were that he was the Messenger of God, that the Qur'an was revealed by God, and that following his example would lead to paradise. If you are a Muslim and are reliant on these promises, be forewarned: "**Allah has sanctioned the dissolution of [Muhammad's] vows.**"

066.003 "**When the Prophet disclosed a matter in confidence to one of his consorts, she then divulged it, and Allah made it known to him. He confirmed part and repudiated part. When he told her, she said, 'Who told you this?' He said, 'He Who knows and is well-acquainted.'**" You've got to give Muhammad credit for one thing—it takes guts to pass off pillow talk for scripture. But it begs the question: what on earth did Muhammad divulge to one of his sex slaves that was so incriminating the rumor had to be squashed by a "divine" ordinance?

Speaking directly to the consorts, the "creator of the universe" gave us a clue as he tried to quell a rift in his aged prophet's harem: *066.004* "**If you two (women) turn in repentance to him, it would be better. Your hearts have been impaired, for you desired (the ban) [on how many girls Muhammad could play with at a time]. But if you back each other up against (Muhammad), truly Allah is his protector, and Gabriel, and everyone who believes—and furthermore, the angels will back (him) up.**" With his insecurities showing, "god" issued another veiled threat. But he also answered the preceding riddle. Muhammad had let his guard down, and while frolicking with one of his captives, said something like: "Stop complaining or I'll make up a Qur'an saying Allah and his angels are with me and against you."

Islam's prophet wants us to believe that his "god" got tough on his unruly brothel. He said that if they continued to bellyache, he would change them out for a fresh batch of virgins. Funny thing, though; Muhammad was the only one who heard Allah say any of this. *066.005* **"Maybe, if he divorces you (all), Allah will give him in exchange consorts better than you—submissive, faithful, obedient, adorers who worship, who travel, and are inclined to fasting—previously married or virgins."**

This verse exposes the true nature of the Qur'an. Muhammad was willing to contrive godly revelations to silence his wives and concubines and to add to his collection of experienced women and playful virgins. He even ran a personal ad: "Seeking girls who were submissive, obedient, hungry, willing to travel and worship me." Even the word "consort" is intriguing. Webster defines it as the spouse of a reigning monarch. The prophet had become king.

While all that is bad, it's not what bothers me the most about Muhammad and Islam. What irks me is that this man put a system in place that ultimately coerced three billion people to their doom. Under penalty of death, his pronouncements assured that everyone living in a conquered land would live in economic, intellectual, and religious poverty—that they would lose their freedoms and their souls. As such, I consider Muhammad to be the most destructive and evil man who ever lived.

Some might object and say that there is sexual indulgence in the Bible. And so there is. But it was not condoned by Yahweh. When David and Solomon let their lust for the ladies get the best of them, God stopped supporting them as he once had. The Israel that had grown great under their leadership became divided, and it was ultimately conquered, with the Jews being led into captivity and then dispersed.

After telling us that he is perverted, Allah says he's demonic as well. He's going to use men's bodies as fagots for hell's fires. This verse is Qur'an 66:6, so Satan might be giving us a clue. For those who may not know, the book of Revelation in the Bible says that the mark of the Beast—the Antichrist—is 666. **"O ye who believe! Save yourselves and your families from a Fire whose fuel is Men and Stones, over which are angels stern (and) severe as wardens, who flinch not (from executing) the commands they receive from Allah, but do (precisely) what they are commanded."** Allah and Satan sure seem to have an awful lot in common—including their interests and the place they spend their time.

You may be wondering if the Qur'an's other 666 is equally Satanic? Opening the Devil's favorite book to Qur'an 6:66 we find wardens and Allah deceiving men—passing off a lie as truth—Satan's favorite vocation. 6:66 reads: **"The people reject this (Book) and call it a lie though it is the truth. Say: 'I am not a warden over you.'"** It goes on to warn: **"When you see men who meddle with Our Revelations, turn away, withdrawing from them. Satan makes you forget."**

Chatting with his victims in hell, Allah proclaims: *066.007* "**O you unbelieving Infidels, make no excuses for yourselves this Day [of Doom]! You are being paid back for what you did!**" Gloating is one of Satan's least admirable qualities.

In the next verse, we have yet another admission. Those who knew Muhammad best ridiculed his feeble attempts at scripture and mocked him for the gross discrepancies between his life and that of a real prophet. *066.008* "**Believers, turn to Allah with repentance: perhaps your Lord may remove your ills, admitting you to Gardens. That Day, He will not permit His Prophet to be humiliated.**"

Giving hate a divine blessing, the Islamic god shares: *066.009* "**O Prophet! Strive hard against the unbelieving Infidels and the Hypocrites; be severe against them. Their abode is Hell, an evil resort.**" If this is tolerant, I'd hate to see intolerant.

To demonstrate his hostility, the Black Stone perverts another Bible story for your reading pleasure: *066.010* "**Allah cites, as an example to the unbelieving Infidels, the wife of Nuh [Noah] and the wife of Lut [Lot]: they were under [not with] two of our righteous slaves, but they betrayed their (husbands), acting treacherously toward them, and they profited nothing. They were told: 'Enter the Fire!'**" Methinks this verse was really made up to scare Muhammad's wives, but that's just a guess.

Then, mixing a little originality with delusion, the Meccan moon god veers away from the Biblical script as he concludes the surah: *066.011* "**And Allah cites, as an example to those who believe, the wife of Firon [Pharaoh]: Behold she said: 'O my Lord! Build for me near You a mansion in the Garden, and save me from Firon [Pharaoh] and his doings, save me from evil-doing folk.' And Mary the daughter of Imran, who guarded her chastity; and We breathed into (her body) Our Spirit; and she testified to the truth of the words of her Lord and of His Scripture Books. She was an obedient (slave).**" The Mary "who guarded her chastity" was the daughter of Heli. Allah would have done well to read the Bible before he tried to elaborate on it.

Returning to intolerance, Muhammad alleges that his lord began the 60th surah, pleading: *060.001* "**Believers, take not my enemies and yours as allies, offering them love, even though they have rejected the truth that has come to you, and have driven out the Prophet and you because you believe in Allah! [That's a lie. The Meccans believed in Allah too. Muhammad was pushing Ar-Rahman when he was driven out.] If you have come out to struggle [fight jihad] in My Cause, and to seek My Pleasure, (take them not as friends), holding secret converse of love with them: for I am aware of all you conceal. And any of you that does this has strayed from the Straight Path. If they were to get the better of you, they would be your foes, and stretch forth their hands and their tongues against you with evil (designs).**" Allah finally gets around to talking about love and he tells Muslims not to do it. If you want to please the Islamic god you have to hate.

Recognizing that the people Muhammad was telling his faithful to hate, on behalf of Allah, were their own family members; he explains: *060.003* "**Your ties to your relatives and to your children will not avail you on the Day of Doom; He will part you.**" This verse contradicts a number of more "family oriented" ones, and that's a problem. Contradictions are evidence something isn't true, or at least isn't godly. And all of the "nice" verses came earlier and were abrogated by this one.

Ever predictable, our illiterate prophet corrupted yet another Bible story—demeaning Abraham to make his case. *060.004* **"There is for you an excellent example, a pattern in Abraham and those with him, when they said to their people: 'We are through with you and with what you worship besides Allah. We reject you. Hostility and hate have come between us forever, unless you believe in Allah only.'"** Hostility and hatred for anyone who does not surrender remains a core motivation for Islamic intolerance. Yet Abraham simply left town and headed to the Promised Land. There is no evidence that he hated anyone, and even less that he spoke of serving a Meccan Moon God. After all, by leaving Ur he was abandoning "Sin," the Chaldean Moon God, from which the Allah cults were derived.

The twisted spirit of Islam uses a triple negative to say that Muslims don't have to hate everybody. *060.008* **"Allah forbids you not, with regard to those who fight you not for (your) Religion nor drive you out of your homes, from dealing kindly and justly with them: for Allah loves those who are just dealers. Allah only forbids you, with regard to those who fight you for (your) Religion, and drive you out of your homes, and support (others) in driving you out, from turning to them (for friendship). Those who turn to them, do wrong."** This verse is used by Islamic clerics to justify attacking America. The United States supports Israel, a nation they wrongly contend has driven Muslims from their homes.

Still getting heat from his fellow militants for having capitulated at Hudaybiyah, Muhammad had his god breach "the right of return" part of the contract. While it's foolish to trust a prophet and god who do not honor their vows, this annulment has far reaching implications. In the second to last surah, Allah will abrogate the entire treaty of Hudaybiyah, and thus justify his messenger's attack during a time of "peace." This set a Muslim precedent: their signature on any peace accord is as meaningless as their prophet's. *060.010* **"Muslims, when there come to you believing women fugitives, examine them: Allah knows best as to their Faith: if you ascertain that they are Believers, then send them not back to the Unbelievers. They are not lawful for them."**

I'm sure this makes sense because it's "scripture" dictated directly from god: *060.011* **"And if any of your wives deserts you to the Unbelievers, and you have an accession (by the coming over of a woman from the other side), afterward you have your turn (of triumph), then give unto those whose wives have gone the like of that which they have spent, and fear Allah."** I know you think you understand what you believe he said but I'm not sure you realize that what you read is not what he meant.

The next verse demonstrates how surahs were jumbled together haphazardly. The oath of women took place after the conquest of Mecca. Yet much of this surah deals with the dissolution of the treaty that ultimately lead to the conquest. And that poses a serious problem for Muslims. It means that their prophet's Companions couldn't remember when something was revealed or the context of the revelation. Thus the book they claim was written perfectly by Allah is out of order—something inconsistent with the nature of God. Moreover, if it is randomly assembled and out of context, there is little chance that it accurately represents what Muhammad claimed he deciphered.

060.012 **"O Prophet! When believing women come to you to take the oath of fealty [allegiance] to you, that they will not associate any other thing with Allah, that they will not steal, that they will not commit adultery, that they will not kill their children, that they will not utter slander, intentionally forging falsehood, and that they will not disobey you (Muhammad) in any matter, then do you receive their allegiance, and pray to Allah for their forgiveness."** As will become abundantly clear when we arrive at this point in the chronology, the oath of allegiance was to Muhammad, not Allah. Muslim women surrendered to him. They were forced to obey his every command. At long last he took his revenge. And while it's a detail, "not associating any other *thing* with Allah" suggests that Allah was one of many things, or idols.

Back to basics…*060.013* **"Believers, turn not to people on whom is the Wrath of Allah, for they are already in despair, just as the Unbelievers are in despair about those (buried) in graves."** The end of this surah is hypocritical. It is Muslims who fret over the fate of their dead, for there is no assurance of paradise (except for martyrs who die killing infidels). This is why all Muslims must blurt out "peace be unto him" every time they say Muhammad's name. The prophet didn't die a martyr and thus may not have been forgiven by his capricious god. In Christianity, by contrast, salvation is assured, it is a gift from Yahweh. All you have to do is accept his gift and paradise is yours.

In the ongoing quest to reveal what Islam says about itself, I want to review two additional Medina surahs before returning to the Hadith. The 48th opens admitting Muhammad was flawed. *048.001* **"Verily We have granted you (Muhammad) a splendid Victory that Allah may forgive you your sins and faults of the past and those to come."** Muslims claim Muhammad was perfect, for he had to be better than Yahshua. But unfortunately, it's hard to imagine a less perfect human than the one described in the Islamic scriptures. If this man were alive today, he would be public enemy number one.

They say that confession is good for the soul. In that light, I'd like to give Muhammad the opportunity to explain how he achieved this **"victory"** of which Allah has spoken and explain what motivated him: *Bukhari:V4B52N220* **"Allah's Apostle said, 'I have been sent with the shortest expressions bearing the widest meanings, and I have been made victorious with *terror*. While I was sleeping the *treasures* of the world were brought to me and put in my hand.'"** Muslims have gall to call Muhammad's legacy a "peaceful religion."

After touting his "heavenly armies" and promising worthless rewards to those who surrender, Muhammad, speaking for Allah, goes on the attack. *048.006* **"And He may punish the Hypocrites who imagine an evil opinion, or have evil thoughts about Allah. It is against them that the wheel of misfortune will turn, a disgraceful** torment: the Wrath of Allah is on them: He has cursed them, and He has prepared Hell for them." How is it *not* possible to think evil thoughts about Allah when he describes himself doing evil things: plotting against men, leading men astray, deceiving them, shackling them, dragging them to hell, using their bodies as kindling, roasting men on a spit, feeding them molten pitch, pouring boiling water over them? Allah confesses to being a terrorist, to murder, to thievery, and to selling children into slavery. His character matches Satan's and rivals Muhammad's in depravity.

Yet Muhammad and Allah believe that this is "good news," also known as "the gospel." Listen: *048.008* **"We have truly sent you (O Muhammad) as a witness, as a bringer of Good News, and as a Warner: In order that you (O men) may believe in Allah and His Messenger, that you may assist him and honor him, and celebrate His praise morning and evening."** Muslims have just been "ordered" to "praise" evil.

The next verse should help freethinking men and women separate themselves from Muhammad's deception. It is another confession. *048.010* **"Verily those who swear allegiance to you (Muhammad), indeed swear their allegiance to Allah."** That is because Muhammad *was* Allah. He not only attributed *his* words to Allah and used his "god" to advance his personal agenda; Muhammad created Allah's persona. This whole charade has been played out to make everyone submissive to an insane megalomaniac so that he could lay claim to what he craved. If Allah's name were erased in each of the hundreds of places throughout the Qur'an that Muslims are ordered to believe in, submit to, and obey Allah *and* His Apostle, nothing would change.

But that is not to say that Muhammad didn't have help. By his own admission he was demon possessed. His behavior and the testimony of his contemporaries confirmed it. He met with Lucifer, albeit disguised as Gabriel. While most of the Qur'an is nothing more than Muhammad whining, threatening, and seducing, some of it was inspired by the Devil. The more rational concepts (the basis of which were stolen from the Hanifs and Jews before they were twisted) were handed down by Lucifer to give him an alias under which he could motivate men to do his bidding. Muhammad used the Black Stone to satiate his cravings. Satan used Allah to deceive and damn mankind. Together they were the demonic duo.

A harsh assessment? What other options do we have? Swimming in this sea of putrid immorality and grotesque criminality, confronted with such an onslaught of deceit, hatred, and violence, how can any other conclusion be drawn? There is no way to make seventy-five terrorist raids and the murder and enslavement of tens of thousands look godly. Piracy isn't good, nor is pedophilia, incest, or rape. Torturing people for money is a bad thing. Armed with the evidence—the Islamic scripture—the verdict is undeniable. Islam was a scam. The religion served a man and a beast, enabling them to lord over mankind, making men beasts.

The perverted founder of the perverse doctrine that forever enslaved the free and peace-loving Bedouins of Arabia, proclaimed: *048.011* **"The desert Arabs who lagged behind [in fighting] will say to you (Muhammad): 'We were engaged in (looking after) our flocks and our families.' They say with their tongues what is not in their hearts."** *048.012* **"Nay, you thought that the Messenger and the Believers would never return to their families [after the raid]; this seemed pleasing in your hearts, and you conceived an evil thought, for you are a people lost (in wickedness), worthless folk doomed to perish. If any believe not in Allah and His Messenger, We have prepared for them a Blazing Fire!"** While it's good to be consistent, being consistently bad isn't good. This is the twentieth time we have been told that Muslims who lead productive lives, who go about their business, who take care of their families, but who are not willing to leave their homes to fight on Muhammad's orders are "lost," "wicked," "worthless," "doomed," and "hell-bound."

Satan, masquerading as the capricious Black Stone of the Ka'aba, shows his true colors: *048.014* **"To Allah belongs the sovereignty of the heavens and the earth: He forgives whom He wills, and He punishes whom He pleases."** Only Lucifer would be "pleased" to "punish" human souls. **"Allah is Oft-Forgiving, Most Merciful."**

Returning to piracy and plunder, the Devil's Advocate preaches: *048.015* **"Those who lagged behind (will say), when you marched forth to capture booty (in war): 'Permit us to follow you.' They wish to change Allah's decree to say: 'You will not march with us: Allah has declared (this) beforehand.' Then they will say, 'Nay, you are jealous and envy us.' Nay, but little do they understand."** I understand: "There is no booty for bad, peace-loving Muslims. Booty is only for good Muslims—the jihad terrorists," so sayeth the Lord. And before we leave this divine pearl, notice the way it began. Muslims **"marched forth to capture booty in war."** They did no go out to share the faith. Muhammad's militants were mercenaries, not missionaries.

048.016 **"Say (Muhammad) to the wandering [thus free] desert Arabs who lagged behind [and were thus productive and peaceful]: 'You shall be invited to fight against a people given to vehement war with mighty prowess. You shall fight them until they surrender and submit. If you obey, Allah will grant you a reward, but if you turn back, as you did before, He will punish you with a grievous torture."** This may be the clearest definition yet of "good" and "bad" Muslims and their relative status. Bad Muslims are peaceful; they are against fighting. They will go to hell. Good Muslims are obedient jihad warriors, fighting until all infidels surrender—submitting to Islam. They are rewarded with booty and Allah's brothel.

Oft-Forgiving and Most-Merciful, Allah grants the blind and the lame a "Get Out of Jihad Free" card. Since one must be blind to follow this lame religion, I'm surprised more Muslims don't take advantage. *048.017* **"There is no blame for the blind, nor is it a sin for the lame, nor on one ill if he joins not in the fighting. But he that obeys Allah and His Messenger will be admitted to Gardens of Bliss. He who retreats, (Allah) will punish him with a painful doom."** Somebody had a one-track mind. Obey me and fight or go to hell. The Qur'an is as repetitive and irritating as a broken record.

048.018 "Allah's Good Pleasure was on the Believers when they swore allegiance to you (Muhammad) under the Tree: He knew what was in their hearts, and He sent down His Sakinah to them; and He rewarded them with a speedy Victory." No he didn't. The swearing of allegiance under the tree preceded the capitulation at Hudaybiyah. There was no speedy victory—only dismay and anguish. The natives were restless—wanting to kill anything that moved. No wonder team Islam can't get their Bible stories right. They can't even remember their own sorry history.

Reconfirming that Islam was all about money, the Qur'an's god makes armed robbery "easy:" *048.019* "He rewarded them with abundant spoils that they will capture. Allah is Mighty, Wise [and disgusting, from a moral perspective]. Allah has promised you much booty that you shall take, and He has made this easy for you. He has restrained the hands of men from you; that it may be a sign for the Believers that He may guide you to a Straight Path [to Hell for stealing and murdering—which is precisely what this was all about]. And other benefits [virgins] which you have not yet obtained." As we shall soon see, the only one who got booty from the victory over Mecca was Muhammad. He inherited his heart's desire—the Ka'aba Inc. All other Muslims lost ground, as future spoils were divided inequitably, unfairly favoring the new converts.

I would be remiss if I didn't highlight the confession. Allah promised the Muslims **"abundant spoils"** and **"much booty."** He did not promise them "many souls." Islam wasn't about salvation or even conversion. It was about conquest and money.

In Islam: war and terror were all in a day's work—standard operating procedure. *048.022* "If the unbelieving infidels fight against you, they will retreat. (Such has been) the practice (approved) of Allah in the past: no change will you find in the ways of Allah."

This next verse was "handed down" to excuse Muhammad's cowardice and capitulation at Hudaybiyah. It was also the Islamic god's way of letting his troops know that peace treaties could be used to lure an enemy into a false sense of security so that Muslims might conquer them more readily. *048.024* "It is He Who restrained their hands from you and your hands from them in the valley of Mecca, after that He gave you the victory over them."

Allah says the Meccans deserved to lose because they had delayed Muhammad from stealing what he coveted: a founder's share of the Ka'aba Inc. *048.025* "They are the ones who denied [Qur'an] Revelation and hindered you from the Sacred Mosque [Allah's House]." The verse goes on to explain that the reason for not trouncing the Meccans right then and there was that some believers were hiding in their huts and Allah didn't want them hurt. **"Had there not been believing men and women whom you did not know that you would have trampled down and on whose account a crime would have accrued to you without knowledge, (Allah would have allowed you to force your way). If they had not been there, We would have punished the unbelievers with a grievous torture."** The moral of the story is: it's good to trample down infidels so long as you are careful not to injure Muslims in the process.

Muhammad's Muslim militants had worked themselves into a lather over not being able to fight the merchants of Mecca and take a spoil. But since that didn't sound religious, Allah claimed: *048.026* **"While the Unbelievers got up in heat and cant [insincerity or false piety]—the zealotry of the Age of Ignorance—Allah sent down His Sakinah to his Messenger and to the Believers, and made them stick close to the command of self-restraint."**

The Islamic terrorists were certain that they were going to conquer Mecca because Muhammad had told them he had envisioned it in his dreams. *048.027* **"Truly did Allah fulfill the vision for His Messenger: you shall enter the Sacred Mosque, if Allah wills, with minds secure, heads shaved, hair cut short, and without fear. For He knew what you knew not, and He granted, besides this, a speedy victory."** This would have been a prophecy if it had actually been *written* prior to the attack on Mecca, not a dozen years later, and if the surah didn't contain post occupation passages.

Then speaking of the Devil: *048.028* **"It is He Who has sent His Messenger with guidance and the Religion of Truth (Islam), that he may make it superior to every other religion, exalting it over them."** Muhammad's agenda was showing. While he was wrong, he saw Judeo-Christianity as a competitive "religion," and his had to be better —to be **"exalted over every other religion"**—"Allahu Akbar." But how can that be if Islam was supposed to be a confirmation of the Torah and Gospels, as Allah has so often claimed? Or is this the serpent's way of competing with Yahweh?

The verse continues to protest: **"Allah is a sufficient Witness. Muhammad is the Prophet of Allah. Those who are with him are severe with Infidel unbelievers, merciful amongst themselves. You will see them bow and prostrate themselves, seeking Allah's acceptance. On their foreheads are marks, the traces of their prostration."** Rub their faces in it, will you? It's so Muhammad to gloat about how he damned so many, forcing them bow to the Devil. And while that's unforgivable, how can a religion that claims its hallmark is tolerance, say: **"be severe with unbelievers?"**

But I'm afraid there is something far more sinister lurking here. Lucifer removed his veil when he said that his *mark* would be on their *foreheads* and that his followers would be known by their *prostrations*. Speaking of how Lucifer will use Islam in the last days, John wrote this in the 13th chapter of Revelation: "I saw another *therion* (poisonous and destructive animal) coming up out of the earth. He had two horns like a lamb and spoke as a *serpent*. He exercised power and caused mankind to *prokuneo* (to *prostrate*, kissing like a dog) themselves to the first *therion* as *protos* (the *greatest* [as in *Allahu Akbar*]) whose death stroke was adored [jihad killers are adored martyrs]. He makes *pur* (fire or lightning) come from the sky in the presence of men. And he *planao* (*deceives*, leads astray, or seduces) mankind by the means of the *signs* which he had power to do [control weather]; saying to the people that they should build a statue to him, showing that he had survived the stroke of the *sword*. The *therion* (poisonous and destructive animal) made the idol come to life, and it said that whoever did not *prostrate* themselves to the image of the *therion* should be slain [kill all non-Muslims]. And he requires all, small and great, rich and poor, *eleutheros* (exempt from obligation [i.e., non-Muslims]) and *doulos* (submissive [Islam means submission]), to receive a *charagma* (scratch or etching, a *mark* of servitude) on their *right hand* (*Qur'an 056.008*) or on their *forehead* (*Qur'an 048.028*). No man may buy or sell, except those who have the *charagma* of the *onoma* (authority or character) of the *therion* (poisonous and destructive animal), or the number of his *onoma*. Let him with understanding calculate the *arithmos* (number or reckoning) of the *therion*: for it is the number of a man; and his number is 666." Rather than invent a new dogma to oppress mankind, the AntiChrist and his False Prophet will use Islam.

While the last Qur'an verse spoke of the **"marks on their foreheads, the traces of their prostration,"** Muslims were also known by their right hand. *Bukhari:V8B76N545* **"Allah's Apostle, said, 'All who are called to account on the Day of Doom will be ruined.' Aisha said, 'O Allah's Apostle! Hasn't Allah said: "For him who will be given his record in his *right hand*, he surely will receive an easy reckoning?"'** (Qur'an 84:7) **The Apostle said, 'That (Verse) means only the presentation of accounts, but anybody whose account is questioned will be punished.'"** A "reckoning" is an "accounting" so Aisha was right. Muhammad had contradicted Allah and confirmed John's prophecy.

Ever desirous of being accepted as a real prophet, our counterfeit proclaimer ended the 28th verse and the 48th surah by errantly suggesting that marks and prostrations are godly identifiers in the Bible. **"This likeness is in the Taurat [Torah]; and their similitude in the Injeel [Gospel]."** Sorry, Mo. Scripture allusions to prostrations and marks are Satanic, not godly. And Christ's "Love your enemy" is the antithesis of **"be severe with unbelievers."** And the distinction is important. Since the Gospels say one thing and the Qur'an says another, they couldn't have been inspired by the same spirit. Loving and afflicting are opposite paths; they cannot both lead to paradise. One path leads in an entirely different direction.

The 47th surah is as warped as the man it was named after—**"Muhammad."** *047.001* **"Those who disbelieve and hinder (men) from Allah's Path, He renders their actions vain and ineffective. But those who believe and work good deeds, and believe in what is revealed to Muhammad—for it is the Truth from their Lord—He will remove from them their ills and improve their condition."**

I'd like to put that to the test—to see if Muhammad is telling the truth for a change. If what he said is accurate, you'd expect Christian and Jewish nations to be impoverished and Muslim nations to be flourishing. How is it then that the productivity per capita in Islamic nations is the lowest in the world? Why doesn't any Muslim country produce a single manufactured product of sufficient quality to sell on world markets? Why doesn't Islam have a single world-class university or boast of a great advancement in literature or science? Why are freedoms and human rights trampled amongst people who have faith in what was revealed to Muhammad? Why are women and minorities abused in such nations if Allah has "improved their condition?" Why isn't there a single Muslim state that succeeds as a democracy? Why hasn't there ever been one? Why is the inverse true in Christian and Jewish countries? Why is the disparity so large, universal, and unflattering between Islam and other creeds? And why did Muhammad's Muslim militants have to live like parasites—plundering their way to infamy—if Allah could improve their condition? You don't suppose that Islam could be at fault because Muhammad was lying, do you?

Muslims will protest that between 750 and 850 A.D. they made great strides in science. But even that is misleading, as all they really did was preserve the Greek manuscripts they had stolen from the Byzantines. During this period literate Persians, not ignorant Arabs, were in control of Islam. And the timing was crucial. Oral recollections of Muhammad's savagery and deception had faded, as five generations had come and gone since his death. The Sira, the first written account of Muhammad's poisonous and destructive dogma, was distributed and Islam's golden age ended. Fundamental Islam damned Muslims and impoverished their condition.

047.003 **"This because those who disbelieve follow vanities, while those who believe follow truth from their Lord: Thus does Allah coin for men their similitudes [resemblances] as a lesson. Whoever denies faith [in Islam and Muhammad], his work is of no account, and in the hereafter he shall be one of the losers."** This is written at the level of a grade-school bully. You'd think that if you were going to claim that the Qur'an was written by God, you'd do a better job. German scholar Salomon Reinach agrees: "From the literary point of view, the Qur'an has little merit. Declamation, repetition, puerility, a lack of logic and coherence strike the unprepared reader at every turn. It is humiliating to the human intellect to think that this mediocre literature has been the subject of innumerable commentaries, and that millions of men are still wasting time in absorbing it."

Yet we must expose it because Allah wants Muslims to smite, wound, kill, overpower, subdue, and imprison infidels. 047.004 **"So, when you clash with the unbelieving Infidels in battle (fighting Jihad in Allah's Cause), smite their necks until you overpower them, killing and wounding many of them. At length, when you have thoroughly subdued them, bind them firmly, making (them) captives. Thereafter either generosity (free them) or ransom (them based upon what benefits Islam) until the war lays down its burdens. Thus are you commanded by Allah to continue carrying out Jihad against the unbelieving infidels until they submit to Islam."** That was vicious.

Pretending to be more powerful than he really is, Lucifer cries: **"But if it had been Allah's will, He Himself could have exacted retribution and punished them (without your help). But He lets you fight in order to test you. But those who are killed in Allah's Cause [Jihad], will never let their deeds go to waste."** Keep in mind that the Qur'an is talking about the deeds of Jihad terrorists. (One doesn't get "killed" in a "spiritual struggle.") The "test" is a Muslim's ability to kill.

The Islamic reward for terror, kidnapping, and murder is Allah's Garden of Bliss. *047.005* **"Soon will He guide them and improve their condition, and admit them to the Garden which He has made known to them. Believers, if you will help [fight] (in the Cause of) Allah, He will help you, and make your foothold firm."**

047.008 **"But those who reject (Allah and Islam), for them is perdition and destruction, and (Allah) will render their deeds ineffective. That is because they hate the (Qur'an and Sunnah) Revelation; so He has made their deeds fruitless. Have they not traveled through the earth to see the fate of those before them? Allah wiped them out, bringing utter destruction, and similar (fates await) them."** Not only is Allah destructive now, he's always been that way. Death litters his path.

So the terrorist rock idol proclaimed: *047.012* **"Allah will admit those who believe and do good deeds to Gardens while those who disbelieve will enjoy and eat as the beasts eat; and the Fire will be their abode."** Muhammad told Muslims that they will always be brutal and vengeful. *Bukhari:V8B76N542* **"Allah's Apostle said, 'The believers, after being saved from the Fire, will be stopped at a bridge between Paradise and Hell and mutual retaliation will be established among them regarding wrongs they have committed in the world against one another. After they are cleansed and purified through the retaliation, they will be admitted into Paradise.'"**

047.012 **"And how many cities, with more power than your city (Muhammad) which has driven you out, have We destroyed?"** I don't know. How many, besides New York and Washington, Beirut and Jerusalem?

Lucky us. Allah is about to share another parable. *047.015* **"(Here is) a Parable of the Garden which those who fear and keep their duty are promised: in it are rivers of unpolluted water; rivers of milk which the taste never changes; rivers of wine, a delicious joy to the drinkers; and rivers of running honey pure and clear. In it there are all kinds of fruits with pardon from their Lord. (Are those in such Bliss) like those who shall dwell forever in the Fire, and are given to drink, boiling water that tears their bowels to pieces, and cutting their intestines to shreds?"** Allah is such a lovely storyteller.

According to the Qur'an, those who lived with Muhammad didn't believe him. *047.016* **"And among them are men who listen to you (Muhammad), but in the end, when they leave you, they say: 'What is this he is saying now?' Such are men whose hearts Allah has sealed, and who follow their own lusts,"** the hypocritical deity declared.

047.020 **"Those who believe say, 'How is it that no surah was sent down (for us)?' But when a categorical [definite, decisive, or uncompromising] surah is revealed, and fighting and war (Jihad, holy fighting in Allah's Cause) are mentioned and ordained, you will see those with diseased hearts looking at you (Muhammad) fainting unto death. Therefore woe unto them!"** "Woe" is a bad thing. It usually precedes destruction or damnation. Here it's being used to warn the "diseased," peaceful Muslims.

The Qur'an's last surahs could be reduced to "obey, pay, and fight." Islam is now completely devoid of peace, prosperity, and freedom. *047.021* **"Were they to obey, showing their obedience in modest speech, after the matter (of preparation for**

Jihad) had been determined for them, it would have been better. Is it to be expected that if you [worthless Muslim] were put in authority and given command that you would do mischief in the land and sever your ties of kinship. Such men are cursed by Allah. He has made them deaf, dumb and blind." Once again, Muhammad/Allah is acting like Satan. He is demeaning his followers by projecting his own flaws onto them. And it's hard to fathom "mischief" worse than that depicted in the Islamic Hadith.

Still rebuking the men he made deaf, dumb, and blind, Muhammad, speaking as Allah, asks: 047.024 "Do they not understand the Qur'an [and its order to obey me and kill for me]? Nay, on the hearts there are locks preventing them from understanding."

Those who translated the Noble Qur'an for the Fahd family dictators in Saudi Arabia wanted us to know that Muhammad intrepreted these verses. Bukhari:V6B60N354 "The Prophet said, 'Allah created His creation, and when He had finished it, the womb got up and caught hold of Allah whereupon Allah said, "What is the matter?" On that, the womb said, "I seek refuge with you from those who sever the ties of kin." On that Allah said, "Will you be satisfied if I bestow My favors on him who keeps your ties?" The womb said, "Yes, my Lord!" Then Allah said, "If you wish, you can recite: 'Would you then if you were given authority do mischief and sever your ties of kinship?'"'"

The Qur'an protests: 047.025 "Those who turn back [retreat] as apostates after guidance was manifest to them, Satan has seduced with false hopes. This, because they said to those who hate what Allah has revealed, 'We will obey you in part of this matter.'" The peaceful Muslims didn't like the fighting and stealing part of Islam. Their consciences couldn't handle the strain. So Allah ordered the good killer Muslims to put the peaceful ones out of their misery. 004.089 "They wish that you would reject Faith, as they have, and thus be on the same footing. Do not be friends with them until they leave their homes in Allah's Cause. But if they turn back from Islam, becoming renegades, seize them and kill them wherever you find them." It's not much of a choice. If you are a good Muslim you're a bad person. If you're a bad Muslim you're a dead person.

The Islamic god continued to terrorize the peaceful Muslims. 047.027 "But how (will it be) when the angels take their souls at death, and smite their faces and their backs? This because they followed that which angered Allah and hated that which pleased him, [Jihad]. So He nullified their deeds. Or do those with diseased hearts think that Allah will not bring to light their rancor and malice?" Living peacefully is now called "rancor and malice." Peace makes Allah angry and Jihad pleases him. Swell.

Allah once again provides the criterion upon which he judges men. 047.031 "And We shall try you until We know those among you who are the fighters; and We shall try your reported (mettle)." A god who knows and sees all doesn't need a "test" to determine which Muslims are the best terrorists. And testing a man's willingness to fight might be a worthy measure for the military but not for God.

047.032 "Those who disbelieve, hinder (men) from the Cause of Allah and resist the Messenger after Guidance has been clearly shown to them will not injure Allah in the least." It's hard to hurt a rock god, I suppose.

Returning to the Qur'anic chorus: *047.033* "Believers, obey Allah and obey the Messenger, and make not vain your deeds! Those who disbelieve and hinder (men) from the Cause of Allah, then die rejecting, Allah will not pardon them. Do not falter; become faint-hearted, or weak-kneed, crying for peace. You have the upper hand, for Allah is with you. He will not grudge (the reward of) your deeds." So why do so many Muslims reject their god's orders and cry: "peace?" Peace is a sign of weakness. Don't they know that such words are an express ticket to the Islamic Hell? The fact is: if you are a peaceful Muslim, your "god" hates you.

Placed in context of the terror these words have inspired, I find this entire Jihad surah repulsive. While Islamic terror was a game to Muhammad, it isn't for his victims. *047.036* "The life of this world is but play and amusement, a sport and frivolity. If you believe and fear Allah, He will not ask for your possessions. But if He were to ask you for all of them, and press you to spend in Allah's Cause, you would hoard it, acting niggardly." But surely, Muhammad wouldn't ask them for their money just to fund some frivolous terrorist campaign. *047.038* "Behold and beware: you are those invited to spend (of your substance) in the Cause of Allah [Jihad]: But among you are some who are niggardly at the expense of their own souls. If you turn back and retreat Allah will substitute other people instead of you!" Muhammad's Jihad fighters were as expendable as his wives. Loyalty was not valued in Islam. And that's not good if you're a suicide bomber, bartering this life for the next.

Moving from the Qur'an to the Hadith we find that the eighth year of the Islamic Era dawned like all others. *Tabari VIII:139* "In this year the Messenger of Allah commanded Ghalib Abdallah to go on a raid to Kadid against the Mulawwih [a confederate of the Banu Bakr]. They traveled until they encountered Harith. Ghalib said, 'We captured Harith,' but he said, 'I came only to become a Muslim. Ghalib replied, 'If you have come as a Muslim, it will not harm you to be bound for a day. If you have come for another purpose, we shall be safe from you.' So he secured him with rope and left a little black man in charge, saying, 'If he gives you any trouble, cut off his head.'"

Tabari VIII:140 "We continued on until we came to the bottomland of Kadid and halted toward evening, after the mid-afternoon prayer. My companions sent me out as a scout. I went to a hill that gave me a view of the settlement and lay face down on the ground. One of their men looked and saw others lying with me on the hill. He said to his wife, 'I see something. Let's see what the dogs have dragged away.' She wasn't missing anything so he asked her for his bow and arrows. He shot twice and hit my side and shoulder, but I did not move. He said, 'If it were a living thing it would have moved.'"

Proving that the religion corrupted the terrorists rather than the other way around: *Tabari VIII:141* "We gave them some time until their herds had come back from pasture. After they had milked their camels and set them out to rest, we launched our raid. We killed some of them, drove away their camels, and set out to return. Meanwhile, the people appealed for aid from the rest of their tribe. But we moved quickly. When we passed Harith [the man they had bound on the way to the raid], we grabbed him. Reinforced, the villagers were too powerful for us. But Allah sent clouds from out of the blue, and there was a torrent that no one could cross so we eluded the tribesmen with what we had taken. The battle cry of the Companions of the Messenger of Allah that night was: 'Kill! Kill! Kill!'" If this were the only Hadith in all of Islam it would be sufficient to prove that Muhammad's scam was responsible for manufacturing terrorists. But it does not stand alone. It is but one of a thousand confirmations shouting out to all who will listen: Islam causes men to: "Kill! Kill! Kill!"

Moving to the next Hadith, we find Muhammad sending another letter. *Tabari VIII:142* "Whoever prays our prayer, eats of our sacrifice, and turns to our Qiblah is a Muslim. Incumbent on whoever refuses is the payment of the jizyah tax." It was all about the money. If you surrender, you pay the zakat. If you don't submit you pay the jizyah. But either way you pay the piper.

Tabari VIII:142 "The Messenger made peace with them on condition that the Zoroastrians should be required to pay the jizyah tax [so onerous, it's akin to economic suicide] that one should not marry their women. The Prophet exacted the zakat tax on the wealth of the two men who [said that they] believed in him and collected the jizyah from all of the Zoroastrians." Khadija's Profitable Prophet Plan was paying dividends.

Tabari VIII:143 "In this year a twenty-four man raiding party led by Shuja went to the Banu Amir. He launched a raid on them and took camels and sheep. The shares of booty came to fifteen camels for each man. Also a raid led by Amr went to Dhat. He set out with fifteen men. He encountered a large force whom he summoned to Islam. They refused to respond so he killed all of them." I do believe that Allah lied in the 2nd surah when he said: *002.256* "There is no compulsion in the matter of religion."

Consistent with the Qur'anic mantra, the Hadith confirms that Islam was about obedience to Muhammad. *Tabari VIII:145* "The Prophet said, 'Amr, swear allegiance; for acceptance of Islam cuts off what went before.' So I swore allegiance to him."

Following this brief "religious" interlude, the Hadith returns to the neverending saga of terrorist raids. *Tabari VIII:146* "The Prophet sent Amr to Salasil with 300 men. The mother of As was a woman from Quda'ah. It has been reported that the Messenger wanted to win them over by that. Amr asked for reinforcements from the Ansar and Emigrants including Bakr and Umar with 200 more men." While it's not clear what happened in Salasil, we soon find the same gang heading for Khabat. *Tabari VIII:147* "During the expedition they suffered such severe dearth and distress that they divided up the dates by number. For three months they ate leaves from trees."

Naturally, that leads us to another raid, this one for sex. *Tabari VIII:149* "Abdallah married a woman but couldn't afford the nuptial gift. He came to the Prophet and asked for his assistance." But the miserly warlord said, "I have nothing with which to help you." So our love starved Muslim accepted a summons from his prophet: "'Go out and spy on the Jusham tribe,' he asked. He gave me an emaciated camel and a companion. We set out armed with arrows and swords. We approached the encampment and hid ourselves. I told my companion, 'If you hear me shout Allahu Akbar and see me attack, you should shout Allah is Greatest and join the fighting.'"

Tabari VIII:150 "When their leader, Rifa'ah, came within range, I shot an arrow into his heart. I leaped at him and cut off his head. Then I rushed toward the encampment and shouted, 'Allahu Akbar!' The families who were gathered there shouted, 'Save yourself.' They gathered what property they could, including their wives and children. We drove away a great herd of camels and many sheep and goats and brought them to the Messenger. I brought him Rifa'ash's head, which I carried with me. The Prophet gave me thirteen camels from that herd as booty, and I consummated my marriage." Page after page, Hadith after Hadith, it's just overwhelming. It's hard to believe that anything could be this destructive—annihilating people, property, and values.

Consistent with that theme, the next Islamic Tradition infers that terror was more profitable than working and that booty came in many forms—some more pleasing than others. *Tabari VIII:151* "The Prophet sent Ibn Abi out with a party of sixteen men. They were away for fifteen nights. Their share of booty was twelve camels for each man, each camel was valued in the accounting as being worth ten sheep. When the people they raided fled in various directions, they took four women, including one young woman who was very beautiful. She fell to Abu Qatadah. The Prophet asked Abu about her. Abu said, 'She came from the spoils.' The Messenger said, 'Give her to me.' So Abu gave her to him, and the Prophet gave her to Mahmiyah."

Kidnapping, selling, and trading humans is an abomination—especially when it entails young women for sex. And while America is not without blame, our forefathers knew slavery was wrong and ultimately 600,000 Americans died trying to settle the matter. No one claimed that he had received scripture revelations approving slavery or rape. And no American founded a religion based upon the capture and sale of humans. Muhammad did.

Tabari VIII:151 "Allah's Apostle sent us to Idam. This was before the conquest of Mecca. As Adbat passed us, he greeted us with the greeting of Islam, 'Peace be upon you.' [Think about how perverted and deceitful that greeting was, and continues to be, in the midst of this barbarism.] So we held back from him. But Muhallim attacked him because of some quarrel, and he killed him. Then he took his camel and his food. When we reported what had happened to the Prophet, he said that the following Qur'an was revealed concerning us: 'Believers, when you are journeying in the path of Allah, be discriminating.'" This was from Qur'an 4:94 which actually dates to the prior year. But by providing this Hadith, Muhammad confirmed that my interpretation was correct.

Tabari VIII:152/Ishaq:531 "While the polytheists supervised the hajj pilgrimage, the Prophet sent out his expedition to Syria and its members met with disaster at Mu'ta." This was supposed to be the first Islamic raid on Christians, but it did not go well. "They equipped themselves and set out with 3,000 men. As they bade farewell, the Commanders of Allah's Apostle saluted him." However, we are told that one of them was crying. "What is making you weep?' someone asked. He said, 'I heard the Prophet recite a verse from the Qur'an in which Allah mentioned the Fires of Hell: "Not one of you there is, that shall not go down to it, that is a thing decreed." I do not know how I can get out of Hell after going down there.'" In other words, Muhammad scared him to death.

Marching off to kill and plunder Christians, the Muslim militants sang the following tune in rajaz meter: *Tabari VIII:153/Ishaq:532* "I ask the Merciful One for a pardon and for a sword that cuts wide and deep, creating a wound that shoots out foaming blood. I ask for a deadly thrust by a thirsty lance held by a zealous warrior that pierces right through the guts and liver, slitting the bowels. People shall say when they pass my grave, 'Allah guided him, fine raider that he was, O warrior, he did well.'" Since Allah was a rock idol, it may have sounded better set to music.

Tabari VIII:153/Ishaq:532 "The men journeyed on and encamped at Mu'an in the land of Syria. They learned that Heraclius come with 100,000 Greeks and Byzantines joined by 100,000 Arabs and that they had camped at Ma'ab." That's not true, but why bicker over facts now. There is much more at stake than errant reporting. *Tabari VIII:154* "The Muslims spent two nights pondering what to do. [Unable to think on their own...] They were in favor of writing to the Prophet to inform him of the number of the enemy. 'Either he will reinforce us or he will give us his command to return.'" Muslims lose their ability to think wisely or independently. These men were outnumbered sixty to one. They were facing, for the first time, a real army. These were not merchants or farmers—these were actual soldiers.

Tabari VIII:153/Ishaq:533 "Abdallah Rawahah encouraged the men, saying, 'By Allah, what you loathe is the very thing you came out to seek—martyrdom. We are not fighting the enemy with number, strength, or multitude, but we are fighting them with this religion with which Allah has honored us. So come on! Both prospects are fine: victory or martyrdom.' So they went forward." These men had been sent out as Jihadists on a Holy War by none other than Islam's lone prophet. Their motivation was to die martyrs and thus gain entry into Allah's whorehouse. Thus fundamental Islam is no different than the Islam that motivated the 9/11 suicide bombers.

Like the victims of every other Islamic terrorist raid, the Byzantines had done nothing to the Muslims. But unlike so many others, these men were prepared. *Tabari VIII:155* "When I heard a verse being recited, I wept. Someone tapped me with a whip and said, 'What's wrong little fellow?' 'Allah is going to reward me with martyrdom, and I am going back between the horns of the camel saddle.'"

Tabari VIII:156/Ishaq:534 "The men journeyed on and were met by Heraclius' armies of Romans and Arabs. When the enemy drew near the Muslims withdrew to Mu'ta, and the two sides encountered each other. Zayd fought with the war banner of the Messenger until he perished among the enemy's javelins. Ja'far took it next but could not extricate himself from difficulties. He fought until he was killed. Abdallah took up the banner, urging his soul to obey. He hesitated and then said, 'Soul, why do you spurn Paradise?' He took up his sword, advanced, and was killed. Then Thabit took the banner. He said, 'O Muslims, agree on a man from among yourselves.' They said, 'You.' I said, 'No.' So they gave it to Khalid. He deflected the enemy in retreat, and escaped."

When the defeated militants returned, Muhammad had no compassion for the families of his fallen comrades. *Ishaq:535* **"The women began to cry after learning about Ja'far's death. Disturbed, Muhammad told Abd-Rahman to silence them. When they wouldn't stop wailing, Allah's Apostle said, 'Go and tell them to be quiet, and if they refuse throw dust in their mouths.'"**

Trying to make hell look like paradise, and stifle the whining: *Tabari VIII:158* **"The Prophet ascended his pulpit and said, 'A gate to good fortune. I bring you news of your campaigning army. They have set out and have met the [Christian] enemy. Zayd has died a martyr's death.' He prayed for his forgiveness. He said, 'Ja'far has died a martyr's death,' and prayed for his forgiveness.".**..and so on down the list. My question is, if Muhammad wanted to fool them with "martyrdom earns paradise," why ask for forgiveness. It weakened his case.

Then in typical Islamic fashion, the head cleric who had ordered men to martyrdom while he remained home in the arms of his consorts, tried once again to quell an angry city. *Tabari VIII:159* **"The people began to throw dust at the army, saying, 'You retreating runaways. You fled in the Cause of Allah!' But the Messenger said, 'They are not fleers. Allah willing, they are ones who will return to fight another day.'"**

A poem recited on this occasion reads: *Ishaq:538* **"While the eyes of others shed tears in the night of sorrows, I wasn't sobbing. I felt the shepherd of Ursa and Pisces [making Muhammad an Occult prophet] between my ribs and bowels, piercing me with pain, afflicting me. Allah bless the martyrs lying dead at Mu'ta. Refresh their bones for they fought for Allah's sake like good Muslims, stallions clad in mail. Their ranks were trapped and now they lay prostrate. The moon lost its radiance at their death. The sun was eclipsed and it became dark. We are a people protected by Allah to whom he has revealed His Book, excelling in glory and honor. Our enlightened minds cover up the ignorance of others. They would not embark on such a vicious enterprise. But Allah is pleased with our guidance and the victorious good fortune of our apostolic Prophet."** Good and bad have been inverted.

Chronologically, the second to last surah revealed to Islam's **"apostolic prophet"** was named **"Repentance"**—something that was beyond his ability. Much of it precedes and validates the conquest of Mecca. As a result of the defeat suffered at the hands of the Byzantines, Muhammad needed to vanquish an easier prey. But there was a problem. Muhammad had given his word, signed his name on a "peace treaty," proclaiming that he would not attack his hometown. So what do you suppose he did?

Foreshadowing what was to come, Muhammad said on behalf of his god: *009.002* **"Go for four months, backwards and forwards, [i.e., travel freely] throughout the land, but know that you cannot weaken Allah or escape. Allah will disgrace the unbelievers and put those who reject Him to shame."**

Then Team Islam reneges on its commitment. *009.003* **"And an announcement from Allah and His Messenger, to the people (assembled) on the day of the Great Pilgrimage,** that Allah and His Messenger dissolve (treaty) obligations with the Pagans. If then, you relent, it is best for you; but if you do not, know you that you cannot escape Allah, weaken or frustrate Him. And proclaim a grievous penalty of a painful doom to those who reject [Islamic] Faith." If you are a Muslim, ask yourself: if your prophet and his god were willing to break their sworn oath on this occasion, why trust them on any other occasion? Might their promises of paradise be equally hollow? Why does anyone trust a *lying* spirit?

The line "Allah and His Messenger dissolve (treaty) obligations" is a repudiation of written testimony. The verse 066.001 "Allah has already sanctioned for you the dissolution of your vows" is an abandonment of sworn oaths, or verbal testimony. Islam's prophet and god said that their word and their scripture was not to be believed. So was Muhammad lying when he said that Allah was God? Did he lie when he claimed to be a prophet? What part of the Qur'an is untrue: some of it or all of it? Does paradise have virgins? Do killers go there? Does God really want his creation to follow the example of a perverted pedophile, a man guilty of incest and rape, a money-grubbing terrorist?

While you are pondering those questions, consider what comes next. Islam's dark spirit declares war on non-Muslims. Allah orders his militants to go out hunting by way of ambush. Muslims are told to fight non-Muslims, to slay them, to enslave them, and to torture them, deploying every strategy of war. Muslims must do this until every non-Muslim surrenders, worships the deceitful deity, and pays the Islamic tax.

I dare say, if this were the only verse in the Qur'an commanding Muslims to fight, enslave, torture, and kill non-Muslims, it would be sufficient to banish Islam: the order is open ended—it's not limited by time or place. Simply stated: they will kill until we stop them. 009.005 "When the sacred forbidden months for fighting are past, *fight* and *kill* the disbelievers wherever you find them, take them *captive* [enslave them], *beleaguer* them [torture them], and lie in wait and *ambush* them using every stratagem of *war*. But if they relent, [and become Muslims by...] performing their devotional obligations and paying the zakat tax, then open the way. Allah is Forgiving, Merciful." The Islamic god said, "I created Islam to start fights that will kill, enslave, and torture people by way of deceptive ambush. Surrender, or I will have Muslims terrorize you."

So that the message would not be lost on the faithful: *Bukhari:V9B84N59* "Allah's Apostle said, 'I have been ordered to fight the people till they say: "None has the right to be worshipped but Allah." Whoever says this will save his property and his life from me.'" Worship the Devil or die.

Then in direct conflict with its doctrine of predestination, the Qur'an says: 009.006 "If a disbeliever seeks protection, grant him asylum so that he may hear the word of Allah; and then escort him to where he can be secure. That is because they are ignorant."

Those who are embarrassed by history rewrite it. This is Islam's feeble yet desperate attempt to justify lying at Hudaybiyah: 009.007 "How can there be a covenant between Allah and His Messenger and the disbelievers with whom you made a treaty near the sacred Mosque? As long as these stand true to you, stand you true to them: for Allah does love those who keep their duty to Him." More directly stated: "Our word only stands if it's in our interest, and if you surrender to and obey us." Moreover, how can Allah gripe about forming a "covenant" with "disbelievers" when he and his Ka'aba were created by them?

Revealing why the surah was named **"Repentance"** we find Muhammad regretting that he had been out-negotiated at Hudaybiyah. *009.008* **"How (can there be such a treaty), seeing that they get an advantage, the upper hand over you? They do not pay you respect, or honor you or the ties of kinship or covenant. With (good words from) their mouths they entice you [out negotiate you], but their hearts are averse to you; and most of them are rebellious and wicked."** Another translation assumes that the words Allah left out, and thus words which had to be inserted by the translator, were **"How (can they be trusted)?"** Ironic, since Muslims, not Meccans, breached the treaty and then disavowed it. The word "hypocrite" comes to mind.

As with most of what flows from Muhammad's mouth, this next verse is a lie. The prophet continues to project his failings onto his foes. He is invariably guilty of what he condemns. *009.010* **"They have no regard to ties of kinship or honor for the covenant with the believers. It is they who have transgressed the bounds and gone beyond the limits."** Because the Qur'an defines fighting, stealing, and kidnapping as "good," the Islamic militants weren't "transgressors."

009.011 **"But if they repent, establish devotional obligations and pay the zakat, they are your brethren in Religion: (thus) do We explain the Signs in detail for those who understand."** These are the "details" of Islam directly from Allah: repent by confessing that Muhammad's message and example are right, perform mindless ritual, and pay a tax. If you do, you get to live (under their tyranny).

Again projecting their faults on others, the Team that dissolved their vows cries: *009.012* **"If they violate their oaths and break treaties, taunting you for your Religion, then fight these specimens of faithlessness, for their vows are nothing to them, that they may be restrained."** Do you suppose **"fighting specimens of faithlessness"** is religious?

As I write these words there is a rumor spreading around the world that the Qur'an is prophetic because verse 9:11 predicts an Arab will destroy an Eagle. While that's a lie, there are lessons here. Muhammad is a hypocrite (the manifistation or behavior of a liar) as he does what he condemns. And treaties with Muslims are useless.

Trying to motivate peaceful Muslims to fight for his personal quest—the acquisition of the Ka'aba Inc.—Muhammad tells them that they have a choice: face his enemy or face his terrorist god. *009.013* **"Will you not fight people who violated their oaths, plotted to expel the Messenger, and became the aggressors by being the first (to assault) you? Do you fear them? Nay, it is Allah Whom you should fear more!"** Not that it's unusual for Allah to lie, but the Muslims were the aggressors. They drew first blood, by their own admission. *Tabari VII:19* **"They plucked up courage and** agreed to kill as many as they could and to seize what they had with them. Waqid shot an arrow at Amr and killed him. Then Abd Allah and his companions took the caravan and the captives back to Allah's Apostle in Medina. This was the first booty taken by the Companions of Muhammad." *Ishaq:289* "Our lances drank of Amr's blood and lit the flame of war." *Ishaq:288* "The Quraysh said, 'Muhammad and his Companions have violated the sacred month, shed blood, seized property, and taken men captive. Muhammad claims that he is following obedience to Allah, yet he is the first to violate the holy month and to kill.'"

Fanning the flames of jihad, the Qur'an bellows: *009.014* "Fight them and Allah will punish them by your hands, lay them low, and cover them with shame. He will help you over them and heal the breasts of Believers." Since neither Allah nor Muhammad ever healed anyone, the promise was as hollow as the pledge of paradise. *009.016* "Do you think you will get away before Allah knows who among you have striven hard and fought?" Islam has but one test to sift the good Muslims from bad ones.

The doctrine masquerading as a tolerant religion says: *009.017* "The disbelievers have no right to visit the mosques of Allah while bearing witness against their own souls to infidelity. These it is whose doings are in vain, and in the fire shall they abide. Only he shall visit the mosques of Allah who believes in Allah and the latter day, and keeps up devotional obligations, pays the zakat, and fears none but Allah." What's particularly intolerant about this is the fact that the Ka'aba had been a pagan mosque, one open for all peace-loving people to visit. Muslims waged an unceasing terrorist campaign against the Meccans because they claimed that they had been prevented from visiting their god's house. So egregious was this crime, Allah said that it was worse than human slaughter. But now that Muslims are on the verge of conquering Mecca, their god does a one-eighty and approves what he once condemned—a lock-out of all non-Muslims.

Muhammad recognized the pickle he had just placed his god in, so he attempted to belittle the services the Quraysh had provided Allah and his pilgrims for centuries. *009.019* "Do you make the giving of drink to pilgrims, or the maintenance of the Sacred Mosque, equal to those who believe in Allah and the Last Day, and fight in the Cause of Allah? They are not comparable in the sight of Allah. Those who believe, and left their homes and strive with might fighting in Allah's Cause [Jihad] with their goods and their lives, have the highest rank in the sight of Allah." Yes, the highest ranking Muslims are those who fight fiercely. Faith is for fools.

The more virgins Muhammad added to his harem, the less he spoke about them in paradise. *009.021* "Their Lord does give them glad tidings of a mercy from Him, of His pleasure, and of gardens for them, wherein are delights that endure."

Then the god who rebuked the Quraysh for breaking family ties, severed them on behalf of Islam. *009.023* "Believers, take not for friends your fathers and your brothers if they love disbelief above belief. If you do, you do wrong. Say: If your fathers, your sons, your families, your wives, relatives and property which you have acquired, and the slackness of trade which you fear and dwellings which you like, are dearer to you than Allah and His Messenger and striving hard and fighting in His Cause, then wait till Allah brings about His decision (torment)." We have been given another insight into Muhammad's insecurity. He craved praise. These Bukhari Hadiths are even more desperate. *Bukhari:V1B2N13* "Allah's Apostle said, 'By Him in Whose Hands my life is, none of you will have faith till he loves me more than his father and his children.'" And: *Bukhari:V1B2N14* "The Prophet said, 'None of you will have faith till he loves me more than his father, his children and all mankind.'" Imagine loving a sexual pervert, a money-grubbing pirate and terrorist, more than your parents and children.

Speaking on behalf of his dark spirit, Muhammad recited: *009.025* "Assuredly, Allah did give you victory on many battlefields and on the day of (the battle of) Hunayn: Behold, your great numbers elated you, but they availed you naught, and you turned back in retreat. But Allah did send down his Sakinah on the Messenger and Believers, and sent down forces (angels) which you saw not. He punished the Infidels. Such is their reward." This "battle" (actually terrorist raid) had not been fought when this surah was allegedly revealed. We will cover Hunayn in the last chapter. The reason it's tossed in here is because the 9th surah has been devoted to Jihad.

Unable to contain his hatred, Muhammad says on behalf of his personal deity: *009.028* "Believers, truly the pagan disbelievers are unclean; so let them not, after this year of theirs, approach the Sacred Mosque [that they built, promoted, and maintained]. And if you fear poverty (from the loss of their merchandise), soon will Allah enrich you, if He wills, out of His bounty [spoils of war]." By booting the Meccans out of Mecca the Muslims knew that they would kill their Golden Goose—their favorite source of booty. Robbing Quraysh caravans had funded the rise of Islam. As parasites, they'd die along with their host.

By calling non-Muslims "unclean," Muhammad confirmed he was a racist. A Hadith in the Noble Qur'an explains: "Their impurity is physical because they lack personal hygiene (filthy as regards urine, stools and blood.)" For Muhammad, cleanliness was next to godliness, so Bukhari devoted an entire book to potty talk. Here is some "inspired scripture" from his *Book of Wudu*: *Bukhari:V1B4N137* "Allah's Apostle said, 'The prayer of a person who does Hadath (passes urine, stool or wind) is not accepted till he performs ablution.'" *Bukhari:V1B4N139* "I asked Allah's Apostle about a person who imagined they passed wind during prayer. He replied: 'He should not leave his prayer unless he hears sound or smells something.'" *Bukhari:V1B4N154* "Whenever Allah's Apostle went to answer the call of nature, I along with another boy used to go behind him carrying a tumbler of water for cleaning the private parts and a spear-headed stick." *Bukhari:V1B4N156* "The Prophet said, 'Whenever anyone makes water he should not hold his penis or clean his private parts with his right hand. While drinking, one should not breathe in the utensil.'" *Bukhari:V1B4N158* "The Prophet went out to answer the call of nature and asked me to bring three stones. I found two stones and searched for the third but could not find it. So I took a dried piece of dung and brought it to him. He took the stones and threw away the dung, saying, 'This is a filthy thing.'" *Bukhari:V1B4N163* "The Prophet said, 'Whoever cleans his private parts with stones should do it with an odd number of stones. And whoever wakes up should wash his hands before putting them in the water for ablution. Nobody knows where his hands were during sleep.'" *Bukhari:V1B4N174* "During the lifetime of Allah's Apostle dogs used to urinate and pass through the mosque. Nevertheless they never used to sprinkle water on it." *Bukhari: V1B4N1229-33* "Aisha said, 'I used to wash the semen off the clothes of the Prophet. When he went for prayers I used to notice one or more spots on them.'" Muslims assure us that these words were inspired by Allah.

Returning to the Qur'an, the peaceful god of the peace-loving religion said: *009.029* "Fight those who do not believe in Allah nor the Last Day, who do not forbid that which has been forbidden by Allah and His Messenger, nor acknowledge the Religion of Truth (Islam), (even if they are) of the People of the Book (Christians and Jews), until they pay the Jizyah tribute tax in submission, feeling themselves subdued and brought low." Everything you need to know about Islam is contained in this one verse. Muslims are ordered to fight Christians and Jews until they either surrender and become Muslims or they commit financial suicide by paying the Jizyah tribute tax in submission. (Paying Muslims the "Jizyah" is not unlike giving the godfather's goons a bribe to keep the mafia from killing you and your family.)

Confirming that Allah is too dumb to be god and that Islam's enemies are Christians and Jews: *009.030* "The Jews call Uzair (Ezra) the son of Allah, and the Christians say that the Messiah is the son of Allah. That is their saying from their mouths; they but imitate what the unbelievers of old used to say. Allah's (Himself) fights against them, cursing them, damning and destroying them. How perverse are they!" God ought to be smarter than this. Ezra was but one of many Hebrew priests. He was neither a prophet nor divine. The Messiah is Yahweh's Anointed and has nothing to do with Allah. No one mouthed these delusional thoughts save Muhammad. But he has revealed the source of his rage. Jews and Christians did not accept his preposterous claim of being a prophet, so his insecurity caused him to hate them, to call them perverse, to curse them, and then to kill them. He was even willing to contradict his scriptures to do it. Remember: *002.286* "We make no distinction between His Messengers." And: *002.285* "Surely those who believe and Jews, and Nazareans [Christians], and the Sabaeans [Zoroastrians], whoever believes in Allah and in the Last Day shall have his reward with his Lord and will not have fear or regret."

The next time you hear a Muslim say that Islam is tolerant because Muslims believe that Jesus was a prophet, you'll know how they define tolerance: "fighting against them, cursing them, damning and destroying them: how perverse are they!" As with everything in Islam, good is bad; truth is deceit; peace is surrender; and tolerance is comprised of hate and violence.

Ignorant, Muhammad claimed his idol said: *009.031* "They (Jews and Christians) consider their rabbis and monks to be gods besides Allah. They also took their Lord Messiah to be a god but they were commanded (in the Taurat and Injeel) to worship only One Ilah (God). There is no ilah (god) but He. Too holy is He for the partners they associate (with Him)." Since God cannot be this poorly informed, Allah cannot be God. Neither rabbis nor monks have ever been considered divine by Jews or Christians. So by reciting these words Muhammad revealed that the Qur'an wasn't inspired.

And while I appreciate the confession, I continue to be skeptical that any thinking person actually believes this foolishness. How can Allah be depicted torturing men in hell, yet be "too holy" to be associated with the Messiah?

Based upon a Hadith footnoted in the Noble Qur'an, it's apparent the first Muslims were better informed than their prophet and god. "Once while Allah's Messenger was reciting this verse, Adi said, 'O Allah's Messenger, they do not worship rabbis and monks.' The Prophet said, 'They certainly do.'"

009.032 "Fain would they extinguish Allah's light with their mouths, but Allah disdaineth (aught) save that He shall perfect His light that His light should be perfected, even though the Unbelievers may detest (it)."...as should everyone.

Anyone who says Islam is tolerant is a liar. *009.033* "It is He Who has sent His Messenger (Muhammad) with guidance and the Religion of Truth (Islam) to make it superior over all religions, even though the disbelievers detest (it)."

In this next verse we learn that monks and rabbis, not Islamic pirates, are money grubbers. *009.034* "Believers, there are many (Christian) monks and (Jewish) rabbis who in falsehood devour the wealth of mankind and hinder (men) from the way of Allah. And there are those who bury gold and silver and spend it not in Allah's Cause. (Muhammad) announce unto them tidings of a painful torture. On the Day [of Doom] heat will be produced out of that (wealth) in the Fire of Hell. It will be branded on their foreheads, their flanks, and their backs. 'This is the (treasure) which you hoarded for yourselves: now taste it!'" Just when you thought Allah couldn't get any nastier...

The Qur'an and Hadith make it abundantly clear that Muhammad hated Jews with a passion, so much so that he became their most bloodthirsty predator. Yet neither explains why, or even how, Muhammad came to detest Christians. His misinformed attacks on their beliefs proved that he didn't know them very well.

This next transition is as flawed as the rest of the Qur'an. The logic of the verse is faulty as well. In reverence to Allah's moon-god heritage, Muhammad established a lunar year without the intercalary month every five years. As a result, the Islamic seasons float aimlessly around the calendar. *009.036* "The number of months in the sight of Allah is twelve—so ordained by Him the day He created the heavens and the earth; of them four are sacred: that is the straight usage and the right religion. [Since Allah's "sacred" months were established by Qusayy, it would make his pagan scam the "right religion."] So wrong not yourselves therein, and wage war on the disbelievers all together as they fight you collectively. But know that Allah is with those who restrain themselves. Verily the transposing (of a prohibited month) is an addition to unbelief: the Unbelievers are led to wrong thereby: for they make it lawful one year, and forbidden another in order to adjust the number of months forbidden by Allah and make such forbidden ones lawful. The evil of their course seems pleasing to them." This is further proof that Allah was too dumb to be divine. For over three thousand years civilized societies had been better informed than he.

Lunacy aside, Muhammad took another swipe at peaceful Muslims who still had a conscience. *009.038* **"Believers, what is the matter with you, that when you are asked to march forth in the Cause of Allah (i.e., Jihad) you cling to the earth? Do you prefer the life of this world to the Hereafter? Unless you march, He will afflict and punish you with a painful torture, and put others in your place. But you cannot harm Him in the least."** According to Allah, if Muslims aren't eager to fight he will replace them and then torture them. But with whom, may I ask? And can you imagine a god so feeble he needs to tell his faithful that they **"cannot harm Him?"**

This next passage, like so many in the Qur'an, makes no sense without the context of the Hadith. *009.040* **"If you help not him (your leader Muhammad), (it is no matter) for Allah did indeed help him, when the Unbelievers drove him out, the second of two when they were in the cave, and he said, 'Be not sad, for Allah is with us.' Then Allah sent down His Sakinah and strengthened him with (angelic) army forces which you saw not, and humbled to the depths the word of the Unbelievers."** Following the Satanic Verse fiasco, Muhammad had to flee Mecca in shame. On the way out of town, he and Abu Bakr had to hide in a cave for fear the Meccans would find them. So Allah is saying that he protected them with an army of killer angels.

Speaking of killers...*009.041* **"March forth, (equipped) with light or heavy arms, and strive with your goods and your lives in the Cause of Allah. That is best for you, if you knew."**

But there were too many "bad" Muslims in the prophet's company who were unwilling to kill for him—unless, of course, it was an easy kill and the booty was plentiful. They were mercenaries, after all. *009.042* **"(O Prophet) had there been immediate gain (in sight with booty in front of them), and the journey easy—a near adventure—they would (all) without doubt have followed you, but the distance was long on them. They would indeed swear, 'If we only could, we would have come out with you.' They cause their own souls to perish; for Allah knows they are liars."** According to Allah, peaceful Muslims lie.

In this series of verses, Allah is speaking about the terrorist raid Muhammad led against the Byzantine Christians at Tabuk. Unfortunately for Islam's credibility, the surah preceded the raid by more than a year. *009.043* **"May Allah forgive you (O Muhammad). Why did you grant them leave (for remaining behind; you should have persisted as regards to your order to them to proceed on Jihad), until those who told the truth were seen by you in a clear light, and you had known the liars."** Speaking of liars, we've just caught Muhammad in the act. If Allah were God and dictating the Qur'an, he would not say **"May Allah forgive you."**

009.044 **"Those who believe in Allah and the Last Day do not ask for an exemption from fighting with your goods and persons. And Allah knows well those who do their duty."** All good Muslims are terrorists. Allah said so. Bad Muslims, on the other hand, just make excuses: *009.045* **"Only those ask for exemption (from Jihad) who believe not in Allah and whose hearts are in doubt, so that they are tossed to and fro. If they had intended to march out to fight, they would certainly have made some preparation and readied their equipment; but Allah was averse to their being sent forth; so He made them lag behind. 'Sit you among those who sit.' If they had marched with you, they would not** have added to your (strength) but only (made for) discord, spying and sowing sedition. There would have been some in your midst who would have listened to them. But Allah knows well those [peace-loving Muslims] who do wrong and are wicked." More than anything, Allah hated peace.

Still rebuking pacifist Muslims…*009.048* "They had plotted sedition before, and upset matters for you until the Decree of Allah [to fight] became manifest, much to their disgust. Among them are many who say: 'Grant me exemption to stay back at home (exempted from Jihad). And do not tempt me [with promises of booty].' Have they not fallen into temptation already? Indeed, Hell surrounds them." Muhammad was "tempting" Muslims to fight for him. Those he couldn't seduce, Allah condemned.

Desperate to beguile his troops: *009.052* "Say: 'Can you expect for us (any fate) other than one of two glorious things (martyrdom or victory)? But we can expect for you that Allah will send his punishment of doom from Himself, or by our hands.' Say: 'Pay your contribution for the Cause willingly or unwillingly: for you are indeed rebellious and wicked.'" "Fight or I will kill you myself," is the message. But since Allah couldn't kill, he opted to have good Muslims kill the bad ones.

After saying that he was going to take their money "willingly or unwillingly," Islam's deceitful spirit claims: *009.054* "The only reasons why their contributions are not accepted are: that they reject Allah and His Messenger; that they come to prayer sluggishly; and that they offer contributions unwillingly." Here's the bottom line: the peaceful Muslims were unwilling to fund Jihad so rather than admit defeat, Muhammad said: "I didn't want their money anyway." But he couldn't help himself. He had to lash out at those who withheld the funds he needed to perpetuate his reign of terror. As we have learned, terrorism isn't cheap. It's no coincidence that the richest Islamic regimes manufacture the most terrorists.

Next we learn that Muhammad was "dazzled by wealth" and "Allah's plan is to punish." *009.055* "Let not their wealth nor their (following in) sons dazzle you or excite your admiration (Muhammad). In reality Allah's plan is to punish them with these things in this life, and make certain that their souls perish in their denial of Allah. They swear that they are indeed with you; but they are not. They do not want (to appear in their true colors) because they are afraid of you." They were "afraid" of their prophet because he was a terrorist. The bad, peace-loving Muslims knew that Muhammad's militants would attack them as they had the Jews—stealing their property, torturing them, raping them, enslaving them, and killing them. It's stunning that the Qur'an would admit that Muslims were afraid of Muhammad. But then again, tyrants the world over are always the same. "He who fears will obey."

If you think this interpretation is too harsh, consider the following Hadith: *Bukhari:V1B11N626* "The Prophet said, 'No prayer is harder for the hypocrites than the Fajr. If they knew the reward they would come to (the mosque) even if they had to crawl. Certainly I decided to order a man to lead the prayer and then take a flame to burn all those who had not left their houses for the prayer, burning them alive inside their homes.'"

The Profit's message was: "Obey and pay or you'll burn." *Bukhari:V8B76N548*

"The Prophet said, 'Protect yourself from the Fire.' He turned his face aside as if he were looking at it and said, 'Protect yourself from the Fire,' and turned his face aside as if he were looking at it, and he said for the third time till we thought he was actually looking at it: 'Protect yourselves from the Fire.'" *Bukhari:V8B76N547* "The Prophet said, 'All of you will be questioned by Allah on the Day of Doom. There will be no interpreter between you and Allah. And the Hell Fire will confront you. So, whoever among you can, save yourself from the Fire.'" Muhammad has once again put Allah in hell.

Slandering and threatening his own, Allah says: *009.057* "If they could find a place to flee to, a cave or hole to hide, they would run away with an obstinate rush. And some slander you, blaming you (of partiality) in the matter of (the distribution of) the offerings [stolen spoils]. If they are given part of these, they are pleased, but if not they are indignant and enraged!" The first Muslims were bickering over the booty.

According to the Hadith, the founders of Islam made nothing and stole everything. As such, these Muslims were squabbling over looted loot. *009.059* "(How much more seemly) if only they had been content with what Allah and His Messenger gave them, and said, 'Sufficient is Allah! His Messenger will soon give us His bounty. We implore Allah to enrich us.'" When you are a miserly pirate, things can get prickly.

Many said Muhammad was too easily swayed, as in the Quraysh Bargain and the Satanic Verses. So the book that claims that it was written before time began, abruptly changes subject and presents a temporal defense of its lone voice: *009.061* "Among them are men who vex, annoy, and molest the Prophet, saying, 'He is (all) ear and believes every thing that he hears.' Say, 'He listens to what is best for you: he believes in Allah, has faith in the Believers, and is a Mercy to those of you who believe.' But those who offend the Messenger will have a grievous torment, a painful doom." It's another insight into the troubled soul of a chronically insecure man. The molested has become a molester.

I'm not sure that this makes any sense, but it does reveal that Islam was perpetrated to please Muhammad. *009.062* "To you they swear in order to please you: but it is more fitting that they should please Allah and His Messenger (Muhammad)."

When there wasn't enough dough to bribe the bullies, Muhammad just threatened them. *009.063* "Know they not that for those who oppose Allah and His Messenger is the Fire of Hell wherein they shall dwell? That is the supreme disgrace."

But the "peaceful Muslim hypocrites" recognized that Muhammad was the biggest Muslim Hypocrite of all. They had observed his willingness to falsify scripture to satiate his desire for money, power, or sex. Acknowledging this problem, his dark spirit says: *009.064* "The Hypocrites are afraid that a surah will be sent down about them, showing them what is (really) in their hearts. Say: 'Go ahead, scoff and mock, will you! Lo, Allah is disclosing what you fear.' If you question them (Muhammad about this), they declare: 'We were only talking idly, jesting in play.' Say: 'Was it at Allah and His proofs, signs, verses, lessons, and Messenger that you were mocking?'" It is as if we have returned to Mecca. Muhammad is being mocked. Those who knew him best were scoffing at his demonic scripture, example, and god.

Muhammad, like all insecure men, was obsessed with rejection. Even after eliminating the Jews, his only literate foe, Arabs continued to be repulsed. Twenty years after the first cave-vision, Muhammad couldn't sell Islam on its merits. *009.066* "**Make no excuses: you have rejected Faith after you had accepted it. If We pardon some of you, We will punish others amongst you, for they are disbelievers.**" Any free and enlightened man or woman exposed to Islam will reject it as did most of those who lived in the prophet's presence. That is why Muhammad had to make rejecting Islam a capital offense.

And it remains so to this day. This news report from WorldNetDaily confirms what happens to Muslims who reject Islam. "Dateline Jerusalem, 2003: After slaughtering a Muslim-turned-Christian, Islamic extremists returned the man's body to his Palestinian family in four pieces. The newly converted man left his friends and family earlier this month bound for a mountainous region of the Palestinian Authority. He took Christian material with him—tapes and a Bible. Ten days later, the body of the man, who left behind a wife and two small children, was returned to his home, having been cut into four pieces. The family believes the act was meant a warning to other Muslims who might consider becoming Christians. Under Muslim Sharia law, any male who leaves Islam faces the death penalty. The terror group Hamas receives funding from Iran specifically for this purpose."

Returning to the surah, we find Muhammad attacking his renegades just as today's Muslims are doing. It's hard to imagine the percentage who must have rejected Muhammad and Islam for the Qur'an to focus so intently on them. *009.067* "**The Hypocrites, men and women, (have an understanding) with each other. They enjoin what is forbidden, and forbid what Islam commands. They withhold their hands (from spending in Allah's Cause [Jihad]). They have forgotten Allah so He has forgotten them. Verily the Hypocrites are oblivious, rebellious and perverse.**" Allah is a very vindictive and nasty spirit. Peaceful Muslims who aren't willing to fund Jihad and terrorize infidels are called "perverse."

Again: *009.068* "**Allah has promised the Hypocrites, both men and women, and the disbelievers the Fire of Hell for their abode: Therein shall they dwell. It will suffice them. On them is the curse of Allah, and an enduring punishment, a lasting torment.**" Fair warning: if you are a peaceful Muslim, your god hates you.

After condemning the vain discourse of those who were not swallowing Muhammad's poison, Allah reprises a worn-out trick: *009.070* "**Has not the story reached them of those before them—the People of Noah, Ad, and Thamud; the folk of Abraham, the men of Midian, and the cities overthrown. To them came their messengers with signs of proof. It is not Allah Who wrongs them, but they wrong their own souls.**" It's been a long time since Muhammad has corrupted a Bible or Hanif story to scare the faithful, but he hasn't forgotten how.

Now that the Islamic god is in the mode of pulverizing "bad" Muslims into submission (a.k.a. Islam), it's time for him to define "good Muslim" and tell them how to behave. *009.071* "The Believers, men and women, are guardians of one another: they enjoin what Islam (orders them to do) and forbid disbelief. They perform their devotional obligations, pay the zakat, and obey Allah and His Messenger." *009.071* "O Prophet, strive hard [fighting] against the unbelievers and the Hypocrites, and be harsh with them. Their abode is Hell, an evil refuge indeed." Islam can thus be defined as: perform, pay, obey, and fight.

Transfixed by the number of Muslims rejecting Muhammad, ritual, taxes, jihad, and piracy, Team Islam said. *009.074* "They swear by Allah that they said nothing, but indeed they uttered blasphemy, and they disbelieved after Surrender (accepting Islam). They meditated a plot (to murder Prophet Muhammad) which they were unable to carry out. The reason for this revenge of theirs was the bounty [of booty] with which Allah and His Messenger had enriched them! If they repent, it will be best for them; but if they turn back, Allah will punish them with a grievous torment in this life and in the Hereafter." While the Hadith doesn't describe the Muslim plot to kill Muhammad, the Qur'an says the motive was money.

It got to the point Muhammad couldn't even bribe his mercenaries: *009.075* "Amongst them are men who made a deal with Allah, that if He bestowed on them of His bounty [booty], they would pay (largely) in zakat tax (for Allah's Cause [Jihad]). But when He did bestow of His bounty, they became niggardly, and turned back (from their bargain), averse (refusing to pay)." All Muhammad really wanted was money. So long as he stole enough, he could buy sex, power, and praise.

But the Muslim militants were as miserly as the man who had beguiled them. So the warlord said that their hypocrisy was a miracle ordained by god: *009.077* "He punished them by putting hypocrisy in their hearts until the Day whereon they shall meet Him, because they lied to Allah and failed to perform as promised [forking over the dough]. Allah knows their secrets. Those who slander and taunt the believers who pay the zakat (for Allah's Cause) voluntarily and throw ridicule on them, scoffing, Allah will throw back their taunts, and they shall have a painful doom. Whether you ask for their forgiveness or not, (their sin is unforgivable). If you ask seventy times for their forgiveness Allah will not forgive them because they have disbelieved Allah and His Messenger." Islam's "unforgivable" sin is: "Not paying Mo da money."

In another translation, Allah confirms that hypocrisy is his fault and that it's the result of a business deal gone bad: *009.075* "Some of you made a deal with Allah, saying, 'If You give us booty we shall pay You the tax.' But when He gave them booty, they became greedy and refused to pay. As a consequence of breaking their promises, Allah filled their hearts with hypocrisy which will last forever." Lest we forget, the business of Allah was terrorism, piracy, and the slave trade.

The broken record that became the Qur'an screeches once again: peaceful Muslims go to hell because they are reluctant to fight. *009.081* "Those who stayed behind (in the Tabuk expedition) rejoiced in their inaction behind the back of the Messenger. They hated to strive and fight with their goods and lives in the Cause of Allah. They said, 'Go not forth in the heat.' Say, 'The fire of Hell is fiercer in heat.' If only they could understand! So let them laugh a little, for they will weep much as a reward for what they did. If Allah brings you back (from the campaign) to a party of the hypocrites and they ask to go out to fight, say: 'You shall never go out to fight with me against a foe. You were content sitting inactive on the first occasion. So sit with the useless men who lag behind.' Do not pray for any of them (Muhammad) that die, nor stand at his grave. They rejected Allah and disbelieved His Messenger. They died in a state of perverse rebellion." Temper, temper. Allah—Oft-Forgiving, Ever-Merciful—isn't being very nice.

Muhammad hated Christians and Jews less than he loathed peace-loving Muslims. He was especially irritated that they were able to make more money than his militants were able to steal. *009.085* "And let not their wealth or (following in) sons dazzle you or excite your admiration. Allah's plan is to punish them with these things in this world, and to make sure their souls perish while they are unbelievers. When a surah comes down enjoining them to believe in Allah and to strive hard and fight along with His Messenger, those with wealth and influence among them ask you for exemption from Jihad. They prefer to be with (their women), who remain behind (at home). Their hearts are sealed and so they understand not." Muhammad stayed behind at home with his harem on fifty of the seventy-five raids he initiated; so he, too, was a hypocrite—the biggest of them all.

Throughout this surah Allah, acting like Lucifer, has said that he wanted people to die as disbelievers so that he could torture them. He claimed to have sealed their hearts and caused their hypocrisy (unwillingness to perform, pay, obey, and fight). But if that's the case, why is the Qur'an so intent on threatening them? Why not just leave them alone and press on with the good militants?

Good Muslims are bad people. Islam makes them that way. *009.088* "The Messenger and those who believe with him, strive hard and fight [jihad] with their wealth and lives (in Allah's Cause)." All Muslims aren't terrorists—just the good ones are.

The Bedouins were peace loving before Islam corrupted them. *009.090* "And there were among the wandering desert Arabs men who made excuses and came to claim exemption (from the battle). Those who lied to Allah and His Messenger sat at home. Soon will a grievous torment seize the Unbelievers." There are Muslims who are excused from fighting. *009.091* "There is no blame on those who are old, weak, ill, or who find no resources to spend (on Jihad, holy fighting), if they are sincere (in duty) to Allah and His Messenger. No ground (of complaint) can there be against them." The only Muslims who don't fight are lame.

Islam isn't complicated. Believe in Allah and become a Jihadist. *Bukhari: V1B2N25* "Allah's Apostle was asked, 'What is the best deed?' He replied, 'To believe in Allah and His Apostle Muhammad.' The questioner then asked, 'What is the next best in goodness?' He replied, 'To participate in Jihad, religious fighting in Allah's Cause.'"

Islam's condemnation of peace marched on: *009.093* "The (complaint) is against those who claim exemption [from fighting] while they are rich. They prefer to stay with the (women) who remain behind (at home). Allah has sealed their hearts. They are content to be useless. Say: 'Present no excuses: we shall not believe you.' It is your actions that Allah and His Messenger will observe. They will swear to you by Allah, when you return hoping that you might leave them alone. So turn away from them, for they are unclean, an abomination, and Hell is their dwelling-place, a fitting recompense for them." This couldn't be any clearer. Allah hates peaceful Muslims. They are called "unclean," an "abomination," and "hell-dwellers."

While we must love Muslims and free the peaceful ones from this perverse doctrine, Allah hates them, especially Arabs. *009.097* "The Arabs of the desert are the worst in unbelief and hypocrisy, and most fitted to be in ignorance of the command which Allah hath sent down to His Messenger. Some of the Bedouins look upon their payments (for Allah's Cause) as a fine and wish disasters to fall on you (so that they might not have to pay). Yet on them be the disaster of evil." The evil disaster that fell upon the Arabs was Islam. The free, productive, and peace-loving Bedouins of Arabia were forced into submission, taxed, and then coerced into fighting.

009.101 "Among the desert Arabs are hypocrites. They, like the people of Medina are obstinate in hypocrisy. We know them. Twice shall We punish them, and in addition they shall be brought back to a horrible torment." While I love Arabs, as does Yahweh, Allah hates them so much he will punish them twice and then torment them.

Continuing to berate those who do not perform, pay, obey, and fight, Allah contradicts himself and tells Muhammad to take their money anyway. *009.103* "Take alms out of their property in order to cleanse and purify them, and invoke Allah for them; surely this is a relief for them." Religion is a wonderful thing if you are a cleric or king. Stealing "cleanses and purifies" your victims.

If you're a Muslim, you'd better die fighting because: *009.106* "There are (yet) others, held in suspense for the command of Allah, whether He will punish them, or turn in mercy to them." Even the builders of mosques are going to hell. *009.107* "And there are those who put up a mosque by way of mischief to disunite the Believers and in preparation for an ambush of him who made war against Allah and His Messenger. They will swear that their intention is good; But Allah declares that they are liars." Their mosque "crumbles to pieces with them in the fire of Hell."

According to the Qur'an, Allah has purchased the believers (bribed them with booty), and all "good" Muslims are killers: *009.111* "Allah has purchased the believers, their lives and their goods. For them (in return) is the Garden (of Paradise). They fight in Allah's Cause, and slay others and are slain, they kill and are killed. It is a promise binding on Him in the Taurat (Torah), the Injeel (Gospel), and the Qur'an. And who is more faithful to his covenant than Allah? Then rejoice in the bargain which you have concluded. It is the achievement supreme." There are no such bargains in the Bible. And that would make Allah a liar. Yahshua never asked men to "slay others." In the Torah, Yahweh only asked once; He asked Moses and Joshua to remove the Canaanites from the land, a people who, like Muhammad's Muslims, were immoral, terrorizing, plundering, enslaving, murdering, worshippers of false gods. Yahweh knew that it was compassionate to exterminate the few who would seduce the many into a doctrine corrosive enough to destroy mankind.

Yes, there are doctrines corrupt enough to deceive and damn all human kind. Such dogmas say: the Garden of Bliss (a.k.a. Allah's Whorehouse) awaits those who **"fight in Allah's Cause, slay others and are slain, kill and are killed."**

As we wind our way to the bitter end of the Qur'an's 113th recital, we find Team Islam spiteful to the last. Muhammad cries in the name of his god: *009.113* **"It is not fitting for the Prophet and those who believe, that they should pray for the forgiveness for disbelievers, even though they be close relatives, after it is clear to them that they are the inmates of the Flaming Hell Fire."** Don't pray to save your family. Allah wants you to kill them so that he can roast them in hell.

Looking for a way to justify his lack of compassion, or at least make it seem holy, Muhammad conjured up a lie about Abraham. *009.114* **"Abraham prayed for his father's forgiveness only because of a promise he had made to him. But when it became clear to him that he was an enemy to Allah, he dissociated himself from him."**

Der prophet proclaimed: *009.120* **"It is not fitting for the people of Medina and the Bedouin Arabs to refuse to follow Allah's Messenger (Muhammad when fighting in Allah's Cause), nor to prefer their own lives to his life. They suffer neither thirst nor fatigue in Allah's Cause, nor do they go without reward. They do not take steps to raise the anger of disbelievers, nor inflict any injury upon an enemy without it being written to their credit as a deed of righteousness."** For those who may have been skeptics as to whether Muhammad created Islam to serve his personal agenda, this verse is reasonably convincing. "Muslims must prefer Muhammad's life to their own." And for any who have mistakenly believed "righteous deeds" were good , you now know that Muslims are given "credit" for "inciting anger and inflicting injury."

Continuing to reinforce the sad reality that Islam was Muhammad's quest to line his pockets, the Qur'an says: *009.121* **"Nor do they spend anything (in Allah's Cause)—small or great, but the deed is inscribed to their credit that Allah may repay their deed with the best."** The Profit gets his in this life; his stooges get theirs in the next. How convenient.

Allah ordered Muslims to evangelize with the sword. Evidently, his words weren't compelling. *009.122* **"It is not proper for the Believers to all go forth together to fight (Jihad). A troop from every expedition should remain behind when others go to war. They should give instruction on the law and religion and warn the folk when they return, so that they may beware."** This, of course, gave the prophet a convenient excuse for staying home and playing house two raids out of every three.

The god of Islam commanded Muslims to fight one last time in the 9th surah, one that should be renamed: "Legacy of Terror." *009.123* **"Believers, fight the unbelievers around you, and let them find harshness in you: and know that Allah is with those who fear Him."** Shame on those in politics and the media who say Islam is a peaceful religion. By doing so, they aid and abet an enemy that grows more numerous, more committed, and more callous everyday. They are accomplices to murder.

23

JIHAD

"Our Prophet, the Messenger of our Lord, ordered us to fight you till you worship Allah Alone."

The conquest of Mecca began in the month in which the Qur'an prohibited fighting. *Tabari VIII:160* **"Allah's Apostle set out on the expedition against the people of Mecca in the month of Ramadan."** The prophet wasn't religious; he knew Islam's "holy months" were a farce. After all, he had stolen the dogma from a pagan.

But why do Muslims follow a prophet who so blatantly ignored his god's orders? *009.005* **"When the sacred forbidden months for fighting are *past*, fight and kill the disbelievers wherever you find them, take them captive, beleaguer them, and lie in wait and ambush them using every stratagem of war.**

The Hadith valiantly tries to explain the reason for the raid, but I'm going to tell you the truth. The Muslim militants were manhandled at Mu'ta. They came home empty-handed, with their tails between their legs. Muhammad was a whisper away from losing control. The mercenary Muslims wanted booty and the peaceful Muslims wanted to be left alone. So he needed an easy kill, and he needed it now.

The last four times he had been in this predicament Muhammad besieged Jewish settlements. But alas, he had over hunted them. There were no more Jews to plunder. So Medina's warlord needed a new patsy, a sure thing, a toothless tiger. And he was in luck. His unrelenting terrorist campaign had destroyed the Meccans economically. And his treaty had deceived them into letting down their defenses. They were vulnerable.

Ishaq:540 **"After sending his expedition to Mu'ta, the Messenger learned that the Banu Bakr had assaulted the Khuza'ah while the latter were at a watering place in lower Mecca."** There was some strife over a merchant who had been robbed and killed. Surprisingly enough, it hadn't been perpetrated by a Muslim.

You may be wondering why the Hadith would bother with such trivia. By this time Muhammad had led scores of terrorist raids. Collectively, Team Islam had robbed, murdered, enslaved, and raped tens of thousands of men, women, and children. So there must have been a reason for highlighting this "assault." Could it be that the Islamic sages were fishing for an excuse to renege on their peace treaty and justify Muhammad's invasion of Mecca?

Tabari VIII:161 "Matters stood thus between the Banu Bakr and the Khuza'ah when Islam intervened to separate them and occupy people's minds. [In other words: they used to be friends before Islam poisoned Arabia.] The Bakr entered into a pact with the Quraysh, and the Khuza'ah entered into a pact with the Muslims. The truce having been concluded, the Banu Bakr took advantage of it against the Khuza'ah. To retaliate, they wanted to kill the persons responsible for killing their men. So the Bakr killed a Khuza'ah man. The Quraysh aided the Bakr with weapons, and some Quraysh fought on their side under the cover of darkness until they drove the Khuza'ah into the sacred territory." Keep in mind, all of this was taking place in Mecca. The Khuza'ah had come bearing arms. The Quraysh didn't go out looking for trouble.

By protecting their town and honoring an alliance they had formed with the Bakr, the Quraysh were accused of attacking the Khuza'ah, a tribe supposedly allied with the Muslims. But there's a problem the Islamic sages didn't count on—we can read. The breach was bogus. If the Bakr were allied with the Quraysh, then the Muslims had violated the treaty, not the Meccans. Tabari documents an Islamic raid against the Bakr after Hudaybiyah, late in the seventh year, along with another dozen Muslim treaty violations.

Ishaq called the affair a "quarrel" over "a man who had gone on a trading journey," a.k.a., a business trip. While the man was mugged and murdered, neither victim nor villain was Meccan or Muslim.

Tabari VIII:162/Ishaq:541 "The Banu Bakr said, 'We have entered the sacred territory. Be mindful of your God.' To which they replied, 'Today we have no God so we'll take our revenge.' That night the Bakr attacked the Khuza'ah and killed a man named Munabbih. He had a weak heart. He said, 'I am as good as dead anyway, whether they kill me or not, for my weak heart has ceased beating.' The others ran away and escaped. Munabbih was caught and killed. ...When the Quraysh leagued together with the Bakr against the Khuza'ah and killed some men [One died of natural causes, not some, and the Bakr caught him, not the Quraysh.], they broke the treaty because of the pact the Khuza'ah had with Muhammad. This was one of the things that prompted the conquest of Mecca." These boys are as predictable as tomorrow's sunrise.

The Muslim militants who had betrayed their fellow Arabs while terrorizing and robbing every neighboring town, explained: *Tabari VIII:175* "Among the terms on which the Messenger and Quraysh had made peace was there should be neither betrayal nor clandestine theft. The Quraysh aided the Bakr with weapons. That is why Muhammad attacked the people of Mecca." Muhammad's excuse was as pathetic as his behavior, and both were as lame as Islamic apologists. Universally, they report that the Meccans had it coming because they aggressively and violently breached the peace treaty that had been steadfastly honored by Muhammad. Nothing could be further from the truth. But truth has never been popular in Islam.

Tabari VIII:163 "Khuza'ah men came to the Messenger and told him how the Quraysh had backed the Bakr against them. The Prophet replied, 'I think you will see Abu Sufyan [the leading Meccan merchant] come to strengthen the pact and extend the term.'" And he did, not knowing that the treaty was just one of Allah's many plots. *Tabari VIII:164/ Ishaq:543* "Abu Sufyan went to Muhammad in Medina to affirm the peace treaty. Upon arriving, he visited his own daughter, Umm. When he was about to sit on the carpet bed of the Prophet, she folded it up to stop him. He said, 'My daughter, I do not know if you think that I am too good for this bed or if this carpet is too good for me.' Umm replied [in the racist style of one infected by Islam], 'You are an unclean polytheist.' Abu answered [insightfully], 'My daughter, by Allah, evil came over you after you left me. You have gone bad.'"

Ishaq:543 "Then Abu Sufyan went to Allah's Messenger, but he refused to speak to him." Muhammad had no interest in peace. He wanted submission, booty, and death. *Tabari VIII:164* "Sufyan went to Abu Bakr and asked him to intercede, but he refused. When Sufyan asked Umar to help [avert war], he replied, 'No way. By Allah, if I had only ant grubs, I would fight you with them!'" Ignorant of Islam, the foolish negotiator went the extra mile to achieve the impossible—peace with an Islamic dictator. Abu Sufyan went to the man who would be Caliph, Ali, and his wife Fatimah— Muhammad's son-in-law and daughter. "Ali said, 'Woe to you, Sufyan. When the Messenger has determined a thing it is useless for anyone to talk to him.'" Islam was, and always has been, dictatorial. The poligious doctrine of "submit and obey" knows nothing of free speech or democracy.

Ishaq:544 "Fatimah said, 'No one can provide any protection against Allah's Apostle.'" And that is the lesson of history. Self-proclaimed tyrants and dictators start wars; freely elected presidents and prime ministers don't. The political doctrines of Islam, Communism, Fascism, and Nazism concentrate power in the hands of a single individual. To maintain their authority, despots establish regimes that are as brutal on their own people as they are violent against their neighbors. Muhammad was a textbook example.

The first Islamic historian confirms: *Tabari VIII:165* "There is nothing that you can do to make peace with him." So Abu Sufyan stood in the mosque and said, 'People, I came to make peace. I promise protection between men.'" But the offer was unilateral so, "He mounted his camel and departed."

Sufyan, like most Arabs before Islam, wanted to live freely and in peace. He wanted to earn a living and care for his family. But those were things Muhammad couldn't tolerate. Islam had to be imposed to survive; it had to plunder to live. Doctrinally bankrupt, he knew his Sunnah and Qur'an would never withstand the scrutiny of a free society. And morally bankrupt, it could not provide the level of trust needed for a free economy. So Muslims were destined to lose their liberties. They were transformed into parasites. Islam conquered them, deceived them, corrupted them, and then damned them.

Tabari VIII:165 "When Abu Sufyan reported back to the Quraysh that Muhammad had given him no reply, they said, 'Woe to you! By Allah, he did no more than play with you.'"

Back in the pirate's den, *Ishaq:544* "Muhammad commanded the people to prepare for the foray [raid, incursion, sortie, attack, or assault]. The Messenger informed his troops that he was going to Mecca. He ordered them to prepare themselves and ready their equipment quickly. He said, 'O Allah, keep spies and news from the Quraysh until we take them by surprise in their land.'" Fundamental Islamic organizations like Hamas, Hezbollah, Islamic Jihad, and al-Qaeda offer the same prayer today.

Ishaq:544 "Hassan incited the men, reciting: 'This is the time for war. Don't feel safe from us. Our swords will open the door to death.'" And so it would be forevermore.

Tabari VIII:168 "He departed on the tenth day of Ramadan. They broke their fast and encamped at Marr Zahran with 10,000 Muslims. No news reached the Quraysh about the Messenger, and they did not know what he would do." I beg to differ. Allah's boy had been a nonstop pirate and an insatiable terrorist for eight years. The Meccans were under no illusions. It was the Muslims who were deceived. In their "prophet's" presence, the first Muslims broke several of Islam's Five Pillars. They ignored the Ramadhan fast. They attacked the town whose people had invented Allah. And they ceased their prostrations so that they could kill.

Tabari VIII:170 "When the Messenger set out for Mecca he appointed no one to military commands and displayed no banners." He was using deceptive tactics. Then he begged for help. "He sent to the Arab tribes, but they hung back from him." In other words, even Muhammad couldn't sell Islam. Given a choice, most Arabs chose not to align themselves with his "religion." Yet sadly, there were enough militants willing to sell their soul for a buck. "When Muhammad reached Qudayd, the Sulaym met him with horses and full armament. Uyaynah joined the Messenger at Arj. Aqra joined in at Suqya." *Tabari VIII:171* "When Muhammad encamped at Marr Zahran, Abbas said, 'Woe to the Quraysh! If Allah's Apostle surprises them in their territory and enters Mecca by force, it means the destruction of the Quraysh.'"

Looking out at the Muslim encampments on the hills surrounding Mecca, "Abu Sufyan said, I have never seen fires like those I see today! These are the fires of men gathered for war. Here is Muhammad, come against us with a force we cannot resist— 10,000 Muslims. If he gets hold of me, he will cut off my head."

Abu Sufyan was captured by a Muslim eager to do just that. He brought him shackled to Muhammad, who demanded: *Tabari VIII:173/Ishaq:547* "Alas, Sufyan, isn't it time for you to admit that I am the Messenger of Allah?' Sufyan replied, 'As to that I have some doubt.'" That wasn't an acceptable answer so Abbas shrieked, "'Woe to you! Submit and recite the testimony that there is no ilah but Allah and that Muhammad is the Apostle of Allah before your head is cut off!'" That was original Islam in action. Submit or die. Testify that there is no ilah but Allah (and that would include Yahweh and Christ) or lose your head. Then recite "Muhammad is the Apostle of Allah" (as opposed to Moses, Peter, Paul, or John) or else...

"Muhammad told Abbas to detain Abu Sufyan by the spur of the mountains in the narrow part of the valley until the troops of Allah passed him." Then Ishaq tells us: *Ishaq:546* "The Apostle punched him in the chest" before he was hauled away.

Tabari VIII:174/Ishaq:548 "Finally, the squadrons of the Messenger, composed of Emigrants and Ansar in iron armor with only their eyes visible, passed by. His company had become great. Woe to you, none can withstand him. It was all due to his prophetic office." The poligious doctrine of Islam had served Muhammad well.

Tradition indicates that Sufyan was freed once the Muslims had taken up their positions surrounding Mecca. *Ishaq:548* "Abu Sufyan ran in haste. When he reached Mecca, he shouted in the sanctuary, 'People of Quraysh, behold Muhammad has come upon us with forces we cannot resist.' Hind [the woman who had lost her son, husband, father, and brother to Islam's butchery at Badr], said, 'Kill this fat greasy bladder of lard! What a rotten protector of the people.' 'Woe to you,' Sufyan replied, 'don't let this woman deceive you, for we cannot resist Islam.'" Muhammad had offered Abu Sufyan a deal he couldn't refuse. Surrender or die. Hind correctly recognized that the Meccan chief had become a traitor.

The prophet was on the warpath. He was now within reach of fulfilling Khadija's aspirations—the Profitable Prophet Plan. The Ka'aba Inc. would soon be his. And all of Mecca would be humbled, humiliated for having rejected him. *Tabari VIII:175* "Heading for Mecca, the Prophet sent Zubayr after the Quraysh. He gave him his banner, and appointed him commander over the cavalry of the Emigrants and Ansar. He ordered: 'Zubayr, plant my banner in the upper part of Mecca. Remain there until I come to you.'"

Ishaq says that the prophet showed his true colors that day. He and his men were festooned in "green and black." Green is symbolic of envy—the root cause of Islam. Black is the color of deceit and death—the result of Islam. Then speaking of the dark spirit that inspired and possessed Muhammad, his biographer reports: *Ishaq:548* "By Allah, the black mass has spread." *Ishaq:548* "Abu Bakr said, 'There is not much honesty among people nowadays.'" One thing led to the other.

Tabari VIII:176/Ishaq:549 "The Prophet sent out his army in divisions. Zubayr was in charge of the left wing. He was ordered to make an entry with his forces from Kuda. Sa'd was commanded to enter with forces by way of Kada. Allah's Apostle said, 'Today is a day for battle and war. Sanctuary is no more. Today the sacred territory is deemed profane [ungodly, irreverent, wicked, and sacrilegious].' When one of the Muhajirs [Emigrants] heard him say this, he warned the Apostle, 'It is to be feared that you would resort to violence.' The Prophet ordered Ali to go after him, to take the flag from him, and fight with it himself."

A less corrupt man suggests that profaning "god" and resorting to violence might not be a very good idea and he was rebuked. The debate between religion and politics, peace and violence, had taken place once again. And as always, Islam's founder made the wrong call. There is no Islam apart from Muhammad and he had spoken. Are you listening?

Bukhari:V4B53N412 "Allah's Apostle said on the day of the conquest of Mecca, 'There is no migration now, only Jihad, holy battle. And when you are called for Jihad, you should come out at once.'" The message is as clear as *Mein Kampf*, as undeniable as Pearl Harbor, as brutal as 9/11: "There is only Jihad." Hitler, interestingly enough, repeated Muhammad's line the morning he invaded Poland: "There is no more emigration now, only war."

This Hadith confirms that Islam's prophet wasn't out being religious. *Muslim: B19N4395* "I said: 'Should I tell you a Hadith from your Traditions?' He gave an account of the Conquest of Mecca, saying: 'Muhammad (may peace be upon him) advanced until he reached Mecca. He assigned Zubayr to his right flank and [killer] Khalid to his left. Then he dispatched Abu with the force that had no armor. They advanced to the interior. The Prophet (may peace be upon him) was in the midst of a large contingent of his fighters. Allah's Messenger (may peace be upon him) said: 'You see the ruffians and the lowly followers of the Quraysh?' He indicated by striking one of his hands over the other that they should be killed. So we went off on his orders and if anyone wanted a person killed; he was slain. No one could offer any resistance. Then [the recently "converted"] Abu Sufyan said: Messenger, the blood of the Quraysh has become very cheap. The Prophet said: 'Kill all who stand in your way.'" If this is the criterion for being God's Messenger, Attila the Hun, Genghis Khan, Lenin, and Adolf Hitler were Prophets, too.

At this point the historian's account conflicts somewhat with Muslim's collection, so we can draw the conclusion that much of this is untrue, as contradiction is proof of deceit. We can view Tabari as an apologist, someone interested in buffing up his prophet's bloody reputation. Or perhaps, Muhammad may have had second thoughts. He may have become more interested in humiliating his prey than devouring them. But either way, we're told Mecca's abandoned orphan dispatched his troops, crying: *Tabari VIII:176* "'Fight only those who fight you.' When Khalid came upon them in the lower part of Mecca, he fought them, and Allah put them to the fight. Zubayr encountered a squadron of Quraysh on the slopes of Kada and killed them." Alas, the debate was moot. "Khalid fought them," and "Zubayr killed them." So..."When the Prophet arrived, the people stood before him to swear allegiance to him, and so the Meccans became Muslims [one who submits]."

And that's all you really need to know about Muhammad and Islam. He had conquered his demon, avenged his childhood. The praise, power, and possessions he had been denied, were now his. Islam had worked like a charm. It had always been about subduing the Meccans, making them pay for abandoning him, making them wish they hadn't kept the family business for themselves. All they needed to do was surrender—to grovel at his feet. Surah 48:28: "You will see them bow and prostrate themselves, seeking Allah's acceptance. On their faces are their marks, the traces of their prostration."

As you no doubt noticed, throughout this disgusting affair, Allah had been nothing more than an implement. The Meccans swore their allegiance to Muhammad. That is what made them Muslims—"one who submits." Allah was used to disavow the treaty, to justify killing, to steal the Ka'aba, and to empower Muhammad.

In conflict with the evidence, Muslim apologists say that the conquest of Mecca was a peaceful affair. Yet many men and women were butchered on this day. *Ishaq:550* "The Muslims met them with their swords. They cut through many arms and skulls. Only confused cries and groans could be heard over our battle roars and snarling."

With his kin confused and in agony: *Tabari VIII:178/Ishaq:550* **"Muhammad ordered that certain men should be assassinated even if they were found behind the curtains of the Ka'aba.** Among them was [a man named Slave-to-Allah] Abdallah bin Sa'd [the Qur'an's one and only scribe]. The reason that Allah's Messenger ordered that he should be slain was because he had become a Muslim and used to write down Qur'an Revelation. Then he apostatized, reverted to being a polytheist, and returned to Mecca." The only man who ever attempted to commit Qur'an surahs to parchment as they left the prophet's lips rejected Islam. That ought to send a shiver up every Muslim's spine. The one and only contemporaneous Qur'an scribe was hunted down by Muhammad. Islam's prophet ordered Muslims to assassinate the first man who attempted to turn the Qur'an into a book. Wow!

Tabari VIII:179 **"Abdallah bin Sa'd fled to Uthman, his brother, who after hiding him, finally surrendered him to the Prophet. Uthman asked for clemency. Muhammad did not respond, remaining silent for a long time. Muhammad explained, 'By Allah, I kept silent so that one of you might go up to him and cut off his head!' One of the Ansar said, 'Why didn't you give me a sign?' Allah's Apostle replied, 'A prophet does not kill by pointing.'"** No. He kills by deceiving, seducing, and coercing. And lest we forget, he kills by establishing false religions—the most virulent and vicious form of mass murder.

Confirming that this had nothing to do with Allah, Muhammad ordered the assassination of another Muslim. *Tabari VIII:179/Ishaq:550* **"Among those who Muhammad ordered killed was Abdallah bin Khatal. The Messenger ordered him to be slain because while he was a Muslim, Muhammad had sent him to collect the zakat tax with an Ansar and a slave of his."** Long story short, the slave disobeyed, so the Muslim tax collector killed him. Rather than face the music by reporting his misdeed to the boss, Abdallah turned tail, rejected Islam, and used his spoils to acquire the talents of a couple of girls. **"The girls used to sing a satire about Muhammad so the Prophet ordered that they should be killed along with Abdullah."** **"Abdallah was killed by Sa'id and Abu Barzah. The two shared in his blood. One of the singing girls was killed quickly but the other fled. So Umar caused his horse to trample the one who fled at Abtah, killing her."**

Muhammad, like his protégé Hitler, suffered from raging insecurities as a result of being abused as a child. Insecure men are enraged by criticism. They will stop at nothing to silence anyone who irritates them. *Ishaq:551* **"Another victim was Huwayrith. He used to insult Muhammad in Mecca. Huwayrith was put to death by Ali."**

The next victim on the "God-Father's" hit list was: *Ishaq:551* **"Miqyas. The Messenger ordered his assassination only because he had killed an Ansar who had killed his brother by mistake and then became a renegade by rejecting Islam."** So much for: **"There should be no compulsion in religion."** **"Miqyas was slain by Numaylah."**

Tabari VIII:180 **"Also among those eliminated were Ikrimah bin Abu Jahl and Sarah, a slave of one of Abd Muttalib's sons. She taunted Muhammad while he was in Mecca."** The prophet had notched his ninth kill in addition to those men and women whose arms and skulls had been cut off in the raid. *Tabari VIII:181* **"According to

Waqidi the Messenger ordered that six men and four women should be assassinated. One of these women was Hind, who swore allegiance and became a Muslim."

His bloodlust satiated, it was time to salve his soul. *Tabari VIII:181* "Having halted by the door of the Ka'aba, the Messenger stood up and said, 'There is no ilah but Allah alone; He has no partner." That's because Muhammad and Allah were one. And now that Muhammad had claimed the founder's share of the Ka'aba Inc., the last thing he wanted was a partner. *Ishaq:553* "Behold, every alleged claim of inherited privilege, blood, wealth, or property is abolished by me except the custody of the Ka'aba and the right to supply water to the pilgrims.'" It's the ultimate confession. The first chance he gets, Muhammad announces that the alleged claims to the Ka'aba, to Qusayy's religious scam, are null and void. Heredity, privilege, property, and wealth will avail the Meccans no longer. Then, Muhammad makes himself an exception—he takes custody of the Ka'aba. It's the fulfillment of Khadija's Profitable Prophet Plan. Islam worked.

Having achieved his life's ambition, the prophet gloats. *Tabari VIII:181* "People of the Quraysh, Allah has taken from you the haughtiness of the Time of Ignorance and its veneration of ancestors.... For now I have humbled you, made you Muslims, submissive unto me.... People of the Quraysh and people of Mecca, what do you think I intend to do with you?" Rub their noses in it, literally. He needed them to grovel at his feet— to bow down and swear allegiance to him. He wanted what he had always craved—to be praised and obeyed, to be empowered, to be enriched. Killing more Meccans wouldn't be any fun. He had done enough of that. No, he wanted to see them *humiliated*.

Tabari VIII:182/Ishaq:553 "The people assembled in Mecca to swear allegiance to the Messenger in submission. They gathered to do homage to the Apostle in Islam. Umar remained below the Prophet, lower than the place where he sat [on his elevated throne], imposing conditions on the people as they paid homage [reverence] to Muhammad, promising to submit and obey. Umar administered the oath, receiving from the Meccans their pledge of allegiance to Muhammad. They promised to heed and obey Allah and His Messenger." And since no one spoke for Allah but Muhammad, there were no orders but Muhammad's and thus no one to be obeyed but him. "That was the oath administered to those who swore allegiance to the Prophet in submission (Islam)."

Tabari VIII:183 "When the Messenger was finished with the men's swearing of allegiance, the women swore allegiance." Having been abandoned by all of the women in his life, Muhammad was particularly harsh on them. "You are swearing allegiance to me on condition that you will associate nothing with Allah [and by default, me].' 'By Allah, you are imposing something on us that you did not impose on the men,' one of the women said." Muhammad paid her no heed and continued his list. When he got to "'Do not kill your children,' the woman said, 'We raised them and you killed them. You know better about killing them than we do.' Umar laughed immoderately at her words." But the Messenger did not think it was funny. The truth hurt. His only response was to call the truth a lie, or at least to sequester the messenger. "He said, 'Do not invent slanderous tales henceforth.'" For a terrorist, Muhammad was very thin-skinned. The woman's line was one of the great comebacks of all time. And she had earned the right to say it. For Muhammad's goons had murdered her father, her brother, her husband, and her son.

"Hind said, 'Bringing slander is ugly. Sometimes it is better to just ignore it.' He said, 'You shall not disobey me in carrying out my orders.' The Messenger told Umar, 'Receive their oath of allegiance and their homage.'" "Now go, for I have accepted your allegiance and praise." The abused became an abuser. And the abused abuser was seeking the one thing he never knew: love.

Before we move on with the narrative, I want you to appreciate the dynamics of this situation. Everything was intensely personal. Mecca was an isolated and shabby collection of mud huts. Every Meccan knew every other Meccan, and most were related. It isn't by chance that Muhammad knew the names of everyone he had killed in each of his raids on the Quraysh, or that his militants were killing their fathers and brothers. This was a family feud, a quarrel over who should inherit Qusayy's scam.

But it was more than that. Islam was a *consequence*. It happened, as did *Mein Kampf*, because a child was denied. I took great pains to expose the true nature of Mecca, Qusayy's adventure, and the circumstances surrounding Muhammad's birth so that you might know *why* the abused boy claimed that he was Allah's Messenger. By sharing what the Qur'an had to say about the pleasures of paradise and the torments of hell, we came to know what pleased and tortured Muhammad—and thus what motivated him. His every word and deed, his Qur'an and Sunnah, were derivatives of the abuse he suffered. And his rage was magnified when his family failed to rescue him. Islam was one man's quest for revenge. Muhammad was powerless, poor, and unloved. Therefore, his Islam was focused on power, money, and sex. It's as simple and sad as that.

Tabari VIII:182/Ishaq:553 "Allah had enabled Muhammad to take the persons of the Quraysh by force, giving him power over them so they were his booty. Their lives were now his spoil, but he emancipated them." No. He enslaved them. That's what an oath of allegiance in submission is all about. But by not selling his possessions—his booty—into slavery, he was perceived as merciful. When a kidnapper stops tormenting victims, they view the reprieve as a form of mercy. In a twisted sort of way it ultimately causes the molested to see their molester as loving. This is why Muslims rewrite their history and revere the man who enslaved them.

But just humiliating the Meccans was insufficient. The "prophet" knew their "praise and homage" was insincere. So he continued to look for love in all the wrong places. *Tabari VIII:187* "The [sixty-two-year old] Messenger of Allah married Mulaykah. She was young and beautiful. One of the Prophet's wives came to her and said, 'Are you not ashamed to marry a man who killed your father during the day he conquered Mecca?' She therefore took refuge from him."

Now that he had conquered his demons, it was time for Muhammad to pay his respects: *Ishaq:552* "When the populace had settled down, Muhammad went to the Ka'aba and compassed it seven times on his camel, touching the Black Stone with a stick. Then he went inside the Temple. There he found a dove made of wood. He broke it in his hands and threw it away." It was perfect. The first idol Muhammad broke was the international symbol of peace.

May the truth be known: *Ishaq:552* "The Ka'aba contained 360 idols which Lucifer had strengthened with lead. The Apostle was standing by them with a stick in his hand, saying, 'The truth has come and falsehood has passed away.' Then he pointed at them with his stick and they collapsed on their backs one after the other." The Ka'aba was a pagan shrine—and a rotten one at that. It had never been anything more. But today, Muhammad helped his dark spirit eliminate the competition. The same stick that had recognized the Black Stone, toppled the *other* false gods.

Ishaq:552 "The Quraysh had put pictures in the Ka'aba including two of Jesus and one of Mary (on both of whom be peace). Muhammad ordered that the pictures should be erased."

So then after stealing the pagan shrine, *Ishaq:554* "Muhammad sat in the mosque and Ali came to him with the key to the Ka'aba asking him to grant his family the rights associated with custodianship." But alas, the Shi'ite didn't measure up. The Mighty Mo handed the key to Uthman for safekeeping. Then, stealing a line from the Scriptures, the dimwitted, delusional degenerate proclaimed: *Ishaq:555* "Mecca is the Holy of Holies." But even Satan knows that's not true, which is why he will desecrate the real "Holy of Holies" on Mount Moriah in the last days.

The blood that had flowed from the broken bodies of the men and women, killed by the Muslims this day, had yet to dry when the Chief Hypocrite said: *Ishaq:555* "It is not lawful for anyone to shed blood in Mecca. It was not lawful to anyone before me and it will not be lawful after me. If anyone should say, "The Apostle killed men in Mecca," say, "Allah permitted his Apostle to do so but He does not permit you.""

In the poetry that accompanied the raid, we discover: *Ishaq:557* "Allah gave you a seal imprinted. [The "Seal of Prophethood" was just a hairy mole.] Allah's proof is great. [Now there's a delusional thought.] I testify that your religion is true and that you are great among men. Allah testifies that Ahmad [the "praised"] is the chosen. You are a noble one, the cynosure [someone who attracts attention or admiration] of the righteous, a prince."

A misguided soul shouted, *Ishaq:558* "Gabriel, Allah's messenger is with us and the Holy Spirit has no equal." Muhammad mistook Lucifer for Gabriel and thus Muslims wrongly believed that Gabriel was the Holy Spirit. One lie simply led to another.

Another orator recited: "Allah said, I have sent an army. Every day they curse, battle and lampoon." Then speaking of the "prince," the poet proclaimed: "He is the pure blessed Hanif, [While Muhammad was once a wannabe Hanif, the Hanifs were never Muslims. They rejected the prophet and his god.] He is Allah's trusted one whose nature is loyalty." Muhammad had just dissolved his vows and reneged on a treaty, so they've got a misguided definition of "trust and loyalty."

Another shared: *Ishaq:560* "We expelled the people and smote them with our swords the day the good Prophet entered Mecca. We pierced their bodies with cuts and thrusts. And we shot them with our feathered shafts. Our ranks went in with lances leveled. We came to plunder as we said we would. We pledged our faith to the Apostle on this day of fear." Now there's an honest Muslim: "We came to plunder as we said we would."

Pledging, piercing, and plundering behind us, Muhammad decided to get religious: *Ishaq:561* "The Apostle sent out troops to the territories surrounding Mecca inviting men to Allah. Among those he sent was Khalid. He was ordered to go as a missionary. Khalid subdued the Jadimah and killed some of them." "Troops" don't deliver "invitations," they deliver ultimatums. Khalid was Muhammad's most vicious terrorist. Calling him a "missionary" is a sick joke. He once defined himself, bragging, "I am the sword of Allah and the sword of His Messenger!"

You'd think that after Muhammad had achieved his life's ambition, he'd tell his militants to lay down their swords. But such was not the case. A man plagued by insecurity can never be satiated. *Tabari VIII:189/Ishaq:561* "Alas for you, Banu Jadimah! It is Khalid. By Allah, after you lay down your weapons, it will be nothing but leather manacles, and after the manacles nothing but the cutting off of heads.' After they had laid down their arms, Khalid ordered that their hands should be tied behind their backs. Then he put them to the sword, smiting their necks, killing them. When the word got to Muhammad as to what Khalid had done, he said, 'I declare that I am innocent of Khalid's deeds.'" Sorry. Muhammad was the responsible party. He preached the sermons and recited the surahs that led to this. His Sunnah and his scripture were clear: good Muslims kill. Jihad is the best deed in Islam. But Muhammad was a weasel. He never accepted responsibility for anything. He had always claimed that it had been his god who had terrorized, robbed, enslaved, and murdered—not him. And Muhammad never disavowed Khalid; he went on to become the Profit's best general and tax collector.

Ishaq:564 "One of the Banu Jadimah [who had been victimized by Khalid] said, 'God take reprisals on the Muslims for the evil they did to us. They stole our goods and divided them. Their spears came at us not once but twice. Their squadrons came upon us like a swarm of locusts. Were it not for the religion of Muhammad, their cavalry would never have attacked." And if not for Muhammad's religion, terrorists wouldn't be terrorizing today.

This brings us to another revealing tale—the assassination of Allah's daughters: *Ishaq:565* "The Apostle sent Khalid to destroy the idol Al-Uzza in the lowland of Nakhlah. The Quraysh used to venerate her temple. When Sulami heard of Khalid's approach, he hung his sword on Al-Uzza, climbed a mountain, and shouted: 'O Uzza, make an annihilating attack on Khalid. Throw aside your veil [Muhammad stole Islam's "veil" from the pagans, too.], and gird up your train. O Uzza, if you do not kill Khalid then bear a swift punishment or become a Christian.'" The custodian of Al-Uzza's temple told his pagan idol to become a Christian. Sure, I believe that. "When Khalid arrived he destroyed her and returned to the Apostle."

Tabari VIII:187 "'I have destroyed it,' he said to Muhammad. 'Did you see anything?' 'No.'

'Then,' Muhammad said, 'go back and kill her.' So Khalid returned to the idol. He destroyed her temple and broke her graven image. The shrine's keeper began saying, 'Rage, O Uzza, display one of your fits of rage!' Whereupon a naked, wailing Ethiopian woman came out before him. Khalid killed her and took the jewels that were on her. Then he went back to Allah's Messenger and gave him a report. 'That was Al-Uzza,' Muhammad said. 'Al-Uzza will never be worshiped again.'" Holy Rock of the Ka'aba! Why didn't somebody put this demented stone worshiper out of his misery? Khalid murdered the wrong idol. He should have slain Muhammad. Islam's lone prophet just confessed that the pagan rock idol Al-Uzza was a real live goddess—she was a naked African woman. It's unfathomable that Muslim militants blow innocents into oblivion based upon this man's testimony.

☆ ✝ ☾ ☄

All bad things must eventually come to an end. Glory be to God. The 5th surah, is the last of a lousy lot. With it, the heavenly fraud was finished.

"The Feast" opens as one would expect from a doctrine named "submission." 005.001 "Believers, fulfill obligations." 005.002 "Believers, violate not the sanctity of the symbols of Allah [the Ka'aba, Crescent Moon, and Black Stone], nor of the sacred month [which Muhammad had violated to acquire Allah's symbols]...fear Allah: for Allah is severe in punishment." Muhammad's mantra never changed.

The Qur'an provides a long list of prohibitions. 005.003 "Forbidden to you are: dead meat, blood, the flesh of swine, and that which has been killed by strangling, or by a violent blow, or by a headlong fall, or by being gored to death; that which hath been eaten by a wild animal... This day those who reject faith give up all hope of your religion. Yet fear them not, fear Me. This day I have perfected your religion and have chosen for you Submission as your religion." Putting the commentary on not eating dead animals aside, the change of voice from "fear Allah for Allah is severe," to "fear Me for I have perfected your religion" is revealing. At best, the shift suggests that the author wasn't skilled at his craft—something that would be inconsistent with God. At worst, it's another confession—Muhammad slipped into first person because he was Allah. And the only thing "perfected" on this day was Muhammad's claim to the Ka'aba. The only thing "religious" about any of this was the tyrant's use of dogma to subdue his people.

The next verse confirms what the Islamic clerics deny and what the American media ignores. Allah is the name of the Islamic god—it was never the Arabic word for "god." 005.004 "Pronounce the Name of Allah: and fear Allah; for Allah is swift in reckoning." Every time you read the word "God" in an Associated Press article emanating from the Islamic world, know that they are unwittingly propagating this deception. Muslims have a perfectly good word for "god" and they use it with great regularity. They say, "There is no ilah but Allah, and Muhammad is His Messenger."

This deception is at the very core of Islam, and thus of Islamic terror. If Allah isn't Yahweh, the Qur'an is rubbish—it's a horrid job of plagiarizing, nothing more. If Allah isn't Yahweh, Muhammad was speaking on his own behalf—and for his own benefit—he could not have been among the line of Biblical prophets. If Allah isn't Yahweh, the god of Islam is fictitious, an impotent mirage. And thus there is no reason to follow his (i.e., Muhammad's) command to prostrate oneself to a false deity.

Ritual is the substance of religion, the control mechanism for obedience, the "opiate of the people." *005.006* "O you who believe, when you prepare for prayer, wash your faces and your hands to the elbows; Rub your heads; and (wash) your feet to the ankles. If you are in a state of sexual discharge, bathe your whole body. But if you are ill, on a journey, come from the privy, or have been in contact with women, and find no water, then take clean dirt and rub it on your faces and hands." But why bother to pray? The very same god that is ordering Muslims to rub dirt in their faces proclaimed: *078.037* "None shall have power to argue with the Lord, none can converse with Him or address Him." If that is true, prayer is a waste of time. If it isn't true, then Allah is a liar, which makes him the wrong god to pray to. And lest I forget, Muhammad just said, "women are dirtier than dirt."

This may be the last surah revealed, but there is no evidence Muhammad and Allah got better with practice. *005.007* "Remember Allah's covenant which He ratified with you, when you said: 'We hear and we obey.' And fear Allah." The "covenant" which they "ratified" was a pledge of allegiance to Muhammad. This is another confession: Allah and Muhammad are one. This man created his god, or at least his god's persona.

And he could have done a better job. The personality Muhammad attributes to Allah is as ugly as his own. *005.010* "Those who reject, disbelieve, and deny Our signs, proofs, verses, and lessons will be companions of Hell-Fire." Returning to familiar religious patter, Muhammad slipped again—Allah was now plural. Could it be that they were a team—partners? Might Allah be to Muhammad what Mickey Mouse was to Walt Disney—a means to fame and fortune? Or did Muhammad know the truth? Did he recognize what he sensed the night all of this began, "I fear that I have been possessed?"

In a desperate attempt to legitimize his counterfeit, Muhammad attempted to usurp Yahweh's authority. Whether deceived, delusional, or just dishonest, these erroneous claims are advanced to cast Allah as Yahweh and to authenticate Islam: *005.012* "Indeed Allah made a covenant of old with the Children of Israel, and We appointed twelve captains among them. And Allah said: 'I am with you if you perform regular prayers [obligatory Islamic worship], pay the zakat tax with regularity [the zakat was from Qusayy, not Abraham], believe in My Messengers...'" Muhammad is referring to himself, not knowing that Yahweh never used humans as "messengers." Angels are Yahweh's messengers; it's what the Hebrew word for "angel" means. Men are called to be rabbis (teachers), prophets, and priests. "...obey and support the Messengers [i.e., fight for them], and loan Allah a beautiful loan [Yahweh didn't need money, but Muhammad did to advance his war machine.], verily I will wipe out from your evils, and admit you to Gardens with rivers flowing; but if any of you, after this [message from Muhammad], resist, you have wandered astray.'" Not only did Muhammad falsely claim that his Islamic mantra was Jewish doctrine, his voice slipped back out of plural to singular (Our to My). He didn't get any better at this, even with practice. Further, the Biblical paradise isn't about rivers, and godly loans aren't equated to forgiveness.

To help us understand these verses, the Noble Qur'an adds: **"The Jews were ordered in the Torah to follow Prophet Muhammad."** It references surah 7:157: **"Those who follow the Messenger (Muhammad), the Prophet who can neither read nor write whom they find written in the Torah (Deuteronomy 18:15) and the Gospel (John 14:16); he commands them to Islam."** We've been through this drill before. While Team Islam couldn't read, I can. And I assure you that no Arab was called a prophet, and no man was called a messenger. But he was right in a way. When the Bible spoke of Satan, it said that he would use prostration, taxation, terror, a new gospel, and a boastful false prophet to deceive mankind.

The Qur'an translators were kind enough to provide the alleged prophetic Torah and Gospel references, so let's check them out. First, Deuteronomy 18:15 "Yahweh [therefore not Allah], your *elohiym* (deity) shall *qum* (raise up or ordain) for you a *nabiy* (man who speaks by inspiration, predicting and teaching) from the *qereb* (midst or heart) of you, from your *awkh* (brethren) [i.e., a Jew] like me. You shall *shama* (hear) him." That was a repudiation of Muhammad's claims, not a confirmation.

A better verse would have been the 18th, but only if taken out of context. "I will raise them up a *nabiy* (an inspired prophet and teacher) from their *qereb* (midst or heart) *awkh* (a brother) like me, and will *nathan* (ascribe) my *dabar* (advice, book, counsel) through his mouth; and he shall speak all I appoint for him. And if anyone fails to heed the words he speaks in my *shem* (name, character, and authority) I will call him to account. But the prophet who *ziyd* (presumptuously) *debar* (subdues (i.e., imposes submission or Islam)) and recites a book in my name which I have not commanded him to utter, or who speaks in the name of other *elohiym* (gods [like Allah]), that prophet shall die."

Team Islam claims John 14:16 contains the Gospel prediction of Muhammad's arrival. So that we don't err by taking Christ's words out of context, I'll begin with the 6th verse: "Iesous [*Strong's Concordance* says "Iesous" was designed to replicate Yahshua or Yehoshua, Hebrew for savior. There was no "Y" in Greek.] said, 'I am ["I Am" means Yahweh] the *hodos* (way or route) and the truth, and the life; no one *erchomai* (appears before or accompanies) the *Pater* (Father), but through Me. [Therefore, not through Muhammad.] If you *ginosko* (know or understand) Me, you *ginosko* My Father also. You have *horao* (seen, experienced, beheld) Him.... He who has *horao* Me has *horao* the

Father. [Yahshua is claiming that he is Yahweh, God in the flesh.] Do you not believe that I am in the Father and the Father is Me? The words that I say to you I do not speak on My own initiative, but the Father *meno* (abiding or dwelling) in Me does His works. *Pisteuo* (trust in or rely upon) Me that I am in the Father and the Father is in Me; otherwise rely upon the account of the works themselves. [Christ performed countless miracles to confirm his deity.] *Amen* (This is trustworthy) what I say to you; he who *pisteuo* (trusts in and relies upon) Me, the works that I do shall he do also; and greater works than these shall he do; because I *poreuomai* (traverse, travel, or go) to the Father. And whatever you *aiteo* (ask, desire, or require) in My *onoma* (name, authority, or character), that will I do, that the Father may be glorified in the Son. If you ask Me anything in My name, I will do it. If you *agapao* (love in a moral sense) Me, you will *tereo* (keep an eye on) My *entole* (prescriptions).'"

That brings us to John 14:16: "And I will ask the Father, and He will *didomi* (give or bestow upon) you *allos* (a) *Parakletos* (Intercessor, Consoler, Advocate, Comforter), that He may *meno* (abide, indwell, or be with) you *aion* (forever); that is the *Pneuma* (Holy Spirit) of Truth, whom the world cannot *lambano* (receive), because it does not *theoreo* (discern, experience, consider, or behold) Him or *ginosko* (know or understand) Him, but you *ginosko* Him because He *meno* (abides or dwells) with you, and will be in you. I will not leave you *orphanos* (bereaved, parentless, comfortless, or fatherless); I will *erchomai* (come back and enter) you. After a little while the world will see Me no more [He's predicting his crucifixion]; but you will *theoreo* (experience, discern, behold, or look upon) Me; because I live [He's predicting his resurrection], you shall live also. [That's the Gospel: we get to live forever with Him because He sacrificed Himself as payment for our sins.] In that day you shall know and understand that I am in My Father, and you in Me, and I in you." The Spirit of the Messiah, Yahshua, is the Holy Spirit, which is Yahweh. They are three manifestations of the same thing, just as our height, width, and depth are three manifestations of our physical body. So, rather than predicting the arrival of an Arab terrorist who is long dead, Yahshua was promising us that his eternal spirit will reside in us. In all of the Bible, it's hard to imagine Islam picking verses more damaging to their claims.

Meanwhile, back in Medina, the mean, angry, intolerant, and racist Lucifer behaved as the Bible predicted: *005.013* **"But because of their breach of their covenant We cursed them, and made their hearts grow hard. They change the words from their (right) places [the illiterate prophet pronounced] and forget and abandon a good part of the message that was sent them. Nor will you cease to find deceit in them."** It's the time bomb of Islam: **"They change the words from their (right) places and forget and abandon a good part of the message that was sent them."** In another translation we find the god who breached the covenant of Hudaybiyah preaching: **"And because of their breaking their covenant We have cursed them and made hard their hearts. They** altered words from their context and they neglected a portion of the message they were reminded of." There is even ambiguity between the translations. The first was written in present tense as if the editing were ongoing. The second was written in past tense as if the alterations were history. So the bottom line is: Islam is clueless. Muhammad didn't know what changed, when it changed, or why it changed because it didn't change.

The Jews told Muhammad that his version of their Torah was preposterous. Christians had done the same with regards to his errant recasting of Yahshua. Both knew that Muhammad wasn't a prophet, that Allah wasn't Yahweh, and that the Qur'an didn't confirm the Judeo-Christian scriptures. This placed Muhammad in an impossible position. Every literate and godly person around was calling him a liar, his god a fraud, and his revelations fictitious.

The Qur'an was clear: Muhammad purchased Talmud stories from the Jews in Medina. When Muhammad "changed the words from their right places and forgot a good part of the message" they held him accountable. They mocked him, rejected him, and disbelieved him. This tormented him.

The Jews knew he hadn't received the surahs from Gabriel or from God. They held the receipts. This is why they had to be eliminated. The evidence, and the people who held it, had to be obliterated before they obliterated Islam. The Nadir and Qurayza were hunted down and slaughtered to keep you and me from knowing the truth. It is why Muhammad mustered the largest raids of his life against Christians.

Muhammad's claim is impossible to defend. The People of the Book, the Children of Israel, the Jews, could not have "changed the words from their right places and forgot a good part of the message" nor could they have "altered words from their context and neglected a portion of the message they were reminded of." Unaltered, unchanged, unforgotten, and rightly placed words scribed on scrolls comprising the Bible were discovered in Qumran dating back to 250 B.C., fully a thousand years before the oldest surviving Qur'an. On them we find Yahweh's name written 6,868 times and Allah's not even once. We find no reference to religion much less to the religion of Abraham, Adam, or Noah. Despite what Allah claims, Lot, Isaac, Jacob, Moses, Joshua, Saul, David, and Solomon weren't Muslims. There is no mention of Mecca or the Ka'aba in the Scriptures, and yet stories of Jerusalem and the Temple abound.

It is absurd to believe that more than a thousand years before an illiterate megalomaniac, a perverted pedophile, a profiteering pirate, a bloodthirsty terrorist, emerged in Arabia that pious Jewish scribes purposely altered the whole of their scriptures just to foil him. The scope of their conspiracy would have had to have gone beyond millions of people plotting together to write Yahweh, Messiah, Jew, Jerusalem, and Temple into the written record and Allah, Muhammad, Muslim, Mecca, and the Ka'aba out—tens of thousands of times. All of Middle Eastern history, four thousand years of it, from Persia to

Egypt, would have had to have been perverted, too, for the Bible to be as errant as the Qur'an requires it to be. Yet no scholar, historian, or archeologist has ever discovered any artifact to suggest that the Bible is in error—not even in the smallest detail. In fact, the opposite is true. So the Qur'an's central claim is impossible. That means Islam cannot possibly be true.

There is a reason Muhammad, Allah, the Qur'an, and Muslim scholars don't explain how, when, or why the Jews **"altered words from their context and neglected part of the message."** They can't, because the Jews didn't.

Some have said, "It doesn't matter what you believe, only that you believe. We all worship the same God and there are many paths to him." That's like saying that it doesn't matter if the bridge over the gorge will carry your weight, only that you believe it will." To say that we all worship the same God is to say that God is schizophrenic. He's so stupid, he can't even remember his own name. And how can opposite paths—"fear and obey" and "choose to love"—lead to the same place? It isn't tolerant to allow or encourage someone to risk his or her life on a bridge that is obviously faulty. Their faith will only get them killed. Faith in the wrong object is deadly.

005.014 **"From those, too, who call themselves Christians, We made a covenant, but they forgot and abandoned a good part of the message that was sent them: so we estranged them, stirred up enmity and hatred among them to the Day of Doom. Soon will Allah show them the handiwork they have done."** The Christian scriptures are comprised of the most prolifically and contemporaneously documented writings in all of antiquity. There are a thousand times more manuscript fragments, dating ten times closer to the events they describe, than there are for the second-best documented book—the *Iliad* by Homer. Further, the central message of the Gospels is salvation through Christ's sacrifice on the cross—something Islam denies. Yahshua preached love, not fear; relationship, not jihad. The Gospel message is as different from the Qur'an as any two books ever written. To say that Allah delivered both messages makes Muhammad too stupid for words —or barring that, as deceitful as the Devil.

You'd think that after twenty-two years of making these things up, Muhammad would have come up with a more believable story. But hey, at least the Bible and Qur'an have one thing in common—they are both focused on the Jews. *005.015* **"O People of the Book! There has come to you Our Apostle, revealing to you much that you used to hide in your Scripture, suppressing and passing over much. There has come to you from Allah a (new) light (Muhammad) and a clear Book [the Qur'an]."** Although it's a detail, it warrants mentioning: not a word of this was *written*. The only man who tried had been murdered. The Qur'an wasn't a book—nor would it become one for quite some time. And even when it was finally committed to paper, it would be poorly written, plagiarized, contradictory, racist, immoral, demented, violent, out of chronological order, devoid of context, and inaccurate. Simply stated: it became the worst book ever written. It inspires the hellish behavior we have come to know as terrorism.

While he was in the mode of shooting himself in the foot, our charlatan said: *005.017* **"Verily they are disbelievers who say, 'The Messiah, son of Mary, is God.'"** This verse condemns both Islam and Christians, but not in the same way. While many Jews question whether Yahshua is the Messiah, there is no question that the Messiah is God. The prophet Isaiah wrote these words about the Messiah six hundred years before he graced our presence: "For unto us a child is born, to us a son is given, and the government will be on his shoulders. And he will be called Wonderful Counselor [the Holy Spirit], Mighty God [Yahweh], Everlasting Father [describes our relationship with Yahweh], Prince of Peace [Yahshua's sacrifice brings peace between a perfect God and sinful man]. He is eternal and will reign on David's throne [Jerusalem] and over his kingdom forever. Yahweh's passion and love will accomplish this." (Isaiah 9:6) By saying that "Jesus" was this Messiah, Muhammad condemned Islam, since Muhammad's message could not be different than, or superior to, God's.

So how does this verse condemn Christians, you ask? Simple. Muhammad had killed every Jew within reach, raided all of Central Arabia, and conquered Mecca. So he redefined his enemy. The "disbelievers" became "Christians." That means each verse that orders Muslims to kill "disbelievers" must now be interpreted as an order to murder "Christians."

Feeling his oats, in the second half of the 17th verse, Muhammad claims Allah told him to…**"Say (O Muhammad): 'Who then has the least power against Allah, if His will were to destroy Christ, the Messiah, the son of Mary, his mother, and everyone else on the earth?"** A self-mutilating god hell-bent on total destruction—it's another Islamic first. But this one is significant. There is nothing Lucifer wants more than to **"destroy Christ, the Messiah,"** for he represents the lone bridge between mankind and Yahweh. Should that bridge be *destroyed*, man would be eternally separated from his creator; Satan wins.

No smarter than the Black Stone which he had the audacity to say was his inspiration, Islam's lone troubadour teaches: *005.018* **"The Jews and the Christians say: 'We are sons of Allah, and his beloved.' Say: 'Why then does He punish you for your sins? Nay, you are but men. He forgives whom He wishes and punishes whom He pleases.'"** Just like Satan, Muhammad was fixated on destroying his competition. Yet to do so he had to rebuke the very doctrines that provided the material for his Qur'an. But he couldn't even get his facts right. While the nature of the *relationship* between man and Yahweh according to the Gospel is father-son, Christians don't go so far as to say that we are Yahweh's biological sons—nor do Jews. Furthermore, and this may come as a surprise, Yahweh doesn't punish men and women for their sins. Sinners who have chosen *not* to accept his gift of eternal life, and who have chosen *not* to form a relationship with him, are kept separate, consistent with their choosing. That place of separation is called Hades or Hell. By definition, hell is where unsaved sinners are and where

Yahweh is not. Therefore, God cannot punish sinners because he will be eternally separated from them. That's what damnation and foresaken means.

Ignorance and arrogance are a deadly combination. This next verse proves Muhammad and his pal Lucifer suffered from both. Moses was a great leader and liberator, but he never considered himself a prophet. Yahweh prepared for Moses the job because he wanted the best-educated Jew on the planet to lead his people. Yahweh wanted to dictate his covenant and instructions to a literate man. *005.020* "Remember, Moses said to his people: 'O my people! Call in remembrance the favor of Allah unto you, when He produced prophets among you and made you kings. [The first Jewish prophet wouldn't write and the first Jewish king wouldn't reign for another 400 years. Moses could not have said what Allah attributes to him.] And He gave you what He had not given to any other among the peoples. O my people! Enter the Holy Land which Allah has assigned unto you [and Muslims want to take from you], and turn not back, for surely you turn back as losers. You will be overthrown, ruined.'" How, pray tell, can Allah be God, Arabs be God's chosen people, Muhammad be God's favored messenger, and Mecca be sacred territory if Yahweh had Moses lead the Jews out of bondage and then ultimately into the "Holy Land" of Israel? Why not Arabia?

This should be a watershed moment for Muslims and those who coddle them in the misguided spirit of political correctness. If you have managed to ignore or justify the mountain of evidence confirming Muhammad's criminal and immoral past, now you have to commit intellectual suicide. Qur'an 5:20 is historically impossible, and thus untrue.

If the Qur'an never mentioned the Bible we would have to render our verdict against Islam based solely upon Allah's demented and delusional nature and Muhammad's grotesque behavior. But the Qur'an refers to the Bible, its patriarchs, and prophets several thousand times. The Qur'an says that the Torah, Psalms, and Gospels were given to Moses, David, and "Jesus" by Allah himself, and yet he can't even plagiarize them intelligently.

You can make several choices without committing intellectual suicide. You can choose to believe that there is *no* God, and that the universe, life, and DNA all spontaneously combusted in perfect order. You can believe that there might be a god, but that he is unknowable. That would make us a chemistry experiment with which he has grown bored. You can believe that *Yahweh* is God, and that he revealed himself in the Scriptures, through Yahshua, and by his spirit, as I do. But you cannot *rationally* believe that Allah, the dimwitted, delusional, and demented spirit depicted in the Qur'an is God.

Thus, Islam's religious credentials are bogus. Since Islam is spiritually bankrupt, the free peoples of the world are actually aiding and abetting murder when they allow an obviously false doctrine to continue poisoning millions of minds. It is a crime to write something that incites men to murder. Islam is criminal. Islam is illegal. Like Nazism, Islam is a scourge on humanity. Islam must be exposed, repudiated, and eliminated.

A dozen verses wallow in a polluted retelling of the Exodus and Cain-and-Abel stories as if one followed the other. They are interesting because they are plagiarized from the same book Muhammad just got through desecrating. Then without an intelligible transition, we leave the Bible and return to the central theme of the Qur'an. In his most pugnacious and inhuman utterance ever, the molested orphan of Mecca orders Muslims to molest the world. *005.033* **"The punishment for those who wage war against Allah and His Messenger and strive after corruption, making mischief in the land [those who refuse to surrender to Islam] is murder, execution, crucifixion, the cutting off of hands and feet on opposite sides, or they should be imprisoned. That is their degradation and disgrace in this world. And a great torment of an awful doom awaits them in the hereafter."**

Qur'an 5:33 is the most torturous verse ever issued in the name of religion. "Making mischief"—a war of words—is sufficient to warrant imprisonment, mutilation, assassination, and crucifixion. Those who reject Islam are to be humiliated and maimed—having their hands and feet cut off—so that they might be disgraced. And this is the last surah. These tortured words weren't abrogated. This is Muhammad's parting shot at the world that had tormented him. The 5th surah is Islam's legacy. And as a result, the Sudan, today's most fundamental Islamic nation, has murdered and mutilated two million Christians over the last fifteen years. Islam remains as Muhammad conceived it.

Muslim apologists argue that repentance prohibits these tortures and that Allah is, "Oft-Forgiving, Most-Merciful." *005.034* **"Except for those who repent (and become Muslims) before you overpower them and they fall into your control. In that case, know that Allah is Oft-Forgiving, Most Merciful."** But consider the price. Consider the context. Repentance requires surrender to Islam, obedience to Muhammad, and the acceptance of his deity. That's why the King Fahd edition of The Noble Qur'an inserted the words "and become Muslims" inside the parenthesis. And capitulation only works if it's done prior to being "overpowered," or conquered by brute force. By ordering his followers to torture men, Allah became nothing more than a molesting thug. He became Muhammad.

Qur'an 5:33-34 provides a synopsis of Islam's message. Men are not persuaded into Islam; they are forced into submission. Allah began his final surah announcing he: **"had chosen submission as man's religion."** Now he is explaining the means he intends to use to impose his choice—terror! Execution, crucifixion, mutilation, and imprisonment are not intellectual or spiritual inducements.

This passage highlights why the real God hates religion. Evil men create perverse and deceitful doctrines to coerce capitulation—to excuse murder and mayhem. And they use religion to control men's lives so that cleric and king might prosper. All the while their coconspirator, Satan, uses religion to deceive mankind, separating us from our creator. The deception, death, and damnation of man is the Devil's life ambition.

Yahweh based his relationship with us on choice. We choose what to believe and in whom to trust. He recognized that love cannot be forced. Submission is the antithesis of the Scriptural message. One cannot love what one fears. (Biblically, the Hebrew *"yare"* means "revere" in reference to God, not fear.) Love cannot be seduced either, as a loving relationship is based upon open disclosure—truth, not deception. This is why Muhammad's cravings were never satisfied. In this regard, Yahweh and Allah could not be more different.

005.035 **"Believers, fear Allah and seek the way to approach Him, striving hard [fighting Jihad] with all your might in His Cause [deception, death, and damnation] that you may be successful. As for the disbelievers [previously defined as Christians], if they had everything on earth, two times over, to give as ransom for the penalty of the Day of Doom, it would never be accepted from them. Theirs will be a painful torment. They will desire to get out of the fire, but they shall not be released from it. They shall have an everlasting punishment."**

The 13th chapter of Paul's first letter to the Corinthians does a better job of explaining why Muhammad failed than any words I could ever write. It serves to expose how dissimilar Muhammad's recital was from Christ's Gospel. The opening line is even prophetic, as Muhammad, the boy who was unloved and never learned to love, claimed to have spoken for angels and to have received his message as a clanging bell: "If I speak with the tongues of men and of angels, but do not have love, I have become a noisy gong, a clanging cymbal. And if I have the gift of prophecy, and know all mysteries and all knowledge; and if I have all faith, so as to remove mountains, but do not have love, I am nothing. If I give all my possessions to feed the poor, and if I deliver my body to be burned, but do not have love, it profits me nothing. Love is patient, love is kind, and is not jealous. Love does not brag and is not arrogant; it does not act unbecomingly. Love does not seek its own, is not provoked, does not take into account a wrong suffered, does not rejoice in unrighteousness, but rejoices in truth. Love bears all things, believes all things, hopes all things, endures all things. Love never fails."

Not fear, fighting, terror, or booty. Neither submission nor obedience. Not painful punishments nor hateful tirades. Love: nothing more, nothing less.

Returning to the Qur'an we discover that Allah prefers torture to love. And while civilized man had advanced three thousand years from the time Hammurabi's laws were first pressed into clay tablets, Allah prefers the Stone Age. Yet it's fitting, as it's where his Black Stone belonged. *005.037* **"The [Christian] disbelievers will long to get out of the Fire, but never will they get out there from; and theirs will be an enduring torture."** *005.038* **"And as to the thief, male or female, cut off his or her hands: a punishment by way of example from Allah. Allah is Mighty, Wise [for a stone]. But if the thief repents after his crime, and amends his conduct, Allah turns to him in forgiveness."** So, if you say you're sorry you can steal all you want.

005.041 **"Messenger, let not those [rejecters and mockers] grieve you. They race each other into unbelief: among those who say 'We believe' with their lips but whose hearts have no** faith." Allah is rebuking the bad Muslims, who like bad Nazis, pretended to go along with the program to keep their heads attached. **"Or it be among the Jews, men who will listen to any lie. They change the context of the words from their (right) times and places."** Muhammad is once again projecting his faults onto the Jews. The Bible is the most historically accurate ancient document the world has ever known. Every story is set within the context of time and place. It is his Qur'an that has no "context" and is devoid of "times and places."

By way of example, I present the second half of the verse: **"They say, 'If you are given this, take it, but if not, beware!' If anyone's temptation is intended by Allah's desires, you have no authority in the least for him against Allah. For such it is not Allah's will to purify their hearts. For them there is disgrace in this world, and in the Hereafter a heavy punishment."** This is gibberish without context.

The most that can be deciphered from the verse is that Allah is once again acting like the Devil. Another translation reads: **"Whomever Allah wants to deceive you cannot help."** It goes on to say: **"Allah does not want them to know the truth because he intends to disgrace them and then torture them."** Lurking behind the veil of Islam is none other than Satan. While that might sound harsh and intolerant, it remains the only rational conclusion. The presentation of Allah's character and ambition in the Qur'an doesn't leave us any other choice. By prostrating themselves to Allah and fighting Jihad in Allah's Cause, Muslims have surrendered to Lucifer; they are doing the Devil's business. While the Qur'anic evidence is overwhelming, the prophet's Sunnah, or example, serves as proof. And the river of blood that has flowed from the mantra of the Black Stone serves as a harsh and vivid confirmation. It isn't by chance that good Muslims are 2000% more violent than the rest of us. It isn't by accident that terror and Islam are irrevocably and undeniably linked. It isn't a coincidence that Allah's enemies are Yahweh's chosen.

Muhammad, speaking of the Jews he had plundered, said on behalf of the spirit that possessed him: *005.042* **"They are fond of listening to falsehood, of devouring anything forbidden; they are greedy for illicit gain!"** If ever a verse was guilty of projecting one's own faults upon a foe, this is it. It defines hypocrite.

The man/god went on to lie: *005.044* **"It was We who revealed the Torah (to Moses). By its standard the prophets judged the Jews, and the prophets bowed (in Islam) to Allah's will, surrendering. For the rabbis and priests: to them was entrusted the protection of Allah's Scripture Book, and they were witnesses of it. Therefore fear not men, but fear Me, and sell not My revelations for a miserable price."** How do you suppose that a god who jumps between first and third person, who can't remember his name, or if he is singular or plural, could have revealed the Torah? And if he revealed it, why couldn't he protect it from change? More important, since Allah claims that his Qur'an was written before time began, and that it was his perfect revelation, why did he bother with the Torah? Moreover, if Allah was such a great and prolific "revealer," why did Muhammad have to buy his scripture "revelations for a miserable price?"

Continuing to prove his lack of divinity, Allah proclaims: *005.046* **"And in their footsteps We sent Jesus, the son of Mary, confirming the Law that had come before him: We sent him the Gospel: therein was guidance and light, and confirmation of the Law that had come before him: a guidance to those who fear Allah."** God has to be smarter than me. The universe is too complex and magnificent to have been formed by a nincompoop. The Gospels were written *about* Christ, not given to him. The first, Mark, was written twenty years after the resurrection. The last, John, was composed some thirty years later. And since the Gospel fulfills the Torah by confirming its prophecies, why does the Qur'an reject that fulfillment in its entirety, and why does it contradict its central message? It is as if the author of the Qur'an were ignorant of the Scriptures he was trying to plagiarize and condemn.

While I do not take my direction from the former Meccan moon god, the following advice is sound up to a point: *005.047* **"Let the people of the Gospel judge by what Allah has revealed therein. If any fail to judge by (the light of) what Allah has revealed, they are (no better than) those who rebel."** If I were a Muslim, I would question why my god, who claims to have personally created "Jesus" by breathing his spirit into him, and then "given him the Gospel," knows nothing of him—or it. While I know why he is ignorant of such things, the paradox ought to trouble Muslims. (The answer: there were few, if any, Christians living in Medina from whom to purchase or purloin Gospel quotes.)

While I have shared many excerpts from the Scriptures in an effort to challenge the foolishness of the Qur'anic corruptions of them, I haven't had to delve into the New Testament in rebuttal simply because Muhammad didn't know it well enough to twist its accounts. His Gospel presentation was wholly his own. In one surah Muhammad makes up a story about Mary being adopted and attributes Moses' father to her; in another he says that Jesus babbled in the cradle and was resurrected but not crucified. In the Hadith, he claims that Christ raised Ham and discussed the problem of poop in the Ark. Muhammad didn't plagiarize or twist these stories; he simply imagined them.

005.048 **"To you [Christians] We sent the Scripture in truth, confirming the scripture that came before it, and guarding it in safety: so judge between them by what Allah has revealed."** Mission accomplished. We *have* judged between them and found Muhammad guilty of counterfeiting scripture. And to add insult to injury, he had his dimwitted deity say that he **"sent the Scripture in truth...and guarded it safely."** If that's true, the Gospel and the Qur'an should be the same, not polar opposites.

Fearing that he had made a fool of himself, Muhammad added a caveat after his second challenge. *005.049* **"And this (He commands): Judge between them by what Allah has revealed and follow not their [Christian] desires, but beware of them lest they beguile you, seducing you away from any of that which Allah hath sent down to you. And if they turn you away [from being Muslims], be assured that for their crime it is Allah's** purpose to smite them. Truly most men are rebellious." This is a very strange passage since Allah claims he revealed the Christian Gospels. Yet in the same breath he tells Muslims not to follow the Christians who have based their faith on them. If Allah had revealed the Gospels, their message could not beguile and seduce Muslims away from Islam. So somebody isn't telling the truth.

If I've told you once, I've told you a thousand times…005.051 "Believers, take not Jews and Christians for your friends. They are but friends and protectors to each other." You'd think that Allah would occasionally get something right. But this is another ignorant mistake. Jews and Christians were antagonistic when this was "revealed," and they remained so for another thousand years. 005.057 "Believers, take not for friends those who take your religion for a mockery or sport, a joke, whether among those who received the Scripture before you or among those who reject Faith; but fear Allah." In other words, don't hang out with rational people. This would be funny if they weren't killing us.

The Islamic god believes he turned Jews into apes and pigs. 005.059 "Say: 'People of the Book! Do you disapprove of us for no other reason than that we believe in Allah, and the revelation that has come to us and that which came before?' Say: 'Shall I point out to you something much worse than this by the treatment it received from Allah? Those who incurred the curse of Allah and His wrath, those of whom He transformed into apes and swine." A Jew must have said that a swine had made monkeys of men.

005.064 "The Jews say: 'Allah's hands are fettered.'" As do I. If Allah is Yahweh, why can't he do any of the miracles with which he so vividly demonstrated his power throughout the Bible? Have Allah's hands become fettered?

For a "new" religion, Islam sure seems fixated on old ones. And for a "tolerant" dogma, it's overly intent on condemning others. Muhammad protests: "Be their hands tied up and be they accursed for the blasphemy they utter. Nay, both His hands are widely outstretched, giving [Muslims Jewish booty] as He pleases. Amongst them we have placed enmity and hatred till the Day of Doom. Every time they kindle the fire of war, Allah does extinguish it. But they strive to do mischief on earth." It had been 1500 years since the Jews had fought offensively, and it would be nearly that long before they would fight again. Banished from the Promised Land by Assyrians, Babylonians, and most recently Romans, the Jews were just trying to survive, to get along. They were among the least "mischievous" people on the planet. It was Muhammad's militants who spiked the mischief scale. They had lied and looted in the process of "kindling the fires of war" seventy-five times in nine bloody years.

005.065 "If only the People of the Book had believed, We should indeed have blotted out their evil deeds [of rejecting and mocking] and admitted them to the Gardens of Bliss." Not knowing enough to be lucid, Muhammad takes a lame swipe at assuaging his conscience by inferring that the plight of the Jews wasn't his fault. "If only they had observed the Torah, the Gospel, and all the revelation that was sent to them from their Lord, they would have enjoyed happiness from every side." While it's true

Jews would have been "happier" if they had followed their Torah and accepted the Gospel, Allah makes a fool of himself by saying it because he repudiates the Torah, dismantling the Ten Commandments, and his prophet's behavior was the antithesis of the message proclaimed in the Gospels. As a result, the Jews were besieged on every side by the Islamic terrorists who, in the name of Allah, stole their homes and possessions, murdered their men, raped their women, and enslaved their children.

Goebbels proposed a theory which states: "If a lie were repeated often enough and long enough, it would come to be perceived as truth." It's true today; virtually everyone—Muslims, Christians, and Jews, political leaders, media spokespeople, and common folk—are befuddled by Islam. They view Qusayy's Ka'aba Inc. and Khadija's Profitable Prophet Plan as a religion. They think that it's peaceful and tolerant because other religions are peaceful and tolerant—it's innocence by association. They believe that Allah is God and that Islam is one of many paths to him. As a result, over a billion Muslims live in religious, economic, intellectual, and political poverty, and five billion others live in fear of them. Islamic terrorism runs amuck because Islam runs amuck. And Islam runs amuck because non-Muslims tolerate it.

005.067 **"Messenger, deliver the (message) which has been sent to you from your Lord. If you do not, you will not have delivered His message. And Allah will protect you from people."** The opening lines are too dumb for words, much less scripture. The last is too sinister to be believed. Why does Allah need to promise to protect his delivery boy? Is Muhammad a coward? Is he so insecure that mocking, ridicule, and rejection have overwhelmed him? Or is the messenger afraid that he who lives by spewing poison will die by being poisoned?

Ever the hypocrite, Allah's poison pen proclaims: *005.068* **"Say: 'O People of the Scripture Book! You have no ground to stand upon unless you observe the Taurat [Torah], the Injeel [Gospel], and all the revelation that has come to you from your Lord [Muhammad's recitals].' It is the revelation [of the Qur'an] that comes to you from your Lord (Muhammad), is certain to increase their rebellion and blasphemy. But grieve you not over (these) unbelieving people."** It's another Islamic first; Allah's scripture *causes* people to rebel against God. And the reason is that Muhammad never understood the Torah's place in the Hebrew Scriptures or the Gospel's role in the Christian Bible, much less their relationship one to the other.

Calling Allah "God" was blasphemy of the first order, but for rebellion, consider this: from the dawn of recorded history (2500 B.C.) to the creation of Islam (620 A.D.) Arabs were among the freest, most self-reliant, tolerant, and least warlike people on earth. There is no record of them conquering or looting neighboring nations. Then everything changed. In the first ten years of the Islamic Era, under the leadership of Muhammad, they initiated scores of terrorist campaigns—pillaging their way to infamy. The following year, Abu Bakr's War of Compulsion forever sealed their fate. He forced every Arab into submission. They lost their freedom, self-reliance, tolerance, and peaceable nature forever. Over the next six years, Arabs—now Muslims—fought six bloody crusades conquering what is today Yemen, Syria, Israel, Jordan, Egypt, Turkey, Iraq, and Iran. They would go on wielding swords over the necks of civilized people from Spain to India. Their victims were always given three choices: surrender and capitulate (accept Islam and pay the zakat tax); surrender and pay the jizyah protection tax in humility; or die. Islam was the sole impetus for the "increase in rebellion." And lest we forget, the collection of spoils and taxes was the motivation. So I challenge you—even dare you—to explain this change of heart any other way.

Muslims take this next verse out of context and use it to promote Islam as peaceful and tolerant. _005.069_ **"Those who believe (in the Qur'an), those who follow the Jewish (Scriptures), and the Sabians and the Christians—whoever believes in Allah and the Last Day, and does right—on them shall be no fear, nor shall they grieve."** The Concise Encyclopedia of Islam says of the Sabians: "A people named in the Qur'an along with Christians, Jews and Zoroastrians (Qur'an 22:17), as having a religion revealed by Allah.... They were Hellenistic pagans with roots to the ancient Babylonian religions." Therefore, since the Sabians worshiped the Greek gods and followed the occult practices of Babylon, it would make Allah Satan if he revealed their religion.

Returning to the core of the verse we discover that by including the **"whoever believes in Allah"** segment between the dashes—Muhammad dashed any semblance of tolerance. Muslims were the first believers listed, thus the dashed portion was established to require Islamic submission from the others to qualify for **"no fear or grief."** Additionally, in context, this verse contradicts any notion of Islamic tolerance. The previous verse said that Jews were blasphemers. Ten verses earlier they were called "apes and swine." And throughout, Christians have been defined as "disbelievers," thus evoking the wrath of the 8th and 9th surahs—the Qur'an's War Manifestos.

Before we press on, I'd like you to consider the 98th surah—one revealed about this same time. Allah said Christianity and Judaism were **"false religions."** _098.001_ **"Those among the People of the Book, who disbelieve and are idolaters, would never have been freed from their false religion if the Clear Proofs had not come to them. An Apostle of Allah came reading out of hallowed pages, containing firm decrees.... They were commanded to serve Allah exclusively, fulfilling their devotional obligations, and paying the zakat. Surely the unbelievers and idolaters from the People of the Book will abide in the Fire of Hell. They are the worst of creatures."**

So I pose this question to the world's cadre of Islamic scholars: if Qur'an 5:69 is testimony to Islamic tolerance, why does Qur'an 98:1 contradict it? Further, if Allah was Yahweh, why isn't there an order for fighting in his cause, for paying the zakat tax, for observing holy months, for performing devotional obligations, for Ramadhan fasting, or for participating in the hajj pilgrimage in the Ten Commandments? And while we are on the subject of Exodus 20, most everything Muhammad did violated Yahweh's commands. How could that be if the Qur'an confirmed the Torah? How can Judeo-Christianity be a false religion if Allah revealed it and then confirmed it?

Preoccupied with the Jews, the Arab god attacks them again: 005.070 **"We took a solemn pledge from the Children of Israel and sent messengers to them; but every time a messenger came bringing something that did not suit their mood—they called one an impostor, another they slew. They imagined that there would be no trial (or punishment); so they became willfully blind and deaf."** Muhammad is inferring that the Jews called him an "imposter" and that they "slew" Christ. But that's a problem for Islam because the Qur'an claims "Jesus" wasn't killed and history confirms that while he was crucified, the Jews didn't do it.

These next two verses, combined with Qur'an 5:17 and 98:1, condemn Christians to endure the cutting edge of Islamic terror—forever. Throughout the Qur'an's most violent surahs (4, 5, 8, 9, 33, 47, 48, 59, 60, and 61) Muhammad used the words "infidel," "unbeliever," and "disbeliever" to describe his enemy. Then in the 5th surah, the prophet defined his terms. "Infidels, unbelievers, and disbelievers" become Christians; and thus they inherited the legacy of Islam's sword.

While it was ingenious and efficient, it was also transparent and immoral. Muhammad had robbed, enslaved, and killed every significant Jewish settlement in Arabia. After enduring ten years of terror, the Quraysh had surrendered, as had most every Arab town within Islam's reach. There was nothing left to steal. But having turned self-sufficient and peaceful men into bloodthirsty pirates, Muhammad needed a new enemy.

So...005.072 **"They are surely infidels who blaspheme and say: 'God is Christ, the Messiah, the son of Mary.' But the Messiah only said: 'O Children of Israel! Worship Allah, my Lord and your Lord.'"** Now that the Qur'an has brought the 14th chapter of John's Gospel to our attention, we know that Christ, the Messiah, claimed that he was God. So Allah is doing what he does best: lie. **"Lo! Whoever joins other gods with Allah or says He has a partner, Allah has forbidden Paradise, and the Hell Fire will be his abode. There will for the wrong-doers be no one to help."** 005.073 **"They are surely disbelievers who blaspheme and say: 'God is one of three in the Trinity,' for there is no ilah (god) except One, Allah. If they desist not from saying this (blasphemy), verily a grievous penalty will befall them—the disbelievers will suffer a painful doom."**

With that said, "Christian" must now be substituted for "infidel" and "disbeliever" in every verse commanding Muslims to fight, kill, terrorize, plunder, or enslave. "Must" because of Qur'anic abrogation. Surah 2:106 proclaims: **"Whenever We cancel a verse or throw it into oblivion, We bring one which is better."** The 5th surah was the last handed down and thus its commands and definitions abrogate all others. The result is as clear as the skies over New York at 8:45 A.M. E.D.T., the 11th of September 2001. I'm sorry to be the bearer of such bad news, but this is why Muslims kill Americans. They believe we are Christians.

The prophet-less profit, the miracle-less apostle, the illiterate messenger of "scripture" felt the need to disparage the Messiah and his mission once more. *005.075* **"The Messiah, Christ, the son of Mary, was no more than a messenger; many were the messengers that passed away before him. His mother was a woman of truth. They had to eat their food. See how Allah does make His signs clear to them; yet see in what ways they are deluded!"** Speaking of deluded, the Qur'an previously revealed that "Jesus" didn't "pass away." We were told that Allah raised him. *004.157* **"'We [Jews] killed the Messiah, Jesus,' but they killed him not, nor crucified him. It appeared so to them (as the resemblance of Jesus was put over another man and they killed that man). Nay, Allah raised him up unto Himself. Those who differ with this version are full of doubts. They have no knowledge and follow nothing but conjecture. For surely they killed him not."**

The impotent Islamic god had the nerve to grumble: *005.076* **"Say: 'Will you serve something which has no power either to harm or benefit you?'"** This is followed by something that, considering the context of the Islamic Hadith, may be the most hypocritical statement yet spoken. *005.077* **"Say (Muhammad): 'People of the Book! Exceed not in your religion the bounds of what is proper, trespassing beyond truth, nor follow the vain desires of people who erred in times gone by, who led many astray."**

Rotten to the bitter end, the Qur'an protests: *005.078* **"Curses were pronounced on the unbelievers, the Children of Israel who rejected Islam, by the tongues of David and of Jesus because they disobeyed and rebelled."** *005.080* **"You see many of them allying themselves with the Unbelievers [other translations read: "Infidels"]. Vile indeed are their souls. Allah's wrath is on them, and in torment will they abide."** *005.081* **"If only they had believed in Allah, in the Prophet, and in what had been revealed to him."** *005.082* **"You will find the Jews and disbelievers [defined as Christians in 5:73] the most vehement in hatred for the Muslims."** Not only are Jews and Christians "vile" according to Allah and thus destined for eternal torment, their leaders, "David and Jesus" will be the ones cursing them. Weird.

The last half of the 82nd verse concludes with these contradictory words. It's as if Muhammad hadn't been listening to his own vitriolic diatribe. **"And nearest among them in affection to the Believers will you find those who say, 'We are Christians,' because amongst these are priests and monks, men devoted to learning who have renounced the world, and are not arrogant."** I can almost hear the False Prophet of Revelation fame, the Pontiff of the one-world religious order that sweeps the globe during the last days, quoting this verse (out of context, of course).

And how, prey tell, can Christians be **"nearest in affection to the Believers"** if: *005.051* **"Believers, take not Jews and Christians for your friends. They are friends to each other. He who befriends them becomes (one) of them. Lo! Allah guides not wrongdoing folk?"** Or how do priests and monks **"renounce the world"** if: *009.034* **"Believers, there are indeed many among the priests who in falsehood devour the wealth of mankind and wantonly debar (men) from the way of Allah. They who hoard gold and silver and spend it not in Allah's Cause, unto them give tidings of a painful doom?"**

Still speaking of Christians—the people he had gleefully called vile and condemned to hell, the schizophrenic god lies: *005.083* **"And when they listen to the revelation received by this Messenger, you will see their eyes overflowing with tears, for they recognize the truth. They pray: 'Our Lord! We believe. Write us down among the witnesses."** I didn't think they had hallucinogenic drugs back then, but somebody must have spiked the water. In this very same surah, we were told: *005.014* **"From those who call themselves Christians, We made a covenant, but they forgot and abandoned a good part of the message that was sent them: so we estranged them, stirred up enmity and hatred among them to the Day of Doom. Soon will Allah show them the handiwork they have done."** Team Islam is very confused.

005.084 **"'What reason can we [Christians] have not to believe in Allah and the truth which has come to us, seeing that we long for our Lord to admit us to the company of the good people?'"** I'll take a stab at that one. Good Muslims are killing Christians because their messenger and his god commanded them to wipe them out to the last. The Qur'an denies Christ's entire mission, his sacrifice, and deity. Then there's the fact that Muhammad was a rotten scoundrel.

005.086 **"But those who reject Islam and are disbelievers, denying our Signs and Revelations—they shall be the owners of the Hell Fire."** Hey, at least Muhammad's Muslims won't steal *everything* from the Christians.

Coming from a man whose father was spared by divination of arrows, a man who cast lots to determine which wife would accompany him on terrorist raids, one who kissed and fondled a Stone, and one who claimed that the rivers of paradise flowed with wine, this verse is entertaining. *005.090* **"Believers! Intoxicants and gambling, (dedication of) stones, and (divination by) arrows, are an abomination. They are Satan's handwork. Shun such (abomination) that you may prosper. Satan's plan is to excite hostility and hatred between you with wine and gambling, and hinder you from the remembrance of Allah, and devotional obligations."** How then can Allah not be Satan if he's responsible for making the rivers of paradise flow with wine? How can Allah not be Satan if his Qur'an **"excites hostility and hatred?"** How can Allah not be Satan if young Muslim boys are commanded to buy into the unholiest of bargains—gambling their lives away betting on martyrdom? How can Allah, the Black Stone, not be Satan if the dedication of stones is Satanic?

To hell with truth, Islam was about obedience. *005.092* **"Obey Allah and obey the Messenger, and beware!"** And Islam was about war: *005.094* **"Believers, Allah will make a test for you in the form of a little game in which you reach out your hands for your lances that He may know who fears. Any who fails this test will have a grievous penalty, a painful punishment."** According to Allah, suicide bombers aren't terrorists; they are just boys playing "games." And Allah's final test for determining salvation or damnation is based upon whether men reach for their lances.

While this verse starts off benign, listen to how it ends. *005.095* **"Believers! Kill not game while in the sacred precincts or in pilgrim garb. If any of you do so intentionally,** the compensation is an offering, brought to the Ka'aba, of a domestic animal equivalent to the one he killed...that he may taste the penalty of his deed. Allah forgives what is past: for repetition Allah will exact a penalty. For Allah is the Lord of Retribution."

Forgetting for a moment that Adam and Abraham are both credited with making the Ka'aba, how can there be asylum during the "Sacred Months" when Muhammad launched his conquest of the Ka'aba during Ramadhan and proceeded to assassinate a dozen or more souls hiding behind its covers? 005.097 "Allah made the Ka'aba, the Sacred House, an asylum of security for men, as also the Sacred Months...." 005.098 "Know you that Allah is severe in punishment and that Allah is Oft-Forgiving, Most Merciful." Since by definition a hypocrite is one who says one thing and does another, Allah has just defined himself. And guess what? He's exactly like Muhammad.

This next passage opens with dialog beneath Sesame Street. 005.100 "Say: 'Not equal are things that are bad and things that are good, even though there is an abundance of bad to dazzle, please, and attract you; so be careful and fear Allah, O you who understand (so) you may prosper.'" Muslims "prosper" according to Allah because "booty is lawful and good." (8:69)

There are two Qur'anic verses in particular that condemn Muslims to live in religious, economic, intellectual, and civil poverty. One says: 004.089 "If they turn back from Islam, becoming renegades, seize them and kill them wherever you find them." The other commands: 005.101 "Believers! Do not ask questions about things which if made plain and declared to you, may vex you, causing you trouble." 005.102 "Some people before you did ask such questions, and on that account they lost their faith and became disbelievers." It's true; the Qur'an is so incomprehensible, so obviously fraudulent, so mean spirited, anyone who even questions it loses their faith. So we need to give Muslims the freedom to ask questions and to make choices.

Questioning minds will reject the Qur'an because it says things like this: 005.104 "When it is said to them: 'Come to what Allah has revealed; come to the Messenger.' They say: 'Enough for us are the ways we found our fathers following.' What! Even though their fathers were void of knowledge and guidance?" Qusayy founded the religious scam that Muhammad promoted as Islam. How could he have been void of guidance if Allah was his god, the Ka'aba was his shrine, the hajj and umrah were his pilgrimages, the prostration, fasts, and the sacred months were his rituals, the zakat tax his means, and holy war his method?

But there was a man without knowledge. His name was Muhammad. 005.109 "One day Allah will gather the messengers together, and ask: 'What was the response you received (from men to your teaching)?' They will say: 'We have no knowledge.'" So all of Allah's messengers will be called together and they will say that they know nothing.

The same surah that says: "Disbelievers are those who say that God is the third in the Trinity," now proclaims: 005.110 "And God will say: 'O Jesus! Recount My favor to you and to your mother. Behold! I strengthened you with the Holy Spirit so that you spoke to the people in the cradle and in the prime of life.'" That's the Trinity: God (Yahweh), Jesus (Yahshua), and the Holy Spirit (Yahweh's/Yahshua's Spirit). So I guess that makes the Islamic god a disbeliever. Can't say that I blame him.

"Behold! I taught you the law and the judgment, the Torah and the Gospel." Actually, Yahweh revealed the Torah, the Gospels are the good news of freedom from judgment, and they were written about him, not taught to him. But even Babe Ruth struck out sometimes.

Not finished swinging wildly away, Allah quotes an obscure and irrelevant story from an Egyptian text falsely attributed to Thomas. "And behold, you made out of clay, as it were, the figure of a bird and you breathed into it and it became a bird by My permission." Trivia aside, Muhammad knew that his god had an embarrassing problem—one he didn't want to talk about—impotence. He couldn't do a miracle. So to help his god out, Muhammad claimed that the Messiah's miracles were really performed by Allah. "And you healed those born blind by My permission and the lepers by My permission. And behold! You raised forth the dead by My permission." Muhammad not only stole Jewish scripture, possessions, homes, property, wives, and children; he stole their miracles, too.

But that was enough. He wanted nothing to do with Christ's sacrifice. According to the Qur'an, that crucifixion thing never happened. "And behold! I did restrain the Children of Israel from harming you when you came with clear proofs." Then to make Christ's situation somewhat analogous to his own, Muhammad said: "And the unbelievers among the Jews said: 'This is nothing but pure magic.'"

Delusional to the last breath, Allah claims that Christ's disciples were Muslims. I wonder why they didn't say so? *005.111* "And behold! I inspired the disciples to have faith in Me and My Messenger. They said, 'We are Believers, and bear witness that we prostrate ourselves to Allah as Muslims.'" Surely you jest.

After claiming credit for Christ's best miracles, Allah says that miracles aren't what they're cracked up to be. *005.112* "Behold! The disciples, said: 'O Jesus, can your Lord send down to us a table well laid out from heaven?' Said Jesus: 'Fear Allah, if you have faith.'" In other words, "No." "When the disciples said: 'O Jesus, son of Mary, is your Lord able to send down for us a table spread with food from heaven?' He said: "Observe your duty to Allah, if you are true believers.'" No miracles for you.

Since the Qur'an claims Christ performed miracles, this is senseless: *005.113* "They said: 'We only wish to eat thereof to satisfy our hearts, and to know you have told us the truth. We want to witness a miracle.' Said Jesus, the son of Mary: 'O Allah our Lord! Send us from heaven a table well laid out, that there may be a feast, a Sign from you."

Ever in character Allah promises and threatens: *005.115* "Allah said: 'I am going to send it down unto you, but if any of you after that disbelieves, resisting Faith [Islam], I will punish him with a torment such as I have not inflicted on any of my creatures, man or jinn.'" The "Feast" for which this surah is named was never described or even mentioned again. Which means it never happened. But, just three verses from the Qur'an's parting salvo Allah tells Christians "I will punish them with a torment such as I have not inflicted on any of my creatures." Pain and punishment, thievery and terror, savagery and slavery, these are the things at which Allah excels. In that regard, nothing has changed. Twenty-two years earlier, the first Qur'an revelations were demonic to a fault, fixated on hellish tortures. One hundred and fourteen surahs later, we haven't progressed very far. We are still mired in the realm of doom and damnation.

As you know by now Muhammad was easily confused. Even the Qur'an said that those around him claimed, **"He was all ear and believes everything he hears."** Well, he must have heard some Catholic say a "Hail Mary" and came to the conclusion that Christians believed she was a goddess. *005.116* **"And behold! Allah will say: 'O Jesus, the son of Mary! Did you say unto men, worship me and my mother as two gods besides Allah?' He will say: 'Glory to You! Never could I utter what I had no right.'"** Wouldn't you know that the man who fancied himself the Messiah, would finish his recital uttering what he had no right.

The second to last verse remains focused on Yahshua, converting him into a Muslim: *005.117* **"I only said what You (Allah) commanded me to say: Worship Allah [Lucifer], my lord and your Lord."** Then, without benefit of the crucifixion, Yahshua was resurrected: **"I was a witness over them while I dwelt amongst them but you took me up."** The Noble Qur'an goes on to say: **"This is a great admonition and warning to the Christians of the whole world."** But once again, salvation is capricious and based upon "god's" whim, not man's choice: *005.118* **"If You punish them, they are Your slaves. If You forgive them, you are the All-Mighty."**

Having damned Christians and Jews, having condemned their Scripture, having ordered Muslims to murder and mutilate them, and having converted David and Jesus to Islam, the Qur'an's final verse explained what motivated Muhammad to perpetrate Islam in the first place: *005.119* **"Allah will say: This is the day on which the Muslims will profit from Islam..."**

Since Islam began by corrupting the Bible, I'd like to give Yahweh the last word: "For what does it profit a man to gain the whole world, and forfeit his soul?" (Mark 8:36)

Now that we have read Allah's war manifesto—the Qur'an—it's time to read Muhammad's. Islam's most respected collector of Hadith entitles the prophet's terrorist dogma: **"Fighting In Allah's Cause—Jihad."** The first Hadith says it all: *Bukhari:V4B52N44* **"A man came to Allah's Apostle and said, 'Instruct me as to such a deed as equals Jihad in reward.' He replied, 'I do not find such a deed.'"** If the best thing a Muslim can do is fight Jihad in Allah's Cause then Islam is the inverse of peaceful. It is a call to war. Maybe somebody should tell the Associated Press —or the White House. The Hadith goes on to define Jihad as **"Muslim fighting."** It claims Jihad is better than obligatory religious ritual. **"Can you, while the Muslim fighter has gone out for Jihad, enter a mosque to perform prayers without ceasing and**

fast forever?' The man said, 'No one can do that.'" So Jihad reigns supreme.

Bukhari:V4B52N46 "I heard Allah's Apostle saying, 'The example of a Mujahid [Muslim fighter] in Allah's Cause—and Allah knows best who really strives in His Cause—is like a person who fasts and prays without ever stopping. Allah guarantees that He will admit the Mujahid in His Cause into Paradise if he is killed, otherwise He will return him to his home safely with rewards and war booty.'" Not only is fighting better than prayer and fasting, jihad is a win-win game. If you die, you get heavenly booty. If you live, you get earthly booty. With a religion like this, who needs Billy Graham?

Bukhari:V4B52N50 "The Prophet said, 'A single endeavor of fighting in Allah's Cause is better than the world and whatever is in it.'" Jihad, therefore, is more important than all of the Five Pillars of Islam combined. It's why Muslims are terrorists.

The Qur'an issued its first order to fight Jihad in the 190th verse of the 2nd surah. The translators of the Noble Qur'an wanted to make certain Muslims understood what "Fighting in the Way of Allah" meant. So they provided this definition which is derived entirely from the Qur'an and Sunnah: "Jihad is holy fighting in Allah's Cause with full force of numbers and weaponry. It is given the utmost importance in Islam and is one of its pillars. By Jihad Islam is established, Allah's Word is made superior (which means only Allah has the right to be worshipped), and Islam is propagated. By abandoning Jihad Islam is destroyed and Muslims fall into an inferior position; their honor is lost, their lands are stolen, their rule and authority vanish. Jihad is an obligatory duty in Islam on every Muslim. He who tries to escape from this duty, or does not fulfill this duty, dies with one of the qualities of a hypocrite."

Bukhari:V4B52N63 "A man whose face was covered with an iron mask of armor came to the Prophet and said, 'Allah's Apostle! Shall I fight or embrace Islam first?' The Prophet said, 'Embrace Islam first and then fight.' So he embraced Islam and was martyred. Allah's Apostle said, 'A Little work, but a great reward.'" Even Muhammad agrees: there is a causal relationship between Islam and terror. One leads to the other.

Bukhari:V4B52N65 "A man came to the Prophet and asked, 'A man fights for war booty; another fights for fame and a third fights for showing off; which of them fights in Allah's Cause?' The Prophet said, 'He who fights that Allah's Word, Islam, should be superior, fights in Allah's Cause.'" Muhammad just defined Jihad as Holy War. And he declared it on all non-Muslims.

The motivation for martyrdom has always been as shocking as a suicide bomber's belt. *Bukhari:V4B52N53* "The Prophet said, 'Nobody who dies and finds Paradise would wish to come back to this life even if he were given the whole world and whatever is in it, except the martyr who, on seeing the superiority of martyrdom, would like to come back to get killed again in Allah's Cause.'" *Bukhari:V4B52N54* "The Prophet said, 'Were it not for the believers who do not want to be without me, I would always go forth in army-units setting out for Jihad. I would love to be martyred in Allah's Cause and then get resurrected and get martyred again only to be resurrected so that I could get martyred again.'" But like the Islamic clerics today, Muhammad sent others out to fight. You never see an Islamic cleric strap on one of the bombs they beguile others to wear.

So what I want to know is this: why don't suicide bombers ask their imams, "If this is such a great idea, why aren't you doing it?"

Bukhari:V4B52N216 "Allah's Apostle said, 'Were it not for fear it would be difficult for my followers, I would not have remained behind any army units. But I don't have riding camels and have no other means of conveyance. No doubt I wish I could fight in Allah's Cause and be martyred and come to life to be martyred again.'" The prophet would have fought nonstop jihad if only he had a riding camel? *Bukhari:V4B52N231* "Allah's Apostle came to Mecca the day of the Conquest riding his she-camel on which Usama was riding behind him." Methinks our boy was a liar, and a coward to boot. Bullies usually are.

Bukhari:V4B52N59 "Allah's Apostle said, 'By Him in Whose Hands my soul is! [And who might that be?] Whoever is wounded in Allah's Cause...and Allah knows well who gets wounded in His Cause...will come with his wound having the color of blood but the scent of musk.'" Sexy blood, only from the mind of Muhammad. And how, pray tell, can "Allah's Cause" be a "spiritual struggle" if one is "wounded and bleeds?"

Bukhari:V4B52N45 "Someone asked, 'Allah's Apostle, who is the best among the people?' He replied, 'A believer who strives his utmost in Allah's Cause with his life and property.'"...said the Imam to the suicide bomber.

Bukhari:V4B52N48 "The people said, 'Allah's Apostle! Acquaint the people with the good news.' He said, 'Paradise has one hundred grades which Allah has reserved for the Mujahidin who fight in His Cause. The distance between each grade is like the distance between the Heaven and the Earth.'" This is where the Islamic establishment concocted the idea that if there were multiple virgins for the garden-variety suicide bomber, there must be at least seventy for the really excellent ones.

Bukhari:V4B52N311 "Allah's Apostle said, 'There is no migration after the Conquest of Mecca, but only Jihad. When you are called by the Muslim ruler for Jihad fighting, you should go forth immediately, responding to the call.'" Calls for jihad echo off the walls of Muslim mosques to this day for in Islam there is "only Jihad."

Bukhari:V4B52N66 "Allah's Apostle said, 'Anyone whose feet get covered with dust in Allah's Cause will not be touched by the Hell Fire.'" Jihad dust is a hell-preserver.

Bukhari:V4B52N137 "The Prophet said, 'Let the slave perish.... Paradise is for him who holds the reins of his horse to strive in Allah's Cause with his hair unkempt and feet covered with dust. If he is appointed in the front line, he is perfectly satisfied with his post, and if he is appointed in the rear, he accepts it.'" Jihad dust is the stuff of destiny.

And I suppose that is why angels are dusty...*Bukhari:V4B52N68* "When Allah's Apostle returned from the battle of the Trench, he put down his arms and took a bath. Then Gabriel whose head was covered with dust, came to him saying, 'You have put down your arms! By Allah, I have not put down my arms yet.' Allah's Apostle said, 'Where to go now?' Gabriel said, 'This way,' pointing towards the tribe of Qurayza. So Allah's Apostle went out towards them." This is why the Qur'an tells us that the Islamicized Gabriel (better known as Lucifer) was the enemy of the Jews. (2:97)

Bukhari:V4B52N280 "When the Qurayza were ready to accept Sa'd's judgment, the Apostle sent for him. Sa'd proclaimed, 'I give the judgment that their men should be killed and their children and women should be taken as prisoners.' The Prophet remarked, 'O Sa'd! You have judged them with the judgment of King Allah.'" And Muslims slaughtered 1,000 Jews in genocidal rage; they raped their women, and sold every child into slavery. King Allah is Most Merciful, Kind.

Bukhari:V4B52N69 "For thirty days the Apostle invoked Allah to curse those who had killed the companions of Bir-Mauna. He invoked evil upon the Arabs of Ral, Dhakwan, and Usaiya who disobeyed Allah and His Apostle. There was revealed about those who were killed a Qur'anic verse we used to recite, but it was cancelled. The Verse was: 'Inform our people that we have met our Lord. He is pleased with us and He has made us pleased.'" It was abrogated because Muhammad alone spoke for Allah. But his curse must have worked because Islam has been an eternal blight on the Arabs.

Bukhari:V4B51N47 "'What causes you to smile, O Allah's Apostle?' He said, 'Some of my followers who in a dream were presented to me as fighters in Allah's Cause on board a ship amidst the sea caused me to smile.'" Allah's Cause made the profiteer money. And boatloads of money made him smile.

Bukhari:V4B51N72 "Our Prophet told us about the message of our Lord: 'Whoever amongst us is killed will go to Paradise.' Umar asked the Prophet, 'Is it not true that our men who are killed will go to Paradise and the Pagan's will go to the Hell Fire?' The Prophet said, 'Yes.'" And they believed him. Pity.

Bukhari:V4B51N73 "Allah's Apostle said, 'Know that Paradise is under the shade of swords.'" Well, his is, anyway.

For a little lighter fare, try this tasteless tidbit. *Bukhari:V4B51N74* "The Prophet said, 'Solomon, son of David said, "By Allah, tonight I will have sexual intercourse with one hundred women each of whom will give birth to a knight who will fight in Allah's Cause." But he did not say, "Allah willing." Therefore only one of those women conceived and gave birth to a half-man. If he had said, "Allah willing," he would have begotten sons, all of whom would have been knights striving in Allah's Cause.'"

Although this begins like the setup to a joke, it isn't funny. *Bukhari:V4B52N80* "Muhammad said, 'Allah welcomes two men with a smile; one of whom kills the other and both of them enter Paradise. One fights in Allah's Cause and gets killed. Later on Allah forgives the killer who also get martyred in Allah's Cause.'"

Bukhari:V4B52N282 "Allah's Apostle said, 'Five are regarded as martyrs: They are those who die because of plague, abdominal disease, drowning, a falling building, and the martyrs in Allah's Cause.'" What would possess a man to say such a thing?

Or why ask someone to scribble this down on a bone… *Bukhari:V4B52N284-5* "When the Divine Inspiration [Qur'an surah]: 'Those of the believers who sit at home,' was revealed, the Prophet sent for Zaid who came with a shoulder blade and wrote on it. Zaid said, 'Maktum came to the Prophet while he was dictating the verse. Maktum said, "O Allah's Apostle! If I were able, I would take part in Jihad." He was a blind man. So Allah sent down revelation to His Apostle while his thigh was on mine. It became so heavy that I feared that my leg would be broken. But the Prophet's state was over after Allah revealed "…except those who are disabled, blind, or lame."'" It was Muhammad's greatest miracle. He made blind men lame and disabled billions more.

Bukhari:V4B52N287 **"The Emigrants and the Ansar said, 'We are those who have given a pledge of allegiance to Muhammad that we will carry on Jihad as long as we live.'"**

Bukhari:V4B52N94 **"The Prophet said, 'Whoever spends two things in Allah's Cause [his life and his wealth], will be called by all the gatekeepers of Paradise. They will say, "O so-and-so! Come here."' Abu Bakr said, 'O Allah's Apostle! Such persons will never be destroyed.' The Prophet said, 'I hope you will be one of them.'"** Without dying a martyr, Muhammad couldn't even guarantee his most loyal comrade, his father-in-law, and future Caliph a ticket to Allah's brothel. No wonder Muslims are willing to kill to get in. I only wish they knew that the Islamic paradise was full.

Bakr's little girl confirmed that her hubby was a passionate Jihadist. *Bukhari:V4B52N130* **"Aisha said, 'Whenever the Prophet intended to proceed on a raid he used to draw lots amongst his wives and would take the one upon whom the lot fell. Once, before setting out for Jihad, he drew lots and it fell on me; so I went with him."** While it's contradictory, the lone "peaceful" Jihad Hadith says: *Bukhari:V4B52N43* **"Aisha said, 'O Apostle! We consider Jihad as the best deed. Should we not fight in Allah's Cause?' He said, 'The best Jihad for women is the Hajj done as I have done it.'"**

Other girls confirmed that they served Islam's leading terrorist: *Bukhari:V4B52N134* **"We used to take part in holy battles with the Prophet, providing his fighters with water and bringing the killed and the wounded back to Medina."** If he were alive today, Muhammad would be a leader of Hamas, Islamic Jihad, or al-Qaeda.

Bukhari:V4B52N175 **"He heard the Prophet saying, 'Paradise is granted to the first batch of my followers who will undertake a naval expedition.' The Prophet then said, 'The first army amongst my followers who will invade Caesar's City will be forgiven their sins.'"** It was quite a bargain. You bring me booty and I will give you paradise.

Bukhari:V4B52N178-9 **"The Prophet said, 'One of the portents of the Hour is that you will fight with people wearing shoes made of hair. And you will fight the Turks, a broad-faced people with small eyes, red faces, and flat noses. Their faces will look like shields coated with leather.'"** That sounds more racist than religious.

The Ku Klux Klan has nothing on these boys. *Bukhari:V4B52N182-4* **"Allah's Apostle invoked evil upon the infidels, saying, 'O Allah! The revealer of the Holy Book, defeat these people and shake them. Fill the infidels' houses and graves with fire as they busied us so that we did not perform the prayer until sunset.'"** With words like these, it's easy to see why Islam has caused so much death and destruction.

Bukhari:V4B52N259 **"Allah's Apostle sent us on a mission as a army unit and said, 'If you find so-and-so and so-and-so, burn both of them with fire.' When we intended to depart, Allah's Apostle said, 'I have ordered you to burn so-and-so and so-and-so, but only Allah punishes with fire, so, if you find them, kill them.'"** The Muhammad-Allah combo continue to do a great Satan impersonation.

Bukhari:V1B11N617 **"Allah's Apostle said, 'I would order someone to collect firewood and another to lead the prayer. Then I would go from behind and burn the houses of men who did not present themselves at the compulsory congregational prayer.'"** Muhammad is

Allah. He loved fire as much as the boss.

Bukhari:V4B52N260 "Ali burnt some people to death and this news reached Abbas, who said, 'Had I been in his place I would not have burnt them, as the Prophet said, 'Don't punish anybody with Allah's Punishment.' No doubt, I would have killed them, for the Prophet said, 'If a Muslim discards his religion, kill him.'" Could somebody please explain how this can be a tolerant or peace-loving religion?

Bukhari:V4B52N196 "Allah's Apostle said, 'I have been ordered to fight with the people till they say, "None has the right to be worshipped but Allah."'" Left unchecked, Muslims will continue to kill until all non-Muslims surrender or die.

Democracy and freedom are in conflict with fundamental Islam. *Bukhari: V4B52N203* "I heard Allah's Apostle saying, 'We are the last but will be the foremost to enter Paradise.' The Prophet added, 'He who obeys me, obeys Allah, and he who disobeys me, disobeys Allah. He who obeys the chief, obeys me, and he who disobeys the chief, disobeys me. The Imam is like a shelter for whose safety the Muslims should fight.'" Whether this Hadith confirms that Muhammad was Allah, or that apart from Muhammad there were no orders from Allah, is immaterial. His agenda was served. And to establish his legacy and damn the world, he ordered Muslims to be obedient to Islamic clerics and kings—forever. The only way to free Muslims from tyranny, and free non-Muslims from Jihad, is to abolish Islam.

According to Muhammad, Islam and Jihad were inseparable. *Bukhari:V4B52N208* "My brother and I came to the Prophet and asked to migrate. He said, 'Migration has passed away.' I replied, 'For what will you accept our pledge of allegiance?" He said, 'I will take the pledge for Islam and Jihad.'" The politically correct crowd and Muslim apologists today would accuse Muhammad of corrupting his religion.

I've shared this Hadith before. It was one of Muhammad's favorites. There are a dozen variations. It's as unambiguous as *Mein Kampf*. *Bukhari:V4B52N220* "Allah's Apostle said, 'I have been sent with the shortest expressions bearing the widest meanings, and I have been made victorious with terror. While I was sleeping, the keys of the treasures of the world were brought to me and put in my hand.' Allah's Apostle has left the world and now we are bringing out those treasures." His motivation was booty; his means was terror.

Bukhari:V4B52N233 "Allah's Apostle forbade people to travel to a hostile country carrying copies of the Qur'an." This proves that every Islamic conquest was about power, control, and money, not religion.

Muhammad didn't care for the Persians. It's amazing that Iranians and Iraqis follow a prophet who wanted them destroyed. *Bukhari:V4B52N190* "Allah's Apostle sent a letter to Khosrau. When he read the letter he tore it. The Prophet then invoked Allah to disperse them with full dispersion, to destroy them severely." Temper, temper.

Showing that he could hate everybody, the religious leader who cursed Arabs, murdered Jews, and condemned Persians went after Byzantine Christians. *Bukhari:V4B52N267* "The Prophet said, 'Khosrau will be ruined. There won't be a Persian King after him. Caesar will be ruined. There will be no Caesar after him. You will spend their treasures in Allah's Cause.' He proclaimed, 'War is deceit.'" As a religion, Islam is bankrupt, since the currency of faith is truth. However, as a war manifesto and terrorist dogma, Islam is perfect. It even comes complete with handy hints. "Use what you steal to equip your militants so they can steal more. And lie all you want; it makes conquering and plundering easier."

Bukhari:V4B52N268 "Allah's Apostle said, 'War is deceit.'" When you combine this with Qur'an 8:7, "Wipe the Infidels out to the last," and Qur'an 8:39, "So fight them till all opposition ends and the only religion is Islam," you get an ongoing state of war that encourages Muslims to continually deceive and murder infidels. That is why they use our media to proclaim: "Jihad is a spiritual struggle," and "Islam is peaceful." Muslims lie to us while their comrades kill us, because their "prophet" and "god" ordered them to do these things.

These next Hadiths demonstrate this principle: *Bukhari:V4B52N270-1* "The Prophet said, 'Who is ready to kill Ka'b bin Al-Ashraf, the Jew, who has really hurt Allah and His Apostle?'" Since the Qur'an says man cannot hurt Allah in any way, Allah is either a liar or a man (or both). "Maslama said, 'O Allah's Apostle! Do you want me to kill him?' He replied in the affirmative. Maslama said, 'Then allow me to deceive him.' The Prophet replied, 'I allow you.' So, Maslama went to Ka'b and said, 'The Prophet has put us to task and asked us for money.' Ka'b replied, 'By Allah, you will get tired of him.' Maslama said, 'We have followed him, so we dislike to leave him till we see how this affair ends.' Maslama went on talking to him this way until he got the chance to kill him." Muslim militants are deploying this same strategy to deceive and kill today.

This next Hadith is also personal. The Meccans had captured a Muslim murderer: *Bukhari:V4B52N281* "They took Khubaib to Mecca after the battle of Badr. He had killed Harith, a Meccan nobleman. The Quraysh gathered to kill him in retribution.... Khubaib wanted to offer two Rakat (prayers). They allowed this and he said, 'O Allah, kill them all with no exception.' He then recited the poetic verse: 'I'm being martyred as a Muslim. I do not mind how I am killed in Allah's Cause. For my killing is for Allah's Sake. If Allah wishes, He will bless the amputated parts of my torn body.' Then the son of Harith [the man Khubaib had murdered] killed him." Live by the sword. Die by the sword. Hopefully Islam will die less violently than it has lived.

For this is how it survived: *Bukhari:V4B53N386* "Umar sent Muslims to great countries to fight pagans. He said, 'I intend to invade Persia and Rome.' So, he ordered us to go to [the Persian King] Khosrau. When we reached the enemy, Khosrau's representative came out with 40,000 warriors, saying, 'Talk to me! Who are you?' Mughira replied, 'We are Arabs; we led a hard, miserable, disastrous life. We used to worship trees and stones. While we were in this state, our Prophet, the Messenger of our Lord, ordered us to fight you till you worship Allah Alone or pay us the Jizyah tribute tax in submission. Our Prophet has informed us that our Lord says: 'Whoever amongst us is killed as a martyr shall go to Paradise to lead such a luxurious life as he has never seen, and whoever survives shall become your master.'"

Islam is a very nasty business.

24

PROFITABLE PROPHET PLAN

"To Allah's lions who fight for His religion go the spoils that come from their prey."

Since the best predictor of future behavior is past behavior, we have been conditioned to expect the eighth year of the Islamic Era to dawn violently. And so it does…*Tabari IX:1* **"The Prophet had been given possession of Mecca following his conquest, but he only stayed a fortnight. He received news that the sheep-herding clans of Hawazin and Thaqif were encamped at Hunayn intending to fight him."** These Arabs knew what you know—Muhammad and Islam spelled trouble. Muslim militants had raided most every village in North, West, and Central Arabia. They would have hammered Eastern Arabia, too, but there was nothing there.

Ishaq:533 / Tabari IX:1 **"These tribes assembled after hearing about how the Messenger had conquered Mecca, thinking that the Muslims were intending to invade them next. When the Prophet heard that they had decided to defend themselves he went out to meet them at Hunayn, and Allah, the Great and Mighty, inflicted defeat on them. Allah has mentioned this battle in the Qur'an."** The reference is from the 9th surah, a "revelation" that must have been dribbled down over a prolonged period. It includes segments that were intended to rally the troops and justify the attack on Mecca all the way through subsequent raids on the Byzantine Christians the following year.

Allah's Hunayn statements were sandwiched between his assault on the family unit and his attack on Christians and Jews. Then the Islamic god called the people who invented him "unclean" and barred them from the "house" they had built for him. Regarding the battle, he cried: *009.025* **"Assuredly, Allah gave you victory on many battlefields and on the day of Hunayn: Behold, your great numbers elated you, but they availed you naught, and you turned back in retreat. But Allah did pour His Sakinah on the Messenger and Believers, and sent down forces which you saw not [Allah's angels]. He punished the Infidels. Such is their reward."** Allah was as eager to take "credit" for the savagery of his followers as Muhammad was to make his butchery appear godly. It was a symbiotic relationship.

The Arabs who had not yet been infected by Islam weren't adept fighters. *Ishaq:566* **"When Malik [the Hawazin chief] decided to fight the Apostle, he had his women, children, and cattle accompany the men. He explained that by bringing them, the men** would have to fight to defend them."

There are some interesting sidebars here. First, Malik, whom the Muslims describe as **"the chief sheep tender,"** *Tabari IX:6* **"sent out spies to obtain intelligence. But they came back with their joints dislocated. When he asked what had happened, they said, 'We saw white men on black horses. Before we could resist, we were struck as you see us now."** Tying men's arms behind their backs and hanging them from meat hooks to dislocate their shoulders is still a preferred form of Islamic torture.

Second, Muhammad also sent out spies. His **"mingled amongst the crowds gathering information,"** much like they do in Europe and America today. *Ishaq:567* **"When the spies had learned Malik's plans they returned and informed the Prophet. Muhammad in turn informed Umar [the second Caliph], who called the Prophet a liar."** Horrified, the Islamic spy said: **"Umar, you may accuse me of lying, but you have denied the truth for a long time."** The fact that he became Caliph proves you don't have to *believe* Islam to benefit from it. Muslim leaders play their subjects like a maestro conducts an orchestra, or more correctly, like a con plays his mark.

Third, the Muslims were overly fixated on booty. The spoils had been divided before the battle was waged. *Tabari IX:3* **"Since the Hawazin and Thaqif had marched with their women, children, and flocks, Allah granted them as booty to His Messenger, who divided the spoils among those Quraysh who had recently embraced Islam."**

I want to thank Muhammad and his Companions for making this so easy. They have, once again, validated my theory. The motivation for Islam was sex, power, and money. Having conquered the Meccans, acquired the Ka'aba Inc., and compelled the pledge of allegiance, it was time to demonstrate Islam. With 2,000 Quraysh in tow, Muhammad raided two tribes. He divided their wealth, enslaved their children, and offered their women as a spoil—as a godly bribe. And by giving preference to the Meccans, he made them mercenaries. While the prophet didn't yet control their minds or hearts, he held sway over their wallets. Tyrants throughout time—political, corporate, and religious—have ruled in like manner.

While marching to attack the Arab tribes, Muhammad conned some pagans out of their armor and swords. *Ishaq:567* **"Lend us your weapons so that we may fight our enemy."** Then Bakr said, *Tabari IX:7* **"Today we will not be overpowered on account of small numbers."** But arrogance soon led to disaster. *Tabari IX:8* **"The Messenger marched with 2,000 Meccans and 10,000 of his Companions who had come with him to facilitate the conquest of Mecca. Thus there were 12,000 in all. Muhammad left Abd Shams in charge of Mecca."** Muhammad liberated Mecca the same way Stalin liberated Eastern Europe. Then, as they marched toward their prey, the great Sulami said: *Ishaq:568* **"This year the ghoul has smitten people in the midst of their tents as the ghoul has many forms.... All wild ass is inedible. The Hawazin tribe is diseased so I think that Allah's Apostle will attack them in the morning."**

The next Hadith reports: *Tabari IX:8/Ishaq:569* **"We descended through a sloping valley at the twilight of daybreak. But the enemy had gotten there before us and we were waylaid** by them in a narrow pass. They had collected themselves and they were fully prepared. By Allah, we were terrified! As we descended, their squadrons made their first assaults on us as if they were one man. Our people were routed and fled, no one turning to look back. Allah's Apostle withdrew and cried, 'Where are you going? Come to me. I am Allah's Apostle! I am Muhammad, son of Abdallah!' It was of no avail. The camels just bumped into one another as the Muslims ran away." Pathetic, isn't it? "Allah's Apostle withdrew and cried, 'Where are you going? Come to me. I am Allah's Apostle!'"

Muhammad's militants were under no illusions. They were out for easy booty, not some religious crusade. They were pirates because stealing was easier than working. They didn't believe Muhammad was an apostle any more than I do. They just ignored him—sage advice, if I do say so myself.

It got so bad... *Tabari IX:8* "When the polytheists overwhelmed the Muslims, the Prophet got off his mount and started reciting verses in the rajaz meter: 'I am the Prophet, it is no lie, I am the son of Abd Muttalib!'" The first line was pathetic. The second was a confession. Abd Muttalib had been the last in Qusayy's line to control all aspects of the Ka'aba Inc. Muhammad was using the scam to establish his authority.

Next we learn that the *previous* prophet's command to "love your neighbor as yourself," didn't apply to this peculiar order of religious stalwarts. *Tabari IX:10/ Ishaq:569* "When the Muslims fled, the uncouth and rude fellows from Mecca who were with us saw that we were in total disarray. Some of them spoke in a manner that disclosed the hatred they harbored against us. Abu Sufyan [the Meccan chief turned Muslim warrior] had divining arrows with him but another Muslim said, 'Sorcery is useless today.' Sufyan replied, 'Shut up! May Allah smash your mouth!'" This episode is alarming. First, we discover, the gambling game of divining arrows that had saved Abd Allah, Muhammad's father, was Satanic. Second, witchcraft was routinely practiced around the Ka'aba. And third, these Meccan Muslims, who had lived next to the Black Stone for decades, knew that Allah was useless. So now they feared that things were so bad that almighty Satan couldn't even rescue them.

Things continued to spiral out of control. *Tabari IX:11/Ishaq:574* "When Muhammad saw his men confused and in disarray, he repeated: 'Where are you going, men?' But not even one of them paid heed to his cries, so he went to the biggest man with the strongest voice and had him shout out to rally the troops." The first Muslims were confused. Neither they, nor their prophet, knew where they were going.

Ultimately, fewer than one percent of the 12,000 fighters responded to the Prophet's plea. *Ishaq:574* "Finally a hundred were gathered around the Prophet. They confronted the enemy, and fought." But their battle cries weren't for Muhammad, Allah, or even Islam. "The first cry was, 'Help the Ansar!' And then, 'For the Khazraj!' Looking down at the mêlée as they were fighting, the Prophet said, 'Now the oven is hot.'"

According to Islamic Tradition, which as we know is a precisely accurate and unbiased account (the narrator intoned with tongue planted firmly in cheek): *Tabari IX:12* "Ali came upon them from behind, hamstrung their camels and they fell on their rumps. He struck the enemy with such blows he cut off feet and shanks. The men fought, and by Allah, when those [Muslims] who had run away returned, they found only prisoners already handcuffed with the Apostle." That means that a force fierce enough to make 12,000 men flee was conquered, bound, and slain by 100.

Ishaq:570 "The Messenger turned to Abu Sufyan, who stood fast fighting that day. He had become an excellent Muslim after embracing Islam." That means it doesn't take much Islam to turn men violent. But it's worse than that. An hour earlier, this "excellent Muslim" was practicing "sorcery."

Tabari IX:13 "Muhammad turned to see Umm, a pregnant woman, who said, 'O Messenger! Kill those [Muslims] who flee from you as you kill those who fight you, for they deserve death. Here is my dagger. If any come near me I will rip them up and slit open their belly with it.'" She had listened to the Qur'an recitals and knew that Allah hated peaceful Muslims who retreated in battle. But Allah loved a good thief...**"Abu Talhah alone took the spoils of twenty men whom he had killed."**

This is such a charming religion. And we know it is a religion because there are killer angels. If Islam were a political doctrine they would be murderous comrades. *Tabari IX:14/Ishaq:572* "While the men were still fighting I saw a black striped garment descending from the sky until it dropped between us and the enemy. I gazed, and lo, it was a mass of black ants strewn everywhere, which filled the valley. I had no doubt that they were angels and that the enemy would be routed." And that would make either Allah or the Muslim a liar, for Allah said: "He sent down forces which you saw not."

One of Muhammad's marauders boasted about how blood and booty had motivated the first Muslims: *Ishaq:571* "I went up to a man and struck off his hand, and he throttled me with the other. He would have killed me if the loss of blood had not weakened him. He fell, and I killed him while he was down. But I was too occupied with fighting to pay any more attention to him. So one of the Meccan Muslims passed by and stripped him. Then when the fighting was over and we had finished with the enemy, the Apostle said that anyone who had killed a foe could have his spoil. I told the Apostle that I had killed a man who was worth stripping but had been too busy killing others at the time to notice who had spoiled him." So Abu Bakr scolded the Muslim who had *wrongly* stolen the mutilated man's clothes: "To Allah's lions who fight for His religion go the spoils that come from their prey. Return the booty to the man who killed him.' The Apostle confirmed Abu Bakr's words. So I was given the property of the man whom I had killed. I sold it and bought a small palm grove with the money. It was the first property I ever owned." Sometimes I don't know if I should scream or just give up. The degree to which Islam's poison corrupts men is hard to fathom. Saving mankind from this "religion" will not be easy.

Old hatreds die hard. *Ishaq:572* "When the Apostle learned that one of the Meccans had died in the battle, he said, 'Allah curse him!' He used to hate the Quraysh." All the while... *Tabari IX:15* "One of the Ansari who was plundering the slain came upon a Thaqif boy. He discovered that he was an uncircumcised Christian. He uncovered others and then yelled out at the top of his voice, 'Allah knows that the Thaqif are uncircumcised.'" Muslims had killed and robbed their first Christians.

This wouldn't be Islam without a sonnet to commemorate the occasion. *Ishaq:572* "Muhammad is the man, an Apostle of my Lord who errs not, neither does he sin. Any who would rival him in goodness must fail. Evil was the state of our enemy so they lost the day. Fortunes change and we came upon them like lions from the thickets. The armies of Allah came openly, flying at them in rage, so they could not get away. We destroyed them and forced them to surrender. In the former days there was no battle like this; their blood flowed freely. We slew them and left them in the dust. Those who escaped were choked with terror. A multitude of them were slain. This is Allah's war in which those who do not accept Islam will have no helper. War destroyed the tribe and fate the clan." With each word, Islam grew ever more violent.

Muhammad's disciples said that their warlord "errs not, neither does he sin," that "none could rival him in goodness." Deceit, sin, and evil have been redefined: it isn't a sin to fight, kill, terrorize, bear false witness, or steal. And that's why the Qur'an and Hadith boast about such things. "Booty is lawful and good." "Wipe the Infidels out to the last." "There is no ilah but Allah and Muhammad is his Messenger."

The second half of Abbas' poem—turned Islamic Tradition—is frightening. It explains what happens to people who are victimized by Islam. The Muslims were the aggressors as they "came upon them like lions." They were an "army" not missionaries. "Rage" consumed them. The first Muslims were "destructive." They "forced surrender." And we know that it was Islam that had done this to them because "in the former days there were no battles like this." Death was the result: "blood flowed freely." Killing meant nothing to the Muslims as they "left them in the dust." The first Muslims were vicious terrorists: "those who escaped were choked with terror. A multitude were slain." And all this death and destruction was perpetrated in the name of their despicable god: "This is Allah's war."

A second poem recited this day was no less harsh. *Ishaq:574* "In faith I do not fear the army of fate. [Islam is fatalistic because Manat was the goddess of fate.] He gave us the blood of their best men to drink when we led our army against them. We were a great army with a pungent smell. And we attack continuously, wherever our enemy is found." Even the most brutal, violent, and ungodly regimes to prowl our planet would have been repulsed by a god who "gave us the blood of their best men to drink." You'd think such "scripture" would prompt a response from those who claim that today's bloodthirsty Islamic terrorists have "corrupted their religion."

Next we find the apostle in a heroic moment. *Ishaq:576* "One of our Companions told us that the Apostle walked past a woman whom Khalid [the perfect Islamic terrorist] had killed. He sent word to Khalid and forbade him to kill more children, women, and slaves." It's hard to sell a corpse into slavery. And this Bukhari Hadith contradicts the moral message: *Bukhari:V4B52N256* "The Prophet passed by and was asked whether it was permissible to attack infidels at night with the probability of exposing their women and children to danger. The Prophet replied, 'Their women and children are from them.'"

While they were out being religious, Allah's cavalry elected to terrorize the good folks of Nakhlah, Awtas, and Sa'd. But they began the fun by capturing and assassinating Bijad first. *Ishaq:576* "Allah's Apostle said, 'If you get hold of Bijad, don't let him escape for he has done something evil.'" *Tabari IX:18* "While fighting the Banu Sa'd, Muslim horsemen seized Bijad. They herded his family around him like cattle, and they treated them roughly." All the while, *Tabari IX:20* "The captives of Hunayn, along with their possessions, were brought to the Messenger. He ordered that their captives, animals, and their possessions be taken to Ji'ranah and held there in custody."

To commemorate their captivity, a Muslim gloated: *Ishaq:576* "Allah and His servant overwhelmed every coward. Allah honored us and made our religion victorious. We were glorified in the worship of the Compassionate God who destroyed them all. He humiliated them in the worship of Satan. By what our Apostle recites from the Book and by our swift horses, I liked the punishment the infidels received. Killing them was sweeter than drink. We galloped among them panting for the spoil. With our loud-voiced army, the Apostle's squadron advanced into the fray." This stuff makes *Mein Kampf* seem mild.

Another Muslim sang: *Ishaq:578* "Crushing the heads of the infidels and splitting their skulls with sharp swords, we continually thrust and cut at the enemy. Blood gushed from their deep wounds as the battle wore them down. We conquered bearing the Prophet's fluttering standard [war banner]. Our cavalry was submerged in rising dust, and our spears quivered, but by us the Prophet gained victory."

Not to be outdone, another of Muhammad's Companions recited some very illuminating lines: *Ishaq:580* "Allah's religion is the religion of Muhammad. We are satisfied with it. It contains guidance and laws. By it he set our affairs right." Once again, I agree with the first Muslims: "Allah's religion is the religion of Muhammad."

Still incriminating themselves: *Ishaq:580* "Our strong warriors obey his orders to the letter. By us Allah's religion is undeniably strong." Islam was not spread by word of mouth, by reason, or by the kind deeds it inspired. Islam was propagated by the sword. "You would think when our horses gallop with bits in their mouths that the sounds of demons are among them." Wherever Muslim militants are found, loud-mouthed demons are close at hand. "The day we trod down the unbelievers there was no deviation or turning from the Apostle's order. During the battle the people heard our exhortations to fight and the smashing of skulls by swords that sent heads flying. We severed necks with a warrior's blow. Often we have left the slain cut to pieces and a widow crying alas over her mutilated husband. 'Tis Allah, not man we seek to please." Just when you thought Islam couldn't get any worse, it spews ever more vitriolic violence in your face. From Sira to Sunnah to Surah, Islam is putrid.

Abbas also composed the following lines. I want you to appreciate the nature of those who, along with Muhammad, invented Islam. While Ibn Ishaq recorded a dozen pages of poetry from this day, I have tried to sift through the rubble to bring you the lines that best illuminate the mentality of the first Muslims. *Ishaq:580* "We helped Allah's Apostle, angry on his account, with a thousand warriors. We carried his flag on the end of our lances. We were his helpers, protecting his banner in deadly combat. We dyed it with blood, for that was its color. We were the Prophet's right arm in Islam. We were his bodyguards before other troops served him.

We helped him against his opponents. Allah richly rewarded that fine Prophet Muhammad."

Islam immortalized one of its best: the woman killing, child abusing, geno-cidal, tax-collecting Khalid. *Ishaq:583* "Since you have made Khalid chief of the army and promoted him, he has become a chief indeed, leading an army guided by Allah. Firmly clad in mail, warriors with lances leveled, we are a strong force not unlike a rushing tor-rent. We smite the wicked while we swear an oath to Muhammad...fighting in the quest of booty." *Ishaq:586* "Red blood flowed because of our rage." No matter the translation, no matter the interpretation, these men were as bad as their religion.

Attacking, killing, enslaving, plundering, and terrorizing the Hawazin, Thaqif, Nakhlah, Awtas, and Sa'd villages was insufficient. *Tabari IX:20* "The Mes-senger and his companions went directly to Ta'if." This was the town between Mecca and Yathrib whose "rabble" had "mocked and stoned the prophet" following the Quraysh Bargain and Satanic Verses. "Muhammad encamped there for a fortnight, waging war. The townsfolk fought the Muslims from behind the fort. None came out in the open. All of the surrounding people surrendered and sent their delegations to the Prophet. After besieging Ta'if for twenty days, Muhammad left and halted at Ji'ranah where the cap-tives of Hunayn were held with their women and children. It is alleged that those captives taken numbered six thousand with women and children." Since only a hundred Mus-lims fought, overcoming sixty to one odds is a little farfetched. But there is an important line in the opening Hadith on the siege of Ta'if. The first Muslims had been so vicious that "all of the surrounding people surrendered."

Tabari IX:21 "Delegations of Hawazin came to the Prophet and embraced Islam. Therefore, he set their women and children free and decided to make the lesser pilgrimage directly from Ji'ranah." Freedom had never been part of this man's vocabulary. "Embracing Islam" was tantamount to surrender, bowing in submission to Muhammad's authority and will. So what's up? Simple economics: there were only four towns within walking distance with enough money to buy slaves: Mecca, Yathrib, Khaybar, and Ta'if. One had been invaded, two con-quered, and the forth was under siege. There simply wasn't a market. Slaves need to be sheltered, fed, and watered. They are a liability to a profiteer who has no means to trade them for money.

Released of his burden, the prophet refocused his rage on Ta'if. After all, this had been the town whose leaders had once said, "If god needed a messenger, he would have chosen somebody better than you." The Hadith reports: *Tabari IX:22* "Muhammad ordered that Ta'if's walled gardens should be torn down and destroyed." Ten years later our boy was still hot under the collar.

But his grudge match was little more than an irritant. *Ishaq:589* "The Muslims were unable to get through the city wall, for the inhabitants had shut the gate." This is as lame as the Meccans being stumped by the trench surrounding Medina. *Tabari IX:22* "The Prophet continued to besiege the town, fighting them bitterly. Both sides shot arrows at each other until one day the wall of Ta'if was stormed. A number of Muhammad's companions went under a testudo [a Roman style siege engine with a roof] and tried to breach it but they were showered with scraps of hot iron. They came out from under their testudo and the Thaqif shot them." Ever mean spirited, "Muhammad then ordered that their vineyards should be cut down."

But all was not war and destruction. The prophet had but two of his two-dozen wives, concubines, and sex slaves with him on the campaign and was now longing for some variety. So... *Tabari IX:24/Ishaq:590* "Muhammad told Bakr, 'I saw in a dream that I was given a large bowl filled with butter. A cock pecked at it and spilt it.' 'O Messenger of Allah, I don't think that you will attain what you desire today.'" Wouldn't you just love to turn Sigmund Freud loose on that one?

Anyway, that was it. The Muslim militants packed up their camels and headed home, grumbling all the way. *Tabari IX:25* "By Allah, I did not come to fight for nothing. I wanted a victory over Ta'if so that I might obtain a slave girl from them and make her pregnant." Lovely.

On the way back home... *Ishaq:587* "Ka'b ibn Malik reacted to the Apostle's decision. He said, 'We put an end to doubt at Khaybar. But we gave our swords a rest. If our swords could have spoken, their blades would have said, "Give us Daus or Thaqif. We will tear off the roofs in Wajj. We will make homes desolate. Our cavalry will come upon you leaving behind a tangled mass. When we assault a town they sound a cry of alarm but our sharp cutting swords flash like lightning. By them we bring death to those who struggle against us. Flowing blood was mingled with saffron the morn the forces met. They were taken by surprise and we surrounded their walls with our troops. Our leader, the Prophet, was firm, pure of heart, steadfast, continent, straightforward, full of wisdom, knowledge, and clemency. He was not frivolous nor light minded. We obey our Prophet and we obey a Lord who is the Compassionate [the Ar-Rahman]. We make you partners in peace and war. If you refuse we will fight you doggedly.'"" The sword of Islam has spoken.

Ka'b continued with these words: *Ishaq:587* "Our onslaught will not be a weak faltering affair. We shall fight as long as we live. We will fight until you turn to Islam, humbly seeking refuge. We will fight not caring whom we meet. We will fight whether we destroy ancient holdings or newly gotten gains. We have cut off every opponent's nose and ears with our fine swords. We have driven them violently before us at the command of Allah and Islam. We will fight until our religion is established. And we will plunder them, for they must suffer disgrace." Nothing more need be said.

This next poem begins as a fairytale; it ends as a nightmare. *Ishaq:588* "Shaddad said this about the Apostle's raid on Ta'if: 'Don't help Al-Lat [one of Allah's pagan daughters] for Allah is about to destroy her. How can one who cannot help herself be helped? She was burned in black smoke and caught fire. Those who fight before her stone are outcasts. When the Apostle descends on your land none of your people will be left when he leaves."

Under the heading, "The Division of Booty Captured at Hunayn and Conciliation Gifts Given to Gain Men's Hearts," we find that the disgruntled mercenaries needed to be appeased. *Ishaq:592* "The Apostle held a large number of captives. There were 6,000 women and children prisoners. He had captured so many sheep and camels they could not be counted." But since there was no market for the slaves, Muhammad asked his mercenaries to free those he had previously divvied up. *Tabari IX:28* **"The Banu Tamim were concerned. They did not want to give up their share. So Muhammad said, 'He who holds a share of these captives shall get six camels for every slave from the next booty we take.' [They were postponing gratification; it was so mature of them.] So the Muslims returned the women and children captives."**

But not every Mujahidun was so mature. The prophet was always an exception to his own rules. *Ishaq:593* **"From the captives of Hunayn, Allah's Messenger gave [his son-in-law] Ali a slave girl called Baytab and he gave [future Caliph] Uthman a slave girl called Zaynab and [future Caliph] Umar another."** As the brain trust of Islam, these fellows knew that there were no babes in paradise, so they got all the fornication they could handle right here on earth.

Umar palmed off his prize on his son Abdallah who scurried off to the Ka'aba to pay tribute to the idol for whom he had been named. He said, **"I will take her when I return."** But alas, the Islamic dictator said, **"Let her go, for her mouth is cold, her breasts are flat. You did not take her as a virgin in her prime nor even full-figured in her middle age!"** Even religious rapists have their standards.

Still bickering, the Muslims who had followed the prophet into battle yelled, *Tabari IX:31/Ishaq:594* **"'Muhammad, divide the spoil and booty of camels and cattle among us.' They forced the Prophet up against a tree, and his robe was torn from him. Muhammad cried, 'Give me back my robe. If there had been more sheep I would have given you some. You have not found me to be niggardly, cowardly or false."** Yes they had; which is why they had so little regard for him. We were just told: *Tabari IX:26* **"He had captured so many sheep and camels they could not be counted."** It is little wonder Muhammad prayed: *Bukhari:V4B52N143* **"O Allah! I seek refuge with you from distress and sorrow, from helplessness and laziness, from miserliness and cowardice, from being heavily in debt and from being overcome by men."**

Let's think about this for a moment. Muhammad had led 12,000 armed militants against a tribe of sheepherders. They had slaughtered the men, stolen their property, and taken 6,000 women and children captive. It came time to pay the pirates their usual share from the spoil and he reneges. He changed the rules and promised to pay them later, out of a future raid. The first Muslims became angry, ganged up on their prophet, forced him up against a tree, and tore off his robe. In response, he lied to them.

Then, to memorialize the event, the warlord of the world's fastest growing religion proclaimed that he was distressed, sorrowful, helpless, and lazy. He confessed to being a coward. Then he said that he was miserly—a death sentence if you're a pirate. No matter how many people he enslaved or how much property he stole, he was so irresponsible, he was always broke. And while that's really bad, how can a man of god be **"overcome by men?"**

As bad as this affair was for Islam's credibility, Muslim apologists cannot wish it away, for Bukhari tells us: *Bukhari:V4B53N376* **"While Allah's Apostle was accompanied by the people on their way back from Hunayn, the Bedouins started begging for** things so aggressively that they forced him to go under a Samura tree where his outer garment was snatched away. On that, Allah's Apostle stood up [in his undies] and said, 'Return my clothes. If I had as many camels as these trees, I would have distributed them amongst you; and you will not find me a miser, liar or coward.'" In what appears to be a related incident, we learn: *Bukhari:V4B53N377* "While I was walking with the Prophet he was wearing a Najrani outer garment with a thick hem. A Bedouin came upon him and pulled his garment so violently that I could see the imprint of the hem on his shoulder caused by the violence of his pull. The Bedouin said, 'Give me something from Allah's Fortune which you have.' The Prophet turned, smiled, and ordered that a gift should be given."

Returning to the historical and biographical accounts, we find Muhammad lying to his troops and contradicting his prayer. *Tabari IX:31/Ishaq:594* "'You have not found me miserly, cowardly, or a liar.' Then he walked over to his camel and took a hair from its hump. Holding it aloft in his fingers he said, 'Men, I do not have anything of your booty, not even as much as this hair. Just filth. And that filth is what is being given to you. [How perceptive. Islam is filth.] So, bring back my cloak, for dishonesty will be a shame, a flame, and a doom to you.'" Since even his own Sunnah proves he was lying through his teeth, Muhammad must be enjoying the shame of the flame.

This wrangling over stolen money continued for a number of pages. Muhammad had lost control; he was "overcome by men." Ever more desperate to buy loyalty, he doled out some of the booty his goons had stolen. But there never seemed to be enough. *Ishaq:594* "The Apostle gave gifts to those whose hearts were to be won over, notably the chiefs of the army, to win them and through them the people." Point, game, set, match. That about wraps it up. Muhammad used stolen property to bribe men. He, like every tyrant who has ever lived, began by greasing the palms of his generals. With the military leadership sufficiently corrupted and induced, there was nothing the people could do. Their fate was sealed. And little has changed in 1400 years. (As an interesting aside, the first and largest bribe listed was paid to the former Meccan chief, occultist, and excellent Muslim, Abu Sufyan.)

But that did not keep the troops from grumbling. The first Muslims weren't very happy with their warlord. *Tabari IX:34/Ishaq:595* "Khuwaysirah came and stood by the Prophet as he was giving gifts to the people and said, 'Muhammad, I have seen what you have done today.' 'Well, what did you see?' He said, 'I don't think you have been fair.' Allah's Messenger became angry. 'Woe to you! If justice is not to be found with me, then with whom is it to be found?'" Might I suggest any of ten billion other choices? "Umar [who got his sex toy] said, 'Muhammad, allow me to kill him.'" *Ishaq:595* "The Apostle said, 'Get him away from me and cut off his tongue.'"

Bukhari reported the naked truth about the nature of fundamental Islam: *Bukhari:V4B53N373* "Allah's Apostle got property and war prisoners and gave them to some people to the exclusion of others. The latter seemed to be displeased by that. The Prophet said, 'I give to some people, lest they should deviate from Islam or lose patience.' Amr bin Taghlib said, 'The statement of Allah's Apostle is dearer to me than red camels.'"

Bukhari:V4B53N374 "The Prophet said, 'I give to the Quraysh so that they will desire Islam, for they are nearer to their life of Ignorance and it is not strong in their hearts.'" The term the mafia uses to describe this situation is "made." A "made man" is someone who has participated in a criminal act like kidnap for ransom or murder for money. Made men continue to embrace the organization to keep the money coming and to keep from being incarcerated for their crime.

Another Bukhari Hadith confirms that the first Muslims were nothing more than bloodthirsty pirates. It also demonstrates that there was no appreciable difference between the Hadiths collected by Ishaq, Tabari, or Bukhari. *Bukhari:V4B53N375* "When Allah favored His Apostle with the properties of the Hawazin tribe as Fai booty, he started giving to some of the Meccan men up to one-hundred camels each. Whereupon some Ansari said, 'May Allah forgive His Apostle! He is giving to the Quraysh and leaving us out, in spite of the fact that our swords are still dripping with the blood of the infidels.' When Muhammad was informed of what they had said, he called for the Ansar and gathered them in a leather tent. 'What is the statement which I have been informed, and that which you have said?' [He meant: "What did you say?"] The smart ones replied, 'O Allah's Apostle! The wise ones did not say anything, but the youngsters said, "May Allah forgive His Apostle; he enriches the Quraysh and leaves the Ansar poor, in spite of the fact that Ansar swords are still dribbling with the blood of the infidels."' The Prophet replied, 'I give them more because they are still close to the period of Infidelity and have just recently embraced Islam. You should be pleased to see them becoming rich.' The Ansar replied, 'Yes, O Allah's Apostle, we are satisfied.'" The moral of the story is: You have to bribe men to make them Muslims and then threaten them to keep them that way. *Bukhari:V4B53N411* "The Prophet said, 'Every betrayer will have a flag which will be fixed to him and displayed on the Day of Doom. This flag will show the betrayal he committed.'" In other words: "Mess with me and you'll go to hell."

This was an unpleasant time for Muhammad. He had bribed men to rob and plunder Arabs and Jews, but now the cupboard was bare. *Tabari IX:36/Ishaq:596* "'Prophet, this group of Ansar have a grudge against you for what you did with the booty and how you divided it among your own people.' After due praise and exaltation of Allah, he addressed them. 'Ansar, what is this talk I hear from you? What is the grudge you harbor in your hearts against me? Do you think ill of me? Did I not come to you when you were erring and needy, and then made rich by Allah?'" It was getting nastier by the moment. There simply wasn't enough plunder to go around. And heaven forbid a Muslim should soil his hands producing something of value.

The Ansar were not satisfied, and they turned the tables on the pirate king—giving him a strong dose of reality. *Tabari IX:37/Ishaq:596* "You came to us discredited, when your message was rejected by the Quraysh, and we believed you. You were forsaken and deserted and we assisted you. You were a fugitive and we took you in, sheltering you. You were poor and in need, and we comforted you." It was all true—every word of it. Muhammad had been "discredited" because he had accepted the Quraysh Bargain. Tempted by sex, power, and money, he had made a deal with the

Devil. He blasphemed his god, reciting Satanic Verses. His demonic message had been "rejected" as delusional. The Quraysh knew that Muhammad was a demon possessed, lying charlatan, forging his scriptures by plagiarizing earlier lore. After telling the Quraysh that he was going to slaughter them, and after duping the Ansar to war against all mankind, Muhammad had become a "fugitive." He was run out of town in shame, "forsaken and deserted" by his own people—his family. He was as "poor" as his religion.

The Yathrib Arabs had foolishly comforted him, believed him, fought for him. Yet none of that fazed the prophet. *Tabari IX:37/Ishaq:596* "Do you hold a grudge against me and are you mentally disturbed because of the worldly things by which I conciliate a people and win them over so that they will embrace Islam and become Muslims?" Case closed. Proof doesn't get any better than this. This is a stunning confession. Muhammad said that he used stolen property to bribe militants so that they would become Muslims. That made the first Muslims mercenaries. They were seduced and lured into Islam just as the Devil had beguiled Muhammad. Islam's warlord bought support with booty. But alas, how can a pirate be a prophet? How can criminal behavior be religious? Stealing is illegal. Bribery is immoral. Venerating a man who advocates both makes one an accomplice. And trusting him with your soul is insane.

Caught between a rock and some hard people, Muhammad chose the rock. "Allah's Apostle left town to make a lesser pilgrimage and ordered that the rest of the booty be held back, although some of the spoil followed him." There's nothing more religious than storing your contraband safely before you rush off to visit your rock god. Then, confirming the new religion was regurgitated paganism: *Ishaq:597* "The people made the pilgrimage that year in the way the pagan Arabs used to do it."

With that two-line religious interlude over, it was time to return the focus to money. Now that Muhammad had admitted to being a lying miser without enough booty to go around, what do you suppose he did? He had already robbed everyone within camel ride, so more piracy wasn't going to work. *Tabari IX:38* "In this year, the Messenger sent Amr to collect the zakat tax from Jayfar and Amr, the clans of Julanda and Azd." And..."He collected the jizyah from the Zoroastrians [an occult religion derived from Babylonian paganism]." He taxed them all. It was Muhammad's version of The New Deal.

Tabari IX:39 "In the same year the [sixty-year old] Prophet married Kilabiyyah. When she was given the choice between this world and the hereafter, and she preferred this world." That means she rejected Islam. She was close enough to Muhammad to know that Allah was impotent even if his prophet wasn't. What's more, this Hadith confirms Muhammad ignored the Qur'an's order not to befriend disbelievers.

The Tradition goes on to report: "Mariyah [a Coptic child-virgin sent as a gift and then turned into a concubine] gave birth to Ibrahim, The Messenger entrusted the infant boy to Umm. Mariyah received Salma, a bond-maid [sex slave] of the Messenger and she announced the good news to Abu. Abu shared the news with Muhammad who gave him a slave as a gift. When Mariyah gave birth to her son, the Prophet's wives became jealous."

Ishaq:597 "When the Apostle returned to Medina after his raid on Ta'if, word spread that he had killed some of the men who had satirized and insulted him. The poets who were left spread in all directions." You've got to give Muhammad credit for one thing, he knew how to control the press.

The next Hadith speaks of "short black men who used to retreat." They "excited anger against them." But then the pacifists became Muslims and turned violent.

Ishaq:601 "The best men launch spears as if they were swords. They peer forward unweariedly with eyes red as burning coals. They devote their lives to their Prophet. On the day of hand-to-hand fighting and cavalry attacks they purify themselves with the blood of infidels. They consider that an act of piety. Their habit is to act like lions. They are accustomed to hunting men." Wow! Good Muslims "purify themselves with the blood of infidels." You don't suppose that this was what the dark spirit of Islam meant when he said: "Allah is the best Baptizer?"

With this "religious" moment over, the curtain came down (most blessedly) on the eighth year of the Islamic Era. We're twenty years into this scam and it remains as ugly as the first night when Muhammad encountered the cave-dwelling demon.

The next day was hotter than usual. It was April 20th 630 A.D. As the sun rose, men gathered to talk about their plight. *Tabari IX:42* "Amr said, 'We have been dealt a situation from which there is no escape. You have seen what Muhammad has done. Arabs have submitted to him and we do not have the strength to fight. You know that no herd is safe from him. And no one even dares go outside for fear of being terrorized." Islam had arrived and conquered. Anarchy was the result. It still is.

So Muhammad and his less-than-inspired band of thugs set out in search of unplundered territory. *Tabari IX:46* "In this year, the Messenger carried out a military expedition to Tabuk." Tabuk was a Christian settlement in Byzantine Syria. They had done nothing to earn Muhammad's wrath. They were simply a target— the nearest untapped source of booty. *Ishaq:602* "The Apostle ordered Muslims to prepare for a military expedition so that he could raid the Byzantines." It would be the largest and best-equipped army Allah's Messenger would ever lead. Thirty thousand militants heeded the call to arms. Muhammad proclaimed: "The treasures of Caesar have been given to me by conquest."

Tabari IX:48 "Muhammad wanted the people to be fully prepared so he informed them that his objective was the Byzantines. The Muslims disliked the idea because of their respect for their fighting ability." But Muhammad had invested much of his last and final surah to demeaning Christians and ordering Muslims to fight them, humiliate them, mutilate them, tax them, enslave them, and even crucify them. He couldn't let all of that wonderful godly inspiration go to waste.

The pirates, however, weren't so inspired. They wanted easy booty, not war. *Tabari IX:49* **"One of the hypocrites, feeling an aversion to battle, being skeptical of the truth, and spreading false rumors about Muhammad, said that they should not go out in the heat. With regard to him, Allah revealed: 'They said, "Do not march out in the heat." Say, "The heat of hell is far more intense."'"** The message was: "Obey my order to fight and plunder or my god will roast you in hell."

Tabari IX:49 **"Muhammad urged the Muslims by way of a meeting to help cover the expenses of Allah's Cause. The men provided mounts in anticipation of Allah's reward."** Once again, we see that neither preaching, evangelism, nor salvation entered the picture. These men weren't off on a religious crusade. **"Allah's Cause"** was armed robbery. And frankly, such behavior would be inexcusable even if it only happened once in the presence of the prophet or during the formation Islam. But Muhammad's militants were in a rut. They had fought for no other reason.

If we were to remove immoral, illegal, hateful, and violent verses from the Hadith and Qur'an, all we'd have left would be an odd collection of plagiarized and twisted Bible stories. Bad simply overwhelms good in Islam. To believe Muhammad is as foolish as protecting the doctrine he inspired.

Ishaq:602 **"The Apostle always referred allusively to the destination which he intended to raid. This was the sole exception, for he said plainly that he was making for the Byzantines because the journey was long, the weather was hot, and the enemy was strong."** No Byzantine had threatened Muhammad. Calling them **"the enemy"** simply confirms that all non-Muslims are Islam's foe. But there is another lesson here. Today, Muslims scream with shrill voices that the Christian Crusaders attacked Muslims without provocation. Yet their own scriptures confirm that Islam drew first blood, and that Muslims invaded and conquered Christians.

But it's worse than that. Christianity had permeated what is now Iraq, Iran, Turkey, Syria, Jordan, Israel, and Egypt by the time Muhammad decided to plunder these people. Christ's message appealed to human hearts and minds by virtue of his words. Within a decade of the Tabuk raid, Islam would lay all of that to ruin, attacking, conquering, and taxing the once free people who occupied these places. Islam imposed its will by violent assault.

On this day, Muhammad discovered that even after promising Allah would reward Muslims with booty beyond their dreams, most Arabs were skeptical. *Tabari IX:50* **"When the Prophet was prepared to set off, a number of Muslims whose intentions had prevented them from following the Messenger, lagged behind without any misgivings."** Those who knew Muhammad much better than we do recognized the obvious. There was no doubt in their minds that Islam's founder was a money-grubbing con, a mean-spirited thug who was out for himself.

Here's an example, up close and personal: *Ishaq:602* **"Jadd told Muhammad, 'Will you allow me to stay behind and not tempt me? Everyone knows that I am strongly addicted to women. I'm afraid that I'll see Byzantine women and will not be able to control myself.'"** This suggests that Muhammad "tempted" Muslims to fight, and that he offered them captured women as booty. **"The Apostle gave him permission to remain behind."** In other words, he didn't want the competition. **"It was about him that Allah sent down: 'There are some who say: "Give me leave to stay behind and do not tempt me." Surely they have fallen into temptation already and hell encompasses these unbelievers.' (9:49) It was not that he feared the temptation from the Byzantine women. The temptation he had fallen into was greater in that he had hung back from the Apostle and sought to please himself rather than Muhammad. Verily hell awaits him."** There are three messages here and all are bad. Being "tempted" to rape is a lesser offense than being a pacifist. The highest calling in Islam is to "please Muhammad." And, if you don't fight, you go to hell.

If you are a peaceful Muslim your god hates you, and he wants to punish you. *Ishaq:603* **"One of the estranged ones said to another, 'Don't go out to fight in this heat.' He disliked strenuous war, doubted the truth, and created misgivings about the Apostle. So Allah sent down regarding them, 'And they said, "Do not go out in this heat." Say, "The fires of hell are hotter. Let them laugh a little now for they will weep a great deal later as a reward for what they did.'"** You will find this gem buried in the 82nd verse of **"The Feast"** surah. A related Hadith says: *Ishaq:603* **"Some Bedouins came to apologize for not going into battle, but Allah would not accept their excuses."**

Ishaq:603 **"The Apostle went forward energetically with his preparations and ordered the men to get ready with all speed. He urged Muslims to help provide the money, mounts, and means to do Allah's work. Those who contributed earned rewards with Allah."** This is why Islamic despots like the Saudi warlords fund terrorism. But those who have tried to cash in their reward aren't happy with the deal they struck.

Like all pirates, Muhammad had to constantly watch his backside. *Tabari IX:51* **"Ali seized his weapons and set off until he caught up with Muhammad. 'The hypocrites allege that you left me behind because you found me burdensome and wanted to get rid of me.' He replied, 'They lied. I left you behind because of what I have left behind. So go back and represent me in my family.'"** The kind of men who were willing to rob were just as likely to pick his pockets. So the pirate king told his son and son-in-law, "Don't let them steal my booty or my babes."

The first Muslims didn't care much for the prophet's company. *Tabari IX:55* **"The Messenger continued his march but his men began to fall behind. The Prophet said, 'Leave them, for if there is any good in them, Allah will unite them [with the rest of his pirates]; if not, Allah has relieved you of them."** So the peaceful Muslims died of exposure, hunger, and thirst—their just dessert.

Tabari IX:57 **"A band of hypocrites...going along with the Prophet as he was marching toward Tabuk said, 'Do you think that fighting these people will be like the others we have fought? It looks to me as if we will be tied with ropes tomorrow.' They said this in order to intimidate and frighten the faithful. But then they said, 'Every one of us would rather be flogged a hundred lashes to escape Allah revealing a verse about us and what we have said.'"** One of the Muslim snitches ratted out these men to his general. So the chief pirate turned in his saddle and confronted the bad Muslims. They protested, "'O Prophet, we were simply playing and speaking nonsense.' Then Allah sent down a Qur'an about them. 'And if you question them, then assuredly they will say, "We were only speaking nonsense and playing."'" (Qur'an 9:65) *Ishaq:607* "Abd Ar-Rahman, the man for whom the Qur'an had been sent down, said, 'O Apostle, my name disgraces me.'" The rock idol Ar-Rahman was no longer vogue. And it's one more proof that Ar-Rahman was not merely a title, or attribute, for Allah.

But this wasn't a game to Muhammad; it was a scam. He had business to conduct. *Tabari IX:58* "When the Messenger reached Tabuk the governor of Aylah [a seaport at the north end of the Gulf of Aqabah] came to him, made a treaty, and agreed to pay the jizyah tax. The people of Jarba and Adhruh also offered to pay him the tax." It was Muhammad's favorite verse: "Gimme da money." Not a word was spoken about summoning them to Islam. Muhammad wasn't out with his troops being religious. He didn't bother calling the lost heathens to faith. No. He just wanted their money. This man wasn't a prophet. He was a pirate. His scam had become what Khadija envisioned: The Profitable Prophet Plan. The Ka'aba Inc. was now paying dividends.

Muhammad summoned additional village leaders to make their contributions. Some: *Tabari IX:59/Ishaq:607* "encountered the Messenger's cavalry which was led by Khalid. Ukaydir was seized and his brother Hassan was killed. Hassan was wearing a silk brocade gown woven with gold in the form of palm leaves. Khalid stripped him of it and sent it to Muhammad. When it arrived, the Muslims felt it with their hands, admiring it." They felt no remorse for the man whose blood they had spilled upon it. They were fundamental Muslims and Islam had corrupted them with words like these: "The Prophet said, 'Are you amazed at it? The kerchiefs in Paradise are better than this.'" He, like Hitler, was incapable of pity.

Later, "Khalid brought Ukaydir to Muhammad. He spared his life and made peace with him on the condition that he pay the zakat tax." Mission accomplished, "they left Tabuk and returned to Medina." *Tabari IX:60* "On the way, Muhammad ordered that whoever got to the first well before him should not drink until he arrived. Some of the hypocrites arrived and drew water. The Prophet cursed them and invoked Allah's curse on them." Nurturing the flock wasn't part of his job description.

The translator of Volume IX of The History of al-Tabari, *The Last Years of the Prophet*, inserted a footnote here to make certain that we understood the nature of these expeditions. "The term *sariyyah* is applied to an army sent by the Prophet in contradistinction to *ghazwah* or *maghazi*, meaning a raiding party wherein the Prophet himself participates." You've got to question a religion that has words for things like this.

Bukhari:V5B59N702 "I heard Kab bin Malik narrating the story of the Ghazwah of Tabuk in which he failed to take part. Kab said, 'I did not abandon Allah's Apostle in any Ghazwa he fought except the Tabuk raid. I failed to take part in the Ghazwa of Badr, but Allah did not admonish anyone who had not participated in it, for in fact, Allah's Apostle had only gone out in search of the Quraysh caravan. I witnessed the night of al-Aqaba with Allah's

Apostle when we pledged [to war against all mankind] for Islam, and I would not exchange it for the Badr battle although Badr is more popular among Muslims than the pledge. As for my news in this battle of Tabuk, I had never been stronger or wealthier than I was when I was with the Prophet in Ghazwas.'" This is a wonderful summation of Islam.

The Bukhari Tradition continues with: "'When I heard that the Prophet was on his way back to Medina. I got concerned, and began to think of false excuses, saying to myself, "How can I avoid his anger?" Those who had failed to join the battle of Tabuk came and started offering excuses. There were more than eighty men from whom Allah's Apostle accepted excuses. Then he took their pledge of allegiance. When I came he smiled a smile of an angry person and then said, "What stopped you from joining us. Had you not purchased an animal for carrying you?" I answered, "Yes. But..."'" The prophet and his militants treated Kab like a pariah, banishing him from the community. They said of the twice-peaceful Muslim, "We never witnessed you sinning like this before." Then "Allah's Apostle forbade all Muslims from talking to him. Kab said, 'I used to go out and pray with the Muslims and roam the markets, but no one would talk to me. This harsh attitude of the people lasted for a long time; even my cousin, who was the dearest person to me, did not return my greetings. Thereupon my eyes flowed with tears.'" It's no fun being a peaceful Muslim.

Muhammad and his militants make Osama bin Laden's al-Qaeda gang look like Boy Scouts. *Tabari IX:64* "Hatim said, 'Adi, whatever you were going to do before Muhammad's cavalry descended upon us, do it now, for I have seen the banners of his army.' When the Islamic cavalry left the settlement they took Hatim's daughter along with other captives. She was brought to the Messenger with slaves from Tayyi. He put her in an enclosure by the door of his mosque where the captives were detained." The mosque was now a prison, a symbol of Muhammad's power and control, not of his religion or faith. This woman was a rape victim in waiting.

Sounding a lot like a Nazi propagandist, Hitler's Goebbels perhaps, a fundamentalist Muslim laid out Islam's agenda: *Tabari IX:69* "Arabs are the most noble people in lineage, the most prominent, and the best in deeds. We were the first to respond to the Prophet's call. We are Allah's helpers and the viziers of His Messenger. We fight people until they believe in Allah. He who believes in Allah and His Messenger has protected his life and possessions from us. As for those who disbelieve, we will fight them forever in the Cause of Allah and killing them is a small matter to us. Peace be onto you." These are terrifying words—words that should be shouted from every political rostrum, from every pulpit, and into every microphone. This man had not corrupted Islam; Islam had corrupted him. Any doctrine that, when properly implemented, inspires such loathing, looting, and lunacy cannot be tolerated. Until Islam is held responsible for the carnage it inspires, terror will continue "forever." "Killing is a small matter" to them.

Tabari dedicates another nine pages to the ninth year of the Islamic Era. They focus on a single theme, money. *Tabari IX:74* "Indeed, Allah has guided you with His guidance. If you wish to do well [capture booty], obey Allah and His Messenger. You must perform the prayers, pay the zakat tax, and give a fifth share of Allah's booty to His Messenger. The required zakat is: from the land one tenth of that watered by springs and rain, and one twentieth of that watered by the leathern bucket. From camels, a milch camel for every forty camels, and a young male camel for every thirty camels. From sheep, one for every five camels; and from cows, one from every fourth... If anyone pays more, it is to his credit. He who professes this, bears witness to his Islam and helps the faithful [fight] against the polytheists, he has the protection of Allah and His Messenger." It was the Profit's pay-me-now and pay-me-later plan. Muhammad used terrorism to confiscate property; then he used Islam to force his victims into submission so that he could tax them, bleeding them dry.

The zakat continues to be an asset-based tax of five to ten percent imposed annually on Muslims. In addition, they are required to give up one fifth of any booty they steal in the name of Islam. Bonus points are awarded for additional contributions to the ongoing war effort—Islamic Imperialism. So long as Muslims pay, they have nothing to fear. If they don't, everything is confiscated and the niggardly Muslim is exterminated. Lenin, Mao, and Hitler imposed a similar regimen.

Now that Muhammad had fleeced his flock, it was time to hammer the infidels. *Tabari IX:75* **"He who holds fast to his religion, Judaism or Christianity, is not to be tempted from it."** Now why do you think that might be? Since Muhammad and his god have said that Christian and Jewish unbelievers are the faggot's of Allah's Hell Fire, why not "tempt" them from their torturous fate? What could be more important to a pirate, I mean profiteer, excuse me, prophet, than souls? **"It is incumbent on them to pay the jizyah protection tax. For every adult, male or female, free or slave, one full denarius, or its value in al-ma'afir [fine cloth]. He who pays that to the Messenger has the protection of Allah and His Messenger, and he who holds back from it is the enemy of Allah and His Messenger."** Sheep were good, camels were better, but when it came to becoming Muhammad's pal, nothing beat the glitter of gold. Al Capone, I mean, the Prophet Muhammad said, "Pay me money and I'll protect you from me." As with the Mafia, it was all about the money. The infidel jizyah tax was imposed at a much higher rate than the Muslim zakat. Muhammad didn't want non-Muslims tempted because it would lower his income. In the choice between religion and revenue, Muhammad had chosen money.

During debates with Islamic clerics I often point out that Muslims were only tolerant because the jizyah was more lucrative than the zakat. While they don't dispute that, as it would make their prophet and god liars as opposed to pirates, they protest that the infidel tax was for their protection. "Protection from whom," I ask without response. Yet they know that the protection was from the sword of Islam as the preceding Hadith confirms. The rules of the game were straightforward: **"He who holds back from paying is the enemy of Allah and His Messenger."** If Christians and Jews coughed up the jizyah they got to keep their heads. It was tolerance, Islam style.

Before we press on, I'd like to highlight Muhammad's choice of words. Jews and Christians, unlike Muslims, weren't to be **"tempted."** By selecting this word, the prophet corroborated my theory. Muslims were seduced into Islam with the same temptations that ensnared Muhammad: sex, power, and money. *Tabari IX:76* **"The Messenger has sent Zur'ah and his Companions to you. 'I commend them to your care. Collect the zakat and jizyah from your districts and hand the money over to my messengers.' The Prophet is the master of your rich and your poor."** Muhammad's use of **"messengers"** was in perfect harmony with the Profitable Prophet Plan. His view of himself as **"master"** is corroboration of his unquenchable lust for power. And this message repudiates his claim of being a Biblical prophet in the line of Moses. Real prophets were neither tax collectors nor masters.

Muhammad said: **"Malik has reported to me that you were the first from Himyar to embrace Islam and that you have killed infidels, so rejoice at your good fortune."** Embrace Islam, kill, and then rejoice. It's the *quid pro quo* of Muslim militancy. It is the reason the Muslim world celebrates death and honors murderers.

But Islam wasn't all money grubbing, power coveting, murderous terror— it was about discrimination, too. *Tabari IX:78* **"No polytheist shall come near the Holy Mosque, and no one shall circumambulate Allah's House naked."** Never mind that pagans built the Ka'aba, that it was a shrine for polytheists, or that each of the pagan rites and rituals they observed were incorporated into Islam; polytheists were no longer welcome under the big tent of the new and improved religion.

Tabari IX:79 **"In this year the zakat was made obligatory, and the Messenger dispatched his agents to collect it. The verse was revealed: 'Take the zakat from their wealth to purify them.'"** Allah was always ready with the perfect scripture revelation for whatever his messenger craved. It's hard to find a god like that. It's also hard to imagine a dogma so transparent it calls stealing "purification."

The poligious doctrine of submission laid down the law. On April 8th 631 A.D., Diman, in the Prophet's presence, prioritized: *Tabari IX:80* **"The obligatory acts of Islam one by one. 'The zakat tax, fasting, pilgrimage, and all the Sunnah or laws of the Prophet.'"** Money was number one. And worshipping Allah didn't even make the list.

Muhammad wouldn't be the "peace-loving" founder of the "tolerant and inclusive" religotic of Islam if he didn't terrorize somebody at the beginning of his final year. *Tabari IX:82* **"The Messenger sent [killer] Khalid with an army of 400 to Harith [a South Arabian tribe] and ordered him to invite them to Islam for three days before he fought them. If they were to respond and submit, he was to teach them the Book of Allah, the Sunnah of His Prophet, and the requirements of Islam [pay Muhammad the money]. If they should decline, then he was to fight them."** Submit or die. Muhammad's Islam wasn't the least bit ambiguous. Nor was this messenger. Khalid was the Islamic militant who bound and butchered an entire Arab village after promising peace. Muhammad pretended to separate himself from the senseless slaughter of innocent families with an ostentatious public prayer. Yet the prophet never repudiated Khalid's behavior, never refused the booty, or refrained from sending the terrorist tax collector out on subsequent raids.

The **"Sunnah of the Prophet"** described in these last two Traditions is nothing more than the use of Muhammad's example—his words and deeds—to establish ideal Islamic behavior. The Sunnah codifies religious rituals, customs, taxation, and law. This is the Hadith's parallel of the 33rd surah, in which Allah commands Muslims to emulate Muhammad's example.

The sole repository of these "virtuous" Islamic behaviors and words is found in the Hadith. And only four collections are credible—Ishaq, Bukhari, Tabari, and Muslim—all tracing back to within 300 years of the prophet's death. By way of confirmation, the Islamic scholar who translated Muslim's Hadith wrote: **"Sahih Muslim is a collection of the sayings and deeds of the Prophet Muhammad (pbuh). It is known as the Sunnah. These reports of the Prophet's sayings and deeds are called Hadith. Muslim lived a couple of centuries after the Prophet's death and worked hard to collect his Hadith. Each report in his collection was checked for compatibility with the Qur'an. The veracity of the chain of reporters, called an isnad, had to be painstakingly established. Muslim's collection is recognized by the overwhelming majority of the Muslim world to be one of the most authentic collections of the Sunnah of the Prophet Muhammad (pbuh)."**

Muslim scholars and imams alike claim that the heinous deeds and immoral words which comprised the Sunnah were inspired by Allah. That makes the Hadith "scripture." That means that pedophilia, incest, polygamy, fornication, rape, deceit, seduction, indoctrination, thievery, the slave trade, racism, fighting, piracy, bribery, intolerance, political assassination, mass murder, and terrorism are authorized Sunnah—the only approved Islamic behaviors. As such, all good Muslims are bad people. To be a good person one has to be a bad Muslim or a non-Muslim. There are no exceptions.

If you believe the world needs more good Muslim rapists who conquer, plunder, terrorize, and murder while indoctrinating others to act in like fashion, continue to ignore the Third Commandment and tolerate Islam's existence. But if you believe these behaviors will lead to death and damnation, you may want to heed the words Yahweh etched in stone 3,200 years ago: "You shall not accept or tolerate in the name or character of Yahweh, your Deity, anything that is false, deceptive, or destructive." I suggest we follow his advice.

In the last year of Muhammad's life, the wannabe prophet turned parasitic tyrant began to sense his mortality. He had more sex, money, and power than he could handle. The only thing left was immortality. So the most vile man who ever lived commanded that his Sunnah, or example, be imposed upon the world by force of arms. The 1,400 year long river of blood that has flowed from Medina is the result.

Tabari IX:83 **"The Messenger commanded me, and I sent riders announcing, 'Arabs, embrace Islam and you will be safe.' They surrendered and did not fight. I stayed, ordering them to fulfill the requirements of Islam."** Then to make certain no one would errantly accept Islam out of some misguided notion that it was a religion inspired by God rather than simply one man's quest for sex, power, and money, Muhammad proclaimed: *Tabari IX:85* **"None but the purified shall touch the Qur'an."** Therefore, one hundred percent of Muslims were compelled into Islam by the sword or seduced by some errant interpretation. Allah's "revelation" persuaded no one. And I believe that is true even today. Very few Muslims understand what the Qur'an actually says. Fewer still know the Sunnah as presented by the first Hadith collectors—Ishaq, Tabari, Bukhari, and Muslim. And that's both good and bad. Good people, exposed to the truth, will reject Muhammad and discard Islam. That's good. But bad people continue to use the poligious doctrine as it was conceived for their own gain.

Tabari IX:86 **"Give the people the good news of [virgins and gluttony in] Paradise and the way to attain it [by killing Christians and Jews]. Warn them of the Hell-Fire and the way to earn it [by being peaceful]. Teach them the rites of the [pagan] pilgrimage, its practices, its obligations [that I usurped from Qusayy] and what Allah has commanded about the hajj and umrah.... He orders you to offer prayer at the appropriate times with proper bowing and humility.... He orders you to give one fifth of Allah's booty and pay the zakat tax. It is enjoined on the faithful from their land and property.... And don't seduce the Jews or Christians for incumbent on them is to pay the jizyah protection tax."** You just can't beat good old-fashioned religion for robbing and controlling folks. **"Allah's Apostle dispersed his representatives to every land where Islam had entered to collect the zakat."** Muhammad has done a swell job of proving that Islam was all about the money. There is no reason to call the Profitable Profit Plan a theory anymore.

Religion is the damnation of mankind. Its rituals are an opiate, deadening the mind, but it's worse than that. Religion is the most powerful and seductive control mechanism ever conceived. From the first religion instituted in Nimrod's Babylon to that imposed by the Egyptians, Assyrians, Greeks, Romans, Catholics, Muslims, Nazis, and Communists, poligious doctrines have been the source of power, control, and wealth for cleric and king. Religions have been the impetus and excuse for thievery and war. While Islam is the worst of a bad lot, most are without merit. The religions of man have served to separate men and women from freedom, prosperity, and God.

For another lesson in fundamental Islam, we turn to: *Tabari IX:88* **"Abdallah Azdi came to the Messenger, embraced Islam, and became a good Muslim. Allah's Apostle invested Azdi with the authority over those who had surrendered and ordered him to fight the infidels from the tribes of Yemen. Azdi left with an army by the Messenger's command. The Muslims besieged them for a month. Then they withdrew, setting a trap. When the Yemenites went in pursuit, Azdi was able to inflict a heavy loss on them."** Muhammad has defined a "good" Muslim as a jihad fighter. And Azdi demonstrates that a little Islam goes a long way.

Skimming over the next twenty pages in al-Tabari we find Arabs poking fun and pretending to be Muhammad. In jest they "revealed surahs in rhyming speech, imitating the Qur'an." They even made paradise on earth "permitting fornication and the drinking of wine." Others were out "trashing" men with "prescribed punishments and lashings." Lots of folks were "deputized," became "good Muslims," and coerced others into "submission." Armies marched, skirmishes were fought, men were killed or banished, cattle were stolen, and young girls were captured and turned into slaves. There was even talk of sorcerers and casting evil spells. One must have worked, because: *Tabari IX:105* "Allah sent a thunderbolt which scorched a man and his camel."

Tabari IX:108 "When Allah's Messenger returned to Medina after performing the hajj of Perfection in Religion, he began to have a complaint of illness." What do you suppose it was—gluttony, venereal disease, or a dead conscience? "News of the Prophet's illness spread, so Musaylimah [a Yemeni "messenger" virtually identical to Muhammad, religiously] leapt at the opportunity to claim the prophethood for himself." Abu Bakr would ultimately slaughter the Yemenites in the War of Compulsion but for now the Muslims were content to rob them. *Tabari IX:111* "Ali returned from Yemen with an army dressed in white linen to meet Muhammad." But the sexy uniforms were stolen; thus they were technically part of the Yemeni booty. So they were stripped off the soldiers who had stolen them and were thrown back in with the rest of the confiscated treasure.

That brings us to Muhammad's "Farewell Sermon." Like the rest of Islam, it was a far cry from Christ's Sermon on the Mount. In the opening stanza, the prophet tried to justify removing the intercalating month. Then, in the most important and revealing line Muhammad ever spoke, he said: *Tabari IX:112* "Beware of Satan in your religion."

Proving that Islam could be as brutal as any occult doctrine, the sexist proclaimed: *Tabari IX:113* "You have a right over your wives and they have a right over you. You have the right that they should not cause anyone of whom you dislike to tread your beds; and that they should not commit any open indecency. If they do, then Allah permits you to shut them in separate rooms and to beat them, but not severely. If they abstain from (evil), they have the right to food and clothing. Treat women well for they are like domestic animals with you and they do not possess anything themselves. Allah has made the enjoyment of their bodies lawful in his Qur'an."

As you might expect, whatever minimal "rights" women might have had in Islam didn't make the list. The abused boy had become an abuser. Women would pay for abandoning him as a child. With this speech, Muhammad condemned over a billion people. Husbands have been told that their wives are their possessions—worth no more than a domesticated animal. Men can beat women. They can strip them and lock them up in a closet. Husbands only have to feed their wives if they behave.

A Muslim Hadith confirms Muhammad's contempt. *Muslim:B1N142* **"'O women-folk, you should ask for forgiveness for I saw you in bulk amongst the dwellers of Hell.' A wise lady said: Why is it, Allah's Apostle, that women comprise the bulk of the inhabitants of Hell? The Prophet observed: 'You curse too much and are ungrateful to your spouses. You lack common sense, fail in religion and rob the wisdom of the wise.' Upon this the woman remarked: What is wrong with our common sense? The Prophet replied, 'Your lack of common sense can be determined from the fact that the evidence of two women is equal to one man. That is a proof.'"** The Qur'an says that the testimony of women, as well as their value, is half that of men. And the Hadith claims that Allah made women stupid. Stupid, no; wrong, yes. Women endure hellish lives in Islam, yet most non-Muslim women simply ignore their plight.

Across America, hundreds of thousands of women have been seduced into Islam. It's presented as a way to rebel against Judeo-Christianity and the godless depravity of the media culture. Yet these women know nothing of Muhammad's life and are offended when I read from the Qur'an and Hadith. The fundamental precepts of the Sunnah are completely alien to them. The nature of Jihad and the prophet's life don't mesh with the politically correct veneer that is used to beguile the media and the masses. Where is the public outcry against this deception, bigotry, and abuse?

I find the following words outrageous. And I'm surprised that no one seems to care. *Bukhari:V3B48N826* **"The Prophet said, 'Isn't the witness of a woman equal to half of that of a man?' The women said, 'Yes.' He said, 'This is because of the deficiency of a woman's mind.'"** *Ishaq:584* **"Tell the men with you who have wives: never trust a woman."** Every aspect of Islam is rotten. It's repressive, racist, sexist, and unforgivably violent. Islam is the most lethal form of religious poison ever concocted.

Yet it's simplistic. It's amazing that something this infantile could wreak such havoc. *Tabari IX:115* **"The Messenger completed the pilgrimage, showed the people its rites, and taught them what was required of them including the stations, the throwing of pebbles, the running around the Ka'aba, and what Allah had permitted them to do [like beating their wives, killing infidels, and stealing booty], and what He had forbidden [like being tolerant, not sharing the booty, and withholding the tax]."** The pilgrimage, the rites, the stations, the throwing of pebbles, and the circumambulation were all part of Qusayy's scam. And the other requirements—fighting and sharing booty—were brutal and immoral.

As the aged prophet was petering out, his companions wanted an accurate accounting of the things that mattered most to Muhammad. The next twenty-seven pages of al-Tabari's History are dedicated to counting the number of terrorist raids the prophet personally led, those he simply commissioned, the people he had assassinated, the times he had humbled the Meccans with his presence, and the number of wives, concubines and sex slaves in his harem. Tabari, Ishaq, Bukhari, and Muslim all cover this same material. But so as to provide a sense of proportion, I am going to stick with one account. And I am going to cover this summation in the order in which it was reported.

Tabari IX:115 **"The military expeditions (Ghazawat) in which the Messenger personally participated were twenty-six. Some say there were twenty-seven."** The victims are listed in the order they were abused, which is puzzling. If Muslims can remember exactly who they robbed and when, but can't remember what comprised a surah or when it was revealed, what does it say about their priorities?

Tabari IX:118 **"The armies and raiding parties sent by the Messenger of Allah between the time he came to Medina and his death (ten years) was thirty-five."** This rather chilling admission is followed by another detailed and chronological listing of tribes. But there was no unanimity of opinion. A subsequent Hadith claims: **"The armies and raiding parties sent by the Messenger were forty-eight."** When you add the number of raids the prophet led to the number he sent, the total becomes alarming. In just over one hundred months he instigated seventy-five assaults. Combined with the three-dozen men and women, he specifically ordered his militants to assassinate, it adds up to at least one slaying or mass murder for each month Muhammad ruled during the Islamic Era. That makes the prophet the most successful Muslim terrorist of all time. "Peace be unto him."

And he wasn't through. After assassinating Yusayr, a Jew from Khaybar, by severing his leg and letting him bleed to death, the prophet sent his Islamic commandoes out to slay another. *Tabari IX:121* **"The Messenger called me and said, 'I suspect that Khalid Sufyan is going to attack me. So go to him and kill him.' 'O Prophet, describe him to me so that I might know him.' He said, 'When you see him he will remind you of Satan.'"** Which is to say, "He will look, act, and talk like Muhammad.

Demonstrating the traits of a good Muslim, the assassin managed to track his victim down, pray, and then murder him in front of his wife and daughters. *Tabari IX:121* **"When it was feasible for me, I struck him with my sword and killed him. Then I departed, leaving his women to throw themselves at him. When I returned to the Prophet, he asked, 'Is your mission accomplished?' 'Yes. I have killed him.'"** Islam might be a religion after all: Muhammad's henchman was on a "mission."

Following more assassinations, there were additional raids. *Tabari IX:122* **"Muhammad sent Uyaynah to raid The Banu Anbar. They killed some people and took others captive. Asma was one of the women taken prisoner."** It was all in a day's work—part of the rites and rituals of Islam. *Tabari IX:123* **"Muhammad sent an expedition to Ghalib and to the land of the Banu Murrah. The expedition of Amr and Abi was sent to the valley of Idam. Another by Aslami was sent to Ghabah. And Abd al-Rahman was ordered by the Messenger to lead an army to the seashore."** Let's just assume that these terrorist attacks were included in the original seventy-five. Enough already.

Tabari IX:126 **"The Messenger of Allah married fifteen women. He combined eleven at a time and left behind nine."** This, of course, does not include rape victims, concubines, and sex slaves but does include pedophilia and incest.

Speaking of pedophilia: *Ishaq:311* **"The Apostle saw Ummu'l when she was a baby** crawling before his feet and said, 'If she grows up, I will marry her.' But he died before he was able to do so." *Tabari IX:128* "Aisha, when he married her was very young and not yet ready for consumption." *Tabari IX:130* "Bakr married Aisha to Muhammad when she was only six years old." *Tabari IX:131* "My mother came to me while I was being swung on a swing between two branches and got me down. My nurse wiped my face with some water and started leading me. When I was at the door she stopped so I could catch my breath. I was then brought in while the Messenger was sitting on a bed in our house. My mother made me sit on his lap. Then the men and women got up and left. The Prophet consummated his marriage with me in my house when I was nine years old." Most rational people prefer to get their spiritual inspiration from someone who isn't a sexual predator and pervert.

Some of the low lights of the stallion's conquests include: *Tabari IX:133* "Juwayriyyah was chosen by the Messenger for himself on the day of the Muraysi raid from the captives." "Muhammad married Umm, who had embraced Christianity." *Tabari IX:134* "Muhammad took Zaynab [his daughter-in-law] but Allah did not find any fault in the [incestuous] relationship and ordered the marriage." *Tabari IX:135* "When the Prophet scrutinized the captives on the day of Khaybar, he threw his cloak over Safayah. Thus she was his chosen one." *Tabari IX:139* "The Messenger married Ghaziyyah after the news of her beauty and skill had reached him." *Tabari IX:137* "Allah granted Rayhanah of the [Jewish] Qurayza to His Messenger as booty [but only after she had been forced to watch him decapitate her father and brother, seen her mother hauled off to be raped, and her sisters sold into slavery]." *Tabari IX:137* "Mariyah, a Copt slave, was presented to the Prophet. She was given to him by Muqawqis, the ruler of Alexandria." Muhammad was one sick puppy.

Tabari IX:138 "The Prophet married Aliyyah, a Bakr woman. He gave her gifts for divorce and left her. He also married Qutaylah, but he died before he could consummate the marriage." *Tabari IX:139* "Layla approached the Prophet while his back was to the sun and clapped him on his shoulder. He asked her who it was and she replied, 'I am the daughter of one who competes with the wind. I am Layla. I have come to offer myself to you.' He replied, 'I accept.'" Layla scampered back home and shared her story with mommy and daddy. "They said, 'What a bad thing you have done! You are a self-respecting girl, but the Prophet is a womanizer.'" Now *there* is an understatement.

The next half-dozen pages provide an accounting of Muhammad's slaves. *Tabari IX:147* "A eunuch named Mubur was presented to Muhammad along with two slave girls. One he took as a concubine, the other he gave to Haasn."

There are twenty-two pages devoted to the collection of the zakat and jizyah taxes in this summation of Islam's formation, twenty-seven pages of accounting notes dedicated to terrorist raids, and sixteen chronicling the prophet's sexual perversity, yet there is only one paragraph devoted to scribes. Since Muhammad was illiterate, and since the Qur'an was supposed to be his miraculous gift from Allah to mankind, how is it that writing scripture received eighty-eight times less attention than money, one hundred and eight times less than terrorist raids or sixty-four times less attention than sex? Islam wasn't about saving mankind and leading them to god. It was about power, sex, and money. Collectively, these things were 260 times more important than scripture. Something to think about if you are a Muslim.

As an interesting aside to Muhammad's scribes, we discovered earlier that one of them, Abdallah bin Sa'd, had quite a story. He was the only person who ever attempted to commit Qur'anic revelations to parchment while they were still fresh in Muhammad's mind. According to the Hadith, he became concerned that some of the phraseology didn't sound godly, so he suggested enhancements. When Muhammad accepted his edits, Abdallah rejected Islam. He recognized that the Qur'an couldn't be from "God" if he, a lowly scribe, could copyedit it. But the story didn't end there. Abdallah had a secret that Muhammad had to conceal. If word got out that he was just making this stuff up as he went along, he would lose everything he had struggled to gain. So...

Tabari VIII:178 **"When the Messenger entered Mecca he ordered that the following men should be killed even if they were under the Ka'aba. First among them was Abdallah bin Sa'd."**

Al-Tabari's Hadiths go on to invest twenty-five times more ink to the pet names Muhammad ascribed to his possessions than to memorializing the Qur'an. We are regaled with the monikers of his horses, mules, camels, sheep, swords, bows, lances, coats of mail, and shields. This list climaxes with the prophet's names for himself. With his insecurities showing, he said: *Tabari IX:156* **"The Messenger of Allah named himself to us in various ways. He said, 'I am Muhammad the one who is praised, Ahmad, the most praiseworthy, al-Aqib, the last in succession, and al-Mahi, the obliterator.'"** They go from bad to worse.

The following physical description sounds more like an ape than a man: *Tabari IX:157* **"The Messenger was neither tall nor short. He had a large head and beard, with big black eyes. His palms and feet were calloused; he had large joints, his face was white with a reddish tinge, his chest hair was long, and when he walked he bent forward as if he were descending a slope."** Maybe Muhammad misspoke when he said that Allah transformed *Jews* into monkeys.

For those in the Nation of Islam trying to seduce disgruntled young black men into Islam by claiming that Muhammad was a man of color, the next Hadith is devastating. *Tabari IX:158* **"He was a white man."**

Muhammad's **"Seal of Prophethood"** was as ugly as his scripture. We have this from a pair of Abu's: *Tabari IX:159* **"The Messenger said, 'O Abu Zayd, come close to me and wipe my back.' I put my finger on the Seal and touched it. The Seal was a collection of hairs on his shoulders." "I asked Abu Said about the Seal which the Prophet had, and he said that it was like a protruding lump of flesh."**

With the prophet's career summarized and his attributes documented, it's time we take a final look at the man who mirrored his character and mission. Only miles and years distinguished Hitler from his mentor.

Der fuhrer's methods for accomplishing his madness were identical to der prophet's: *Mein Kampf:676* "*Spiritual terror...men must threaten and dominate men by compulsion. Compulsion is only broken by compulsion and terror by terror.*" On the road to power, compulsion follows seduction. And the lever that coerces compulsion is terror. Hitler simply followed Muhammad's path. *Bukhari:V4B52N220* **"Allah's Apostle said, 'I have been made victorious with terror.'"**

Mein Kampf:677 "*Since our view of life will never share power with another, it cannot co-operate with the existing doctrines it condemns. It is obliged to fight by all available means until the entire world of hostile ideas collapses.*" Throughout the entirety of the Islamic era we have heard a singular battle cry: *Bukhari:V4B53N386* **"Our Prophet, the Messenger of our Lord, ordered us to fight you till you worship Allah Alone."** Both men envisioned an eternal battle and total submission.

Mein Kampf:677 "*This corrosive fight...for the new program and new view of life demands determined fighters...and a forceful fighting organization. The recipe for a favorable result requires the formulation of a declaration of war against all existing orders, and against all existing conceptions of life in general.*" Just like Islam, it was the Nazis against the world. The "House of Islam" forever battles the "House of War." *Tabari IX:69* **He who believes in Allah and His Messenger has protected his life and possessions from us. As for those who disbelieve, we will fight them forever in the Cause of Allah. Killing them is a small matter to us.**"

The Nazis usurped Muhammad's dogma. The recipe of "submit and obey" was perfect for empowering their tyrant. *Mein Kampf:679* "*The strength of a party lies in the disciplined obedience of the members to follow their leadership. The decisive factors are leadership and discipline. When troops battle one another, the victorious one will be that which is blindly obedient to the Superior Leader.*" Islam says: *Ishaq:601* **"The best men launch spears as if they were swords. They peer forward unweariedly. They devote their lives to their Prophet. In hand-to-hand fighting and cavalry attacks they purify themselves with the blood of the infidels. They consider that an act of piety."**

It is hard to distinguish which poligious doctrine was more fixated on violence. *Mein Kampf:680* "*In order to lead a view of life to victory, we have to transform it into a fighting movement.*" *Ishaq:587* **"Our onslaught will not be a weak faltering affair. We shall fight as long as we live. We will fight until you turn to Islam, humbly seeking refuge. We will fight not caring whom we meet. We will fight whether we destroy ancient holdings or newly gotten gains. We have cut off every opponent's nose and ears with our swords. We have driven them violently before us at the command of Allah and Islam. We will fight until our religion is established. And we will plunder them for they must suffer disgrace."**

Like Muhammad, Hitler seduced men before he coerced them. He made promises but never delivered. *Mein Kampf:683* "*The Party with its program of twenty-five points is unshakable.*" Ten of the twenty-five Nazi pillars were financial inducements, bribes if you will. Twelve were control mechanisms. Three were focused on fighting. The following Islamic concepts made Hitler's list in *Mein Kampf:* "*abrogation,*" "*duty,*" "*annulment of treaties,*" the "*confiscation of war booty,"* profit sharing or *"distribution of spoils,"* the party's cut or *"fifth,"* *"conquest," "expulsion of nonbelievers," "alms"* or pensions for believers, *"Jewish businesses to be looted and divided," "Jewish land to become communal,"* a *"ban on Jewish usury," "Jews to be punished by death," "the establishment of the laws"* of der Fuhrer, the formation of *"an army," "restrictions on journalists,"* and a *"recasting of Christianity."* Apart from time and place, der fuhrer's list was an awful lot like der prophet's.

Both men were serious about their personal views. It was their way or the highway. *Mein Kampf:698 "The N.S.G.W.P. must not become a bailiff of public opinion, but its ruler. It must not be the masses' slave, but their master!"* Muhammad wasn't much of a listener either. *047.021* **"Were they to obey, showing their obedience in modest speech, after the matter of preparation for Jihad had been determined for them, it would have been better."**

If the definition of propaganda is artful deceit, Hitler and Muhammad were grand masters. *Mein Kampf:701 "On behalf of our view of life I will strike the weapon of reply from the enemy's hand personally."* And how might der fuhrer accomplish this? *Mein Kampf:702 "Skillful propaganda.... The best proof of this was furnished by the success of the propaganda, introduced by me, against the peace treaty of Versailles. I had before me a surging crowd filled with most sacred indignation and utter wrath. A great lie had been torn out of the brains and hearts of a multitude, and in its stead, a truth had been implanted.... In this meeting I became familiar with the pathos and the gestures which mesmerizing a thousand people demands."* Islam and Nazism share an unhealthy trait, the willingness to link "sacred" to "wrath." And neither can be trusted as they are willing to abrogate treaties which they do not like. *Qur'an 009.003* **"And a declaration from Allah and His Messenger to all mankind: 'Allah is free from all treaty obligations with non-Muslims and so is His Messenger."**

Confirming the role of seductive verbal expression in achieving victory, der fuhrer shared: *Mein Kampf:704 "The emphasis was put on the spoken word because only it is in a position to bring about great changes for general psychological reasons. Enormous world revolutionary events have not been brought about by the written word, but by the spoken word."* *Mein Kampf:704 "The agitatory activity of speech is bound to have mass influence."* Hitler went on to say that spoken words were like pictures because they communicate more vividly and faster than text. His mentor never allowed his words to be written or read, only spoken. And that's because: *Bukhari:V6B60N662* **"Allah's Apostle said, 'Some eloquent speech is as effective as magic.'"** *Bukhari:V9B87N127* **"The Prophet said, 'I have been given the keys of eloquent speech and given victory with terror so the treasures of the earth were given to me.'"**

Expounding upon the merits of Muhammad's situational scriptures, der fuhrer said, *Mein Kampf:706 "The great speaker senses the words that he needs to use in order to impassion his audience. If he errs he has the opportunity for correction. He can read his listeners' expressions to see if they understand, and can repeat his message until he has convinced them of the correctness of what he has said."* This reminds me of the 8th surah in which Muhammad changed his presentation of the power of Islamic terror on the fly. When his militants appeared displeased with Allah's proclamation, Muhammad corrected the error and lessened the odds. *Ishaq:326* **"Abdullah told me that when this verse came down it was a shock to the Muslims who took it hard. They were afraid, as the odds were too great. So Allah relieved them and cancelled the verse with another: 'Now has Allah relieved you and He knows that there is a weakness among you, so if there are 100 [rather than 20] they shall vanquish 200.'"** The 66th verse corrected the 65th. Instant abrogation. Just add grumbling.

Der fuhrer also explained why an oral recital had to be as repetitive as the Qur'an—a word which means "to recite." *Mein Kampf:706* *"The great speaker will repeat his message so often, with so many examples, he will overcome objections and refute them before they are even raised."* While the Mecca surahs were fixated on pain and punishment, with the vast majority of the 1,000 repetitions occurring therein, the Medina themes were no less repetitive. They bellowed: submit, obey, perform, pay, and fight.

Hitler and Muhammad learned that their demonic message was most effective when it was revealed in the darkness of night. *Mein Kampf:710* *"I was astonished by how much better my message was received at night.... It's a mysterious magic that allows an encroachment upon man's free will. In the evening they succumb more easily to the dominating force of a stronger will. The domineering apostolic nature weakens their resistance."* Islam's apostle used the same psychologist to weaken men's resistance: *Qur'an 073.001* **"Keep watch all the night except a little, reciting the Qur'an as it ought to be recited in slow, measured rhythmic tones. We will soon entrust you with Our weighty Word. Surely the night is the most devout way when the soul is most receptive and the words are the most telling."** The most telling line, *"magic allows an encroachment upon man's free will,"* exposes the dark spirit's agenda. This is why Islam and Nazism are fatalistic and why they are devoted to submission and obedience. If deceit encroaches on man's free will, we lose our ability to choose Yahweh and to accept his gift of eternal life. When we lose our free will, we lose the ability to love and to know God. When we lose the ability to choose, we die. It isn't a coincidence that history's least-free poligious communities have succumbed to doctrines of submission. Death and destruction was not only predictable, it was a predetermined consequence.

Hitler, like his mentor, despised scribes. *Mein Kampf:712* *"The average sparrow brain of the scribbler produces intellectual babble."* Muhammad dispensed with the verbal assault. He simply killed them.

Mein Kampf:715 *"The [mosque] meeting is necessary if only because new adherents of a new movement feel lonely and are easily seized with the fear of being alone. Brought together they sense a greater community.... They are carried away by the powerful effect of the suggestive intoxication and enthusiasm of the others. The crowd confirms the correctness of the new doctrine in his mind and removes doubt. He then succumbs to the magic seductive influence of the [mosque] meeting."* *Mein Kampf:717* *"God be praised and thanked that unspoilt people avoid bourgeois mass meetings as the Devil avoids holy water."* Togetherness can be as seductive as it is coercive. It is the essence of mob mentality. An evil person with a bad idea can be parlayed into an eruption of uncontrollable rage. *Ishaq:580* **"Our strong warriors obey his orders to the letter. By us Allah's religion is undeniably strong. You would think when our horses gallop with bits in their mouths that the sounds of demons are among them. The day we trod down the unbelievers, there was no deviation or turning from the Apostle's order. During the battle the people heard our exhortations to fight and the smashing of skulls by swords that sent heads flying. We severed necks with a warrior's blow. Often we have left the slain cut to pieces and a widow crying 'alas' over her mutilated husband."** The study of Islam, like Nazism, is an exposé on gang mentality. Uncorrupted by Islam, or left free to choose, few if any Arabs would have been capable of perpetrating such horrific deeds. Yet as part of Muhammad's gang of ghouls, they fed off each other's rage. Terror and piracy became good because everyone they knew was a terrorizing pirate.

Then sounding like Muhammad in Mecca, der fuhrer preached these words in Munich, *Mein Kampf:715 "The man who is the first representative of a new doctrine is exposed to serious oppression and urgently needs the strengthening that lies in the conviction of being a fighter in an embracing body."* Muhammad found his soul mates in Medina. *Ishaq:596* **"You came to us discredited, when your message was rejected and we believed you. You were forsaken and deserted and we assisted you. You were a fugitive and we took you in, sheltering you. You were poor and in need and we comforted you."**

Mein Kampf:720 "It was important to introduce blind discipline into our meetings and to safeguard the authority of the leader. The brutal recklessness of our guards were able to thwart the enemy's hecklers." Speaking as if he were Muhammad, Hitler said, *Mein Kampf:726 "Anyone who provoked us was thrown out ruthlessly. We would not tolerate any provocation." Mein Kampf:728 "Before they could finish a sentence they would find themselves thrown outside the hall."* It was no different in Muhammad's day. *Ishaq:246* **"Hypocrites used to assemble in the mosque and listen to the stories of the Muslims and laugh and scoff at their religion. So Muhammad ordered that they should be ejected. They were thrown out with great violence. Abu went to Amr, took his foot and dragged him out of the mosque. Another Muslim slapped a man's face while dragging him forcefully, knocking him down. One was pulled violently by his hair. 'Don't come near the Apostle's mosque again, for you are unclean.'"**

Der fuhrer and der prophet had security detachments. Hitler called the first of these "Storm Troops." *Mein Kampf:729 "I had a protective detachment as a supervision service. They were all young Party comrades who were instructed and trained to the effect that terror can be broken only by terror. By fighting for our idea, they protected me with their last drop of blood. They were saturated with the doctrine. We found that the best weapon of defense was the attack. We became known not as a debating club but as a fighting community. My boys shined when I made clear to them the necessity of their mission, assuring them again and again that all the wisdom in the world will*

remain futile if force does not enter its service, defending and protecting it. The Goddess of Peace can only march side by side with the God of War."
Muhammad's thugs weren't quite as articulate, but they were no less loyal. *Ishaq:580* "We helped Allah's Apostle, angry on his account, with a thousand warriors. We carried his flag on the end of our lances. We were his helpers, protecting his banner in deadly combat. We dyed it with blood, for that was its color. We were the Prophet's right arm in Islam. We were his bodyguards before other troops served him. We helped him against his opponents. Allah richly rewarded that fine Prophet Muhammad."

Like the good Muslims who left their homes to fight jihad for Muhammad, Hitler had helpers too: *Mein Kampf:730* "*And how these boys stood up! Like a swarm of hornets they stormed upon the mockers at our meeting incurring wounds and making sacrifices so that they made a path for the holy mission of our movement.*" *Mein Kampf:747* "*The boys of the Storm Troop performed their duty. They attacked like wolves.... Our opponents learned a lesson they will never forget.*" This is reminiscent of the 8th surah which says: "Inflict upon them such a defeat as will be a lesson for others, that they may be warned." And the Hadith which substituted one pest for another. *Ishaq:564* "The Muslims stole our goods and divided them. Their spears pierced us not once but twice. Their squadrons came at us like a swarm of locusts. Were it not for the religion of Muhammad's people, their cavalry would never have attacked us."

Hitler dedicates a number of pages to his personal involvement in choosing the Nazi colors (black and red, symbolizing deceit and blood) and his swastika. Der fuhrer's fixation on his flag was no different than the prophet's fixation on his war banners which we were told were white, black, and blood red. *Mein Kampf:733* "*They became a symbol for the fight of the future.... It had the effect of a flaming torch.*" Just as Muhammad had usurped the concept of war banners from his pagan ancestor Qusayy, Hitler recycled an old tradition. *Mein Kampf:736* "*The swastika had been used as a symbol of the Germanic [pagan] religion by folkish groups in primitive cults.*" Even in the details, they were indistinguishable.

This next passage encapsulates Muhammad's reason for founding Islam. *Mein Kampf:752* "*Destiny [Fate, a.k.a. Satan] chooses the Man and Destiny gives him the final victory. Dissatisfied with the religious life of his people, he longs for a renovation. Based upon his inspiration he is called upon to present a solution for this religious distress, appearing like a prophet of a new doctrine and as a fighter against the existing ones.*" There is no more effective means to rule people than to claim that you are called to be "god's" *prophet*, and then to mix your poison with the passion of a pugilist. *Ishaq:530* "Get out of his way, you infidel unbelievers. Every good thing goes with His Apostle. O Lord, I believe in his word. I know Allah's [Fate's, a.k.a. Satan's] truth in accepting it. We will fight you about its interpretations as we have fought you about its revelation with strokes that will remove heads from shoulders and make enemies of friends."

If you were to replace Nature with Allah, this Hitlerism could be Qur'anic. *Mein Kampf:752* "*The strongest man is chosen for fulfilling the great mission. One Man is the One who is exclusively called upon.*" *Mein Kampf:753* "*They have the purest faith in their own mission, they consider themselves obliged to go their own way without considering others. Nature Herself, in Her inexorable logic, makes the decision by prompting fights and by leading that movement to the goal that has been chosen by the clearest, shortest, and surest way."* Qur'an 059.006 **"Allah gives his Messenger Lordship and Power over whomever He wills."** Qur'an 049.007 **"And know that among you is Allah's Messenger: were he to follow your (wishes), you would fall into misfortune....""**

By promising "Valhalla," a seductive, pagan, and hedonistic "paradise" to those who sacrificed their lives for the "cause," the second tyrant mirrored the first. Mein Kampf:768 *"It is certain that each hero who comes forward voluntarily, and dies the sacred death of martyrdom climbs the steps to Valhalla."* This is no different than: Qur'an 004.074 **"Let those who fight in the Cause of Allah sell the life of this world for the hereafter. To him who fights in the Cause of Allah, whether he is slain or gets victory— soon shall We give him a great reward."**

Speaking of the Germans who rejected him, Hitler's never-ending argument replicates Muhammad's. Mein Kampf:768 *"They are 'scum,' 'rabble, deserters, and pimps who shunned the light,' 'hyenas,' 'freeloaders,' 'thieves, and duty shirkers,' 'traitors,' and an 'undisciplined gang of looters, criminals, and evil rabble.'"*

But alas, even Hitler had to outmaneuver and threaten the peaceful hypocrites. Mein Kampf:756 *"Some people merely pretend that they are fighting for the same goal, but they do not honestly place themselves into the ranks of our movement."* Qur'an 008.005 **"Your Lord ordered you out of your homes to fight for the true cause even though some Muslims disliked it, and were averse to fighting. They argued with you concerning this matter even after it was made clear to them. It was as if they were being driven to their death."**

Der fuhrer was as humble as der prophet. Mein Kampf:763 *"One must never forget that everything that is actually great in this world has not been fought for and won by coalitions, but always by the success of One Individual victor. The religious State will never be created by compromise but only by the steel-hard willpower of one sole movement which has struggled its way against all others."* Qur'an 048.001 **"Verily We have granted you (Muhammad) a splendid Victory."** Qur'an 048.008 **"We have truly sent you (Muhammad) as a witness, as a bringer of Good News, and as a Warner: In order that you (men) may believe in Allah and His Messenger, that you may assist him and honor him, and celebrate His praise morning and evening."**

Islam and Nazism seduced a sufficient number of men to become popular enough to build a coercive militant force. Both usurped pagan traditions to condition adherents and then established absolute authority over them. Mein Kampf:765 *"If popularity and force unite then authority can be established more solidly based upon tradition. When popularity, force, and tradition combine, authority becomes unshakable."* This is Islam in a nutshell.

Writing words that would come to haunt the world fifteen and then again seventy-seven years after they were scribed by Hitler's hand, we discover: Mein Kampf:787 *"Terror which is derived from a religion can never be broken by a formal State power. It will only succumb to a new view of life that proceeds with equal boldness and determination. The State may for centuries apply the strongest means of power against a terror by which it is threatened, but in the end it will be powerless and will succumb."* Hitler and Muhammad were unaware of a power stronger than hate, and of a tool more effective than terror. That force is love and its implement is truth. And that is how we must fight *"terror which is derived from a religion."* We must love the victims of Islam enough to free them from deceit. By emancipating mankind from Muhammad's legacy we free everyone from its scourge.

But Hitler was right in a way. Nations like America are unable to break the back of religious terror. We are unwilling to confront a religion, because we don't think that's nice. But by not understanding the source of the terrorists' rage, we eliminate them far more slowly than the religotic manufactures new ones. And even if we were to shed our ignorance, conventional defensive and offensive military tactics are counterproductive. Offensively, massive armaments and air superiority only prevail against conventional forces. Terrorists scatter, lying in wait to strike another day. And defensively, the freedoms we usurp from our citizens under the guise of "Homeland Security" only serve to create the totalitarian climate in which religious terrorists thrive.

While there is good news, I'm afraid it may be too late. To combat poligious terror we don't have to become like them, as Hitler attests. All we have to do is come to understand the deceit that drives men to such madness. Collectively, if we were to see Muhammad and his terrorist dogma Islam as we now see Hitler and Nazism, we would win the war on terror by freeing Muslims from Islam. Light extinguishes darkness, and courageous, sacrificial love overwhelms fear, hate, and terror.

While Hitler's argument was wrong, it remains seductive. A time will come, according to Bible prophets, in which America and Europe will tire of their governments' inability to thwart the continued onslaught of Islamic terror. They will be tempted, as were 1930s Germans, to employ the services of a similarly-minded tyrant to protect them. Like Hitler, this evil man will rise to prominence promising "peace." But once empowered, he'll unleash hell's fury—literally. The religotic he'll deploy will be as demonic as Nazism and Islam. *Mein Kampf:981 "To end this eternal shame, people will prefer to accept the terror of the moment rather than bear an endless terror any longer."*

Hitler went on to plagiarize two of Allah's favorite words. *Mein Kampf:798 "What we need is not one hundred daring plotters, but many hundreds of thousands of fanatical fighters for our view of life." Mein Kampf:801 "Give the German nation six million bodies, faultlessly trained, all of them glowing with passion for the highest spirit of attack, and we will have an army." Qur'an 047.004* **"Therefore, when you clash with the unbelieving Infidels in battle, strike them and overpower them. At length, when you have thoroughly subdued them, make them prisoners in bondage until the war lays down its burdens. Thus are you commanded. He lets you fight in order to test you. But those who are slain in Allah's Cause will never have their deeds go to waste."** *Qur'an 047.031* **"We shall** try you until We know those among you who are the fighters; and We shall try your reported mettle." *Qur'an 047.033* "**Believers, obey Allah, and obey the Messenger! Those who disbelieve and hinder men from the Cause of Allah [Jihad], He will not pardon. Do not falter; become faint-hearted, or weak-kneed, crying for peace. You have the upper hand.**"

Muhammad's contemporaries saw him as a lying thief and a murdering bandit. We know this because their criticisms are chronicled in the Qur'an. Hitler was not immune. His contemporaries: *Mein Kampf:807* "*Lovingly showered upon us the pet names: 'murderers, bandits, robbers, and criminals.' But the S.A. [Storm Troop] maintained perfect order...daring to smash the skulls in of those who resisted.*" The translators of *Mein Kampf* provided the grim details. During the formation period of Nazism (1923-1931): "The Hitlerites killed 323 Marxists and seriously wounded 750. Other Nazi rivals lost 48 men. The perpetrators of Mein Kampf suffered 86 dead and 25 wounded." But as with the initial Islamic terrorist raids perpetrated by Muhammad, one murder quickly led to another. Death became an avalanche. Scores of rotting corpses became hundreds, then thousands, then millions.

Returning to one of der prophet's favorite themes, der fuhrer protests: *Mein Kampf:827* "*Systematically, Jewish parasites ravish our innocent young blonde girls and thus destroy the Aryan race. Yet both Christian denominations disregard the desecration and annihilation of the noble and unique race God gave the earth. It is not important whether Protestants vanquish Catholics or Catholics vanquish Protestants, but whether Aryans survive. Any who reject his work thereby declares war on the Lord's creation and upon his divine will.*" *Ishaq:262* "**Some Muslims remained friends with the Jews, so Allah sent down a Qur'an forbidding them to take Jews as friends. From their mouths hatred has already shown itself and what they conceal is worse.**" *Qur'an 002.059* "**We sent a plague upon the Jews from heaven, for their evil-doing.**" *Bukhari:V4B56N679* "**Allah's Apostle said, 'Plague was a means of torture sent on the Israelis.'**" *Qur'an 005.051* "**Believers, take not Jews and Christians for your friends. They are but friends and protectors to each other.**" *Qur'an 005.082* "**You will find the Jews and disbelievers [defined as Christians in 5:73] the most vehement in hatred for the Muslims.**"

Mein Kampf:845 "*Nazism must claim the right to force its principles on the whole and educate everyone about its ideas and thoughts without regard to previous boundaries.*" This is an order to impose Nazism on the world and then to indoctrinate the victims. *Bukhari:V4B52N196* "**Allah's Apostle said, 'I have been ordered to fight the people till they say, "None has the right to be worshipped but Allah."'**"

Speaking immodestly of how he created his religotic, Hitler shares some extremely relevant insights: *Mein Kampf:848* "*Great theorists are only in the rarest cases great organizers. The Greatness of the program-maker [religious founder] lies in the recognition and in the establishment of abstractly correct rules, while the organizer has to be a psychologist. He has to take man as he is, and thus must know him. He must not over evaluate him. He must try to account for his weakness and bestial nature so that the program becomes a strong, constant force, suitable for carrying an idea and paving its way to success."* Hitler's words bind him to Muhammad and separate both men from Moses and Christ. Islam and Nazism see man as lowly and replaceable. They appeal to man's weakness and bestial nature. They seduce men into becoming a militant force for the benefit of the program-maker. Hitler was even suggesting that Islam was made dimwitted and bestial on purpose. It was as dumb and visceral as the men it was perpetrated upon.

The reason the word "religion" can't be found in the Old Testament and is only used negatively in the New Testament is that Judeo-Christianity is not a religion, a movement, a cause, a mission, or a program. It's a relationship that focuses on the spirit, not the flesh.

Mein Kampf:848 "Rarely is a great theorist a great leader. More usually he is an agitator who shows the ability of imparting an idea to the masses as a psychologist and demagogue. For to lead means to be able to move [seduce] the masses." While I wouldn't go so far as to say that Muhammad was a great theorist, leader, or psychologist, he was certainly an agitator and demagogue. And two out of five was sufficient to "move the masses."

Hitler glorified himself using similar terms to those used by Islamic apologists to elevate Muhammad's status. *Mein Kampf:849 "The combination of the theorist [prophet], organizer [politician], and leader [general] in one person is the rarest thing to be found on this globe. This combination makes the Great Man."*

By calling his message "propaganda," Hitler was being more honest with his audience than was Muhammad. Both knew that they were lying; one had the courtesy to tell us. *Mein Kampf:851 "The first task of propaganda [Qur'an recitals] is the winning of people for the future organization [Islam]. The first task of the organization [Islam] is the winning of people for the continuation of propaganda. The second task of propaganda [the Qur'an] is the destruction of existing doctrines [Judeo-Christianity]. The second task of the organization must be the fight for power [Muslim militancy] so that by it will achieve the final success of the doctrine [world religious conquest—total submission]."* Tabari IX:82 **"The Messenger sent Khalid with an army of 400 and ordered him to invite people to Islam before he fought them. If they were to respond and submit, he was to teach them the Book of Allah, the Sunnah of His Prophet, and the requirements of Islam. If they should decline, then he was to fight them."** Ishaq:245 **"The Apostle used to say, 'Their religion will never march with ours.'"**

Mein Kampf:851 "The most striking success of the revolution of a view of life will always be won whenever the new view of life [religotic] is taught [dictated] to all people, and if necessary, is forced upon them." Neville Chamberlain gave this man the high ground of Czechoslovakia thinking that it would satiate his cravings. That proved as fatal as George Bush's "Road Map to Peace," in which he proposed to give the high ground of Israel to the Muslims. One doctrine has, and the other doctrine will, force its view of life on everyone within its reach. Tabari IX:86 **"Give the people the good news of Paradise and the way to attain it. Warn them of the Hell-Fire and the way to earn it. Teach them the rites of the hajj.... He orders you to offer** prayer at the appropriate times with proper bowing and humility.... He orders you to give one fifth of Allah's booty and pay the zakat tax. It is enjoined on the faithful from their land and property." *Qur'an 008.039* "Fight them until the only religion is Islam." When will we learn to read the words on the page? When will we come to understand that tolerating evil leads to disaster?

Islam and Nazism are intolerant, dictatorial fighting machines. *Mein Kampf:852* *"The highest task of the organization is to see to it that no kind of internal disagreements among the members of the movement weaken the work of the movement. The spirit of determined aggression must not die out. It must be constantly renewed and fortified. It must never lose its fighting force and must propagate the idea with determination and attack."* *Mein Kampf:855* *"The more radical and inciting my propaganda was, the more it frightened off the weaklings [hypocrites] and prevented them from pushing into the nucleus of our organization."* Hitler would have loved this poem: *Ishaq:572* "Muhammad is the man, an Apostle of my Lord who errs not. Any who would rival him must fail. Evil was the state of our enemy so they lost the day. We came upon them like lions from the thickets. The armies of Allah came openly, flying at them in rage, so they could not get away. We destroyed them and forced them to surrender. In the former days there was no battle like this; their blood flowed freely. We slew them and left them in the dust. Those who escaped were choked with terror. A multitude of them were slain. This is Allah's war in which those who do not accept Islam will have no chance."

Mein Kampf:856 *"Folkish [religious] visionaries procure leadership for themselves and collapse the plots that swirl around them. I was unanimously given the entire leadership of the movement. New articles were accepted which entrusted me with full responsibility and this proved its value in the most blissful manner,"* *Mein Kampf:858* *"All collaborators were made subordinate to me."* *Muslim:C22B20N4604* "We used to take oath to the Messenger of Allah that we would listen to and obey his orders. He would tell us to say in the oath: As far as it lies in my power." *Qur'an 048.010* "Verily those who swear allegiance to you (Muhammad), indeed swear their allegiance to Allah."

Nazism was as peaceful as Islam. *Mein Kampf:891* *"To forge the sword is the task of leadership. The mission is to seek comrades in arms."* *Mein Kampf:892* *"The correct road is to strengthen our power by winning new soil and territory."* *Mein Kampf:950* *"We Nazis say: 'The right to soil and territory is a duty for a great nation must extend its boundaries."* The clues in *Mein Kampf* that the Nazis were intent on world conquest were no less vague than those found in the Qur'an. *Mein Kampf:953* *"The German needs only to be given land by the sword."* *Bukhari:V4B52N288* "Expel disbelievers from the Arabian Peninsula.'" *Qur'an 002.191* "Slay them wherever you find and catch them, and drive them out from where they have turned you out; for persecution and oppression are worse than slaughter." *Qur'an 033.025* "Allah drove the disbelievers back...and helped the believers in battle.... He terrorized the People of the Book so that you killed some and made many captive. He made you inherit their lands, their homes, and their wealth. He gave you a country you had not traversed before."

Chamberlain wasn't the only fool. Stalin also signed a "peace treaty" with

Hitler years after *Mein Kampf* was written. *Mein Kampf:959* *"The conclusion of a treaty with Russia embodies the declaration of the next war."* Der fuhrer, like der prophet, enjoyed projecting his faults on his foes. *"We must never forget that the rulers of present-day Russia are common bloodstained criminals, the scum of humanity. They butchered and rooted out millions of leading intellectuals with savagery. They have imposed the most frightful regime of tyranny of all time. The Marxist and their Jewish comrades combine bestial horror and an inconceivable gift for lying. They intend to impose bloody oppression on the whole world. One does not conclude a treaty with someone whose sole interest is destruction."* The only difference between Hitler and Muhammad in the application of this strategy was, Hitler was right.

Der Fuhrer went on to share: *"The struggle against the Jewish Marxist conquest of the world requires a clear attitude towards Soviet Russia. You cannot drive out the Devil with Beelzebub [another name for Satan]."* This is similar to Lucifer impersonating Gabriel while speaking for Allah and condemning Satan.

Mein Kampf:920 *"Peace treaties whose demands are a scourge to a people, frequently beat the first drum roll for a coming rebellion. The boundless extortion and shameful abasement are a means of whipping up national passions to the boiling point. The propagandistic utilization of these sadistic atrocities can remove indifference and raise indignation to the most blazing anger! Every point should be burned into the brain and heart of men until sixty million share the same hate, causing a sea of flames out of whose glow a steely will arises and the cry: 'We want more arms!' Yes, a peace treaty could do that. It becomes the greatest propaganda weapon for re-arousing the dormant spirits of a cause."* *Mein Kampf:920* *"We must reimplant in the people the spirit of proud self-respect, manly defiance, and wrathful hate."* The first Muslims didn't take kindly to peace treaties either. *Tabari VIII:87/Ishaq:505* **"The Companions of the Prophet had set out not doubting that they would conquer, because of a vision Muhammad had seen. Therefore, when they saw the negotiations for peace, the retreat, and the obligations the Messenger agreed to—the Muslims felt so grieved about it that they were close to despair. Some were depressed to the point of death."** So...*Qur'an 009.003* **"An announcement from Allah and His Messenger to the people assembled on the day of the Great Pilgrimage, that Allah and His Messenger dissolve treaty obligations with the Pagans."** And then...*Qur'an 009.005* **"Fight and kill the disbelievers wherever you find them, take them captive, torture them, lie in wait and ambush them using every stratagem of war."**

Telling us how Nazi and Islamic tyrannies would use land-for-peace roadmaps to propagate their fury and lead the world to war, der fuhrer explained: *Mein Kampf:921* *"Everything, beginning with the child's primer down to the last newspaper, every theater and every picture, every billboard and every wall, must be placed at the service of this single great mission, until the prayer of fear of our patriots cry, 'Lord deliver us!' The burning plea must come from even the smallest child: 'Almighty God, bless our arms! Lord, bless our battle!'"* The Muslims also had such a "prayer." *Bukhari:V5B59N512* **"The Prophet offered the Prayer of Fear when it was still dark and said, 'Allahu-Akbar! Khaybar is destroyed, for whenever we approach a hostile nation to fight,** then evil will be the morning for those who have been warned.' The inhabitants came out running. The Prophet had their men killed, their children and women taken as captives." *Bukhari:V5B59N516* "When Allah's Apostle fought or raided people we raised our voices saying, 'Allahu-Akbar! Allahu-Akbar! None has the right to be worshipped but Allah.'"

And they went off to wage holy war: *Mein Kampf:932* *"May Reason be our leader, The sacred duty to act gives us determination, and our highest Protector remains our faith." Mein Kampf:925 "We may suffer many bitter woes but this isn't grounds for abandoning Reason with squabbling instead of standing up with a concentrated force against the enemy." Qur'an 008.060* "And make ready against the infidels all of the power you can, including steeds of war [the Noble Qur'an says these are: tanks, planes, missiles, and artillery] to threaten the enemy of Allah and your enemy. And whatever you spend in Allah's Cause shall be repaid unto you." *Qur'an 061.014* "O Muslims! Be helpers of Allah...We gave power to those who believed against their enemies, and they became the ones that prevailed." *Ishaq:441* "A sharp sword in the hand of a brave man kills his adversary."

Muhammad called his dark spirit a "Protector," too, even when his armed force was preparing to swoop down, terrorize, and plunder innocents. *Ishaq:510* "When the Apostle looked down he said, 'O Allah, Lord of the heavens and what they overshadow, and Lord of the Devils and what into error they throw, and Lord of the winds and what they winnow, we ask Thee for the booty of this town and its people. We take refuge in Thee from its evil and the evil of its people. Forward in the name of Allah.' He used to say this of every town he raided."

Mein Kampf ends as it begins, by praising martyrs, and wrapping overtly religious themes around their death. *Mein Kampf:993* *"At the end of this volume I want to bring before the eyes of our adherents and of the crusaders for our doctrine those eighteen heroes to whom I dedicated the first volume of my work, as those heroes who consciously sacrificed themselves for all of us. They must always recall the fulfillment of duty, a duty which they fulfilled with the best faith despite the consequences. I want to reckon men who by words, thoughts, and deeds dedicated their lives to the awakening of our nation. I quote from Eckard's poem: 'Father in Heaven, resolved to the death, bow we before Thee. Does any other people follow thine awful command more loyally than do we Germans? Then Eternal One, send us the victory, Mighty with Fate. Thou smilest with joy at our holy crusade."*

I could give you any of a thousand Qur'an and Hadith quotes to match this, but instead, I'd like you to contemplate the overwhelming similarity of the message, the motivation, and the means Hitler and Muhammad used to attack mankind. Then consider the consequence of ignoring, or even tolerating, Hitler's "holy crusade" during the fifteen years between the time he wrote it and the time he enacted it.

If we behave similarly today, now that Muhammad's mantra has been revealed, a billion people will remain enslaved by Islam. And within a quarter century, a quarter of earth's people will die because of it.

25

PROPHET OF DOOM

"I have ordered you to kill them."

Muhammad was a terrorist to the bitter end. *Tabari IX:166* **"The Prophet ordered the expedition of Usamah, but it did not go well because of his illness and because two other Arabs had proclaimed themselves prophets and renounced his authority. The Prophet's head was wrapped around because of the pain."**

Superstitious, and a believer in occult spells, Muhammad tried to cure himself by going to a magic spring. When that proved insufficient, he blew knots out of a tangle, something that sorcerers practiced as part of their black arts. Desperate, he tried praying to Allah, but needless to say, he only got sicker. Allah had never answered prayers to keep folks alive, only to kill them.

This prophet's fixation on Satan and his demonic cast of killer angels tells us a great deal about the nature of the man who invented Islam. Many if not all of these Hadith, were revealed during the waning days of his life as he struggled vainly to cheat death. *Bukhari:V4B54N491* **"Allah's Apostle said, 'While you sleep, Satan ties three knots at the back of your head. He blows the following words at each knot, "The night is long so keep sleeping." If that person wakes up and praises Allah, then one knot is undone. When he performs ablution the second is undone. When he prays, all the knots are undone, and he gets up in the morning lively and gay, otherwise he is dull and gloomy.'"** Satan's ugly spirit permeates this hideous cult. But I assure you, Satan cannot, and does not, tie knots. All he can do is play havoc with weather and men's minds. He, like Allah, is otherwise impotent.

In this next treasure, we discover that Muhammad believed in magic spells. He sought cures identical to the remedies prescribed by the occultists of his day. As you read this angelic encounter, keep in mind that this is how Muhammad alleges the Qur'an was revealed to him. *Bukhari:V7B71N660* **"Magic was worked on Allah's Apostle so that he used to think that he had sexual relations with his wives while he actually had not. [Apparently, Muhammad had become like his god in yet another way.] That is the hardest kind of magic as it has such an effect. One day he said, 'O Aisha, do you know that Allah has instructed me concerning the matter I asked Him about? Two men came to me and one of them sat near my head and the other near my** feet. The one asked, "What is wrong with this man?" "He is under the effect of magic." "Who cast the magic spell on him?" "Labid, an Arab ally of the Jews and a hypocrite." "What material did he use to cast the spell?" "A comb with hair stuck to it." "Where is that comb and hair?" "In a skin of pollen of a male palm tree kept under a stone in the well of Dharwan."' So the Prophet went to that well and took out those things, saying, 'That was the well shown to me in the dream. Its water looked red and its palms looked like the heads of devils. My companions removed those things.' I said, 'Why didn't you just treat your-self?' He said, 'Allah has cured me, and I don't want to spread evil among my people.'"

Well, it's a little late for that now. And the evil spell that possessed the prophet was not cured by Allah. He will die of this illness.

A similar Bukhari Hadith confirms that Muhammad was possessed by evil, that he was a fraud who believed in magic spells, and that his spiritual under-standing and medical prowess rendered him more voodoo witchdoctor than prophet. *Bukhari:V7B71N661* "**Magic was worked on Allah's Apostle so that he began to imagine he had done something although he had not. While he was with me, he invoked Allah for a long period and then said, 'Aisha! Do you know what Allah has instructed me to do regarding the matter I asked Him about?' 'What is that?' He said, 'Two men came to me. One said, "What is the disease of this man?" The other replied, "He is under the effect of magic." "Who has worked magic on him?" "Labid, a Jew from the Zuraiq tribe."'"** By saying that his "disease" was spiritual, not biological, Muhammad became a witchdoctor. By contradicting himself and saying that the perpetrator was a Jew, rather than a Muslim hypocrite, he demonstrated that he couldn't be trusted.

Back a couple of chapters, I shared some inspired scripture from Bukhari's *Book of Wudu*; I saved this one because of its reference to demons. *Bukhari:V5B58N200* "**I carried a water pot for the Prophet's ablution and for cleaning his private parts. While following him with the pot, the Prophet turned and said, 'Who are you?' 'I am Abu.' The Prophet said, 'Bring me stones in order to clean my private parts, but do not bring any bones or animal dung.' So I brought some stones, carrying them in the corner of my robe till I put them by his side. When he finished, I walked with him and asked, 'What can you tell me about the bones and the animal dung?' He said, 'They are of the food of Jinns [Devils]. A delegate of Jinns of the city of Nasibin came to me—and how nice those Jinns were—and asked me for the remains of human food. I invoked Allah for them that they would never pass by a bone or animal dung but find food on them.'"** I'm not surprised Muhammad thought demons were nice. Nor am I surprised he believes they eat dung and bones. In fact, that pretty much sums up Islam. Muhammad had been, by his own admission, possessed by a demon.

As we mosey down this trail of discovery, occasionally something catches our eye that is particularly revealing. *Muslim:C14B39N6759* "**Aisha, the wife of Allah's Apostle (may peace be upon him), reported: 'Allah's Messenger (may peace be upon him) left my apartment during the night. Then he came and he saw me in an agitated state.' He said: "Aisha, what has happened to you? Do you feel jealous?" I said: "How can it be that** a girl like me would not feel jealous in regard to a husband like you?" You've got to admire her wit. She was sharing a sixty-two year old pervert, I mean prophet, with twenty-four other children, sex slaves, concubines, and wives of every faith and description. It's only reasonable that she should express some anxiety "in regard to a husband like" him. "Thereupon Allah's Messenger said: "It is your devil who has come to you." [Bingo! Her "devil" had indeed come to her.] I said: "Allah's Messenger, is there a devil with me?" He said: "Yes." I said: "Is there a devil attached to everyone?" He said: "Yes." I said: "Allah's Messenger, is there a devil attached to you also?" [Now for the moment of truth...] He said: "Yes."'" Muhammad finally got something right. But alas, even *that* was wrong.

The Hadith ends with the Prophet saying: "But my Lord has helped me against my devil and as such I am absolutely safe from his mischief." The spirit that controls demons is Lucifer. They stopped reporting to Yahweh at least 6,000 years ago. As we have learned, "mischief" has a peculiar Islamic definition. A "mischief maker" is someone who rejects Muhammad, Allah, the Qur'an, Sunnah, and Islam. No doubt Lucifer, as Muhammad's Lord, ordered the devil who possessed his prophet to keep him from such *mischief*.

Demons provide the bookends for Islam. Twenty-two years earlier, Islam was born when Muhammad received a recital from a demonic spirit late one night. The experience was horrible, nearly pressing the life out of him. The new "prophet" tried to commit suicide. Terrorized, he ran home to his sixty-year-old wife, crying, "I fear that something bad has happened to me. I have been possessed." Now, in the throes of death, days from his last breath, Allah's messenger tells his teenage wife that the devil never left him. He had become comfortable enough with his demonic spirit to explain that the "devil" was "attached to him."

There was no one closer to Islam's "Godfather" than Aisha. Every Hadith reporting the circumstances surrounding the birth of Islam and the death of its prophet, come from her lips. She alone reported the nature of Qur'an revelations, saying that the inspiration process was like the clanging of a bell in her husband's head. She also said, "Anyone who claims Muhammad saw Gabriel more than twice is a liar." And that's a serious problem because a "devil" was "attached" to him. It is little wonder he was morally bankrupt and vicious.

But more important than all of that, Lucifer, by controlling Muhammad's devil, was able to control his prophet. It's why his example was so abysmal (as in "from the abyss"). It's why his Sunnah was a terrorist manifesto and why the Qur'an was so mean spirited. Lucifer knows nothing of choice, thus Islam was all about submission and obedience. Lucifer knows nothing of love, thus Islam focused on hate and fear. Lucifer despises truth, life, and especially salvation, thus Islam was about deceit, death, and especially damnation. The reason why has just been.

Next, Muhammad confirmed publicly what he had revealed privately to Aisha. *Muslim:C14B39N6757* "Allah's Messenger said: 'There is none amongst you with whom is not an attaché from amongst the jinn, a devil.' The Companions said: 'Allah's Messenger, is there a devil with you too?' Thereupon he said: 'Yes, but Allah helps me against him so I am safe from his hand and he does not command me but for good.'" The first thing that Team Islam did was to redefine its terms. Most bad things are considered good. For example, terrorism is good. So is jihad, holy fighting in Allah's Cause. Stealing booty is good. So is incest, rape, and slavery.

While we're on the subject of demons in Islam, I want to provide a variety of supporting confessions. The first is troubling because the Qur'an's initial revelation was a nightmare. *Bukhari:V4B54N513* "The Prophet said, 'A good dream is from Allah, and a bad or evil dream is from Satan; so if anyone of you has a bad dream of which he is afraid, he should spit on his left side.'" Speaking of nocturnal deceptions: *Bukhari:V4B54N533* "The Prophet said, 'Cover your utensils and tie your water skins, close your doors and keep your children close at night as Jinn spread out and snatch things. When you go to bed put out your lights, for the mischief-doer may drag away the candle and burn your house with you in it. Ata said, 'The prophet actually said "devils" instead of "Jinn."'"

Occult soothsayers are demonic messengers. As such, Muhammad knew all about them. *Bukhari:V4B54N508* "The Prophet said, 'While angels talk amidst the clouds about things that are going to happen, devils hear what they say and pour it in the ears of soothsayers as one pours something in a bottle, and they add one hundred lies to it.'"

While that's troubling, this Hadith should send a jolt of terror up every Muslim's spine. Muhammad's Qur'an was revealed and recited in rhymed speech called rajaz poetry. So were many of these Hadiths. *Muslim:C10B16N4168* "Allah's Messenger said: 'He seems to be one of the soothsayers on account of the rhymed speech which he has composed.'" So would that make Muhammad a soothsayer or just the father of rap?

Lucifer's name is derived from the morning star, better known as the sun. *Bukhari:V4B54N494* "Allah's Apostle said, 'When the edge of the sun appears, don't perform a prayer till the sun appears in full. And when the lower edge of the sun sets, don't perform prayer till it sets completely. And you should not seek to pray at sunrise or sunset for the sun rises between two sides of the head of the devil Satan.'"

In his witchdoctor mode, the prophet proclaimed: *Bukhari:V4B54N484* "Fever is from the heat of the Hell Fire; so cool it with water.'"

A devil must have disobeyed Lucifer's command so...*Bukhari:V4B54N634* "The Prophet said, 'A strong demon from the Jinn came to me yesterday suddenly, so as to spoil my prayer, but Allah enabled me to overpower him, and so I caught him and intended to tie him to one of the pillars of the mosque so that all of you might see him.'"

With each Satanic Verse, Islam continued to self destruct. *Bukhari:V1B11N582* "Allah's Apostle said, 'When the Adhan [the call to prayer] is announced, Satan takes to his heels and passes wind with noise during his flight in order not to hear the Adhan.'" While Satan is an ass in the figurative sense, he lacks human anatomy and thus a digestive system and anus. *Bukhari:V3B33N254* "Satan circulates in the human being as blood circulates. I was afraid lest Satan might insert an evil thought in your minds." While Satan hasn't "circulated" within anyone, including Muham-mad, the damage he did was far worse. Islam corrodes its victim's minds so that they lose the ability to think rationally.

Then moving from back to front, and inside out, we find: *Bukhari:V4B54N509* **"The Prophet said, 'Yawning is from Satan and if anyone of you yawns, he should check his yawning as much as possible. If anyone during the act of yawning should say: "Ha," Satan will laugh at him.'"** Our Satanic journey continues with: *Bukhari:V2B21N245* **"A person slept in and missed the morning prayer, so the Prophet said, 'Satan urinated in his ears.'"** If Satan and Allah were not the same, Satan would have no reason to be trou-bled by a Muslim missing a prayer to Allah.

Not a moment too soon, our anatomical voyage ends with: *Bukhari:V4B54N516* **"The Prophet said, 'If anyone rouses from sleep and performs ablution, he should wash his nose by putting water in it and then blow it out thrice because Satan has stayed in the upper part of his nose all night.'"** If Muhammad had aspired to being nothing more than a witchdoctor, his patients would have sued him for malpractice. How is it then that a billion people trust this false prophet with their souls?

This next Hadith requires some thinking. It opens with a prophetic order to protect the prophet's booty and closes with a conundrum. *Bukhari:V6B61N530* **"Allah's Apostle ordered me to guard the Zakat revenue of Ramadan. Then somebody came and started stealing the foodstuff. I caught him and said, 'I'm going to take you to Allah's Apostle!' He replied, 'Please don't take me to him. If you spare me that fate I will tell you a few words by which Allah will benefit you.' So then he said, 'When you go to bed recite Ayat-al-Kursi, (Qur'an 2:255) for then a guard from Allah will protect you all night long, and Satan will not be able to come near you till dawn.' When the Prophet heard the story he said to me, 'He who came to you at night told you the truth although he is a liar; and it was Satan.'"** Starting at the beginning, the zakat was called "revenue," not charity. By this time there were only Muslims in Medina, so the order to guard the storehouse means the first Muslims couldn't be trusted. The thief couldn't be Satan, for why would a spirit steal food? Further, why would someone trust a thief *or* Satan to share Qur'anic insights? The referenced verse (2:255) says that Allah is God and that everything belongs to him. Quot-ing it makes no sense if Satan is Allah's enemy. But it makes perfect sense if Satan is using Allah as a disguise. Yet by saying that it will protect one from Satan, it no longer makes sense. But speaking of senseless, how can one who told the truth be a liar?

So that I don't leave you in the same quandary Muhammad left his stooge, the answer is simple. Satan is everywhere in Islam. He's in the Qur'an, in the prophet, in the bodies of believers, in their homes, in Muhammad's harem, and in his booty. Lucifer is a liar, so each time the Qur'an says: verily, truth-fully, truly, surely, the right path, or the true religion, rest assured, he's lying. There is a reason the Sunnah says: *Tabari VI:107* **"Satan Cast a False Qur'an Revelation on the Messenger of Allah's Tongue."** And it's the same reason surah 22:52 claims:

"Every Messenger or Prophet before you recited the message Satan cast into his recitation."

Returning to Islam's death bed: *Tabari IX:166* "May Allah curse those who make the tombs of their prophets places of worship," the dying man grumbled, not knowing that Jews don't have shrines and Christians celebrate the fact that Christ *doesn't have* a tomb. Yet...*Bukhari:V2B23N414* "The Prophet in his fatal illness said, "Allah cursed Jews and Christians because they took their Prophets' graves as places for praying.'"

Tabari IX:167 "Muhammad waged war against the false prophets [slitting his own wrists would have done nicely] by sending messengers with instructions to get rid of them by artful contrivance [plot, machination, or device]." Hitler had a word for "artful contrivance." He called it propaganda. Con men don't like competition. Even today, Islam deceives its non-Muslim enemies using *"Al Takeya,"* which means "The Legal Lie." Calling Jihad a "Spiritual Struggle" is a *"Takeya."*

His rivals eliminated, the Prophet turned his attention to weightier matters. *Tabari IX:168* "He turned to me, saying, 'Abu Muwayhibah, I have been given the keys of the treasuries of this world.'" It was always about the money. While demons provide the bookends for history's most "artful contrivance," nothing but money and blood lies in between.

Knowing that the Grim Reaper was calling his name, Muhammad decided to visit his final accommodation. *Tabari IX:169* "Aisha said, 'When the Messenger returned from the Baqi cemetery he found me. He was suffering from a headache and crying. 'Alas, O my head!' He moaned, 'Nay, by Allah, O Aisha, rather alas, O my head!'" While his pain brings me no pleasure, to know he suffered is some small consolation to the billions he has made suffer.

"Then he said, 'Would it distress you if you were to die before me so that I could take care of your body, wrap you in a shroud, pray over you, and bury you?'" The Hadith says that Aisha was just eighteen years old, so she was a little young to be buried. However, Muslims were never very good with math. Since we are in the eleventh year of the Islamic Era and the fifty-three year old prophet married his child bride at its onset, she must have been seven, not nine, when she was removed from the swing, plucked from childhood and thrust into his lap. "Aisha replied, 'It seems to me that if you were to do that you would return to my apartment and would party with another one of your wives.'" Out of the mouths of babes.

While out visiting his future quarters, the prophet revealed this racist verse: *Bukhari:V2B23N457* "The Prophet went out after sunset and heard a dreadful voice. He said, 'The Jews are being punished in their graves.'"

Bukhari:V5B59N727 "When the ailment of Allah's Apostle became aggravated, he requested his wives to permit him to be nursed in my apartment. They gave him permission. He came out between two men with his feet dragging on the ground."

Reverting to witchcraft: *Tabari IX:121/Bukhari:V5B59N727* "The Messenger's illness intensified, the pain became fierce, so he said after entering my apartment, 'Pour seven skins of water over me from different wells, and from skins whose mouths have not been untied, so that I may give advice to the people.'" Feeling guilty and dreading his own encounter with eternity, he said, "Your rights are dear to me so whomever I have flogged on his back with a whip, here is my back—let him avenge. Whomever I have reviled, here is my honor—let him retort...that he should absolve me from it so that I shall meet the Lord while I am exonerated.'" Yes, it's true. Muhammad was concerned about meeting his Lord. Islam's lone prophet was unsure of his own salvation.

Bukhari:V5B59N727 "When Allah's Apostle became seriously sick, he started covering his face with a woolen sheet. When he felt short of breath, he removed it, and said, 'That is so! Allah's curse be on Jews and Christians.'" I don't think he had a nice bone in his body.

Tabari IX:174 "The Messenger's pain became so severe he said, 'Give me pen and paper so I may write a document for you so you will never go astray after me.'" He knew that the Qur'an was rubbish and was trying to make amends. Yet there's a time bomb lurking in Muhammad's unguarded words. His timeless document was going to be from him, not his ilah. There was no pretense of receiving a divine revelation. His final masterpiece was going to be from his own hand.

Speaking of the Qur'an, guess what? Muhammad never asked or ordered anyone to collect his surahs and write them down in a book. Not one, ever. With a thousand "obey me," "pay me," and "go fight for me," there wasn't one "write for me." He knew the Qur'an was revealed to serve his interests and that it would be of no value to anyone once he was gone.

Recognizing that their prophet was illiterate and about to make a fool of himself: "His companions wangled over it. But it did not befit them to carry on a dispute before a prophet. Some people said, 'What's the matter with him? Is he talking nonsense? He is delusional.' [It's a shame it took them so long to figure it out.] Others said, 'We must ask him for an explanation.' So they went back to him and repeated what had been said. The prophet replied, 'Leave me alone.'"

Bukhari reports it this way: *Bukhari:V5B59N716-V4B52N288* "The ailment of Allah's Apostle became worse. He said, 'Fetch me something so I may write something to keep you from going astray.' The people differed in this matter, and it was not right to differ before a prophet. Some said, 'What is wrong with him? Do you think he's delirious? Let's ask him.' So they went to the Prophet and asked. He said, 'Leave me, for my present state is better than what you question me about.' Then he ordered them to do three things. He said, 'Turn the pagans out of the Arabian Peninsula; give gifts to the foreign delegations as you have seen me dealing with them.'" Like I said, Muslims were never good at math.

Another Hadith reports: *Tabari IX:175* "Bring me a tablet, or a plank of the shoulder blade and an inkpot, so that I can write for you a document, after which you will not go astray.' Some said, 'The Messenger of Allah is out of his mind.'"

This confirms my speculation. Muhammad was proposing a new revelation from himself to keep his followers obedient even after his death. *Bukhari:V5B59N717* "When the Prophet was on his deathbed and there were some men in the house, he said, 'Come near, I will write something to keep you obedient.' His Companions said, Allah's Apostle is seriously ill and we have the Qur'an. Allah's Book is sufficient.' So they started disputing. Some said, 'Give him writing material.' Others said the other way round. So when their differences increased, Allah's Apostle said, 'Get out.' No doubt, it was very unfortunate and a great disaster that he was prevented from writing that writing because of their differences and noise.'" It wouldn't have made a difference because it wouldn't have been different. Muhammad was Allah, which is why the Qur'an and Hadith speak with one voice.

Bukhari:V5B59N713 "The Prophet in his ailment used to say, 'Aisha! I feel the pain caused by the food I ate at Khaybar. My aorta is being cut from that poison.'" If it were true, Muhammad would be elevated to "martyr status." He'd gain a direct pass into Allah's brothel and earn seventy virgins rather than the regular allotment.

I dare say, Muhammad was no fun to nurse: *Bukhari:V5B59N735* "We poured medicine in one side of the Prophet's mouth and he started pointing to us, meaning to say, 'Don't pour medicine in me.' When he felt a little better, he said, 'Didn't I forbid you to pour medicine in my mouth?' We said, 'We thought it was because of the dislike patients have for them.' He said, 'Let everyone in the house be given medicine by pouring it in his mouth while I am looking at him.'"

"Blowing" and "cupping" were both prescribed Islamic cures and Satanic practices. The prophet preferred them. *Bukhari:V6B61N536* "Aisha said, 'Whenever the Prophet went to bed he used to cup his hands together and blow over them, rubbing his hands over whatever parts of his body he was able to rub. He used to do that three times.'"

Bukhari:V5B59N714 "Whenever Allah's Apostle became ill he used to recite the last two Suras of the Qur'an and then blow his breath and pass his hands over himself. When he had his fatal illness, I started reciting and blowing my breath over him as he used to do. Then I rubbed the hand of the Prophet over his body." The Qur'an had not yet been ordered, and I use that term loosely, so there was know way of knowing the first surah from the last. But, should Aisha have been right, Muhammad ended his life speaking of himself. The 114th surah says: "I seek refuge with the Lord of men, the King of men, from the evil of the whispering devil who blows temptations into the minds of men, who suggests evil thoughts to the hearts of men—from among the demons and men." It's hard to imagine a more incriminating way for a "prophet," especially this one, to end his life.

Bukhari:V5B59N715 "I heard the Prophet while he was lying on his back say, 'O Allah! Forgive me.'" Even Muhammad could have been forgiven, but not by Allah. And that's why this false prophet was in such agony. *Bukhari:V5B59N731* "Aisha said, 'Allah's Apostle in his fatal illness, used to ask, "Where will I be tomorrow? Where will I be tomorrow?"'"

This Hadith is as nonsensical as the rest of Islam: *Bukhari:V5B59N719* "I used to hear the Prophet say that no Prophet dies until he is given the option to select either the worldly life or the life of the Hereafter." Sorry, not all prophets are scum, and they certainly aren't this stupid. Muhammad is saying that after a lifetime of dedicating oneself to God's calling and to revealing his truth, prophets are asked if they want to renounce their mission.

The first Muslims were a conniving and covetous lot. *Bukhari:V5B59N728* "Ali came out of the house of Allah's Apostle during his fatal illness. The people asked, 'How is the health of Muhammad this morning?' Ali replied, 'He has recovered with the Grace of Allah.' 'Abbas bin Abdul Muttalib held him by the hand and said, 'He will die from this ailment, for I know how the faces of the offspring of Abdul Muttalib look at the time of their death. So let us go to him and ask who will take over the Caliphate. If it is given to us we will know, and if it is given to somebody else, we will inform him so that he may tell the new ruler to take care of us.' Ali said, 'If we asked him for the Caliphate and he denies it to us, the people will never give it to us after that.'"

Loitering in the mosque, just outside the doorway to Aisha's apartment, some Muslims... *Tabari IX:178* "said they were afraid that he might have pleurisy. He said, 'Pleurisy is from Satan and Allah would not inflict it on me.'" *Tabari IX:181* "Before Muhammad died, he cried, 'O my Lord, help me overcome the severity of the agony of death.'" *Bukhari:V5B59N730* "Aisha said, 'It was one of the favors of Allah towards me that His Apostle expired in my apartment on the day of my turn while he was leaning on my chest and Allah made my saliva mix with his at his death. Abd-Rahman entered upon me with a Siwak in his hand and I was supporting Muhammad against my chest. I saw the Prophet looking at it and I knew that he loved the Siwak, so I said, 'Shall I take it for you?' He nodded. It was too stiff for him to use and I softened it as He nodded his approval. He cleaned his teeth with it, crying, "Death has its tortures."'"

Tabari IX:183 "Aisha said, 'Muhammad rubbed his teeth with it more energetically than I had ever seen him doing before. Then he put it down, and I found him getting heavy in my lap...and he died.'" He knew that he had dispensed some of the most revolting poison ever spoken. Millions would die, and billions would be damned, as a result of the words that had left his mouth. So seeing Muhammad use his last measure of life to scrub his mouth of death is the perfect way to say goodbye to the most evil man who ever lived.

Only one problem: Muhammad wasn't supposed to die. Allah had promised. And then there was the Messianic problem. "Jesus" had raised men from the dead; and Christ had *not* died, according to Allah. And what about the Night's Journey? All of the prior prophetic big shots, Adam, Abraham, Moses, and Jesus were alive, joining Islam's hallucinogenic prophet in the temple that wasn't there for a prayer and a glass of milk. Muhammad was supposed to be better than all of them.

Bukhari:V5B59N733 "Abu Bakr came from his [stolen] house at As-Sunh on a [stolen] horse. He dismounted and entered the mosque, but did not speak to the people till he entered upon Aisha and went straight to Allah's Apostle who was covered with a [stolen] Yemenite cloth. He uncovered the Prophet's face and bowed over him and kissed him and wept, saying, 'Let my father and mother be sacrificed for you. Allah will never cause you to die twice. As for the death which was written for you, has come upon you.'" It's telling that Bakr "bowed over him." The spirit that had made Bakr rich and powerful had been Muhammad's, not Allah's. Bakr's willingness to **"sacrifice his father and mother"** to save the soul of his fallen comrade is also telling. The first Muslims had been corrupted to the point they had willingly and gleefully killed their closest relatives. And Muhammad had never given Muslims a plan of salvation. They lack a rational solution to the problem of sin even today. There is no sacrifice to accept or perform to obtain forgiveness and thus come into the presence of a holy God. But, then again, that's not a problem for Islam. Their god is anything but holy.

Tabari IX:187 **"When the Prophet died, Umar stood up threatening the people, saying, 'Some of the hypocrites allege that the Messenger of Allah is dead. I swear by Allah that he is alive, not dead. By Allah the Prophet will return and he will go after those who are spreading lies about him. He will cut off the hands and the feet of those who claim that he is dead. He will crucify them.'"** Sorry pal; he was certifiably and undeniably dead. And not a moment too soon.

Bukhari:V5B59N733 **"While Umar was talking to the people, Abu Bakr said, 'Sit down, Umar!' But he refused. So the people came to Abu and left him. Bakr said, 'To proceed, if you used to worship Muhammad, then Muhammad is dead, but if anyone of you used to worship Allah, then Allah is alive and shall never die. Allah said, 'Muhammad is no more than an Apostle, and indeed apostles have passed away before him.' (3:144) By Allah, it was as if the people never knew Allah had revealed this Verse before Abu recited it. Umar said, 'When I heard Bakr, my legs could not support me and I fell down, declaring that the Prophet had died.'"** Abu Bakr just confirmed what I have been saying from the beginning. Muslims **"used to worship Muhammad."** Not out of respect, mind you. They worshiped Muhammad for the same reasons they would come to worship Allah. They feared him. They knew good Muslims would kill them the moment they stopped. And let's not forget: Islam had its rewards. Jihad had become holy, and booty had been made lawful and good.

Islam's first historian paints the drama like this: *Tabari IX:187* **"Bakr saw that Umar would not listen. He went forward. 'I swear by the Lord of the Ka'aba that Muhammad is gone. Those people who formerly worshipped Muhammad must know that the deity you worshiped is dead. Those who formerly worshipped Allah must know that Allah is still alive and immortal.'"** In death, Muhammad had given birth to the god he had conceived in life. They were separate and distinct for the first time.

Bukhari:V5B59N736 **"It was mentioned in the presence of Aisha that the Prophet had appointed Ali as successor by will. She said, 'Who says so? I was with the Prophet, supporting him against my chest, when he expired. I didn't hear anything. So how do the people say he appointed Ali as successor?'"** Aisha had never forgiven Ali, when, after her little indiscretion, he had told Muhammad, **"Women are plentiful. You can always exchange her for another one."**

Bukhari:V5B59N737 **"I asked Abdallah, 'Did the Prophet make a will?' He replied, 'No.' I asked, 'How come?'"** Because Lucifer had deceived his prophet. But his promise of eternal life was useless (as are his promises of virgins for jihadists).

Umar and Bakr were at their wits' end to be sure, but so was Ali. He craved the power others were swooshing in to grab. Before the body was cold, they were assembling their allies. *Tabari IX:188* **"Zubayr drew his sword saying, 'I will not put it back until the oath of allegiance is rendered to Ali.' When this news reached Abu Bakr and Umar, the latter said, 'Hit him with a stone and seize the sword.'"** Recognizing that Islam had been Muhammad's ticket to babes, booty, and power, the boys were ruthless. *Tabari IX:196* **"Fatimah [Muhammad's daughter] and Ali [Muhammad's adopted son and Fatimah's husband] came to Bakr demanding their share of inheritance of the Messenger. They demanded Muhammad's land in Fadak and his share of Khaybar's tribute."** But Bakr was unmoved. He had sacrificed his six-year-old daughter to make sure no one would cheat him out of what Muhammad had stolen. **"Fatimah shunned him and did not speak to Bakr until she died. Ali buried her at night and did not permit Abu Bakr to attend her burial."** This spat over money was not without consequence. It caused the rift that separated Sunni from Shi'ite. The scam that had been conceived to enrich its prophet had split over booty. How poetic.

Bukhari covers the financial feud this way: *Bukhari:V5B59N368* **"Fatimah came to Abu Bakr, claiming her inheritance of the Prophet's land of Fadak and his share from Khaybar. Abu said, 'I heard the Prophet say, "Our property is not inherited."'"** Muslims the world over are brainwashed to believe that their prophet died broke, with nothing more than his robe and sandals. But that, like so much of Islam, is simply not true. For example: *Bukhari:V4B52N308* **"There was a man who looked after the family and the belongings of the Prophet called Karkara. He died and Allah's Apostle said, 'He is in the Hell Fire.' He had stolen a cloak from the Prophet's war booty."**

Buried among the money grubbing Hadiths are two that contradict a score of others. *Bukhari:V5B59N743* **"The Prophet died while his armor was mortgaged to a Jew for thirty Sa's of barley."** Sorry, I'm not buying that. Muhammad and his pals had murdered, enslaved, and exiled every Jew worth robbing. And...*Bukhari:V5B59N738* **"Allah's Apostle did not leave a Dinar or a Dirham or a male or a female slave. He left only his white mule on which he used to ride, and his weapons, and a piece of land which he gave in charity for the needy travelers.'"** So for argument's sake, let's say this one is right and all the others are wrong. It really doesn't matter if he died covered in stolen plunder or not. The fact he stole it is what's important. Criminal behavior destroys his credibility. The fact he had owned and used slaves, especially female slaves, speaks to his depraved character as well. And the fact that the most inspired Sunnah scriptures in Islam conflict with one another suggest that none of this can be trusted. And that's important too.

Bukhari:V5B59N546 **"Fatimah, the daughter of the Prophet, sent someone to Bakr, asking for her inheritance of what Allah's Apostle had left of the property taken from the Fai booty gained without fighting in Medina and Fadak, and what remained of the Khumus [Muhammad's fifth of the booty gained through fighting] of the Khaybar booty. On that, Abu said, 'Our property is not inherited. Whatever we leave is Sadaqa, but the family of Muhammad can eat of this property. I will not make any change in the estate of the Apostle and will** dispose of it as he used to [bribing men to fight].' So Bakr refused to give anything to Fatimah. She became angry. When she died, her husband Ali buried her at night without informing Bakr and he said the funeral prayer by himself. When Fatimah was alive, the people used to respect Ali, but after her death, Ali noticed a change in people's attitude towards him. So he sought reconciliation with Bakr. [The warlord is dead; long live the warlord.] Ali sent someone to Bakr saying, 'Come to me, but let nobody come with you,' as he disliked Umar. But Umar said, 'No, not alone.' 'What do you think he will do to me? I will go to him.' Ali uttered, 'Tashah-hud [a ritual prayer],' and said, 'I know your superiority and am not jealous, but you did not consult me in the question of rulership and I thought that I had a right to rule because of my near relationship to Allah's Apostle.'

"Thereupon Bakr's eyes flowed with tears. 'As for the trouble which arose between me and you about his property, I will spend it according to what is good, and will not leave any rule or regulation which I saw Allah's Apostle following in disposing of it.' [In other words: "You're out of luck kid. I've already grabbed the power and the money and I'm not giving you either."] Ali added, 'I believed that I had some rights in this affair and when you did not consult me in these matters, it caused me to feel sorry.'"

Even Aisha wasn't keen on the idea of her dad running the Islamic war machine. *Bukhari:V5B59N727* "Aisha added, 'I had argued with Allah's Apostle repeatedly about his order that Abu Bakr should lead the people in his place. What made me argue so much was that it never occurred to my mind that after the Prophet, the people would ever love a man who had taken his place. I felt that anybody standing in his place would be a bad omen to the people, so I wanted him to give up the idea of choosing dad."

And that wasn't the worst of it. The Meccans wanted to return the Ka'aba's custodianship back to the line of Qusayy. Bakr didn't qualify. And with the warlord dead, Arabs stopped paying the zakat tax. That was a problem because there was no village in Arabia left to rob. Islam was teetering on financial ruin. So Bakr did what any good fundamentalist Muslim would have done. He grabbed his sword, called his fellow militants, and forced the entire subcontinent into submission. He called it, "The War of Compulsion."

Bakr, like Muhammad, was in it for the money. This Hadith is very incriminating. There is no suggestion of salvation; religious ritual is discounted, but money reigns supreme. *Bukhari:V9B84N59* "When the Prophet died, Arabs reverted to disbelief. Umar said, 'Abu, should we fight these people? Allah's Apostle said, "I have been ordered to fight everyone until they say: 'None has the right to be worshipped but Allah,"' Bakr said, 'By Allah! I will fight whoever differentiates between prayers and Zakat, as Zakat is the right to be taken from property according to Allah's Orders. If they refuse to pay me even so little as a kid they used to pay, I will fight with them for withholding it.' Umar said, 'I noticed that Allah opened Bakr's chest towards the decision to fight.'"

All the while the pungent aroma of Muhammad's rotting body was fouling his mosque. So the decision was made to bury the dead prophet as he had lived—beneath the bed upon which he had died morally a decade earlier. *Tabari IX:204* "They buried him where he died. Aisha's bed was removed and a grave was dug beneath it." The profiteer whose religious scam that had been conceived when, terrified and suicidal, he had crawled into bed with his sixty-year-old wife died in the bed of his child bride. Mission accomplished: he had become rich, loved, and powerful. But at what cost?

I was not the only American troubled by the senseless acts of violence that preceded the destruction of the World Trade Towers or by the carnage that followed. The lethality of the poison required for men to believe slaughtering innocent souls is a service to God is beyond comprehension. Now, two years after having met personally with terrorists from al-Qaeda, Hamas, al-Aqsa Martyrs' Brigade, and Islamic Jihad, and having studied the Islamic scriptures they quoted, I am repulsed but no longer unaware. I recognize that the terrorists have not corrupted their religion; Islam has corrupted them. And I know that Muslim militants will continue to slaughter Christians and Jews, peaceful Muslims and atheists alike, until there are no more. So we can either eliminate Islam so that there is no longer an incentive for them to kill, or we can let Muslims eliminate us. Those are the only two options we have been given. They have declared holy war, and we must respond.

Sadly, all we have done thus far is to parade Islam's most articulate clerics and politicos on television and let them deceive our nation. Our president has lied to us. Our pastors, priests, and rabbis don't seem to care. Fact is, many have been willing to sacrifice your life for money and power. It's like Islam in a way. Muslims threaten clerics, politicians, and the media with angry demonstrations, protestations, boycotts, and even death if they speak out honestly about the obvious correlation between Islam and terror.

Thus far, I have shared hundreds of Qur'an verses commanding Muslims to fight. Muhammad, speaking for Allah made himself perfectly clear. *008.007* **"Allah wished to confirm the truth by His words, 'Wipe the disbelieving infidels out to the last."** *008.039* **"So fight them until all opposition to Islam ends and all are obedient to Allah."**

Speaking for himself, he unsheathed the same sword. Muhammad has blessed us with countless Jihad Hadiths chronicled by the likes of Ishaq, Tabari, and Bukhari. *Ishaq:618* **"Kill the disbelievers wherever you find them. Lie in wait for them, ambush them, overwhelm them. I have ordered you to kill them."** *Tabari VIII:141* **"The battle cry of Muhammad's Companions was, 'Kill! Kill! Kill!'"** *Bukhari:V4B52N196* **"Allah's Apostle said, 'I have been ordered to fight people until they say, "None has the right to be worshipped but Allah."'"** The four most important and holy books in Islam speak with the same voice. So what about the fifth? What does Muslim have to say about the first Muslims? His voice must be heard too, as no Islamic scholar disputes the authenticity of his inspired collection of Sunnah.

By way of background, Muslim was born in 202 A.H. and died in 933 A.D.

"He traveled widely to gather his collection of Hadith, including to Iraq, Saudi Arabia, Syria, and Egypt. Out of 300,000 Hadith which he evaluated, only 4,000 were extracted for inclusion into his collection based on stringent acceptance criteria. Muslim was a student of Bukhari." He had a great deal to report on the subject of Jihad. In fact, what he had to say is hard to miss.

Muslim begins his dissertation under the title: "**Command For Fighting Against People So Long As They Do Not Profess That There Is No Ilah But Allah And Muhammad Is His Messenger.**" The first Tradition is a bolder version of a Bukhari Hadith, confirming that the first Islamic Caliphs fought for money, not souls. *Muslim:C9B1N29* "**When the Messenger breathed his last and Bakr was appointed Caliph, many Arabs chose to become apostates [leaving Islam, rejecting Muhammad, Allah, and the Qur'an]. Umar said: 'Why would you fight against these people? The Messenger declared: "I have been directed to fight against everyone who does not say: 'There is no god but Allah.'"' Bakr replied: 'I would definitely fight against anyone who stopped paying the Zakat, for it is an obligation. I would fight against them even to secure the cord used for hobbling the feet of a camel which they used to pay if they withheld it now.' Umar remarked: 'Allah had opened the heart of Abu for understanding the justification of fighting against those who refused to pay Zakat.'**" The War of Compulsion enslaved all Arabs. The reason for fighting was money. Islam stole Arab property and freedom.

Muslim:C9B1N30 "**The Messenger said: 'I have been commanded to fight against people so long as they do not declare that there is no god but Allah.'**" That means Muslims must fight and kill non-Muslims until there are no more non-Muslims. No matter how you translate or interpret this Hadith, that is what these words mean. The only way to avoid the sword of Islam, and the loss of life and property, is to become one. Even then, if you don't pay the zakat tax and obey their every command, Muslims will hunt you down and kill you. And should you decide to leave the cult, they'll kill you for that too.

There will be no peace until there is no Islam. *Muslim:C9B1N31* "**The Messenger said: 'I have been commanded to fight against people until they testify that there is no god but Allah, and they believe in me (that) I am the Messenger and in all that I have brought [the Sunnah/Hadith]. And when they do it, their blood and riches are protected.'**" Muslims are commanded to follow Muhammad's example. They are ordered to fight non-Muslims in the Qur'an. Now, all people on earth, you and me included, are required to "**believe in Muhammad,**" and to "**believe Muhammad was the God's Messenger**" if we want to live. And then to add insult to injury, if we want Muslims to spare our "**blood and riches**" we must believe in "**all that Muhammad brought.**" All would include the entirety of the deeds and words recorded by Bukhari, Muslim, Ishaq, Tabari, and Allah. Go back and read Muhammad's creation accounts if you need to be reminded as to how insane such capitulation would be. And continue to read this collection of what "**Muhammad brought**" if you would like to know how lethal Islam can be.

Lest you think that this dire threat is an aberration, an isolated warning, consider this: *Muslim:C9B1N33* **"The Prophet said: 'I have been commanded to fight against people till they testify that there is no god but Allah, that Muhammad is the Messenger of Allah, and they establish prostration prayer, and pay Zakat. If they do it, their blood and property are protected.'"** And if they don't submit, obey, and pay, they lose their blood and property.

Muslim:C10B1N176 **"Muhammad (may peace be upon him) sent us in a raiding party. We raided Huraqat in the morning. I caught hold of a man and he said: 'There is no god but Allah,' but I attacked him with a spear anyway. It once occurred to me that I should ask the Apostle about this. The Messenger said: 'Did he profess "There is no god but Allah," and even then you killed him?' I said: 'He made a profession out of the fear of the weapon I was threatening him with.' The Prophet observed: 'Did you tear out his heart in order to find out whether it had professed truly or not?' 'By Allah, I would never kill any Muslim so long as a person with a heavy belly would not kill.' Upon this a person remarked: 'Did Allah not say: "And fight them until there is no more mischief and religion is wholly for Allah?"'"**

While I do not understand Muhammad's question regarding cutting out the man's heart, nor the reference to obesity, I know what Allah had to say about this specific subject. *005.033* **"The punishment for those who wage war against Allah and His Messenger and strive after corruption, making mischief in the land [those who refuse to surrender to Islam] is murder, execution, crucifixion, the cutting off of hands and feet on opposite sides, or they should be imprisoned. That is their degradation and disgrace in this world. And a great torment of an awful doom awaits them in the hereafter. Except for those who repent (and become Muslims) before you overpower them and they fall into your control."** According to Allah, the Muslim militant who overpowered his victim and then impaled him after a confession of faith was justified. Since Muhammad revealed this surah, and since it was his last, and thus the most current in his memory, he should have known this as well. But he didn't recite it even though it provided a direct answer to the man's question. Instead he proposed a ghoulish question.

The following is similar yet contradictory, all at the same time. *Muslim:C10B1N177* **"The Messenger (may peace be upon him) sent us to raid Huraqat, a tribe of Arabs. We attacked the tribe early in the morning and defeated them. I and an Ansar man caught hold of a person of the defeated tribe. When we overcame him, he said: 'There is no ilah but Allah.' At that moment the Ansari spared him, but I attacked him with my spear and killed him. The news had already reached the Apostle, so when we came back he said: 'Usama, did you kill him after he had made the profession: "There is no ilah but Allah?"' I said. 'He did it only as a shelter.' 'Did you kill him after he had made the profession?' He went on repeating this to me till I wished I had not embraced Islam."** Keep in mind that contradictory scripture is untrustworthy scripture. Liars lie, that's what liars do.

And speaking of liars, Muhammad demonstrated an inability to recall or apply his own scriptures. If I know them, why didn't he?

Those who lie and say "Islam is a peaceful religion," or "Jihad is a spiritual struggle," should have this verse tattooed on their foreheads. Like the "Scarlet

Letter" in days gone by, we could use it to more readily recognize those who would deceive us so that others might kill us more readily. *Muslim:C20B1N4597* **"The Prophet (may peace be upon him) said at the conquest of Mecca: 'There is no migration now, but only Jihad, fighting for the Cause of Islam. When you are asked to set out on a Jihad expedition, you should readily do so.'"** There is only Jihad. When Muslims are called to Jihad, they must go without hesitation. If they don't, they become hypocrites or apostates, who must be killed as a way of encouraging future Jihadists.

Muslim:C22B20N4604 **"We used to take oaths to Muhammad that we would listen to and obey his orders."** Islam was an oath to serve and obey Muhammad. Period. Since he is dead now, why are so many people enslaved by his words?

Muslim:C26B20N4614 **"I saw Allah's Messenger (may peace be upon him) twisting the fore-lock of a horse with his fingers as he was saying: 'A great benefit. A reward for rearing them for Jihad. The spoils of war have been tied to the forelocks of horses.'"** Just imagine what was going through his twisted mind as he was lying to his people.

The 28th chapter of Muslim is entitled: **"Merit Of Jihad And Campaigning In The Way Of Allah."** There is nothing moral or spiritual in it. The first Hadith lets us know that Jihad is a selfish act, that Jihad is a call to war, and that Muhammad was a liar. *Muslim:C28B20N4626* **"Allah's Apostle (mpbuh) said: 'Allah has undertaken to look after the affairs of one who goes out to fight in His Way believing in Him and affirming the truth of His Apostle. He is committed that He will either admit him to Paradise or bring him back to his home with a reward or his share of booty. By the Being [Satan] in Whose Hand is the life of Muhammad, if a person gets wounded in Allah's Cause he will arrive on the Day of Judgment with his wound in the same condition as it was when it was first inflicted; its color will be blood but its smell will be musk perfume. If it were not too hard on Muslims I would not lag behind any raid going out to fight in the Cause of Allah. But I do not have abundant means to provide them (the Mujahids [Islamic terrorists]) with riding beasts, nor have they all the means (to provide themselves with the weapons of Jihad). I love to fight in the Way of Allah and be killed, to fight and again be killed and to fight and be killed.'"** That was the "Value Meal" of Jihad Traditions. It included a little bit of everything and had something for everybody.

For those on a diet, this is the slimed-down version: *Muslim:C28B20N4628* **"Allah has undertaken to provide for one who leaves his home to fight for His Cause and to affirm the truth of His word; Allah will either admit him to Paradise or will bring him back home with his reward and booty."**

For our next tasteless treat, Islam serves up: *Muslim:C28B20N4629* **"The Messenger (may peace be upon him) [**Don't you love the knee-jerk, brain-dead, idiocy of adding "(may peace be upon him)" every time these buffoons mention their warlord?**] said: 'One who is wounded in the Way of Allah—and Allah knows better who is wounded in His Way—will appear on the Day of Judgment with his wound still bleeding. The color (of its discharge) will be blood, (but) its smell will be musk.'"** If it was dumb to say once, it's dumber to say twice. So, what would you call a man who mumbled such foolishness a third time? (Muslims called him Muhammad.) *Muslim:C28B20N4630* "**Muhammad (mpbuh) said: 'Every wound received by a Muslim in the Way of Allah will appear on the Day of Judgment in the same condition as it was when it was inflicted, and would be bleeding profusely. The color…**" You know the rest. But then… "**By the Being in Whose Hand is Muhammad's life, if it were not hard on Muslims, I would not lag behind any expedition undertaken for Jihad. But I do not possess means to provide Mujahids with riding animals to follow me, nor would it please them to stay behind me.'**"

Since Muhammad called himself a coward, and since he remained home with his harem on two out of every three Islamic raids, someone must have asked: "If this Jihad stuff is such a great idea, why aren't you doing it?" So he repeated: *Muslim:C28B20N4631* "**I heard Muhammad (mpbuh) say: 'I would not stay behind when an expedition for Jihad was being mobilized unless it was going to be too hard on the believers.'** This is followed by the same words as in the previous Traditions, but this Hadith has a slight difference in the wording. '**I love that I should be killed in the way of Allah; then I should be brought back to life and be killed again.'**"

That brings us to the bastardization of what was once a noble word. Martyr is derived from the Greek "*martus.*" It means "witness," not "murderer." Muslim, using the corrupted connotation, devoted his next chapter to: "**The Merit Of Martyrdom.**" It begins: *Muslim:C29B20N4634* "**The Messenger of Allah (mpbuh) said: 'Nobody who dies and has something good for him with Allah will (like to) return even though he were offered the whole world and all that is in it (as an inducement), except the martyr who desires to return and be killed for the merit of martyrdom.'**" Anyone who believes that "martyrdom," by Islam's definition, earns "merit" is corrupted beyond words or reason. They are too lost to recognize truth, much less choose it. While we can, and should, reach and hopefully save "bad," peaceful Muslims from the spirit who hates them, our best hope for Jihadists is to prevent them from killing us and corrupting others.

Same tune, different lyric: *Muslim:C29B20N4635* "**The Prophet said: 'Nobody who enters Paradise wants return even if he were offered everything on the surface of the earth [as a bribe] except the martyr who will desire to return and be killed ten times for the sake of the great honor that has been bestowed upon him.'**"

By presenting the Muslim Jihad collection along with compilations contained in the books by Bukhari, Ishaq, Tabari, and Allah, I have revealed a thousand Islamic scriptures glorifying fighting and booty. Yet the following Hadith alone is sufficient to justify the extermination of Islam. *Muslim:C29B20N4636* "**The Messenger of Allah (mpbuh) was asked: 'What deed could be equivalent to Jihad in the Way of Allah? He answered: 'You do not have the strength to do that deed.' The question was repeated twice or thrice. Every time he answered: 'You do not have the strength to do it.' When the question was asked for the third time, he said: 'One who goes out for Jihad is like a person who keeps fasts and stands in prayer forever, (obeying) Allah's Verses, and never exhibiting any weariness in fasting and prayer until the Mujihid returns from Jihad.'**" You can die as a Jihadist, of starvation, or sleep deprivation. But with Islam you are going to die. *Muslim:C29B20N4638* "As I was (sitting) near the pulpit of the Messenger (mpbuh) [which was a large chair raised high on a platform, i.e., a throne] a man said: 'I do not care if, after embracing Islam, I do not do any good deed (except) distributing drinking water to pilgrims.' Another said: 'I do not care if I do not do any good deed beyond maintenance service to the Sacred Mosque.' Yet another said: 'Jihad in the Way of Allah is better than what you have said.' Umar reprimanded them: 'Don't raise your voices near the pulpit of the Messenger. When prayer was over, I entered (the apartment of the Prophet) and asked his verdict about the matter. It was upon this that Allah, the Almighty and Exalted, revealed the Qur'anic Verse: 'Do you make the giving of drinking water to the pilgrims and the maintenance of the Sacred Mosque equal to (the service of those) who believe in Allah and strive hard and fight Jihad in His Cause. They are not equal. Those who believed and fought Jihad in Allah's Cause with their wealth and their lives are far higher in degree with Allah.'" (Qur'an 9:19) No matter where you turn, the best deed remains Jihad.

It's hard to believe, but Muslim has a chapter entitled: "The Merit Of Leaving For Jihad In The Morning And Evening." *Muslim:C30B20N4639* "The Messenger of Allah (peace be unto him) said: 'Leaving for Jihad in the Way of Allah in the morning or in the evening will merit a reward better than the world and all that is in it.'" As such, Jihad is better than Islam's Five Pillars combined. Jihad is Islam's foundation. Jihad is better than every treasure Muslims plundered, better than every man they murdered, better than every woman they raped, better even than every child they sold into slavery. And while there is no question he said this, it's a lie. Yet it was not his biggest lie, or even his worst lie. Claiming that Allah was the God of the Bible, the Creator of the universe, and that he spoke for Him, was a far more egregious sin.

In Muslim's version of the greatest lie ever told, we are confronted by: "The High Position Reserved By Allah For Muhahids [Islamic Fighters] In Paradise." *Muslim:C31B20N4645* "The Prophet said: 'Whoever cheerfully accepts Allah as his Lord, Islam as his Religion and Muhammad as his Apostle is necessarily entitled to enter Paradise.' Abu wondered at it and said: 'Messenger of Allah, repeat that for me.' He did that and said: 'There is another act which elevates the position of a man in Paradise to a grade one hundred (higher), and the elevation between one grade and the other is equal to the height of the heaven from the earth.' Abu said: 'What is that act?' He replied: 'Jihad in the Way of Allah! Jihad in Allah's Cause!'" The reason the Abu asked for clarification was that he knew Muhammad was lying. *Bukhari:V8B76N550* "I heard Allah's Apostle saying, 'From my followers there will be a crowd of 70,000 in number who will enter Paradise all together.'" There have been 3 billion Muslims. That means the prophet oversold paradise. It's a *real* bad idea to trust a lying prophet. It's an even worse idea to murder for one.

Muslim:C32B20N4646 "Muhammad [may he not be believed] stood up among his Companions to deliver his sermon in which he told them that Jihad in the way of Allah and belief in Allah were the most meritorious of acts. A man stood up and said: 'Messenger of Allah, do you think that if I am killed in the way of Allah, my sins will be blotted out from me?' The Messenger said: 'Yes, in case you are killed in the Way of Allah and you were patient and sincere and you always fought facing the enemy, never turning your back upon him.' The man asked (again).' The Messenger said: 'Yes, if you always fought facing the enemy and never retreated, except debt. Gabriel has told me this.'" In Islam two things are certain: death and taxes. Even if you die gloriously, murdering innocent infidels for Allah, you still have to pay the piper. Lucifer told him so.

And I suppose Lucifer taught his disciple how to lie as well. But not very well...*Muslim:C33B20N4651* "We asked Abdallah about the Qur'anic Verse: 'Think not of those who are slain in Allah's way as dead. Nay, they are alive, finding their sustenance in the presence of their Lord.' (Qur'an 3:169) He said: 'We asked the Holy Prophet the meaning of the verse and he said: "The souls of martyrs live in the bodies of green birds who have their nests in chandeliers hung from the throne of the Almighty. They eat the fruits of Paradise from wherever they like and then nestle in these chandeliers. Once their Lord cast a glance at them and said: 'Do you want anything?' They said: 'What more shall we desire? We eat the fruit of Paradise from wherever we like.' Their Lord asked them the same question thrice. When they saw that they would continue to be asked and not left, they said: 'O Lord, we wish that Thou mayest return our souls to our bodies so that we may be slain in Thy Way once again.' When He (Allah) saw that they had no need, they were left (to their joy)."'" Souls live in the bodies of green birds who nest in chandeliers. So if that's true, how, pray tell, do they frolic with their virgins, why do the rivers flow with wine, and why does Allah provide fowl to eat? And one other little thing: if Allah knows all, why did he have to pester the little birdies?

Under the heading, "The Merit Of Jihad And Of Keeping Vigilance Over The Enemy," we find Muhammad reconfirming that Jihadists are the best Muslims. *Muslim: C34B20N4652-3* "A man came to the Holy Prophet [may he have flown the coop sooner] and said: 'Who is the best of men?' He replied: 'A man who fights staking his life and spending his wealth in Allah's Cause.' The man asked: 'Who is next to him (in excellence)? He said: 'Next to him is a believer who lives isolated in a mountain gorge worshipping his Lord and sparing men from his mischief.'" Whose mischief: Allah's or the second-best Muslims? Either way it's not good.

The Sunnah, like the Qur'an, teaches that those who encourage, harbor, and equip terrorists are as "good" as the terrorists themselves. *Muslim:C38B20N4665* "A man came to the Messenger of Allah (mpbuh) and said: 'My riding beast has been killed, so give me some animal to ride upon.' The Prophet said: 'I have none with me.' A man said: 'I can guide him to a riding beast.' Muhammad said: 'One who guides to something good has a reward similar to that of its doer.'" *Muslim:C34B20N4668* "The Messenger said: 'Anybody who equips a warrior going to fight in the Way of Allah is like one who actually fights. And anybody who looks after his family in his absence is also like one who actually fights." If this were true, the Fahd family thugs ruling Saudi Arabia would have earned a few billion virgins by now.

With scripture like this it's easy to see why Muslims raise martyrs. It's clear why they celebrate their murderous deeds. Sending a son or daughter off to die terrorizing non-Muslims is selfish. *Muslim:C34B20N4669* **"The Prophet (may peace be upon him) said: 'He who equips a warrior in the Way of Allah is like one who actually fights and he who looks after the family of a warrior in the Allah's Cause in fact participated in the battle.'"** Not that we need reminding, but fighting, war, the Way of Allah, and Allah's Cause remain synonymous.

But there is an escape clause for those who are blind and lame. All others must fight, for..."**Jihad Is Compulsory."** *Muslim:C40B20N4676* **"Bara was talking about the Qur'anic Verse: 'Believers who sit home and those who go out for Jihad in Allah's Cause are not equal.' (Qur'an 4:95). He said that the Messenger ordered Zaid and he brought a shoulder blade of a camel and inscribed it thereon. The son of Umm complained of blindness to the Prophet. At this descended the revelation: 'Those believers who sit without any trouble.'"** Team Islam benched the blind and lame rather than heal them.

Muslim claims that there is: **"Proof Of The Martyr's Attaining Paradise."** *Muslim: C41B20N4678* **"Jabir said that a man said: 'Messenger of Allah, where shall I be if I am killed?' He replied: 'In Paradise.' The man threw away the dates he had in his hand and fought until he was killed."** In Islam, that's considered "proof." *Muslim:C41B20N4681* **"Abdallah heard it from his father who, while facing the enemy, reported that the Messenger (mpbuh) said: 'Surely, the gates of Paradise are under the shadow of the swords.' A man in a shabby condition got up and said: 'Abu, did you hear the Prophet say this?' He said: 'Yes.' He returned to his friends and said: 'I greet you (a farewell greeting).' Then he broke the sheath of his sword, threw it away, advanced with his (naked) sword towards the enemy and fought with it until he was slain."**

I believe that we have stumbled upon something profound. Muhammad is the sole repository of Islamic proof. He testified that the Qur'an was given to him by Gabriel, who in turn got it from Allah. If he lied, Islam vaporizes. And that's why it's crucial to investigate what the Sunnah has to say about his trustworthiness. Were his words believable? Or did he say things like, **"Martyr's souls live in green birds who nest in chandeliers," "War is deceit,"** and **"Paradise is under the shadows of swords?"** Were his deeds exemplary? Or did he lead a criminal and immoral life? Should the words of a man be trusted who was a rapist and an incestuous pedophile? If all we have is one man's witness and he bragged about being a terrorist, a thief, and a slave trader, why would anyone in their right mind trust him?

And then you have his Qur'an itself—the worst "book" ever recited. It's filled with contradictions, historical and scientific errors, and laughably absurd claims. There are grammatical errors, inconsistencies of voice, missing words, and meaningless words. It's gibberish without context and hellish with it. It's out of order, jumbled together haphazardly. And that's the good news. The bad news is what it actually says. It claims that paradise is a drunken orgy and that hell is Allah's personal torture chamber. Early on, its most repetitive theme is pain and punishment. That message evolves to perform, obey, and pay. It defines "good" as "fighting" and "bad" as "peace."

Bottom line: proof is abundant; it's undeniable. Islam is the most heinous and thinly disguised fraud ever perpetrated on mankind.

Muslim:C42B20N4684 "A desert Arab came to the Prophet (may peace be upon him) and said: 'Messenger, one man fights for the spoils of war; another fights that he may be remembered, and one fights that he may see his (high) position (achieved as a result of his valor in fighting). Which of these is fighting in the Cause of Ilah?' The Messenger of Allah (mpbuh) said: 'Who fights so that the word of Allah is exalted is fighting in the Way of Allah.'" If a Muslim "fights" non-Muslims to *force* Islam on them, he is "exalted."

Islam was never about salvation; it was always about power, control, and especially money. Muslim dedicates a chapter to the Muslim mercenaries. (In case you're curious, there isn't one for Muslim missionaries.) Under "**The Reward Of One Who Fought And Got His Share Of The Booty And Of One Who Fought But Did Not Get Any Booty**," we find: *Muslim:C44B20N4690* "The Messenger (mpbuh) said: 'A troop of soldiers who fight in Allah's Cause and get their share of the booty receive in advance two-thirds of their reward, and in the Hereafter one-third will remain (to their credit). If they do not receive any booty, they will get their full reward.'" Muhammad was trying to keep Allah from looking like a liar. His god had previously promised to reward all surviving jihadists with booty.

Islam teaches that Jihadists get it now and later. *Muslim:C44B20N4691* "Muhammad said: 'A troop of soldiers, large or small, who fight get their share of the booty and return safe and sound, receive in advance two-thirds of their reward; and a troop of soldiers who return empty-handed and are afflicted or wounded will receive their full reward.'"

Muslim:C49B20N4699 "Allah's Apostle used to visit Umm Haram, daughter of Milhan (the sister of his foster-mother). She was the wife of Ubada. One day the Messenger paid her a visit. She entertained him with food and then sat down to rub his head. The Prophet dozed off and when he woke he was laughing. She asked: 'What made you laugh?' He said: 'Some people from my Umma [Islamic commune] were fighters in the Way of Allah and were sailing in this sea. Gliding smoothly on the water, they appeared to be kings on thrones.' She said: 'Messenger, pray to Allah that He may include me among these warriors.' He prayed for her then he placed his head and dozed off." It's hard to believe this is Islamic scripture—a divinely inspired revelation.

Muslim:51B20N4705 "Muhammad said, 'A man walks along a path, finds a thorny twig lying on the way, and puts it aside. Allah would appreciate it and forgive him [for what?].' The Prophet said: 'The martyrs are of five kinds: 'One who dies of plague; one who dies of diarrhoea; one who is drowned; one who is buried under debris [making the victims of 9/11 martyrs]; and one who dies fighting in Allah's Cause.'" *Muslim:51B20N4706* "Allah's Messenger said: 'Whom do you consider to be a martyr among you?' The Companions said: 'One who is slain in Allah's Cause is a martyr.' He said: 'Then (if this is the definition of a martyr) the martyrs of my Umma [Islamic community] will be small in number.' They asked: 'Prophet, who are martyrs then?' He said: 'One who is slain in Allah's Cause is a martyr; one who dies in the way of Allah is a martyr; one who dies of plague is a martyr; one who dies of cholera is a martyr.'" It's nice to see Muhammad being inclusive. Now if he could only be consistent. What happened to those who were buried under debris and drowned?

Muslim:52B20N4711 **"I heard the Messenger delivering a sermon from the pulpit: 'Prepare to meet them with as much strength as you can afford. Beware, strength consists in archery. Beware, strength consists in archery. Beware, strength consists in archery.'"** *Muslim: 52B20N4712* **"I heard the Messenger of Allah (mpbuh) say: 'Lands shall be thrown open to you and Allah will suffice you against your enemies, but none of you should give up playing with his arrows.'"** The man who mumbled these words from his lofty perch amid the apartments of his concubines said that he was the closest to the Messiah of all men who ever lived. Yet in the Gospels, Christ said, "I say to you, love your enemies; do good to those who hate you, bless those who curse you, pray for those who mistreat you. Whoever hits you on the cheek; offer him the other also. And whoever steals your coat; do not withhold your shirt from him either. Treat others the same way you want to be treated." (Luke 6:27) If one "messenger's" message was the opposite of the other then they couldn't have been speaking for the same God.

It bears mention here that "archery" doesn't appear in the New Testament. There is no command to fight or to take to booty. Jihadists aren't mentioned, much less rewarded. Yet the Qur'an has a chapter named, "The Spoils of War," and dozens of surahs promote war and booty. The Hadith features scores of chapters on Jihad. But like the Qur'an, there isn't a single Hadith chapter focused on promoting either peace or love.

Muslim:52B20N4714 **"Abd al-Rahman said to Uqba: 'You frequent between these targets but you are an old man. Hitting them is hard.' Uqba said: 'But for a thing I heard from the Prophet, I would not strain myself.' 'What was that?' The Prophet said, 'Who learnt archery and then gave it up is not from us and is guilty of disobedience to Allah's Apostle.'"** Islam's "prophet" said that if a Muslim stopped shooting arrows he was being disobedient to *him*, and he was therefore no longer a Muslim.

The Jihadists have, and will continue to fight a holy war until the end of time, Islam, or infidels. *Muslim:C53B20N4717* **"The Holy Prophet (mpbuh) said: 'This religion will continue to exist, and a group of people from the Muslims will continue to fight for its protection until the Hour is established.'"** By "fighting" they are "protecting" Islam. It wouldn't endure if left to reason and choice. And that is why we, if we wish to go on living, must create choice by removing Islam's sword.

Muslim:C53B20N4721 **"Abd al-Rahman said: 'I was in the company of Maslama [the murderer] and Abdallah [the assassin]. Abdallah said: "The Hour shall some when the worst type of people are left on earth. They will be worse than the people of pre-Islamic days. They will get whatever they ask of Allah." Maslama said: "Listen to what Abdallah says. He knows better. So far as I'm concerned, I heard the Messenger say: 'A group of people from my Umma will continue to fight in obedience to the Command of Allah, remaining dominant over their enemies. Those who will oppose them shall not do them any harm. They will** remain in this condition until the Hour overtakes them.'" Abdullah said: "Yes. Then Allah will raise a wild [?] which will be fragrant like musk and whose touch will be like silk. It will cause the death of all persons, not leaving behind a single person with an iota of faith in his heart. Then only the worst of men will remain to be overwhelmed by the Hour." This sounds like a prophecy. But since Muhammad said that the "Hour" would come 500 years after his "prophetic ministry," he either goofed or all true Muslims are dead, having been wiped out by the fragrant and soft wild [?].

If errant prophecy isn't troublesome enough, consider this contradiction from the preceding Hadith: Muslim:C53B20N4720 "Abu Sufyan quoted a Tradition from the Prophet which he related his sermon from the pulpit, saying, 'He grants him an understanding of religion. A group of people from the Muslims will remain on the Right Path and continue until the Day of Judgment to triumph over those who oppose them.'"

Bukhari and Muslim both reported: Muslim:C24B20N4607 "Allah's Messenger forbade that one should travel to the land of the enemy taking the Qur'an with him." Under the chapter heading, "It Is Forbidden To Take The Qur'an To The Land Of The Infidels When It Is Feared That It Might Fall Into Their Hands," imam Muslim provides clarification: Muslim:C24B20N4608 "Muhammad used to forbid anyone from traveling to the land of the enemy taking the Qur'an lest it should fall into the hands of the enemy." And...Muslim: C24B20N4609 "The Messenger said: 'Do not take the Qur'an on a journey with you, for I am afraid lost it would fall into the hands of the enemy.' Ayyub, one of the narrators in the chain of transmitters, said: 'The enemy may seize it and may quarrel with you over it.'"

I would like to ponder the devastating consequence of this final Hadith to the mission and message of Islam's lone prophet. It confirms that the Qur'an was not a godly revelation designed to reveal truth or to save mankind. Non-Muslims weren't to see it. Therefore, the sole purpose of the armed assaults against the infidels was for power, land, and money. Religion didn't play into the equation. The scriptures were not to be shared. That also means that no one became a Muslim based upon Muhammad's Qur'an recitals. All Muslims submitted to the sword of Islam. They were indoctrinated later.

There are some other troubling sidebars here. The Qur'an didn't exist as a book and there was no divine or prophetic order to turn it into one. To say that it could not be taken is to say that Muslim militants had to wipe the poisonous poetry from their minds before they set off to slay the infidels. So then, why were they fighting if not for booty?

Most troubling of all is that Muhammad knew he had perpetrated a scam. He knew his Qur'an recitals would not stand up to scrutiny. Literate people, godly people, would make a farce of them. So Muhammad didn't want his Qur'an seen by anyone who was free to think, free to speak, free to choose. It was only after Islam eliminated these freedoms that Islam's message was to be revealed. And then it was too late.

✡ ✝ ☾ 💣

Before we part company, I want to expose one of the most obscure details of the Qur'an to demonstrate the direct correlation between Islam and the tragic events unfolding before our eyes. Between two thousand and three thousand years ago, real prophets named Daniel, Ezekiel, and Isaiah, and a former fisherman named John foretold the events that would shadow our days. Central to their prognostications was that an international coalition led by Gog, the leader of Magog, would attack Israel. They also warned that a nation known for its wings and naval prowess, a land across the sea divided by rivers, an aggressive fair-skinned people who had separated themselves from God—America—would be pruned back like a diseased grapevine.

So what? Israel has been invaded more times than Muhammad had consorts and America remains the undisputed heavyweight champ of the world. Well, the first snip of the pruning sheers was 9/11. The second was the trillion-dollar impact on the nation's economy. The third was the bloodletting in Iraq—where America engendered the wrath of the world.

This predicted war isn't Badr—a skirmish between militants and merchants—it's World War III. To borrow a phrase from a former tyrant, "This will be the mother of all battles." The prophets appear to be saying that Gog, perhaps the leader of Iran at the time, will form an alliance entirely comprised of Islamic nations—the legacy of Muhammad. Egypt, Syria, Ethiopia, Libya, Sudan, Iraq, and Turkey will join the southern tier of Islamic nations that comprise the Russian Federation (the "stans" and Chechens). Collectively they will unleash hell's fury, beginning with their normal pincer attack. Egypt and Syria will break a peace treaty to simultaneously assault Israel from the north and south. The conflict will devolve into chemical, biological, and nuclear warfare. But the Muslims will lose. A billion of Muhammad's followers and 500,000,000 infidels will die over the course of a year and a half. One third of the Earth's surface will be scorched. America, weakened and humiliated, will protest. A United Europe will answer the call and defend Israel, but not for the sake of the Jews, of course. An unholy trinity will covet what belongs to Yahweh—his promised land and his people.

The catalyst for this war will be as all others. A wolf in sheep's clothing will use the peace process to broker the first and only treaty between many nations and Israel "guaranteeing security" for Jews in the Promised Land. This world leader will arise from what was once the Roman Empire. He will become the Antichrist. His allies will be Satan and the False Prophet. You know who Satan is, so a word about the other guy. He will be an ecumenical religious leader uniting much of the world into one universal and tolerant doctrine. His religion will be closely aligned with that of ancient Babylon— the same religion that forms the basis of both Catholicism and Islam.

The pruning of America—because we've separated ourselves from Yahweh —sounds bad, as does the death of a quarter of the earth's population. But what obscure detail in the Qur'an, you may be asking, led us to this horrific peek at our destiny? The answer is "Gog and Magog." Allah mentions them twice: in Qur'an 18:94 and then again in 21:96. Since Muhammad was illiterate and Allah was dumb as a stone, the source of this material is obvious. It came from Yathrib rabbis. They knew Yahweh's prophecies, and they understood their implications. But not knowing any better, Muhammad included within his own scriptures the very event that would one day lay his legacy to ruin.

In a surah insightfully named **"The Prophets,"** we find this jewel: *021.092* **"Verily, this Brotherhood of Islam is a single Religion, and I am your Lord: therefore worship Me. But (later generations) broke into fragments as regards to their religion, one from another."** This generation of Muslims has spent more time fighting amongst themselves than attacking infidels. But the Bible (and through it the Qur'an), predicts that this will soon change…**"(Yet) they will all return to Us [to make war on Israel]. Therefore whoever shall do good [fighting] deeds as a believer, there shall be no denying of his exertion, and surely We will write (it) down for him (in his book of deeds)."**

Then speaking of the Jews: **"But there is a ban on any population which We have destroyed: that they shall not return until Gog and Magog are let loose (from their barrier) and they swoop down, swarming from every hill, letting loose and breaking forth from every elevated place. Then will the true promise of Doom draw nigh. Behold, the disbelieving Infidels will be terrorized, staring in horror. 'Woe to us! Alas! We made a state heedless of this. We did wrong!'"** Wise and cunning as ever, the Jews who sold Muhammad his scripture, infused it with a admonition: "Do not build a state without heeding this warning." But this is exactly what Israel has done.

Yet fourteen hundred years ago, Yathrib Jews hooked Muhammad. He took the bait and swam with it, not knowing that he was being used to predict his own demise. *021.098* **"Verily you (disbelieving Infidels), and the gods that you worship besides Allah, are the fuel for Hell, faggots for the fire! Certainly you will enter it! Had their (idols) been (real) alihah (gods), they would have kept them out of Hell. Therein, sobbing will be your lot. Breathing with deep sighs, roaring. You will hear nothing but wailing and groaning."** He calls this: *021.103* **"The Greatest Terror," "The Supreme Horror," "The Fearful Event. The angels will meet them. 'This is the Day [of Doom] which you were promised. The Day that We shall roll up the world like a scroll; a promise (binding on Us); surely We will bring it about."** Amongst all of this hate speech, there is a tiny little problem. Allah is allegedly talking to disbelieving infidels, but they, according to Muhammad, were never to see this book. So why are these threats here? What purpose do they serve?

Dumb to the bitter end, Muhammad ends "his" prophecy by confessing that the source of the inspiration was the Bible, although he got the section wrong: *021.105* **"Certainly, We wrote this prophecy before in the Scripture (given to Moses). The Message: 'My righteous slaves shall inherit the earth.'"** The Gog prophecy is in Ezekiel, not the Books of Moses. And Muslims will never inherit the earth—

although they will die trying. It will be a **"Day of Doom."**

Remember, the words and phrases inside parenthesis are not mine. They were added by translators so we might understand what Allah was saying. *021.106* **"Verily in this (Qur'an) is a Message, a plain statement for folks who worship Allah (and for those who act practically on the Sunnah—legal ways of the Prophet). And We sent you (Muhammad) not but as a mercy for mankind and jinn [demons]. Say: (Muhammad) 'It is revealed to me that your Ilah (God) is only one Ilah (God). Will you submit to His Will (and become Muslims)? But if they (disbelievers, Christians, and Jews) turn away (from Islam) say: 'I give notice (of war) to be known to all. But I know not whether the (torment which you are) promised and threatened is nigh or far."** It is nigh.

The second prophecy of **"The Great Terror"** proceeding from the Magog **"sweeping swarm"** comes from a surah entitled **"The Cave."** But before we read the story I'd like to turn your attention to a footnote in the Ahmed Ali translation. It says: **"Qur'an commentators identify Dhu'l-Qarnain with Alexander the Great of Macedonia as he is the closest in his travels, wisdom, and [Islamic] prophethood to the description."** The problem with that theory is Alexander was a pagan. He said that he was a sun god, and he died in a drunken stupor. He never mentioned Allah, the moon god of Mecca, nor visited his rock pile of a house.

So as not to let facts get in our way, let's listen to what Muhammad claims Allah had to say in his perfect book. *018.083* **"They will ask you of Dhu'l-Qarnain. Say: 'I shall recite something of his story.' Verily We established his power on earth and gave him the ways and means to all ends. He followed a course until he reached the setting place of the sun. He found it setting in a spring of hot, black, muddy water."** Remember, Muhammad wasn't very smart, and his god's inspiration wasn't of any value. Earlier in the Hadith we read that the sun set each night in a muddy spring. The Qur'an is verifying that "truth."

The Islamic "scripture" goes on to say: **"And he found near the murky spring a people thereabout."** In an adjoining Hadith, Muhammad explained that the "people" who lived near the sun's muddy-spring-setting-place were extraterrestrials: *Tabari I:236* **"Allah created two cities out in space.... Were those people not so many and noisy, all the inhabitants of this world would hear the loud crash made by the sun falling when it rises and when it sets. Gabriel took me to them during my Night Journey from the Sacred Mosque [the Ka'aba] to the Farthest Mosque [the Jewish Temple which was no longer on Mount Moriah]. I told the people of these cities to worship Allah but they refused to listen to me."** This proves that extraterrestrials are more advanced than humans.

Now that you know which "people" Alexander was visiting and that neither Allah nor Muhammad can be trusted, we'll return to the Qur'anic fairytale: **"We (Allah) said (by inspiration): 'O Dhu'l-Qarnain, either you punish them or treat them with kindness.'"** For a frame of reference: Allah is offering this capricious advice to Alexander the Great as he surveys people living around the murky spring in which the sun goes to bed at night. *018.087* **"He said: 'Whoever does wrong** (a disbeliever in Allah), as for him [the extraterrestrial] we [Alexander's Greek troops] shall punish; then shall he be sent back to his Lord and He will punish him with a terrible torture unheard of (before). But as for him who believes [in what?] and works good, he shall have the best reward [from whom], and we (Dhu'l-Qarnain) shall speak mild words unto him." So he couldn't have quoted from the Qur'an.

018.089 "Then followed he (another) way until he came to the rising place of the sun. [And where might that be?] He found it rising on a people for whom We (Allah) had provided no covering protection against the sun. So (it was)! And We knew all about him (Dhu'l-Qarnain),"...said Professor Allah. Proof the Qur'an wasn't inspired by a rational being.

But this brings us back to Islam's poison pill, albeit more colorfully this time. *018.092* "Then he followed (another) course until, when he reached (a tract) between two mountains, he found beneath them a people who scarcely understood a word [Meccans, perhaps?]. They said: 'O Dhu'l-Qarnain, verily the Gog and Magog do great mischief on earth and they are spoiling our land.'" In the previous surah, Gog was not to arrive until the Last Day, now they are making mischief in a time long past. And by the way, the Qur'an doesn't describe these critters as people. Qur'an 21:92 said: "Gog and Magog are let loose (from their barrier) and they swoop down, swarming." And that may be why these mischief makers are associated with Alexander's extraterrestrial activities.

The 94th verse continues with the "people who scarcely understood a word" saying "'Shall we then pay you tribute in order that thou might erect a barrier between us and them? He said: 'That (the wealth, authority, and power [a.k.a. Islam]) in which my Lord has established me is better (than your tribute). So help me therefore with strength (of men and labor); I will erect a strong barrier between you and them." As an interesting aside, The Jewish rabbis would have known that Arabia wouldn't join Magog's attack on Israel and that the mischief they unleashed would spoil the land. Further, the pagan Dhu'l-Qarnain/Alexander was being presented as an Islamic prophet to help validate Muhammad's claim that he, David, and Solomon were Muslims. But alas, there is no record of Alexander building a "great barrier" anywhere, ever.

The Islamic Alexander the Great said, *018.096* "'Bring me (blocks) of iron;' then, when he had filled up the gap between the two mountainsides, he said, 'Blow.' Then when he had made them (red) as fire [by blowing on an iron wall], he said: 'Bring me molten lead-copper-brass to pour over them. Thus Gog and Magog were made powerless to scale it or dig a hole in it. (Dhu'l-Qarnain) said: 'This is a mercy from my Lord. But when the promise of my Lord comes to pass, He will make it into dust; and the promise of my Lord is ever true.' On that day (the day of Gog and Magog will come out) We shall leave them to surge like waves on one another: the trumpet will be blown, and We shall collect them (the creatures) all together in one gathering in conflict. And We shall present Hell that day for disbelievers to see, all spread out in plain view.... Verily We have prepared Hell for the hospitality of the Infidels; Hell is for the disbeliever's entertainment." At least Allah hasn't lost his touch. He remains the most devilishly demonic deity ever devised. But then I suppose a god who would call hell "entertainment," is much like a warlord who entertains himself torturing men and raping women.

018.103 **"Say: 'Shall we inform you of who will be the greatest losers? ...Those who reject my Revelations... Hell is their reward, because they rejected Islam, and took My proofs, verses, and lessons, and those of My Messengers by way of jest in mockery.'"** In all fairness, it's pretty hard not to mock such foolishness.

There is a Magog Hadith. *Bukhari:V9B88N249* **"One day Allah's Apostle entered upon her in a state of fear and said, 'None has the right to be worshipped but Allah! Woe to the Arabs from the Great evil that has approached (them). Today a hole has been opened in the dam [Alexander's iron barrier between the mountains] of Gog and Magog like this.' The Prophet made a circle with his index finger and thumb. Zainab added: I said, 'O Allah's Apostle! Shall we be destroyed though there will be righteous people among us?' The Prophet said, 'Yes, if the (number) of evil (persons) increases.'"** Somebody had a very rich imagination—one might even call it hallucinogenic.

Enough with the fairytale. According to the Bible, Islam will lead to the destruction of much of the world. I share this with you so that you might appreciate the cost of tolerating the terrorist dogma rather than freeing Muslims from it. And equally important, I want you to be prepared for what is to come, because while it will happen, millions can be saved from it.

I know the future because—unlike Muhammad—Isaiah, Daniel, Ezekiel, and John were real prophets. By putting their predictions together, one can reasonably deduce that six thousand years after Adam and Eve made the wrong choice, Yahweh will put an end to man's rolling in the mud, of false doctrines, ignorance, and sin. He wants to establish a new world order, one without disease, death, or separation.

Yet, true to his character and purpose, he wants the final choice to remain ours, not his. Yahweh simply removes his spirit from the earth, enabling those who remain to plot their own course. Totally separated from God, the prophets predict, humanity will choose poorly. The world will plummet into chaos.

The story of Islam's ultimate demise is but one of many tragic tales that collectively comprise what the Bible calls the "Tribulation"—the last seven years of man's rule on planet earth. Isaiah, in addition to writing about the arrival and nature of the Messiah, was inspired by Yahweh to foretell how Lucifer would form Islam. Then he predicted the events that would lead the Nation of Islam to attack Israel, engulfing the world in war. Daniel explains that it will begin, as did World War II, with a "peace treaty." Foolishly, the world trusts nations whose official god and prophet order them to disavow such oaths. As a result, a third of the earth's surface is scorched (Revelation 8:7), a quarter of its people die (Revelation 6:8)—including the annihilation of five out of every six Muslims (Ezekiel 39:2). I want to provide you with an overview of this battle so that you might be saved from its devastation.

Starting in the 9th chapter, Isaiah speaks of rebuilding Jerusalem with dressed stone, which is exactly what has happened. Every building is covered in white limestone. Then describing martyrdom parades in Gaza, he says the Philistines, the people after whom the "Palestinians" derive their name, will devour Israel from the west with open mouths. Speaking of Israelis who want to trade land for peace, he proclaims, "Those who guide, mislead. They have not sought Yahweh." Consistent with the couplet nature of the Psalms, most all of these prophecies have a dual fulfillment—one relatively near, and one destined for our time. Isaiah presents them in parallel, much the same way he predicted the first and second coming of the Messiah.

Then, stealing a page from yesterday's newspaper, Isaiah reveals that Yahweh will judge Assyria, today's Iraq. He is angry because they are a "godless people seizing loot and snatching plunder. They will be trampled down in the streets." God promises to punish its leader and waste its warriors—all in advance of World War III. Yahweh summons a "noisy" army to carry out his wrath against Babylon. But, Isaiah predicts, "There will be an uproar amongst the kingdoms as this army musters for war. Terror will seize them." While I cannot say for certain, this sure seems an awful lot like what America is doing today, in 2003, as I write these words.

For Israel there is good and bad news. More Jews will settle in the Promised Land and they will ultimately prevail because: "Aliens will join them, uniting with Israel...and her captors will become her captives. On that day Yahweh provides relief from suffering, turmoil, and cruel bondage." Unfortunately, one of Israel's allies will be the Antichrist, the human embodiment of Satan. But not for long: "The morning star [Lucifer], fallen from heaven and cast down to earth, who once laid low the nations...will be brought to the depths of the pit."

While the Palestinians will rejoice, Isaiah predicts their partnership with the Devil will bite them. "Do not rejoice, all you Philistines...a shifty and venomous serpent will spring up.... Wail at the gate. Howl, O City, Melt away, all you Philistines. The answer shall be given to the envoys of that nation that Yahweh has established Israel and her afflicted people will find refuge."

Jordan opts out of the war, but it makes no difference. The Islamic armies march through, ravaging the nation. Describing some of Islam's most obvious ritual rites, a thousand years before they were invented, Isaiah says, "Every head is shaved, every beard is cut off. They wear sackcloth in the streets and public squares. They all wail, prostrating themselves." The Jordanians will actually flee into Israel as the attacking nations ravage their land.

In the 17th chapter, Isaiah says that today's oldest continuously occupied city will be laid to waste. "Damascus will no longer be a city but will become a heap of ruins." Moving on to Israel, he predicts: "In that day the glory of Jacob [Israel] will fade. The fat body will waste away." The thinning of Israel

could well be a "land-for-peace" accord that thins Israel at the waist by giving
Muslims the West Bank—a move that will lead to the death of millions of
Jews. The timing follows what Isaiah refers to as the "harvest." This is the
removal of the believers, thus Yahweh's spirit, from the earth. (I will not be
here to see any of this happen. I pray that you are with me.)

The survivors of this dreadful time will finally "turn back to their Creator." Perhaps speaking of America, the prophet predicts: "In that day their
strong cities, which they left because of the Israelites, will be like places abandoned to thickets and undergrowth. And all will be desolation." Much of the
reason Muslims laid New York and Washington buildings to waste, and will
ultimately waste entire American cities with biological and nuclear devices, is
because the United States supports Israel.

Isaiah says of this country: "You have forgotten God, your Savior; you
have separated yourself from your fortress. Though you set out the finest
plants [the U.S. is the world's leading food producer], and plant imported
vines [Christians], though you make them grow, when it is time for the final
harvest, there will be nothing but incurable disease and pain."

Next, the prophet relays something that sounds like he was been watching
the worldwide uproar against America following the invasion of Iraq: "Oh,
the raging of many nations—they rage like the raging sea! Oh the uproar of
the people, they roar like the roaring of great waters! Although the people
roar like surging waters, when rebuked they flee, driven before the wind like
the chaff on hill, like tumbleweeds before a gale." Describing the methods of
the Islamic Jihadists, and America's inability to see them for what they are,
Isaiah reports: "In the evening, sudden terror! Before morning, they are gone!
This is the portion of those who loot us, the lot of those who plunder us."

While Muslims see America as Israel's best friend, this nation has actually
been the only country to loot the young state—and the U.S. has done it
repeatedly. Following each Arab Israeli conflict, America has taken the lead
in demanding that Israel abandon the Sinai, Lebanon, the Golan, East
Jerusalem, and the West Bank. This was done to improve America's relationship with Islamic nations so that their dictators would either buy American military hardware or sell oil more cheaply. The U.S. required Israel to give
up something they possessed to gain something America wanted.

Continuing to speak about this nation, Isaiah says: "Woe to the land of
whirring wings [ancient Hebrew for airplane or helicopter, perhaps—the symbols of America's might] past the rivers of Cush [west of Africa from the perspective of Israel] that sends envoys and ambassadors by sea in ships. They
are swift messengers from a tall and smooth-skinned people feared far and
wide, an aggressive nation of strange speech whose land is divided by rivers."
From the perspective and vocabulary of a man writing nearly three thousand
years ago, that's a pretty respectable description of America circa the dawn of

the 21st century.

Perhaps speaking of the power of television, Isaiah shares a vision that was impossible until recently: "All you people of the world, you who live on the earth, when a banner is raised on the mountains, you will see it, and when a trumpet sounds, you will hear it. This is what Yahweh said to me: 'I will remain quiet and will look on from my dwelling place like shimmering heat in the sunshine, like a cloud of dew in the heat of harvest.'" That is to say, the calamity that is to come will come from man not God. Yahweh is just reporting what will occur. His truth is illuminating, and he is as close to us as dew is to the harvest.

The harvest, in Biblical nomenclature could be the reaping of souls in the rapture—when those with God's spirit are harvested from the earth and called to him. This rapture is the final predicted event prior to the peace treaty and the beginning of the Tribulation. "For, before the harvest, when the blossom is gone and the flower becomes a ripening grape, he will cut off the shoots with pruning knives and cut down and take away the spreading branches. They will all be left to the birds of prey." If this is a description of America, then we are being told that before the rapture, the nation will be pruned and that our influence around the globe will be cut back.

The prophet goes on to speak about Egypt—the nation that starts the war. He says that the Nile will dry up, that brother will fight brother, and that they will lose heart. Egypt is the center of Islamic scholarship today. He says, "Where are your wise men now? Let them show you and make known what Yahweh has planned for Egypt. The officials have become fools, the leaders are deceived, and have led many astray—pouring into them a spirit of dizziness. They make Egypt stagger as a drunkard in his own vomit." The land of Israel will bring terror to the Egyptians. Fortunately a remnant of Egyptians and Assyrians will return to Yahweh, and he will bless them.

Following Muhammad's example, the Saudis will consider themselves too important to fight. "They flee from the sword and the heat of battle. Their warriors will be few."

Isaiah reports what will ultimately occur in the Middle East—the heart of the Nation of Islam. "Like the whirlwinds sweeping through the southland, an invader comes from the desert, from the land of terror. A dire vision has been shown to me: the traitor betrays, the looter loots. Iran's alliance lays siege. I will bring to an end all the groaning she caused." Speaking in first person about Israel, Isaiah predicts: "At this my body is racked with pain, like a woman in labor. I am staggered by what I hear; I am bewildered by what I see. Fear makes me tremble. The twilight I longed for has become a horror to me." Ultimately he predicts: "The earth will be laid waste and plundered, defiled by its people. They have disobeyed the instructions and broken the covenant. Therefore, they must bear the guilt. The earth's inhabitants are burned up and very few are left—all the merrymakers groan. The cities are desolate, the doors to homes are barred, all joy turns to gloom." Islam does this to humankind. So finally: "With treachery the treacherous betray. Terror, pit and snare await you, people of the earth. Whoever flees at the sound of terror will fall into a pit; whoever climbs out of the pit will be caught in a snare."

Collectively, these dire predictions of the winds of war should be sufficient for you to want to be part of the solution rather than the problem. For ultimately, Yahweh prevails. He wins the final battle—Armageddon—where all of the world's armies, led by two hundred million Chinese march into Israel only to be thwarted. Death loses its sting: disease exists no more. Suffering is abolished. Evil is removed from the earth and man lives in the very presence of his maker for one thousand years. Eternity follows.

Yes, unwittingly, Islam predicted its own demise. It will be extinguished as it was born. Muhammad was unable to give his followers a reason to live, so he gave Muslims a reason to die. And tragically, they shall. Allah's prophet sacrificed three billion souls upon the altar of his selfish ambitions.

The Messiah was the inverse of Muhammad. He made himself a living sacrifice, building a bridge between our polluted world and his perfect one. He died that we might live. He lives that we might never die.

EPILOGUE

WHAT ARE YOU GOING TO DO?

"All of us like sheep have gone astray."

You have survived a perilous journey into a frightening realm. You have explored the dark recesses of man's soul, examined our worst nature, surveyed our most heinous behavior. You have probed hell and have met demons, both real and imagined. On behalf of the billion souls ensnared by Islam, and the millions who have been victimized by it, thank you for caring enough to endure.

So what are you going to do?

I suppose the answer to that question depends upon who you are—what you believe. Knowing that Islam is rotten to the core is better than not knowing, but knowledge alone won't save lives or make the world any better.

If you'll bear with me a few more pages, I'd like to suggest a course of action for folks who, like me, know Yahweh and have accepted Yahshua's gift of eternal life; for agnostics and atheists, secular humanists practicing the false religion of Political Correctness; for bad Muslims; and then for good ones.

But first a word for everyone: all religions are poisonous; some are just more lethal than others. Islam is the worst of a bad lot. Islam has no redeeming qualities. Those who submit are destined to live and die in civil, economic, intellectual, and religious poverty. Collectively, the Islamic nations rank as the least free, least prosperous, and least enlightened places on earth. One fifth of the world's population is responsible for over four fifths of the world's armed conflicts. In life, Muslims are damned by a false prophet. In death, a demonic spirit claims their soul. And they do not suffer alone. Terror is the legacy of Islam.

If you were looking for a summary of Muhammad's creation, a way to shortcut 700 pages of study, you won't find it here. The religion of a billion people isn't something to trifle with. A little knowledge is always dangerous. A handful of quotes used out of context will do more harm than good. If you want to study what Islam has to say about Jihad, Muhammad's indiscretions, the history and nature of Allah, or Satan's role in establishing the religion, an Index and a Quotations appendix has been provided to assist you.

It all comes down to this: the Hadith Collections of Ishaq, Tabari, Bukhari, and Muslim contain all that is known about Muhammad and his formation of Islam. If they are not accurate then Islam ceases to exist as the Qur'an is jibberish without the context and chronology they provide. No Muslim could follow the Qur'an's command to emulate the prophet's example. Muslims would be unable to emplement the Qur'an's incessant demands to follow the messenger's orders, as they would be unknown. The substance behind all five pillars vanish. *But* if the Hadith Collections of Ishaq, Tabari, Bukhari, and Muslim are accurate then Islam is nothing more than a sadistic fraud—a scam perpetrated by an immoral pirate, a terrorist, and warlord. Either way, Islam's wrong.

With that said, let's get down to business. I'd like to begin with the practitioners of the liberal and atheistic poligious doctrine of Political Correctness. You may be gloating. You have been taught to believe that religions are opiates, duping people into fighting holy wars. You think all fundamentalists are religious whackos, ever ready to bludgeon nonbelievers into submission. You believe that your tolerant, pacifist beliefs are more civil and enlightened. But don't smile too quickly. The last century occurred under your watch, under your tutelage; and it was the bloodiest in human history. In it, atheists decimated more people in the name of their poligious doctrines than those who served false gods. Good Communists practiced genocide, murdering all they couldn't seduce or coerce. Lenin's revolution left a sea of corpses in its wake. Stalin killed 20 million Russians. Mao killed or starved 40 million in China. Pol Pot obliterated a quarter of his country. Atheists have murdered Americans by the tens of thousands in Korea and Vietnam.

In practice, there is no difference between worshiping no god and serving a false one. The Communist Manifesto enshrines man while *Mein Kampf* and the Qur'an put Satan on a pedestal. From their throne they deceive, beguiling the masses to perpetrate murder and mayhem. Draconian dictatorships are imposed. All people are indoctrinated, starting in grade school. All freedoms are obliterated. Only poverty survives. The mantra is always submit and obey. A thin veneer of order is maintained through fear.

Throughout time man has demonstrated an aptitude for behaviors both heavenly and hellish. Liberals, preaching the dogma of Political Correctness, seem to believe that man can be conditioned to behave more angelically. But that is not what the empirical evidence suggests. Man indoctrinated and separated from God becomes a more demonic creature. The central-control, universal-conditioning experiment has been run in Nazi, Communist, and Islamic nations, always with the same result. All things we hold dear are eliminated: prosperity, liberty, justice, opportunity, and peace. Yet such nations always seem to develop the perfect culture in which to breed killers. And that isn't easy. To corrupt men to the point that they believe it's good to murder innocent people takes a total commitment. Schools, mosques, party councils, courtrooms, meeting halls, and media outlets must work in harmony with a singular state religotic to deceive the masses on this massive scale.

The common denominator that makes this possible, and that makes false and atheistic poligious doctrines indistinguishable, is a liberal use of government. Individual liberty—choice—must be obliterated. Freedom is sacrificed on the altar of control. Power is concentrated and then abused by godless men. The masses are discounted, emasculated, indoctrinated, and conditioned to serve the few. The victors call themselves cleric and king, comrade and secretary general.

Ultimately, good men are made bad. Deceived, they plunder and kill. They mutilate and terrorize; they rob, enslave, and destroy. And they continue to do these things until someone who hasn't been victimized, who still knows freedom, *cares* enough to expose them. But that's a problem. Not enough people care. Thanks in large part to the false poligious doctrine of Political Correctness, most don't even know what the problem is, much less how to fix it.

Worst of all, those in a position to make a difference are the most deceived. Media darlings and political actors are the most self-centered people on the planet. They crave attention, revel in power, and will do and say most anything if it makes them more popular. Together they are the practitioners of Political Correctness. Dispensing a jaundiced view of the world, they prohibit free expression and thus rational thought.

Step so much as an inch outside the constraints of the PC agenda, and you're yesterday's news. Your character is mutilated. You'll be raped, spit upon, and then discarded, after having been kicked and shamed by those who preach tolerance. I know. I've been there. I spoke out against the culture that was destroying corporate America and found myself on the cover of *Business Week* being torn apart limb from limb. Nothing the media said over the course of their pictorial spread was true, but it didn't matter. The damage was done. The point was made. Step outside the circle and you're burnt alive.

It's just like Islam's carrot and stick. No matter how wrong, submission and obedience are rewarded with booty and babes. But if a Muslim steps outside the circle they're ostracized, often murdered, and then they're sent to hell to roast on Allah's spit.

The carrot and stick is why I believe there isn't a single media spokesperson from any major network or national syndicate willing to expose the least beneficial, most deceitful, and vicious poligious doctrine ever conceived. It might be a career-ending move. To a person, the media darlings crave the adulation, power, and money their microphones and cameras provide. Such things are prioritized over truth, over life itself. And their co-conspirators, the political actors who depend upon the media, are no different. Insecurity drives them into the public arena. They do it for themselves, for the perks of power. They will tell any lie or embrace any falsehood if it serves their interests.

But hopefully, somewhere, there is someone with a microphone or a bully pulpit who is willing to step outside the line and reveal Islam's sinister and violent nature. Hope burns eternal. If only ten percent of those who hold the levers of public opinion demonstrate the compassion and courage needed to tell the truth, we could change the world.

But alas, that kind of sacrificial love, that sense of purpose and mission comes from but one place—God. While I am not your judge, polls taken of those in the national media show that ninety percent classify themselves as politically liberal and religiously agnostic. Knowing that politicians have a propensity to lie, the pollsters didn't even bother taking their pulse. Yet as atheists and agnostics, you should be agitated, haunted, even bewildered. How is it that Yahweh predicted the mess we are in, and the remedy, if he were not God?

Fortunately, you can find God and truth in the same place: the Bible. Unfortunately, most of you don't have an interest in looking. So to kindle a spirit of curiosity, I encourage political actors in the gilded arena of egos, and media darlings in the make-believe world of artificial lights and cameras, to read *In the Company of Good and Evil* and *Tea With Terrorists*. (If you're in politics or the media, send me an email at www.TeaWithTerrorists.com and I'll *give* them to you.) In the first book, you'll come to appreciate the nature of insecurity in a contemporary setting, and you'll witness the media dispense its poison from a different perspective. In the second, you'll confront errant reporting again, and then face the deceitful nature of politics from the vantage point of one outside the arena. You'll discover the true nature of modern-day Islam and its link to terror in a geopolitical and historic perspective. And in *Tea With Terrorists*, you'll meet the Messiah, truth incarnate, up close and personal. You'll discover just how liberating stepping outside the circle can be, especially if you're in the right company. As one who has done so and survived, I assure you, the sense of purpose and satisfaction that comes as a result, is more rewarding than winning a ratings sweep or an election.

While some may venture outside the confines of Political Correctness, most will not. America will indoctrinate another generation of godless, and thus amoral, thoughtless, and directionless people, as has Europe before us. Our culture and economy will suffer. We will be terrorized. And then, like 1930's Germany, we will long for a dictator who will pull us out of the morass—only to find that he will push us into the abyss. After announcing that we have achieved peace in our time, the world will erupt in global war. And all because media darlings and political actors were afraid to step outside the circle. But I have done my part. I have left you without excuse.

Moving on, I'd like to speak to Christians—actually I'd like to wake you up. Speaking of this generation of believers, Yahweh said, "You are neither hot nor cold so I spew you out of my mouth." We've lost our passion, our courage, our faith. Most Christians don't know God's name, much less what He is like or what He wants. And that is why I believe the world is in such a mess. We're in a position to make a difference, but we've been sleeping on the job.

History tell us that bad overwhelms good until good cares. Islam will continue to poison its faithful and deceive its foes until the planet is embroiled in World War. That is what it was born to do. And while we could stop it, we won't. All of us could make the right choice; we could discard that which is false and rely on that which is true. But not enough of us are going to make the right call to make a difference.

So why bother? Why did I write, and why did you read, *Prophet of Doom*? Because while we collectively will continue to embrace the lie, deny the truth, and march like lemmings toward our doom, all will not jump into the pit. There is salvation, a bridge to paradise, but it's single file. As Christians, it's our job to point as many people as possible in the right direction. And often that means showing them that the direction they are currently going is wrong.

If you have chosen Yahweh, if you know Yahshua personally, you have been given your marching orders. The Third Commandments proclaims: "You shall not *nasa* (advance or accept) the *shem* (character or mark) of Yahweh (I Am—the Creator's name) your *elohiym* (deity) in *shav* (an evil, destructive, deceptive, or false manner), for Yahweh will not hold him *naqah* (clean, innocent, or blameless) who *nasa* (advances or accepts) His *shem* (character or mark) *shav* (evilly, destructively, deceptively, or falsely)." You have been instructed to confront Islam, to save Muslims and non-Muslims from it.

Now, before I share the location of the bridge to eternity and the rules regarding its passage with bad Muslims, the peaceful and loving ones, I'd like to review the nature of this strange place Islam has taken us. God has been reshaped to look like the Devil. Allah leads men astray; he seals hearts, blinds eyes, and plots against human kind. He is depicted interrogating and torturing the inhabitants of hell, a place created for his entertainment. Humans are turned on a spit and given fresh skin each time one burns off so that the torment might be eternal. Allah pours boiling water down our throats, makes us eat pitch and thorns. And this painful punishment isn't for the few but for the many. Only one in a thousand avoids being tortured. Yet even they go to a place of decadence—a four-star brothel with the best foods, free-flowing wine, and virginal attendants. Allah loves warriors; he craves death and destruction. He brags about his participation in terror, mass murder, the enslavement of women and children, and thievery. Allah claims booty is lawful and good. Unable to give Muslims a reason to live, Allah gave them a reason to die.

And as evil as the Islamic "god" is, his prophet was worse. His resume reads: demon possession, suicidal, bearing false witness, hate speech, taking and offering bribes, pedophilia, terrorism, piracy, slave trading, incest, rape, torture, genocide, warmongering, plagiarism, womanizing, sexism—well, you know the list. Muhammad was hardly a model citizen. Fact is, he and his god had a lot in common—too much in common.

But worst of all, Allah and Muhammad prohibit choice. They not only named their doctrine submission, they chose it for mankind, not the other way around. Allah determined who would burn in lust or roast in hell based upon a backrub, predestining all men and women to their fate. The theme of the Qur'an's last score of surahs is simply: submit and obey, perform and pay, fight and slay. It's no wonder Islam has bred hell on earth. Muslims are unable to rise above the depraved character of their prophet and god. And those who do are killed.

For Muslims who believe paradise lies under the shade of swords, for those trying to emulate the life of Muhammad the Terrible, there is no longer hope. Your iniquity is full, which means you have been corrupted beyond salvation. While my evangelical Christian friends will chafe at these words, they are nonetheless true. Yahweh provided the proof when he caused the flood, when he dealt with Sodom, and when he ordered the annihilation of the Canaanites (people extraordinarily similar to Jihadist Muslims). Christ told his disciples to shake the dust off their sandals if the gift they were offering, the good news of the Gospels, was rejected. All we can do with good Muslims is to remove the sword from their hands so that bad Muslims might know the truth and be freed to make the right choice.

If you *were* a bad Muslim you know the truth. Muhammad was the most evil man who ever lived. Allah was the most demonic god ever conceived. The Qur'an was the nastiest book ever written. Islam was the most hateful and violent fraud ever perpetrated on humankind. The path to damnation has been revealed. As a former Muslim you are free of the deceptions that have led you astray. So what now?

First, I want to commiserate with you. You probably feel dirty, like your soul needs a good scrubbing. You've got to feel lonely, isolated, afraid. Allah orders Muslims to kill renegades. Rejecting Islam takes courage. I admire yours.

Second, I want to tell you about the bridge to eternity. But understand, I cannot take you across it. The choice is yours alone, and passage is single file.

Choice! Ultimately, that's all that really matters. Not good deeds, certainly not jihad, not prayer, ritual, religion, fear, fasting, pilgrimages, taxes, or prophets. No. This is a one on one thing between you and your Maker. He has a gift He wants to give you. You can't earn it or pay Him for it. He alone earned the right to give it to you; He alone paid the price. Now He's calling your name, knocking at the door to your heart. If you hear him knocking and open that door He will come to you and be with you. All you have to do is accept his gift of eternal life; He'll do the rest.

I want you to understand, I have nothing to do with this gift. It's not mine to give. I can't save you. I get no bonus points for you accepting. All I can do is point you in the right direction, explain the rules of passage, and let you know how wonderful it is on the other side. Working for the Boss is the greatest joy of my life. Every day is a grand adventure. You see, I'm on a first name basis with the Creator of the universe. Craig and Yahweh: He's my friend and my father. And we're a lot alike because He created me in His image. Sure I'm a little rough around the edges, but He loves me in spite of that. I'm sure I make Him laugh, as He does me. I can almost hear Him cheer as I battle the Devil. I can see Him smile when I figure something out that He put in His Scriptures 3,000 years ago, knowing I'd find it.

Yes, this is all very personal with me, as I hope it will be with you someday. That said, it's time to make introductions. God's name is Yahweh. It means I Am. His name answers the most important question we can ask. His book, the Bible, was given to us so that we might know Him. It's comprised of 66 books with a singular message: "I love you. And I created you in My image so that we might enjoy a personal relationship."

The message is simple enough, but it's hard to develop a relationship with someone you don't know—especially when you don't even know yourself very well. So the Bible serves many purposes. It introduces us to Yahweh. It explains what He is like so that we can love Him, not fear Him. That was half of Yahshua's mission. God incarnate came to earth in the form of a man to show us what He is like. And what an example He set: He's loving, approachable, knowable, talkative, caring, brilliant, powerful, funny, creative, even humble—something we don't think of God being.

The Bible is also an "Owner's Manual." In it we learn how to operate all of our really advanced features. It tells us that faith is trust and that love is power. It explains each of the spiritual gifts that we have been given and how to use them effectively. But there is a problem. Sin separates us from our Creator. He is perfect and we aren't. So what to do?

Fortunately, Yahweh recognized the problem and provided a cure. Centuries before Christ came into our world in the form of a man, Isaiah wrote: "All of us like sheep have gone astray. Each has turned to his own way. But Yahweh has caused the iniquity of us all to fall on Him. He was pierced for our transgressions and by his scourging we are healed. He Himself bore the sin of many, and interceded [became a bridge] for our transgressions." Yahweh told us how He was going to solve the problem of sin; how He was going to build a bridge from our polluted world to His perfect one. He said that He would sacrifice Himself for our iniquity. The bridge is His gift to us.

Paul, centuries later, in his letter to the Ephesians wrote: "You were dead in your trespasses and sins in which you did according to Satan and his spirit working through the sons of disobedience. Among them we too all formerly lived in the lusts of our flesh, indulging the desires of the world and of our mind. But Yahweh, being rich in mercy, and because of His great love for us, made us alive together with Christ. By grace you have been saved through faith, and that not of yourselves; it is the gift of God, not as a result of works that no one should boast. By the blood of Yahshua, the Messiah, we have been brought near Yahweh."

John, the most passionate of Christ's disciples, composed these stirring words: "In the beginning was the Word, and the Word was with God, and the Word was God. And the Word became flesh, and dwelt among us, and we beheld His glory, the glory of the only begotten from the Father, full of grace and truth. Whoever receives Him, He gives the right to become His children, even to those who believe in Him. For God so loved the world that He gave His only begotten Son, that whoever believes in Him should not perish, but have eternal life. For God did not send the Son into the world to judge the world; but that the world should be saved through Him. He who believes in Him is no longer judged."

Therefore, according to the Bible, there is no day of judgment for those washed by Christ's blood. There are no rituals that earn passage on his bridge —one built entirely out of the timbers upon which He hung. There are no taxes, no tolls, no devotional obligations, no pilgrimages, or prayer performances. Your salvation isn't dependent upon the submission to, or acknowledgement of, any prophet. Fear and fighting have no role. A simple "I do" will suffice. Yahshua said, "I am the way the truth and the life; no one comes to the Father but by me." He sacrificed himself so that your sins would all be forgiven, abrogated, in Islamic parlance. His blood on the cross of history, at the crossroads of civilization, frees you to enter a personal and eternal relationship with Yahweh in paradise.

To cross that bridge, you don't need to get on your knees, close your eyes, bring your hands together, bow your head, or face Jerusalem. You do, however, need to make a choice.

Thirty years ago I was confronted with the Bible prophecies revealed in the last chapter. I came to the only rational conclusion possible: the prophets knew the future because they spoke for God. So I did what I encourage you to do. I prayed: "God, I'm a sinner. Thank you for sacrificing yourself so that I might know you. I accept your gift of eternal life. Thanks for forgiving me. Please reveal yourself so that I might understand who you are and what you want."

Then, just as He promised, His spirit entered me. He changed me. He did not make me perfect (although I am in his eyes); He made me better. I began to read the Bible and His words pierced my soul, they leapt off the page and into my mind and heart. I speak to you today as His son, as a child born again in His image.

May the truth set you free...

SOURCE MATERIAL

ISLAM'S DARK PAST

"The Qur'an escapes from the hearts of men faster than a runaway camel."

Islam provides only one prime source of information on Muhammad and the formation of Islam written within two centuries of the time he lived and it was conceived. Ishaq's Sira, or Biography, stands alone—a singular and tenuous thread connecting us to a very troubled man and time. Over the next two hundred years, other Hadith Collections were compiled by the likes of Tabari, Bukhari, and Muslim. Their assemblages of oral reports, or Traditions, were said to have been inspired by Allah. They purport to convey Muhammad's words and example. They also explain the Qur'an—a book so deficient in context and chronology, it can only be understood when seen through the eyes of the Sunnah writers.

Throughout *Prophet of Doom*, I have been less concerned with the validity of these sources than with what they have to say. Their message is all Muslims have. Together, the Sunnah and Qur'an *are* Islam. Therefore, I was willing to take them at face value.

But you don't have to dig very deep to find the truth. Even a cursory reading of the Qur'an is sufficient to prove that it is a fraud. There is no way the creator of the universe wrote a book devoid of context, without chronology or intelligent transitions. Such a creative spirit wouldn't need to plagiarize. He would know history and science and thus wouldn't have made such a fool of himself. The God who created man wouldn't deceive him or lead him to hell as Allah does. Nor would he order men to terrorize, mutilate, rob, enslave, and slaughter the followers of other Scriptures he claims he revealed, wiping them out to the last. One doesn't need a scholastic review of the Qur'anic text to disprove its veracity. It destroys itself quite nicely.

While that remains true, I believe that I owe it to readers, especially Muslims, to explore the textual evidence for the Sunnah and Qur'an. I'll start with what the Hadith has to say about the Qur'an's origins, but I'm going to dispense in short order with the circular reasoning Islamic scholars use in that they all quote the Sunnah. While there are Hadiths that say Bakr tried to assemble the Qur'an and others that credit Uthman, Muhammad's third successor, it's like using the results of Carbon-14 dating to prove the validity of Carbon-14 dating. The source is the same.

In Bukhari's Hadith Collection alone we find a sea of disturbing and contradictory claims regarding the compilation of Allah's book. We discover there were differing versions, even in Muhammad's day: **"Ibn Abbas asked, 'Which of the two readings of the Qur'an do you prefer?' The Prophet answered, 'The reading of Abdallah ibn Mas'ud.' Then Abdallah came to him, and he learned what was altered and abrogated."** This is reasonably clear. The Hadith says that portions of the Qur'an were conflicting, changed, and cancelled.

Tradition tells us that Muhammad had not foreseen his death, and so he had made no preparations for gathering his revelations. He left it up to his followers to sift through the conflicting versions. That's astonishing. Islam's lone "prophet" left his Qur'an as vapor, sound waves that had long since faded.

Bragging one day, the imposter called his surahs a miracle: *Bukhari:V6B61N504* **"Muhammad said, 'Every Prophet was given miracles because of which people believed. But what I have been given is Divine Inspiration which Allah has revealed to me. So I hope that my followers will outnumber the followers of the other Prophets.'"** If the Qur'an was his only "miracle," why would he leave it in such horrid condition? I believe the answer is clear. Muhammad knew his recitals had been nothing more than a figment of his less-than-admirable imagination, situational scriptures designed to satiate *his* cravings. Preserving these recitals would only serve to incriminate him, as this Hadith suggests. *Muslim: C24B20N4609* **"The Messenger said: 'Do not take the Qur'an on a journey with you, for I am afraid lest it would fall into the hands of the enemy.' Ayyub, one of the narrators in the chain of transmitters, said: 'The enemy may seize it and may quarrel with you over it.'"**

A number of Bukhari Hadith suggest that Muhammad's companions tried to remember what they could of what he had said, but there was a problem. Like today, those who *knew* the Qur'an were militants. So Abu Bakr feared that large portions would be forgotten. The best Muslims were dying on the battlefield subduing fellow Arabs. In one battle alone, most of the Qur'an's most knowledgeable reciters were lost, and many Qur'anic passages along with them. *Bukhari:V6B60N201* **"Zaid bin Thabit, the Ansari said, 'Abu Bakr sent for me after the (heavy) casualties among the warriors (of the battle) of Yamama (where a great number of Muhammad's Companions were killed). Umar was present with Bakr. "The people have suffered heavy casualties at Yamama, and I am afraid that there will be more casualties among those who can recite the Qur'an on other battlefields. A large part of the Qur'an may be lost unless you collect it." I replied to Umar, "How can I do something which Allah's Apostle has not done?" Umar kept on pressing, trying to persuade me to accept his proposal.' Zaid bin Thabit added, 'Umar was sitting with Abu Bakr and was speaking (to) me. "You are a wise young man and we do not suspect you of telling lies or of forgetfulness. You used to write the Divine Inspiration for Allah's Apostle. Therefore, look for the Qur'an and** collect it (in one manuscript)." By Allah, if Abu Bakr had ordered me to shift one of the mountains (from its place) it would have been easier for me than the collection of the Qur'an. I said to both of them, "How dare you do a thing which the Prophet has not done?"

Zaid declared that collecting the Qur'an's surahs would be an impossible task. He said that it would be easier to move mountains than to turn Muhammad's string of oral recitals into a book. The reason for this rather odd statement becomes obvious. Zaid's search for Qur'anic passages forced him to rely upon carvings on the leg or thigh bones of dead animals, as well as palm leaves, skins, mats, stones, and bark. But for the most part, he found nothing better than the fleeting memories of the prophet's Companions, many of whom were dead or dying.

This shows that there were no Muslims at that time who had memorized the entire Qur'an, otherwise the collection would have been a simple task. Had there been individuals who knew the Qur'an, Zaid would only have had to write down what they dictated. Instead, Zaid was overwhelmed by the assignment, and was forced to "search" for the passages from men who believed that they had memorized certain segments and then compare what he heard to the recollection of others. Therefore, even the official Islamic view of things, the one recorded in their scripture, is hardly reassuring.

And, as is typical of the Islamic Traditions, the more one digs, the worse it gets. *Bukhari:V6B61N511* **"Zaid bin Thabit said, 'I started searching for the Qur'an till I found the last two Verses of Surat At-Tauba with Abi but I could not find them with anyone other than him. They were: 'Verily there has come to you an Apostle from amongst yourselves.'"** [9:128] This is incriminating. The 9th surah was the second to last revealed. If only one person could remember it, there is no chance those revealed twenty-five years earlier were retained. Furthermore, this Tradition contradicts the most highly touted Islamic mantra: Most Muslims contend Uthman, not Bakr, ordered the collection of the Qur'an a decade later.

And who knows what version they finally committed to paper, if in fact they ever did? *Bukhari:V6B61N513*: **"Allah's Apostle said, 'Gabriel [whom Muhammad said had 600 wings] recited the Qur'an to me in one way. Then I requested him and continued asking him to recite it in other ways, and he recited it in several ways till he ultimately recited it in seven different ways.'"** So there were at least seven Qur'ans.

And that wasn't the end of the confusion. In version two of the angelic recital, Muhammad was the reciter, not Gabriel. *Bukhari:V6B61N519*: **"In the month of Ramadan Gabriel used to meet Muhammad every night of the month till it elapsed. Allah's Apostle used to recite the Qur'an for him."** Then, we go from every night to once a year. *Bukhari:V6B61N520*: **"Gabriel used to repeat the recitation of the Qur'an with the Prophet once a year, but he repeated it twice with him in the year he died."**

No wonder they couldn't remember who said what to whom. *Bukhari:V6B61N549* **"Allah's Apostle said, "The example of the person who knows the Qur'an by heart is like the owner of tied camels. If he keeps them tied, he will control them, but if he releases them,**

they will run away." To release something you have memorized you would have to share it. So this Hadith is apparently telling Muslims not to recite surahs for fear of losing them. And speaking of losing it: *Bukhari:V6B61N550* **"The Prophet said, 'It is a bad thing that some of you say, "I have forgotten such-and-such verse of the Qur'an." For indeed, I have been caused to forget it. So you must keep on reciting the Qur'an because it escapes from the hearts of men faster than a runaway camel.'"**

This frivolity is important because it exposes a lie that sits at the heart of Islam. Why did God shift all of a sudden from his reliance on literate Jewish prophets to an illiterate Arab? The foundation of Islamic teaching is based upon the notion that God chose Arabs because they had good memories. Therefore, they reason, the Qur'an wouldn't be changed the way the Bible was corrupted. All Islamic schools from Alazahr to Pakistan are centered around this obvious lie. The Qur'an was forgotten; it was changed and recited by so many people it was corrupted beyond hope before it ever found paper. And since the Bible started out as words on a page, it has remained true to its initial inspiration.

But it's worse than that. Muslims insist on confining the Qur'an to Religious Arabic—a language which is so hard to learn with its complex grammar and antiquated vocabulary, it's ranked second by linguists after Chinese, as the world's least hospitable communication medium. Worse still, even in Arabic much of the Qur'an cannot be understood because many words are missing and others are nonsensical. It's not rational to think that God would choose illiterate people and such a difficult language if he wished to communicate his message to the whole world. It's like using diesel to fuel a lamp and then hiding it in a swamp.

But there is a method to their madness. By confining the Qur'an to Religious Arabic, Islamic clerics and kings can say whatever they want—and they do. An Egyptian doctor who edited *Prophet of Doom* wrote: "You would be amazed how they can distort facts to deceive others."

In keeping with the camel theme, Allah's divinely inspired messenger announced: *Bukhari:V6B61N552* **"The Prophet said, 'Keep on reciting the Qur'an, for Qur'an runs away (is forgotten) faster than camels that are released from their tying ropes.'"** In the interest of full disclosure, I present: *Bukhari:V6B61N559* **"The Prophet said, 'Why does anyone of the people say, "I have forgotten such-and-such Verses (of the Qur'an)?" I am, in fact, caused (by Allah) to forget.'"** It's a wonder anyone takes Islam seriously.

Continuing to cripple its own claim that the Qur'an was retained as Allah's Pen wrote it: *Bukhari:V6B61N561* **"Umar bin Khattab [the second Caliph] said, 'I heard Hisham bin Hakim bin Hizam reciting Surat Al-Furqan ["Al-Furqan," the title of the 25th surah, has no meaning in any language.] during the lifetime of Allah's Apostle. I listened to his recitation and noticed that he recited it in several ways which Allah's Apostle had not taught me. So I was on the point of attacking him in the prayer, but I waited till he finished, and then I seized him by the collar. "Who taught you this Surah which I have** heard you reciting?" He replied, "Allah's Apostle taught it to me." I said, "You are lying. Allah's Apostle taught me in a different way this very Surah which I have heard you reciting." So I led him to Muhammad. "O Allah's Apostle! I heard this person reciting Surat-al-Furqan in a way that you did not teach me." The Prophet said, "Hisham, recite!" So he recited in the same way as I heard him recite it before. On that Allah's Apostle said, "It was revealed to be recited in this way." Then the Prophet said, "Recite, Umar!" So I recited it as he had taught me. Allah's Apostle said, "It was revealed to be recited in this way, too." He added, "The Qur'an has been revealed to be recited in several different ways, so recite of it that which is easier for you." If Muhammad were alive today and made this statement, he would be branded an apostate, hunted down and murdered. As we shall soon discover, he just contradicted Islam's holy grail.

Examining these Hadith we discover that the first "manuscript" wasn't even in Muhammad's tongue, requiring it to be translated. *Bukhari:V4B56N709* "Uthman called Zaid, Abdallah, Said, and 'Abd-Rahman. They wrote the manuscripts of the Qur'an in the form of a book in several copies. Uthman said to the three Quraishi persons, 'If you differ with Zaid bin Thabit on any point of the Qur'an, then write it in the language of the Quraysh, as the Qur'an was revealed in their language.' So they acted accordingly." Because there was such confusion, Uthman ordered competing versions to be burned. But by destroying the evidence, he destroyed the Qur'an's credibility. Now all Muslims have is wishful thinking.

Since "wishful thinking" isn't sufficient, and since the Islamic Hadith is more conflicting than helpful, I am going to turn to reason and fact to determine what is true and what is not.

First, let's establish what Muslims believe so that we can direct our attention to determining whether or not it is accurate, or even reasonable. As evidenced by the official Islamic introduction to the Qur'an, Islamic scholars contend: "The Qur'an is one leg of two which form the basis of Islam. The second leg is the Sunnah of the Prophet. What makes the Qur'an different from the Sunnah is its form. Unlike the Sunnah, the Qur'an is quite literally the Word of Allah, whereas the Sunnah was inspired by Allah but the wording and actions are the Prophet's. The Qur'an has not been expressed using any human words. Its wording is letter for letter fixed by Allah. Prophet Muhammad was the final Messenger of Allah to humanity, and therefore the Qur'an is the last Message which Allah has sent to us. Its predecessors, such as the Torah, Psalms, and Gospels have all been superceded." Funny thing, though, the Allah-inspired Sunnah just confirmed that the Qur'an used "human words" and that it wasn't "fixed letter for letter by Allah." Muslims ought to read their own scriptures.

Despite all evidence to the contrary, including their own, Islamic scholars contend that today's Qur'an is an identical copy of Allah's Eternal Tablets, even so far as the punctuation, titles, and divisions of chapters are concerned. Maududi, one of the most esteemed Qur'anic scholars said, "The Qur'an exists in its original text, without a word, syllable nor even letter having been changed." (*Towards Understanding Islam*, Maududi) Abu Dhabi, another leading Muslim said, "No other book in the world can match the Qur'an. The astonishing fact about this Book of Allah is that it has remained unchanged, even to a dot, over the last fourteen hundred years. No variation of text can be found in it." That's factually untrue, every word of it.

The Qur'an says of itself: "Nay this is a glorious Qur'an, (inscribed) on a Preserved Tablet." (85:21) "A Scripture Book, whereof the verses are explained in detail; a Qur'an in Arabic." (41:3) "We have coined for man in this Qur'an. (It is) a Qur'an in Arabic, without any crookedness (therein)." (39:27) Richard Nixon tried that line too. It didn't work any better for him than it does for Allah. Over the course of these pages you'll discover why.

This appendix follows twenty-five chapters of Islamic scripture, all punctuated by my analysis, so I thought you'd be best served if this section was driven by most qualified Islamic scholars. And while their findings are shocking, don't say you weren't warned. I dedicated the opening of the "Heart of Darkness" chapter (pages 115-8) to this very problem.

The best-researched scholastic analysis of the validity of the Qur'an and Sunnah was presented in 1995 by Jay Smith. In his debate at Cambridge University, he said, "Most Westerners have accepted Islamic claims at face value. They have never had the ability to argue their veracity, because the claims could neither be proved nor disproved, as their authority was derived solely from the Qur'an itself. There has also been a reticence to question the Qur'an and the prophet due to the adverse response directed upon those who were brave enough to attempt it in the past. [Muslims kill their critics.] So Westerners have been content to assume that Muslims have some evidence to substantiate their beliefs." We are about to discover that they have no such data. And what little exists serves only to destroy Islam's credibility.

According to Wansbrough, Schacht, Rippin, Crone, and Humphreys: "Almost universally, independent scholars studying the Qur'an and Hadith, have concluded that the Islamic scripture was not revealed to just one man, but was a compilation of later redactions and editions formulated by a group of men, over the course of a few hundred years. The Qur'an which we read today is not that which was in existence in the mid-seventh century, but is a product of the eighth and ninth centuries. It was not conceived in Mecca or Medina, but in Baghdad. It was then and there that Islam took on its identity and became a religion. Consequently, the formative stage of Islam was not within the lifetime of Muhammad but evolved over a period of 300 years." While these are strong words, rest assured: the scholars prove their case.

What's interesting here is that apart from the Islamic Hadith, virtually nothing is known about the formation of Islam and the creation of the Qur'an. The scholars agree: "Source material for this period is sparse. The only manuscripts available to historians are Muslim sources. What is more, outside the

Qur'an, the sources are all late. Prior to 750 A.D., and Ishaq's *Sirat Rasul Allah*, we have no verifiable Muslim documents which can provide a window into Islam's formative period. Even then, his manuscript has been lost so we are dependent upon those who wrote fifty to one hundred years thereafter. And no independent secular document exists with which to corroborate any Hadith," says Smith on behalf of Crone, Humphreys, Schacht, and Wansbrough.

"During the ninth century, Islamic sages in Baghdad attempted to describe Islam's beginnings from their viewpoint. But much like an adult writing about their childhood, the account is colored and biased. The picture that Islam was fully developed religiously, politically, and legally by an illiterate man in one of the most primitive places on earth isn't feasible," Smith claimed in his Cambridge debate.

Sure, Muhammad's scripture was feeble—equal parts delusional, dimwitted, and demented, regurgitated, plagiarized, and twisted—but there was too much of it to have been comprised and retained in the vacuum of the Hijaz. Central Arabia wasn't part of, or even known to, the civilized world at the time. And the Islamic Traditions themselves refer to this period as *Jahiliyyah*, or Period of Ignorance, implying its backwardness. "Arabia did not have an urbanized culture, nor could it boast of having the sophisticated infrastructure needed to create, let alone maintain the scenario painted by the later Traditions. There is no historical precedence for such a scenario."

Fortunately, historical experts have recently converged on Islam. They include: Dr. John Wansbrough of the University of London, Michael Cook, Patricia Crone of Oxford, now lecturing at Cambridge, Yehuda Nevo from the University of Jerusalem, Andrew Rippin from Canada, and others, including Joseph Schacht. They sought out, examined, and probed every source concerning the Qur'an and Sunnah to ascertain clues as to their origins.

In his debate, Smith said, "In order to critique the Qur'an we must go back to the beginning, to the earliest sources which we have at our disposal, to pick up clues as to its authenticity. One would assume that this should be quite easy to do, as it is a relatively new piece of literature, having appeared on the scene, according to Muslims, a mere '1,400 years ago.'"

However, the first century of Islam is dark, a veritable black hole from which nothing emerges. "The primary sources which we possess are 150 to 300 years after the events which they describe, and therefore are quite distant from those times and characters," say Nevo, Wansbrough, and Crone. "For that reason they are, for all practical purposes, secondary sources, as they rely on hearsay material. The first and largest of these sources is what is called the 'Islamic Traditions' or 'Hadith.' Because of the importance of these Sunnah Collections, it is crucial that we deal with them first."

Jay Smith was kind enough to publish his research in advance of his Cambridge debate. So as not to turn this appendix into a book, I have elected to abridge his findings. While I have come to the same conclusions, the words that follow are either his or quoted from cited sources. "Islamic Traditions are comprised of writings which were compiled by Muslims in the late eighth to early tenth centuries concerning what the prophet Muhammad said and did back at the dawn of the seventh century. There is also one early commentary on the Qur'an. These comprise the sole body of material which we have on Islam's formation.

"The Qur'an by itself is difficult to follow, as it leaves readers confused while it jumps from story to story, with little background narration or explanation. So the Traditions are critical as they provide the context of place, circumstance, and time which otherwise would be lost. In some instances the Hadith prevails over the Qur'an. For example, the Qur'an refers to three daily prayers (surahs 11:114, 17:78, 30:17)." The Hadith demands five. Muslims prostrate themselves in accordance with Muhammad's Sunnah orders rather than Allah's Qur'anic command.

"A number of genres exist within the Islamic Traditions. Their authors were not writers themselves, but were compilers and editors who drew together information passed to them. There are many compilers, but the four who are considered by Muslims to be the most authoritative in each genre lived and assembled their material between 750-923 A.D. (or 120-290 years after Muhammad's death). Here is a list of their works, along with their dates: The Sira (Arabic for "Biography") is comprised of accounts concerning the life of the prophet, including his raids. The earliest and most comprehensive Sira was written by Ibn Ishaq, who died 765 A.D. His manuscript has been lost. Consequently, we are dependent on the Sira of Ibn Hisham, who died in 833. He edited Ishaq, and by his own admission, he omitted Hadiths which he thought might have caused offense."

While Smith quoted Crone as his source, I'd like you to see the original. Hisham said: *Ishaq:691* **"For the sake of brevity, I am confining myself to the Prophet's biography and omitting some of the things which Ishaq recorded in this book in which there is no mention of the Apostle and about which the Qur'an says nothing. I have omitted things which are disgraceful to discuss, matters which would distress certain people, and such reports as al-Bakkai [Bukhari?] told me he could not accept as trustworthy—all of these things I have omitted."** Since the character, deeds, and words of Muhammad presented in Hisham's edits of Ishaq are revolting, I can't even imagine what would have been too **"disgraceful to discuss."** And in case you're wondering, the **"matters that would distress certain people"** comment speaks volumes. Hisham is telling us that Wansbrough, Cook, Crone, Humphries, Rippin, Margoliouth, and Muir are right. The Hadith that comprise the Sunnah were composed and compiled in a highly politicized environment 200 years after Muhammad's death. A compiler's life was dependant upon not offending the cleric-kings.

While the Sira is nothing more than a collection of Hadith arranged in chronological order, the most official Islamic "Hadith" Collection was compiled by al-Bukhari, who died in 870 A.D. "These include two thousand short reports or narratives (*akhbar* [news]) on the sayings and deeds of the prophet. They were all collected by Muslims in the ninth and tenth centuries. Of the six most famous collections of Hadith, those of al-Bukhari and Muslim are considered to be the most authoritative.

"The Ta'rikh (which means "History" in Arabic) provide chronologies of the prophet's life and the formation of Islam. The earliest and most famous was written by al-Tabari, who died in 923 A.D." Some portions of Ishaq's original manuscript, discarded by Hisham, were retained by Tabari. Of particular interest is Ishaq's recording of Muhammad's Islamic creation accounts and his entanglement in the Quraysh Bargain and Satanic Verses. As such, the Ta'rikh, or History of al-Tabari is the oldest surviving uncensored account of Muhammad and Islam.

According to the Islamic scholars, "The Tafsir [which means explanation or interpretation in Arabic] comprise the fourth most reliable Islamic source documents. They are commentaries and exegesis on the Qur'an. The earliest and best known was also written by Tabari."

As an interesting aside; I am routinely threatened by Muslims who assail my character in colorful ways. They claim that I know nothing about Islam and that my words are offensive, repulsive, disgraceful, bigoted, hateful, intolerant, mean spirited, #%$&*.... But little do they know, they are not my words. All I have done is report what Islam has to say about itself. Apart from the Sira-Ta'rikh-Hadith collections of Ishaq, Tabari, Bukhari, and Muslim, nothing is known about Muhammad or Islam. The Qur'an literally disintegrates without them, since without context and chronology, it is gibberish.

This puts Muslims in a hellish predicament. If the Hadith compilations of Ishaq, Tabari, Bukhari, and Muslim are true, their prophet was the most evil man who ever lived—a bloodthirsty pirate, a ruthless terrorist, and a sexual pervert. His Islam was nothing more than the Profitable Prophet Plan. Allah was just one of many moon rocks. That's not good. But if the Hadith compilations of Ishaq, Tabari, Bukhari, and Muslim are not true, Islam evaporates.

Returning to Smith's debate paper, we find: "Obviously, the first question which we must ask is why these Traditions were written so late, 150 to 300 years after the fact? We simply do not have any account from the Islamic community during the initial 150 years or so. Not a single document has been found that can be traced to the period between the first Arab conquests of the early seventh century and the appearance of the Sira-Ta'rikh-Hadith collections of Ishaq, Tabari, Bukhari, and Muslim towards the late eighth and ninth century. 'As historians and scholars, we would expect to find, in those intervening two centuries, at least remnants of evidence for the development of Islam; yet we find nothing,' say Nevo, Crone, and Wansbrough.

"A few Muslims disagree, maintaining that there is evidence of an earlier Tradition called the *Muwatta* by Malik ibn Anas. He died in 795 A.D. Yet even a cursory review shows this collection was comprised of 'schooled texts,' transmitted and developed over several generations. More incriminating still, they follow 'Shafi'i's law' which demands that all Hadith be traced to Muhammad by way of isnad. Yet the law and its observance did not come into effect until after 820 A.D."

Shafi'i was one of four Islamic Imams, along with Malik Ibn Anas, Abu Hanefa, and Ibn Hanbul, they are credited with creating Islamic Law, or Feqh. Each had their own interpretation of the Qur'an and Hadith. The most extreme, militant, and radical was Ibn Hanbul, nicknamed Hunbali. In the Middle East, his name is used to describe a highly religious or obsessed person. The Hunbali School, which is similar to that of Ibn Taymea, forms the basis of Saudi Arabian Wahabism.

Returning to the dearth of source material, Humphreys says: "Muslims, we would suppose, would have taken great care to record their spectacular achievements, and the highly literate and urbanized societies which they subjugated could hardly avoid coming to grips with what had happened to them. Yet all we find from this early period are sources which are either fragmentary or represent very specific or even eccentric perspectives, completely annulling any possibility of reconstructing Islam's first century." "We have no reliable proof that any Hadith Tradition actually speaks of the life of Muhammad, or even of the Qur'an," Joseph Schacht attests after putting the Hadith through the most rigorous scholastic investigation in history.

Schacht was ingenious. He used the court records from the early ninth century to show that neither defense nor prosecution used Hadiths that have since become the backbone of Islamic law. There is no chance men would have been convicted or exonerated in an Islamic court without referencing the most appropriate Hadith unless they simply didn't exist at the time. Schacht, therefore, dates the creation of a Hadith to the time they were first used at trial. Not only did he find late dates for most Hadiths, he discovered something very sinister. Hadith with the best isnads were the most suspect.

Quoting Humphreys, Smith said: "We are asked to believe that these documents written hundreds of years later are accurate, though we are not presented with any evidence for their veracity, outside of isnads, which are nothing more than lists purporting to give the names of those from whom the oral traditions were passed down. Yet even the isnads lack any supportive documentation with which to corroborate their authenticity." Simply stated, insights into Islam's formation, the Qur'an's creation, and Muhammad's life are as black as the message they proclaim.

"Muslims maintain that the late dates of the primary sources can be attributed to the fact that writing was simply not used in such an isolated area or at that time. This assumption is completely unfounded, however, as writing on paper began long before the seventh century. Paper was invented in the fourth century, and used extensively throughout the civilized world thereafter. The Umayyad dynasty of Islam's first one hundred years was headquartered in the former Byzantine area of Syria, not Arabia. Thus, unlike Arabia, it was a sophisticated society which used secretaries in the Caliphal courts, proving that manuscript writing was well developed. Yet nothing has been found to support the religion of Islam. Not a single Hadith or Qur'an fragment dates to this time or place. The Muslims who had managed to conquer and tax much of the world during Islam's first 100 years couldn't manage to write a single scroll, surah, Sira, or Sunnah during those same 100 years.

"So we must ask how we came by the Qur'an if there was no Muslim scribe, cleric, or scholar capable of putting pen to paper before the eighth or ninth century? Muslims claim the existence of a number of codices of the Qur'an shortly after the death of Muhammad. The Uthmanic text, for example, had to have been written, otherwise it wouldn't be a text. Writing was available, but for some reason, no record was written prior to 750 A.D." As I am sure you are aware, these are very serious accusations. And ultimately they will lead us to a singular, undeniable, and very dire conclusion.

"Muslim scholars maintain that the absence of early documentation can be blamed on old age. They believe that the material upon which the primary sources were written either disintegrated over time, leaving us with no examples, or wore out and so were destroyed. But this argument is dubious. In the British Library we have ample examples of documents written by individuals in communities near Arabia. And they predate Islam by centuries. On display are New Testament manuscripts such as the Codex Syniaticus and the Codex Alexandrinus, both of which were written in the fourth century, 400 years before the period in question! Why have they not disintegrated with age?

"Where this argument is especially weak, however, is when we apply it to the Qur'an itself. The 'Uthman text,' the final canon supposedly compiled by Zaid ibn Thabit under the direction of the third Caliph, is considered by all Muslims to be the most important piece of literature ever written. According to surah 43:2, it is the **'Mother of all Books.'** It is considered to be an exact replica of the **'Eternal Tablets'** which exist in heaven (surah 85:22). Muslim Traditions claim that all other competing codices and manuscripts were destroyed after 650 A.D. Even Hafsah's copy, from which the final recension was taken was burned. If this Uthmanic text was so important, why then was it not written on paper, or other material which would have lasted? And if the earliest manuscripts wore out with usage, why were they not replaced with others written on skin, like so many other older documents which have managed to survive?

"'We have absolutely no evidence of the original Qur'an,' say Schimmel, Gilchrist, Ling, and Safadi. 'Nor do we have a surviving fragment from the four copies which were made of this recension and sent to Mecca, Medina, Basra and Damascus.' Even if these copies had somehow disintegrated with time, there would surely be some fragments we could refer to. By the end of the seventh century Islam had expanded right across North Africa and up into Spain, and east as far as India. The Qur'an (according to tradition) was the centerpiece of their faith. Within that enormous sphere of influence, there should be some Qur'anic documents or manuscripts which have survived. Yet, there isn't even a scrap from that period. There is literally nothing from the first three generations of Islam to suggest that the Qur'an existed.

"While Christianity can claim more than 5,500 known Greek manuscripts of the New Testament, 10,000 Latin Vulgates and at least 9,500 other early versions, adding up to 25,000 New Testament manuscripts still in existence (McDowell, *Evidence that Demands a Verdict*), most of which were written between 25 to 350 years after the death and resurrection of Christ (or between the 1st and 4th centuries), Islam cannot provide a single manuscript until well into the eighth century (Lings, Safadi, Schimmel). If Christians could retain so many thousands of ancient manuscripts, all of which were written centuries earlier, at a time when paper had not yet been introduced, forcing the dependency on papyrus which disintegrated more rapidly, then one wonders why Muslims were unable to forward a single manuscript from this much later period? This renders the argument that all the earliest Qur'ans simply disintegrated with age, absurd to the extreme."

The evidence, or lack thereof, leads us to a solitary rational conclusion. The reason no one has found a single surviving Qur'an or Hadith fragment, manuscript, or scroll dating to within a hundred years of the time they were allegedly revealed is they never existed. The Qur'an and Hadith, and therefore Islam, were born in Baghdad, not Mecca or Medina in the late eighth and early ninth centuries, not at the cusp of the seventh.

If you waited to read this appendix until you were finished with much or all of *Prophet of Doom*, you may be horrified knowing that what you have read from the Qur'an and Sunnah was fabricated. While that's true, it has been my contention all along that it doesn't matter. First, something happened to turn good men bad. For the first 3,000 years of recorded history the Bedouins of Arabia were self-reliant, peace- and freedom-loving peoples. They conquered no one. Then at the dawn of the seventh century everything changed. These Arabs, now Muslims, became the planet's most ruthless militants. They conquered the civilized world, plundering and taxing it for booty. They left oceans of blood and dictatorial tyrannies in their wake. Someone and something obviously changed them.

Second, it doesn't matter what happened in the searing sands of the Arabian Desert. What counts is what Muslims *believe* happened. It is why they terrorize us, shouting: *"Allahu Akbar!"* While neither the Qur'an nor Sunnah are accurate reflections of Muhammad, Allah, and Islam, they are the only reflections. The faith of a billion people is based upon them. If we want to understand why they kill, if we want to stop them, we must come to understand what they believe.

I have, therefore, taken the Qur'an and Sunnah at face value, sharing the Hadith as if it were an accurate accounting of Muhammad's words and deeds. I have exposed the Qur'an as if Muhammad actually recited it. I did this for many reasons. First, it is the only means we have to understand the motivation for terror. Second, the words contained in these books are sufficient in and of themselves to demonstrate the deceitful, hateful, intolerant, immoral, and vicious nature of Muhammad, Allah, and Islam. So by reviewing them we have killed three birds with the same stone. I have proved that Islam is without merit, rotten to its core. The motivation for Islamic terror has been exposed. We know why good Muslims are 2,000% more violent than the rest of us. And by comparing the Islamic scriptures to *Mein Kampf*, we have been warned: we ignore Islam at our peril.

Returning to the Cambridge debate, Smith said: "In response, Muslims contend that they have a number of the Uthman Qur'ans, original copies from the seventh century, still in their possession. I have heard Muslims claim that there are originals in Mecca, in Cairo, and in almost every ancient Islamic settlement. I have often asked them to furnish me with the data which would substantiate their antiquity; a task which, to date, nobody has been able to do." Smith's experience is typical. Islam has bread a community of liars.

"There are two documents, however, which hold some credibility, and to which many Muslims refer. These are the Samarkand Manuscript, which is located in the State Library at Tashkent, Uzbekistan (in the southern part of the Russian Federation), and the Topkapi Manuscript, which can be found in the Topkapi Museum in Istanbul, Turkey. These two documents are old, and there has been ample etymological and paleographical analysis on them by scriptologists, as well as experts in Arabic calligraphy to warrant discussion.

"The Samarkand Manuscript is not a complete document. Out of the 114 surahs found in today's Qur'ans, only parts of suras 2 to 43 are included. Of these much of the text is missing. The actual inscription of the text in the Samarkand codex presents a real problem, as it is very irregular. According to Gilchrist's research, 'Some pages are neatly and uniformly copied while others are quite untidy and imbalanced. On some pages the text is expansive, while on others it is severely cramped and condensed. At times the Arabic letter KAF has been excluded, while on other pages it is the dominant letter on the page. Because so many pages differ so extensively from one another, the assumption is that we have a composite text, compiled from portions of different manuscripts. Also within the text, one finds artistic illuminations between the surahs, usually made up of colored bands of red, green, blue and orange medallions.' 'These illuminations have compelled the scriptologists to give the codex a ninth century origin, as it is grossly unlikely that such embellishments would have accompanied a seventh century Uthmanic manuscript sent out to the various provinces,' say Lings, Safadi, and Gilchrist.

"The Topkapi Manuscript in Istanbul is also written on parchment. It is devoid of the diacritical points needed for vocalization and word discernment. Like the Samarkand text, it is supplemented with ornamental medallions indicating a later age. Some Muslims claim that it must be one of the original copies, if not the original one compiled by Zaid ibn Thabit. Yet one only needs to compare it with the Samarkand codex to realize that they most certainly cannot both be Uthmanic originals. For instance, the Istanbul's Topkapi codex has 18 lines to the page whereas the Samarkand codex in Tashkent has only half that many; the Istanbul codex is inscribed throughout in a very formal manner, while the text of the Samarkand codex is often haphazard and considerably distorted. One cannot believe that both were copied by the same scribes.

"Experts in manuscript analysis use three tests for ascertaining age. They test the age of the paper on which the manuscript is written, using such chemical processes as carbon-14 dating. Precise dating of between +/-20 years is possible. There has been a reticence to use it, however, even though a refined form of carbon-14, known as Accelerator Mass Spectometry, requires only 0.5 mg. of material for testing. Yet, to date, neither of these manuscripts have been tested by either method.

"Experts also study ink, analyzing its makeup, discerning where it originated, or if it had been erased and copied over. But the inaccessibility of these manuscripts for detailed research has precluded that. Those who guard them are afraid of what the tests will reveal. Thus specialists must go to the script itself to determine whether the manuscript is recent or old. This study is known as paleography. 'Styles of letter formation change over time. These changes tend to be uniform as manuscripts are written by professional scribes. Thus penmanship tends to follow easy to delineate conventions, with only gradual modifications,' says Vanderkam, an expert in the field. 'By examining handwriting in texts whose dates are known and noting their development over time, a paleographer can compare them with other undated texts and thereby ascertain the time period to which they belong.'

"When experts apply the paleographical test to the Samarkand and Topkapi manuscripts they arrive at some interesting conclusions. The evidence proves that neither could be from Uthman's time. What most Muslims do not realize is that both manuscripts were written in Kufic Script, a script which according to modern Qur'anic experts, such as Martin Lings and Yasin Hamid Safadi, did not appear until late into the eighth century (790s or later). It was not in use at all in Mecca or Medina in the seventh century.

"The reasons for this are quite simple. The Kufic script, properly known as al-Khatt al-Kufi, derives its name from the city of Kufa in Iraq. It would be rather odd for this to be the official script of an Arabic Qur'an as it takes its name from a city that had just been conquered by Muslims." Arabic was a foreign language to the Persians. Further, for most of Islam's first century, the new empire was ruled from Syria, the very place where written Arabic had recently evolved from Aramaic. Baghdad and Damascus were vying for power, and at the time, the Syrians were in charge.

"We know in fact, that the Kufic script reached its perfection during the late eighth century, one hundred and fifty years after Muhammad's death. Thereafter it became widely used throughout the Muslim world. This makes sense, since after 750 A.D. the Abbasids controlled Islam, and due to their Persian background, they moved the Islamic capital to Kufa and then Baghdad. They would thus have wanted their script to dominate, having been themselves dominated by the Umayyads who were based in Damascus for 100 years. It would be quite understandable that an Arabic script which originated in their area of influence, such as the Kufic script, would evolve into that which we find in these two documents mentioned here. (Kufa, Najaf, and Karbala are the most important towns for Shia Muslims even today.)

"Another factor which points to the late dates for these manuscripts are the format in which they are written. Due to the elongated style of the Kufic script, they both use sheets which are wider than they are tall. This 'landscape' format was borrowed from Syriac and Iraqi Christian documents of the eighth and ninth centuries. 'Earlier Arabic manuscripts were all written in the upright format,' explained Dr. Hugh Goodacre of the Oriental and India Office of Collections. 'Because the Topkapi and Samarkand Manuscripts were written in the Kufic script, and because they use the landscape format, they could not have been written earlier than 150 years after Uthman's Recension was supposedly compiled,' Gilchrist confirmed.

"So what script would have been used in Central Arabia at that time? 'The first Arabic scripts in Mecca and Medina were al-Ma'il and Mashq,' say Lings and Safadi. The Ma'il Script came into use at the end of the seventh century and is easily identified, as it was written at a slight angle.' The word al-Ma'il means 'slanting.' The Mashq Script emerged at the same time. It is more horizontal and can be distinguished by its cursive and leisurely style. If a Qur'an had been compiled in Mecca or Medina in the seventh century, it would have had to be written in the Ma'il or Mashq script.

"Interestingly, we have a Qur'an written in the Ma'il script, and many considered it to be the earliest Qur'an in our possession. Yet it is not found in either Istanbul or Tashkent, but, ironically, resides in the British Library in London. It has been dated towards the end of the eighth century by Martin Lings, the former curator for the manuscripts of the British Library, who is himself a practicing Muslim. Therefore, with the help of script analysis, scholars are certain that there is no known manuscript of the Qur'an which can be dated to within a century of the time it was allegedly revealed.

"Furthermore, none of the earliest Qur'an manuscript fragments can be dated earlier than 100 years after the time of Muhammad, either. In her book *Calligraphy and Islamic Culture*, Annemarie Schimmel underlines this point as she talks about the recently discovered Sana'a Qur'ans. 'The earliest datable fragments go back to the first quarter of the eighth century.'

"The Sana'a Qur'ans still remain a mystery, as the Yemen government has not permitted the Germans who were called to investigate them to publish their findings. There have been suggestions that the actual words in these early eighth century Qur'ans do not correspond to those which we have today. We still wait to know the whole truth." I will cover the Sana'a fragments and deal with the most recent findings surrounding them later in this appendix. Jay Smith's intuition was proved correct.

"Let's return to the Islamic Traditions and continue our discussion on whether the earliest Hadith can provide an adequate assessment of the Qur'an's authority. There is much discussion amongst secular historians and Islamic clerics as to the credibility of the Hadith compilations. 'It now seems obvious that the early ninth century schools of law authenticated their own agenda by asserting that their doctrines came initially from the companions of the prophet and then from the prophet himself,' Joseph Schacht reported.

"Joseph Schacht maintains that the inspiration for his investigation was Islamic scholar al-Shafi'i, who died in 820 A.D. He stipulated that all Traditions of law must be traced back to Muhammad in order to retain their credibility. Schacht explains: 'A great mass of legal traditions invoking the authority of the prophet originated during the time of Shafi'i and later. Consequently, they all express Iraqian doctrines, and not those from early Arabia or even Syria. The Iraqi legal and political agenda imposed by each school demonstrates that most Hadith were conceived in the ninth and tenth centuries, invalidating the authenticity of the Sunnah.'

"Wansbrough agrees with Humphreys and Schacht. 'Take the example of the Shi'ites. Their agenda is quite transparent. They maintain that of the 2,600 valid Hadith in Bukhari, the majority (1,750) were derived from Ali, the cousin, adopted son, and son-in-law of the prophet, to whom all Shi'ites look for inspiration. This looks rather suspect. If the premise for authenticity for the Shi'ites was purely political, then why should we not deduce the same premise was likewise at work with the other compilers of the traditions? In this light, Ishaq's Sira, which gives us the best material on the prophet's life, holds little credibility. The slightly earlier material doesn't help us either as it's focused on Ghazwatt raids, which are stories of the prophet's battles. [Actually, Ghazwaat, the plural of Ghazwa, means "invasion." *Ghazwaat Alrasool* in Arabic literally means "the prophet's invasions!] They tell us nothing of Islam's teachings and don't even venerate Muhammad as a man of God!'"

In his debate, Smith explained something readers of *Prophet of Doom* already know. "Certain compilers wrote reports which contradict other reports which they had themselves collected. Tabari, for instance, often gives conflicting accounts of the same incidents. Ishaq informs us that Muhammad stepped into a political vacuum upon entering Yathrib, but then later tells us that he snatched away authority from an established ruler. He says the Jews in Medina were supportive of their Arab neighbors, and yet were molested by them. Which are we to believe? Crone points out, 'The stories are told with complete disregard for what the actual situation in Medina may have been.'

"Contradictory accounts are also given by different compilers. Many are variations on a common theme. For example, there are fifteen different versions of Muhammad being blessed by a representative of a non-Islamic religion who 'recognized' him as a future prophet. Some place this encounter during his infancy, others when he was nine; some say he was twenty-five at the time. One Tradition maintains he was recognized by Ethiopian Christians, several by a Syrian monk, many by Yathrib Jews, one by a local Hanif, while others maintain it was a sorcerer. Some even suggest it was the belly of a dead animal. Crone concludes: 'What we have here is nothing more than fifteen equally fictitious versions of an event that never took place.'

"To make matters worse, the later the Hadith, the more detail it contains. Take for instance of the death of Abdallah, Muhammad's father. Ishaq and Tabari were agreed that Abdallah died early enough to leave Muhammad an orphan; but as to the specific details of his death, 'Allah knows best.' Waqidi, who wrote a half-century later, tells us not only when Abdallah died, but how he died, where he died, what his age was, and the exact place of his burial. According to Michael Cook, 'This evolution in the course of fifty years from uncertainty to a profusion of precise detail suggests that a fair amount of what Waqidi knew was not knowledge. This is rather typical of Waqidi. He was always willing to give precise dates, locations, names where Ishaq had none. But given that this information was all unknown earlier to Ishaq and Tabari its value is doubtful in the extreme. And if spurious information accumulated at this rate in the three generations between Ishaq and Waqidi, it is hard to avoid the conclusion that even more must have accumulated in the four generations between Muhammad and Ishaq.'

"The sheer number of Hadith which suddenly appear create a good deal of skepticism. Bukhari claims that by 850 A.D. there were 600,000 Hadith about the prophet. They were so numerous the ruling Caliph asked him to pick the 'true' sayings of the prophet out of the sea of false ones. Bukhari never spelled out the criteria which guided his choice, except for vague pronouncements of 'unreliability' or 'unsuitability.' But in the end, he retained only 2,602 Hadith (9,082 with repetition)—a mere 0.5%! Of the 600,000 Hadith 597,398 were false, and had to be scrapped." Thus, by the time they were collected, 99.5% of the Oral Traditions upon which Islam was based were considered spurious.

Muslim scholars maintain that the primary means for choosing between authentic and spurious Hadith was a process of oral transmission called an isnad. This, Muslims contend, was the science which was used by Bukhari, Tabari and other ninth and tenth century compilers to authenticate their compilations. The compilers provided a list of names, which supposedly traced back the authorship through time to the prophet himself. For the early Muslim, an isnad was considered essential, because it was considered to be the signature of those from whom the document came. "Unfortunately, we have no evidence the isnads are legitimate. Rather it seems that isnads were simply applied to Hadith that approved or outlawed matters of interest to the Iraqi community in generations after Muhammad had died. These isnads, and the Hadith that they supposedly authenticate, merely testify to what the exegetes chose to enact rather than to what can be deemed historical fact. Isnads weaken that which they sought to confirm. We are left with the realization that without any continuous transmission between the seventh and eighth centuries, the Traditions can only be considered a snapshot of the later ninth and tenth centuries and nothing more.

"Humphreys asserts: 'The "science" of isnad set about to authenticate isnads in the tenth century, long after the isnads in question had already been compiled, and have little relevance. Consequently, the larger the list, which includes the best known historical names, the more suspect its authenticity.'"

Therefore, from a credibility standpoint, the Islamic Hadith is no better than the Qur'an. There isn't a single glimmer of light from Islam's first one hundred and fifty years. Archeologists haven't found a scrap of paper, a papyrus scroll, a parchment, even a rock carving to suggest a single Hadith was coined within a century of Muhammad's death. Then, all of a sudden, two hundred and fifty years later, there are 600,000 of them that emerge out of thin air. Once again there is a singular rational explanation. They didn't exist previously. The Islamic Sunnah upon which Islam is based, upon which the Five Pillars are comprised, upon which suicide bombers blast their way into infamy is a farce. Like the Qur'an, the Sunnah was created in Baghdad.

But that does not mean that they are completely untrue. I believe much of what has come down to us in the Sunnah and Qur'an is a somewhat accurate depiction of what Muhammad said and did. First, it is inconceivable that Islamic clerics just made it all up. Somebody conquered them, and something made them Muslims. Second, somebody and something motivated Arabs to stream out of Arabia wielding swords. The portrayal of Muhammad presented in the Hadith provides a perfect explanation of what caused the first

Muslims to behave so badly. While the glove was woven in Mecca and decorated in Baghdad, the hand that fits inside belongs to the real Muhammad.

Third, attributing rape, incest, pedophilia, deceit, thievery, kidnapping, ransom, the slave trade, torture, and terrorist raids to a religious prophet in a land subjected to his doctrine, is unimaginable if not true. If you were going to conceive a "prophet" out of thin air, you wouldn't include the Quraysh Bargain, the Satanic Verses, the Pledge of War at Aquaba, the Naklah raid, the real motivation for Badr, the Qurayza genocide, the Khaybar rape, or Bakr's pan-Arabian war over taxes. The Persians were way too smart for that.

What I believe happened is embellishment. The Qur'an was insufficient religiously, so eighth century scholars buffed it up. You'll soon discover where they got their material. The Hadith gained fables, miracles, exaggerations, laws, religious rituals and dogma—the kind of stuff the ruling elite in Baghdad needed to control and fleece those who were now under their spell.

Having demonstrated that there isn't a shred of credible evidence (outside of Islamic behavior) to support the validity of the Qur'an and Hadith historically, scientifically, archeologically, or rationally, Smith turned his attention to its content. He began by positioning the Islamic claims so that his rebuttal would be on target. He said: "Muslims claim that the superiority of the Qur'an over all other revelations is due to its sophisticated structure and eloquent literary style. They quote from suras 10:37-8, 2:23, or 17:88, which say: 'Will they say Muhammad has forged it? Answer: Bring therefore a surah like it, and call whom you may to your assistance, besides Allah, if you speak truth.' This boast is echoed in the Hadith: 'The Qur'an is the greatest wonder among the wonders of the world. This book is second to none in the world according to the unanimous decision of the learned men in points of diction, style, rhetoric, thoughts and soundness of laws and regulations to shape the destinies of mankind.'

"Muslims conclude that since there is no literary equivalent in existence, this proves that the Qur'an is a miracle sent down from God, and not simply written by any man. It is this inimitability, or uniqueness, termed i'jaz in Arabic, which Muslims believe proves its divine authorship and thus its status as a miracle. It confirms Muhammad's prophetic claims as well as the entire veracity of Islam."

Yet, the Qur'an is a horrid book by any criterion. It promotes terrorism. It condones rape, incest, thievery, kidnapping for ransom, the slave trade, mass murder, and worst of all, world conquest by way of the sword. It is nauseatingly repetitive, foolishly plagiarized, contradictory, and false scientifically and historically. And it's a literary disaster with grammatical errors, missing words, and meaningless words. One out of every five verses is senseless. The speaker ducks in and out of first, second and third person and doesn't know if he is one or many. He doesn't even know his name. There are no intelligent transitions. And it's jumbled together haphazardly, lacking any pretense of sensible organization by subject, context, or chronology. It's little more than a childish rant revealing the demented, decadent, and delusional nature of its author. It is unsound in every way.

Pfander reports, "It is by no means the universal opinion of unprejudiced Arabic scholars that the literary style of the Qur'an is superior to that of other books in the Arabic language. Many doubt whether in eloquence and poetry it surpasses the *Mu'allaqat* by Imraul Quais, or the *Maqamat* of Hariri, though in Muslim lands few people are courageous enough to express such an opinion." Pfander elaborates by comparing the Qur'an with the Bible. He states, "When we read the Old Testament in the original Hebrew, scholars hold that the eloquence of Isaiah and the Psalms, for instance, is far greater than that of any part of the Qur'an. Hardly anyone but a Muslim would deny this." Although, that isn't saying much. Any coherent writing would be superior to the Qur'an.

"A comparison with the Bible brings other problems to light. When anyone familiar with it begins to read the Qur'an, it becomes immediately apparent that the Qur'an is an entirely different kind of literature, whatever its poetic merits. Whereas the Bible provides a historical context for everything, the Qur'an contains almost none. Whereas the Bible goes out of its way to explain unfamiliar terminology or territory, the Qur'an remains silent. In fact, the very structure of the Bible, consisting of a library of 66 books, written over a period of 1,500 years reveals that it is ordered according to chronology, subject, and theme. The Qur'an, on the other hand, reads more like a jumbled and confused collection of statements and ideas, many of which bear little relationship to preceding chapters and verses. Many scholars admit that the Qur'an is so haphazard in its make-up that it requires the utmost sense of duty for anyone to plow through it."

The German secular scholar Salomon Reinach states: "From the literary point of view, the Qur'an has little merit. Declamation, repetition, puerility, a lack of logic and coherence strike the unprepared reader at every turn. It is humiliating to the human intellect to think that this mediocre literature has been the subject of innumerable commentaries, and that millions of men are still wasting time in absorbing it." I have also struggled with this thought. Muhammad and his scripture are so moronic and repulsive, I feel like I am wasting my time. Then I think of the billion people who are victimized by Islam. Without a voice willing to proclaim the truth, no matter how disgusting it is, they will never be freed from its clutches. Then I think of victims of Islamic terror and my soul cries out, hoping to limit future carnage. Finally, I read Isaiah's prophecies, and those by Ezekiel, Daniel, and John. If I am interpreting them correctly, within a quarter century one quarter of the earth's people are going to die as a result of Islam. That's motivation enough.

McClintock and Strong's Encyclopedia maintains: "The Qur'an is exceedingly incoherent and sententious, the book being without any logical order of thought either as a whole or in its parts. This agrees with the desultory and incidental manner in which it is said to have been delivered." Even the Muslim scholar Dashti laments the literary defects: "Unfortunately the Qur'an was badly edited and its contents are very obtusely arranged. All students of the Qur'an wonder why the editors did not use the natural and logical method of ordering by date of revelation."

Fortunately, you know the answer. By arranging the Qur'an in the order it was revealed and by infusing it with the context of the Sira, the message becomes very dark and sinister. With a correctly ordered Qur'an, it becomes obvious that the whole of Muhammad's recital was composed to serve a covetous, immoral, criminal, and murderous agenda.

"Another problem is that the reader of the Qur'an must endure endless repetition of the same material." The stories of Adam, Noah, Abraham, Lot, Moses, Pharaoh, Jesus, and Mary are collectively retold one hundred times. "The frequency with which we find alternative versions of the same passage in different surahs is troublesome."

The Qur'an has other literary difficulties. "The subject matter within surahs jumps from one topic to the next, with duplications and inconsistencies in grammar, law, and theology," Rippin suggests. "The language is semi-poetical, while its grammar, due to omission, is so elliptical as to be obscure and ambiguous. There is grammatical discord such as the use of plural verbs with singular subjects, and variations in the treatment of the gender nouns (2:177; 3:59; 4:162; 5:69; 7:160; & 63:10). Many times sentences leave verbs out, and it is replete with dangling modifiers. It has few explanations and consequently the Qur'an is difficult to read and impossible to comprehend."

As an example, Qur'an 3:60 omits the words "This is." The verse begins: **"the truth from your Lord, so be not from those who doubt."** But it gets worse. The Arabic "word" used for "doubt" is *"momtreen."* It is not used anywhere else in the Arabic language except in this verse. Islamic Imams are clueless as to what *momtreen* means so the translators simply guessed "doubt." In Qur'an 7:160 *"Fanbagesat"* is a nonexistent, and thus meaningless word, as well.

Similarly, *"al Sa'boon"* in Qur'an 5:69 isn't a word. The only place it's used in all of the Arabic language is in this one verse. No one knows what *al Sa'-boon* means. What's more, the oft quoted and superficially tolerant: 005.069 **"Surely, those who believe and those who are Jews, Sabians and Christians, whosoever believed in Allah and the Last Day, and worked good, on them shall be no fear, nor shall they grieve,"** verse was abrogated. The Noble Qur'an says: **"This verse should not be misinterpreted. It was abrogated by 3:85 [which is impossible since the 3rd surah was revealed before the 5th surah]. After the coming of Prophet Muhammad no other religion except Islam will be accepted from anyone."**

An example of a grammatical error can be found in Qur'an 63:11. *"Ethny*

Asher Asbatan" according to Arabic grammar rules should be: *"Ethny Asher Sebtan"* not *"Asbatan."* As it was written is says: **"Allah will not delay in taking a soul in it is time."** He meant to say: "when it dies."

All of this serves to contradict everything the Qur'an says about itself. This Qur'an and its Arabic are senseless.

These aren't the only problems. Patricia Crone points out: "Within blocks of verses trivial dislocations are surprisingly frequent. Allah may appear in the first and third persons in the same sentence. There are omissions, which if not made good by interpretation, render the sense unintelligible."

In response to these accusations, the theologian-grammarian al-Rummani argued that the ellipses and grammatical irregularities were really positive rhetorical devices rather than evidence of rushed or sloppy writing. It's another Islamic first: the Qur'an is so poorly written only god could have bungled it.

Muir discovered: "Al-Kindi, a Christian polemicist employed in the Caliphal court, had discussions with Muslims as early as 830 A.D., immediately after the Qur'an was canonized based upon the historical evidence. He seemed to understand the agenda and the problem. Anticipating the claim that the Qur'an itself was proof for its divine inspiration he responded by saying: 'The result of all of this process by which the Qur'an has come into being is that it's patently obvious to those who have read these scriptures that your histories are all jumbled together and intermingled. It is an evidence that many different hands have been at work therein, and caused discrepancies, adding or cutting out whatever they liked or disliked. As such, the conditions are right for a new revelation to be sent down from heaven.'" Interestingly, Al-Kindi's pronouncement as early as the ninth century agrees with the conclusion of Wansbrough over eleven hundred years later; both maintaining that the Qur'an was the result of a haphazard compilation by later redactors a century or more after the alleged revelation.

"Another difficulty with the Qur'an is scope. Some verses state that it is a book only for Arabs (surahs 14:4; 42:7; 43:3 & 46:12), while others imply it's a revelation for all mankind (34:28; 33:40). Did this universal application come later on, appended after the expansion of Islam into foreign lands, and among foreign peoples? If so, it then puts added doubt upon its reliability as an early source. This also speaks to the problem of choosing Arabic. If God wanted to communicate to mankind in the seventh century, Greek or Latin would have been vastly superior choices.

According to Dr. Crone, "There were other people in existence at that time, who lived close by and have left us material which we can use to evaluate the Qur'an. The non-Muslim evidence is found in Greek, Syriac, Armenian, Hebrew, Aramaic, and Coptic literature from the time of the conquests in the seventh century onwards," Nevo shares, "We also have a large body of Arabic inscriptions, which pre-date the Muslim Traditions. Yet, these materials all seem to contradict much of what the Islamic Hadith and Qur'an say." This evidence is particularly troubling. If Muslims wish to save Islam, they will need to come up with a ready defense. Attacking the messenger and putting their heads in the sand will not suffice.

Patricia Crone discovered: "A papyrus dated 643 A.D. speaks of the year "twenty-two," suggesting that something happened in 622 A.D. This coincides with the year of the Hijra according to Islamic Traditions." But in reality, all the papyrus did was undermine Islam. It demonstrated that written Arabic existed by 643, eleven years after Muhammad's death. And it proves that a fragment could have survived from that period. So, since we have this meaningless fragment, why don't we have even a single document referencing the Qur'an or Hadith?

At Cambridge, Smith revealed: "Crone finds interesting support for a Hijra outside Arabia. She documents 57 attestations which come from within and without the Muslim Tradition, which point to a Hijra, or exodus, not from Mecca to Medina, but from more prominent places to garrison cities in the north. This is indeed interesting, as much of what we will learn from here on will parallel and corroborate her findings." What we are about to discover is that the Sunnah and Qur'an are not the only things to have disappeared in time. There is no evidence for Mecca either.

"According to archaeological research carried out by Creswell and Fehervari, the floor-plans of the Umayyad mosques in Iraq, one built by the governor Hajjaj in Wasit (the oldest surviving mosque), and another attributed to roughly the same period near Baghdad, have Qiblahs (the direction the mosques face to accommodate prayer) which do not point to Mecca, but are oriented to the north. The Wasit and Baghdad mosques are off by 33 and 30 degrees, respectively."

As an interesting aside, Hajjaj (Al Hajjaj Ibn Yoseef Althaqafi) was one of the most brutal Islamic governors, even by Muslim admission. He ruled at the time of Omar Ibn Abd Al Azez, and appointed Kora Ibn Shoreek Alasady as his correspondent in Egypt. They extracted the money used to build the Dome of the Rock. To "encourage" Christians to pay "their fair share" they killed all those they felt were miserly. Al Hajjaj speeches still echo throughout the Islamic world. They remain as famous and as menacing as Hitler's maniacal diatribes in Nazi Germany.

Returning to the misaligned Qiblahs, Baladhuri testifies: "The Qiblah of the first mosque in Kufa, Iraq, supposedly constructed in 670 A.D., lay to the west, when it should have pointed almost directly south. The original floor plan of the Fustat mosque of Amr b. al As, outside Cairo, shows a Qiblah pointed too far north. If you take a map you will soon find where all these mosques were pointing. The Qiblah was not towards Mecca, but to Jerusalem." Yet Muslims, ever ready with an excuse, say one should not take these findings too seriously as many mosques have misdirected Qiblahs. But then one must ask why, if the Muslims were so incapable of ascertaining directions, they should all happen to be pointing to a singular location: Jerusalem?

"We find further corroboration for this direction of prayer by the Christian traveler Jacob of Edessa, who, writing in Syriac as late as 705 A.D., was a contemporary eyewitness in Egypt. In a letter, which can be found in the British Museum, he refers to the Mahgraye [the name applied to Muslims before the creation of the Qur'an and Hadith in the eighth century], saying, 'It is clear that it is not to the south that Jews and Mahgraye here in the regions of Syria pray, but towards Jerusalem their Ka'aba, the patriarchal places of their races.' (The mention of a Ka'aba does not infer Mecca since there were other Ka'abas at the time, usually in market towns. It was profitable to build a Ka'aba in trading centers so that people coming to market could also do their pilgrimage or penitence to the idols contained within.)

"The Ka'aba Jacob of Edessa was referring to in his letter was situated at 'the patriarchal places of the races.' Both the Jews and Muslims (Mahgraye) maintain a common descent from Abraham who was known to have lived and died just outside Jerusalem, as has been corroborated by recent archaeological discoveries. Therefore, according to Jacob of Edessa, as late as 705, the direction of prayer towards Mecca had not yet been established." It was to Jerusalem instead. If this is correct, as all of the archeological evidence seems to indicate, there is no chance the Qur'an was canonized before 705 A.D., as the 2nd surah expressly forbids the Jerusalem Qiblah and mandates that all Muslims turn to Mecca.

This is devastating for Islam. If there is no historical or archeological evidence for the existence of a seventh century Qur'an ordaining Mecca, or even a seventh century Mecca, what is left of Muhammad and Islam besides blood, taxes, fables, and folklore?

"New research carried out by Patricia Carlier on the Umayyad Caliphal summer palaces notes that the mosques at these palaces also had Qiblahs pointing towards Jerusalem. According to Dr. Hawting, who lectures on Islam at the University of London, no mosques have been found from the seventh century which face towards Mecca. Yet, the Qur'an devotes a score of verses on the importance of Mecca as the only acceptable Qiblah. And the 2nd surah was allegedly revealed in 623 A.D.

"According to Crone, Cook, Carlier, and Hawting, the combination of the archaeological evidence from Iraq along with the literary evidence from Syria and Egypt points unambiguously to a sanctuary in Jerusalem, not Mecca. So why is there such a glaring discrepancy between the Qur'an and that which archaeology has revealed, especially as late as 705 A.D?" Smith asks.

"Muslims argue that perhaps the early Muslims didn't know the direction of Mecca. Yet these were desert traders, caravaneers! Their livelihood was dependant on traveling the desert, which has few landmarks, and, because of the sandstorms, no roads. They, above all, knew how to follow the stars. Their lives depended on it. Certainly they knew the difference between north and south. Furthermore, the mosques in Iraq and Egypt were built by civilized and sophisticated people who were well adept at finding directions. It is highly unlikely that they would have miscalculated their Qiblahs by so many degrees. How else did they perform the obligatory Hajj, which we are told was also dictated eighty years earlier? And why are all of the earliest mosques facing Jerusalem?"

Muslims maintain that Mecca is the center of Islam, and the center of history. "It's Allah's Home on Earth." According to Qur'an 3:96: **"The first sanctuary appointed for mankind was in Mecca, a blessed place, a guidance for the peoples."** In surahs 6:92 and 42:5 we find that Mecca is the **"Mother of all Settlements."** The Hadith claims Adam placed the Black Stone in the original Ka'aba, while according to the Qur'an (2:125) it was Abraham and Ishmael who built/rebuilt the Ka'aba. Thus, by implication, Mecca is considered by Muslims to be the first and most important holy city in the world. But there is no documentary or archaeological evidence that Abraham ever went to Mecca. In fact, there is no evidence the little town even existed before the creation of the Islamic scriptures in Baghdad during the eighth, ninth, and tenth centuries of our era.

"From research carried out by Crone and Cook, the first and only pre-Islamic allusion to a town some have mistakenly thought was Mecca is a reference to a city called 'Makoraba' by the Greco-Egyptian geographer Ptolemy in the mid-2nd century A.D. Though it appears that this citation by Ptolemy didn't actually refer to Mecca, because the three Arabic root letters for Mecca (MKK) do not correspond with the three Arabic root letters for Makoraba (KRB), as the letters 'ma,' which precede 'koraba,' signify 'the place of.' With that report thereby discredited, there is absolutely no other mention of Mecca or its Ka'aba in any authenticated ancient document prior to the eighth century. In fact, says Crone and Cook, 'The earliest references are those found in one Syriac version of the Apocalypse of Pseudo-Methodius.' However, while the Apocalypse itself dates from the very late seventh century, the references to Mecca are only found in much more recent copies. They are not present in the European or older Syrian traditions, and make no appearance in the Vatican Codex,' which is considered by etymologists to be the earliest text.

"The next allusion to Mecca occurs in the *Continuatio Byzantia Arabica*. It dates from the reign of the Caliph Hisham, who ruled between 724-743 A.D. Therefore, the earliest corroborative evidence we have for the existence of Muhammad's home town is a century after Islam was allegedly formed. If it was so important a city, someone, somewhere would have mentioned it; yet we find nothing prior to the eighth century." How is it possible that three of Islam's four most enduring symbols—Mecca, Qur'an, and Sunnah—show no indication whatsoever that they existed at the time they were said to exist? The trail simply vanishes the closer one gets—just like a mirage.

For Muslims, the dilemma only gets worse. Their "scriptures" fall apart at the seams if Mecca wasn't a thriving trade center. Otherwise Muhammad and Allah wouldn't have been justified in rebuking the Quraysh for their money-grubbing behavior. If the Meccans weren't rolling in riches while neglecting the needy, the Qur'an's first 90 surahs serve no purpose. If Mecca wasn't on a major trading route, if the Quraysh weren't mighty merchants, if Allah's Ka'aba wasn't something special, then the Qur'an and Sunnah are tales of a pirate and terrorist, nothing more.

Trying to salvage their illusion, Muslims the world over steadfastly maintain that Mecca was a great and prosperous city, a thriving commercial center at the crossroads of world trade—a place on par with Jerusalem. Yet, according to all historical and archeological research, none of that is true. Bulliet, an expert on the history of trade in the ancient Middle-East, claims that Mecca wasn't on any trading route. The reason for this, he contends, is: 'Mecca is tucked away at the edge of the Peninsula. Only by the most tortured map reading can it be described as a natural crossroads for any north-south traffic and it could never have been used going from east to west.'"

His findings are corroborated by the research of Groom and Muller, who contend that Mecca simply could not have been on a trading route, as it would have entailed a detour from the natural course. In fact, they maintain the trade route must have bypassed Mecca by some one hundred miles. A great distance across jagged mountains and searing desert sands.

Patricia Crone, in her *Meccan Trade and the Rise of Islam*, adds a practical reason which is too often overlooked. "Mecca was a barren place, and barren places do not make natural halts. This is especially true when there are famously green environments close by. Why should caravans have made a steep descent into the barren valley of Mecca when they could have stopped at Ta'if? Mecca may have had a modest well and humble sanctuary, but Ta'if not only had vastly superior ones, they had a ready food supply, too."

"Furthermore," Crone says, "there was no commodity available in Arabia that could be transported such a distance, through such an inhospitable environment, and still be sold at a profit large enough to support the growth of a city in a peripheral site bereft of natural resources." Dr. Crone points out: "Some Muslims maintain it was camel herding; yet that's not possible in a barren environment." Jay Smith agreed: "According to the latest research by Kister and Sprenger, the Arabs engaged in the trade of leather and clothing; hardly items which could have founded a commercial empire of international dimensions. Moreover, Mecca couldn't have been a center for either as there is insufficient pasture and water for animals or crops. But the real problem with Mecca is that there simply was no international trade taking place in Arabia, let alone in Mecca, in the centuries prior to Muhammad's birth.

"The Greek and Roman trade between India and the Mediterranean was entirely maritime after the first century A.D. One need only look at a map to understand why. It made no sense to ship goods across such distances by land when a waterway was available close by. Patricia Crone shares: 'In Diocletian's Rome it was cheaper to ship wheat 1,250 miles by sea than to transport it fifty miles by land. The distance from Najran, Yemen in the south, to Gaza in the north was roughly 1,250 miles. Why would the traders ship their goods from India by sea, and unload it Aden, where it would be put on the backs of much slower and more expensive camels to trudge across the inhospitable Arabian desert to Gaza, when they could simply have left it on the ships and followed the Red Sea route up the west coast of Arabia?'

"There were other problems as well. Greco-Roman trade collapsed by the third century A.D., so that by Muhammad's time there simply was no overland route, and no Roman market to which the trade was destined. Of even more significance, the Romans and Greeks to whom the trade went had never even heard of a place called Mecca. If, according to the Islamic Hadith, Mecca was so important, certainly those to whom the trade was going would have noted its existence. Yet, we find nothing."

Crone says: "Greek trading documents refer to the towns of Ta'if (which is close to present-day Mecca), and to Yathrib (later Medina), as well as Khaybar in the north, but no mention is ever made of Mecca. Even the Persian Sassanids, who had incursions into Arabia between 300 and 570 A.D. mentioned the towns of Yathrib and Tihama, but not Mecca. That indeed is troubling. The fact is, the overland route was not used after the first century A.D., it certainly was not in use in the fifth or sixth centuries, and much of what has been written concerning Mecca should have been corrected long before now."

We are left in a quandary. If Mecca was not the great commercial center the Muslim Traditions would have us believe, if it was not known by the people who lived and wrote from that period, and, if it could not even qualify as a city during the time of Muhammad, it certainly could not have been the center of the Muslim world, much less Allah's world. What city, therefore, was? The answer is not difficult to guess. It seems Jerusalem, not Mecca, was the center and sanctuary of the Maghrebites until around 700 A.D.

"In the center of Jerusalem sits an imposing structure called the Dome of the Rock, built by Abd al-Malik in 691 A.D. One will note, however, that the shrine is not a mosque, as it has no Qiblah (no direction for prayer). It is built as an octagon with eight pillars, suggesting it was used for circumambulation. Thus, it was built as a sanctuary—a Ka'aba. Today it is considered to be the third most holy site in Islam, after Mecca and Medina. Muslims contend that it was built to commemorate the night when Muhammad went up to heaven to speak with Moses, Abraham, Jesus, and Allah concerning the number of prayers required of believers. The wild ride is known as the Mi'raj.

"Yet according to the research carried out on the inscriptions by Van Berchem and Nevo, the earliest dated writings in the edifice say nothing of the Mi'raj, but relate merely polemical quotations which are somewhat Qur'anic, and aimed primarily at Christians. In defense, Muslims are quick to point out that both surahs 17:1 and 2:143, which speak of the 'inviolable place' and the 'change of Qiblah', can be found on the inscriptions on the drum of the dome and the doorway facing south. But they would do well to read the history of those inscriptions. What they will find is that neither are original, nor are they old. The entire dome was rebuilt by al Zaher Li-L'zaz in 1022 A.D. due to an earthquake in 1016. It was rebuilt again in 1318. But the inscriptions (both the lower surah 36 and the upper surah 17) were not added until 1876 by Abdul Hamid II. The present doors (where surah 2:144 is found) were not erected until 1545. The southern portico where surah 2:143 is written was not built until 1817 by the Sultan Mahmud.

Van Berchem and Nevo attest: "The earliest inscriptions speak of the Messianic status of Jesus, the acceptance of prophets, Muhammad's receipt of revelation, and the use of the terms 'Islam' and 'Muslim.' It must be noted, however, that even their early dates are in doubt due to a different design attributed to the supporting pillars from an account by the Persian Nasir Khusran in 1047 A.D."

"If the sanctuary was built to commemorate such an important event in the history of the prophet's life (the Mi'raj), why don't any of the earliest inscriptions refer to it? They don't mention of the Night Journey, Heaven, the Winged Buraq, nor Abraham, Moses, Gabriel, or Allah. There isn't even a mention of the required five prayers, which was the purpose of the event. How can this be rationalized?"

Driving home his point, Jay Smith said, "The best explanation is that the story of the Mi'raj either didn't exist or wasn't known at this time, but was redacted later on during the Abbasid period. This becomes apparent when one realizes that the idea of five prayers also emanated from this time. The only Qur'anic references to prayer occur in suras 11:114; 17:78; 20:130; and 30:17, and they require three, not five prayers. If the Qur'an is the word of Allah, why doesn't he know how many prayers a Muslim is required to pray? And why, if the Dome of the Rock were built to commemorate that momentous event, does it say nothing about it until a 1000 years later?

"It's obvious this building was originally constructed for purposes other than commemorating the Mi'raj. The fact that such an imposing structure was built so early suggests that this was deemed to be Allah's House and therefore the center of the Islamic world up until at least the dawn of the eighth century. From what we read earlier of Muhammad's intention to fulfill his and Ishmael's birthright, by taking back the land of Abraham—Israel—it makes sense that Abd al-Malik would build this structure as the centerpiece of that fulfillment. Is it no wonder then, that when Abd al-Malik built the dome in which he proclaimed the prophetic mission of Muhammad, he placed it over the temple rock itself. [Actually he built it upon the foundation of the Temple to Jupiter, the Roman sun god, but that's another story.]

"According to Islamic Tradition, the Caliph Suleyman, who reigned as late as 717 A.D., went to Mecca to ask about the Hajj. Hadiths composed in the ninth century claim that he was not satisfied with the response he received there, and so chose to follow 'abd al-Malik's ritual rite of circumambulating the Dome of the Rock.' This fact alone, according to Dr. Hawting at the University of London, points out: 'There was considerable confusion as to where Allah's Ka'aba was as late as the early eighth century.'"

Having seen three of Islam's four most enduring symbols vanish, we are about to lose the fourth. Apart from the Sunnah, Muhammad is yet another mirage. "The earliest Islamic documents," according to Dr. John Wansbrough, "say nothing of Muhammad's prophethood. The Maghazi, stories of the prophet's battles and campaigns, are the earliest Islamic documents we possess. Yet they tell us little about Muhammad's life or teachings. In fact, nowhere in these documents is there a veneration of Muhammad as a prophet!" The earliest comprehensive history of Muhammad's life, Ibn Ishaq's Sira consistently refrains from calling Muhammad a "prophet," too.

"In order to know who Muhammad was, and what he did, we must, therefore, go back to the time he lived, and look at the evidence which existed then, and still exists, to see what it can tell us about this infamous figure. The most prolific artifacts are Arabic rock inscriptions scattered all over the Syro-Jordanian deserts and the Peninsula, especially in the Negev. The man who has done the greatest research on these rock inscriptions is Yehuda Nevo. In his *Towards a Prehistory of Islam*, he explains that the Arab religious carvings dating from this period show a monotheistic creed. However, he contends that this creed 'is demonstrably not Islam, but a dogma from which Islam could have developed.'" Sounds like Qusayy's religious scam to me.

Nevo found: "In the Arab religious documents during the Sufyani period [661-684] there is a complete absence of any reference to Muhammad. Neither the name Muhammad nor any Muhammadan formulae (that he is the prophet of Allah) appears in any inscription dated before the Dome of the Rock—and even those are dubious. This is true whether the purpose of the inscription is religious, or whether it was used as a commemorative carving."

Muhammad's name is absent from all seventh century inscriptions, even religious ones. Since the Sira, Ta'rikh, and Hadith, which comprise the Sunnah, are made up almost entirely of narratives on the prophet's life, making him the example all Muslims must follow, why don't we find this same emphasis in earlier Arabic inscriptions which are closer to the time he lived? Even more troubling, why is there no mention of him at all? His name isn't found in Arab inscriptions until the eighth century. What's more, the first dated occurrence of the phrase *"Muhammad Rasul Allah"* (Muhammad is the Prophet of Allah) was discovered on an Sassanian coin of Xalid from the year 690, which was struck in Damascus, not Arabia.

The first occurrence of what Nevo calls the "'Triple Confession of Faith,' which includes the *Tawhid* (Allah is one), the phrase, *Muhammad Rasul Allah*, and the denial of Christ's divinity (*Rasul Allah Wa-Abduhu*), is in Jerusalem, not Arabia. Before this inscription, the Muslim confession cannot be attested at all." So neither Muhammad, his prophetic status, his god, nor their profession of faith are even so much as mentioned in their land or in their century.

Nevo explains, "Religious content on rock inscriptions does not become pronounced until after 700 A.D. And though they bear religious messages, they don't mention the prophet or his message. This means that the official Arab religious confession did not include Muhammad or his claim to being a prophet within 100 years or more after his death. What they did contain was a monotheistic form of belief, belonging to a certain body of sectarian literature with developed Judeo-Christian conceptions in a particular literary style, but one which contained no features specific to any known monotheistic religion, including Islam.

"The Muhammadan formulae only began to be used on rock inscriptions of the Negev around 740 A.D. And even these," according to Nevo, "though they are Muhammadan, are not Muslim. The Muslim texts only begin to appear at the beginning of the ninth century, around 820 A.D., coinciding with the first written Qur'ans, as well as the first written Sunnah compilations."

The terms "Muslim" and "Islam" are also an enigma. While the Qur'an says in surah 33:35, that the faithful were Muslims and their religion was Islam, neither term was used until the late seventh century. According to Crone and Cook: "Islam and Muslim in the sense of 'submission' and 'one who submits' was borrowed from the Samaritans. The verb *aslama* has cognates in Hebrew, Aramaic, and Syriac, but whereas neither Jewish nor Christian literature provides satisfactory precedent for the Islamic usage, we find exact parallels in the *Memar Marqah*, which is the most important Samaritan text of the pre-Islamic period. The sense of submission can readily be seen as intended to differentiate the Hagarene covenant from Judaism."

While hunting for archeological inscriptions, Cook found: "The quotations from the Qur'an on both the 690 coin and Dome of the Rock differ from that which we find in today's Qur'an." Van Berchem and Grohmann are etymologists who have done extensive research on the Dome inscriptions. They maintain: "The earliest contain variant verbal forms, extensive deviances, as well as omissions from the current Qur'anic text. If these inscriptions had been derived from the Qur'an, the variants they contain prove that the Qur'an could not have been canonized prior to the late seventh century."

These sources also seem to suggest that the Qur'an was put together rather hurriedly. Dr. John Wansbrough reports, "The book is strikingly lacking in overall structure, frequently obscure and inconsequential in both language and content, perfunctory in its linking of disparate materials, and given to the repetition of whole passages in variant versions. On this basis it must be argued that the book is the product of the belated and imperfect editing of materials from a plurality of traditions."

I believe the reason is obvious. Muhammad's companions plundered the world on verbal instructions. And the next two generations of Muslims were too busy wielding swords and accumulating booty to be bothered with scripture. But then things settled down. The war capital of Islam moved to the more civil city of Baghdad. There, the new Caliphs had to control and fleece those others had conquered. The best way to do that was with religion. So they invented one, complete with a prophet, god, and scripture. They took the pirate who had inspired the conquests and dressed him up in fancier clothes.

Crone and Cook say, "It was under governor Hajjaj of Iraq in 705 A.D. that we have the most logical historical context for the formation of the Qur'an. In an account attributed to Leo by Levond, the governor is shown to have collected all the old Hagarene writings and replaced them with others 'according to his own taste, and disseminated them everywhere among his nation.'" This is particularly provocative considering that Hajjaj was ruthless. Some would say he was Hitleresque is his behavior and demeanor.

"All these findings give us good reason to question the authority of the Qur'an as the word of God. Archaeology, as well as documentary and manuscript evidence indicates that much of what the Qur'an maintains does not coincide with the factual data at our disposal. From the material amassed from external sources in the seventh and eighth centuries, we can conclude: that the Qiblah was initially toward Jerusalem and not fixed toward Mecca until the eighth century; that the Dome of the Rock was the first Islamic shrine; that Muhammad was not classified as Allah's prophet until the late seventh century; that the terms Muslim and Islam were not used until the end of the seventh century; that five daily prayers as well as the Hajj were not standardized until the eighth century; that the earliest Qur'an does not appear until the mid-eighth century; and that the earliest Qur'anic writings do not coincide with the current text." Besides that Mrs. Lincoln, how did you like the play?

"All scientific, historical, and archeological data contradicts the Qur'an. The ramifications of this assertion are astounding indeed. Whichever way one chooses to interpret the facts, they leave no doubt that the Qur'an was the product of an evolving revelation, canonized during the early Abbasid period towards the mid to end of the eighth century, in what is today Iraq." It gives an altogether different insight into Revelation's "Whore of Babylon."

"Wansbrough takes the position that the Qur'an was compiled even later than the Hadith, and was used as an authoritative stamp to authenticate later rites and laws by those who were responsible for imposing Islam. If he is correct, then one would wonder whether Muhammad would even recognize the Qur'an which we possess today."

Jay Smith concluded by quoting Wansbrough: "Readers are faced with many structural and literary difficulties which bode ill for a document claiming to be the final and perfect word of God. We are presented with spurious Biblical accounts, which parallel known second century heretical Talmudic and Apocryphal documents. And while we wonder how these very human documents found their way into a supposedly non-human scripture, we are introduced to scientific peculiarities which have also found their way into its pages. These problems all point away from a divine authorship and toward a more plausible explanation: the Qur'an is simply a collection of disparate sources borrowed from surrounding pieces of literature, folk tales, and oral traditions present during the seventh and eighth centuries, and accidentally grafted in by unsuspecting later compilers of the Abbasid period."

The oldest surviving Qur'an fragments were discovered by accident in 1972, during the restoration of the Great Mosque of Sana'a in Yemen. Workers found a paper grave between the mosque's inner and outer roofs. While it looked to be an unappealing pile of old parchment in Arabic, fused together over the millennia, and gnawed at by rats and insects, it was really a stash containing Qur'ans. Seven years later, the curator of the mosque managed to interest a German scholar in the discovery.

The best investigative study of the Sana'a find was conducted by Toby Lester. Writing for the *Atlantic Monthly*, he reports: "Some of the parchment pages from the paper grave seem to date back to the eighth century, making them the oldest Qur'ans in existence. What's more, some of these fragments reveal intriguing aberrations from the standard text—devastating in that Muslims are told that the Qur'an, as it has reached us today, is the perfect and unchanging Word of God—letter for letter how he wrote it."

The first scholar to examine the Yemeni fragments was Gerd Puin, a specialist in Arabic calligraphy and Qur'anic paleography. His inspection revealed unconventional verse orderings, textual variations, and artistic embellishments. Scripture was written in a rare and early Hijaz Arabic script. And newer scripts were very clearly written over earlier, worn-out versions. Therefore, the text evolved. It wasn't simply revealed in its entirety to the prophet

Muhammad in the early seventh century, as alleged.

More than 15,000 sheets of the Yemeni Qur'an's have been flattened, cleaned, treated, sorted, and assembled. They await further examination in Yemen's House of Manuscripts. Yet that is something Islamic authorities seem unwilling to allow. Puin suggests, "They want to keep this thing low-profile, as we do, although for different reasons."

Puin, and his colleague Graf von Bothmer, an Islamic historian, have published short essays on what they discovered. They continue to feel that when the Yemeni authorities realize the implications of the find, they will refuse further access. Von Bothmer, however, in 1997 shot 35,000 microfilm pictures of the fragments, and has brought the pictures back to Germany. The texts will soon be scrutinized and the findings published freely—a prospect that pleases Puin. "So many Muslims have this belief that everything between the two covers of the Qur'an is Allah's unaltered word. They like to quote the textual work that shows that the Bible has a history and did not fall straight out of the sky, but until now the Qur'an has been out of this discussion. The only way to break through this wall is to prove that the Qur'an has a history too. The Sana'a fragments will help us accomplish this."

In his article on the Yemeni fragments, Toby Lester quoted many of the same scholars Jay Smith referenced in his Cambridge debate. A second perspective on their insights, and what this find might mean for Islam, is important as we are navigating perilous waters. One such expert was Andrew Rippin, a professor of religious studies at the University of Calgary, and a man at the forefront of Qur'anic studies. He said, "The impact of the Yemeni manuscripts is still to be felt. Their variant readings and verse orders are all very significant. Everybody agrees on that. These manuscripts say that the early history of the Qur'anic text is much more of an open question than most have suspected. The text was less stable, and therefore had less authority, than has been claimed."

Stephen Humphreys, a professor of Islamic studies at the University of California at Santa Barbara, says, "To historicize the Qur'an would in effect delegitimize the whole experience of the Muslim community. The Qur'an is the charter for the community, the document that called it into existence. If the Qur'an is a historical document, then the whole Islamic struggle of fourteen centuries is effectively meaningless."

The *Encyclopedia of Islam* says: "The closest analogue in Christian belief to the role of the Qur'an in Islam is not the Bible, but Christ. If Christ is the Word of God made flesh, the Qur'an is the Word of God made text." Questioning its sanctity or authority is thus considered an outright attack on Islam.

The prospect of a Muslim backlash has not completely deterred the critical and historical study of the Qur'an. In 1996 the Qur'anic scholar Günter Lüling wrote in *The Journal of Higher Criticism*: "The wide extent to which both the text of the Qur'an and the official Muslim account of Islamic origins have been distorted has been unsuspectingly accepted by Western Islamicists until now." In 1994, the journal *Jerusalem Studies in Arabic and Islam* published a study by Yehuda Nevo of the Hebrew University, detailing seventh- and eighth-century religious inscriptions on stones in the Negev Desert. Dr. Nevo said, "These pose considerable problems for the traditional Muslim account of the history of Islam." That same year, and in the same journal, Patricia Crone, a historian of early Islam currently based at the Institute for Advanced Study, in Princeton, published an article in which she argued that elucidating problematic passages in the Qur'anic text is only possible by "abandoning the conventional account of how the Qur'an was born."

Patricia Crone collaborated on a book with Michael Cook, called *Hagarism: The Making of the Islamic World*. They claim that the Qur'an came into being later than is now believed. "There is no hard evidence for the existence of a Qur'an in any form before the last decade of the seventh century, and that only includes inconsistent and sparse quotations from inside the Dome of the Rock." *Hagarism*, however, came under immediate attack from Muslims for its heavy reliance on hostile, non-Islamic sources.

Gerd Puin says, "My idea is that the Qur'an is a kind of cocktail of texts that were not understood even at the time of Muhammad. Many may even be a hundred years older than Islam itself. Within the Islamic traditions there is a huge body of contradictory information."

Crone agrees: "The Qur'an is a scripture with a history like any other, except we don't know this history and tend to provoke howls of protest when we study it. Nobody would mind the howls if they came from Westerners, but Westerners feel deferential when the howls come from other people. Muslims shout: 'Who are you to tamper with our legacy?'"

Personally, I share William Muir's perspective. Many consider Muir to be Islam's foremost scholar. He contends: "The Qur'an is the most stubborn enemy of Civilization, Liberty, and Truth which the world has yet known."

But Muslims would rather be indoctrinated than investigate. The truth frightens them, as do facts and rational thought. They routinely reject all non-Islamic study of the Qur'an. Unable to refute the assault on their holy books with facts, history, or reason they simply assail the messengers of news they do not want to hear.

An Egyptian doctor who edited *Prophet of Doom* explained: "Their response is psychological. It is what you'd expect from someone who has been told that their religion is a delusion. The revelation triggers a defense mechanism of anger. This what I faced every time I tried to discuss Islam with them. Our only hope is that Muslims learn to contain their anger and then make use their minds. But I'm afraid that will not be tolerated by those who benefit from imposing Islam. If Islam suddenly disappears, Muslim clerics and kings, dictators and terrorists, would lose their power and funding. A million Islamic clergy, dictators, and terrorists would instantly be out of work."

Here is an example of how they respond. In 1987, in the *Muslim World Book Review,* an Islamic apologist, Parvez Manzoor, wrote: "The Western enterprise of Qur'anic studies is a project born of spite, bred in frustration and nourished by vengeance. The Western man, coordinating the powers of the State, Church and Academia [now there's a delusional thought], launched his most determined assault on the citadel of Muslim faith with arrogance, reckless rationalism, and a world-domineering fantasy of sectarian fanaticism, joined in an unholy conspiracy to dislodge the Muslim Scripture from its firmly entrenched position as the epitome of authenticity and moral unassailability. The ultimate trophy that the Western man sought by his daredevil venture was the Muslim mind itself. [Yes, we would like to open it.] In order to rid the West forever of the 'problem' of Islam, Muslim consciousness must be made to despair of the cognitive certainty of the Divine message revealed to the Prophet. Only a Muslim confounded of the historical authenticity or doctrinal autonomy of the Qur'anic revelation would abdicate his universal mission and hence pose no challenge to the global domination of the West. Such, at least, seems to have been the tacit, if not the explicit, rationale of the assault on the Qur'an."

These boys have a vivid imagination. Like their prophet and god, they see conspiratorial plots being hatched everywhere. And nowhere is there a word of reason to refute any adverse claim. Muslims are so used to lying and being lied to they have become paranoid and delusional. It is part of their every day life, the perceived cause of all their troubles. If Western doctors inoculated Muslim children against disease, imams preach that they are infecting them with HIV. When Americans deliver food to feed starving families, the clerics claim the food is drugged so as to make Muslims barren. When it doesn't rain, it's a CIA plot. It's pathetic. Yet to believe a scheme as deceptive and delusional as Islam one's mind has to be corroded, so it's not surprising.

But in a way, Manzoor was right. The motivation for exposing the Qur'an (at least mine) was "spite, bred in frustration and nourished by vengeance." The spiteful and frustrated vengeance of the 9/11 terrorists motivated me to learn why Muslims were killing us. And Manzoor was also correct in displaying his panicked paranoia over the Qur'an. By showing it to be a fraud, the curse of Islam can be removed from the world. But then, alas, Manzoor and clerics like him would have to get a real job.

Another Muslim scholar, Abu Zaid, protests: "The Qur'an is a literary text, and the only way to understand, explain, and analyze it is through a literary approach. This is essentially a theological issue. The Qur'an must be read literally as the absolute and unchanging Word of God." While Zaid may not like *Prophet of Doom*, that was precisely the tact I took—analyzing the

Qur'an based upon what it said theologically. But free speech is not tolerated in Islam, nor are contrarian views. In 1995 Abu Zaid was officially branded an apostate, a ruling that was upheld by Egypt's highest court. Yet Zaid stead-fastly maintains that he is a pious Muslim. He simply contends that the Qur'an's archaic laws about the treatment of women, for which Islam is infa-mous, is much less important than its "complex, regenerative, and spiritually nourishing latent content. The orthodox Islamic view," Zaid claims, "is stul-tifying; it reduces a divine, eternal, and dynamic text to a fixed human inter-pretation with no more life and meaning than a trinket or an ornament."

Abu Zaid sought to refute the charges of apostasy, but in the face of death threats and relentless public harassment he fled Cairo for Holland, calling the whole affair: "a macabre farce." Sheikh Youssef Badri, the cleric whose preach-ing inspired much of the opposition to Zaid, was ecstatic. He said, "We are not terrorists; we have not used bullets or machine guns, but we have stopped an enemy of Islam from poking fun at our religion.... No one will even dare to think about harming Islam again." Sorry sheikh, not everyone is so easily dissuaded.

While death threats emanating from religious clerics are hardly humorous, it's hard not to laugh. Muhammad's statements regarding the Qur'an were more damning than Abu's: *Bukhari:V6B61N561* **"The Prophet said, 'The Qur'an has been revealed to be recited in several different ways, so recite of it that which is easier for you.'"**

Returning to Lester's report: "Abu Zaid seems to have been justified in fearing for his life and fleeing. In 1992 the Egyptian journalist Farag Foda was assassinated by Islamists for criticizing Egypt's [terrorist organization called the] Muslim Brotherhood. In 1994 the Nobel Prize-winning novelist Naguib Mahfouz was stabbed for writing an allegorical novel, structured like the Qur'an, but presenting 'heretical' conceptions of Allah and Muhammad." Algerian Mohammed Arkoun, a professor emeritus of Islamic Thought at the University of Paris, said: "Deviating from the orthodox interpretation of the Qur'an is a very sensitive business with serious implications. Millions refer to the Qur'an to explain their actions and to justify their aspirations." And therein lies the problem.

I agree with Lester and all those who have tried to study the Qur'an objec-tively. "Despite its repeated assertions to the contrary, the Qur'an is extremely difficult for contemporary readers—even highly educated speakers of Arabic —to understand. It makes dramatic shifts in style, voice, and subject matter from verse to verse. It assumes a familiarity with language, stories, and events that seem to have been lost even to the earliest Muslims, which is typical of a text that initially evolved through oral tradition. Its inconsistencies are easy to find: Allah is referred to in the first and third person in the same sentence; divergent versions of the same story are repeated at different points in the text; and divine rulings contradict one another. The Qur'an, anticipating this criticism, defends itself by asserting the right to abrogate its own message: 'Allah blots out or confirms what He pleases.'" It's interesting that every independent scholastic review of the Qur'an gives Allah failing marks.

Toby Lester went on to write: "As Muslims came into contact with literate people during the eighth century, the wars of conquest were accompanied by theological challenges, in which Christians and others latched on to the confusing literary state of the Qur'an as proof of its human origins." It's too dimwitted and demented to be from a sane human, much less God. "So Muslim scholars found themselves fastidiously cataloguing the problematic aspects of Allah's Book. These include: incomprehensible vocabulary, omitted words, foreign words, grammatical incongruities, contradictions, historical inaccuracies, scientific errors, and deviant texts. Yet for complicated political reasons, the official Islamic doctrine became that of *i'jaz*, or the 'inimitability' of the Qur'an. As a result, 'Allah's Book' is recited in Religious Arabic by Muslims worldwide, the overwhelming majority of whom do not understand any form of the language."

After studying the Yemenite parchments, Gerd Puin speaks with disdain about the traditional willingness, on the part of Muslim and Western scholars, to accept the conventional understanding: "The Qur'an claims for itself that it is *'mubeen,'* or clear, but if you look at it, you will notice that every fifth sentence or so simply doesn't make sense. Many Muslims will tell you otherwise, of course, but the fact is that a fifth of the Qur'anic text is just incomprehensible. This is what has caused the traditional anxiety regarding translation. If the Qur'an is not comprehensible, if it can't even be understood in Arabic, then it's not translatable into any language. That is why Muslims are afraid. Since the Qur'an claims repeatedly to be clear but is not—there is an obvious and serious contradiction. Something else must be going on." You would have to search long and hard for a better summary of the Qur'an from a more knowledgeable source.

Stephen Humphreys, writing in *Islamic History: A Framework for Inquiry*, concisely presented the nature of the historical vacuum surrounding the formation of Islam. "If our goal is to comprehend the way in which Muslims of the late 8th and 9th centuries understood the origins of their society, then we are very well off indeed. But if our aim is to find out what really happened in terms of reliably documented answers about the first century of Islamic society, then we are in trouble."

In his *Atlantic Monthly* article, Toby Lester reported: "The person who, more than anyone, has shaken up Qur'anic studies in the past few decades is John Wansbrough, formerly of the University of London. Puin is 're-reading him now' as he prepares to analyze the Yemeni fragments. Patricia Crone says that she and Michael Cook 'did not say much about the Qur'an in *Hagarism* that was not based on Wansbrough.' Anybody engaged in the critical

study of the Qur'an must contend with Wansbrough's two main works—
Qur'anic Studies: Sources and Methods of Scriptural Interpretation and *The Sectarian Mileu: Content and Composition of Islamic Salvation History.*

"Wansbrough applied an entire arsenal of what he called the 'instruments and techniques of Biblical scholarship—form, source, and redaction criticism —to the text.' He concluded: 'The Qur'an evolved only gradually in the eighth century, during a long period of oral transmission when Jewish and Christian sects were arguing volubly with one another well to the north of Mecca and Medina, in what are now parts of Syria, Jordan, Israel, and Iraq. The reason that no Islamic source material from the first century or so of Islam has survived,' Wansbrough said, 'is that it never existed.' Wansbrough's theories have been contagious in scholarly circles, but Muslims have found them deeply offensive. Parvez Manzoor has described Wansbrough and others as 'a naked outburst of psychopathic vandalism.'" Another messenger lies wounded by Islam's intolerant tongue while his facts lay undisputed.

The hostility experienced by the exiled Egyptian professor, Nasr Abu Zaid, was not unique. One of his most famous predecessors was a prominent Egyptian government minister, and university professor, Taha Hussein. He is considered by many Muslims to be the Dean of Arabic Studies. "Hussein devoted himself to understanding pre-Islamic Arabian poetry and ended up concluding that much of that body of work had been fabricated well after the establishment of Islam in order to lend outside support to Qur'anic mythology." Recently, the Iranian journalist and diplomat Ali Dashti, in his *Twenty Three Years: A Study of the Prophetic Career of Muhammad*, took his fellow Muslims to task for not questioning the traditional accounts of Muhammad's life, much of which he called "myth-making and miracle-mongering." Ali is right. What's more, it's obvious.

Lester explains: "Such work has not come without cost, however: Taha Hussein, like Nasr Abu Zaid, was declared an apostate in Egypt; Ali Dashti died mysteriously just after the 1979 Iranian revolution. Muslims interested in challenging doctrine must tread carefully. 'I would like to get the Qur'an out of this prison,' Abu Zaid has said of the prevailing Islamic hostility, 'so that it becomes productive for our culture, which is now being strangled.' Yet the majority of Muslims are unlikely to question the orthodox approach to the Qur'an and Islamic history." There is something distasteful about being killed, I suppose.

The first thing Muslims would discover if they exposed the Qur'an to rational, factual, historic, scientific, and linguistic scrutiny is that Arabic didn't exist when the Qur'an was allegedly scribed by the Pen on Heavenly Tablets. Scholars have determined that written Arabic evolved relatively recently from

Aramaic. The earliest trace of Aramaic turned Arabic is found, ever so appropriately, on a gravestone. The earliest document is the Qur'an itself.

By way of background, the Aramaic language has fewer consonants than Arabic; so, during the 7th century new letters were created by adding dots to existing ones in order to avoid ambiguities. Diacritics indicating short vowels were introduced, but they are only used so that the Qur'an can be recited. There are two types of written Arabic. Classical or Religious Arabic is the language of the Qur'an. It differs from Modern Standard Arabic in style and vocabulary, much of which is archaic—antiquated beyond understanding.

Arabic inscriptions were virtually unknown prior to the birth of Islam in the seventh century. The Nabataeans, living in modern-day Jordan, wrote with a highly cursive Aramaic alphabet that some believe eventually evolved into Classical Arabic. The first inscriptions in what could be called an Arabic alphabet are also found in Jordan. They were carved by Syriac Christians. Scholars suggest that a range of inscriptions in northern Arabia, datable to the fifth century A.D., exhibit a group of dialects which may be the ancestors of Arabic as we know it, although they cannot be termed Arabic any more than Anglo-Saxon could be termed English. The dialects of pre-Islamic South Arabia are a separate language within the Semitic family, and are not in any sense ancestors of the Qur'anic language. Around A.D. 600 there were a number of dialects, but our information about these remains scattered and unorganized in remarks by later Muslim philologists.

As evidence that written Arabic was unknown in Mecca during Muhammad's lifetime, Ishaq, the first to write on behalf of Islam, tells us: *Ishaq:85* **"The Quraysh found in the corner [of the Ka'aba's foundation] a writing in Syriac. They could not understand it until a Jew read it for them. It read: 'I am Allah the Lord of Mecca. I created it on the day that I created heaven and earth and formed the sun and moon.'"** This was "found" as the crumbling Ka'aba was being remodeled. The Tradition is the final Sunnah event prior to Muhammad's battle with the cave-dwelling spirit that became the Qur'an's initial revelation. Yet no Arab could read the script from which written Arabic was derived and Allah's "Book" was allegedly written. As always, the Islamic scripture does a better job destroying Islam than does any scholar.

Here's the bottom line: Arabic, especially in written form, is a recent phenomenon linguistically. Not only wasn't it one of man's earliest languages, it was derived from a language that predated it by at least 3,000 years. There is no evidence that written Arabic existed in Mecca when the Qur'an was handed down. Therefore, it couldn't have been the language of Allah if, as the Qur'an and Hadith attest, written scrolls were given to Adam, Abraham, Moses, and Jesus prior to the time written Arabic was conceived. And that would make Allah a liar and the Qur'an a fraud.

So that you are not confused, there is more you should know about the difference between the Classical Arabic of the Qur'an and the language spoken by Arabs today. First, there is a wide gap between written Arabic and all varieties of the spoken language. None of the spoken dialects are used in writing. The modern colloquial dialects are not mutually intelligible. In nations where Modern Standard Arabic (MSA) is used, speakers must learn a local colloquial Arabic dialect to communicate as their native language and then gain a greater or lesser fluency with MSA as an educated and commercial language.

Second, there are major differences between Modern Standard Arabic and Religious Arabic. Classical Arabic only survives in poetry and in the Qur'an. Being schooled in MSA does not prepare a student to understand the Qur'an, as its form of Arabic is substantially different than MSA and massively different than spoken dialects. For example, Muslims are required to take classes called *Tagweed*, every year for ten years just to learn how to read and recite the Qur'an. But even then, they don't know what the words mean. The situation is similar to contemporary Italian and Latin. Being literate in one does not make one literate in the other.

The biggest differences between Religious and Standard Arabic are word order, grammar, and vocabulary. Classical Arabic is always verb-subject-object, rather than the more familiar subject-verb-object. If someone aims to learn Arabic he or she would have to learn MSA, Classical, and at least one local dialect. To make matters worse, Arabic has a wicked property—diglossia—a phenomenon in which two forms of one language are used side by side. One variety is formal; the other is mostly oral.

This brings us to a shocking conclusion. Less than three percent of the world's population speaks Arabic, and almost all of them need to have the Qur'an translated before they can understand it. Thus the Islamic apologists who scream that the Qur'an must only be written in its original Arabic are saying that they only want an infinitesimal fraction of three percent of the world's population to understand it. I wonder why?

The Qur'anic headaches get worse, not better. During the Qur'an's first century, the emerging Arabic alphabet did not have diacritical points, and some of its letters were omitted. The text Uthman canonized, if this actually occurred, was a bare consonantal text with no marks to show verse endings, to distinguish consonants, or vowels. Without them it is impossible to comprehend the intended meaning of the text. In the introduction to his translation of the Qur'an, Dawood said, **"Owing to the fact that the Kufic script in which the eighth and ninth century Qur'ans were originally written contained no indication of vowels or diacritical points, variant readings are recognized by Muslims as of equal authority."**

For example, without the diacritical points the following words would be indistinguishable: repent, plant, house, girl, and abide, as are rich and stupid. There are thousands of Arabic words like these in which the meaning changes depending upon the placement of the diacritical marks. Yet the Qur'an was neither revealed nor initially scribed with these designations. Thus men had to guess as to what Allah was trying to say. The Qur'an cannot be letter for letter as Allah revealed it, because without the diacritical points and vowels, the identity of many letters is missing.

The principles of sound Arabic demand that words have diacritical points and their letters should be written in complete form. It is inconceivable that God would have revealed a book in such an inferior condition. To demonstrate the magnitude of this problem, try to establish the meaning of the following sentences extracted from this page with vowels removed along with one out of every five consonants and punctuation: *f th ltrs r ssng h smlst pncpls snd rc lngg mnd tt wrd hv dctcl pts nd hr ltrs shd be wttn n mplt fm t s nmprhnbl th gd wl hv rvd bk n ch n nrr cndn t.* Now, imagine trying to do this without having an intelligible text right before your eyes. Then, to equate this challenge to deciphering the Qur'an, remove every fifth word and replace some of those that remain with an unknown vocabulary. This is what you would have left: *f ltrs r ssng h* ♋♒♑♒ *snd rc lngg tt wrd hv dctcl nd hr ltrs shd be n mplt fm* @$%&*! *th wl hv rvd bk n ch n nrr cndn.* Try to make sense of that.

Our Muslim brethren claim the eloquence of the Qur'an, the supremacy of its language and the beauty of its expression, is conclusive evidence that it was revealed by Allah. "Forget the content," they say. "The inimitability of the Qur'an lies in its stylistic use of the Arabic language." Yet how can this be if there are so many omissions and errors pertaining to acceptable principles of style, literary expression, and grammatical rules? We even find many words that don't have any meaning whatsoever and aren't found in any language. Simply stated: much of the vocabulary no one understands, and much of the text is so oblique and obscure, it's senseless.

But even so, the eloquence of any book cannot be an evidence of the greatness of the scripture or proof that it was revealed by God. What must be important to God in communicating to man is not manifest in style, but rather the power, truth, clarity, and usefulness of the spiritual meaning contained in his revelation. And this is where the Qur'an fails so miserably. What's more, the Classical Arabic language in which the Qur'an was recited is so outdated, even Arabic speaking peoples have considerable difficulty understanding it themselves.

Speaking of style over substance, in his *A Comprehensive Commentary on the Qur'an,* E.M. Wherry, wrote: "Though it be written in prose, the Qur'an's sentences generally conclude in a long continued rhyme. And for the sake of rhyme the sense of what is being communicated is often interrupted. Unnecessary repetitions too frequently made, appear still more ridiculous in a translation, where the ornament, such as it is, for whose sake they were made, cannot be perceived. However, the Arabians are so mightily delighted with this jingling, that they employ it in their most elaborate compositions, which they also embellish with frequent passages of, and allusions to, the Qur'an. It is probable the harmony of expression which the Arabians find in the Qur'an considerably contributes to making them relish the doctrine and efficacy of argument which, had they been nakedly proposed without this rhetorical dress, might not have so easily prevailed." He is saying that Muhammad's militants, like Hitler's minions, were stupefied. Beguiled by a twist of phrase, they were unable to see the base and vile nature of the words themselves. The Qur'an is Islam's equivalent of rap music.

Stealing a page from *Mein Kampf,* Wherry concludes: "Very extraordinary effects are related to the power of words well chosen and artfully placed, whose power can ravish or amaze. Wherefore much has been ascribed to the best orators. He must have a very bad ear who is not uncommonly moved with the very cadence of a well-turned sentence; and Muhammad seems not to have been ignorant of the enthusiastic operation of rhetoric on the minds of men. For this reason he has not only employed his utmost skill in reciting his pretend revelations. The sublimity of style might seem worthy of the majesty of that being whom he gave out to be the author of them as he tried to imitate the prophetic manner of the Old Testament. Yet it was only in the art of oratory wherein he succeeded, strangely captivating the minds of his audience. Some thought it the effect of witchcraft and enchantment, as the Qur'an itself so often complains."

Wherry's conclusion squares quite nicely with Muhammad's confessions: *Bukhari:V6B60N662* **"Allah's Apostle said, 'Some eloquent speech is as effective as magic.'"** *Bukhari:V9B87N127* **"The Prophet said, 'I have been given the keys of eloquent speech and given victory with terror so the treasures of the earth were given to me.'"**

The Qur'an is like a Christmas tree. Decorated in its holiday finery it appears beautiful, but the tree is dead. Worse, everything it stands for is pagan, even Satanic. The Messiah was born on the Feast of the Tabernacles, in September. The Winter Solstice was the birthday of Tammuz, the Babylonian sun god—and all sun gods thereafter. Lucifer wasn't called the Morning Star for nothing. The festival, its date, tree, ornaments, and exchange of presents all date back to the time when they were used to celebrate Lucifer's birthday. Trimmings can be deceiving.

But the ornamentation of the Qur'an was only superficial. The document is severely flawed. Jalal al-Suyuti dedicated a hundred pages of his *Itqan,* to explain the difficult words included therein. Under the title **"Foreign Words of the Qur'an,"** he critiques the obscure vocabulary of Religious Arabic: **"No one can have a comprehensive knowledge of the language except the Prophet."** (*Itqan II*: p 106)

Jalal al-Suyuti states: **"Muhammad's Companions, in whose dialect the Qur'an was given, failed to understand the meaning of many words, and thus they said nothing about them. When Bakr was asked about the Qur'anic statement 'and fruits and fodder,' he said,**

'What sky would cover me or what land would carry me if I say what I do not know about the book of Allah?' Umar read the same text from the rostrum, then said, 'This fruit we know, but what is fodder?' Then he was asked about the Qur'anic text in chapter 13 discussing Mary and he had no response. Ibn Abbas [the most prolific source of Islamic Hadith] said that he did not know the meanings of Qur'an verses like 69:36, 9:114, and 18:9." Suyuti suggests that only Muhammad knew what they meant.

Next we learn that the Arabic found in the Qur'an was not as sound as Muslims infer. In *Itqan*, Suyuti speaks explicitly about things which no one expected to find in the Qur'an—defects which shouldn't occur in any Arabic book. "The word 'after' was used twice in the Qur'an so as to mean 'before.' As in this saying: 'We have written in the Psalms after the reminder' (Qur'an 21:105) while He meant 'before.' Also in this saying, 'The earth after that He has extended' (Qur'an 79:30) while Allah meant 'before'" Suyuti went on to say: "The Qur'an means: 'Do not those who believe "know" that had Allah willed, He could have guided all mankind', but Allah said, 'Do not those who believe "despair" instead of writing "know" as He meant. The Qur'an says in chapter 2:23: '... your martyrs', but it means, '... your partners.' The martyr is supposed to be the person who is killed, but here it means 'your partners.' In chapter 20 on Joseph the word 'bakhs' (too little) is meant to be 'haram' (forbidden or sacred). In surah 46, Mariam, the phrase, 'I certainly will stone you' is interpreted to mean, 'I certainly will curse you', and not, 'I will kill you' as its literal meaning suggests."

In another illustration from *Itqan*, Jalal al-Suyuti claims, "In the Rahman chapter the Qur'an says: 'The "nagm" stars and the trees bow themselves.' Here the Qur'an does not mean by 'the stars' but the plants which do not have trunks. This is the far-fetched meaning." There are many hundreds of examples, but there is no need to belabor the point.

As you have read, the Qur'an claims that it is pure Arabic. But this is not true. First the erroneous claim: 046.002 "And before it the Book of Musa was a guide: and this [Qur'an] is a Book verifying (it) in the Arabic language." 039.027 "We have coined for man in this Qur'an every kind of parable in order that they may receive admonition. (It is) a Qur'an in Arabic, without any crookedness (therein)." 041.003 "A Scripture Book, whereof the verses are explained in detail; a Qur'an in Arabic, for people who have knowledge." Then...041.044 "Had We sent this as a Qur'an (in the language) other than Arabic, they would have said: 'Why are not its verses explained in detail? What! (a foreign tongue, a Book) not in Arabic and (a Messenger) an Arab?' Say (to them, Muhammad): 'It is a Guide to those who believe; and for those who do not believe it, there is a deafness in their ears, and a blindness in their (eyes)!'" While the purpose of these Qur'an quotes was to confirm Allah's Arabic claims, consider the number of words the translators had to add inside the parenthesis for Allah's message to make any sense.

The Qur'an's pure Arabic assertion is not true. There are many foreign words or phrases which are employed in the Qur'an. Arthur Jeffrey, in his book *Foreign Vocabulary of the Qur'an* devoted 300 pages to this study. One must wonder why these words were borrowed, as they refute the "pure Arabic" claim and put doubt on whether "Allah's language" was sufficient to explain what he intended. Some of the foreign words include: pharaoh, an Egyptian word which means king or potentate. There is an Arabic equivalent yet the foreign word was repeated eighty times. That would be no big deal if the Qur'an didn't claim to be pure Arabic, but it does.

Adam and Eden are Akkadian words from Mesopotamia. A more correct term for "Adam" in Arabic would be *basharan* or *insan*, meaning "mankind." "Eden" should have been *janna* in Arabic, which means "garden." Yet the foreign words were repeated over twenty times. Abraham, sometimes recorded as Ibrahim, comes from the Assyrian language. The correct Arabic equivalent is *Abu Raheem*.

Harut and *Marut* are Persian names for angels. The Persian "*sirat*" meaning "the path" was repeated thirty times yet it has an Arabic equivalent, *alta-reeq*, which was not used. The Persian "*hoor*" meaning "disciple" has the Arabic equivalent, *tilmeeth*. Guess which one Allah selected?

The Persian word "*Jinn*" meaning "demon" is used consistently throughout the Qur'an. Entire surahs are dedicated to Satan's allies. Yet there is an Arabic equivalent, *Ruh*. Going the other way, Islam's decadent heaven is called by the Persian word "*firdaus*" meaning "the highest or seventh heaven" rather than the Arabic equivalent, *jannah*.

The Syriac Christians also helped Allah out with his vocabulary. They coined the word *qura*, from which qur'an was derived. Additional Syriac words include: *haboot, taghouth, malakout,* and the infamous *zakat* tax. Some of the Hebrew words are: *heber, Sakinah* for Yahweh's presence, *maoon, taurat, jehannim,* and *tufan,* which means deluge. The Greek word "*Injil*," which means "gospel" was borrowed, even though there is an Arabic equivalent, *bisharah*. *Iblis*, the Qur'anic name for Lucifer or Satan, is not Arabic. It is a corruption of the Greek word *Diabolos*. Muhammad said that believing in the "Day of Resurrection" was a third of his message, yet he chose a Christian Aramaic word, *Qiyama*, for resurrection rather than the Arabic one.

The Qur'an is fixated on stripping the Messiah of his divinity and of the sacrifice he made to save mankind. You'd think that Allah could at least get his name right. But Christ's Qur'anic name, "*Issa*," is erroneously applied. *Issa* is the Arabic equivalent of Esau, the name for the twin brother of Jacob. The correct Arabic name for Yahshua would be *Yesuwa*, yet the "all-knowing" Allah doesn't mention it. And this mistake is unlike the erroneous translations of the Bible. God got his name right in Hebrew; the English translators messed it up. Even Arabic speaking Christians in the Middle East use the name Yesuwa for "Jesus." Only Muslims use Issa.

By way of recap, we have learned that the Qur'an wasn't, as Allah claims, a book memorialized on heavenly tablets, but instead was comprised of an evolving text. The oldest Qur'ans differ from one another and from today's version. We discovered that the original written copies were devoid of the diacritical points, so most words had to be chosen and their meaning interpreted two centuries after the Qur'an was revealed orally. It's not pure Arabic as Allah claims, and there are a plethora of foreign words. There are also missing words, wrong words, and meaningless words, too. And most important of all, the leading authority of the initial script of the Qur'an, studying the oldest fragments says: "One out of every five verses is indecipherable—meaningless in any language."

Moving on, lets see if what is left is accurate. For that let's review some of the most glaring historic and scientific errors. Allah's claim, **"This Qur'an must be the Word of Allah or they would have found fault in it"** is torn asunder if it contains obvious errors of fact.

A number of online websites were kind enough to chronicle many of these errors, so I have elected to present their findings. Let's start with the historical blunders. For example, the Qur'an claims that the Samaritans enticed Israel to make the golden calf when Moses was receiving the Ten Commandments on Mt. Sinai. Yet the term "Samaritan" hadn't even been coined when the events depicted in Exodus unfolded. The Samaritan people could not have existed during the life of Moses as they didn't become a nation until 800 years later. The city of Samaria was founded by King Omri in about 875 B.C. and the Samaritans became a "people" just after the tribes of Israel were dispersed by the Assyrians in the seventh century B.C. Thus Qur'an 20:85-7, and 95-7 are erroneous.

In surahs 7:124 and 26:49 we find Pharaoh admonishing his sorcerers because they believed in the superiority of Moses' power over them. Pharaoh threatens his magicians with cutting off their hands and feet on opposite sides (Qur'an 5:33), and then says they will all die on the cross by crucifixion. But there were no crosses in those days. Crucifixion was first practiced by the Assyrians in 519 B.C. under the rule of Darius I. *Encyclopedia Britannica* reports: "Crucifixion did not exist any earlier than about 500 B.C." Muslim scholar, Malik Farid, in his translation of the Qur'an, says in footnote 1033, **"Incidentally, the verse shows that even as early as in the time of Moses the punishment of death by crucifixion was in vogue"** Rather than admit the "perfect" Qur'an had made a huge historical blunder, Muslim's merely rewrite history in an attempt to bail their god out.

Another interesting historical glitch occurs when Allah erroneously calls Mary the sister of Aaron in surah 19:28, and the daughter of Imran (the Biblical Amran) in 66:12. While Miriam and Mary are the same name, the first Miriam, the sister of Aaron and the daughter of Amran, died 1500 years before Mary, the mother of Yahshua, was born. (18:28; 66:12; 20:25-30) Hearing Muslims explain away the spectacular coincidence that both Mary and Miriam had a brother named Aaron and a father named Amram sounds identical to the way Catholics perform etymological gymnastics to explain away the fourteen Bible passages that clearly state Mary had other children.

Another difficult passage concerns Haman. In the Qur'an he is a servant of Pharaoh and built a high tower to ascend up to the God of Moses (surah 28:38; 29:38; 40:25,38). Yet the Babel tower dates 750 years earlier and is Babylonian, not Egyptian. The name Haman is brought to us by Esther. She writes about what became Persia 1,100 years after Pharaoh. While Muslim apologists say it is simply another Haman, the name is not Egyptian, but uniquely Babylonian.

This ignorance of history and earlier scriptures speaks of a certain isolationism, which one would expect if the stories had been transmitted orally in an environment distant from that in which they originated. Although Muslims attempt to talk their way out of Mary being called a brother of Aaron, the misplaced and mistimed tower of Babel, and Samaritans at the time of Moses, they just throw in the towel without a fight and proclaim world history wrong when it comes to crucifixion. Therefore, crucifixion in Egypt represents a spectacular challenge for any honest Muslim to research for himself.

As impossible as it is to reconcile these Qur'anic mumblings with the historical record, the "setting place of the sun" and the tales of Alexander the Great are more challenging still. Surah 18:86 states, "Until, when he reached the setting of the sun, he found it set in a spring of murky water: Near it he found a people: We said: O Dhu al Qarnayn..." The sun does not set in a muddy spring. There are no extraterrestrials living where the sun goes to bed, and no human—and that would include Alexander the Great—has ever visited with such creatures.

In the continuing story of the Islamicized version of the Greek conqueror, we learn that Alexander's power was given to him by Allah. Muslims contend, as the Hadith confirms, that he was an Islamic prophet. He was even credited with building an enormous wall of iron and brass between two mountains, which was tall enough and wide enough to keep an entire army at bay. Muhammad claimed that a hole was cut in the wall during his lifetime. Yet it is simple to test these claims because Alexander lived in the full light of history. We know that he was a great general whose debauchery and drunkenness contributed to his untimely death. He was an idolater, actually claiming to be the son of the Egyptian sun god Amun. The temple drawing depicting Alexander worshiping the sun god Amun is still present in Egypt. How, therefore, could he be considered an Islamic prophet, or say that Allah was the agent for his power? And why is there is no evidence anywhere that Alexander built a wall of iron and brass between two mountains, a feat which would have proven him to be one of the greatest builders and engineers in history? It's one thing that the Qur'an has no prophecies—predictions of things that are to come—but it can't even get the past right.

Moving from history to science, surahs 16:15; 21:31; 31:10; 78:6; 88:19

tell us that Allah threw down mountains like tent pegs to keep the earth from shaking. For illiterate men this would sound logical, since mountains are large and therefore, their weight would seemingly have a stabilizing effect. Yet the opposite is true. Mountains were built up, not thrown down. Rather than create stability they are the result of instability. Colliding tectonic plates push up the earth's surface forming all non-volcanic mountains.

Surah 16:66 says that cow's milk comes from between the excrement and the blood of the cow's abdomen. That doesn't make sense. In surah 16:69 we're told that honey comes out of a bee's abdomen. That's not true either. Then, surah 6:38 claims *all* animals and flying beings form communities like humans. While some do, most don't. Take for example spiders, where in some species the female eats the male after mating. That's not exactly a community like ours. Qur'an 25:45 maintains that the sun moves to create shadows. In other surahs it is shown orbiting and swimming. Even the moon was said to be effaced and racing the sun.

Surah 17:1 claims Muhammad went to the "farthest mosque" during his Night's Journey. Consistent with the Hadith, Muslims believe this was the either the Jewish Temple or the Dome of the Rock, in Jerusalem. But neither existed in 620 A.D. The last Temple was destroyed in 70 A.D., and the Dome of the Rock was not built until 691, 59 years after Muhammad's death!

Other statements make no sense at all. Surah 4:59 states, **"Greater surely than the creation of man is the creation of the heavens and the earth; but most men know it not."** This implies that greatness is only measured by size. Yet we have learned that the complexity of life is much greater than the simplicity of all stars and dirt combined. Surah 65:12 reads, **"It is Allah who has created seven heavens and as many earths."** Where might we find the other six earths? If these refer to the planets in our solar system, then they are short by two or three depending upon how one looks at Pluto.

Meteors, and even stars are said to be missiles fired at eavesdropping Satans and Jinn who seek to listen to the reading of the Qur'an in Heaven (15:16-8; 37:6-10; 55:33-5; 67:5; 72:6-9 & 86:2-3). Are we to believe that Allah throws meteors (which are made up of carbon dioxide or iron-nickel) at non-material devils who listen to heavenly council? Are we to believe that there is a Jinn convention each time there's a meteor shower? I don't think so.

Adlibbing on the Bible, Allah stammers. He claims king Solomon was taught the speech of birds and the language of ants (27:16-9). In addition to birds and ants, Jinn were forced to work for Solomon, making him whatever he pleased, such as palaces, statues, large dishes, and brass fountains (34:11-3). A malignant jinn was even commissioned to bring the Queen of Sheba's throne in the twinkling of an eye (27:38-44).

Following Solomon's lead, in the 105th surah, Allah claims to have used birds to drop clay pebbles on Abraha's army. But according to the historical record, his troops withdrew after smallpox broke out, not because they were dirty.

Qur'an 18:9-25 tells the story of **"some youths and a dog who sleep for 309 years with their eyes open and their ears closed"** which is a cleaver trick in itself. The object was to show how Allah keeps those who trust him, including the dog, without food or water for as long as he likes. In surahs 2:65-6 and 7:163-7, Allah turns people who break the Sabbath into apes for their disobedience. Darwin must have been confused because he had it the other way around.

In Qur'an 11:81 and 15:74 the cities of Sodom and Gomorrah are turned upside-down with angelic wings. There are as many errors in the accounting as there are sentences. We know this because these cities have been unearthed. The Bible's account is accurate. The Qur'an's is not.

In addition to factual errors, grammatical mistakes also abound. And while that wouldn't be a big deal if we were talking about the Bible, it destroys the Qur'an. Yahweh never claimed that the Bible was inerrant. He knew better because he inspired men to write it with an imprecise tool called language. Allah wasn't that smart. He claimed that his Qur'an was perfect because he says he wrote it himself. A single deficiency in a book claiming to be written by God, and dictated letter for letter as Muhammad memorialized it, is sufficient to destroy its credibility. But as you have grown to expect, grammatical errors abound. In surah 2:177, the word *sabireen* should be *sabiroon* because of its position in the sentence. In 7:160, the phrase **"We divided them into twelve tribes,"** is written in the feminine plural: *"Uthnati ashrat asbaataan."* To be grammatically correct, it should have been written in the masculine plural: *"Uthaiy ashara sibtaan,"* as all human plurals are automatically male in Arabic.

In surah 4:162, the phrase **"And (especially) those who establish regular prayer"** is written as *"al Muqiyhina al salaat,"* which again is in the feminine plural form, instead of the masculine plural. It is important to note that the following phrases, **"(those who) practice regular zakat, and believe in Allah"** are both correctly written in the masculine plural form. So the first phrase is simply a grammatical error. Qur'an 5:69 uses the title *al Sabioon*, referring to the Sabians, but it should be *al Sabieen*. And then we have schizophrenia. Allah refers to himself in first and third person, singular and plural, in the same surah.

While there are scores of examples, copyediting Allah is hardly entertaining. So for those who are still in doubt as to whether the Qur'an is subject to grammatical errors, consider the insights of one of the last Muslim scholars to write before such revelations became deadly. Commenting on the problem of grammatical miscues, Dashti said: **"The Qur'an contains sentences which are incomplete and not intelligible; foreign words, unfamiliar Arabic words, and words used with other than the normal meaning; adjectives and verbs inflected without observance of the concords of gender and number; illogically and ungrammatically applied pronouns which sometimes have no referent [dangling modifiers]; and predicates which in rhymed passages are often remote from the subjects... To sum up, more than one hundred**

Qur'anic aberrations from the normal rules and structure of Arabic have been noted." (Ali Dashti, *Twenty Three Years: A Study of the Prophetic Career of Muhammad*, p 48)

The Qur'an contains so many grammatical errors, Muslim's defend it by finding similar errors in pre-Islamic poetry. What they don't know, however, is that much of this poetry is a forgery. It was actually fabricated for the specific purpose of defending the miracle of the Qur'an. Egyptian Muslim scholar Taha Hussein, said, "The vast quantity of what is called pre-Islamic poetry has nothing to do with the pre-Islamic literature, but it is fabricated after Islam. Thus our research will lead us to a very strange conclusion; that this poetry cannot be used in interpreting the Qur'an." (*Fil-Adab al-Jaheli,* Taha Hussein, Dar al-Ma'aref, p. 65-7)

Moving on to theological errors, Qur'an 5:116 represents Christians as worshipping Mary as the third member of the Trinity. The Qur'an says: "Allah will say, O Jesus, son of Mary, did you say to the people, Make me and my mother idols beside Allah?" It was not until the seventeenth century—a thousand years after the Qur'anic revelation—that Alphonsus Liguori, (1696-1787) wrote his book, *The Glories of Mary*, in which he hoodwinked Catholics into promoting Mary to her present-day status. Interestingly, an insignificant and heretical sect called the Cholloridians held this view, and lived in the Middle East at the time of the Qur'an's compilation in the eighth century. While this might have been be the source for such a gross error, an all-knowing God should have been aware of a core tenet of the Christian faith.

In an effort to show the scientific accuracy of the Qur'an, Muslim's are quick to say that the embryology revealed in it was beyond what man had discovered for himself. However, Muslims are completely unaware that all of the information in the Qur'an about embryology had already been revealed many centuries before. Furthermore, most of the information has been shown to be scientifically inaccurate—as is the totality of the Sunnah on this subject. The alleged genius of the Qur'an is found in its repetitive stories concerning the stages of formation of a fetus (surahs 22:5; 23:12-4; 40:67; 75:37-9; & 96:1-2). According to these surahs it passes through four stages, starting with *torab*, which means dust. Using a little hocus pocus, Muslims scholars translate *torab* as sperm, just to keep Allah from looking foolish. It becomes *nutfah* and *alaqa*. Though no one seems to know what the words *"nutfah"* or *"alaqa"* mean. Many have tried, contending that they are something which clings, a clot, an adhesion, an embryonic lump, and even chewed-up meat. The *alaqa* then creates *motgha* and uncreated *motgha*. But no one has a clue what *motgha* means. So some brilliant scholar suggested: "bones that are finally covered by flesh." The *alaqa* to bone stage is also in Qur'an 23:13-4 which introduces us to: "We made him a *nutfah* (mixed drops of male and female sexual discharge) in the safe lodging. Then We made the *nutfah* into an *alaqa* (piece of thick coagulated blood), then a *motgha* (little lump of bones clothed in flesh)." A more accurate translation would be: "I haven't got a clue."

Yet even the translators' wishful interpretations are inaccurate. Neither sperm nor dust becomes a "lump or adhesion." There is no clotting stage during the formation of a fetus. "The thing which clings" does not stop clinging to become "chewed meat," but remains clinging for nine months. And the skeleton is not formed independent of flesh. In fact, muscles form several weeks before there are calcified bones, rather than arriving later as the Qur'an implies. It is, therefore, ironic to hear the above accounts cited as proof by modern day apologists of the Qur'an's divine authority, when in fact, once the truth is known, the very science which they hope to harness for their cause proves to be their undoing.

Before we leave professor Allah's lecture on gestation, I'd like to repeat what Muhammad had to say about such things: *Bukhari:V4B55N549* **"Allah's Apostle, the true and truly inspired said, 'As regards to your creation, every one of you is collected in the womb of his mother for the first forty days, and then he becomes a clot for another forty days, and then a piece of flesh for forty days. [Four months, not nine.] Then Allah sends an angel to write four words: He writes his deeds, time of his death, means of his livelihood, and whether he will be wretched or blessed. Then the soul is breathed into his body. So a man may do deeds characteristic of the people of the Hell Fire...but he enters Paradise. A person may do deeds characteristic of Paradise...but he will enter the Hell Fire.'"** It's easy to see where Allah got his material and why he was so confused.

In surah 16:4, one of Allah's twenty-five variant creation accounts, says, **"He has created man from a sperm-drop,"** But this was understood 2,000 years before Allah's book was revealed. The Bible says, "Onan knew that the offspring would not be his; so when he went in to his brother's wife, he wasted his seed on the ground in order not to give offspring to his brother." (Genesis 38:9) Another Qur'anic assertion, that **"man was created from the dust of the earth"** was recorded in Genesis a few millennia before Muhammad ennobled his town's rock idol.

Muslim doctors, like Ibn-Qayyim, were first to blow the whistle when they saw the Qur'anic material mirrored by a much earlier Greek doctor named Galen. He lived in 150 A.D. In 1983 Basim Musallam, Director of the Center of Middle Eastern Studies at the University of Cambridge, concluded, **"The stages of development which the Qur'an and Hadith established for believers agreed perfectly with Galen's account. In other words when it comes to embryology, the Qur'an merely echoes the scientific knowledge man had already discovered 450 years earlier."**

The Qur'an is wrong when it states: **"He is created from a drop emitted, proceeding from between the backbone and the ribs."** This echoes the error of Hippocrates who believed semen originated from all the fluid in the body, starting from the brain down the spinal chord, before passing through the kidneys and finally the testicles into the penis. While Hippocrates error is understandable, Allah's is not.

✡ ✟ ☾ ☄

As we analyzed the Qur'an's bastardization of the Biblical patriarchs, I suggested that Muhammad garnered much of his errant material from Jewish oral traditions—the *Talmud, Midrash, Targum,* and other apocryphal works. Here is the proof as revealed by Abraham Geiger in 1833, and further documented by Jay Smith and Dr. Abraham Katsh, of New York University (*The Concise Dictionary of Islam,* Katsh; *The Bible and the Qur'an,* Jomier; *Studies,* Sell; *Islam,* Guillaume).

I'll begin with Smith's analysis. "Possibly the greatest puzzlement for Christians who pick up the Qur'an and read it are the numerous Biblical stories which bear little similarity to the original accounts. The Qur'anic versions include distortions, amendments, and some bizarre twists. So where did these stories come from, if not from the previous scriptures?

"Upon investigation we discover that much of it came from Jewish apocryphal literature, the *Talmud* in particular. These books date from the second century A.D.—about seven hundred years before the Qur'an was canonized. By comparing stories we destroy the myth that the Qur'an was inspired by God. The similarities between these fables, or folk tales, and the stories which are recounted in the Qur'an, are stunning."

It's ironic in a way. By plagiarizing fairytales and claiming that they were divinely inspired histories, Muslims actually destroyed the credibility of the book they were trying to bolster. And by writing such nonsense, the Jews loaded the gun Muslims are using to kill them.

The Talmudic writings were compiled from oral folklore in the second century. They evolved like the Islamic Hadith. As Jews became more numerous and urbanized, clerics and kings desired a more comprehensive set of laws and religious traditions to help them control their subjects. So Jewish rabbis set an example for Islamic imams. They created laws and traditions and artificially traced them back to Moses via the Torah. Then to help make the medicine go down, the rabbis coated their new commands in a syrupy slew of fanciful tales. Very few Jews consider the Talmudic writings authoritative, and none consider them inspired. They are only read for the light they cast on the times in which they were conceived.

Smith asks: "So how did these uninspired Jewish Talmudic writings come to be included in the Qur'an?" There are two ways, equally likely. After being hauled into captivity by the Babylonians, many Jews elected to stay. In fact, in 1948 when Israel became a state, the fourth largest concentration of Jews was in Iraq. So the Persians who canonized the Qur'an in the eighth and ninth century would have had ample access to them. And we know that Yathrib was principally a Jewish community. According to the Qur'an and Sunnah, Muhammad bought oral scripture recitals from the Jews before he killed, robbed, banished, and enslaved them.

"Some scholars believe that when the Islamic compilers came onto the

scene in the eighth to ninth centuries, they merely added this body of literature to the nascent Qur'anic material to fill it out and make it seem more like
scripture. Scores of Qur'anic tales have their roots in second century Jewish
apocryphal literature." Smith highlights three of them. Since the devil is in
the details, I beg your patience as we work our way through them.

One of the Qur'an's Cain and Abel stories is found in surah 5:30. It begins
much as it does in the Biblical account with Cain killing his brother Abel,
though Allah doesn't seem to recall their names in this rendition. Yet the
moment one unnamed brother kills the other, the story changes and no longer
follows the Biblical trail. The Qur'an's variant was plagiarized from books
drafted centuries after the Old Testament had been canonized, after even the
New Testament was written: the *Targum of Jonathan-ben-Uzziah*, *The Targum of
Jerusalem*, and *The Pirke-Rabbi Eleazar*. All three are Jewish myths composed
from oral traditions between 150 to 200 A.D.

The Qur'an says: *005.031* **"Then Allah sent a raven who scratched the ground to show
him how to hide the shame of the dead body of his brother. 'Woe is me!' said he; 'Was I
not even able to be as this raven, and to hide the dead body of my brother?' Then he
became full of regrets."** We find a striking parallel to the Talmudic sources. The
Targum of Jonathan-ben-Uzziah says: "Adam and Eve, sitting by the corpse,
wept not knowing what to do, for they had no knowledge of burial. A raven
came up, took the dead body of its fellow, and having scratched at the ground,
buried it thus before their eyes. Adam said, 'Let us follow the example of the
raven,' so taking up Abel's body, buried it at once." Apart from the contrast
between who buried whom, the two stories are otherwise uncannily similar.
We can only conclude that it was from here that Muhammad, or a later compiler, obtained his "scripture." A Jewish fable came to be repeated as a historical fact in the Qur'an.

Yet that is not all. We find further proof of plagiarism of apocryphal Jewish literature; this time in the Jewish *Mishnah Sanhedrin*. The Qur'an reads:
005.032 **"On that account: We ordained for the Children of Israel that if anyone slew a person—unless it be in retaliation for murder or for spreading mischief in the land—it would
be as if he slew all mankind: and if anyone saved a life, it would be as if he saved the life
of all humanity."** The *Mishnah Sanhedrin* 4:5 says: "We find it said in the case of
Cain who murdered his brother, the voice of thy brother's blood cries out [this
is a quote from Genesis 4:10, but not the rest…], and he says, it does not say
he has blood in the singular, but bloods in the plural. It was singular in order
to show that to him who kills a single individual, it should be reckoned that
he has slain all humanity. But to him who has preserved the life of a single
individual, it is counted that he has preserved all mankind."

Jay Smith asserts: "There is no Qur'anic connection between the previous
verse, 31, and that which we find in the 32nd. What does the murder of Abel
by Cain have to do with the slaying or saving of the whole people? Ironically,

the 32ⁿᵈ verse, supports the basis of the Old Testament hope for the finished work of the Messiah, who was to take away the sins of the world (John 1:29). Yet, in the Qur'an it doesn't flow from the verse which preceded it. And remember, the *Mishnah* is nothing but the speculation of one rabbi commenting on a fable. Yet this rabbi's comments are repeated almost word-for-word in the Qur'an. The muses of a mere human become the Qur'anic holy writ, and were attributed to God." That's *real* embarrassing.

Speaking of embarrassing, I'd like to share something directly related to this Qur'an passage. The largest commercial radio station in the United Kingdom asked me to spend two hours speaking about the relationship between fundamental Islam and terrorism. Over the course of the interview, the station received several hundred phone calls and emails from irate Muslims. One woman, toward the end of the program, said, "You are typical of Americans who speak about things that you know nothing about. You don't understand Islam or the Qur'an. You've taken everything out of context and have interpreted it too literally." She went on to explain, "Islam is nonviolent because the Qur'an says: 'If anyone kills a person, it is as if he killed all mankind and if anyone saves a life, it is as if he saves all of mankind.'"

Forgetting for a moment that the entire quote was pilfered verbatim from *Mishnah Sanhedrin* 4:5, proving that Qur'an 5:32 was plagiarized not inspired, the Islamic apologist omitted the core of the verse and all of what follows. She misquoted the Qur'an by omitting from the verse, its exemption for murder: "except in retaliation or the spread of mischief." The "spread of mischief" is "non-Islamic behavior" and a "mischief maker" is anyone who does not "submit to and obey Allah and his Apostle." Then she took the verse out of context by not completing the point Allah was making. The next verse flows from the previous one. And Qur'an 5:33 is violent, murderous, and intolerant: "The punishment for those who wage war against Allah and His Messenger and who do mischief in the land is only that they shall be killed or crucified, or their hands and their feet shall be cut off on opposite sides, or they shall be exiled. That is their disgrace in this world, and a dreadful torment is theirs in Hell." Then: Qur'an 5:34 "Except for those who came back (as Muslims) with repentance *before* they fall into your power."

In trying to defend Islam and the Qur'an, the Muslim woman quoted a verse that was inspired by Jewish folklore rather than an Arab god. Then she did what she falsely accused me of doing; she misquoted the Qur'an and took it out of context. But worst of all she tried to deceive the millions who were listing to the show into believing that Islam, the Qur'an, and its god were peaceful when the very passage she selected required Muslims to "punish" and "disgrace" non-Muslims with: murder, torture, mutilation, enslavement, or exile so that Allah might "torment them in Hell."

It's hard to know if the woman had been deceived or if she was intent on deceiving. Both are equally bad, and both are symptomatic of Islam. And lest

I forget, the next caller angrily told me, "I pledge to kill you to save mankind from you." Trying to save Muslims from the deception of Islam and non-Muslims from the terror it inspires, requires patience and love.

Moving on, in surah 21:51-71, we find one of the Qur'an's many stories of Abraham. It says that Abraham confronted his people and his father because of the idols they worshiped. After an argument between Abraham and the people, they depart and Abraham breaks the smaller idols, leaving the largest one intact. When folks see this, they call Abraham and ask if he's responsible, to which he replies that it must have been the larger idol who axed the little guys. After challenging the mutilated idols to speak, the locals reply, "You know full well that these idols do not speak!" Abraham gives a taunting retort, and they throw him into a fire. Then in the 69th verse, Allah commands the fire to be cool, making it safe for Abraham, and he miraculously walks out unscathed.

"There are no parallels to this story in the Bible. But there is an equivalent in a second century book of Jewish folktales called *The Midrash Rabbah*. In this account, Abraham breaks all the idols except the biggest one. His father and the others challenged him on this, and he claims the bigger idol smashed the smaller ones. The enraged father does not believe Abraham's account, and takes him to a man named Nimrod, who throws him into a fire. But God made it cool for him and he walked out unscathed. The similarity between these stories is unmistakable. Second century Jewish folklore and myth is repeated in the Qur'an as if it were divinely inspired scripture."

The next example is even more incriminating. In the 27th surah, named **"Ants,"** the Qur'an makes up a story along the lines of something you'd expect to see in a children's fairytale. Come to find out, that's where it came from. "In 27:17-44 Allah tells a story about Solomon, a Hoopoe bird, and the Queen of Sheba. Let's compare the Qur'anic account with one taken from Jewish folklore, the *II Targum of Esther*, which was written nearly five hundred years before the creation of the Qur'an (Tisdall and Shorrosh)."

027.017 **"And before Solomon were marshaled his hosts of Jinns and men, and birds, and they were all kept in order and ranks. And he took a muster of the Birds; and he said: 'Why is it I see not the Hoopoe? Or is he among the absentees? I will certainly punish him with a severe penalty, or execute him, unless he brings me a clear reason (for absence).' But the Hoopoe tarried not far: he (came up and) said: 'I have compassed (territory) which you have not compassed, and I have come to you from Saba with tidings true. I found (there) a woman ruling over them and provided with every requisite; and she has a magnificent throne.' (Solomon) said: 'Soon shall we see whether you have told the truth or lied! Go you, with this letter of mine, and deliver it to them: then draw back from her, and (wait to) see what answer she returns.' (The queen) said: 'You chiefs! Here is delivered to me—a letter worthy of respect. It is from Solomon, and is as follows: "In the name of Allah, Ar-Rahman, Ar-Rahim: Be you not arrogant against me, but come to me in submission**

(Islam, the true Religion)."' She said: 'You chiefs! Advise me in (this) my affair: no affair have I decided except in your presence.' They said: 'We are endued with strength, and given to vehement war: but the command is with you; so consider what you will command.' She said, 'But I am going to send him a present, and (wait) to see with what (answer) return (my) ambassadors.' So when she arrived, she was asked to enter the lofty Palace: but when she saw it, she thought it was a lake of water, and she (tucked up her skirts), uncovering her legs. He said: 'This is but a palace paved smooth with slabs of glass.'"

II Targum of Esther: "Solomon gave orders 'I will send King and armies against you (of) Genii [jinn] beasts of the land the birds of the air.' Just then the Red-cock bird, enjoying itself, could not be found; King Solomon said that they should seize it and bring it by force, and indeed he sought to kill it. But just then, the cock appeared in the presence of the King and said, 'I had seen the whole world (and) know the city and kingdom of Sheba which is not subject to you, My Lord King. They are ruled by a woman called the Queen of Sheba. Then I found the fortified city in the Eastlands (Sheba) and around it are stones of gold and silver in the streets.' By chance the Queen of Sheba was out in the morning worshipping the sea, the scribes prepared a letter, which was placed under the bird's wing, and away it flew, and (it) reached the Fort of Sheba. Seeing the letter under its wing Sheba opened it and read it. 'King Solomon sends to you his Salaams. Now if it please you to come and ask after my welfare, I will set you high above all. But if it please you not, I will send kings and armies against you.' The Queen of Sheba heard it, she tore her garments, and sending for her Nobles asked their advice. They knew not Solomon, but advised her to send vessels by the sea, full of beautiful ornaments and gems...also to send a letter to him. When at last she came, Solomon sent a messenger to meet her...Solomon, hearing she had come, arose and sat down in the palace of glass. When the Queen of Sheba saw it, she thought the glass floor was water, and so in crossing over lifted up her garments. When Solomon seeing the hair about her legs, (He) cried out to her..."

There are only two rational options available to us. If Solomon really marshaled devils, spoke to birds, and castles were made of glass, then both the Qur'an and Targum could have been inspired writings. But if this is not historically or scientifically accurate, then the Qur'an is a fake, a rotten job of plagiarism and nothing more. This counterfeit alone is sufficient to prove that the Qur'an is a colossal forgery.

One of the most documented and damaging facts about the Qur'an is that Muhammad used heretical Gnostic Gospels and their fables to create his "scripture." The *Encyclopedia Britannica* comments: "The Gospel was known to him chiefly through apocryphal and heretical sources."

The odd accounts of the early childhood of Jesus in the Qur'an can be traced to a number of Christian apocryphal writings: the Palm tree which provides for the anguish of Mary after Jesus' birth (surah 19:22-6) comes from *The Lost Books of the Bible*; while the account of the infant Jesus creating birds from clay (surah 3:49) comes from *Thomas' Gospel*. The story of the baby 'Jesus' talking (surah 19:29-33) can be traced to an Arabic apocryphal fable from Egypt named *The first Gospel of the Infancy of Christ*.

The source of surah 3:35 is the fanciful book called *The Protevangelion's James the Lesser*. From it, Allah has Moses' father beget Mary and then show his disappointment for having a girl. The source of surah 87:19's fictitious **"Books of Abraham"** comes from the apocryphal *Testament of Abraham*. The fantastic tale in surah 2:259 that God made a man **"die for a hundred years"** with no ill effects on his food, drink, or donkey was from *The Jewish Fable*. The false notion in surah 2:55-6 and 67 that Moses was resurrected came from the *Talmud*. The errant account of Abraham being delivered from Nimrod came from the *Midrash Rabbah* (surahs 21:51-71; 29:16; 37:97).

In surah 17:1 we have the report of Muhammad's **"journey by night from the sacred mosque to the farthest mosque."** From later Traditions we know this verse refers to him ascending up to the seventh heaven, after a miraculous night journey (the Mi'raj) from Mecca to Jerusalem, on an "ass" called Buraq. Yet we can trace the story back to *The Testament of Abraham*, written around 200 B.C., in Egypt, and then translated into Greek and Arabic centuries later.

The source of the devilish encounter in the Jewish court depicted in the 2nd surah is found in chapter 44 of the *Midrash Yalkut*. The Qur'anic myth in 7:171 of God lifting up Mount Sinai and holding it over the heads of the Jews as a threat to squash them if they rejected the law came from the apocryphal book *Abodah Sarah*.

The making of the golden calf in the wilderness, in which the image jumped out of the fire fully formed and actually mooed (7:148; 20:88), came from *Pirke Rabbi Eleazer*. The seven heavens and hells described in the Qur'an came from the *Zohar* and the *Hagigah*. Muhammad utilized the *Testament of Abraham* to teach that a scale or balance will be used on the day of judgment to weigh good and bad deeds in order to determine whether one goes to heaven or hell (42:17; 101:6-9).

Neither the Jewish nor Christian apocryphal material is canonical or inspired. They have always been considered to be heretical by believers and literate people everywhere. For this reason scholars find it suspicious that the apocryphal accounts should have made their way into a book claiming to be the final revelation from the God of Abraham, Isaac and Jacob.

Another analogous account is that of *The Secrets of Enoch* (chapter 1:4-10 and 2:1), which predates the Qur'an by four centuries. What Allah didn't steal from the Jewish fable, he borrowed from an old Persian book entitled *Arta-i Viraf Namak*. It tells how a pious young Zoroastrian ascended to the skies, and, on his return, related what he had seen, or professed to have seen.

The Qur'anic description of Hell resembles the portrayals in the *Homilies of Ephraim,* a Nestorian preacher of the sixth century," according to Sir John Glubb, although I'm convinced most of hell's torments came from the abuse Muhammad suffered in the desert as a youth. The description of Paradise in suras 55:56, 56:22, and 35-7, which speak of the righteous being rewarded with wide-eyed *houris,* or virgins, who have eyes like pearls has interesting parallels in the Zoroastrian religion of Persia, where the maidens are quite similar. The rivers in the Persian Paradise flow with wine as well.

And I would be remiss if I didn't confirm Muhammad's rendition of Paradise, as it wasn't divine. *Bukhari:V4B54N469* **"Allah's Apostle said, 'The first batch who will enter Paradise will be like a full moon; and those who will enter next will be like the brightest star. Their hearts will be as the heart of a single man, for everyone of them shall have two wives from the houris, each of whom will be so beautiful, pure and transparent that the marrow of the bones of their legs will be seen through the flesh. They will never fall ill, and they will neither blow their noses, nor spit. Their utensils are silver, their combs are gold, the fuel used in their centers will be aloe, and their sweat will smell like musk.'"**

Muhammad, or whoever compiled the Qur'an, incorporated parts of the religion of the Sabeans, Zoroastrianism, and Hinduism into Islam. He adopted such pagan rituals as: worshiping at the Ka'aba, praying five times a day towards Mecca, the zakat tax, and fasting in Ramadhan. The Qur'an ascribes things to Muhammad and Islam beyond the wild ride to the seventh heaven and the virgins from previously known concepts in earlier doctrines: Azazil and other spirits coming up from Hades, the "light" of Muhammad, the bridge of Sirat, and the angel of death.

The original Arabic in surah 3:106-7 says: **"On Judgment Day, people who made good deeds will have white faces and they will go to Paradise. People who did bad deeds will have black faces and they will go to hell."** But to be fair, the Islamic scriptures also say: *Bukhari:V9B89N256* **"Allah's Apostle said, 'You should listen to and obey your ruler even if he is an Ethiopian black slave whose head looks like a raisin.'"**

This caustic brew of uninspired ingredients may be why Clair Tisdall, in her *Original Sources of the Qur'an,* wrote: "Islam is not an invention, but a concoction; there is nothing novel about it except Mohammed's mixing old ingredients in a new panacea for human ills and forcing it down by means of the sword." She went on to say: "Islam's scriptures came to reflect the carnal and sensual nature of its founder. Islam therefore may aptly be compared with: 'that bituminous lake where Sodom flamed,' which, receiving into its bosom the waters of many streams that united form a basin that turns them into one great Sea of Death, from whose shores flee pestilential exhalations destructive to all life within reach of their malign influence. Such is Islam. Originating from many different sources, it has assumed its form from the character and disposition of Muhammad; and thus the good in it serves only to recommend and preserve the evil which renders it a false and delusive faith, a curse to men and not a blessing. Muhammad's concoction has turned many of the fairest regions of the earth into deserts, deluged many a land with innocent blood, and has smitten with a moral, intellectual, and spiritual blight every nation of men which lies under its iron yoke and groans beneath its pitiless sway."

It's hard to imagine a more adept description of the poisons that oozed from Muhammad's soul or a more adept summation of Islam's legacy. Tisdall went on to write: "While the devout Muslim believes that the rituals and doctrines of Islam are entirely heavenly in origin and thus cannot have any earthly sources, scholars have demonstrated beyond all doubt that every ritual and belief in Islam can be traced back to pre-Islamic Arabian culture. In other words Muhammad did not preach anything new. Everything he taught had been believed and practiced in Arabia long before he was ever born. Even the idea of 'only one God' was borrowed from the Jews and Christians."

Carlyle's dictum on the Qur'an was also enlightened: "It is as toilsome reading as I ever undertook, a wearisome, confused jumble, crude, incondite. Nothing but a sense of duty could carry any European through it." Samuel Zwemer, in *The Influence of Animism on Islam* wrote: "In no monotheistic religion are magic and sorcery so firmly entrenched as they are in Islam; for in the case of this religion they are based on the teaching of the Qur'an and the practice of the Prophet." In other words, it's Satan's book.

Official Islamic dictionaries, websites, and holy books are consistent when they describe the nature of the elements which compose Islam. The scholastic summation proclaims: "As Islam solidified as a religious and political entity, a vast body of exegetical and historical literature evolved to explain the Qur'an and the rise of the empire. The most important elements of which are Hadith, or the collected sayings and deeds of the Prophet Muhammad; Sunnah, or the body of Islamic social and legal custom; Sira, or biographies of the Prophet; and Tafsir, or Qur'anic commentary and explication. It is from these Traditions—compiled in written form in the eighth to tenth centuries—that all accounts of the revelation of the Qur'an and the early years of Islam are ultimately derived."

You've seen the following clerical proclamation before, but it's worth repeating: "The Qur'an is one leg of two which form the basis of Islam. The second leg is the Sunnah of the Prophet. What makes the Qur'an different from the Sunnah is its form. Unlike the Sunnah, the Qur'an is quite literally the Word of Allah, whereas the Sunnah was inspired by Allah but the wording and actions are the Prophet's. The Qur'an has not been expressed using any human words. Its wording is letter for letter fixed by Allah. Prophet Muhammad was the final Messenger of Allah to humanity, and therefore the Qur'an is the last Message which Allah has sent to us."

This is what Islamic clerics and scholars had to say about Bukhari's Hadith Collection: "Sahih Bukhari is a collection of sayings and deeds of Prophet Muhammad (pbuh), also known as the Sunnah. The reports of the Prophet's sayings and deeds are called Hadith. Bukhari lived a couple of centuries after the Prophet's death and worked extremely hard to collect his Hadith. Each report in his collection was checked for compatibility with the Qur'an, and the veracity of the chain of reporters had to be painstakingly established. Bukhari's collection is recognized by the overwhelming majority of the Muslim world to be one of the most authentic collections of the Sunnah of the Prophet (pbuh). Bukhari Abu Abdallah Muhammad bin Ismail bin Ibrahim bin al-Mughira al-Ja'fai was born in 194 A.H. and died in 256 A.H. His collection of Hadith is considered second to none. He spent sixteen years compiling it, and ended up with 2,602 Hadith (9,082 with repetition). His criteria for acceptance into the collection were amongst the most stringent of all the scholars of Hadith."

While there is no question Bukhari's Collection is as sound as Muslim's, its complete lack of chronology limits its usefulness. If you are interested in a subject like taxes or jihad you could turn to the appropriate chapter and read what Muhammad had to say about such things. But without the grounding of time, circumstance, constituents, and place, you'd be forced to take everything you read out of context. That's why every accurate and unbiased presentation of the Muhammad of Islam must be based upon the only biographical and historical Hadith Collections compiled within three centuries of Muhammad's death—Ishaq and Tabari. They, and they alone, enable a person to speak with authority about Islam without taking Muhammad's example and scriptures out of context.

Quite recently, however, there has been a new movement afoot in the Islamic world. Cleric and king have come to recognize they have a problem. The Qur'an and Sunnah are repulsive—so are their prophet, god, and religion. They do not stand up to scrutiny. While they have been able to fool politicians and the media by repeating "Islam is a peaceful religion," and they have been able to cower religious leaders by threatening them, it hasn't worked on everyone. Enough Americans have learned the truth to put the Islamic power brokers in a terrible bind.

So those who benefit from Islam have deployed a new strategy. They proclaim that the Qur'an may not be translated out of the arcane language only 0.0003% understand. Imagine that, 99.9997% of those who listen to the surahs being recited have no earthly idea of what is being said. In Classic Arabic, the verses have a good beat and the rhyme sounds heavenly. But if the only people who are authorized to interpret them all benefit from Islam, who is going to confess that the words are hellish?

In this regard, the Qur'an is no different than rap music. Its cadence and rhyme are seductive while its lyrics are often corrupting. And the Qur'an works the same way, too. Those who recite it rake in the bucks, babes, and power privilege provides. Those who listen are fleeced.

While disguising the Qur'an's evil intent via a language few understand solves one problem, the Islamic establishment still needs to deal with the vile message of the Sunnah. It's one thing to say Allah's jingle is too majestic to be translated, but Muhammad's words were written in prose.

To fix this problem, Islamic officials unveiled a different strategy during my earliest debates with them. They said that they were "unaware" of Tabari's History. When that didn't fly, they protested saying, Tabari isn't "approved." Then they claimed that it was just a "history book and not a collection of Hadith." Some even said that it contained "unauthorized material." While that's not true, it created confusion and served their interests.

Their rejection of Tabari is unsound for several reasons. First, Ishaq's original manuscripts have been lost, so Tabari is the oldest unedited account of Muhammad's life and the formation of Islam. Second, Tabari is nothing but a collection of Hadiths. Everything I quoted came complete with a chain of transmitters. In fact, Tabari's isnads are more complete than Bukhari's. And third, the Hadith Tabari compiled are no different than those arranged a century earlier by Ishaq, or by his near contemporary, Bukhari. They were all pumping from the same well—digging out of the same pit.

So why do you suppose Islamic officials ganged up on their best source? Because it was translated into English and available, while the others were not; that's why. In each debate I urged listeners to go to the S.U.N.Y. Press website and buy Tabari and then read it for themselves. That was easy enough. If what I was quoting was accurate, everything Muslims were saying about their religion was a lie. America would know the truth. And if I misrepresented Tabari's message, I promised to go away, never to be heard from again.

The Islamic apologists knew what I was saying was not only true but devastating. They stopped debating me and started discrediting Tabari because they were aware of what I had discovered: the only English translation of Ishaq's Sira was out of print and nearly impossible to find. I searched for a year, ordering it from the largest booksellers, the publisher, even used bookstores. I searched libraries, too, but to no avail. Muslims check Ishaq out and burn it. Fortunately, a Christian couple who had listened to one of my debates found a copy in a university library. They photocopied the Sira—all 900 pages—and sent it to me.

The reason this is important is because those who benefit from Islam know that without a chronological presentation of Muhammad's words and deeds, they can get away with murder—literally. They can say whatever they like, and they do. Without Ishaq or Tabari, the Qur'an is senseless. Muslims can claim that the god of the Qur'an is the same as the God of the Bible when they are opposites. They can say Islam is peaceful even though it condemns peace and promotes war. They can argue that Muhammad only fought defensive battles, when his scriptures say he was a terrorist. They can posture the notion that Islam made the Bedouins better, when in fact it transformed them into bloody pirates and immoral parasites. They can claim that the Qur'an is Allah's perfect book; when, by any rational criterion, it's hideous.

To put this in perspective, being a Muslim without the information contained in the only chronological presentations of Muhammad's words and deeds would be like being a Christian without the Gospels. It would be impossible to be Christ-like without knowing Christ, his message and example. It would be like being a Jew without the Torah and the other historical books. All you'd have are prophets and psalms, and that's just not enough, not even remotely.

As you have discovered, the Qur'an isn't like any intelligent book. It's jumbled together without context or chronology, rendering it nothing more than a mean-spirited rant, a demented, delusional, and dimwitted tirade. Without the chronological Hadith collections of Ishaq and Tabari, Islam becomes whatever Islamic clerics and kings want it to be. So in their fiefdoms it's all about jihad. In the free world, it's all about peace.

To prove my point, I'd like to review Islam's Five Pillars to see if they stand without the Hadith Collections found in the Sunnah. But before we begin, Islam provides an important clue. To find the Pillars, we must turn to the Hadith, not the Qur'an. And while I will conduct this analysis using the "approved" version of Islam's Five Pillars, there are competing scenarios we must consider. As you might expect, Muhammad himself couldn't decide what his priorities were—much less Allah's.

The most famous Islamic proclamations echo the Qur'an's incessant command to fight jihad in Allah's Cause. Muhammad established jihad's preeminence, claiming that fighting was the foundation upon which Islam's other pillars must stand. Under the title **"Fighting In Allah's Cause—Jihad,"** we read: **"Jihad is holy fighting in Allah's Cause with full force of numbers and weaponry. It is given the utmost importance in Islam and is one of its pillars. By Jihad Islam is established, Allah's Word is made superior (which means only Allah has the right to be worshiped), and Islam is propagated. By abandoning Jihad Islam is destroyed and Muslims fall into an inferior position; their honor is lost, their lands are stolen, their rule and authority vanish. Jihad is an obligatory duty in Islam on every Muslim. He who tries to escape from this duty, or does not fulfill this duty, dies with one of the qualities of a hypocrite."**

The reason jihad supercedes the other pillars is because: *Bukhari:V4B52N44* **"A man came to Allah's Apostle and said, 'Instruct me as to such a deed as equals Jihad in reward.' He replied, 'I do not find such a deed. Can you, while the Muslim fighter has gone out for Jihad, enter a mosque to perform prayers without ceasing and fast forever?' The man said, 'No one can do that.'"** So Jihad is superior to endless prayer and fasting. But there was more: *Bukhari:V4B52N46* **"I heard Allah's Apostle saying, 'The example of a Mujahid [Muslim fighter] in Allah's Cause—and Allah knows best who really strives in His Cause—is like a person who fasts and prays without ever stopping. Allah guarantees that**

He will admit the Mujahid in His Cause into Paradise if he is killed, otherwise He will return him to his home safely with rewards and war booty.'" It's the Devil's rendition of the win-win scenario. And that leads us to the capper, the line that confirmed jihad was better than all of the Five Pillars combined: *Bukhari:V4B52N50* "**The Prophet said, 'A single endeavor of fighting in Allah's Cause is better than the world and whatever is in it.'"**

From the very beginning, there was always a direct causal link between the religion of Islam and Islamic terror: *Bukhari:V4B52N63* "**A man whose face was covered with an iron mask of armor came to the Prophet and said, 'Allah's Apostle! Shall I fight or embrace Islam first?' The Prophet said, 'Embrace Islam first and then fight.' So he embraced Islam, and was martyred. Allah's Apostle said, 'A Little work, but a great reward.'"** Consistent with this message, *Bukhari:V1B2N25* "**Allah's Apostle was asked, 'What is the best deed?' He replied, 'To believe in Allah and His Apostle Muhammad.' The questioner then asked, 'What is the next (in goodness)?' He replied, 'To participate in Jihad (religious fighting) in Allah's Cause.' The questioner again asked, 'What is the next (in goodness)?' He replied, 'To perform Hajj (Pilgrim age to Mecca in accordance with the Traditions of the Prophet.'"** This is important because it establishes Three Pillars, with Jihad being the second most important.

The next rendition of Pillars eliminates the Hajj, which was number three above, and replaces it with the Khumus—Muhammad's share of stolen booty. *Bukhari:V1B2N50* "**They said, 'O Allah's Apostle, order us to do some religious deeds that we may enter Paradise.' The Prophet ordered them to believe in Allah Alone and asked them, 'Do you know what is meant by believing in Allah Alone?' They replied, 'Allah and His Apostle know better.' Thereupon the Prophet said, 'It means: 1. To testify that none has the right to be worshipped but Allah and Muhammad is Allah's Apostle. 2. To offer prayers perfectly. 3. To pay the Zakat obligatory tax. 4. To observe fast during Ramadhan. 5. And to pay the Khumus (one fifth of the booty to be given in Allah's Cause) to Allah's Apostle.'"**

That said, I promised to resolve Islam's absolute reliance on the Sunnah by analyzing the "officially recognized" Pillars. To begin: *Bukhari:V1B2N7* "**Allah's Apostle said: 'Islam is based on (the following) five (principles): 1. To testify that none has the right to be worshipped but Allah and Muhammad is Allah's Apostle.'"** Let's tackle them one at a time. In its present order, the Qur'an's initial surah, the 2nd, (the 1st is an invocation, not a revelation as it speaks to god not to man) makes a transition from Ar-Rahman to Allah. But as we read on, this changes. The Qur'anic God becomes Ar-Rahman again and then a nameless Lord. Without the chronology the Sira's Hadith provide, Muslims don't know who God is or how many of them there are. Furthermore, they know nothing about the "Apostle." Without the Sunnah, acknowledging him in the profession of faith is like a tape recorder asking to be credited for bringing you the songs of your favorite artist.

But it gets worse. The Qur'an orders Muslims to obey the Messenger. If you don't know what *he* said that's impossible. The Qur'an alleges that it's entirely composed of Allah's orders, not Muhammad's, so you'd be out of luck. The Qur'an also tells Muslims that they must follow the Messenger's example, yet the only place that example is established is in the Sunnah. Therefore, Islam's First Pillar is utterly meaningless, and impossible to implement, without Ishaq and Tabari.

The Second Pillar is: "**2. To offer the (compulsory congregational) prayers dutifully and perfectly.**" Once again, that's not feasible. The "**compulsory congregational prayer**" isn't described in the Qur'an. There aren't even any clues. In fact, the Qur'an says that there should be three prayers, none of which it depicts, and the Hadith demands five. The only explanation of the obligatory prostration is found in the Sunnah—and even then it's never described by the prophet himself. Muslims are performing a ritual without Qur'anic precedence. As such, the Second Pillar is rubble.

Let's see if the Third Pillar survives without the Sunnah. To find out, we turn to the Hadith: *Bukhari:V1B2N7* "**3. To pay Zakat.**" How is that possible when the terms of the Zakat are omitted from the Qur'an? The first to commit them to paper was Ishaq. A century later, Tabari referenced Ishaq's Hadith. The only reason Muslims can pay the Zakat is that Ishaq explained it to them. The Profitable Prophet Plan is bankrupt without the Sira.

Surely the Fourth Pillar will fare better: "**4. To perform Hajj.**" Nope. That's impossible too. The only explanations of the Hajj are in the Sunnah. No aspect of the pilgrimage can be performed without referencing the Hadith. Muslims would be lost without it.

Do you suppose Allah will redeem himself and explain the final pillar in his "perfect, detailed, and final revelation to mankind?" *Bukhari:V1B2N7* "**5. To observe fast during the month of Ramadan.**" Guess what? Allah forgot to explain the nature of the fast. Without the Hadith, Muslims would be expected to forgo eating during the entire month of Ramadhan. But that's not the way they observe the fast, for it's not the way it's explained in the Sunnah. As a matter of fact, without the Hadith, Muslims wouldn't know why Ramadhan was special. The only account of the initial revelation is in their Traditions— initially chronicled by Ishaq and then copied by Bukhari, Muslim, and Tabari.

Without Ibn Ishaq and those who copied and edited his arrangement of Hadith concerning Muhammad's words and deeds, there would be no Islam. The Qur'an is senseless and the Five Pillars are meaningless. Faith is folly. And that's especially true since the lone individual responsible for Islam, Allah, and the Qur'an, preached: *Bukhari:V9B88N174* "**Allah's Apostle said, 'Far removed from mercy are those who change the religion of Islam after me! Islam cannot change!'**"

The penalty for escaping Muhammad's clutches has always been high. *Bukhari:V4B52N260* "**The Prophet said, 'If a Muslim discards his religion, kill him.'**" This was no ordinary prophet or religion. No, Muhammad was special. He was a terrorist and a pirate, and you don't find too many of those in religious circles. *Bukhari:V4B52N220* **"Allah's Apostle said, 'I have been made victorious with terror. The treasures of the world were brought to me and put in my hand.'"**

Yes, Islam was the Profitable Prophet Plan. It was all about Muhammad, and he knew it. That is why he required his Sunnah, or example to be enacted as law. *Tabari IX:82* **"The Messenger sent [killer] Khalid out to collect taxes with an army of 400 and ordered him to invite people to Islam before he fought them. If they were to respond and submit, he was to teach them the Book of Allah, the Sunnah of His Prophet, and the requirements of Islam. If they should decline, then he was to fight them."**

So it all comes down to this: If the Hadith Collections of Ishaq, Tabari, Bukhari and Muslim are true, Muhammad was the most evil man who ever lived, Allah was the most demented god ever conceived, and Islam was the most vile doctrine ever imposed on humankind. If, however, the Hadith Collections are untrue, then nothing is known of Muhammad, the conception of his god, or his formation of Islam. There is no rational reason to believe it, observe it, suffer under it, or die for it.

TOPICAL QUOTATIONS

MUHAMMAD'S OWN WORDS

"The Prophet said, 'If I take an oath and later find something else better, then I do what is better and expiate my oath.'"

Prophet of Doom was written to expose what Islam's founder had to say about himself, his ambition, religion, and god. Here are some examples:

FIGHTING:

Bukhari:V4B52N50 "The Prophet said, 'A single endeavor of fighting in Allah's Cause is better than the world and whatever is in it.'"

Qur'an 9:88 "The Messenger and those who believe with him, strive hard and fight with their wealth and lives in Allah's Cause."

Qur'an 9:5 "Fight and kill the disbelievers wherever you find them, take them captive, harass them, lie in wait and ambush them using every stratagem of war."

Qur'an 9:111 "The Believers fight in Allah's Cause, they slay and are slain, kill and are killed."

Qur'an 9:29 "Fight those who do not believe until they all surrender, paying the protective tax in submission."

Ishaq:325 "Muslims, fight in Allah's Cause. Stand firm and you will prosper. Help the Prophet, obey him, give him your allegiance, and your religion will be victorious."

Qur'an 8:39 "Fight them until all opposition ends and all submit to Allah."

Qur'an 8:39 "So fight them until there is no more Fitnah (disbelief [non-Muslims]) and all submit to the religion of Allah alone (in the whole world)."

Ishaq:324 "He said, 'Fight them so that there is no more rebellion, and religion, all of it, is for Allah only. Allah must have no rivals.'"

Qur'an 9:14 "Fight them and Allah will punish them by your hands, lay them low, and cover them with shame. He will help you over them."

Ishaq:300 "I am fighting in Allah's service. This is piety and a good deed. In Allah's war I do not fear as others should. For this fighting is righteous, true, and good."

Ishaq:587 "Our onslaught will not be a weak faltering affair. We shall fight as long as we live. We will fight until you turn to Islam, humbly seeking refuge. We will fight not caring whom we meet. We will fight whether we destroy ancient holdings or newly gotten gains. We have mutilated every opponent. We have driven them violently before us at the command of Allah and Islam. We will fight until our religion is established. And we will plunder them, for they must suffer disgrace."

Qur'an 8:65 "O Prophet, urge the faithful to fight. If there are twenty among you with determination they will vanquish two hundred; if there are a hundred then they will slaughter a thousand unbelievers, for the infidels are a people devoid of understanding."

Ishaq:326 "Prophet exhort the believers to fight. If there are twenty good fighters they will defeat two hundred for they are a senseless people. They do not fight with good intentions nor for truth."

Bukhari:V4B52N63 "A man whose face was covered with an iron mask came to the Prophet and said, 'Allah's Apostle! Shall I fight or embrace Islam first?' The Prophet said, 'Embrace Islam first and then fight.' So he embraced Islam, and was martyred. Allah's Apostle said, 'A Little work, but a great reward.'"

Bukhari:V4B53N386 "Our Prophet, the Messenger of our Lord, ordered us to fight you till you worship Allah alone or pay us the Jizyah tribute tax in submission. Our Prophet has informed us that our Lord says: 'Whoever amongst us is killed as a martyr shall go to Paradise to lead such a luxurious life as he has never seen, and whoever survives shall become your master.'"

Muslim:C34B20N4668 "The Messenger said: 'Anybody who equips a warrior going to fight in the Way of Allah is like one who actually fights. And anybody who looks after his family in his absence is also like one who actually fights."

Qur'an 9:38 "Believers, what is the matter with you, that when you are asked to go forth and fight in Allah's Cause you cling to the earth? Do you prefer the life of this world to the Hereafter? Unless you go forth, He will afflict and punish you with a painful doom, and put others in your place."

Qur'an 9:123 "Fight the unbelievers around you, and let them find harshness in you."

Qur'an 8:72 "Those who accepted Islam and left their homes to fight in Allah's Cause with their possessions and persons, and those who gave (them) asylum, aid, and shelter, those who harbored them—these are allies of one another. You are not responsible for protecting those who embraced Islam but did not leave their homes [to fight] until they do so." [Another translation reads:] "You are only called to protect Muslims who fight."

Muslim:C9B1N31 "I have been commanded to fight against people till they testify to the fact that there is no god but Allah, and believe in me (that) I am the Messenger and in all that I have brought." *Bukhari:V9B84N59* "Whoever says this will save his property and life from me.'"

Qur'an 8:73 "The unbelieving infidels are allies. Unless you (Muslims) aid each other (fighting as one united block to make Allah's religion victorious), there will be confusion and mischief. Those who accepted Islam, left their homes to fight in Allah's Cause (al-Jihad), as well as those who give them asylum, shelter, and aid—these are (all) Believers: for them is pardon and bountiful provision (in Paradise)."

Tabari IX:69 "Arabs are the most noble people in lineage, the most prominent, and the best in deeds. We were the first to respond to the call of the Prophet. We are Allah's helpers and the viziers of His Messenger. We fight people until they believe in Allah. He who believes in Allah and His Messenger has protected his life and possessions from us. As for one who disbelieves, we will fight him forever in the Cause of Allah. Killing him is a small matter to us."

Qur'an 48:16 "Say (Muhammad) to the wandering desert Arabs who lagged behind: 'You shall be invited to fight against a people given to war with mighty prowess. You shall fight them until they surrender and submit. If you obey, Allah will grant you a reward, but if you turn back, as you did before, He will punish you with a grievous torture.'"

Qur'an 48:22 "If the unbelieving infidels fight against you, they will retreat. (Such has been) the practice (approved) of Allah in the past: no change will you find in the ways of Allah."

Qur'an 47:4 "When you clash with the unbelieving Infidels in battle (fighting Jihad in Allah's Cause), smite their necks until you overpower them, killing and wounding many of them. At length, when you have thoroughly subdued them, bind them firmly, making (them) captives. Thereafter either generosity or ransom (them based upon what benefits Islam) until the war lays down its burdens. Thus are you commanded by Allah to continue carrying out Jihad against the unbelieving infidels until they submit to Islam."

Qur'an 47:31 "And We shall try you until We know those among you who are the fighters."

Tabari VI:138 "Those present at the oath of Aqabah had sworn an allegiance to Muhammad. It was a pledge of war against all men. Allah had permitted fighting."

Tabari VI:139 "Allah had given his Messenger permission to fight by revealing the verse 'And fight them until persecution is no more, and religion is all for Allah.'" [Qur'an 8:39]

Qur'an 9:19 "Do you make the giving of drink to pilgrims, or the maintenance of the Mosque, equal to those who fight in the Cause of Allah? They are not comparable in the sight of Allah. Those who believe, and left their homes, striving with might, fighting in Allah's Cause with their goods and their lives, have the highest rank in the sight of Allah."

Ishaq:550 "The Muslims met them with their swords. They cut through many arms and skulls. Only confused cries and groans could be heard over our battle roars and snarling."

Qur'an 5:94 "Believers, Allah will make a test for you in the form of a little game in which you reach out for your lances. Any who fails this test will have a grievous punishment."

Ishaq:578 "Crushing the heads of the infidels and splitting their skulls with sharp swords, we continually thrust and cut at the enemy. Blood gushed from their deep wounds as the battle wore them down. We conquered bearing the Prophet's fluttering war banner. Our cavalry was submerged in rising dust, and our spears quivered, but by us the Prophet gained victory."

Tabari IX:22 "The Prophet continued to besiege the town, fighting them bitterly."

Tabari IX:25 "By Allah, I did not come to fight for nothing. I wanted a victory over Ta'if so that I might obtain a slave girl from them and make her pregnant."

Tabari IX:82 "The Messenger sent Khalid with an army of 400 to Harith [a South Arabian tribe] and ordered him to invite them to Islam for three days before he fought them. If they were to respond and submit, he was to teach them the Book of Allah, the Sunnah of His Prophet, and the requirements of Islam. If they should decline, then he was to fight them."

Tabari IX:88 "Abdallah Azdi came to the Messenger, embraced Islam, and became a good Muslim. Allah's Apostle invested Azdi with the authority over those who had surrendered and ordered him to fight the infidels from the tribes of Yemen. Azdi left with an army by the Messenger's command. The Muslims besieged them for a month. Then they withdrew, setting a trap. When the Yemenites went in pursuit, Azdi was able to inflict a heavy loss on them."

Ishaq:530 "Get out of his way, you infidel unbelievers. Every good thing goes with the Apostle.

Lord, I believe in his word. We will fight you about its interpretations as we have fought you about its revelation with strokes that will remove heads from shoulders and make enemies of friends."

Muslim:C9B1N29 "Command For Fighting Against People So Long As They Do Not Profess That There Is No Ilah (God) But Allah And Muhammad Is His Messenger: When the Messenger breathed his last and Bakr was appointed Caliph, many Arabs chose to become apostates [rejected Islam]. Abu Bakr said: 'I will definitely fight against anyone who stops paying the Zakat tax, for it is an obligation. I will fight against them even to secure the cord used for hobbling the feet of a camel which they used to pay if they withhold it now.' Allah had justified fighting against those who refused to pay Zakat."

Muslim:C9B1N33 "The Prophet said: 'I have been commanded to fight against people till they testify there is no god but Allah, that Muhammad is the Messenger of Allah, and they establish prostration prayer, and pay Zakat. If they do it, their blood and property are protected.'"

Muslim:C10B1N176 "Muhammad (may peace be upon him) sent us in a raiding party. We raided Huraqat in the morning. I caught hold of a man and he said: 'There is no god but Allah,' but I attacked him with a spear anyway. It once occurred to me that I should ask the Apostle about this. The Messenger said: 'Did he profess "There is no god but Allah," and even then you killed him?' I said: 'He made a profession out of the fear of the weapon I was threatening him with.' The Prophet said: 'Did you tear out his heart in order to find out whether it had professed truly or not?'"

Muslim:C20B1N4597 "The Prophet said at the conquest of Mecca: 'There is no migration now, but only Jihad, fighting for the Cause of Islam. When you are asked to set out on a Jihad expedition, you should readily do so.'"

Muslim:C28B20N4628 "Allah has undertaken to provide for one who leaves his home to fight for His Cause and to affirm the truth of His word; Allah will either admit him to Paradise or will bring him back home with his reward and booty."

Muslim:C28B20N4629 "The Messenger said: 'One who is wounded in the Way of Allah—and Allah knows best who is wounded in His Way—will appear on the Day of Judgment with his wound still bleeding. The color (of its discharge) will be blood, (but) its smell will be musk.'"

Muslim: C34B20N4652-3 "The Merit Of Jihad And Of Keeping Vigilance Over The Enemy: A man came to the Holy Prophet and said: 'Who is the best of men?' He replied: 'A man who fights staking his life and spending his wealth in Allah's Cause.'"

Muslim:C42B20N4684 "A desert Arab came to the Prophet and said: 'Messenger, one man fights for the spoils of war; another fights that he may be remembered, and one fights that he may see his (high) position (achieved as a result of his valor in fighting). Which of these is fighting in the Cause of Allah?' The Messenger of Allah said: 'Who fights so that the word of Allah is exalted is fighting in the Way of Allah.'"

Muslim:C53B20N4717 "The Prophet said: 'This religion will continue to exist, and a group of people from the Muslims will continue to fight for its protection until the Hour is established.'"

Bukhari: V5B59N288 "I witnessed a scene that was dearer to me than anything I had ever seen. Aswad came to the Prophet while Muhammad was urging the Muslims to fight the pagans. He said, 'We shall fight on your right and on your left and in front of you and behind you.' I saw the face of the Prophet getting bright with happiness, for that saying delighted him."

Bukhari:V5B59N290 "The believers who did not join the Ghazwa [Islamic raid or invasion] and those who fought are not equal in reward."

Qur'an 2:193 "Fight them until there is no more Fitnah (disbelief) and religion is only for Allah. But if they cease/desist, let there be no hostility except against infidel disbelievers."

Qur'an 2:217 "They question you concerning fighting in the sacred month. Say: 'Fighting therein is a grave (matter); but to prevent access to Allah, to deny Him, to prevent access to the Sacred Mosque, to expel its members, and polytheism are worse than slaughter. Nor will they cease fighting you until they make you renegades from your religion. If any of you turn back and die in unbelief, your works will be lost and you will go to Hell. Surely those who believe and leave their homes to fight in Allah's Cause have the hope of Allah's mercy."

Qur'an 2:244 "Fight in Allah's Cause, and know that Allah hears and knows all."

Qur'an 2:246 "He said: 'Would you refrain from fighting if fighting were prescribed for you?' They said: 'How could we refuse to fight in Allah's Cause?'"

Ishaq:280 "The Apostle prepared for war in pursuance of Allah's command to fight his enemies and to fight the infidels who Allah commanded him to fight."

Qur'an 61:2 "O Muslims, why say one thing and do another? Grievously odious and hateful is it in the sight of Allah that you say that which you do not. Truly Allah loves those who fight in His Cause in a battle array, as if they were a solid cemented structure."

Bukhari:V4B52N61 "Allah's Apostle! We were absent from the first battle you fought against the pagans. If Allah gives us a chance to do battle, no doubt, He will see how bravely we fight."

Ishaq:398 "Ask them for their help. Thereby make the religion of Islam agreeable to them. And when you are resolved in the matter of religion concerning fighting your enemy you will have the advantage."

Qur'an 3:146 "How many prophets fought in Allah's Cause? With them (fought) myriads of godly men who were slain. They never lost heart if they met with disaster in Allah's Cause, nor did they weaken nor give in. Allah loves those who are firm and steadfast [warriors]."

Ishaq:393 "How many prophets has death in battle befallen and how many multitudes with him? They did not show weakness toward their enemies and were not humiliated when they suffered in the fight for Allah and their religion. That is steadfastness. Allah loves the steadfast."

Qur'an 3:153 "Behold! You ran off precipitately, climbing up the high hill without even casting a side glance at anyone, while the Messenger in your rear is calling you from your rear, urging you to fight. Allah gave you one distress after another by way of requital, to teach you not to grieve for the booty that had escaped you and for (the ill) that had befallen you."

Qur'an 3:154 "Say: 'Even if you had remained in your houses, those ordained to be slaughtered would have gone forth to the places where they were to slain."

Ishaq:440 "Helped by the Holy Spirit we smited Muhammad's foes. The Apostle sent a message to them with a sharp cutting sword."

Ishaq:470 "We attacked them fully armed, swords in hand, cutting through heads and skulls."

Qur'an 61:4 "Surely Allah loves those who fight in His Cause."

Qur'an 61:11 "Come to believe in Allah and His Apostle and struggle in the Cause of Allah with your wealth and person. This will be good for you.... Allah will give you an early victory."

Qur'an 8:5 "Your Lord ordered you out of your homes to fight for the true cause, even though some Muslims disliked it, and were averse (to fighting)."

Qur'an 24:53 "They swear their strongest oaths saying that if only you would command them. They would leave their homes (and go forth fighting in Allah's Cause). Say: 'Swear not; Obedience is (more) reasonable.'"

Qur'an 4:74 "Let those who fight in Allah's Cause sell this world's life for the hereafter. To him who fights in Allah's Cause, whether he is slain or victorious, We shall give him a reward."

Qur'an 4:75 "What reason have you that you should not fight in Allah's Cause?" [Another translation says:] "What is wrong with you that you do not fignt for Allah?"

Qur'an 4:76 "Those who believe fight in the Cause of Allah."

Qur'an 4:77 "Have you not seen those to whom it was said: Withhold from fighting, perform the prayer and pay the zakat. But when orders for fighting were issued, a party of them feared men as they ought to have feared Allah. They say: 'Our Lord, why have You ordained fighting for us, why have You made war compulsory?'"

Qur'an 4:78 "Wherever you are, death will find you, even if you are in towers strong and high! So what is wrong with these people, that they fail to understand these simple words?"

Qur'an 4:84 "Then fight (Muhammad) in Allah's Cause. Incite the believers to fight with you."

Qur'an 4:94 "Believers, when you go abroad to fight wars in Allah's Cause, investigate carefully, and say not to anyone who greets you: 'You are not a believer!' Coveting the chance profits of this life (so that you may despoil him). With Allah are plenteous spoils and booty."

Qur'an 4:95 "Not equal are believers who sit home and receive no hurt and those who fight in Allah's Cause with their wealth and lives. Allah has granted a grade higher to those who fight with their possessions and bodies to those who sit home. Those who fight He has distinguished with a special reward."

Qur'an 4:100 "He who leaves his home in Allah's Cause finds abundant resources and many a refuge. Should he die as a refugee for Allah and His Messenger His reward becomes due and sure with Allah. When you travel through the earth there is no blame on you if you curtail your worship for fear unbelievers may attack you. In truth the disbelievers are your enemy."

Qur'an 4:102 "When you (Prophet) lead them in prayer, let some stand with you, taking their arms with them. When they finish their prostrations, let them take positions in the rear. And let others who have not yet prayed come—taking all precaution, and bearing arms. The Infidels wish, if you were negligent of your arms, to assault you in a rush. But there is no blame on you if you put away your arms because of the inconvenience of rain or because you are ill; but take precaution. For the Unbelieving Infidels Allah hath prepared a humiliating punishment."

Qur'an 4:104 "And do not relent in pursuing the enemy."

TERRORISM:

Bukhari:V4B52N220 "Allah's Apostle said, 'I have been made victorious with terror.'"

Qur'an 8:12 "I shall terrorize the infidels. So wound their bodies and incapacitate them because they oppose Allah and His Apostle."

Qur'an 8:57 "If you gain mastery over them in battle, inflict such a defeat as would terrorize them, so that they would learn a lesson and be warned."

Ishaq:326 "If you come upon them, deal so forcibly as to terrify those who would follow, that they may be warned. Make a severe example of them by terrorizing Allah's enemies."

Qur'an 8:67 "It is not fitting for any prophet to have prisoners until he has made a great slaughtered in the land."

Ishaq:588 "When the Apostle descends on your land none of your people will be left when he leaves."

Tabari IX:42 "We have been dealt a situation from which there is no escape. You have seen what Muhammad has done. Arabs have submitted to him and we do not have the strength to fight. You know that no herd is safe from him. And no one even dares go outside for fear of being terrorized."

Ishaq:326 "Allah said, 'No Prophet before Muhammad took booty from his enemy nor prisoners for ransom.' Muhammad said, 'I was made victorious with terror. The earth was made a place for me to clean. I was given the most powerful words. Booty was made lawful for me. I was given the power to intercede. These five privileges were awarded to no prophet before me.'"

Ishaq:327 "Allah said, 'A prophet must slaughter before collecting captives. A slaughtered enemy is driven from the land. Muhammad, you craved the desires of this world, its goods and the ransom captives would bring. But Allah desires killing them to manifest the religion.'"

Qur'an 7:3 "Little do you remember My warning. How many towns have We destroyed as a raid by night? Our punishment took them suddenly while they slept for their afternoon rest. Our terror came to them; Our punishment overtook them."

Ishaq:510 "When the Apostle looked down on Khaybar he told his Companions, 'O Allah, Lord of the Devils and what into error they throw, and Lord of the winds and what they winnow, we ask Thee for the booty of this town and its people. Forward in the name of Allah.' He used to say this of every town he raided."

Bukhari:V5B59N512 "The Prophet offered the Fajr Prayer [Prayer of Fear] near Khaybar when it was still dark. He said, 'Allahu-Akbar!' [Allah is Greatest] Khaybar is destroyed, for whenever we approach a hostile nation to fight, then evil will be the morning for those who have been warned.' Then the inhabitants came out running on their roads. The Prophet had their men killed; their children and woman were taken as captives."

Bukhari:V9B87N127 "The Prophet said, 'I have been given the keys of eloquent speech and given victory with terror.'"

Ishaq:517 "Khaybar was stormed by the Apostle's squadron, fully armed, powerful and strong. It brought certain humiliation with Muslim men in its midst. We attacked and they met their doom. Muhammad conquered the Jews in fighting that day as they opened their eyes to our dust."

Tabari VIII:116/Ishaq:511 "So Muhammad began seizing their herds and their property bit by bit. He conquered home by home. The Messenger took some people captive, including Safiyah and her two cousins. The Prophet chose Safiyah for himself."

Bukhari:V5B59N512 "The Prophet had their men killed, their children and woman taken captive."

Tabari VIII:129 "After the Messenger had finished with the Khaybar Jews, Allah cast terror into the hearts of the Jews in Fadak when they received news of what Allah had brought upon Khaybar. Fadak became the exclusive property of Allah's Messenger."

Tabari VIII:133 "The raiding party went to Tha'labah. One of Muhammad's slaves, said, 'Prophet, I know where Tha'labah can be taken by surprise.' So Muhammad sent him with 130 men. They raided the town and drove off camels and sheep, bringing them back to Medina."

Tabari VIII:138 "Muhammad carried arms, helmets, and spears. He led a hundred horses, appointing Bahir to be in charge of the weapons and Maslamah to be in charge of the horses. When the Quraysh received word of this, it frightened them."

Qur'an 33:26 "Allah made the Jews leave their homes by terrorizing them so that you killed some and made many captive. And He made you inherit their lands, their homes, and their wealth. He gave you a country you had not traversed before."

Qur'an 59:2 "It was Allah who drove the [Jewish] People of the Book from their homes and into exile. They refused to believe and imagined that their strongholds would protect them against Allah. But Allah came at them from where they did not suspect, and filled their hearts with terror. Their homes were destroyed. So learn a lesson, O men who have eyes. This is My warning...they shall taste the torment of Fire."

Qur'an 33:60 "Truly, if the Hypocrites stir up sedition, if the agitators in the City do not desist, We shall urge you to go against them and set you over them. Then they will not be able to stay as your neighbors for any length of time. They shall have a curse on them. Whenever they are found, they shall be seized and slain without mercy—a fierce slaughter—murdered, a horrible murdering."

Tabari VIII:143 "In this year a twenty-four man raiding party led by Shuja went to the Banu Amir. He launched a raid on them and took camels and sheep. The shares of booty came to fifteen camels for each man. Also a raid led by Amr went to Dhat. He set out with fifteen men. He encountered a large force whom he summoned to Islam. They refused to respond so he killed all of them."

Bukhari:V4B52N256 "The Prophet passed by and was asked whether it was permissible to attack infidels at night with the probability of exposing their women and children to danger. The Prophet replied, 'Their women and children are from them.'"

Tabari IX:20 "The captives of Hunayn, along with their possessions, were brought to the Messenger. He ordered that their captives, animals, and their possessions be taken to Ji'ranah and held there in custody."

Ishaq:576 "Allah and His servant overwhelmed every coward. Allah honored us and made our religion victorious. We were glorified and destroyed them all. Allah humiliated them in the worship of Satan. By what our Apostle recites from the Book and by our swift horses, I liked the punishment the infidels received. Killing them was sweeter than drink. We galloped among them panting for the spoil. With our loud-voiced army, the Apostle's squadron advanced into the fray."

Ishaq:580 "Our strong warriors obey his orders to the letter. By us Allah's religion is undeniably strong. You would think when our horses gallop with bits in their mouths that the sounds of demons are among them. The day we trod down the unbelievers there was no deviation or turning from the Apostle's order. During the battle the people heard our exhortations to fight and the smashing of skulls by swords that sent heads flying. We severed necks with a warrior's blow. Often we have left the slain cut to pieces and a widow crying alas over her mutilated husband. 'Tis Allah, not man we seek to please."

Tabari IX:122 "Muhammad sent Uyaynah to raid The Banu Anbar. They killed some people and took others captive. Asma was one of the women taken prisoner."

Tabari IX:123 "Muhammad sent an expedition to Ghalib and to the land of the Banu Murrah. The raid on Amr and Abi was sent to the valley of Idam. Another by Aslami was sent to Ghabah. And Abd al-Rahman was ordered by the Messenger to lead an army to the seashore."

Tabari IX:69 "He who believes in Allah and His Messenger has protected his life and possessions from us. As for those who disbelieve, we will fight them forever in the Cause of Allah. Killing them is a small matter to us."

Bukhari:V5B59N516 "When Allah's Apostle fought or raided people we raised our voices saying, 'Allahu-Akbar! Allahu-Akbar! None has the right to be worshipped but Allah.'"

Tabari VII:10 "In Ramadhan, seven months after the Hijrah, Muhammad entrusted a white war banner to Hamzah with the command of thirty Emigrants. Their aim was to intercept a Quraysh caravan."

Ishaq:281 "The Raid on Waddan was the first Maghazi [invasion]. The Expedition of Harith was second. They encountered a large number of Quraysh in the Hijaz. Abu Bakr composed a poem about the raid: 'When we called them to the truth they turned their backs and howled like bitches. Allah's punishment on them will not tarry. I swear by the Lord of Camels [Allah?] that I am no perjurer. A valiant band will descend upon the Quraysh which will leave women husbandless. It will leave men dead, with vultures wheeling round. It will not spare the infidels.'"

Ishaq:285 "Then the Apostle went raiding in the month of Rabi u'l-Awwal making for the Quraysh. Then he raided the Quraysh by way of Dinar." *Tabari VII:11* "In this year the Messenger entrusted to Sa'd a white war banner for the expedition to Kharrar. Sa'd said, 'I set out on foot at the head of twenty men. We used to lie hidden by day and march at night, until we reached Kharrar on the fifth morning. The caravan had arrived in town a day before. There were sixty men with it." *Tabari VII:11* "The Messenger of Allah went out on a raid as far as Waddan, searching for Quraysh."

Tabari VII:15 "Expeditions Led by Allah's Messenger: In this year, according to all Sira writers, the Messenger personally led the Ghazwa of Alwa. [A Ghazwa is an Islamic Invasion in Allah's Cause consisting of an army unit led by the Prophet himself.] He left Sa'd in command of Medina. On this raid his banner was carried by Hamzah. He stayed out for fifteen days and then returned to Medina. The Messenger went on a Ghazwa at the head of two hundred of his companions in October, 623 and reached Buwat. His intention was to intercept a Quraysh caravan with a hundred men and twenty-five hundred camels."

Ishaq:286 "Meanwhile the Apostle sent Sa'd on the raid of Abu Waqqas. The Prophet only stayed a few nights in Medina before raiding Ushayra and then Kurz."

Bukhari:V5B57N51 "The Apostle said, 'Tomorrow I will give the flag to a man whose leadership

Allah will use to grant a Muslim victory."

Bukhari:V5B59N569 "I fought in seven Ghazwat battles along with the Prophet and fought in nine Maghazi raids in armies dispatched by the Prophet."

Bukhari:V5B57N74 "I heard Sa'd saying, 'I was the first Arab to shoot an arrow in Allah's Cause.'"

Bukhari:V5B59N401 "Allah's Wrath became severe on anyone the Prophet killed in Allah's Cause."

Bukhari:V5B59N456 "Muhammad led the Fear Prayer [Allahu Akbar!] with one batch of his army while the other (batch) faced the enemy."

Bukhari:V5B59N440 "Allah's Apostle used to say, 'None has the right to be worshipped except Allah Alone because He honored His Warriors and made His Messenger victorious. He defeated the clans; so there is nothing left.'"

Ishaq:287 "The Muslim raiders consulted one another concerning them. One of the Muslims said, 'By Allah, if we leave these people alone, they will get into the sacred territory and will be safely out of our reach. If we kill them we will have killed in the sacred month.'" *Tabari VII:19* "They hesitated and were afraid to advance, but then they plucked up courage and agreed to kill as many as they could and to seize what they had with them. Waqid shot an arrow at Amr and killed him. Uthman and al-Hakam surrendered. Then Waqid and his companions took the caravan and the captives back to Allah's Apostle in Medina. This was the first booty taken by the Companions of Muhammad."

Ishaq:289 "Our lances drank of Amr's blood and lit the flame of war." *Tabari VII:20/Ishaq:287* "Abd Allah told his Companions, 'A fifth of the booty we have taken belongs to the Apostle.' This was before Allah made surrendering a fifth of the booty taken a requirement."

Tabari VII:20/Ishaq:288 "The Quraysh said, 'Muhammad and his Companions have violated the sacred month, shed blood, seized property, and taken men captive.' The polytheists spread lying slander concerning him, saying, 'Muhammad claims that he is following obedience to Allah, yet he is the first to violate the holy month and to kill our people.'"

Ishaq:288 "When the Qur'an passage concerning this matter was revealed, and Allah relieved Muslims from their fear and anxiety, Muhammad took possession of the caravan and prisoners. The Quraysh sent him a ransom and the Prophet released the prisoners on payment. When the Qur'an authorization came down to Muhammad, Abd Allah and his Companions were relieved and they became anxious for an additional reward. They said, 'Will this raid be counted as part of the reward promised to Muslim combatants?' So Allah sent down this Qur'an: 'Those who believe and have fought in Allah's Cause may receive Allah's mercy.' Allah made the booty permissible. He divided the loot, awarding four-fifths to the men He had allowed to take it. He gave one-fifth to His Apostle."

Ishaq:288 "Allah divided the booty stolen from the first caravan after he made spoils permissible. He gave four-fifths to those He had allowed to take it and one-fifth to His Apostle."

Tabari VII:29/Ishaq:289 "The Apostle heard that Abu Sufyan [a Meccan merchant] was coming from Syria with a large caravan containing their money and their merchandise. He was accompanied by only thirty men." *Ishaq:289* "Muhammad summoned the Muslims and said, 'This is the Quraysh caravan containing their property. Go out and attack it. Perhaps Allah will give it to us as prey."

Tabari VII:29 "Abu Sufyan and the horsemen of the Quraysh were returning from Syria following the coastal road. When Allah's Apostle heard about them he called his companions together and told them of the wealth they had with them and the fewness of their numbers. The Muslims set out with no other object than Sufyan and the men with him. They did not think that this raid would be anything other than easy booty."

Bukhari:V5B59N702 "Allah did not admonish anyone who had not participated in the Ghazwa [raid] of Badr, for in fact, Allah's Apostle had only gone out in search of the Quraysh caravan so that he could rob it. But Allah arranged for the Muslims and their enemy to meet by surprise. I was at the Aqaba pledge with Allah's Apostle when we gave our lives in submission, but the Badr battle is more popular amongst the people. I was never stronger or wealthier than I was when I followed the Prophet on a Ghazwa.'"

Tabari VII:29 "They did not suppose that there would be a great battle. Concerning this Allah revealed a Qur'an: *Qur'an 8:7* 'Behold! Allah promised you that one of the two parties would be yours. You wished for the unarmed one, but Allah willed to justify His truth according to His words and to cut off the roots of the unbelievers.'"

Tabari VII:29 "When Abu Sufyan heard that Muhammad's Companions were on their way to intercept his caravan, he sent a message to the Quraysh. 'Muhammad is going to attack our caravan, so protect your merchandise.' When the Quraysh heard this, the people of Mecca hastened to defend their property and protect their men as they were told Muhammad was lying in wait for them." *Ishaq:290* "Some Meccans got up to circumambulate the Ka'aba.... Sitting around the mosque, they wondered why they had allowed this evil rascal to attack their men."

Ishaq:292 "Setting out in Ramadhan, Muhammad was preceded by two black flags. His companions had seventy camels." *Tabari VII:38* "I have been informed by authorities that Muhammad set out on 3 Ramadhan at the head of 310 of his companions. The war banner of the Messenger was carried by Ali. The banner of the Ansar was carried by Sa'd."

Ishaq:293/Tabari VII:30 "The prophet marched forward and spent the night near Badr with his Companions. While the Prophet was standing in prayer [asking Allah to help him steal] some Quraysh water-carriers came to the well. Among these was a black slave. Muhammad's men seized him and brought him to the Messenger's bivouac. They ordered him to salute Allah's Apostle. Then they questioned him about Abu Sufyan. When the slave began to tell them about the protecting force, it was unwelcome news, for the only object of their raid was the caravan." *Tabari VII:30* "Meanwhile the Prophet was praying, bowing and prostrating himself, and also seeing and hearing the treatment of the slave. They beat him severely and continued to interrogate him but they found that he had no knowledge of what they were looking for."

Ishaq:294 "The Apostle was afraid the Ansar would not feel obliged to help him fight without the enemy being the aggressor and attacking in Medina. Sa'd said, 'We hear and obey. We are experienced in war, trustworthy in combat. Allah will let us show you something that will bring you joy. The Apostle was delighted at Sa'd's words which greatly encouraged him. Muhammad shouted, 'It is as if I see the enemy lying prostrate.'"

Tabari VII:32 "When the Quraysh advanced, Muhammad threw dust in the direction of their faces, and Allah put them to flight.... The Meccan [merchant] force and the Prophet's [pirates] met and Allah gave victory to His Messenger, shamed the unbelievers, and satisfied the Muslims' thirst for revenge." *Ishaq:297* "When the Apostle saw them he cried, 'Allah, they called me a liar. Destroy them this morning.'"

Bukhari:V5B59N330/Ishaq:300 "Here is Gabriel holding the rein of a horse and leading the charge. He is equipped with his weapons and ready for the battle. There is dust upon his front teeth." *Bukhari:V5B59N327* "Gabriel came to the Prophet and said, 'How do you view the warriors of Badr?' The Prophet said, 'I see the fighters as the best Muslims.' On that, Gabriel said, 'And so are the Angels who are participating in the Badr battle.'"

Tabari VII:55 "Mihaja, the mawla [slave] of Umar [the future Caliph] was struck by an arrow and killed. He was the first Muslim to die."

Tabari VII:55 "Allah's Messenger went out to his men and incited them to fight. He promised, 'Every man may keep all the booty he takes.' Then Muhammad said, 'By Allah, if any man fights today and is killed fighting aggressively, going forward and not retreating, Allah will cause him to enter Paradise.' Umayr, who was holding some dates in his hand and eating them, said, 'Fine, fine. This is excellent! Nothing stands between me and my entering Paradise except to be killed by these people!' He threw down the dates, seized his sword, and fought until he was slain."

Tabari VII:56 "'Messenger of Allah, what makes the Lord laugh with joy at his servant?' He replied, 'When he plunges his hand into the midst of an enemy without armor.' So Auf took off the coat of mail he was wearing and threw it away. Then he took his sword and fought the enemy until he was killed."

Ishaq:301 "Muhammad picked up a handful of pebbles and faced the Quraysh. He shouted, 'May their faces be deformed!' He threw the pebbles at them and ordered his companions to attack. The foe was routed. Allah killed Quraysh chiefs and caused many of their nobles to be taken captive. While the Muslims were taking prisoners, the Messenger was in his hut."

Bukhari:V5B59N290 "The Prophet said, 'The believers who failed to join the Ghazwa of Badr and those who took part in it are not equal in reward.'"

Bukhari:V5B59N333 "Az-Zubair said, 'I attacked him with my spear and pierced his eye. I put my foot over his body to pull the weapon out, but even then I had to use great force. Later on Allah's Apostle asked me for that spear and I gave it to him.'"

Ishaq:301 "As the Muslims were laying their hands on as many prisoners as they could catch, the Prophet, saw disapproval in the face of Sa'd. He said, 'Why are you upset by the taking of captives?' Sa'd replied, 'This was the first defeat inflicted by Allah on the infidels. Slaughtering the prisoners would have been more pleasing to me than sparing them.'"

Tabari VII:59 "On the day of Badr I passed Umayyah as he was standing with his son Ali, holding his hand. I had with me some coats of mail which I had taken as plunder. Umayyah said, 'Abd al-Ilah, would you like to take me as a prisoner? I will be more valuable to you as a captive to be ransomed than the coats of mail that you are carrying.' I said, 'Yes. Come here then.' I flung away the armor and bound Umayyah and his son Ali, taking them with me. Muslims encircled us. Then they restrained us physically. One of the Muslims drew his sword and struck Ali in the leg, severing it so that he fell down. Umayyah gave a scream the like of which I have never heard. I said, 'Save yourself, for there is no escape for your son. By Allah, I cannot save him from these men.' Then the Muslims hacked Ali to pieces. Abd al-Rahman used to say, 'May Allah have mercy on Bial [a slave turned Muslim marauder]! I lost my coats of mail, and he deprived me of my captives.'"

Bukhari:V5B59N297 "The Prophet faced the Ka'aba and invoked evil on the Quraysh people."

Bukhari: V5B59N397 "Allah's Apostle raised his head after bowing the first Rak'a of the morning prayer. He said, 'O Allah! Curse so-and-so and so-and-so.' After he had invoked evil upon them, Allah revealed: 'Your Lord will send thousands of angels riding upon chargers sweeping down as a form of good tidings to reassure you that victory comes from Him. He will cut off parts of the unbelievers, overthrow them, and turn them back in frustration. For Allah is forgiving and kind.'" [3:124]

Ishaq:303 "A cousin and I mounted a hill from which we could overlook Badr and see who would be defeated, so that we could join in the plundering afterwards. I was pursuing one of the Meccan polytheists in order to smite him, when his head suddenly fell off before my sword touched him. Then I knew that someone other than I had killed him."

Tabari VII:61 "When the Prophet had finished with his enemy, he gave orders that Abu Jahl should be found among the dead. He said, 'O Allah, do not let him escape!' The first man who encountered Abu Jahl yelled out and I made him my mark. When he was within my reach, I attacked him and struck him a blow which severed his foot and half his leg. By Allah, when it flew off I could only compare it to a date-stone which flies out of a crusher when it is struck. Then his son hit me on the shoulder and cut off my arm. It dangled at my side from a piece of skin. The fighting prevented me from reaching him after that. I fought the whole day, dragging my arm behind me. When it began to hurt me, I put my foot on it and stood until I pulled it off.'" *Ishaq:304* "Abd Allah bin Mas'ud said, 'I found Abu Jahl in the throws of death. I put my foot on his neck because he had grabbed me once at Mecca and had hurt me. Then I said, Has Allah disgraced you and put you to shame, O enemy of Allah?' 'In what way has he disgraced me?' he asked. 'Am I anything more important than a man whom you have killed?'" *Bukhari:V5B59N298* "Abu Jahl said, 'You should not be proud that you have killed me.'"

Ishaq:304/Tabari VII:62 "I cut off Abu Jahl's head and brought it to the Messenger. 'O Allah's Prophet, this is the head of the enemy of Allah.' Muhammad said, 'Praise be to Allah.'"

Ishaq:305 "Ukkasha fought until he broke his sword. He came to the Apostle who gave him a wooden cudgel telling him to fight with that. He brandished it and it became a brilliant weapon. Allah gave him victory while he wielded it. He took that weapon with him to every raid he fought with Allah's Apostle until he was killed in the rebellion. These were his dying words: 'What do you think about when you kill people? Are these not men just because they are not Muslims?'"

Ishaq:315 "It was so criminal, men could hardly imagine it. Muhammad was ennobled because of the bloody fighting. I swear we shall never lack soldiers, nor army leaders. Driving before us infidels until we subdue them with a halter above their noses and a branding iron. We will drive them to the ends of the earth. We will pursue them on horse and on foot. We will never deviate from fighting in our cause. We will bring upon the infidels the fate of the Ad and Jurhum. Any people that disobey Muhammad will pay for it. If you do not surrender to Islam, then you will live to regret it. You will be shamed in Hell, forced to wear a garment of molten pitch forever!"

Ishaq:310 "A Meccan said, 'As soon as we were confronted by the raiding party, we turned our backs and they started killing and capturing us at their pleasure. Some of our men turned tail humiliated. Allah smote some of us with pustules from which we died.'" *Ishaq:311* "When the Quraysh began to bewail their dead, consumed in sorrow, one said, 'Do not do this for Muhammad and his companions will rejoice over our misfortune.'"

Ishaq:340 "Surely Badr was one of the world's great wonders. The roads to death are plain to see. Disobedience causes a people to perish. They became death's pawns. We had sought their caravan, nothing else. But they came to us and there was no way out. So we thrust our shafts and swung our swords severing their heads. Our swords glittered as they killed. The banner of error was held by Satan. He betrayed the evil ones, those prone to treachery. He led them to death crying, 'Fear Allah. He is invincible!' On that day a thousand spirits were mustered on excited white stallions. Allah's army fought with us. Under our banner, Gabriel attacked and killed them."

Ishaq:341 "Allah favored His Apostle and humiliated the unbelievers. They were put to shame in captivity and death. The Apostle's victory was glorious. Its message is plain for all to see. The Lord brought repeated calamities upon the pagans, bringing them under the Apostle's power. Allah's angry army smote them with their trusty swords. Many a lusty youngster left the enemy lying prone. Their women wept with burning throats for the dead were lying everywhere. But now they are all in Hell."

Ishaq:342 "I wonder at foolish men like these who sing frivolously and vainly of the slain at Badr. This was nothing more than an impious and odious crime. Men fought against their brothers, fathers, and sons. Any with discernment and understanding recognize the wrong that was done here."

Ishaq:344 "I wonder at Allah's deed. None can defeat Him. Evil ever leads to death. We unsheathed our swords and testified to the unity of Allah, and we proved that His Apostle brought truth. We smote them and they scattered. The impious met death. They became fuel for Hell. All who aren't Muslims must go there. It will consume them while the Stoker [Allah] increases the heat. They had called Allah's Apostle a liar. They claimed, 'You are nothing but a sorcerer.' So Allah destroyed them."

Ishaq:348 "They retreated in all directions. They rejected the Qur'an and called Muhammad a liar. But Allah cursed them to make his religion and Apostle victorious. They lay still in death. Their throats were severed. Their foreheads embraced the dust. Their nostrils were defiled with filth. Many a noble, generous man we slew this day. We left them as meat for the hyenas. And later, they shall burn in the fires of Hell."

Ishaq:349 "The battle will tell the world about us. Distant men will heed our warning. The infidels may cut off my leg, yet I am a Muslim. I will exchange my life for one with virgins fashioned like the most beautiful statues."

Ishaq:357 "Their leaders were left prostrate. Their heads were sliced off like melons. Many an adversary have I left on the ground to rise in pain, broken and plucked. When the battle was joined I dealt them a vicious blow. Their arteries cried aloud, their blood flowed."

Ishaq:308 "Muhammad halted on a sandhill and divided the booty Allah had given him. They congratulated him on the victory Allah had granted. But one of the warriors replied, 'What are you congratulating us about? We only met some bald old women like the sacrificial camels who are hobbled, and we slaughtered them!' The Apostle smiled because he knew that description fit ."

Tabari VII:81 "The next day I went to the Prophet. He was sitting with Abu Bakr, and they were weeping. I said, 'O Messenger of Allah, tell me, what has made you weep? If I find cause to weep, I will weep with you, and if not, I will pretend to weep because you are weeping.' The Prophet said, 'It is because of the taking of ransoms. It was laid before me that I should punish them instead.' Allah revealed: 'It is not for any Prophet to have captives until he has made slaughter in the land.' After that Allah made booty lawful for them."

Tabari VII:98 "The Messenger ordered Zayd [the prophet's former slave turned adoptive son] out on a raid in which he captured a Quraysh caravan led by Abu Sufyan at a watering place in Najd…. A number of their merchants set out with a large amount of silver since this was the main part of their merchandise. They hired a man to guide them along this route. Zayd captured the caravan and its goods but was unable to capture the men. He brought the caravan to the Prophet." [If this isn't piracy and terror the words need to be redefined.]

Tabari VII:98 "The reason for this expedition was the Quraysh said, 'Muhammad has damaged our trade, and sits astride our road. If we stay in Mecca we will consume our capital.' …The news of the caravan reached the Prophet, as did the information that it contained much wealth and silver vessels. Zayd therefore intercepted it and made himself master of their caravan. The fifth (khums) was twenty thousand dirhams; Allah's Apostle took it and divided the other four fifths among the members of the raiding party. Furat was taken captive. They said to him. 'If you accept Islam the Messenger will not kill you.'"

Qur'an 3:150 "Soon We shall strike terror into the hearts of the Infidels, for that they joined companions with Allah, for which He had sent no authority: their abode will be in the Fire!"

Ishaq:395 "Muslims, if you listen to the unbelievers you will retreat from the enemy and become losers. Ask Allah for victory and do not retreat, withdrawing from His religion. 'We will terrorize those who disbelieve. In that way I will help you against them.'"

Qur'an 33:9 "O ye who believe! Remember the Grace of Allah, on you, when there came down an army. But We sent against them a hurricane and forces that ye saw not. Behold! They came on you from above you and from below you, and behold, the eyes became dim and the hearts gaped up to the throats, stupefied with terror, and ye imagined various vain thoughts about Allah!"

Ishaq:461 "Muhammad besieged them for twenty-five nights. When the siege became too severe for them, Allah terrorized them. Then they were told to submit."

WAR:

Ishaq:208 "When Allah gave permission to his Apostle to fight, the second Aqaba contained conditions involving war which were not in the first act of submission. Now we bound ourselves to war against all mankind for Allah and His Apostle. He promised us a reward in Paradise for faithful service. We pledged ourselves to war in complete obedience to Muhammad no matter how evil the circumstances."

Ishaq:472 "Muhammad's Companions are the best in war."

Qur'an 8:7 "Allah wished to confirm the truth by His words: 'Wipe the infidels out to the last.'"

Qur'an 8:12 "Your Lord inspired the angels with the message: 'I am with you. Give firmness to the Believers. I will terrorize the unbelievers. Therefore smite them on their necks and every joint and incapacitate them. Strike off their heads and cut off each of their fingers and toes."

Qur'an 8:15 "Believers, when you meet unbelieving infidels in battle while you are marching for war, never turn your backs to them. If any turns his back on such a day, unless it be in a stratagem of war, a maneuver to rally his side, he draws on himself the wrath of Allah, and his abode is Hell, an evil refuge!"

Qur'an 8:39 "So, fight them till all opposition ends and the only religion is Islam."

Qur'an 8:45 "O believers! When you meet an army, be firm, and think of Allah's Name much; that you may prosper."

Qur'an 8:57 "If you meet them in battle, inflict on them such a defeat as would be a lesson for those who come after them, that they may be warned."

Qur'an 8:58 "If you apprehend treachery from any group on the part of a people (with whom you have a treaty), retaliate by breaking off (relations) with them. The infidels should not think that they can bypass (the law or punishment of Allah). Surely they cannot get away." [Another translation reads:] "The unbelieving infidels should not think that they can bypass Islam; surely they cannot escape."

Qur'an 8:59 "The infidels should not think that they can get away from us. Prepare against them whatever arms and weaponry you can muster so that you may terrorize them. They are your enemy and Allah's enemy."

Qur'an 8:60 "And make ready against the infidels all of the power you can, including steeds of war [the Noble Qur'an says these are: tanks, planes, missiles, and artillery] to threaten the enemy of Allah and your enemy. And whatever you spend in Allah's Cause shall be repaid unto you." [Another translation reads:] *Qur'an 8:60* "Prepare against them whatever arms and cavalry you can muster that you may strike terror in the enemies of Allah, and others besides them not known to you. Whatever you spend in Allah's Cause will be repaid in full, and no wrong will be done to you."

Qur'an 8:71 "He will give you mastery over them."

Ishaq:204 "'Men, do you know what you are pledging yourselves to in swearing allegiance to this man?' 'Yes. In swearing allegiance to him we are pledging to wage war against all mankind.'"

Ishaq:471 "We are steadfast trusting Him. We have a Prophet by whom we will conquer all men."

Qur'an 4:77 "Lord, why have You ordained fighting for us, why have You made war compulsory?"

Qur'an 4:71 "Believers, take precautions and advance in detachments or go (on expeditions) together in one troop.'"

Ishaq:322 "Allah said, 'Do not turn away from Muhammad when he is speaking to you. Do not contradict his orders. And do not be a hypocrite, one who pretends to be obedient to him and then disobeys him. Those who do so will receive My vengeance. You must respond to the Apostle when he summons you to war."

Ishaq:544 "Hassan incited the men, reciting: 'This is the time for war. Don't feel safe from us. Our swords will open the door to death.'"

Bukhari:V5B57N1 "Allah's Apostle said, 'A time will come when a group of Muslims will wage a Holy War and it will be said, "Is there anyone who has accompanied Allah's Apostle?" They will say, "Yes." And so victory will be bestowed on them.'"

Ishaq:574 "In faith I do not fear the army of fate. He gave us the blood of their best men to drink when we led our army against them. We are a great army with a pungent smell. And we attack continuously, wherever our enemy is found."

Qur'an 9:5 "When the sacred forbidden months for fighting are past, fight and kill disbelievers wherever you find them, take them captive, beleaguer them, and lie in wait and ambush them using every stratagem of war.

Qur'an 67:20 "Who is he that will send an army to assist you besides Ar-Rahman?"

Tabari IX:115 "The military expeditions (Ghazawat) in which the Messenger personally participated were twenty-six. Some say there were twenty-seven." *Tabari IX:118* "The armies and raiding parties sent by the Messenger of Allah between the time he came to Medina and his death (ten years) was forty-eight."

Qur'an 48:15 "Those who lagged behind (will say), when you marched forth to capture booty in war: 'Permit us to follow you.'"

Qur'an 47:20 "Those who believe say, 'How is it that no surah was sent down (for us)?' But when a categorical [definite or uncompromising] surah is revealed, and fighting and war (Jihad, holy fighting in Allah's Cause) are ordained, you will see those with diseased hearts looking at you (Muhammad) fainting unto death. Therefore woe to them!"

Tabari VIII:159 "The people began to throw dust at the army, saying, 'You retreating runaways. You fled in the Cause of Allah!' But the Messenger said, 'They are not fleers. Allah willing, they are ones who will return to fight another day.'"

Qur'an 9:25 "Assuredly, Allah did give you victory on many battlefields.... Allah did send down His forces (angels) which you saw not. He punished the Infidels. Such is their reward."

Qur'an 9:41 "March forth (equipped) with light or heavy arms. Strive with your goods and your lives in the Cause of Allah. That is best for you."

Ishaq:548 "The squadrons of the Messenger, composed of Emigrants and Ansar in iron armor with only their eyes visible, passed by. His company had become great. Woe to you, none can withstand him. It was all due to his prophetic office."

Tabari IX:20 "The Messenger and his companions went directly to Ta'if. They encamped there for a fortnight, waging war. The townsfolk fought the Muslims from behind the fort. None came out in the open. All of the surrounding people surrendered and sent their delegations to the Prophet. After besieging Ta'if for twenty days, Muhammad left and halted at Ji'ranah where the captives of Hunayn were held with their women and children. It is alleged that those captives taken numbered six thousand with women and children."

Tabari VIII:176 "The Prophet sent out his army in divisions. Zubayr was in charge of the left wing. He was ordered to make an entry with his forces from Kuda. Sa'd was commanded to enter with forces by way of Kada. Allah's Apostle said, 'Today is a day for battle and war. Sanctuary is no more. Today the sacred territory is deemed profane [ungodly and sacrilegious].' When one of the Muhajirs [Emigrants] heard him say this, he warned the Apostle, 'It is to be feared that you would resort to violence.' The Prophet ordered Ali to go after him, to take the flag from him, and fight with it himself."

Tabari IX:8 "The Messenger marched with 2,000 Meccans and 10,000 of his Companions who had come with him to facilitate the conquest of Mecca. Thus there were 12,000 in all."

Bukhari:V5B59N320 "Allah's Apostle said, 'When your enemy comes near shoot at them but use your arrows sparingly (so that they are not wasted).'"

Ishaq:572 "Muhammad is the man, an Apostle of my Lord. Evil was the state of our enemy so they lost the day. Fortunes change and we came upon them like lions from the thickets. The armies of Allah came openly, flying at them in rage, so they could not get away. We destroyed them and forced them to surrender. In the former days there was no battle like this; their blood flowed freely. We slew them and left them in the dust. Those who escaped were choked with terror. A multitude of them were slain. This is Allah's war in which those who do not accept Islam will have no helper. War destroyed the tribe and fate the clan."

Ishaq:580 "We helped Allah's Apostle, angry on his account, with a thousand warriors. We carried his flag on the end of our lances. We were his helpers, protecting his banner in deadly combat. We dyed it with blood, for that was its color. We were the Prophet's right arm in Islam. We were his bodyguards before other troops served him. We helped him against his opponents. Allah richly rewarded that fine Prophet Muhammad."

Ishaq:583 "Since you have made Khalid chief of the army and promoted him, he has become a chief indeed, leading an army guided by Allah. Firmly clad in mail, warriors with lances leveled, we are a strong force not unlike a rushing torrent. We smite the wicked while we swear an oath to Muhammad...fighting in the quest of booty."

Ishaq:586 "Red blood flowed because of our rage."

Ishaq:587 "Ka'b reacted to the Apostle's decision. He said, 'We put an end to doubt at Khaybar. If our swords could have spoken, their blades would have said, "Give us Daus or Thaqif. We will tear off the roofs in Wajj. We will make homes desolate. Our cavalry will come upon you leaving behind a tangled mass. When we assault a town they sound a cry of alarm but our sharp cutting swords flash like lightning. By them we bring death to those who struggle against us. Flowing blood was mingled with saffron the morn the forces met. They were taken by surprise and we surrounded their walls with our troops. Our leader, the Prophet, was firm, steadfast, and full of wisdom. He was not frivolous nor light minded. We obey our Prophet and we obey a Lord who is Compassionate [Ar-Rahman]. We make you partners in peace and war. If you refuse we will fight you doggedly."'"

Ishaq:602 "The Apostle ordered Muslims to prepare for a military expedition so that he could raid the Byzantines."

Qur'an 47:4 "When you clash with unbelieving Infidels in battle, strike and overpower them. At length, when you have thoroughly subdued them, make them prisoners in bondage until the war lays down its burdens. Thus are you commanded. He lets you fight in order to test you. Those who are slain in Allah's Cause will never have their deeds go to waste."

Qur'an 61:14 "O Muslims! Be helpers of Allah...We gave power to those who believed against their enemies, and they prevailed."

Ishaq:441 "A sharp sword in the hand of a brave man kills his adversary."

Muslim:C34B20N4669 "The Prophet said: 'He who equips a warrior in the Way of Allah is like one who actually fights and he who looks after the family of a warrior in the Allah's Cause in fact participated in the battle.'"

Muslim:52B20N4711 "I heard the Messenger delivering a sermon from the pulpit: 'Prepare to meet them with as much strength as you can afford. Beware, strength consists in archery. Beware, strength consists in archery. Beware, strength consists in archery.'"

Muslim: 52B20N4712 "I heard the Messenger of Allah say: 'Lands shall be thrown open to you and Allah will suffice you against your enemies, but none of you should give up playing with his arrows.'"

Qur'an 100:1 "I call to witness the (cavalry steeds), the (snorting courses), that run breathing pantingly (rushing off to battle), striking sparks of fire, scouring to the raid at dawn, raising clouds of dust as they penetrate deep into the midst of a foe en masse."

Qur'an 21:44 "Do they see Us advancing, gradually reducing the land (in their control), curtailing its borders on all sides? It is they who will be overcome."

Ishaq:322 "I will cast terror into the hearts of those who reject Me. So strike off their heads and cut off their fingers. All who oppose Me and My Prophet shall be punished severely."

Qur'an 13:41 "Do they not see Us advancing from all sides into the land (of the disbelievers), reducing its borders (by giving it to believers in war victories)?"

Qur'an 33:22 "When the faithful saw the retreating allied armies this enhanced their faith and obedience...Allah drove the infidels back in their fury so that their resistance was futile."

Ishaq:404 "War has distracted me, but blame me not, 'tis my habit. Struggling with the burdens it imposes, I bear arms bestride my horse at a cavalry's gallop, running like a wild ass in the desert."

Ishaq:405 "It is your folly to fight the Apostle, for Allah's army is bound to disgrace you. Leaders of the infidels, why did you not learn?"

Tabari VIII:12/Ishaq:451 "I have heard some stories about the digging of the trench in which there is an example of Allah justifying His Apostle and confirming his prophetic office. For example, Muhammad spat on a rock, sprinkled water on it, and it crumbled. Then the Apostle said, 'I struck the first blow and what you saw flash out was that Iraq and Persia would see dog's teeth. Gabriel informed me that my nation would be victorious over them. Then I struck my second blow, and what flashed out was for the pale men in the land of the Byzantines to be bitten by the dog's teeth. Gabriel informed me that my nation would be victorious over them. Then I struck my third blow and Gabriel told me that my nation would be victorious over Yemen. Rejoice, victory shall come. This increased the Muslims faith and submission."

Tabari VIII:13 "These cities were conquered in the time of Umar, Uthman, and others, Muslims used to say, 'Conquer for yourselves whatever seems good to you; for by Allah you have conquered no city but that Muhammad was given its keys beforehand.'"

Ishaq:475 "Allah commanded that horses should be kept for His enemy in the fight so they might vex them. We obeyed our Prophet's orders when he called us to war. When he called for violent efforts we made them. The Prophet's command is obeyed for he is truly believed. He will give us victory, glory, and a life of ease. Those who call Muhammad a liar disbelieve and go astray. They attacked our religion and would not submit."

Ishaq:489 "War is kindled by passing winds. Our swords glitter, cutting through pugnacious heads. Allah puts obstacles in our victims' way to protect His sacred property and our dignity."

Qur'an 24:55 "Allah has promised to those among you who believe and do good work that He will make them rulers of the earth. He will establish in authority their religion—the one which He has chosen for them."

Ishaq:594 "The Apostle gave gifts to those whose hearts were to be won over, notably the chiefs of the army, to win them and through them the people."

Qur'an 5:33 "The punishment for those who wage war against Allah and His Messenger and strive after corruption, making mischief in the land [those who refuse to surrender to Islam] is murder, execution, crucifixion, the cutting off of hands and feet on opposite sides, or they should be imprisoned. That is their degradation and disgrace in this world. And a great torment of an awful doom awaits them in the hereafter. Except for those who repent (and become Muslims) before you overpower them and they fall into your control."

JIHAD:

Qur'an 2:216 "Jihad (holy fighting in Allah's Cause) is ordained for you (Muslims), though you dislike it. But it is possible that you dislike a thing which is good for you, and like a thing which is bad for you. But Allah knows, and you know not." [Another translation reads:] "Warfare is ordained for you."

Qur'an 4:95 "Not equal are those believers who sit at home and receive no injurious hurt, and those who strive hard, fighting Jihad in Allah's Cause with their wealth and lives. Allah has granted a rank higher to those who strive hard, fighting Jihad with their wealth and bodies to those who sit (at home). Unto each has Allah promised good, but He prefers Jihadists who strive hard and fight above those who sit home. He has distinguished his fighters with a huge reward."

Bukhari:V4B52N44 "A man came to Allah's Apostle and said, 'Instruct me as to such a deed as equals Jihad in reward.' He replied, 'I do not find such a deed.'"

Bukhari:V1B2N25 "Allah's Apostle was asked, 'What is the best deed?' He replied, 'To believe in Allah and His Apostle Muhammad.' The questioner then asked, 'What is the next best in goodness?' He replied, 'To participate in Jihad, religious fighting in Allah's Cause.'"

Qur'an 33:22 "Among the Believers are men who have been true to their covenant with Allah and have gone out for Jihad (holy fighting). Some have completed their vow to extreme and have been martyred fighting and dying in His Cause, and some are waiting, prepared for death in battle."

Bukhari:V4B53N412 "Allah's Apostle said on the day of the conquest of Mecca, 'There is no migration now, only Jihad, holy battle. And when you are called for Jihad, you should come out at once.'" *Bukhari:V4B52N311* "Allah's Apostle said, 'There is no migration after the Conquest of Mecca, but only Jihad. When you are called by the Muslim ruler for Jihad fighting, you should go forth immediately, responding to the call.'"

Muslim:C28B20N4631 "I heard Muhammad say: 'I would not stay behind when a raid for Jihad was being mobilized unless it was going to be too hard on the believers. I love that I should be killed in Allah's Cause; then I should be brought back to life and be killed again.'"

Qur'an 9:111 "Allah has purchased the believers, their lives and their goods. For them (in return) is the Garden (of Paradise). They fight in Allah's Cause, and they slay and are slain; they kill and are killed."

Bukhari:V4B52N196 "Allah's Apostle said, 'I have been ordered to fight with the people till they say, "None has the right to be worshipped but Allah."'"

Qur'an 47:4 "So, when you clash with the unbelieving Infidels in battle (fighting Jihad in Allah's Cause), smite their necks until you overpower them, killing and wounding many of them. At length, when you have thoroughly subdued them, bind them firmly, making (them) captives. Thereafter either generosity or ransom (them based upon what benefits Islam) until the war lays down its burdens. Thus are you commanded by Allah to continue carrying out Jihad against the unbelieving infidels until they submit to Islam."

Qur'an 9:91 "There is no blame on those who are old, weak, ill, or who find no resources to spend (on Jihad, holy fighting), if they are sincere (in duty) to Allah and His Messenger."

Qur'an 9:122 "It is not proper for the Believers to all go forth together to fight Jihad. A troop from every expedition should remain behind when others go to war."

Bukhari:V4B52N46 "I heard Allah's Apostle saying, 'The example of a Mujahid [Muslim fighter] in Allah's Cause—and Allah knows best who really strives in His Cause—is like a person who fasts and prays without ever stopping. Allah guarantees that He will admit the Mujahid in His Cause into Paradise if he is killed, otherwise He will return him to his home safely with rewards and war booty.'"

Bukhari:V4B52N50 "The Prophet said, 'A single endeavor of fighting in Allah's Cause is better than the world and whatever is in it.'"

Noble Qur'an 2:190 Footnote: "Jihad is holy fighting in Allah's Cause with full force of numbers and weaponry. It is given the utmost importance in Islam and is one of its pillars. By Jihad Islam is established, Allah's Word is made superior (which means only Allah has the right to be worshiped), and Islam is propagated. By abandoning Jihad Islam is destroyed and Muslims fall into an inferior position; their honor is lost, their lands are stolen, their rule and authority vanish. Jihad is an obligatory duty in Islam on every Muslim. He who tries to escape from this duty, or does not fulfill this duty, dies as a hypocrite."

Bukhari:V4B52N65 "A man came to the Prophet and asked, 'A man fights for war booty; another fights for fame and a third fights for showing off; which of them fights in Allah's Cause?' The Prophet said, 'He who fights that Allah's Word, Islam, should be superior, fights in Allah's Cause.'"

Muslim:C40B20N4676 "Jihad Is Compulsory."

Bukhari:V4B52N284-5 "When the Divine Inspiration [Qur'an surah]: 'Those of the believers who sit at home,' was revealed, Maktum came to the Prophet while he was dictating the verse. 'O Allah's Apostle! If I were able, I would take part in Jihad.' So Allah sent down revelation to His Apostle: '...except those who are disabled, blind, or lame.'"

Muslim:C40B20N4676 "Believers who sit home and those who go out for Jihad in Allah's Cause are not equal."

Bukhari:V4B52N54 "The Prophet said, 'Were it not for the believers who do not want to be without me, I would always go forth in army-units setting out for Jihad.'"

Bukhari:V4B52N216 "Allah's Apostle said, 'Were it not for fear it would be difficult for my followers, I would not have remained behind any army units. But I don't have riding camels and have no other means of conveyance. No doubt I wish I could fight in Allah's Cause and be martyred and come to life to be martyred again.'" *Bukhari:V4B52N231* "Allah's Apostle came to Mecca the day of the Conquest riding his she-camel on which Usama was riding behind him." [Muhammad was lying.]

Bukhari:V4B52N59 "Allah's Apostle said, 'By Him in Whose Hands my soul is! Whoever is wounded in Allah's Cause...and Allah knows well who gets wounded in His Cause...will come with his wound having the color of blood but the scent of musk.'"

Bukhari:V4B52N45 "Someone asked, 'Allah's Apostle, who is the best among the people?' He replied, 'A believer who strives his utmost in Allah's Cause with his life and property.'"

Bukhari:V4B52N48 "The people said, 'Allah's Apostle! Acquaint the people with the good news.' He said, 'Paradise has one hundred grades which Allah has reserved for the Mujahidin who fight in His Cause.'"

Bukhari:V4B52N66 "Allah's Apostle said, 'Anyone whose feet get covered with dust in Allah's Cause will not be touched by the Hell Fire.'"

Bukhari:V4B52N137 "The Prophet said, 'Paradise is for him who holds the reins of his horse to strive in Allah's Cause with his hair unkempt and feet covered with dust. If he is appointed in the front line, he is perfectly satisfied with his post, and if in the rear, he accepts it.'"

Bukhari:V4B51N47 "'What causes you to smile, O Allah's Apostle?' He said, 'Some of my followers who in a dream were presented to me as fighters in Allah's Cause on board a ship amidst the sea caused me to smile.'"

Bukhari:V4B51N72 "Our Prophet told us about the message of our Lord: 'Whoever amongst us is killed will go to Paradise.' Umar asked the Prophet, 'Is it true that our men who are killed will go to Paradise and the Pagan's will go to the Hell Fire?' The Prophet said, 'Yes.'"

Bukhari:V4B51N73 "Allah's Apostle said, 'Know that Paradise is under the shade of swords.'"

Bukhari:V4B52N80 "Muhammad said, 'Allah welcomes two men with a smile; one of whom kills the other and both of them enter Paradise. One fights in Allah's Cause and gets killed. Later on Allah forgives the killer who also get martyred in Allah's Cause.'"

Bukhari:V4B52N287 "The Emigrants and the Ansar said, 'We are those who have given a pledge of allegiance to Muhammad that we will carry on Jihad as long as we live.'"

Bukhari:V4B52N94 "The Prophet said, 'Whoever spends two things in Allah's Cause [his life and his wealth], will be called by all the gatekeepers of Paradise. They will say, "O so-and-so! Come here."' Abu Bakr said, 'O Allah's Apostle! Such persons will never be destroyed.'

The Prophet said, 'I hope you will be one of them.'"

Bukhari:V4B52N130 "Aisha said, 'Whenever the Prophet intended to proceed on a raid he used to draw lots amongst his wives and would take the one upon whom the lot fell. Once, before setting out for Jihad, he drew lots and it fell on me; so I went with him."

Bukhari:V4B52N43 "Aisha said, 'Apostle! We consider Jihad as the best deed. Should we not fight in Allah's Cause?' He said, 'The best Jihad for women is the Hajj done as I have done it.'"

Bukhari:V4B52N134 "We used to take part in holy battles with the Prophet, providing his fighters with water and bringing the killed and the wounded back to Medina."

Bukhari:V4B52N175 "He heard the Prophet saying, 'Paradise is granted to the first batch of my followers who will undertake a naval expedition.' The Prophet then said, 'The first army amongst my followers who will invade Caesar's City will be forgiven their sins.'"

Bukhari:V4B52N178-9 "The Prophet said, 'One of the portents of the Hour is that you will fight people wearing shoes made of hair. And you will fight the Turks, a broad-faced people with small eyes, red faces, and flat noses. Their faces will look like shields coated with leather.'"

Bukhari:V4B52N182-4 "Allah's Apostle invoked evil upon the infidels, saying, 'O Allah! The revealer of the Holy Book, defeat these people and shake them. Fill the infidels' houses and graves with fire.'"

Bukhari:V4B52N259 "Allah's Apostle sent us on a mission as a army unit and said, 'If you find so-and-so and so-and-so, burn both of them with fire.'"

Bukhari: V4B52N203 "I heard Allah's Apostle saying, 'We are the last but will be the foremost to enter Paradise.' The Prophet added, 'He who obeys me, obeys Allah, and he who disobeys me, disobeys Allah. He who obeys the chief, obeys me, and he who disobeys the chief, disobeys me. The Imam is like a shelter for whose safety the Muslims should fight.'"

Bukhari:V4B52N208 "My brother and I came to the Prophet and asked to migrate. He said, 'Migration has passed away.' I replied, 'For what will you accept our pledge of allegiance?' He said, 'I will take the pledge for Islam and Jihad.'"

Bukhari:V4B52N220 "Allah's Apostle said, 'I have been sent with the shortest expressions bearing the widest meanings, and I have been made victorious with terror. While I was sleeping, the keys of the treasures of the world were brought to me and put in my hand.' Allah's Apostle has left the world and now we are bringing out those treasures."

Bukhari:V4B52N267 "The Prophet said, 'Khosrau will be ruined. There won't be a Persian King after him. Caesar will be ruined. There will be no Caesar after him. You will spend their treasures in Allah's Cause.' He proclaimed, 'War is deceit.'"

Bukhari:V4B53N386 "Umar sent Muslims to great countries to fight pagans. He said, 'I intend to invade Persia and Rome.' So, he ordered us to go to [the Persian King] Khosrau. When we reached the enemy, Khosrau's representative came out with 40,000 warriors, saying, 'Talk to me! Who are you?' Mughira replied, 'We are Arabs; we led a hard, miserable, disastrous life. We used to worship trees and stones. While we were in this state, our Prophet, the Messenger of our Lord, ordered us to fight you till you worship Allah Alone or pay us the Jizyah tribute tax in submission. Our Prophet has informed us that our Lord says: 'Whoever amongst us is killed as a martyr shall go to Paradise to lead such a luxurious life as he has never seen, and whoever survives shall become your master.'"

Tabari IX:49 "Muhammad urged the Muslims by way of a meeting to help cover the expenses of Jihad in Allah's Cause. The men provided mounts in anticipation of Allah's reward."

Ishaq:602 "The Apostle always referred allusively to the destination which he intended to raid. This was the sole exception, for he said plainly that he was making for the Byzantines because the journey was long, the weather was hot, and the enemy was strong." *Ishaq:603* "The Apostle went forward energetically with his preparations and ordered the men to get ready with all speed. He urged Muslims to help provide the money, mounts, and means to do Allah's work. Those who contributed earned rewards with Allah."

Tabari IX:76 "Malik has reported to me that you were the first from Himyar to embrace Islam and that you have killed infidels, so rejoice at your good fortune."

Qur'an 047.033 "Believers, obey Allah, and obey the Messenger! Those who disbelieve and hinder men from the Cause of Allah, He will not pardon. Do not falter; become faint-hearted, or weak-kneed, crying for peace. You have the upper hand."

Muslim:C29B20N4636 "The Messenger of Allah was asked: 'What deed could be equivalent to Jihad in the Cause of Allah? He answered: 'You do not have the strength to do that deed.' The question was repeated twice or thrice. Every time he answered: 'You do not have the strength to do it.' When the question was asked for the third time, he said: 'One who goes out for Jihad is like a person who keeps fasts and stands in prayer forever, never exhibiting any weariness until the Mujihid returns from Jihad.'"

Muslim:C29B20N4638 "As I was (sitting) near the pulpit of the Messenger a man said: 'I do not care if, after embracing Islam, I do not do any good deed (except) distributing drinking water to pilgrims.' Another said: 'I do not care if I do not do any good deed beyond main-tenance service to the Sacred Mosque.' Yet another said: 'Jihad in the Way of Allah is bet-ter than what you have said.' When prayer was over, I entered (the apartment of the Prophet) and asked his verdict about the matter. It was upon this that Allah, the Almighty and Exalted, revealed the Qur'anic Verse: 'Do you make the giving of drinking water to the pilgrims and the maintenance of the Sacred Mosque equal to (the service of those) who believe in Allah and strive hard and fight Jihad in His Cause. They are not equal. Those who believed and fought Jihad in Allah's Cause with their wealth and their lives are far higher in degree with Allah.'"

Muslim:C30B20N4639 "The Messenger said: 'Leaving for Jihad in the Way of Allah in the morn-ing or in the evening will merit a reward better than the world and all that is in it.'"

Muslim:C32B20N4646 "Muhammad stood up among his Companions to deliver his sermon in which he told them that Jihad in Allah's Cause and belief in Allah were the most meritorious of acts. A man stood and said: 'Messenger, do you think that if I am killed in the Way of Allah, my sins will be blotted out?' The Messenger said: 'Yes, in case you are killed in Allah's Cause and you always fought facing the enemy, never turning your back upon him.' The man asked (again).' The Messenger said: 'Yes, if you always fought facing the enemy and never retreated. Gabriel has told me this.'"

Bukhari:V4B52N104 "The Prophet said, 'Good will remain in the foreheads of horses for Jihad for they bring about a reward in Paradise or booty.'" *Bukhari:V4B52N105* "The Prophet said, 'If somebody keeps a horse in Allah's Cause motivated by His promise, then he will be rewarded for what the horse has eaten or drunk and for its dung and urine.'"

Ishaq:470 "We attacked them fully armed, swords in our hand, cutting through heads."

Ishaq:385 "Amr Jamuh was a very lame man. He had four lion-like sons who were present at the Apostle's battles. At Uhud he came to the Prophet and told him that his sons wanted to keep him back and prevent his joining the army. 'Yet, by Allah, I hope to tread in the Heavenly Garden of Paradise despite my lameness. The Apostle said, 'Allah has excused you, and Jihad is not incumbent on you.' Then Muhammad turned to his sons and said, 'You need not prevent him. Perhaps Allah will favor him with martyrdom.' So the lame old man went into battle and was killed."

Tabari VII:144/Ishaq:426 "The Muslims bivouacked for the night and were taken by surprise. So the Muslims took up their swords [not Qur'ans] to fight them, but the Lihyans said, 'We do not want to kill you. We only want to get some money by selling you to the Meccans. We swear by Allah's Covenant that we will not kill you.' 'By Allah,' Asim said, 'we will never accept a an agreement from an unbelieving infidel.' They fought until they were killed."

Bukhari:V4B52N153 "The properties of the Nadir which Allah had transferred to His Apostle as Booty were not gained by the Muslims with their horses and camels. The properties therefore, belonged especially to Allah's Apostle who used to give his family their yearly expenditure and spend what remained thereof on arms and horses to be used in Allah's Cause."

Tabari VII:162 "There is a difference of opinion as to which of his expeditions [terrorist raids] took place after the one against the Nadir. Some say Muhammad remained in Yathrib for two months before leading a raid on Najd."

Ishaq:445 "The rules of the Prayer of Fear were revealed during this raid [4:102]. The Messenger divided the Companions into two groups; one stood facing the enemy while the other stood behind the Prophet. He magnified Allah by shouting 'Allahu Akbar.' Then he and those behind him performed a rak'ah and prostrated themselves." [Magnifying Allah is "The Prayer of Fear"—appropriate for a terrorist dogma. It is comprised of shouting: Allahu Akbar—Allah is Greatest!]

Ishaq:455 "'I summon you to Allah, to His Messenger, and to Islam.' Amr replied, 'I have no use for these.' So Ali said, 'Then I summon you to fight.' Amr replied, 'Why, son of my brother? By Allah, I do not want to kill you.' Ali shouted, 'But I, by Allah, want to kill you.' Amr jumped from his horse and advanced toward Ali. The two fought until Ali killed Amr. He shouted, 'Allahu Akbar!'" *Ishaq:456* "As he returned to the Apostle smiling with joy [for having killed his uncle] Jumar asked him if he had stripped Amr of his armor. 'No,' Ali answered. 'I saw his private parts and was ashamed.'"

Bukhari:V4B52N68 "When Allah's Apostle returned from the battle of the Trench, he put down his arms and took a bath. Then Gabriel whose head was covered with dust, came to him saying, 'You have put down your arms! By Allah, I have not put down my arms yet.' Allah's Apostle said, 'Where to go now?' Gabriel said, 'This way,' pointing towards the tribe of Qurayza. So Allah's Apostle went out towards them." *Bukhari:V4B52N280* "When the Qurayza were ready to accept Sa'd's judgment, the Apostle sent for him. Sa'd proclaimed, 'I give the judgment that their men should be killed and their children and women should be taken as prisoners.' The Prophet remarked, 'O Sa'd! You have judged them with the judgment of King Allah.'"

Ishaq:485 "Muhammad found that the Lihyan had been warned. They had taken secure positions on the mountaintops. After he failed to take them by surprise as he intended, he said, 'If we go down to Usfan, the Meccans will think we have come to [terrorize] them.'" *Ishaq:486* "If the Lihyan had remained in their homes they would have met bands of fine fighters, audacious warriors who terrorize. They would have confronted an irresistible force glittering like stars. But they were weasels, sticking to the clefts of rocks instead."

Ishaq:489 "Do the bastards think that we are not their equal in fighting? We are men who believe there is no shame in killing. We don't turn from piercing lances. We smite the heads of the haughty with blows that quash the zeal of the unyielding [non-Muslims]. We're heroes, protecting our war banner. We are a noble force, as fierce as wolves. We preserve our honor and protect our property by smashing heads."

Tabari VIII:48 "Then he set out at full speed after the enemy—he was like a beast of prey."

Ishaq:490/Tabari VIII:51 "When Allah's Messenger heard about the Mustaliq gathering against him he set out and met them at one of their watering holes near the coast. The people advanced and fought fiercely. Allah caused the Mustaliq to fight and killed some of them. Allah gave the Apostle their children, women, and property as booty."

Muslim:B19N4292 "Aun inquired whether it was necessary to extend an invitation to submit to Islam before murdering infidels in the fight. Nafi told me that it was necessary in the early days of Islam. The Messenger made a raid upon Mustaliq while they were unaware and their cattle were having a drink at the water. He killed those who fought and imprisoned others. This Tradition was related by one who was among the raiding troops."

Tabari VIII:56/Ishaq:493 "According to Aisha: 'A great number of Mustaliq were wounded. The Messenger took many captives, and they were divided among all the Muslims.'"

Muslim:C26B20N4614 "I saw Allah's Messenger twisting the forelock of a horse with his fingers as he was saying: 'A great benefit. A reward for rearing them for Jihad. The spoils of war have been tied to the forelocks of horses.'"

Muslim:C28B20N4626 "Merit Of Jihad And Campaigning In Allah's Cause: The Apostle said: 'Allah has undertaken to look after the affairs of one who goes out to fight in His Way believing in Him and affirming the truth of His Apostle. He is committed that He will either admit him to Paradise or bring him back to his home with a reward or his share of booty. If a person gets wounded in Allah's Cause he will arrive on the Day of Judgment with his wound in the same condition as it was when it was first inflicted; its color will be blood but its smell will be musk perfume. If it were not too hard on Muslims I would not lag behind any raid going out to fight in the Cause of Allah. But I do not have abundant means to provide them (the Mujahids [Islamic terrorists]) with riding beasts, nor have they all have the means (to provide themselves with the weapons of Jihad). I love to fight in the Way of Allah and be killed, to fight and again be killed and to fight and be killed.'"

Tabari VIII:123/Ishaq:515 "Allah's Apostle besieged the final [Jewish] community until they could hold out no longer. Finally, when they were certain that they would perish, they asked Muhammad to banish them and spare their lives, which he did. The Prophet took possession of all their property."

Bukhari:V5B59N510 "Allah's Apostle reached Khaybar at night. It was his habit that, whenever he reached an enemy at night, he would not attack them till it was morning. When morning came, the Jews came out with their spades and baskets. When they saw the Prophet, they said, 'Muhammad! O dear God! It's Muhammad and his army!' The Prophet shouted, 'Allahu-Akbar! Khaybar is destroyed, for whenever we approach a nation, evil will be the morning for those who have been warned.'"

Bukhari:V5B59N516 "When Allah's Apostle fought the battle of Khaybar, or when he raided any other people, we raised voices crying, 'Allahu-Akbar! Allahu-Akbar!'"

Tabari VIII:130 "The Prophet conquered Khaybar by force after fighting. Khaybar was something that Allah gave as booty to His Messenger. He took one-fifth of it and divided the remainder among the Muslims."

MARTYRS/MERCENARIES:

Muslim:C31B20N4645 "The Prophet said: 'Whoever cheerfully accepts Allah as his Lord, Islam as his Religion and Muhammad as his Apostle is necessarily entitled to enter Paradise.' Abu wondered at it and said: 'Messenger of Allah, repeat that for me.' He did that and said: 'There is another act which elevates the position of a man in Paradise to a grade one hundred (higher), and the elevation between one grade and the other is equal to the height of the heaven from the earth.' Abu said: 'What is that act?' He replied: 'Jihad in the Way of Allah! Jihad in Allah's Cause!'"

Bukhari:V4B52N53 "The Prophet said, 'Nobody who dies and finds Paradise would wish to come back to this life even if he were given the whole world and whatever is in it, except the martyr who, on seeing the superiority of martyrdom, would like to come back to get killed again in Allah's Cause.'"

Bukhari:V4B52N54 "The Prophet said, 'Were it not for the believers who do not want me to leave them, I would certainly and always go forth in army units setting out in Allah's Cause. I would love to be martyred in Allah's Cause and then get resurrected and then get martyred, and then get resurrected again and then get martyred and then get resurrected again and then get martyred.'"

Qur'an 33:22 "The Believers said: 'This is what Allah and his Messenger promised us.' It added to their faith, obedience, and submission. Among the Believers are men who have been true to their covenant with Allah and have gone out for Jihad (holy fighting). Some have completed their vow to extreme (and have been martyred) fighting and dying in His Cause, and some are waiting, prepared for death in battle."

Bukhari:V4B53N386 "Our Prophet has informed us that our Lord says: 'Whoever amongst us is killed as a martyr shall go to Paradise to lead such a luxurious life as he has never seen, and whoever survives shall become your master."

Bukhari V4B52N46 "I heard Allah's Apostle saying, 'Allah guarantees that He will admit the Muslim fighter into Paradise if he is killed, otherwise He will return him to his home safely with rewards and booty.'"

Ishaq:518 "Masud was one of those who found martyrdom at Khaybar. Muhammad said, 'He has with him now his two dark-eyed virgins. When a martyr is slain, his two virgins pet him, wiping the dust from his face. They say, "May Allah throw dust on the face of the man who did this to you, and slay him who slew you!"'"

Tabari VIII:153/Ishaq:533 "Abdallah Rawahah encouraged the men, saying, 'By Allah, what you loathe is the very thing you came out to seek—martyrdom. We are not fighting the enemy with number, strength, or multitude, but we are fighting them with this religion with which Allah has honored us. So come on! Both prospects are fine: victory or martyrdom.'"

Qur'an 9:111 "Allah has purchased the believers, their lives and their goods. For them (in return) is the Garden (of Paradise). They fight in Allah's Cause, and slay others and are slain, they kill and are killed. It is a promise binding on Him in the Taurat (Torah), the Injeel (Gospel), and the Qur'an. And who is more faithful to his covenant than Allah? Then rejoice in the bargain which you have concluded. It is the achievement supreme."

Qur'an 4:74 "Let those who fight in the Cause of Allah sell the life of this world for the hereafter. To him who fights in the Cause of Allah, whether he is slain or gets victory—soon shall We give him a great reward."

Muslim:C29B20N4634 "The Messenger of Allah said, 'Nobody who dies and has something good for him with Allah will (like to) return even though he were offered the whole world and all that is in it (as an inducement), except the martyr who desires to return and be killed for the merit of martyrdom.'"

Muslim:C29B20N4635 "The Prophet said: 'Nobody who enters Paradise wants return even if he were offered everything on the surface of the earth except the martyr who will desire to return and be killed ten times for the sake of the great honor that has been bestowed upon him.'"

Bukhari:V8B76N550 "I heard Allah's Apostle saying, 'From my followers there will be a crowd of 70,000 in number who will enter Paradise all together.'"

Muslim:C33B20N4651 "We asked Abdallah about the Qur'anic Verse: 'Think not of those who are slain in Allah's way as dead. Nay, they are alive, finding their sustenance in the presence of their Lord.' (Qur'an 3:169) He said: 'We asked the Holy Prophet the meaning of the verse and he said: "The souls of martyrs live in the bodies of green birds who have their nests in chandeliers hung from the throne of the Almighty. They eat the fruits of Paradise from wherever they like and then nestle in these chandeliers. Once their Lord cast a glance at them and said: 'Do you want anything?' They said: 'What more shall we desire? We eat the fruit of Paradise from wherever we like.' Their Lord asked them the same question thrice. When they saw that they would continue to be asked and not left, they said: 'O Lord, we wish that Thou mayest return our souls to our bodies so that we may be slain in Thy Way once again.' When He (Allah) saw that they had no need, they were left (to their joy)."'"

Ishaq:400 "One whom I do not suspect told me that he was asked about these verses and he said, 'We asked Muhammad about them and we were told that when our brethren were slain at Uhud Allah put their spirits in the crops of green birds which come down to the rivers of the Garden and eat of its fruits. They say, "We should like our spirits to return to our bodies and then return to the earth and fight for You until we are killed again."'"

Muslim: C41B20N4678 "Proof Of The Martyr's Attaining Paradise: Jabir said that a man said, 'Messenger of Allah, where shall I be if I am killed?' He replied: 'In Paradise.' The man threw away the dates he had in his hand and fought until he was killed."

Muslim:C41B20N4681 "Abdallah heard it from his father who, while facing the enemy, reported that the Messenger said: 'Surely, the gates of Paradise are under the shadows of the swords.' A man in a shabby condition got up and said: 'Abu, did you hear the Prophet say this?' He said: 'Yes.' He returned to his friends and said: 'I greet you (a farewell greeting).' Then he broke the sheath of his sword, threw it away, advanced with his (naked) sword towards the enemy and fought with it until he was slain."

Muslim:C44B20N4690 "The Messenger said, 'A troop of soldiers who fight in Allah's Cause and get their share of the booty receive in advance two-thirds of their reward, and in the Hereafter one-third will remain (to their credit). If they do not receive any booty, they will get their full reward.'" *Muslim:C44B20N4691* "Muhammad said: 'A troop of soldiers, large or small, who fight get their share of the booty and return safe and sound, receive in advance two-thirds of their reward; and a troop of soldiers who return empty-handed and are afflicted or wounded will receive their full reward.'"

Muslim:51B20N4706 "Allah's Messenger said: 'Whom do you consider to be a martyr among you?' The Companions said: 'One who is slain in Allah's Cause is a martyr.' He said: 'Then (if this is the definition of a martyr) the martyrs of my Umma [Islamic community] will be small in number.' They asked: 'Prophet, who are martyrs then?' He said: 'One who is slain in Allah's Cause is a martyr; one who dies in the Way of Allah is a martyr; one who dies of plague is a martyr; one who dies of cholera is a martyr.'" *Bukhari:V4B52N282* "Allah's Apostle said, 'Five are regarded as martyrs: They are those who die because of plague, abdominal disease, drowning, a falling building, and the martyrs in Allah's Cause.'"

Ishaq:208 "Uhud commanded the Apostles archers. He was killed in the battle of Yemen as a martyr. Abu was present at all of the Apostle's battles and died in Byzantine territory as a martyr. Mu'adh was present at every raid. He was killed at Badr as a martyr. Mu'awwidh, his brother, shared the same glory. Umara was at every battle and died a martyr in Yemen. As'ad died before Badr when the Prophet's mosque was being built. The Apostle put Amr in command of the rearguard. He died at Uhud as a martyr. Abdallah led many raids and was slain as a martyr at Muta. He was one of Muhammad's commanders. Khallad fought at Badr, Uhud, and Khandaq. He was martyred fighting the [Jewish] Qurayza. The Apostle said that he would have the reward of two martyrs."

Bukhari: V5B59N377 "A man came to the Prophet and said, 'Can you tell me where I will go if I get martyred?' The Prophet replied, 'To Paradise.' The man fought till he was martyred."

Tabari VII:55 "Allah's Messenger went out to his men and incited them to fight. He promised, 'Every man may keep all the booty he takes.' Then Muhammad said, 'By Allah, if any man fights today and is killed fighting aggressively, going forward and not retreating, Allah will cause him to enter Paradise.' Umayr said, 'Fine, fine. This is excellent! Nothing stands between me and my entering Paradise except to be killed by these people!' He seized his sword, and fought until he was slain."

Ishaq:306 "When the Allah's Apostle said, '70,000 of my followers shall enter Paradise like the full moon,' Ukkasha asked if he could be one of them. Then a lesser Ansari asked to be included, but the Prophet replied, 'Ukkasha beat you to it and my prayer is now cold.'"

Bukhari:V5B59N379 "When we wrote the Qur'an, I missed one of the verses I used to hear Allah's Apostle reciting. Then we searched for it and found it. The verse was: 'Among the Believers are men who have been true to their Covenant with Allah. Of them, some have fulfilled their obligations to Allah (i.e. they have been killed in Allah's Cause), and some of them are (still) waiting to be killed.' (Surah 33.23) So we wrote this in its place in the Qur'an."

Qur'an 61:10 "Believers, shall I lead you to a bargain or trade that will save you from a painful torment? That you believe in Allah and His Messenger (Muhammad), and that you strive and fight in Allah's Cause with your property and your lives: That will be best for you!" *Qur'an 61:12* "He will forgive you your sins, and admit you to Gardens under which rivers flow, and to beautiful mansions in Eden: that is indeed the Supreme Achievement. And another (favor) which you love: help from Allah for a speedy victory over your enemies."

Bukhari:V4B52N72 "The Prophet said, 'Nobody who enters Paradise likes to go back to the world even if he got everything on the earth, except a Mujahid [Islamic fighter] who wishes to return so that he may be martyred ten times because of the dignity he receives.' Our Prophet told us about the message of Allah: 'Whoever among us is killed will go to Paradise.' Umar asked the Prophet, 'Is it not true that our men who are killed will go to Paradise and those of the Pagan's will go to Hell?' The Prophet said, 'Yes.'"

Bukhari:V4B52N63 "A man came to the Prophet and said, 'Shall I fight or embrace Islam first?' The Prophet said, 'Embrace Islam and then fight.' He became a Muslim and was martyred. The Prophet said, 'A little work, but a great reward."

Ishaq:388 "Abu Qasim [Muhammad] said, 'I testify concerning these that all wounded for Allah's sake will be raised with his wounds bleeding, the color of blood, the smell of musk. Look for the one who has remembered the most surahs and put him in front of his Companions in one mass grave.'"

Qur'an 3:140 "If you have received a blow and have been wounded, be sure a similar wound has hurt others. Such days We give to men and men by turns: that Allah may know those who believe, and that He may take to Himself from your ranks Martyrs."

Qur'an 3:156 "If you are slain, or die, in Allah's Cause [as a martyr], pardon from Allah and mercy are far better than all they could amass."

Ishaq:397 "There is no escape from death, so death for Allah's sake in battle is better than all one can amass in life while holding back from fighting in fear of death. Let not the world deceive you and be not deceived by it. Let fighting and the reward which Allah holds out to you be the most important thing."

Qur'an 3:169 "Think not of those who are slain in Allah's Cause as dead. Nay, they live, finding their provision from their Lord. Jubilant in the bounty provided by Allah: and with regard to those left behind, who have not yet joined them (in their bliss), the Martyrs glory in the fact that on them is no fear, nor have they cause to grieve. Allah will not waste the reward of the believers."

Qur'an 3:172 "Of those who answered the call of Allah and the Messenger, even after being wounded (in the fight), those who do right and ward off have a great reward."

Ishaq:400 "'If our fellow Muslims knew what Allah has done for us they would not dislike fighting or shrink from war!' And Allah said, 'I will tell them of you,' so He sent down to His Apostle these verses." *Ishaq:400* "The Apostle swore that there was no believer who had parted from the world and wanted to return to it for a single hour even if he could possess it with all it has except the martyr who would like to return and fight for Allah and be killed a second time."

Bukhari:V8B75N417 "Allah's Messenger said, 'Allah has some angels who look for those who think about Allah while they're out [fighting] and they encircle them with their wings. Allah [who hears all] asks these angels, 'What do my slaves say?' The angels reply, 'Allahu Akbar!' Allah [who sees all] asks, 'Can they see Me?' The angels answer, 'No. They can't see you.' Allah [who knows all] says, 'How would it have been if they had seen Me?' 'If they had seen You [one spirit said to another] they would have worshiped you more.' Allah [who created a brothel] asks, 'What do they desire?' 'They ask for your Paradise.' 'Have they seen it?' 'No. But if they had they would covet it all the more.' 'What do they fear?' 'Hell Fire.' 'Have they seen it?' 'No. If they had seen it they would flee it with extreme fear.' Allah said, 'I will not reduce every Companion to misery.'"

Ishaq:468 "Then Allah said, 'Some of you have fulfilled your vow to Me by dying; you have finished your work and returned to Me like those who sought martyrdom in prior battles. And some are still waiting to capitalize on Allah's promise of martyrdom. You do not hesitate in your religion and never doubt.'"

Ishaq:469 "On the day the Qurayza Jews were slain, one Muslim was martyred. A stone was thrown on him and it inflicted a shattering wound. The Apostle said, 'He will have the reward of two martyrs.'"

Tabari VIII:46 "Akhram said, 'If you believe in Allah and know that Paradise is real and that the Fire is real, don't stand between me and martyrdom!' But Abd-Rahman dismounted and thrust his spear into Akhram. So I shot Abd-Rahman with an arrow, and said, 'Take that!'"

MUSLIM MILITANTS:

Qur'an 47:4 "But if it had been Allah's will, He Himself could have exacted retribution and punished them (without your help). But He lets you fight in order to test you. But those who are killed in Allah's Cause, will never let their deeds go to waste."

Qur'an 8:72 "Those who accepted Islam and left their homes to fight in Allah's Cause with their possessions and persons, and those who gave them shelter and aided them are your allies. You are only called to protect Muslims who fight." *Qur'an 8:73* "The infidels aid one another. Unless you do the same there will be anarchy in the land. Those who accepted Islam and left their homes to fight in Allah's Cause are good Muslims."

Ishaq:406 "Among us was Allah's Apostle whose command we obey. When he gives an order we do not examine it. The spirit descends on him from his Lord. We tell him about our wishes and our desires which is to obey him in all that he wants. Cast off fear of death and desire it. Be the one who barters his life. Take your swords and trust Allah. With a compact force holding lances and spears we plunged into a sea of men.... and all were made to get their fill of evil. We are men who see no blame in him who kills."

Ishaq:414 "If you kill us, the true religion is ours. And to be killed for the truth is to find favor with Allah. If you think that we are fools, know that the opinion of those who oppose Islam is misleading. We are men of war who get the utmost from it. We inflict painful punishment on those who oppose us.... If you insult Allah's Apostle, Allah will slay you. You are a cursed, rude fellow! You utter filth, and then throw it at the clean-robed, godly, and faithful One."

Tabari VIII:153 "I ask the Merciful One for a pardon and for a sword blow that makes a wide wound that shoots out foaming blood. For a deadly thrust by a thirsty sword, and a lance that pierces right through the guts and liver. People shall say, when they pass my grave, 'Allah guided you the right way, O warrior.'"

Tabari VIII:141 "We gave them some time until their herds had come back from pasture. After they had milked their camels and set them out to rest, we launched our raid. We killed some of them, drove away their camels, and set out to return. Meanwhile, the people appealed for aid from the rest of their tribe. But we moved quickly. Reinforced, the villagers were too powerful for us. But Allah sent clouds from out of the blue, and there was a torrent that no one could cross so we eluded the tribesmen with what we had taken. The battle cry of the Companions of the Messenger of Allah that night was: 'Kill! Kill! Kill!'"

Tabari VIII:117 "The next morning Allah opened the township of Sa'b bin Mu'adh for them to conquer. There was no stronghold in Khaybar more abounding in food. After the Prophet had defeated some of their settlements and taken their property, they reached the communities of Watib and Sulalim, which were the last of the Khaybar neighborhoods to be conquered. Muhammad besieged the inhabitants between thirteen and nineteen nights."

Tabari VIII:133 "A raiding party led by Bahir went to Yumn. The Muslims went out and captured camels and sheep. A slave belonging to Uyaynah met them, and they killed him."

Tabari VIII:149 "Abdallah married a woman but couldn't afford the nuptial gift. He came to the Prophet and asked for his assistance. He said, 'Go out and spy on the Jusham tribe.' He gave me an emaciated camel and a companion. We set out armed with arrows and swords. We approached the encampment and hid ourselves. I told my companion, 'If you hear me shout Allahu Akbar and see me attack, you should shout Allah is Greatest and join the fighting.'"

Tabari VIII:150 "When their leader, Rifa'ah, came within range, I shot an arrow into his heart. I leaped at him and cut off his head. Then I rushed toward the encampment and shouted, 'Allahu Akbar!' The families who were gathered there shouted, 'Save yourself.' They gathered what property they could, including their wives and children. We drove away a great herd of camels and many sheep and goats and brought them to the Messenger. I brought him Rifa'ash's head, which I carried with me. The Prophet gave me thirteen camels from that herd as booty, and I consummated my marriage."

Tabari VIII:151 "The Prophet sent Ibn Abi out with a party of sixteen men. They were away for fifteen nights. Their share of booty was twelve camels for each man, each camel was valued in the accounting as being worth ten sheep. When the people they raided fled in various directions, they took four women, including one young woman who was very beautiful. She fell to Abu Qatadah. The Prophet asked Qatadah about her. He said, 'She came from the spoils.' The Messenger said, 'Give her to me.' So he gave her to him."

Ishaq:538 "Allah bless the martyrs lying dead at Mu'ta. Refresh their bones for they fought for

Allah's sake like good Muslims, stallions clad in mail. We are a people protected by Allah to whom he has revealed His Book, excelling in glory and honor. Our enlightened minds cover up the ignorance of others. They would not embark on such a vicious enterprise. *Tabari VII:19* "They plucked up courage and agreed to kill as many as they could and to seize what they had with them. Waqid shot an arrow at Amr and killed him. Then Abd Allah and his companions took the caravan and the captives back to Allah's Apostle in Medina. This was the first booty taken by the Companions of Muhammad."

Ishaq:289 "Our lances drank of Amr's blood and lit the flame of war."

Ishaq:288 "The Quraysh said, 'Muhammad and his Companions have violated the sacred month, shed blood, seized property, and taken men captive. Muhammad claims that he is following obedience to Allah, yet he is the first to violate the holy month and to kill.'"

Qur'an 9:23 "Believers, take not for friends your fathers and your brothers if they love disbelief above belief. If you do, you do wrong. Say: If your fathers, your sons, your families, your wives, relatives and property which you have acquired, and the slackness of trade which you fear and dwellings which you like, are dearer to you than Allah and His Messenger and striving hard and fighting in His Cause, then wait till Allah brings about His torment."

Muslim:B19N4395 "I said: 'Should I tell you a Hadith from your Traditions?' He gave an account of the Conquest of Mecca, saying: 'Muhammad advanced until he reached Mecca. He assigned Zubayr to his right flank and Khalid to his left. Then he dispatched the force that had no armor. They advanced to the interior. The Prophet was in the midst of a large contingent of his fighters. Allah's Messenger said: 'You see the ruffians and the lowly followers of the Quraysh?' He indicated by striking one of his hands over the other that they should be killed. So we went off on his orders and if anyone wanted a person killed; he was slain. No one could offer any resistance. Then [the recently "converted"] Abu Sufyan said: Messenger, the blood of the Quraysh has become very cheap. The Prophet said: 'Kill all who stand in your way.'"

Tabari VIII:171 "Muhammad said, 'Woe to the Quraysh! If Allah's Apostle surprises them in their territory and enters Mecca by force, it means the destruction of the Quraysh.'"

Ishaq:570 "The Messenger turned to Abu Sufyan, who stood fast fighting that day. He had become an excellent Muslim after embracing Islam."

Ishaq:576 "Allah's Apostle said, 'If you get hold of Bijad, don't let him escape for he has done something evil.'" *Tabari IX:18* "While fighting the Banu Sa'd, Muslim horsemen seized Bijad. They herded his family around him like cattle, and they treated them roughly."

Ishaq:558 "Allah said, I have sent an army. Every day they curse, battle and lampoon."

Ishaq:560 "We expelled the people and smote them with our swords the day the good Prophet entered Mecca. We pierced their bodies with cuts and thrusts. And we shot them with our feathered shafts. Our ranks went in with lances leveled. We came to plunder as we said we would. We pledged our faith to the Apostle on this day of fear."

Ishaq:561 "The Apostle sent out troops to the territories surrounding Mecca inviting men to Allah. Among those he sent was Khalid. He was ordered to go as a missionary. Khalid subdued the Jadimah and killed some of them." *Tabari VIII:189* "Alas for you, Banu Jadimah! It is Khalid. By Allah, after you lay down your weapons, it will be nothing but leather manacles, and after the manacles nothing but the cutting off of heads.' After they had laid down their arms, Khalid ordered that their hands should be tied behind their backs. Then he put them to the sword, smiting their necks, killing them."

Ishaq:564 "One of the Banu Jadimah [who had been victimized by Khalid] said, 'God take reprisals on the Muslims for the evil they did to us. They stole our goods and divided them. Their spears came at us not once but twice. Their squadrons came upon us like a swarm of locusts. Were it not for the religion of Muhammad, their cavalry would never have attacked."

Ishaq:580 "Our strong warriors obey his orders to the letter. By us Allah's religion is undeniably strong. You would think when our horses gallop with bits in their mouths that the sounds of demons are among them."

Bukhari:V5B59N702 "I heard Kab bin Malik narrating the story of the Ghazwah of Tabuk in which he failed to take part. Kab said, 'I did not abandon Allah's Apostle in any Ghazwa he fought except the Tabuk raid. I failed to take part in the Ghazwa of Badr, but Allah did not admonish anyone who had not participated in it, for in fact, Allah's Apostle had only gone out in search of the Quraysh caravan. I witnessed the night of al-Aqaba with Allah's Apostle when we pledged [to war against all mankind] for Islam, and I would not exchange it for the Badr battle although Badr is more popular among Muslims than the pledge. As for my news in this battle of Tabuk, I had never been stronger or wealthier than I was when I was with the Prophet in Ghazwas.'"

Tabari IX:64 "Hatim said, 'Adi, whatever you were going to do before Muhammad's cavalry descended upon us, do it now, for I have seen the banners of his army.' When the Islamic cavalry left the settlement they took Hatim's daughter along with other captives. She was brought to the Messenger with slaves from Tayyi. He put her in an enclosure by the door of his mosque where the captives were detained."

Ishaq:601 "The best men launch spears as if they were swords. They peer forward unweariedly. They devote their lives to their Prophet. In hand-to-hand fighting and cavalry attacks they purify themselves with the blood of the infidels. They consider that an act of piety."

Tabari VIII:87 "The Companions of the Prophet had set out not doubting that they would conquer, because of a vision Muhammad had seen. Therefore, when they saw the negotiations for peace, the retreat, and the obligations the Messenger agreed to—the Muslims felt so grieved about it that they were close to despair. Some were depressed to the point of death."

Ishaq:131 "Hamzah came with his bow slung over his shoulder. He was a great hunter, the strongest man of the Quraysh. A woman rose up and said, 'If only you had seen what your nephew Muhammad had to endure just now before you came. Abu Jahl spoke to him offensively. Hamzah was carried away by a fury, as it was Allah's will to honor him this way. [In Islam, it is an honor to be furious.] He went off quickly, not stopping to speak to anyone. Instead of circumambulating the Ka'aba, he was ready to attack Abu Jahl when he saw him. When he entered the mosque, he saw him sitting among the people. Hamzah raised his bow and gave Abu Jahl a blow which split his head open in an ugly way. He said, 'Do you insult him when I am a member of his religion? Hit me back if you can.'"

Tabari VI:103 "Hamza's Islam was complete. He followed the Prophet's every command. The

Quraysh recognized that by Hamzah's acceptance of Islam Muhammad had been made strong. Hamzah would protect him."

Tabari VI:103 "Umar bin al-Khattab [the Caliph who ruled during Islam's bloodiest conquests] was a staunch and mighty warrior. He accepted Islam, as had Hamzah before him. The Messenger's Companions began to feel stronger." *Ishaq:155* "Umar became a Muslim, he being a strong, stubborn man whose protégés none dare attack. The prophet's companions were so fortified by him and Hamza that they got the upper hand on the Quraysh. 'We could not pray at the Ka'aba until Umar became a Muslim, and then he fought the Quraysh until we could pray there.'"

Tabari VII:109/Ishaq:372 "The Messenger called for his coat of armor and put it on. When they saw this they repented, 'What an evil deed we have done. We have given him advice when inspiration comes to him!' Muhammad replied, 'It is not fitting for a prophet to put on his coat of mail and take it off before fighting.' So the Prophet went out to Uhud at the head of a thousand of his Companions, having promised them victory."

Ishaq:373 "The Apostle, wearing two coats of mail, drew up his troops for battle, about 700 men. There were 50 archers. Muhammad said, 'Keep their cavalry away with your arrows.' Then he asked, 'Who will take my sword with its right and use it as it deserves to be used?' Abu Dujana asked, 'What is its right, Apostle?' 'That you should smite the enemy with it until it bends.' When Dujana took the sword from the Apostle's hand he walked toward the fight reciting: 'I'm the man who took the sword when "Use it right" was the Prophet's word for the sake of Allah.' When Muhammad saw Dujana strutting, he said, 'This is a gait which Allah hates except on an occasion like this.'"

Muslim:B20N4678 "Before the battle of Uhud a Muslim asked, 'Messenger, where shall I be if I am killed?' He replied: 'In Paradise.' The man fought until he was killed."

Ishaq:375 "Abu Dujana said, 'I saw a person inciting the enemy, shouting violently. When I made for him, I lifted my sword and he shrieked, and lo, it was a woman. I respected the Prophet's sword too much to use it on a girl.'" *Ishaq:380* "We attacked them thrusting, slaying, chastising, and driving them before us with blows on every side. Had not women seized their war banner they would have been sold in the markets like chattel."

Ishaq:379 "Then Allah sent down His help to the Muslims and fulfilled His promise. They slew the enemy with the sword until they cut them off from their camp and there was a rout."

Ishaq:380 "The Muslims were put to the fight and the Meccans slew many of them. It was a day of trial and testing in which Allah honored several with martyrdom."

Ishaq:375 "'Come here you son of a female circumciser.' His mother was Umm Anmar, a female circumciser in Mecca. Hamza smote and killed him."

Bukhari:V4B52N276 "By Allah, we saw the Meccan women running, revealing their leg-bangles. So, we cried out, 'The booty! O Muslims, the booty! Our Companions have become victorious. What are we waiting for? By Allah! We will go to the pagans and collect our share of the war booty.'"

Tabari VII:121 "I saw Hamzah cutting down men with his sword, sparing no one. He yelled out to us, 'Come here, you son of a cutter-off of clitorises.' He hit Siba so swiftly, his sword could not be seen striking his head. So I balanced my javelin until I was satisfied. Then I hurled it at Hamzah. It struck him in the lower part of the belly with such force it came out between his legs. He came toward me, but was overcome and fell. I waited until he was dead and recovered my javelin. I returned to the camp since there was nothing else I wanted." *Muslim:B19N4413* "When the enemy got the upper hand at Uhud, the Messenger was left with only seven Ansar and two Emigrants. When the enemy overwhelmed him, he said: 'Whoso turns them away will be my companion in Paradise.' An Ansar man fought until he was killed. The enemy advanced and overwhelmed them again so Muhammad repeated: 'Whoever turns them away will attain Paradise.' Another Ansar fought until he was slain. This state continued until all seven Ansari were killed, one after the other. The Prophet said to the Muslims: We have not done justice to them."

Tabari VII:120 "When the enemy overwhelmed the Holy Prophet he said, 'Who will sell his life for me?'"

Muslim:B19N4420 "The Prophet said: 'Great is the wrath of Allah upon a people who have done this to the Messenger.' At that time he was pointing to his front teeth. The Apostle said: 'Great is the wrath of Allah upon a person who has been killed by me in Allah's Cause.'"

Bukhari:V4B52N70 "Some people drank alcohol in the morning of the day of the battle of Uhud and were martyred on the same day."

Bukhari:V4B52N147 "Allah's Apostle and the pagans faced each other and started fighting. When the Apostle returned to his camp somebody talked about Quzman, a Muslim who had killed many pagans. The Apostle said of him, 'Nobody did his job of fighting as well as that man. Indeed, he is amongst the people of the Hell Fire."

Tabari VII:136/Ishaq:383 "During Uhud, Quzman fought hard and killed seven to nine polytheists with his own hands, being brave, bold, and strong. But he got wounded so seriously, he had to be carried off by his comrades. They said, 'Rejoice, you fought valiantly.' He replied, 'For what have I fought?'"

Ishaq:383 "Perhaps Allah will grant us martyrdom.' So they took their swords and sallied out until they mingled with the [retreating] army. One was killed by the Meccans, the other by his fellow Muslims who failed to recognize him. One of the young men's fathers confronted Muhammad and said, 'You have robbed my son of his life by your deception and brought great sorrow to me.'"

Bukhari:V4B52N69 "For thirty days Allah's Apostle invoked Allah to curse those who had killed his companions. He invoked evil upon the tribes who disobeyed Allah and His Apostle. There was revealed about those who were killed a Qur'anic Verse we used to recite, but it was cancelled later on. The Verse was: 'Inform our people that we have met our Lord. He is pleased with us and He has made us pleased.'"

Tabari VII:120 "May Allah's anger be intense against those who have bloodied the face of His Prophet." "By Allah, I never thirsted to kill anyone as I thirst to kill a Meccan."

Tabari VII:127 "The Messenger said, 'Hamzah is being cleansed by the angels. He went into battle in a state of ritual impurity when he heard the call to arms. That is why the angels are cleansing him.'" *Ishaq:386* "Our dead are in Paradise; your dead are in Hell."

Tabari VII:129 "If you had seen what Muhammad did at the pit of Badr you would have been terror struck for as long as you lived. I requited Badr with its like."

Ishaq:385 "Hind [a Meccan woman who had lost her father, husband, son, and brother to Muhammad's raiders at Badr] stopped to mutilate the Muslim dead, cutting off their ears and noses until she was able to make anklets and necklaces of them. Then she ripped open Hamzah's body for his liver and chewed it. Then she climbed a high rock and screamed rajaz poetry at the top of her voice, taunting us. 'We have paid you back for Badr. A war that follows a war is always violent. I could not bear the loss of Utba nor my brother, his uncle, or my first-born son. I have slaked my vengeance and fulfilled my vow.' Umar [the future leader of the Islamic world] recited these verses back to her: 'The vile woman was insolent, and she was habitually base with disbelief. May Allah curse Hind, she with the large clitoris. ...Her backside and her genitals are covered with ulcers as a result of spending too much time in the saddle. Did you set out seeking to avenge our killing of your father and your son at Badr? And for your husband, who was wounded in the backside, lying in his blood, and your brother, all of them coated in the grime of the pit. What a foul deed you committed. Woe to you Hind, the shame of the age.'"

Tabari VII:133 "When Muhammad saw Hamzah he said, 'If Allah gives me victory over the Quraysh at any time, I shall mutilate thirty of their men!' When the Muslims saw the rage of the Prophet they said, 'By Allah, if we are victorious over them, we shall mutilate them in a way which no Arab has ever mutilated anybody."

Ishaq:389 "When the Apostle came home he handed his sword to his daughter Fatima, saying, 'Wash the blood from this, daughter, for by Allah it has served me well today.'"

Tabari VII:139/Ishaq:389 "The battle was fought on the Sabbath. On the following day, Sunday, 16 Shawwal (March 24, 625) the Messenger of Allah's crier called out to the people to go in pursuit of the enemy. His only purpose was to lower the morale of the Quraysh; by going in pursuit of them, he wanted to give the impression that his strength [not his god's or his faith's] was unimpaired, and that the Muslim casualties had not weakened their ability [...to be religious? ...to be faithful to their god? Alas, no...] to engage in fighting."

Ishaq:391 "The day of Uhud was a day of trial, calamity, and heart-searching on which Allah tested the believers. He put the hypocrites [peaceful Muslims] on trial, those who professed faith with their tongue and hid unbelief in their hearts. And it was a day in which Allah honored with martyrdom those whom He willed."

Qur'an 3:121 "Remember that morning [of Uhud]? You left your home to post the faithful at their stations for battle at the encampments for war. Remember two of your parties were determined to show cowardice and fell away. Allah had helped you at Badr, when you were a contemptible little force." *Qur'an 3:124* "Remember you (Muhammad) said to the faithful: 'Is it not enough for you that Allah should help you with three thousand angels (specially) sent down? Yea, if you remain firm, and act aright, even if the enemy should rush here on you in hot haste, your Lord would help you with five thousand havoc-making angels for a terrific onslaught."

Qur'an 3:126 "Allah made it but a message of hope, and an assurance to you, a message of good cheer, that your hearts might be at rest. Victory comes only from Allah that He might cut off a fringe of the unbelievers, exposing them to infamy. They should then be turned back overwhelmed so that they retire frustrated." *Qur'an 3:140* "If you have received a blow (at

Uhud) and have been wounded, be sure a similar wound has hurt others. Such days We give to men and men by turns: that Allah may know those who believe, and that He may take to Himself from your ranks Martyrs."

Ishaq:392 "Allah helped you at Badr when you were contemptible, so fear Allah. Fear Me, for that is gratitude for My kindness. Is it not enough that your Lord reinforced you with three thousand angels? Nay, if you are steadfast against My enemies, and obey My commands, fearing Me, I will send five thousand angels clearly marked. Allah did this as good news for you that your hearts might be at rest. The armies of My angels are good for you because I know your weakness. Victory comes only from Me."

Ishaq:394 "Allah said, 'I let them get the better of you to test you. So fear Me and obey Me. If you had believed in what My Prophet brought from Me you would not have received a shock from the Meccan army. But We cause days like this so that Allah may know those who believe and may choose martyrs from among you. Allah must distinguish between believers and hypocrites so that He can honor the faithful with martyrdom."

Ishaq:394 "Did you think that you would enter Paradise and receive My reward before I tested you so that I might know who is loyal? You used to wish for martyrdom before you met the enemy. You wished for death before you met it. Now that you have seen with your own eyes the death of swords...will you go back on your religion, Allah's Book, and His Prophet as disbelievers, abandoning the fight with your enemy? He who turns back [from fighting] in his religion will not harm Allah.'"

Qur'an 3:141 "This is so that Allah may test the faithful and destroy the unbelieving infidels." [Another translation proclaims:] "Allah's object is to purge those that are true in Faith and blight the disbelievers. Did you think that you would enter Paradise while Allah does not know those of you who really fights hard (in His Cause) and remains steadfast? You wished for death before you met it (in the field of battle). Now [that] you have seen it with your own eyes, (you flinch!)"

Qur'an 3:152 "Allah did indeed fulfill His promise to you when you; with His permission were about to annihilate your enemy, until you flinched and fell to disputing about the order, and disobeyed it after He brought you in sight (of the booty) which you covet. Among you are some that hanker after this world and some that desire the Hereafter."

Ishaq:396 "I promise to give you victory over your enemy. You routed them with the sword, killing them by My permission. Then you deserted Me and disobeyed My order and disputed about the order of My Prophet. He told the archers to stay put. But after I showed you what you were desiring, the Meccan wives and property, you desired the spoil and abandoned the order to fight. Only those who fought for religion did not transgress in going after the booty. Allah reproached the hypocrites for running away from their Prophet and paying no heed when he called to them."

Tabari VIII:116 "After his return from Hudaybiyah, Allah's Messenger marched against Khaybar. He halted with his army in a valley between the people of Khaybar and the Ghatafan tribe to prevent the latter from assisting the Jews."

Ishaq:515 "Allah's Apostle besieged the final [Jewish] community of Khaybar until they could hold out no longer. Finally, when they were certain that they would perish, they asked Muhammad to banish them and spare their lives, which he did. The Prophet took possession of all their property."

Ishaq:500 "The Messenger said, 'Woe to the Quraysh! War has devoured them! What harm would they suffer if they left me to deal with the rest of the Arabs? [Besides having their property seized and their people terrorized and killed?] If the Arabs defeat me, that will be what they want. If Allah makes me prevail over the Arabs [not save them], the Quraysh can enter Islam [surrender] en masse. Or they can fight. I shall not cease to fight against them for the mission which Allah has entrusted me until Allah makes me victorious or I perish."

Tabari VIII:76 "Urwah went to the Prophet. 'Muhammad, tell me, if you exterminate your tribesmen—have you ever heard of any of the Arabs who has destroyed his own race before you?'"

Ishaq:502 "Muhammad, you have collected a mixed group of people and brought them to your kin to destroy them. By Allah, I see both prominent people and rabble who are likely to flee, deserting you tomorrow.' Now Abu Bakr who was standing behind the Apostle, said, 'Go suck the clitoris of Al-Lat!'"

Tabari VIII:76/Ishaq:502 "He began speaking to the Prophet again, stroking his beard. Mughira, clad in mail, was standing next to him with his sword. Whenever Urwah extended his hand toward the Prophet's beard, Mughira struck his hand with the lower end of the scabbard and said, 'Take your hand away from his beard before you lose it!' Urwah raised his head and asked, 'Who is this?' They said, 'Mughira.' Urwah said, 'Rude man, I am trying to rectify your act of treachery.' During the Time of Ignorance [pre-Islam] Mughira had accompanied some men and killed them, taking their money. The Apostle just smiled."

Ishaq:503/Tabari VIII:82 "When Muhammad received a report that Uthman had been killed, he said, 'We will not leave until we fight it out with the enemy.' He summoned the people to swear allegiance. The Prophet's crier announced: People, an oath of allegiance! The Holy Spirit has descended!'"

Ishaq:503/Tabari VIII:83 "On the day of Hudaybiyah we swore allegiance to the Messenger while Umar was holding his hand under the acacia tree. It was a pledge unto death."

Ishaq:503 "Allah saw what was in their hearts so he rewarded them with victory and with as much spoil as they could take. Allah promised that they would soon capture a great deal of booty."

Ishaq:505 "Umar jumped up, walking beside Jandal, saying, 'Be patient. They are only pagans, and the blood of any of them is no more than the blood of a dog!' Umar held the hilt of his sword close to him. He said, 'I hoped he would take the sword and kill his father with it.' But Jandal was too attached to his father to kill him."

Ishaq:508/Tabari VIII:91 "Abu Jandal, Suhayl's son, escaped and joined Abu Basir. Nearly seventy Muslim men gathered around them and they harassed the Quraysh. Whenever they heard of a Meccan caravan setting out for Syria, they intercepted it, and killed everyone they could get a hold of. They tore every caravan to pieces and took the goods. The Quraysh, therefore, sent to the Prophet, imploring him for the sake of Allah and the bond of kinship to send word to them."

Tabari VIII:93 "In this year, according to Waqidi, the Messenger dispatched the raiding party of Abu Ubaydah with forty men. They traveled through the night on foot and reached Qassah just before dawn. They raided the inhabitants, who escaped them by fleeing to the mountains. They took cattle, old clothes, and a man."

Tabari VIII:93 "In this year a raiding party led by Zayd went to Jamum. He captured a Muzaynah woman named Halimah. She guided them to an encampment of the Banu Sulaym where they captured cattle, sheep, and prisoners."

Tabari VIII:94 "In this year a raiding party led by Zayd went to al-Is. During it, Abu As'b's property was taken." *Tabari VIII:94* "A fifteen-man raiding party led by Zayd went to Taraf against the Banu Thalabah. The Bedouins fled, fearing that Allah's Messenger had set out against them. Zayd took twenty camels from their herds. He was away four nights."

Tabari VIII:96 "Muhammad sent him with an army against the Fazarah settlement. He met them in Qura and inflicted casualties on them and took Umm Qirfah prisoner. He also took one of Umm's daughters and Abdallah bin Mas'adah prisoner."

Tabari VIII:97 "The Messenger appointed Abu Bakr as our commander, and we raided some of the Banu Fazarah. When we came near the watering place, Bakr ordered us to rest. After we prayed the dawn prayer, Abu ordered us to launch the raid against them. We went down to the watering hole and there we killed some people. I saw women and children among them, who had almost outstripped us; so I sent an arrow between them and the mountain. When they saw the arrow they stopped, and I led them back to Abu Bakr. Among them was a woman of the Banu Fazarah. She was wearing a worn-out piece of leather. With her was her daughter, among the fairest of the Arabs. Abu Bakr gave me her daughter as booty."

MURDER:

Tabari IX:69 "Killing disbelievers is a small matter to us."

Tabari VIII:141 "The battle cry of the Companions of the Messenger of Allah that night was: 'Kill! Kill! Kill!'"

Bukhari:V5B59N512 "The Prophet had their men killed, their woman and children taken captive."

Ishaq:489 "Do the bastards think that we are not their equal in fighting? We are men who think that there is no shame in killing."

Qur'an 2:191 "And kill them wherever you find and catch them. Drive them out from where they have turned you out; for Al-Fitnah (polytheism, disbelief, oppression) is worse than slaughter."

Qur'an 33:60 "Truly, if the Hypocrites stir up sedition, if the agitators in the City do not desist, We shall urge you to go against them and set you over them. Then they will not be able to stay as your neighbors for any length of time. They shall have a curse on them. Whenever they are found, they shall be seized and slain without mercy—a fierce slaughter—murdered, a horrible murdering."

Bukhari:V4B52N270 "Allah's Messenger said, 'Who is ready to kill Ashraf? He has said injurious things about Allah and His Apostle.' Maslama got up saying, 'Would you like me to kill him?' The Prophet proclaimed, 'Yes.' Maslama said, 'Then allow me to lie so that I will be able to deceive him.' Muhammad said, 'You may do so.'"

Ishaq:368 "Ka'b's body was left prostrate [humbled in submission]. After his fall, all of the

Nadir Jews were brought low. Sword in hand we cut him down. By Muhammad's order we were sent secretly by night. Brother killing brother. We lured him to his death with guile [cunning or deviousness]. Traveling by night, bold as lions, we went into his home. We made him taste death with our deadly swords. We sought victory for the religion of the Prophet."

Tabari VII:97/Ishaq:368 "We carried Ka'b's head and brought it to Muhammad during the night. We saluted him as he stood praying and told him that we had slain Allah's enemy. When he came out to us we cast Ashraf's head before his feet. The Prophet praised Allah that the poet had been assassinated and complimented us on the good work we had done in Allah's Cause. Our attack upon Allah's enemy cast terror among the Jews, and there was no Jew in Medina who did not fear for his life.'"

Tabari VII:97 "The morning after the murder of Ashraf, the Prophet declared, 'Kill any Jew who falls under your power.'"

Ishaq:369 "Thereupon Mas'ud leapt upon Sunayna, one of the Jewish merchants with whom his family had social and commercial relations and killed him. The Muslim's brother complained, saying, 'Why did you kill him? You have much fat in you belly from his charity.' Mas'ud answered, 'By Allah, had Muhammad ordered me to murder you, my brother, I would have cut off your head.' Wherein the brother said, 'Any religion that can bring you to this is indeed wonderful!' And he accepted Islam."

Bukhari:V1B1N6 "Just issue orders to kill every Jew in the country."

Ishaq: 676 "'You obey a stranger who encourages you to murder for booty. You are greedy men. Is there no honor among you?' Upon hearing those lines Muhammad said, 'Will no one rid me of this woman?' Umayr, a zealous Muslim, decided to execute the Prophet's wishes. That very night he crept into the writer's home while she lay sleeping surrounded by her young children. There was one at her breast. Umayr removed the suckling babe and then plunged his sword into the poet. The next morning in the mosque, Muhammad, who was aware of the assassination, said, 'You have helped Allah and His Apostle.' Umayr said. 'She had five sons; should I feel guilty?' 'No,' the Prophet answered. 'Killing her was as meaningless as two goats butting heads.'"

Bukhari:V1B11N626 "The Prophet said, 'No prayer is harder for the hypocrites than the Fajr. If they knew the reward they would come to (the mosque) even if they had to crawl. I decided to order a man to lead the prayer and then take a flame to burn all those who had not left their houses for the prayer, burning them alive inside their homes.'"

Tabari VIII:178/Ishaq:550 "Muhammad ordered that certain men should be assassinated even if they were found behind the curtains of the Ka'aba. Among them was Abdallah bin Sa'd [the Qur'an's one and only scribe]. The reason that Allah's Messenger ordered that he should be slain was because he had become a Muslim and used to write down Qur'an Revelation. Then he apostatized [rejected Islam]."

Tabari VIII:179 "Abdallah bin Sa'd fled to Uthman, his brother, who after hiding him, finally surrendered him to the Prophet. Uthman asked for clemency. Muhammad did not respond, remaining silent for a long time. Muhammad explained, 'By Allah, I kept silent so that one of you might go up to him and cut off his head!' One of the Ansar said, 'Why didn't you give me a sign?' Allah's Apostle replied, 'A prophet does not kill by pointing.'"

Tabari VIII:179/Ishaq:550 "Among those who Muhammad ordered killed was Abdallah bin Khatal. The Messenger ordered him to be slain because while he was a Muslim, Muhammad had sent him to collect the zakat tax with an Ansar and a slave of his.... His girls used to sing a satire about Muhammad so the Prophet ordered that they should be killed along with Abdullah. He was killed by Sa'id and Abu Barzah. The two shared in his blood. One of the singing girls was killed quickly but the other fled. So Umar caused his horse to trample the one who fled, killing her."

Ishaq:551 "Another victim was Huwayrith. He used to insult Muhammad in Mecca. Huwayrith was put to death by Ali. The Messenger ordered Miqyas' assassination only because he had killed an Ansar who had killed his brother by mistake and then became a renegade by rejecting Islam."

Tabari VIII:180 "Also among those eliminated were Ikrimah bin Abu Jahl and Sarah, a slave of one of Abd Muttalib's sons. She taunted Muhammad while he was in Mecca."

Tabari VIII:181 "The Messenger ordered six men and four women to be assassinated. One of these women was Hind, who swore allegiance and became a Muslim."

Bukhari:V4B52N281 "They took Khubaib to Mecca after the battle of Badr. He had killed Harith, a Meccan nobleman. The Quraysh gathered to kill him in retribution.... Khubaib wanted to offer two Rakat (prayers). They allowed this and he said, 'O Allah, kill them all with no exception.' He then recited the poetic verse: 'I'm being martyred as a Muslim. I do not mind how I am killed in Allah's Cause. For my killing is for Allah's Sake. If Allah wishes, He will bless the amputated parts of my torn body.' Then the son of Harith [the man Khubaib had murdered] killed him."

Ishaq:597 "When the Apostle returned to Medina after his raid on Ta'if, word spread that he had killed some of the men who had satirized and insulted him. The poets who were left spread in all directions."

Tabari IX:76 "Malik has reported to me that you were the first from Himyar to embrace Islam and that you have killed infidels, so rejoice at your good fortune."

Tabari IX:121 "When it was feasible for me, I struck him with my sword and killed him. Then I departed, leaving his women to throw themselves at him. When I returned to the Prophet, he asked, 'Is your mission accomplished?' 'Yes. I have killed him.'"

Ishaq:308/Tabari VII:65 "When the Apostle was in Safra, Nadr was assassinated. When Muhammad reached Irq al-Zabyah he killed Uqbah. When the Prophet ordered him to be killed, Uqbah said, 'Who will look after my children, Muhammad?' "Hellfire,' the Apostle replied, and he was killed."

Tabari VII:85 "Muhammad killed many Quraysh polytheists at Badr."

Tabari VII:99 "In this year, the killing of Abu Rafi the Jew took place. The Messenger sent some Ansar under the command of Abd Allah and Abd Allah against the Jew. Abu Rafi used to injure and wrong the Prophet.... Abd Allah said to the others, 'Stay where you are, and I will go and ingratiate myself with the doorkeeper to gain entrance.'"

Tabari VII:100 "Every time I opened a door, I shut it behind me from the inside, saying to myself, 'If they become aware, they will not have time to stop me from killing him.' When I reached Rafi, he was in a dark room with his family. As I did not know where he was in the room, I said, 'O Abu Rafi.' When he replied, I proceeded toward the voice and gave him a blow with my sword. He shouted and I came back, pretending to be a helper. I said, 'O Abu,' changing the tone of my voice. He asked me, 'I don't know who came to strike me with his sword.' Then I drove my sword into his belly and pushed it forcibly till it touched the bone. I hit him again and covered him with wounds, but I could not kill him, so I thrust the point of my sword into his stomach until it came out through his back. At that, I knew that I had killed him [in front of his wife and children]. I came out, filled with puzzlement, and went towards a ladder in order to get down but I fell into a moonlit night and sprained my foot. I bound it with my turban and moved on. I came to my companions and said, 'By Allah, I will not leave till I hear the wailing of their women.' So, I did not move till I heard them crying for the Jewish merchant. I said, 'Deliverance! Allah has killed Abu Rafi.' I got up, feeling no ailment, and proceeded till we came upon the Prophet and informed him."

Tabari VII:101 "The Khazraj asked the Prophet for permission to kill Sallam Huqayq, who was in Khaybar. He granted this." *Ishaq:482* "One of the favors which Allah conferred upon his Prophet was that these two tribes of the Ansar, the Aws and the Khazraj, used to vie with one another like stallions to carry out the will of Muhammad. The Aws did not do anything which benefited him without the Khazraj saying, 'By Allah they will not gain superiority over us in Islam in the eyes of the Messenger by doing this.' And they would not cease until they had done something similar. Thus when the Aws killed Ka'b Ashraf on account of his hostility to Muhammad, the Khazraj conferred to find a man comparable to Ka'b in hostility and called to mind Sallam Huqayq in Khaybar. They asked the Prophet for permission to kill him, and it was granted."

Tabari VII:101/Ishaq:483 "Sallam's wife came out and we told her that we were Arabs in search of supplies. When we entered, we bolted the door on her so she gave a shout to warn him of our presence. We rushed upon him with our swords as he lay in his bed. He took his pillow and tried to fend us off. Abd Allah thrust his sword into his stomach and transfixed him while he was shouting, 'Enough! Enough!' At once we went out but Abd Allah had bad eyesight, and he fell off the stairway, bruising his leg or arm. 'How shall we know that the enemy of Allah is dead?' one of us asked. 'I will go and look,' one replied. He set off and mingled with the people. He said, 'I found him with the men of the Jews, and with his wife, who had a lamp in her hand, peering into his face. She said, 'By the God of the Jews, he is dead.' I never heard any more pleasing words than these. We went to the Messenger of Allah and told him that we had killed the enemy of Allah. We disagreed in his presence about the killing of Sallam, each of us claiming to have done it. The Prophet said, 'Bring me your swords.' We did and he looked at them. He said, 'This sword of Abd Allah killed him. I can see the marks left by bones on it.'"

Ishaq:483 "Allah, what a fine band you have, one willing to kill Sallam and Ashraf! We went with sharp swords, like fighting lions. We came upon their homes and made them drink death with our swift-slaying swords. Looking for the victory of our Prophet's religion, we ignored every risk."

Tabari VII:112/Ishaq:372 "When a blind Jew became aware of the presence of the Messenger and the Muslims he rose and threw dust in their faces, saying, 'Even if you are a prophet, I will not allow you into my garden!' I was told that he took a handful of dirt and said, 'If only I knew that I would not hit anyone else, Muhammad, I would throw it in your face.' Sa'd rushed in and hit him on the head with his bow and split the Jew's head open."

Ishaq:403 "Allah killed twenty-two polytheists at Uhud."

Tabari VII:147 "Amr was sent by Muhammad to kill Abu Sufyan [the Quraysh leader and merchant]. The Prophet said, 'Go to Abu Sufyan and kill him.' ...When I entered Mecca I had a dagger ready to slay anybody who laid hold of me. My Ansar companion asked, 'Should we start by circumambulating the Ka'aba seven times and praying two rak'ahs?' I said, 'I know the Meccans better than you do.' But he kept pestering me until in the end we went to the Ka'aba, circumambulated it seven times, and prayed." *Tabari VII:148* "One of the Meccans recognized me and shouted, 'That is Amr!' They rushed after us, saying, 'By Allah, Amr has not come here for any good purpose! He has come for some evil reason.' Amr had been a cutthroat and a desperado before accepting Islam."

Tabari VII:148 "Amr said, 'Let's wait here until the cry has died down. They are sure to hunt for us tonight and tomorrow. I was still in the cave when Uthman bin Malik came riding proudly on his horse. He reached the entrance to our cave and I said to my Ansar companion, 'If he sees us, he will tell everyone in Mecca.' So I went out and stabbed him with my dagger. He gave a shout and the Meccans came to him while I went back to my hiding place. Finding him at the point of death, they said, 'By Allah we knew that Amr came for no good purpose.' The death of their companion impeded their search for us, for they carried him away."

Tabari VII:149 "I went into a cave with my bow and arrows. While I was in it, a one-eyed man from the Banu Bakr came in driving some sheep. He said, 'Who's there?' I said [lied], 'I'm a Banu Bakr.' 'So am I.' Then he laid down next to me, and raised his voice in song: 'I will not believe in the faith of the Muslims.' I said, 'You will soon see!' Before long the Bedouin went to sleep and started snoring. So I killed him in the most dreadful way that anybody has ever killed. I leant over him, struck the end of my bow into his good eye, and thrust it down until it came out the back of his neck. After that I rushed out like a wild beast and took flight. I came to the village of Naqi and recognized two Meccan spies. I called for them to surrender. They said no so I shot and arrow and killed one, and then I tied the other up and took him to Muhammad." *Tabari VII:150* "I had tied my prisoner's thumbs together with my bowstring. The Messenger of Allah looked at him and laughed so that his back teeth could be seen. Then he questioned me and I told him what had happened. 'Well done!' he said, and prayed for me to be blessed."

Ishaq:434 "Amr and an Ansari waited until they were asleep. Then Amr killed them, thinking that he had taken vengeance for the Muslims who had been slain. When he came to the Messenger, he told him what had happened. The Prophet said, 'You have killed men for whom I shall have to pay blood-money.'"

Tabari VIII:22 "Hassan was with the women and children. A Jew passed by and began to walk around his settlement. There was no one to protect them while the Apostle and his Companions were at the Meccans' throats. So I said: 'Hassan, this Jew is walking around. I fear he will point out our weakness while the Muslims are too busy to attend to us. So go down to him and kill him."

Tabari VIII:22 / Ishaq:458 "'Allah forgive you, daughter of Abd al-Muttalib,' Hassan said. 'You know that I am not the man to do it.' When he said that to me I saw that nothing could be expected from him. I girded myself, took a club, and, having gone down from the fortress to the man, I struck him with the club until I killed him. When I had finished with him, I returned to the fortress and said, 'Hassan, go down to him and strip him—only his being a man kept me from taking his clothes.' Hassan replied, 'I have no need for his spoils.'"

Ishaq:464 "The Jews were made to come down, and Allah's Messenger imprisoned them. Then the Prophet went out into the marketplace of Medina, and he had trenches dug in it. He sent for the Jewish men and had them beheaded in those trenches. They were brought out to him in batches. They numbered 800 to 900 boys and men." *Tabari VIII:40* "The Messenger commanded that furrows should be dug in the ground for the Qurayza. Then he sat down. Ali and Zubayr began cutting off their heads in his presence."

Tabari VIII:38 "The Messenger of Allah commanded that all of the Jewish men and boys who had reached puberty should be beheaded. Then the Prophet divided the wealth, wives, and children of the Banu Qurayza Jews among the Muslims."

Tabari VIII:90 "Abu Basir went out with his companions. When they stopped to rest he asked one of them, 'Is this sword of yours sharp?' 'Yes,' he replied. 'May I look at it?' Basir asked. 'If you wish.' Basir unsheathed the sword, attacked the man, and killed him. The other Muslim ran back to the Messenger, saying, 'Your Companion has killed my friend.' While the man was still there, Abu Basir appeared girded with the sword. He halted before Muhammad and said, 'Messenger, your obligation has been discharged.'"

TORTURE:

Qur'an 5:33 "The punishment for those who wage war against Allah and His Prophet and make mischief in the land, is to murder them, crucify them, or cut off a hand and foot on opposite sides...their doom is dreadful. They will not escape the fire, suffering constantly."

Tabari VIII:122 / Ishaq:515 "The Prophet gave orders concerning Kinanah to Zubayr, saying, 'Torture him until you root out and extract what he has. So Zubayr kindled a fire on Kinanah's chest, twirling it with his firestick until Kinanah was near death. Then the Messenger gave him to Maslamah, who beheaded him."

Bukhari:V4B54N487 "The Prophet said, 'The Hell Fire is 69 times hotter than ordinary worldly fires.' So someone said, 'Allah's Apostle, wouldn't this ordinary fire have been sufficient to torture the unbelievers?'"

Bukhari:V4B52N260 "Ali burnt some [former Muslims alive] and this news reached Ibn Abbas, who said, 'Had I been in his place I would not have burnt them, as the Prophet said, "Don't punish with Allah's Punishment." No doubt, I would have killed them, for the Prophet said, "If a Muslim discards his Islamic religion, kill him."'"

Qur'an 48:27 "If the Muslims had not been there, We would have punished the unbelievers with a grievous torture."

Qur'an 9:5 "When the sacred forbidden months for fighting are past, fight and kill the disbelievers wherever you find them, take them captive, torture them, and lie in wait and ambush them using every stratagem of war."

Ishaq:550 "The Muslims met them with their swords. They cut through many arms and skulls. Only confused cries and groans could be heard over our battle roars and snarling."

Qur'an 5:37 "The [Christian] disbelievers will long to get out of the Fire, but never will they get out there from; and theirs will be an enduring torture."

Tabari IX:6 "The chief sheep tender sent out spies to obtain intelligence. But they came back with their joints dislocated. When he asked what had happened, they said, 'We saw white men on black horses. Before we could resist, we were struck as you see us now."

Ishaq:595 "The Apostle said, 'Get him away from me and cut off his tongue.'"

Ishaq:312 "Umar said to the Apostle, 'Let me pull out Suhayl's two front teeth. That way his tongue will stick out and he will never be able to speak against you again.'"

Ishaq:316 "Following Badr, Muhammad sent a number of raiders with orders to capture some of the Meccans and burn them alive."

Qur'an 8:12 "Your Lord inspired the angels with the message: 'I will terrorize the unbelievers. Therefore smite them on their necks and every joint and incapacitate them. Strike off their heads and cut off each of their fingers and toes."

Tabari VII:133/Ishaq:387 "When Muhammad saw Hamzah he said, 'If Allah gives me victory over the Quraysh at any time, I shall mutilate thirty of their men!' When the Muslims saw the rage of the Prophet they said, 'By Allah, if we are victorious over them, we shall mutilate them in a way which no Arab has ever mutilated anybody."

Tabari VIII:96 "A raiding party led by Zayd set out against Umm in Ramadan. During it, Umm suffered a cruel death. Zyad tied her legs with rope and then tied her between two camels until they split her in two. She was a very old woman. Then they brought Umm's daughter and Abdallah to the Messenger. Umm's daughter belonged to Salamah who had captured her. Muhammad asked Salamah for her, and Salamah gave her to him."

THIEVERY & SLAVERY:

Qur'an 8:1 "They ask you about the benefits of capturing the spoils of war. Tell them: 'The benefits belong to Allah and to His Messenger.'"

Ishaq:510 "We ask Thee for the booty of this town and its people. Forward in the name of Allah.' He used to say this of every town he raided."

Ishaq:327 "Allah said, 'A prophet must slaughter before collecting captives. A slaughtered enemy is driven from the land. Muhammad, you craved the desires of this world, its goods and the ransom captives would bring. But Allah desires killing them to manifest the religion.'"

Tabari VII:64/Ishaq:307 "The Messenger of Allah gave orders concerning the contents of the camp which the people had collected, and it was all brought together. Among the Muslims, however, there was a difference of opinion concerning it. Those who had collected it said, 'It is ours. Muhammad promised every man that he could keep the booty he took.' Those who were fighting said, 'If it had not been for us, you would not have taken it. We distracted the enemy from you so that you could take what you took.' Those who were guarding the Prophet for fear the enemy would attack him said, 'By Allah, you have no better right to it than we have. We wanted to kill the enemy when Allah gave us the opportunity and made them turn their backs, and we wanted to take property when there was no one to protect it; but we were afraid that the Meccans might attack the Prophet. We protected him so you have no better right to it than we have.' When we quarreled about the booty we became very bad tempered. So Allah removed it from us and handed it over to His Messenger."

Bukhari:V5B59N360 "The total number of Muslim fighters from Mecca who fought at Badr and were given a share of the booty, were 81. When their shares were distributed, their number was 101. But Allah knows it better."

Ishaq:307 "The 'Spoils of War' Surah came down from Allah to His Prophet concerning the distribution of the booty when the Muslims showed their evil nature. Allah took it out of their hands and gave it to the Apostle." *Tabari VII:65* "Allah's Messenger came back to Medina, bringing with him the booty which had been taken from the polytheists.... There were forty-four captives in the Messenger of Allah's possession. There was a similar number of dead."

Bukhari:V5B59N512 "The captives of Khaybar were divided among the Muslims. Then the Messenger began taking the homes and property that were closest to him."

Tabari VIII:116/Ishaq:511 "So Muhammad began seizing their herds and their property bit by bit. He conquered home by home. The Messenger took some of its people captive, including Safiyah and her two cousins. The Prophet chose Safiyah for himself."

Ishaq:511 "When Dihyah protested, wanting to keep Safiyah for himself, the Apostle traded for Safiyah by giving Dihyah her two cousins. The women of Khaybar were distributed among the Muslims."

Tabari VIII:130 "The Prophet conquered Khaybar by force after fighting. Khaybar was something that Allah gave as booty to His Messenger. He took one-fifth of it and divided the remainder among the Muslims."

Bukhari V4B52N46 "I heard Allah's Apostle saying, 'Allah guarantees that He will admit the Muslim fighter into Paradise if he is killed, otherwise He will return him to his home safely with rewards and booty.'"

Tabari VIII:117 "The Banu Sahm of Aslam [newly recruited Muslim militants] came to the Messenger and complained, 'Muhammad, we have been hurt by drought and possess nothing.' Although they had fought for the Prophet they found he had nothing [he was willing] to give them. The Apostle said, 'O Allah, You know their condition—I have no strength and nothing [I want] to give them [from the booty I have stolen]. So conquer for them the wealthiest of the Khaybar homes, the ones with the most food and fat meat.'"

Ishaq:515 "Allah's Apostle besieged the final [Jewish] community of Khaybar until they could hold out no longer. Finally, when they were certain that they would perish, they asked Muhammad to banish them and spare their lives, which he did. The Prophet took possession of all their property."

Tabari VIII:128 "Khaybar was divided among the people who had been at Hudaybiyah."

Ishaq:521 "Khaybar was apportioned among the men of Hudaybiyah without regard to whether they were present at Khaybar or not. The spoil was divided into 1,800 shares."

Ishaq:521 "When the spoil of Khaybar was apportioned, the settlements of Shaqq and Nata were given to the Muslims while Katiba was divided into five sections: Allah's fifth [which Muhammad was custodian]; the Prophet's fifth; the share to the kindred [Muhammad's kin]; maintenance of the Prophet's wives [now there's an honest report]; and payment to the men who acted as intermediaries in the peace negotiation with Fadak [which enabled the prophet to steal the entire spoil]."

Ishaq:522 "Then the Apostle distributed the booty between his relatives, his wives, and to other men and women. He gave his daughter Fatima 200 shares, Ali 100, Usama 250, Aisha 200, Bakr 100.... In the name of Allah—this is a memorandum of what Muhammad the Apostle gave his wives from the dates and wheat: 180 loads."

Bukhari:V5B59N537 "Allah's Apostle divided the war booty with the ratio of two shares for the horse and one-share for the foot soldier."

Bukhari:V5B59N541 "When we conquered, we gained neither gold nor silver as booty, but we gained cows, camels, goods and gardens."

Tabari VIII:12 "When cities were conquered Muslims used to say, 'Conquer for yourselves whatever seems good to you because all treasures were given to Muhammad.'"

Qur'an 48:19 "He rewarded them with abundant spoils that they will capture. Allah has promised you much booty that you shall take, and He has made this easy for you."

Qur'an 9:103 "Take alms out of their property in order to cleanse and purify them, and invoke Allah for them; surely this is a relief for them."

Tabari IX:3 "Since the Hawazin and Thaqif had marched with their women, children, and flocks, Allah granted them as booty to His Messenger, who divided the spoils among those Quraysh who had recently embraced Islam."

Tabari IX:13 "Abu Talhah alone took the spoils of twenty men whom he had killed."

Ishaq:571 "I went up to a man and struck off his hand. He fell and I killed him while he was down. But I was too occupied with fighting to pay any more attention to him. So one of the Meccan Muslims passed by and stripped him. Then when the fighting was over and we had finished with the enemy, the Apostle said that anyone who had killed a foe could have his spoil. I told the Apostle that I had killed a man who was worth stripping but had been too busy killing others at the time to notice who had spoiled him. Abu Bakr said, "To Allah's lions who fight for His religion go the spoils that come from their prey. Return the booty to the man who killed him.' The Apostle confirmed Abu Bakr's words. So I was given the property of the man whom I had killed. I sold it and bought a small palm grove with the money. It was the first property I ever owned."

Ishaq:592 "The Apostle held a large number of captives. There were 6,000 women and children prisoners. He had captured so many sheep and camels they could not be counted."

Tabari IX:31/Ishaq:594 "'Muhammad, divide the spoil and booty of camels and cattle among us.' They forced the Prophet up against a tree, and his robe was torn from him. Muhammad cried, 'Give me back my robe. If there had been more sheep I would have given you some. You have not found me to be niggardly, cowardly or false."

Tabari IX:31/Ishaq:594 "'You have not found me miserly, cowardly, or a liar.' Then he walked over to his camel and took a hair from its hump. Holding it aloft in his fingers he said, 'Men, I do not have anything of your booty, not even as much as this hair. Just filth. And that filth is what is being given to you. So, bring back my cloak.'"

Ishaq:594 "The Apostle gave gifts to those whose hearts were to be won over, notably the chiefs of the army, to win them and through them the people."

Bukhari:V4B53N373 "Allah's Apostle got property and war prisoners and gave them to some people to the exclusion of others. The latter seemed to be displeased by that. The Prophet said, 'I give to some people, lest they should deviate from Islam or lose patience.'"

Bukhari:V4B53N374 "The Prophet said, 'I give to the Quraysh so that they will desire Islam, for they are nearer to their life of Ignorance and it is not strong in their hearts.'"

Tabari IX:36/Ishaq:596 "'Prophet, this group of Ansar have a grudge against you for what you did with the booty and how you divided it among you own people.' 'Ansar, what is this talk I hear from you? What is the grudge you harbor against me? Do you think ill of me? Did I not come to you when you were erring and needy, and then made rich by Allah?" *Tabari IX:37/Ishaq:596* "Do you hold a grudge against me and are you mentally disturbed because of the worldly things by which I conciliate a people and win them over so that they will embrace Islam and become Muslims?"

Tabari IX:38 "In this year, the Messenger sent Amr to collect the zakat tax from Jayfar and Amr, the clans of Julanda and Azd…. He collected the jizyah from the Zoroastrians."

Tabari IX:74 "Indeed, Allah has guided you with His guidance. If you wish to do well [capture booty], obey Allah and His Messenger. You must perform the prayers, pay the zakat tax, and give a fifth share of Allah's booty to His Messenger. The required zakat is: from the land one tenth of that watered by springs and rain, and one twentieth of that watered by the leathern bucket. From camels, a milch camel for every forty camels, and a young male camel for every thirty camels. From sheep, one for every five camels; and from cows, one from every fourth… If anyone pays more, it is to his credit. He who professes this, bears witness to his Islam and helps the faithful [fight] against the polytheists, he has the protection of Allah and His Messenger."

Tabari IX:75 "He who holds fast to his religion, Judaism or Christianity, is not to be tempted from it. It is incumbent on them to pay the jizyah protection tax. For every adult, male or female, free or slave, one full denarius, or its value in al-ma'afir [fine cloth]. He who pays that to the Messenger has the protection of Allah and His Messenger, and he who holds back from it is the enemy of Allah and His Messenger."

Tabari IX:76 "The Messenger has sent Zur'ah and his Companions to you. 'I commend them to your care. Collect the zakat and jizyah from your districts and hand the money over to my messengers.' The Prophet is the master of your rich and your poor."

Ishaq:564 "The Muslims stole our goods and divided them. Their spears pierced us not once but twice. Their squadrons came at us like a swarm of locusts. Were it not for the religion of Muhammad's people, their cavalry would never have attacked us."

Bukhari:V9B84N59 "When the Prophet died, Arabs reverted to disbelief. Umar said, 'Should we fight these people?' Bakr said, 'By Allah! I will fight whoever differentiates between prayers and Zakat, as Zakat is to be taken from property according to Allah's Orders. If they refuse to pay me even so little as a kid they used to pay, I will fight with them for withholding it.'"

Qur'an 59:6 "What Allah gave as booty to His Messenger He has taken away from them [the Jews]. For this you made no raid. Allah gives His Messenger Lordship over whomsoever He wills. Whatever booty Allah has given to His Messenger and taken away from the [Jewish] people of the townships, belongs to Allah and to His Messenger.... So take what the Messenger assigns to you, and deny yourselves that which he withholds from you."

Tabari VII:26 "In this year Muhammad ordered people to pay the zakat tax. It is said that the Prophet commanded them to do this."

Ishaq:309 "'Bind Abu Aziz tight for his mother is rich and she may ransom him for a great deal of money.'" *Tabari VII:71* "Among the captives was Abu Wada. Muhammad said, 'He has a son who is a shrewd merchant with much money." [The son] "slipped away at night, went to Medina, ransomed his father for 4,000 dirhams."

Ishaq:312 "The Prophet said, 'Abbas, you must ransom yourself, your two nephews, Aqil and Nawfal, and your confederate, Utbah, for you are a wealthy man.' 'Muhammad,' Abbas said, 'I was a Muslim, but the people compelled me to fight against my will.' Allah knows best concerning your Islam,' Muhammad said. 'As for your outward appearance, you have been against us, so pay to ransom yourself.' The Messenger had previously taken twenty ounces of gold from him following the battle. So Abbas said, 'Credit me with this amount towards my ransom.' 'No,' Muhammad replied. 'That money Allah has already taken from you and given to us.'"

Ishaq:313 "The Muslims told Abu Sufyan to pay them a ransom to free his son, Amr. He replied, 'Am I to suffer the double loss of my blood and my money? After you have killed my son Hanzala, you want me to pay you a ransom to save Amr?'"

Bukhari:V5B59N357 "The Badr warriors were given five thousand dirhams each, yearly. Umar [the future Caliph] said, 'I will always give them more than what I will give to others.'"

Tabari VII:80 "When the events of Badr were over, Allah revealed the 8th surah, 'The Spoils of War,' in its entirety. The two armies met [there were no armies—just merchants and militants] and Allah defeated the Meccans [with Muslim swords]. Seventy of them were killed, and seventy were taken captive. Abu Bakr said, 'O Prophet of Allah, these are your people, your family; they are your cousins, fellow clansmen, and nephews. I think that you should accept ransoms for them so that what we take from them will strengthen us.'" *Tabari VII:81* "'What do you think Khattab?' Muhammad asked. 'I say you should hand them over to me so that I can cut off their heads. Thus Allah will know that there is no leniency in our hearts toward the unbelievers.' The Messenger liked what Bakr said and did not like what I said, and accepted ransoms for the captives."

Ishaq:316 "On the Badr expedition, the Messenger took the sword of Dhu al-Faqar as booty. It had belonged to Munabbih. On that day he also took Abu Jahl's camel as booty. It was a Mahri dromedary on which he used to go on raids. It is said that he wrote 'Ma'aqil' [Blood-Money] on his sword."

Qur'an 8:1 "They question you about (windfalls taken as) spoils of war. Say: 'Booty is at the disposal of Allah and the Messenger; they belong to Us and are for Our benefit. So fear Allah, and adjust your way of thinking in this matter. Obey Allah and His Messenger.'"

Ishaq:321 "The Spoils of War surah was handed down because we quarreled about the booty.

So Allah took it away from us and gave it to His Apostle. When He did, we learned to fear Allah and obey his Messenger.... For in truth, our army had gone out with the Prophet seeking the caravan because we wanted its booty."

Ishaq:324 "Allah taught them how to divide the spoil. He made it lawful and said, 'A fifth of the booty belongs to the Apostle.'

Qur'an 8:40 "If people are obstinate, and refuse to surrender, know that Allah is your Supporter. And know that one fifth of all the booty you take belongs to Allah, and to the Messenger, and for the near relatives (of the Messenger)."

Qur'an 8:68 "Had it not been for a previous agreement from Allah, a severe penalty would have reached you for the (ransom) that you took as booty." *Qur'an 8:69* "So enjoy what you took as booty; the spoils are lawful and good."

Ishaq:327 "Allah made booty lawful and good. He used it to incite the Muslims to unity of purpose. So enjoy what you have captured."

Bukhari:V4B52N276 "By Allah, we saw the Meccan women running, revealing their leg-bangles. So, we cried out, 'The booty! O Muslims, the booty! Our Companions have become victorious. What are we waiting for? By Allah! We will go to the pagans and collect our share of the war booty.'"

Tabari VIII:38 "The Messenger divided the wealth, wives, and children of the Banu Qurayza Jews among the Muslims." *Ishaq:465* "When their wrists were bound with cords, the Apostle was a sea of generosity to us. Allah's Messenger took his fifth of the booty. He made known on that day the extra shares for horses and their riders —giving the horse two shares and the rider one. A Muslim without a horse got one share of the spoil. It was the first booty in which lots were cast."

Tabari VIII:39 "Then the Messenger of Allah sent Sa'd bin Zayd with some of the Qurayza captives to Najd, and in exchange for them he purchased horses and arms."

Ishaq:503 "Allah saw what was in their hearts [what they coveted] so he rewarded them with victory and with as much spoil as they could take. Allah promised that they would soon capture a great deal of booty."

Ishaq:508/Tabari VIII:91 "Abu Jandal, Suhayl's son, escaped and joined Abu Basir. Nearly seventy Muslim men gathered around them and they harassed the Quraysh. Whenever they heard of a Meccan caravan setting out for Syria, they intercepted it, and killed everyone they could get a hold of. They tore every caravan to pieces and took the goods."

Tabari VIII:93 "According to Waqidi, in this month, the Messenger sent out Ukkashah with forty men to raid Ghamr. He traveled quickly, but the enemy became aware and fled. He sent out scouts and they captured a spy who guided them to some of their cattle. They took two hundred head back to Medina."

Tabari IX:28 "The Muslims were concerned. They did not want to give up their share. So Muhammad said, 'He who holds a share of these captives shall get six camels for every slave from the next booty we take.' So the Muslims returned the women and children captives."

Qur'an 4:94 "Believers, when you go abroad to fight wars in Allah's Cause, investigate carefully, and say not to anyone who greets you: 'You are not a believer!' Coveting the chance profits of this life (so that you may despoil him). With Allah are plenteous spoils and booty."

PEACE, ISLAM STYLE:

Bukhari:V9B84N59 "Allah's Apostle said, 'I have been ordered to fight the people till they say: "None has the right to be worshipped but Allah." Whoever says this will save his property and his life from me.'"

Qur'an 8:58 "If you apprehend treachery from any group on the part of a people (with whom you have a treaty), retaliate by breaking off (relations) with them. The infidels should not think they can bypass (Islamic law or the punishment of Allah). Surely they cannot escape."

Tabari VII:86 "Gabriel brought down the following verse to the Messenger: 'If you apprehend treachery from any people (with whom you have a treaty), retaliate by breaking off (relations).' When Gabriel had finished delivering this verse, the Prophet said, 'I fear the Banu Qaynuqa.' It was on the basis of this verse that Muhammad advanced upon them."

Tabari VII:158 "Judayy went to Abd Allah Ibn Ubayy to ask for support. He said, 'I found him sitting among a number of his companions while the Prophet's crier was calling men to arms. He said, 'This is a clever trick of Muhammad's.' The Messenger of Allah besieged the Nadir Jews for fifteen days. In the end they made peace with him on the condition that the Prophet would not kill them and that their property and their coats of mail would be his."

Tabari VII:159 "The Messenger of Allah besieged the Nadir for fifteen days until he had reduced them to a state of utter exhaustion, so that they would give him what he wanted. The terms in which the Prophet made peace with the Jews were: he would not shed their blood, he would expel them from their lands and settlements, providing for every three of them a camel and a water-skin."

Tabari VII:159 "The Prophet fought them until he made peace with them on condition that they evacuated Yathrib. He expelled them to Syria but allowed them to keep what their camels could carry, except for their coats of mail and weapons."

Qur'an 47:33 "Believers, obey Allah, and obey the Messenger. Do not falter; become faint-hearted, or weak-kneed, crying for peace."

Qur'an 9:3 "Allah is not bound by any contract or treaty with non-Muslims, nor is His Apostle."

Qur'an 97:5 "There is peace until the dawning of the day!"

Ishaq:515 "When the people of Fadak heard what had happened, they sent word to the Messenger, asking him to banish them and spare their lives, saying they too would leave him their property. When the people of Khaybar surrendered on these conditions, the survivors asked Muhammad to employ them on their farms for a half share of whatever they produced. They said, 'We know more about farming [seeing that you are terrorists and all].' So Muhammad made peace with them for a half share, provided that: 'If we want to expel you, we may.' He made a similar arrangement with Fadak. So Khaybar became the prey of the Muslims, while Fadak belonged exclusively to the Messenger of Allah, becoming his personal property, because the Muslims had not attacked its people with cavalry."

Qur'an 9:3 "And an announcement from Allah and His Messenger to the people on the day of the Pilgrimage is that Allah and His Messenger dissolve treaty obligations with the Pagans."

Tabari VIII:104 "Peace to whoever follows the right guidance! To proceed; Submit yourself, and you shall be safe.'"

Qur'an 49:9 "If two parties among the Believers fall into fighting, make peace: but if one becomes aggressive, then fight against the one that transgresses until it complies."

Tabari VIII:142 "The Messenger made peace with them on condition that the Zoroastrians should be required to pay the jizyah tax [so onerous, it's akin to economic suicide] that one should not marry their women."

Qur'an 9:7 "How can there be a covenant between Allah and His Messenger and the disbelievers with whom you made a treaty near the sacred Mosque?" *Qur'an 9:8* "How (can there be such a treaty), seeing that they get an advantage, the upper hand over you? They do not pay you respect, or honor you or the ties of kinship or covenant. With (good words from) their mouths they entice you [out negotiate you], but their hearts are averse to you."

Qur'an 9:12 "If they violate their oaths and break treaties, taunting you for your Religion, then fight these specimens of faithlessness."

Tabari VIII:163 "The Prophet said, 'I think you will see Abu Sufyan [the leading Meccan merchant] come to strengthen the pact and extend the term.'" *Ishaq:543* "Abu Sufyan went to Muhammad in Medina to affirm the peace treaty, but Muhammad refused to speak to him." *Tabari VIII:164* "Sufyan went to Abu Bakr and asked him to intercede, but he refused. When Sufyan asked Umar to help [avert war], he replied, 'No way. By Allah, if I had only ant grubs, I would fight you with them! Ali said, 'Woe to you, Sufyan. When the Messenger has determined a thing it is useless for anyone to talk to him.'"

Tabari VIII:165 "There is nothing that you can do to make peace with him." *Tabari VIII:165* "When Abu Sufyan reported back to the Quraysh that Muhammad had given him no reply, they said, 'Woe to you! By Allah, he did no more than play with you.'"

Ishaq:544 "Muhammad commanded the people to prepare for the foray [raid, incursion, sortie, attack, or assault]. The Messenger informed his troops that he was going to Mecca. He ordered them to prepare themselves and ready their equipment quickly. He said, 'O Allah, keep spies and news from the Quraysh until we take them by surprise in their land.'"

Tabari VIII:182 "Allah had enabled Muhammad to take the persons of the Quraysh by force, giving him power over them so they were his booty. Their lives were now his spoil."

Ishaq:552 "When the populace settled down, Muhammad went to the Ka'aba and compassed it seven times on his camel, touching the Black Stone with a stick. Then he went inside the Temple. There he found a dove made of wood. He broke it in his hands and threw it away." [The first idol Muhammad broke was the international symbol of peace.]

Tabari IX:58 "When the Messenger reached Tabuk the governor of Aylah [a seaport at the north end of the Gulf of Aqabah] came to him, made a treaty, and agreed to pay the jizyah tax. The people of Jarba and Adhruh also offered to pay him the tax."

Ishaq:607 "The Byzantines encountered the Messenger's cavalry which was led by Khalid. Ukaydir was seized and his brother Hassan was killed. Muhammad spared his life and made peace with him on the condition that he pay the zakat tax."

Tabari IX:79 "In this year the zakat was made obligatory, and the Messenger dispatched his agents to collect it. The verse was revealed: 'Take the zakat from their wealth to purify them.'"

Ishaq:316 "In peace you are wild asses—rough and coarse. And in war you are like women wearing corsets. But I care not so long as my hand can grasp my trusty blade."

Qur'an 8:61 "But if the enemy inclines toward peace, do you (also) incline to peace, and trust in Allah. Should they intend to deceive or cheat you, verily Allah suffices: He strengthened you with His aid and with Believers." [The small print is real important. "Should they intend to deceive or cheat" is an open invitation to invoke 8:57 to 60. The first to interpret this surah said:] *Ishaq:326* "If they ask you for peace on the basis of Islam (submission), make peace on that basis. Be of one mind by His religion."

Tabari VIII:17 "The Muslims and polytheists stayed in their positions for twenty nights with no fighting except for the shooting of arrows and the siege. When the trial became great for the people, the Messenger sent for the leaders of the Ghatafan [Meccan comrades]. He offered them a third of the date harvest of Medina on condition that they leave. The truce between the sides progressed to the point of drawing up a written document, but there was no witnessing or firm determination to make peace; it was only a matter of maneuvering."

Ishaq:454 "Now that Allah has conferred Islam on us, and made us famous, shall we give them our property? By Allah, we will offer them only the sword until Allah judges between us.' 'As you wish,' said Allah's Messenger."

Tabari VIII:100 "Abu Sufyan said, 'We were merchants but the fighting between us and Muhammad has prevented us from journeying, so our wealth is depleted. [This is the purpose of terrorism.] Even after the truce with the Muslims, we fear that we still are not safe. [Muslims, continuing to plunder Meccan caravans, violated the treaty twenty times.]'"

Qur'an 4:90 "For those who join a group between you and whom there is a treaty, or (those who become) weary of fighting you, had Allah had willed, He could have given them power over you, and they would have fought you. Therefore if they withdraw and wage not war, and send you (guarantees of) peace, then Allah has not given you a way (to war) against them." [The purpose of terror is to cause people to become so "weary of fighting" they surrender.]

Qur'an 4:91 "You will find others who, while wishing to live in peace and being safe from you to gain the confidence of their people; thrown back to mischief headlong; therefore if they do not withdraw from you, and offer you peace besides restraining their hands, then seize them and kill them wherever you find them; and against these We have given you a clear sanction and authority." [So if you wish to live in peace, but are *perceived* as being mischievous (i.e., non-Muslim), Allah has given his Jihad warriors "a clear sanction and authority to seize and kill" you.]

PEACEFUL MUSLIM HYPOCRITES:

Qur'an 48:11 "The desert Arabs who lagged behind [in fighting] will say to you (Muhammad): 'We were engaged in (looking after) our flocks and our families.' We have prepared for them a Blazing Fire!" *Qur'an 48:17* "There is no blame for the blind, nor is it a sin for the lame, nor on one ill if he joins not in the fighting. But he who retreats, (Allah) will punish him with a painful doom."

Qur'an 4:77 "Have you not seen those to whom it was said: Withhold your hands from fighting, perform the prayer and pay the zakat. But when orders for fighting were issued, a party of them feared men as they ought to have feared Allah. They say: 'Our Lord, why have You ordained fighting for us, why have You made war compulsory?'" *Qur'an 4:78* "Wherever you are, death will find you, even if you are in towers built up strong and high! If some good befalls, they say, 'This is from Allah;' but if evil, they say, 'This is from you (Muhammad).' Say: 'All things are from Allah.' So what is wrong with these people, that they fail to understand these simple words?"

Qur'an 4:88 "What is the matter with you that you are divided about the Hypocrites? Allah has cast them back (causing their disbelief). Would you guide those whom Allah has thrown out of the Way? For those whom Allah has thrown aside and led astray, never shall they find the Way." *Qur'an 4:89* "They wish that you would reject Faith, as they have, and thus be on the same footing: Do not be friends with them until they leave their homes in Allah's Cause. But [and this is a hell of a but...] if they turn back from Islam, becoming renegades, seize them and kill them wherever you find them."

Qur'an 47:20 "Those who believe say, 'How is it that no surah was sent down (for us)?' But when a categorical [decisive or uncompromising] surah is revealed, and fighting and war (Jihad, holy fighting in Allah's Cause) are ordained, you will see those with diseased hearts looking at you (Muhammad) fainting unto death. Therefore woe unto them!" *Qur'an 47:21* "Were they to obey, showing their obedience in modest speech, after the matter (of preparation for Jihad) had been determined for them, it would have been better. Is it to be expected that if you were put in authority and given command that you would do mischief in the land and sever your ties of kinship. Such men are cursed by Allah. He has made them deaf, dumb and blind."

Qur'an 4:97 "Verily, when angels take the souls of those who die wronging themselves (by staying home), they say: 'In what (plight or engagement) were you?' They reply: 'Weak on the earth.' Such men will find their abode in Hell, an evil resort!" *Qur'an 4:8* "Except those who are feeble—men, women and children—who cannot devise a plan nor have the means or power. These are those whom Allah is likely to forgive."

Qur'an 9:16 "Do you think you will get away before Allah knows who among you have striven hard and fought?"

Qur'an 9:38 "Believers, what is the matter with you, that when you are asked to march forth in the Cause of Allah (i.e., Jihad) you cling to the earth? Do you prefer the life of this world to the Hereafter? Unless you march, He will afflict and punish you with a painful torture, and put others in your place. But you cannot harm Him in the least."

Qur'an 9:43 "May Allah forgive you (Muhammad). Why did you grant them leave (for remaining behind; you should have persisted as regards to your order to them to proceed on Jihad), until you had known the liars." *Qur'an 9:44* "Those who believe in Allah and the Last Day do not ask for an exemption from fighting with your goods and persons. And Allah knows well those who do their duty."

Qur'an 9:45 "Only those ask for exemption (from Jihad) who believe not in Allah and whose hearts are in doubt, so that they are tossed to and fro. If they had intended to march out to fight, they would certainly have made some preparation and readied their equipment; but Allah was averse to their being sent forth; so He made them lag behind. 'Sit you among those who sit.' If they had marched with you, they would not have added to your (strength) but only (made for) discord, spying and sowing sedition. There would have been some in your midst who would have listened to them. But Allah knows well those [peace-loving

Muslims] who do wrong and are wicked."

Qur'an 9:48 "They had plotted sedition before, and upset matters for you until the Decree of Allah [to fight] became manifest, much to their disgust. Among them are many who say: 'Grant me exemption to stay back at home (exempted from Jihad). And do not tempt me [with promises of booty].' Have they not fallen into temptation already? Indeed, Hell surrounds them."

Qur'an 9:67 "The Hypocrites enjoin what is forbidden, and forbid what Islam commands. They withhold their hands (from spending in Allah's Cause [Jihad]). They have forgotten Allah so He has forgotten them. Verily the Hypocrites are oblivious, rebellious and perverse." *Qur'an 9:68* "Allah has promised the Hypocrites, both men and women, and the disbelievers the Fire of Hell for their abode: Therein shall they dwell. It will suffice them. On them is the curse of Allah, and an enduring punishment, a lasting torment."

Qur'an 9:74 "The Hypocrites swear by Allah that they said nothing, but indeed they uttered blasphemy, and they disbelieved after Surrender (accepting Islam). They meditated a plot (to murder Prophet Muhammad) which they were unable to carry out. The reason for this revenge of theirs was the bounty [of booty] with which Allah and His Messenger had enriched them! If they repent, it will be best for them; but if they turn back, Allah will punish them with a grievous torment in this life and in the Hereafter." *Qur'an 9:75* "Some of you made a deal with Allah, saying, 'If You give us booty we shall pay You the tax.' But when He gave them booty, they became greedy and refused to pay. As a consequence of breaking their promises, Allah filled their hearts with hypocrisy which will last forever."

Qur'an 9:77 "He punished them by putting hypocrisy in their hearts until the Day whereon they shall meet Him, because they lied to Allah and failed to perform as promised. Allah knows their secrets. Those who slander and taunt the believers who pay the zakat (for Allah's Cause) voluntarily and throw ridicule on them, scoffing, Allah will throw back their taunts, and they shall have a painful doom. Whether you ask for their forgiveness or not, (their sin is unforgivable). If you ask seventy times for their forgiveness Allah will not forgive them."

Qur'an 9:81 "Those who stayed behind rejoiced in their inaction behind the back of the Messenger. They hated to strive and fight with their goods and lives in the Cause of Allah. They said, 'Go not forth in the heat.' Say, 'The fire of Hell is fiercer in heat.' If only they could understand! So let them laugh a little, for they will weep much as a reward for what they did. If Allah brings you back (from the campaign) to a party of the hypocrites and they ask to go out to fight, say: 'You shall never go out to fight with me against a foe. You were content sitting inactive on the first occasion. So sit with the useless men who lag behind.' Do not pray for any of them (Muhammad) that die, nor stand at his grave. They rejected Allah and disbelieved His Messenger. They died in a state of perverse rebellion."

Qur'an 9:85 "And let not their wealth or (following in) sons dazzle you or excite your admiration. Allah's plan is to punish them with these things in this world, and to make sure their souls perish while they are unbelievers. When a surah comes down enjoining them to believe in Allah and to strive hard and fight along with His Messenger, those with wealth and influence among them ask you for exemption from Jihad. They prefer to be with (their women), who remain behind (at home). Their hearts are sealed and so they understand not."

Qur'an 9:88 "The Messenger and those who believe him, strive hard and fight jihad with their wealth and lives (in Allah's Cause)." *Qur'an 9:90* "And there were among the wandering desert Arabs men who made excuses and came to claim exemption (from the battle). Those who lied to Allah and His Messenger sat at home. Soon will a grievous torment seize them."

Qur'an 9:93 "The (complaint) is against those who claim exemption [from fighting] while they are rich. They prefer to stay with the (women) who remain behind (at home). Allah has sealed their hearts. They are content to be useless. Say: 'Present no excuses: we shall not believe you.' It is your actions that Allah and His Messenger will observe. They will swear to you by Allah, when you return hoping that you might leave them alone. So turn away from them, for they are unclean, an abomination, and Hell is their dwelling-place, a fitting recompense for them."

Qur'an 9:97 "The Arabs of the desert are the worst in unbelief and hypocrisy, and most fitted to be in ignorance of the command which Allah hath sent down to His Messenger. Some of the Bedouins look upon their payments (for Allah's Cause) as a fine and wish disasters to fall on you (so that they might not have to pay). Yet on them be the disaster of evil."

Qur'an 9:101 "Among the desert Arabs are hypocrites. They, like the people of Medina are obstinate in hypocrisy. We know them. Twice shall We punish them, and in addition they shall be brought back to a horrible torment."

Qur'an 9:120 "It is not fitting for the people of Medina and the Bedouin Arabs to refuse to follow Allah's Messenger (Muhammad when fighting in Allah's Cause), nor to prefer their own lives to his life. They suffer neither thirst nor fatigue in Allah's Cause, no do they go without reward. They do not take steps to raise the anger of disbelievers, nor inflict any injury upon an enemy without it being written to their credit as a deed of righteousness."

Tabari IX:13 "Muhammad turned to see Umm, a pregnant woman, who said, 'O Messenger! Kill those [Muslims] who flee from you as you kill those who fight you, for they deserve death. Here is my dagger. If any come near me I will rip them up and slit open their belly with it.'"

Tabari IX:49 "One of the hypocrites, feeling an aversion to battle, being skeptical of the truth, and spreading false rumors about Muhammad, said that they should not go out in the heat. With regard to him, Allah revealed: 'They said, "Do not march out in the heat." Say, "The heat of hell is far more intense."'"

Ishaq:602 "Jadd told Muhammad, 'Will you allow me to stay behind and not tempt me? Everyone knows that I am strongly addicted to women. I'm afraid that I'll see Byzantine women and will not be able to control myself.' The Apostle gave him permission to remain behind. It was about him that Allah sent down: 'There are some who say: "Give me leave to stay behind and do not tempt me." Surely they have fallen into temptation already and hell encompasses these unbelievers.' (9:49) It was not that he feared the temptation from the Byzantine women. The temptation he had fallen into was greater in that he had hung back from the Apostle and sought to please himself rather than Muhammad. Verily hell awaits him."

Ishaq:603 "One of the estranged ones said to another, 'Don't go out to fight in this heat.' He disliked strenuous war, doubted the truth, and created misgivings about the Apostle. So Allah sent down regarding them, 'And they said, "Do not go out in this heat." Say, "The fires of hell are hotter. Let them laugh a little now for they will weep a great deal later as a reward for what they did.'" (5:82) *Ishaq:603* "Some Bedouins came to apologize for not going into battle, but Allah would not accept their excuses."

Ishaq:246 "The surah of the Hypocrites came down because some men sent secret messages to the Nadir Jews when the Apostle besieged them. So Allah sent down, "Have you not considered the Hypocrites who say to their brethren, the People of the Book [Jews], 'We shall never obey anyone against you. If you are attacked and driven out we will help you. Allah bears witness that they are liars.'"

Qur'an 59:11 "Have you not observed the Hypocrites saying to their unbelieving brethren among the People of the Book, 'If you are expelled [from your homes by the Muslims], we will go with you?' But Allah is witness that they are liars. If the Jews are expelled, never will the Hypocrites go with them; if they are attacked, they will not help them defend themselves. In truth you [jihadist Muslims] are more fearful and awful (than they) because they are afraid of you. This is a result of the terror (sent) by Allah. They are men devoid of understanding." *Qur'an 59:14* "They are a divided people devoid of sense. There is a grievous punishment awaiting them. Satan tells them not to believe so both of them will end up in Hell."

Qur'an 8:20 "O you who believe! Obey Allah and His Messenger. Do not turn away from him when you hear him speak. Do not be like those who say, 'We hear,' but do not listen. Those who do not obey are the worst of beasts, the vilest of animals in the sight of Allah. They are deaf and dumb. Those who do not understand are senseless. If Allah had seen any good in them, He would have made them listen. And even if He had made them listen, they would but have turned away and declined submission."

Qur'an 8:47 "Be not as those who came from their homes full of their own importance, trying to turn men away from [fighting] in Allah's Cause. Allah is encircling them. Satan made their acts seem alluring to them, and said: 'No one can conquer you this day, while I am near you.' But when the two armies came in sight of each other, he turned on his heels, and said: 'Lo! I am not with you. I see what you cannot. Verily, I fear Allah: for Allah is severe in punishment.'" *Qur'an 8:49* "When the hypocrites and those in whose hearts is a disease said: 'The religion has deceived and misled them.'"

Qur'an 8:55 "Verily the worst of creatures, the vilest of beasts in the sight of Allah are those who reject Him and will not believe. They are those with whom you make an agreement, but they break their covenant every time, and they keep not their duty [to fight]."

Qur'an 61:2 "O Muslims, why say one thing and do another? Grievously odious and hateful is it in the sight of Allah that you say that which you do not. Truly Allah loves those who fight in His Cause in a battle array, as if they were a solid cemented structure."

Qur'an 63:1 "When the Hypocrites come to you they say, 'We bear witness that you are indeed the Messenger of Allah.' Allah knows you are His Messenger, and Allah bears witness the Hypocrites are indeed liars." *Qur'an 63:2* "They have made their oaths a screen, thus they obstruct (men) from the Path of Allah: truly evil are their deeds. That is because they believed, then they rejected Faith: So a seal was set on their hearts."

Qur'an 63:4 "When you look at the Hypocrites, their bodies please you; and when they speak, you listen to their words. They are pieces of wood propped up. They think every cry is against them. They are the enemies; so beware of them. The curse of Allah is on them!

Allah will destroy them. How are they deluded and perverted?" *Qur'an 63:6* "It is equal to them whether you ask forgiveness or not. Allah will never forgive them. Allah does not forgive the transgressing people."

Qur'an 63:7 "The Hypocrites are the ones who say, 'Spend nothing on those who are with Allah's Messenger so that they will desert him.' But to Allah belong the treasures of the earth; but the Hypocrites understand not. They say, 'If we return to Medina, surely the more honorable (element) will expel the meaner (i.e., Muhammad).'"

Ishaq:372 ""When he went out, Abd Allah bin Ubayy [the man who had advised against leaving town] came back with 300 men, saying, 'We do not know why we should get ourselves killed here.' So he went back to Medina with the Hypocrites and doubters who followed him. Abd Allah bin Amr said, 'Allah curse you, enemies of Allah. Allah will let us manage without you.'"

Ishaq:391 "The day of Uhud was a day of trial, calamity, and heart-searching on which Allah tested the believers. He put the hypocrites on trial, those who professed faith with their tongue and hid unbelief in their hearts. And it was a day in which Allah honored with martyrdom those whom He willed."

Qur'an 3:141 "Did you think that you would enter Paradise while Allah does not know those of you who really fights hard (in His Cause) and remains steadfast? You wished for death before you met it (in the field of battle). Now [that] you have seen it with your own eyes, (you flinch!)" [Another translation reads:] "Did you think you would enter Paradise without Allah testing those of you who fight in His Cause?"

Ishaq:393 "Then Allah said: 'Obey Allah and the Apostle and maybe you will attain mercy. Reproaching those who disobeyed the Apostle in the orders he gave them that day [to fight] He said, 'Vie with one another for forgiveness from your Lord and for the Garden of Bliss prepared for those who fear, a dwelling for those who obey Me and obey My Apostle.... They have wronged themselves by disobedience. But they must not continue disobeying Me for I have prohibited the worship of any but Myself."

Ishaq:398 "Show them that you listen to them and ask them for their help. Thereby make the religion of Islam agreeable to them. And when you are resolved in the matter of religion concerning fighting your enemy you will have the advantage."

Ishaq:393 "Allah loves the steadfast [fighters]. How many a prophet has death in battle befallen and how many multitudes with him? They did not show weakness toward their enemies and were not humiliated when they suffered in the fight for Allah and their religion. That is steadfastness, and Allah loves the steadfast." *Ishaq:395* "Practice your religion as they did, and be not renegades, turning back on your heels, retreating. Those who retreat and turn away from the battle are losers in this world and in the next."

Qur'an 3:152 "Allah did indeed fulfill His promise to you when you, with His permission were about to annihilate your enemy, until you flinched and fell to disputing about the order, and disobeyed it after He brought you in sight (of the booty) which you covet. Among you are some that hanker after this world and some that desire the Hereafter."

Ishaq:396 "I promise to give you victory over your enemy. You routed them with the sword, killing them by My permission. Then you deserted Me and disobeyed My order and dis-puted about the order of My Prophet. He told the archers to stay put. But after I showed you what you were desiring, the Meccan wives and property, you desired the spoil and abandoned the order to fight. Only those who fought for religion did not transgress in going after the booty. Allah reproached the hypocrites for running away from their Prophet and paying no heed when he called to them."

Qur'an 3:154 "Say: 'Even if you had remained in your houses, those ordained to be slaughtered would have gone forth to the places where they were to slain.'"

Qur'an 3:155 "Those who turned back the day the two armies clashed, Satan caused them to backslide, fail in their duty, and run away from the battlefield." *Qur'an 3:156* "O you who believe! Be not like the Unbelievers, who say of their brethren when they are traveling through the land engaged in raids and fighting: 'If they had stayed with us, they would not have died or been slain.' This is that Allah may make it anguish, a cause of sighs and regrets. It is Allah that gives Life and causes Death by His power, as He wishes. And if you are slain, or die, in Allah's Cause [as a martyr], pardon from Allah and mercy are far bet-ter than all they could amass."

Qur'an 3:165 "What! When a single disaster smites you, although you smote with one twice as great, do you say: 'Whence is this?' Say: 'It is from yourselves.' What you suffered on the day the armies clashed was by permission of Allah; that He might know the true believers."

Qur'an 3:167 "And that He might know the Hypocrites, unto whom it was said: 'Come, fight in Allah's Cause, or (at least) drive (the foe from your city).' They said: 'Had we known how to fight, we should certainly have followed you.' They were that day nearer to Unbelief than to Faith, saying with their lips what was not in their hearts but Allah hath full knowledge of all they conceal." *Qur'an 3:168* "Those who, while they sat at home, said (of their brethren slain fighting for the cause of Allah), while they themselves sit (at home at ease): 'If only they had listened to us they would not have been killed.' Say: 'Avert death from your own selves, if you speak the truth.'"

Ishaq:399 "You had smitten your enemy with a double dose of torment at Badr, slaying them and taking prisoners. Yet you disobeyed your Prophet's orders and brought the defeat of Uhud on yourselves. And it was said to them: 'Come, fight for Allah's sake.' The hypocrites stopped fighting for Allah's sake, eager to survive, fleeing death. So Allah said to His Prophet to make the Muslims wish to fight and to desire battle: 'And do not think that those who were killed for Allah's sake are dead. Nay, they are alive with their Lord being nourished, glad with the bounty Allah has brought them and rejoicing for those who have not yet joined them that they have nothing to fear or grieve over."

Qur'an 33:11 "In that situation the Believers were sorely tried and shaken as by a tremendous shaking. And behold! The Hypocrites and those in whose hearts is a disease said: 'Allah and His Messenger promised us nothing but delusion!' [Or...] "Allah and His Messenger promised only to deceive us." *Qur'an 33:13* "Behold! A party among them said: 'Men of Yathrib! You cannot stand (the attack); therefore go back!' And a band of them asked for leave of the Prophet, saying, 'Our houses are bare and exposed,' though they were not exposed. They intended nothing but to run away." [In a second translation:] "And verily they had already sworn to Allah that they would nct turn their backs (to a foe). An oath to Allah must be adhered to. Say: 'Running away will not profit you if you are running away from death or slaughter; and even if (you escape), no more than a brief (respite) will you be allowed!'" [A third translation:] "Say: Flight will not avail you if you flee from death, killing, or slaughter. In that case you will not be allowed to enjoy yourselves but a little while. Say, 'Who will screen you, saving you from Allah if he intends to harm and injure you?'"

Qur'an 33:18 "Verily Allah already knows those among you who keep back and those who say to their brethren, 'Come along to us,' but come not to the fight in the stress of battle except for just a little while. Being covetous and niggardly with respect to you; but when fear comes, you will see them looking to you, their eyes rolling like one swooning because of death. But when the fear is gone they smite you with sharp tongues, covetous of goods, in their greed for wealth (from the spoil). Such men have no faith, and so Allah has made their deeds of none effect: and that is easy for Allah." *Qur'an 33:20* "They...wish the allied clans were (wandering) in the desert among the Bedouins. But if they were in your midst, they would only battle or fight with them for moment."

Qur'an 33:60 "Truly, if the Hypocrites, those in whose hearts is a disease, those who stir up sedition, the agitators in the City, do not desist, We shall urge you (Muhammad) to go against them and set you over them. Then they will not be able to stay as your neighbors for any length of time. They shall have a curse on them. Whenever they are found, they shall be seized and slain without mercy—a fierce slaughter—murdered, a horrible murdering. (Such was) the practice (approved) of Allah among those who lived before. No change wilt thou find in the practice of Allah."

Qur'an 4:137 "Those who believe, then reject faith, then believe and reject faith, and go on increasing in unbelief, Allah will never pardon them, nor guide them. To the Hypocrites give the glad tidings that there is for them a grievous penalty, a painful doom."

Qur'an 4:140 "You have been commanded in the Book that whenever you hear Verses of Allah denied, derided, ridiculed, or mocked [as is the only reasoned response], do not sit with them and engage them in this talk or you will be no different from them. Indeed, Allah will collect the Hypocrites and Infidels together and put them all in Hell."

Qur'an 4:142 "The Hypocrites try to deceive Allah, but it is He Who deceives them. When they stand up performing the prayer, they stand sluggishly, to be seen, but they are mindful of Allah but little. (They are) distracted in mind even in the midst of it, swaying between this and that, one group or the another. Those who Allah causes to go astray and err will not find a way. Believers, take not for friends unbelieving infidels rather than believers [because rational thought is contagious]. Do you want to offer Allah an open proof against you? The Hypocrites will be in the lowest depths of the Fire."

NO FREEDOM, NO CHOICE:

Qur'an 3:19 "Lo! religion with Allah (is) Surrender."

Ishaq:322 "Allah said, 'Do not turn away from Muhammad when he is speaking to you. Do not contradict his orders. And do not be a hypocrite, one who pretends to be obedient to him and then disobeys him. Those who do so will receive My vengeance. You must respond to the Apostle when he summons you to war."

Qur'an 8:24 "O Believers! Answer Allah and (His) Messenger when he calls you to that which will give you life [martyrdom].... Fear the affliction and trial that awaits those who do not obey. Allah is severe."

Qur'an 4:80 "He who obeys the Messenger obeys Allah."

Tabari VIII:182 "The people assembled in Mecca to swear allegiance to the Messenger in submission. He received from them the oath of allegiance to himself, to heed and obey."

Bukhari:V4B52N203 "I heard Allah's Apostle saying, 'He who obeys me, obeys Allah, and he who disobeys me, disobeys Allah. He who obeys the chief, obeys me, and he who disobeys the chief, disobeys me.'"

Qur'an 33:36 "It is not fitting for a Muslim man or woman to have any choice in their affairs when a matter has been decided for them by Allah and His Messenger. They have no option. If any one disobeys Allah and His Messenger, he is indeed on a wrong Path."

Qur'an 87:10 "He who fears will mind."

Qur'an 47:21 "Were they to obey, showing their obedience in modest speech after a matter had been determined for them, it would have been better."

Qur'an 47:33 "Believers, obey Allah, and obey the Messenger. Do not falter; become faint-hearted, or weak-kneed, crying for peace."

Qur'an 4:114 "He who disobeys the Apostle after guidance has been revealed will burn in Hell."

Qur'an 49:14 "The desert Arabs say, 'We believe.' Say: 'You have no faith; but you (only) say, "We submit." For not yet has Faith entered you. But if you obey Allah and His Messenger, He will not belittle your deeds.' Only those are Believers who have believed in Allah and His Messenger, and have never since doubted, and have striven with their belongings and lives in the Cause of Allah."

Qur'an 49:16 "Say: 'What! Will you instruct Allah about your religion?' They impress you (Muhammad) that they have Surrendered (Islam). Say, 'Count not your Surrender as a favor to me: Nay, Allah lays you under an obligation."

Qur'an 9:53 "Say: 'Pay your contribution for the Cause willingly or unwillingly.'"

Qur'an 5:4 "This day those who reject faith give up all hope of your religion. Yet fear them not, fear Me. This day I have perfected your religion and have chosen for you Submission as your religion." *Qur'an 5:7* "Remember Allah's covenant which He ratified with you, when you said: 'We hear and we obey.' And fear Allah."

Qur'an 5:92 "Obey Allah and obey the Messenger, and beware!"

Muslim:C22B20N4604 "We used to take oath to the Messenger of Allah that we would listen to and obey his orders. He would tell us to say in the oath: As far as it lies in my power."

Qur'an 48:10 "Verily those who swear allegiance to you (Muhammad), indeed swear their allegiance to Allah."

Qur'an 56:57 "It is We Who have created you: admit the truth and then surrender."

Bukhari: V9B89N256 "Allah's Apostle said, 'You should listen to and obey your ruler even if he is a black African slave whose head looks like a raisin.'"

Bukhari:V9B89N258 "The Prophet said, 'A Muslim has to listen to and obey the order of his ruler whether he likes it or not.'"

Qur'an 58:46 "Obey Allah and His Messenger; and do not dispute!"

Qur'an 64:12 "So obey Allah, and obey His Messenger (Muhammad)."

Qur'an 3:131 "Fear the Fire, which is prepared for those who reject Faith: and obey Allah and the Messenger."

Qur'an 24:51 "The only response of the (true) Believers when summoned to Allah and His Messenger in order to judge between them, is no other than this: they say, 'We hear and we obey.' Such are successful. Those who obey Allah and His Messenger, fear Allah and do right, such are the victorious. Whoever obeys Allah and His Messenger fears Allah and keeps his duty."

Qur'an 24:53 "They swear their strongest oaths saying that if only you would command them. They would leave their homes (and go forth fighting in Allah's Cause). Say: 'Swear not; Obedience is (more) reasonable.' Say: 'Obey Allah, and obey the Messenger.'"

Qur'an 4:59 "Believers, obey Allah, and obey the Messenger, and those charged with authority. If you dispute any matter, refer it to Allah and His Messenger. That is best, and most suitable for final determination."

Qur'an 4:64 "We sent not a messenger but to be obeyed, in accordance with the will of Allah."

Qur'an 4:65 "But no, by the Lord, they can have no Faith until they make you (Muhammad) judge in all disputes, and find in their souls no resistance against Your decisions, and accept them with complete submission."

Qur'an 4:66 "If We had ordered them to sacrifice their lives or to leave their homes [to fight], very few of them would have done it: But if they had done what they were told, it would have been best for them, and would have strengthened their (faith)." *Qur'an 4:69* "All who obey Allah and the Messenger are the ones whom Allah has bestowed favors [war booty]."

Qur'an 4:83 "When there comes to them some matter regarding war, they discuss it. If only they had referred it to the Messenger, or to those charged with authority, the proper investigators would have understood it."

Qur'an 4:115 "If anyone contradicts or opposes the Messenger [not Allah] after guidance has been conveyed to him, and follows a path other than the way, We shall burn him in Hell!"

Bukhari:V9B92N384 "Allah's Apostle said, 'Whoever obeys me will enter Paradise, and whoever disobeys me will not.'"

DECEPTION:

Bukhari:V7B67N427 "The Prophet said, 'If I take an oath and later find something else better than that, then I do what is better and expiate my oath.'"

Qur'an 9:3 "Allah and His Messenger dissolve obligations."

Qur'an 66:1 "Allah has already sanctioned for you the dissolution of your vows."

Bukhari:V4B52N268 "Allah's Apostle said, 'War is deceit.'"

Qur'an 4:142 "Surely the hypocrites strive to deceive Allah. He shall retaliate by deceiving them."

Bukhari:V7B71N661 "Magic was worked on Allah's Apostle and he was bewitched so that he began to imagine doing things which in fact, he had not done."

Bukhari:V6B60N8 "Umar said, 'Our best Qur'an reciter is Ubai. And in spite of this, we leave out some of his statements because Allah's Apostle himself said, "Whatever verse or revelation

We abrogate or cause to be forgotten We bring a better one."

Qur'an 33:11 "In that situation the Believers were sorely tried and shaken as by a tremendous shaking. And behold! The Hypocrites and those in whose hearts is a disease said: 'Allah and His Messenger promised us nothing but delusion; they have promised only to deceive us."

Qur'an 33:14 "Say: Flight will not avail you if you flee from death, killing, or slaughter. In that case you will not be allowed to enjoy yourselves but a little while. Say, 'Who will screen you, saving you from Allah if he intends to harm and injure you?'"

Qur'an 33:21 "You have in (Muhammad) the Messenger of Allah a beautiful pattern of conduct for any one to follow."

Qur'an 74:31 "We have appointed nineteen angels to be the wardens of the Hell Fire. We made a stumbling-block for those who disbelieve and We have fixed their number as a trial for unbelievers in order that the people of the Book may arrive with certainty, and that no doubts may be left for the people of the Book, those in whose hearts is a disease. And for those to whom the Scripture Book has been given, and the believers, there should be no doubt. The unbelievers may say, 'What does the Lord intend by this?' The Lord will lead astray whomever He pleases, and He will guide whomever He pleases: and none can know the armies of your Lord except He, and this is no other than a warning to mankind."

Qur'an 74:52 "Each one of them wants to be given scrolls of revelation spread out! No! By no means! Nay, this is an admonishment. Let them keep it in remembrance! But they will not heed unless the Lord wants them to. He is the fountain of fear."

Bukhari:V2B24N555 "I heard the Prophet say, 'Allah hates for you for asking too many questions.'"

Qur'an 89:5 "There surely is an oath for thinking man."

Qur'an 92:8 "We will make smooth for him the path to misery."

Ishaq:519 "Hajjaj said to the Apostle, 'I have money scattered among the Meccan merchants, so give me permission to go and get it.' Having got Muhammad's permission, he said, 'I must tell lies.' The Apostle said, 'Tell them.'"

Qur'an 8:58 "If you apprehend treachery from a people with whom you have a treaty, retaliate by breaking off relations with them."

Qur'an 47:24 "Do they not understand the Qur'an? Nay, on the hearts there are locks preventing them from understanding."

Ishaq:548 "By Allah, the black mass has spread. Abu Bakr said, 'There is not much honesty among people nowadays.'"

Qur'an 5:41 "Whomever Allah wants to deceive you cannot help. Allah does not want them to know the truth because he intends to disgrace them and then torture them."

Qur'an 5:101 "Believers! Do not ask questions about things which if made plain and declared to you, may vex you, causing you trouble." *Qur'an 5:102* "Some people before you did ask such questions, and on that account they lost their faith and became disbelievers."

Ishaq:567 "Muhammad informed Umar [the second Caliph], and he called the Prophet a liar."

Tabari IX:36/Ishaq:596 "'Prophet, this group of Ansar have a grudge against you for what you did with the booty and how you divided it among you own people.' 'Ansar, what is this talk I hear from you? What is the grudge you harbor against me? Do you think ill of me? Did I not come to you when you were erring and needy, and then made rich by Allah?' 'You came to us discredited, when your message was rejected by the Quraysh, and we believed you. You were forsaken and deserted and we assisted you. You were a fugitive and we took you in, sheltering you. You were poor and in need, and we comforted you."

Bukhari:V6B60N662 "Allah's Apostle said, 'Some eloquent speech is as effective as magic.'"

Tabari VI:110 "When Muhammad brought a revelation from Allah canceling what Satan had cast on the tongue of His Prophet, the Quraysh said, 'Muhammad has repented of [reneged on] what he said concerning the position of our gods with Allah. He has altered [the bargain] and brought something else.' Those two phrases which Satan had cast on Muhammad's tongue of were in the mouth of every polytheist. The Messenger said, 'I have fabricated things against Allah and have imputed to Him words which He has not spoken.'"

Qur'an 40:32 "O my People! I fear a Day when there will be mutual wailing. No one shall defend you against Allah. Any whom Allah causes to err, there is no guide. That is how Allah leads the skeptic astray."

Ishaq:248 "Allah has sealed their hearts and their hearing, blinding them so that they will never find guidance. And that is because they have declared you a liar and they do not believe in what has come down from their Lord to you even though they believe in all that came down before you. For opposing you they will have an awful punishment."

Qur'an 2:6 "As for the disbelievers, it is the same whether you warn them or not; they will not believe. Allah has set a seal upon their hearts, upon their hearing, and a covering over their eyes. There is a great torment for them."

Qur'an 2:9 "They deceive Allah and those who believe, but they only deceive themselves, and realize (it) not! In their hearts is a disease; and Allah has increased their disease. Grievous is the painful doom they (incur) because they (lie)."

Qur'an 8:18 "This and surely; Allah weakens the deceitful plots of unbelieving infidels."

Qur'an 8:30 "Remember how the unbelievers plotted against you (Muhammad). They plotted, and Allah too had arranged a plot; but Allah is the best schemer." *Ishaq:323* "I am the best of plotters. I deceived them with My guile so that I delivered you from them."

Qur'an 8:49 "When the hypocrites and those in whose hearts is a disease said: 'The religion has deceived and misled them.'"

Qur'an 8:71 "If they try to deceive you, remember they have deceived Allah before."

Tabari VII:85/Ishaq:363 "The Jews of the Qaynuqa replied, 'Muhammad, do you think that we are like your people? Do not be deluded by the fact that you met a people with no knowledge and you made good use of your opportunity.'"

Ishaq:365/Tabari VII:94 "Muhammad bin Maslamah said, 'O Messenger, we shall have to tell lies.' 'Say what you like,' Muhammad replied. 'You are absolved, free to say whatever you must.'"

Bukhari:V5B59N369 "Allah's Apostle said, 'Who is willing to kill Ka'b bin Ashraf who has hurt Allah and His Apostle?' Thereupon Muhammad bin Maslamah got up saying, 'O Allah's Apostle! Would you like me to kill him?' The Prophet said, 'Yes,' Maslamah said, 'Then allow me to say false things in order to deceive him.' The Prophet said, 'You may say such things.'"

Qur'an 61:5 "Moses said: 'O my people, why do you annoy and insult me, when you well know I am Allah's Messenger?' Then when they turned away, Allah caused them to be deceived."

Bukhari:V4B52N233 "Allah's Apostle forbade the people to travel to a hostile country carrying copies of the Qur'an. [He said:] Unbelievers will never understand our signs and revelations."

Ishaq:248 "Allah increases their sickness. A tormented doom awaits the Jews. Allah said, 'They are mischief makers. They are fools. The Jews deny the truth and contradict what the Apostle has brought. I will mock them and let them continue to wander blindly.'"

Bukhari:V4B52N147 "Allah's Apostle said, 'A man may seem as if he were practicing the deeds of Paradise while in fact he is from the people of Hell.'"

Qur'an 13:27 "Say, 'God leads whosoever He wills astray.'"

Ishaq:383 "One of the young men's fathers confronted Muhammad and said, 'You have robbed my son of his life by your deception and brought great sorrow to me.'"

Qur'an 3:24 "They have been deceived by the lies they have themselves fabricated; their religion has deceived them."

Ishaq:397 "Then Allah said, 'It is not for any prophet to deceive."

Ishaq:442 "By Muhammad's order we beguiled them."

Tabari VIII:23 "The Messenger and his Companions continued in the fear and distress that Allah has described in the Qur'an. Then Nu'aym came to the Prophet. 'I 've become a Muslim, but my tribe does not know of my Islam; so command me whatever you will.' Muhammad said, 'Make them abandon each other if you can so that they will leave us; for war is deception.'"

Ishaq:496 "'By Allah you lie,' one said to another. 'Liar yourself!' 'You are a disaffected person arguing on behalf of the diseased."

Bukhari:V4B53N408 "When the Prophet wanted to perform the Umrah, the Quraysh stipulated that he could not preach (Islam). So Ali started writing a treaty. 'This is what Muhammad, Apostle of Allah, has agreed to.' The (Meccans) said, 'If we believed that you were the Apostle of Allah we would have followed you. So write, 'This is what Muhammad bin Abdallah has agreed to.' The Apostle could not write, so he asked Ali to erase the expression: 'Apostle of Allah.' On that Ali said, 'I will never erase it.' Muhammad said, 'Let me see the paper.' The Prophet erased the expression with his own hand."

INTOLERANCE:

Qur'an 9:71 "O Prophet, strive hard [fighting] against the unbelievers and the Hypocrites, and be harsh with them. Their abode is Hell, an evil refuge indeed."

Qur'an 8:59 "The infidels should not think that they can get away from us. Prepare against them whatever arms and weaponry you can muster so that you may terrorize them."

Qur'an 4:168 "Those who reject [Islamic] Faith, Allah will not forgive them nor guide them to any path except the way to Hell, to dwell therein forever. And this to Allah is easy."

Qur'an 4:114 "He who disobeys the Apostle after guidance has been revealed will burn in Hell."

Ishaq:344 "We smote them and they scattered. The impious met death. They became fuel for Hell. All who aren't Muslims must go there. It will consume them while the Stoker [Allah] increases the heat. They had called Allah's Apostle a liar. They claimed, 'You are nothing but a sorcerer.' So Allah destroyed them."

Qur'an 33:60 "Truly, if the Hypocrites stir up sedition, if the agitators in the City do not desist, We shall urge you to go against them and set you over them. They shall have a curse on them. Whenever they are found, they shall be seized and slain without mercy—a fierce slaughter—murdered, a horrible murdering."

Qur'an 33:64 "Verily Allah has cursed the Unbelievers [whom he defines as Christians in the 5th surah] and has prepared for them a Blazing Fire to dwell in forever. No protector will they find, nor savior. That Day their faces will be turned upside down in the Fire. They will say: 'Woe to us! We should have obeyed Allah and obeyed the Messenger!' 'Our Lord! Give them double torment and curse them with a very great Curse!'"

Qur'an 5:10 "Those who reject, disbelieve and deny Our signs, proofs and verses will be companions of Hell-Fire."

Qur'an 88:1 "Has the narration reached you of the overwhelming (calamity)? Some faces (all disbelievers, Jews and Christians) that Day, will be humiliated, downcast, scorched by the burning fire, while they are made to drink from a boiling hot spring."

Bukhari:V1B11N617 "I would order someone to collect firewood and another to lead prayer. Then I would burn the houses of men who did not present themselves at the compulsory prayer and prostration."

Bukhari:V1B11N626 "The Prophet said, 'No prayer is harder for the hypocrites than the Fajr. If they knew the reward they would come to (the mosque) even if they had to crawl. Certainly I decided to order a man to lead the prayer and then take a flame to burn all those who had not left their houses for the prayer, burning them alive inside their homes.'"

Bukhari:V4B52N260 "The Prophet said, 'If a Muslim discards his religion, kill him.'"

Qur'an 5:51 "Believers, take not Jews and Christians for your friends."

Qur'an 74:31 "We have appointed nineteen angels to be the wardens of the Hell Fire. We made a stumbling-block for those who disbelieve and We have fixed their number as a trial for unbelievers in order that the People of the Book may arrive with certainty, and that no doubts may be left for the People of the Book, those in whose hearts is a disease."

Bukhari:V4B54N487 "The Prophet said, 'The Hell Fire is 69 times hotter than ordinary worldly fires.' So someone said, 'Allah's Apostle, wouldn't this ordinary fire have been sufficient to torture the unbelievers?'"

Qur'an 72:15 "The disbelievers are the firewood of hell."

Qur'an 72:17 "If any turns away from the reminder of his Lord (the Qur'an), He will thrust him into an ever growing torment, and cause for him a severe penalty."

Qur'an 72:25 "Whoever disobeys the Lord and His Messenger then there is for him the fire of Hell where they shall abide forever."

Qur'an 88:21 "You are not a warden over them; except for those who turn away and disbelieve, in which case, he will be punished with the severest punishment. Verily to Us they will return."

Qur'an 90:19 "But those who reject Our Signs, Proofs, and Verses, they are the unhappy Companions of the Left Hand. Fire will be their awning, vaulting over them."

Qur'an 95:4 "We have indeed created man in the best molds. Then do We abase him, reducing him to be the lowest of the low, except such as believe."

Tabari VIII:130 "The Messenger said, 'Two religions cannot coexist in the Arabian Peninsula.' Umar investigated the matter, then sent to the Jews, saying: 'Allah has given permission for you to be expelled.'"

Qur'an 2:64 "But you [Jews] went back on your word and were lost losers. So become apes, despised and hated. We made an example out of you."

Qur'an 66:9 "O Prophet! Strive hard against the unbelieving Infidels and the Hypocrites; be severe against them. Their abode is Hell, an evil resort."

Qur'an 60:1 "Believers, take not my enemies and yours as allies, offering them love, even though they have rejected the truth that has come to you, and have driven out the Prophet and you because you believe in Allah! If you have come out to struggle [fight jihad] in My Cause, and to seek My Pleasure, (take them not as friends), holding secret converse of love with them: for I am aware of all you conceal. And any of you that does this has strayed from the Straight Path. If they were to get the better of you, they would be your foes, and stretch forth their hands and their tongues against you with evil (designs)."

Qur'an 60:5 "We reject you. Hostility and hate have come between us forever, unless you believe in Allah only.'"

Qur'an 48:13 "If any believe not in Allah and His Messenger, We have prepared a Blazing Fire for them!"

Qur'an 48:28 "It is He Who has sent His Messenger with guidance and the Religion of Truth (Islam), that he may make it superior to every other religion, exalting it over them. Allah is a sufficient Witness. Muhammad is the Prophet of Allah. Those who are with him are severe with Infidel unbelievers."

Qur'an 47:3 "Those who disbelieve follow vanities, while those who believe follow truth from their Lord: Thus does Allah coin for men their similitudes [resemblances] as a lesson. Whoever denies faith [in Islam and Muhammad], his work is of no account, and in the hereafter he shall be one of the losers."

Qur'an 9:2 "You cannot weaken Allah or escape. Allah will disgrace the unbelievers and put those who reject Him to shame." *Qur'an 9:4* "You cannot escape Allah, weaken or frustrate Him. And proclaim a grievous penalty of a painful doom to those who reject [Islamic] Faith."

Qur'an 9:17 "The disbelievers have no right to visit the mosques of Allah while bearing witness against their own souls to infidelity. These it is whose doings are in vain, and in the fire shall they abide. Only he shall visit the mosques of Allah who believes in Allah and the latter day, and keeps up devotional obligations, pays the zakat, and fears none but Allah."

Qur'an 9:28 "Believers, truly the pagan disbelievers are unclean."

Qur'an 9:30 "The Jews call Uzair (Ezra) the son of Allah, and the Christians say that the Messiah is the son of Allah. That is their saying from their mouths; they but imitate what the unbelievers of old used to say. Allah's (Himself) fights against them, cursing them, damning and destroying them. How perverse are they!"

Qur'an 9:33 "He has sent His Messenger (Muhammad) with guidance and the Religion of Truth (Islam) to make it superior over all religions, even though the disbelievers detest (it)."

Qur'an 9:63 "Know they not that for those who oppose Allah and His Messenger is the Fire of Hell wherein they shall dwell? That is the supreme disgrace."

Qur'an 9:66 "Make no excuses: you have rejected Faith after you had accepted it. If We pardon some of you, We will punish others amongst you, for they are disbelievers."

Qur'an 9:113 "It is not fitting for the Prophet and those who believe, that they should pray for the forgiveness for disbelievers, even though they be close relatives, after it is clear to them that they are the inmates of the Flaming Hell Fire."

Qur'an 5:78 "Curses were pronounced on the unbelievers, the Children of Israel who rejected Islam, by the tongues of David and of Jesus because they disobeyed and rebelled." *Qur'an 5:80* "You see many of them allying themselves with the Unbelievers [other translations read: "Infidels"]. Vile indeed are their souls. Allah's wrath is on them, and in torment will they abide." *Qur'an 5:82* "You will find the Jews and disbelievers [defined as Christians in 5:73] the most vehement in hatred for the Muslims."

Qur'an 5:86 "Those who reject Islam and are disbelievers, denying our Signs and Revelations —they shall be the owners of the Hell Fire."

Tabari IX:78 "No polytheist shall come near the Holy Mosque, and no one shall circumambulate Allah's House naked."

Ishaq:246 "Hypocrites used to assemble in the mosque and listen to the stories of the Muslims and laugh and scoff at their religion. So Muhammad ordered that they should be ejected. They were thrown out with great violence. Abu went to Amr, took his foot and dragged him out of the mosque. Another Muslim slapped a man's face while dragging him forcefully, knocking him down. One was pulled violently by his hair. 'Don't come near the Apostle's mosque again, for you are unclean.' The first hundred verses of the Cow surah came down in reference to these Jewish rabbis and Hypocrites."

Ishaq:262 "Some Muslims remained friends with the Jews, so Allah sent down a Qur'an forbidding them to take Jews as friends. From their mouths hatred has already shown itself and what they conceal is worse."

Qur'an 5:51 "Believers, take not Jews and Christians for your friends. They are but friends and protectors to each other."

Ishaq:245 "The Apostle used to say, 'Their religion will never march with ours.'"

Bukhari:V4B52N288 "Expel disbelievers from the Arabian Peninsula.'"

Qur'an 2:191 "Slay them wherever you find and catch them, and drive them out from where they have turned you out; for persecution and oppression are worse than slaughter."

Qur'an 33:25 "Allah drove the disbelievers back...and helped the believers in battle.... He terrorized the People of the Book so that you killed some and made many captive."

Tabari IX:167 "Muhammad waged war against the false prophets [slitting his own wrists would have done nicely] by sending messengers with instructions to get rid of them by artful contrivance [plot or machination]."

Bukhari:V5B59N727 "When Allah's Apostle became seriously sick, he started covering his face with a woolen sheet. When he felt short of breath, he removed it, and said, 'That is so! Allah's curse be on Jews and Christians.'"

Qur'an 21:98 "Verily you (disbelieving Infidels), and the gods that you worship besides Allah, are the fuel for Hell, faggots for the fire! Certainly you will enter it! Had their (idols) been (real) alihah (gods), they would have kept them out of Hell. Therein, sobbing will be your lot. Breathing with deep sighs, roaring. You will hear nothing but wailing and groaning."

Qur'an 18:103 "Say: 'Shall we inform you of who will be the greatest losers? ...Those who reject my Revelations... Hell is their reward, because they rejected Islam, and took My proofs, verses, and lessons, and those of My Messengers by way of jest in mockery.'"

Qur'an 52:9 "On the Day when heaven will heave in dreadful shaking, trembling, and mountains will fly hither and thither, woe to those who reject [me], that play in shallow trifles and sport in vain discourses. That Day they will be pushed down by force, thrust with a horrible thrust into the Fire of Hell. Unable to resist, they shall be driven to the fire with violence."

Qur'an 40:10 "Lo, those who disbelieve will be informed by proclamation: 'Verily Allah's abhorrence is more terrible than your aversion to yourselves. Allah's hatred of you is terrible, seeing that you were called to the Faith [of submission] and you refused.'"

Qur'an 40:35 "Those who dispute the Signs and Verses of Allah without any authority, grievous and odious, hateful and disgusting, is it in the sight of Allah and the Believers.'"

Ishaq:185 "Adam reviewed the spirits of his offspring. The infidels excited his disgust. I saw men with lips like camels. In their hands were pieces of fire like stones which they thrust into their mouths. They came out their posteriors."

Qur'an 20:48 "Verily it has been revealed to us that the Penalty of Doom awaits those who reject and deny."

Qur'an 20:100 "Whoever turns from it, he shall bear a burden on the Day of Doom. Grievous evil will the load on them. We shall gather the Mujrimun (disbeliever) blue or blind-eyed with thirst.... My Lord will blast them and scatter them as dust."

Qur'an 21:06 "Not one of the populations which We destroyed believed: will these believe? ...So we saved whom We pleased, and We destroyed the disbelievers." *Qur'an 21:10* "Verily, We have sent down for you a Book in which is your reminder. Have you then no sense? How many towns have We utterly destroyed because of their wrongs, exchanging them for other people? When they (felt) Our Torment, behold, they (began to) fly. Fly not, but return to that which emasculated you so that you may be interrogated. They cried: 'Woe to us!' Their crying did not cease till We mowed them down as ashes silent and quenched."

Qur'an 21:98 "Verily you (unbelievers), and that which you worship besides Allah, are faggots for the Hell Fire! And come to it you will! There, sobbing and groaning will be your lot."

Qur'an 46:20 "On that Day the unbelievers will be placed before the Fire: 'You squandered your good things in this life and you sought comfort from them, but today shall you be rewarded with a penalty of humiliation.'"

Qur'an 59:4 "If any one resists Allah, verily Allah is severe in Punishment, stern in reprisal."

Ishaq:249 "Fear Hell, whose fuel is men and stones prepared for the infidels.'"

Qur'an 2:39 "Those who reject and deny Our Signs will be inmates of the Hell Fire and will abide there forever."

Qur'an 2:99 "We have sent down to you Manifest Signs; and none reject them but those who are perverse."

Qur'an 2:71 "The semblance of the infidels is one who shouts to one who cannot hear. They are deaf, dumb, and blind. They make no sense." *Qur'an 2:174* "Those who conceal Allah's revelations in the [Bible] Scripture Book, and thus make a miserable profit thereby [selling it to Muhammad], swallow Fire into themselves; Allah will not address them. Grievous will be their doom." *Qur'an 2:175* "They are the ones who bartered away guidance for error and Torment in place of Forgiveness. Ah, what boldness (they show) for the Fire! (Their doom is) because Allah sent down the Book in truth but those who seek causes of dispute in the Book are in a schism of great opposition."

Qur'an 2:256 "There is no compulsion in religion." *Qur'an 4:90* "If they turn back from Islam, becoming renegades, seize them and kill them wherever you find them."

Bukhari:V5B59N572 "O Muslims, take not My enemies as friends, offering them kindness when they reject Allah, the Prophet Muhammad, and his Qur'an. And whoever does that, then indeed he has gone (far) astray. You have come out to fight in My Cause, seeking My acceptance so do not be friendly with them, even in secret." [60:1]

Qur'an 8:12 "I will terrorize the unbelievers. Therefore smite them on their necks and every joint and incapacitate them. Strike off their heads and cut off each of their fingers and toes." *Qur'an 8:13* "This because they rejected Allah and defied His Messenger. If anyone opposes Allah and His Messenger, Allah shall be severe in punishment. That is the torment: 'So taste the punishment. For those infidels who resist there is the torment of Hell.'"

Qur'an 8:20 "Those who do not obey are the worst of beasts, the vilest of animals in the sight of Allah. They are deaf and dumb. Those who do not understand are senseless."

Qur'an 8:36 "The unbelievers spend their wealth to hinder (man) from the Way of Allah, and so will they continue to spend; but in the end they will have intense regrets and sighs. It will become an anguish for them, then they will be subdued. The unbelievers shall be driven into hell in order that Allah may distinguish the bad from the good and separate them. Allah wants to heap the wicked one over the other and cast them into Hell. They are the losers."

Qur'an 8:39 "So fight them until there is no more Fitnah (disbelief [non-Muslims]) and all submit to the religion of Allah alone (in the whole world)."

Qur'an 8:40 "If people are obstinate, and refuse to surrender, know Allah is your Supporter."

Qur'an 8:50 "If you could have seen the infidels when the angels drew away their souls, striking their faces and smiting their backs. The angels said: 'Taste the penalty of the blazing Fire.'"

Qur'an 8:52 "They denied and rejected the revelations of Allah, and Allah destroyed them, punishing them for their crimes: for Allah is strict, severe in punishment."

Ishaq:231 "Muslims are one ummah (community) to the exclusion of all men. Believers are friends of one another to the exclusion of all outsiders."

Ishaq:363 "Say to those who do not believe you: 'You will be vanquished and gathered into Hell, an evil resting place.'"

Qur'an 61:7 "Who does greater wrong than one who invents falsehood against Allah, even as he is being summoned to Submission? And Allah guides not the disbelievers. Their intention is to extinguish Allah's Light (by blowing) with their mouths: But Allah will complete His Light, even though the Unbelievers detest (it). It is He Who has sent His Messenger with Guidance and the Religion of Truth (Islam), that he may make it conquer all religion, even though the disbelievers hate (it)."

Qur'an 2:104 "To those who don't submit there is a grievous punishment."

Qur'an 3:4 "As a guidance to mankind, He sent down the criterion (to judge between right and wrong). Truly, for those who deny the proofs and signs of Allah, the torture will be severe; Allah is powerful, the Lord of Retribution."

Qur'an 3:10 "As for those who deny [Islam], neither their wealth nor their children will help them in the least against Allah. They shall be faggots for the fire of Hell." *Qur'an 3:11* "The punishment of Allah is severe. So tell the unbelieving infidels: 'You will surely be vanquished, seized by Allah, and driven to Hell. How bad a preparation.'"

Qur'an 3:26 "You [Allah] exalt whom You please and debase and humiliate whom You will. Those who believe should not take unbelievers as their friends...guard yourselves from them.... Allah commands you to beware of Him."

Qur'an 3:32 "Say: 'Obey Allah and His Messenger;' If they refuse, remember Allah does not like unbelieving infidels."

Qur'an 3:55 "Allah said, 'Jesus, I will take you and raise you to Myself and rid you of the infidels (who have forged the lie that you are My son).... Those who are infidels will surely receive severe torment both in this world and the next; and none will they have as a savior for them."

Qur'an 3:61 "If anyone disputes with you about Jesus being divine, flee them and pray that Allah will curse them."

Qur'an 3:62 "This is the true account, the true narrative, the true explanation: There is no Ilah (God) except Allah; and Allah—He is the Mighty. And if they turn away, then lo! Allah is aware of the corrupters, the mischief-makers. Say: 'People of the Book, come to common terms as an agreement between us and you: That we all shall worship none but Allah.'"

Qur'an 3:84 "Say (Muhammad): 'We believe in Allah and that which is revealed to us and that which was revealed unto Abraham and Ishmael and Isaac and Jacob and the tribes [of Israel], and in (the Books) given to Moses, Jesus, and the prophets, from their Lord. We make no distinction between any of them, and unto Him we have surrendered, bowing our will (in Islam).'" *Qur'an 3:85* "If anyone desires a religion other than Islam (Surrender), never will it be accepted of him; and in the Hereafter He will be in the ranks of those who are losers." *Qur'an 3:87* "Of such, the reward is the curse of Allah, of His angels, and of all men, all together. Their penalty of doom will not be lightened."

Qur'an 3:118 "Believers! Take not into your intimacy those outside your religion (pagans, Jews, and Christians). They will not fail to corrupt you. They only desire your ruin. Rank hatred has already appeared from their mouths. What their hearts conceal is far worse. When they are alone, they bite off the very tips of their fingers at you in their rage. Say unto them: 'Perish in your rage.'"

Qur'an 3:141 "This is so that Allah may test the faithful and destroy the unbelieving infidels." [Another translation:] "Allah's object is to purge those that are true in Faith and blight the disbelievers. This is so that Allah may test the faithful and destroy the unbelieving infidels."

Qur'an 3:150 "Soon We shall strike terror into the hearts of the Infidels, for that they joined companions with Allah, for which He had sent no authority: their abode will be in the Fire!"

Qur'an 33:8 "He has prepared for the Unbelievers a grievous Penalty."

Qur'an 33:58 "And those who annoy or malign Muslims bear (on themselves) a crime of calumny and a glaring sin."

Qur'an 24:39 "For those who disbelieve, their deeds are like a mirage in the desert. There is no water for the thirsty. He only finds Allah, who will pay him his due in Hell."

Qur'an 23:40 "Soon they will regret. Torment and an awful cry will overtake them. We have made such men rubbish, like rotting plants. So away with the people."

Qur'an 24:57 "Never think that the unbelievers can escape in the land. Their abode is Fire!"

Qur'an 4:12 "Those who disobey Allah and His Messenger and transgress His limits will be admitted to a Fire, to abide therein: And they shall have a humiliating punishment."

EYE WITNESSES:

Qur'an 38:3 "They wonder that a warner has come to them from among themselves. And the disbelievers say, 'This (Prophet Muhammad) is a sorcerer, a charlatan, an wizard telling lies. He has made the alihah (gods) into one Ilah (God). This is a curious and strange thing to be sure!' Their leaders said, 'Walk away from him...there is surely some motive behind this—something sought after—a thing he has designed against us...It is surely a forgery.'"

Qur'an 38:7 "'We have not heard of this in the religion of later days. This is nothing but an invention! What! Has this been sent to him?' Nay, but they are in doubt about My reminder (this Qur'an). Nay, but they have not tasted (My) Torment yet! Let them climb up the ladders to the heavens. They will be one more army vanquished among the many routed hordes.... They rejected my Messengers so My Torment was justified."

Qur'an 52:29 "Therefore remind: By the grace of your Lord you are no vulgar soothsayer, nor are you a possessed madman." [Another translation reads:] "Therefore warn (Muhammad). By the grace of Allah you are neither soothsayer nor madman." *Qur'an 52:30* "Or do they say: 'A Poet! We await for him some evil accidental calamity (hatched) by time!' Do they say: He is a poet from whom we expect an adverse turn of fortune?"

Qur'an 52:32 "Is it that their mental faculties of understanding urge them to this, or are they an outrageous folk, transgressing beyond the bounds?" *Qur'an 52:33* "Or do they say, 'He fabricated it (the Qur'an)?' Nay, they will never believe. Let them then produce a recital like unto it, if they speak the truth!" *Qur'an 52:38* "Or have they a ladder, by which they can (climb up to heaven and) listen (to its secrets)? Then let (such a) listener of theirs produce a warrant manifesting proof."

Qur'an 52:40 "Or is it that you demand a reward or fee from them (for preaching Islam), so that they are burdened with expense and a load of debt? Or that the Ghaib (unseen) is in their hands that they have it written down? Or do they intend a plot (against you), staging a deception? But those who defy and seek to ensnare (the messenger) are themselves being plotted against and will be tricked!"

Ishaq:155 "Khadija was the first to believe in Allah and His Apostle. By her Allah lightened the burden on His prophet. He never met with contradiction and charges of falsehood but he was comforted by her when he went home. She strengthened him and belittled the opposition."

Bukhari:V4B54N440 "The Prophet said, 'Aisha, this is Gabriel. He sends his greetings and salutations to you.' Aisha replied, 'Salutations and greetings to him.' Then addressing the Prophet she said, 'You see what I don't see.'"

Qur'an 74:21 "Again, woe to them; may they be cursed for how they plotted. They looked around, frowned, and scowled with displeasure. Then they turned back and were haughty with pride. They said: 'This is nothing but magical enchantment, derived and narrated from others. This is nothing but the words of a mortal man!'"

Qur'an 74:49 "What is the matter with them that they turn away from admonition as if they were freighted asses!"

Qur'an 74:52 "Each one of them wants to be given scrolls of revelation spread out! No! By no means! They fear not the hereafter. Nay, this is an admonishment. Let them keep it in remembrance! But they will not heed unless the Lord wants them to. He is the fountain of fear. He is the fount of mercy."

Ishaq:118 "Muhammad is trying to bewitch you."

Ishaq:119 "'Abu Tabib, your nephew Muhammad has cursed our gods [at this point he had cursed all of them, including Allah], insulted our religion [more correctly, insulted them by trying to steal their religion], mocked our way of life and accused our forefathers of error. Either you stop him or let us get to him. For you, like us, are in opposition to him. He gave them a conciliatory reply. They returned a second time and said, 'We have asked you to put a stop to your nephew's activities but you have not done so. By Allah, we cannot endure having our fathers reviled and our customs mocked.' Muhammad thought that his uncle had the idea of abandoning and betraying him, and that he was going to lose his support. The Apostle broke into tears."

Tabari VI:93 "The Quraysh went to Abu Talib and said, 'Your nephew [Muhammad] has reviled our gods, denounced our religion, derided our traditional values, and told us that our forefathers were misguided [and burning in hell]. Either curb his attacks on us or give us a free hand to deal with him, for you are as opposed to him as we are.' They said, 'We asked you to forbid your nephew from attacking us, but you did nothing. By Allah, we can no longer endure this vilification of our forefathers, this derision of our traditional values, and this abuse of our gods.' This breach and enmity with his tribe weighed heavily on Talib. 'Abu Talib, you are our elder and our chief, so give us justice against your nephew and order him to desist from reviling our gods, and we will leave him to his god.'"

Tabari VI:95 "Abu Talib sent for Muhammad. 'Nephew, here are the shaykhs and nobles of your tribe. They have asked for justice against you. You should desist from reviling their gods and they will leave you to your god.'"

Tabari VI:96 "Abu Talib said to Muhammad, 'Nephew, how is it that your tribe is complaining of you and claiming that you are reviling their gods and saying this, that, and the other?' The Messenger said, 'I want them to utter one saying. If they say it, the Arabs will submit to them and the non-Arabs will pay the jizyah [submission tax] to them.'"

Ishaq:121 "'If we say contradictory things about Muhammad, we might lose our credibility [and thus the financial benefits of being heir to Qusayy's religious scam]. Therefore, let us agree upon one criticism, which we can all claim without dispute. Some say that we should call Muhammad a deranged soothsayer. But is his the incoherent speech of a madman? [Yes] Some say he is possessed. But there is no choking, spasmodic movements, or whispering.' [Actually, this is how Muhammad said that he endured revelations.] Others said, 'Then let's say he is a poet.' 'No, he is no poet. We know poetry in its forms.' [They knew that the Hanif Zayd, among others, was a far better poet than Muhammad and his god.] Then they said: 'He is a sorcerer.' 'No, we have seen sorcerers and their sorcery. With him there is no spitting and no blowing. [There are dozens of Hadiths depicting Muhammad spitting and blowing to exorcize illness and evil spells.]"

Ishaq:121 "'The nearest thing to the truth is that he is a sorcerer who has brought a message by which he separates a man from his father, brother, wife, children and family.' They all agreed. Then, according their scheme, the men of Quraysh spread the word that 'this is nothing but ancient sorcery among the pilgrims in the hajj season. They warned everyone they met that Muhammad was a possessed sorcerer, stirring up divisions in the families."

Ishaq:130 "When the Quraysh became distressed by the trouble caused by the Apostle they called him a liar, insulted him, and accused him of being a poet, a sorcerer, a diviner [occult soothsayer], and of being possessed. However, the Apostle continued to proclaim what Allah had ordered him to proclaim. He excited their dislike by condemning their religion."

Ishaq:116 "I heard the Apostle say, 'I have never invited anyone to accept Islam who hasn't has shown signs of reluctance, suspicion and hesitation.'"

Qur'an 69:38 "But nay! I swear that this is truly the word of an honored, illustrious, and noble Messenger; it is not the word of a poet, nor is it the word of a soothsayer."

Qur'an 70:36 "What is the matter with the disbelievers that they rush madly to listen to you (Muhammad in order to belie you and mock you and Allah's Book)? Doesn't every man long to enter the Garden of Delight?"

Qur'an 68:1 "I call to witness the Pen and what it writes. You are not a demented madman or possessed."

Qur'an 68:4 "You are an exalted character of tremendous morality. Soon you will see, and they will see, which of you is afflicted with madness. Surely the Lord knows best who errs from His way, and who follows the right course. So don't listen to those who deny, or those who would form compromises with you to get you to relent. Heed not despicable men or contemptible swearers or back-biters, neither obey feeble oath-mongers, or slanderers, going about defaming, hindering good, transgressing beyond bounds, crude, deep in sin, violent and cruel, greedy, and intrusive, ignoble, and besides all that, mean and infamous."

Qur'an 68:15 "When you recite Our (Qur'an) proofs and verses they cry, 'Tales of the ancients, mere fables of long ago.' Soon shall We muzzle them and brand the beast on the snout!"

Ishaq:180 "According to my information, the Apostle often sat by a young Christian slave named Jabr. The Meccans said, 'He is the one who teaches Muhammad most of what he brings.' Then Allah revealed, *Qur'an 16:103* 'We know what they (pagans) say: "It is only a mortal man who teaches him (Muhammad). But the tongue of the man they wickedly point to is notably foreign, while this (Qur'an) is pure Arabic.'"

Qur'an 16:103 "When we replace a message with another, and Allah knows best what He reveals, they say: 'You have made it up.'"

Qur'an 68:51 "And the unbelievers would almost smite you (Muhammad) with their eyes, tripping you when they hear the Message. And they say: 'Surely he is possessed!'"

Qur'an 81:22 "And people, your comrade is not one who is possessed, or one who has gone mad."

Qur'an 6:66 "The people reject this (Book) and call it a lie though it is the truth.' ...When you see men who meddle with Our Revelations, turn away, withdrawing from them. Satan makes you forget."

Qur'an 66:8 "Believers, turn to Allah with repentance. That Day, He will not permit His Prophet to be humiliated."

Qur'an 47:16 "And among them are men who listen to you (Muhammad), but in the end, when they leave you, they say: 'What is this he is saying now?'"

Qur'an 9:61 "Among them are men who vex, annoy, and molest the Prophet, saying, 'He is (all) ear and believes every thing that he hears.' ...But those who offend the Messenger will have a grievous torment, a painful doom."

Qur'an 9:64 "The Hypocrites are afraid that a surah will be sent down about them, showing them what is (really) in their hearts. Say: 'Go ahead, scoff and mock, will you! Lo, Allah is disclosing what you fear.' If you question them (Muhammad about this), they declare: 'We were only talking idly, jesting in play.' Say: 'Was it at Allah and His proofs, signs, verses, lessons, and Messenger that you were mocking?'"

Tabari VIII:173/Ishaq:547 "Alas, Sufyan, isn't it time for you to admit that I am the Messenger of Allah?' Sufyan replied, 'As to that I have some doubt.' 'Woe to you! Submit and recite the testimony that there is no Ilah (God) but Allah and that Muhammad is the Apostle of Allah before your head is cut off!'"

Qur'an 5:64 "The Jews say: 'Allah's hands are fettered.'" [i.e., Allah is powerless.]

Qur'an 5:104 "When it is said to them: 'Come to what Allah has revealed; come to the Messenger.' They say: 'Enough for us are the ways we found our fathers following.' What! Even though their fathers were void of knowledge and guidance?"

Tabari IX:36/Ishaq:596 "'Prophet, this group of Ansar have a grudge against you for what you did with the booty and how you divided it among you own people.' 'Ansar, what is this talk I hear from you? What is the grudge you harbor in your hearts against me? Do you think ill of me? Did I not come to you when you were erring and needy, and then made rich by Allah?' 'You came to us discredited, when your message was rejected by the Quraysh, and we believed you. You were forsaken and deserted and we assisted you. You were a fugitive and we took you in, sheltering you. You were poor and in need, and we comforted you."

Tabari IX:187 "When the Prophet died, Umar stood up threatening the people, saying, 'Some of the hypocrites allege that the Messenger of Allah is dead. I swear by Allah that he is alive, not dead. By Allah, the Prophet will return and he will go after those who are spreading lies about him. He will cut off the hands and the feet of those who claim that he is dead. He will crucify them.'"

Bukhari:V5B59N733 "While Umar was talking to the people, Abu Bakr said, 'Sit down, Umar!' But he refused. So the people came to Abu and left him. Bakr said, 'To proceed, if you used to worship Muhammad, then Muhammad is dead, but if anyone of you used to worship Allah, then Allah is alive and shall never die.'"

Qur'an 76:4 "For the rejecters We have prepared chains, iron collars, manacles, and a blazing fire." *Qur'an 77:39* "If you have a trick or plot, use it against Me! If you have any wit, outwit Me. Woe to the rejecters!" *Qur'an 78:28* "They called Our proofs, signs, and verses false with strong denial. We have recorded everything in a book, so taste (that which you earned). We give you nothing but torment."

Qur'an 83:10 "Woe to those who deny, reject Our message, and repudiate. When Our Verses are rehearsed they say, 'Tales of the ancients! Mere fables of old.'"

Qur'an 83:29 "The disbelievers used to laugh at believers. When they passed by them, they winked at one another (in mockery). When they returned to their folk, they would jest...but soon the believers will laugh at the unbelievers sitting on high thrones, gazing. The unbelievers will be paid back for what they did."

Qur'an 84:22 "The unbelievers reject (Muhammad and the Qur'an); they deny and lie. Allah has full knowledge of what they secrete. So announce to them tidings of a terrible torment."

Qur'an 84:20 "What is the matter with them that they do not believe, and when the Qur'an is recited to them, they do not fall prostrate in adoration."

Qur'an 85:10 "Those who try or tempt the believers will have the penalty of Hell: They will have the doom of the burning fire. Verily, the Seizure of the Lord is severe and painful.... Allah will encompass them from behind! He will punish them. Nay! This is a Glorious Qur'an."

Qur'an 86:15 "They are plotting a scheme against you, but I am also planning a scheme against them."

Tabari VI:98 "The situation deteriorated, hostility became bitter, and people withdrew from one another, displaying open hatred. The Meccan chiefs conspired to seduce their sons, brothers, and clansmen away from the new religion. It was a trial which severely shook the Muslims who had followed the Prophet. Some were seduced. Muhammad commanded Muslims to emigrate to Abyssinia." *Tabari VI:98* "The main body went to Abyssinia because of the coercion they were being subjected to in Mecca. His fear was that they would be seduced from their religion. There is a difference of opinion as to the number of those who emigrated in stealth and secret. Some say there were eleven men and four women. ...Ibn Ishaq claims there were ten."

Tabari VI:101 "The Messenger remained in Mecca preaching in secret and openly, protected by his uncle Abu Talib. When the Quraysh saw that they had no means of attacking him physically, they accused him of sorcery, soothsaying, and madness, and of being a poet. They began to keep those away from him whom they feared might listen and follow him."

Ishaq:130/Tabari VI:101 "'The nastiest thing I saw the Quraysh do to the Messenger occurred when their nobles assembled in the Hijr [standing place]. They discussed Muhammad, saying, "We have never seen the kind of trouble we have endured from this fellow. He has derided our traditional values, declared our way of life foolish, abused and insulted our forefathers, reviled our religion, caused division among us, divided the community, and cursed our gods. We have endured a great deal from him.' While they were saying this, the Apostle walked up and kissed the Black Stone. Then he performed the circumambulation of the Ka'aba. As he did they said some injurious things about him. I could see from the Messenger's face that he had heard them. When he passed a second time they made similar remarks. When he passed them the third time, the Prophet stopped and said, 'Hear me, O Quraysh. By Him who holds Muhammad's life in his hand, I will bring you slaughter.'"

Tabari VI:102 "'They were gripped by what he had said. The word he used struck the people so not one could move. It was as though everyone had a bird perched on his head. Even those of them who had been urging the severest measures against him, now spoke in a conciliatory way, using the politest expressions they could muster. They said, "Depart Abu al-Qasim [Muhammad's real name]; for by Allah, you were never violent [before Islam].'"'

Tabari VI:102 "The Prophet left, and the next day they gathered in the Hijr, and I [Abdallah] was again present. 'You were talking about the unpleasantness which you endured and the things Muhammad has done, but when he said something disagreeable you shrank from him.'" *Ishaq:131/ Bukhari:V5B57N27* "'Then I saw Uqba coming to the Prophet while he was praying. He seized his robe. Abu Bakr came crying and pulled Uqba away. Then they left him. That is the worst that I ever saw the Quraysh do to him.'"

Ishaq:143 "When they heard the Qur'an they said in mockery, 'Our hearts are veiled, we do not understand what he is saying. There is a load in our ears.' Then Allah revealed, 'And when you recite the Qur'an we put between you and those who do not believe a hidden veil. They turn in aversion.' In secret counsels the mockers say, 'They are following a man bewitched.'"

Tabari VI:106 "The revelation from Allah was coming to the Prophet continuously, commanding and threatening those who showed open hostility to him, and vindicating him against those who opposed him."

Qur'an 21:2 "Never comes to them a renewed reminder from their Lord, but they listen to it in jest, playing in sport, their hearts toying with trifles. The wrongdoers conceal their private counsels, conferring in secret, 'He is just a man like yourselves—a mortal. Will you succumb to his witchcraft with your eyes open?' Say: 'My Lord is the One that hears and knows.' 'Nay,' they say, 'these are merely medleys of muddled dreams! He forged it! He is just a poet! Let him then bring us a miracle like the ones that were sent to (prophets) of old!'"

Qur'an 21:24 "Say, 'Bring your proof: this is the Reminder Book for those before me but most do not know and are adverse.'"

Qur'an 21:36 "When the disbelievers see you (Muhammad), they treat you with ridicule, choosing you out for mockery: 'Is this he who mentions your gods? Yet they disbelieve at the mention of Ar-Rahman."

Qur'an 21:41 "Mocked were messengers before you, but their scoffers were hemmed in by what they mocked. Say: 'Who can protect you from (the wrath of) Ar-Rahman?' Yet they turn away from the mention of their Lord. Have they alihah (gods) who can defend them against Us?"

Ishaq:132-3 "Utba, who was a chief, said while sitting in a Quraysh assembly, 'Why don't I go to Muhammad and make some proposals to him? If he accepts, we will give him whatever he wants, and he will leave us in peace.' They thought it was a good idea, because if they tried to negotiate with him they would no longer be blamed for his actions. So Utba went to the Prophet, who was sitting in the mosque by himself, and said, 'My nephew, you are one of us yet you have come to our people with a matter that is dividing the community. You are ridiculing our customs. You have insulted our gods and our religion. You have even declared that our forefathers were infidels. So listen to me and I will make some suggestions, and perhaps you will be able to accept one of them.' The Apostle agreed. Utba said, 'If what you want is money, we will gather for you some of our property so that you may be the richest man in town. If you want honor, we will make you a chief so that no one can decide anything apart from you. If you want sovereignty, we will make you king. And if this demonic spirit which has possession of you is such that you cannot get rid of him, we will find a physician for you, and exhaust our means trying to cure you. For often a demonic spirit gets possession of a man, but he can be rid of it.' The apostle listened patiently."

Ishaq:134 "'Muhammad if you don't accept our offer then ask your Lord to give us the land and water we lack, for we are shut in by these mountains, we have no river, and none live a harder life than we do. If you speak the truth, resurrect Qusayy for us for he was a true shaikh, so that we may ask him whether what you say is accurate. If you do this we will believe you and know that God has sent you as an apostle as you claim. Well then at least ask your god to send an angel to confirm your depictions of paradise and give you the mansions and gold you obviously crave. If not that, then send us the Day of Doom you threaten us with, for we will not believe you until you perform a miracle. Why doesn't your god help you? Didn't he know that we were going to present you with these opportunities to prove yourself? Listen, Muhammad; we know the truth. Information has reached us that you are taught by this fellow in Yemen called al-Rahman. By Allah, we will never believe in Ar-Rahman. Alright then, our conscience is clear.' When they said this the Prophet got up and left."

Ishaq:135 "'Muhammad, your people have made certain propositions.... They asked you for things so that they might know that your position with God is as you say it is so that they might believe and follow you, and yet you did nothing. They even asked you to hasten the punishment you are frightening them with, but you could not do it.' The Prophet went to Khadija, sad and grieving."

Ishaq:136 "Ask him about the Mighty Traveler who reached the confines of both East and West. Ask him what the spirit is. And ask him what happened to the men who disappeared in ancient days. If he does not know he is a rogue, a forger, so treat him as you will. So Muhammad said to the emissaries, 'I will give you the answers tomorrow.' But the Apostle waited for fifteen days without a revelation from God on the matter, nor did Gabriel come to him, so the people of Mecca began to spread evil reports."

Tabari VI:106 "The Quraysh promised Muhammad that they would give him so much wealth that he would become the richest man in Mecca [money], they would give him as many wives as he wanted [sex], and they would submit to his commands [power].... The Quraysh said, 'This is what we will give you, Muhammad, so desist from reviling our gods and do not speak evilly of them.'" *Tabari VI:107* "'If you will do so, we offer you something which will be to your advantage and to ours.' 'What is it,' Muhammad asked. They said, 'If you will worship our gods, Al-Lat and Al-Uzza, for a year, we shall worship your god for a year."

Ishaq:162 "Abu Jahl met the Apostle and said, 'By Allah, Muhammad, you will either stop cursing our gods or we will curse the god you serve.' So the Qur'an verse was revealed, 'Do not insult those [gods] to whom they pray lest they curse God wrongfully through lack of knowledge.' [Qur'an 6:108] I have been told that the Apostle then refrained from cursing their gods, and *began* to call them to Allah [rather than Ar-Rahman]."

Tabari VI:107/Ishaq:165 "Walid, As, Aswad, and Umayyah said, 'Muhammad, come and let us worship that which you worship and you worship what we worship. We shall combine in the matter and shall make you a partner in all our undertakings. [The Ka'aba Inc.—the legacy of Qusayy's religious scam was still the principle game in town.] If what you have brought is better than what we already have, we will be partners with you and take our share, and if what we have is better than what you have, you shall be a partner with us in what we have, and you shall have your share of it.' 'Let me see what revelation comes to me from my Lord [not Allah],' he replied."

Tabari VI:107 "Satan Cast a False Revelation on the Messenger of Allah's Tongue: The Messenger was eager for the welfare of his people and wished to effect reconciliation with them in whatever way he could. It is said he wanted to find a way to do this, and what happened was as follows: *Tabari VI:108/Ishaq:165* "The Messenger saw his tribe turn on him. He was pained to see them shunning the message he had brought. So he [abandoned both his message and his god because he] longed for something that would reconcile his tribe to him. With his anxiety over this it would have delighted him if the obstacle which had made his task so difficult could be removed [so he could accept their offer of power, sex, and money]. So Muhammad debated with himself and fervently desired such an outcome. Then Allah revealed: 'By the Star when it sets, your comrade does not err, nor is he deceived; nor does he speak out of his own desire. [In truth, he did all three and was about to prove his guilt.] And when he came to the words: "Have you thought about Al-Lat, Al-Uzza and Manat," Satan, when he was meditating upon it and desiring to bring reconciliation, cast on his tongue, because of his inner longings and what he desired, the words: "These are exalted high-flying cranes (goddesses). Verily their intercession is accepted with approval."'"

Tabari VI:108/Ishaq:166 "When the Quraysh heard this, they rejoiced and were delighted at the way in which he spoke of their gods, and they listened to him. While the Muslims, trusting their Prophet in respect to the messages which he brought, did not suspect him of a vain desire or slip. When he came to the prostration, having completed the surah, he prostrated himself and the Muslims did likewise, obeying his command and following his example."

Tabari VI:108/Ishaq:166 "Those polytheists of the Quraysh and others who were in the mosque likewise prostrated themselves because of the reference to their gods which they had heard, so that there was no one in the mosque, believer or unbeliever, who did not prostrate himself. Then they all dispersed from the mosque."

Tabari VI:109/Ishaq:167 "The news of this prostration reached those of the Messenger's Companions who were in Abyssinia. The people said, 'The Quraysh have accepted Islam.' Some rose up to return. Then angel Gabriel came to the Messenger and said, 'Muhammad, what have you done?'" *Ishaq:166* "'You have recited to the people that which I did not bring to you from Allah, and you have said that which He did not say to you.' The Messenger was grieved and feared Allah greatly. So Allah sent a revelation to him, consoling him and making light of the affair [of worldly bargains and Satanic indulgences]. He informed him that there had never been a prophet or messenger before who desired as he desired and wished as he wished but that Satan had cast words into his recitation, as he had interjected them on Muhammad's tongue and into his desires."

Ishaq:166 "Then Allah annulled what Satan had cast, and established his verses by telling him that he was like other prophets and messengers.' Every Messenger or Prophet before you recited the message Satan cast into his recitation. Allah abrogates what Satan casts.

Then Allah established his verses.'"

Qur'an 22:52 "Never did We send a messenger or a prophet before you, but, when he framed a desire, Satan threw some vanity into his desire: but Allah will cancel anything that Satan throws in." *Qur'an 53:1* "I call to witness the Star when it dips. Your Companion (Muhammad) is neither confused, deceived, nor misled [except by Satan, in the guise of Allah]. Nor does he speak out of (his own) desire [unless he is tempted with money, sex, and power]. It is a revelation revealed, He was taught (this Qur'an) by the Supreme Intellect (Gabriel [actually Lucifer]), One free from any defect in body or mind: for he rose and became stable (in stately form), clear to view."

Qur'an 53:10 "So He did reveal to His slave whatever He revealed. The (Prophet's) heart did not falsify what he perceived he saw. Will you then dispute with him about what he saw? For indeed he saw him [him who] at a second descent. [A "descent" is a journey down.] Near the Lote Tree beyond which none may pass. Near it is the Garden of Abode (the Seventh Haven). [Muhammad's heaven is down, not up.]"

Qur'an 53:25 "They follow nothing but conjecture and what they themselves desire! Whereas guidance has come to them from their Lord!"

Qur'an 53:56 "Do you then wonder at this recital? And will you laugh at it and not weep, wasting your time in amusements? So fall you down in prostration to Allah, and serve [me]!"

Tabari VI:110 "When Muhammad brought a revelation from Allah canceling what Satan had cast on the tongue of His Prophet, the Quraysh said, 'Muhammad has repented of [reneged on] what he said concerning the position of our gods with Allah. He has altered [the bargain] and brought something else.' Those two phrases which Satan had cast on Muhammad's tongue of were in the mouth of every polytheist. They became even more ill-disposed and more violent in their persecution of those of them who had accepted Islam and followed the Messenger."

Tabari VI:115 "The deaths of Abu Talib and Khadija were a great affliction to the Messenger. After the death of Abu Talib, the Quraysh went to greater lengths in molesting him than they had ever done during his lifetime. One of them even poured dust upon his head. The Prophet said, 'The Quraysh never did anything unpleasant to me until Abu Talib died.'"

Ishaq:192 "When Abu Talib died, the Messenger went to Ta'if to seek support and protection against his own people. He spoke to them about the requests which he had come to make, (that is,) that they should come to his aid in defense of Islam and take his side against those of his own tribe who opposed him." *Tabari VI:116/Ishaq:192* "One of them said, 'If Allah has sent you, I will tear off the covering of the Ka'aba.' Another said, 'Couldn't God find somebody better than you to send?' The third added, 'I shall not speak to you, for if you are Allah's messenger as you say, you're too important for me to reply to, and if you're lying, you're too despicable to address.'"

Tabari VI:116/Ishaq:192 "Muhammad left them, despairing of getting any good out of the Thaqif. I have been told that he said to them, 'If that is your decision, keep it secret and do not tell anyone about it,' for he did not want his tribe to hear about this matter and be emboldened against him. However, they did not comply with his request, and incited against him their ignorant rabble who reviled him, shouted at him and hurled stones."

Tabari VI:118 "The Messenger came back to Mecca and found that its people were more determined to oppose him and to abandon his religion, except for a few weak people who believed in him."

Qur'an 40:4 "None can argue or dispute about the Signs of Allah or His Revelations but the Unbelievers. Let not their strutting about or their turn of fortune deceive you (for their ultimate end will be the Fire of Hell)!" *Qur'an 40:5* "Before them, folk denied, the People of Noah, and the Confederates (of Evil) after them; and every nation has plotted against their prophet, to seize and destroy him. They disputed by means of falsehood to condemn the truth. So I seized and destroyed them! How (terrible) was My punishment! In this way the sentence [behavior] of your Lord against the disbelieving infidels was justified. They will be the inmates of the Hell Fire!"

Bukhari:V4B56N830-1 "The Meccan people requested Allah's Apostle to show them a miracle, and so during the lifetime of the Prophet the moon was split into two parts. On that the Prophet said, 'Bear witness [to my god].'"

Ishaq:184 "The Apostle went on no journey except while he was in my house. He slept in my home that night after he prayed the final night prayer. A little before dawn he woke us, saying, 'Umm, I went to Jerusalem.' He got up to go out and I grabbed hold of his robe and laid bare his belly. I pleaded, 'O Muhammad, don't tell the people about this for they will know you are lying and will mock you.'"

Ishaq:183 "Upon hearing this many became renegades who had prayed and joined Islam. Many Muslims gave up their faith. Some went to Abu Bakr and said, 'What do you think of your friend now? He alleges that he went to Jerusalem last night and prayed there and came back to Mecca.' Bakr said that they were lying about the Apostle. But they told him that he was in the mosque at this very moment telling the Quraysh about it. Bakr said, 'If he says so then it must be true. I believe him. And that is more extraordinary than his story at which you boggle.' Then Allah sent down a Qur'an surah concerning those who left Islam for this reason: 'We made the vision which we showed you only, a test for men. We put them in fear, but it only adds to their heinous error.'" [Qur'an 13:33]

Qur'an 13:7 "The unbelievers say, 'Why was no sign or miracle sent down to him by his Lord?'"
Qur'an 13:27 "The unbelievers say, 'How is it that no sign miracle was sent down to him by his Lord?' Say, 'God leads whosoever He wills astray.'" *Qur'an 13:32* "Many an Apostle have they mocked before you; but I seized them. How awful was My punishment then! ...The unbelievers plot, but for them is torment in this life and a far more severe torture in Hell."

Qur'an 13:38 "It was not for any Apostle to come up with a miracle or sign unless it was granted by Our permission. For every age there is a Book revealed. Ar-Rahman abrogates, blots out, or confirms (whatever He wants)."

Qur'an 13:41 "Do they not see Us advancing from all sides into the land (of the disbelievers), reducing its borders (by giving it to believers in war victories)? (When) Allah dooms there is none who can postpone His doom. Sure, they devised their plots, but We are the best schemers." *Qur'an 13:43* "Yet the disbelievers say: 'You are not a Messenger.' Tell them: 'This Scripture is sufficient witness between me and you.'"

Qur'an 17:59 "Nothing stops Us from sending signs and proofs except that earlier people rejected them as lies. We sent to Thamud the she-camel as a clear sign, but they treated her cruelly."

Qur'an 17:90 "They say, 'We shall not believe you (Muhammad), until you cause a spring to gush forth from the earth [like Moses]. Or until you have a garden, and cause rivers to flow in their midst [like you claim Allah does]. Or you cause the sky to fall upon us in chunks, as you say will happen [like Yahweh did to Sodom and Gomorrah]. Or you bring angels before us face to face [like Abraham]. Or you have a house adorned with gold [like David or Solomon], or you ascend up into the skies [like Jesus]. No, we shall not have faith in you unless you send down to us a book that we can read [like the Bible].'"

Ishaq:194 "The Apostle offered himself to the Arab tribes at the fairs whenever an opportunity arose. He used to ask them to believe in him and protect him." *Ishaq:195* "The Apostle stopped by the Arab encampments and told them that he was the Prophet of Allah ordering them to worship Him, to believe in His Messenger, and protect him until Allah made plain His purpose. He went to the tents of the Kinda and offered himself to them, but they declined. He went to the Abdallah clan with the same message, but they would not heed. The Apostle went to the Hanifa, where he met with the worst reception of all. He tried the Amir, but one of them said to him, 'I suppose you want us to protect you from the Arabs with our lives and then if you prevail, someone else will reap the benefits. Thank you, No!'"

Ishaq:197 "The Apostle heard about Abdul. He asked them if they would like to get something more profitable than their present errand. Their leader took a handful of dirt and threw it in Muhammad's face."

Tabari VI:125 "After the Messenger had spoken to the group from Yathrib they said, 'Take note. This is the very prophet whom the Jews are menacing us with. Don't let them find him before we accept him.' Because of this, they responded to his call and became Muslims."

Ishaq:212 "The Quraysh persecuted his followers, seducing some from their religion and exiling others. They became insolent towards Muhammad's God. They accused His prophet of lying. So He gave permission to His Apostle to fight those who had wronged him. He said in his Qur'an: 'Fight them so that there will be no more seduction [i.e., no more exposing Islam's faults], until no Muslim is seduced from Islam. Fight them until the only religion is Islam and Allah alone is worshiped.'" [22:40 & 2:198]

Tabari VI:140 "The Quraysh were now anxious about Muhammad going there as they knew he had decided to join them in order to make war on them."

Ishaq:221 "They deliberated as to what to do about Muhammad as they had come to fear him. 'Keep him in fetters, lock him up, and wait for the same kind of death to overtake him which overtook other poets of his sort.' 'If you imprison him, his followers will attack and snatch him away. Then their numbers will grow so large, they will destroy the authority of the Quraysh.' 'Let us expel him from among us and banish him from the land. The harm which he has been doing will disappear, and we shall be rid of him. We shall be able to put our affairs back in order and restore our social harmony.'"

Tabari VI:143/Ishaq:222 "Among those who had gathered against him was Abu Jahl. He said, while waiting at his door, 'Muhammad alleges that if we follow him, we shall be kings over the Arabs and Persians. Then after we die fighting for him, we shall be brought back to life and live in gardens like those in Jordan. He also claims that if we do not submit to him, we shall be slaughtered. And after his followers kill us, we shall be brought back to life and thrown into the fires of hell in which we shall burn.' Allah's Messenger came out and took a handful of dust and said, 'Yes, I do say that; and you are one of them.' Allah took away their sight so that they could not see him. [Just as we have been blinded today.] And Muhammad began to sprinkle the dust [of ignorance and complacency] on their heads while reciting the following verses: 'Ya Sin. I call to witness the Qur'an. You are one sent on a straight path...The sentence is justified against most of them, for they do not believe. We will certainly put iron collars on their necks which will come up to their chins so that they will not be able to raise their heads. And We have set a barrier before them, and cover them so that they will not be able to see.'" [Qur'an 36:1]

Qur'an 20:133 "They say: 'Why does he not bring us a sign or miracle from his Lord?' Has not a Clear Sign come to them in the former scripture Books of revelation?"

Qur'an 46:6 "And when men are gathered they will be hostile enemies and reject worship!" "When Our Clear Signs are rehearsed to them, the unbelievers say: 'This is evident sorcery! It is a fabrication.'" *Qur'an 46:8* "Or do they say, 'He has forged it?' Say: 'If I fabricated it, still you have no power to support me against Allah. He knows best of that whereof you talk (so glibly)! Sufficient is He a witness between me and you!'" *Qur'an 46:9* "Say: 'I am no bringer of new-fangled doctrine among the messengers,'"

Qur'an 46:10 "Bethink you: If (this) be from Allah, and you reject it, and a witness from among the Children of Israel testifies to its similarity (of Allah's Qur'an with earlier Torah), and believed while you are arrogant and spurn it. Lo! Allah guides not wrong-doing folk.'" *Qur'an 46:11* "The disbelievers say to the believers: 'Had this (Islam) been a good thing, (such men as) they would not have gone to it before us!' And seeing that they do not guide themselves thereby, they will say, 'This is an ancient falsehood, the same old lie!'"

Qur'an 46:22 "They said: 'If you have come in order to turn us away from our gods then bring upon us the (calamity) you threaten us with, if you are telling the truth.' He [Muhammad] said: 'The knowledge (of when it will come) is only with Allah. I proclaim to you the mission on which I have been sent: But I see that you are a people in ignorance!'"

Ishaq:191 "Abu Jahl with sundry other notables went to Abu Talib and said, 'We acknowledge your rank with us, but now that you are at the point of death we are deeply concerned. You know the trouble that exists between us and your nephew, so call him and let us make an agreement that he will leave us alone and we will leave him alone.' The Messenger arrived and Abu said, 'Nephew, these noble men have come to give you something and gain something in return.' Muhammad said, 'Can you give me words by which you can rule the Arabs and subject the Persians to you?' 'How about ten words,' Abu Jahl said [knowing the drill]. Muhammad replied, 'You must say, "There is no ilah but Allah" and "Muhammad is his Messenger."' They clapped their hands and said, 'Do you want to make all the Gods into one Ilah, Muhammad? That would be an extraordinary thing.'"

Ishaq:284 "I am amazed at the causes of anger and folly and at those who stir up strife by lying controversy. They abandon our fathers' ways. They come with lies to twist our minds.

But their lies cannot confound the wise. If you give up your raids we will take you back for you are our cousins, our kin. But they chose to believe Muhammad and became obstinately contentious. All their deeds became evil."

Tabari VII:20/Ishaq:288 "The Quraysh said, 'Muhammad and his Companions have violated the sacred month, shed blood, seized property, and taken men captive.' The polytheists spread lying slander concerning him, saying, 'Muhammad claims that he is following obedience to Allah, yet he is the first to violate the holy month and to kill our companion in Rajab.'"

Tabari VII:21 "The Muslims who were still in Mecca refuted this."

Ishaq:288 "The Jews, seeing in this an omen unfavorable to Muhammad, said, 'Muslims killing Meccans means war is kindled.' There was much talk of this. However, Allah turned it to their disadvantage. When the Muslims repeated what the Jews had said, Allah revealed a Qur'an to His Messenger: 'They question you with regard to warfare in the sacred month. Say, "War therein is serious, but keeping people from Islam, from the sacred mosque, and driving them out is more serious with Allah.' [2:217] The Muslims now knew that seduction [speaking out against Islam] was worse than killing."

Ishaq:239 "About this time Jewish rabbis showed hostility to the Apostle in envy, hatred, and malice, because Allah had chosen His Apostle from the Arabs. The Jews considered the Prophet a liar and strove against Islam." "The Aus and Khazraj joined the Jews by obstinately clinging to their heathen religion. They were hypocrites. When Islam appeared and their people flocked to it, they were compelled to pretend to accept it to save their lives."

Ishaq:239 "Jewish rabbis used to annoy the Apostle with questions, introducing confusion."

Ishaq:244 "Hatib was a sturdy man steeped in paganism. Yazid, his son, was one of the best Muslims when he was disabled by wounds. At the point of death, Muslims said, 'Rejoice, son of Hatib, in the thought of Paradise!' Then his father's hypocrisy showed it self. He said, 'Humph! It is a Garden of Rue. You have sent my son to his death by your deception.' Concerning him, Allah said: 'Argue not on behalf of those who deceive themselves.'" [4:107]

Ishaq:256 "The Jews used to ask Muhammad questions which annoyed and confused him."

Ishaq:257 "Your situation seems obscure to us, Muhammad."

Ishaq:257 "'O Jews, fear Allah and submit, for you used to hope for the Messiah's help against the Arabs when we were pagans. You told us that he would be sent and then told us about him.' A Jew responded, 'Muhammad has not shown us anything we recognize as prophetic. He is not the one we spoke to you about.' So Allah revealed, 'We confirmed what they had, and We sent one they recognized, but they rejected him so We are cursing them.' The Jews replied, 'No Covenant was ever made with us about Muhammad.'"

"'Muhammad, you have not brought anything we recognize. And God has not sent down any sign or miracle suggesting that we should believe you.' So Allah said, 'We have sent down to you plain signs and only evildoers disbelieve them.'"

Ishaq:257 "The Jews told Allah's Messenger, 'Bring us a book. Bring us something down from heaven that we might read it.'"

Ishaq:258 "The Jews used to turn men away from Islam. So Allah said, 'Many Scripture folk wish to make you unbelievers after you have believed. They are envious. But be indulgent until Allah gives you his orders [to rob them and murder them.]"

Qur'an 2:12 "They are mischief-mongers, but they realize not. When it is said to them: 'Believe as the others believe:' They say: 'Shall we believe as the fools?' Nay, surely they are the fools, but they know not. When they meet the faithful, they say: 'We believe;' but when they are alone with the devils, they say: 'We are really with you: We (were) only mocking.'" *Qur'an 2:15* "Allah mocks them, paying them back, increasing their wrong-doing so they wander blindly."

Qur'an 2:23 "If you are in doubt of what We have revealed to Our Votary, then bring a surah like this, and call any witnesses apart from Allah. But you cannot, as indeed you cannot guard yourselves against the Hell Fire whose fuel is men and rocks, which has been prepared for the infidels."

Qur'an 2:43 "Perform prayer; pay the zakat tax; bow down and prostrate yourself with Ar-Raki'un (the obedient bowers). You read, recite and study the Scripture. Why don't you understand? [Why don't you capitulate?] Nay, seek [Islamic prostration] prayer: It is indeed hard, heavy, and exacting, except for those who obey in submission."

Tabari VII:63 "The Messenger uttered these words: 'O people of the pit, you were evil fellow tribesmen to your Prophet! You disbelieved me when other people believed me. You drove me out when other people gave me shelter. You fought me when other people came to my aid.'"

Qur'an 8:30 "Remember how the unbelievers plotted against you (Muhammad), to get you out (of your home). They plotted, and Allah too had arranged a plot; but Allah is the best schemer."

Qur'an 8:31 "When Our Verses are rehearsed to them, they say: 'We have heard this (before) [i.e., it's plagiarized]. If we wished, we could say (words) like these. These are nothing but stories of the ancients.'"

Qur'an 8:32 "Remember how they said: 'O Allah, if this (Qur'an) is indeed the Truth (revealed) from You, rain down on us a shower of stones from the sky, or send us a painful doom!' But Allah was not going to send them a penalty while you (Muhammad) were among them. But what plea have they that Allah should not punish them; what makes them so special?"

Tabari VII:85/Ishaq:363 "The Jews of the Qaynuqa replied, 'Muhammad, do you think that we are like your people? Do not be deluded by the fact that you met a people with no knowledge and you made good use of your opportunity.'"

Qur'an 61:5 "Moses said: 'O my people, why do you annoy and insult me, when you well know I am Allah's Messenger?' Then when they turned away, Allah caused them to be deceived."

Qur'an 64:5 "Has not the story reached you of those who disbelieved before? They tasted the ill effects of their unbelief. They tasted a painful torment because there came to them messengers with Clear Proofs, but they said: 'Shall (mere) human beings direct us?' So they rejected and turned away. But Allah can do without (them): Allah is Rich, the Owner of Praise. Those who reject Faith and treat Our Signs as falsehoods, they will be Companions of the Fire, to dwell therein forever: an evil resort."

Ishaq:383 "One of the young men's fathers confronted Muhammad and said, 'You have robbed my son of his life by your deception and brought great sorrow to me.'"

Qur'an 3:19 "Lo! religion with Allah (is) Surrender. Nor did the People of the Book differ except out of envy after knowledge had come to them. But if any deny the proofs, signs and lessons of Allah, Allah is swift in reckoning." *Qur'an 3:20* "If they argue with you, (Muhammad), say: 'I have surrendered to Allah (in Islam) and those who follow me.' And say to those who were given the Scripture (Jews and Christians) and to the illiterates (Arabs): 'Do you also submit? If they surrender, then they are rightly guided."

Qur'an 3:69 "It is the wish of the followers of the People of the Book to lead you astray. But they make none to go astray except themselves. You People of the Book! Why reject you the signs, proofs, and verses of Allah, of which you are witnesses? You People of the Book! Why do you clothe Truth with falsehood, and conceal the Truth?"

Qur'an 3:77 "As for those who sell for a small price the covenant and faith they owe to Allah and their own plighted word for a small price, they shall have no portion in the Hereafter. Nor will Allah speak to them or look at them on the Day of Judgment, nor will He cleanse them: They shall have a grievous torment, a painful doom. There is among them a section who distort the Book with their tongues. (As they read) you would think it is from the Book, but it is not from the Book; and they say, 'That is from God,' but it is not from Allah: It is they who tell a lie against Allah, and (well) they know it!"

Ishaq:395 "Muslims, if you listen to the unbelievers you will retreat from the enemy and become losers. Ask Allah for victory and do not retreat, withdrawing from His religion. 'We will terrorize those who disbelieve. In that way I will help you against them.'"

Qur'an 3:184 "Then if they reject you (Muhammad), so were rejected messengers before you, who came with miracles and with the prophetic Psalms and with the Scripture giving light."

Qur'an 33:11 "In that situation the Believers were sorely tried and shaken as by a tremendous shaking. And behold! The Hypocrites and those in whose hearts is a disease said: 'Allah and His Messenger promised us nothing but delusion!'"

Ishaq:459 "Allah sent against them bitter cold winter nights and a wind that overturned their cooking pots, blowing away their tents. This combined with the disagreement and how Allah had disrupted their unity sowed distrust. [So...] Muhammad began to wonder what they were doing." *Tabari VIII:26* "The Prophet asked, 'Who will go and spy on the enemy?' The Messenger stipulated that should he come back, Allah would cause him to enter paradise. But no one stood up. The Prophet prayed and then uttered the same words, but no one volunteered. Again he asked, 'Whoever goes may be my companion in paradise.' Yet none stood, so intense was the fear, hunger, and cold."

Ishaq:475 "Those who call Muhammad a liar disbelieve and go astray. They attacked our religion and would not submit."

Tabari VIII:52/Ishaq:491 "Jahjah and Juhani fought. Juhani shouted, 'People of the Ansar [Medina Muslims].' Jahjah shouted, 'People of the Emigrants [Meccan Muslims].' Abdallah bin Ubayy [the leader of the Ansar] became enraged and said, 'Why are they doing this? Are they trying to outrank us and outnumber us in our own land? The proverb "Feed a dog and it will devour you" fits these Quraysh vagabonds [Muhammad's Muslims]. When we go back to Medina, those who are stronger will drive out the weaker. Then he turned to his tribe and said, 'This is what you have done to yourselves! You have allowed them [the Meccan Muslims] to settle in your land [Yathrib/Medina] and divide your wealth. Had you kept from them what you had, they would have moved to another place.'" *Tabari VIII:53* "Abdallah said, 'Those who are stronger will drive out the weaker from Medina.'"

Ishaq:499 "Many Bedouins were slow in coming to him.

Qur'an 24:47 "They say, 'We believe in Allah and in the Messenger, and we obey,' but even after that, some of them turn away: they are not (really) Believers. When they are summoned to Allah and His Messenger, in order that He may judge between them, behold some of them decline (to come) and are averse." *Qur'an 24:50* "Is there is a disease in their hearts, do they have doubts? Do they in fear that Allah and His Messenger will deal unjustly, acting wrongfully toward them?"

Qur'an 24:11 "Those who brought forward the lie are a body among you: but think it not an evil to you; on the contrary, it is good for you. Every man among them (will get the punishment) their sin earned. For him who took the lead in the slander, his will be an awful doom. Why did not the believers, when you heard of the affair, put the best construction on it in their minds and say, 'This is an obvious lie?' Why did they not bring four witnesses to prove it? Since they produce not witnesses, they are liars in the sight of Allah. Were it not for His mercy a grievous penalty would have seized you in that you rushed glibly into this affair. You said out of your mouths things of which you had no knowledge; and you thought it to be a light matter, while it was most serious in the sight of Allah, a grave offense. And why did you not, when you heard it, say? 'It is not right of us to speak of this: this is a most serious slander, an awful calumny!' Those who love scandal to be broadcast among the Believers will have a painful punishment in this life and the hereafter."

Tabari VIII:89 "When the Messenger had finished his pact, he said to his Companions, 'Arise, sacrifice, and shave.' Not a man stood even after he had said it three times. When no one stood up, went into Umm's tent and told her what he had encountered from the Muslims. She said, 'Do you approve of this?"

Qur'an 4:81 "They have obedience on their lips; but when they leave you, a section of them plots things that are different from what you commanded them. So keep clear of them."

Qur'an 4:140 "You have been commanded in the Book that whenever you hear Verses of Allah denied, derided, ridiculed, or mocked [as is the only reasoned response], do not sit with them and engage them in this talk or you will be no different from them. Indeed, Allah will collect the Hypocrites and Infidels together and put them all in Hell."

Qur'an 4:142 "The Hypocrites try to deceive Allah, but it is He Who deceives them. When they stand up performing the prayer, they stand sluggishly, to be seen, but they are mindful of Allah but little. (They are) distracted in mind even in the midst of it, swaying between this and that, one group or the another."

Qur'an 4:153 "The people of the Book ask you to cause (an actual) book to descend to them from heaven. Indeed they asked Moses for an even greater (miracle), for they said: 'Show us Allah in public,' but they were dazed for their presumption."

MEGALOMANIA:

Ishaq:233 "Allah's Apostle: the Lord of the Muslims, Leader of the Allah Fearing, Messenger of the Lord of the Worlds, the Peerless and Unequalled."

Qur'an 4:65 "They can have no Faith, until they make you (Muhammad) judge in all disputes, and find in their souls no resistance against Your decisions, accepting them with complete submission."

Bukhari:V1B7N1331 "The Prophet said, 'I have been given five things which were not given to any one else before me. 1. Allah made me victorious by awe by His terrorizing my enemies. 2. The earth has been made for me. 3. Booty has been made lawful for me yet it was not lawful for anyone else before me. 4. I have been given the right of intercession. 5. Every Prophet used to be sent to his nation only but I have been sent to all mankind.'"

Qur'an 33:21 "You have indeed a noble paradigm in the Apostle of Allah." [A second translation reads:] "You have in (Muhammad) the Messenger of Allah a beautiful pattern of conduct for anyone to follow." [A third reads:] "Verily in the Messenger of Allah you have a good example for him who looks unto Allah and the Last Day." [A fourth reads:] "Certainly you have in the Messenger of Allah an excellent prototype." [A fifth says:] "You have indeed a noble paradigm [archetype, exemplar, standard, model, or pattern] to follow in Allah's Apostle."

Bukhari:V7B63N1891 "Indeed in the Apostle of Allah you have a good example to follow."

Ishaq:467 "Allah addressed the believers and said, 'In Allah's Apostle you have a fine example for anyone who hopes to be in the place where Allah is.'"

Bukhari:V1B3N65 "The Prophet got a silver ring made with 'Muhammad Allah's Apostle' engraved on it. The ring glittered on his hand."

Bukhari:V4B56N732 "Allah's Apostle said, 'I have five names: I am Muhammad and Ahmad, the praised one; I am al-Mahi through whom Allah will eliminate infidelity [by killing every infidel]; I am al-Hashir who will be the first to be resurrected [beating Jesus]; and I am also al-Aqib, because there will be no prophet after me.'"

Bukhari:V4B55N651-2 "I heard Allah's Apostle saying, 'I am the nearest of all the people to Jesus. All the prophets are paternal brothers—their mothers are different, but their religion is one. There has been no prophet between me and Jesus.'"

Bukhari:V6B61N504 "Allah's Apostle said, 'Every Prophet was given miracles because of which people believed, but what I have been given is Divine Inspiration which Allah has revealed to me. So I hope that my followers will outnumber the followers of the other Prophets.'"

Bukhari:V1B3N68 "The Prophet preached at a suitable time so that we might not get bored. He abstained from pestering us with sermons and knowledge.'"

Bukhari:V9B92N384 "Allah's Apostle said, 'Whoever obeys me will enter Paradise, and whoever disobeys me will not enter it.'"

Qur'an 49:1 "Believers, be not forward in the presence of Allah and His Messenger, and fear Allah. Raise not your voices above the voice of the Prophet, nor speak loudly around him, as you speak to one another, lest your deeds become nullified unconsciously. Those that lower their voices in the presence of the Messenger have their hearts tested by Allah. Theirs will be an immense reward."

Qur'an 33:36 "No Muslim has any choice after Allah and His Apostle have decided a matter."

Qur'an 33:56 "Allah and His angels shower blessings on the Prophet. So believers, send your blessings on him, and salute him with all respect—a worthy salutation. Those who annoy Allah and His Messenger and speak evil things of them—Allah has cursed them and prepared a humiliating torment."

Qur'an 33:57 "Those who speak negatively of Allah and His Apostle shall be cursed."

Bukhari:V8B78N628 "The Prophet was holding Umar's hand. 'O Allah's Apostle! You are dearer to me than everything except my own self.' The Prophet said, 'No, by Him in Whose Hand my soul is, you will not have faith till I am dearer to you than your own self.' Then Umar said, 'However, now, by Allah, you are dearer to me than my own self.' The Prophet said, 'Now, Umar, you are a believer.'"

Bukhari:V9B88N174 "I heard the Prophet saying, 'Islam cannot change!'"

Tabari VI:70 "He went to Khadija and said, 'I think that I have gone mad.'"

Ishaq:155 "Khadija was the first to believe in Allah and His Apostle. By her Allah lightened the burden on His Prophet. He never met with contradiction and charges of falsehood but he was comforted by her when he went home. She strengthened him and belittled the opposition."

Qur'an 94:4 "We have exalted your fame, raising high the esteem in which you are held."

Ishaq:118 "'Muhammad is trying to bewitch you.' With that the Quraysh got up and left before the Messenger could speak. The following day they gathered again. This time the Apostle said, 'Kinsmen, I know of no Arab who has come to his people with a nobler message than mine. I have brought you the best of this world and the next.'"

Qur'an 109:3 "To you you're Way, and to me my way. You shall have your religion and I shall have mine."

Qur'an 108:3 "For he who insults you (Muhammad) will be cut off."

Qur'an 24:62 "Only those are believers in Allah and His Messenger who, when they are with him on a matter requiring collective action, do not depart until they have asked for his permission. Deem not the summons of the Messenger like the summons of one of you. Allah knows those who slip away, making excuses. Beware of rejecting the Messenger's orders lest a grievous penalty be inflicted."

Qur'an 67:1 "Blessed is He who holds the reins of Kingship."

Qur'an 68:4 "You are an exalted character of tremendous morality. Soon you will see, and they will see, which of you is afflicted with madness."

Bukhari:V9B87N127 "The Prophet said, 'I have been given the keys of eloquent speech and given victory with terror.'"

Qur'an 81:19 "Verily this is the Word (brought by) a most honorable Messenger imbued with power, the Lord of the Throne, Mighty, One to be obeyed."

Qur'an 81:24 "Neither is he a concealer, withholding knowledge of the unseen. Nor is it (the Qur'an) the Word of an evil spirit accursed, the utterance of a devil, the curses of Satan."

Ishaq:471 "We were steadfast trusting in Him. We have a Prophet by whom we will conquer all men."

Bukhari:V4B52N203 "I heard Allah's Apostle saying, 'He who obeys me, obeys Allah, and he who disobeys me, disobeys Allah. He who obeys the chief, obeys me, and he who disobeys the chief, disobeys me.'"

Bukhari:V9B87N127 "The Prophet said, 'I have been given the keys of eloquent speech and given victory with terror so the treasures of the earth were given to me.'"

Ishaq:391 "O people, this is Allah's Apostle among you. Allah has honored and exalted you by him. So help him and strengthen him. Listen to his commands and obey them."

Tabari VIII:182 "The people assembled in Mecca to swear allegiance to the Messenger in submission. He received from them the oath of allegiance to himself, to heed and obey."

Muslim:C22B20N4604 "We pledged an oath to the Messenger of Allah that we would listen to and obey his orders."

Tabari VI:24/Ishaq:53 "His authority among the Quraysh was like a religion which the people followed and which could not be infringed; they always acted in accordance with its laws. They recognized his superiority and nobility."

Qur'an 4:114 "He who disobeys the Apostle after guidance has been revealed will burn in Hell."

Qur'an 49:4 "Those who shout out to you from behind the private apartments have no sense."

Qur'an 49:7 "And know that among you is Allah's Messenger: were he to follow your (wishes), you would fall into misfortune...."

Qur'an 66:1 "O Prophet! Why forbid yourself that which Allah has made lawful to you? You seek to please your consorts. And Allah is Forgiving, Most Kind. Allah has already sanctioned for you the dissolution of your vows."

Qur'an 48:8 "We have truly sent you (Muhammad) as a witness, as a bringer of Good News, and as a Warner: In order that you (men) may believe in Allah and His Messenger, that you may assist him and honor him, and celebrate His praise morning and evening."

Qur'an 48:10 "Verily those who swear allegiance to you (Muhammad), indeed swear their allegiance to Allah."

Qur'an 48:18 "Allah's Good Pleasure was on the Believers when they swore allegiance to you (Muhammad) under the Tree: He rewarded them with a speedy Victory."

Bukhari:V1B2N13 "Allah's Apostle said, 'By Him in Whose Hands my life is, none of you will have faith till he loves me more than his father and his children.'" *Bukhari:V1B2N14* "The Prophet said, 'None of you will have faith till he loves me more than his father, his children and all mankind.'"

Bukhari:V1B4N154 "Whenever Allah's Apostle went to answer the call of nature, I along with another boy used to go behind him carrying a tumbler of water for cleaning the private parts and a spear-headed stick." *Bukhari:V1B4N158* "The Prophet went out to answer the call of nature and asked me to bring three stones."

Qur'an 9:62 "To you they swear in order to please you: but it is more fitting that they should please Allah and His Messenger (Muhammad)."

Tabari VIII:181 "People of the Quraysh, Allah has taken from you the haughtiness of the Time of Ignorance and its veneration of ancestors.... For now I have humbled you, made you Muslims, submissive unto me.... People of the Quraysh and people of Mecca, what do you think I intend to do with you?"

Ishaq:553 "The people assembled in Mecca to swear allegiance to the Messenger in submission. They gathered to do homage to the Apostle in Islam. Umar remained below the Prophet, lower than the place where he sat, imposing conditions on the people as they paid homage [reverence] to Muhammad, promising to submit and obey. Umar administered the oath, receiving from the Meccans their pledge of allegiance to Muhammad. They promised to heed and obey Allah and His Messenger."

Tabari VIII:183 "When the Messenger was finished with the men's swearing of allegiance, the women swore allegiance." "He said, 'You shall not disobey me in carrying out my orders.' The Messenger told Umar, 'Receive their oath of allegiance and their homage.... Now go, for I have accepted your allegiance and praise."

Ishaq:555 "It is not lawful for anyone to shed blood in Mecca. It was not lawful to anyone before me and it will not be lawful after me. If anyone should say, 'The Apostle killed men in Mecca,' say, 'Allah permitted his Apostle to do so but He does not permit you.'"

Ishaq:557 "Allah gave you a seal imprinted. [The "Seal of Prophethood" was a hairy mole.] Allah's proof is great. [Now there's a delusional thought.] I testify that your religion is true and that you are great among men. Allah testifies that Ahmad [it means "praised"] is the chosen. You are a noble one, the cynosure [someone who attracts attention or admiration] of the righteous, a prince."

Tabari IX:8/Ishaq:569 "Our people were routed and fled, no one turning to look back. Allah's Apostle withdrew and cried, 'Where are you going? Come to me. I am Allah's Apostle! I am Muhammad, son of Abdallah!' It was of no avail. The camels just bumped into one another as the Muslims ran away."

Tabari IX:8 "When the polytheists overwhelmed the Muslims, the Prophet got off his mount and started reciting verses in the rajaz meter: 'I am the Prophet, it is no lie."

Tabari IX:11/Ishaq:574 "When Muhammad saw his men confused and in disarray, he repeated: 'Where are you going, men?' But not even one of them paid heed to his cries."

Ishaq:580 "Allah's religion is the religion of Muhammad. We are satisfied with it."

Tabari IX:76 "The Prophet is the master of your rich and your poor."

Tabari IX:156 "The Messenger of Allah named himself to us in various ways. He said, 'I am Muhammad the one who is praised, Ahmad, the most praiseworthy, al-Aqib, the last in succession, and al-Mahi, the obliterator.'"

Qur'an 59:6 "Allah gives his Messenger Lordship and Power over whomever He wills." *Qur'an*

Qur'an 56:92 "But if he (the dying person), be of the denying, erring (away from Islam), then for him is the entertainment with boiling water and roasting in hell fire. Verily. this is the absolute truth with certainty, so celebrate (Muhammad)."

Qur'an 33:51 "You may have whomever you desire; there is no blame."

Ishaq:182 "While I was in the Hijr, Gabriel came and stirred me with his foot. He took me to the door of the mosque and there was a white animal, half mule, half donkey, with wings on its sides yet it was propelled by its feet. He mounted me on it. When I mounted, he shied. Gabriel placed his hand on its mane and said [to the jackass], 'You should be ashamed to behave this way. By God, you have never had a more honorable rider than Muhammad.' The animal was so embarrassed, it broke into a cold sweat."

Muslim:C75B1N309 "The Messenger said: 'I was brought on al-Buraq, an animal white and long. I mounted it and came to the Temple in Jerusalem. I tethered it to the ring used by the prophets and entered the mosque, praying two rak'ahs in it. Then I came out [of the non-existent building] and Gabriel brought me a vessel of wine and one of milk. I chose the milk, and he said: "You have chosen the natural thing," and took me to heaven.'"

Ishaq:182 "When we arrived at the Temple in Jerusalem, we found Abraham, Moses, and

Jesus, along with a company of prophets. I acted as their imam in prayer."

Ishaq:184 "After the completion of my business in Jerusalem, a ladder was brought to me finer than any I have ever seen. An angel was in charge of it and under his command were 12,000 angels each of them having 12,000 angels under his command."

Bukhari:V4B54N429/ Muslim:C75B1N309 "'Then we ascended to the second heaven. The guard at the gate asked, "Who is it?" Gabriel said, "Gabriel." The gatekeeper asked, "Who is with you?" He said, "Muhammad" "Has he been sent for?" He said, "Yes." The guard said, "He is welcomed. What a wonderful visit his is!" and opened the gate. Then I met Jesus and Yahya (John) who said, "You are welcomed, O brother and Pious Prophet.... Then we ascended to the sixth heaven and again the same questions and answers were exchanged. There I met and greeted Moses. When I proceeded on, he started weeping and on being asked why, he said, "Followers of this youth who was sent after me will enter Paradise in greater number than my followers.'"

Bukhari:V8B77N610 "We granted the vision of the ascension to the heavens, Miraj, which We showed you as an actual eye witness but as a trial for people.' [17:60] Allah's Apostle actually saw with his own eyes the vision of all the things which were shown to him on the Night Journey to Jerusalem. It was not a dream."

Ishaq:203 "'Choose what you want for yourself and your Lord.' The Messenger recited [lurid tales of virgins from] the Qur'an and made us desirous of Islam. Then he said, 'I will enter a contract of allegiance with you, provided that you protect me as you would your women and children.'" *Tabari VI:133* "We pledge our allegiance to you and we shall defend you as we would our womenfolk. Administer the oath of allegiance to us, Messenger of Allah, for we are men of war possessing arms and coats of mail."

Tabari VI:134 "'Men of the Khazraj, do you know what you are pledging yourselves to in swearing allegiance to this man?' 'Yes,' they answered. 'In swearing allegiance to him we are pledging ourselves to wage war against all mankind.'"

Ishaq:205 "'If you are loyal to this undertaking it will profit you in this world and the next.' They said, 'We will accept you as a Prophet under these conditions, but we want to know specifically what we will get in return for our loyalty.' Muhammad said, 'I promise you Paradise.'"

Ishaq:256 "Do you find in what He has sent down to you that you should believe in Muhammad? If you do not find that in your scripture then there is no compulsion upon you. 'The right path has been plainly distinguished from error'" [2:257]

Qur'an 2:104 "You of Faith, say not (to the Prophet) words of ambiguous import like 'Listen to us,' but words of respect; and obey (him): To those who don't submit there is a grievous punishment."

Ishaq:235 "When the Apostle was settled in Medina and his comrades were gathered to him, the affairs of the workers were arranged, and Islam became firmly established. Prayer was instituted, the zakat tax was prescribed, legal punishments were fixed, as were all things permitted and forbidden."

Tabari VII:54 "Muhammad turned toward his new Qiblah and said. 'Allah, if this band perishes today, you will be worshipped no more.' Abu Bakr picked up his cloak and put it on him, grasping him from behind. 'Prophet whom I value more than my father and mother, this constant calling on your Lord is annoying.' Then Allah revealed, 'When you sought the help of your Lord he answered, "I will help you with a thousand angels, rank on rank."'" [8:9]

Ishaq:306 "Allah's Apostle ordered the dead to be thrown into a pit. All were thrown in except Umayyah. He had swollen up in his coat of mail and filled it. They went to move him, but he fell apart, so they left him where he was and flung some rocks over him. As the dead were being thrown in, Muhammad stood over them and said, 'O people of the pit, have you found what your Lord promised you to be true? For I have found what my Lord promised me to be true.' The Muslims said to him. 'Allah's Messenger, are you speaking to dead people who have been putrefied?' He replied, 'They know what I promised them is the truth.' You hear what I say no better than they, but they cannot answer me."

Bukhari:V5B58N193 "The Prophet cursed those that had teased him. He said, 'O Allah! Destroy the chiefs of Quraysh, Abu Jahl, Utba, Shaba, Umaiya, and Ubai.' I saw these people killed on the day of Badr battle and thrown in the pit except Ubai whose body parts were mutilated."

Bukhari:V5B59N314-7 "At Badr, the Prophet ordered the corpses of twenty-four Quraysh leaders to be thrown into a pit. It was a habit of the Prophet that whenever he conquered some people, he used to stay at the battlefield for three nights [to gloat]. So, on the third day he ordered that his she-camel be saddled and he set out. His Companions followed, saying: 'The Prophet is proceeding for some great purpose.' When he halted at the edge of the pit, he addressed the corpses of the Quraysh infidels by their names, 'O so-and-so, son of so-and-so! Why didn't you obey Allah's Apostle?' Umar said, 'Apostle! You are speaking to the dead!' Muhammad said, 'Allah brought them to life (again) to let them hear me, to reprimand them, to slight them, and so that I might take my revenge over them.' Then he quoted the Holy Verse out of the Qur'an: 'You cannot make the dead listen or the deaf hear your call...until they believe Our Signs and come into submission." [30:52]

Ishaq:231 "Whenever you differ about a matter it must be referred to Allah and Muhammad."

Qur'an 61:6 "And Jesus, the son of Mary, said: 'Children of Israel, I am the Messenger of Allah (sent) to you, confirming that (which was revealed) before me in the Torah, and giving Glad Tidings of a Messenger to come after me, whose name shall be Ahmad, the Praised One.' But when he came to them with Clear Signs, they said, 'this is sorcery!'"

Qur'an 62:2 "It is He Who has sent to the unlettered ones a Messenger from among them, to rehearse and recite to them His Verses, to purify them, and to instruct them in the Book and Sunnah (of Muhammad); they had been in manifest error."

Tabari VII:126 "The Prophet went up the mountain. He had become stout and heavy with age. When he tried to climb up, he could not manage on his own. Talba Ubaydullah squatted beneath him and lifted him up until he settled comfortably on a rock." *Ishaq:383* "That day I heard the Prophet saying, 'Talha earned paradise when he did what he did for me.'"

Ishaq:391 "O people, Allah's Apostle is among you. Allah has honored and exalted you by him. So help him and strengthen him. Listen to his commands and obey them.'"

Ishaq:398 "Allah sent you an Apostle of your own, reciting to you His verses concerning what you did, and teaching you good and evil that you might know what is good and do it, and know what is bad and refrain from it, and so that you might gain much from obeying Him and avoid His wrath proceeding from disobedience and thereby escape His vengeance."

Bukhari:V4B52N220 "Allah's Apostle said, 'I have been sent with the shortest expressions bearing the widest meanings, and I have been made victorious with terror. While I was sleeping [besieging], the keys to the treasures of the world were brought to me and put in my hand.'"

Ishaq:440 "Helped by the Holy Spirit we smited Muhammad's foes. He is a true Messenger from the Compassionate, an Apostle reciting Allah's Book. He became honored in rank and station. So the Apostle sent a message to them with a sharp cutting sword."

Qur'an 33:53 "O ye who believe! Enter not the Prophet's apartments until leave is given you for a meal. (And then) not (so early as) to wait for its preparation. But when you are invited, enter; and, when your meal is ended, then disperse. Linger not for conversation. Lo! that would cause annoyance to the Prophet. Such (behavior) bothers him. He is ashamed to dismiss you, but Allah is not ashamed (to tell you) the truth. And when ye ask (his ladies) for anything, ask them from behind a screen: that makes for greater purity for your hearts and for theirs. Nor is it right for you that you should annoy Allah's Messenger, or that you should marry his widows after him at any time. Truly such a thing is in Allah's sight an enormous offense."

Tabari VIII:40 "Aisha, the Mother of the Faithful, was asked, 'How did the Messenger of God behave?' She replied, 'His eye did not weep for anyone.'"

Qur'an 4:12 "Those who obey Allah and His Messenger will be admitted to Gardens to abide therein and that will be the supreme achievement. But those who disobey Allah and His Messenger and transgress His limits will be admitted to a Fire, to abide therein: And they shall have a humiliating punishment."

Qur'an 4:80 "He who obeys the Messenger obeys Allah."

INSPIRATION:

Bukhari:V1B1N2 "'Allah's Messenger! How is the Divine Inspiration revealed to you?' He replied, 'Sometimes it is like the ringing of a bell. This form of Inspiration is the hardest of all and then this state passes off after I have grasped what is inspired. Sometimes the angel comes in the form of a man and talks to me and I grasp whatever he says.'"

Bukhari:V7B67N427 "The Prophet said, 'If I take an oath and later find something else better than that, then I do what is better and expiate my oath.'"

Bukhari:V6B60N8 "Umar said, 'Our best Qur'an reciter is Ubai. And in spite of this, we leave out some of his statements because Allah's Apostle himself said, "Whatever verse or revelation We abrogate or cause to be forgotten We bring a better one."

Bukhari:V4B54N457 "Whoever claims the Prophet Muhammad saw his Lord is committing a great fault for he only saw Gabriel in his genuine shape in which he was covering the horizon."

Bukhari:V6B60N378 "'O Mother of the faithful, did Muhammad see his Lord?' Aisha said, 'What you have said makes my hair stand on end! Know that if somebody tells you the following things, he is a liar. Whoever tells you that Muhammad saw his Lord, is a liar. [i.e., the Qur'an isn't from God] Whoever tells you that the Prophet knows what is going to happen tomorrow, is a liar.[i.e., Muhammad wasn't a prophet] Aisha added. 'The Prophet saw Gabriel in his true form twice.'" [i.e., the Qur'an is 112 surahs too long]

Bukhari:V4B54N455 "So (Allah) conveyed the Inspiration to His slave (Gabriel) and then he

(Gabriel) conveyed (it to Muhammad)."

Ishaq:558 "Gabriel, Allah's messenger is with us and the Holy Spirit has no equal."

Bukhari:V4B54N440 "The Prophet said, 'Aisha, this is Gabriel. He sends his greetings and salutations to you.' Aisha replied, 'Salutations and greetings to him.' Then addressing the Prophet she said, 'You see what I don't see.'"

Bukhari:V4B54N455 "The Prophet informed us that he had seen Gabriel and he had 600 wings."

Qur'an 74:43 "Each one of them wants to be given scrolls of revelation spread out! No! By no means!"

Qur'an 2:106 "When we cancel a Verse or throw it into oblivion, We replace it with a better one." [Or:] "Whatever Revelation We abrogate or cause to be forgotten, We substitute something better."

Qur'an 16:103 "When we replace a message with another, and Allah knows best what He reveals, they say: 'You have made it up.'"

Qur'an 4:82 "Do they not ponder over the Qur'an? Had it been the word of any other but Allah they would surely have found a good deal of variation in it, much discrepancy and incongruity...those who check and scrutinize will know it."

Ishaq:326 "Abdullah told me that when this verse came down it was a shock to the Muslims who took it hard. They were afraid, as the odds were too great. So Allah relieved them and cancelled the verse with another: 'Now has Allah relieved you and He knows that there is a weakness among you, so if there are 100 [rather than 20] they shall vanquish 200.'"

Bukhari:V6B60N478 "The commencement of divine inspiration to Allah's Messenger was in the form of dreams.... The Prophet loved the seclusion of a cave in Hira. The angel came to him and asked him to read. The Prophet replied, 'I do not know how to read.' The Prophet added, 'Then the angel caught me forcefully and pressed me so hard that I could not bear it any more. He released me and asked me to read. I replied, "I do not know how to read." Thereupon he caught me again and pressed me till I could not bear it any more. He asked me to read but I replied, "I do not know how to read or what shall I read?" Thereupon he caught me for the third time and pressed me, "Read in the name of your Lord who has created man from a clot. Read!" Then the Apostle returned from that experience; the muscles between his neck and shoulders were trembling, and his heart beating severely. He went to Khadija and cried, 'Cover me! Cover me!' She did until his fear subsided. He said, 'What's wrong with me? I am afraid that something bad has happened to me.'"

Tabari VI:67 "The Prophet said, 'I had been standing, but fell to my knees; and crawled away, my shoulders trembling. I went to Khadija and said, "Wrap me up!" When the terror had left me, he came to me and said, "Muhammad, you are the Messenger of Allah.'" Muhammad said, 'I had been thinking of hurling myself down from a mountain crag, but he appeared to me as I was thinking about this and said, "I am Gabriel and you are the Messenger." Then he said, "Recite!" I said, "What shall I recite?" He took me and pressed me three times. I feared for my life.'"

Ishaq:106 "When I thought I was nearly dead I said, 'What shall I read;' only to deliver myself from him, lest he should do the same thing to me again. He said, 'Read in the name of your Lord who created man of blood coagulated. Read! Your Lord taught by the pen.' So I read it, and he departed from me. I awoke from my sleep. These words were written on my heart. None of Allah's creatures was more hateful to me than an ecstatic poet or a man possessed.' I thought, 'Woe is me, I'm a possessed poet.'"

Ishaq:105 "Aisha said that when Allah desired to honor Muhammad, the first sign of prophethood was a vision in brightness of day shown to him in his sleep. He liked nothing better than to be alone. When he left Mecca and there was no house in sight, every stone and tree that passed by said, 'Peace be unto you, Allah's Apostle.' Muhammad would turn around and see naught but trees and stones. He stayed seeing and hearing things as long as it pleased Allah."

Bukhari:V9B87N113 "The Prophet said, 'A good dream is from Allah, and a bad dream is from Satan.'"

Tabari VI:76 "The inspiration ceased to come to the Messenger for a while, and he was deeply grieved. He began to go to the tops of mountain crags, in order to fling himself from them; but every time he reached the summit of a mountain, Gabriel appeared to him and said to him, 'You are Allah's Prophet.' Thereupon his anxiety would subside and he would come back to himself. [Muhammad explains:] I was walking one day when I saw the angel who used to come to me at Hira. I was terror-stricken by him."

Qur'an 73:1 "O you who have been wrapped in your garments! Who said, 'Cover me, cover me. I'm afraid of the angel.' Keep watch all night except a little. And recite the Qur'an as it ought to be recited, in slow, measured rhythmic tones. Surely We will soon entrust you with Our weighty Word. Surely the night is the most devout way when the soul is most receptive and the words most telling."

Ishaq:115 "Now Muhammad did not want his secret to be divulged before he applied himself to the publication of his message."

Ishaq:155 "The revelations stopped for some time so that the Apostle was distressed and grieved. Then Gabriel brought him the 'Morning,' in which he swore that he had not forsaken him and did not hate him."

Qur'an 93:1 "I swear by the early hours of the day, and the night when it covers with darkness. Your Lord hath not forsaken thee, nor doth He despisith thee."

Ishaq:117 "Three years elapsed from the time that Muhammad concealed his state until Allah commanded him to publish his religion according to information that has reached me. 'Proclaim what you have been ordered and turn away from the polytheists.' [15:94] 'Warn your family, your nearest relations.' [26:214] When these words came down to the Apostle he said, 'Allah has ordered me to warn my family and the task is beyond my strength. When I make my message known to them I will meet with great unpleasantness so I have kept silent. But Gabriel has told me that if I do not do as ordered my Lord will punish me.'"

Bukhari:V6B61N550 "The Prophet said, 'It is a bad thing that some of you say, "I have forgotten such-and-such verse of the Qur'an." For indeed, I have been caused to forget it. So you must keep on reciting the Qur'an because it escapes from the hearts of men faster than a runaway camel.'" [Contradicting himself, Allah tells his illiterate messenger...] *Qur'an 87:4* "We shall make you read so that you will not forget."

Tabari VI:75 "'Messenger, how did you first know with absolute certainty that you were a prophet?' He replied, 'Two angels came to me while I was somewhere in Mecca.... One angel said, "Open his breast and take out his heart." He opened my chest and heart, removing the pollution of Satan and a clot of blood, and threw them away. Then one said, "Wash his breast as you would a receptacle." He summoned the Sakinah, which looked like the face of a white cat, and it was placed in my heart. Then one said, "Sew up his breast." So they sewed up my chest and placed the seal between my shoulders.'"

Qur'an 94:1 "Have We not opened up your chest and removed your burden which left you hopeless?"

Qur'an 75:6 "Move not your tongue concerning the Qur'an to make haste. It is for Us to collect it, put it together, and promulgate it. When We have read it, follow its recital as promulgated. It is for Us to explain it."

Qur'an 47.024 "Do they not understand the Qur'an? Nay, on the hearts there are locks preventing them from understanding."

Qur'an 5:101 "Believers! Do not ask questions about things which if made plain and declared to you, may vex you, causing you trouble." *Qur'an 5:102* "Some people before you did ask such questions, and on that account they lost their faith and became disbelievers."

Qur'an 5:109 "One day Allah will gather the messengers together, and ask: 'What was the response you received (to your teaching)?' They will say: 'We have no knowledge.'"

Bukhari:V2B24N555 "I heard the Prophet say, 'Allah has hated for you for asking too many questions.'"

Qur'an 3:7 "He it is Who has sent down to you the Book. In it are entirely clear verses, decisive, or fundamental (with established meaning); they are the foundation of the Book: others are unclear or allegorical. As for those who are perverse, they follow the part that is not entirely clear, trying (to cause) dissension by seeking to explain it and searching for hidden meanings. But no one knows its explanation or meaning except Allah. And those who are firmly grounded in knowledge say: 'We believe in the Book; the whole of it (clear and unclear) is from our Lord.' None will grasp the Message except men of understanding."

Qur'an 69:38 "But nay! I swear that this is truly the word of an honored, illustrious, and noble Messenger; it is not the word of a poet, nor is it the word of a soothsayer."

Qur'an 69:43 "This is a Message sent down from the Lord of men and jinn [demons]. And if the Messenger were to attribute any false words to Us, We would seize him and cut his aorta. None of you would be able to stop Us. So truly this is a Message for those who fear. Yet We know that there are those who deny and belie (this Qur'an). But truly this (Qur'an) revelation is a cause of sorrow and anguish; the nemesis of unbelievers."

Ishaq:180 "According to my information, the Apostle often sat by a young Christian slave named Jabr. The Meccans said, 'He is the one who teaches Muhammad most of what he brings.' Then Allah revealed, *Qur'an 16:103* 'We know what they (pagans) say: "It is only a mortal man who teaches him (Muhammad). But the tongue of the man they wickedly point to is notably foreign, while this (Qur'an) is pure Arabic.'"

Bukhari:V4B56N814 "There was a Christian who embraced Islam and he used to write the revelations for the Prophet. Later on he returned to Christianity again he used to say:

'Muhammad knows nothing but what I have written for him.'"

Bukhari:V4B55N554 "Allah's Apostle said, 'Shall I not tell you about the a story of which no prophet told his nation? Someone will bring with him what will resemble Hell and Paradise, and what he will call Paradise will be actually Hell.'"

Qur'an 72:1 "Say (Muhammad): 'It has been revealed to me that a group of Jinn [demons or devils] listened (to the Qur'an). They said, "We have heard a really wonderful recital (of this Qur'an)! It guides to the Right Path. We have come to believe it. We shall not associate anything with our Lord."

Bukhari:V5B58N199 "'Who informed you Prophet about the Jinn [Demons] when they heard the Qur'an?' He said, 'A tree informed me about them.'"

Qur'an 72:13 "So, since we [Jinn/Devils] have listened to the guidance (of the Qur'an), we have accepted (Islam): and any who believes in his Lord has no fear of loss, force, or oppression."

Qur'an 81:24 "Neither is he a concealer, withholding knowledge of the unseen. Nor is it (the Qur'an) the Word of an evil spirit accursed, the utterance of a devil, the curses of Satan."

Qur'an 81:26 "Then where are you going? Verily this (Qur'an) is no less than a reminder to all the Alamin (men and jinn [demons or devils])."

Qur'an 91:1 "I swear by the sun and its brilliance, and by the moon when she follows him."

Muslim:C14B39N6757 "Allah's Messenger said: 'There is none amongst you with whom is not an attaché from amongst the jinn, a devil.' The Companions said: 'Allah's Messenger, is there a devil with you too?' Thereupon he said: 'Yes, but Allah helps me against him so I am safe from his hand and he does not command me but for good.'"

Tabari VI:107 "Satan Cast a False Qur'an Revelation on the Messenger of Allah's Tongue."

Qur'an 22:52 "Every Messenger or Prophet before you recited the message Satan cast into his recitation."

Bukhari:V5B59N716-V4B52N288 "The ailment of Allah's Apostle became worse. He said, 'Fetch me something so I may write something to keep you from going astray.' The people differed in this matter, and it was not right to differ before a prophet. Some said, 'What is wrong with him? Do you think he's delirious? Let's ask him.' So they went to the Prophet and asked. He said, 'Leave me, for my present state is better than what you question me about.' Then he ordered them to do three things. He said, 'Turn the pagans out of the Arabian Peninsula; give gifts to the foreign delegations as you have seen me dealing with them.'"

Tabari IX:175 "Bring me a tablet, or a plank of the shoulder blade and an inkpot, so that I can write for you a document, after which you will not go astray.' Some said, 'The Messenger of Allah is out of his mind.'"

Muslim:C24B20N4607 "Allah's Messenger forbade that one should travel to the land of the enemy taking the Qur'an with him."

Tabari IX:85 "None but the purified shall touch the Qur'an."

Muslim:C24B20N4608 "It Is Forbidden To Take The Qur'an To The Land Of The Infidels When It Is Feared That It Might Fall Into Their Hands: Muhammad used to forbid anyone from traveling to the land of the enemy taking the Qur'an lest it should fall into the hands of the enemy."

Muslim: C24B20N4609 "The Messenger said: 'Do not take the Qur'an on a journey with you, for I am afraid lost it would fall into the hands of the enemy.' Ayyub, one of the narrators in the chain of transmitters, said: 'The enemy may seize it and may quarrel with you over it.'"

Qur'an 56:75 "Furthermore I call to witness the falling Stars, and that is indeed a mighty adjuration, a tremendous oath, if only you knew, that this is indeed a noble recitation (of the Qur'an). In a Book kept hidden that is protected which none shall touch but those who are clean, the purified ones. A Revelation from the Lord of men and jinn [devils]. Is it such a talk that you would hold in light esteem, a statement to scorn? Do you then hold this announcement in contempt?"

Qur'an 12:1 "These are verses of the immaculate Book, a clear discourse." *Qur'an 12:3* "Through the Qur'an We narrate the best of histories." *Qur'an 2:1* "This is a book free of doubt." *Qur'an 10:37* "This Qur'an is such a writing that none but Allah could have composed it. It confirms what has been revealed before."

Ishaq:141/Tabari VI:104 "The first to recite the Qur'an aloud in Mecca after the apostle was Abdallah bin Mas'ud. One day the companions of the Prophet were assembled together [all five of them] and remarked, 'The Quraysh have never heard this Qur'an recited aloud to them. Who will make them listen to it?'" *Ishaq:141* "The next day Ibn Mas'ud went to the Ka'aba in the late morning when the Quraysh were gathered in groups. He turned toward them as he recited: *Qur'an 55:1* "Ar-Rahman bestowed the Qur'an. He created man. He has taught man eloquent speech (and intelligence). The sun and moon are made punctual, following courses, they revolve to a computation."

Qur'an 13:38 "It was not for any Apostle to come up with a miracle or sign unless it was granted by Our permission. For every age there is a Book revealed. Ar-Rahman abrogates, blots out, or confirms (whatever He wants)." *Qur'an 13:42* "Sure, they devised their plots, but We are the best schemers." *Qur'an 13:43* "Yet the disbelievers say: 'You are not a Messenger.' Tell them: 'This Scripture is sufficient witness between me and you.'"

Bukhari:V4B56N667 "The Messenger said, 'Convey to the people even if it were a single sentence, and tell others the stories of Israel (which have been taught to you), for it is not sinful to do so. And whoever tells a lie on me intentionally, will surely take his place in the Hell Fire.'"

Qur'an 87:18 "Verily, this is in the Books of the earliest Revelation, in the former scrolls and Scriptures, The Books of Abraham and Moses."

Qur'an 46:12 "Before this was the Scripture Book of Moses [the Torah] as a guide. This Book [the Qur'an] confirms and verifies (it) in the Arabic tongue; to admonish the unjust, and as glad tidings to the good-doers."

Qur'an 3:1 "Alif-Lam-Mim. (These letters are one of the miracles of the Qur'an but only Allah knows their meaning.)" *Qur'an 3:3* "He has verily revealed to you this Book, in truth and confirmation of the Books revealed before, as indeed He had revealed the Taurat (Torah) and the Injeel (Gospel)."

Tabari VII:167 "The Prophet commanded Zayd bin Thabit to study the Book of the Jews, saying, 'I fear that they may change my Book.'"

Qur'an 20:113 "Thus we have sent the Qur'an down as a Lecture in Arabic and explained the intimidations and different threats that they might fear Allah."

Qur'an 21:18 "Nay, We fling the true against the false, and it knocks out its brains. [In a way, it's true. Hurl enough of this stuff at someone and they'll lose their mind.] Behold, it is vanished! Ah! woe be to you for that thing you ascribe. To Him belong all men and jinn."

Bukhari:V6B60N13 "The Prophet prayed facing Jerusalem but he *wished* that his Qiblah would be the Ka'aba at Mecca *so Allah revealed* a Qur'an."

Qur'an 59:21 "Had We sent down this Qur'an on a mountain, verily, you would have seen it humble itself, turn desolate and cleave asunder, splitting in two for fear of Allah. Such are these parables which We propound to men, that they may reflect."

ALLAH, ISLAM'S ILAH:

Ishaq:324 "Allah said, 'Leave Me to deal with the liars. I have fetters, fire, and food which chokes."

Qur'an 68:44 "Then leave Me alone with such as reject this Message and call Our pronouncements a lie. Systematically by degrees, step by step, We shall punish them in ways they can not even imagine."

Qur'an 73:11 "Leave Me alone to deal with the beliers (those who deny My Verses). Respite those who possess good things for a little while. Verily, with Us are heavy shackles (to bind), a raging fire (to burn), food that chokes, and a torturous penalty of a painful doom."

Qur'an 104:4 "He will be sure to be thrown into that which breaks him into pieces, flung to the Consuming One. And what will explain that which Breaks him into Pieces, the Consuming One? It is the fire kindled by Allah." [Allah is in hell, kindling the fire.]

Qur'an 89:12 "All made mischief so your Lord poured on them the disaster of His torment, a scourge of diverse chastisements. Most surely your Lord is in laying in wait, watching."

Qur'an 89:21 "Nay, when the earth is made to crumble the Lord comes, His angels rank upon rank, and Hell is brought face to face, man will remember, but how will that avail him? For His Chastisement will be such as no other can inflict. None punishes as He will punish! None can bind as He will bind."

Qur'an 67:16 "Are you so unafraid that He will not open the earth to swallow you, pelt you with showers of stones, or let loose on you a violent wind so that you shall know how terrible is My warning? But indeed men before them rejected My warning. They denied, so then how terrible will be My punishment of them and My wrath."

Qur'an 91:13 "The Messenger said: 'Be cautious. It is a She-camel of God! And bar her not from having her drink!' But they rejected him as a false prophet, and they hamstrung her. So Allah on account of their crime, obliterated their traces, doomed them, desolated their dwellings, leveling them to the ground, crushing them for their sin."

Qur'an 48:6 "He may punish the Hypocrites who imagine an evil opinion, or have evil thoughts about Allah. It is against them that the wheel of misfortune will turn, a disgraceful torment: the Wrath of Allah is on them: He has cursed them, and He has prepared Hell for them."

Qur'an 47:12 "And how many cities, with more power than your city (Muhammad) which has driven you out, have We destroyed?"

Qur'an 53:49 "He is the Lord of Sirius (the Mighty Star the pagan Arabs used to worship). It is

He Who destroyed the (powerful) ancient Ad (people) [who never existed], and (the tribe of) Thamud He spared not; And before them, the folk of Noah, for that they were (all) most unjust and rebellious; and He destroyed the Overthrown Cities."

Qur'an 40:1 "Ha Mim. (These letters are one of the miracles of the Qur'an and none but Allah understands their meaning.) The revelation of this Book is from Allah, Exalted in Power, the All-Knower, The Forgiver, the Accepter, the Severe in Punishment."

Qur'an 40:21 "Do they not travel through the earth and see the end of those before them? They were superior to them in strength, and in the traces (they have left) in the land, yet Allah seized and destroyed them, and they had no one to defend them against Allah. That was because their Messengers kept bringing them Clear (Signs and Proofs) (of Allah's Sovereignty), but they rejected them: So Allah seized and destroyed them: for He is Strong, Severe in Punishment and Retribution."

Tabari VII:3 "I recommend to you the fear of Allah, for the best thing which a Muslim can enjoin upon a Muslim is that he should...fear Allah. [*Qur'an 87:10* "He who fears will obey."] Beware of what Allah has warned you concerning himself. The fear of Allah, for whoever acts according to it in fear and dread of his Lord is a trusty aid to what you desire. Allah says, 'The sentence that comes from me cannot be changed, and I am in no wise a tyrant unto the slaves.' The fear of Allah will ward off Allah's hatred, retribution, and wrath."

Qur'an 33:26 "Allah made the Jews leave their homes by terrorizing them so that you killed some and made many captive. And He made you inherit their lands, their homes, and their wealth. He gave you a country you had not traversed before."

Qur'an 59:2 "It was He [Allah] who drove the People of the Book from their [Medina] homes and into exile. They refused to believe. They imagined that their settlement would protect them against Allah. But Allah's (torment) came at them from where they did not suspect and terrorized them. Their homes were destroyed. So learn a lesson men who have eyes. This is My warning. Had Allah not decreed the expulsion of the Jews, banishing them into the desert, He would certainly have punished them in this world, and in the next they shall taste the torment of Hell Fire."

Qur'an 8:2 "The only believers are those who feel fear and terror when Allah is mentioned."

Ishaq:322 "Allah said concerning the pebbles thrown by the Apostle, 'I threw them not you. Your tossing them would have had no effect without My help. But working together, We terrorized the enemy and put them to flight."

Qur'an 8:17 "It is not you who slew them; it was Allah who killed them. It was not you (Muhammad) who threw (a handful of dust), it was not your act, but it was Allah who threw (the sand into the eyes of the enemy at Badr) in order that He might test the [Muslim] Believers by doing them a gracious favor of His Own: for Allah is He Who hears and knows."

Ishaq:327 "Allah said, 'A prophet must slaughter before collecting captives. A slaughtered enemy is driven from the land. Muhammad, you craved the desires of this world, its goods and the ransom captives would bring. But Allah desires killing them to manifest the religion.'"

Qur'an 64:11 "No calamity occurs, no affliction comes, except by the decision and preordainment of Allah."

Qur'an 3:62 "This is the true account, the true explanation: There is no Ilah (God) except Allah." *Qur'an 3:102* "You who believe! Fear Allah as He should be feared."

Ishaq:392 "It is not your affair whether Allah changes His attitude to them or punishes them.... I may change My mind toward them. Punishing them is my prerogative. They deserve this for their disobedience to Me.'"

Ishaq:393 "Fear Allah that you may be prosperous. Obey Allah and perhaps you may escape from His punishment of which He has warned you and attain His reward which He has made you desire. And fear the fire which He has prepared for the disbelievers, a resort for those who disbelieve Me."

Qur'an 78:37 "None shall have power to argue with the Lord, none can converse with Him or address Him."

Qur'an 3:98 "Allah is self-sufficient, standing not in need, independent of any of His creatures."

Qur'an 21:16 "Not for sport did We create the heavens, earth and all that is between! It wasn't a plaything. If it had been Our wish to take a pastime, to make a diversion or hobby (like a wife or a son), We surely could have made it Ourselves, in Our presence, if We would do."

Qur'an 52:43 "Have they an ilah (god) other than Allah? [An odd question to ask the Meccans since their primary deity was Allah.]"

Qur'an 5:4 "Pronounce the Name of Allah: and fear Allah; for Allah is swift in reckoning."

Qur'an 21:107 "Say: (Muhammad) 'It is revealed to me that your Ilah (God) is only one Ilah (God). Will you submit to His Will? But if they (disbelievers, Christians, and Jews) turn away (from Islam) say: 'I give notice (of war) to be known to all. But I know not whether the (torment which you are) promised and threatened is nigh or far."

Qur'an 114:1 "Say: I seek refuge in the Lord of men and jinn [demons], the King of men and jinn, the Ilah (God) of men and jinn."

Qur'an 20:8 "Allah! There is no Ilah (God) save Him. His are the most beautiful Names. To Him belong the most beautiful attributes."

Qur'an 20:14 "Verily, I am Allah. No Ilah (God) may be worshiped but I. So serve you Me, and perform regular prostration prayer for My praise. Verily the Hour is coming. I am almost hiding it from Myself."

Qur'an 20:96 "Now look at your ilah (god), of whom you have become devoted. We will (burn) it and scatter it in the sea! But your Ilah (God) is Allah: there is no ilah (god) but He. Thus do We relate to you some stories of what happened before from Our own Remembrance."

Qur'an 2:132 "And this was the legacy that Abraham left to his sons by Yah'qub (Jacob); 'Oh my sons! Allah has chosen the Faith for you—the true religion; then die not except in the faith of Islam as Muslims. He said to his sons: 'What will you worship after me?' They said: 'We shall worship your Ilah (God), the Ilah (God) of your fathers, of Abraham, Ishmael and Isaac, the one Ilah (God): To Him we submit in Islam.'"

Ishaq:324 "He said, Fight them so that there is no more rebellion, and religion, all of it, is for Allah only. Allah must have no rivals."

Qur'an 8:45 "O believers! When you meet an army, be firm, and think of Allah's Name much; that you may prosper."

Qur'an 73:8 "But keep in remembrance the name of your Lord and devote yourself to Him whole-heartedly. Lord of the East and West: there is no Ilah (God) but He."

Qur'an 87:1 "Glorify the Name of your Lord, the Most High, Who creates, then proportions, Who has measured; and then guided."

Qur'an 87:14 "He indeed shall be successful who purifies himself, and magnifies the Name of his Lord and prays." [Allahu Akbar!]

Qur'an 59:22 "Allah is He, no other Ilah (God) may be worshiped; Who knows both secret and open; He, Most Gracious, Most Merciful. He is Allah, Whom there is no other Ilah (God); the Sovereign, the Holy One, the Source of Security, the Guardian of Faith, the Majestic, the Irresistible, the Superb, the Compeller: Glory to Allah! He is Allah, the Creator, the Evolver, the Bestower of Forms (or Colors). To Him belong the Best Names: whatever is in the heavens and on earth declares His Praises and Glory: and He is the Mighty, the Wise."

Ishaq:162 "Abu Jahl met the Apostle and said, 'By Allah, Muhammad, you will either stop cursing our gods or we will curse the god you serve.' So the Qur'an verse was revealed, 'Do not insult those [gods] to whom they pray lest they curse God wrongfully through lack of knowledge.' [Qur'an 6:108] I have been told that the Apostle then refrained from cursing their gods, and *began* to call them to Allah [rather than Ar-Rahman]."

AR RAHMAN, THE OTHER ILAH:

Qur'an 67:28 "Say: 'He is Ar-Rahman; in Him we believed, and in Him we have placed our trust: Soon will you know which one of us is in manifest error.'"

Qur'an 67:20 "Who is he that will send an army to assist you besides Ar-Rahman? The unbelievers are lost in delusion."

Qur'an 55:1 "Ar-Rahman bestowed the Qur'an. He created man. He has taught man eloquent speech (and intelligence). The sun and moon are made punctual, following courses, they revolve to a computation."

Qur'an 55:6 "Ar-Rahman created the herbs (or stars) and the trees all of which prostrate themselves." *Qur'an 55:14* "He created man of fermented clay dried tinkling hard like earthen ware, and created jinn from the white-hot flame of fire. How many favors of your Lord will you both (men and jinn) deny?"

Qur'an 55:31 "Soon We [Ar-Rahman] will dispose of you by applying Our two armies. How many favors of your Lord will you both deny?" *Qur'an 55:35* "There will be let loose on you white-hot flames of fire and smoke that chokes so that you will not be able to defend yourselves. How many favors of your Lord will you both deny?" [Ar-Rahman makes jinn out of the same material he will use to torture men. He intends to send his demons after us, and he considers torture a favor.] *Qur'an 55:41* "The sinners will be seized by their forelock and feet. This is the Hell the sinners called a lie. They will go round and round between its fierce fires and boiling water. Which of the favors of your Lord will you then deny?" *Qur'an 55:46* "For him who lives in terror of his Lord [Ar-Rahman] are two Gardens."

Qur'an 13:30 "They do not believe in Ar-Rahman. Tell them, 'He is my Lord. There is no other Ilah (God) but He. In Him I have placed my trust.'"

Qur'an 13:38 "It was not for any Apostle to come up with a miracle or sign unless it was granted by Our permission. For every age there is a Book revealed. Ar-Rahman abrogates, blots out, or confirms (whatever He wants)."

Qur'an 20:90 "'O my people, you are being misled with this. Surely your Lord is Ar-Rahman. So follow me and obey my command."

Qur'an 20:108 "Their voices will be hushed before Ar-Rahman. You will not hear a sound but faint shuffling. That day no intercession will matter other than his whom Ar-Rahman grants permission."

Qur'an 21:25 "Not a messenger did We send before you but We revealed to him: La ilaha illa Ana (No gods but I), so worship Me." [Incredibly, this assertion of a singular divinity is followed by:] *Qur'an 21:26* "And yet they say: 'Ar-Rahman has begotten a son.' Too exalted his He." [Most translations, trying to hide their god's duplicity, mistranslate the passage:] "(Allah) Most Gracious has begotten offspring." [Muslims have to deceive us to keep their god together.] *Qur'an 21:29* "If any of them should say, 'I am an ilah (god) besides Him,' such a one We should reward with Hell."

Qur'an 21:36 "When the disbelievers see you (Muhammad), they treat you with ridicule, choosing you out for mockery: 'Is this he who mentions your gods? Yet they disbelieve at the mention of Ar-Rahman."

Qur'an 21:41 "Mocked were messengers before you, but their scoffers were hemmed in by what they mocked. Say: 'Who can protect you from (the wrath of) Ar-Rahman?' Yet they turn away from the mention of their Lord. Have they alihah (gods) who can defend them against Our Torment?"

Ishaq:302/Tabari VII:60 "Umayyah [a merchant] was a friend of mine in Mecca. My name was Abd Amr, but when I became a Muslim I was called Abd al-Rahman. Umayyah used to meet me when we were in Mecca and would say, 'Abd Amr, do you dislike the name your father gave you?' I would reply, 'Yes.' Umayyah would then say, 'I do not recognize Ar-Rahman [as a god], so adopt a name that I can call you by when we meet.... Well then, you are Abd al-Ilah [Slave-to-the-God].' I agreed."

DEMONS & DEVILS:

Muslim:C14B39N6759 "Aisha, the wife of Allah's Apostle, reported: 'Allah's Messenger left my apartment during the night. Then he came and he saw me in an agitated state.' He said: "Aisha, what has happened to you? Do you feel jealous?" I said: "How can it be that a girl like me would not feel jealous in regard to a husband like you? Thereupon Allah's Messenger said: "It is your devil who has come to you." I said: "Allah's Messenger, is there a devil with me?" He said: "Yes." I said: "Is there a devil attached to everyone?" He said: "Yes." I said: "Allah's Messenger, is there a devil attached to you also?" He said: "Yes.""

Muslim:C14B39N6757 "Allah's Messenger said: 'There is none amongst you with whom is not an attaché from amongst the jinn, a devil.' The Companions said: 'Allah's Messenger, is there a devil with you too?' Thereupon he said: 'Yes, but Allah helps me against him so I am safe from his hand and he does not command me but for good.'"

Bukhari:V6B60N475 "Allah's Apostle became sick and could not offer his prayer. A lady came and said, 'Muhammad! I think that your Satan has forsaken you, for I have not seen him with you for two or three nights!' On that Allah revealed: 'By the night when it darkens, your Lord has neither forsaken you, nor hated you.'" [93:1]

Ishaq:166 "'You have recited to the people that which I did not bring to you from Allah, and you have said that which He did not say to you.' The Messenger was grieved and feared Allah greatly. So Allah sent a revelation to him, consoling him and making light of the affair [of worldly bargains and Satanic indulgences]. He informed him that there had never been a prophet or messenger before who desired as he desired and wished as he wished but that Satan had cast words into his recitation, as he had interjected them on Muhammad's tongue and into his desires."

Ishaq:166 "Then Allah annulled what Satan had cast, and established his verses by telling him that he was like other prophets and messengers. Every Messenger or Prophet before you recited the message Satan cast into his recitation. Allah abrogates what Satan casts. Then Allah established his verses.'"

Qur'an 22:52 "Never did We send a messenger or a prophet before you, but, when he framed a desire, Satan threw some vanity into his desire: but Allah will cancel anything (vain) that Satan throws in." [Another translation reads:] "He recited (the message) Satan proposed. But Allah abolishes that which Satan proposes." [A third claims:] "Satan made a suggestion respecting his desire; but Allah annuls that which Satan casts," [A fourth:] "whose recitations Satan tampered with, yet Allah abrogates what Satan interpolates; and Allah will confirm His Signs/Revelations."

Qur'an 22:53 "He may make the suggestions thrown in by Satan, the Devil's proposals, but a trial and temptation for those in whose hearts is a disease. Verily the wrong-doers are in a schism. And those on whom knowledge has been bestowed may learn that the (Qur'an) is the truth from your Lord, that they may believe, and their hearts may submit lowly before it."

Tabari VI:110 "Thus Allah removed the sorrow from his Messenger, reassured him about that which he had feared, and cancelled the words which Satan had cast on his tongue, that their gods were exalted high-flying cranes (goddesses) whose intercession was accepted with approval. He now revealed, following the mention of 'Al-Lat, Al-Uzza, and Manat,' the words: 'are yours the males and his the females? That indeed is an unfair division!'"

Qur'an 53:1 "I call to witness the Star when it dips. Your Companion (Muhammad) is neither confused, deceived, nor misled [except by Satan, in the guise of Allah]. Nor does he speak out of (his own) desire [unless he is tempted with money, sex, and power]. It is a revelation revealed, He was taught (this Qur'an) by the Supreme Intellect (Gabriel [actually Lucifer]), One free from any defect in body or mind: for he rose and became stable (in stately form), clear to view. While he was in the highest part of the horizon, then he approached and came closer, then he prostrated. He was at a distance of but two bow-lengths or nearer."

Qur'an 53:19 "Have you then seen or thought upon Al-Lat and Al-Uzza (two idols of the pagan Arabs), and considered another, the third (goddess), Manat (of the pagan deities)? What! for you sons, the male sex, and for Him, daughters, the female? Are yours the males and His the females? Behold, such would be indeed a division most unfair!"

Tabari VI:110 "When Muhammad brought a revelation from Allah canceling what Satan had cast on the tongue of His Prophet, the Quraysh said, 'Muhammad has repented of what he said concerning the position of our gods with Allah."

Tabari VI:116/Ishaq:193 "When the Messenger despaired of getting any positive response from the Thaqif, he left Ta'if to return to Mecca. When he was at Nakhlah, he rose in the middle of the night to pray, and, as Allah has told [in the Qur'an], a number of the jinn [devils] passed by. They listened to him, and when he had completed his prayer they went back to their people to warn them, having believed and responded to what they had heard. Allah mentioned their story when he said: *Qur'an 46:29* "Behold, We turned towards you (Muhammad) a company of Jinn who wished to hear the Qur'an: when they stood in the presence thereof, they said, 'Give ear!'"

Qur'an 46:30 "We [Jinns/Demons] have heard a Book revealed after Moses, confirming what came before it: it guides to the Truth and to a Straight Path.' 'O our people, hearken to the one who invites (you) to Allah, and believe in him. He will forgive you your sins, and deliver you from a Penalty Grievous.'"

Bukhari:V2B21N245 "A person slept in and missed the morning prayer. So the Prophet said, 'Satan urinated in his ears.'"

Bukhari:V4B54N494 "Allah's Apostle said, 'When the upper edge of the sun appears in the morning, don't perform a prayer till it has risen. When the lower edge of the sun sets, don't perform a prayer till it has set, for the sun rises between two sides of the Satan's head.'"

Bukhari:V4B54N509 "The Prophet said, 'Yawning is from Satan and if anyone of you yawns, he should check his yawning as much as possible, for if anyone of you during the act of yawning should say: "Ha," Satan will laugh at him.'"

Bukhari:V4B54N513 "Allah's Apostle said, 'A good dream is from Allah, and a bad dream is from Satan; so if anyone of you has a bad dream and is afraid, he should spit on his left side, for then it will not harm him.'"

Bukhari:V4B54N516 "The Prophet said, 'If anyone rouses from sleep and performs ablution, he should wash his nose by putting water in it and then blow it out thrice because Satan has stayed in the upper part of his nose all the night.'"

Bukhari:V4B54N522 "Allah's Apostle said, 'When you hear the crowing of cocks seek blessings, their crowing indicates that they have seen an angel. When you hear the braying of donkeys, seek refuge, for their braying indicates that they have seen Satan.'"

Ishaq:72 "Some months after Muhammad's return to the desert two men in white seized the boy, threw him down and opened up his belly, stirring it up. His wet nurse said, 'I am afraid that this child has had a stroke, so I want to take him back before the result appears.' She carried him back to Muhammad's mother and said, 'I am afraid that ill will befall him, so I have brought him back to you.' She asked what had happened. I said, 'I fear that a demon has possessed him.'"

Ishaq:90 "Jewish rabbis, Christian monks, and Arab soothsayers had spoken about the Apostle of Allah before his mission when his time drew near. The rabbis and monks found his description in their scriptures. The Arab occultists had been visited by satans from the jinn with reports which they had secretly overheard before they were prevented form hearing by being pelted with stars."

Ishaq:91 "The Prophet explained the nature of shooting stars. 'Allah shut off the satans by these stars which pelted them. So satans tried to steal information, listening in, mingling what they heard with conjecture and false intelligence. They conveyed it to the soothsayers.'"

Qur'an 67:5 "Your gaze turns back dazed and tired. We have adorned the lowest skies with lamps, and We have made them missiles to drive away the devils and against the stone Satans, and for them We have prepared the doom of Hell and the penalty of torment in the most intense Blazing Fire."

Qur'an 37:6 "We have decked the lower heaven with stars to protect them against all rebellious evil spirit, and provide security from every forward devil. So they cannot listen to the highest chiefs for they are pelted from every side, repulsed; they are under a perpetual torment, being driven off. Except such as they snatch away something by stealth, but then they are pursued by a flaming fire of piercing brightness."

Bukhari:V4B54N508 "The Prophet said, 'While angels talk amidst the clouds about things that are going to happen, devils hear what they say and pour it in the ears of soothsayers as one pours something in a bottle, and they add one hundred lies to it.'"

Muslim:C10B16N4168 "Allah's Messenger said: 'He seems to be one of the soothsayers on account of the rhymed speech which he has composed.'"

Qur'an 72:1 "Say (Muhammad): 'It has been revealed to me that a group of (three to ten) Jinn [demons or devils] listened (to the Qur'an). They said, "We have heard a really wonderful recital (of this Qur'an)! It guides to the Right Path. We have come to believe it. We shall not associate anything with our Lord."

Qur'an 72:3 "There were some foolish ones among us, who used to utter preposterous things, atrocious lies against the Lord; We Jinn [Devils] had thought that no man or jinn would ever say anything untrue about the Lord. But there were men who took shelter with the male jinn. But they (jinn) increased them in waywardness, folly, and revolt. And surely they came to think as you thought, that the Lord would not raise up any Messenger. We jinn pried into the secrets of heaven; but we found it filled with fierce guards, stern wardens and flaming fires. We used to sit there in, hidden in observatories, trying to steal a hearing; but any who listen now will find a shooting star and a flaming fire watching him, lying in wait as an ambush for him. And we Jinn know not whether harm or evil is the intended fate of all men on earth, or whether the Lord intends to give them some guidance."

Bukhari:V6B60N332 "The Prophet said, 'Last night a demon from the Jinn came to me to disturb my prayer, but Allah gave me the power to overcome him. I intended to tie him to one of the pillars of the mosque till the morning so that all of you could see him.'"

Bukhari:V5B58N199 "'Who informed you Prophet about the Jinn [Demons] when they heard the Qur'an?' He said, 'A tree informed me about them.'"

Bukhari:V9B93N650 "Some people asked the Prophet about soothsayers. 'Allah's Apostle! Some of their talks come true.' The Prophet said, 'That word which happens to be true is what a Jinn snatches away by stealth (from Heaven) and pours it in the ears of the soothsayer with a sound like the cackling of a hen. The soothsayer mixes it with one hundred lies.'"

Tabari VI:73/Ishaq:107 "'Cousin, can you tell me when this visitor comes to you?' Muhammad replied, 'Yes.' She said, 'Tell me then, when he comes.' Gabriel came to him as before, and Muhammad said, 'Here is Gabriel who has just come to me.' She said, 'Yes? Come, cousin, and sit by my left thigh.' He came, and she said, 'Can you see him?' 'Yes.' 'Move around and sit by my right thigh.' He did so and she said, 'Can you see him?' 'Yes.' She said, 'Sit in my lap.' He did so, and she said, 'Can you see him?' He replied, 'Yes.' She was grieved, and flung off her veil and disclosed her body while the Apostle was sitting in her lap, inside her shift next to her body. Then she said, 'Can you see him?' 'No.' At that she said, 'Rejoice cousin. By Allah, this spirit is an angel and not Satan.'"

Qur'an 74:32 "Truly: I swear by the Moon as a witness, and by the darkness of night."

Ishaq:510 "When the Apostle looked down on Khaybar he told his Companions, 'O Allah, Lord of the heavens and what they overshadow, and Lord of the Devils and what into error they throw, and Lord of the winds and what they winnow, we ask Thee for the booty of this town and its people. Forward in the name of Allah.'"

Ishaq:106 "None of Allah's creatures was more hateful to me than an ecstatic poet or a man possessed. I thought, 'Woe is me, I'm a possessed poet.'" *Ishaq:106* "I will go to the top of the mountain and throw myself down that I may kill myself and be at rest."

Ishaq:106 "I stood gazing at him and that distracted me from committing suicide. I couldn't move. Khadija sent her messengers in search of me and they gained the high ground above Mecca so I came to her and sat by her thigh. She said, 'O Abu'l-Qasim [Muhammad's actual name], where have you been?' I said, 'Woe is me. I am possessed.'"

Tabari VI:70 "He went to Khadija and said, 'I think that I have gone mad.'"

Ishaq:132-3 "If this demonic spirit which has possession of you is such that you cannot get rid of him, we will find a physician for you, and exhaust our means trying to cure you. For often a demonic spirit gets possession of a man, but he can be rid of it.' The Apostle listened patiently."

Qur'an 74:32 "No, truly: I swear by the Moon as a witness, and by the darkness of night as it wanes. And by the dawn as it is unveiled, surely Hell is one of the greatest signs and gravest misfortunes, a warning to men."

Qur'an 75:1 "I swear by the the self-reproaching spirit, the accusing soul."

Qur'an 69:38 "But nay! I swear that this is truly the word of an honored, illustrious, and noble Messenger; it is not the word of a poet, nor is it the word of a soothsayer."

Qur'an 69:43 "This is a Message sent down from the Lord of men and jinn [demons]. And if the Messenger were to attribute any false words to Us, We would seize him and cut his aorta. None of you would be able to stop Us. So truly this is a Message for those who fear. Yet We know that there are those who deny and belie (this Qur'an). But truly this (Qur'an) revelation is a cause of sorrow and anguish; the nemesis of unbelievers."

Qur'an 70:26 "Fear the torment of the Lord, for the Lord's torment is such none can feel secure."

Qur'an 68:1 "I call to witness the Pen and what it writes. You are not a demented madman or possessed."

Qur'an 68:44 "Then leave Me alone with such as reject this Message and call Our pronouncements a lie. Systematically by degrees, step by step, We shall punish them in ways they can not even imagine."

Qur'an 68:51 "And the unbelievers would almost smite you (Muhammad) with their eyes, tripping you when they hear the Message. And they say: 'Surely he is possessed!'"

Bukhari:V6B60N662 "Allah's Apostle said, 'Some eloquent speech is as effective as magic.'"

Bukhari:V9B87N127 "The Prophet said, 'I have been given the keys of eloquent speech.'"

Bukhari:V6B60N658 "A man worked magic on Allah's Apostle until he started imagining that he had done a thing that he had not really done."

Muslim:B001N0244/Bukhari:V4B54N496 "The Messenger of Allah observed: 'Satan comes to everyone of you and says, "Who created this and that," until he asks, "Who created your Lord?" When he comes to that, one should seek refuge and keep away from such idle thoughts.'"

Bukhari:V4B54N533 "Muhammad preached, 'Cover your utensils, tie your water skins, close your doors, and keep your children close at night, as Jinn spread out at such time and snatch things away. When you go to bed put out your lights, for they may use a candle to burn you and your house.' Ata added, 'The Prophet actually said, Devils, instead of Jinn.'"

Qur'an 72:13 "So, since we [Jinn/Devils] have listened to the guidance (of the Qur'an), we have accepted (Islam): and any who believes in his Lord has no fear of loss, force, or oppression."

Qur'an 79:1 "I swear by those who violently tear out (the souls), and drag them to destruction."

Bukhari:V4B54N506 "When a human being is born, Satan touches him at both sides of the body with his two fingers. That is why it cries.'"

Qur'an 81:24 "Neither is he a concealer, withholding knowledge of the unseen. Nor is it (the Qur'an) the Word of an evil spirit accursed, the utterance of a devil, the curses of Satan."

Qur'an 81:26 "Then where are you going? Verily this (Qur'an) is no less than a reminder to all the Alamin (men and jinn [demons or devils])."

Qur'an 89:1 "I swear by the dawn, and the ten nights, and the even and the odd, and the night when it departs."

Qur'an 89:21 "Nay, when the earth is made to crumble the Lord comes, His angels rank upon rank, and Hell is brought face to face, man will remember, but how will that avail him? For His Chastisement will be such as no other can inflict. None punishes as He will punish! None can bind as He will bind."

Qur'an 92:1 "I swear by the night when it draws a veil."

Qur'an 6:66 "The people reject this (Book) and call it a lie though it is the truth. Say: 'I am not a warden over you.' ...When you see men who meddle with Our Revelations, turn away, withdrawing from them. Satan makes you forget."

Ishaq:548 "By Allah, the black mass has spread. Abu Bakr said, 'There is not much honesty among people nowadays.'"

Ishaq:569 "When the Muslims fled, the uncouth and rude fellows from Mecca who were with us saw that we were in total disarray. Some of them spoke in a manner that disclosed the hatred they harbored against us. Abu Sufyan [the Meccan chief turned Muslim warrior] had divining arrows with him but another Muslim said, 'Sorcery is useless today.' Sufyan replied, 'Shut up! May Allah smash your mouth!'"

Tabari IX:14/Ishaq:572 "While the men were still fighting I saw a black striped garment descending from the sky until it dropped between us and the enemy. I gazed, and lo, it was a mass of black ants strewn everywhere, which filled the valley. I had no doubt that they were angels and that the enemy would be routed."

Ishaq:580 "Our strong warriors obey his orders to the letter. By us Allah's religion is undeniably strong. You would think when our horses gallop with bits in their mouths that the sounds of demons are among them."

Tabari IX:121 "The Messenger called me and said, 'I suspect that Khalid Sufyan is going to attack me. So go to him and kill him.' 'O Prophet, describe him to me so that I might know him.' He said, 'When you see him he will remind you of Satan.'"

Bukhari:V4B54N491 "Allah's Apostle said, 'While you sleep, Satan ties three knots at the back of your head. He blows the following words at each knot, "The night is long so keep sleeping." If that person wakes up and praises Allah, then one knot is undone. When he performs ablution the second is undone. When he prays, all the knots are undone, and he gets up in the morning lively and gay, otherwise he is dull and gloomy.'"

Bukhari:V7B71N660 "Magic was worked on Allah's Apostle so that he used to think that he had sexual relations with his wives while he actually had not. That is the hardest kind of magic as it has such an effect. One day he said, 'O Aisha, do you know that Allah has instructed me concerning the matter I asked Him about? Two men came to me and one of them sat near my head and the other near my feet. The one asked, "What is wrong with this man?" "He is under the effect of magic." "Who cast the magic spell on him?" "Labid, an Arab ally of the Jews and a hypocrite." "What material did he use to cast the spell?" "A comb with hair stuck to it." "Where is that comb and hair?" "In a skin of pollen of a male palm tree kept under a stone in the well of Dharwan."' So the Prophet went to that well and took out those things, saying, 'That was the well shown to me in the dream. Its water looked red and its palms looked like the heads of devils. My companions removed those things.' I said, 'Why didn't you just treat yourself?' He said, 'Allah has cured me, and I don't want to spread evil among my people.'"

Bukhari:V7B71N661 "Magic was worked on Allah's Apostle so that he began to imagine he had done something although he had not. While he was with me, he invoked Allah for a long period and then said, 'Aisha! Do you know what Allah has instructed me to do regarding the matter I asked Him about?' 'What is that?' He said, 'Two men came to me. One said, "What is the disease of this man?" The other replied, "He is under the effect of magic." "Who has worked magic on him?" "Labid, a Jew from the Zuraiq tribe."'"

Bukhari:V5B58N200 "I carried a water pot for the Prophet's ablution and for cleaning his private parts. While following him with the pot, the Prophet turned and said, 'Who are you?' 'I am Abu.' The Prophet said, 'Bring me stones in order to clean my private parts, but do not bring any bones or animal dung.' So I brought some stones, carrying them in the corner of my robe till I put them by his side. When he finished, I walked with him and asked, 'What can you tell me about the bones and the animal dung?' He said, 'They are of the food of Jinns [Devils]. A delegate of Jinns of the city of Nasibin came to me—and how nice those Jinns were—and asked me for the remains of human food. I invoked Allah for them that they would never pass by a bone or animal dung but find food on them.'"

Bukhari:V4B54N484 "I heard Muhammad saying, 'Fever is from the heat of the Hell Fire; so cool it with water.'"

Bukhari:V1B11N582 "Allah's Apostle said, 'When the Adhan [the call to prayer] is announced, Satan takes to his heels and passes wind with noise during his flight in order not to hear the Adhan.'"

Bukhari:V3B33N254 "Satan circulates in the human being as blood circulates. I was afraid lest Satan might insert an evil thought in your minds."

Bukhari:V6B61N530 "Allah's Apostle ordered me to guard the Zakat revenue. Then somebody came and started stealing food. I caught him and said, 'I'm going to take you to Allah's Apostle!' He replied, 'Please don't take me to him. If you spare me that fate I will tell you a few words by which Allah will benefit you.' So then he said, 'When you go to bed recite Ayat-al-Kursi, (2:255) for then a guard from Allah will protect you from Satan.' When the Prophet heard the story he said, 'He who came to you at night told you the truth although he is a liar; and it was Satan.'"

Tabari VI:107 "Satan Cast a False Qur'an Revelation on the Messenger of Allah's Tongue."

Qur'an 113:1 "Say: I seek refuge with the Lord of the Dawn from the mischief of the evil He created." *Qur'an 113:3* "From the mischievous evil of Darkness as it becomes intensely dark, and from the mischief of those who practice the evil of malignant witchcraft and blowing on knots, and from the mischievous evil of the envier when he covets."

Bukhari:V7B71N643 "I heard the Prophet saying, 'If anyone sees something he dislikes, he should blow three times on his left side and its evil will not harm him.'" *Bukhari:V6B61N535* "Whenever the Prophet became ill he used to blow his breath over his body hoping for its blessing." *Bukhari:V6B61N536* "When the Prophet went to bed he would cup his hands together and blow over them reciting surahs. He would then rub his hands over whatever parts of his body he could reach, starting with his head, face and frontal areas."

Qur'an 114:1 "Say: I seek refuge in the Lord of men and jinn [demons], the King of men and jinn, the Ilah (God) of men and jinn." *Qur'an 114:4* "From the evil of the sneaking Devil who Whispers Evil and withdraws after his whisper, the slinking Satan, the same who whispers into the hearts of mankind from among the jinn and men."

Qur'an 52:29 "Therefore remind: By the Grace of your Lord, you are no vulgar soothsayer, nor are you a possessed madman."

Qur'an 55:35 "There will be let loose on you white-hot flames of fire and smoke that chokes so that you will not be able to defend yourselves." *Qur'an 55:41* "The sinners will be seized by their forelock and feet. Which of the favors of your Lord will you then deny? This is the Hell the sinners called a lie. They will go round and round between its fierce fires and boiling water. Which of the favors of your Lord will you then deny?"

Ishaq:205/Tabari VI:133 "When we had all sworn the oath of allegiance to the Messenger, Satan shouted from the top of Aqabah in the most piercing and penetrating voice I have ever heard. 'People of the [pagan ritual] stations [of the idolatrous hajj] of Mina, do you want to follow a blameworthy reprobate?' The Messenger said, 'What does the Enemy of God say?' 'I am the Devil, and I shall deal with you!'"

Ishaq:262 "'To arms! To arms!' the Muslims said quarreling and boasting among themselves. When this reached the Prophet, he said, 'Muslims, will you act as pagans while I am with you?' They realized that their dissension was due to Satan and the guile of their enemy. Then they went off with the Apostle attentive and obedient."

Qur'an 2:102 "They follow what Satan chanted and gave out during the lifetime of Solomon. Though Solomon never disbelieved, the devils denied and taught sorcery to men, which they said had been revealed to the angels of Babylon, Harut, and Marut. However, these two (angels) never taught without saying: 'We have been sent to deceive you.'"

Qur'an 8:10 "Allah made the victory [killing, kidnapping, and stealing] but a message of hope, a glad tiding, to reassure you. Victory [of this kind] comes only from Allah. Lo! Allah is Almighty. He covered you with slumber, as a security from Him. He sent down rain to clean you of the plague of evil suggestions of Satan, that you might plant your feet firmly."

Ishaq:327 "Allah said, 'A prophet must slaughter before collecting captives. A slaughtered enemy is driven from the land. Muhammad, you craved the desires of this world, its goods and the ransom captives would bring. But Allah desires killing them to manifest the religion.'"

Qur'an 3:175 "It is the Devil who would make (men) fear his messengers and frighten you. Fear them not; fear Me, if you are believers. And let not those grieve you who fall into unbelief hastily; surely they can do no harm to Allah; they cannot injure Him; Allah intends that He should not give them any portion in the hereafter, and they shall have a grievous doom."

PREDESTINATION:

Tabari I:202 "There are people who consider predestination untrue. Then they consider the Qur'an untrue.... People merely carry out what is a foregone conclusion, decided by predestination and written down by the Pen."

Qur'an 97:1 "We have revealed it (the Qur'an) in the Night of Predestination."

Bukhari:V6B60N473 "Every created soul has his place written for him either in Paradise or in the Hell Fire. His happy or miserable fate is predetermined for him."

Bukhari:V6B60N473 "While we were in a funeral procession, Allah's Apostle said, 'Every created soul has his place written for him either in Paradise or in Hell. They have a happy or miserable fate predestined for them.' A man said, 'Apostle! Shall we depend upon what is written and give up doing deeds? For whoever is destined to be fortunate, will join the fortunate and whoever is destined to be miserable will go to Hell.'"

Tabari I:306 "The Messenger said, "Allah created Adam and then rubbed Adam's back with his right hand and brought forth his progeny. Then He said, 'I have created these as the inhabitants of Paradise.' Then he rubbed his back with His left hand and said, 'I have created those for the Fire, and they will act as the inhabitants of the Fire.' A man asked, 'O Messenger, how is that?' Muhammad replied, 'When Allah creates a human being for Paradise, He employs him to act as the inhabitants of Paradise, and he will enter Paradise. And when Allah creates a human being for the Fire, He will employ him to act as the inhabitants of the Fire, and will thus make him enter the Fire.'"

Tabari I:305 "Then Allah rubbed Adam's back and brought forth his progeny. And every living being to be created by Allah to the Day of Resurrection came forth. He scattered them in front of him like tiny ants. He took two handfuls and said to those on the right, 'Enter Paradise! And He said to the others, 'Enter the Fire! I do not care.'"

Qur'an 70:1 "A questioner questioned concerning the doom about to fall upon the infidels, which none can avert or repel."

Bukhari:V4B55N550 "The Prophet said, 'Allah has appointed an angel in the womb, and the angel says, "Lord, a drop of semen discharge. Lord, a clot, Lord, a piece of flesh." And then, if Allah wishes to complete the child's creation, the angel will say. Lord, male or a female? Lord, wretched or blessed in religion? What will his livelihood be? What will his age be?" The angel writes all this while the child is in the womb of its mother.'"

Bukhari:V4B54N430 "Allah's Apostle, the true and truly inspired said, 'Regarding the matter of the creation of a human being: humans are put together in the womb of the mother in forty days. Then he becomes a clot of thick blood for a similar period. He becomes a piece of flesh for forty days. Then Allah sends an angel who is ordered to write four things: the new creature's deeds, livelihood, date of death, and whether he will be blessed or wretched. He will do whatever is written for him.'"

Bukhari:V7B71N665 "The Prophet said, 'No contagious disease is conveyed without Allah's permission.'"

Qur'an 48:14 "To Allah belongs the sovereignty of the heavens and the earth: He forgives whom He wills, and He punishes whom He pleases."

Qur'an 52:7 "Verily the Doom and torment of your Lord will surely come to pass; there is none that can avert it or ward it off."

Qur'an 64:11 "No calamity occurs, no affliction comes, except by the decision and preordainment of Allah."

Qur'an 3:145 "No person can ever die except by the permission of Allah, the term being fixed as by writing."

Ishaq:395 "No soul can die but by Allah's permission in a term that is written."

MUHAMMAD'S MORALITY:

Qur'an 66:1 "O Prophet! Why forbid yourself that which Allah has made lawful to you? You seek to please your consorts. And Allah is Forgiving, Most Kind. Allah has already sanctioned for you the dissolution of your vows."

Bukhari:V4B52N143 "The Prophet told an Ansar, 'Choose one of your slave boys to serve me in my expedition to Khaybar.' So, he chose me, even though I was just nearing puberty. I served Muhammad when he stopped to rest. I heard him saying repeatedly, 'Allah! I seek refuge with you from distress and sorrow, from helplessness and laziness, from miserliness and cowardice, from being heavily in debt and from being overcome by men.'"

Qur'an 8:29 "O you who believe! If you obey and fear Allah, He will grant you a criterion to judge between right and wrong, or a way to overlook your evil thoughts and deeds."

Ishaq:288 "The Quraysh said, 'Muhammad and his Companions have violated the sacred month, shed blood, seized property, and taken men captive. Muhammad claims that he is following obedience to Allah, yet he is the first to violate the holy month and to kill.'"

Qur'an 8:68 "Had it not been for a previous agreement from Allah, a severe penalty would have reached you for the (ransom) that you took as booty." *Qur'an 8:69* "So enjoy what you took as booty; the spoils are lawful and good."

Ishaq:327 "Allah made booty lawful and good. He used it to incite the Muslims to unity of purpose. So enjoy what you have captured."

Qur'an 8:40 "If people are obstinate, and refuse to surrender, know that Allah is your Supporter. And know that one fifth of all the booty you take belongs to Allah, and to the Messenger, and for the near relatives (of the Messenger)."

Tabari VI:89 "Utaibah came before the Prophet and said: 'I repudiate Islam.' Then he spat at him, but his spital did not fall on him. The Prophet prayed: 'O Allah, subject him to the power of a dog from among Your dogs.'"

Ishaq:106 "I will go to the top of the mountain and throw myself down that I may kill myself and be at rest."

Qur'an 70:28 "Preserve their chastity except with their wives and the slave girls they possess—for which there is no blame."

Tabari VIII:116/Ishaq:511 "So Muhammad began seizing their herds and their property bit by bit. He conquered home by home. The Messenger took some of its people captive, including Safiyah, and her two cousins. The Prophet chose Safiyah for himself."

Tabari VIII:121/Ishaq:515 "Safiyah was brought to him, and another woman with her. Bilal led them past some of the Jews we had slain including the woman's dead husband. When she saw them, the woman with Safiyah cried out, slapped her face, and poured dust on her head. When Allah's Prophet saw her, he said, 'Take this she-devil away from me!'"

Tabari VIII:123/Ishaq:515 "Allah's Apostle besieged the final [Jewish] community until they could hold out no longer. Finally, when they were certain that they would perish, they asked Muhammad to banish them and spare their lives, which he did. The Prophet took possession of all their property."

Tabari VIII:124/Ishaq:516/Bukhari:V5B59N541 "Having finished with Khaybar, the Apostle went to Wadi Qura and besieged its people for a while. Then we headed back to Medina, halting at Qura toward sunset. With Muhammad was a slave lad of his whom Rifa'ah had given him. Suddenly, as we were setting down the saddle of the Prophet, a stray arrow came and hit the slave boy, killing him. We congratulated him, saying, 'May he enjoy Paradise!' But Allah's Apostle said, 'Certainly not! The sheet of cloth on his back is now being burnt on him in the Hell Fire!' He pilfered it from the booty of the Muslims following the Khaybar raid before it was duly distributed."

Tabari VIII:12 "'Rejoice, Allah has promised us victory after tribulation.' This increased the Muslims faith and submission. When cities were conquered Muslims used to say, 'Conquer for yourselves whatever seems good to you because all treasures were given to Muhammad."

Qur'an 24:58 "Believers, let your slave girls, and those who have not come to puberty, ask permission (before they come in your presence) on three occasions: before dawn, while you take off your clothes at midday, and after the night prayer. These are your times of undress—times of privacy for you. Outside those times it is not wrong for them to move about: Thus does Allah make clear the Signs."

Ishaq:535 "The women began to cry after learning about Ja'far's death. Disturbed, Muhammad told Abd-Rahman to silence them. When they wouldn't stop wailing, Allah's Apostle said, 'Go and tell them to be quiet, and if they refuse throw dust in their mouths.'"

Qur'an 64:14 "Believers, truly, among your wives and your children there are enemies for you: so beware of them! ... Your wealth and your children are only a trial."

Qur'an 8:28 "And know that your property and your children are just a temptation."

Qur'an 4:135 "Believers, stand out for justice as witnesses for Allah even against yourselves, your parents, your family, and relatives whether it be against rich or poor."

Qur'an 9:23 "Believers, take not for friends your fathers and your brothers if they love disbelief above belief. If you do, you do wrong. Say: If your fathers, your sons, your families, your wives, relatives and property which you have acquired, and the slackness of trade which you fear and dwellings which you like, are dearer to you than Allah and His Messenger and striving hard, fighting in His Cause, then wait till Allah brings about His torment."

Tabari VIII:183 "When the Messenger was finished with the men's swearing of allegiance, the women swore allegiance. You are swearing allegiance to me.... 'Do not kill your children.' A woman said, 'We raised them and you killed them. You know better about killing them than we do.' Umar laughed immoderately at her words."

Bukhari:V1B4N1229-33 "Aisha [who was 9] said, 'I used to wash semen off the Prophet's [who was 53] clothes. When he went for prayers I used to notice one or more spots on them.'"

Ishaq:572 "When the Apostle learned that one of the Meccans had died in the battle, he said, 'Allah curse him!' He used to hate the Quraysh."

Ishaq:594 "The Apostle gave gifts to those whose hearts were to be won over, notably the chiefs of the army, to win them and through them the people."

Ishaq:499 "The Apostle provided some compensation that included a castle, some property, a portion of the zakat tax, and a Copt slave girl."

Tabari IX:34 "Khuwaysirah came and stood by the Prophet as he was giving gifts to the people and said, 'Muhammad, I have seen what you have done today.' 'Well, what did you see?' He said, 'I don't think you have been fair.' Allah's Messenger became angry. 'Woe to you! If justice is not to be found with me, then with whom is it to be found?'" "Umar said, 'Muhammad, allow me to kill him.'" *Ishaq:595* "The Apostle said, 'Get him away from me and cut off his tongue.'"

Bukhari:V4B53N374 "The Prophet said, 'I give to the Quraysh so that they will desire Islam, for they are nearer to their life of Ignorance and it is not strong in their hearts.'"

Ishaq:596 "'Prophet, this group of Ansar have a grudge against you for what you did with the booty and how you divided it among you own people.' After due praise and exaltation of Allah, he addressed them. 'Ansar, what is this talk I hear from you? What is the grudge you harbor in your hearts against me? Do you think ill of me? Did I not come to you when you were erring and needy, and then made rich by Allah?' 'You came to us discredited, when your message was rejected by the Quraysh, and we believed you. You were forsaken and deserted and we assisted you. You were a fugitive and we took you in, sheltering you. You were poor and in need, and we comforted you."

Tabari IX:37/Ishaq:596 "Do you hold a grudge against me and are you mentally disturbed because of the worldly things by which I conciliate a people and win them over so that they will embrace Islam and become Muslims?"

Tabari IX:60 "On the way, Muhammad ordered that whoever got to the first well before him should not drink until he arrived. Some of the hypocrites arrived and drew water. The Prophet cursed them and invoked Allah's curse on them."

Tabari VIII:38 "The Prophet selected for himself from among the Jewish women of the Qurayza, Rayhanah. She became his concubine. When he predeceased her, she was still in his possession. When the Messenger of Allah took her as a captive, she showed herself averse to Islam and insisted on Judaism."

Ishaq:466 "The Apostle [taking first dibs] chose one of the Jewish women for himself. Her name was Rayhanah. She remained with him until she died, in his power."

Tabari VIII:56/Ishaq:493 "According to Aisha: 'A great number of Mustaliq were wounded. The Messenger took many captives, and they were divided among all the Muslims. Juwayriyah was one of the slaves. When the Prophet divided the captives by lot [a gambling game], Juwayriyah fell to the share of Thabit, Muhammad's cousin. Juwayriyah was the most beautiful woman and she captivated anyone who looked at her. She came to the Apostle seeking his help. As soon as I saw her at the door of my chamber, I took a dislike to her, and I knew that he would see in her what I saw.'"

Tabari VIII:97 "When I returned to Medina, the Prophet met me in the market and said, 'Give me the woman.' I said, 'Holy Prophet of Allah, I like her, and I have not uncovered her garment.' Muhammad said nothing to me until the next day. He again met me in the market and said, 'Salamah, give me the woman.' I said, 'Prophet, I have not uncovered her garment but she is yours.'"

Ishaq:467 "Allah addressed the believers and said, 'In Allah's Apostle you have a fine example for anyone who hopes to be in the place where Allah is.'"

LOVE OF MONEY:

Qur'an 64:16 "Fear Allah as much as you can; listen and obey. Pay the zakat. Those saved from covetousness prosper. If you loan to Allah a beautiful loan, He will double it. He will grant Forgiveness: for Allah is most ready to appreciate."

Tabari VI:82 "I asked Abbas, 'What is this religion?' He answered, 'This is Muhammad bin Abdallah, who claims that Allah has sent him as His Messenger with this religion and that the treasures of Chusroes and Caesar will be given to him by conquest.'"

Ishaq:113 "When I was a merchant I came to Mecca during the hajj pilgrimage. While I was there a man came out to pray and stood facing the Ka'aba. I asked, 'What is their religion? It is something new to me.' Abbas said, 'This is Muhammad who alleges that Allah has sent him with it so that the treasures of Chusroes and Caesar will be open to him."

Bukhari:V4B52N267 "The Prophet said, 'Khosrau will be ruined, and there will be no Khosrau after him, and Caesar will surely be ruined and there will be no Caesar after him, and you will spend their treasures in Allah's Cause.'"

Bukhari:V4B56N793 "The Prophet said, 'If you live long enough the treasures of Khosrau will be opened and taken as spoils. You will carry out handfuls of gold and silver.'"

Bukhari:V4B56N795 "I have been given the keys of the treasures of the world by Allah."

Tabari VIII:16/Ishaq:454 "Soon the trial became great for the Muslims and fear intensified. One said, 'Muhammad was promising us that we should eat up the treasures of Chosroes and Caesar, and now none of us even can go out to relieve himself!'"

Qur'an 93:4 "Soon will your Lord give you so much you shall be well pleased.... Did He not find you poor and made you rich?"

Qur'an 108:1 "To you have We granted Kausar, the fountain of abundance."

Tabari VI:95 "Abu Talib said to Muhammad, 'Nephew, how is it that your tribe is complaining about you and claiming that you are reviling their gods and saying this, that, and the other?' The Allah's Apostle said, 'Uncle, I want them to utter one saying. If they say it, the Arabs will submit to them and the non-Arabs will pay the jizyah tax.'"

Qur'an 9:29 "Fight against those People of the Book [Christians and Jews] who do not follow what Allah and His Messenge acknowledge as the true religion (Islam), nor accept Our law, until they pay the Jizyah tribute tax in submission."

Qur'an 68:3 "Nay, truly for you is a never-ending reward."

Bukhari:V5B59N512 "The Prophet had their men killed, their children and woman taken as captives. The captives were divided among the Muslims. Then the Messenger began taking the homes and property that were closest to him."

Tabari VIII:122/Ishaq:515 "Abi Huqayq held the treasure of the Nadir. He was brought to Allah's Messenger, and he questioned him. But Huqayq denied knowing where it was. So the Prophet questioned other Jews. One said, 'I have seen Kinanah walk around a ruin.' Muhammad had Kinanah brought to him and said, 'Do you know that if we find it, I shall kill you.' 'Yes,' Kinanah answered. The Prophet commanded that the ruin should be dug up. Some treasure was extracted. Then Muhammad asked Kinanah for the rest. He refused to surrender it; so Allah's Messenger gave orders concerning him to Zubayr, saying, 'Torture him until you root out and extract what he has. So Zubayr kindled a fire on Kinanah's chest, twirling it with his firestick until Kinanah was near death. Then the Messenger gave him to Maslamah, who beheaded him."

Ishaq:515 "When the people of Fadak heard of what had happened, they sent word to the Messenger, asking him to banish them and spare their lives, saying they too would leave him their property. So Khaybar became the prey of the Muslims, while Fadak belonged exclusively to the Messenger of Allah, becoming his personal property."

Qur'an 8:1 "They ask you about the benefits of capturing the spoils of war. Tell them: 'The benefits belong to Allah and to His Messenger.' So fulfill your duty to Allah and the Prophet."

Tabari VIII:142 "Whoever prays our prayer and turns to our Qiblah is a Muslim. Incumbent on whoever refuses is the payment of the jizyah tax."

Qur'an 9:42 "(Prophet) had there been immediate gain (in sight with booty in front of them), and the journey easy—a near adventure—they would (all) have followed you."

Qur'an 9:55 "Let not their wealth nor their sons dazzle you or excite your admiration (Muhammad)." *Qur'an 9:57* "Some slander you, blaming you (of partiality) in the matter of (the distribution of) the offerings [stolen spoils]. If they are given part of these, they are pleased, but if not they are indignant and enraged!"

Qur'an 9:59 "(How much more seemly) if only they had been content with what Allah and His Messenger gave them, and said, 'Sufficient is Allah! His Messenger will soon give us His bounty. We implore Allah to enrich us.'"

Qur'an 9:75 "Amongst them are men who made a deal with Allah, that if He bestowed on them of His bounty [booty], they would pay (largely) in zakat tax (for Allah's Cause [Jihad]). But when He did bestow of His bounty, they became niggardly, and turned back (from their bargain), averse (refusing to pay)."

Qur'an 5:13 "Loan Allah a beautiful loan, verily I will wipe out from your evils, and admit you to Gardens."

Qur'an 5:119 "Allah will say: This is the day on which the Muslims will profit from Islam...''

Bukhari:V4B53N376 "While Allah's Apostle was accompanied by the people on their way back from Hunayn, the Bedouins started begging for things so aggressively that they forced him to go under a Samura tree where his outer garment was snatched away. On that, Allah's Apostle stood up and said, 'Return my clothes. If I had as many camels as these trees, I would have distributed them amongst you; and you will not find me a miser.'"

Bukhari:V4B53N377 "While I was walking with the Prophet he was wearing a Najrani outer garment with a thick hem. A Bedouin came upon him and pulled his garment so violently that I could see the imprint of the hem on his shoulder caused by the violence of his pull. The Bedouin said, 'Give me something from Allah's Fortune which you have.' The Prophet turned, smiled, and ordered that a gift should be given."

Tabari IX:34/Ishaq:595 "Khuwaysirah came and stood by the Prophet as he was giving gifts to the people and said, 'Muhammad, I have seen what you have done today.' 'Well, what did you see?' He said, 'I don't think you have been fair.' Allah's Messenger became angry."

Bukhari:V4B53N374 "The Prophet said, 'I give to the Quraysh so that they will desire Islam, for they are nearer to their life of Ignorance and it is not strong in their hearts.'"

Bukhari:V4B53N375 "When Allah favored His Apostle with the properties of the Hawazin tribe as Fai booty, he started giving to some of the Meccan men up to one-hundred camels each. Whereupon some Ansari said, 'May Allah forgive His Apostle! He is giving to the Quraysh and leaving us out, in spite of the fact that our swords are still dripping with the blood of the infidels.' When Muhammad was informed of what they had said, he called for the Ansar and gathered them in a leather tent. 'What is the statement which I have been informed?' The smart ones replied, 'O Allah's Apostle! The wise ones did not say anything, but the youngsters said, "May Allah forgive His Apostle; he enriches the Quraysh and leaves the Ansar poor, in spite of the fact that Ansar swords are still dribbling with the blood of the infidels."' The Prophet replied, 'I give them more because they are still close to the period of Infidelity and have just recently embraced Islam. You should be pleased to see them becoming rich.'"

Tabari IX:36/Ishaq:596 "'Prophet, this group of Ansar have a grudge against you for what you did with the booty and how you divided it among your own people.' 'Ansar, what is this talk

I hear from you? What is the grudge you harbor? Do you think ill of me? Did I not come to you when you were erring and needy, and then made rich by Allah? Do you hold a grudge against me and are you mentally disturbed because of the worldly things by which I conciliate a people and win them over so that they will embrace Islam and become Muslims?"

Tabari IX:79 "In this year the zakat was made obligatory, and the Messenger dispatched his agents to collect it. The verse was revealed: 'Take the zakat from their wealth to purify them.'"

Tabari IX:86 "He orders you to give one fifth of Allah's booty and pay the zakat tax. It is enjoined on the faithful from their land and property.... And don't seduce the Jews or Christians for incumbent on them is to pay the jizyah protection tax. Allah's Apostle dispersed his representatives to every land where Islam had entered to collect the zakat."

Tabari IX:196 "Fatimah [Muhammad's daughter] and Ali [Muhammad's adopted son and Fatimah's husband] came to Bakr demanding their share of inheritance of the Messenger. They demanded Muhammad's land in Fadak and his share of Khaybar's tribute."

Bukhari:V5B59N546 "Fatimah, the daughter of the Prophet, sent someone to Bakr, asking for her inheritance of what Allah's Apostle had left of the property taken from the Fai booty gained without fighting in Medina and Fadak, and what remained of the Khumus [Muhammad's fifth of the booty gained through fighting] of the Khaybar booty."

Bukhari:V9B84N59 "When the Prophet died, Arabs reverted to disbelief. Umar said, 'Should we fight these people?'" Bakr said, 'By Allah! I will fight whoever differentiates between prayers and Zakat, as Zakat is the right to be taken from property according to Allah's Orders. If they refuse to pay me even so little as a kid they used to pay, I will fight with them for withholding it.'"

Qur'an 20:131 "Do not covet what we have granted other people. Nor strain your eyes in longing for the things We have given for their enjoyment, the splendor of the life, through which We tempt them."

Bukhari:V5B57N119 "The people used to send presents to the Prophet on the day of Aisha's turn [to have sex with him]. Aisha said, 'His other wives gathered in the apartment of Um Salama and said, "Um, the people send presents on the day of Aisha's turn and we too, love the good presents just as much as she does. You should tell Allah's Apostle to order the people to send their presents to him regardless of whose turn it may be." Um repeated that to the Prophet and he turned away from her. When the Prophet returned to Um, she repeated the request again. The Prophet again turned away. After the third time, the Prophet said, "Um, don't trouble me by harming Aisha, for by Allah, the Divine Inspiration [Qur'an surahs] never came to me while I was under the blanket of any woman among you except her."'"

Qur'an 2:195 "Spend your wealth in Allah's Cause [fighting infidels]...send such gifts as you can afford." *Qur'an 2:215* "They ask you what they should spend. Say: Whatever they spend is good.... Allah is aware of it."

Qur'an 2:245 "Who is he that will loan Allah a beautiful loan, which Allah will double to his credit and multiply many times?"

Bukhari: V9B87N127 "The Prophet said, 'I have been awarded victory by terror so the treasures of the earth are mine.'"

Qur'an 59:8 "The spoils are for the Emigrants who were expelled from their homes and from their belongings while seeking the bounty of Allah, and aiding His Messenger: such are the sincere ones. They are loyal."

Qur'an 63:10 "Spend out of the substance [booty] which We gave you before death comes and you say, 'My Lord, why didn't You give me respite for a little while? I wish I had given (more).'" [The Noble Qur'an footnotes a Bukhari Hadith to explain this verse.] "The Prophet said, 'Everyday two angels come down from heaven. One says, "O Allah, reward every person who spends in Your Cause." The other says, "O Allah, destroy every miser."'"

Tabari VII:106 "Abu Azzah, you are a poet, so aid us with your tongue. Join our expedition and I swear before Allah I will make you a rich man.'"

Qur'an 3:14 "Beautified for men is the love of the things they covet, desiring women, hoards of gold and silver, attractive horses, cattle and well-tilled land. These are the pleasures of this world's life."

Qur'an 3:181 "Verily Allah heard the taunt of those who said, (when asked for contributions for the war): 'Allah is poor, and we are rich!' We shall record their saying and We shall say: Taste you the penalty of the Scorching Fire!"

Qur'an 8:69 "So enjoy what you took as booty; the spoils are lawful and good."

Ishaq:327 "Allah made booty lawful and good. He used it to incite the Muslims to unity of purpose. So enjoy what you have captured."

Ishaq:324 "Allah taught them how to divide the spoil. He made it lawful and said, 'A fifth of the booty belongs to the Apostle.'

LUST:

Qur'an 33:51 "You may have whomever you desire; there is no blame."

Tabari VIII:187 "The [sixty-two-year old] Messenger of Allah married Mulaykah. She was young and beautiful. One of the Prophet's wives came to her and said, 'Are you not ashamed to marry a man who killed your father during the day he conquered Mecca?" She therefore took refuge from him."

Qur'an 66:1 "O Prophet! Why forbid yourself that which Allah has made lawful to you? You seek to please your consorts."

Qur'an 66:4 "If you (women) turn in repentance to him, it would be better. Your hearts have been impaired, for you desired (the ban) [on how many girls Muhammad could play with at a time]. But if you back each other up against (Muhammad), truly Allah is his protector, and Gabriel, and everyone who believes—and furthermore, the angels will back (him) up."

Qur'an 66:5 "Maybe, if he divorces you (all), Allah will give him in exchange consorts better than you—submissive, faithful, obedient, adorers who worship, who travel, and are inclined to fasting—previously married or virgins."

Tabari VIII:117 "Dihyah had asked the Messenger for Safiyah when the Prophet chose her for himself. Muhammad gave Dihyah her two cousins instead." *Ishaq:511* "When he protested, wanting to keep Safiyah for himself, the Apostle traded for Safiyah by giving Dihyah her two cousins. The women of Khaybar were distributed among the Muslims."

Bukhari:V5B59N524 "The Muslims said among themselves, 'Will Safiyah be one of the Prophet's wives or just a lady captive and one of his possessions?'"

Tabari VIII:110 "When Abu Sufyan learned that the Prophet had taken her, he said, 'That stallion's nose is not to be restrained!'"

Bukhari:V4B52N143/V5B59N523 "When we reached Khaybar, Muhammad said that Allah had enabled him to conquer them. It was then that the beauty of Safiyah was described to him. Her husband had been killed [by Muhammad], so Allah's Apostle selected her for himself. He took her along with him till we reached a place where her menses were over and he took her for his wife, consummating his marriage to her, and forcing her to wear the veil.'"

Tabari VIII:122/Ishaq:515 "Muhammad commanded that Safiyah should be kept behind him and he threw his cloak over her. Thus the Muslims knew that he had chosen her for himself."

Ishaq:517 "When the Apostle took Safiyah on his way out of town, she was beautified and combed, putting her in a fitting state for the Messenger. The Apostle passed the night with her in his tent. Abu Ayyub, girt with his sword, guarded the Apostle, going round the tent until he saw him emerge in the morning. Abu said, 'I was afraid for you with this woman for you have killed her father, her husband, and her people.'"

Qur'an 33:30 "O Consorts of the Prophet! If...any of you are devout, obedient, and submissive in the service to Allah and His Messenger, and does good, to her shall We grant her reward twice. We have prepared for her a generously rich provision."

Tabari IX:126 "The Messenger of Allah married fifteen women. He combined eleven at a time and left behind nine."

Ishaq:311 "The Apostle saw Ummu'l when she was a baby crawling before his feet and said, 'If she grows up, I will marry her.' But he died before he was able to do so."

Tabari VII:7 "The Prophet married Aisha in Mecca three years before the Hijrah, after the death of Khadija. At the time she was six." *Ishaq:281* "When the Apostle came to Medina he was fifty-three." *Tabari IX:128* "When the Prophet married Aisha she very young and not yet ready for consummation."

Bukhari:V9B87N139-40 "Allah's Apostle told Aisha, 'You were shown to me twice in my dreams [a.k.a. sexual fantasies]. I beheld a man or angel carrying you in a silken cloth. He said to me, "She is yours, so uncover her." And behold, it was you. I would then say to myself, "If this is from Allah, then it must happen."'"

Tabari IX:131 "My mother came to me while I was being swung on a swing between two branches and got me down. My nurse wiped my face with some water and started leading me. When I was at the door she stopped so I could catch my breath. I was then brought in while the Messenger was sitting on a bed in our house. My mother made me sit on his lap. Then the men and women got up and left. The Prophet consummated his marriage with me in my house when I was nine years old."

Tabari IX:133 "Juwayriyyah was chosen by the Messenger for himself on the day of the Muraysi raid from the captives." "Muhammad married Umm, who had embraced Christianity."

Tabari IX:134 "Muhammad took Zaynab [his daughter-in-law] but Allah did not find any fault in the [incestuous] relationship and ordered the marriage."

Tabari IX:135 "When the Prophet scrutinized the captives on the day of Khaybar, he threw his cloak over Safayah. Thus she was his chosen one." *Tabari IX:139* "The Messenger married Ghaziyyah after the news of her beauty and skill had reached him."

Tabari IX:137 "Allah granted Rayhanah of the [Jewish] Qurayza to His Messenger as booty [but only after she had been forced to watch him decapitate her father and brother, seen her mother hauled off to be raped, and her sisters sold into slavery]."

Tabari IX:137 "Mariyah, a Copt slave, was presented to the Prophet. She was given to him by Muqawqis, the ruler of Alexandria."

Tabari IX:138 "The Prophet married Aliyyah, a Bakr woman. He gave her gifts for divorce and left her. He also married Qutaylah, but he died before he could consummate the marriage."

Tabari IX:139 "Layla approached the Prophet while his back was to the sun and clapped him on his shoulder. He asked her who it was and she replied, 'I am the daughter of one who competes with the wind. I am Layla. I have come to offer myself to you.' He replied, 'I accept.'" [Layla shared her story with her parents.] "They said, 'What a bad thing you have done! You are a self-respecting girl, but the Prophet is a womanizer.'"

Tabari IX:147 "A eunuch named Mubur was presented to Muhammad along with two slave girls. One he took as a concubine, the other he gave to Haasn."

Ishaq:186 "He took me into Paradise and there I saw a damsel with dark red lips. I asked her to whom she belonged, for she pleased me much when I saw her."

Bukhari:V4B52N211 "I participated in a Ghazwa [raid] with the Prophet. I said, 'Apostle, I am a bridegroom.' He asked me whether I had married a virgin or matron. I answered, 'A matron.' He said, 'Why not a virgin who would have played with you? Then you could have played with her.' 'Apostle! My father was martyred and I have some young sisters, so I felt it not proper that I should marry a young girl as young as them.'"

Tabari VIII:100 "The Messenger sent Hatib to Muqawqis, the ruler of Alexandria. Hatib delivered the letter of the Prophet, and Muqawqis gave Allah's Apostle four slave girls."

Bukhari:V9B86N98 "The Prophet said, 'A virgin should not be married till she is asked for her consent.' 'O Apostle! How will the virgin express her consent?' He said, 'By remaining silent.'"

Bukhari:V5B59N342 "Umar said, 'When my daughter Hafsa lost her husband in the battle of Badr, Allah's Apostle demanded her hand in marriage and I married her to him.'"

Tabari VIII:1 "In this year the Messenger married Zaynab bt. Jahsh [a first cousin: Allah's Messenger came to the house of Zayd bin [son of] Muhammad. Perhaps the Messenger missed him at that moment. Zaynab, Zayd's wife, rose to meet him. She was dressed only in a shift.... She jumped up eagerly and excited the admiration of Allah's Messenger, so that he turned away murmuring something that could scarcely be understood. However, he did say overtly, 'Glory be to Allah Almighty, who causes hearts to turn!' So Zayd went to Muhammad. 'Prophet, I have heard that you came to my house. Why didn't you go in? [Dad,] Perhaps Zaynab has excited your admiration, so I will leave her.'"

Tabari VIII:4 "One day Muhammad went out looking for Zayd. Now there was a covering of haircloth over the doorway, but the wind had lifted the covering so that the doorway was uncovered. Zaynab was in her chamber, undressed, and admiration for her entered the heart of the Prophet. After that Allah made her unattractive to Zayd.'"

Tabari VIII:3 "Zayd left her, and she became free. While the Messenger of Allah was talking with Aisha, a fainting overcame him. When he was released from it, he smiled and said, 'Who will go to Zaynab to tell her the good news? Allah has married her to me.' Then the Prophet recited [Qur'an 33] to the end of the passage. Aisha said, 'I became very uneasy because of what we heard about her beauty and another thing, the loftiest of matters, what Allah had done for her by personally giving her to him in marriage. I said that she would boast of it over us.'"

Qur'an 33:4 "Allah has not made your wives whom you divorce your mothers: nor has He made your adopted sons your sons. Such is (only) your (manner of) speech by your mouths."

Qur'an 33:6 "The Prophet has a greater claim on the faithful than they have on themselves, and his wives are their mothers.... This is written in the Book."

Qur'an 33:37 "You hid in your mind and your heart that which Allah was about to manifest: you feared the people, but it is more fitting that thou shouldst fear Allah. Then when Zayd had dissolved (his marriage) with her, with the necessary (formality), We gave her to you, joining her in marriage to you: in order that there may be no difficulty or sin for the Believers in the wives of their adopted sons, when the latter have dissolved with the necessary (formality) (their marriage) with them. And Allah's command must be fulfilled."

Qur'an 33:38 "There can be no difficulty, harm, or reproach to the Prophet in doing what Allah has ordained to him as a duty. It was the practice (approved) of Allah amongst those of old that have passed away. And the commandment of Allah is a decree determined. (It is the practice of those) who deliver the Messages of Allah, and fear Him. Allah keeps good account. Muhammad is not the father of any of your men, but (he is) the Messenger of Allah, and the Last of the Prophets with the Seal: and Allah has full knowledge of all things."

Qur'an 33:48 "And obey not (the behests) of the Unbelievers and the Hypocrites. Disregard their noxious talk and heed not their annoyances, but put thy trust in Allah. For enough is Allah as a Disposer of affairs."

Qur'an 33:50 "O Prophet! We have made lawful to you all the wives to whom you have paid dowers; and those whom your hands possess out of the prisoners of war spoils whom Allah has assigned to you; and daughters of your paternal uncles and aunts, and daughters of your uncles and aunts, who migrated with you; and any believing woman if the Prophet wishes her; this is a privilege for you only, and not for the rest of the Believers; We know what We have appointed for them as to their wives and the captives whom they possess; in order that there should be no difficulty for you and that you should be free from blame."

Qur'an 33:51 "You may put off whom you please, and you may take to you whomever you desire. You may defer any of them you please, and you may have whomever you desire; there is no blame on you if you invite one who you had set aside. It is no sin."

Qur'an 33:28 "O Prophet, say to your wives and consorts: 'If you desire this world's life and its glittering adornment, then come! I will provide them for your enjoyment and set you free in a handsome manner. And if you desire Allah and His Messenger and the latter abode, then lo! Allah hath prepared for the good-doers an immense reward."

Qur'an 33:30 "O Consorts of the Prophet! If any of you are guilty of unseemly conduct, shamelessness, or lewdness, the punishment will be doubled, and that is easy for Allah. But any of you that is devout, obedient, and submissive in the service to Allah and His Messenger, and does good, to her shall We grant her reward twice. We have prepared for her a generously rich provision."

Qur'an 33:32 "Consorts of the Prophet! You are not like any of the (other) women. Fear and keep your duty, lest one in whose heart is a disease should be moved with desire. Stay quietly in your apartment. Make not a dazzling display like that of the former times of Ignorance. Perform the devotion, pay the zakat; and obey Allah and His Messenger. And Allah wishes to cleanse you with a thorough cleansing. And bear in mind that which is recited in your houses of the revelations of Allah and the wisdom."

Qur'an 33:36 "It is not fitting for a Muslim man or woman to have any choice in their affairs when a matter has been decided for them by Allah and His Messenger. They have no option. If any one disobeys Allah and His Messenger, he is indeed on a wrong Path."

Qur'an 4:23 "Prohibited to you are: your mothers, daughters, sisters.... Also (prohibited are) women already married, except slaves who are captives." [Rape is okay with Team Islam.]

Bukhari:V5B59N459 "I entered the Mosque, saw Abu, sat beside him and asked about sex. Abu Said said, 'We went out with Allah's Apostle and we received female slaves from among the captives. We desired women and we loved to do coitus interruptus.'"

MUHAMMAD'S PARADISE:

Qur'an 56:8 "Those of the right hand-how happy will be those of the right hand! ...Who will be honored in the Garden of Bliss; *Qur'an 56:13* "A multitude of those from among the first, and a few from the latter, (will be) on couch-like thrones woven with gold and precious stones. Reclining, facing each other. Round about them will (serve) boys of perpetual (freshness), of never ending bloom, with goblets, jugs, and cups (filled) with sparkling wine. No aching of the head will they receive, nor suffer any madness, nor exhaustion. And with fruits, any that they may select: and the flesh of fowls, any they may desire. And (there will be) Hur (fair females) with big eyes, lovely and pure, beautiful ones, like unto hidden pearls, well-guarded in their shells. A reward for the deeds."

Qur'an 56:33 "Unending, and unforbidden, exalted beds, and maidens incomparable. We have formed them in a distinctive fashion and made them virgins, loving companions matched in age, for the sake of those of the right hand." [Another translation reads:] "On couches or thrones raised high. Verily, We have created them (maidens) incomparable: We have formed their maidens as a special creation, and made them to grow a new growth. We made them virgins—pure and undefiled, lovers, matched in age."

Bukhari:V8B76N550 "I heard Allah's Apostle saying, 'From my followers there will be a crowd of 70,000 in number who will enter Paradise whose faces will glitter as the moon.'"

Qur'an 37:40 "Fruits, Delights; they will be honored in the Gardens of Pleasure, on thrones facing one another. Round them will be passed a cup of pure white wine, delicious to the drinkers, free from ghoul (hurt), nor shall you be made mad or exhausted thereby. And with them will be Qasirat-at-Tarf (virgin females), restraining their glances (desiring none but you), with big, beautiful eyes. As if they were (sheltered) eggs, preserved."

Qur'an 88:8 "Faces will be joyful, glad with their endeavour. In a lofty Garden they hear no harmful speech." *Qur'an 88:12* "Therein will be a bubbling spring, raised throne-like couches, drinking cups ready placed, cushions set in rows, and rich silken carpets all spread out."

Bukhari:V4B55N544 "Allah's Apostle said, 'The first group who will enter Paradise will be glittering like the moon and those who will follow will glitter like the most brilliant star. They will not urinate, relieve nature, spit, or have any nasal secretions. Their combs will be gold and their sweat will smell like musk. Their companions will be houris [virgins]. All of them will look alike and will be sixty cubits (180 feet) tall.'"

Bukhari:V8B76N542 "Allah's Apostle said, 'The believers, after being saved from the Fire, will be stopped at a bridge between Paradise and Hell and mutual retaliation will be established among them regarding wrongs they have committed against one another. After they are cleansed and purified through the retaliation, they will be admitted into Paradise.'"

Qur'an 47:15 "(Here is) a Parable of the Garden which those who fear and keep their duty are promised: in it are rivers of unpolluted water; rivers of milk which the taste never changes; rivers of wine, a delicious joy to the drinkers; and rivers of running honey pure and clear. In it there are all kinds of fruits with pardon from their Lord."

Qur'an 76:5 "As for the righteous, they will drink a cup of wine from a spring, making it gush forth abundantly." *Qur'an 76:19* "And round them shall serve immortal boys of perpetual freshness, never altering in age. If you saw them, you would think they were scattered pearls."

Qur'an 76:21 "Upon them will be green garments of fine green silk and heavy gold brocade. They will be adorned with bracelets of silver; their Lord will slack their thirst with wine."

Qur'an 77:41 "The righteous shall be amidst cool shades, springs, and fruits—all they desire. Eat and drink to your heart's content."

Qur'an 78:31 "Verily for those who follow Us, there will be a fulfillment of your desires: enclosed Gardens, grapevines, voluptuous full-breasted maidens of equal age, and a cup full to the brim of wine. There they never hear vain discourse nor lying—a gift in payment—a reward from your Lord."

Qur'an 83:22 "The believers will be in Delightful Bliss: On couch-like thrones, gazing, their thirst will be slaked with pure wine." *Qur'an 85:11* "For those who believe and do good deeds will be Gardens; the fulfillment of all desires."

Bukhari:V7B69N494 "I heard the Prophet saying, 'From among my followers there will be some who will consider illegal sexual intercourse, the wearing of silk, the drinking of alcoholic drinks and the use of musical instruments, to be lawful. Allah will destroy them during the night and will let mountains fall on them. He will transform the rest into monkeys and pigs and they will remain so till the Day of Doom.'"

Bukhari:V4B54N476-544 "The Prophet said, 'In Paradise they will not urinate, relieve nature, spit, or have any nasal secretions. Everyone will have two virgins who will be so beautiful and transparent the bones of their legs will be seen through their flesh.'"

Qur'an 52:17 "Verily, the Muttaqun (those who fear) will be in Gardens and Delight. Enjoying the (bliss) which their Lord has provided, and their Lord saved them from the torment of the blazing Fire. 'Eat and drink with glee, because of what you used to do.' They will recline (with ease) on Throne Couches (of dignity) arranged in ranks; and We shall join them to beautiful Hur (female maidens) with big, lustrous eyes."

Qur'an 52:21 "Those who believe and whose families follow them in Faith, to them shall We join their offspring: Nor shall We deprive them of their works: (Yet) each individual is in pledge for his deeds. [Imagine that. Wives and children will be joined with husbands and fathers who are cavorting with virgins. That ought to be entertaining.] And We shall provide fruit and meat, anything they desire. There they shall pass from hand to hand a (wine) cup free of frivolity, free of all taint of vanity or cause of sin. Round about them will serve, (devoted) to them, young boy servants of their own (handsome) as well-guarded pearls. They will advance to each other, drawing near, engaging in mutual enquiry. They will say: 'We used to be afraid (of the punishment) in the midst of our families, but Allah has been good to us, and has delivered us from the torment of the Scorching Wind and Breath of Fire."

Qur'an 55:46 "For him who lives in terror of his Lord are two Gardens containing delights: shade, two fountains flowing, fruits in pairs. Reclining on carpets lined with silk brocade, fruits hanging low. In them virginal females with averted glances (desiring none but you), undeflowered by men or jinn. Is the reward of goodness aught but goodness?"

Qur'an 55:62 "And beside this, there are two other Gardens, rich green in color from plentiful watering. In them will be two springs, gushing forth, and fruits. And beautiful companions, virgins cloistered in pavilions, undefiled by men and jinn, reclining on green cushions and rich mattresses. Which of the favors of you Lord will you both deny?"

ALLAH'S HELL:

Qur'an 56:41 "But those of the left hand-how unhappy those of the left hand. They will be in the scorching hot wind and boiling water, under the shadow of thick black smoke, neither cool nor agreeable. ...They will be gathered together on a certain day which is predetermined. Then you, the erring and the deniers will eat Zaqqoom [a thorn tree]. Fill your bellies with it, and drink scalding water, lapping it up like female camels raging of thirst and diseased. Such will be their entertainment, their welcome on the Day of Doom...the welcome of boiling water and the entertainment of roasting in Hell. This is the ultimate truth."

Bukhari:V8B76N537 "The Prophet said, 'Allah will say, "Adam!" "I am obedient to Your orders." Allah will say, "Bring out the people of the Fire." "How many are the people of the Fire?" Allah will say, "Out of every thousand take out nine-hundred and ninety-nine persons." At that time children will become hoary-headed and every pregnant female will drop her load. You will see the people as if they were drunk. Allah's punishment will be very severe.'"

Qur'an 37:19 "They will say, 'Woe to us! This is the Day of Doom.' Assemble the wrong-doers and their wives and the things they worshipped besides Allah, then lead them to the fierce flaming fires of Hell."

Qur'an 37:63 "For We have truly made it as a trial to torment the disbelievers. Zaqqum is a horrible thorn tree that grows in Hell. The shoots of its fruit-stalks are like the heads of devils. Truly they [non-Muslims] will eat it and fill their bellies with it. On top of that they will be given a mixture made of boiling water to drink especially prepared. Then they shall be returned to the Blazing Fire."

Qur'an 74:8 "The trumpet shall sound a day of anguish for disbelievers. Leave Me alone to deal with the creature whom I created bare and alone! Leave Me to deal with those I granted wealth and sons."

Qur'an 96:15 "Let him beware! If he does not desist, We will seize him, smite his forehead, and drag him by the forelock, a lying, sinful forelock! Then, let him call upon his henchmen for help and summon his council of comrades. We will call on the angels of punishment to deal with him!"

Qur'an 74:15 "They have offered stubborn opposition to Our Signs. Soon I will visit them with a mountain of calamities, imposing a fearful doom and a distressing punishment. For these men thought and plotted; so woe to them! They shall be cursed for their plots."

Qur'an 74:26 "Soon will I fling them into the burning Hell Fire! And what will explain what Hell Fire is? It permits nothing to endure, and nothing does it spare! It darkens and changes the color of man, burning the skin! It shrivels and scorches men."

Qur'an 74:31 "We have appointed nineteen angels to be the wardens of the Hell Fire. We made a stumbling-block for those who disbelieve and We have fixed their number as a trial for unbelievers in order that the People of the Book [Christians and Jews] may arrive with certainty, and that no doubts may be left for the people of the Book, those in whose hearts is a disease."

Qur'an 75:20 "Some faces will be gloomy knowing that some great back-breaking calamity is about to be inflicted on them. Yes, when their soul comes up their throat and reaches their collarbone they will cry, 'Is there a magician or wizard who can save us?' But they will know that it is the hour of parting and one leg will be joined with another, agony heaped on agony, affliction combined with affliction."

Qur'an 67:7 "We have prepared the doom of Hell and the penalty of torment in the most intense Blazing Fire. For those who reject their Lord is the punishment of Hell: Evil, it is such a wretched destination. When they are flung therein, they will hear the terrible drawing in of their breath and loud moaning even as the flame blazes forth, roaring with rage as it boils up, bursting with fury. Every time a fresh crowd is cast in, Hell's wardens will ask, 'Did no Warner come to you?'"

Qur'an 69:27 "'I wish death had put an end to me. The stern command will say: 'Seize him, manacle him, chain him and cast him into the Blazing Fire of Hell. String him to a chain the length of which is seventy cubits. This is the fate of those who do not believe in the Lord Most Supreme or feed the poor. They have no friend today. They will have no food save filthy refuse which the hellish eat."

Qur'an 70:10 "The Mujrim (disbeliever) desire will be to free himself from the Punishment by sacrificing his children as a ransom to save himself from the torment."

Qur'an 70:12 "He would sacrifice his wife and his brother, and his kin who sheltered him, and all that is on earth to deliver himself from the Doom. By no means! For them it is the Fire of Hell! Plucking apart his body right to the skull! Taking away the head skin. Eager to roast; dragged by the head, hell shall claim all who flee."

Qur'an 70:42 "So let them chat vainly and play about, with their idle disputes until they encounter that Day of Doom which they have been threatened! They will rise from their sepulchers in sudden haste as if they were rushing to a goal, their eyes lowered in dejection and disgrace, aghast, abasement stupefying them—ignominy shall overtake them! Such is the Day that they are threatened with!"

Qur'an 80:33 "At length, when the deafening cry comes, that Day shall a man flee from his own brother, and from his mother and father, and he will abandon his wife and children. Each one of them will have enough concern to make him indifferent to others."

Qur'an 68:42 "On the day when the great calamity of doom befalls them in earnest, and they are ordered to prostrate themselves, they will not. There shall be a severe affliction. Their eyes will be downcast, abasement stupefying them; ignominy will cover them. Seeing that they had been summoned beforehand to bow in adoration, while they were still whole and unhurt, they refused."

Qur'an 68:44 "Then leave Me alone with such as reject this Message and call Our pronouncements a lie. Systematically by degrees, step by step, We shall punish them in ways they can not even imagine. [Hell is where Allah resides.]"

Qur'an 73:11 "Leave Me alone to deal with the beliers (those who deny My Qur'an). Respite those who possess good things for a little while. Verily, with Us are heavy shackles (to bind), a raging fire (to burn them), food that chokes, and a torturous penalty of painful doom."

Bukhari:V4B54N487 "The Prophet said, 'The Hell Fire is 69 times hotter than ordinary worldly fires.' So someone said, 'Allah's Apostle, wouldn't this ordinary fire have been sufficient to torture the unbelievers?'"

Qur'an 72:15 "But the Qasitun (disbelievers) are the firewood of hell."

Qur'an 7:41 "They shall have a bed on the floor of Hell and coverings of fire; this is how We reward them."

Qur'an 104:4 "He will be sure to be thrown into that which breaks him into pieces, flung to the Consuming One. And what will explain to you that which Breaks him into Pieces, Consuming and Crushing? It is the fire kindled by Allah which leaps up over them penetrating the hearts of men." [Allah is in hell, kindling the fire.]

Qur'an 79:1 "I swear by those who violently tear out (the souls), and drag them to destruction."

Qur'an 87:12 "They will be flung in to burn in the great Fire (and be made to taste its burning, in which they will then neither die nor live?"

Qur'an 88:1 "Has the narration reached you of the overwhelming (calamity)? Some faces (all disbelievers, Jews and Christians) that Day, will be humiliated, downcast, scorched by the burning fire, while they are made to drink from a boiling hot spring."

Qur'an 88:6 "They shall have no food but a poisonous plant with bitter thorns, which will neither nourish nor satisfy hunger."

Qur'an 90:19 "But those who reject Our Signs, Proofs, and Verses, they are the unhappy Companions of the Left Hand. Fire will be their awning, vaulting over them."

Qur'an 66:6 "Believers! Save yourselves and your families from a Fire whose fuel is Men and Stones, over which are angels stern (and) severe as wardens, who flinch not (from executing) the commands they receive from Allah, but do (precisely) what they are commanded."

Qur'an 47:15 "Those who shall dwell forever in the Fire are given to drink boiling water that tears their bowels to pieces, and cutting their intestines to shreds."

Bukhari:V8B76N548 "The Prophet said, 'Protect yourself from the Fire.' He turned his face aside as if he were looking at it and said, 'Protect yourself from the Fire,' and turned his face aside as if he were looking at it, and he said for the third time till we thought he was actually looking at it: 'Protect yourselves from the Fire.'"

Bukhari:V8B76N547 "The Prophet said, 'All of you will be questioned by Allah on the Day of Doom. There will be no interpreter between you and Allah. And the Hell Fire will confront you. So, whoever among you can, save yourself from the Fire.'"

Qur'an 21:98 "Verily you (disbelieving Infidels), and the gods that you worship besides Allah, are the fuel for Hell, faggots for the fire! Certainly you will enter it! Had their (idols) been (real) alihah (gods), they would have kept them out of Hell. Therein, sobbing will be your lot. Breathing with deep sighs, roaring. You will hear nothing but wailing and groaning."

Qur'an 18:108 "And We shall present Hell that day for disbelievers to see, all spread out in plain view…. Verily We have prepared Hell for the hospitality of the Infidels; Hell is for the disbeliever's entertainment."

Qur'an 77:29 "It will be said: Depart to the doom those who used to deny! Depart to a shadow of smoke (from the Hell Fire) ascending in three columns, which yields no relief or shelter and is of no use against the fierce blaze. Verily, (Hell) throws off sparks huge as castles as if they were yellow camels."

Qur'an 78:21 "Truly Hell is as a place of ambush, a resort for the rebellious. A dwelling place for the disbelievers. They will abide there forever. Therein they taste neither coolness nor any drink save a boiling water and a fluid, dark, murky, intensely cold, paralyzing, a dirty wound discharge. It is a fitting reward for them."

Qur'an 84:10 "Soon will He cry for perdition, invoking destruction, throwing them into the scorching fire. They shall enter the fire and be forced to taste its burning."

Qur'an 85:1 "I swear by the Zodiacal Signs, woe to the makers of the pit of fire. Cursed were the people." *Qur'an 85:5* "The Fire is supplied abundantly with fuel."

Qur'an 101:8 "He whose balance is light will abide in a bottomless Pit. And what will make you know what it is? It is a fire blazing fiercely!"

Qur'an 56:92 "But if he (the dying person), be of the denying (on the Day of Doom), erring (away from Islam), then for him is the entertainment with boiling water and roasting in hell fire. Verily. this is the absolute truth with certainty, so celebrate (Muhammad)."

Qur'an 52:14 "'This,' it will be said, 'is the Fire, which you used to deny! Is this a magic fake? Burn therein, endure the heat; taste it. It's the same whether you bear it patiently, or not. This is My retaliation for what you did.'"

Qur'an 55:41 "The sinners will be seized by their forelock and feet. This is the Hell the sinners called a lie. They will go round and round between its fierce fires and boiling water. Which of the favors of your Lord will you then deny?"

Qur'an 40:18 "Warn them of the Day of (Doom) that is drawing near, when hearts will jump up and choke their throats, filling them with anguish. And they can neither return their hearts to their chests nor throw them out. No friend nor intercessor will the disbelievers have.

(Allah) knows of (the tricks) that deceive with treachery, and all that the bosoms conceal."

Qur'an 40:46 "In front of the Fire will they be brought and exposed morning and evening: And (the sentence will be): 'Cast the People of Pharaoh into the severest torment, the most awful doom!' Behold, they will argue noisily with each other while they wrangle in the Fire! The weak ones (who followed) will say to those who had been arrogant, 'We but followed you. Can you then take (on yourselves) from us some share of the Fire? The arrogant will say: 'We are all in this (Fire)! Truly, Allah has judged between slaves!'"

Qur'an 40:9 "Those in the Fire will say to the guards and keepers of Hell: 'Pray to your Lord to lighten the torment for a day!' They will say: 'Did there not come to you your Messengers with Clear Signs?' They will say, 'Yes.' 'Then pray (as you like)! But the prayer of the disbelievers is futile (and will go unanswered)!' They will present their excuses, but they will (only) have the curse and the home of misery."

Qur'an 13:5 "Those who deny will wear collars and chains, yokes (of servitude) tying their hands to their necks; they will be the inmates of Hell.... They will witness Our (many) exemplary punishments! Verily, your Lord is severe in retribution."

Qur'an 21:37 "I will show you My Signs; then you will not ask Me to hasten them! They say: 'When will this (come to pass) if you are telling the truth?' If only the unbelievers knew (when) they will not be able to ward off the fire from their faces, nor from their backs! Nay, it will come to them all of a sudden and stupefy them, and they will be unable to repel it or avert it."

Qur'an 4:55 "Sufficient for them is Hell and the Flaming Fire! Those [Jews] who disbelieve Our Revelations shall be cast into Hell. When their skin is burnt up and singed, We shall give them a new coat that they may go on tasting the agony of punishment."

JEWS:

Qur'an 2:61 "Humiliation and wretchedness were stamped on the Jews and they were visited with Allah's wrath."

Qur'an 4:44 "Have you not considered those to whom a portion of the Book has been given? They traffic in error and desire that you should go astray. But Allah has full knowledge of your enemies. Of the Jews there are those who displace words from their (right) places, saying, 'We hear and we disobey' with a twist of their tongues they slander Faith.... Allah has cursed them for disbelief."

Qur'an 4:47 "O you People of the Book to whom the Scripture has been given, believe in what We have (now) revealed, confirming and verifying what was possessed by you, before We destroy your faces beyond all recognition, turning you on your backs, and curse you as We cursed the Sabbath-breakers, for the decision of Allah Must be executed."

Qur'an 4:160 "For the iniquity of the Jews We made unlawful for them certain (foods) in that they hindered many from Allah's Way, that they took usury, though they were forbidden, and that they devoured men's wealth on false pretenses, We have prepared for those among them who reject [Islamic] Faith a painful doom."

Qur'an 5:59 "Say: 'People of the Book! Do you disapprove of us for no other reason than that we believe in Allah, and the revelation that has come to us and that which came before?'

Say: 'Shall I point out to you something much worse than this by the treatment it received from Allah? Those who incurred the curse of Allah and His wrath, those of whom He transformed into apes and swine."

Qur'an 2:64 "But you [Jews] went back on your word and were lost losers. So become apes, despised and hated. We made an example out of you."

Ishaq:240 "The Jews are a nation of liars.... The Jews are a treacherous, lying, and evil people."

Qur'an 33:26 "Allah made the Jews leave their homes by terrorizing them so that you killed some and made many captive. And He made you inherit their lands, their homes, and their wealth. He gave you a country you had not traversed before."

Ishaq:250 "The bestial transformation occurred when Allah turned Jews into apes, despised."

Qur'an 59:14 "The Jews are devoid of sense. There is a grievous punishment awaiting them. Satan tells them not to believe so they will end up in Hell."

Ishaq:254/Qur'an 2:96 "We will not remove a Jew from the punishment. They know the shameful thing that awaits them."

Qur'an 4:55 "Sufficient for the Jew is the Flaming Fire!"

Qur'an 88:1 "Has the narration reached you of the overwhelming (calamity)? Some faces (all disbelievers, Jews and Christians) that Day, will be humiliated, downcast, scorched by the burning fire, while they are made to drink from a boiling hot spring."

Tabari VIII:116 "After his return from Hudaybiyah, Allah's Messenger marched against Khaybar. He halted with his army in a valley between the people of Khaybar and the Ghatafan tribe to prevent the latter from assisting the Jews."

Ishaq:264 "A notable Jew spoke to the Apostle, twisting his tongue. He attacked Islam and reviled it, so Allah sent down, 'Allah knows best about your enemies. Some of the Jews change words from their contexts and say: "We hear and disobey," twisting their tongues and attacking the religion so Allah cursed them.'"

Tabari VIII:121 "Ali struck the Jew with a swift blow that split his helmet, neck protector, and head, landing in his rear teeth. And the Muslims entered the city. Muhammad conquered the [Jewish] neighborhood. Safiyah was brought to him, and another woman with her. Bilal led them past some of the Jews we had slain including the woman's dead husband. When she saw them, the woman with Safiyah cried out, slapped her face, and poured dust on her head. When Allah's Prophet saw her, he said, 'Take this she-devil away from me!'"

Bukhari:V4B53N380 "Umar expelled all the Jews and Christians from Arabia. Allah's Apostle after conquering Khaybar thought of expelling the Jews from the land which, after he conquered it, belonged to Allah, Allah's Apostle and the Muslims. But the Jews requested Allah's Apostle to leave them there on the condition that they would do the labor and get half of the fruits (the land would yield). Allah's Apostle said, 'We shall keep you on these terms as long as we wish.' Thus they stayed till the time of Umar's Caliphate when he expelled them." *Tabari VIII:130* "The Messenger said during his final illness, 'Two religions cannot coexist in the Arabian Peninsula.' Umar investigated the matter, then sent to the Jews, saying: 'Allah has given permission for you to be expelled; for I have received word that the Prophet said that two religions cannot coexist in Arabia."

Ishaq:517 "Khaybar was stormed by the Apostle's squadron, fully armed, powerful, and strong. It brought certain humiliation with Muslim men in its midst. We attacked and they met their doom. Muhammad conquered the Jews in fighting that day as they opened their eyes to our dust."

Ishaq:524 "We cannot accept the oaths of Jews. Their infidelity is so great they swear falsely."

Qur'an 59:14 "They [Jews] will not fight against you save in fortified townships. Their hostility and hatred amongst themselves is strong: you would think they were united, but their hearts they are divided. That is because these [Jews] are a people devoid of sense."

Ishaq:245 "Do you love Jews and their religion, you liver-hearted ass, and not Muhammad? Their religion will never march with ours.... Jews make false professions about Islam. So Allah sent down: 'Satan wishes to lead them astray."

Ishaq:248 "Allah increases their sickness. A tormented doom awaits the Jews. Allah said, 'They are mischief makers. They are fools. The Jews deny the truth and contradict what the Apostle has brought. I will mock them and let them continue to wander blindly.'"

Tabari VII:158 "The Messenger of Allah besieged the Nadir Jews for fifteen days. In the end they made peace with him on the condition that the Prophet would not shed their blood and that their property and possessions would be his."

Qur'an 5:13 "But because of their breach of their covenant We cursed the Jews, and made their hearts grow hard. They change the words from their (right) places [the illiterate prophet pronounced] and forget and abandon a good part of the message that was sent them. Nor will you cease to find deceit in them. And because of their breaking their covenant We have cursed them. They altered words from their context and they neglected a portion of the message they were reminded of."

Qur'an 5:41 "Or it be among the Jews, men who will listen to any lie. They change the context of the words from their (right) times and places.... For them there is disgrace in this world, and in the Hereafter a heavy punishment."" *Qur'an 5:42* "They are fond of listening to falsehood, of devouring anything forbidden; they are greedy for illicit gain!"

Qur'an 5:44 "It was We who revealed the Torah. By its standard the prophets judged the Jews, and the prophets bowed (in Islam) to Allah's will, surrendering. For the rabbis and priests: to them was entrusted the protection of Allah's Scripture Book; they were witnesses of it. Therefore fear not men, but fear Me, and sell not My revelations for a miserable price."

Qur'an 5:64 "The Jews say: 'Allah's hands are fettered.' Be their hands tied up and be they accursed for the blasphemy they utter. Nay, both His hands are widely outstretched, giving [Muslims Jewish booty] as He pleases. Amongst them we have placed enmity and hatred till the Day of Doom. Every time they kindle the fire of war, Allah does extinguish it. But they strive to do mischief on earth."

Qur'an 98:1 "Those among the People of the Book, who disbelieve and are idolaters, would never have been freed from their false religion if the Clear Proofs had not come to them. An Apostle of Allah came reading out of hallowed pages.... They were commanded to serve Allah exclusively, fulfilling their devotional obligations, and paying the zakat. Surely the unbelievers and idolaters from the People of the Book will abide in the Fire of Hell. They are the worst of creatures."

Qur'an 5:78 "Curses were pronounced on the unbelievers, the Children of Israel who rejected Islam, by the tongues of David and of Jesus because they disobeyed and rebelled." *Qur'an 5:80* "You see many of them allying themselves with the unbelieving infidels. Vile indeed are their souls. Allah's wrath is on them, and in torment will they abide." *Qur'an 5:81* "If only they had believed in Allah, in the Prophet, and in what had been revealed to him." *Qur'an 5:82* "You will find the Jews and disbelievers [defined as Christians in 5:73] the most vehement in hatred for the Muslims."

Ishaq:262 "Some Muslims remained friends with the Jews, so Allah sent down a Qur'an forbidding them to take Jews as friends. From their mouths hatred has already shown itself and what they conceal is worse."

Qur'an 2:59 "We sent a plague upon the Jews from heaven, for their evil-doing."

Bukhari:V4B56N679 "Allah's Apostle said, 'Plague is a means of torture sent on the Israelis.'"

Bukhari:V2B23N457 "The Prophet went out after sunset and heard a dreadful voice. He said, 'The Jews are being punished in their graves.'"

Qur'an 17:7 "We shall rouse Our (Muslim) slaves to shame and ravage you (Jews), disfiguring your faces. They will enter the Temple as before and destroy, laying to waste all that they conquer."

Bukhari:V1B4N147 "People say, 'Whenever you sit for answering the call of nature, you should not face the Qiblah of Jerusalem.' I told them. 'Once I went up the roof of our house and I saw Allah's Apostle answering the call of nature while sitting on two bricks facing Jerusalem."

Ishaq:239 "About this time Jewish rabbis showed hostility to the Apostle in envy, hatred, and malice, because Allah had chosen His Apostle from the Arabs. The Jews considered the Prophet a liar and strove against Islam."

Ishaq:239 "Jewish rabbis used to annoy the Apostle with questions, introducing confusion." "Qur'ans used to come down in reference to their questions."

Ishaq:240 "Labid bewitched Allah's Apostle so that he could not come at his wives. These Jewish rabbis opposed the apostle, they asked questions and stirred up trouble against Islam trying to extinguish it."

Ishaq:240 "I concealed the matter from the Jews and then went to the Apostle and said, 'The Jews are a nation of liars and I want you to give me a house and hide me from them. If they learn I've become a Muslim, they'll utter slanderous lies against me.' So the prophet gave me a house, and when the Jews came, I emerged and said, 'O Jews, fear Allah and accept what He has sent you. For you know that he is the Apostle of Allah. You will find him described in your Torah and even named.' They accused me of lying and reviled me. I told Muhammad, 'The Jews are a treacherous, lying, and evil people.'"

Ishaq:241 "Mukhayriq was a learned rabbi owning much property in date palms. He recognized the Apostle by his description and felt a predilection for his religion. He violated the Sabbath to fight on behalf of Islam and was killed in battle. I am told the Prophet used to say, 'Mukhayriq is the best of the Jews [a dead one].' The Apostle took his property."

Ishaq:242 "Julas the Jew used to say, 'If Muhammad is right we are worse than donkeys.' Allah sent down concerning him: 'They swear that they did not say it, when they did say the words of unbelief.... Allah will afflict them with a painful punishment in this world and in the next.' [Surah 9:75] *Ishaq:242* "The Apostle ordered Umar to kill him, but he escaped to Mecca."

Ishaq:246 "The surah of the Hypocrites came down because some men sent secret messages to the Nadir Jews when the Apostle besieged them.... Allah bears witness that they are liars. Like Satan when he says to men, "Disbelieve."' [59:11]

Qur'an 59:14 "They are a divided people devoid of sense. There is a grievous punishment awaiting them. Satan tells them not to believe so both of them will end up in Hell."

Qur'an 59:2 "It was He [Allah] who drove the [Jewish] People of the Book from their [Medina] homes and into exile. They refused to believe. You did not think that they would go away. And they imagined that their settlement would protect them against Allah. But Allah's [actually Muhammad's] (torment) came at them from where they did not suspect and terrorized them. Their homes were destroyed. So learn a lesson O men who have eyes. This is My warning. Had Allah not decreed the expulsion of the Jews, banishing them into the desert, He would certainly have punished them in this world, and in the next they shall taste the torment of Hell Fire."

Ishaq:251 "Moses commanded them to prostrate themselves and his Lord spoke to him and they heard His voice giving them commands and prohibitions so that they understood what they heard. But when Moses went back to the Jews a party of them changed the Commandments they had been given." [2:75]

Ishaq:252 "Have you no understanding? Why do you maintain that he is not a prophet since you know that Allah has made a Covenant with you that you should follow him? While he tells you that he is the prophet whom you are expecting, and that you will find him in Our book, you oppose him and do not recognize him. You reject his prophethood on mere opinion."

Ishaq:253 "Allah cursed them for their unbelief. When a scripture comes to them from Allah confirming what they already have, they deny it. Allah's curse is on them."

Ishaq:254 "In the pagan era the Jews were scripture folk and we were pagans. They used to say, 'Soon a prophet will be sent whom we shall follow.' When Allah sent his Apostle from the Quraysh and we followed him they denied him. Allah revealed, 'When there comes to him one they recognize, they deny him. They are wretched, so Allah cursed them, and He will give them a shameful punishment.' The double anger is His wrath because they have disregarded the Torah and anger because they disbelieved in this Prophet whom Allah has sent to them." [2:89]

Ishaq:254 "Long for death [Jews], if you are truthful. Pray that God will kill whichever one of us is the most false. The Jews refused the Prophet's dare." "Allah said to His Prophet, 'They will never accept your dare because of their past deeds. But they recognize you from the knowledge they have. Yet they deny. Had they accepted your dare, not a single Jew would have remained alive on the earth." [2:94]

Ishaq:254 "We will not remove a Jew from the punishment. The Jew knows the shameful thing that awaits him in the next life because he has wasted the knowledge he has." [2:96]

Ishaq:255 "Jewish rabbis came to the Apostle and asked him to answer four questions saying, 'If you do so we will follow you, testify to your truth, and believe in you.' They began, 'Why does a boy resemble his mother when the semen comes from the father?' Muhammad replied, 'Do you not know that a man's semen is white and thick and a woman's is yellow and thin? The likeness goes with that which comes to the top.' 'Agreed,' the rabbis proclaimed.... The rabbis said. 'But Muhammad, your spirit is an enemy to us, an angel who comes only with violence and the shedding of blood, and were it not for that we would follow you."

Ishaq:255 "So Allah sent down concerning them: 'When the Apostle comes to them from Allah confirming that which they have received in scripture, they put it behind their backs as if they did not know it. They follow that which Satan read concerning the kingdom of Solomon—sorcery.' One of the rabbis said, 'Don't you wonder at Muhammad? He alleges that Solomon was a prophet, and yet he was nothing but a sorcerer.' So Allah sent down, 'Solomon did not disbelieve but Satan did, practicing sorcery.'" [2:101]

Ishaq:256 "The Apostle wrote a letter to the Jews of Khaybar [before he annihilated them]. In the name of Allah, from Muhammad the Apostle of Allah, friend and brother of Moses who confirms what Moses brought [the Torah]. Allah says to you, 'O Scripture folk, and you will find it in your scripture "Muhammad is the Apostle of Allah. Those with him are severe against the unbelievers. You see them bowing, falling prostrate, seeking bounty, and acceptance. The mark of their prostrations is on their foreheads." That is their likeness in the Torah and in the Gospels.'"

Ishaq:256 "The Jews used to ask Muhammad questions which annoyed and confused him."

Ishaq:257 "Your situation seems obscure to us, Muhammad."

Ishaq:257 "'O Jews, fear Allah and submit, for you used to hope for the Messiah's help against the Arabs when we were pagans. You told us that he would be sent and then told us about him.' A Jew responded, 'Muhammad has not shown us anything we recognize as prophetic. He is not the one we spoke to you about.' So Allah revealed, 'We confirmed what they had, and We sent one they recognized, but they rejected him so We are cursing them.' The Jews replied, 'No Covenant was ever made with us about Muhammad.'"

"'Muhammad, you have not brought anything we recognize. And God has not sent down any sign or miracle suggesting that we should believe you.' So Allah said, 'We have sent down to you plain signs and only evildoers disbelieve them.'"

Ishaq:257 "The Jews told Allah's Messenger, 'Bring us a book. Bring us something down from heaven that we might read it.'"

Ishaq:258 "The Jews used to turn men away from Islam. So Allah said, 'Many Scripture folk wish to make you unbelievers after you have believed. They are envious. Be indulgent until Allah gives you his orders [to rob them, rape them, sell them into slavery, and murder them.]"

Ishaq:262 "Some Muslims remained friends with Jews, so Allah sent down a Qur'an forbidding them to take Jews as friends. From their mouths hatred has already shown itself and what they conceal is worse." "You believe in their Book [though you don't have a clue what it says] while they deny your book, so you have more right to hate them than they have to hate you."

Ishaq:263 "Abu Bakr went into a Jewish school [there is no mention of him ever going into a Muslim school] and found many pupils gathered around Finhas, a learned rabbi. Bakr told the Jews to fear Allah and submit. He told them that they would find that Muhammad was an Apostle written in the Torah and Gospels. Finhas replied, 'Why does your god ask us to lend him money as your master pretends.' Abu was enraged and hit Finhas hard in the face [for telling the truth]. Were it not for the treaty between us I would cut off your head, you enemy of Allah. So Allah said, 'They will taste Our punishment of burning.'"

Ishaq:264 "Allah revealed concerning Finhas and the other rabbis: 'Allah issued orders to those who had received the Book: 'You are to make it clear to men and not conceal it, yet they cast the Torah behind their backs and sold it for a small price. Wretched was their exchange. They will therefore receive a painful punishment.'"

Ishaq:264 "The Torah confirms what Muhammad brought. Rifa'a, a notable Jew, spoke to the Apostle, twisting his tongue: 'Give us your attention, Muhammad, so that we can make you understand.' Then he attacked Islam and reviled it. So Allah sent down, 'Allah knows about your enemies. Some Jews change words from their contexts and say: "We hear and disobey," twisting their tongues and attacking the religion. But Allah cursed them.'" [2:59 & 4:47]

Ishaq:264 "The Jewish rabbis knew that Muhammad had brought them the truth, but they denied that they knew it. They were obstinate. So Allah revealed, 'People of the Book, believe in what we have sent down in confirmation of what you had been given before or We will efface your features and turn your face into your ass, cursing you.'"

Ishaq:269 "'Tell us when the Day of Doom will be, Muhammad, if you are a prophet as you say.' So Allah sent down, 'They will ask you about the hour when it will come to pass. Say, only my Lord knows of it. None but He will reveal it at its proper time. Say, 'Only Allah knows about it but most men do not know.' How can we follow you, Muhammad, when you have abandoned our Qiblah? And you do not allege that Uzayr [who knows?] is the son of God.' So Allah revealed, 'The Jews say that Uzayr is the son of God [no they don't] and the Christians say the Messiah is the son of God. That is what they say with their mouths, copying the speech of those who disbelieved in the earlier times. Allah fight them! How perverse are they?'"

Ishaq:269 "'For our part we don't see how your Qur'an recitals are arranged anything like our Torah is.' [So Muhammad who couldn't read said,] 'You know quite well that the Qur'an is from Allah. You will find it written in the Torah which you have.'"

Ishaq:269 "'If men and jinn [demons] came together to produce its like they could not.' Finhas said, 'Did men or jinn tell you this, Muhammad?' 'You know full well that the Qur'an is from Allah and that I am the Apostle of Allah. You will find it written in the Torah you have.' The rabbi replied, 'When God sends a prophet, He provides for him, so bring us a book that is divinely inspired that we may read it and determine if you are telling the truth. We can produce *our* Book.' So Allah revealed, concerning their words, 'Though men and jinn should meet to produce this Qur'an, they would not produce its like, even working together.'"

Qur'an 2:40 "O Children of Israel, remember the favors I bestowed on you. So keep My Covenant so that I fulfil your covenant. Fear Me. And believe in what I sent down, confirming and verifying the Scripture which you possess already." *Qur'an 2:41* "Be not the first to deny or sell My Verses for a small price; and fear Me, and Me alone." [Another translation reads:] "Part not with My Revelations for a trifling price, getting a small gain by selling My Verses."

Qur'an 2:43 "[Jews] Perform prayer; pay the zakat tax; bow down and prostrate yourself with Ar-Raki'un (the obedient bowers). You read, recite, and study the Scripture. Why don't you understand? Nay, seek [Islamic prostration] prayer: It is indeed hard, heavy, and exacting, except for those who obey in submission."

Qur'an 2:59 "The [Jewish] transgressors changed and perverted the word from that which had been spoken to them to a word distorted; so We sent a plague upon them from heaven, for their evil-doing."

Qur'an 2:61 "Humiliation and wretchedness were stamped upon the Jews and they were visited with wrath from Allah. That was because they disbelieved Allah's Proofs, Signs and Verses and killed the prophets. They disobeyed and rebelled."

Qur'an 2:64 "But you [Jews] went back on your word and were lost losers. You know that you have broken the sanctity of the Sabbath, so We said: 'Become monkeys despised and hated.' We made this punishment an example and a warning for those who fear Allah."

Qur'an 2:79 "But woe to the Jews who fake the Scriptures and say, 'This is from God,' so that they might earn some profit thereby.' And woe to them for what their hands have written, and woe to them for what they earn from it.'"

Qur'an 2:80 "Yet they (Jews) say: 'The Fire will not touch us for more than a few days...but they are enclosed in error and are inmates of Hell."

Qur'an 2:85 "Do you [Jews] believe a part of the Book and reject a part? There is no reward for them who so act but disgrace in the world, and on the Day of Doom, the severest of punishment...their torment will never decrease!"

Qur'an 2:89 "The Book was sent to them (the Jews) by Allah verifying and confirming what had been revealed to them already (the Torah and Gospel). They used to pray for victory over the unbelievers—and even though they recognized it when it came to them, they renounced it. The curse of Allah be on those who deny!"

Qur'an 2:101 "When there came a messenger from Allah confirming what was with them, a party of the people of the (Torah and Gospel) Scripture Book fling away the Book of Allah, tossing it behind their backs, as if they did not know!"

Qur'an 2:109 "Quite a number of the People of the Book wish they could turn you [Muslim] (people) back to infidelity after you have believed [submitted], through selfish envy, even after the Truth has become manifest to them. Indulge them until Allah issues his orders."

Tabari VII:26 "When the Prophet came to Yathrib he saw the Jews fasting on Ashura day. He questioned them, and they said it was the day upon which God drowned Pharaoh and saved Moses from the Egyptians. He said, 'We have a better right to Moses than you do.'"

Tabari VII:85 "After Muhammad killed many Quraysh polytheists at Badr, the Jews were envious and behaved badly toward him, saying, 'Muhammad has not met anyone who is good at fighting. Had he met us, he would have had a real battle.' They also infringed the treaty in various ways."

Ishaq:232 "The Jews shall contribute to the cost of war so long as they are fighting alongside the believers. The Jews have their religion, the Muslims have theirs. None of them shall go out to war unless they have Muhammad's permission. The Jews must pay, however, for as long as the war lasts. If any dispute or controversy should arise it must be referred to Allah and Muhammad, His Apostle. If the Jews are called to make peace they must, except in the case of Holy War. Allah approves of this document."

Tabari VII:85 "What happened to the Qaynuqa [the wealthiest Jewish tribe in Yathrib] was that Muhammad assembled them in their Marketplace and said, 'Jews, beware lest Allah brings on you the kind of vengeance which He brought on the Quraysh. Accept Islam [submit] and become Muslims [surrender]. You know that I am a Prophet. You will find me in your Scriptures and in Allah's Covenant with you.'"

Ishaq:363 "The Jews of the Qaynuqa replied, 'Muhammad, do you think that we are like your people? Do not be deluded by the fact that you met a people with no knowledge and you made good use of your opportunity.'"

Tabari VII:85 "The Qaynuqa were the first Jews to infringe the agreement between them and the Messenger." [We are not told how they "infringed."] "The campaign of the Prophet against the Banu Qaynuqa was in Shawwal (March 27, 624) in the second year of the Hijrah [migration from Mecca]."

Tabari VII:86 "Gabriel brought down the following verse to the Messenger: 'If you apprehend treachery from any people (with whom you have a treaty), retaliate by breaking off (relations) with them.' [8:58] When Gabriel had finished delivering this verse, the Prophet said, 'I fear the Qaynuqa.' It was on the basis of this verse that Muhammad advanced on them."

Ishaq:363 "Allah's Apostle besieged the Qaynuqa until they surrendered at his discretion unconditionally."

Tabari VII:86 "Abd Allah [a Yathrib chief] rose up when Allah had put them in his power, and said, 'Muhammad, treat my ally well, for the Qaynuqa are a confederate of the Khazraj.' The Prophet ignored him, so Abd Allah repeated his request." *Ishaq:363* "The Prophet turned away from him so Abd Allah put his hand on the collar of the Messenger's robe. Muhammad said, 'Let go of me!' He was so angry his face turned black. Then he said, 'Damn you, let me go!' Abd Allah replied, 'No, by God, I will not let you go until you treat my ally humanely. There are seven hundred men among them who defended me from my foes when I needed their help. And now, you would mow them down in a single morning? By God I do not feel safe around here any more. I am afraid of what the future may have in store.' So the Messenger said, 'You can have them.'"

Tabari VII:87 "The Prophet said, 'Let them go; may Allah curse them, and may he curse Abd Allah with them.' So the Muslims let them go. Then Muhammad [went back on his word and] gave orders to expel the Jews. Allah gave their property as booty to his Messenger. The Qaynuqa did not have any farmland, as they were goldsmiths. The Prophet took many weapons belonging to them and the tools of their trade. The person who took charge of their expulsion from Yathrib along with their children was Ubadah. He accompanied them as far as Dhubab, saying: 'The farther you go the better.'"

Bukhari:V5B59N362 "He exiled all the Qaynuqa Jews from Medina."

Ishaq:364 "Muslims, take not Jews and Christians as friends. Whoever protects them becomes one of them, they become diseased, and will earn a similar fate."

Ishaq:364 "'I fear this change of circumstance may end up overtaking us.' So Allah replied, 'He will be sorry for his thoughts. True believers perform prostrations, they pay the tax, they bow in homage, and renounce their agreements with the Jews. They are Hezbollah—Allah's Party.'"

Qur'an 59:2 "It was Allah who drove the (Jewish) People from their [Yathrib] homes and into exile. They refused to believe. They imagined that their strongholds would protect them against Allah. But Allah's Torment came at them from where they did not suspect. He terrorized them. Their homes were destroyed. So learn a lesson. This is My warning. Had I not decreed the expulsion of the Jews, banishing them to the desert, I would have punished them. They shall taste the torment of Hell Fire." *Qur'an 59:4* "That is because they resisted Allah and His Messenger. If any one resists Allah, verily Allah is severe in Punishment."

Qur'an 59:6 "What Allah gave as booty to His Messenger, He has taken away from the Jews. Allah gives His Messenger Lordship over whom He will. Whatever booty Allah has given to Muhammad and taken away from the (Jewish) people of the townships, belongs to Allah and to His Apostle."

Tabari VII:94 "The Murder of Ka'b bin Ashraf, The Evil Genius of the Jews: The Prophet sent messengers to the people of Medina announcing the good news of the victory granted to him by Allah at Badr. They listed the names of the polytheists they had killed." *Ishaq:365* "Ka'b bin Ashraf was from the Jewish clan of Nadir. When he heard the news, he said, 'Can this be true? Did Muhammad actually kill these people? These were fine men. If Muhammad has slain them, then the belly of the earth is a better place for us than its surface!'"

Ishaq:365 "When the enemy of Allah became convinced the report was true, he set out for Mecca. He began to arouse people against Muhammad [i.e., he exposed him]. He recited verses in sympathy for the Quraysh men Muhammad had cast into the pit. Ka'b Ashraf composed the following poetic lines: 'The blood spilled at Badr calls to its people. They cry and weep. The best men were slain and thrown into a pit.'" *Ishaq:365* "Drive off that fool of yours so that you might be safe from talk that makes no sense. Why do you taunt those who mourn over their dead? They lived good lives, and as such we must remember them. But now you have become like jackals."

Tabari VII:94 "The Prophet said, 'Who will rid me of Ashraf?' Muhammad bin Maslamah, said, 'I will rid you of him, Messenger of Allah. I will kill him.' 'Do it then,' he said, 'if you can.'" *Bukhari:V4B52N270* "The Prophet said, 'Who is ready to kill Ka'b bin Ashraf who has really hurt Allah and His Apostle?' Muhammad bin Maslama said, 'O Allah's Apostle! Do you want me to kill him?' He replied in the affirmative." *Ishaq:365* "'Who will rid me of Ashraf?' Maslama said, 'I will deal with him for you. O Apostle, I will kill him.' Muhammad said, 'Do so if you can.'"

Ishaq:365 / Tabari VII:94 "Muhammad bin Maslamah said, 'O Messenger, we shall have to tell lies.' 'Say what you like,' Muhammad replied. 'You are absolved, free to say whatever you must.'"

Tabari VII:94 / Ishaq:367 "Maslamah made a plan to kill Ka'b, the enemy of Allah. Before they went to him, they sent Abu ahead. When he arrived, they spoke together for a while. They recited verses, for Abu was something of a poet. Then Abu said, 'Ka'b, I have come to you about a matter which I want you to keep secret.' 'Go ahead,' he replied. 'The arrival of the

Prophet Muhammad has been an affliction for us.' Abu said, 'Most Arabs are now hostile to us. We cannot travel along the roads, and the result is that our families are facing ruin. We are all suffering.' Ka'b replied, 'I warned you that things would turn out like this.' Abu said, 'I would like you to sell us some food. We will give you some collateral and make a firm contract. Please treat us generously.'"

Tabari VII:95 "Abu said, 'We will deposit sufficient weapons with you to guarantee the payment of our debt.' Abu wanted to fool the Jew so that he would not be suspicious about the weapons when they came bearing them. Abu went back to his companions, informed them of what had happened. He told them to grab their swords and join him. Before leaving, they went to the house of the Messenger. Muhammad walked with them as far as Baqi al-Gharqad. Then he sent them off, saying, 'Go in Allah's name; O Allah, help them [assassinate the outspoken Jew]!' Then the Prophet went back home. It was a moonlit night, and they went forward until they reached Ka'b's house."

Ishaq:368 "Then Abu called out to him. He had recently married, and he leapt up in his bed. His wife took hold of the sheets, and said to the strange voice, 'You are a fighting man; as only a man of war leaves his house at an hour like this." *Bukhari:V5B59N369* "His wife asked him, 'Where are you going?' Ka'b replied, 'Out with Muhammad bin Maslamah and my brother Abu.' His wife said, 'I hear evil in his voice as if his words are dripping blood.' Ka'b said. 'They are my brother and my foster brother. A generous man should respond to a call at night even if invited to be killed.'"

Muslim:B19N4436 "Muhammad said to his companions: 'As he comes down, I will extend my hands towards his head, I will touch his hair and smell it. When you see that I have got hold of his head, strip him. When I hold him fast, you do your job.'" *Bukhari:V5B59N369* "Muhammad said. 'I have never smelt a better perfume than this,' so that Ka'b would relax his guard. 'Will you allow me to smell your head?' Then Abu thrust his hand into the hair near his temple. When Muhammad got a strong hold of him, he said, 'Strike the enemy of Allah!' So they smote him."

Ishaq:368 "Their swords rained blows upon him, but to no avail. Muhammad bin Maslamah said, 'When I saw that they were ineffective, I remembered a long, thin dagger which I had in my scabbard. I took hold of it. By this time the enemy of Allah had shouted so loudly lamps had been lit in the homes around us. I plunged the dagger into his breast and pressed upon it so heavily that it reached his pubic region. Allah's enemy fell to the ground.'"

Tabari VII:97/Ishaq:368 "We carried Ka'b's head and brought it to Muhammad during the night. We saluted him as he stood praying and told him that we had slain Allah's enemy. When he came out to us we cast Ashraf's head before his feet. The Prophet praised Allah that the poet had been assassinated and complimented us on the good work we had done in Allah's Cause. Our attack upon Allah's enemy cast terror among the Jews, and there was no Jew in Medina who did not fear for his life.'"

Ishaq:368 "Ka'b's body was left prostrate. After his fall, all the Nadir Jews were brought low. Sword in hand we cut him down. By Muhammad's order we were sent secretly by night. Brother killing brother. We lured him to his death with guile [cunning or deviousness].

Traveling by night, bold as lions, we went into his home. We made him taste death with our deadly swords. We sought victory for the religion of the Prophet."

Tabari VII:97 "The next morning, the Jews were in a state of fear on account of our attack upon the enemy of Allah. After the assassination, the Prophet declared, 'Kill every Jew.'"

Bukhari:V1B1N6 "Just issue orders to kill every Jew in the country."

Tabari VII:97/Ishaq:369 "Thereupon Mas'ud leapt upon Sunayna, one of the Jewish merchants with whom his family had social and commercial relations and killed him. The Muslim's brother complained, saying, 'Why did you kill him? You have much fat in you belly from his charity.' Mas'ud answered, 'By Allah, had Muhammad ordered me to murder you, my brother, I would have cut off your head.' Wherein the brother said, 'Any religion that can bring you to this is indeed wonderful!'"

Qur'an 59:14 "The Jews will not unite and fight against you except from behind walls. They hate themselves. You would think they were united, but their hearts are divided. That is because these [Jews] are a people devoid of sense. Like those who recently preceded them [the Meccans at Badr], they [the Jews who were just sent into the desert to die] have tasted the evil result of their conduct. And for them a grievous punishment."

Qur'an 59:16 "They [the Jews] are like Satan when he tells man, 'Not to believe,' When (man) denies, Satan says, 'I have nothing to do with you. I fear Allah, the Lord of men and jinn!'"

Qur'an 59:17 "Both [Jews and Satan] will go into the Fire of Hell, dwelling therein forever. Such is the reward of the Zalimun (disbelievers and polytheists)."

Qur'an 62:5 "The likeness of those who are entrusted with the Taurat (Torah), who subsequently failed in those (obligations), is that of an ass which carries huge books (but understands them not). Wretched is the likeness of folk who deny the Verses of Allah."

Qur'an 62:6 "Say: 'You Jews! If you think that you are friends to Allah, to the exclusion of (other) men, then desire death, if you are truthful!' But never will they long (for death), because of what their hands have done before them! Allah knows well the polytheists! Say: 'The Death from which you flee will truly overtake you.'"

Qur'an 3:65 "You People of the Book! Why dispute you about Abraham, when the Law and the Gospel were not revealed till after him? Have you no understanding? Ah! You are those who fell to disputing (even) in matters of which you had some knowledge! But why dispute in matters of which you have no knowledge? It is Allah Who knows, and you who know not!" *Qur'an 3:67* "Abraham was not a Jew nor yet a Christian; but he was a true Muslim, surrendered to Allah (which is Islam), and he joined not gods with Allah."

Qur'an 3:77 "As for those who sell for a small price the covenant and faith they owe to Allah and their own plighted word for a small price, they shall have no portion in the Hereafter. Nor will Allah speak to them or look at them on the Day of Judgment, nor will He cleanse them: They shall have a grievous torment, a painful doom. There is among them a section who distort the Book with their tongues. (As they read) you would think it is from the Book, but it is not from the Book; and they say, 'That is from God,' but it is not from Allah: It is they who tell a lie against Allah, and (well) they know it!"

Qur'an 3:84 "Say (Muhammad): 'We believe in Allah and that which is revealed to us and that which was revealed unto Abraham and Ishmael, Isaac and Jacob and the tribes [of Israel], and in (the Books) given to Moses, Jesus, and the prophets, from their Lord. We make no distinction between any of them, and unto Him we have surrendered, bowing our will (in Islam).'" *Qur'an 3:85* "If anyone desires a religion other than Islam (Surrender), never will it be accepted of him; and in the Hereafter He will be in the ranks of those who are losers." *Qur'an 3:87* "Of such the reward is that on them (rests) the curse of Allah, of His angels, and of all men, all together. In that will they dwell; nor will their penalty of doom be lightened." *Tabari VII:156/Ishaq:437* "In the fourth year of the Islamic Era the Prophet expelled the Nadir [a large Jewish community in Yathrib] from their homes.

Tabari VII:158 "Call Muhammad bin Maslamah to me.' When Muhammad came, he was told to go to the Jews and say, 'Leave my country. You have intended treachery.' He went and said, 'The Messenger orders you to depart from his country.' They replied, 'We never thought that an Aws would come with such a message.' 'Hearts have changed,' Muhammad said. 'Islam has wiped out our old covenants.'"

Ishaq:437 "The Apostle ordered them to prepare for war and to march against them. Muhammad personally led his men against the Nadir and halted in their quarter. The Jews took refuge against him in their homes, so he ordered their date palms to be cut down and burnt. They shouted, 'Muhammad, you have forbidden wonton destruction of property and have blamed those who perpetrated it. Why are you doing this?'" *Qur'an 59:5* "The palm trees you cut down or left standing intact was by Allah's dispensation so that He might disgrace the transgressors."

Ishaq:437 "So Allah cast terror into the hearts of the Jews. Then the Prophet said, 'The Jews have declared war.'"

Tabari VII:159 "The Messenger of Allah besieged the Banu Nadir for fifteen days until he had reduced them to a state of utter exhaustion, so that they would give him what he wanted. The terms in which the Prophet made peace with the Jews were: he would not shed their blood, he would expel them from their lands and settlements, providing for every three of them a camel and a water-skin."

Ishaq:438 "The Jews loaded their camels with their wives, children, and property. There were tambourines, pipes and singing. They went to Khaybar with such splendor as had never been seen from any tribe." *Ishaq:438* "The Nadir left their property to Muhammad and it became his personal possession, to do with it as he wished."

Ishaq:438 "Allah wreaked His vengeance on the Jews and gave His Apostle power over them and control to deal with them as he wished. Allah said, 'I turned out those who disbelieved of the Scripture People from their homes. And in the next world I will torment them again with a painful punishment in Hell. The palm trees you cut down were by Allah's permission; they were uprooted on My order. It was not destruction but it was vengeance from Allah to humble the evildoers. The spoil which Allah gave the Apostle from the Nadir belongs to him.'"

Bukhari:V4B52N153 "The properties of Nadir which Allah had transferred to His Apostle as Booty were not gained by the Muslims with their horses and camels. The properties therefore, belonged especially to Allah's Apostle who used to give his family their yearly expenditure and spend what remained thereof on arms and horses to be used in Allah's Cause."

Bukhari:V4B52N176 "Allah's Apostle said, 'You Muslims will fight the Jews till some of them hide behind stones. The stones will betray them saying, "O Abdullah (slave of Allah)! There is a Jew hiding behind me; so kill him.""

Bukhari:V4B52N177 "Allah's Apostle said, 'The Hour will not be established until you fight with the Jews, and the stone behind which a Jew will be hiding will say. "O Muslim! There is a Jew hiding behind me, so kill him.""

Ishaq:441 "A man who had neither shown treachery nor bad faith haply had a change of fortune and took revenge, cutting down their palm trees and killing the Nadir. A sharp sword in the hand of a brave man kills his adversary. The rabbis were disgraced for they denied mighty Lord Allah." *Ishaq:442* "Sword in hand we brought down the Nadir. By Muhammad's order we beguiled them."

Tabari VIII:7 "The Quraysh said: 'Jews, you are the people of the first Scripture, and you have knowledge about the subject on which we and Muhammad have come to differ. Is our religion better or his?' 'Your religion is better,' they said. 'You are closer to the truth than he.'"

Ishaq:450 "They are the ones concerning whom Allah revealed: 'Have you not seen those to whom a portion of the Scripture has been given? They believe in idols and false deities. They say, "These are more rightly guided than those who believe?"—until the words, "Hell is sufficient for their burning. They are jealous and Allah has cursed them.""" [4:51]

Tabari VIII:15 "When the news reached Muhammad, he sent Sa'd, chief of the Aws to Ka'b. 'If it is true, speak to me in words that we can understand but that will be unintelligible to others. So he went out and found them engaged in the worst of what had been reported. They slandered the Messenger and said, 'There is no treaty between us.' Sa'd reviled them, and they reviled him. Sa'd was a man with a sharp temper. He told the Jews, 'Stop reviling him for the disagreement between us is too serious for an exchange of taunts.'"

Ishaq:461 "Just before the noon prayers, Gabriel came to the Apostle wearing a gold turban. He was riding a mule. He said, 'Have you laid down your weapons and stopped fighting, Muhammad?' 'Yes,' he replied. Gabriel said, 'The angels have not laid down their arms! I've just returned from pursuing the enemy. Allah commands you to march to the Qurayza. I, too, will attack the Jews and shake them out of their homes.'"

Bukhari:V5B59N443-8 "When the Prophet returned from the Trench, laid down his arms and took a bath, Gabriel came to him covered in dust. "Why have you laid down your sword? We angels have not set them down yet. It's time to go out against them.' The Prophet said, 'Where to go?' Gabriel said, 'This way,' pointing towards the Qurayza. So the Prophet went out to besiege them."

Bukhari:V5B59N444 "The dust rose in the streets of Medina as Gabriel's regiment marched through. The angels joined Allah's Apostle in attacking the Qurayza Jews."

Ishaq:461 "The Messenger commanded a crier to announce that all should heed and obey. He ordered that none should perform the afternoon prayer until after they reached the Qurayza settlement. The Prophet sent Ali ahead with his war banner against the Jews, and the Muslims hastened to it. Ali advanced toward their homes and heard insulting language from the Jews about Allah's Messenger. Ali ran back and told the Prophet that the

Jews were rascals and that there was no need for him to go near those wicked men. 'Why?' Muhammad asked. 'Have you heard them insult me?' 'Yes,' Ali answered. 'Had they seen me,' Allah's Apostle replied, 'they would not have said anything of the sort.'"

Tabari VIII:28 "Before reaching the Qurayza, Muhammad greeted his Companions. 'Has anyone passed you?' he asked. 'Yes, Prophet,' they replied. 'Dihyah ibn Khalifah passed us on a white mule with a brocade covered saddle.' Allah's Apostle said, 'That was Gabriel. He was sent to the Qurayza to shake their homes and terrorize them.'"

Tabari VIII:29 "The Prophet said, 'No one should pray the afternoon prayer until they are in the territory of the Qurayza because warfare against the Jews is incumbent upon Muslims.'"

Ishaq:461 "The Muslims had been totally occupied with warlike preparations. They refused to pray until they had come upon the Jews in accordance with Muhammad's order. Allah did not find fault with them in His Book, nor did the Messenger reprimand them for it."

Tabari VIII:28 "When the Messenger approached the Jews, he said, 'You brothers of apes! Allah shamed you and cursed you.'"

Bukhari:V5B59N449 "On the day of the Qurayza siege, Allah's Apostle said to Hassan, 'Abuse them with your poems, for Gabriel is with you.'"

Ishaq:461 "Muhammad besieged them for twenty-five nights. When the siege became too severe, Allah terrorized them. After the siege exhausted and terrorized them, the Jews felt certain that the Apostle would not leave them until he had exterminated them. So they decided to talk to Ka'b Asad. He said, 'Jews, you see what has befallen you. I shall propose three alternatives. Take whichever one you please.' He said, 'Swear allegiance to Muhammad and accept him; for it has become clear to you that he is a prophet sent from Allah. It is he that you used to find mentioned in your scripture book. Then you will be secure in your lives, your property, your children, and your wives.'" *Tabari VIII:30* "The Jews said, 'We will never abandon the Torah or exchange it for the Qur'an.' Asad said, 'Since you reject this proposal, then kill your children and your wives and go out to Muhammad and his Companions as men who brandish swords, leaving behind no impediments to worry you. If you die, you shall have left nothing behind; if you win you shall find other women and children.' The Jews replied, 'Why would we kill these poor ones? What would be the good of living after them?'"

Ishaq:462 "Then the Jews asked, 'Send us Abu Lubaba, one of the Aws,' for they were confederates, 'so that we can ask his advice.' The Prophet complied and the Jews grabbed hold of him. The women and children were crying, so he felt pity for them. They said, 'Lubaba, do you think we should submit to Muhammad's judgment?' 'Yes,' he said. But he pointed with his hand to his throat, indicating that it would be slaughter. Lubaba later said, 'As soon as my feet moved, I knew that I had betrayed Allah's Apostle. He rushed away and tied himself to a pillar in the mosque. He cried, 'I will not leave this spot until Allah forgives me for what I've done. I betrayed His Apostle.'" *Ishaq:462/Tabari VIII:32* "I heard Allah's Apostle laughing at daybreak; so I said, 'Why are you laughing, Prophet? May Allah make you laugh heartily!' He replied, 'Lubaba has been forgiven.'" *Ishaq:463* "He vanished into the night. It is not known to this day what happened to him. Some allege that he was bound with a rotten rope and cast away."

Tabari VIII:33 "In the morning, the Jews submitted to the judgment of Allah's Messenger. The Aws [Medina Muslims] leapt up and said, 'Muhammad, they are our allies. You know what you did the other day with the allies of the Khazraj [another tribe of Medina Muslims]!' Before besieging the Qurayza, the Messenger had besieged the Qaynuqa, who were the confederates of the Khazraj. They had submitted to his judgment and were banished."

Bukhari:V5B59N448 "Sa'd said, 'O Allah! You know that there is nothing more beloved to me than to fight in Your Cause against those who disbelieve Your Apostle. If there remains any fight with the infidels, then keep me alive till I fight against them for Your sake.'"

Ishaq:463 "En route to Muhammad, the Aws said, 'Treat our client well for the Prophet has put you in charge of this matter. After many requests, Sa'd said, 'The time has come for Sa'd, in the Cause of Allah, not to be influenced by anyone's reproach.' Some of the people who heard him, announced the impending death of the Qurayza before Sa'd Mu'adh reached them because of the words he had said."

Ishaq:463/Tabari VIII:34 "When Sa'd reached the Messenger of Allah and the Muslims, the Prophet said, 'Pass judgment on them.' Sa'd replied, 'I pass judgment that their men shall be killed, their women and children made captives, and their property divided.' Allah's Apostle proclaimed, 'You have passed judgment on the Jews with the judgment of Allah and the judgment of His Messenger.'"

Bukhari:V5B59N362 "So the Prophet killed the Qurayza men. He distributed their women, children and property among the Muslims."

Tabari VIII:39 "After the affair of the Qurayza ended, the wound of Sa'd broke open. He prayed saying, 'O Allah, You know that there are no men whom I would rather fight and kill than men who called Your Messenger a liar.'"

Qur'an 33:26 "Allah took down the People of the Scripture Book. He cast terror into their hearts. Some you slew, and some you made prisoners. And He made you heirs of their lands, their houses, and their goods, giving you a land which you had not traversed before." [Version two:] "And He drove the People of the Scripture down from their homes and cast panic into their hearts. Some you killed, and you made some captive. And He caused you to inherit their farms, houses, wealth, and land you have not trodden."

Ishaq:464 "The Jews were made to come down, and Allah's Messenger imprisoned them. Then the Prophet went out into the marketplace of Medina (it is still its marketplace today), and he had trenches dug in it. He sent for the Jewish men and had them beheaded in those trenches. They were brought out to him in batches. They numbered 800 to 900 boys and men. As they were being taken in small groups to the Prophet, they said to one another, 'What do you think will be done to us?' Someone said, 'Do you not understand. On each occasion do you not see that the summoner never stops? He does not discharge anyone. And that those who are taken away do not come back. By God, it is death!' The affair continued until the Messenger of Allah had finished with them all."

Tabari VIII:40 "Allah's Apostle commanded that furrows should be dug in the ground for the Qurayza. Then he sat down. Ali and Zubayr began cutting off their heads in his presence."

Tabari VIII:35/Ishaq:464 "Huyayy, the enemy of Allah, was brought out. He was wearing a rose-colored suit of clothes that he had torn all over with fingertip-sized holes so that it would not be taken as booty. His hands were bound to his neck with a rope. When he looked at Muhammad he said, 'I do not regret opposing you. Whoever forsakes God will be damned.' He sat down and was beheaded."

Ishaq:464/Tabari VIII:36 "According to Aisha, one Jewish woman was killed. She was by my side, talking with me while Allah's Messenger was killing her men in the marketplace."

Tabari VIII:38 "The Messenger of Allah commanded that all of the Jewish men and boys who had reached puberty should be beheaded. Then the Prophet divided the wealth, wives, and children of the Qurayza Jews among the Muslims." *Ishaq:465* "When their wrists were bound with cords, the Apostle was a sea of generosity to us."

Ishaq:465 "Then the Apostle divided the property, wives, and children of the Qurayza among the Muslims. Allah's Messenger took his fifth of the booty. He made known on that day the extra shares for horses and their riders—giving the horse two shares and the rider one. It was the first booty in which lots were cast."

Tabari VIII:38 "According to this example (Sunnah), the procedure of the Messenger of Allah in the divisions of booty became a precedent which was followed in subsequent raids."

Tabari VIII:39 "Then the Messenger of Allah sent Zayd with some of the Qurayza captives to Najd, and in exchange for them he purchased horses and arms."

Tabari VIII:38 "The Prophet selected for himself from among the Jewish women of the Qurayza, Rayhanah. She became his concubine. When he predeceased her, she was still in his possession. When the Messenger of Allah took her as a captive, she showed herself averse to Islam and insisted on Judaism."

Ishaq:466 "The Apostle chose one of the Jewish women for himself. Her name was Rayhanah. She remained with him until she died, in his power. The Apostle proposed to marry her and put the veil on her but she said, 'Leave me under your power, for that will be easier. She showed a repugnance towards Islam when she was captured."

Ishaq:466 "Allah sent down [a surah] concerning the Trench and Qurayza raid. The account is found in the Allied Troops. In it He mentions their trial and His kindness to the Muslims."

Ishaq:468 "Allah brought down the People of the Scripture Book. I forced the Qurayza from their homes and cast terror into their hearts. Some you slew, and some you took captive. You killed their men and enslaved their women and children. And I caused you to inherit their land, their dwellings, and their property. Allah can do all things.'"

Ishaq:479 "Slain in Allah's religion, Sa'd inherits Paradise with the martyrs. His was a noble testimony. When he pronounced his verdict on the Qurayza, he did not judge on his own volition. His judgment and Allah's were one. Sa'd is among those who sold his life for the Garden of Bliss." *Ishaq:469* "An Ansar [Muslim] recited this poem: 'The throne of Allah shook for only one man: Sa'd the brave and bold, a glorious leader, a knight ever ready. Stepping into the battle, he cut heads to pieces."

Ishaq:469 "On the day the Qurayza Jews were slain, one Muslim was martyred. A stone was thrown on him and it inflicted a shattering wound. The Apostle said, 'He will have the reward of two martyrs.'"

Ishaq:475 "Allah commanded that horses should be kept for His enemy in the fight so they might vex them. We obeyed our Prophet's orders when he called us to war. When he called for violent efforts we made them. The Prophet's command is obeyed for he is truly believed. He will give us victory, glory, and a life of ease. Those [Jews] who call Muhammad a liar disbelieve and go astray. They attacked our religion and would not submit."

Ishaq:481 "The Apostle slew them in their own town. With our troops he surrounded their homes. We shouted out cries in the heat of battle. The Jews were given the Scripture and wasted it. Being blind, [the illiterate man said] they strayed from the Torah. You Jews disbelieved the Qur'an and yet you have tasted the confirmation of what it said. May Allah make our raid on them immortal. May fire burn in their quarter. They will no longer ruin our lands. You [Jews] have no place here, so be off!"

Ishaq:480 "The Qurayza met their misfortune [now there's an understated word]. In humiliation they found no helper. A calamity worse than that which fell upon the Nadir befell them. On that day Allah's Apostle came to them like a brilliant moon. We left them with blood upon them like a pool. They lay prostrate with the vultures circling round."

CHRISTIANS:

Qur'an 5:17 "Verily they are disbelievers and infidels who say, 'The Messiah, son of Mary, is God.'"

Qur'an 5:51 "Believers, take not Jews and Christians for your friends. They are but friends and protectors to each other."

Qur'an 5:72 "They are surely infidels who blaspheme and say: 'God is Christ, the Messiah, the son of Mary.' But the Messiah only said: 'O Children of Israel! Worship Allah, my Lord and your Lord.'"

Qur'an 74:31 "We have appointed nineteen angels to be the wardens of the Hell Fire. We made a stumbling-block for those who disbelieve and We have fixed their number as a trial for unbelievers in order that the People of the Book may arrive with certainty, and that no doubts may be left for the People of the Book, those in whose hearts is a disease."

Ishaq:180 "According to my information, the Apostle often sat by a young Christian slave named Jabr. The Meccans said, 'He is the one who teaches Muhammad most of what he brings.' Then Allah revealed, *Qur'an 16:103* 'We know what they (pagans) say: "It is only a mortal man who teaches him (Muhammad). But the tongue of the man they wickedly point to is notably foreign, while this (Qur'an) is pure Arabic.'"

Qur'an 72:15 "But the Qasitun (disbelievers) are the firewood of hell."

Qur'an 88:1 "Has the narration reached you of the overwhelming (calamity)? Some faces (Jews and Christians) that Day, will be humiliated, downcast, scorched by the burning fire, while they are made to drink from a boiling hot spring."

Qur'an 9:29 "Fight those who do not believe in Allah or the Last Day, who do not forbid that which has been forbidden by Allah and His Messenger, or acknowledge the Religion of Truth (Islam), (even if they are) People of the Book (Christians and Jews), until they pay the Jizyah tribute tax in submission, feeling themselves subdued and brought low." [Another translation says:] "pay the tax in acknowledgment of our superiority and their state of subjection."

Ishaq:552 "The Quraysh had put pictures in the Ka'aba including two of Jesus and one of

Mary. Muhammad ordered that the pictures should be erased."

Qur'an 5:14 "From those, too, who call themselves Christians, We made a covenant, but they forgot and abandoned a good part of the message that was sent them: so we estranged them, stirred up enmity and hatred among them to the Day of Doom. Soon will Allah show them the handiwork they have done."

Qur'an 5:15 "O People of the Book! There has come to you Our Apostle, revealing to you much that you used to hide in your Scripture, suppressing and passing over much. There has come to you from Allah a (new) light (Muhammad) and a clear Book [the Qur'an]."

Qur'an 5:17 "...Say (Muhammad): 'Who then has the least power against Allah, if His will were to destroy Christ, the Messiah, the son of Mary, his mother, and everyone else on earth?"

Qur'an 5:18 "The Jews and the Christians say: 'We are sons of Allah, and his beloved.' Say: 'Why then does He punish you for your sins? Nay, you are but men. He forgives whom He wishes and punishes whom He pleases.'"

Qur'an 5:35 "Believers, fear Allah and seek the way to approach Him, striving hard, fighting Jihad with all your might in His Cause that you may be successful. As for the disbelievers [previously defined as Christians], if they had everything on earth, two times over, to give as ransom for the penalty of the Day of Doom, it would never be accepted from them. Theirs will be a painful torment. They will desire to get out of the fire, but they shall not be released from it. They shall have an everlasting torture."

Qur'an 5:47 "Let the people of the Gospel judge by what Allah has revealed therein. If any fail to judge by what Allah has revealed, they are (no better than) those who rebel."

Qur'an 5:48 "To you [Christians] We sent the Scripture in truth, confirming the scripture that came before it, and guarding it in safety: so judge between them by what Allah has revealed."

Qur'an 5:49 "And this (He commands): Judge between them by what Allah has revealed and follow not their [Christian] desires, but beware of them lest they beguile you, seducing you away from any of that which Allah hath sent down to you. And if they turn you away [from being Muslims], be assured that for their crime it is Allah's purpose to smite them. Truly most men are rebellious."

Qur'an 5:57 "Believers, take not for friends those who take your religion for a mockery or sport, a joke, whether among those who received the Scripture before you or among those who reject Faith; but fear Allah."

Qur'an 5:68 "Say: 'People of the Scripture Book! You have no ground to stand upon unless you observe the Taurat [Torah], the Injeel [Gospel], and all the Revelation that has come to you from your Lord.' It is certain to increase their rebellion and blasphemy. But grieve you not over unbelieving people."

Qur'an 5:72 "...Lo! Whoever joins other gods with Allah or says He has a partner, Allah has forbidden Paradise, and the Hell Fire will be his abode. There will for the wrong-doers be no one to help." *Qur'an 5:73* "They are surely disbelievers who blaspheme and say: 'God is one of three in the Trinity for there is no Ilah (God) except One, Allah. If they desist not from saying this (blasphemy), verily a grievous penalty will befall them—the disbelievers will suffer a painful doom."

Qur'an 5:75 "The Messiah, Christ, the son of Mary, was no more than a messenger; many were the messengers that passed away before him. His mother was a woman of truth. They had to eat their food. See how Allah does make His signs clear to them; yet see in what ways they are deluded!"

Qur'an 4:157 "'We [Jews] killed the Messiah, Jesus,' but they killed him not, nor crucified him. It appeared so to them (as the resemblance of Jesus was put over another man and they killed that man). Nay, Allah raised him up unto Himself. Those who differ with this version are full of doubts. They have no knowledge and follow nothing but conjecture. For surely they killed him not."

Qur'an 4:171 "O People of the Book! Do not exaggerate in your religion; nor speak lies of Allah. The Messiah, Christ Jesus, the son of Mary was (no more than) a messenger of Allah, and His Word, which He bestowed on Mary, and a Spirit proceeding from Him. So believe in Allah and His messengers. Say not 'Trinity.' Cease and Desist: (it is) better for you: for Allah is one Ilah (God). (Far it is removed from him of) having a son. To Him belong all things in the heavens and on earth. And enough is Allah as a Disposer of affairs. The Messiah is proud to be a slave of Allah, as are the angels, those nearest. Those who disdain His worship and are arrogant. He will gather them all together unto Himself to (answer)…. He will punish with a painful doom; Nor will they find, besides Allah, any to protect or save them." *Qur'an 4:159* "And there is none of the People of the Book but will believe in him (Jesus as only a messenger of Allah and a human being) before his (Jesus') death. He will be a witness against them."

Qur'an 5:77 "Say (Muhammad): 'People of the Book, do not overstep the bounds in your religion, or follow the people who erred and led many astray. Cursed are the unbelievers among the Children of Israel by David and Jesus…. They do vile things, allying themselves with the infidels so that Allah's indignation is upon them and in torment they will suffer for all eternity." [Another translation reads:] "Curses were pronounced on the unbelievers, the Children of Israel who rejected Islam, by the tongues of David and of Jesus because they disobeyed and rebelled."

Qur'an 5:80 "You see many of them allying themselves with the unbelieving infidels. Vile indeed are their souls. Allah's wrath is on them, and in torment will they abide." *Qur'an 5:81* "If only they had believed in Allah, in the Prophet, and in what had been revealed to him."

Qur'an 5:82 "You will find the Jews and disbelievers [defined as Christians in 5:73] the most vehement in hatred for the Muslims."

Qur'an 5:110 "And God will say: 'O Jesus! Recount My favor to you and to your mother. Behold! I strengthened you with the Holy Spirit so that you spoke to the people in the cradle and in the prime of life. Behold! I taught you the law and the judgment, the Torah and the Gospel. And behold, you made out of clay, as it were, the figure of a bird and you breathed into it and it became a bird by My permission. And you healed those born blind by My permission and the lepers by My permission. And behold! You raised forth the dead by My permission. And behold! I did restrain the Jews from harming you when you came with clear proofs. And the unbelievers among the Jews said: 'This is nothing but magic.'"

Qur'an 5:111 "Behold! I inspired the [Christian] disciples to have faith in Me and My Messenger. They said, 'We are believers, and bear witness that we prostrate ourselves to Allah as Muslims.'" *Qur'an 5:112* "Behold! The disciples, said: 'O Jesus, can your Lord send down to us a table well laid out from heaven?' Said Jesus: 'Fear Allah, if you have faith.' When the disciples said: 'O Jesus, son of Mary, is your Lord able to send down for us a table spread with food from heaven?' He said: "Observe your duty to Allah, if you are true believers.'" *Qur'an 5:113* "They said: 'We only wish to eat thereof to satisfy our hearts, and to know that you have told us the truth. We want to witnesses a miracle.' Said Jesus, the son of Mary: 'O Allah our Lord! Send us from heaven a table well laid out, that there may be for us a feast, a Sign from you." *Qur'an 5:115* "Allah said: 'I am going to send it down unto you, but if any of you after that disbelieves, resisting Faith [Islam], I will punish him with a torment such as I have not inflicted on any one of my creatures, man or jinn. I will punish them with a torment such as I have not inflicted on any one of my creatures."

Qur'an 5:116 "And behold! Allah will say: 'O Jesus, the son of Mary! Did you say unto men, worship me and my mother as two gods besides Allah?' He will say: 'Glory to You! Never could I utter what I had no right." *Qur'an 5:117* "I only said what You (Allah) commanded me to say: Worship Allah, my lord and your Lord. I was a witness over them while I dwelt amongst them but you took me up. (This is a great admonition and warning to the Christians of the whole world.)"

Tabari IX:15 "One of the Ansari who was plundering the slain came upon a Thaqif boy. He discovered that he was an uncircumcised Christian. He uncovered others and then yelled out at the top of his voice, 'Allah knows that the Thaqif are uncircumcised."

Tabari IX:86 "Don't seduce the Jews or Christians for incumbent on them is to pay the jizyah protection tax."

Bukhari:V2B23N414 "The Prophet in his fatal illness said, "Allah cursed Jews and Christians because they took their Prophets' graves as places for praying.'"

Bukhari:V5B59N727 "When Allah's Apostle became seriously sick, he started covering his face with a woolen sheet. When he felt short of breath, he removed it, and said, 'That is so! Allah's curse be on Jews and Christians.'"

Bukhari:V4B55N607 "Allah's Apostle said, 'On the night of my Ascension to Heaven, I saw Jesus with a red face as if he had just come out of a bathroom. And I resemble Abraham more than any of his offspring.'"

Qur'an 2:111 "They say: 'None shall enter Paradise unless he be a Jew or a Christian.' Those are their (vain) desires. Say: 'Produce your proof if you are truthful.' Nay, whoever submits His face to Allah and surrenders, he will get his reward; on such shall be no fear, nor shall they grieve. The Jews say: 'The Christians follow nothing; and the Christians say: 'the Jews follow nothing (true);' Yet they (profess to) recite the (same) Scripture Book. But Allah will judge between them in their quarrel."

Qur'an 9:30 "The Jews call Uzair the son of Allah, and the Christians say that the Messiah is the son of Allah. That is their saying from their mouths; they but imitate what the unbelievers of old used to say. Allah's (Himself) fights against them, cursing them, damning and destroying them. How perverse are they!"

Qur'an 9:31 "They (Jews and Christians) consider their rabbis and monks to be gods besides Allah. They also took their Lord Messiah to be a god but they were commanded (in the Taurat and Injeel) to worship only One Ilah (God). There is no ilah (god) but He. Too holy is He for the partners they associate (with Him)."

Qur'an 9:34 "Believers, there are many (Christian) monks and (Jewish) rabbis who in falsehood devour the wealth of mankind and hinder (men) from the way of Allah. And there are those who bury gold and silver and spend it not in Allah's Cause. (Muhammad) announce unto them tidings of a painful torture. On the Day [of Doom] heat will be produced out of that (wealth) in the Fire of Hell. It will be branded on their foreheads, their flanks, and their backs. 'This is the (treasure) which you hoarded for yourselves: now taste it!'"

Qur'an 2:116 "They say: 'Allah hath begotten a son: glory be to Him.' Nay, to Him belongs all that is in heavens and on earth: All are subservient and obedient to Him."

Qur'an 2:145 "Even if you were to bring to the people of the Scripture Book all the Signs, they would not follow Your Qiblah; nor are you going to follow their Qiblah; nor indeed will they follow each other's Qiblah." *Qur'an 2:146* "The People of the Book, unto whom We gave the Scripture, know/recognize this revelation/him as they know/recognize their own sons; But lo! a party of them knowingly conceals truth."

Qur'an 2:71 "The semblance of the infidels is one who shouts to one who cannot hear. They are deaf, dumb, and blind. They make no sense." *Qur'an 2:174* "Those who conceal Allah's revelations in the [Bible] Scripture Book, and thus make a miserable profit thereby [selling it to Muhammad], swallow Fire into themselves; Allah will not address them. Grievous will be their doom." *Qur'an 2:175* "They are the ones who bartered away guidance for error and Torment in place of Forgiveness. Ah, what boldness (they show) for the Fire! (Their doom is) because Allah sent down the Book in truth but those who seek causes of dispute in the Book are in a schism of great opposition."

Tabari VIII:98 "Between the truce of Hudaybiyah and his death, the Messenger dispersed his Companions with letters. 'I have been sent as a mercy and for all. Therefore, convey the message from me, and Allah shall have mercy on you. Do not become disobedient to me as the Disciples became disobedient to Jesus. He called them to the like of what I called you to. Those whom he sent close by were pleased and accepted; those whom he sent far off were refused. Jesus complained of their behavior to Allah, and when they awoke the next morning, each could speak the language of the people to whom he had been sent. Then Jesus said, 'This is an affair that Allah has determined for you; so go forth!'"

Qur'an 8:50 "If you could have seen the infidels when the angels drew away their souls, striking their faces and smiting their backs. The angels said: 'Taste the penalty of the blazing Fire.'"

Qur'an 8:52 "They brought this on themselves. Their case is like that of Pharaoh and of those before them. They denied and rejected the revelations of Allah, and Allah destroyed them, punishing them for their crimes: for Allah is strict, severe in punishment."

Qur'an 61:6 "And Jesus, the son of Mary, said: 'Children of Israel, I am the Messenger of Allah (sent) to you, confirming that (which was revealed) before me in the Torah, and giving Glad Tidings of a Messenger to come after me, whose name shall be Ahmad, the Praised One.'

But when he came to them with Clear Signs, they said, 'this is sorcery!'"

Qur'an 61:14 "O Muslims! Be helpers of Allah: As Jesus the son of Mary said to the Disciples, 'Who will be my helpers (in the Cause) of Allah?' Said the disciples, 'We are Allah's helpers!' Then a portion of the Children of Israel believed, and a portion disbelieved: But We gave power to those who believed against their enemies, and they became the victorious."

Qur'an 3:37 "Mariam was given into the care of Zacharyah. Whenever he came to see her in her chamber he found her provided with food, and he asked, 'Where has this come from Mary?' She said, 'From Allah who gives in abundance to whomsoever He will. Zacharyah prayed, 'Bestow on me offspring that is good [i.e., not a girl]. As he stood in the chamber the angels said, 'Allah sends you tidings of Yahya (John) who will confirm a thing from Allah (the creation of Isa (Jesus), the Word of Allah) and be a noble prophet, one who is upright and does good [a Muslim]." *Qur'an 3:42* "Behold! the angels said: 'Mariam! Allah has chosen you and purified you above the women of all nations and creation (including jinn). Mary! submit with obedience to your Lord (Allah). Prostrate yourself, and bow down with those [Muslims] who bow down." *Qur'an 3:44* "This is part of the tidings of the things unseen, which you have no knowledge and We reveal unto you (Messenger!) by inspiration. You were not with them when they cast lots with arrows, as to which of them should be charged with the care of Mariam. Nor were you with them when they disputed."

Qur'an 3:45 "Behold, the angels said: 'O Mariam! Allah gives you glad tidings of a Word from Him: his name will be the Messiah, Isa (Jesus), the son of Mariam, held in honor in this world and the Hereafter and of those nearest to Allah."

Qur'an 4.171 "O people of the Book (Christians), do not be fanatical in your faith, and say nothing but the truth about Allah. The Messiah who is Isa (Jesus), son of Mariam, was only a messenger of Allah, nothing more. He bestowed His Word on Mariam and His Spirit. So believe in Allah and say not Trinity for Allah is one Ilah (God)...far be it from His Glory to beget a son."

Qur'an 3:46 "And he shall speak to the people when in the cradle and when of old age, and shall be one of the good ones."

Bukhari:V4B55N645 "The Prophet said, 'None spoke in cradle but three: The first was Jesus, the second was an Israeli called Juraij. While he was offering his prayers, his mother called him. He said, "Shall I answer her or keep on praying?" He went on praying and did not answer her. His mother said, "O Allah! Do not let him die till he sees the faces of prostitutes."

Qur'an 3:47 "Mary said: 'O my Lord! How shall I have a son when no man has touched me?' He said: 'Even so: Allah creates what He wills: When He has decreed a plan, He but says to it, 'Be,' and it is!" *Qur'an 3:48* "And Allah will teach him the Scripture Book and Wisdom, the Torah and the Gospel, and appoint him a messenger to the Children of Israel, with this message: 'Lo! I come unto you with a Sign from your Lord. Lo! I fashion for you out of clay the likeness of a bird, and I breathe into it and it is a bird, by Allah's leave. I heal him who was born blind, and the leper, and I raise the dead, by Allah's leave." [As if reading a different Arabic text, the Ali translation says:] "He will teach him the Law and the Judgment, the Torah and the Gospel, and he will be Apostle to the children of Israel, (saying) 'I have come to you with a prodigy from your Lord that I will fashion the state of destiny out of the mire for you and breathe (a new spirit) into it, and (you) will rise by the will of Allah."

Bukhari:V4B55N657 "Allah's Messenger said, 'Isa (Jesus), the son of Mariam, will shortly descend amongst you Muslims and will judge mankind by the law of the Qur'an. He will break the cross and kill the swine [Jews] and there will be no Jizyah tax taken from non-Muslims. Money will be so abundant no one will accept it. So you may recite this Holy Verse: "Isa (Jesus) was just a human being before his death. On the Day of Resurrection he (Jesus) will be a witness against the Christians."'"

Bukhari:V4B55N658 "Allah's Apostle said 'How will you be when the son of Mary (i.e. Jesus) descends amongst you and he will judge people by the Law of the Qur'an and not by the law of Gospel.'"

Bukhari:V4B55N651-2 "I heard Allah's Apostle saying, 'I am the nearest of all the people to Jesus. There has been no prophet between me and Jesus. All the prophets are paternal brothers; their mothers are different, but their religion is one.'"

Qur'an 3:50 "(I [Isa/Jesus] have come) to attest the Torah which was before me. And to make lawful to you part of what was forbidden; I have come to you with a Sign from your Lord. So fear Allah, and obey me. Lo! Allah is my Lord and your Lord, so worship Him. That is a straight path."

Bukhari:V4B56N814 "There was a Christian who embraced Islam and he used to write the revelations for the Prophet. Later on he returned to Christianity again he used to say: 'Muhammad knows nothing but what I have written for him.'"

Qur'an 3:52 "But when Jesus became conscious of their disbelief, he cried: 'Who will be my helpers in the Allah's Cause? The disciples said: We will be Allah's helpers. We believe in Allah, and do you bear witness that we are Muslims." *Qur'an 3:54* "And they (the disciples from the previous verse) schemed, and Allah schemed and plotted (against them): and Allah is the best of schemers." [Another translation reads:] *Qur'an 3:54* "'Lord, we believe in Your revelations [the Torah and Gospels] and follow this Apostle [Jesus]. Enroll us among the witnesses.' But the Christians contrived a plot and Allah did the same; but Allah's plot was the best." [A third translation says that "they" refers to "disbelievers," not the disciples and they plotted to kill Jesus.] "And they (disbelievers) plotted (to kill Isa [Jesus]) and Allah plotted too."

Qur'an 3:55 "Allah said, 'Jesus, I will take you and raise you to Myself and rid you of the infidels (who have forged the lie that you are My son).... Those who are infidels will surely receive severe torment both in this world and the next; and none will they have as a savior for them." [Interesting, considering...] *Qur'an 5:72* "They are surely infidels who say; 'God is the Christ, the Messiah, the son of Mary." [Another translation reads:] *Qur'an 3:55* "Behold! Allah said: 'O Jesus! I will take you and raise you to Myself and clear you (of the falsehoods) of those who blaspheme; I will make those who follow you superior to those who reject faith. Then shall you all return unto me, and I will judge between you on the matters wherein you dispute." [Another:] "(Remember) when Allah said: 'Jesus! Lo! I am gathering you and causing you to ascend unto Me. I am cleansing you of those who disbelieve." [A fourth reads:] "When Allah said: 'Jesus, I am going to terminate the period of your stay (on earth) and cause you to ascend unto Me and purify you of those who disbelieve.... I will decide between you concerning that which you differed."

Qur'an 3:56 "As for those disbelieving infidels, I will punish them with a terrible agony in this world and the next. They have no one to help or save them." *Qur'an 3:58* "This is what We rehearse to you of the Signs and Message, a wise reminder. The similitude (likeness) of Jesus before Allah is as that of Adam; He created him from dust, then said to him: 'Be.' And he was." *Qur'an 3:60* "The Truth (comes) from Allah alone. So be not of those who doubt, waver or dispute. If any one disputes in this matter with you, now after knowledge has come to you, say: 'Come! Let us gather together our sons and women among ourselves. Then let us earnestly pray, and invoke the curse of Allah on those who lie!'"

Qur'an 3:61 "If anyone disputes with you about Jesus being divine, flee them and pray that Allah will curse them." *Qur'an 3:62* "This is the true account, the true explanation: There is no Ilah (God) except Allah; and Allah—He is the Mighty, the Wise. And if they turn away, then lo! Allah is aware of the corrupters, the mischief-makers. Say: 'O People of the Book, come to common terms as an agreement between us and you: That we all shall worship none but Allah; that we associate no partners with him; and that none of us shall take others for lords beside Allah.' If then they turn back, say you: 'Bear witness that we (at least) are Muslims surrendered."

Qur'an 3:67 "Abraham was not a Jew nor yet a Christian; but he was a true Muslim, surrendered to Allah (which is Islam), and he joined not gods with Allah." *Qur'an 3:69* "It is the wish of the followers of the People of the Book to lead you astray. But they make none to go astray except themselves, but they perceive not. You People of the Book! Why reject you the signs, proofs, and verses of Allah, of which you are witnesses? You People of the Book! Why do you clothe Truth with falsehood, and conceal the Truth?"

Qur'an 3:118 "O you who believe! Take not into your intimacy those outside your religion (pagans, Jews, and Christians). They will not fail to corrupt you. They only desire your ruin. Rank hatred has already appeared from their mouths. What their hearts conceal is far worse. When they are alone, they bite off the very tips of their fingers at you in their rage. Say unto them: 'Perish in your rage.'"

Qur'an 4:48 "Allah forgives not that partners [Christ as God] should be set up with Him; but He forgives anything else, to whom He please; to set up partners with Allah is to devise a sin most heinous." *Qur'an 4:50* "Behold! how they invent lies against Allah! That is flagrant sin."

Qur'an 4:51 "Have you not seen those to whom a portion of the Book has been given? They believe in sorcery and false deities and say of those who disbelieve: these are better guided than those who believe. They are (men) whom Allah has cursed: And those whom Allah has cursed, you will find that they have no savior."

Qur'an 4:54 "Are they jealous and envious what Allah has given them of his bounty? But We had already given the house of Abraham the Book, and conferred upon them a grand kingdom. Some of them believed, and some of them averted their faces from him. And Hell is sufficient for their burning. Those who reject our Signs, We shall soon cast into the Fire. As often as their skin is burnt and singed, roasted through, We shall change it for fresh skin, so that they may go on tasting the torment."

RACISM:

Ishaq:243 "I heard the Apostle say: 'Whoever wants to see Satan should look at Nabtal!' He was a black man with long flowing hair, inflamed eyes, and dark ruddy cheeks.... Allah sent down concerning him: 'To those who annoy the Prophet there is a painful doom." [9:61] "Gabriel came to Muhammad and said, 'If a black man comes to you his heart is more gross than a donkey's.'"

Ishaq:144 "A rock was put on a slave's chest. When Abu Bakr complained, they said, 'You are the one who corrupted him, so save him from his plight.' I will do so,' said Bakr. 'I have a black slave, tougher and stronger than Bilal, who is a heathen. I will exchange him. The transaction was carried out."

Qur'an 9:97 "The Arabs of the desert are the worst in unbelief and hypocrisy, and most fitted to be in ignorance of the command which Allah hath sent down to His Messenger."

Tabari II:11 "Shem, the son of Noah was the father of the Arabs, the Persians, and the Greeks; Ham was the father of the Black Africans; and Japheth was the father of the Turks and of Gog and Magog who were cousins of the Turks. Noah prayed that the prophets and apostles would be descended from Shem and kings would be from Japheth. He prayed that the African's color would change so that their descendants would be slaves to the Arabs and Turks."

Tabari II:21 "Ham [Africans] begat all those who are black and curly-haired, while Japheth [Turks] begat all those who are full-faced with small eyes, and Shem [Arabs] begat everyone who is handsome of face with beautiful hair. Noah prayed that the hair of Ham's descendants would not grow beyond their ears, and that whenever his descendants met Shem's, the latter would enslave them."

Tabari IX:69 "Arabs are the most noble people in lineage, the most prominent, and the best in deeds. We were the first to respond to the call of the Prophet. We are Allah's helpers and the viziers of His Messenger. We fight people until they believe in Allah. He who believes in Allah and His Messenger has protected his life and possessions from us. As for one who disbelieves, we will fight him forever in Allah's Cause. Killing him is a small matter to us."

Bukhari: V9B89N256 "Allah's Apostle said, 'You should listen to and obey your ruler even if he is a black African slave whose head looks like a raisin.'"

Ishaq:405 "It is your folly to fight the Apostle, for Allah's army is bound to disgrace you. We brought them to the pit. Hell was their meeting place. We collected them there, black slaves, men of no descent. *Ishaq:374* "The black troops and slaves of the Meccans cried out and the Muslims replied, 'Allah destroy your sight, you impious rascals.'"

Bukhari:V4B52N137 "The Prophet said, 'Let the negro slave of Dinar perish. And if he is pierced with a thorn, let him not find anyone to take it out for him.... If he [the black slave] asks for anything it shall not be granted, and if he needs intercession [to get into paradise], his intercession will be denied.'"

WOMEN IN ISLAM:

Tabari IX:113 "Allah permits you to shut them in separate rooms and to beat them, but not severely. If they abstain, they have the right to food and clothing. Treat women well for they are like domestic animals and they possess nothing themselves. Allah has made the enjoyment of their bodies lawful in his Qur'an."

Tabari I:280 "Allah said, 'It is My obligation to make Eve bleed once every month as she made this tree bleed. I must also make Eve stupid, although I created her intelligent.' Because Allah afflicted Eve, all of the women of this world menstruate and are stupid."

Qur'an 4:3 "If you fear that you shall not be able to deal justly with orphans, marry women of your choice who seem good to you, two or three or four; but if you fear that you shall not be able to do justice (to so many), then only one, or (a slave) that you possess, that will be more suitable. And give the women their dower as a free gift; but if they, of their own good pleasure, remit any part of it to you, eat it with enjoyment, take it with right good cheer and absorb it (in your wealth)."

Qur'an 4:11 "Allah directs you in regard of your Children's (inheritance): to the male, a portion equal to that of two females.... These are settled portions ordained by Allah."

Bukhari:V1B22N28 "The Prophet said: 'I was shown the Hell Fire and the majority of its dwellers were women who are disbelievers or ungrateful.' When asked what they were ungrateful for, the Prophet answered, 'All the favors done for them by their husbands.'"

Muslim:B1N142 "'O womenfolk, you should ask for forgiveness for I saw you in bulk amongst the dwellers of Hell.' A wise lady said: Why is it, Allah's Apostle, that women comprise the bulk of the inhabitants of Hell? The Prophet observed: 'You curse too much and are ungrateful to your spouses. You lack common sense, fail in religion and rob the wisdom of the wise.' Upon this the woman remarked: What is wrong with our common sense? The Prophet replied, 'Your lack of common sense can be determined from the fact that the evidence of two women is equal to one man. That is a proof.'"

Qur'an 4:43 "Believers, approach not prayers with a mind befogged or intoxicated until you understand what you utter. Nor when you are polluted, until after you have bathed. If you are ill, or on a journey, or come from answering the call of nature, or you have touched a woman, and you find no water, then take for yourselves clean dirt, and rub your faces and hands. Lo! Allah is Benign, Forgiving." [The Qur'an claims women are unclean and polluted—worse than dirt.]

Bukhari:V4B55N547 "The Prophet said, 'But for the Israelis, meat would not decay, and if it were not for Eve, wives would never betray their husbands.'"

Qur'an 33:59 "Prophet! Tell your wives and daughters and all Muslim women to draw cloaks and veils all over their bodies (screening themselves completely except for one or two eyes to see the way). That will be better."

Qur'an 4:15 "If any of your women are guilty of lewdness, take the evidence of four witnesses from amongst you against them; if they testify, confine them to houses until death [by starvation] claims them."

Bukhari:V4B52N143/V5B59N523 "When we reached Khaybar, Muhammad said that Allah had enabled him to conquer them. It was then that the beauty of Safiyah was described to him. Her husband had been killed, so Allah's Apostle selected her for himself. He took her along with him till we reached a place called Sad where her menses were over and he took her for his wife, consummating his marriage to her, and forcing her to wear the veil.'"

Bukhari:V5B59N524 "The Muslims said among themselves, 'Will Safiyah be one of the Prophet's wives or just a lady captive and one of his possessions?'"

Ishaq:593 "From the captives of Hunayn, Allah's Messenger gave [his son-in-law] Ali a slave girl called Baytab and he gave [future Caliph] Uthman a slave girl called Zaynab and [future Caliph] Umar another."

Bukhari:V3B48N826 "The Prophet said, 'Isn't the witness of a woman equal to half of that of a man?' The women said, 'Yes.' He said, 'This is because of the deficiency of a woman's mind.'"

Ishaq:584 "Tell the men with you who have wives: never trust a woman."

Ishaq:185 "In hell I saw women hanging by their breasts. They had fathered bastards."

Qur'an 24:31 "Say to the believing women that they should lower their gaze and guard their modesty; that they should not display their beauty except what (must) appear; that they should draw their veils over their bosoms and not display them except to their husbands..."

Qur'an 24:34 "Force not your slave-girls to whoredom (prostitution) if they desire chastity, that you may seek enjoyment of this life. [And here's the freedom-to-pimp card:] But if anyone forces them, then after such compulsion, Allah is oft-forgiving."

Ishaq:469 "The Apostle said, 'Every wailing woman lies except those who wept for Sa'd.'"

Tabari VIII:62/Ishaq:496 "Ali [Muhammad's adopted son, son-in-law, and future Caliph] said, 'Prophet, women are plentiful. You can get a replacement, easily changing one for another.'"

Ishaq:496 "Ask the slave girl; she will tell you the truth.' So the Apostle called Burayra to ask her. Ali got up and gave her a violent beating first, saying, 'Tell the Apostle the truth.'"

Qur'an 24:1 "(This is) a surah which We have revealed and made obligatory and in which We have revealed clear communications that you may be mindful. For the woman and the man guilty of adultery or fornication, flog each of them with a hundred stripes. Let not compassion move you in their case, in a matter prescribed by Allah. And let a party of the Believers witness their punishment." *Qur'an 24:6* "And for those who launch a charge against their wives, accusing them, but have no witnesses or evidence, except themselves; let the testimony of one of them be four testimonies, (swearing four times) by Allah that he is the one speaking the truth."

STUPIDITY:

Bukhari:V6B61N550 "The Prophet said, 'It is a bad thing some of you say, "I have forgotten such-and-such verse of the Qur'an." For truly, I have been caused by Allah to forget it. So you must keep on reciting the Qur'an because it escapes faster than a runaway camel.'"

Tabari I:299 "Scholars of the nation of our Prophet say, 'The tree which Allah forbade Adam and his spouse to eat was wheat.'"

Tabari I:321 "When Eve became heavy with her first pregnancy, Satan came to her before she gave birth and said, 'Eve, what is that in your womb?' She said, 'I do not know.' He asked, 'Where will it come out from-your nose, your eye, or your ear?' She replied, 'I do not know.'"

Tabari I:299 "It was the cover of fingernails that had kept their secret parts concealed."

Tabari I:275 "Satan wanted to meet them in Paradise, but the keepers prevented him from entering. He went to a snake, an animal with four feet like a camel. Satan tried to persuade it to let him enter its mouth and take him to Adam. The snake agreed, passed by the keepers, and entered without their knowledge, because that was Allah's plan."

Tabari I:278 "Adam went inside the tree to hide. Eve cut the tree and it bled. Then feather that covered Adam and Eve dropped off. So Allah said, 'Now Eve, as you caused the tree to bleed, you will bleed every new moon, and you, snake, I will cut off your feet and you will walk slithering on your face.'"

Tabari I:279 "It was a tree which made whoever ate from it defecate. But there must be no faeces in Paradise."

Tabari I:281 "I heard him swear by Allah unequivocally, 'As long as Adam was in his right mind, he would never have eaten from the tree. Eve gave him wine and got him drunk. She led him to the tree."

Tabari I:267 "And Allah taught Adam all the names as follows: He taught him the name of everything, down to fart and little fart."

Bukhari:V1B4N137 "Allah's Apostle said, 'The prayer of a person who does Hadath (passes urine, stool or wind) is not accepted till he performs ablution.'"

Bukhari:V1B4N139 "I asked Allah's Apostle about a person who imagined they passed wind during prayer. He replied: 'He should not leave his prayer unless he hears sound or smells something.'"

Bukhari:V1B4N156 "The Prophet said, 'Whenever anyone makes water he should not hold his penis or clean his private parts with his right hand. While drinking, one should not breathe in the utensil.'"

Bukhari:V1B4N163 "The Prophet said, 'Whoever cleans his private parts with stones should do it with an odd number of stones. And whoever wakes up should wash his hands before putting them in the water for ablution. Nobody knows where his hands were during sleep.'"

Bukhari:V1B4N174 "During the lifetime of Allah's Apostle dogs used to urinate and pass through the mosque. Nevertheless they never used to sprinkle water on it."

Tabari I:367 "The Apostles said to Jesus, 'Would you send us a man who saw the ark and could tell us about it.' He took a handful of the earth in his palm and asked, 'Do you know what this is?' 'Allah and His prophet know best!' they replied. Jesus said, 'This is the grave of Noah's son, Ham.' He struck the hill with his staff and said, 'Rise with Allah's permission!' And behold there was Ham, with gray hair, shaking the earth from his head. Jesus asked him whether he had perished in that state with gray hair. Ham replied, 'No when I died, I was a young man, but I thought the Day of Doom had come, and my hair turned gray.' Jesus said, 'Tell us about Noah's ark.' He said, 'It was 1,200 cubits long [nearly 4,000 feet] and 600 cubits wide. It had three stories, one for domestic and wild animals, another for human beings, and a third for birds. When the dung of the animals became excessive, Allah inspired Noah to tickle the elephant's tail. He did, and a male and female hog fell down and attacked the dung. When the rat fell down into the seams of the planks of the ark and gnawed at them, Allah inspired Noah to strike the lion between its eyes and a male and female cat came out from its nose and attacked the rat.'"

Tabari I:360 "The first animal to be put aboard was the ant, and the last the donkey. When Noah brought the donkey in, Lucifer attached himself to its tail, so that it could not lift its legs. Noah started to say, 'Woe to you. Go in.' The donkey rose but was unable to move.

Noah said, 'Woe to you. Go in even if Satan is with you.' It was a slip of the tongue, but when Noah said it, Satan let the donkey proceed. It went in, and Satan went in with it. Noah said, 'How did you get in here with me?' Satan replied, 'You cannot escape from having me on board. Satan stayed in the rear of the boat. Noah also carried along Adam's corpse, making it a barrier between the women and men."

Tabari II:106 "Allah sent gnats against the Babylonians, and they ate their flesh and drank their blood, and nothing but their bones were left. But Allah gave Nimrod a single gnat which entered his nostril and went on beating the inside of his head with hammers for four hundred years. The most merciful of his friends was he who bunched up his hands and beat Nimrod's head with them."

Tabari II:107 "Nimrod vowed to seek out Abraham's God. So he took four eagle fledglings and nurtured them on meat and wine so that they grew up tough and strong. Then he tied them to a chest and sat in it. He suspended a piece of meat over them and they flew up trying to reach it. When they had risen high in the sky, Nimrod looked down and beheld the earth. He saw the mountains crawling below like creeping ants. When they had risen still higher he looked and saw the earth with a sea surrounding it. After climbing still higher, he came into a region of darkness and could not see what was above him nor what was below him. He became frightened and threw the meat down. The eagles followed it, darting downward. When the mountains saw them coming near and heard their noise, they became afraid and almost moved from their places, but did not do so. As Allah says in the Qur'an, 'Verily they have plotted their plot, and their plot is with Allah, even if their plot were one whereby the mountains should be moved.'"

Tabari II:78 "And everything that heard him-stones, trees, hills, and dust said, 'Here I am, my Allah, here I am.'"

Tabari II:99 "Abraham was tested with ten Islamic practices: rinsing the mouth, cleansing nostrils with water, trimming the mustache, using a toothstick, plucking the armpit, paring nails, washing finger joints, circumcision, shaving pubic hair, and washing the rear and vulva."

Qur'an 2:138 "(Our religion is) the Baptism of Allah: And who can baptize better than Allah?"

Tabari VI:21 "Qusayy purchased the custodianship of the Ka'aba for a skin full of wine and a lute."

Bukhari:V4B55N585 "'O Allah's Apostle! Which mosque was first built on the surface of the earth?' He said, 'The mosque Haram in Mecca.' 'Which was built next?' He replied 'The mosque of Al-Aqsa in Jerusalem.' 'What was the period of construction between the two?' He said, 'Forty years.'"

Tabari VI:66 "Umar said, 'By Allah I was by one of the idols of the Jahiliyyah. An Arab sacrificed a calf to it, and we were waiting for it to be divided up in order to receive a share. I heard coming from the belly of the calf a voice which was more penetrating than any I've heard. The dead calf's belly said, 'There is no ilah but Allah.'"

Ishaq:85 "The people were afraid to demolish the temple and withdrew in terror from it. Al-Walid said, 'I will begin the demolition.' He took up his pickaxe and walked up to Allah's House saying, 'O Ka'aba, do not be afraid. O Allah we intend nothing but good.' The he demolished part of it near the two corners."

Bukhari:V4B54N52 "The Prophet said, 'Kill the snake with two white lines on its back, for it blinds the onlooker and causes abortion.'"

Tabari VI:75 "'Messenger, how did you first know with absolute certainty that you were a prophet?' He replied, 'Two angels came to me while I was somewhere in Mecca.... One angel said, "Open his breast and take out his heart." He opened my chest and heart, removing the pollution of Satan and a clot of blood, and threw them away. Then one said, "Wash his breast as you would a receptacle." He summoned the Sakinah, which looked like the face of a white cat, and it was placed in my heart. Then one said, "Sew up his breast." So they sewed up my chest and placed the seal between my shoulders.'"

Qur'an 33:69 "Believers, be not like those who annoyed Moses. Allah proved his innocence of that which they alleged." *Bukhari:V4B55N616* "Allah's Apostle said, 'The Prophet Moses was a shy person and used to cover his body. An Israeli insulted him, saying, "He covers it because of some defect like leprosy or scrotal hernia." Allah wished to clear Moses of this allegation, so one day he took off his clothes, put them on a stone and started taking a bath. When he moved towards his clothes the stone took them and fled. Moses picked up his staff and ran after the stone saying, "O stone! Give me back my clothes!" He reached some Israelis who saw him naked, and found him to be the best of what Allah had created. The stone stopped there and Moses took his garments and started hitting the stone with his stick. By Allah, the stone still has some traces of the hitting, three, four or five marks. This was what Allah meant when he revealed the surah saying: "Believers! Be you not like those who annoyed Moses. Allah proved his innocence of that which they alleged."'"

Bukhari:V7B71N643 "I heard the Prophet saying, 'If anyone of you dreams something he dislikes, when you get up, blow thrice on your left.'"

Bukhari:V9B87N115 "If you spit on the left side of your bed the bad dream will not harm you."

Bukhari:V6B60N373 "The Prophet explained, 'Paradise and Hell argued.... Allah said to the Hell Fire, "You are my (means of) punishment by which I torment whoever I wish of my slaves. You will have your fill. As for the Fire, it will not be filled until I put My Foot over it.'"

Bukhari:V7B71N590 "The climate of Medina did not suit some people so the Prophet ordered them to drink camel urine as a medicine."

Bukhari:V7B71N592 "I heard Allah's Apostle saying, 'There is healing in black cumin for all diseases except death.'"

Bukhari:V7B71N673 "Allah's Apostle said, 'If a fly falls in your drink, dip all of it into the cup and then throw it away, for in one of its wings there is a disease and in the other there is healing, an antidote or treatment for that disease.'"

Qur'an 49:12 "Spy not behind the backs of others. Would any of you like to eat the flesh of his dead brother?"

Ishaq:565 "The Apostle sent Khalid to destroy the idol Al-Uzza in the lowland of Nakhlah. The Quraysh used to venerate her temple. When Sulami heard of Khalid's approach, he hung his sword on Al-Uzza, climbed a mountain, and shouted: 'O Uzza, make an annihilating attack on Khalid. Throw aside your veil and gird up your train. O Uzza, if you do not kill Khalid then bear a swift punishment or become a Christian.' When Khalid arrived he destroyed her and returned to the Apostle." *Tabari VIII:187* "'I have destroyed it,' he said to

Muhammad. 'Did you see anything?' 'No.' 'Then,' Muhammad said, 'go back and kill her.' So Khalid returned to the idol. He destroyed her temple and broke her graven image. The shrine's keeper began saying, 'Rage, O Uzza, display one of your fits of rage!' Whereupon a naked, wailing Ethiopian woman came out before him. Khalid killed her and took the jewels that were on her. Then he went back to Allah's Messenger and gave him a report. 'That was Al-Uzza,' Muhammad said. 'Al-Uzza will never be worshiped again.'"

Bukhari:V1B3N68 "Muhammad used to take care of us in preaching by selecting a suitable time, so that we might not get bored. He abstained from pestering us with sermons and knowledge."

Muslim:B40N6837 "Allah's Messenger delivered an address, mentioning a camel and a bad person who cut off its hind legs, reciting: 'When the basest of them broke forth with mischief.' He then delivered instruction saying: 'There are amongst you those who beat their women. They flog them like slave girls. Then after flogging them like slaves they comfort them in their beds as a result at the end of the day.' He then advised in regard to people laughing at the breaking of wind and said: 'You laugh at that which you yourself do.'"

Bukhari:V3B33N254 "Satan circulates in human beings as blood flows in our bodies."

Tabari II:121 "Gabriel spread out his wings and gouged out their eyes. Gabriel seized Sodom's girdle, snatching it up so high into the sky the angels could hear their dogs. He threw rocks at the laggards, one after the other. There were three towns called Sodom that lay between Medina and Syria. It has been mentioned that there were four million people in the town."

Qur'an 79:1 "I swear by those (angels) who violently tear out (the souls), and drag them forth to destruction, by those who gently take out, by those meteors rushing by, swimming along (angels or planets), and by those who press forward as in a race (the angels, or stars, or horses [the translators added, clueless as to what "god" was trying to say]), and by those who regulate the affair."

Bukhari:V7B71N665 "The Prophet said, 'No contagious disease is conveyed without Allah's permission.'" *Bukhari:V4B54N484* "I heard the Prophet saying, 'Fever is from the heat of the Hell Fire.'" *Bukhari:V8B77N616* "Allah's Apostle said, 'Plague is a means of torture which Allah sends upon whom-so-ever He wishes.'"

Qur'an 38:17 "We endued Our slave David with power. It was We who subdued the hills to sing Our praises with him at nightfall. And the birds were assembled, all obedient to him."

Qur'an 89:6 "Saw you not how your Lord dealt with [the mythical] Ad, possessors of lofty buildings, the likes of which were not produced in all the land?"

Qur'an 91:11 "Thamud rejected (their prophet) through inordinate wrong-doing. Behold, the most-wicked wretch among them broke forth but the Messenger said: 'Be cautious. It is a She-camel of Allah! And bar her not from having her drink!' But they rejected him as a false prophet and hamstrung her. So Allah on account of their crime, obliterated their traces, doomed them, desolated their dwellings, leveling them to the ground for their sin."

Qur'an 78:37 "The Lord with Whom they cannot dare to speak, none can converse with Him, none are able to address Him."

Qur'an 86:13 "Lo this (Qur'an) is a conclusive Word; it is not a thing for amusement. It is no pleasantry. And it is no joke."

ISLAMIC SCIENCE:

Bukhari:V4B55N546 "Allah's Apostle said, 'Gabriel has just now told me of the answer. If a man has sexual intercourse with his wife and gets discharge first, the child will resemble him, and if the woman gets discharge first, the child will resemble her.'"

Tabari I:258/Qur'an 15:26 "Allah created Adam from sticky clay, meaning viscous and sweet smelling slime, being stinking. It became stinking slime after having been compact soil."

Qur'an 80:17 "Be cursed man! He has self-destructed. From what stuff did He create him? From nutfa (male and female semen drops) He created him and set him in due proportion."

Tabari I:258 "Allah sent Gabriel to the earth to bring Him some clay. The earth said, 'I take refuge in Allah against you mutilating me. Then He sent the angel of death. He took some soil from the earth and made a mixture. He did not take it from a single place but took red, white, and black soil. Therefore, the children of Adam came out different."

Bukhari:V4B54N430 "Allah's Apostle, the true and truly inspired said, 'Regarding the matter of the creation of a human being: humans are put together in the womb of the mother in forty days. Then he becomes a clot of thick blood for a similar period. He becomes a piece of flesh for forty days. Then Allah sends an angel who is ordered to write four things: the new creature's deeds, livelihood, date of death, and whether he will be blessed or wretched. He will do whatever is written for him.'"

Tabari I:293 "When Allah cast Adam down from Paradise, Adam's feet were on earth while his head was in heaven. He became too familiar with the angels and they were in awe of him so much so that they complained to Allah in their various prayers. Allah, therefore, lowered Adam. But Adam missed what he used to hear from the angels and felt lonely. He complained to Allah and was sent to Mecca. On the way every place where he set foot became a village, and the interval between his steps became a desert until he reached Mecca."

Bukhari:V4B54N482 "Allah's Apostle said, 'The Hell Fire complained to its Lord saying, "O my Lord! My different parts are eating each other up." So, He allowed it to take two breaths, one in winter, the other in summer. This is the reason for the severe heat and bitter cold you find in weather.'"

Bukhari:V1B10N510 "Allah's Apostle said, 'If it is very hot, the severity of the heat is from the raging of the Hell Fire.'"

Qur'an 56:58 "Then tell Me the semen that you emit, throwing out. Is it you who create it, or are We the Creators? [It's only natural—the god of lust is the god of semen.] We have decreed/predestined/ordained Death for you all, and We are not to be frustrated from replacing you with others in (forms) that you know not."

Ishaq:255 "Jewish rabbis came to the Apostle and asked him to answer four questions saying, 'If you do so we will follow you, testify to your truth, and believe in you.' They began, 'Why does a boy resemble his mother when the semen comes from the father?' Muhammad replied, 'Do you not know that a man's semen is white and thick and a woman's is yellow and thin? The likeness goes with that which comes to the top.' 'Agreed,' the rabbis said. 'Tell us about your sleep.' 'Do you not know that a sleep which you allege I do not have is when the eye sleeps but the heart is awake?' 'Tell us about what Israel [Jacob] forbade himself.' 'Do you not know that the food he loved best was the flesh and milk of camels or perhaps two lobes of liver, kidneys, and fat?' 'Tell us about the spirit.' 'Do you not know that it is Gabriel, he who comes to me?' 'Agreed,' the rabbis said. 'But Muhammad, your spirit is an enemy to us, an angel who comes only with violence and the shedding of blood."

Qur'an 33:72 "We did indeed offer the opportunity to the Heavens, the Earth, the Mountains, but they refused to take it, being afraid (of Allah's torment). But man undertook it. He was unjust and foolish. Lo, he has proved a tyrant and fool, ignorant. Allah has to punish the Hypocrites, men and women, and the Unbelievers."

ALLAH'S ASTRONOMY:

Tabari I:232 "Gabriel brings to the sun a garment of luminosity from the light of Allah's Throne according to the measure of the hours of the day. The garment is longer in the summer and shorter in the winter, and of intermediate length in autumn and spring. The sun puts on that garment as one of you here puts on his clothes."

Tabari I:233 "When the Messenger was asked about that, he replied, 'When Allah was done with His creation He created two suns from the light of His Throne. His foreknowledge told Him that He would efface one and change it to a moon; so the moon is smaller in size."

Tabari I:234 "Allah thus sent Gabriel to drag his wing three times over the face of the moon, which at the time was a sun. He effaced its luminosity and left the light in it. This is what Allah means: [in Qur'an 17:12] 'We have blotted out the sign of the night, and We have made the sign of the day something to see by.' The blackness you can see as lines on the moon is a trace of the blotting."

Tabari I:244 "Allah then created for the sun a chariot with 360 handholds from the luminosity of the light of the Throne and entrusted 360 of the angels inhabiting the lower heaven with the sun and its chariot, each of them gripping one of those handholds. Allah also entrusted 360 angels with the moon."

Tabari I:234 "Then the Prophet said: 'For the sun and the moon, Allah created easts and wests on the two sides of the earth and the two rims of heaven. There are 180 springs in the west of black clay-this is why Allah's word says: "He found the sun setting in a muddy spring." [18:86] The black clay bubbles and boils like a pot when it boils furiously.'"

Qur'an 18:83 "They ask you about Dhu'l-Qarnain [Alexander the Great]. Say, 'I will cite something of his story. We gave him authority in the land and means of accomplishing his goals. So he followed a path until he reached the setting place of the sun. He saw that it set in black, muddy, hot water. Near it he found people."

Tabari I:236 "'When the sun rises upon its chariot from one of those springs it is accompanied by 360 angels with outspread wings.... When Allah wishes to test the sun and the moon, showing His servants a sign and thereby getting them to obey, the sun tumbles from the chariot and falls into the deep end of that ocean. When Allah wants to increase the significance of the sign and frighten His servants severely, all of the sun falls and nothing of it remains in the chariot. That is a total eclipse of the sun. It is a misfortune for the sun.'"

Tabari I:235 "Allah's Apostle said, 'Allah created an ocean three farakhs (918 kilometers) removed from heaven. Waves contained, it stands in the air by the command of Allah. No drop of it is spilled. All the oceans are motionless, but that ocean flows at the speed of an arrow. The sun, moon and retrograde stars [planets] by which Allah swears in the Qur'an [81:15], run like the sun and moon and race. All of the other stars are suspended from heaven as lamps are from mosques, and circulate together praising Allah. The Prophet said, 'If you wish to have this made clear, look to the circulation of the sphere alternately here and there.'"

Tabari I:236 "Allah created two cities out in space, each with ten thousand gates, each 6 kilometers distant from the other. By Allah, were those people not so many and so noisy, all the inhabitants of this world would hear the loud crash made by the sun falling when it rises and when it sets. Gabriel took me to them during my Night Journey from the Sacred Mosque [the Ka'aba] to the Farthest Mosque [the Jewish Temple in Jerusalem]. I told the people of these cities to worship Allah but they refused to listen to me."

Bukhari:V4B54N421 "I walked hand in hand with the Prophet when the sun was about to set. We did not stop looking at it. The Prophet asked, 'Do you know where the sun goes at sunset?' I replied, 'Allah and His Apostle know better.' He said, 'It travels until it falls down and prostrates Itself underneath the Throne. The angels who are in charge of the sun prostrate themselves, also. The sun asks permission to rise again. It is permitted. Then it will prostrate itself again but this prostration will not be accepted. The sun then says, "My Lord, where do You command me to rise, from where I set or from where I rose?" Allah will order the sun to return whence it has come and so the sun will rise in the west. And that is the interpretation of the statement of Allah in the Qur'an.'"

Qur'an 36:38 "The sun keeps revolving in its orbit at the dispensation of the All-Knowing. And the Moon, We have measured for her mansions till she returns like dried date stalks. It is not permitted for the Sun to overtake the Moon, nor can the Night outstrip the Day. Each (just) swims along, floating in (its own) orbit as a Sign as in a race. And we made similar vessels [chariots] for them to ride. But we could have drowned them if we pleased."

Tabari I:332 "The sun and the moon were in eclipse for seven days and nights."

Qur'an 67:3 "We created seven heavens, one above the other. Muhammad, can you see any fault in Ar-Rahman's creation? Look again: Can you see any rifts or fissures? Then look again and yet again. Your gaze turns back dazed and tired. We have adorned the lowest skies with lamps, and We have made them missiles to drive away the devils and against the stone Satans, and for them We have prepared the doom of Hell and the penalty of torment in the most intense Blazing Fire."

Qur'an 38:27 "We have not created the heavens and earth and all that lies between for nothing."

Qur'an 21:26 "Don't the unbelievers see that the heavens and earth were joined together in one piece before we clove them asunder? ...Will they not believe? And We have set on the earth mountains as stabilizers, lest the earth should convulse without them. And We have made therein broad highways for them to pass through, that they may be guided. We have made the heaven a roof well guarded. Yet they turn away from its Signs! All (the celestial bodies) swim along, on a course, floating."

Qur'an 2:189 "They ask you about the New Moons. Say: They are but signs to mark fixed seasons in (the affairs of) men, and for Hajj Pilgrimage."

Tabari I:204 "I asked the Prophet, 'Where was Allah before His creation?' Muhammad replied: 'He was in a cloud with no air underneath or above it.'"

Tabari I:219 "When Allah wanted to create the creation, He brought forth smoke from the water. The smoke hovered loftily over it. He called it 'heaven.' Then He dried out the water and made it earth. He split it and made it seven earths on Sunday. He created the earth upon a big fish, that being the fish mentioned in the Qur'an. By the Pen, the fish was in the water. The water was upon the back of a small rock. The rock was on the back of an angel. The angel was on a big rock. The big rock was in the wind. The fish became agitated. As a result, the earth quaked, so Allah anchored the mountains and made it stable. This is why the Qur'an says, 'Allah made for the earth firmly anchored mountains, lest it shake you up.'"

The documented references in *Prophet of Doom* were derived from English translations of the following ancient Islamic manuscripts. I encourage you to purchase and read them. The *Sirat Rasul Allah* was written by Ibn Ishaq in 750 A.D. It was edited and abridged by Ibn Hisham in 830 and translated by Alfred Guillaume under the title, *The Life of Muhammad* in 1955 by Oxford Press. Referred to as the Sira, or Biography, Ishaq's Hadith Collection is comprised of oral reports from Muhammad and his companions. It provides the only written account of Muhammad's life and the formation of Islam within two centuries of the prophet's death. There is no earlier or more accurate source.

The *History of al-Tabari,* called the Ta'rikh, was written by Abu Muhammad bin al-Tabari between 870 and 920 A.D. His monumental work was translated and published in 1987 through 1997 by the State University of New York Press. I quote from volumes I, II, VI, VII, VIII, and IX. Tabari's History is comprised entirely of Islamic Hadith. It is arranged chronologically. Tabari is Islam's oldest uncensored source.

Al-Bukhari's Hadith, titled: *Sahih Al-Bukhari—The True Traditions* was collected by Imam Bukhari in 850 A.D. I have used the collector's original nomenclature because the only printed English translation (Publisher-Maktaba Dar-us-Salam, Translator-Muhammad Khan) was abridged and erroneously numbered. Muslim was a student of Bukhari. His Hadith Collection was translated into English and is available online. Most Muslims consider these Hadith Collections to be inspired scripture. They are arranged by topic.

I have blended the following Qur'an translations to convey its message as clearly as possible: Ahmed Ali, Pikthal, Noble by Muhsin Khan, Yusuf Ali, and Shakir. The oldest Qur'an fragments date to 725 A.D.—a century after they were first recited. The Qur'an lacks context and chronology so it must be read in conjunction with Ishaq and Tabari.

Before using passages in this appendix, read *Prophet of Doom.* Each quote is explained and presented in the context of Muhammad's life.

INDEX

Qur'an Surah References:
  042: SMxxii, SMxxv, SMlvi
  043: SMxi, SMxxii
  046: 12, 30, 189, 255, 281-3, SMxxii, SMxliii
  047: Pix, 554, 572-576, 660, 665
  048: 504, 506, 567-572, 600, 664, 668
  049: 561-3, 664
  050: 11
  051: 11
  052: Pxxii, 223-8
  053: 248, 250-2
  054: 343
  055: 28, 30, 236-7, 507, SMlvii, SMlvii
  056: 39-40, 97, 220-3, 572, SMlvii
  059: 312, 374, 379-80, 382, 398, 443, 445, 478, 485, 489, 546, 547, 664
  060: 270, 348, 565-7
  061: Pix, 382-3, 481, 490, 670
  062: 382-4
  063: 384-5, SMxxi
  064: 385-6
  065: SMxlvii
  066: 509, 563-5, SMxlv
  067: Pxxiii, 171-4, 177, SMxlvii
  068: Pxxii, 13, 97, 143, 185-6, 187-8
  069: 178-80, SMxliii
  070: 180-2
  071: 48-9
  072: 189-90, 193-5, SMxlvii
  073: 146-7, 150, 188-9, 661
  074: Pxix, Pxxiii, 10, 145, 152-6, 486
  075: 168-70, SMxlix
  076: 216, 217
  077: 216-7
  078: 97, 216, 217, 607, SMxlvi
  079: 197-9, SMxliii
  080: 6, 199-200, 201-2
  081: 21, 202-4
  083: 216, 217
  084: 216, 217, 572
  085: Pxix, 216, 217, SMvi, SMxi
  086: 216, 217, SMxlvii
  087: 47, 204-6, 287

TOPICAL QUOTATIONS: MUHAMMAD'S OWN WORDS

BIBLIOGRAPHY

The documented references in *Prophet of Doom* were derived from English translations of ancient Islamic manuscripts. While hundreds of scholars and researchers have written about Muhammad, his god Allah, and his religion Islam, only five sources can be considered prime, authentic, and to the extent possible, unbiased. All other writings present a cleric's or scholar's opinion, one drawn directly or indirectly from the original sources. So rather than study someone's interpretation of Muhammad, Allah, and Islam, read what Islam's lone prophet had to say about himself, his god, and his religion. If Muhammad got Islam wrong, no one has it right. And without Muhammad, there would be no Qur'an and no Islam. Allah would be completely unknown.

The *Sirat Rasul Allah* was written by Ibn Ishaq in 750 A.D. It was edited and abridged by Ibn Hisham in 830 and translated by Alfred Guillaume under the title, *The Life of Muhammad* in 1955 by Oxford Press. Referred to as the Sira, or Biography, Ishaq's Hadith Collection is comprised of oral reports from Muhammad and his companions. It provides the only written account of Muhammad's life and the formation of Islam composed within two centuries of the prophet's death. There is no earlier or more accurate source.

The *History of al-Tabari,* called the Ta'rikh, was written by Abu Muhammad bin al-Tabari between 870 and 920 A.D. His monumental work was translated and published in 1987 through 1997 by the State University of New York Press. I quote from volumes I, II, VI, VII, VIII, and IX. Tabari's History is comprised entirely of Islamic Hadith. It is arranged chronologically. Tabari is Islam's oldest uncensored source.

Al-Bukhari's Hadith, titled: *Sahih Al-Bukhari—The True Traditions* was collected by Imam Bukhari in 850 A.D. I have used it's original nomenclature because the only printed English translation (Publisher-Maktaba Dar-us-Salam, Translator-Muhammad Khan) was abridged and erroneously numbered. Muslim was a student of Bukhari. His Hadith Collection was translated into English and is available online. Most Muslims consider their Hadith to be inspired scripture. They are arranged by topic.

I have blended five Qur'an translations together to convey its message as clearly as possible: Ahmed Ali, Pikthal, Noble by Muhsin Khan, Yusuf Ali, and Shakir. The oldest Qur'an fragments date to 725 A.D.—a century after they were recited. The Qur'an lacks organization and context so it must be read in conjunction with the chronological Hadith Collections of Ishaq and Tabari.

Also from Craig Winn

Tea With Terrorists is a taut thriller with a haunting message: the link between Islam and terrorism in today's world is more than coincidental. Terrorism is the very essence of Islam's earliest history, and it continues to be its driving force. *Tea With Terrorists* is rich with detail and buttressed with documentation both ancient and modern.

Each of the following statements is a lie. Do you know why?

1. Islam is a peace-loving and tolerant religion.
2. The Bible and the Qur'an present the same God.
3. We are not at war with Islam.
4. Muhammad was a prophet.
5. Terrorists like bin Laden have corrupted their religion.
6. Islam doesn't promote killing innocent women and children.
7. Al-Qaeda is a fringe group of radical extremists.
8. It was wise to invade Afghanistan and Iraq.
9. Our politicians and media tell us the truth.
10. The world is safer now than it has ever been.

Most people think all these statements are true, but they're not. Our politicians, media, and even well-meaning but ill-informed clergy promote a view of Islam that is totally out of step with what their scriptures teach.

Tea With Terrorists takes the reader on a voyage of discovery, and the destination is truth. It's message is as haunting as it is controversial: the source of terror is Islam—not a radical fringe group, not some fanatical terrorist organization, but Islam itself. *Tea With Terrorists* predicts what could happen to America as a result of our ignorance of Islam.

Though written as a novel, *Tea With Terrorists* contains more factual information on who the terrorists are and what can be done to stop them than any other book ever written. It provides a contemporary analysis of the threat of Islam and should be considered a companion volume to *Prophet of Doom*. The two books cover the same subject but from a different perspective.

The bizarre and revealing interview with members of al-Qaeda, Hamas, al-Aqsa Martyrs' Brigade, and Islamic Jihad recounted in the title chapter actually happened. The authors know first hand how these men think and why they do what they do.

www.ProphetOfDoom.net
Order Direct: 1(800)487-0568

Also from Craig Winn

Long before Craig Winn became one of America's foremost experts on the root causes of Islamic terrorism, he was a successful manufacturer and innovative entrepreneur. *In The Company of Good and Evil* is the story of the rise and fall of his last and greatest business venture—one brought to it's knees by the same kind of insecure minds that conquered seventh-century Arabia.

In the Company of Good and Evil reveals what it takes to build a business—and how little it can take to destroy one. The true story of ill-fated online retailer Value America, this amazing book provides insight into other recent corporate disasters like Enron, Global Crossing, K-Mart, and WorldCom. By reading *In the Company of Good and Evil*, you will come to understand the sinister nature of insecurity—how it causes destructive, abusive behavior. Muhammad was a textbook example of an insecure leader; the people who brought Value America down followed the same devastating path.

The authors were insiders. They founded the company, nurtured it, helped it grow, gave it wings—and then watched it die a very painful, very public death. Winn and Power shed light on both the entrepreneurial spirit that builds reality out of dreams, and the kind of self-serving ambition that is threatening to destroy the very fabric of our society. They chronicle the brash self-confidence and remarkable coincidences that shaped Value America into the most promising star of the dot-com era, and they examine the methods and motivations of those who brought the company to its knees.

Value America was an idea whose time had come. In three short years, it grew from nothing into one of the largest businesses of its kind in the world, worth over three billion dollars. But sixteen months later it was bankrupt, a worthless shell of its former self. *In The Company of Good and Evil* is the story of what really happened: flashes of inspiration capping months of grueling work, games of "chicken" won and lost, blackmail schemes, white knights, dire corporate poverty, and billion-dollar IPOs. They're all part of the drama. You'll meet some of the most powerful people in America, in technology and in politics, in business and labor, in finance and faith. They all left their fingerprints on The Company.

These events actually happened. If the story reads like a novel, maybe it's because truth can be more exciting than fiction.